ULTIMATE KITCHEN COMPANION

ULTIMATE KITCHEN COMPANION

OVER 2000 RECIPES FOR EVERYDAY COOKING

DETAILED CONTENTS LIST AND EASY-TO-USE INDEX

bay books

CONTENTS

INTRODUCTION

OF THE MYRIAD WAYS IN WHICH TODAY'S HOME KITCHEN MIGHT BE DESCRIBED, 'CHOICE' IS THE WORD THAT COMES QUICKEST TO MIND. NO LONGER BOUND BY BORDERS OR TRADITION, WE ARE FREE BOTH TO EXPLORE THE CULINARY WONDERS OF THE WORLD AND ALSO TO ENJOY THE FAMILIAR AND COMFORTING FLAVOURS OF A MUCH-LOVED RECIPE.

There's choice, too, in the world of cookbooks—a choice which is seemingly endless and sometimes overwhelming. That's where this book comes in. Here between its covers you'll find over 2000 recipes to cater to your every culinary whim and inspire you on even the weariest of weekdays. Contained in this one volume are chapters on soups and salads, finger foods and first course meals. The chapters on chicken and turkey, beef, lamb and pork offer a wide variety of recipes ranging from noodle and rice-based dishes to time-honoured roasts and casseroles. There's a chapter dedicated to vegetarian recipes, too, and our 'World cuisine' chapter offers you the chance to sample flavours from all corners of the

globe. If you're looking for something to serve on the side, we have oven-baked treats, sauces and dressings, and plenty of inspiration for simple yet tasty side dishes and vegetables. And not forgetting everyone's favourite part of the meal, there are three whole chapters of sweet delights to indulge in. There are classic recipes, old favourites, exotic tastes, Christmas treats, and a collection of recipes just for children.

Whether you're looking for a speedy weekday meal or a feast for a special occasion, *The Ultimate Kitchen Companion* will fast become your new best friend in the kitchen.

SOUPS

SNOW PEA (MANGETOUT), PRAWN AND PASTA SOUP

Preparation time: 30 minutes
Total cooking time: 15 minutes
Serves 4

12 raw king prawns
100 g (3½ oz) snow peas (mangetout)
1 tablespoon oil
2 onions, chopped
6 cups (1.5 litres) chicken stock
½ teaspoon grated fresh ginger
200 g (6½ oz) angel hair pasta or
    spaghettini
fresh basil leaves, to garnish

1 Peel and devein the prawns, leaving the tails intact. Trim the snow peas and if they are big ones, slice them into smaller pieces.
2 Heat the oil in a pan, add the onion and cook over low heat until soft. Add the chicken stock to the pan and bring to the boil.
3 Add the fresh ginger, snow peas, prawns and pasta. Cook over medium heat for 4 minutes. Season with salt and pepper and serve immediately, garnished with fresh basil leaves.

CHICKEN AND SWEET CORN SOUP

Preparation time: 15 minutes
Total cooking time: 10 minutes
Serves 4

200 g (6½ oz) chicken breast fillets
1 teaspoon salt
2 egg whites
3 cups (750 ml/24 fl oz) chicken stock
1 cup (250 g/8 oz) creamed corn
1 tablespoon cornflour
2 teaspoons soy sauce
2 spring onions, diagonally sliced

1 Wash the chicken under cold water and pat dry with paper towels. Place the chicken in a food processor and process until finely chopped. Add the salt.
2 Lightly beat the egg whites in a small bowl until foamy. Fold the egg whites into the chicken mince.
3 Bring the chicken stock to the boil and add the creamed corn. Dissolve the cornflour in a little water and add to the soup, stirring until the mixture thickens.
4 Reduce the heat and add the chicken mixture, breaking it up with a whisk. Allow to heat through, without boiling, for about 3 minutes. Season to taste with soy sauce. Serve immediately, sprinkled with the spring onion.

AVGOLEMONO SOUP WITH CHICKEN

Preparation time: 20 minutes
Total cooking time: 30 minutes
Serves 4

1 onion, halved
2 cloves
1 carrot, cut into chunks
1 bay leaf
500 g (1 lb) chicken breast fillets
⅓ cup (75 g/2½ oz) short-grain rice
3 eggs, separated
3 tablespoons lemon juice
2 tablespoons chopped fresh flat-leaf
    parsley
4 thin lemon slices, to garnish

1 Stud the onion with the cloves and place in a large saucepan with 1.5 litres water. Add the carrot, bay leaf and chicken and season with salt and freshly ground black pepper. Slowly bring to the boil, then reduce the heat and simmer for 10 minutes, or until the chicken is cooked.
2 Strain the stock into a clean saucepan, reserving the chicken and discarding the vegetables. Add the rice to the stock, bring to the boil, then reduce the heat and simmer for 15 minutes, or until the rice is tender. Meanwhile, tear the chicken into shreds.
3 Whisk the egg whites in a clean dry bowl until stiff peaks form, then beat in the yolks. Slowly beat in the lemon juice. Gently stir in about 150 ml (5 fl oz) of the hot (not boiling) stock and beat thoroughly. Add the egg mixture to the stock and heat gently, but do not let it boil otherwise the eggs may scramble. Add the chicken and season with salt and black pepper.
4 Set aside for 2–3 minutes to allow the flavours to develop, then sprinkle the parsley

SEAFOOD SOUP

Preparation time: 30 minutes
Total cooking time: 40 minutes
Serves 6

500 g (1 lb) firm white fish fillets
500 g (1 lb) raw prawns
1 tablespoon oil
5 cm (2 inch) piece fresh ginger, grated
3 tablespoons finely chopped lemon grass (white part only)
3 small red chillies, finely chopped
2 medium onions, chopped
4 medium tomatoes, peeled, seeded and chopped
3 cups (750 ml/24 fl oz) fish stock
3 cups (750 ml/24 fl oz) water
4 kaffir lime leaves, finely shredded
1 cup (160 g/5¼ oz) chopped fresh pineapple
1 tablespoon tamarind concentrate
1 tablespoon grated palm sugar or soft brown sugar
2 tablespoons lime juice
1 tablespoon fish sauce
2 tablespoons chopped fresh coriander leaves

1 Cut the fish fillets into 2 cm (¾ inch) cubes. Peel and devein the prawns.
2 Heat the oil in a large pan; add the ginger, lemon grass, chilli and onion and stir over medium heat for 5 minutes or until the onion is golden.
3 Add the tomatoes to the pan and cook for 3 minutes. Stir in the fish stock, water, lime leaves, pineapple, tamarind, palm sugar, lime juice and fish sauce; cover, bring to the boil, reduce heat and simmer for 15 minutes.
4 Add the fish fillets, prawns and coriander to the pan, and simmer for 10 minutes or until the seafood is tender. Serve immediately.

PLAIN CONGEE WITH ACCOMPANIMENTS

Preparation time: 15 minutes
Total cooking time: 2 hours
Serves 4

1 cup (220 g/7 oz) short-grain rice, rinsed and drained
2.5 litres (80 fl oz) chicken stock or water
light soy sauce, to taste
roasted sesame oil, to taste

Toppings
3 spring onions (scallions), chopped
4 tablespoons chopped coriander (cilantro)
30 g (1 oz) sliced pickled ginger
4 tablespoons finely chopped preserved turnip
4 tablespoons roasted peanuts
2 one-thousand-year-old eggs, cut into slivers
2 tablespoons sesame seeds, toasted
2 fried dough sticks, diagonally sliced

1 Put the rice in a clay pot, casserole dish or saucepan and stir in the stock or water. Bring to the boil, then reduce the heat and simmer very gently, stirring occasionally, for 1¾–2 hours, or until it has a porridge-like texture and the rice is breaking up.
2 Add a sprinkling of soy sauce, sesame oil and white pepper to season the congee. The congee can be served plain, or choose a selection from the toppings listed and serve in bowls alongside the congee for guests to help themselves.

NOTE: You'll need access to an Asian or Chinese grocery store to acquire preserved turnip, one-thousand-year-old eggs and fried dough sticks; if you don't have one nearby, choose some of the more easily available toppings instead.

BEAN SOUP WITH SAUSAGE

Preparation time: 25 minutes
Total cooking time: 40 minutes
Serves 4–6

4 Italian sausages
2 teaspoons olive oil
2 leeks, sliced
1 clove garlic, crushed
1 large carrot, chopped into small cubes
2 celery sticks, sliced
2 tablespoons plain flour
2 beef stock cubes, crumbled
8 cups (2 litres) hot water
½ cup (125 ml/4 fl oz) white wine
125 g (4 oz) conchiglie (shell pasta)
440 g (14 oz) can three-bean mix, drained

1 Cut the sausages into small pieces. Heat the oil in a large heavy-based pan and add the sausage pieces. Cook over medium heat for 5 minutes or until golden, stirring regularly. Remove from the pan and drain on paper towels.
2 Add the leek, garlic, carrot and celery to the pan and cook for 2–3 minutes or until soft, stirring occasionally.
3 Add the flour and stir for 1 minute. Gradually stir in the combined stock cubes and water and the wine. Bring to the boil, reduce the heat and simmer for 10 minutes.
4 Add the pasta and beans to the pan. Increase the heat and cook for 8–10 minutes, or until the pasta is tender. Return the sausage to the pan and season with salt and pepper, to taste. Serve with chopped fresh parsley, if desired.

NOTE: Use dried beans, if preferred. Put them in a bowl, cover with water and soak overnight. Drain and add to a large pan with enough water to cover the beans well. Bring to the boil, reduce the heat and simmer for 1 hour. Drain well before adding to the soup.

LOBSTER BISQUE

Preparation time: 20 minutes
Total cooking time: 1 hour
Serves 4–6

1 raw lobster tail, about 400 g (13 oz)
90 g (3 oz) butter
1 large onion, chopped
1 large carrot, chopped
1 stick celery, chopped
¼ cup (60 ml/2 fl oz) brandy
1 cup (250 ml/8 fl oz) white wine
6 sprigs fresh parsley
1 sprig fresh thyme
2 bay leaves
1 tablespoon tomato paste (tomato purée)
1 litre (32 fl oz) fish stock
2 ripe tomatoes, chopped
2 tablespoons rice flour or cornflour
½ cup (125 ml/4 fl oz) cream

1 Remove the meat from the lobster tail. Wash the shell and crush into large pieces with a mallet or rolling pin, then set aside. Chop the meat into small pieces, cover and chill.
2 Melt the butter in a large pan, add the onion, carrot and celery and cook over low heat for 20 minutes, stirring occasionally, until the vegetables are softened but not brown.

3 In a small pan, heat the brandy, set alight with a long match and carefully pour over the vegetables. Shake the pan until the flame dies down. Add the white wine and the lightly crushed lobster shell. Increase the heat and boil until the liquid is reduced by half. Add the parsley, thyme, bay leaves, tomato paste, fish stock and chopped tomato. Simmer, uncovered, for 25 minutes, stirring occasionally.
4 Strain the mixture through a fine sieve or dampened muslin, pressing gently to extract all the liquid. Discard the vegetables and shell.
5 Return the liquid to the cleaned pan. Blend the rice flour or cornflour with the cream in a small bowl. Add to the liquid and stir over medium heat until the mixture boils and thickens. Add the lobster meat and season, to taste. Cook, without boiling, for 10 minutes, or until the lobster is just cooked. Serve hot.

NOTE: If you don't dampen the muslin when straining the mixture, it will soak up too much of the liquid.

KAKAVIA

Preparation time: 20 minutes
Total cooking time: 20 minutes
Serves 6

2 onions, finely sliced
400 g (13 oz) can good-quality chopped
   tomatoes
750 g (1½ lb) potatoes, cut into 5 mm
   (¼ inch) slices
1 teaspoon chopped fresh oregano
150 ml (5 fl oz) olive oil
2 litres fish or vegetable stock
1.5 kg (3 lb) white fish fillets, such as cod,
   jewfish or snapper, cut into chunks
500 g (1 lb) raw prawn meat
½ cup (125 ml/4 fl oz) lemon juice
chopped fresh flat-leaf parsley, to
   garnish

1 Layer the onion, tomato and potato in a large heavy-based saucepan, seasoning with salt, pepper and oregano between each layer. Add the oil and stock and bring the mixture to the boil. Reduce the heat and simmer for 10 minutes, or until the potato is cooked through and tender.
2 Add the fish and prawn meat and cook for 5 minutes, or until the seafood is cooked. Add the juice, spoon into bowls and top with parsley.

VIETNAMESE COMBINATION SEAFOOD SOUP
(CANH CHUA)

Preparation time: 30 minutes
Total cooking time: 30 minutes
Serves 4

1 tablespoon vegetable oil
1 stem lemon grass, white part only, finely chopped
1 fresh red chilli, finely chopped
2 cloves garlic, finely chopped
2 litres (64 fl oz) home-made fish or chicken stock (see page 23) or 1.5 litres (48 fl oz) purchased stock diluted with 2 cups (500 ml/16 fl oz) water
1 tablespoon tamarind purée
1 tablespoon fish sauce
400 g (13 oz) black mussels, scrubbed and debearded
500 g (1 lb) raw medium prawns, peeled and deveined, with tails intact
500 g (1 lb) firm white fish fillets (e.g. ling, blue eye or snapper), cut into 2.5 cm (1 inch) pieces
1 ripe tomato, cut into thin wedges
3 tablespoons fresh coriander leaves
1 tablespoon fresh Vietnamese mint
1 cup (90 g/3 oz) bean sprouts, tailed

1 Heat a non-stick wok over high heat, add the oil and swirl to coat the side of the wok. Add the lemon grass, chilli and garlic, then cook for 2 minutes, or until softened and fragrant. Add the stock, tamarind and fish sauce, bring to the boil, then reduce the heat to low and simmer for 15 minutes.
2 Discard any broken mussels. Increase the heat to medium–high, add the mussels, cover with a lid and cook for 2–3 minutes, tossing occasionally. Remove the lid and add the prawns, fish pieces and tomato wedges. Cook for a further 3 minutes, or until the seafood is completely cooked. Discard any unopened mussels. Stir in the coriander leaves and mint.
3 Divide the bean sprouts among four soup bowls, ladle in the soup and serve.

CORN CHOWDER

Preparation time: 15 minutes
Total cooking time: 30 minutes
Serves 8

90 g (3 oz) butter
2 large onions, finely chopped
1 clove garlic, crushed
2 teaspoons cumin seeds
4 cups (1 litre) vegetable stock
2 medium potatoes, peeled and chopped
1 cup (250 g/8 oz) canned creamed-style corn
2 cups (400 g/12⅔ oz) fresh corn kernels
3 tablespoons chopped fresh parsley
1 cup (125 g/4 oz) grated Cheddar cheese
salt and freshly ground black pepper
3 tablespoons cream (optional)
2 tablespoons chopped fresh chives, to garnish

1 Heat the butter in large heavy-based pan. Add the onions and cook over medium-high heat for 5 minutes or until golden. Add garlic and cumin seeds, cook 1 minute, stirring constantly. Add vegetable stock, bring to boil. Add potatoes and reduce heat. Simmer, uncovered, 10 minutes.
2 Add the creamed corn, corn kernels and parsley. Bring to the boil, reduce heat, simmer for 10 minutes. Stir through the cheese, salt and pepper, to taste, and cream. Heat gently until the cheese melts. Serve immediately, sprinkled with chopped chives.

MONGOLIAN HOTPOT

Preparation time: 15 minutes + 10 minutes soaking
Total cooking time: 5 minutes
Serves 6

⅓ cup (80 ml/2¾ fl oz) light soy sauce
2 tablespoons Chinese sesame paste
3 tablespoons Chinese rice wine
1 teaspoon chilli and garlic paste
250 g (8 oz) dried rice vermicelli
600 g (1¼ lb) lamb backstraps or loin fillet, thinly sliced across the grain
4 spring onions (scallions), sliced
1.5 litres (48 fl oz) chicken stock
6 thin slices of ginger
300 g (10 oz) silken firm tofu, cut into 1.5 cm (⅝ inch) cubes
300 g (10 oz) Chinese broccoli (gai lan), cut into 4 cm (1½ inch) lengths
2 cups (75 g/2½ oz) shredded Chinese cabbage (wom bok)

1 To make the sauce, combine the soy sauce, sesame paste, 1 tablespoon of the rice wine and the chilli and garlic paste in a small bowl.
2 Put the vermicelli in a large heatproof bowl, cover with boiling water and soak for 6–7 minutes. Drain well and divide among six serving bowls. Top with the lamb slices and spring onion.
3 Put the stock, ginger and remaining rice wine in a 2.5 litre (80 fl oz) flameproof hotpot or large saucepan. Cover and bring to the boil over high heat. Add the tofu, Chinese broccoli and Chinese cabbage and simmer, uncovered, for 1 minute, or until the broccoli has wilted. Divide the tofu, broccoli and cabbage among the serving bowls, then ladle on the hot stock—it should be hot enough to cook the lamb. Drizzle a little of the sauce on top and serve the rest on the side.

BACON AND PEA SOUP

Preparation time: 20 minutes
Total cooking time: 15 minutes
Serves 4–6

4 bacon rashers
50 g (1¾ oz) butter
1 large onion, finely chopped
1 celery stick, thinly sliced
8 cups (2 litres) chicken stock
1 cup (155 g/5 oz) frozen peas
250 g (8 oz) rissoni
2 tablespoons chopped fresh parsley

1 Trim the rind and excess fat from the bacon and chop into small pieces.
2 Melt the butter in a large heavy-based pan and cook the bacon, onion and celery over low heat for 5 minutes, stirring occasionally. Add the stock and peas and simmer, covered, for 5 minutes. Increase the heat, add the rissoni and cook, uncovered, stirring occasionally, for 5 minutes, or until the rissoni is tender.
3 Add the chopped fresh parsley and season with salt and pepper, to taste, just before serving.

SWEET RED BEAN SOUP WITH MOCHI

Preparation time: 5 minutes
Total cooking time: 3 hours 10 minutes
Serves 4

1 cup (220 g/7 oz) azuki beans
⅔ cup (145 g/5 oz) caster (superfine) sugar
pinch of salt
4 squares of mochi (see Note)

1 Rinse the beans, then place in a large saucepan of water and bring to the boil. Drain, then return the beans to the pan with 1 litre (32 fl oz) fresh water. Bring to the boil again, cover, reduce the heat to low and cook for 2 hours, or until the beans are tender and almost all the water has been absorbed. Check the beans occasionally as you may need to add a little more water.
2 Add the sugar and 1.5 litres (48 fl oz) water and stir to combine. Increase the heat to high and cook for about 40 minutes, or until the beans are soft but not mushy. You should have a thin but chunky 'soup'; if you prefer, you can make the soup thicker by mashing some of the beans with a fork or make it thinner by adding a little extra water. Remove the pan from the heat, cover and set aside.
3 Preheat the grill (broiler) to high. Line a baking tray with foil and place the mochi on top. Cook, turning frequently, for 10 minutes, or until mottled golden and puffed up to about twice their size. Place a rice cake in the base of four small, deep serving bowls and ladle the soup over the top. Traditionally the chewy mochi is eaten with chopsticks, then the soup is drunk directly from the bowl.

NOTE: Mochi cakes, often sold as kirimochi are glutinous rice cakes. They are available at Japanese speciality stores and Asian supermarkets. Mochi cakes are traditional celebratory fare at New Year.

STILTON SOUP

Preparation time: 20 minutes
Total cooking time: 30 minutes
Serves 4–6

Thyme pitta croutons
2 large Lebanese breads
1½ tablespoons fresh thyme leaves
½ cup (50 g/1½ oz) grated Parmesan

30 g (1 oz) butter
2 leeks, white part only, chopped
1 kg (2 lb) potatoes, chopped into chunks
1.25 litres (40 fl oz) chicken stock
½ cup (125 ml/4 fl oz) cream
100 g (3½ oz) Stilton cheese
fresh thyme sprigs, to garnish

1 Preheat the oven to moderate 180°C (350°F/Gas 4). Split each Lebanese bread into two, then cut each half into 8 wedges. Put on baking trays, sprinkle with the combined thyme and Parmesan and bake in batches for 5–8 minutes each batch, or until golden and crisp.
2 Melt the butter in a large saucepan, add the leek and cook until softened. Add the potato and chicken stock and bring to the boil. Simmer, covered, for 15 minutes, or until the potato is tender (pierce with the point of a knife—if the potato comes away easily, it is cooked).
3 Transfer the mixture, in batches if necessary, to a blender or food processor and blend until smooth. Return to the saucepan and add the cream and cheese, to taste. Stir over low heat until the cheese has melted, being careful not to let the mixture boil. Ladle into individual dishes and garnish with sprigs of fresh thyme. Serve with the thyme pitta croutons.

SOUPE AU PISTOU
(VEGETABLE SOUP WITH BASIL SAUCE)

Preparation time: 45 minutes
Total cooking time: 35 minutes
Serves 8

3 stalks fresh flat-leaf parsley
1 large sprig of fresh rosemary
1 large sprig of fresh thyme
1 large sprig of fresh marjoram
¼ cup (60 ml/2 fl oz) olive oil
2 onions, thinly sliced
1 leek, thinly sliced
1 bay leaf
375 g (12 oz) pumpkin, cut into small pieces
250 g (8 oz) potato, cut into small pieces
1 carrot, cut in half lengthways and thinly sliced
2 litres vegetable stock or water
½ cup (90 g/3 oz) fresh or frozen broad beans
½ cup (80 g/2¾ oz) fresh or frozen peas
2 small zucchinis (courgettes), finely chopped
2 ripe tomatoes, peeled and roughly chopped
½ cup (60 g/2 oz) short macaroni or shell pasta

Pistou
½ cup (25 g/¾ oz) fresh basil leaves
2 large cloves garlic, crushed
⅓ cup (35 g/1¼ oz) grated Parmesan
⅓ cup (80 ml/2¾ fl oz) olive oil

1 Tie the parsley, rosemary, thyme and marjoram together with string. Heat the oil in a heavy-based saucepan and add onion and leek. Cook over low heat for 10 minutes, or until soft.
2 Add the herb bunch, bay leaf, pumpkin, potato, carrot, 1 teaspoon salt and the stock. Cover and simmer 10 minutes, or until vegetables are almost tender.
3 Add the broad beans, peas, zucchini, tomato and pasta. Cover and cook for 15 minutes, or until the vegetables are very tender and the pasta is cooked. Add more water if necessary. Remove the herbs, including the bay leaf.
4 For the pistou, finely chop the basil and garlic in a food processor. Pour in the oil gradually, processing until smooth. Stir in the Parmesan and ½ teaspoon freshly ground black pepper and serve spooned over the soup.

NOTE: The flavour of this soup improves if refrigerated overnight, then gently reheated.

BEEF PHO
(VIETNAMESE BEEF SOUP)

Preparation time: 15 minutes +
    40 minutes freezing
Total cooking time: 30 minutes
Serves 4

400 g (13 oz) rump steak, trimmed
½ onion
1½ tablespoons fish sauce
1 star anise
1 cinnamon stick
pinch of ground white pepper
1.5 litres (48 fl oz) beef stock
300 g (10 oz) fresh thin rice noodles
3 spring onions (scallions), thinly sliced
30 Vietnamese mint leaves
90 g (3 oz) bean sprouts, tailed
1 small white onion, cut in half and thinly sliced
1 small red chilli, thinly sliced on the diagonal
lemon wedges, to serve

1 Wrap the steak in plastic wrap and freeze for 40 minutes—this will make it easier to slice.
2 Meanwhile, put the onion, fish sauce, star anise, cinnamon stick, pepper, stock and 2 cups (500 ml/16 fl oz) water in a large saucepan. Bring to the boil, then reduce the heat, cover and simmer for 20 minutes. Discard the onion, star anise and cinnamon stick.
3 Cover the noodles with boiling water and gently separate. Drain and refresh under cold water. Thinly slice the meat across the grain.
4 Divide the noodles and spring onion among four deep bowls. Top with the beef, mint, bean sprouts, onion and chilli. Ladle the hot broth over the top and serve with the lemon wedges.

CLAM CHOWDER

Preparation time: 35 minutes + soaking
Total cooking time: 45 minutes
Serves 4

1.5 kg (3 lb) clams (vongole) or pipis,
  in shell
2 teaspoons oil
3 rashers bacon, chopped
1 onion, chopped
1 clove garlic, crushed
750 g (1½ lb) potatoes, cut into small dice
1¼ cups (315 ml/10 fl oz) fish stock
2 cups (500 ml/16 fl oz) milk
½ cup (125 ml/4 fl oz) cream
3 tablespoons chopped fresh parsley

1 Discard any clams that are broken,
already open or do not close when tapped
on the bench. If necessary, soak in cold
water for 1–2 hours to remove sand. Drain
and put in a large heavy-based pan with
1 cup (250 ml/8 fl oz) water. Cover and
simmer over low heat for 5 minutes, or
until open. Discard any that do not open.
Strain and reserve the liquid. Remove the
clam meat from the shells.
2 Heat the oil in the cleaned pan. Add the
bacon, onion and garlic and cook, stirring,
over medium heat until the onion is soft
and the bacon golden. Add the potato and
stir well.
3 Measure the reserved liquid and add
water to make 1¼ cups (315 ml/10 fl oz).
Add to the pan with the stock and milk.
Bring to the boil, reduce the heat, cover
and simmer 20 minutes, or until the
potato is tender. Uncover and simmer for
10 minutes, or until slightly thickened.
4 Add the cream, clam meat and parsley
and season, to taste, with salt and pepper.
Heat through gently before serving, but do
not allow to boil or the liquid may curdle.

LENTIL AND SILVERBEET/ SWISS CHARD SOUP

Preparation time: 20 minutes
Total cooking time: 3 hours 30 minutes
Serves 6

Chicken stock
1 kg (2 lb) chicken trimmings (necks, ribs,
  wings), fat removed
1 small onion, roughly chopped
1 bay leaf
3–4 sprigs fresh flat-leaf parsley
1–2 sprigs fresh oregano or thyme

1½ cups (280 g/9 oz) brown lentils,
  washed
850 g (1 lb 12 oz) silverbeet
¼ cup (60 ml/2 fl oz) olive oil
1 large onion, finely chopped
4 cloves garlic, crushed
1/2 cup (35 g/1¼ oz) finely chopped fresh
  coriander leaves
⅓ cup (80 ml/2¾ fl oz) lemon juice
lemon wedges, to serve

1 For the stock, put all the ingredients in
a large saucepan, add 3 litres water and
bring to the boil. Skim any scum from the
surface. Reduce the heat and simmer for
2 hours. Strain the stock, discarding the
trimmings, onion and herbs. You will
need 1 litre of stock.
2 Skim any fat from the stock. Place the
lentils in a large saucepan, add the stock
and 1 litre water. Bring to the boil, then
reduce the heat and simmer, covered, for
1 hour.
3 Meanwhile, remove the stems from the
silverbeet and shred the leaves. Heat the
oil in a saucepan over medium heat and
cook the onion for 2–3 minutes, or until
transparent. Add the garlic and cook for
1 minute. Add the silverbeet and toss for
2–3 minutes, or until wilted. Stir the
mixture into the lentils. Add the coriander
and lemon juice, season, and simmer,
covered, for 15–20 minutes. Serve with
the lemon wedges.

CLEAR SOUP WITH SALMON QUENELLES

Preparation time: 20 minutes
Total cooking time: 25 minutes
Serves 6

400 g (13 oz) salmon cutlets
1 litre (32 fl oz) fish stock
½ cup (125 ml/4 fl oz) dry white wine
2 teaspoons lemon juice
1 small carrot, finely chopped
2 spring onions, sliced
2 sprigs fresh dill
2 sprigs fresh parsley
3 black peppercorns
1 egg white, well chilled
½ cup (125 ml/4 fl oz) cream, well chilled
2 tablespoons fresh chervil leaves

1 Remove the skin and bones from the
salmon and set aside. For the quenelles,
weigh 150 g (5 oz) of the fish, chop
roughly, cover and chill well. For the
soup, in a large pan, combine the skin and
bones with the remaining salmon, fish
stock, wine, lemon juice, carrot, spring
onion, dill, parsley and peppercorns. Slowly
bring to the boil, then reduce the heat,
cover and simmer for 15 minutes. Strain
and discard the vegetables. (You won't be
using the cooked salmon for this recipe, but
you can use it as a sandwich filling.)
2 Pour the soup into a clean pan, bring to
the boil, then reduce the heat to just
simmering. Season, to taste.
3 To make the quenelles, process the
reserved salmon in a food processor until
finely chopped. Gradually add the egg white
and process until smooth. Transfer to a
chilled bowl and season well with salt and
ground white pepper. Whip the cream and
quickly fold into the salmon. Shape
quenelles using 2 teaspoons dipped in cold
water. Add to the soup in two batches and
poach for 2 minutes, or until cooked.
Transfer the quenelles to warm soup bowls.
4 Heat the soup to almost boiling and
carefully ladle over the quenelles. Sprinkle
with chervil leaves and serve.

CHINESE NOODLE SOUP

Preparation time: 30 minutes
Total cooking time: 15 minutes
Serves 6

300 g (10 oz) pork mince
4 spring onions, sliced
3 cloves garlic, roughly chopped
2 teaspoons grated fresh ginger
2 teaspoons cornflour
110 ml (3½ fl oz) light soy sauce
¼ cup (60 ml/2 fl oz) Chinese rice wine
30 won ton wrappers
 2.25 litres (70 fl oz) stock diluted with 3
  cups (750 ml/24 fl oz) water
20 g (¾ oz) fresh ginger, thinly sliced
200 g (6½ oz) dried flat egg noodles
2 spring onions, extra, sliced diagonally
1 teaspoon sesame oil

1 Put the mince, spring onion, garlic, ginger, cornflour, 1½ tablespoons of the soy sauce and 1 tablespoon of the rice wine in a food processor and process until combined.
2 Place 2 teaspoons of the mixture in the centre of a won ton wrapper and brush the edges with water. Lift sides up tightly and pinch around the filling to form a pouch. Repeat with the remaining wrappers.
3 Pour the chicken stock into a large wok, add the ginger and bring to a simmer over medium–high heat. Stir in the remaining soy sauce and wine.
4 Meanwhile, bring a large saucepan of water to the boil. Reduce the heat, add the won tons and simmer for 1 minute, or until they float to the surface. Remove the won tons with a slotted spoon and set aside. Return the water to the boil, add the egg noodles and cook for 3 minutes, or until just tender. Drain and rinse.
5 Remove the ginger slices from the broth, then add the won tons and simmer for 2 minutes, or until they float to the top and are heated through. Add the noodles to the soup to reheat.
6 Divide the soup and won tons among six large serving bowls, sprinkle with extra spring onion and drizzle with sesame oil.

SPICY CHICKEN BROTH WITH CORIANDER PASTA

Preparation time: 1 hour
Total cooking time: 50 minutes
Serves 4

350 g (11 oz) chicken thighs or wings, skin
  removed
2 carrots, finely chopped
2 celery sticks, finely chopped
2 small leeks, finely chopped
3 egg whites
6 cups (1.5 litres) chicken stock
Tabasco sauce

Coriander pasta
½ cup (60 g/2 oz) plain flour
1 egg
½ teaspoon sesame oil
90 g (3 oz) coriander leaves

1 Put the chicken pieces, carrot, celery and leek in a large heavy-based pan. Push the chicken to one side and add the egg whites to the vegetables. Using a wire whisk, beat for a minute or so, until frothy (take care not to use a pan that can be scratched by the whisk).
2 Warm the stock in another pan, then add gradually to the first pan, whisking continuously to froth the egg whites. Continue whisking while slowly bringing to the boil. Make a hole in the froth on top with a spoon and leave to simmer for 30 minutes, without stirring.
3 Line a large strainer with a damp tea towel or double thickness of muslin and strain the broth into a clean bowl (discard the chicken and vegetables). Season with salt, pepper and Tabasco sauce, to taste. Set aside until you are ready to serve.

4 To make the coriander pasta, sift the flour into a bowl and make a well in the centre. Whisk the egg and oil together and pour into the well. Mix together to make a soft pasta dough and knead on a lightly floured surface for 2 minutes, until smooth.
5 Divide the pasta dough into four even portions. Roll one portion out very thinly and cover with a layer of evenly spaced coriander leaves. Roll out another portion of pasta and lay this on top of the leaves, then gently roll the layers together. Repeat with the remaining pasta and coriander.
6 Cut out squares of pasta around the leaves. The pasta may then be left to sit and dry out if it is not needed immediately. When you are ready to serve, heat the chicken broth gently in a pan. As the broth simmers, add the pasta and cook for 1 minute. Serve immediately.

NOTE: The egg whites added to the vegetable and chicken stock make the broth very clear, rather than leaving it with the normal cloudy appearance of chicken stock. This is called clarifying the stock. When you strain the broth through muslin or a tea towel, don't press the solids to extract the extra liquid or the broth will become cloudy. It is necessary to make a hole in the froth on top to prevent the stock boiling over.

TOM KHA GAI
(CHICKEN AND GALANGAL SOUP)

Preparation time: 20 minutes
Total cooking time: 20 minutes
Serves 4

5 cm (2 inch) piece fresh galangal
2 cups (500 ml/16 fl oz) coconut milk
1 cup (250 ml/8 fl oz) chicken stock
600 g (1¼ lb) chicken breast fillets, cut
   into thin strips
1–2 teaspoons finely chopped red chilli
2 tablespoons fish sauce
1 teaspoon soft brown sugar
¼ cup (7 g/¼ oz) fresh coriander leaves

1 Cut the galangal into thin slices.
Combine the galangal, coconut milk and
stock in a medium pan. Bring to the boil,
then reduce the heat and simmer over
low heat for 10 minutes, stirring
occasionally.
2 Add the chicken and chilli to the pan and
simmer for 8 minutes. Add the fish sauce
and sugar and stir to combine.
3 Add the coriander leaves and serve
immediately, garnished with extra sprigs
of coriander if you like.

BOURRIDE
(GARLIC SEAFOOD SOUP)

Preparation time: 25 minutes
Total cooking time: 1 hour 10 minutes
Serves 8

1 tablespoon butter
1 tablespoon olive oil
4 slices good white bread, trimmed of
   crusts and cut into 1.5 cm (⅝ inch) cubes
2 kg (4 lb) white-fleshed whole fish
   (preferably three varieties, in any
   proportion, such as bass, whiting, cod,
   flounder)
1 quantity aïoli (see page 741)
3 egg yolks

Stock
⅓ cup (80 ml/2¾ fl oz) olive oil
1 large onion, chopped
1 carrot, sliced
1 leek, white part only, chopped
1⅔ cups (410 ml/13 fl oz) dry white wine
1 teaspoon dried fennel seed
2 cloves garlic, bruised
2 bay leaves
1 large strip orange peel
2 sprigs of fresh thyme

1 Heat the butter and oil in a heavy-based
frying pan. When the butter begins to
foam, add the bread cubes and cook for
5 minutes, or until golden. Drain on
crumpled paper towels.
2 Fillet the fish (or ask your fishmonger to
do it), reserving the heads and bones for
the stock.
3 For the stock, heat the olive oil in large
saucepan or stockpot and add the onion,
carrot and leek. Cook over low heat for

12–15 minutes, until the vegetables are
soft. Add the fish heads and bones, wine,
fennel seed, garlic, bay leaves, orange
peel, thyme, black pepper and ½ teaspoon
salt. Cover with 2 litres water. Bring to the
boil and skim off the froth. Reduce the
heat and simmer for 30 minutes. Strain
into a pot, crushing the bones well to
release as much flavour as possible.
Return to the stove.
4 Cut the fish fillets into large pieces
about 9 cm (3½ inches) long. Add them to
the stock and slowly bring to simmering
point, putting the heavier pieces in first
and adding the more delicate pieces later.
Poach for 6–8 minutes, until the flesh
starts to become translucent and begins
to flake easily. Transfer the fish pieces to
a serving platter and moisten with a little
stock. Cover with foil and keep warm in a
low oven.
5 Place 8 tablespoons of the aïoli in a
large bowl and slowly add the egg yolks,
stirring constantly. Ladle a little stock
into the aïoli mixture, blend well and
return slowly to the rest of the stock and
cook over very low heat. Stir continuously
with a wooden spoon for 8–10 minutes, or
until the soup has thickened and coats the
back of a spoon. Do not boil or the
mixture will curdle.
6 Serve the croutons in the soup and the
fish and the remaining aïoli separately.

BROCCOLI SOUP

Preparation time: 15 minutes
Total cooking time: 20 minutes
Serves 4

2 tablespoons olive oil
1 large onion, thinly sliced
50 g (1¾ oz) diced prosciutto or
  unsmoked ham
1 clove garlic, crushed
5 cups (1.25 litres) chicken stock
50 g (1¾ oz) stellini or other miniature
  pasta shapes
250 g (8 oz) broccoli, tops cut into small
  florets and the tender stems julienned
freshly grated Parmesan, for serving

1 Heat the oil in a large pan over low heat,
add the onion, prosciutto and garlic and
cook for 4–5 minutes.
2 Pour in the chicken stock, bring to the
boil, reduce the heat slightly and simmer
for 10 minutes with the lid three-quarters
on.
3 Add the stellini and broccoli and cook
until the pasta is al dente and the broccoli
is crisp but tender. Season, to taste, with
salt and freshly ground black pepper.
Serve in warm bowls with the grated
Parmesan.

PUMPKIN, PRAWN AND COCONUT SOUP

Preparation time: 15 minutes
Total cooking time: 20 minutes
Serves 4–6

500 g (1 lb) pumpkin, diced
4 tablespoons lime juice
1 kg (2 lb) raw large prawns
2 onions, chopped
1 small fresh red chilli, finely chopped
1 stem lemon grass, white part only,
  chopped
1 teaspoon shrimp paste
1 teaspoon sugar
1½ cups (375 ml/12 fl oz) coconut milk
1 teaspoon tamarind purée
½ cup (125 ml/4 fl oz) coconut cream
1 tablespoon fish sauce
2 tablespoons fresh Thai basil leaves

1 Combine the pumpkin with half the lime
juice in a bowl. Peel the prawns and pull
out the dark vein from each back, starting
at the head end.
2 Process the onion, chilli, lemon grass,
shrimp paste, sugar and 3 tablespoons of
the coconut milk in a food processor until
a paste forms.
3 Combine the paste with the remaining
coconut milk, tamarind purée and 1 cup
(250 ml/8 fl oz) water in a large pan and
stir until smooth. Add the pumpkin with
the lime juice to the pan and bring to the
boil. Reduce the heat and simmer,
covered, for about 10 minutes or until the
pumpkin is just tender.
4 Add the raw prawns and coconut
cream, then simmer for 3 minutes, or
until the prawns are just pink and cooked
through. Stir in the fish sauce, the
remaining lime juice and the Thai basil
leaves. Pour the soup into warmed bowls
and garnish with Thai basil leaves or
sprigs.

YOGHURT SOUP

Preparation time: 15 minutes
Total cooking time: 20 minutes
Serves 4–6

1.5 litres vegetable stock
⅓ cup (75 g/2¼ oz) short-grain white rice
80 g (2¾ oz) butter
50 g (1¾ oz) plain flour
250 g (8 oz) natural yoghurt
1 egg yolk
1 tablespoon finely sliced fresh mint
¼ teaspoon cayenne pepper

1 Put the stock and rice in a saucepan and
bring to the boil over high heat. Reduce
the heat to medium-low and simmer for
10 minutes, then remove from the heat
and set aside.
2 In another saucepan, melt 60 g (2 oz) of
the butter over low heat. Stir in the flour
and cook for 2–3 minutes, or until pale
and foaming. Gradually add the stock and
rice mixture, stirring constantly, and cook
over medium heat for 2 minutes, or until
the mixture thickens slightly. Reduce the
heat to low.
3 In a small bowl, whisk together the
yoghurt and egg yolk, then gradually pour
into the soup, stirring constantly. Remove
from the heat and stir in the mint and ½
teaspoon salt.
4 Just before serving, melt the remaining
butter in a small saucepan over medium
heat. Add the cayenne pepper and cook
until the mixture is lightly browned. Pour
over the soup.

ITALIAN TOMATO BREAD SOUP

Preparation time: 25 minutes
Total cooking time: 25 minutes
Serves 4

750 g (1½ lb) vine-ripened tomatoes
1 loaf (450 g/14 oz) day-old crusty Italian
  bread
1 tablespoon olive oil
3 cloves garlic, crushed
1 tablespoon tomato paste (tomato purée)
1.25 litres hot vegetable stock or water
⅓ cup (20 g/¾ oz) torn fresh basil leaves
2–3 tablespoons extra virgin olive oil
extra virgin olive oil, extra, for serving

1 Score a cross in the base of each
tomato. Place the tomatoes in a bowl of
boiling water for 10 seconds, then plunge
into cold water and peel the skin away
from the cross. Cut the tomatoes in half
and scoop out the seeds with a teaspoon.
Roughly chop the tomato flesh.
2 Discard most of the crust from the
bread and tear the bread into 3 cm (1¼
inch) pieces.
3 Heat the oil in a large saucepan. Add the
garlic, tomato and tomato paste, then
reduce the heat and simmer, stirring
occasionally, for 10–15 minutes, or until
reduced. Add the stock and bring to the
boil, stirring for 2–3 minutes. Reduce the
heat to medium, add the bread pieces and
cook, stirring, for 5 minutes, or until the
bread softens and absorbs most of the
liquid. Add more stock or water if the
soup is too thick. Remove the saucepan
from the heat.
4 Stir in the basil leaves and extra virgin
olive oil, and leave for 5 minutes so the
flavours have time to develop. Serve
drizzled with a little extra virgin olive oil.

TOFU MISO SOUP

Preparation time: 15 minutes
Total cooking time: 7 minutes
Serves 4

250 g (8 oz) firm tofu
1 spring onion
4 cups (1 litre) water
½ cup (80 g/2⅔ oz) dashi granules
100 g (3⅓ oz) miso
1 tablespoon mirin

1 Use a sharp knife to cut the tofu into 1
cm (½ inch) cubes. Slice the spring onion
diagonally into 1 cm (½ inch) lengths.
2 Using a wooden spoon, combine the
water and dashi granules in a small pan,
then bring the mixture to the boil.
3 Reduce the heat to medium, add the
miso and mirin and stir to combine, being
careful the mixture does not boil
(overheating will result in the loss of miso
flavour). Add the tofu cubes to the hot
stock and heat, without boiling, over
medium heat for 5 minutes, until the tofu
is warmed through. Serve in individual
soup bowls, garnished with the spring
onion.

THAI LEMON GRASS BROTH WITH MUSSELS

Preparation time: 20 minutes
Total cooking time: 25 minutes
Serves 4

1.5 kg (3 lb) black mussels, scrubbed and
  debearded
1 tablespoon vegetable oil
5 spring onions, thinly sliced on the
  diagonal
2 cloves garlic, crushed
3 cups (750 ml/24 fl oz) good-quality
  chicken or fish stock (see Notes)
2½ tablespoons sliced fresh galangal or
  ginger
4 stems lemon grass, white part only,
  bruised
2 long fresh red chillies, halved
  lengthways
6 fresh kaffir lime leaves, crushed
2 tablespoons roughly chopped fresh
  coriander leaves

1 Discard any broken mussels, or open
ones that don't close when tapped on the
bench. Rinse them well.
2 Heat a wok over medium heat, add the
oil and swirl to coat the side of the wok.
Cook the spring onion and garlic for
1 minute, or until softened. Add the stock,
galangal, lemon grass, chilli, lime leaves
and 3 cups (750 ml/24 fl oz) water and
rapidly simmer for 15 minutes.
3 Add the mussels, cover with a lid, bring
to the boil over high heat and cook for
7–8 minutes, or until the mussels open,
tossing occasionally. Discard any
unopened mussels.
4 Stir in half the coriander, then divide the
broth and mussels among four large
serving bowls. Sprinkle with the
remaining coriander, then serve
immediately.

PRAWN BISQUE

Preparation time: 25 minutes
Total cooking time: 15–20 minutes
Serves 4–6

500 g (1 lb) raw medium prawns
60 g (2 oz) butter
2 tablespoons plain flour
2 litres (64 fl oz) fish stock
½ teaspoon paprika
1 cup (250 ml/8 fl oz) cream
⅓ cup (80 ml/2¾ fl oz) dry sherry
1–2 tablespoons cream, extra, for serving
paprika, extra, to garnish

1 Peel the prawns and gently pull out the dark vein from each prawn back, starting at the head end. Reserve the heads and shells. Heat the butter in a pan, add the prawn heads and shells and cook, stirring, over medium heat for 5 minutes, lightly crushing the heads with a wooden spoon.
2 Add the flour to the pan and stir until combined. Add the fish stock and paprika and stir over the heat until the mixture boils. Reduce the heat and simmer, covered, over low heat for 10 minutes. Strain the mixture through a fine sieve set over a bowl, then return the liquid to the pan. Add the prawns and cook over low heat for 2–3 minutes. Allow to cool slightly, then process in batches in a blender or food processor until smooth. Return the mixture to the pan.
3 Add the cream and sherry to the pan and stir to heat through. Season, to taste, with salt and freshly ground black pepper. Serve topped with a swirl of cream and sprinkled with paprika.
Note: The prawn heads and shells give the bisque its rich flavour. A few of the small cooked prawns can be reserved for garnishing.

SZECHWAN SOUP

Preparation time: 20 minutes +
  40 minutes soaking
Total cooking time: 15 minutes
Serves 6–8

4 dried Chinese mushrooms
45 g (1½ oz) thick dried rice stick noodles
4 cups (1 litre) chicken stock
1 cup (175 g/5⅔ oz) chopped cooked chicken
230 g (7⅓ oz) can bamboo shoots, drained and chopped
1 teaspoon grated fresh ginger
1 tablespoon cornflour
⅓ cup (80 ml/2¾ oz) water
1 egg, lightly beaten
1 teaspoon tomato sauce
1 tablespoon soy sauce
1 tablespoon vinegar
2 teaspoons sesame oil
2 spring onions, finely chopped

1 Cover the mushrooms with hot water and soak for 20 minutes; drain thoroughly and chop. Soak the noodles in hot water for 20 minutes; drain and cut into short lengths.
2 Heat the stock in a large pan and bring to the boil. Add the mushrooms, noodles, chicken, bamboo shoots and ginger. Reduce the heat and simmer gently.
3 Combine the cornflour and water in a small bowl and mix to a smooth paste. Add the cornflour mixture to the soup and stir until clear. Add the egg to the soup in a fine stream, stirring the mixture constantly.
4 Remove the pan from the heat. Add the tomato sauce, soy sauce, vinegar, sesame oil and spring onion. Season with salt and black pepper to taste. Serve topped with extra spring onion, if desired.

FIVE-SPICE DUCK AND SOMEN NOODLE SOUP

Preparation time: 10 minutes
Total cooking time: 30 minutes
Serves 4

4 duck breasts, skin on
1 teaspoon five-spice powder
1 teaspoon peanut oil
200 g (6½ oz) dried somen noodles

Star anise broth
2 litres (64 fl oz) good-quality chicken stock
3 star anise
5 spring onions, chopped
3 tablespoons chopped fresh coriander leaves

1 Preheat the oven to moderately hot 200°C (400°F/Gas 6). Trim the duck breast of excess fat, then lightly sprinkle both sides with the five-spice powder.
2 Heat a wok over high heat, add the oil and swirl to coat the side of the wok. Add the duck breasts, skin-side down, and cook over medium heat for 2–3 minutes, or until browned and crisp. Turn and cook the other side for 3 minutes. Transfer to a baking tray and roast, skin-side-up, for a further 8 minutes for medium–rare, or until cooked to your liking.
3 Meanwhile, put the chicken stock and star anise in a clean non-stick wok. Bring to the boil, then reduce the heat and simmer, covered, for 5 minutes. Add the spring onion and coriander and simmer for a further 5 minutes.
4 Cook the noodles in a saucepan of boiling water for 2 minutes, or until tender. Drain and divide among four large bowls. Ladle the broth on the noodles and top each bowl with one sliced duck breast.

WILD RICE SOUP

Preparation time: 15 minutes
Total cooking time: 1 hour
Serves 6

½ cup (95 g/3 oz) wild rice
1 tablespoon oil
1 onion, finely chopped
2 celery stalks, finely chopped
1 green capsicum (pepper), finely
   chopped
4 back bacon rashers, finely chopped
4 open cap mushrooms, thinly sliced
1 litre (32 fl oz) chicken stock
½ cup (125 ml/4 fl oz) cream
1 tablespoon finely chopped parsley

1 Put the wild rice in a saucepan with
plenty of water and bring to the boil. Cook
for 40 minutes, or until the rice is tender.
Drain.
2 Heat the oil in a large saucepan and add
the onion, celery, capsicum and bacon.
Fry for 8 minutes, or until the onion has
softened and the bacon browned. Add the
mushroom and cook for 1–2 minutes.
Pour in the chicken stock and bring to the
boil, then add the rice, stir and cook the
mixture for 2 minutes. Remove the pan
from the heat.
3 Stir in the cream and parsley, then
reheat until the soup is almost boiling.
Serve in deep bowls with bread.

LEEK AND POTATO SOUP

Preparation time: 20 minutes
Total cooking time: 45 minutes
Serves 4

cooking oil spray
2 leeks, white part only, sliced
3 cloves garlic, crushed
1 teaspoon ground cumin
1 kg (2 lb) potatoes, chopped
5 cups (1.25 litres) vegetable stock
½ cup (125 ml/4 fl oz) skim milk

1 Lightly spray a non-stick frying pan
with oil. Add the leek, garlic and
1 tablespoon water to prevent sticking,
then cook over low heat, stirring
frequently, for 25 minutes, or until the
leek turns golden. Add the cumin and
cook for 2 minutes.
2 Put the potato in a large pan with the
leek mixture and stock, bring to the boil,
reduce the heat and simmer for 10–15
minutes, or until tender. Purée in a
processor or blender until smooth.
Return to the pan.
3 Stir in the milk, season and heat
through before serving.

PIE-CRUST MUSHROOM
SOUP

Preparation time: 25 minutes
Total cooking time: 35 minutes
Serves 4

400 g (13 oz) large field mushrooms
60 g (2 oz) butter
1 onion, finely chopped
1 clove garlic, crushed
¼ cup (30 g/1 oz) plain flour
3 cups (750 ml/24 fl oz) chicken stock
2 tablespoons fresh thyme leaves
2 tablespoons sherry
1 cup (250 ml/8 fl oz) cream
1 sheet frozen puff pastry, thawed
1 egg, lightly beaten

1 Preheat the oven to moderately hot
200°C (400°F/Gas 6). Peel and roughly
chop the mushrooms, including the
stems. Melt the butter in a large
saucepan, add the onion and cook over
medium heat for 3 minutes, or until soft.
Add the garlic and cook for another
minute. Add the mushrooms and cook
until soft. Sprinkle with the flour and stir
for 1 minute.
2 Stir in the stock and thyme and bring to
the boil. Reduce the heat and simmer,
covered, for 10 minutes. Cool before
processing in batches. Return the soup to
the pan, stir in the sherry and cream, then
pour into 4 ovenproof bowls (use small
deep bowls rather than wide shallow
ones, or the pastry may sag into the
soup).
3 Cut rounds of pastry slightly larger than
the bowl tops and cover each bowl with
pastry. Seal the pastry edges and brush
lightly with the egg. Place the bowls on a
baking tray and bake for 15 minutes, or
until golden and puffed.

LAMB AND FUSILLI SOUP

Preparation time: 25 minutes
Total cooking time: 40 minutes
Serves 6–8

500 g (1 lb) lean lamb meat, cut into
   cubes
2 onions, finely chopped
2 carrots, diced
4 celery sticks, diced
425 g (14 oz) can crushed tomatoes
8 cups (2 litres) beef stock
500 g (1 lb) fusilli
chopped fresh parsley, for serving

1 Heat a little oil in a large pan and cook
the cubed lamb, in batches, until golden
brown. Remove each batch as it is done
and drain on paper towels. Add the onion
to the pan and cook for 2 minutes or until
softened. Return the meat to the pan.
2 Add the carrot, celery, tomato, and beef
stock. Stir to combine and bring
to the boil. Reduce the heat to low and
simmer, covered, for 15 minutes.
3 Add the fusilli to the pan. Stir briefly
to prevent the pasta from sticking to the
pan. Simmer, uncovered, for another
10 minutes or until the lamb and pasta are
tender. Sprinkle with chopped fresh
parsley before serving.

HOT AND SOUR LIME SOUP WITH BEEF

Preparation time: 20 minutes
Total cooking time: 35 minutes
Serves 4

1 litre beef stock
2 stems lemon grass, white part only,
   halved
3 cloves garlic, halved
2.5 cm x 2.5 cm (1 inch x 1 inch) piece
   fresh ginger, sliced
95 g (3 oz) fresh coriander, leaves and
   stalks separated
2 1.5 cm x 4 cm (5/8 inch x 1½ inch) strips
   lime rind
2 star anise
3 small fresh red chillies, seeded and
   finely chopped
4 spring onions, thinly sliced on the
   diagonal
500 g (1 lb) fillet steak, trimmed
2 tablespoons fish sauce
1 tablespoon grated palm sugar
2 tablespoons lime juice
fresh coriander leaves, extra, to garnish

1 Place stock, lemon grass, garlic, ginger,
coriander stalks, rind, star anise, 1 teaspoon
chopped chilli, half the spring onion, and 1
litre water in a saucepan. Bring to the boil
and simmer, covered, for 25 minutes.
Strain and return the liquid to the pan.
2 Heat a chargrill pan until very hot.
Brush with olive oil and sear the steak on
both sides until browned on the outside,
but very rare in the centre.
3 Reheat soup, adding the fish sauce and
palm sugar. Season and add the lime
juice to taste (you may want more than 2
tablespoons)—you should achieve a hot
and sour flavour.
4 Add the remaining spring onion and the
chopped coriander leaves to the soup.
Slice the beef across the grain into thin
strips. Curl the strips into a decorative
pattern, then place in four deep serving
bowls. Pour the soup over the beef and
garnish with the chilli and coriander.

SPICY TOMATO AND PEA SOUP

Preparation time: 15 minutes
Total cooking time: 20–25 minutes
Serves 6

5 large very ripe tomatoes, chopped
2 cups (500 ml/16 fl oz) water
2 tablespoons ghee or butter
1 large onion, thinly sliced
1 clove garlic, crushed
2 teaspoons ground coriander
2 teaspoons ground cumin
½ teaspoon fennel seeds
2 bay leaves
1 green chilli, seeded and sliced
1½ cups (375 ml/12 fl oz) coconut cream
1½ cups (240 g/7½ oz) frozen peas
1 tablespoon sugar
1 tablespoon chopped fresh mint

1 Simmer the tomato in the water until
very tender, then blend the tomato and
water in a food processor.
2 Heat the ghee in a large pan; add the
onion and garlic and cook over medium
heat until very soft. Add the coriander,
cumin, fennel seeds, bay leaves and chilli,
and cook, stirring, for 1 minute.
3 Add the coconut cream and the puréed
tomatoes, and bring to the boil. Reduce
the heat, add the peas and cook until
tender. Remove the bay leaves, add the
sugar and mint, and season with freshly
ground pepper to taste. Serve with hot
toasted chapattis brushed with ghee.

MINESTRONE WITH PESTO

Preparation time: 25 minutes +
  overnight soaking
Total cooking time: 2 hours
Serves 6

125 g (4 oz) dried borlotti beans
¼ cup (60 ml/2 fl oz) olive oil
1 large onion, finely chopped
2 cloves garlic, crushed
60 g (3 oz) pancetta, finely chopped
1 stick celery, halved lengthways, then
  cut into 1 cm (½ inch) slices
1 carrot, halved lengthways, then cut into
  1 cm (½ inch) slices
1 potato, diced
2 teaspoons tomato paste (tomato purée)
400 g (13 oz) can good-quality crushed
  tomatoes
6 fresh basil leaves, roughly torn
2 litres chicken or vegetable stock
2 thin zucchini (courgettes), cut into
  1.5 cm (5/8 inch) slices
¾ cup (115 g/4 oz) shelled fresh peas
60 g (2 oz) green beans, cut into short
  lengths
80 g (2¾ oz) silverbeet (Swiss chard)
  leaves, shredded
3 tablespoons chopped fresh flat-leaf
  parsley
75 g (2½ oz) ditalini or other small pasta

Pesto

1 cup (30 g/1 oz) fresh basil leaves
20 g (¾ oz) lightly toasted pine nuts
2 cloves garlic
100 ml (3½ fl oz) olive oil
¼ cup (25 g/¾ oz) grated Parmesan

1 Soak the borlotti beans in plenty of cold water overnight. Drain and rinse thoroughly under cold water.
2 Heat the oil in a large deep saucepan, add the onion, garlic and pancetta and cook over low heat, stirring occasionally, for 8–10 minutes, until softened.
3 Add the celery, carrot and potato to the saucepan and cook for 5 minutes. Stir in the tomato paste, tomato, basil and drained borlotti beans. Season, to taste, with freshly ground black pepper. Add the stock and bring slowly to the boil. Cover and simmer, stirring occasionally, for 1 hour 30 minutes.
4 Add the remaining vegetables, parsley and the pasta. Simmer for 8–10 minutes, or until the vegetables and pasta are al dente. Check for seasoning and adjust if necessary.
5 For the pesto, combine the fresh basil, pine nuts and garlic with a pinch of salt in a food processor. Process until finely chopped. With the motor running, slowing add the olive oil. Transfer to a bowl and stir in the Parmesan and ground black pepper, to taste. Spoon on top of the soup.

CORN AND CRAB SOUP WITH CORIANDER

Preparation time: 15 minutes
Total cooking time: 10 minutes
Serves 4

1½ tablespoons oil
6 cloves garlic, chopped
6 Asian shallots, chopped
2 stems lemon grass, white part only,
  chopped
1 tablespoon grated fresh ginger
1 litre (32 fl oz) chicken stock
1 cup (250 ml/8 fl oz) coconut milk
2½ cups (375 g/12 oz) frozen corn kernels
2 x 170 g (5½ oz) cans crab meat, drained
2 tablespoons fish sauce
2 tablespoons lime juice
1 teaspoon grated palm sugar or brown
  sugar
fresh coriander leaves, to garnish

1 Heat the oil in a large pan. Add the chopped garlic, Asian shallots, lemon grass and grated ginger to the pan and stir over medium heat for 2 minutes.
2 Add the stock and coconut milk to the pan and bring to the boil. Add the corn and cook for 5 minutes.
3 Add the crab meat, fish sauce, lime juice and sugar to the pan and stir. Season with salt and pepper and serve immediately, topped with coriander leaves, and sliced chillies if you like.

NOTES: For a variation, 2 eggs, beaten with 2 tablespoons of water, can be whisked into the soup before serving.
  Red-skinned Asian shallots grow like garlic, in a clump. They are used extensively in Southeast Asian cookery.

SICHUAN BEEF NOODLE SOUP

Preparation time: 10 minutes
Total cooking time: 3 hours
Serves 4

1.5 litres (48 fl oz) good-quality beef stock
1 tablespoon peanut oil
400 g (13 oz) piece chuck steak
½ cinnamon stick
2 star anise
1½ teaspoons Sichuan peppercorns, crushed
1 tablespoon julienned fresh ginger
2 tablespoons dark soy sauce
1 tablespoon Chinese rice wine
1 tablespoon brown bean sauce
3 x 5 cm (1¼ x 2 inch) piece dried mandarin peel
125 g (4 oz) fresh thin egg noodles
3 spring onions, thinly sliced on the diagonal

1 Pour the beef stock and 2 litres (64 fl oz) water into a stockpot and simmer over low heat; keep warm until needed.
2 Heat a wok over high heat, add the oil and swirl to coat. Add the steak and sear it for 2–3 minutes on each side. Add the cinnamon stick, star anise, peppercorns, ginger, soy sauce, rice wine, bean sauce and mandarin peel. Pour in the hot broth, then cover and bring to simmering point over medium heat. Reduce the heat to low and simmer, covered, for 2–2½ hours, or until the steak is tender—you should be able to shred it; if not, return to the simmer until tender.
3 Remove the steak and discard the mandarin peel. Meanwhile, cook the noodles in a large saucepan of boiling water for 1 minute to separate them. Drain. Just before serving, add the noodles to the broth and let them stand for 1–2 minutes, or until heated through. Shred the steak into bite-sized pieces and divide evenly among four large serving bowls. Ladle on the broth and noodles, sprinkle with spring onion and serve.

SPINACH AND LENTIL SOUP

Preparation time: 10 minutes
Total cooking time: 1 hour 25 minutes
Serves 4–6

2 cups (370 g/11¾ oz) brown lentils
5 cups (1.25 litres) water
2 teaspoons olive oil
1 medium onion, finely chopped
2 cloves garlic, crushed
20 English spinach leaves, stalks removed and leaves finely shredded
1 teaspoon ground cumin
1 teaspoon finely grated lemon rind
2 cups (500 ml/16 fl oz) vegetable stock
2 cups (500 ml/16 fl oz) water
2 tablespoons finely chopped fresh coriander

1 Place the lentils in a large pan with water. Bring to the boil and then simmer, uncovered, for 1 hour. Rinse and drain, then set aside. In a separate pan heat the oil; add the onion and garlic. Cook over medium heat until golden. Add spinach and cook for another 2 minutes.
2 Add the lentils, cumin, lemon rind, stock and water to the pan. Simmer, uncovered, for 15 minutes. Add the coriander and stir through. Serve immediately.

RED PEPPER (CAPSICUM) SOUP

Preparation time: 20 minutes
Total cooking time: 30 minutes
Serves 6

4 medium red peppers (capsicums)
4 medium tomatoes
¼ cup (60 ml/2 fl oz) oil
½ teaspoon dried marjoram
½ teaspoon dried mixed herbs
2 cloves garlic, crushed
1 teaspoon mild curry paste
1 medium red (Spanish) onion, sliced
1 medium leek, sliced (white part only)
250 g (8 oz) green cabbage, chopped
4 cups (1 litre) water
1 teaspoon sweet chilli sauce
salt and freshly ground black pepper

1 Cut the red peppers into quarters. Remove the seeds and membrane. Grill until the skin blackens and blisters. Place on a cutting board, cover with a tea towel and allow to cool before peeling. Mark a small cross on the top of each tomato. Place in a bowl and cover with boiling water for about 2 minutes. Drain and cool. Peel skin off downwards from the cross and discard. Cut the tomatoes in half and gently scoop out the seeds using a small spoon.
2 Heat the oil in a large pan; add the herbs, garlic and curry paste. Stir over low heat for 1 minute, or until aromatic. Add the onion and leek and cook for 3 minutes or until golden. Add the cabbage, tomatoes, red peppers and water. Bring to the boil, reduce heat and simmer for 20 minutes. Remove from the heat; allow to cool slightly.
3 Place the soup in small batches in a food processor bowl. Process for 30 seconds or until smooth. Return the soup to a clean pan, stir through chilli sauce and season with salt and pepper. Reheat gently and serve hot.

BOUILLABAISSE WITH ROUILLE

Preparation time: 35 minutes soaking
Total cooking time: 1 hour 10 minutes
Serves 6

500 g (1 lb) ripe tomatoes
3 tablespoons olive oil
1 large onion, chopped
2 leeks, sliced
4 cloves garlic, crushed
1–2 tablespoons tomato paste (tomato
    purée)
6 sprigs fresh flat-leaf parsley
2 fresh bay leaves
2 sprigs of fresh thyme
1 sprig of fresh fennel
2 pinches of saffron threads
2 kg (4 lb) fish trimmings (such as heads,
    bones, shellfish remains, etc.)
1 tablespoon Pernod or Ricard
4 potatoes, cut into 1.5 cm (⅝ inch) slices
1.5 kg (3 lb) mixed fish fillets and steaks
    (such as rascasse, snapper, red fish,
    blue eye and bream), cut into large
    chunks (see Note)
2 tablespoons chopped fresh flat-leaf
    parsley

Toasts
12 slices of baguette
2 large cloves garlic, sliced in half

Rouille
3 slices white bread, crusts removed
1 red pepper (capsicum), seeded, cut into
    quarters
1 small red chilli, seeded, chopped
3 cloves garlic, crushed
1 tablespoon shredded fresh basil
⅓ cup (80 ml/23/ 4 fl oz) olive oil

1 Score a cross in the base of each
tomato and place the tomatoes in boiling
water for 10 seconds, then plunge into
cold water and peel away from the cross.
Roughly chop
the flesh.
2 Heat the oil in a large saucepan over
medium heat, add the onion and leek and
cook for 5 minutes without browning. Add
the garlic, tomato and 1 tablespoon
tomato paste, reduce the heat and
simmer for 5 minutes. Stir in 2 litres cold
water, then add the parsley, bay leaves,
thyme, fennel, saffron and fish
trimmings. Bring to the boil, then reduce
the heat and simmer for 30 minutes.
Strain into a large saucepan, pressing the
juices out of the ingredients.

EIGHT TREASURE SOUP

Preparation time: 15 minutes +
    20 minutes soaking
Total cooking time: 1 hour
Serves 4–6

4 dried shiitake mushrooms
1 tablespoon vegetable oil
1 teaspoon sesame oil
2 teaspoons finely chopped fresh ginger
1 tablespoon finely chopped spring onion
60 g (2 oz) Chinese bacon or ham, cut into
    thin strips (see Note)
1 litre (32 fl oz) good-quality chicken stock
1 tablespoon soy sauce
1 tablespoon rice wine
250 g (8 oz) chicken breast fillet
1 carrot, cut into 1 cm (½ inch) slices
12 small raw prawns, peeled and
    deveined
200 g (6½ oz) firm tofu, cut into 2 cm
    (¾ inch) cubes
50 g (1¾ oz) sliced bamboo shoots
100 g (3½ oz) English spinach, chopped
2 spring onions, thinly sliced on the
    diagonal, extra

1 Soak the mushrooms in ½ cup (125 ml/ 4
fl oz) boiling water for 20 minutes.
Squeeze dry, reserving the soaking liquid.
Discard the woody stalks and cut the caps
into quarters.
2 Heat a wok over high heat. Add the oils
and swirl to coat the side of the wok, then
add the ginger, spring onion and bacon.
Cook for about 10 seconds before adding
the stock, soy sauce, rice wine, mushroom
liquid and ½ teaspoon salt. Bring to the
boil, then add the chicken. Reduce the heat
to low, cover with a lid and poach the
chicken for 40 minutes. Remove the
chicken from the stock and, when cool
enough to handle, shred the meat.
3 Return the stock to the boil, add the
carrot and cook for 5 minutes. Add the
prawns, tofu, bamboo shoots, spinach
and chicken meat to the wok and cook
over low heat for a further 5 minutes.
Serve with the extra spring onion.

RICE SOUP WITH PRAWN AND EGG

Preparation time: 15 minutes
Total cooking time: 15 minutes
Serves 4

3 teaspoons dashi granules
¼ cup (60 ml/2 fl oz) Shoyu (Japanese soy sauce)
2 tablespoons sake
1 tablespoon mirin
4 cups (740 g/1½ lb) cold cooked Japanese short-grain rice, rinsed well
12 raw prawns (shrimp), peeled and deveined
3 eggs, beaten
2 teaspoons ginger juice (see Notes)
2 spring onions (scallions), finely chopped
mitsuba or shiso, to garnish (optional)

1 Dissolve the dashi granules in 1.5 litres (48 fl oz) hot water, then combine with the Shoyu, sake, mirin and ½ teaspoon salt in a large saucepan and bring to the boil over high heat. Reduce the heat to low, then add the rice and simmer for 4 minutes, or until heated through. Add the prawns and cook for a further 3 minutes, or until the prawns are pink and starting to curl.
2 Remove the pan from the heat and drizzle the eggs over the top, place the lid on the pan and allow to sit for 1 minute before stirring the eggs through the soup along with the ginger juice and the spring onions. Season to taste, garnish with mitsuba or shiso if using and serve immediately as the eggs should not be allowed to set completely.

POTATO, BROCCOLI AND CORIANDER SOUP

Preparation time: 15 minutes
Total cooking time: 30 minutes
Serves 6

500 g (1 lb) broccoli
cooking oil spray
2 onions, finely chopped
2 cloves garlic, finely chopped
2 teaspoons ground cumin
1 teaspoon ground coriander
750 g (1½ lb) potatoes, cubed
2 small chicken stock cubes
1½ cups (375 ml/12 fl oz) skim milk
3 tablespoons finely chopped fresh coriander

1 Cut the broccoli into small pieces. Lightly spray the base of a large saucepan with cooking oil, then place over medium heat and add the onion and garlic. Add 1 tablespoon water to prevent sticking. Cover and cook, stirring occasionally, over low heat for 5 minutes, or until the onion has softened and is lightly golden. Add the ground cumin and coriander and cook for 2 minutes.
2 Add the potato and broccoli to the pan, stir well and add the stock cubes and 1 litre of water. Slowly bring to the boil, reduce the heat, cover and simmer over low heat for 20 minutes, or until the vegetables are tender. Allow to cool slightly.
3 Blend the soup in batches in a food processor or blender until smooth. Return to the pan and stir in the milk. Slowly reheat, without boiling. Stir the chopped coriander through and season well before serving.

ZUPPA DI COZZE

Preparation time: 25 minutes
Total cooking time: 35 minutes
Serves 6

200 g (6½ oz) ripe tomatoes
1 kg (2 lb) black mussels
2 tablespoons olive oil
40 g (1¼ oz) butter
1 leek, white part only, finely chopped
3 cloves garlic, crushed
pinch of saffron threads or powder
1 tablespoon finely chopped fresh coriander or parsley
1 small fresh red chilli, finely chopped
⅔ cup (170 ml/5½ fl oz) dry white wine

1 Score a cross in the base of each tomato. Place in a heatproof bowl and cover with boiling water. Leave for 30 seconds, transfer to cold water, drain and peel away from the cross. Cut the tomatoes in half, scoop out the seeds with a teaspoon and finely chop the flesh.
2 Scrub the mussels with a stiff brush and pull out the hairy beards. Discard any broken mussels, or open ones that don't close when tapped on the bench. Rinse well.
3 Heat the oil and butter in a large saucepan and cook the leek and garlic over low heat until the leek is soft but not brown. Add the saffron, coriander or parsley and chilli and cook, stirring, for 1–2 minutes. Increase the heat and add the wine. Bring to the boil and cook for 1–2 minutes, then add the chopped tomato and 1 cup (250 ml/8 fl oz) water. Cover and simmer for 20 minutes.
4 Add the mussels to the pan and cook, covered, until they are opened. After 4–5 minutes, discard any unopened mussels. So the soup is not too crowded with shells, remove one third of the remaining mussels, remove the mussel meat and add to the soup. Discard the empty shells. Season, to taste, with salt and pepper. Serve immediately with crusty bread.

MEAT DUMPLING SOUP

Preparation time: 45 minutes
Total cooking time: 35 minutes
Serves 4–6

1 tablespoon white sesame seeds
2 tablespoons oil
2 cloves garlic, finely chopped
150 g (4¾ oz) lean pork mince
200 g (6½ oz) lean beef mince
⅓ cup (80 ml/2¾ fl oz) water
200 g (6½ oz) Chinese cabbage, finely
   shredded
100 g (3⅓ oz) bean sprouts, chopped,
   scraggly ends removed
100 g (3⅓ oz) mushrooms, finely chopped
3 spring onions, finely chopped
150 g (4¾ oz) gow gee wrappers

Soup
2.5 litres beef stock
2 tablespoons soy sauce
3 cm (1¼ inch) piece fresh ginger, very
   finely sliced
4 spring onions, chopped

1 Toast the sesame seeds in a dry pan
over medium heat for 3 to 4 minutes,
shaking the pan gently, until the seeds
are golden brown; remove from the pan
at once to prevent burning. Crush the
seeds in a food mill or with a mortar and
pestle.

2 Heat the oil in a pan. Cook the garlic
and mince over medium heat until the
meat changes colour, breaking up any
lumps with a fork. Add the water,
cabbage, sprouts and mushrooms. Cook,
stirring occasionally, for 5 to 6 minutes or
until the water evaporates and the
vegetables soften. Add the spring onion,
crushed seeds and season with salt and
pepper to taste; set aside.
3 Work with one gow gee wrapper at a
time and keep the extra wrappers
covered with a damp tea towel. Place 1
teaspoon of filling on a wrapper, just off-
centre, and gently smooth out the filling a
little. Brush the edges of the wrapper
with a little water and fold it over the
filling to form a semicircle. Press the
edges together to seal. Repeat with the
extra wrappers and filling.
4 To make Soup: Combine the stock, soy
sauce, ginger and half the spring onion in
a large pan; bring to the boil and simmer
for 15 minutes.
5 Drop the dumplings into the soup and
cook gently for 5 minutes, or until they
change colour and look plump. Garnish
with the remaining spring onion and
serve immediately.

CARROT AND ORANGE SOUP

Preparation time: 20 minutes
Total cooking time: 35 minutes
Serves 4

500 g (1 lb) carrots
30 g (1 oz) butter
½ cup (125 ml/4 fl oz) orange juice
4–5 cups (1–1.25 litres) vegetable stock
1 small onion, roughly chopped
3–4 teaspoons chopped fresh thyme, or
   1 teaspoon dried
salt and pepper
sour cream and nutmeg, for serving

1 Peel and slice the carrots. Place carrots
and butter in a large heavy-based pan and
cook over medium heat for 10 minutes,
stirring occasionally.
2 Add the orange juice, stock and onion.
Bring to the boil, add thyme, salt and
pepper. Reduce heat; cover and cook for
20 minutes, or until the carrots are
tender. Allow to cool.
3 Process the mixture in batches, in a
food processor or blender, until smooth.
Return mixture to the pan and reheat.
Serve in individual bowls. Top each with
a dollop of sour cream sprinkled with
nutmeg. Garnish with a small sprig of
thyme, if desired.

MARMITE DIEPPOISE

Preparation time: 45 minutes
Total cooking time: 30 minutes
Serves 4

500 g (1 lb) raw medium prawns
600 g (1¼ lb) black mussels
350 g (11 oz) scallops
300 g (10 oz) assorted skinless fish fillets
    (eg. monkfish, snapper, orange roughy,
    salmon)
½ medium leek, white part only, sliced
½ small fennel bulb, sliced
1½ cups (375 ml/12 fl oz) dry white wine
2 sprigs fresh thyme
1 bay leaf
150 g (5 oz) button mushrooms, sliced
1 cup (250 ml/8 fl oz) cream
1 tablespoon chopped fresh flat-leaf
    parsley

1 Peel the prawns and gently pull out the dark vein from each prawn back, starting at the head end.
2 Scrub the mussels with a stiff brush and pull out the hairy beards. Discard any broken mussels, or open ones that don't close when tapped on the bench. Rinse well.
3 Slice or pull off any vein, membrane or hard white muscle from the scallops, leaving any roe attached. Cut the fish into bite-sized cubes.

4 In a large heavy-based pan, combine the leek, fennel, wine, thyme, bay leaf and mussels. Bring to the boil, cover and simmer for 4–5 minutes, stirring occasionally, until the mussels are cooked. Remove the mussels from the pan with tongs, discarding any unopened ones. Remove the mussels from their shells and discard the shells.
5 Bring the cooking liquid to simmering point. Add the prawns and scallops, cover and simmer for 2 minutes, or until cooked. Remove the prawns and scallops and set aside.
6 Return the cooking liquid to simmering point and add the fish. Poach for 3 minutes, or until cooked, then remove and set aside. Line a sieve with a double layer of dampened muslin and strain the liquid into a clean pan. Bring to the boil, add the mushrooms and cook, uncovered, over high heat for 3 minutes. Stir in the cream, bring to the boil and simmer for about 5 minutes, stirring occasionally, until thick enough to coat the back of a spoon. Add the mussels, prawns, scallops and fish and simmer until heated through. Season, stir in the parsley and serve.

RATATOUILLE AND PASTA SOUP

Preparation time: 25 minutes + standing
Total cooking time: 40 minutes
Serves 6

1 medium eggplant (aubergine)
2 tablespoons olive oil
1 large onion, chopped
1 large red pepper (capsicum), chopped
1 large green pepper (capsicum),
    chopped
2 cloves garlic, crushed
3 zucchini (courgettes), sliced
2 x 400 g (13 oz) cans crushed tomatoes
1 teaspoon dried oregano leaves
½ teaspoon dried thyme leaves
4 cups (1 litre) vegetable stock
½ cup (45 g/1½ oz) fusilli
Parmesan shavings, for serving

1 Chop the eggplant. To remove any bitterness, spread the eggplant pieces out in a colander and sprinkle generously with salt. Set aside for 20 minutes and then rinse thoroughly and pat dry with paper towels.
2 Heat the oil in a large heavy-based pan and cook the onion over medium heat for 10 minutes, or until soft and lightly golden.
Add the peppers, garlic, zucchini and eggplant and stir-fry for 5 minutes.
3 Add the tomato, herbs and vegetable stock to the pan. Bring to the boil, reduce the heat and simmer for 10 minutes, or until the vegetables are tender. Add the fusilli and cook for another 15 minutes, or until the fusilli is tender. Serve with shavings of Parmesan.

NOTE: This delicious soup can be served with Italian bread.

MANHATTAN-STYLE SEAFOOD CHOWDER

Preparation time: 30 minutes
Total cooking time: 30 minutes
Serves 4–6

60 g (2 oz) butter
3 rashers bacon, chopped
2 onions, chopped
2 cloves garlic, finely chopped
2 sticks celery, sliced
3 potatoes, diced
1.25 litres (40 fl oz) fish or chicken stock
3 teaspoons chopped fresh thyme
12 raw large prawns
1 tablespoon tomato paste (tomato purée)
425 g (14 oz) can chopped tomatoes
375 g (12 oz) skinless white fish fillets
    (eg. ling, cod, flake, hake), cut into bite-
    sized pieces
310 g (10 oz) can baby clams, undrained
2 tablespoons chopped fresh parsley
grated orange rind, to garnish

1 Melt the butter in a large pan and cook the bacon, onion, garlic and celery over low heat, stirring occasionally, for 5 minutes, or until soft but not brown.
2 Add the potato, stock and thyme to the pan and bring to the boil. Reduce the heat and simmer, covered, for 15 minutes.
3 Meanwhile, peel the prawns and pull out the dark vein from each prawn back, starting at the head end. Add the tomato paste and tomato to the pan, stir through and bring back to the boil. Add the fish pieces, prawns and clams with juice and simmer over low heat for 3 minutes. Season, to taste, and stir in the parsley. Serve garnished with the grated orange rind.

SEAFOOD LAKSA

Preparation time: 45 minutes
Total cooking time: 45 minutes
Serves 4–6

1 kg (2 lb) raw medium prawns
⅓ cup (80 ml/2¾ fl oz) oil
2–6 fresh red chillies, seeded, finely
    chopped
1 onion, roughly chopped
3 cloves garlic, halved
2 cm (¾ inch) piece ginger or galangal,
    chopped
1 teaspoon ground turmeric
1 tablespoon ground coriander
3 stems lemon grass, white part only,
    chopped
1–2 teaspoons shrimp paste
2½ cups (600 ml/20 fl oz) coconut cream
2 teaspoons grated palm sugar or brown
    sugar
4 kaffir lime leaves, lightly crushed
1–2 tablespoons fish sauce
200 g (6½ oz) packet fish balls
190 g (6½ oz) packet tofu puffs
250 g (8 oz) dried rice vermicelli
250 g (8 oz) bean sprouts
4 tablespoons chopped fresh mint, for
    serving
2 teaspoons fresh coriander leaves, for
    serving

1 Peel the prawns and gently pull out the dark vein from each prawn back, starting at the head end. Set the shells, heads and tails aside. Cover the prawn meat and refrigerate.
2 To make the prawn stock, heat 2 tablespoons of the oil in a large, heavy-based pan or wok and add the prawn shells, heads and tails. Stir until the heads are bright orange, then add 1 litre (32 fl oz) water. Bring to the boil, reduce the heat and simmer for 15 minutes. Strain through a fine sieve, discarding the shells. Clean the pan.

3 Put the chilli, onion, garlic, ginger (or galangal), turmeric, coriander, lemon grass and ¼ cup (60 ml/2 fl oz) of the prawn stock in a food processor and process until finely chopped.
4 Heat the remaining oil in the clean pan and add the chilli mixture and shrimp paste. Stir over low heat for 3 minutes, or until fragrant. Pour in the remaining stock and simmer for 10 minutes. Add the coconut cream, sugar, lime leaves and fish sauce. Simmer for 5 minutes.
5 Add the prawns and simmer for 2 minutes, until just pink. Add the fish balls and tofu puffs and simmer gently until just heated through.
6 Soak the rice vermicelli in a bowl of boiling water for 2 minutes, drain and divide among serving bowls. Top with bean sprouts and ladle the soup over the top. Sprinkle with the mint and coriander.

NOTE: Fish balls and tofu puffs are available in the refrigerator section at Asian supermarkets.

CALDO VERDE
(PORTUGUESE GREEN SOUP)

Preparation time: 15 minutes
Total cooking time: 1 hour
Serves 6

150 g (5 oz) chorizo sausage, thinly sliced
2 tablespoons olive oil
1 large onion, thinly sliced
4 garlic cloves, very finely chopped
2 teaspoons finely chopped oregano
1 large all-purpose potato (e.g. desiree),
  peeled and diced
1 cup (200 g/6½ oz) long-grain rice
1 litre (32 fl oz) chicken stock
1 small green chilli, split down the centre
6 cups (270 g/9 oz) very finely shredded
  kale, silverbeet (Swiss chard) or
  English spinach (see Notes)
1 cup (20 g/¾ oz) flat-leaf (Italian)
  parsley, chopped
extra virgin olive oil, for drizzling
lemon wedges, to serve

1 Fry the chorizo in a frying pan over medium heat for about 5 minutes, or until slightly crispy, then set aside. Heat the olive oil in a large saucepan, then add the onion, garlic and oregano and cook over medium heat for 8 minutes, or until the onion is softened but not browned. Add the potato and rice and cook for a few more minutes, stirring to make sure it doesn't catch on the bottom of the pan.

2 Pour in the stock, 1 litre (32 fl oz) water and the chilli, increase the heat and bring to the boil, stirring occasionally. Reduce the heat and simmer for about 20 minutes, or until the rice is tender and the potato is starting to fall apart, skimming as needed. Discard the chilli. Lightly crush the potato with a vegetable masher, then add the kale and chorizo. Cook for a further 15 minutes, or until kale is softened and loses its raw flavour.
3 Stir in the chopped parsley and season to taste. Ladle into bowls and drizzle with extra virgin olive oil, if desired. Serve with lemon wedges to squeeze over the top.

NOTES: Kale is a relative of the cabbage, with a similar but stronger flavour and, depending on the variety, dark green or purple, smooth or curly leaves. Also known as cole, colewart or curly kale.

  Originating in the northern Portuguese province of Minho, this hearty soup is popular throughout the country. The authentic recipe calls for couve tronchuda, a dark green cabbage, and linguica, a spicy Portuguese sausage; however, as both are difficult to obtain outside the Iberian peninsula, we have used kale and chorizo instead.

TOM YUM GOONG
(HOT AND SOUR PRAWN SOUP)

Preparation time: 25 minutes
Total cooking time: 45 minutes
Serves 4–6

500 g (1 lb) raw prawns
1 tablespoon oil
2 litres water
2 tablespoons Red Curry Paste (page 112)
  or ready-made paste
2 tablespoons tamarind concentrate
2 teaspoons ground turmeric
1 teaspoon chopped red chilli, optional
4–8 kaffir lime leaves, whole or shredded
2 tablespoons fish sauce
2 tablespoons lime juice
2 teaspoons soft brown sugar
¼ cup (7 g/¼ oz) fresh coriander leaves

1 Peel and devein the prawns, leaving the tails intact. Heat the oil in a large pan; add the prawn shells and heads to the pan and cook for 10 minutes over moderately high heat, tossing frequently, until the shells and heads are deep orange.
2 Add 1 cup (250 ml/8 fl oz) of the water and the curry paste to the pan. Boil for 5 minutes, until reduced slightly. Add the remaining water and simmer for 20 minutes. Drain the stock, discarding the heads and shells.
3 Return the drained stock to the pan. Add the tamarind, turmeric, chilli and lime leaves, bring to the boil and cook for 2 minutes. Add the prawns to the pan and cook for 5 minutes or until the prawns turn pink. Add the fish sauce, lime juice and sugar and stir to combine. Serve immediately, sprinkled with coriander leaves.

WON TON SOUP

Preparation time: 40 minutes
Total cooking time: 5 minutes
Serves 6

250 g (8 oz) raw prawns
4 dried Chinese mushrooms
250 g (8 oz) pork mince
1 teaspoon salt
1 tablespoon soy sauce
1 teaspoon sesame oil
2 spring onions, finely chopped
1 teaspoon grated fresh ginger
2 tablespoons finely sliced water
  chestnuts
1 x 250 g (8 oz) packet won ton wrappers
5 cups (1.25 litres) chicken or beef stock
4 spring onions, very finely sliced, for
  garnish

1 Peel, devein and finely chop the prawns.
2 Cover the mushrooms with hot water
and soak them for 20 minutes. Drain and
squeeze to remove excess liquid. Remove
stems and chop the caps finely.
Thoroughly combine the prawn meat,
mushrooms, pork, salt, soy sauce,
sesame oil, spring onion, ginger and
water chestnuts.
3 Work with 1 won ton wrapper at a time,
keeping the remainder covered with a
clean, damp tea towel to stop them drying
out. Place heaped teaspoons of mince
mixture in the centre of each square.
Moisten the edges of the wrapper, fold it
in half diagonally and bring the 2 points
together. Place the won tons on a plate
dusted with flour to prevent sticking.
4 Cook the won tons in rapidly boiling
water for 4 to 5 minutes. Bring the stock
to the boil in a separate pan. Remove the
won tons from the water with a slotted
spoon and place them in a serving bowl.
Garnish with the extra spring onion and
pour the simmering stock over them.
Serve immediately.

CHICKEN MULLIGATAWNY

Preparation time: 25 minutes +
  overnight refrigeration
Total cooking time: 4 hours
Serves 6

Stock
1.5 kg (3 lb) chicken
1 carrot, chopped
2 celery stalks, chopped
4 spring onions (scallions), cut into 3 cm
  (1¼ inch) lengths
2 cm (¾ inch) piece of ginger, sliced

2 tomatoes, peeled
20 g (¼ oz) ghee
1 large onion, finely chopped
3 garlic cloves, crushed
8 curry leaves
¾ cup (60 g/2 oz) Madras curry paste
1 cup (250 g/8 oz) red lentils, washed and
  drained
⅓ cup (75 g/2½ oz) short-grain rice
1 cup (250 ml/8 fl oz) coconut cream
2 tablespoons coriander (cilantro) leaves,
  chopped
mango chutney, to serve

1 To make the stock, put all the
ingredients and 4 litres (128 fl oz) cold
water in a large stockpot or saucepan.
Bring to the boil, removing any scum that
rises to the surface. Reduce the heat to
low and simmer, partly covered, for
3 hours. Continue to remove any scum
from the surface.
2 Carefully remove the chicken and cool.
Strain the stock into a bowl and cool.
Cover and refrigerate overnight. Discard
the skin and bones from the chicken and
shred the flesh into small pieces. Cover
and refrigerate overnight.

3 Score a cross in the base of the
tomatoes. Put in a heatproof bowl and
cover with boiling water. Leave for 30
seconds then transfer to a bowl of cold
water and peel the skin away from the
cross. Chop the flesh.
4 Remove the fat from the surface of the
stock. Melt the ghee in a large saucepan
over medium heat. Cook the onion for 5
minutes, or until softened but not
browned. Add the garlic and curry leaves
and cook for 1 minute. Add the curry
paste, cook for 1 minute, then stir in the
lentils until coated. Pour in the stock and
bring to the boil over high heat, removing
any scum on the surface. Reduce the
heat, add the tomato and simmer for 30
minutes, or until the lentils are
completely soft.
5 Bring a large saucepan of water to the
boil. Add the rice and cook for 12 minutes,
stirring once or twice. Drain. Stir the rice
into the soup with the chicken and
coconut cream until warmed through—
don't allow it to boil or it will curdle.
Season. Sprinkle with the coriander and
serve with the mango chutney.

SPLIT PEA AND HAM SOUP

Preparation time: 15 minutes
Total cooking time: 2 hours 15 minutes
Serves 8

500 g (1 lb) yellow split peas
leftover ham bone, about 650 g (1 lb 5 oz)
2 carrots, chopped
2 celery sticks, chopped
1 onion, chopped
2 bay leaves

1 Rinse the split peas in cold water, then drain. Place the peas, ham bone, carrot, celery, onion, bay leaves and 3 litres (96 fl oz) water in a pan. Cover and bring to the boil. Reduce the heat and simmer, partly covered, for 2 hours, or until the peas are tender. Skim off any scum that rises to the surface.
2 Remove the ham bone and cut the meat from the bone, discarding any fat or skin. Finely chop the ham and set aside. Remove the bay leaves. Cool the soup slightly, then blend in batches in a blender until smooth, adding a little more water if necessary. Stir in the ham and season with salt and pepper, to taste.

NOTE: This soup thickens on standing. Add vegetable or chicken stock to thin to the desired consistency. The soup can be frozen.

PORK BALL SOUP WITH NOODLES

Preparation time: 25 minutes
Total cooking time: 30 minutes
Serves 4

250 g (8 oz) pork bones
5 cm (2 inch) piece fresh ginger, thinly sliced
1 teaspoon salt
1 teaspoon pepper
4 cups (1 litre) water
6 spring onions, chopped
300 g (92/ 3 oz) Shanghai noodles
250 g (8 oz) pork mince
2 tablespoons fish sauce
150 g (4¾ oz) fresh pineapple, cut into small chunks
100 g (3⅓ oz) bean sprouts, scraggly ends removed
2 tablespoons shredded fresh mint

1 Place the pork bones, ginger, salt, pepper and water in a pan, and bring it to the boil. Skim off any scum, add the spring onion and simmer for 20 minutes. Remove and discard the bones and set the stock aside.
2 Cook the noodles in a pan of boiling water for 5 minutes. Drain and rinse in cold water.
3 Chop the mince very finely with a cleaver or large knife for 3 minutes or until the meat feels very soft and spongy. Wet your hands and roll
2 teaspoons of mince at a time into small balls.
4 Return the stock to the heat and bring it to the boil. Add the pork balls and cook for 4 minutes. Add the fish sauce and pineapple.
5 Place the noodles in individual soup bowls and ladle the hot stock over them, making sure each bowl has pork balls and pineapple. Scatter the bean sprouts and mint over the soup, and serve immediately.

SOBA NOODLE SOUP

Preparation time: 15 minutes +
 5 minutes standing
Total cooking time: 10 minutes
Serves 4

250 g (8 oz) packet soba noodles
2 dried shiitake mushrooms
2 litres (64 fl oz) vegetable stock
120 g (4 oz) snow peas, cut into thin strips
2 small carrots, cut into thin strips
2 cloves garlic, finely chopped
6 spring onions, cut into 5 cm (2 inch) lengths and sliced lengthways
3 cm (1 inch) piece ginger, cut into julienne strips
⅓ cup (80 ml/2¾ fl oz) soy sauce
¼ cup (60 ml/2 fl oz) mirin or sake
1 cup (90 g/3 oz) bean sprouts
fresh coriander, to garnish

1 Cook the noodles according to the packet instructions. Drain.
2 Soak the mushrooms in ½ cup (125 ml/ 4 fl oz) boiling water until soft. Drain, reserving the liquid. Remove the stalks and finely slice the mushrooms.
3 Combine the vegetable stock, mushrooms, reserved liquid, snow peas, carrot, garlic, spring onion and ginger in a large saucepan. Bring slowly to the boil, then reduce the heat to low and simmer for 5 minutes, or until the vegetables are tender. Add the soy sauce, mirin and bean sprouts. Cook for a further 3 minutes.
4 Divide the noodles among four large serving bowls. Ladle the hot liquid and vegetables over the top and garnish with coriander.

JAPANESE VEGETABLE RAMEN NOODLE SOUP

Preparation time: 15 minutes
Total cooking time: 15 minutes
Serves 6

250 g (8 oz) fresh ramen noodles
1 tablespoon vegetable oil
1 tablespoon finely chopped fresh ginger
2 cloves garlic, crushed
150 g (5 oz) oyster mushrooms, halved
1 small zucchini (courgette), thinly sliced
1 leek, halved lengthways and thinly sliced
100 g (3½ oz) snow peas (mangetout), halved on the diagonal
100 g (3½ oz) fried tofu puffs, cut into julienne strips
⅓ cup (80 g/2¾ oz) white miso paste
⅓ cup (80 ml/2¾ fl oz) light soy sauce
¼ cup (60 ml/2 fl oz) mirin
1 cup (90 g/3 oz) bean sprouts, tailed
½ teaspoon sesame oil
4 spring onions, thinly sliced
100 g (3½ oz) enoki mushrooms

1 Bring a large saucepan of lightly salted water to the boil. Add the noodles and cook, stirring to prevent them sticking together, for 2 minutes, or until just tender. Drain, rinse under cold running water, then drain again.
2 Heat a wok over medium heat, add the vegetable oil and swirl to coat. Add the ginger and garlic and stir-fry for 30 seconds, then add the oyster mushrooms, zucchini, leek, snow peas and sliced tofu puffs and stir-fry for 4 minutes. Pour in 1.5 litres (48 fl oz) water and bring to the boil, then reduce the heat and simmer. Stir in the miso paste, soy sauce and mirin until heated through, but don't let it boil. Just before serving, stir in the bean sprouts and sesame oil.
3 Place the noodles in the bottom of six serving bowls, then pour the broth over the top. Sprinkle with the sliced spring onion and enoki mushrooms.

CREAMY CORN AND TOMATO SOUP

Preparation time: 20 minutes
Total cooking time: 15 minutes
Serves 4–6

1 teaspoon olive oil
1 teaspoon vegetable stock powder
1 medium onion, finely chopped
3 medium tomatoes
425 g (13½ oz) canned tomato purée
310 g (9¾ oz) canned creamed-style corn
125 g (4 oz) canned corn kernels, drained
chilli powder
sour cream and tortillas, for serving

1 Heat the oil in a large pan. Add stock powder and onion and cook until onion is soft.
2 Peel tomatoes, remove seeds with a spoon and chop flesh. Add to the pan with the tomato purée, creamed corn and corn kernels. Season with chilli. Stir until heated through. Serve with a dollop of sour cream and some warm tortillas.

CHINESE MUSHROOM AND CHICKEN SOUP

Preparation time: 20 minutes +
 10 minutes soaking
Total cooking time: 10 minutes
Serves 4

3 dried Chinese mushrooms
185 g (6 oz) thin dried egg noodles
1 tablespoon oil
4 spring onions, julienned
1 tablespoon soy sauce
2 tablespoons rice wine, mirin or sherry (see Note)
1.25 litres chicken stock
½ small barbecued chicken, shredded
50 g (1¾ oz) sliced ham, cut into strips
1 cup (90 g/3 oz) bean sprouts
fresh coriander leaves, to serve
thinly sliced red chilli, to serve

1 Soak the mushrooms in boiling water for 10 minutes to soften them. Squeeze dry then remove the tough stem from the mushrooms and slice them thinly.
2 Cook the noodles in a large pan of boiling water for 3 minutes, or according to the manufacturer's directions. Drain and cut the noodles into shorter lengths with scissors.
3 Heat the oil in a large heavy-based pan. Add the mushrooms and spring onion. Cook for 1 minute, then add the soy sauce, rice wine and stock. Bring slowly to the boil and cook for 1 minute. Reduce the heat then add the noodles, shredded chicken, ham and bean sprouts. Heat through for 2 minutes without allowing the soup to boil.
4 Use tongs to divide the noodles among four bowls, ladle in the remaining mixture, and garnish with coriander leaves and sliced chilli.

PASTA AND BEAN SOUP

Preparation time: 20 minutes +
   overnight soaking
Total cooking time: 1 hour 25 minutes
Serves 4–6

250 g (8 oz) borlotti beans, soaked in
   water overnight
1 ham hock
1 onion, chopped
pinch of ground cinnamon
pinch of cayenne pepper
2 teaspoons olive oil
2 cups (500 ml/16 fl oz) chicken stock
125 g (4 oz) tagliatelle (plain or spinach),
   broken into short lengths

1 Drain and rinse the borlotti beans, cover with cold water in a pan and bring to the boil. Stir, lower the heat and simmer for 15 minutes.
2 Drain the beans and transfer to a large pan, with a tight-fitting lid. Add the ham hock, onion, cinnamon, cayenne, olive oil and stock, and cold water to cover. Cover the pan and simmer over low heat for 1 hour, or until the beans are cooked and have begun to thicken the stock. Remove the hock and cut off any meat. Chop the meat and return to the pan, discarding the bone.
3 Taste for seasonings and add salt, if necessary. Bring the soup back to the boil, toss in the tagliatelle and cook until al dente. Remove the pan from the heat and set aside for 1–2 minutes before serving. Can be garnished with fresh herbs.

SPICY VIETNAMESE BEEF AND PORK NOODLE SOUP (BUN BO HUE)

Preparation time: 20 minutes +
30 minutes freezing
Total cooking time: 40 minutes
Serves 4

300 g (10 oz) beef fillet steak
¼ cup (60 ml/2 fl oz) vegetable oil
300 g (10 oz) pork leg fillet, cut into 3 cm
   (1¼ inch) cubes
1 large onion, cut into thin wedges
2 litres (64 fl oz) good-quality beef stock
2 stems lemon grass
2 tablespoons fish sauce
1 teaspoon ground dried shrimp
1 teaspoon sugar
2 large fresh red chillies, sliced
400 g (13 oz) fresh round rice noodles
2 cups (180 g/6 oz) bean sprouts, tailed
½ cup (10 g/¼ oz) fresh mint
½ cup (15 g/½ oz) fresh coriander leaves
thinly sliced fresh chilli, to serve
   (optional)
lemon wedges, to serve

1 Place the beef in the freezer for 20–30 minutes, or until partially frozen, then cut into paper-thin slices across the grain. Set aside.
2 Heat a wok until hot, add 1 tablespoon of the oil and swirl to coat the side of the wok. Stir-fry the pork in batches for 2–3 minutes, or until browned. Remove from the wok. Add another tablespoon of oil and stir-fry the onion for 2–3 minutes, or until softened. Pour in the stock and 2 cups (500 ml/16 fl oz) water. Bruise one of the lemon grass stems and add it to the wok. Return the pork to the wok and bring the liquid to the boil, then reduce the heat and simmer for 15 minutes, or until the pork is tender, periodically skimming off any scum that rises to the surface. Meanwhile, thinly slice the white part of the remaining lemon grass stem.

3 Remove the whole lemon grass stem from the broth and stir in the fish sauce, dried shrimp and sugar and keep at a simmer.
4 Heat the remaining oil in a small frying pan over medium heat and cook the sliced lemon grass and chilli for 2–3 minutes, or until fragrant. Stir into the broth. Just before serving, bring the broth to the boil over medium–high heat.
5 Place the rice noodles in a large heatproof bowl, cover with boiling water and gently separate the noodles. Drain immediately and rinse. Divide the noodles among four warm serving bowls. Top with the bean sprouts and cover with the boiling broth. Add the beef to the soup— the heat of the soup will cook it. Sprinkle with the mint and coriander, and fresh chilli, if desired. Serve immediately with some wedges of lemon.

HARIRA
(CHICKPEA, LAMB AND
CORIANDER SOUP)

Preparation time: 15 minutes
Total cooking time: 2 hours 25 minutes
Serves 4

2 tablespoons olive oil
2 small brown onions, chopped
2 large cloves garlic, crushed
500 g (1 lb) lamb shoulder steaks,
    trimmed of excess fat and sinew, cut
    into small chunks
1½ teaspoons ground cumin
2 teaspoons paprika
½ teaspoon ground cloves
1 bay leaf
2 tablespoons tomato paste (tomato purée)
1 litre beef stock
3 x 300 g (10 oz) cans chickpeas, rinsed
    and drained
800 g (1 lb 10 oz) can diced good-quality
    tomatoes
½ cup (30 g/1 oz) finely chopped fresh
    coriander
fresh coriander leaves, extra, to garnish
small black olives, for serving

1 Heat the oil in a large heavy-based
saucepan or stockpot, add the onion and
garlic and cook for 5 minutes, or until
softened. Add the meat, in batches, and
cook over high heat until the meat is
browned on all sides. Return all the meat
to the pan.
2 Add the spices and bay leaf to the pan
and cook until fragrant. Add the tomato
paste and cook for about 2 minutes,
stirring constantly. Add the stock to the
pan, stir well and bring to the boil.
3 Add the chickpeas, tomato and chopped
coriander to the pan. Stir, then bring to the
boil. Reduce the heat and simmer for
2 hours, or until the meat is tender. Stir
occassionally. Season, to taste.
4 Serve garnished with coriander leaves
and small black olives. Can be served with
toasted pitta bread drizzled with a little
extra virgin olive oil.

SCALLOP AND EGG
FLOWER SOUP

Preparation time: 30 minutes +
    10 minutes chilling
Total cooking time: 45 minutes
Serves 4

300 g (10 oz) scallops
1 tablespoon dry sherry
¼ teaspoon ground white pepper
1 teaspoon grated fresh ginger
7 spring onions
2 tablespoons oil
1 tablespoon cornflour
3 cups (750 ml/24 fl oz) chicken stock
2 tablespoons soy sauce
⅓ cup (75 g/2½ oz) canned straw
    mushrooms, cut in halves
⅓ cup (50 g/1¾ oz) frozen peas
1 egg, lightly beaten
dry sherry, extra, to taste
2 teaspoons soy sauce, extra

1 Slice or pull off any vein, membrane or
hard white muscle from the scallops,
leaving any roe attached. Combine with
the sherry, pepper and ginger in a bowl
and refrigerate for 10 minutes.
2 Finely chop the spring onions, keeping
the green and white parts separate.
3 Heat the oil in a wok or heavy-based
frying pan, swirling gently to coat the base
and side. Add the white part of the spring
onion and cook for 30 seconds. Add the
scallops and their liquid and cook, turning,
over high heat until the scallops turn
milky white. Transfer to a bowl.
4 Blend the cornflour in a little of the
stock until smooth, add to the wok with
the remaining stock and soy sauce and
bring to the boil, stirring until the mixture
boils and thickens. Add the straw
mushrooms and peas and cook for
2 minutes. Return the scallops to the
wok, stirring the soup constantly.
5 Pour in the egg and cook, stirring until
it turns opaque. Stir the spring onion
greens through and add a little more
sherry and soy sauce, to taste.

GREEN PEA SOUP

Preparation time: 20 minutes +
    2 hours soaking
Total cooking time: 1 hour 40 minutes
Serves 4–6

1½ cups (330 g/10 1/2 oz) green split peas
2 tablespoons oil
1 medium onion, finely chopped
1 celery stick, finely sliced
1 medium carrot, finely sliced
1 tablespoon ground cumin
1 tablespoon ground coriander
2 teaspoons grated fresh ginger
5 cups (1.25 litres) vegetable stock
2 cups (310 g/9¾ oz) frozen green peas
salt and freshly ground black pepper
1 tablespoon chopped fresh mint
4 tablespoons plain yoghurt or sour
    cream

1 Soak the split peas in cold water for
2 hours. Drain peas well. Heat oil in a
large heavy-based pan and add onion,
celery and carrot. Cook over medium heat
for 3 minutes, stirring occasionally, until
soft but not browned. Stir in cumin,
coriander and ginger, then cook for
1 minute.
2 Add split peas and stock to pan. Bring to
the boil; reduce heat to low. Simmer,
covered, for 1½ hours, stirring
occasionally.
3 Add frozen peas to pan and stir to
combine; set aside to cool. When cool,
purée soup in batches in a blender or food
processor until smooth. Return to pan,
gently reheat. Season with salt and
pepper and then stir in mint. Serve in
bowls with a swirl of yoghurt or sour
cream.

RASAM

Preparation time: 15 minutes
Total cooking time: 45 minutes
Serves 4

¼ cup (80 g/2¾ oz) tamarind purée
1½ tablespoons coriander seeds
2 tablespoons cumin seeds
1 tablespoon black peppercorns
1 tablespoon oil
5 garlic cloves, skins on, roughly
    pounded
1 red onion, thinly sliced
2–3 dried chillies, torn into pieces
2 stalks of curry leaves
200 g (6½ oz) skinless, boneless chicken
    thighs, cut into small pieces
⅓ cup (65 g/2¼ oz) basmati rice

1 Mix the tamarind purée with 3 cups (750 ml/ 24 fl oz) water. Put a small frying pan over low heat and dry-fry the coriander seeds until fragrant. Remove, then dry-fry the cumin seeds, followed by the black peppercorns. Grind them together using a spice grinder or a mortar and pestle.
2 Heat the oil in a large, heavy-based saucepan over low heat, add the garlic and onion and fry until golden. Add the chilli and the curry leaves and fry for 2 minutes, or until they are fragrant. Add the tamarind water, the ground spices and season with salt. Bring to the boil, reduce the
heat and simmer for 10 minutes.
3 Add the chicken pieces and rice to the saucepan with 1 cup (250 ml/8 fl oz) water and simmer for 20 minutes, gradually adding another 1 cup (250 ml/ 8 fl oz) water as the soup reduces and thickens. Remove any garlic skin which has floated to the top. Season with salt, to taste, then serve.

PENANG FISH LAKSA

Preparation time: 20 minutes +
    20 minutes soaking
Total cooking time: 40 minutes
Serves 4

1 whole snapper (750 g/11/2 lb), scaled
    and cleaned
3 cups (750 ml/24 fl oz) chicken stock
6 Vietnamese mint stalks
4 dried red chillies
2 x 3 cm (¾ x 11/4 inch) piece of galangal,
    finely chopped
4 red Asian shallots, finely chopped
2 stems lemon grass, white part only,
    finely chopped
1 teaspoon ground turmeric
1 teaspoon shrimp paste
4 tablespoons tamarind purée
1 tablespoon sugar
500 g (1 lb) fresh round rice noodles
1 small Lebanese (short) cucumber,
    seeded and cut into strips
½ cup (10 g/¼ oz) Vietnamese mint
1 large green chilli, sliced

1 Trim the fins and tail off the fish with kitchen scissors. Make several deep cuts through the thickest part of the fish on both sides.
2 Pour the stock and 3 cups (750 ml/24 fl oz) water into a non-stick wok. Add the mint stalks and bring to the boil over high heat. Put the fish in the wok and simmer for 10 minutes, or until cooked. The fish should remain submerged during cooking; you might need to add some more boiling water. Lift the fish out of the wok and allow to cool.

3 Soak the chillies in 1 cup (250 ml/8 fl oz) boiling water for 20 minutes. Drain and chop. To make the laksa paste, put the chilli, galangal, shallots, lemon grass, turmeric and shrimp paste in a food processor or blender and blend to a smooth paste, adding a little water if needed.
4 Flake the flesh off the fish and remove all the bones, reserving both. Add the bones and tamarind to the stock in the wok and bring to the boil. Simmer for 10 minutes, then strain and return the liquid to a clean wok—make sure no bones slip through. Stir the laksa paste into the liquid and simmer over medium heat for 10 minutes. Stir in the sugar, add the fish flesh and simmer for 1–2 minutes, or until the fish is heated through.
5 Put the noodles in a heatproof bowl, cover with boiling water, then gently separate. Drain immediately and refresh under cold water. Divide the noodles among four bowls. Ladle on the fish pieces and broth, then sprinkle with cucumber, mint and chilli and serve.

BEEF SOUP WITH RICE NOODLES

Preparation time: 30 minutes +
    1 hour marinating
Total cooking time: 1 hour
Serves 4

350 g (11¼ oz) fillet steak
2 teaspoons soy sauce
¼ cup (60 ml/2 fl oz) coconut milk
1 tablespoon crunchy peanut butter
1 tablespoon grated palm sugar or soft
    brown sugar
2 teaspoons sambal oelek
1 teaspoon oil
125 g (4 oz) dried rice vermicelli
1.5 litres beef stock
2 tablespoons grated palm sugar or soft
    brown sugar, extra
2 tablespoons fish sauce
1 small Lebanese cucumber
1 cup (90 g/3 oz) bean sprouts, scraggly
    ends removed
2 lettuce leaves, cut in small pieces
6 tablespoons finely chopped fresh mint
1/ 2 cup (80 g/2⅔ oz) unsalted roasted
    peanuts, finely chopped

1 Trim the meat of fat and sinew and slice it
evenly across the grain into thin slices.
2 Combine the meat, soy sauce, coconut
milk, peanut butter, sugar and sambal
oelek. Cover and marinate in the
refrigerator for 1 hour.
3 Heat the oil in a frying pan and cook the
meat in small batches over high heat for
3 minutes, or until browned. Remove from
heat and cover. Soak the vermicelli in hot
water for 10 minutes. Drain.
4 Place the stock in a large pan and bring
to the boil. When the stock is boiling add
the extra sugar and fish sauce.
5 Cut the cucumber in quarters lengthways
and then into thin slices. Place 1 tablespoon
cucumber slices in each bowl; divide the
bean sprouts, lettuce and mint evenly
between bowls. Place vermicelli and a
ladleful of stock in each. Top with slices of
beef, sprinkle with peanuts and serve.

INDONESIAN SPICY CHICKEN SOUP (SOTO AYAM)

Preparation time: 30 minutes +
    overnight refrigeration
Total cooking time: 2 hours 15 minutes
Serves 6

2 teaspoons coriander seeds
2 tablespoons vegetable oil
1.4 kg (2 lb 13 oz) whole chicken, jointed
    into 8 pieces
4 cloves garlic
1 onion, chopped
2 teaspoons julienned fresh ginger
1 dried red chilli, halved
2 stems lemon grass, white part only,
    roughly chopped
50 g (1¾ oz) coriander roots and stems,
    well rinsed, roughly chopped
2 teaspoons ground turmeric
1 teaspoon galangal powder
1 teaspoon sugar
1 litre (32 fl oz) good-quality chicken stock
2 tablespoons lemon juice
120 g (4 oz) cellophane noodles
1½ tablespoons fish sauce
1 cup (90 g/3 oz) bean sprouts, tailed
3 tablespoons chopped fresh coriander
    leaves
4 spring onions, thinly sliced on the
    diagonal
¼ cup (20 g/¾ oz) crisp fried onions
1 tablespoon sambal oelek

1 Toss the coriander seeds in a small, dry
frying pan over medium heat for 1 minute,
or until fragrant. Cool, then finely grind.
2 Heat a wok to very hot, add 2 teaspoons
of the oil and swirl to coat. Add the
chicken pieces and cook in batches for
3–4 minutes, or until browned all over.
Remove from the wok.

3 Heat the remaining oil in the same wok,
then add the garlic, onion, ginger and
chilli and stir-fry for 5 minutes, or until
softened. Add the lemon grass, coriander
root and stem, turmeric, galangal, sugar
and ground coriander and cook for 5
minutes. Return the chicken to the wok
and pour in the stock, lemon juice and 2
cups (500 ml/16 fl oz) water to cover the
chicken.
4 Cover the wok with a lid and simmer for
20 minutes, skimming the surface
periodically to remove any fat and scum
that rises to the surface. Remove only the
chicken breast pieces, then cover the wok
and simmer (still skimming the surface
occasionally) for 20 minutes before
removing the rest of the chicken pieces.
Cover and refrigerate the chicken until
needed. Return the lid to the wok and
simmer the broth over low heat for a
further 1 hour.
5 Strain the broth through a fine sieve,
and allow to cool to room temperature
before covering with plastic wrap and
refrigerating overnight.
6 Soak the cellophane noodles in boiling
water for 3–4 minutes, then drain and
rinse.
7 Remove any fat from the top of the cold
broth. Remove the flesh from the chicken
and shred with a fork. Place the broth and
chicken flesh in the wok, and place over
medium heat. Bring to the boil, then stir
in the fish sauce, bean sprouts, coriander
leaves and noodles. Season well, then
ladle into large bowls. Sprinkle with
spring onion and crisp fried onion, and
then serve with sambal oelek.

SMOKED HADDOCK CHOWDER

Preparation time: 20 minutes
Total cooking time: 35 minutes
Serves 4–6

500 g (1 lb) smoked haddock or cod
1 potato, diced
1 stick celery, chopped
1 onion, finely chopped
50 g (1¾ oz) butter
1 rasher bacon, finely chopped
2 tablespoons plain flour
½ teaspoon dried mustard
½ teaspoon Worcestershire sauce
1 cup (250 ml/8 fl oz) milk
3 tablespoons chopped fresh parsley
¼ cup (60 ml/2 fl oz) cream, optional

1 To make the fish stock, put the fish in a deep frying pan, add 1.25 litres (40 fl oz) water and bring to the boil. Reduce the heat and simmer for 8 minutes, or until the fish flakes easily. Drain; reserve the stock. Discard the skin and bones and flake the fish. Set aside.
2 Put the potato, celery and onion in a pan with 3 cups (750 ml/24 fl oz) reserved stock. Bring to the boil, reduce the heat and simmer for 8 minutes, or until the vegetables are tender. Set aside.
3 Melt the butter in a large pan over low heat, add the bacon and stir for 3 minutes. Stir in the flour, mustard and Worcestershire sauce and cook for 1 minute, or until pale and foaming. Remove from the heat and gradually stir in the milk. Return to the heat and stir until the chowder boils and thickens. Reduce the heat and simmer for 2 minutes. Stir in the vegetables and stock mixture, then add the parsley and fish. Simmer over low heat for 5 minutes, or until heated through. Season and serve with cream.

ASIAN-STYLE SEAFOOD SOUP

Preparation time: 30 minutes
Total cooking time: 40 minutes
Serves 6

4 ripe tomatoes
1 tablespoon oil
5 cm (2 inch) piece fresh ginger, grated
3 stems lemon grass, white part only, finely chopped
3 small fresh red chillies, finely chopped
2 onions, chopped
3 cups (750 ml/24 fl oz) fish stock
4 kaffir lime leaves, finely shredded
160 g (5½ oz) fresh pineapple, chopped
1 tablespoon tamarind concentrate
1 tablespoon grated palm sugar or brown sugar
2 tablespoons lime juice
1 tablespoon fish sauce
500 g (1 lb) raw medium prawns
500 g (1 lb) skinless white fish fillets (eg. snapper, ocean perch, red rock cod, red mullet), cut into bite-sized pieces
2 tablespoons chopped fresh coriander

1 Score a cross in the base of each tomato. Place in a heatproof bowl and cover with boiling water. Leave for 30 seconds, transfer to cold water, drain and peel away from the cross. Cut the tomatoes in half, scoop out the seeds with a teaspoon and finely chop the flesh.
2 Heat the oil in a large pan, add the ginger, lemon grass, chilli and onion and stir over medium heat for 5 minutes, or until the onion is golden brown.
3 Add the tomato to the pan and cook for 3 minutes. Stir in the fish stock, kaffir lime leaves, pineapple, tamarind, sugar, lime juice, fish sauce and 3 cups (750 ml/24 fl oz) water. Cover and bring to the boil. Reduce the heat and simmer for 15 minutes.
4 Meanwhile, peel the prawns and gently pull out the dark vein from each prawn back, starting at the head end. Add the prawns, fish and coriander to the pan and simmer for 10 minutes, or until the seafood is tender. Season, to taste.

RED GAZPACHO
(COLD TOMATO SOUP)

Preparation time: 40 minutes +
    5 minutes soaking + 2 hours
    refrigeration
Total cooking time: Nil
Serves 4

1 kg (2 lb) vine-ripened tomatoes
2 slices day-old white Italian bread, crust removed, broken into pieces
1 red pepper (capsicum), seeded, roughly chopped
2 cloves garlic, chopped
1 small fresh green chilli, chopped, optional
1 teaspoon sugar
2 tablespoons red wine vinegar
2 tablespoons extra virgin olive oil
8 ice cubes

Garnish
½ Lebanese cucumber, seeded, diced
½ red pepper (capsicum), seeded, diced
½ green pepper (capsicum), seeded, finely diced
½ red onion, finely diced
½ ripe tomato, diced

1 Score a cross in the base of each tomato. Place in a bowl of boiling water for 10 seconds, then plunge into cold water and peel away from the cross. Cut the tomatoes in half and scoop out the seeds with a teaspoon. Chop the tomatoes.
2 Soak the bread in cold water for 5 minutes, then squeeze out any excess liquid. Place the bread in a food processor with the tomato, pepper, garlic, chilli, sugar and vinegar, and process until combined and smooth.
3 With the motor running, add the oil to make a smooth creamy mixture. Season, to taste. Refrigerate for at least 2 hours. Add a little extra vinegar, if desired.
4 For the garnish, mix the ingredients in a bowl. Put 2 ice cubes in each bowl of soup and serve the garnish in separate bowls.

FRAGRANT CORN, COCONUT AND CHICKEN NOODLE SOUP

Preparation time: 20 minutes + 10 minutes soaking
Total cooking time: 20 minutes
Serves 4

100 g (3½ oz) dried rice vermicelli
1 cup (250 ml/8 fl oz) coconut cream
2 cups (500 ml/16 fl oz) coconut milk
1 cup (250 ml/8 fl oz) chicken stock
130 g (4½ oz) creamed corn
500 g (1 lb) chicken thigh fillets, diced into 2 cm (¾ inch) squares
200 g (6½ oz) baby corn, halved lengthways
5 cm (2 inch) piece of galangal, thinly sliced
6 makrut (kaffir) lime leaves, finely shredded
2 stems lemon grass, white part only, bruised and cut into 5 cm (2 inch) pieces
2 tablespoons fish sauce
2 tablespoons lime juice
1 tablespoon grated palm sugar
½ cup (15 g/½ oz) coriander (cilantro) leaves

1 Soak the vermicelli in boiling water for 6–7 minutes, or until soft. Drain.
2 Put the coconut cream, coconut milk, chicken stock and creamed corn in a large saucepan and bring to the boil, then reduce the heat and simmer.
3 Add the chicken, baby corn, galangal, lime leaves and lemon grass and simmer until the chicken is tender.
4 Season with fish sauce, lime juice and palm sugar. Stir through half the coriander leaves and serve topped with the remaining leaves.

OXTAIL SOUP

Preparation time: 20 minutes + chilling
Total cooking time: 3 hours 20 minutes
Serves 4

1 tablespoon plain flour
1 kg (2 lb) oxtail, chopped into 5 cm (2 inch) pieces (ask your butcher to do this)
1 tablespoon oil
2 litres beef stock
1 onion, chopped
1 celery stick, chopped
2 carrots, chopped
1 swede or turnip, peeled and chopped
3 whole cloves
12 peppercorns
2 bay leaves
1 tablespoon plain flour, extra
2 tablespoons port
1 tablespoon tomato paste
⅓ cup (20 g/¾ oz) finely chopped fresh parsley

1 Season the flour, put it in a plastic bag with the oxtail and shake to coat. Shake off excess flour. Heat the oil in a large pan, add the oxtail and cook in batches, tossing continually, for 5 minutes, or until evenly browned. Return all the oxtail to the pan.
2 Add the stock, 1½ cups (375 ml/12 fl oz) water, vegetables, cloves, peppercorns, bay leaves and ½ teaspoon salt. Bring slowly to the boil then reduce the heat and simmer, covered, for 3 hours.
3 Strain the vegetables and meat, reserving the liquid. Discard the vegetables and leave the meat to cool. Pull the meat from the bone, shred and refrigerate. Meanwhile, refrigerate the stock until the fat has solidified on the surface and can be removed with a spoon. Add the meat.
4 Put the soup in a clean pan. Mix together the extra flour, port and tomato paste, and add to the pan. Bring to the boil, stirring, until the soup thickens slightly. Simmer for 10 minutes, then stir in the parsley.

COUNTRY PUMPKIN AND PASTA SOUP

Preparation time: 25 minutes
Total cooking time: 20 minutes
Serves 4–6

1 large onion
750 g (1½ lb) pumpkin
2 medium potatoes
1 tablespoon olive oil
30 g (1 oz) butter
2 cloves garlic, crushed
12 cups (3 litres) vegetable stock
125 g (4 oz) miniature pasta or risoni
1 tablespoon chopped fresh parsley, for serving (optional)

1 Peel the onion and chop finely. Peel pumpkin and potatoes and chop into small cubes. Heat oil and butter in a large pan. Add onion and garlic and cook, stirring, for 5 minutes over low heat.
2 Add the pumpkin, potatoes and stock. Increase heat, cover pan and cook for 10 minutes or until vegetables are tender.
3 Add pasta and cook, stirring occasionally, for 5 minutes or until just tender. Serve immediately. Sprinkle with chopped parsley, if desired.

FISH AND NOODLE SOUP

Preparation time: 15 minutes
Total cooking time: 20 minutes
Serves 4

200 g (6½ oz) dried rice vermicelli
1 tablespoon oil
2.5 cm (1 inch) piece fresh ginger, grated
3 small red chillies, finely chopped
4 spring onions, chopped
3½ cups (875 ml/28 fl oz) coconut milk
2 tablespoons fish sauce
2 tablespoons tomato paste (tomato purée, double concentrate)
500 g (1 lb) firm white fish fillets, cubed
2 ham steaks, diced
150 g (5 oz) snake beans, chopped
180 g (6 oz) bean sprouts, trimmed
1 cup (20 g/⅔ oz) fresh mint
½ cup (80 g/2⅔ oz) unsalted roasted peanuts

1 Soak the vermicelli in boiling water for 5 minutes; drain well. Heat the oil in a large, heavy-based pan and cook the ginger, chilli and spring onion and for 3 minutes, or until golden.
2 Stir in the coconut milk, fish sauce and tomato paste, cover and simmer for 10 minutes. Add the fish, ham and snake beans and simmer for 10 minutes, or until the fish is tender.
3 Divide the vermicelli among four bowls and top with bean sprouts and mint. Spoon the soup into the bowls and sprinkle with peanuts.

RAINBOW CONGEE

Preparation time: 15 minutes +
  30 minutes soaking
Total cooking time: 2 hours 15 minutes
Serves 6

200 g (61/2 oz) short-grain rice
2 dried Chinese mushrooms
85 g (3 oz) snow peas (mangetout), trimmed
2 Chinese sausages (lap cheong)
2 tablespoons oil
¼ red onion, finely diced
1 carrot, cut into 1 cm (½ inch) dice
2 litres (64 fl oz) chicken stock or water
3 teaspoons light soy sauce

1 Put the rice in a bowl and, using your fingers as a rake, rinse under cold running water to remove any dust. Drain the rice in a colander.
2 Soak the dried mushrooms in boiling water for 30 minutes, then drain and squeeze out any excess water. Remove and discard the stems and chop the caps into 5 mm (¼ inch) dice. Cut the snow peas into 1 cm (½ inch) pieces.
3 Place the sausages on a plate in a steamer. Cover and steam over simmering water in a wok for 10 minutes, then cut them into 1 cm (½ inch) pieces.

4 Heat a wok over medium heat, add the oil and heat until hot. Stir-fry the sausage until it is brown and the fat has melted out of it. Remove with a wire sieve or slotted spoon and drain. Pour the oil from the wok, leaving 1 tablespoon.
5 Reheat the reserved oil over high heat until very hot. Stir-fry the red onion until soft and transparent. Add the mushrooms and carrot and stir-fry for 1 minute, or until fragrant.
6 Put the mushroom mixture in a clay pot, casserole dish or saucepan and stir in the soy sauce, rice, 2 litres (64 fl oz) stock or water and ¼ teaspoon salt. Bring to the boil, then reduce the heat and simmer very gently, stirring occasionally, for 1¾–2 hours, or until it has a porridge-like texture and the rice is breaking up. If it is too thick, add the remaining stock and return to the boil. Toss in the snow peas and sausage, cover and stand for 5 minutes before serving.

MEDITERRANEAN FISH SOUP

Preparation time: 30 minutes
Total cooking time: 45 minutes
Serves 4

½ teaspoon saffron threads
3 teaspoons oil
2 large onions, thinly sliced
1 leek, white part only, chopped
4 cloves garlic, finely chopped
1 bay leaf, torn
½ teaspoon dried marjoram
1 teaspoon grated orange rind
2 tablespoons dry white wine
1 red pepper (capsicum), cut into bite-sized pieces
500 g (1 lb) ripe tomatoes, chopped
½ cup (125 ml/4 fl oz) tomato passata
2 cups (500 ml/16 fl oz) fish stock
2 tablespoons tomato paste (tomato purée)
2 teaspoons soft brown sugar
500 g (1 lb) skinless fish fillets (eg. snapper, red mullet, red rock cod, ocean perch), cut into bite-sized pieces
3 tablespoons chopped fresh parsley

1 In a small bowl, soak the saffron threads in 2 tablespoons boiling water.
2 Heat the oil in a large heavy-based pan, over low heat. Add the onion, leek, garlic, bay leaf and marjoram. Cover and cook for 10 minutes, shaking the pan occasionally, until the onion is soft. Add the rind, wine, pepper and tomato, cover and cook for 10 minutes.
3 Add the tomato passata, fish stock, tomato paste, sugar and saffron (with the liquid) to the pan. Stir well and bring to the boil, then reduce the heat to low and simmer, uncovered, for 15 minutes.
4 Add the fish to the soup, cover and cook for 8 minutes, or until tender. Add salt and pepper, to taste, and half the parsley. Discard the bay leaf. Sprinkle the soup with the remaining parsley just before serving. Delicious served with slices of crusty bread.

CURRIED CHICKEN NOODLE SOUP

Preparation time: 15 minutes
Total cooking time: 50 minutes
Serves 4

175 g (6 oz) dried thin egg noodles
¼ cup (60 ml/2 fl oz) peanut oil
2 x 250 g (8 oz) chicken breast fillets
1 onion, sliced
1 small fresh red chilli, seeded and finely chopped
1 tablespoon finely chopped fresh ginger
2 tablespoons Indian curry powder
3 cups (750 ml/24 fl oz) good-quality chicken stock
800 ml (26 fl oz) coconut milk
300 g (10 oz) baby bok choy, cut into long strips
4 tablespoons torn fresh basil

1 Cook the egg noodles in a large saucepan of boiling water for 3 minutes. Drain and rinse.
2 Heat a wok over medium heat, add 1 tablespoon oil and swirl to coat. Add the chicken and cook on each side for 5 minutes, or until cooked. Remove the chicken and keep warm. Clean the wok.
3 Return the wok to the heat, add the rest of the oil and swirl to coat. Add the onion and cook over low heat for 4–6 minutes, or until soft but not brown. Add the chilli, ginger and curry powder and cook for a further 1–2 minutes. Pour in the stock and bring to the boil. Reduce the heat and simmer for 10 minutes. Thinly slice the chicken on the diagonal.
4 Add the coconut milk to the wok and simmer for 8 minutes, then add the bok choy and cook for 3 minutes. Stir in the basil just before serving.
5 To serve, divide the noodles among four deep serving bowls. Top with slices of chicken and ladle in the soup. Serve immediately.

PRAWN AND UDON NOODLE SOUP

Preparation time: 20 minutes
Total cooking time: 30 minutes
Serves 6

500 g (1 lb) raw medium prawns
1½ tablespoons oil
1 stem lemon grass, white part only, chopped
2 cloves garlic, chopped
2 small fresh red chillies, cut in half
2 fresh kaffir lime leaves
1 lime, quartered
4 spring onions, sliced on the diagonal
500 g (1 lb) dried udon noodles
2 tablespoons soy sauce
100 g (3½ oz) shiitake mushrooms, halved
1 tablespoon fresh coriander leaves
500 g (1 lb) baby bok choy, trimmed, leaves separated

1 Peel the prawns, reserving the heads and shells. Gently pull out the dark vein from each prawn back, starting at the head end.
2 Heat the oil in a large pan, add the prawn heads and shells and cook over high heat until pink. Add the lemon grass, garlic, red chillies, kaffir lime leaves, lime quarters, half the spring onion and 2 litres (64 fl oz) water. Bring to the boil, reduce the heat and simmer for 20 minutes. Pour through a fine strainer into a bowl and discard the solids. Rinse the pan and return the stock to the pan.
3 Add the noodles to a large pan of boiling salted water and cook for 5 minutes, or until tender. Drain well.
4 Bring the stock to the boil. Add the soy sauce and prawns to the pan and cook for 5 minutes, or until the prawns turn pink and are cooked through. Add the remaining ingredients and season with salt and pepper, to taste.
5 Divide the cooked noodles among the soup bowls, then ladle the soup over them. The soup can be served garnished with extra lime wedges if you wish.

SPANISH-STYLE RICE, MUSSEL, PRAWN AND CHORIZO SOUP

Preparation time: 45 minutes
Total cooking time: 45 minutes
Serves 4

1 kg (2 lb) black mussels
1 cup (250 ml/8 fl oz) dry sherry
1 tablespoon olive oil
1 red onion, chopped
200 g (6½ oz) chorizo sausage, thinly
   sliced on the diagonal
4 garlic cloves, crushed
½ cup (100 g/3½ oz) long-grain rice
400 g (13 oz) tin chopped tomatoes
2 litres (64 fl oz) chicken stock
½ teaspoon saffron threads
2 bay leaves
1 tablespoon chopped oregano
500 g (1 lb) raw prawns (shrimp), peeled
   and deveined, tails intact
3 tablespoons chopped flat-leaf (Italian)
   parsley

1 Scrub the mussels with a stiff brush and pull out the hairy beards. Discard any broken mussels or open ones that don't close when tapped on the bench. Rinse well. Put the mussels in a saucepan with the sherry and cook, covered, over high heat for 3 minutes,
or until the mussels have opened. Strain the liquid into a bowl. Discard any unopened mussels. Remove all but 8 mussels from their shells and discard the empty shells.

2 Heat the oil in a large saucepan over medium heat, add the onion and cook for 5 minutes, or until softened but not browned. Add the chorizo and cook for 3–5 minutes, or until browned, then add the garlic and cook for a further 1 minute.
3 Add the rice to the mixture and stir to coat with the chorizo mixture. Add the reserved mussel cooking liquid and cook for 1 minute before adding the chopped tomatoes, stock, saffron, bay leaves and oregano. Bring to the boil, then reduce the heat and simmer, covered, for 25 minutes.
4 Add the prawns and the mussels (except the ones in their shells) to the soup, cover with a lid, and cook for 3 minutes, then stir in the parsley. Ladle into four bowls, then top each bowl with 2 mussels still in their shells.

TOMATO SOUP WITH PASTA AND BASIL

Preparation time: 25 minutes
Total cooking time: 35 minutes
Serves 4

3 large ripe tomatoes (750 g/1½ lb)
2 tablespoons olive oil
1 medium onion, finely chopped
1 clove garlic, crushed
1 small red pepper (capsicum), finely
   chopped
4 cups (1 litre) vegetable stock
3 tablespoons tomato paste
salt and pepper
1 teaspoon sugar
¼ cup (7 g/¼ oz) basil leaves, or 1½
   teaspoons dried basil
1 cup (155 g/5 oz) small shell pasta or
   macaroni
fresh basil leaves, extra

1 Cut a small cross in the top of each tomato. Place in a bowl and cover with boiling water for about 2 minutes; drain and cool. Peel skin downward from the cross and discard. Roughly chop flesh. Heat oil in a large heavy-based pan. Add onion, garlic and red pepper; cook, stirring, for 10 minutes or until all ingredients are soft. Add tomatoes and cook another 10 minutes.
2 Add the stock, tomato paste, salt, pepper and sugar. Cover and simmer for 15 minutes. Remove from the heat, add the basil. Allow to cool. Process in batches, in a food processor or blender, until smooth. Return the mixture to the pan and reheat gently.
3 Cook the pasta separately in boiling salted water until tender; drain. Add to soup and heat through. Serve sprinkled with fresh basil leaves.

CHILLI, CORN AND RED CAPSICUM SOUP

Preparation time: 20 minutes
Total cooking time: 45 minutes
Serves 4

1 coriander sprig
4 corn cobs
30 g (1 oz) butter
2 red capsicums, diced
1 small onion, finely chopped
1 small red chilli, finely chopped
1 tablespoon plain flour
2 cups (500 ml/16 fl oz) vegetable stock
½ cup (125 ml/4 fl oz) cream

1 Trim the leaves off the coriander and finely chop the root and stems. Cut the kernels off the corn cobs.
2 Heat the butter in a large saucepan over medium heat. Add the corn kernels, capsicum, onion and chilli and stir to coat the vegetables in the butter. Cook, covered, over low heat, stirring occasionally, for 10 minutes, or until the vegetables are soft. Increase the heat to medium and add the coriander root and stem. Cook, stirring, for 30 seconds, or until fragrant. Sprinkle with the flour and stir for a further minute. Remove from the heat and gradually add the vegetable stock, stirring together. Add 2 cups (500 ml/16 fl oz) water and return to the heat. Bring to the boil, reduce the heat to low and simmer, covered, for 30 minutes, or until the vegetables are tender. Cool slightly.
3 Ladle about 2 cups (500 ml/16 fl oz) of the soup into a blender and purée until smooth. Return the purée to the soup in the saucepan, pour in the cream and gently heat until warmed through. Season to taste with salt. Sprinkle with the coriander leaves to serve. Delicious with grilled cheese on pitta bread.

RICE NOODLE SOUP WITH DUCK

Preparation time: 40 minutes
Total cooking time: 25 minutes
Serves 4–6

1 whole Chinese roast duck
4 coriander (cilantro) roots and stems, well rinsed
5 slices galangal
4 spring onions (scallions), sliced on the diagonal into 3 cm (1¼ inch) lengths
400 g (13 oz) Chinese broccoli, cut into 5 cm (2 inch) lengths
2 garlic cloves, crushed
3 tablespoons fish sauce
1 tablespoon hoisin sauce
2 teaspoons grated palm sugar
½ teaspoon ground white pepper
500 g (1 lb) fresh rice noodles
crisp fried shallots, to garnish (optional)
coriander (cilantro) leaves, to garnish

1 To make the stock, cut off the duck's head with a sharp knife and discard. Remove the skin and fat from the duck, leaving the neck intact. Carefully remove the flesh from the bones and set aside. Cut any visible fat from the carcass along with the parson's nose, then discard. Break the carcass into large pieces, then put in a large stockpot with 2 litres (64 fl oz) water.
2 Bruise the coriander roots and stems with the back of a knife. Add to the pot with the galangal and bring to the boil. Skim off any foam that floats on the surface. Boil over medium heat for 15 minutes. Strain the stock through a fine sieve—discard the carcass and return the stock to a large clean saucepan.
3 Slice the duck flesh into strips. Add to the stock with the spring onion, Chinese broccoli, garlic, fish sauce, hoisin sauce, palm sugar and white pepper. Gently bring to the boil.
4 Cook the noodles in boiling water for 2–3 minutes, or until tender. Drain well. Divide the noodles and soup evenly among the serving bowls. If desired, garnish. Serve immediately.

CREAMY FISH SOUP

Preparation time: 10 minutes
Total cooking time: 35 minutes
Serves 4–6

¼ teaspoon saffron threads
1 litre (32 fl oz) fish stock
½ cup (125 ml/4 fl oz) dry white wine
1 onion, finely chopped
1 small carrot, finely chopped
1 stick celery, chopped
1 bay leaf
45 g (1½ oz) butter
2 tablespoons plain flour
300 g (10 oz) skinless fish fillets (eg. snapper, orange roughy, bream), in bite-sized pieces
1 cup (250 ml/8 fl oz) cream
2 teaspoons chopped fresh chives, to garnish

1 In a small bowl, soak the saffron threads in 2 tablespoons boiling water.
2 Put the fish stock, wine, onion, carrot, celery and bay leaf in a large saucepan and slowly bring to the boil. Cover and simmer for 20 minutes. Strain and discard the vegetables. Stir the saffron (with the liquid) into the hot stock.
3 In a clean saucepan, melt the butter and stir in the flour for 2 minutes, or until pale and foaming. Remove from the heat and gradually stir in the fish stock. Return to the heat and stir until the mixture boils and thickens.
4 Add the fish and simmer for 2 minutes, or until the fish is cooked. Stir in the cream and heat through without boiling. Season with salt and ground white pepper, to taste. Serve garnished with chives.

NOTE: Saffron threads are quite costly, but they add a subtle flavour and vivid yellow touch to food. The bright orange threads are sold in small glass jars or tiny plastic packets. Some people squeeze the threads after soaking, to release more colour into the water.

CHINESE CHICKEN AND CORN SOUP

Preparation time: 10 minutes
Total cooking time: 15 minutes
Serves 4

3 cups (750 ml/24 fl oz) good-quality
  chicken stock
2 x 200 g (6½ oz) chicken breast fillets
3–4 corn cobs
1 tablespoon vegetable oil
4 spring onions, thinly sliced, greens
  chopped and reserved for garnish
1 clove garlic, crushed
2 teaspoons grated fresh ginger
310 g (10 oz) can creamed corn
2 tablespoons light soy sauce
1 tablespoon Chinese rice wine
1 tablespoon cornflour
2 teaspoons sesame oil

1 Bring the stock to simmering point in a small saucepan. Add the chicken and remove the pan from the heat. Cover the pan and leave the chicken to cool in the liquid. Remove the chicken with a slotted spoon, then finely shred the meat using your fingers. Cut the corn kernels from the cobs—you should get about 2 cups (400 g/13 oz).
2 Heat a wok over medium–high heat, add the oil and swirl to coat. Add the spring onion, garlic and ginger and stir-fry for 30 seconds before adding the stock, corn kernels, creamed corn, soy sauce, rice wine and 1 cup (250 ml/8 fl oz) water. Stir until the soup comes to the boil, then reduce the heat and simmer for 10 minutes. Add the chicken meat.
3 Stir the cornflour, sesame oil and 1 tablespoon water together in a small bowl until smooth. Add a little of the hot stock, stir together, then pour this mixture into the soup. Bring to simmering point, stirring constantly for 3–4 minutes, or until slightly thickened. Season to taste. Garnish with the chopped reserved spring onion greens.

COCONUT AND LEMON GRASS SOUP WITH PRAWN WON TONS

Preparation time: 30 minutes +
  overnight refrigeration
Total cooking time: 1 hour 10 minutes
Serves 4

Stock
1.5 kg (3 lb) chicken bones, washed
1 onion, roughly chopped
1 cup (125 g/4 oz) roughly chopped celery

Won tons
325 g (11 oz) raw small prawns, peeled
  and deveined, finely chopped
2 tablespoons finely chopped fresh
  coriander leaves
1 tablespoon shredded fresh Thai basil
2 tablespoons finely chopped celery
2 spring onions, finely chopped
12 won ton wrappers
1 egg, lightly beaten

Broth
2 tablespoons tom yam paste
3 stems lemon grass, white part only,
  thinly sliced
6 fresh kaffir lime leaves
2 small fresh red chillies, finely chopped
200 ml (6½ fl oz) coconut milk
1 tablespoon grated palm sugar
1 tablespoon lime juice
1 tablespoon fish sauce
fresh coriander leaves, to garnish

1 To make the stock, put the chicken bones, onion, celery and 3 litres (96 fl oz) water in a large saucepan and bring slowly to a simmer over medium heat. Skim off any scum that rises to the surface. Reduce the heat and simmer for 1 hour, skimming the surface when necessary. Strain the stock through a fine sieve and allow to cool. Cover with plastic wrap and refrigerate overnight. Remove the layer of fat from the surface once it has solidified.

2 To make the won tons, combine the prawn meat, coriander, basil, celery and spring onion. Lay the won ton wrappers out on a clean work surface. Place a heaped teaspoon of prawn mixture in the centre of each wrapper. Brush the edge of each wrapper with a little of the beaten egg. Lift the sides up tightly and pinch around the filling to form a pouch. Repeat with the remaining wrappers and filling to make 20 won tons in total. Cover and refrigerate.
3 Heat a wok over medium heat, add the tom yam paste and cook for 10 seconds, or until fragrant. Gradually whisk in 1 litre (32 fl oz) of the chicken stock until combined, then bring to the boil over high heat. Reduce the heat to medium, then add the lemon grass, lime leaves, chilli and coconut milk and simmer for 5 minutes. Stir in the sugar, lime juice and fish sauce. Gently add the won tons and simmer for 2 minutes, or until cooked through. Remove the won tons with a slotted spoon and place five in each serving bowl. Ladle the broth into the bowls and garnish with fresh coriander leaves.

NOTE: Freeze the remaining stock.

TOMATO DITALINI SOUP

Preparation time: 15 minutes
Total cooking time: 20 minutes
Serves 4

2 tablespoons olive oil
1 large onion, finely chopped
2 celery sticks, finely chopped
3 vine-ripened tomatoes
1.5 litres chicken or vegetable stock
½ cup (90 g/3 oz) ditalini pasta
2 tablespoons chopped fresh
   flat-leaf parsley

1 Heat the oil in a large saucepan over medium heat. Add the onion and celery and cook for 5 minutes, or until they have softened.
2 Score a cross in the base of each tomato, then place them in a bowl of boiling water for 1 minute. Plunge into cold water and peel the skin away from the cross. Halve the tomatoes and scoop out the seeds. Roughly chop the flesh. Add the stock and tomato to the onion mixture and bring to the boil. Add the pasta and cook for 10 minutes, or until al dente. Season and sprinkle with parsley. Serve with crusty bread.

CHICKEN LAKSA

Preparation time: 30 minutes +
   10 minutes soaking
Total cooking time: 35 minutes
Serves 4–6

1½ tablespoons coriander seeds
1 tablespoon cumin seeds
1 teaspoon ground turmeric
1 onion, roughly chopped
1 tablespoon roughly chopped ginger
3 garlic cloves, peeled
3 stems lemon grass (white part only),
   sliced
6 candlenuts or macadamias (see Notes)
4–6 small red chillies
2–3 teaspoons shrimp paste, roasted
   (see Notes)
1 litre (32 fl oz) chicken stock
¼ cup (60 ml/2 fl oz) oil
400 g (13 oz) chicken thigh fillets, cut into
   2 cm (¾ inch) pieces
3 cups (750 ml/24 fl oz) coconut milk
4 makrut (kaffir) lime leaves
2½ tablespoons lime juice
2 tablespoons fish sauce
2 tablespoons grated palm sugar or soft
   brown sugar
250 g (8 oz) dried rice vermicelli
90 g (3 oz) bean sprouts, tailed
4 fried tofu puffs, julienned
3 tablespoons roughly chopped
   Vietnamese mint
⅔ cup (20 g/¾ oz) coriander (cilantro)
   leaves
lime wedges, to serve

1 Roast the coriander and cumin seeds in a dry saucepan or frying pan over medium heat for 1–2 minutes, or until fragrant, tossing the pan constantly to prevent them burning. Grind finely in a mortar and pestle or a spice grinder.
2 Put all the spices, onion, ginger, garlic, lemon grass, candlenuts, chillies and shrimp paste in a food processor or blender. Add about ½ cup (125 ml/4 fl oz) of the stock and blend to a paste.

3 Heat the oil in a wok or large saucepan over low heat and gently cook the paste for 3–5 minutes, stirring constantly to prevent it burning or sticking to the bottom. Add the remaining stock and bring to the boil over high heat. Reduce the heat to medium and simmer for 15 minutes, or until reduced slightly. Add the chicken and simmer for 4–5 minutes, or until cooked through.
4 Add the coconut milk, lime leaves, lime juice, fish sauce and palm sugar and simmer for 5 minutes over medium–low heat. Do not bring to the boil or cover with a lid, as the coconut milk will split.
5 Meanwhile, put the vermicelli in a heatproof bowl, cover with boiling water and soak for 6–7 minutes, or until softened. Drain and divide among large serving bowls with the bean sprouts. Ladle the hot soup over the top and garnish with some tofu strips, mint and coriander leaves. Serve with a wedge of lime.

NOTES: Raw candlenuts are slightly toxic so must be cooked before use.
   To roast the shrimp paste, wrap the paste in foil and put under a hot grill (broiler) for 1 minute.

SOUPE DE POISSON

Preparation time: 30 minutes
Total cooking time: 45 minutes
Serves 6

1 large ripe tomato
1½ kg (3 lb) chopped fish bones from
  white-fleshed fish
1 leek, white part only, chopped
1 carrot, chopped
1 stick celery, chopped
1 large clove garlic, chopped
1 bay leaf
3 fresh parsley stalks
6 black peppercorns
1 cup (250 ml/8 fl oz) dry white wine
1 tablespoon lemon juice
250 g (8 oz) skinless fish fillets (eg.
  snapper, perch, cod, red mullet), cut
  into bite-sized pieces
2 tablespoons chervil leaves
¼ lemon, cut into very fine slices

1 Score a cross in the base of the tomato.
Place in a heatproof bowl and cover with
boiling water. Leave for 30 seconds,
transfer to cold water, drain and peel
away from the cross. Cut the tomato in
half, scoop out the seeds with a teaspoon
and finely chop the flesh.
2 Rinse the bones well in cold water and
combine in a large pan with the leek,
carrot, celery, garlic, bay leaf, parsley,
peppercorns, wine, lemon juice and
2 litres (64 fl oz) water. Slowly bring to
the boil, skimming off any scum that
forms on the surface. Reduce the heat
and simmer for 20 minutes.
3 Strain and discard the fish and
vegetables. Strain the soup again, through a
sieve lined with dampened muslin, into a
clean pan. Simmer, uncovered, for 10 minutes.
4 Add the fish pieces and simmer for
2 minutes, or until tender. Season, to
taste, with salt and ground white pepper.
5 Divide the chopped tomato and chervil
among six warm bowls and ladle the hot
soup over them. Float lemon slices on top
and serve immediately.

TWELVE VARIETIES SOUP

Preparation time: 45 minutes +
20 minutes soaking
Total cooking time: 20 minutes
Serves 8

300 g (9⅔ oz) pork liver or lamb liver
200 g (6½ oz) chicken breast fillet
30 g (1 oz) dried Chinese mushrooms
3 tablespoons oil
3 medium onions, finely sliced
4 cloves garlic, finely chopped
1 teaspoon finely chopped fresh ginger
2 tablespoons fish sauce
⅓ cup (40 g/1⅓ oz) diagonally and thinly
  sliced green beans
⅓ cup (40 g/1⅓ oz) small cauliflower
  florets
⅓ cup (30 g/1 oz) sliced button
  mushrooms
8 cups (2 litres) water
⅓ cup (25 g/¾ oz) shredded Chinese
  cabbage
⅓ cup (20 g/⅔ oz) shredded spinach
⅓ cup (30 g/1 oz) bean sprouts
3 spring onions, finely sliced
1 tablespoon fresh coriander leaves
3 eggs
1 tablespoon soy sauce
¼ teaspoon ground black pepper
wedges of lime, to serve

1 Cook the liver in simmering water
for 5 minutes, cool and slice thinly.
Cut the chicken into thin slices. Place
the Chinese mushrooms in a
heatproof bowl, cover with boiling
water and soak for 20 minutes; drain
well and slice.
2 Heat the oil in a wok, add the onion
and cook over medium heat for about
5 minutes, until lightly golden. Add
the slices of liver and chicken and
stir to combine. Add the garlic and
ginger and cook for another minute,
then pour in the fish sauce and cook
for 2 more minutes.
3 Place the Chinese mushrooms,
beans, cauliflower, button
mushrooms and onion mixture in a
large pan. Add the water, bring to the
boil and cook until the vegetables are
just tender. Add the cabbage, spinach
and bean sprouts and cook a further
5 minutes, until just tender. Stir in
the spring onion and coriander.
4 Break the eggs into the boiling
soup and stir immediately. (The eggs
will break up and cook.) Add the soy
sauce and pepper and serve
immediately with the wedges of lime
to squeeze into the soup.

SALADS

GARDEN SALAD

Preparation time: 15 minutes
Total cooking time: Nil
Serves 4–6

1 green oak-leaf lettuce
150 g (4¾ oz) rocket
1 small radicchio lettuce
1 large green pepper (capsicum), cut into thin strips
zest of 1 lemon

Dressing
2 tablespoons roughly chopped fresh coriander
¼ cup (60 ml/2 fl oz) lemon juice
2 teaspoons soft brown sugar
2 tablespoons olive oil
1 clove garlic, crushed (optional)

1 Wash and dry the salad greens thoroughly; tear into bite-size pieces. Combine salad greens, green pepper and lemon zest in a large serving bowl.
2 To make Dressing: Whisk all ingredients in a small mixing bowl for 2 minutes or until well combined. Pour dressing over salad and toss to combine. Serve chilled.

NOTE: Make dressing and salad just before serving. Choose a selection of your favourite salad greens for this recipe. This is delicious served in summer with a chilled frascati or a light red wine.

COLESLAW

Preparation time: 20 minutes
Total cooking time: Nil
Serves 10

½ green (savoy) cabbage
¼ red cabbage
3 carrots, coarsely grated
6 radishes, coarsely grated
1 red pepper (capsicum), chopped
4 spring onions, sliced
3 tablespoons chopped fresh flat-leaf parsley
1 cup (250 g/8 oz) good-quality mayonnaise

1 Remove the hard cores from the cabbages and thinly shred the leaves with a sharp knife. Place in a large bowl and add the carrot, radish, red pepper, spring onion and parsley.
2 Add the mayonnaise, season with salt and freshly ground black pepper and toss well.

NOTE: The vegetables can be chopped and refrigerated for up to 3 hours before serving. Add the mayonnaise just before serving.

SALATA HORIATIKI
(GREEK SALAD)

Preparation time: 20 minutes
Total cooking time: Nil
Serves 4

1 telegraph cucumber, peeled
2 green peppers (capsicums)
4 vine-ripened tomatoes, cut into wedges
1 red onion, finely sliced
16 Kalamata olives
250 g (8 oz) Greek feta, cubed
24 fresh flat-leaf parsley leaves
12 whole fresh mint leaves
½ cup (125 ml/4 fl oz) good-quality olive oil
2 tablespoons lemon juice
1 clove garlic, crushed

1 Cut the cucumber in half lengthways and discard the seeds. Cut into bite-sized pieces. Cut each pepper in half lengthways, remove the membrane and seeds and cut the flesh into 1 cm (½ inch) wide strips. Gently mix the cucumber, green pepper, tomato, onion, olives, feta, parsley and mint leaves in a large salad bowl.
2 Place the oil, lemon juice and garlic in a screw top jar, season and shake well. Pour over the salad and serve.

CHICKPEA AND OLIVE SALAD

Preparation time: 20 minutes +
overnight soaking
Total cooking time: 25 minutes
Serves 6

1½ cups (330 g/10½ oz) dried chickpeas
1 small Lebanese cucumber
2 medium tomatoes
1 small red (Spanish) onion
3 tablespoons chopped fresh parsley
½ cup (60 g/2 oz) pitted black olives
1 tablespoon lemon juice
3 tablespoons olive oil
1 clove garlic, crushed
1 teaspoon honey

1 Place the chickpeas in a large bowl and cover with cold water. Leave to soak overnight. Drain the chickpeas, place in a pan, cover with fresh water and cook for 25 minutes or until just tender. Drain and allow to cool.
2 Cut the cucumber in half lengthways, scoop out seeds and cut into 1 cm (½ inch) slices. Cut the tomatoes into cubes roughly the same size as the chickpeas, and chop onion finely. Combine the chickpeas, cucumber, tomato, onion, parsley and olives in a serving bowl.
3 Place the lemon juice, oil, garlic and honey in a small screw-top jar and shake well. Pour the dressing over the salad and toss lightly to combine. Serve at room temperature.

GREEN OLIVE, WALNUT AND POMEGRANATE SALAD

Preparation time: 10 minutes
Total cooking time: Nil
Serves 4

1 cup (100 g/3½ oz) walnut halves
½ cup (125 ml/4 fl oz) olive oil
1½ tablespoons pomegranate syrup
½ teaspoon chilli flakes
2 cups (350 g/11 oz) green olives, pitted
  and cut in halves
1 cup (175 g/6 oz) pomegranate seeds
1 large red onion, chopped
1 cup (20 g/¾ oz) fresh flat-leaf parsley
  leaves

1 Soak the walnut halves in boiling water for 3–4 minutes, or until the skins peel off readily. Drain, peel and pat dry. Lightly toast under a medium grill and when cool, roughly chop.
2 Combine the olive oil, pomegranate syrup and chilli flakes in a screw top jar and shake well.
3 Place the olives, pomegranate seeds, onion, walnuts and parsley in a bowl and toss. Just before serving, pour the dressing over, season, to taste, and combine well.

WILD RICE SALAD

Preparation time: 20 minutes + cooling
Total cooking time: 1 hour
Serves 4

½ cup (95 g/3 oz) wild rice
1 cup (250 ml/8 fl oz) chicken stock
20 g (¾ oz) butter
½ cup (100 g/3½ oz) basmati rice
½ cup (60 g/2 oz) slivered almonds
1 tablespoon olive oil
2 back bacon rashers, chopped
125 g (4 oz) currants
1 cup (30 g/1 oz) chopped parsley
6 thinly sliced spring onions (scallions)
grated zest and juice of 1 lemon
olive oil, to drizzle
lemon wedges, to serve

1 Put the wild rice and stock in a saucepan, add the butter, bring to the boil, then cook, covered, over low heat for 1 hour. Drain.
2 Meanwhile, put the basmati rice in a separate saucepan with cold water and bring to the boil. Cook at a simmer for 12 minutes, then drain.
3 Mix the rices together in a bowl and leave to cool to room temperature.
4 Lightly toast the slivered almonds in a dry frying pan for a few minutes, or until lightly golden, watching carefully to make sure they don't burn. Heat the oil in the same pan and cook the bacon for 5 minutes, or until cooked. Remove from the pan and cool.
5 Combine the rice with the bacon, currants, almonds, parsley, spring onion and lemon zest and juice. Season with salt and freshly ground black pepper, drizzle with olive oil and serve with lemon wedges.

BEEF AND NOODLE SALAD

Preparation time: 25 minutes +
    5 minutes soaking
Total cooking time: 10 minutes
Serves 4

500 g (1 lb) beef fillet, 5 cm (2 inches)
    in diameter
1½ tablespoons vegetable oil
1 teaspoon dried shrimp
1 teaspoon jasmine rice
1 stem lemon grass (white part only),
    finely chopped
1 small red chilli, seeded and finely
    chopped
2 coriander (cilantro) roots, finely
    chopped
2 makrut (kaffir) lime leaves, finely
    shredded
1–2 tablespoons lime juice
2 teaspoons finely chopped ginger
300 g (10 oz) dried rice vermicelli
1 Lebanese (short) cucumber, peeled,
    cut in half lengthways and cut into
    1 cm (½ inch) pieces
1 vine-ripened tomato, cut into 1 cm
    (½ inch) wedges
1 red onion, cut into thin wedges
3 tablespoons torn Thai basil
3 tablespoons Vietnamese mint
1 tablespoon crisp fried shallots
2 tablespoons coriander (cilantro) leaves

Dressing
⅓ cup (80 ml/2¾ fl oz) lime juice
2 tablespoons grated palm sugar
1 tablespoon fish sauce
1 small red chilli, seeded and finely
    chopped
1 teaspoon sesame oil
½ teaspoon tamarind purée

1 Heat a chargrill plate or frying pan over
high heat. Brush the beef with the
vegetable oil and season generously with
salt and black pepper. Sear on all sides
for 3–4 minutes, ensuring the meat
remains rare in the centre. Remove from
the plate and allow to rest.
2 Dry-fry the dried shrimp and rice in a
clean frying pan for 1–2 minutes, or until
fragrant. Put in a spice grinder or mortar
and pestle and grind to a fine powder.
Mix the powder with the lemon grass,
chilli, coriander roots, lime leaves, lime
juice and ginger in a non-metallic bowl.
Add the beef and turn to coat well on all
sides. Cover with plastic wrap and
marinate for at least 5 minutes, then cut
into 1 cm (½ inch) thick slices across
the grain.
3 To make the dressing, combine all the
ingredients in a small bowl.
4 Put the vermicelli in a heatproof bowl,
cover with boiling water and soak for
6–7 minutes, or until softened. Drain,
rinse under cold water and drain again.
Transfer the noodles to a large bowl, then
add the beef, cucumber, tomato, onion,
basil, mint and dressing and toss well.
Serve garnished with the crisp fried
shallots and coriander leaves.

CAESAR SALAD

Preparation time: 25 minutes
Total cooking time: 20 minutes
Serves 6

1 small French bread stick
2 tablespoons olive oil
2 cloves garlic, halved
4 rashers bacon (trimmed of fat)
2 cos lettuces
10 anchovy fillets, halved lengthways
1 cup (100 g/3½ oz) shaved Parmesan
Parmesan shavings, extra, for serving

Dressing
1 egg yolk
2 cloves garlic, crushed
2 teaspoons Dijon mustard
2 anchovy fillets
2 tablespoons white wine vinegar
1 tablespoon Worcestershire sauce
¾ cup (185 ml/6 fl oz) olive oil

1 Preheat the oven to moderate 180°C
(350°F/Gas 4). To make the croutons, cut
the bread stick into 15 thin slices and brush
both sides of each slice with oil. Spread
them all on a baking tray and bake for
10–15 minutes, or until golden brown.
Leave to cool slightly, then rub each side of
each slice with the cut edge of a garlic
clove. The baked bread can then be broken
roughly into pieces or cut into small cubes.
2 Cook the bacon under a hot grill until
crisp. Drain on paper towels until cooled,
then break into chunky pieces.
3 Tear the lettuce into pieces and put in a
large serving bowl with the bacon,
anchovies, croutons and Parmesan.
4 For the dressing, place the egg yolks,
garlic, mustard, anchovies, vinegar and
Worcestershire sauce in a food processor
or blender. Season and process for
20 seconds, or until smooth. With the motor
running, add enough oil in a thin stream to
make the dressing thick and creamy.
5 Drizzle the dressing over the salad and
toss gently. Sprinkle the Parmesan shavings
over the top and serve immediately.

TUNA AND CANNELLINI BEAN SALAD

Preparation time: 25 minutes
Total cooking time: 5 minutes
Serves 4–6

400 g (13 oz) tuna steaks
1 tablespoon olive oil
1 small red onion, thinly sliced
1 ripe tomato, seeded and chopped
1 small red pepper (capsicum), thinly sliced
2 x 400 g (13 oz) cans cannellini beans
2 cloves garlic, crushed
1 teaspoon chopped fresh thyme
4 tablespoons chopped fresh flat-leaf parsley
1½ tablespoons lemon juice
⅓ cup (80 ml/2¾ floz) extra virgin olive oil
1 teaspoon honey
100 g (3½ oz) rocket (arugula)
1 teaspoon lemon zest

1 Heat the grill or barbecue. Place the tuna steaks on a plate, brush with the oil and sprinkle with cracked black pepper on both sides. Cover with plastic wrap and refrigerate until needed.
2 Combine the onion, tomato and red pepper in a large bowl. Rinse the cannellini beans under cold running water for 30 seconds, drain and add to the bowl with the garlic, thyme and 3 tablespoons of the parsley.
3 Place the lemon juice, oil and honey in a small saucepan, bring to the boil, then reduce the heat to low and simmer, stirring, for 1 minute, or until the honey dissolves. Remove from the heat.
4 Sear the tuna for 1 minute on each side. The meat should still be pink in the middle. Slice into 3 cm (11/4 inch) cubes and combine with the salad. Pour on the warm dressing and toss well.
5 Place the rocket on a large platter. Top with the salad, season and garnish with the lemon zest and remaining parsley. Serve immediately.

CONCHIGLIE SALAD WITH BOCCONCINI, ASPARAGUS AND OREGANO

Preparation time: 25 minutes
Total cooking time: 10–15 minutes
Serves 4–6

350 g (11 oz) conchiglie (shell pasta)
155 g (5 oz) fresh asparagus
200 g (6½ oz) bocconcini cheese, thinly sliced
100 g (3½ oz) cherry tomatoes, quartered
2 tablespoons fresh oregano leaves
4 tablespoons walnut oil
1 tablespoon white wine vinegar
1 tablespoon balsamic vinegar
¼ teaspoon each salt and freshly ground black pepper

1 Cook the conchiglie in a large pan of rapidly boiling salted water until al dente. Drain, rinse under cold water and drain again. Allow to cool.
2 Cut the asparagus into short lengths. Bring a small pan of water to the boil, add the asparagus and blanch for 1 minute. Drain, transfer to a bowl of iced water to cool and then drain again.
3 In a large bowl, combine the conchiglie, asparagus, bocconcini, tomato and oregano. In a small bowl, whisk together the walnut oil, vinegars, salt and pepper until well combined.
4 Drizzle the dressing over the salad and toss thoroughly before serving.

MUSSEL SALAD WITH SAFFRON DRESSING

Preparation time: 40 minutes
Total cooking time: 30 minutes
Serves 4–6

500 g (1 lb) new potatoes, unpeeled
1 kg (2 lb) black mussels
⅔ cup (170 ml/5½ fl oz) dry white wine
1 small onion, sliced
2 sprigs fresh thyme
2 bay leaves
large pinch of powdered saffron or threads
4 tablespoons sour cream
2 teaspoons chopped fresh parsley

1 Place the potatoes in a pan of cold, lightly salted water. Bring to the boil, then reduce the heat and simmer for 20 minutes, or until tender. (When pierced with the point of a small knife, the potato will come away easily.) Drain and leave to cool.
2 Scrub the mussels with a stiff brush and pull out the hairy beards. Discard any broken mussels, or open ones that don't close when tapped on the bench. Rinse well. Place the wine, onion, thyme sprigs, bay leaves and half the mussels in a saucepan with a tight-fitting lid. Cover and cook over high heat, stirring once, for about 4–5 minutes, or until the mussels start to open. Remove the mussels as they open, using tongs. Discard any unopened mussels. Cook the remaining mussels the same way, and leave to cool.
3 Strain the mussel cooking liquid and reserve ½ cup (125 ml/4 fl oz) of the liquid. While it is still warm, stir in the saffron. Whisk in the sour cream and season well with salt and cracked pepper.
4 Cut the potatoes into quarters if large, or halves if small. Remove the mussels and discard the shells. Combine the potatoes and mussels in a bowl and add the saffron dressing. Sprinkle with chopped parsley and serve immediately.

HOT POTATO SALAD

Preparation time: 15 minutes
Total cooking time: 25 minutes
Serves 8

4 rashers bacon
1.5 kg (3 lb) small waxy red potatoes,
   unpeeled
4 spring onions, sliced
3 tablespoons chopped fresh flat-leaf
   parsley

Dressing
⅔ cup (170 ml/5½ fl oz) extra virgin
   olive oil
1 tablespoon Dijon mustard
⅓ cup (80 ml/2¾ fl oz) white wine vinegar

1 Trim the rind and any excess fat from
the bacon, then cook under a hot grill
until crisp. Chop into small pieces.
2 Steam or boil the potatoes for
10–15 minutes, or until just tender
(pierce with the point of a small sharp
knife—if the potato comes away easily
it is ready). Don't let the skins break
away. Drain and cool slightly.
3 For the dressing, whisk all the
ingredients together in a jug.
4 Cut the potatoes into quarters and place
in a bowl with half the bacon, the spring
onion, parsley and some salt and freshly
ground black pepper. Pour in half the
dressing and toss to coat the potatoes
thoroughly. Transfer to a serving bowl,
drizzle with the remaining dressing and
sprinkle the remaining bacon over the top.

NOTE: The cooking time will depend on
the size of the potatoes. The potatoes can
be diced instead of quartered if you
prefer.

THAI PORK NOODLE SALAD
(YUM WOON SEN)

Preparation time: 20 minutes
Total cooking time: 35 minutes
Serves 4–6

Broth
1 cup (250 ml/8 fl oz) chicken stock
3 coriander roots
2 fresh kaffir lime leaves
3 x 3 cm (1¼ x 1¼ inch) piece fresh ginger,
   sliced

30 g (1 oz) fresh black fungus
100 g (3½ oz) cellophane noodles or dried
   rice vermicelli
1 small fresh red chilli, seeded and thinly
   sliced
2 red Asian shallots, thinly sliced
2 spring onions, thinly sliced
2 cloves garlic, crushed
1 tablespoon vegetable oil
250 g (8 oz) pork mince
2½ tablespoons lime juice
2½ tablespoons fish sauce
1½ tablespoons grated palm sugar
¼ teaspoon ground white pepper
½ cup (15 g/½ oz) fresh coriander leaves,
   chopped
oakleaf or coral lettuce, torn or shredded
lime wedges, to garnish
fresh red chilli, extra, cut into strips, to
   garnish
fresh coriander leaves, extra, to garnish
   (optional)

1 To make the broth, put the chicken
stock, coriander roots, lime leaves,
ginger and 1 cup (250 ml/8 fl oz) water in
a wok. Simmer for 25 minutes, or until it
has reduced to ¾ cup (185 ml/6 fl oz).
Strain.
2 Discard the woody stems from the
fungus, then thinly slice. Soak the noodles
in boiling water for 3–4 minutes, or until
pliable. Rinse, drain, then cut into 3 cm (1¼
inch) lengths. Combine the noodles,
fungus, chilli, shallots, spring onion and
garlic.
3 Heat a clean, dry wok over high heat,
add the oil and swirl to coat. Add the pork
mince and stir-fry, breaking up any
lumps, for 1–2 minutes, or until the pork
changes colour and is cooked. Add the
broth and bring the mixture to the boil
over high heat. Boil for 1 minute, then
drain, and add the pork to the noodle
mixture.
4 Combine the lime juice, fish sauce,
palm sugar and white pepper, stirring
until the sugar is dissolved. Add to the
pork mixture with the coriander and mix
well. Season to taste with salt.
5 Arrange the lettuce on a serving dish,
spoon on the pork and noodle mixture
and garnish with the lime, chilli and, if
desired, fresh coriander leaves.

SOUTH-WESTERN BEAN SALAD

Preparation time: 20 minutes +
   overnight soaking
Total cooking time: 50 minutes
Serves 4–6

1 cup (220 g/7 oz) dried black beans
1 cup (200 g/6½ oz) white cannellini beans
1 medium red (Spanish) onion
1 medium red pepper (capsicum)
270 g (8⅔ oz) canned corn kernels,
   drained
3 tablespoons chopped fresh coriander
1 clove garlic, crushed
½ teaspoon ground cumin
½ teaspoon French mustard
2 tablespoons red wine vinegar
¼ cup (60 ml/2 fl oz) olive oil
salt and pepper

1 Soak the beans in separate bowls in
cold water overnight. Drain the beans;
place them in separate pans and cover
with water. Bring both pans of water to
the boil, reduce heat and simmer for
45 minutes or until tender. Drain, rinse
and allow to cool.
2 Chop the onion and red pepper. Place in
a bowl and add the beans, corn and
coriander. Stir until well combined.
3 Combine the garlic, cumin, mustard and
vinegar in a small jug; gradually whisk in
the oil. Season lightly with salt and
pepper. Pour over the bean mixture and
toss lightly to combine.

NOTE: South-Western Bean Salad can be
made up to a day in advance. It is a great
dish to serve at a barbecue or take on a
picnic, as it can be made ahead of time
and will carry well. Black beans are also
known as turtle beans and are available
at good delicatessens. They are not to be
confused with Chinese black beans.

SMOKED TROUT WITH WARM CHILLI AND RASPBERRY DRESSING

Preparation time: 25 minutes
Total cooking time: 10 minutes
Serves 4–6

250 g (8 oz) sorrel
310 g (10 oz) fresh asparagus
1 smoked trout (about 400 g/13 oz)
1 red onion, thinly sliced
250 g (8 oz) teardrop tomatoes, cut in
   halves
200 g (6½ oz) fresh raspberries

Warm chilli and raspberry dressing
125 g (4 oz) fresh raspberries
1 teaspoon chilli paste
2 cloves garlic, crushed
½ cup (125 ml/4 fl oz) olive oil
2 tablespoons raspberry vinegar or white
   wine vinegar

1 Trim the stalks from the sorrel, rinse
well, then dry and refrigerate to crisp.
2 For the dressing, gently stir all the
ingredients in a small pan over low heat
until the raspberries begin to break up
and colour the liquid. Transfer to a bowl,
whisk together well and season with salt
and freshly ground black pepper.
3 Boil, steam or microwave the asparagus
until just tender. Drain and refresh under
cold water. Peel away and discard the
skin and bones from the trout. Break the
flesh into pieces.
4 Divide the sorrel among individual
plates. Arrange the asparagus, trout,
onion, tomatoes and raspberries on top.
Drizzle with the dressing.

FRESH BEETROOT AND GOAT'S CHEESE SALAD

Preparation time: 20 minutes
Total cooking time: 30 minutes
Serves 4

1 kg (2 lb) fresh beetroot (4 bulbs with
   leaves)
200 g (6½ oz) green beans
1 tablespoon red wine vinegar
2 tablespoons extra virgin olive oil
1 clove garlic, crushed
1 tablespoon drained capers, coarsely
   chopped
100 g (3½ oz) goat's cheese

1 Trim the leaves from the beetroot. Scrub
the bulbs and wash the leaves well. Add
the whole bulbs to a large saucepan of
salted water, bring to the boil, then
reduce the heat and simmer, covered, for
30 minutes, or until tender when pierced
with the point of a knife.
2 Meanwhile, bring a saucepan of water
to the boil, add the beans and cook for
3 minutes, or until just tender. Remove
with a slotted spoon and plunge into a
bowl of cold water. Drain well. Add the
beetroot leaves to the same saucepan of
water and cook for 3–5 minutes, or until
the leaves and stems are tender. Drain,
plunge into a bowl of cold water, then
drain well.
3 Drain and cool the beetroots, then peel
the skins off and cut the bulbs into thin
wedges.
4 For the dressing, put the red wine
vinegar, oil, garlic, capers, ½ teaspoon
each of salt and pepper in a screw top jar
and shake.
5 To serve, divide the beans, beetroot
leaves and bulbs among four serving
plates. Crumble goat's cheese over the
top of each and drizzle with dressing.
Delicious served with fresh crusty bread.

RED-RICE SALAD

Preparation time: 20 minutes + cooling
Total cooking time: 50 minutes
Serves 4

1 cup (220 g/7 oz) Camargue red rice
1 red capsicum (pepper)
1 yellow capsicum (pepper)
⅓ cup (80 ml/2¾ fl oz) olive oil
1 red onion, cut into slivers
2 zucchini (courgettes), diced
1 tablespoon butter
1 garlic clove, crushed
1 chicken breast with skin on
2 tablespoons lemon juice
2 tablespoons chopped basil
2 tablespoons chopped parsley

1 Put the rice in a saucepan with plenty of boiling water and cook for 30 minutes, or until tender. Drain well, then cool.
2 Cut the red and yellow capsicums in half lengthways. Remove the seeds and membrane, then cut the flesh into large, flattish pieces. Grill or hold over a gas flame until the skin blackens and blisters. Place on a cutting board, cover with a tea towel and allow to cool. Peel the skin off and cut the flesh into smaller pieces. Add the capsicum strips to the rice.
3 Heat the oil in a frying pan, then cook the onion and zucchini until lightly charred around the edges. Add the onion and zucchini to the rice.
4 Mix the butter with the garlic. Push the mixture under the skin of the chicken breast so it is evenly distributed. Grill (broil) the chicken on both sides until the skin is crisp and the breast is cooked through. Leave the chicken to rest for 2 minutes, then slice it into strips (you can discard the skin, if you like).
5 Add the chicken slices to the rice with any juices. Add the lemon juice, any remaining olive oil and the herbs, and toss together. Season well and serve immediately.

FARFALLE SALAD WITH SUN-DRIED TOMATOES AND SPINACH

Preparation time: 20 minutes
Total cooking time: 12 minutes
Serves 4–6

500 g (1 lb) farfalle (butterfly pasta) or spiral pasta
3 spring onions
60 g (2 oz) sun-dried tomatoes, cut into strips
500 g (1 lb) English spinach, stalks trimmed and leaves shredded
4 tablespoons toasted pine nuts
1 tablespoon chopped fresh oregano

Dressing
¼ cup (60 ml/2 fl oz) olive oil
1 teaspoon chopped fresh chilli
1 clove garlic, crushed
salt and pepper

1 Add the pasta to a large pan of rapidly boiling water and cook until just tender. Drain the pasta and rinse well under cold water. Transfer to a large salad bowl.
2 Trim the spring onions and chop finely. Add to the pasta with the tomatoes, spinach, pine nuts and oregano.
3 To make Dressing: Combine the oil, chilli, garlic, salt and pepper in a small screw-top jar and shake until well combined. Pour the dressing over the top of the salad; toss well and serve immediately.

ORANGE AND DATE SALAD

Preparation time: 30 minutes + refrigeration
Total cooking time: Nil
Serves 4–6

6 navel oranges
2 teaspoons orange blossom water
8 dates, pitted and thinly sliced lengthways
90 g (3 oz) slivered almonds, lightly toasted
1 tablespoon shredded fresh mint
¼ teaspoon ras el hanout or cinnamon

1 Peel the oranges, removing all the pith. Section them by cutting away all the membranes from the flesh. Place the segments in a bowl and squeeze the juice from the remainder of the orange over them. Add the orange blossom water and stir gently to combine. Cover with plastic wrap and refrigerate until chilled.
2 Place the segments and the juice on a large flat dish and scatter the dates and almonds over the top. Sprinkle the mint and ras el hanout over the orange segments. Serve chilled.

COOKED VEGETABLE SALAD

Preparation time: 45 minutes +
   20 minutes standing
Total cooking time: 15 minutes
Serves 4

1 small turnip, peeled, cut into fine strips
2 teaspoons salt
½ cup (80 g/2⅔ oz) pine nuts
2 tablespoons sesame oil
1 tablespoon oil
2 cloves garlic, finely chopped
1 large onion, thinly sliced into rings
2 sticks celery, sliced
200 g (6½ oz) button mushrooms, sliced
1 large carrot, cut into fine strips
½ red pepper (capsicum), cut into fine strips
4 spring onions, chopped

Dressing
¼ cup (60 ml/2 fl oz) soy sauce
1 tablespoon white vinegar
3 cm (1¼ inch) piece fresh ginger, very
   finely sliced and cut into fine strips
1–2 teaspoons soft brown sugar

1 Place the turnip on a plate lined with a paper towel. Sprinkle with salt, and set aside for at least 20 minutes. Rinse the turnip under cold water and pat dry with paper towels.
2 Toast the pine nuts in a dry pan over medium heat for 3 to 4 minutes, shaking the pan gently, until the seeds are golden brown; remove from the pan at once to prevent burning and set aside.
3 Heat the combined oils in a large frying pan or wok. Stir-fry the turnip, garlic and onion for 3 minutes over medium heat until lightly golden. Add the celery, mushrooms, carrot, red pepper and spring onion and toss well; cover and steam for 1 minute. Remove the vegetables from the wok and cool.
4 To make Dressing: Combine the soy sauce, vinegar, ginger and sugar in a bowl.
5 Pour the dressing over the cooled vegetables and toss. Arrange them on a serving plate and sprinkle over the pine nuts. Serve with steamed rice, if you like.

SALAD NICOISE

Preparation time: 30 minutes
Total cooking time: 15 minutes
Serves 4

3 eggs
2 vine-ripened tomatoes
175 g (6 oz) baby green beans, trimmed
½ cup (125 ml/4 fl oz) olive oil
2 tablespoons white wine vinegar
1 large clove garlic, halved
325 g (11 oz) iceberg lettuce heart, cut
   into 8 wedges
1 small red pepper (capsicum), seeded
   and sliced thinly
1 Lebanese cucumber, cut into thin 5 cm
   (2 inch) lengths
1 stick celery, cut into thin 5 cm (2 inch)
   lengths
¼ large red onion, thinly sliced
2 x 185 g (6 oz) cans tuna, drained,
   broken into chunks
12 Kalamata olives
45 g (1½ oz) can anchovy fillets, drained
2 teaspoons baby capers
12 small fresh basil leaves

1 Place the eggs in a saucepan of cold water. Bring to the boil, then reduce the heat and simmer for 10 minutes. Stir during the first few minutes to centre the yolks. Cool under cold water, then peel and cut into quarters. Meanwhile, score a cross in the base of each tomato and place in a bowl of boiling water for 10 seconds. Plunge into cold water and peel away from the cross. Cut each tomato into eight.
2 Cook the beans in a saucepan of boiling water for 2 minutes, rinse under cold water, then drain.
3 For the dressing, place the oil and vinegar in a jar and shake to combine.
4 Rub the garlic over the base and sides of a platter. Arrange the lettuce over the base. Layer the egg, tomato, beans, red pepper, cucumber and celery over the lettuce. Scatter the onion and tuna over them, then the olives, anchovies, capers and basil. Drizzle with dressing and serve.

TOFU SALAD

Preparation time: 20 minutes +
   1 hour marinating
Total cooking time: Nil
Serves 4

2 teaspoons Thai sweet chilli sauce
½ teaspoon grated fresh ginger
1 clove garlic, crushed
2 teaspoons soy sauce
2 tablespoons oil
250 g (8 oz) firm tofu
105 g (3½ oz) snow peas (mangetout), cut
   into 3 cm (1¼ inch) lengths
2 small carrots, cut into matchsticks
105 g (3½ oz) red cabbage, finely
   shredded
2 tablespoons chopped peanuts

1 Place the chilli sauce, ginger, garlic, soy sauce and oil in a small screw-top jar and shake well. Cut the tofu into 2 cm (¾ inch) cubes. Place the tofu in a medium bowl, pour the marinade over and stir. Cover with plastic wrap and refrigerate for 1 hour.
2 Place the snow peas in a small pan, pour boiling water over and leave to stand for 1 minute, then drain and plunge into iced water. Drain well.
3 Add the snow peas, carrots and cabbage to tofu and toss lightly to combine. Transfer to a serving bowl or individual plates, sprinkle with peanuts and serve immediately.

MIXED SEAFOOD SALAD

Preparation time: 1 hour + 1 hour chilling
Total cooking time: 20 minutes
Serves 8

1.25 kg (2½ lb) large cooked prawns
12 cooked yabbies or crayfish
500 g (1 lb) scallops
½ cup (125 ml/4 fl oz) white wine
pinch of dried thyme
pinch of dried tarragon or a bay leaf
400 g (13 oz) salmon, trout or firm white
   fish fillets (eg. flake, hake, ling)

Vinaigrette
½ cup (125 ml/4 fl oz) extra virgin olive oil
2 tablespoons white wine vinegar
1 teaspoon sugar
2 teaspoons Dijon mustard
1 tablespoon chopped fresh dill

6 hard-boiled eggs
150 g (5 oz) mixed lettuce leaves
2 tablespoons chopped fresh flat-leaf
   parsley
2 ripe avocados, sliced
2 tablespoons lemon juice

Green goddess dressing
1¼ cups (310 g/10 oz) whole-egg
   mayonnaise
4 canned anchovy fillets, drained, finely
   chopped
1 clove garlic, crushed
¼ cup (60 g/2 oz) sour cream
3 tablespoons chopped fresh herbs
   (chives, parsley, dill)

1 Peel the prawns and pull out the dark
vein from each prawn back, starting at the
head end.
2 Cut down each side of the shell on the
underside of each yabby with kitchen
scissors, starting at the head and working
towards the tail. Pull back the flap and
remove the meat from each shell. Gently
pull out the vein from each back and
discard each shell.

3 Slice or pull off any vein, membrane or
hard white muscle from the scallops.
4 Put 1 cup (250 ml/8 fl oz) water with the
wine, herbs, and a pinch each of salt and
pepper, in a pan. Bring to the boil, then
reduce the heat and simmer for 5
minutes. Add the scallops and poach for
a few minutes, or until they have just
turned white, then remove with a slotted
spoon and drain on a wire rack. Add the
fish fillets to the gently simmering liquid.
Poach until cooked and just tender,
remove with a slotted spoon and drain on
a wire rack. Break into large pieces.
5 Combine the prawns, yabbies, scallops
and fish in a bowl. Whisk together the oil,
vinegar, sugar, mustard and dill, and
season, to taste. Pour over the seafood,
cover and refrigerate for 1 hour.
6 Peel and slice the eggs, reserving
2 yolks. Put half the lettuce leaves in a
deep serving bowl. Arrange half the
seafood over the lettuce, reserving the
vinaigrette. Sprinkle with half the parsley,
top with half the avocado, drizzle with half
the lemon juice, then finish with half the
sliced eggs, including the extra whites.
Season with salt and pepper. Repeat the
layers and season, to taste. Drizzle with
the reserved vinaigrette. Crumble the
reserved egg yolks over the top. Serve
with the green goddess dressing.
7 For the green goddess dressing, mix all
the ingredients in a bowl and season, to
taste.

CUCUMBER SALAD WITH PEANUTS AND CHILLI

Preparation time: 25 minutes +
   45 minutes marinating
Total cooking time: Nil
Serves 4–6

3 medium cucumbers
2 tablespoons white vinegar
2 teaspoons white sugar
1–2 tablespoons sweet chilli sauce
12 French shallots, chopped
½ cup (15 g/½ oz) fresh coriander leaves
185 g (6 oz) roasted peanuts, chopped
2 tablespoons crisp fried garlic
1 tablespoon fish sauce (optional)

1 Peel the cucumber, cut in half
lengthways, scoop out the seeds and
slice thinly.
2 Combine the vinegar and sugar in a
small bowl and stir until sugar has
dissolved. Transfer to a large bowl and
add cucumber, vinegar mixture, chilli
sauce, shallots and coriander leaves.
Allow to marinate for 45 minutes.
3 Just before serving, sprinkle with
peanuts, fried garlic and fish sauce.

NOTE: If French shallots are unavailable,
use red (Spanish) onions.

GREEN TEA NOODLE SALAD WITH LAMB AND TOMATO

Preparation time: 20 minutes +
  2 hours marinating
Total cooking time: 20 minutes
Serves 4

1 teaspoon hot mustard
2 tablespoons vegetable oil
¼ cup (60 ml/2 fl oz) balsamic vinegar
400 g (13 oz) lamb loin fillets, thinly
  sliced across the grain
250 g (8 oz) chasoba noodles (see Note)
¼ cup (60 ml/2 fl oz) light soy sauce
2 tablespoons mirin
1–2 teaspoons sesame oil
½ teaspoon sugar
2 Lebanese cucumbers, cut in half
  lengthways and thinly sliced on the
  diagonal
2 large tomatoes, cut into 1 cm (1/2 inch)
  cubes
½ cup (15 g/½ oz) fresh coriander leaves
2 spring onions, thinly sliced on the
  diagonal
1 tablespoon sesame seeds, lightly
  toasted

1 Combine the mustard, 1 tablespoon of
the oil, 1 tablespoon of the vinegar and
½ teaspoon pepper in a large non-
metallic bowl. Add the lamb and toss.
Cover, then refrigerate for 2 hours.

2 Add the noodles to a large saucepan of
boiling water and stir to separate. Return
to the boil, adding 1 cup (250 ml/8 fl oz) cold
water and repeat this step three times, as it
comes to the boil. Drain and rinse under
cold water. Place in a large bowl.
3 Combine the soy sauce, mirin, sesame
oil, sugar, the remaining balsamic
vinegar and 1/2 teaspoon salt and stir
until the sugar dissolves. Toss half of the
dressing through the noodles.
4 Place the cucumber, tomato and
½ teaspoon salt in a bowl and toss well.
Add to the noodles with the coriander and
spring onion and toss well.
5 Heat a wok over high heat, add the
remaining oil and swirl to coat. Drain the
lamb, then, using tongs or a slotted
spoon, add the lamb to the wok in two
batches, and stir-fry each batch for 2–3
minutes, or until the lamb is seared and
cooked to your liking. Divide the noodle
salad among serving plates, then top with
the lamb. Drizzle with as much of the
dressing as you like. Sprinkle with the
sesame seeds and serve.

NOTE: Chasoba noodles are soba noodles
that have had green tea powder added to
them.

WARM LAMB SALAD

Preparation time: 15 minutes +
  3 hours refrigeration
Total cooking time: 15 minutes
Serves 4–6

2 tablespoons Thai red curry paste
3 tablespoons chopped fresh coriander
  leaves
1 tablespoon finely grated fresh ginger
3–4 tablespoons peanut oil
750 g (1½ lb) lamb loin fillets, thinly sliced
  across the grain
200 g (6½ oz) snow peas (mangetout)
600 g (1¼ lb) fresh thick rice noodles
1 red pepper (capsicum), thinly sliced
1 Lebanese cucumber, thinly sliced
6 spring onions, thinly sliced

Mint dressing
1½ tablespoons peanut oil
¼ cup (60 ml/2 fl oz) lime juice
2 tablespoons soft brown sugar
3 teaspoons fish sauce
3 teaspoons soy sauce
4 tablespoons chopped fresh mint leaves
1 clove garlic, crushed

1 Combine the curry paste, coriander,
ginger and 2 tablespoons oil in a non-
metallic bowl. Add the lamb and coat well.
Cover with plastic wrap and marinate in
the refrigerator for 2–3 hours.
2 Steam or boil the snow peas until tender,
then refresh under cold water. Drain.
3 Cover the noodles with boiling water.
Drain immediately and gently separate
the noodles with your fingers.
4 To make the mint dressing, put all the
ingredients in a screw-top jar and shake.
5 Heat a wok over high heat, add
1 tablespoon of the oil and swirl to coat
the side of the wok. Add half the lamb and
stir-fry for 5 minutes, or until tender.
Repeat with the remaining lamb.
6 Place the lamb, snow peas, noodles,
pepper, cucumber and spring onion in a
large bowl, drizzle with the dressing and
toss to combine.

INSALATA CAPRESE
(TOMATO AND BOCCONCINI SALAD)

Preparation time: 10 minutes
Total cooking time: Nil
Serves 4

3 large vine-ripened tomatoes
250 g (8 oz) bocconcini
12 fresh basil leaves
¼ cup (60 ml/2 fl oz) extra virgin olive oil
4 fresh basil leaves, roughly torn, extra

1 Slice the tomato into twelve 1 cm (½ inch) slices. Slice the bocconcini into 24 slices the same thickness as the tomato.
2 Arrange the tomato slices on a serving plate, alternating them with 2 slices of bocconcini and placing a basil leaf between the bocconcini slices.
3 Drizzle with the olive oil, sprinkle with the torn basil and season well with salt and freshly ground black pepper.

NOTE: You could use whole cherry tomatoes and toss them with the bocconcini and basil.

POACHED SALMON SALAD WITH CAPER DILL DRESSING

Preparation time: 20 minutes
Total cooking time: 10 minutes
Serves 6–8

300 g (10 oz) small new potatoes
200 g (6½ oz) mixed salad leaves, rinsed and dried
100 g (3½ oz) watercress
400 g (13 oz) cooked poached salmon, broken into large flakes
2 Lebanese cucumbers, sliced
½ red onion, thinly sliced
6 gherkins, sliced
6 hard-boiled eggs, quartered
200 g (6½ oz) semi-dried tomatoes, roughly chopped
200 g (6½ oz) feta cheese, crumbled
Caper dill dressing
1 tablespoon drained bottled capers, finely chopped
2 tablespoons chopped fresh dill
1 teaspoon finely grated lime rind
2 tablespoons lime juice
1 tablespoon honey mustard
1 tablespoon white wine vinegar
½ cup (60 ml/2 fl oz) olive oil

1 Steam or boil the new potatoes for 10 minutes, or until just tender (pierce with the point of a small knife—if the potato comes away easily it is ready). Drain well and cut into quarters.
2 Combine the salad leaves and the watercress and arrange on a large chilled salad plate.
3 Combine the potato, salmon, cucumber, onion, gherkins, hard-boiled eggs, semi-dried tomatoes and feta in a bowl and toss very gently. Arrange on top of the salad greens.
4 Place the dressing ingredients in a small bowl and whisk until well combined. Drizzle over the salad and serve immediately.

CHEF'S SALAD

Preparation time: 25 minutes
Total cooking time: Nil
Serves 4

Dressing
½ cup (125 ml/4 fl oz) extra virgin olive oil
2 tablespoons white wine vinegar
1 teaspoon sugar

1 iceberg lettuce
2 tomatoes, cut into wedges
2 celery sticks, cut into julienne strips
1 cooked chicken breast fillet, cut into thin strips
200 g (6½ oz) ham, cut into thin strips
60 g (2 oz) Swiss cheese, cut into strips
3 hard-boiled eggs, cut into wedges
6 radishes, sliced

1 Whisk the dressing ingredients together in a small jug until well combined. Season, to taste, with salt and freshly ground black pepper.
2 Coarsely shred the lettuce leaves and divide among serving plates. Top with layers of the tomato, celery, chicken, ham, cheese, egg and radish. Drizzle the dressing over the salad and serve immediately.

HALOUMI WITH SALAD AND GARLIC BREAD

Preparation time: 20 minutes
Total cooking time: 5 minutes
Serves 4

4 firm, ripe tomatoes
1 Lebanese cucumber
140 g (4½ oz) rocket (arugula)
½ cup (80 g/2¾ oz) Kalamata olives
1 loaf crusty unsliced white bread
5 tablespoons olive oil
1 large clove garlic, cut in half
400 g (13 oz) haloumi cheese
1 tablespoon lemon juice
1 tablespoon chopped fresh oregano

1 Preheat the oven to moderate 180°C (350°F/ Gas 4). Heat the grill to high.
2 Cut the tomatoes and cucumber into bite-sized chunks and place in a serving dish with the rocket and olives. Mix well.
3 Slice the bread into eight 1.5 cm (⅝ inch) slices, drizzle 1½ tablespoons of the olive oil over the bread and season with salt and pepper. Grill until lightly golden, then rub each slice thoroughly with a cut side of the garlic. Wrap loosely in foil and keep warm in the oven.
4 Cut the haloumi into 8 slices. Heat ½ tablespoon of the oil in a shallow frying pan and fry the haloumi slices for 1–2 minutes on each side, until crisp and golden brown.
5 Whisk together the lemon juice, oregano and remaining olive oil to use as a dressing. Season, to taste. Pour half the dressing over the salad and toss well. Arrange the haloumi on top and drizzle with dressing. Serve immediately with the warm garlic bread.

MEXICANA SALAD

Preparation time: 40 minutes
  + overnight standing
Total cooking time: 45 minutes
Serves 10–12

250 g (8 oz) dried black-eyed beans
250 g (8 oz) dried red kidney beans
500 g (1 lb) sweet potato
1 large red onion, chopped
1 large green pepper (capsicum), chopped
3 ripe tomatoes, chopped
3 tablespoons chopped fresh basil
3 flour tortillas
1 tablespoon oil
2 tablespoons grated Parmesan
¼ cup (60 g/2 oz) sour cream

Dressing
1 clove garlic, crushed
1 tablespoon lime juice
2 tablespoons olive oil

Guacamole
3 ripe avocados
2 tablespoons lemon juice
1 clove garlic, crushed
1 small red onion, finely chopped
1 small red chilli, seeded and chopped
¼ cup (60 g/2 oz) sour cream
2 tablespoons hot taco sauce

1 Soak the beans in a large bowl of cold water overnight. Drain and cook in a large pan of rapidly boiling water for 30 minutes, or until just tender. Skim off any scum that appears on the surface during cooking. Do not overcook or the beans will be mushy. Drain and set aside to cool.
2 Chop the sweet potato into small cubes and cook in boiling water for 5 minutes, or until tender. Drain and allow to cool, then combine with the onion, pepper, tomato and beans. Stir in the basil.
3 For the dressing, combine all the ingredients in a jar and shake well until combined. Pour over the salad and toss gently to coat.
4 Preheat the oven to moderate 180°C (350°F/Gas 4). Using a small knife or shaped cutter, cut Christmas tree shapes out of the tortillas, brush lightly with the oil, place on baking trays and and sprinkle with grated Parmesan. Bake for 5–10 minutes, or until crisp and golden.
5 To make the guacamole, mash the avocados with the lemon juice. Add the garlic, onion, chilli, sour cream and taco sauce and mix well.
6 Put the salad in a large bowl or on a platter, pile the guacamole in the centre, top with the sour cream and arrange the Christmas tree shapes on top.

LENTIL SALAD

Preparation time: 15 minutes +
  30 minutes standing
Total cooking time: 30 minutes
Serves 4–6

1 small onion
2 cloves
1½ cups (300 g/10 oz) puy lentils
  (see Note)
1 strip lemon rind
2 cloves garlic, peeled
1 fresh bay leaf
2 teaspoons ground cumin
2 tablespoons red wine vinegar
¼ cup (60 ml/2 fl oz) olive oil
1 tablespoon lemon juice
2 tablespoons finely chopped fresh mint
  leaves
3 spring onions, finely chopped

1 Stud the onion with the cloves and place
in a saucepan with the lentils, rind, garlic,
bay leaf, 1 teaspoon cumin and 3½ cups
(875 ml/28 fl oz) water. Bring to the boil
and simmer gently over medium heat for
25–30 minutes, or until the lentils are
tender. Drain off any excess liquid and
discard the onion, rind and bay leaf.
Reserve the garlic and finely chop.
2 Whisk together the vinegar, oil, juice,
garlic and remaining cumin. Stir the
dressing through the lentils with the mint
and spring onion. Season well, then leave
for 30 minutes to allow the flavours to
develop. Serve at room temperature.

NOTE: Puy lentils are small green lentils,
available from gourmet food stores.

CHICKEN AND VEGETABLE SALAD

Preparation time: 30 minutes
Total cooking time: 20 minutes
Serves 4–6

400 g (12⅔ oz) chicken breast fillets
1 cup (250 ml/8 fl oz) water
3 slices fresh ginger
2 stems lemon grass (white part only),
  roughly chopped
2 tablespoons fish sauce
250 g (8 oz) broccoli, cut into florets
150 g (4¾ oz) fresh baby corn
100 g (3⅓ oz) snow peas (mangetout),
  trimmed
1 red pepper (capsicum), cut into strips
3 spring onions, cut into strips
½ cup (125 ml/4 fl oz) sweet chilli sauce
2 tablespoons honey or 2 tablespoons
  grated palm sugar mixed with a little
  warm water
2 tablespoons lime juice
2 teaspoons grated lime rind
¼ cup (7 g/¼ oz) fresh coriander leaves

1 Slice the chicken into short, thin strips.
2 Place the water, ginger, lemon grass
and fish sauce in a frying pan. Bring the
mixture to the boil, reduce the heat
slightly and simmer for 5 minutes.
3 Add the chicken to the pan and cook in
the hot liquid for 5 minutes, stirring
occasionally. Drain and allow to cool.
Discard liquid.
4 Bring a large pan of water to the boil
and cook the broccoli, corn, snow peas,
red pepper and spring onion for
2 minutes. Drain and plunge into iced
water; drain again.
5 Combine the sweet chilli sauce, honey,
lime juice and rind in a small bowl and
mix well. Arrange the vegetables and
chicken on a serving platter. Pour the
sauce over the top and toss gently.
Sprinkle over the coriander leaves.

WARM BEEF AND WATERCRESS SALAD

Preparation time: 25 minutes +
  30 minutes marinating
Total cooking time: 10 minutes
Serves 4

350 g (11¼ oz) fillet steak, partially frozen
  (see Note)
1 tablespoon green peppercorns, roughly
  chopped
4 cloves garlic, crushed
3 stems lemon grass (white part only),
  very finely sliced
3 tablespoons oil
¼ teaspoon salt
¼ teaspoon freshly ground black pepper
250 g (8 oz) watercress
125 g (4 oz) cherry tomatoes, halved
4 spring onions, chopped
2 tablespoons lime juice

1 Cut the steak into thin slices. Place the
steak, peppercorns, garlic, lemon grass,
2 tablespoons oil, salt and pepper in a
bowl. Mix well, cover and marinate in the
refrigerator for 30 minutes.
2 Remove the watercress sprigs from the
tough stems, break them into small
pieces, and wash and drain them well.
Arrange the watercress on a serving
platter and place the tomatoes on top,
around the outside edge.
3 Heat the remaining oil in a wok or
heavy-based frying pan until very hot and
lightly smoking. Add the beef mixture and
stir-fry it quickly until the meat is just
cooked. Add the spring onion and toss
through. Remove the beef mixture from
the pan, pile it up in the centre of the
watercress and sprinkle lime juice over
the top. Serve immediately.

NOTE: If time allows, partially freezing the
meat for about 30 minutes makes it firm
and therefore easier to slice very finely.

WILD RICE SALAD WITH CHINESE ROAST DUCK

Preparation time: 15 minutes
Total cooking time: 50 minutes
Serves 4–6

1 cup (200 g/6½ oz) wild rice
1 cup (200 g/6½ oz) basmati or jasmine rice
16 thin asparagus spears, sliced
8 spring onions (scallions), thinly sliced
100 g (3½ oz) pecans, roughly chopped
100 g (3½ oz) dried cranberries
zest and juice 1 orange
1 whole Chinese roast duck

Dressing
½ cup (125 ml/4 fl oz) soy sauce
2 tablespoons sugar
1½ tablespoons balsamic vinegar
1½ tablespoons peanut oil
2 teaspoons sesame oil
2 teaspoons grated ginger
2 small red chillies, finely chopped

1 Put the wild rice in a saucepan of cold, salted water, bring to the boil and cook for 30 minutes. Add the basmati or jasmine rice and continue to cook for a further 10 minutes, or until both rices are just cooked. Drain and refresh under cold water, then drain again and transfer to a large bowl.
2 Blanch the asparagus in a saucepan of boiling water, then drain and refresh under cold water. Add to the bowl with the rice.
3 Add the spring onions, pecans, dried cranberries and orange zest to the rice and mix together well.
4 Combine all the dressing ingredients and the orange juice in a screw-top jar and shake well.
5 Heat the oven to 200°C (400°F/Gas 6). Remove the skin from the duck and break it into rough pieces. Shred the duck meat and add it to the salad. Place the skin on a baking tray and bake for 5 minutes, or until crispy. Drain on paper towel, then slice.
6 Pour the dressing over the salad. Toss everything together. Serve the salad in bowls, topped with pieces of crispy duck skin.

ROASTED FENNEL AND ORANGE SALAD

Preparation time: 30 minutes
Total cooking time: 45 minutes
Serves 4

8 baby fennel bulbs
5 tablespoons olive oil
2 oranges
1 tablespoon lemon juice
1 red onion, halved and thinly sliced
100 g (3½ oz) Kalamata olives
2 tablespoons roughly chopped fresh mint
1 tablespoon roughly chopped fresh flat-
   leaf parsley

1 Preheat the oven to moderately hot 200°C (400°F/Gas 6). Trim the fronds from the fennel and reserve. Remove the stalks and cut a slice off the base of each fennel about 5 mm (¼ inch) thick. Slice each fennel into 6 wedges, place in a baking dish and drizzle with 3 tablespoons olive oil. Season well. Bake for 40–45 minutes, or until the fennel is tender and slightly caramelized. Turn once or twice during cooking. Allow to cool.
2 Cut a thin slice off the top and bottom of each orange. Using a small sharp knife, slice the skin and pith off the oranges. Remove as much pith as possible. Slice down the side of a segment between the flesh and the membrane. Repeat with the other side and lift the segment out. Do this over a bowl to catch the juices. Repeat with all the segments on both. Squeeze out any juice remaining in the membranes.
3 Whisk the remaining oil into the orange juice and the lemon juice until emulsified. Season well. Combine the orange segments, onion and olives in a bowl, pour on half the dressing and add half the mint. Mix well. Transfer to a serving dish. Top with the roasted fennel, drizzle with the remaining dressing, and scatter the parsley and remaining mint over the top. Chop the reserved fronds and sprinkle over the salad.

PRAWN AND PAPAYA SALAD WITH LIME DRESSING

Preparation time: 25 minutes
Total cooking time: 5 minutes
Serves 4

750 g (1½ lb) cooked medium prawns
1 large papaya, chopped
1 small red onion, finely sliced
2 sticks celery, finely sliced
2 tablespoons shredded fresh mint

Lime dressing
½ cup (125 ml/4 fl oz) oil
¼ cup (60 ml/2 fl oz) lime juice
2 teaspoons finely grated fresh ginger
1 teaspoon caster sugar

1 Peel the prawns, leaving the tails intact. Gently pull out the dark vein from each prawn back, starting at the head end. Put the prawns in a bowl.
2 For the lime dressing, put the oil, lime juice, ginger and sugar in a small bowl and whisk to combine. Season, to taste, with salt and freshly ground black pepper.
3 Add the lime dressing to the prawns and toss gently to coat the prawns. Add the papaya, onion, celery and fresh mint and gently toss to combine. Serve the salad at room temperature, or cover and refrigerate for up to 3 hours before serving. Can be served garnished with extra sprigs of fresh mint.

SPANISH-STYLE SEAFOOD SALAD

Preparation time: 40 minutes
  + 2 hours chilling
Total cooking time: 10 minutes
Serves 6

750 g (1½ lb) raw medium prawns
200 g (6½ oz) scallops
12–15 black mussels
2 slices lemon
2 bay leaves
pinch of dried thyme
250 g (8 oz) broccoli, cut into small
  florets
3 teaspoons capers
20 dry-cured black olives
3 spring onions, chopped
½ green pepper (capsicum), diced
¼ cup (60 ml/2 fl oz) olive oil
2 tablespoons lemon juice
1 teaspoon Dijon mustard
1 clove garlic, crushed

1 Peel the prawns and pull out the dark
vein from each prawn back, starting at
the head end.
2 Slice or pull off any vein, membrane or
hard white muscle from the scallops,
leaving any roe attached.
3 Scrub the mussels with a stiff brush
and pull out the hairy beards. Discard any
broken mussels, or open ones that don't
close when tapped on the bench. Rinse
well.

4 Put the lemon, bay leaves, thyme and
3 cups (750 ml/24 fl oz) water in a large
pan and bring to the boil. Add the scallops
and cook for 30 seconds to 1 minute, or
until opaque. Remove with a slotted
spoon and drain on crumpled paper
towels. Add the prawns to the pan and
cook for 2–3 minutes, or until cooked.
Remove with a slotted spoon and drain on
paper towels. Add the mussels to the pan,
cover and cook for 4–5 minutes, or until
they have opened, shaking the pan
occasionally. Drain the mussels on
crumpled paper towels, discarding any
that haven't opened. Discard one half
shell from each mussel. Put all the
seafood in a bowl.
5 Cook the broccoli in boiling water for 2
minutes. Refresh in cold water. Drain and
add to the seafood with the capers, olives,
spring onion and diced green pepper.
6 Whisk the oil, lemon juice, mustard,
garlic and some salt and freshly ground
black pepper in a bowl. Pour over the
seafood and gently toss to coat the
seafood. Cover and refrigerate for about 2
hours before serving.

ROAST DUCK, LIME, HERB AND NOODLE SALAD

Preparation time: 25 minutes +
  20 minutes soaking
Total cooking time: 10 minutes
Serves 4

Dressing
¼ cup (60 ml/2 fl oz) fish sauce
2 tablespoons lime juice
1 tablespoon grated palm sugar
1 small red chilli, finely chopped

250 g (8 oz) dried flat rice stick noodles
  (5 mm/¼ inch thick)
1 Chinese roast duck
1 tablespoon julienned fresh ginger
90 g (3 oz) bean sprouts, tailed
1 small red onion, thinly sliced
3 tablespoons fresh coriander (cilantro)
  leaves
3 tablespoons fresh Thai basil or basil
1 lime, cut into wedges

1 To make the dressing, combine the fish
sauce, lime juice, palm sugar and chilli in
a small bowl.
2 Put the noodles in a large heatproof
bowl, cover with warm water and soak for
about 20 minutes, or until soft and pliable.
Drain, then return to the bowl.
3 Preheat the oven to moderate 180°C
(350°F/ Gas 4). Remove the flesh and skin
from the duck in large pieces, then cut
into thin strips, trying to keep some skin
on every piece. Put the pieces of duck on
a baking tray and heat in the oven for
10 minutes, or until the flesh is warmed
through.
4 Add the ginger, bean sprouts, onion,
coriander, basil and the dressing to the
noodles and toss until well combined.
Serve the salad on a platter, or on
individual serving plates or bowls, and
arrange the duck strips on top. Serve with
lime wedges.

VIETNAMESE SALAD

Preparation time: 30 minutes +
    10 minutes standing + 30 minutes
    refrigeration
Total cooking time: Nil
Serves 4–6

200 g (6½ oz) dried rice vermicelli
1 cup (140 g/4½ oz) crushed peanuts
½ cup (10 g/¼ oz) fresh Vietnamese mint
    leaves, torn
½ cup (15 g/½ oz) firmly packed fresh
    coriander leaves
½ red onion, cut into thin wedges
1 green mango, cut into julienne strips
1 Lebanese cucumber, halved lengthways
    and thinly sliced on the diagonal

Lemon grass dressing
½ cup (125 ml/4 fl oz) lime juice
1 tablespoon shaved palm sugar
¼ cup (60 ml/2 fl oz) seasoned rice
    vinegar
2 stems lemon grass, finely chopped
2 red chillies, seeded and finely chopped
3 kaffir lime leaves, shredded

1 Place the rice vermicelli in a bowl and
cover with boiling water. Leave for
10 minutes, or until soft, then drain, rinse
under cold water and cut into short
lengths.
2 Place the vermicelli, three-quarters of
the peanuts, the mint, coriander, onion,
mango and cucumber in a large bowl and
toss together.
3 To make the dressing, place all the
ingredients in a jar with a lid and shake
together.
4 Toss the salad and dressing and
refrigerate for 30 minutes. Sprinkle with
the remaining nuts to serve.

TURKEY, POTATO AND APPLE SALAD

Preparation time: 25 minutes
Total cooking time: 15 minutes
Serves 6

4 spring onions
2 tablespoons oil
750 g (1½ lb) new baby potatoes
1 red apple
1 tablespoon lemon juice
2 zucchini (courgettes), thickly sliced
400 g (13 oz) cooked turkey meat
2 tablespoons chopped fresh flat-leaf
    parsley

Dressing
½ cup (125 g/4 oz) whole-egg mayonnaise
3 teaspoons Dijon mustard
1 tablespoon wholegrain mustard
2 tablespoons lemon juice

1 Cut the spring onions into thin strips.
Heat the oil in a small frying pan and
shallow-fry the spring onion until crisp.
Remove and drain on crumpled paper
towels.
2 Steam or boil the potatoes for 10
minutes, or until just tender (pierce with
the point of a small knife—if the potato
comes away easily, it is ready). Drain and
allow to cool, then cut in halves.
3 Cut the unpeeled apple into thin wedges
and toss with the lemon juice in a bowl
(this prevents the apple from
discolouring).
4 Boil, steam or microwave the zucchini
until tender, then drain and refresh in
cold water.
5 For the dressing, stir the ingredients
together in a small bowl, then season, to
taste.
6 Cut the leftover cooked turkey meat into
thin strips and put in a large bowl. Add
the potato, apple, zucchini and parsley to
the turkey, drizzle the dressing over the
top and gently toss until well combined.
Serve topped with the crispy spring onion.

SNOW PEA SALAD
(MANGETOUT SALAD)

Preparation time: 25 minutes
Total cooking time: 5 minutes
Serves 4–6

200 g (6½ oz) snow peas (mangetout),
    sliced diagonally
1 large red pepper (capsicum), sliced
4 leaves oak leaf lettuce
5 leaves green coral lettuce
250 g (8 oz) cherry tomatoes
60 g (2 oz) watercress sprigs
Parmesan cheese, to serve

Garlic croutons
3 slices white bread
¼ cup (60 ml/2 fl oz) olive oil
1 clove garlic, crushed

Dressing
2 tablespoons olive oil
1 tablespoon mayonnaise
1 tablespoon sour cream
2 tablespoons lemon juice
1 teaspoon soft brown sugar
cracked black pepper

1 Wash the lettuce and tomatoes.
Combine the snow peas, red pepper,
watercress, lettuces and tomatoes in a
large bowl.
2 To make Garlic Croutons: Remove the
crusts from the bread slices. Cut the
bread into 1 cm (1/ 2 inch) squares. Heat
the olive oil in small, heavy-based pan and
add the crushed garlic. Stir in the
prepared bread cubes and cook until
golden and crisp. Remove from the heat
and leave to drain well on paper towels.
3 To make Dressing: Whisk all the
ingredients in a small bowl for 2 minutes
or until combined. Just before serving,
pour the dressing over the salad, stirring
until well combined. Top with the Garlic
Croutons and thin shavings of Parmesan
cheese.

ESCABECHE

Preparation time: 20 minutes + overnight
  chilling
Total cooking time: 15 minutes
Serves 4

plain flour, for dusting
500 g (1 lb) skinless fish fillets (eg. red
  mullet, whiting, redfish, garfish)
5 tablespoons extra virgin olive oil
1 red onion, thinly sliced
2 cloves garlic, thinly sliced
2 sprigs fresh thyme
1 teaspoon ground cumin
2 spring onions, chopped
½ teaspoon finely grated orange rind
¼ cup (60 ml/2 fl oz) orange juice
¾ cup (185 ml/6 fl oz) white wine
¾ cup (185 ml/6 fl oz) white wine vinegar
60 g (2 oz) pitted green olives, roughly
  chopped
½ teaspoon caster sugar

1 Mix a little salt and pepper into the flour
and dust the fish lightly with the flour.
Heat 2 tablespoons of the oil in a frying
pan over medium heat and add the fish in
batches. Cook on both sides until lightly
browned and cooked through (the fish
should flake easily when tested with a
fork). Remove from the pan and place in a
single layer in a large shallow, non-
metallic dish.
2 Heat the remaining oil in the same pan,
add the onion and garlic and cook, stirring
over medium heat for about 5 minutes, or
until soft.
3 Add the thyme, cumin and spring onion
and stir until fragrant. Add the orange
rind, juice, wine, vinegar, olives and sugar
and salt and pepper, to taste. Bring to the
boil and pour over the fish. Allow to cool
in the liquid, or refrigerate overnight.
Serve at room temperature. Can be
served on a bed of watercress sprigs and
finely sliced spring onion.

TABBOULEH

Preparation time: 20 minutes +
  1 hour 30 minutes soaking +
  30 minutes drying
Total cooking time: Nil
Serves 6

¾ cup (130 g/4½ oz) burghul
3 ripe tomatoes
1 telegraph cucumber
4 spring onions, sliced
4 cups (120 g/4 oz) chopped fresh flat-
  leaf parsley
1/2 cup (25 g/¾ oz) chopped fresh mint

Dressing
⅓ cup (80 ml/2¾ fl oz) lemon juice
¼ cup (60 ml/2 fl oz) olive oil
1 tablespoon extra virgin olive oil

1 Place the burghul in a bowl, cover with
2 cups (500 ml/16 fl oz) water and leave
for 1½ hours.
2 Cut the tomatoes in half, squeeze gently
to remove any excess seeds and cut into
1 cm (½ inch) cubes. Cut the cucumber in
half lengthways, remove the seeds with a
teaspoon and cut the flesh into 1 cm
(½ inch) cubes.
3 To make the dressing, place the lemon
juice and 1½ teaspoons salt in a bowl and
whisk until well combined. Season well
with freshly ground black pepper and
slowly whisk in the olive oil and extra
virgin olive oil.
4 Drain the burghul and squeeze out any
excess water. Spread the burghul out on
a clean tea towel or paper towels and
leave to dry for about 30 minutes. Put the
burghul in a large salad bowl, add the
tomato, cucumber, spring onion, parsley
and mint, and toss well to combine. Pour
the dressing over the salad and toss until
evenly coated.

ASPARAGUS AND MUSHROOM SALAD

Preparation time: 20 minutes
Total cooking time: 10 minutes
Serves 4

155 g (5 oz) asparagus spears
1 tablespoon wholegrain mustard
¼ cup (60 ml/2 fl oz) orange juice
2 tablespoons lemon juice
1 tablespoon lime juice
1 tablespoon orange zest
2 teaspoons lemon zest
2 teaspoons lime zest
2 cloves garlic, crushed
¼ cup (90 g/3 oz) honey
400 g (13 oz) button mushrooms, halved
150 g (5 oz) rocket
1 red capsicum, cut into strips

1 Snap the woody ends from the
asparagus spears and cut in half on the
diagonal. Cook in boiling water for 1
minute, or until just tender. Drain, plunge
into cold water and set aside.
2 Place the mustard, citrus juice and zest,
garlic and honey in a large saucepan and
season with pepper. Bring to the boil,
then reduce the heat and add the
mushrooms, tossing for 2 minutes. Cool.
3 Remove the mushrooms from the sauce
with a slotted spoon. Return the sauce to
the heat, bring to the boil, then reduce
the heat and simmer for 3–5 minutes, or
until reduced and syrupy. Cool slightly.
4 Toss the mushrooms, rocket leaves,
capsicum and asparagus. Put on a plate
and drizzle with the sauce.

WARM GARLIC PRAWN AND FETTUCINE SALAD

Preparation time: 30 minutes
Total cooking time: 25 minutes
Serves 4–6

300 g (10 oz) fettucine
2 tablespoons olive oil
4 cloves garlic, crushed
300 g (10 oz) raw prawn meat
2 tablespoons whisky
½ cup (125 ml/4 fl oz) cream
3 spring onions, chopped

1 Cook the fettucine in a large pan of rapidly boiling salted water until al dente. Drain, rinse under cold water and drain again. Allow to cool and set aside.
2 Heat the olive oil in a heavy-based frying pan. Add the garlic and cook for 30 seconds. Add the prawns and stir-fry over high heat until they change colour. Add the whisky and cook until it evaporates. Add the cream and spring onion and simmer for 2 minutes.
3 Drizzle the sauce over the pasta. Season with plenty of salt and pepper.

LEEK AND CAPER SALAD

Preparation time: 20 minutes
Total cooking time: 20 minutes
Serves 6

5 leeks, white part only
⅓ cup (80 ml/2¾ fl oz) olive oil
2 tablespoons sherry vinegar
2 tablespoons baby capers, rinsed

1 Cut the leeks in half lengthways and wash under cold running water. Cut them into 5 cm (2 inch) lengths, then cut in half again lengthways. Heat the oil in a large heavy-based pan, add the leeks and stir until coated with the oil. Cover and cook over low heat for 15–20 minutes, or until the leeks are soft and tender (but don't let them brown or burn). Cool for 10 minutes.
2 Stir through the vinegar and season to taste with salt and pepper. Transfer to a serving dish and scatter with the baby capers (if baby capers are unavailable, use chopped ordinary-sized capers).

WARM CHICKPEA AND SILVERBEET(SWISS CHARD) SALAD WITH SUMAC

Preparation time: 30 minutes +
    overnight soaking
Total cooking time: 2 hours
Serves 4

250 g (8 oz) dried chickpeas
½ cup (125 ml/4 fl oz) olive oil
1 onion, cut into thin wedges
2 ripe tomatoes
1 teaspoon sugar
¼ teaspoon ground cinnamon
2 cloves garlic, chopped
1.5 kg (3 lb) silverbeet (Swiss chard)
3 tablespoons chopped fresh mint
2–3 tablespoons lemon juice
1½ tablespoons ground sumac

1 Place the chickpeas in a large bowl, cover with water and leave to soak overnight. Drain and place in a large saucepan. Cover with water and bring to the boil, then simmer for 1¾ hours, or until tender. Drain thoroughly.
2 Heat the oil in a heavy-based frying pan, add the onion and cook over low heat for 5 minutes, or until softened and just starting to brown.
3 Cut the tomatoes in half, scrape out the seeds with a teaspoon and dice the flesh. Add the tomato flesh to the pan with the sugar, cinnamon and garlic, and cook for 2–3 minutes, or until softened.
4 Thoroughly wash the silverbeet and pat dry with paper towels. Trim the stems and finely shred the leaves. Add to the tomato mixture with the chickpeas and cook for 3–4 minutes, or until the silverbeet wilts. Add the mint, lemon juice and sumac, season, and cook for 1 minute. Serve immediately.

PRAWN AND RICE NOODLE SALAD

Preparation time: 15 minutes +
  10 minutes soaking
Total cooking time: 15 minutes
Serves 4

Dressing
2 tablespoons lime juice
2 tablespoons dark soy sauce
1 tablespoon fish sauce
1 teaspoon grated lime zest
1 teaspoon caster (superfine) sugar
1 red chilli, seeded and finely chopped
2 teaspoons finely chopped ginger

Salad
150 g (5 oz) dried rice vermicelli
100 g (3½ oz) snow peas (mangetout),
  trimmed, cut in half widthways
¼ cup (60 ml/2 fl oz) peanut oil
⅔ cup (100 g/3½ oz) raw cashews,
  chopped
24 raw prawns (shrimp), peeled,
  deveined and tails intact
½ cup (10 g/¼ oz) mint, chopped
½ cup (15 g/½ oz) coriander (cilantro)
  leaves, chopped

1 To make the dressing, combine the
ingredients in a small bowl.
2 Soak the dried rice vermicelli in boiling
water for 6–7 minutes. Drain and set
aside.
3 Blanch the snow peas in boiling salted
water for 10 seconds. Drain and refresh in
cold water.
4 Heat the oil in a wok and swirl to coat.
Add the cashews and stir-fry for 2 minutes,
or until golden. Remove with a slotted
spoon and drain on paper towels. Stir-fry
the prawns over high heat for 2–3 minutes,
or until just pink. Transfer to a bowl, pour
on the dressing and toss. Chill.
5 Add the noodles, snow peas, mint,
coriander and cashews, toss well and
serve immediately.

WATERCRESS SALAD

Preparation time: 35 minutes
Total cooking time: Nil
Serves 4–6

500 g (1 lb) watercress
3 celery sticks
1 cucumber
3 medium oranges
1 red (Spanish) onion, thinly sliced and
  separated into rings
¾ cup (35 g/1¼ oz) chopped fresh chives
½ cup (60 g/2 oz) chopped pecans or
  walnuts

Dressing
¼ cup (60 ml/2 fl oz) olive oil
¼ cup (60 ml/2 fl oz) lemon juice
2 teaspoons grated orange rind
1 teaspoon seeded mustard
freshly ground black pepper
1 tablespoon honey

1 To make Salad: Wash and drain all
vegetables. Break the watercress into
small sprigs, discarding the coarser
stems. Cut the celery into thin 5 cm
(2 inch) long sticks. Peel, halve and seed
the cucumber and cut into thin slices.
Peel the oranges, remove all the white
pith and cut the oranges into segments
between the membrane. Refrigerate until
needed.
2 To make Dressing: Combine oil, juice,
rind, mustard, pepper and honey in a
screw-top jar. Shake vigorously to
combine.
3 Combine all the salad ingredients
except nuts in a serving bowl. Pour
dressing over and toss. Sprinkle with
pecans or walnuts.

WARM PRAWN, ROCKET AND FETA SALAD

Preparation time: 30 minutes
Total cooking time: 10 minutes
Serves 4–6

1 kg (2 lb) raw medium prawns
4 spring onions, chopped
4 Roma (egg) tomatoes, chopped
1 red pepper (capsicum), chopped
425 g (14 oz) can chickpeas, drained
1 tablespoon chopped fresh dill
3 tablespoons finely shredded fresh basil
¼ cup (60 ml/2 fl oz) extra virgin olive oil
60 g (2 oz) butter
2 small fresh red chillies, finely chopped
4 cloves garlic, crushed
2 tablespoons lemon juice
300 g (10 oz) rocket leaves
150 g (5 oz) feta cheese

1 Peel the prawns, leaving the tails intact.
Gently pull out the dark vein from each
prawn back, starting at the head end.
2 Combine the spring onion, tomato,
pepper, chickpeas and herbs in a bowl.
3 Heat the oil and butter in a large frying
pan or wok, add the prawns and cook,
stirring over high heat for 3 minutes. Add
the chilli and garlic, and continue cooking
until the prawns turn pink. Remove from
the heat and stir in the lemon juice.
4 Arrange the rocket leaves on a large
platter, top with the tomato mixture, then
the prawn mixture. Crumble the feta
cheese over the top.

LAOTIAN BEEF SALAD

Preparation time: 15 minutes +
  2 hours marinating
Total cooking time: 10 minutes
Serves 4

500 g (1 lb) rump steak
4 tablespoons water
3 tablespoons lemon juice
2 tablespoons finely chopped lemon
  grass (white part only)
1 tablespoon fish sauce
1 medium onion, finely sliced
2 tablespoons chopped fresh coriander
  leaves
1 tablespoon chopped fresh mint
2 Lebanese cucumbers, chopped
½ small Chinese cabbage, shredded

1 Char-grill the steak for 3 minutes on
each side or until cooked to medium-rare.
Remove, cover and set aside for 5
minutes. Use a sharp knife to cut the
steak into 5 mm (¼ inch) thick slices.
2 Heat the water in a wok, add the sliced
beef and cook over medium heat for
2 minutes. Do not overcook. Transfer the
beef and liquid to a non-metallic bowl.
3 Add the lemon juice, lemon grass, fish
sauce, onion, coriander and mint and mix
until well combined. Cover and leave in
the refrigerator for 2 hours to marinate.
4 Stir in the chopped cucumber. Serve the
salad on a bed of shredded cabbage,
garnished with extra mint leaves if you
like.

NOTE: If you prefer your steak more well
done, increase the char-grilling time.

SPINACH AND AVOCADO SALAD WITH WARM MUSTARD VINAIGRETTE

Preparation time: 15 minutes
Total cooking time: 2 minutes
Serves 8

30 English spinach leaves (90 g/3 oz)
1 red or green curly-leafed lettuce
2 medium avocados
3 tablespoons olive oil
2 teaspoons sesame seeds
1 tablespoon lemon juice
2 teaspoons wholegrain mustard

1 Wash and thoroughly dry the spinach
and lettuce leaves. Tear leaves into bite-
size pieces. Place in a large serving bowl.
2 Peel the avocados and cut into thin
slices. Scatter over the leaves. Heat 1
tablespoon of oil in a small pan. Add the
sesame seeds and cook over low heat
until they just start to turn golden.
Remove from the heat immediately and
allow to cool slightly.
3 Add the lemon juice, remaining oil and
mustard to the pan and stir to combine.
While still warm, pour over the salad and
toss gently to coat leaves. Salad is best
served immediately.

GREEN PAWPAW AND PEANUT SALAD

Preparation time: 25 minutes
Total cooking time: 5 minutes
Serves 4–6

50 g (1⅔ oz) dried shrimp
100 g (3⅓ oz) green beans, cut into short
  pieces
1 medium lettuce
½ medium green pawpaw, peeled and
  grated
¼ cup (60 ml/2 fl oz) lime juice
2 tablespoons fish sauce
2 teaspoons soft brown sugar
1–2 teaspoons chopped red chilli
½ cup (80 g/2⅔ oz) unsalted roasted
  peanuts, chopped
1 red chilli, extra, finely chopped

1 Pound the dried shrimp in a mortar and
pestle, or chop finely.
2 Cook the beans in a pan of boiling water
for 2 minutes. Drain and then plunge
them into iced water; drain again. Shred
the lettuce and arrange it on a serving
plate. Top with the shrimp, beans, and
pawpaw.
3 Combine the lime juice, fish sauce,
sugar and chilli in a small bowl; mix well.
Pour over the salad and sprinkle the
peanuts and extra chilli over the top.

NOTE: Green pawpaw and dried shrimp
are available at Asian food speciality
stores—there are no substitutes. When
grating pawpaw, lightly oil your hands or
wear gloves. Pawpaw can be very sticky
and hard to wash off.

LEMON AND VEGETABLE PASTA SALAD

Preparation time: 20 minutes
Total cooking time: 15 minutes
Serves 4

250 g (8 oz) farfalle
⅓ cup (80 ml/2¾ fl oz) olive oil
250 g (8 oz) broccoli, cut into small
    florets
125 g (4 oz) snow peas (mangetout),
    topped and tailed
150 g (5 oz) small yellow button squash,
    cut into quarters
2 tablespoons sour cream
1 tablespoon lemon juice
2 teaspoons finely grated lemon rind
1 celery stick, finely sliced
1 tablespoon chopped chervil
chervil sprigs, to garnish

1 Cook the farfalle in a large pan of rapidly boiling salted water until al dente. Drain well, toss with 1 tablespoon of the olive oil and set aside to cool.
2 Combine the broccoli, snow peas and squash in a large bowl, cover with boiling water and leave for 2 minutes. Drain, plunge into iced water, drain again and pat dry with paper towels.
3 Put the sour cream, lemon juice, rind and the remaining oil in a screw top jar and shake for 30 seconds, or until combined. Season with salt and pepper, to taste.
4 Combine the cooled pasta, sliced celery and drained vegetables in a large bowl; sprinkle with chervil. Drizzle the dressing over and toss to combine. Garnish with chervil sprigs. Serve at room temperature.

CUCUMBER, FETA, MINT AND DILL SALAD

Preparation time: 15 minutes
Total cooking time: Nil
Serves 4

120 g (4 oz) feta cheese
4 Lebanese cucumbers
1 small red onion, thinly sliced
1½ tablespoons finely chopped fresh dill
1 tablespoon dried mint
3 tablespoons olive oil
1½ tablespoons lemon juice

1 Crumble the feta into 1 cm (½ inch) pieces and place in a large bowl. Peel and seed the cucumbers and cut into 1 cm (½ inch) dice. Add to the bowl along with the onion and dill.
2 Grind the mint in a mortar and pestle, or force through a sieve, until powdered. Combine with the oil and juice, then season with salt and black pepper. Pour over the salad and toss well.

TOMATO AND BOCCONCINI SALAD

Preparation time: 15 minutes
Total cooking time: Nil
Serves 6–8

12 ripe Roma (egg) tomatoes
10 bocconcini
1⅓ cups (40 g/1½ oz) fresh basil leaves

Dressing
½ cup (125 ml/4 fl oz) extra virgin olive oil
⅓ cup (80 ml/2¾ fl oz) balsamic vinegar

1 Cut the tomatoes lengthways into 3–4 slices (discard the outside slices, which won't lie flat). Slice each bocconcini lengthways into 3–4 slices.
2 Arrange some tomato slices on a serving plate, place a bocconcini slice on top of each and scatter with some basil leaves. Repeat until all the tomato, bocconcini and basil have been used. Season with salt and pepper.
3 For the dressing, whisk the oil and vinegar together. Drizzle over the salad.

NOTE: This salad can also be served with a pesto dressing. Finely chop 1 cup (50 g/1¾ oz) fresh basil leaves, 2 tablespoons pine nuts, ½ cup (50 g/1¾ oz) grated Parmesan and 2 crushed garlic cloves in a food processor. With the motor running, add ½ cup (125 ml/4 fl oz) olive oil and 2 tablespoons lemon juice in a steady stream.

HERBED FETA SALAD

Preparation time: 20 minutes +
    30 minutes
Total cooking time: 10 minutes
Serves 6–8

2 slices thick white bread
200 g (6½ oz) feta cheese
1 clove garlic, crushed
1 tablespoon finely chopped fresh
    marjoram
1 tablespoon finely chopped fresh chives
1 tablespoon finely chopped fresh basil
2 tablespoons white wine vinegar
⅓ cup (80 ml/2¾ fl oz) olive oil
1 red coral lettuce
1 butter, coral or oak-leaf lettuce

1 Preheat oven to moderate 180°C
(350°F/ Gas 4). Remove crusts from
bread and cut bread into cubes. Place on
an oven tray in a single layer; bake for
10 minutes, or until crisp and lightly
golden; cool completely.
2 Cut feta into small cubes; place in a
bowl. Combine garlic, marjoram, chives,
basil, vinegar and oil in small screw-top
jar and shake for 30 seconds. Pour over
feta and cover with plastic wrap. Leave for
at least 30 minutes, stirring occasionally.
Wash and dry lettuces. Tear leaves into
pieces and place in a bowl. Add feta with
dressing, and bread cubes; toss.

SALMON AND GREEN BEAN SALAD

Preparation time: 20 minutes
Total cooking time: 30 minutes
Serves 4–6

350 g (11 oz) skinless salmon fillet
oil, for deep-frying
4 cloves garlic, thinly sliced
200 g (6½ oz) white sweet potato, thinly
    sliced
100 g (3½ oz) green beans, halved
    lengthways
1 red onion, thinly sliced
20 g (¾ oz) sesame seeds, toasted
1 mizuna lettuce, stems trimmed

Dressing
2 cloves garlic, crushed
2 tablespoons tahini
1 tablespoon rice vinegar
2 tablespoons lime juice
1 tablespoon soy sauce
¼ cup (60 ml/2 fl oz) olive oil

1 Chargrill or grill the fish fillet until
medium-rare or cooked to your taste.
Allow to cool slightly before cutting into
large pieces.
2 Heat the oil in a deep heavy-based
saucepan to 180°C (350°F), or until a cube
of bread dropped into the oil browns in
15 seconds. Deep-fry the garlic and sweet
potato separately until crisp and golden.
Drain on crumpled paper towels.
3 Cook the beans in boiling water until
tender. Rinse, plunge into iced water and
drain. Combine with the onion, sesame
seeds, sweet potato, garlic and mizuna.
Divide among serving plates. Top with the
fish.
4 For the dressing, whisk the ingredients
together in a bowl. Drizzle over the salad
and serve immediately.

GREEK SALAD

Preparation time: 20 minutes
Total cooking time: Nil
Serves 6–8

6 tomatoes, cut into thin wedges
1 red onion, cut into thin rings
2 Lebanese cucumbers, sliced
1 cup (185 g/6 oz) Kalamata olives
200 g (6½ oz) feta cheese
½ cup (125 ml/4 fl oz) extra virgin olive oil
dried oregano, to sprinkle

1 Combine the tomato wedges with the
onion rings, sliced cucumber and
Kalamata olives in a large bowl. Season
to taste with salt and freshly ground black
pepper.
2 Break up the feta into large pieces with
your fingers and scatter over the top of
the salad. Drizzle with the olive oil and
sprinkle with some oregano.

HAM AND BEAN SALAD

Preparation time: 30 minutes
Total cooking time: 1 minute
Serves 6

200 g (6½ oz) green beans
200 g (6½ oz) sugar snap peas
200 g (6½ oz) frozen broad beans
200 g (6½ oz) sliced ham
250 g (8 oz) cherry tomatoes, cut in
   halves
¾ cup (115 g/4 oz) toasted cashews
2 tablespoons chopped fresh parsley
2 tablespoons chopped fresh chives
¼ cup (60 ml/2 fl oz) olive oil
2 tablespoons cider vinegar
½ teaspoon sugar
2 tablespoons chopped fresh mint

1 Top and tail the green beans and sugar
snap peas, then cut the beans diagonally
into short lengths. Put the beans, peas
and broad beans in a pan of boiling water
and cook for 1 minute. Drain and refresh
in cold water. Discard the outer skin from
the broad beans.
2 Cut the ham into thin strips and
combine in a large bowl with the beans
and peas, cherry tomatoes, cashews,
parsley and chives.
3 For the dressing, combine the oil,
vinegar, sugar and mint in a screw top jar,
shake, then season, to taste. Pour over
the salad and toss well.

MIXED VEGETABLE SALAD

Preparation time: 40 minutes
Total cooking time: 3 minutes
Serves 4–6

300 g (9⅔ oz) chopped fresh pineapple
1 long cucumber, chopped
1 punnet cherry tomatoes, halved
155 g (5 oz) green beans, finely sliced
155 g (5 oz) bean sprouts, scraggly ends
   removed
⅓ cup (80 ml/2¾ fl oz) rice vinegar
2 tablespoons lime juice
2 red chillies, seeded and very finely
   chopped
2 teaspoons sugar
30 g (1 oz) dried shrimp, to garnish
small fresh mint leaves, to garnish

1 Toss together the pineapple, cucumber,
tomatoes, beans and sprouts in a bowl,
cover and refrigerate until chilled.
Combine the vinegar, lime juice, chilli and
sugar in a small bowl and stir until the
sugar dissolves.
2 Dry-fry the shrimp in a frying pan,
shaking the pan constantly until the
shrimp are light orange and fragrant.
Process the shrimp in a food processor
until finely chopped.
3 Arrange the chilled salad on a serving
platter, drizzle the dressing over the top
and garnish with the chopped shrimp and
mint leaves. Serve immediately.

SPROUT AND PEAR SALAD WITH SESAME DRESSING

Preparation time: 30 minutes
Total cooking time: Nil
Serves 6

250 g (8 oz) snow pea (mangetout)
   sprouts
250 g (8 oz) fresh bean sprouts
30 g (1 oz) fresh chives
100 g (3⅓ oz) snow peas (mangetout)
1 celery stick
2 firm pears, not green
fresh coriander sprigs
sesame seeds, for garnish

Sesame Dressing
2 tablespoons soy sauce
1 teaspoon sesame oil
1 tablespoon soft brown sugar
2 tablespoons peanut oil
1 tablespoon rice vinegar

1 Wash and drain the snow pea sprouts.
Remove the brown tips from the bean
sprouts. Cut the chives into 4 cm (1½ inch)
lengths and cut the snow peas and celery
into thin matchstick strips. Peel and core
the pears. Cut them into thin strips,
slightly wider than the celery and snow
peas. Place in a bowl and cover with
water to prevent discoloration.
2 To make Sesame Dressing: Combine all
the ingredients in a small screw-top jar
and shake them well.
3 Drain the pears. Combine all salad
ingredients and the coriander sprigs in a
large serving bowl. Pour the dressing
over and toss lightly. Sprinkle with
sesame seeds and serve immediately.

GRILLED PEPPERS (CAPSICUMS) AND ANCHOVY SALAD

Preparation time: 15 minutes
Total cooking time: 25 minutes
Serves 6

500 g (1 lb) penne or spiral pasta
2 large red peppers (capsicums)
1 small red onion, finely chopped
1 cup (20 g/¾ oz) fresh flat-leaf parsley
   leaves
2–3 anchovies, whole or chopped
¼ cup (60 ml/2 fl oz) olive oil
2 tablespoons lemon juice

1 Cook the pasta in a large pan of rapidly boiling salted water until al dente. Drain, rinse under cold water and drain again.
2 Cut the peppers in half and remove seeds and membrane. Place skin-side-up under a hot grill and cook for 8 minutes, or until the skin is black and blistered. Remove from the heat and cover with a damp tea towel. When cool, peel away the skin and cut the flesh into thin strips.
3 In a large salad bowl, combine the pasta, pepper strips, onion, parsley, anchovies, oil, lemon juice, and salt and pepper, to taste. Toss until well combined and serve immediately.

NOTE: To prevent pasta sticking together, after rinsing under cold water add a little of the oil to pasta and toss well.

FISH AND HERB SALAD

Preparation time: 40 minutes
Total cooking time: 15 minutes
Serves 4–6

500 g (1 lb) smoked cod
3 tablespoons lime juice
½ cup (30 g/1 oz) flaked coconut
1 cup (200 g/6½ oz) jasmine rice, cooked
   and cooled
½ cup (25 g/¾ oz) chopped fresh
   Vietnamese mint
3 tablespoons chopped fresh mint
½ cup (25 g/¾ oz) chopped fresh
   coriander leaves
8 kaffir lime leaves, very finely shredded

Dressing
1 tablespoon chopped fresh coriander
   root
2 cm (¾ inch) piece fresh ginger, finely
   grated
1 red chilli, finely chopped
1 tablespoon chopped lemon grass (white
   part only)
3 tablespoons chopped fresh Thai basil
1 avocado, chopped
⅓ cup (80 ml/2¾ fl oz) lime juice
2 tablespoons fish sauce
1 teaspoon soft brown sugar
½ cup (125 ml/4 fl oz) peanut oil

1 Preheat the oven to slow 150°C (300°F/ Gas 2). Place the cod in a large frying pan and cover with water. Add the lime juice and simmer for 15 minutes, or until the fish flakes when tested with a fork. Drain and set aside to cool slightly before breaking it into bite-sized pieces.
2 Spread the coconut onto an oven tray and toast in the oven for 10 minutes or until it is golden brown, shaking the tray occasionally. Remove the coconut from the tray to prevent it burning.
3 Place the fish, coconut, rice, Vietnamese mint, mint, coriander and kaffir lime leaves in a large bowl and mix to combine.
4 To make Dressing: Place the coriander root, ginger, chilli, lemon grass and basil in a food processor and process until combined. Add the avocado, lime juice, fish sauce, sugar and peanut oil and process until creamy.
5 Pour the dressing over the salad and toss to coat the rice and fish. Serve immediately.

CARAMELIZED ONION AND POTATO SALAD

Preparation time: 20 minutes
Total cooking time: 50 minutes
Serves 10–12

2 tablespoons oil
6 red onions, thinly sliced
1 kg (2 lb) kipfler, desiree or pontiac potatoes
4 rashers bacon
6 tablespoons chopped fresh chives

Mayonnaise
1 cup (250 g/8 oz) whole-egg mayonnaise
1 tablespoon Dijon mustard
2–3 tablespoons lemon juice
2 tablespoons sour cream

1 Heat the oil in a large heavy-based frying pan, add the onion and cook over low-medium heat for 40 minutes, or until caramelized.
2 Cut the potatoes into large chunks (if small, leave them whole) and steam or boil for 5–10 minutes until just tender (pierce with the point of a small knife— if the potato comes away easily, it is ready). Drain and cool slightly.
3 Remove the rind from the bacon and grill until crisp. Drain on crumpled paper towels and cool slightly before roughly chopping.
4 Put the potato, onion and chives in a large bowl, reserving a few chives for garnish, and toss to combine.
5 For the mayonnaise, whisk the ingredients together in a bowl. Pour over the salad and toss to coat. Sprinkle with the bacon and garnish with the reserved chives.

NOTE: Ideal boiling potatoes are waxy in texture with a high moisture content and low starch content. Examples other than those given in the recipe are sebago, coliban, pink fir apple and jersey royals.

PEARS WITH BRIE AND PECANS

Preparation time: 15 minutes
Total cooking time: Nil
Serves 4

200 g (6½ oz) brie cheese, at room temperature
3 medium pears
1 butter or mignonette lettuce
4 tablespoons finely chopped pecans

Vinaigrette Dressing
3 tablespoons oil
1 tablespoon tarragon vinegar

1 Cut the brie into thin wedges. Do not peel the pears, but cut them into quarters; remove the cores and slice the pears thinly. Wash and dry the lettuce thoroughly, then separate the leaves and arrange on individual serving plates. Top with the brie and pears.
2 To make Vinaigrette Dressing: Place the oil and vinegar in a small screw-top jar and shake well. Drizzle the dressing over the salad and sprinkle with pecans. Serve immediately.

NOTE: Camembert can be used instead of brie in this recipe. Ripe brie or camembert give the best flavour. Make sure that the cheese is at room temperature to serve.

TOMATO, HALOUMI AND SPINACH SALAD

Preparation time: 15 minutes +
  2 hours marinating
Total cooking time: 1 hour
Serves 4

200 g (6½ oz) haloumi cheese
¼ cup (60 ml/2 fl oz) olive oil
2 cloves garlic, crushed
1 tablespoon chopped fresh oregano
1 tablespoon chopped fresh marjoram
8 egg (Roma) tomatoes, halved
1 small red onion, cut into 8 wedges with base intact
¼ cup (60 ml/2 fl oz) olive oil, extra
2 tablespoons balsamic vinegar
150 g (5 oz) baby English spinach leaves

1 Cut the haloumi into 1 cm (½ inch) slices lengthways and put in a shallow dish. Mix together the oil, garlic and herbs and pour over the haloumi. Marinate, covered, for 1–2 hours.
2 Preheat the oven to moderately hot 200°C (400°F/Gas 6). Place the tomato and onion in a single layer in a roasting tin, drizzle with 2 tablespoons of the extra olive oil and 1 tablespoon of the vinegar and sprinkle with salt and cracked black pepper. Bake for 50–60 minutes, or until golden.
3 Meanwhile, heat a non-stick frying pan over medium heat. Drain the haloumi and cook for 1 minute each side, or until golden brown.
4 Divide the spinach leaves among four serving plates and top with the tomato and onion. Whisk together the remaining olive oil and balsamic vinegar in a small bowl and drizzle over the salad. Top with the haloumi.

FRISEE (CURLY ENDIVE) AND GARLIC CROUTON SALAD

Preparation time: 20 minutes
Total cooking time: 10 minutes
Serves 4–6

Vinaigrette
1 French shallot, finely chopped
1 tablespoon Dijon mustard
¼ cup (60 ml/2 fl oz) tarragon vinegar
⅔ cup (170 ml/5½ fl oz) extra virgin olive oil

1 tablespoon olive oil
250 g (8 oz) speck, rind removed, cut into 5 mm x 2 cm (¼ x ¾ inch) pieces
½ medium bread stick, sliced
4 whole cloves garlic
1 baby frisee (curly endive), washed and dried
½ cup (100 g/3½ oz) walnuts, toasted

1 For the vinaigrette, whisk together in a bowl the shallot, mustard and vinegar. Slowly add the oil, whisking constantly until thickened. Set aside.
2 Heat the oil in a large frying pan, add the speck, bread and garlic cloves and cook over medium–high heat for 5–8 minutes, until the bread and speck are both crisp. Remove the garlic from the pan.
3 Place the frisee, bread, speck, walnuts and vinaigrette in a large bowl. Toss together well and serve.

INSALATA DI FRUTTI DI MARE (SEAFOOD SALAD)

Preparation time: 45 minutes + 40 minutes marinating
Total cooking time: 25 minutes
Serves 4

500 g (1 lb) small squid
1 kg (2 lb) large clams
1 kg (2 lb) mussels
5 tablespoons chopped fresh flat-leaf parsley (reserve the stalks)
500 g (1 lb) raw medium prawns, peeled, deveined, tails intact
2 tablespoons lemon juice
⅓ cup (80 ml/2¾ fl oz) olive oil
1 clove garlic, crushed

1 Grasp each squid body in one hand and the head and tentacles in the other. Pull to separate. Cut the tentacles from each head below the eyes. Discard the heads. Push out the beaks and discard. Pull the quill from inside each body and discard. Under cold running water, pull away the skin (the flaps can be used). Rinse, then slice into 7 mm (¼ inch) rings.
2 Scrub the clams and mussels with a stiff brush and remove the hairy beards. Discard any that are cracked or don't close when tapped. Rinse under cold water. Fill a wide shallow pan with 1 cm (½ inch) water, add the parsley stalks, cover the pan and bring the water to simmering point. Add the clams and mussels in batches, being careful not to overcrowd the pan. Cover and steam over high heat for 2–3 minutes, or until the shells begin to open. Remove with a slotted spoon and place in a colander over a bowl. Return any drained juices to the pan before cooking the next batch. Continue until all the clams and mussels are cooked. Reserve the cooking liquid. Allow the clams and mussels to cool before removing them from the shells. Discard any unopened ones.

3 Add 1 litre water to the pan with the cooking liquid. Bring to the boil, then add the prawns and cook for 3–4 minutes, or until the water returns to the boil. Remove with a slotted spoon and drain in a colander. Add the squid and cook for 30–40 seconds, until the flesh becomes white and opaque. Remove immediately and drain.
4 Whisk the lemon juice, oil and garlic in a bowl, then season. Pour over the seafood with 4 tablespoons parsley, then toss. Adjust the seasoning if necessary. Marinate for 30–40 minutes to allow the flavours to develop. Sprinkle with parsley. Serve with crusty bread.

CHICKPEA AND ROAST VEGETABLE SALAD

Preparation time: 25 minutes
  + 30 minutes standing
Total cooking time: 40 minutes
Serves 8

500 g (1 lb) butternut pumpkin, cut
  into chunks
2 red peppers (capsicums), halved
4 slender eggplants (aubergines), sliced
  in half lengthways
4 zucchini (courgettes), sliced in half
  lengthways
4 onions, cut into quarters
olive oil, for brushing
2 x 300 g (10 oz) cans chickpeas, rinsed
  and drained
2 tablespoons chopped fresh flat-leaf
  parsley
Dressing
⅓ cup (80 ml/2¾ fl oz) olive oil
2 tablespoons lemon juice
1 clove garlic, crushed
1 tablespoon chopped fresh thyme

1 Preheat the oven to hot 220°C
(425°F/Gas 7). Brush two baking trays
with oil and spread the vegetables in a
single layer over the trays. Brush the
vegetables lightly with the olive oil.
2 Bake for 40 minutes, or until the
vegetables are tender and begin to brown
slightly on the edges. Remove and set
aside to cool. Remove the skins from the
red peppers if you wish. Chop the red
peppers, eggplant and zucchini into large
pieces, then put all the vegetables in a
bowl with the chickpeas and half the
parsley.
3 Whisk together all the dressing
ingredients in a bowl. Season, then toss
through the vegetables. Set aside for
30 minutes to marinate. Spoon into a
serving bowl and sprinkle with the rest of
the parsley before serving.

STUFFED MUSHROOM SALAD

Preparation time: 25 minutes
Total cooking time: Nil
Serves 4

20 button mushrooms
¼ cup (60 g/2 oz) pesto, chilled
100 g (3½ oz) rocket leaves
1 green oakleaf lettuce
12 small black olives
⅓ cup (50 g/1¾ oz) sliced semi-dried or
  sun-dried tomatoes
1 tablespoon roughly chopped basil
Parmesan shavings, to serve

Dressing
1/3 cup (80 ml/2¾ fl oz) olive oil
1 tablespoon white wine vinegar
1 teaspoon Dijon mustard

1 Trim the mushroom stalks level with
the caps and scoop out the remaining
stalk with a melon baller. Spoon the
pesto into the mushrooms.
2 To make the dressing, whisk together
all the ingredients. Season with salt and
pepper, to taste.
3 Arrange the rocket and lettuce leaves
on a serving plate and top with the
mushrooms, olives, tomato and basil.
Drizzle the dressing over the salad and
top with the Parmesan shavings. Serve
immediately.

HINT: Home-made pesto is preferable for
this recipe. To make your own, process
1 cup (30 g/1 oz) loosely packed basil
leaves, 2 tablespoons pine nuts and ¼ cup
(25 g/¾ oz) grated Parmesan in a food
processor to form a smooth paste.
Gradually pour in ¼ cup (60 ml/2 fl oz)
olive oil in a steady stream with the motor
running. Process until combined.

CRAB AND PAPAYA NOODLE SALAD

Preparation time: 20 minutes +
  10 minutes soaking + 15 minutes
  refrigeration
Total cooking time: Nil
Serves 4

80 g (2¾ oz) dried rice vermicelli
250 g (8 oz) green papaya
300 g (10 oz) fresh, cooked crab meat
2 tablespoons thinly sliced Chinese celery
  or celery
½ cup (10 g/¼ oz) mint
4 tablespoons finely chopped Thai basil
2 tablespoons crisp fried shallots
30 g (1 oz) roasted peanuts, crushed

Dressing
2 tablespoons peanut oil
155 ml (5 fl oz) lime juice
1½ tablespoons fish sauce
2 tablespoons sugar
2 small red chillies, seeded and finely
  chopped

1 Put the vermicelli in a heatproof bowl,
cover with boiling water and soak for
6–7 minutes, or until tender. Drain well,
rinse in cold water and drain again.
2 Meanwhile, peel the green papaya, cut in
half lengthways and scoop out the seeds
with a spoon. Cut the fruit into julienne
strips and put in a non-metallic bowl. Add
the crab meat and Chinese celery.
3 To make the dressing, whisk together
the peanut oil, lime juice, fish sauce, sugar
and chopped chillies in a small bowl.
4 Pour the dressing over the crab and
papaya mixture and toss well. Add the
noodles, mint and Thai basil and toss
again, coating well in the dressing. Cover
with plastic wrap and refrigerate for
15 minutes to allow the flavours to
develop.
5 Sprinkle the salad with the crisp fried
shallots and crushed roasted peanuts just
before serving.

ASPARAGUS AND RED CAPSICUM SALAD

Preparation time: 20 minutes
Total cooking time: 15 minutes
Serves 4

2 red capsicums
⅓ cup (80 ml/2¾ fl oz) virgin olive oil
1 clove garlic, crushed
2 tablespoons lemon juice
2 tablespoons chopped basil
2 tablespoons pine nuts
310 g (10 oz) fresh asparagus
small black olives

1 Cut the capsicums into large pieces, removing the seeds and white membrane. Place, skin-side-up, under a hot grill until the skin blackens and blisters. Cool under a tea towel or in a plastic bag, then carefully peel away and discard the skin. Finely dice the capsicum flesh.
2 Put the olive oil, garlic, lemon juice and basil in a small bowl and whisk to combine. Add the capsicum and pine nuts, and season with salt and pepper.
3 Remove the woody ends from the asparagus (hold each spear at both ends and bend gently—the woody end will snap off at its natural breaking point). Plunge the asparagus into a large frying pan of boiling water and cook for 3 minutes, or until just tender. Drain and plunge into a bowl of iced water, then drain again and gently pat dry with paper towels.
4 Arrange the asparagus on a large serving platter and spoon the dressing over the top. Garnish with the black olives and perhaps a few lemon wedges to squeeze over the top.

LEBANESE TOASTED BREAD SALAD

Preparation time: 15 minutes
Total cooking time: 10 minutes
Serves 6

2 pitta bread rounds (17 cm/7 inch diameter)
6 cos lettuce leaves, shredded
1 large Lebanese cucumber, cut into 1 cm (½ inch) cubes
4 ripe tomatoes, cut into 1 cm (½ inch) cubes
8 spring onions, chopped
4 tablespoons chopped fresh flat-leaf parsley
1 tablespoon chopped fresh mint
2 tablespoons chopped fresh coriander

Dressing
2 cloves garlic, crushed
100 ml (3½ fl oz) extra virgin olive oil
100 ml (3½ fl oz) lemon juice

1 Preheat the oven to moderate 180°C (350°F/ Gas 4). Split the bread into two through the centre and bake on a baking tray for about 8 minutes, or until golden and crisp, turning halfway through. Break into small pieces.
2 For the dressing, whisk all the ingredients together in a bowl until combined.
3 Place the bread pieces and remaining salad ingredients in a bowl and toss. Pour on the dressing and toss well. Season, to taste, with salt and ground black pepper. Serve immediately.

WARM BEAN SALAD

Preparation time: 10 minutes
Total cooking time: 8 minutes
Serves 4

2 tablespoons olive oil
1 medium onion, finely chopped
1 clove garlic, crushed
1 small red pepper (capsicum), cut into short strips
90 g (3 oz) green beans
60 g (2 oz) button mushrooms, sliced
1 tablespoon balsamic vinegar
440 g (14 oz) canned mixed beans
chopped fresh parsley, for serving

1 Heat half the oil in a medium pan. Add the onions and cook for 2 minutes over medium heat. Add the garlic, red pepper, green beans, mushrooms and vinegar. Cook for another 5 minutes, stirring occasionally.
2 Thoroughly rinse and drain the mixed beans. Add to the vegetables with the remaining oil and stir until just warmed through. Sprinkle with chopped parsley for serving.

BARBECUED CHICKEN AND PASTA SALAD

Preparation time: 15 minutes
Total cooking time: 15 minutes
Serves 6

1 barbecued chicken
500 g (1 lb) penne
¼ cup (60 ml/2 fl oz) olive oil
2 tablespoons white wine vinegar
200 g (6½ oz) cherry tomatoes, halved
⅓ cup (20 g/¾ oz) chopped fresh basil
  leaves
½ cup (75 g/2½ oz) chopped pitted black
  olives
freshly ground black pepper, to taste

1 Pull the meat and skin from the barbecued chicken. Cut into fine shreds.
2 Cook the penne in a large pan of rapidly boiling salted water until al dente. Drain and transfer to a serving bowl. Combine the oil and vinegar and toss through while the pasta is still warm.
3 Add the chicken, cherry tomatoes, basil and olives to the pasta, and toss thoroughly to combine. Sprinkle with freshly ground black pepper. Serve warm, as a main meal, or at room temperature as part of a selection of salads.

NOTE: The salad can be prepared up to 2 hours in advance. Refrigerate the chicken until close to serving time and add it to the salad at the last minute. Chop and add the basil close to serving time as well, as it discolours when cut.

SMOKED SALMON, DILL AND EGG PASTA SALAD

Preparation time: 20 minutes
Total cooking time: 15 minutes
Serves 4–6

350 g (11 oz) farfalle or fusilli
2 eggs
200 g (6½ oz) smoked salmon, cut into
  thin strips
1 tablespoon finely chopped fresh dill
3 tablespoons sour cream
2 tablespoons lemon juice
¼ teaspoon each salt and freshly ground
  black pepper
1 tablespoon chopped fresh parsley, to
  garnish

1 Cook the pasta in a large pan of rapidly boiling salted water until al dente. Drain, rinse under cold water and drain again. Allow to cool.
2 While the pasta is cooking, cook the eggs for 12 minutes, or until hard-boiled. Allow to cool and then peel, finely grate or chop and set aside.
3 Place the pasta in serving bowls and scatter the strips of smoked salmon and the chopped fresh dill over the top.
4 In a small bowl, whisk together the sour cream, lemon juice, salt and pepper. Drizzle the dressing over the pasta. Sprinkle the egg and parsley over the top and serve immediately.

TUNISIAN CARROT SALAD

Preparation time: 10 minutes
Total cooking time: 10 minutes
Serves 6

500 g (1 lb) carrots, thinly sliced
3 tablespoons finely chopped fresh flat-
  leaf parsley
1 teaspoon ground cumin
⅓ cup (80 ml/2¾ fl oz) olive oil
¼ cup (60 ml/2 fl oz) red wine vinegar
2 cloves garlic, crushed
¼ to ½ teaspoon harissa
12 black olives
2 hard-boiled eggs, quartered

1 Bring 2 cups (500 ml/16 fl oz) water to the boil in a saucepan. Add the carrot and cook until tender. Drain and transfer to a bowl. Add the parsley, cumin, olive oil, vinegar and garlic. Season with harissa and salt and pepper. Stir well.
2 To serve, place the carrots in a serving dish and garnish with the olives and eggs.

NOTE: If the carrots are not sweet, you can add a little honey to the dressing.

SALMON AND FENNEL SALAD

Preparation time: 15 minutes
Total cooking time: Nil
Serves 4

2 teaspoons Dijon mustard
1 teaspoon caster sugar
½ cup (125 ml/4 fl oz) olive oil
2 tablespoons lemon juice
2 fennel bulbs, thinly sliced
200 g (6½ oz) smoked salmon, cut into
    strips
2 tablespoons chopped fresh chives
1 tablespoon chopped fresh fennel fronds
    from the top of the fennel, or chopped
    fresh dill
fresh rocket leaves, for serving
lemon wedges, for serving

1 For the dressing, whisk together the
mustard, sugar, olive oil and lemon juice
in a large bowl.
2 Add the sliced fennel, salmon, chives
and fennel fronds to the bowl. Season
with salt and pepper and toss gently.
Serve with the rocket leaves, lemon
wedges and maybe some toast.

SPICY FUN SEE NOODLE SALAD

Preparation time: 20 minutes + 5 minutes
    soaking + 2 hours refrigeration
Total cooking time: 5 minutes
Serves 4

125 g (4 oz) mung bean vermicelli (fun
    see)
1 teaspoon sesame oil
1 large carrot, julienned
2 sticks celery, julienned
100 g (3½ oz) snow peas, julienned
2 small Lebanese cucumbers
3 spring onions, thinly sliced into long
    diagonal strips
½ cup (15 g/½ oz) fresh coriander leaves
½ cup (10 g/¼ oz) fresh mint

Dressing
⅓ cup (70 g/2 oz) Chinese sesame paste
2 teaspoons chilli oil
¼ cup (60 ml/2 fl oz) light soy sauce
1 tablespoon white vinegar
1 tablespoon sugar
¼ teaspoon cayenne pepper
2½ tablespoons chicken stock

1 Place the noodles in a large heatproof
bowl, cover with boiling water and soak
for 3–4 minutes, or until softened. Drain.
Cut in half with scissors, place in a large
bowl, add the sesame oil and mix well.
Cover and refrigerate for 1 hour, or until
needed.

2 Bring a large saucepan of water to the
boil, add the carrot, celery, snow
peas and 2 teaspoons salt and cook
for 30 seconds. Drain and refresh
in icy cold water. Drain again and
pat dry, making sure that as little
moisture as possible remains. Seed and
julienne the cucumber, and combine with
the vegetables and spring onion.
Refrigerate for 1 hour.
3 To make the dressing, place the
sesame paste in a bowl and stir well.
Slowly mix in the chilli oil, soy sauce,
vinegar, sugar, cayenne pepper and
chicken stock.
4 Just before serving, add three quarters
of the blanched vegetables and three
quarters of the herbs to the chilled
noodles. Pour the dressing on top, then
toss well. Season to taste with salt and
pepper. Transfer to a serving platter and
top with the remaining vegetables and
herbs.

BARBECUED CHICKEN AND PASTA SALAD

Preparation time: 15 minutes
Total cooking time: 15 minutes
Serves 6

1 barbecued chicken
500 g (1 lb) penne
¼ cup (60 ml/2 fl oz) olive oil
2 tablespoons white wine vinegar
200 g (6½ oz) cherry tomatoes, halved
⅓ cup (20 g/¾ oz) chopped fresh basil
   leaves
½ cup (75 g/2½ oz) chopped pitted black
   olives
freshly ground black pepper, to taste

1 Pull the meat and skin from the
barbecued chicken. Cut into fine shreds.
2 Cook the penne in a large pan of rapidly
boiling salted water until al dente. Drain
and transfer to a serving bowl. Combine
the oil and vinegar and toss through while
the pasta is still warm.
3 Add the chicken, cherry tomatoes, basil
and olives to the pasta, and toss
thoroughly to combine. Sprinkle with
freshly ground black pepper. Serve warm,
as a main meal, or at room temperature
as part of a selection of salads.

NOTE: The salad can be prepared up to
2 hours in advance. Refrigerate the
chicken until close to serving time and
add it to the salad at the last minute. Chop
and add the basil close to serving time as
well, as it discolours when cut.

SMOKED SALMON, DILL AND EGG PASTA SALAD

Preparation time: 20 minutes
Total cooking time: 15 minutes
Serves 4–6

350 g (11 oz) farfalle or fusilli
2 eggs
200 g (6½ oz) smoked salmon, cut into
   thin strips
1 tablespoon finely chopped fresh dill
3 tablespoons sour cream
2 tablespoons lemon juice
¼ teaspoon each salt and freshly ground
   black pepper
1 tablespoon chopped fresh parsley, to
   garnish

1 Cook the pasta in a large pan of rapidly
boiling salted water until al dente. Drain,
rinse under cold water and drain again.
Allow to cool.
2 While the pasta is cooking, cook the
eggs for 12 minutes, or until hard-boiled.
Allow to cool and then peel, finely grate
or chop and set aside.
3 Place the pasta in serving bowls and
scatter the strips of smoked salmon and
the chopped fresh dill over the top.
4 In a small bowl, whisk together the sour
cream, lemon juice, salt and pepper.
Drizzle the dressing over the pasta.
Sprinkle the egg and parsley over the top
and serve immediately.

TUNISIAN CARROT SALAD

Preparation time: 10 minutes
Total cooking time: 10 minutes
Serves 6

500 g (1 lb) carrots, thinly sliced
3 tablespoons finely chopped fresh flat-
   leaf parsley
1 teaspoon ground cumin
⅓ cup (80 ml/2¾ fl oz) olive oil
¼ cup (60 ml/2 fl oz) red wine vinegar
2 cloves garlic, crushed
¼ to ½ teaspoon harissa
12 black olives
2 hard-boiled eggs, quartered

1 Bring 2 cups (500 ml/16 fl oz) water to
the boil in a saucepan. Add the carrot and
cook until tender. Drain and transfer to a
bowl. Add the parsley, cumin, olive oil,
vinegar and garlic. Season with harissa
and salt and pepper. Stir well.
2 To serve, place the carrots in a serving
dish and garnish with the olives and eggs.

NOTE: If the carrots are not sweet, you
can add a little honey to the dressing.

PIQUANT POTATO SALAD

Preparation time: 10 minutes
Total cooking time: 10 minutes
Serves 4

500 g (1 lb) baby chat potatoes
2 teaspoons chopped fresh dill
2 spring onions, chopped
1 tablespoon capers, coarsely chopped
2 tablespoons extra virgin olive oil
1½ tablespoons lemon juice
1 teaspoon finely grated orange rind

1 Place the potatoes in a large saucepan of salted water and bring to the boil. Cook for 10 minutes, or until tender when pierced with a knife. Drain well.
2 Place the potatoes in a bowl with the dill, onion, capers and some salt and pepper. Mix well to combine. Whisk together the oil, lemon juice and orange rind in a small jug and pour over the hot potatoes. Toss to coat the potatoes and serve warm.

NOTE: Any small, waxy potato works well in this delicious salad. You can choose from those which are readily available such as pink fir, bintje or kipfler.

MIDDLE EASTERN HUMMUS, TOMATO AND OLIVE PASTA SALAD

Preparation time: 25 minutes
Total cooking time: 15 minutes
Serves 6

350 g (11 oz) macaroni elbows or conchiglie (shell pasta)
200 g (6½ oz) cherry tomatoes, cut into quarters
1 large zucchini (courgette), grated
1 small onion, grated
50 g (1¾ oz) black olives, pitted and chopped

Hummus dressing
2 tablespoons hummus
2 tablespoons natural yoghurt
1 tablespoon olive oil
1 clove garlic, finely chopped
1 teaspoon finely grated lemon rind
1 tablespoon chopped fresh parsley

1 Cook the pasta in a large pan of rapidly boiling salted water until al dente. Drain, rinse under cold water and drain again. Allow to cool. Place the pasta in a large bowl with the tomato, zucchini, onion and olives.
2 To make the hummus dressing, in a blender or food processor, combine the hummus, yoghurt, olive oil, garlic and lemon rind. Add plenty of salt and pepper and process again briefly.
3 Pour the dressing over the salad, add the parsley and toss well to combine.

SPAGHETTI TOMATO SALAD

Preparation time: 25 minutes
Total cooking time: 15 minutes
Serves 6

500 g (1 lb) spaghetti or bucatini
1 cup (50 g/1¾ oz) fresh basil leaves, shredded
250 g (8 oz) cherry tomatoes, halved
1 clove garlic, crushed
½ cup (75 g/2½ oz) chopped black olives
¼ cup (60 ml/2 fl oz) olive oil
1 tablespoon balsamic vinegar
½ cup (50 g/1¾ oz) freshly grated Parmesan

1 Cook the pasta in a large pan of rapidly boiling salted water until al dente. Drain, rinse under cold water and drain again.
2 Combine the basil, tomato, garlic, olives, oil and vinegar in a salad bowl. Set aside for about 15 minutes. Mix in the drained pasta.
3 Add the Parmesan and salt and pepper, to taste. Toss well and serve immediately.

RUSSIAN SALAD

Preparation time: 40 minutes
Total cooking time: 40 minutes
Serves 4–6

Mayonnaise
2 egg yolks
1 teaspoon Dijon mustard
½ cup (125 ml/4 fl oz) extra virgin olive oil
2 tablespoons lemon juice
2 small cloves garlic, crushed

3 canned artichoke hearts (about 120 g/4 oz)
3 waxy potatoes such as desiree, unpeeled
100 g (3½ oz) baby green beans, trimmed
    and cut into 1 cm (½ inch) lengths
1 large carrot, cut into 1 cm (½ inch) dice
125 g (4 oz) fresh peas
30 g (1 oz) cornichons, chopped
2 tablespoons baby capers, rinsed
10 black olives cut into 3 slices
4 anchovy fillets, finely chopped
5 whole black olives, to garnish

1 For the mayonnaise, using electric beaters, beat the egg yolks with the mustard and ¼ teaspoon salt until creamy. Gradually add the oil in a fine stream, beating constantly until all the oil has been added. Add the lemon juice, garlic and 1 teaspoon boiling water and beat for 1 minute until well combined. Season, to taste.

2 Cut each artichoke into quarters. Rinse the potatoes, cover with cold, salted water and bring to a gentle simmer. Cook for 15–20 minutes, or until tender when pierced with a knife. Drain and allow to cool slightly. Peel and set aside. When the potatoes are completely cool, cut into 1 cm (½ inch) dice.
3 Blanch the beans in boiling salted water until tender but still firm to the bite. Refresh in cold water, then drain thoroughly. Repeat with the carrot and peas.
4 Set aside a small quantity of each vegetable, including the cornichons, for the garnish and season, to taste. Place the remainder in a bowl with the capers, anchovies and sliced olives. Add the mayonnaise, toss to combine and season, to taste. Arrange on a serving dish and garnish with the reserved vegetables and the whole olives.

NOTE: This Russian salad can be prepared up to 2 days in advance and stored in the refrigerator but should be served at room temperature.

AVOCADO AND BLACK BEAN SALAD

Preparation time: 15 minutes +
    overnight soaking
Total cooking time: approximately 1½
    hours
Serves 4

250 g (8 oz) dried black beans
1 red (Spanish) onion, chopped
4 egg (Roma) tomatoes, chopped
1 red pepper (capsicum), chopped
375 g (12 oz) canned corn kernels,
    drained
90 g (3 oz) fresh coriander, roughly
    chopped
2 avocados, peeled and chopped
1 mango, peeled and chopped
150 g (4¾ oz) rocket, leaves separated

Dressing
1 clove garlic, crushed
1 small red chilli, finely chopped
2 tablespoons lime juice
¼ cup (60 ml/2 fl oz) olive oil

1 Soak the beans in cold water overnight. Rinse; drain. Place the beans into a large heavy-based pan, cover with water and bring to the boil. Reduce the heat and simmer for 1½ hours, or until tender. Drain and cool slightly.
2 Place the beans, onion, tomatoes, pepper, corn, coriander, avocado, mango and rocket into a large bowl and toss to combine.
3 To make Dressing: Place all ingredients in a bowl, whisk, pour over the salad and toss.

PENNE SALAD WITH SUN-DRIED TOMATOES

Preparation time: 20 minutes
Total cooking time: 10 minutes
Serves 6

500 g (1 lb) penne pasta
1 tablespoon olive oil
150 g (4¾ oz) sun-dried tomatoes, drained
½ cup (25 g/¾ oz) fresh basil leaves
½ cup (70 g/2⅓ oz) black pitted olives, halved
2 tablespoons olive oil, extra
2 teaspoons white wine vinegar
1 clove garlic, cut in half
60 g (2 oz) Parmesan, shaved

1 Cook pasta in a large pan of boiling water until just tender. Drain and rinse under cold water; drain again. Place in a large serving bowl and combine with oil to prevent sticking.
2 Thinly slice sun-dried tomatoes. Mix basil leaves and tomatoes into pasta with the olives.
3 Place the extra oil, vinegar and garlic in a small screw-top jar and shake well. Leave for 5 minutes then discard garlic. Shake dressing again and then pour over salad. Stir gently to combine. Garnish with shavings of Parmesan and serve immediately.

CITRUS WALNUT SALAD

Preparation time: 20 minutes
Total cooking time: Nil
Serves 8

2 oranges
2 grapefruit
125 g (4 oz) sugar snap peas
75 g (2½ oz) rocket, leaves torn
½ oak leaf lettuce, leaves torn
1 large Lebanese cucumber, sliced
⅓ cup (40 g/1⅓ oz) walnut pieces

Walnut Dressing
2 tablespoons walnut oil
2 tablespoons oil
2 teaspoons tarragon vinegar
2 teaspoons seeded mustard
1 teaspoon sweet chilli sauce

1 Peel the oranges and grapefruit, removing all the white pith. Cut the fruit into segments between the membrane, removing the seeds. Cover the sugar snap peas with boiling water and leave to stand for 2 minutes. Plunge the peas into iced water. Drain and pat dry with sheets of paper towel. Combine the fruit, peas, rocket, lettuce, cucumber and walnut pieces in a large bowl.
2 To make Walnut Dressing: Combine all the ingredients in a screw-top jar and shake well.
3 Pour the dressing over the salad ingredients and toss until combined.

MARINATED FISH SALAD WITH CHILLI AND BASIL

Preparation time: 30 minutes + several hours marinating
Total cooking time: Nil
Serves 4

500 g (1 lb) skinless firm white fish fillets (eg. mahi mahi, coral trout, snapper, red emperor)
¼ cup (60 ml/2 fl oz) lime juice
¼ cup (60 ml/2 fl oz) coconut milk
3 tomatoes, diced
3 Lebanese cucumbers, diced
5 spring onions, finely sliced
2 fresh red chillies, seeded and sliced
2 cloves garlic, crushed
1 teaspoon grated fresh ginger
½ cup (15 g/½ oz) fresh basil leaves, torn
mixed salad leaves, for serving

1 Slice the fish into thin strips and place in a glass or ceramic bowl.
2 For the marinade, combine the lime juice, coconut milk, 1 teaspoon salt and ¼ teaspoon cracked black pepper in a jug. Mix well, then pour over the fish. Cover and refrigerate for several hours or overnight, turning once or twice.
3 Add the tomato, cucumber, spring onion, chilli, garlic, ginger and basil to the fish. Mix well and serve spooned over salad leaves.

NOTES: The action of acid in the lime juice 'cooks' the fish, firming the flesh and turning it opaque.
When mangoes are in season, dice roughly and toss through the finished salad for extra flavour and sweetness.

SPICY LENTIL SALAD

Preparation time: 30 minutes
Total cooking time: 1 hour 10 minutes
Serves 6

1 cup (220 g/7 oz) brown rice
1 cup (185 g/6 oz) brown lentils
1 teaspoon turmeric
1 teaspoon ground cinnamon
6 cardamom pods
3 star anise
2 bay leaves
¼ cup (60 ml/2 fl oz) sunflower oil
1 tablespoon lemon juice
250 g (8 oz) broccoli florets
2 carrots, cut into julienne strips
1 onion, finely chopped
2 cloves garlic, crushed
1 red capsicum, finely chopped
1 teaspoon garam masala
1 teaspoon ground coriander
1½ cups (250 g/8 oz) fresh or frozen peas,
   thawed

Mint and Yoghurt Dressing
1 cup (250 g/8 oz) plain yoghurt
1 tablespoon lemon juice
1 tablespoon chopped fresh mint
1 teaspoon cumin seeds

1 Put 3 cups (750 ml/24 fl oz) water with the rice, lentils, turmeric, cinnamon, cardamom, star anise and bay leaves in a pan. Stir well and bring to the boil. Reduce the heat, cover and simmer gently for 50–60 minutes, or until the liquid is absorbed. Remove the whole spices. Transfer the mixture to a large bowl. Whisk 2 tablespoons of the oil with the lemon juice and fork through the rice mixture.
2 Boil, steam or microwave the broccoli and carrots until tender. Drain and refresh in cold water.
3 Heat the remaining oil in a large pan and add the onion, garlic and capsicum. Stir-fry for 2–3 minutes, then add the garam masala and coriander, and stir-fry for a further 1–2 minutes. Add the vegetables and toss to coat in the spice mixture. Add to the rice and fork through to combine. Cover and refrigerate until cold.
4 To make the dressing mix the yoghurt, lemon juice, mint and cumin seeds together, and season with salt and pepper. Spoon the salad into individual serving bowls or onto a platter and serve with the dressing.

TUSCAN WARM PASTA SALAD

Preparation time: 15 minutes
Total cooking time: 15 minutes
Serves 6

500 g (1 lb) rigatoni
⅓ cup (80 ml/2¾ fl oz) olive oil
1 clove garlic, crushed
1 tablespoon balsamic vinegar
425 g (14 oz) can artichoke hearts,
   drained and quartered
8 thin slices prosciutto, chopped
½ cup (80 g/2¾ oz) sun-dried tomatoes in
   oil, drained and thinly sliced
¼ cup (15 g/½ oz) fresh basil leaves,
   shredded
2 cups (70 g/2¼ oz) rocket leaves,
   washed and drained well
¼ cup (40 g/1¼ oz) pine nuts, lightly
   toasted
¼ cup (45 g/1½ oz) small black Italian
   olives

1 Add the rigatoni to a large pan of rapidly boiling water and cook until al dente. Drain the pasta thoroughly and transfer to a large serving bowl.
2 While the pasta is cooking, whisk together the oil, garlic and balsamic vinegar.
3 Toss the dressing through the hot pasta. Allow the pasta to cool slightly. Add the artichoke hearts, prosciutto, sun-dried tomato, basil, rocket, pine nuts and olives.
4 Toss all the ingredients together until well combined. Season, to taste, with salt and freshly ground black pepper.

NOTE: To toast the pine nuts, cook in a dry frying pan over medium heat for 1–2 minutes, until lightly golden. Allow to cool.

GOAT'S CHEESE SALAD

Preparation time: 20 minutes
Total cooking time: 15 minutes
Serves 4

12 slices white bread
4 x 100 g (3⅓ oz) rounds goat's cheese
60 g (2 oz) mixed salad leaves (mesclun)
60 g (2 oz) rocket
250 g (8 oz) cherry tomatoes, halved
1 tablespoon white wine vinegar
¼ cup (60 ml/2 fl oz) olive oil
½ teaspoon wholegrain mustard

1 Preheat the oven to moderate 180°C
(350°F/Gas 4). Using a biscuit cutter, cut a
round out of each slice of bread. (The
bread must not be larger than the cheese
or the edges will burn under the grill.)
Place the bread on a baking tray and bake
for 10 minutes. Slice each cheese into
three.
2 Place a slice of cheese on each piece of
bread. Arrange a bed of salad leaves and
rocket on small individual serving plates;
top with several tomato halves. Cook
cheese and bread rounds under a
preheated hot grill for 5 minutes or until
the cheese turns golden and bubbles.
Drizzle salad leaves with dressing and
place 3 cheese rounds on top of each
salad. Sprinkle with chopped chives to
serve, if desired.
3 To make dressing: Combine vinegar, oil
and mustard in a small screw-top jar;
shake vigorously for a minute or so until
well combined.

WARM STIR-FRIED SALAD

Preparation time: 15 minutes
Total cooking time: 5 minutes
Serves 2

2 tablespoons olive oil
1 red onion, sliced
1 red capsicum, cut into small squares
2 cloves garlic, thinly sliced
250 g (8 oz) cherry tomatoes, halved
150 g (5 oz) baby English spinach leaves
½ cup (15 g/½ oz) basil leaves
125 g (4 oz) feta cheese, crumbled

1 Heat the wok until very hot, add the oil
and swirl it around to coat the base and
side of the wok. Add the onion, capsicum
and garlic to the wok and stir-fry for 2
minutes, or until just beginning to soften.
Add the tomatoes, spinach and basil and
stir-fry until the leaves have just wilted.
2 Transfer the salad to a serving plate
and top with the crumbled feta cheese.
Serve immediately.

NOTE: Serve as a main course with crusty
bread or pasta or heap onto crostini as a
starter.

RED CABBAGE SALAD

Preparation time: 15 minutes
Total cooking time: Nil
Serves 6

155 g (5 oz) red cabbage, finely shredded
125 g (4 oz) green cabbage, finely
   shredded
2 spring onions, finely chopped
3 tablespoons olive oil
2 teaspoons white wine vinegar
½ teaspoon French mustard
1 teaspoon caraway seeds

1 Combine the red and green cabbage and
spring onions in a serving bowl.
2 Place the oil, vinegar, mustard and
caraway seeds in a small screw-top jar
and shake well.
3 Pour the dressing over the salad, toss
lightly to combine and serve immediately.

CHICKEN AND NOODLE SALAD WITH CASHEWS

Preparation time: 20 minutes +
    2 hours marinating
Total cooking time: 20 minutes
Serves 4

2 garlic cloves, peeled
¼ cup (60 ml/2 fl oz) fish sauce
¼ cup (60 ml/2 fl oz) lime juice
2 teaspoons chilli paste
2 tablespoons soft brown sugar
2 cups (60 g/2 oz) firmly packed
    coriander (cilantro) leaves
1 cup (155 g/5 oz) unsalted roasted
    cashews, chopped
¼ cup (60 ml/2 fl oz) oil
650 g (1 lb 5 oz) chicken thigh fillets
370 g (12 oz) rice noodle sticks
200 g (61/2 oz) tomatoes, diced
3 tablespoons coriander (cilantro) leaves,
    extra

1 To make the dressing, combine the garlic, fish sauce, lime juice, chilli paste, sugar, coriander and half the cashews in a food processor until smooth. With the motor running, slowly add the oil and mix well.
2 Put the chicken in a bowl with ½ cup (125 ml/4 fl oz) of the dressing. Cover and marinate in the refrigerator for at least 2 hours.
3 Cook the chicken in a non-stick frying pan for 5 minutes on each side, or until cooked through. Rest for 5 minutes, then cut into thin strips.
4 Cook the noodles in a saucepan of boiling water for 4 minutes, or until tender. Rinse and drain. Toss with the tomato and the remaining dressing.
5 Arrange the noodles on a platter. Top with the chicken, the remaining cashews and extra coriander leaves. Serve warm.

WILD RICE AND WALNUT SALAD

Preparation time: 10 minutes
    + 1 hour standing
Total cooking time: 5 minutes
Serves 6

1½ cups (285 g/9½ oz) wild rice
3 oranges
6 spring onions, finely sliced
¾ cup (90 g/3 oz) walnut pieces, toasted
1 tablespoon chopped fresh flat-leaf
    parsley

Dressing
⅓ cup (80 ml/2¾ fl oz) walnut oil
1 tablespoon olive oil
2 tablespoons white wine vinegar
1 tablespoon soy sauce
2 teaspoons honey

1 Thoroughly rinse the wild rice under cold running water, then put in a saucepan and fill with water to come 2.5 cm (1 inch) above the rice. Bring to the boil and cook for 5 minutes. Remove from the heat, cover and leave for 1 hour. Drain well, transfer to a bowl and leave to cool.
2 Peel the oranges, reserving the skin from one of them. Separate the flesh into segments and cut into small pieces. Cut the white pith off the reserved skin, cut the rind into julienne strips and reserve for garnish.
3 Add the orange pieces to the cooled rice with the spring onion, walnut pieces and parsley and lightly toss.
4 For the dressing, whisk all the ingredients together in a bowl until combined. Pour over the rice mixture and toss gently until well distributed. Garnish with the julienned orange rind.

NACHOS SALAD

Preparation time: 20 minutes
Total cooking time: Nil
Serves 4

440 g (14 oz) canned red kidney beans
1 large tomato, cut into cubes
½ cup (125 g/4 oz) bottled mild salsa
280 g (9 oz) packet plain corn chips
8 lettuce leaves, shredded
1 small avocado, sliced
20 g (⅔ oz) Cheddar cheese, grated

1 Empty the beans into a colander or strainer and rinse under running water. Drain well and combine with the tomato and salsa.
2 Arrange a bed of corn chips on each plate and top with lettuce, bean mixture and avocado. Sprinkle with the grated cheese and serve.

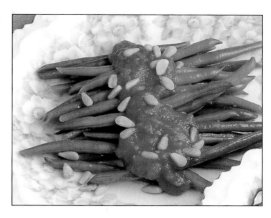

CITRUS AND AVOCADO SALAD

Preparation time: 10 minutes
Total cooking time: Nil
Serves 4

2 ripe avocados, sliced into 1 cm (½ inch)
   slices
2 oranges, segmented, reserving
   1 tablespoon juice
1 grapefruit (preferably pink), segmented
90 g (3 oz) baby rocket leaves
1 teaspoon finely grated orange rind
1 tablespoon orange juice
75 ml (2½ fl oz) extra virgin olive oil
1 tablespoon red wine vinegar
½ teaspoon Dijon mustard
1 teaspoon sugar
1 tablespoon chopped fresh mint

1 Place the avocado and citrus fruit in a
serving bowl or platter and toss gently
with the rocket leaves.
2 In a separate bowl, place the orange
rind and juice, oil, vinegar, mustard and
sugar. Season with salt and pepper and
whisk together. Pour over the salad and
cover all the leaves and the fruit. Sprinkle
with the chopped mint and serve
immediately.

TUNA SALAD WITH GARLIC MAYONNAISE

Preparation time: 25 minutes
Total cooking time: 10 minutes
Serves 6

6 medium potatoes such as pontiac,
   sebago, coliban
150 g (5 oz) snow peas (mangetout)
200 g (6½ oz) asparagus
250 g (8 oz) cherry tomatoes
2 x 425 g (14 oz) cans tuna, drained

Garlic mayonnaise
3 egg yolks
1 clove garlic, crushed
½ teaspoon French mustard
2 tablespoons lemon juice
1 cup (250 ml/8 fl oz) olive oil

1 Cut the peeled potatoes into 2 cm
(¾ inch) cubes and steam or boil for
8–10 minutes, or until just tender (pierce
with the point of a small knife—if the
potato comes away easily, it is ready).
Drain and set aside.
2 Cook the snow peas in a pan of boiling
water for 1 minute, remove from the
water with a slotted spoon and plunge
into iced water. Drain and set aside.
3 Trim the woody ends from the
asparagus and blanch as for snow peas.
4 To make garlic mayonnaise, place the
yolks, garlic, mustard and juice in a
bowl and beat with electric beaters for
1 minute. Add the oil in a thin steady
stream, about 1 teaspoon at a time,
beating constantly until thick and creamy.
Start to add the oil more quickly as the
mayonnaise thickens. Continue beating
until all the oil is incorporated. Season, to
taste, with salt and cracked black pepper.
5 Arrange the potato, snow peas,
asparagus, tomatoes and chunks of tuna
on individual plates. Place a spoonful of
mayonnaise on each plate or serve
separately. Serve immediately.

GREEN BEAN SALAD

Preparation time: 15 minutes
Total cooking time: 15 minutes
Serves 4

280 g (9 oz) green beans
1 tablespoon olive oil
2 teaspoons lemon juice
1 tablespoon pine nuts
⅓ cup (80 ml/2¾ fl oz) tomato juice
1 clove garlic, crushed
few drops Tabasco sauce

1 Top and tail beans; place in a pan of
boiling water. Boil for 1 minute, drain and
plunge into iced water; drain well; toss
with oil and lemon juice. Preheat oven to
moderate 180°C (350°F/ Gas 4). Spread
nuts on a foil-covered oven tray and cook
for 5 minutes. Do not allow to burn.
2 Combine tomato juice, garlic and
Tabasco in a small pan. Bring to boil;
simmer, uncovered, over low heat for
8 minutes or until reduced by half. Allow
to cool. Arrange beans on a serving plate;
pour tomato mixture over. Sprinkle with
nuts.

ITALIAN-STYLE PRAWN AND PASTA SALAD

Preparation time: 15 minutes
Total cooking time: 15 minutes
Serves 4

Dressing
⅓ cup (80 ml/2¾ fl oz) olive oil
1½ tablespoons white wine vinegar
1½ tablespoons pine nuts, toasted
1 tablespoon roughly chopped fresh basil
1 tablespoon roughly chopped fresh flat-
   leaf parsley
1 clove garlic
1 tablespoon grated Parmesan
pinch of sugar

400 g (13 oz) large pasta shells
1 tablespoon olive oil, extra
500 g (1 lb) small cooked prawns
100 g (3½ oz) bocconcini, thinly sliced
125 g (4 oz) chargrilled red capsicum, cut
   into thin strips
125 g (4 oz) cherry tomatoes, halved
fresh basil leaves, to garnish

1 For the dressing, process all the ingredients together in a blender or food processor until smooth.
2 Cook the pasta in a large pan of rapidly boiling salted water until al dente. Drain well, return to the pan and toss with the extra olive oil. Allow to cool.
3 Peel the prawns and gently pull out the dark vein from each prawn back, starting at the head end.
4 Put the pasta, prawns, bocconcini, capsicum and tomatoes in a serving bowl and pour on the dressing. Toss together well and garnish with basil leaves to serve.

PORK NOODLE SALAD

Preparation time: 20 minutes +
   10 minutes soaking
Total cooking time: 35 minutes
Serves 4–6

Broth
1 cup (250 ml/8 fl oz) chicken stock
3 coriander (cilantro) roots
2 makrut (kaffir) lime leaves
3 x 3 cm (1¼ x 1¼ inch) piece of ginger,
   sliced

100 g (3½ oz) dried rice vermicelli
30 g (1 oz) fresh wood ear (see Note)
1 small red chilli, seeded and thinly
   sliced
2 red Asian shallots, thinly sliced
2 spring onions (scallions), thinly sliced
2 garlic cloves, crushed
250 g (8 oz) minced (ground) pork
¼ cup (60 ml/2 fl oz) lime juice
¼ cup (60 ml/2 fl oz) fish sauce
1½ tablespoons grated palm sugar
¼ teaspoon ground white pepper
½ cup (15 g/½ oz) coriander (cilantro)
   leaves, chopped, plus extra, to garnish
oakleaf or coral lettuce, to serve
lime wedges, to garnish
chilli strips, to garnish

1 To make the broth, combine the stock, coriander roots, lime leaves, ginger and 1 cup (250 ml/8 fl oz) water in a saucepan. Simmer for 25 minutes, or until the liquid has reduced to ¾ cup (185 ml/6 fl oz). Strain and return to the pan.
2 Soak the vermicelli in boiling water for 6–7 minutes. Drain, then cut into 3 cm (1¼ inch) lengths. Discard the woody stems from the wood ear, then thinly slice. Combine the vermicelli, wood ear, chilli, red Asian shallots, spring onion and garlic.
3 Return the stock to the heat and bring to the boil. Add the pork mince and stir, breaking up any lumps, for 1–2 minutes, or until the pork changes colour and is cooked. Drain, then add to the vermicelli mixture.
4 Combine the lime juice, fish sauce, palm sugar and white pepper, stirring until the sugar has dissolved. Add to the pork mixture with the coriander and mix well. Season with salt.
5 To assemble, tear or shred the lettuce, then arrange on a serving dish. Spoon on the pork and noodle mixture and garnish with the lime wedges, chilli and extra coriander.

NOTE: Wood ear (also called black fungus) is a cultivated wood fungus. It is mainly available dried; it needs to be reconstituted in boiling water for a few minutes until it expands to five times its dried size.

THAI BEEF SALAD

Preparation time: 20 minutes + cooling
Total cooking time: 5 minutes
Serves 6

2 tablespoons peanut oil
500 g (1 lb) lean beef fillet, thinly sliced
    across the grain
2 cloves garlic, crushed
1 tablespoon grated palm sugar
3 tablespoons finely chopped fresh
    coriander roots and stems
⅓ cup (80 ml/2¾ fl oz) lime juice
2 tablespoons fish sauce
2 small fresh red chillies, seeded and
    thinly sliced
2 red Asian shallots, thinly sliced
2 telegraph cucumbers, sliced into thin
    ribbons
1 cup (20 g/¾ oz) fresh mint leaves
1 cup (90 g/3 oz) bean sprouts, tailed
¼ cup (40 g/1¼ oz) chopped roasted
    peanuts

1 Heat a wok over high heat, add
1 tablespoon of the oil and swirl to
coat the side of the wok. Add half the
beef and cook for 1–2 minutes, or until
medium–rare. Remove from the wok and
put on a plate. Repeat with the remaining
oil and beef.
2 Put the garlic, palm sugar, coriander,
lime juice, fish sauce, ¼ teaspoon ground
white pepper and ¼ teaspoon salt in a
bowl, and stir until all the sugar has
dissolved. Add the chilli and shallots, and
mix well.
3 Pour the sauce over the hot beef, mix
together well, then allow the beef to cool
to room temperature.
4 In a separate bowl, toss together the
cucumber and mint leaves, and
refrigerate until required.
5 Pile up a bed of the cucumber and mint
on a serving platter, then top with the
beef, bean sprouts and peanuts.

ESCALIVADA
(GRILLED VEGETABLE SALAD)

Preparation time: 15 minutes +
    30 minutes cooling
Total cooking time: 10 minutes
Serves 4

1 red onion
6 small eggplants (aubergines), not
    pencil eggplant, about 16 cm (6½
    inches) long
4 red peppers (capsicums)
4 orange peppers (capsicums)
1 tablespoon baby capers
⅓ cup (80 ml/2¾ fl oz) good-quality
    olive oil
1 tablespoon chopped fresh flat-leaf
    parsley
2 cloves garlic, finely chopped

1 Without slicing through the base, cut the
onion from top to base into 6 sections,
leaving it attached at the base. Place on a
barbecue, or over an open-flamed grill or
gas stovetop, with the eggplants and
peppers. Cook over moderate heat for
about 10 minutes, turning occasionally,
until the eggplants and pepper skins are
blackened and blistered. Cool the
peppers in a plastic bag for 10 minutes
and set the onion and eggplant aside.
2 Dry-fry the capers with a pinch of salt
until crisp. Cut the onion into its 6 sections
and discard the charred outer skins. Peel
the skins off the eggplants and remove
the stalk. Cut from top to bottom into
slices. Peel the peppers and remove the
seeds. Cut into wide slices. Arrange all
the vegetables on a large serving platter.
Drizzle the olive oil over them and season
with salt and pepper. Scatter the parsley,
garlic and capers over the top. Serve cold
as a salad or warm as an accompaniment
to grilled meats.

CRAB AND MANGO SALAD

Preparation time: 25 minutes
Total cooking time: 5 minutes
Serves 4

Dressing
⅓ cup (80 ml/2¾ fl oz) light olive oil
¼ cup (60 ml/2 fl oz) lime juice
1 teaspoon fish sauce
½ small green chilli, finely chopped
1 tablespoon finely chopped fresh
    coriander
2 teaspoons grated fresh ginger

2 x 4 cm (1½ inch) squares of fresh
    coconut
1 teaspoon olive oil
2 cups (60 g/2 oz) trimmed watercress
100 g (3½ oz) snow pea (mangetout)
    sprouts
100 g (3½ oz) small cooked prawns
400 g (13 oz) cooked fresh or canned crab
    meat, drained
1 firm ripe mango, cut into thin strips
fresh coriander leaves, to garnish
1 lime, cut into slices, to garnish

1 For the dressing, combine the
ingredients and season with salt and
freshly ground black pepper. Set aside to
allow the flavours to develop.
2 Peel the coconut into wafer-thin slices
with a vegetable peeler. Heat the olive oil
in a pan and gently fry the coconut,
stirring, until golden. Drain on crumpled
paper towels.
3 Combine the watercress and snow pea
sprouts and arrange on a platter.
4 Peel the prawns and gently pull out the
dark vein from each prawn back, starting
at the head end. Lightly toss the crab
meat, prawns, mango and three-quarters
of the toasted coconut and dressing
together. Pile in the centre of the
watercress and snow pea sprout mixture,
scatter the remaining coconut over the
top and garnish with the coriander leaves
and lime slices.

WATERCRESS AND DUCK SALAD WITH LYCHEES

Preparation time: 25 minutes
Total cooking time: 30 minutes
Serves 4

2 large duck breasts, skin on
1 tablespoon Golden Mountain sauce
½ each red, green and yellow pepper (capsicum)
250 g (8 oz) watercress
12 fresh or canned lychees
2 tablespoons pickled shredded ginger
1–2 tablespoons green peppercorns, optional
1 tablespoon white vinegar
2 teaspoons soft brown sugar
1–2 teaspoons chopped red chilli
½ cup (15 g/½ oz) fresh coriander leaves

1 Preheat the oven to hot 210°C (415°F/ Gas 6–7). Brush the duck breasts with the Golden Mountain sauce and place on a rack in a baking tray. Bake for 30 minutes. Remove from the oven and allow to cool.
2 Remove the membrane and seeds from the peppers and slice the flesh into thin strips. Discard any tough woody stems from the watercress. Peel the fresh lychees and remove the seeds or, if you are using canned lychees, drain them thoroughly.
3 Arrange the pepper strips, watercress, lychees and ginger on a large serving platter. Slice the duck into thin pieces and toss gently through the salad. In a small bowl, mix together the peppercorns, if using, vinegar, sugar, chilli and coriander. Serve this on the side for spooning over the salad.

PEAR AND WALNUT SALAD WITH LIME VINAIGRETTE

Preparation time: 25 minutes
Total cooking time: 20 minutes
Serves 4

1 small baguette, cut into 16 thin slices
soy bean oil, for brushing
1 clove garlic, cut in half
1 cup (100 g) walnuts
200 g soy cheese
400 g mesclun leaves
2 pears, cut into 2 cm cubes, mixed with 2 tablespoons lime juice
Lime vinaigrette
3 tablespoons soy bean oil
¼ cup (60 ml) lime juice
2 tablespoons raspberry vinegar

1 Preheat the oven to moderate 180°C (350°F/Gas 4). Brush the baguette slices with a little oil, rub with the cut side of the garlic, then place on a baking tray. Bake for 10 minutes, or until crisp and golden. Place the walnuts on a baking tray and roast for 5–8 minutes, or until slightly browned—shake the tray to ensure even colouring. Allow to cool for 5 minutes.
2 To make the lime vinaigrette, whisk together the oil, lime juice, raspberry vinegar, 1 teaspoon salt and ½ teaspoon freshly ground black pepper in a small bowl. Set aside until ready to use.
3 Spread some of the soy cheese on each crouton, then cook under a hot grill for 2–3 minutes, or until hot.
4 Place the mesclun, pears and walnuts in a bowl, add the vinaigrette and toss through. Divide the salad among four serving bowls and serve with the soy cheese croutons.

WARM CURRIED CHICKEN SALAD

Preparation time: 15 minutes + overnight marinating
Total cooking time: 10 minutes
Serves 4–6

3 tablespoons mild Indian curry paste
¼ cup (60 ml/2 fl oz) coconut milk
750 g (1½ lb) chicken breast fillets, sliced
150 g (5 oz) green beans, halved
2 tablespoons peanut oil
⅓ cup (30 g/1 oz) flaked almonds, toasted
1 red pepper (capsicum), sliced
240 g (7½ oz) rocket (arugula)
100 g (3½ oz) fried egg noodles

Lemon dressing
⅓ cup (80 ml/2¾ fl oz) olive oil
2 tablespoons lemon juice
2 cloves garlic, crushed
1 teaspoon soft brown sugar

1 Combine the curry paste and coconut milk in a bowl. Add the chicken, toss to coat in the mixture, then cover with plastic wrap and marinate in the fridge overnight.
2 Cook the beans in a saucepan of boiling water for 30 seconds, or until just tender. Refresh under cold running water. Drain thoroughly.
3 Heat a wok over high heat, add half the oil and swirl to coat the side of the wok. Stir-fry the chicken in two batches for 5 minutes per batch, adding the remaining oil in between batches. Remove from the wok. Repeat with the remaining chicken and oil.
4 To make the dressing, place the ingredients in a screw-top jar and shake thoroughly.
5 Place the chicken, beans, almonds, pepper, rocket and dressing in a large bowl, and mix well. Stir in the noodles and serve.

SUNOMONO
(PRAWN AND CUCUMBER SALAD)

Preparation time: 20 minutes +
    1 hour marinating
Total cooking time: 5 minutes
Serves 4

1 Lebanese cucumber
375 g (12 oz) raw prawns
¼ cup (60 ml/2 fl oz) rice vinegar
1 tablespoon caster sugar
1 tablespoon Japanese soy sauce
1 teaspoon finely grated fresh ginger
1 tablespoon Japanese white sesame
    seeds

1 Peel the cucumber with a vegetable peeler, halve it lengthways and remove any seeds with a teaspoon. Cut the cucumber into thin slices, sprinkle thoroughly with salt and set aside for 5 minutes. Rinse to remove salt, and pat dry with paper towels.
2 Place the prawns in a pan of lightly salted boiling water and simmer for 2 minutes, or until just cooked. Drain the prawns and plunge them into cold water. When the prawns are cool, peel and devein them, leaving the tails intact.
3 Place the vinegar, sugar, soy sauce and ginger in a large bowl and stir until the sugar dissolves. Add the prawns and cucumber, cover and marinate in the refrigerator for 1 hour.
4 Toast the sesame seeds in a dry pan over medium heat for 3 to 4 minutes, shaking the pan gently, until the seeds are golden brown; remove the seeds from the pan at once to prevent burning.
5 Drain the prawns and cucumber from the marinade. Arrange on serving plates, sprinkle with the sesame seeds and serve.

WILD RICE AND ROAST CHICKEN SALAD

Preparation time: 15 minutes
Total cooking time: 40 minutes
Serves 8

1 cup (190 g/6½ oz) wild rice
1 cup (200 g/6½ oz) jasmine rice
1 Chinese barbecued chicken (see Note)
3 tablespoons chopped mint
3 tablespoons chopped coriander (cilantro)
1 large Lebanese (short) cucumber
6 spring onions (scallions)
½ cup (80 g/2¾ oz) roasted peanuts,
    roughly chopped
⅓ cup (80 ml/2¾ fl oz) mirin
2 tablespoons Chinese rice wine
1 tablespoon soy sauce
1 tablespoon lime juice
2 tablespoons sweet chilli sauce, plus
    extra, to serve

1 Bring a large saucepan of water to the boil and add the wild rice and 1 teaspoon salt. Cook for 30 minutes, then add the jasmine rice and cook for a further 10 minutes, or until tender. Drain the rice, refresh under cold water and drain again.
2 Shred the chicken (both the skin and flesh) into bite-sized pieces, place in a large bowl and add the mint and coriander. Cut the cucumber through the centre (do not peel) and slice thinly on the diagonal. Slice the spring onions on the diagonal. Add the cucumber, spring onion, rice and peanuts to the bowl.
3 Mix together the mirin, rice wine, soy sauce, lime juice and sweet chilli sauce in a small jug, pour over the salad and toss to combine. Pile the salad onto serving platters and serve with a little extra chilli sauce.

NOTE: It is important to use an Asian barbecued chicken, available from Asian barbecue shops, as the flavours of five spice and soy used to cook it will add to the flavour of the salad.

COTTAGE CHEESE SALAD

Preparation time: 20 minutes
Total cooking time: 5 minutes
Serves 4

1 sheet lavash bread
2 teaspoons canola oil
mild paprika, to sprinkle
16 red oak leaf lettuce leaves
2 tablespoons chopped fresh chives
500 g (1 lb) cottage cheese
200 g (6½ oz) red grapes
1 medium carrot, grated
3 tablespoons alfalfa sprouts

1 Preheat oven to moderate 180°C (350°F/Gas 4). Brush lavash with oil, and sprinkle lightly with paprika. Cut in half lengthways, then across into 16 strips. Place on a baking tray and bake for 5 minutes or until golden. Cool on a rack.
2 Wash and dry lettuce thoroughly. Combine chives with cottage cheese. Arrange with other ingredients on individual plates, with four lavash crisps on the side. Serve immediately.

NOTE: Lavash is rectangular flat bread. It is available from supermarkets.

PATES, DIPS AND DIPPERS

TAPENADE
(PROVENÇAL OLIVE, ANCHOVY AND CAPER PASTE)

Preparation time: 10 minutes
Total cooking time: Nil
Makes 1½ cups

400 g (13 oz) Kalamata olives, pitted
2 cloves garlic, crushed
2 anchovy fillets in oil, drained
2 tablespoons capers in brine, rinsed,
    squeezed dry
2 teaspoons chopped fresh thyme
2 teaspoons Dijon mustard
1 tablespoon lemon juice
¼ cup (60 ml/2 fl oz) olive oil
1 tablespoon brandy, optional

1 Process all the ingredients together in a food processor until they form a smooth consistency. Season with freshly ground black pepper. Spoon into a sterilized, warm jar (see Note), seal and refrigerate for up to 2 weeks.

NOTES: To prepare a sterilized storage jar, preheat the oven to very slow 120°C (250°F/ Gas ½). Wash the jar and lid in hot soapy water and rinse with hot water. Put the jar in the oven for 20 minutes, or until fully dry. Do not dry with a tea towel.
 If refrigerated, the olive oil may solidify, making it white. This will not affect the flavour of the dish. Bring to room temperature before serving and the oil will return to a liquid state.

SMOKED TROUT DIP

Preparation time: 25 minutes
Total cooking time: Nil
Serves 4–6

250 g (8 oz) smoked rainbow trout
1½ teaspoons olive oil
½ cup (125 ml/4 fl oz) cream
1 tablespoon lemon juice
pinch of cayenne pepper

1 Remove the skin and bones from the smoked trout. Put the flesh in a food processor or blender with the olive oil, 2 teaspoons of the cream and the lemon juice. Blend to a thick paste, then slowly add the remaining cream until well mixed. Season, to taste, with salt and the cayenne pepper. Serve with grissini or water crackers and baby radishes or other vegetables, for dipping.

NOTE: This dip can be made a few days ahead and kept, covered, in the refrigerator.

PRAWN, CORN AND SWEET CHILLI DIP

Preparation time: 1 hour + 2 hours chilling
Total cooking time: 3 minutes
Serves 8

1 kg (2 lb) cooked medium prawns
¼ cup (60 ml/2 fl oz) lime juice
¾ cup (110 g/3½ oz) frozen corn kernels
3 teaspoons finely grated lime rind
250 g (8 oz) cream cheese, softened
3 tablespoons finely chopped chives
1 tablespoon sweet chilli sauce
4 cooked large prawns, to garnish

1 Peel the prawns and gently pull out the dark vein from each prawn back, starting at the head end. Pat them dry with paper towels and place in a bowl. Add the lime juice to the prawns, cover and refrigerate for 10 minutes.
2 Cook the corn in boiling water for 2–3 minutes, or until tender. Drain and plunge the kernels into iced water to prevent further cooking, then drain and pat dry with paper towel.
3 Process the prawns and lime juice in a food processor in short bursts for 2–3 seconds, until the prawns are finely chopped but not minced. Transfer to a bowl and stir in the corn, lime rind, cream cheese and chives. Add the chilli sauce and mix well. Cover with plastic wrap and refrigerate for at least 2 hours.
4 Just before serving, peel the large prawns, leaving the tails intact. Gently pull out the dark vein from each prawn back, starting at the head end. Transfer the dip to a serving bowl and garnish with the peeled prawns. Serve with some extra cooked and peeled prawns, or Melba toast or pitta bread, for dipping.

CHEESE CRACKERS

Preparation time: 10 minutes+
   1 hour refrigeration
Total cooking time: 15 minutes
Makes about 60

1 cup (125 g) plain (all-purpose) flour
2 tablespoons self-raising flour
1 teaspoon curry powder
125 g butter
½ cup (50 g) grated Parmesan
⅔ cup (85 g) grated Cheddar
20 g crumbled blue-vein cheese
1 tablespoon lemon juice
¼ cup (25 g) finely grated Parmesan,
   extra

1 Place the flours, curry powder and
butter in a food processor. Process until
the mixture resembles fine breadcrumbs.
2 Stir in the cheeses and the lemon juice.
Bring the mixture together into a ball.
3 Roll into a 30 cm (12 inch) log. Wrap in
plastic wrap and chill for 1 hour. Slice into
5 mm (¼ inch) slices. Reshape if
necessary. Preheat the oven to
moderately hot 200°C (400°F/Gas 6).
4 Place on a baking paper-lined oven
tray, allowing some room for spreading.
Sprinkle the tops with Parmesan. Bake
for 15 minutes, or until the biscuits are
golden. Cool on the trays.

TZATZIKI
(CUCUMBER AND YOGHURT DIP)

Preparation time: 10 minutes +
   15 minutes standing
Total cooking time: Nil
Makes 2 cups

2 Lebanese cucumbers (about 300 g/
   13 oz)
400 g (13 oz) Greek-style natural yoghurt
4 cloves garlic, crushed
3 tablespoons finely chopped fresh mint
1 tablespoon lemon juice
chopped fresh mint, extra, to garnish

1 Cut the cucumbers in half lengthways,
scoop out the seeds with a teaspoon and
discard. Leave the skin on and coarsely
grate the cucumber into a small
colander. Sprinkle with a little salt and
leave to stand over a large bowl for 15
minutes to drain off any bitter juices.
2 Meanwhile, stir together the yoghurt,
garlic, mint and lemon juice in a bowl.
3 Rinse the cucumber under cold water
then, taking small handfuls, squeeze out
any excess moisture. Combine the
cucumber with the yoghurt mixture and
season, to taste. Serve immediately or
refrigerate until ready to serve. Garnish
with mint. Can be served as a dip with
flatbread or as a sauce for seafood and
meat.

SPINACH DIP

Preparation time: 10 minutes +
   3 hours refrigeration
Total cooking time: Nil
Serves 6–8

250 g (8 oz) frozen chopped spinach
300 g (10 oz) ricotta
¾ cup (185 g/6 oz) sour cream
30 g (1 oz) packet spring vegetable soup
   mix
4 spring onions, finely chopped

1 Thaw the spinach and squeeze out as
much liquid as possible with your hands.
2 Process the spinach, ricotta, sour
cream, soup mix and spring onions in a
food processor or blender until smooth.
Cover and refrigerate for 2–3 hours.
Serve with crisp lavash bread, biscuits
or assorted crisp vegetables such as
blanched snow peas (mangetout),
cauliflower and carrots.

NOTE: Can be made a week in advance.

BABA GHANNOUJ
(EGGPLANT/AUBERGINE DIP)

Preparation time: 20 minutes +
    30 minutes cooling
Total cooking time: 50 minutes
Makes 1¾ cups

2 large eggplants (aubergines)
3 cloves garlic, crushed
½ teaspoon ground cumin
⅓ cup (80 ml/2¾ fl oz) lemon juice
2 tablespoons tahini
pinch of cayenne pepper
1½ tablespoons olive oil
1 tablespoon chopped fresh flat-leaf
    parsley
black olives, to garnish

1 Preheat the oven to moderately hot
200°C (400°F/Gas 6). Prick the eggplants
several times with a fork, then cook over
an open flame for about 5 minutes, until
the skin is black and blistered. Transfer to
a baking tin and bake for 40–45 minutes,
or until the eggplants are very soft and
wrinkled. Place in a colander over a bowl
to drain off any bitter juices, leaving them
for 30 minutes, or until cool.
2 Carefully peel the skin from the
eggplants, chop the flesh and put it in a
food processor with the garlic, cumin,
lemon juice, tahini, cayenne pepper and
olive oil. Process until smooth and
creamy. Alternatively, use a potato
masher or fork. Season with salt and stir
in the parsley. Spread in a flat bowl or on
a plate and garnish with the olives. Serve
with flatbread or pide for dipping.

NOTE: If you prefer, you can bake the
eggplant in a baking tin in a moderately
hot (200°C/ 400°F/Gas 6) oven for 1 hour,
or until very soft.

TARAMOSALATA
(FISH ROE PUREE)

Preparation time: 10 minutes + soaking
Total cooking time: Nil
Makes 1½ cups

5 slices white bread, crusts removed
⅓ cup (80 ml/2¾ fl oz) milk
100 g can tarama (grey mullet roe)
1 egg yolk
½ small onion, grated
1 clove garlic, crushed
2 tablespoons lemon juice
⅓ cup (80 ml/23 4 fl oz) olive oil
pinch of ground white pepper

1 Soak the bread in the milk for 10
minutes. Press in a strainer to extract
excess milk, then mix in a food processor
with the tarama, egg yolk, onion and
garlic for 30 seconds, or until smooth.
Mix in 1 tablespoon lemon juice.
2 With the motor running, slowly pour in
the olive oil. The mixture should be
smooth. Add the remaining lemon juice
and white pepper. If the dip tastes too
salty, add another piece of bread.

NOTE: Grey mullet roe is traditional but
smoked cod's roe also gives a lovely
flavour.

CHILLI CRAB AND TOMATO
DIP

Preparation time: 25 minutes
Total cooking time: Nil
Serves 6

1 small ripe tomato
2 x 170 g (5½ oz) cans crab meat, drained
200 g (6½ oz) neufchatel cheese (see
    Note)
2 tablespoons chilli sauce
2 teaspoons tomato paste (tomato purée)
1 teaspoon grated lemon rind
2 teaspoons lemon juice
1 small onion, finely grated
2 spring onions, finely sliced

1 Score a cross in the base of the tomato.
Place in a heatproof bowl and cover with
boiling water. Leave for 30 seconds,
transfer to cold water, drain and peel
away from the cross. Cut the tomato in
half, scoop out the seeds with a teaspoon
and finely chop the flesh.
2 Squeeze any liquid from the crab meat
with your hands. Beat the neufchatel in a
bowl with a wooden spoon until smooth,
then stir in the crab meat, chilli sauce,
tomato paste, lemon rind, lemon juice and
grated onion. Season well with salt and
pepper. Mix together and spoon into a
serving bowl.
3 Scatter the sliced spring onion and
chopped tomato over the top. Refrigerate,
covered, before serving. Can be served
with thinly sliced or lightly toasted bread.
A small serving spoon makes it easier for
guests.

NOTE: Neufchatel is a smooth, mild,
good-quality cream cheese available from
delicatessens. If it is not available,
another cream cheese can be used
instead.

HERB CHEESE LOG

Preparation time: 25 minutes
+ 3 hours refrigeration
Total cooking time: Nil
Serves 12

500 g (1 lb) cream cheese, at room
temperature
1 tablespoon lemon juice
1 clove garlic, crushed
2 teaspoons chopped fresh thyme
2 teaspoons chopped fresh tarragon
1 tablespoon chopped fresh flat-leaf
parsley
1 cup (50 g/1¾ oz) snipped fresh chives

1 Beat the cream cheese in a large bowl
with electric beaters until soft and
creamy. Mix in the lemon juice and garlic.
In a separate bowl, combine the thyme,
tarragon and parsley.
2 Line a 20 x 30 cm (8 x 12 inch) shallow
tin with foil. Spread the chives over the
base, then dollop the cream cheese over
the chives. Using a palette knife, gently
join the dollops, spreading the mixture
and pushing it into any gaps. Sprinkle the
herbs over the cheese. Lift the foil from
the tin and place on a work surface. Roll
into a log, starting from the longest edge,
then cover and place on a baking tray.
3 Refrigerate for at least 3 hours, or
preferably overnight. Serve with crackers
or crusty bread.

CHEESE AND CHILLI SHAPES

Preparation time: 10 minutes +
30 minutes refrigeration
Total cooking time: 20 minutes
Makes 12

155 g (1¼ cups) plain flour
pinch dry hot mustard
90 g (3 oz) butter, roughly chopped
60 g (½ cup) grated vintage Cheddar
cheese
4 red chillies, seeded and sliced
1 egg yolk

1 Process the flour, mustard and butter
until they resemble fine breadcrumbs.
Add the cheese and chilli, then the egg
yolk and 1 tablespoon water, and process
until the mixture comes together. Gather
into a ball, cover with plastic wrap and
refrigerate for 30 minutes.
2 Preheat the oven to 190°C (375°F/Gas 5).
On a lightly floured surface, roll out the
dough to a 5 mm thickness. Cut into 5 cm
rounds.
3 Place on lightly greased baking trays
and bake for 15–20 minutes, or until
golden. Cool.

SMOKED FISH PATE

Preparation time: 10 minutes + several
hours chilling
Total cooking time: Nil
Serves 4–6

4 smoked mackerel or smoked trout
fillets
2–3 tablespoons lemon or lime juice
125 g (4 oz) cream cheese, softened
200 g (6½ oz) butter, melted
sprigs of fresh herbs (dill, fennel, flat-
leaf parsley)
lemon slices, to garnish

1 Remove the skin and bones from the
fish and roughly flake the flesh. Place the
flesh in a blender or food processor with
the juice, cream cheese and butter. Blend
or process until smooth. Season, to taste,
with pepper.
2 Spread into a 2-cup (500 ml/16 fl oz)
capacity serving dish and chill for several
hours. Garnish with sprigs of fresh herbs
and lemon slices. Serve with Melba toast
or crackers.

NO OCCASION WOULD BE QUITE COMPLETE WITHOUT A STYLISH PATE.

GRAND MARNIER PATE

Melt 90 g (3 oz) butter in a pan and cook 1 chopped onion and 1 crushed clove of garlic until the onion is tender. Add 250 g (4 oz) trimmed duck or chicken livers and cook for 5–10 minutes. Spoon into a food processor or blender with 2 tablespoons orange juice, 1 tablespoon Grand Marnier (or port or liqueur of your choice), 1 tablespoon sour cream and freshly ground pepper, to taste. Process until smooth. To prepare the topping, arrange 2 orange slices (cut into quarters if you wish), and fresh chives or parsley in the base of a 2-cup (500 ml/ 16 fl oz) capacity serving dish. Sprinkle 1½ teaspoons gelatine over ½ cup (125 ml/4 fl oz) hot chicken stock and whisk vigorously with a fork to dissolve. Pour over the oranges to a depth of 1 cm (½ inch). Refrigerate until set. Spoon the pâté over the gelatine layer, tap gently and smooth the top. Refrigerate until set. Unmould onto a serving plate. Serve with crackers or Melba toast. (Pâté can also be made without the gelatine topping, and served on cracker biscuits.)
Serves 12–15.

SMOKED TROUT PATE

Mix 250 g (8 oz) skinned and boned smoked trout, 125 g (4 oz) softened butter and 125 g (4 oz) softened cream cheese in a food processor for 20 seconds, or until smooth. Add 1 tablespoon lemon juice, 1 teaspoon horseradish cream, 15 g (½ oz) each of finely chopped fresh parsley and fresh chives and process for 10 seconds. Add salt and freshly ground black pepper, to taste, and more lemon juice, if liked. Transfer to a small serving dish. Serve with hot toasted brown bread.
Serves 8–10.

LEMON PRAWN PATE

Melt 100 g (3½ oz) butter in a frying pan. When it sizzles, add 3 crushed cloves garlic and 750 g (1½ lb) peeled and deveined raw prawns and stir for 3–4 minutes, or until the prawns are pink and cooked through. Cool. Transfer to a food processor, add 1 teaspoon grated lemon rind, 3 tablespoons lemon juice and ¼ teaspoon grated nutmeg and process for 20 seconds, or until roughly puréed. Season and add 2 tablespoons each of mayonnaise and finely chopped fresh chives, then process for 20 seconds, or until combined. Spoon into a dish and chill for at least 1 hour, or until firm. Serves 6–8.

MUSHROOM PATE

Melt 40 g (1¼ oz) butter and 1 tablespoon oil in a large frying pan. Add 400 g (13 oz) chopped field mushrooms and 2 crushed cloves garlic. Cook until the mushrooms have softened and the mushroom liquid has evaporated. Stir in 3 chopped spring onions. Allow to cool, then process with 1 tablespoon lemon juice, 100 g (3½ oz) ricotta cheese, 100 g (3½ oz) soft cream cheese and 2 tablespoons chopped fresh coriander leaves. Process until smooth. Season, to taste, then spoon into a serving dish, cover and chill for 2 hours. Serves 8–10.

SOFT CHEESE PATE

Roughly chop 150 g (5 oz) toasted pine nuts in a food processor, add 500 g (1 lb) crumbled feta cheese, ¾ cup (185 ml/6 fl oz) cream and 2 teaspoons coarsely ground pepper and mix until smooth. Add 30 g (1 oz) each of chopped fresh mint, dill and parsley and process until just combined. Line a 3-cup (750 ml/24 fl oz) capacity bowl with plastic wrap. Transfer the mixture to the bowl and press in firmly. Refrigerate, covered, for at least 1 hour, or until firm. Turn out onto a plate and smooth the surface with a knife. Serve with toast triangles. Serves 12–15.

PATES, CLOCKWISE, FROM LEFT: Grand Marnier; Smoked trout; Lemon prawn; Soft cheese; Mushroom

SALMON AND CHIVE LOG

Preparation time: 10 minutes + several
  hours chilling
Total cooking time: Nil
Serves 4–6

250 g (8 oz) cream cheese, softened
2 tablespoons sour cream
1 tablespoon lemon juice
3 spring onions, chopped
420 g (14 oz) can red salmon, drained,
  skin and bones removed, flaked
1 teaspoon freshly ground black pepper
⅓ cup (40 g/1¼ oz) finely chopped pecan
  nuts
80 g (23/ 4 oz) fresh chives, finely
  chopped

1 Beat the cream cheese, sour cream and
lemon juice in a bowl until smooth. Stir in
the spring onion, salmon, pepper, pecan
nuts and a quarter of the chives until
combined. Refrigerate for several hours
to firm.
2 Place the mixture on a sheet of plastic
wrap and roll into a log shape. Roll the
log in the remaining chives and
refrigerate until needed. Serve with
crackers or bread.

ARTICHOKE DIP

Preparation time: 10 minutes
Total cooking time: 15 minutes
Serves 8

2 x 400 g (13 oz) cans artichoke hearts,
  drained
1 cup (250 g/8 oz) mayonnaise
¾ cup (75 g/2½ oz) grated Parmesan
2 teaspoons onion flakes
2 tablespoons grated Parmesan, extra
paprika, to sprinkle

1 Preheat the oven to 180°C (350°F/
Gas 4). Gently squeeze the artichokes to
remove any remaining liquid. Chop and
place in a bowl. Stir through the
mayonnaise, Parmesan and the onion
flakes.
2 Spread into a 1-litre capacity shallow
ovenproof dish. Sprinkle with the extra
Parmesan and a little paprika. Bake for
15 minutes, or until heated through and
lightly browned on top. Serve with crusty
bread.

CREAMY BLUE CHEESE DIP WITH PEARS

Preparation time: 25 minutes +
  20 minutes refrigeration
Total cooking time: Nil
Serves 4

150 g (5 oz) creamy blue cheese (see
  NOTE)
200 ml (6½ fl oz) thick cream
3 tablespoons thick plain yoghurt
2 tablespoons finely chopped chives
4 ripe pears, cored and cut into wedges

1 Mash the blue cheese with a fork to
soften it slightly. Add the cream and
yoghurt and season with black pepper,
mixing until smooth and well blended—
do not overmix or it will become grainy
and curdled. Spoon into a serving bowl,
cover and refrigerate for 20 minutes, or
until firm.
2 Scatter the chives over the dip. Serve
with the pear wedges.

NOTE: A creamy cheese such as
Dolcelatte, Gorgonzola or King Island
Blue will give the best result.

CHICKEN LIVER AND GRAND MARNIER PATE

Preparation time: 20 minutes +
2 hours 30 minutes refrigeration
Total cooking time: 10 minutes
Serves 8

750 g (1½ lb) chicken livers, well trimmed
1 cup (250 ml/8 fl oz) milk
200 g (6½ oz) butter, softened
4 spring onions, finely chopped
1 tablespoon Grand Marnier
1 tablespoon frozen orange juice
concentrate, thawed
½ orange, very thinly sliced

Jellied layer
1 tablespoon orange juice concentrate
1 tablespoon Grand Marnier
1¼ cups (315 ml/10 fl oz) canned chicken
consommé, undiluted
2½ teaspoons powdered gelatine

1 Put the chicken livers in a bowl, add the milk and stir to combine. Cover and refrigerate for 1 hour. Drain the livers and discard the milk. Rinse in cold water, drain and pat dry with paper towels.
2 Melt a third of the butter in a frying pan, add the spring onion and cook for 2–3 minutes, or until tender, but not brown. Add the livers and cook, stirring, over medium heat for 4–5 minutes, or until just cooked. Remove from the heat and cool a little.

3 Transfer the livers to a food processor and process until very smooth. Chop the remaining butter, add to the processor with the Grand Marnier and orange juice concentrate and process until creamy. Season, to taste, with salt and freshly ground black pepper. Transfer to a 1.25 litre (40 fl oz) serving dish, cover the surface with plastic wrap and chill for 1½ hours, or until firm.
4 For the jellied layer, whisk together the orange juice concentrate, Grand Marnier and ½ cup (125 ml/4 fl oz) of the consommé in a jug. Sprinkle the gelatine over the liquid in an even layer and leave until the gelatine is spongy—do not stir. Heat the remaining consommé in a pan, remove from the heat and add the gelatine mixture. Stir to dissolve the gelatine, then leave to cool and thicken to the consistency of uncooked egg white, but not set.
5 Press the orange slices lightly into the surface of the pâté and spoon the thickened jelly evenly over the top. Refrigerate until set. Serve at room temperature with toast or crackers.

NOTE: Grand Marnier is a cognac-based liqueur with an orange flavour.

CHEESE FRUIT LOG

Preparation time: 15 minutes +
refrigeration
Total cooking time: 5 minutes
Serves 6

¼ cup (35 g/1¼ oz) shelled pistachio nuts
250 g (4 oz) cream cheese, at room
temperature
50 g (1¾ oz) dried apricots, finely chopped
3 spring onions, finely chopped
¼ cup (45 g/1½ oz) sun-dried tomatoes,
drained, finely chopped
3 tablespoons finely chopped fresh flat-
leaf parsley

1 Preheat the oven to moderately hot 200°C (400°F/Gas 6). Bake the pistachio nuts on a lined baking tray for 5 minutes, or until golden brown. Cool, then finely chop.
2 Beat the cream cheese in a bowl until smooth. Fold in the dried apricots, spring onion and sun-dried tomatoes, and some pepper, to taste.
3 Sprinkle the combined pistachio nuts and parsley over a sheet of baking paper, shaping into a 20 cm x 6 cm (8 x 2½ inch) rectangle. Form the mixture into a 20 cm (8 inch) log and roll in the nut mixture. Wrap in plastic wrap and refrigerate for 2–3 hours, or until firm. Serve with plain savoury biscuits.

BROAD BEAN DIP

Preparation time: 10 minutes +
   overnight soaking
Total cooking time: 6 hours
Serves 6

1 cup (200 g/6½ oz) dried broad beans
   (fava or ful nabed—see Note)
2 cloves garlic, crushed
¼ teaspoon ground cumin
1½ tablespoons lemon juice
up to 75 ml (2½ fl oz) olive oil
2 tablespoons chopped fresh flat-leaf
   parsley
flatbread, for serving

1 Rinse the beans well, then place in a
large bowl and cover with 2 cups (500
ml/16 fl oz) of water and leave to soak
overnight.
2 If using peeled beans (see Note),
transfer them and their soaking water to
a large heavy-based saucepan. If using
the unpeeled brown beans, drain, then
add to the pan with 2 cups (500 ml/16 fl oz)
fresh water. Bring to the boil, cover, and
simmer over low heat for 5–6 hours.
Check the water level from time to time
and add a little boiling water, as
necessary, to keep the beans moist. Do
not stir, but shake the pan occasionally to
prevent the beans sticking. Set aside to
cool slightly.
3 Purée the contents of the pan in a food
processor, then transfer to a bowl and stir
in the garlic, cumin and lemon juice.
Gradually stir in enough olive oil to give a
dipping consistency, starting with about
50 ml (1½ fl oz). As the mixture cools it
may become thick, in which case you can
stir through a little warm water to return
the mixture to dipping consistency.
4 Spread over a large dish and sprinkle
the parsley over the top. Serve with the
flatbread, cut into triangles.

NOTE: The dried fava beans can be the
ready-peeled white ones or the small,
brown ones.

BLUE CHEESE AND
PORT PATE

Preparation time: 10 minutes
   + 3–4 hours refrigeration
Total cooking time: Nil
Serves 8

350 g (11 oz) cream cheese, at room
   temperature
60 g (2 oz) unsalted butter, softened
⅓ cup (80 ml/2¾ fl oz) port
300 g (10 oz) blue cheese, at room
   temperature, mashed
1 tablespoon chopped fresh chives
½ cup (50 g/1¾ oz) walnut halves

1 Beat the cream cheese and butter in a
small bowl with electric beaters until
smooth, then stir in the port. Add the blue
cheese and chives and stir until just
combined. Season, to taste. Spoon into a
serving dish and smooth the surface.
Cover with plastic wrap and refrigerate
for 3–4 hours, or until firm.
2 Arrange the walnuts over the top and
press in lightly. Serve at room
temperature. Delicious with crusty bread,
crackers, celery sticks or wedges of firm
fruit such as apple and pear.

HUMMUS
(CHICKPEA DIP)

Preparation time: 20 minutes +
   overnight soaking
Total cooking time: 1 hour 15 minutes
Makes 3 cups

1 cup (220 g/6½ oz) dried chickpeas
2 tablespoons tahini
4 cloves garlic, crushed
2 teaspoons ground cumin
⅓ cup (80 ml/2¾ fl oz) lemon juice
3 tablespoons olive oil
large pinch of cayenne pepper
extra lemon juice, optional
extra virgin olive oil, to garnish
paprika, to garnish
chopped fresh flat-leaf parsley, to
   garnish

1 Put the chickpeas in a bowl, add 1 litre
water, then soak overnight. Drain and
place in a large saucepan with 2 litres
water, or enough to cover the chickpeas
by 5 cm (2 inches). Bring to the boil, then
reduce the heat and simmer for 1 hour
15 minutes, or until the chickpeas are very
tender. Skim any scum from the surface.
Drain well, reserving the cooking liquid
and leave until cool enough to handle.
Pick through for any loose skins and
discard them.
2 Combine the chickpeas, tahini, garlic,
cumin, lemon juice, olive oil, cayenne
pepper and 1½ teaspoons salt in a food
processor until thick and smooth. With
the motor running, gradually add enough
of the reserved cooking liquid, about
¾ cup (185 ml/6 fl oz), to form a smooth
creamy purée. Season with salt or some
extra lemon juice.
3 Spread onto flat bowls or plates, drizzle
with the extra virgin olive oil, sprinkle with
paprika and scatter parsley over the top.
Delicious served with warm pita bread
or pide.

BEETROOT HUMMUS

Preparation time: 25 minutes + overnight
  soaking
Total cooking time: 1 hour 15 minutes
Serves 8

250 g (8 oz) dried chickpeas
1 large onion, chopped
500 g (1 lb) beetroot
½ cup (125 ml/4 fl oz) tahini (sesame seed
  paste)
3 cloves garlic, crushed
¼ cup (60 ml/2 fl oz) lemon juice
1 tablespoon ground cumin
¼ cup (60 ml/2 fl oz) olive oil

1 Put the chickpeas in a large bowl, cover
with cold water and soak overnight. Drain.
2 Place the chickpeas and onion in a large
heavy-based pan, cover with water and
bring to the boil. Cook for 1 hour or until
chickpeas are very soft. Drain, reserving
1 cup of cooking liquid; allow to cool.
3 Cook the beetroot in a large pan of
boiling water until tender. Drain and allow
to cool slightly before removing skins.
4 Chop the beetroot and place in a food
processor, in batches if necessary. Add
the chickpea and onion mixture, tahini,
garlic, lemon juice and cumin; process
until smooth. Slowly add reserved
cooking liquid and olive oil while the
machine is running. Process until mixture
is thoroughly combined. Drizzle with a
little olive oil and serve with Lebanese
bread.

PESTO

Preparation time: 10 minutes
Total cooking time: 5 minutes
Serves 6

50 g (1¾ oz) pine nuts
50 g (1¾ oz) small fresh basil leaves
2 cloves garlic, crushed
½ teaspoon sea salt
½ cup (125 ml/4 fl oz) olive oil
30 g (1 oz) Parmesan, finely grated
20 g (¾ oz) pecorino cheese, finely grated

1 Preheat the oven to 180°C (350°F/
Gas 4). Spread the pine nuts on a baking
tray and bake for 2 minutes, or until
lightly golden. Cool.
2 Chop the pine nuts, basil, garlic, salt
and oil in a food processor until smooth.
Transfer to a bowl and stir in the cheeses.
Serve as a dip with bread, crackers or
crudités, or as a sauce for barbecued
meat, chicken or seafood.

WHITE BEAN, CHICKPEA AND HERB DIP

Preparation time: 20 minutes +
  overnight soaking
Total cooking time: 1 hour
Serves 12

180 g (6 oz) dried cannellini beans
100 g (3½ oz) dried chickpeas
3 slices white bread
3 tablespoons milk
2 spring onions, finely chopped
4 tablespoons thick plain yoghurt
1 tablespoon lemon juice
2 teaspoons finely grated lemon rind
1 tablespoon chopped fresh parsley
2 teaspoons chopped fresh oregano
2 tablespoons olive oil

1 Soak the beans and chickpeas in cold
water overnight. Rinse well and transfer
to a pan. Cover with cold water and bring
to the boil. Reduce the heat and simmer
for 1 hour, or until very tender, adding
more water if needed. Skim any froth
from the surface. Drain well, cool and
mash.
2 Remove the crusts from the bread,
place in a bowl and drizzle with the milk.
Leave for 2 minutes, then mash with your
fingertips until very soft. Mix together
with the beans.
3 Add the spring onion, yoghurt, lemon
juice, rind, fresh herbs and oil and season
well. Mix together well and serve at room
temperature.

GUACAMOLE

Preparation time: 30 minutes
Total cooking time: Nil
Serves 6

3 ripe avocados
1 tablespoon lime or lemon juice (see HINT)
1 tomato
1–2 red chillies, finely chopped
1 small red onion, finely chopped
1 tablespoon finely chopped fresh coriander leaves
2 tablespoons sour cream
1–2 drops Tabasco or habanero sauce

1 Roughly chop the avocado flesh and place in a bowl. Mash lightly with a fork and sprinkle with the lime or lemon juice to prevent the avocado discolouring.
2 Cut the tomato in half horizontally and use a teaspoon to scoop out the seeds. Finely dice the flesh and add to the avocado.
3 Stir in the chilli, onion, coriander, sour cream and Tabasco or habanero sauce. Season with freshly cracked black pepper.
4 Serve immediately or cover the surface with plastic wrap and refrigerate for 1–2 hours. If refrigerated, allow to come to room temperature before serving.

HINT: You will need 1–2 limes to produce 1 tablespoon of juice, depending on the lime. A heavier lime will probably be more juicy. To get more juice from a citrus fruit, prick it all over with a fork and then heat on High (100%) in the microwave for 1 minute. Don't forget to prick it or the fruit may burst.

MARINATED ROASTED VEGETABLE DIP

Preparation time: 55 minutes +
  marinating
Total cooking time: 50 minutes
Serves 8

1 small eggplant (aubergine), sliced
2 zucchini (courgettes), sliced
3 red peppers (capsicums)
½ cup (125 ml/4 fl oz) extra virgin olive oil
2 cloves garlic, sliced
2 Roma tomatoes
200 g (6½ oz) canned artichoke hearts, drained
7 g (¼ oz) fresh oregano leaves
250 g (8 oz) ricotta cheese
45 g (1½ oz) black olives, pitted and sliced

1 Place the eggplant and zucchini in a colander over a bowl, sprinkle generously with salt and leave for 15–20 minutes. Meanwhile, cut the red peppers into large flat pieces, removing the seeds and membrane. Cook, skin-side-up, under a hot grill until the skin is black and blistered. Cool in a plastic bag, then peel. Reserve about a quarter of the peppers to use as a garnish and place the rest in a large non-metallic bowl.
2 Place half the olive oil in a bowl, add 1 garlic clove and a pinch of salt and mix. Rinse the eggplant and zucchini and pat dry with paper towels. Place the eggplant on a non-stick or foil-lined tray and brush with the garlic oil. Cook under a very hot grill for 4–6 minutes each side, or until golden brown, brushing both sides with oil during grilling. The eggplant will burn easily, so keep a close watch. Allow to cool while grilling the zucchini in the same way. Add both to the red pepper in the bowl.

3 Slice the tomatoes lengthways, place on a non-stick or foil-lined baking tray and brush with the garlic oil. Reduce the temperature slightly and grill for 10–15 minutes, or until soft. Add to the bowl with the other vegetables.
4 Cut the artichokes into quarters and add to the bowl. Mix in any remaining garlic oil along with the remaining olive oil. Stir in the oregano and remaining garlic. Cover with a tight-fitting lid or plastic wrap and refrigerate for at least 2 hours.
5 Drain the vegetables and place in a food processor. Add the ricotta and process for 20 seconds, or until smooth. Reserve a tablespoon of olives to garnish. Add the rest to the processor. Mix in a couple of short bursts, then transfer to a non-metallic bowl and cover with plastic wrap. Chill for at least 2 hours.
6 Slice the reserved roasted red pepper into fine strips and arrange over the top of the dip with the reserved olives.

POTTED CHICKEN

Preparation time: 15 minutes + 2 hours
    refrigeration
Total cooking time: 1 hour
Serves 6

6 chicken thighs, skin removed
1 onion, sliced
1 carrot, sliced
6 peppercorns
1 bay leaf
pinch ground mace
pinch cayenne pepper
¼ teaspoon freshly grated nutmeg
200 g (6½ oz) unsalted butter, softened

1 Place the chicken thighs, onion, carrot,
peppercorns and bay leaf in a pan and add
2 cups (500 ml/16 fl oz) of water. Bring to
the boil, skimming off any foam. Reduce
the heat, then cover and simmer for
30 minutes, or until the chicken is tender
and cooked through.
2 Remove the chicken, then rapidly boil
the remaining liquid until it has reduced
to about ¼ cup (60 ml/ 2 fl oz). Strain
through a fine sieve and allow to cool.
3 Remove the chicken flesh from the
bones. Place the flesh in a food processor
with the liquid and process until smooth.
Add the mace, cayenne pepper, nutmeg
and 150 g (5 oz) of the butter. Season to
taste with salt and pepper and process
until combined and smooth.
4 Put the chicken mixture in a 3-cup
(750 ml/24 fl oz) ceramic dish. Melt the
remaining butter in a small pan and pour
the yellow clarified butter onto the
surface of the chicken, leaving the white
milk solids in the pan. Refrigerate for
2 hours, or until the butter sets.

HERB PEPPER CRISPS
WITH BLUE CHEESE DIP

Preparation time: 30 minutes
Total cooking time: 5 minutes
Serves 10

4 sheets lavash bread
90 g (3 oz) butter, melted
1 small jar herb pepper seasoning
1 tablespoon finely chopped fresh chives

Blue Cheese Dip
250 g (8 oz) blue vein cheese, chopped
60 g (2 oz) butter, softened
1 tablespoon sweet white wine
2 teaspoons chopped fresh mint
1 teaspoon chopped fresh rosemary
2 teaspoons chopped fresh oregano
⅓ cup (90 g/3 oz) crème fraîche or sour
    cream
salt and pepper

1 Preheat the oven to moderate 180°C
(350°F/Gas 4). Brush each sheet of lavash
bread with butter. Sprinkle with herb
pepper seasoning and chives.
2 Cut each sheet into twenty squares.
Cut each piece in half to make triangles.
Place triangles on baking trays. Bake for
5 minutes or until crisp. Remove and cool.
Serve with Blue Cheese Dip.
3 To make Blue Cheese Dip: Using
electric beaters, beat the cheese and
butter in a small bowl until smooth and
creamy. Add the wine, mint, rosemary and
oregano; mix well. Fold through the
crème fraîche or sour cream. Season to
taste. Spoon the mixture into serving
dishes.

NOTE: Crisps may be stored in an airtight
container for up to 2 weeks. For a
variation, combine 2 cloves crushed garlic
with melted butter before brushing over
lavash bread. Sprinkle with grated
Parmesan cheese and chives, cut into
squares and triangles and bake.

MEXICAN LAYERED DIP

Preparation time: 1 hour + chilling
Total cooking time: Nil
Serves 12

Guacamole
3 ripe avocados
1 small tomato
1–2 red chillies, finely chopped
1 small red onion, finely chopped
1 tablespoon chopped fresh coriander
1 tablespoon lime or lemon juice
2 tablespoons sour cream
1–2 drops habanero or Tabasco sauce

450 g (14 oz) can refried beans
35 g (1¼ oz) packet of taco seasoning mix
300 g (10 oz) sour cream
200 g (6½ oz) ready-made salsa sauce
60 g (2 oz) Cheddar, grated
2 tablespoons chopped pitted black olives
200 g (6½ oz) corn chips
chopped fresh coriander leaves, to
    garnish

1 For the guacamole, roughly chop the
avocado flesh, then mash lightly with a
fork. Cut the tomato in half horizontally.
Using a teaspoon, scoop out the seeds and
discard. Finely dice the flesh and add to the
avocado. Stir in the chilli, onion, coriander,
lime juice, sour cream and sauce. Season
with salt and cracked black pepper. Cover
and refrigerate until required.
2 Using a fork, mix the refried beans and
taco seasoning together in a small bowl.
3 To assemble, spread the beans in the
centre of a large platter (we used a
30 x 35 cm/12 x 14 inch dish), leaving a
border for the corn chips. Spoon the sour
cream on top, leaving a small border of
bean mixture showing. Repeat with the
guacamole and salsa sauce so that you
can see each layer. Sprinkle the top with
cheese and olives.
4 Arrange some of the corn chips around
the edge just before serving and garnish
with the coriander. Serve with the
remaining corn chips.

DIPS

THESE ARE A FAVOURITE AT ANY GATHERING. SERVE THEM UP WITH CRUDITES, CRACKERS OR CRUSTY BREAD AND WATCH YOUR GUESTS HOVERING AROUND THE BOWL TRYING NOT TO LOOK TOO GREEDY.

CREAMY SALMON

Combine 200 g (6½ oz) cream cheese with 100 g (3½ oz) chopped smoked salmon and 5 tablespooons cream in a food processor and mix until smooth. Season with pepper and sprinkle with a few chopped chives. Keep refrigerated until ready to use. Makes about 1½ cups.

HOT APPLE CHUTNEY

Beat ¼ cup (60 g/2 oz) sour cream, ½ cup (125 g/4 oz) natural yoghurt, ¼ cup (70 g/2¼ oz) ready-made hot apple chutney and 1 teaspoon maple syrup together until smooth. Season, to taste, with salt and pepper and refrigerate until ready to serve. Makes about 1½ cups.

BLUE CHEESE AND CREAM

Mix 250 g (8 oz) blue cheese in a food processor with ½ cup (125 ml/4 fl oz) cream until smooth. Transfer to a bowl, stir in another ½ cup (125 ml/4 fl oz) cream and 2 teaspoons apple cider vinegar and mix well. Season with salt and pepper, cover and refrigerate until ready to use. Makes about 1½ cups.

SWEET AND SOUR

Beat 1 cup (250 g/4 oz) natural yoghurt and ⅓ cup (80 ml/2¾ fl oz) bottled sweet and sour sauce together until smooth. Add 1 tablespoon finely chopped fresh chives and season, to taste, with salt and pepper. Cover and keep refrigerated until ready to use. Makes about 1½ cups.

CUCUMBER AND PEAR

Beat 2 tablespoons whole egg mayonnaise, 2 tablespoons natural yoghurt, 1 tablespoon sour cream and 1 teaspoon Dijon mustard together until well combined and smooth. Finely dice half a pear and ¼ of a small cucumber and stir into the mixture with 1 teaspoon of lemon juice. Season, to taste, with salt and freshly ground black pepper. Cover and keep refrigerated until ready to use. Makes about 1 cup.

REFRIED BEANS

Combine a 460 g (14 oz) can refried beans and ¼ cup (60 g/2 oz) sour cream in a food processor and mix until smooth, adding salt and pepper, to taste. Cover and keep at room temperature until ready to use. Makes about 1½ cups.

AVOCADO AND HERB

Place 1 avocado, 1 tablespoon each of sour cream, lemon juice and light olive oil, 1 small seeded tomato and ¾ cup (25 g/¾ oz) coriander leaves in a food processor and mix until smooth. Season with salt and pepper. Transfer to a glass bowl, lay plastic wrap directly onto the surface of the dip (to prevent a skin forming) and keep refrigerated until ready to use. Try to make this dip close to serving time, so it doesn't discolour. Makes about 2 cups.

CORN AND BACON

Cut the corn kernels from 2 cobs of corn and cook in boiling water, covered, for about 10 minutes, then drain. Meanwhile cook 250 g (8 oz) lean finely chopped bacon in a non-stick pan until very crispy and drain on paper towels. Put the corn in a food processor with 1 crushed clove garlic and mix until quite smooth. Add 250 g (8 oz) spreadable cream cheese and process until well combined. Spoon into a serving dish, cool to room temperature and sprinkle the bacon and some chopped chives over the top. Makes about 2 cups.

CLOCKWISE, FROM TOP LEFT: Creamy salmon; Blue cheese and cream; Cucumber and pear; Avocado and herb; Corn and bacon; Refried beans; Sweet and sour; Hot apple chutney

CHICKEN LIVER PATE WITH PISTACHIOS AND PROSCIUTTO

Preparation time: 20 minutes + 3 hours refrigeration
Total cooking time: 15 minutes
Serves 10

8–10 very thin slices prosciutto
500 g (1 lb) chicken livers
30 g (1 oz) butter
¼ cup (60 ml/2 fl oz) olive oil
2 rashers bacon, finely diced
1 onion, finely chopped
2 cloves garlic, crushed
3 bay leaves
⅓ cup (80 ml/2¾ fl oz) sherry or brandy
125 g (4 oz) butter, softened
⅓ cup (50 g/1¾ oz) pistachio nuts, toasted

1 Line a 25 x 11 cm (10 x 4½ inch) loaf tin with foil, then line with the prosciutto slices so that the prosciutto hangs over the sides, making sure each slice overlaps slightly. Trim the chicken livers of any fat and veins.
2 Heat the butter and oil in a frying pan and cook the bacon, onion and garlic for 5 minutes, or until the onion is soft but not brown.
3 Add the chicken livers to the frying pan with the bay leaves. Increase the heat to hot and cook for 3–4 minutes, or until the livers are brown on the outside, but still slightly pink on the inside.
4 Add the sherry or brandy to the frying pan and simmer, stirring constantly, for 3 minutes, or until the liquid has almost all evaporated. Remove the bay leaves. Put the mixture in a food processor and blend to a very fine texture. Gradually add the butter to the food processor and blend until the mixture is smooth. Season, to taste, then stir in the nuts.
5 Spoon the mixture into the loaf tin and fold the prosciutto over the top. Cover with plastic wrap and refrigerate for at least 3 hours, or overnight. Cut into slices for serving

TANGY TOMATO DIP WITH PITTA CRISPS

Preparation time: 20 minutes
Total cooking time: 20 minutes
Makes 2 cups

2 tablespoons oil
1 onion, chopped
2 cloves garlic, crushed
2 small red chillies, chopped
425 g (13½ oz) canned tomatoes, crushed
2 pimientos, chopped
2 tablespoons lemon juice
4 tablespoons chopped fresh parsley
3 pitta bread pockets
3 tablespoons sour cream

1 Preheat the oven to moderate 180°C (350°F/Gas 4). Heat oil in a medium pan and add onion, garlic and chillies. Stir over medium heat for 2 minutes or until onion is tender.
2 Add the tomatoes, pimientos and lemon juice; bring to the boil. Reduce heat to low; simmer, uncovered, for 5 minutes or until reduced and thickened. Remove from heat; stir in parsley.
3 Split the pitta pockets in half and cut each half into eight wedges; brush with a little oil. Place in a single layer on an oven tray and bake for 10 minutes or until golden and crisp. Spoon the tomato dip into a bowl and top with sour cream. Serve warm or cold, as a dip for pitta crisps.

PANISSES (CHICKPEA CHIPS)

Preparation time: 20 minutes + cooling
Total cooking time: 30 minutes
Serves 6

170 g (5½ oz) chickpea flour
1½ tablespoons olive oil
vegetable oil, for frying

1 Spray six saucers with cooking oil spray. Place the flour in a bowl and stir in 2¾ cups (685 ml/22 fl oz) cold water. Whisk with a wire whisk for about 2 minutes, or until smooth. Stir in the olive oil and season, to taste, with salt and finely ground black pepper.
2 Pour into a heavy-based saucepan and cook over low heat for about 8 minutes, stirring constantly, until thickened. Cook and stir until the mixture goes lumpy and starts to pull away from the sides of the pan, about 10–12 minutes. Remove from the heat and beat until smooth. Working quickly before the mixture sets, distribute among the saucers and spread to an even thickness. Allow to cool and set.
3 Preheat the oven to very slow 120°C (250°F/ Gas ½). Remove the mixture from the saucers and cut into sticks 5 cm (2 inches) long and 2 cm (¾ inch) wide. Pour vegetable oil into a large heavy-based saucepan to a depth of about 2.5 cm (1 inch). Heat to very hot and fry the sticks in batches until crisp and golden, about 2 minutes on each side. Remove with a slotted spoon and drain on crumpled paper towels. Transfer cooked batches to trays and keep warm in the oven while the rest are being fried. Serve hot, sprinkled with salt and freshly ground black pepper and perhaps some grated Parmesan.

NOTE: For a sweet snack, sprinkle with sugar while still hot.

TEX-MEX CHEESE CRISPS

Preparation time: 20 minutes + chilling
Total cooking time: 12 minutes
Makes 80

1¾ cups (215 g/7 oz) plain flour
1 teaspoon chilli powder
1 teaspoon garlic salt
½ teaspoon ground paprika
200 g (6½ oz) butter, chopped
1 egg, lightly beaten
200 g (6½ oz) Cheddar, grated

1 Preheat the oven to hot 210°C (415°F/
Gas 6–7). Lightly brush two baking trays
with melted butter.
2 Sift the flour, chilli powder, garlic salt
and paprika into a large bowl. Rub the
butter into the flour with your fingertips
until the mixture resembles fine
breadcrumbs. Add the egg and cheese
and stir until the mixture comes together.
Turn onto a lightly floured surface and
gather together into a ball. Cover the
dough with plastic wrap and refrigerate
for 20 minutes.
3 Roll the dough on a lightly floured
surface to 3 mm (⅛ inch) thickness. Cut
into shapes with a 6 cm (2½ inch) star-
shaped biscuit cutter. Place on the trays,
allowing room for spreading. Bake for
12 minutes, or until crisp and golden
brown. Leave on the trays for 2 minutes
before transferring to a wire rack to cool.

EGG AND CAVIAR MOULDED DIP

Preparation time: 1 hour + chilling
Total cooking time: 7 minutes
Serves 8–12

7 eggs
3 tablespoons finely chopped fresh
  parsley
3 tablespoons whole egg mayonnaise
80 g (2¾ oz) chives, finely chopped
500 g (1 lb) cream cheese, softened to
  room temperature
90 g (3 oz) black caviar
300 g (10 oz) sour cream
extra chives, snipped, and black caviar,
  for serving

1 Fill a pan with cold water and gently add
the eggs. Bring to the boil, then reduce the
heat and simmer for 7 minutes. Drain and
plunge the eggs in cold water to stop the
cooking process. Cool thoroughly and drain.
2 Line a deep loose-based fluted flan tin
(about 18 cm/7 inches in diameter) with
plastic wrap, leaving a wide overhang to
help you remove the moulded dip from
the tin.
3 Peel and mash the eggs, add the
parsley and mayonnaise, and season with
salt and pepper.
4 Divide the egg mixture in half. Spoon
one half into the lined tin. Firmly press
down and smooth the surface with a
spatula or the back of a spoon, pressing
well into the side of the tin. Sprinkle with
half the chives, pressing them down into
the dip. Using a clean, warm spatula,
spread with half the cream cheese to form
another layer. Spoon half the caviar over
the cream cheese and press down gently.
5 Repeat the layering with the remaining
egg mixture, chives, cream cheese and
caviar. Cover the moulded dip with plastic
wrap, pressing down firmly so the layers
stick together, and refrigerate for 2 hours.
6 Remove the top cover of plastic wrap
and place a plate over the mould. Flip
over onto the plate while holding the tin
and gently ease the tin off. Carefully
remove the plastic wrap, trying not to
damage the fluted edges.
7 Spoon dollops of sour cream over the
top of the mould and spread a little.
Decorate with the extra snipped chives
and a few spoonfuls of caviar. Serve with
water crackers.

VEGETABLE CHIPS

PAPER-THIN OR SAW-TOOTHED AND CHUNKY, CHIPS ARE LOVED BY EVERYONE—AND THEY DON'T HAVE TO BE MADE FROM POTATOES, AS THESE CLEVER AND SURPRISING SUGGESTIONS PROVE.

BEETROOT CHIPS

Using a sharp vegetable peeler or a knife, cut 500 g (1 lb) of peeled beetroot into paper-thin slices. Heat 3 cups (750 ml/ 24 fl oz) of oil in a pan and cook the beetroot chips in hot oil, in batches, until they are crisp and browned. Drain on paper towels and keep warm in a preheated moderate 180°C (350°F/Gas 4) oven while cooking the remainder. Serve beetroot chips with a blend of whole egg mayonnaise and chopped fresh herbs of your choice.

CRISPY SWEET POTATO (KUMERA) DISCS

Peel 500 g (1 lb) of orange sweet potato (kumera) and cut into thin slices using a sharp vegetable peeler or a knife. Heat 3 cups (750 ml/24 fl oz) of oil in a pan and cook the sweet potato discs in batches until crisp and golden. Drain on paper towels and keep warm in a preheated moderate 180°C (350°F/ Gas 4) oven while cooking remainder. Serve with a mixture of mayonnaise, lime juice and curry powder.

ZUCCHINI (COURGETTE) RIBBONS

Using a sharp vegetable peeler, cut 500 g (1 lb) of large zucchinis (courgettes) into ribbons by running the peeler horizontally along the zucchinis. Dip the zucchini ribbons into a bowl of 4 lightly beaten eggs, then dip into a mixture of 1 cup (100 g/3⅓ oz) of dried breadcrumbs and 1 tablespoon of chopped fresh herbs. Cook the crumbed zucchini ribbons in batches in 3 cups (750 ml/24 fl oz) of hot oil until the ribbons are golden. Drain on paper towels and keep warm in a preheated moderate 180°C (350°F/ Gas 4) oven while cooking the remaining zucchini ribbons. Zucchini ribbons are delicious served with a dipping sauce made from chopped sun-dried tomatoes and natural yoghurt.

GOLDEN POTATO CHIPS

Cut 500 g (1 lb) washed old potatoes into thick country-style chips (wedges). Heat 3 cups (750 ml/24 fl oz) of oil in a pan and cook potatoes in batches until lightly golden; drain on paper towels. Repeat with remaining potatoes. Just before serving, re-fry the potatoes in batches until crisp and golden. Sprinkle with sea salt and malt vinegar, if desired.

PUMPKIN CRISPS

Peel 500 g (1 lb) butternut pumpkin and cut into crinkle-cut slices. Heat 3 cups (750 ml/24 fl oz) of oil in a pan and cook slices in batches until they are crisp and golden. Drain on paper towels and keep warm in a preheated moderate 180°C (350°F/Gas 4) oven while cooking the remaining pumpkin chips.

CARROT AND HERB RIBBONS

Peel 500 g (1 lb) carrots into ribbons by running a sharp peeler horizontally along the length of the carrot. Rinse and dry 1 cup (50 g/1⅔ oz) of large basil leaves. Heat 3 cups (750 ml/24 fl oz) of oil in a pan and cook carrot ribbons and basil leaves in batches until crisp. Drain on paper towels and keep warm in a preheated moderate 180°C (350°F/ Gas 4) oven while cooking remaining carrot and basil. Serve with a dipping sauce of sweet chilli sauce, lime juice and chopped fresh coriander.

CLOCKWISE, FROM TOP LEFT: Golden Potato Chips; Zucchini Ribbons; Beetroot Chips; Pumpkin Crisps; Carrot and Herb Ribbons; Crispy Sweet Potato Discs

FINGER FOOD

SPICY NUTS

Preparation time: 10 minutes + cooling
Total cooking time: 20 minutes
Serves 6

2 tablespoons olive oil
½ teaspoon ground cumin
½ teaspoon ground coriander
½ teaspoon garlic powder
¼ teaspoon chilli powder
¼ teaspoon ground ginger
¼ teaspoon ground cinnamon
⅔ cup (65 g/2¼ oz) pecans
⅔ cup (100 g/3½ oz) raw cashews
1½ cups (240 g/7½oz) raw almonds

1 Preheat the oven to slow 150°C
(300°F/Gas 2). Heat the oil over low heat
in a pan and stir in the spices for
2 minutes, or until fragrant. Remove from
the heat, add the nuts and stir with a
wooden spoon until the nuts are well
coated. Spread over a baking tray and
bake for 15 minutes, or until golden.
Sprinkle with salt and cool.

POTATO NOODLE NIBBLES

Preparation time: 30 minutes + cooling
Total cooking time: 40 minutes
Serves 6

450 g (14 oz) floury potatoes, peeled and
   chopped
40 g (1¼ oz) butter, softened
2 tablespoons grated Parmesan or
   Pecorino cheese
100 g (3½ oz) besan (chickpea flour)
2 teaspoons ground cumin
2 teaspoons garam masala
1 teaspoon ground coriander
1 teaspoon chilli powder
1 teaspoon cayenne pepper
1½ teaspoons ground turmeric
oil, for deep-frying

1 Boil or steam the potato until tender.
Drain and cool for 15–20 minutes, then
mash with the butter and cheese. Add the
besan, cumin, garam masala, coriander,
chilli powder, cayenne, turmeric and
¾ teaspoon of salt and mix with a wooden
spoon until a soft, light dough forms.
Turn out and knead lightly 10–12 times,
until quite smooth.
2 Fill a deep heavy-based pan one third
full of oil and heat to 180°C (350°F). Test
the temperature by dropping a small ball
of dough into the oil. The oil is ready if the
dough rises immediately to the surface.
3 Using a piping bag with a 1 cm (½ inch)
star nozzle, pipe short lengths of dough
into the oil, cutting the dough off with a
knife. Cook in manageable batches. They
will rise to the surface and turn golden
quickly. Remove with a slotted spoon and
drain on crumpled paper towels. Serve
the nibbles within 2 hours of cooking.

FRIED CHICKPEAS

Preparation time: 30 minutes +
   overnight soaking
Total cooking time: 15 minutes
Serves 6

1¼ cups (275 g/9 oz) dried chickpeas
oil, for deep-frying
½ teaspoon paprika
¼ teaspoon cayenne pepper

1 Soak the chickpeas overnight in plenty
of cold water. Drain well and pat dry with
paper towels.
2 Fill a deep saucepan one third full of oil
and heat to 180°C (350°F), or until a cube
of bread dropped into the oil browns in
15 seconds. Deep-fry half the chickpeas
for 3 minutes. Remove with a slotted
spoon, drain on crumpled towels and
repeat with the rest of the chickpeas.
Partially cover the saucepan as some of
the chickpeas may pop. Don't leave the oil
unattended.
3 Deep-fry the chickpeas again in batches
for 3 minutes each batch, or until
browned. Drain well again on crumpled
paper towels. Combine the paprika and
cayenne pepper with a little salt and
sprinkle the mixture over the hot
chickpeas. Allow to cool before serving.

SEAFOOD PARCELS

Preparation time: 25 minutes
Total cooking time: 35 minutes
Makes 20

250 g (8 oz) skinless white fish fillets (eg.
   cod, snapper, coley, ocean perch)
100 g (3½ oz) scallops
400 g (13 oz) cooked medium prawns
30 g (1 oz) butter
1 tablespoon lemon juice
1 tablespoon plain flour
1 cup (250 ml/8 fl oz) milk
60 g (2 oz) Cheddar, grated
1 tablespoon chopped fresh chives
1 tablespoon chopped fresh dill
10 sheets filo pastry
60 g (2 oz) butter, melted
2 teaspoons poppy seeds or sesame
   seeds

1 Preheat the oven to moderate 180°C
(350°F/Gas 4). Line a baking tray with
baking paper.
2 Cut the fish into 1 cm (½ inch) wide
strips. Wash the scallops and slice or pull
off any vein, membrane or hard white
muscle, leaving any roe attached. Peel the
prawns and pull out the dark vein from
each prawn back, starting at the head.
3 Melt the butter in a heavy-based pan. Add
the fish, scallops and lemon juice. Cook
over medium heat for 1 minute, or until
tender. Remove from the pan with a slotted
spoon, place in a bowl and keep warm.

4 Stir the flour into the butter and cook
for 1 minute, or until pale and foaming.
Remove from the heat and gradually stir
in the milk. Return to the heat and stir
constantly until the mixture boils and
thickens. Reduce the heat and simmer for
2 minutes. Stir in the Cheddar, chives,
dill, fish, scallops and prawns. Remove
from the heat and season, to taste, with
salt and pepper. Cover the surface with
plastic wrap.
5 Layer 2 sheets of pastry together with
melted butter, then cut into 4 equal
strips. Cover unused pastry with a damp
tea towel. Place 2 tablespoons of seafood
mixture on one short end of each pastry
strip. Fold in the edges and roll up.
Repeat with the remaining pastry,
seafood and some of the remaining
butter. Place the parcels seam-side-
down on the baking tray. Brush with the
remaining melted butter, sprinkle with
poppy seeds and bake for 20 minutes.

NOTE: You can make the sauce a day
ahead and refrigerate until required.

CAJUN POTATO WEDGES

Preparation time: 10 minutes
Total cooking time: 25–30 minutes
Serves 4

vegetable oil
4 medium potatoes
1–2 tablespoons Cajun spice mix

1 Preheat the oven to moderately hot
190°C (375°F/Gas 5). Pour 1 cm (½ inch) of
oil into a baking dish and place in the
oven until hot (about 5 minutes).
2 Cut the potatoes into wedge shapes or
chunks. Roll the wedges in the Cajun
spice mix until well coated.
3 Add the potatoes to the hot oil and toss
to coat. Bake for 20–25 minutes or until
golden brown, turning occasionally. Drain
on paper towels. Serve immediately with
ready-made tomato salsa and sour
cream, if desired.

NOTE: Cajun spice mix is available from
supermarkets, or you can make up your
own.

TURKEY AND CRANBERRY PIKELETS

Preparation time: 25 minutes + standing
Total cooking time: 15 minutes
Makes about 30

1 cup (125 g/4 oz) self-raising flour
1 egg, plus 1 egg yolk
1¼ cups (315 ml/10 fl oz) milk
25 g (¾ oz) butter, melted
3 tablespoons mayonnaise
150 g (5 oz) cooked turkey, shredded
3 tablespoons cranberry sauce
60 g (2 oz) alfalfa sprouts
3 hard-boiled eggs, sliced

1 Sift the flour and a pinch of salt into a bowl and make a well in the centre. Lightly whisk together the egg, egg yolk, milk and melted butter in a jug and gradually add to the flour, whisking to make a smooth, lump-free batter. Cover and leave for 30 minutes.
2 Heat a frying pan and brush lightly with melted butter or oil. Drop tablespoons of the batter into the pan, allowing room for spreading. Cook over medium heat until small bubbles begin to appear on the surface and the undersides are golden. Turn the pikelets over and cook the other sides. Transfer to a plate, cover with a tea towel and leave to cool while cooking the remaining batter.
3 Spread mayonnaise over each pikelet and top with turkey, cranberry sauce, alfalfa sprouts and a slice of egg.

IN ADVANCE: Pikelets can be made a day ahead and stored, covered, in the refrigerator. They can be frozen if you prefer, in single layers, for up to 2 months.

HOT CORN CAKES WITH AVOCADO AND PRAWNS

Preparation time: 25 minutes
Total cooking time: 15–20 minutes
Makes 32

¾ cup (110 g/3½ oz) frozen corn kernels, thawed, roughly chopped
1½ canned chipotle peppers, roughly chopped, and 2 teaspoons of the sauce
½ cup (60 g/2 oz) plain flour
⅓ cup (50 g/1¾ oz) polenta (cornmeal)
½ teaspoon baking powder
¼ teaspoon bicarbonate of soda
1 teaspoon salt
½ teaspoon sugar
1 cup (250 ml/8 fl oz) buttermilk
20 g (¾ oz) butter, melted
1 egg
32 cooked medium prawns, peeled, deveined
32 fresh coriander leaves, to garnish

Avocado sauce
1 ripe avocado, roughly chopped
2 tablespoons lime juice
1 canned chipotle pepper, in sauce
½ cup (15 g/½ oz) fresh coriander leaves
1 clove garlic, chopped
½ teaspoon salt
1 teaspoon ground cumin
2 tablespoons sour cream

1 Roughly chop the corn and chipotle peppers, using short bursts of a food processor.
2 Combine the dry ingredients in a large bowl and make a well. Whisk the buttermilk, butter and egg together in a jug, gradually add to the dry ingredients and whisk until thoroughly incorporated. Stir in the chopped corn and chipotle pepper. (The batter should have the consistency of pancake batter.) Add a tablespoon of water to thin the batter if necessary. Set aside.
3 Purée all the sauce ingredients in a food processor until very smooth. Season.
4 Heat a lightly greased frying pan over medium heat. Spoon tablespoons of the corn cake batter into the pan, forming 5 cm (2 inch) cakes, cooking in batches. Cook until golden brown, about 1 minute per side. Remove from the pan and repeat with the remaining batter. Keep the cakes warm until ready to serve. Alternatively, you can make the corn cakes up to 2 days ahead of time, wrap well in plastic wrap and refrigerate. Place a single layer on a baking sheet and reheat in a warm 170°C (325°F/Gas 3) oven for 5 minutes, or until warmed through. (Corn cakes can also be served at room temperature.)
5 To assemble, dollop a heaped teaspoon of avocado sauce on the warmed corn cakes. Place one cooked prawn on top of the avocado sauce. Garnish with coriander leaves.

PROSCIUTTO WITH MELON

Preparation time: 20 minutes
Total cooking time: Nil
Makes 16

1 rockmelon or honeydew melon
16 slices prosciutto
extra virgin olive oil

1 Remove the seeds from the melon, cut into thin wedges and wrap a slice of prosciutto around each. Drizzle with oil and grind black pepper over each. Refrigerate until required.

LABNEH MAKBUR
(MARINATED YOGHURT CHEESE BALLS)

Preparation time: 35 minutes +
  3 days draining + 3 hours refrigeration
Total cooking time: Nil
Makes 18 balls

1.5 kg (3 lb) thick natural yoghurt
2 clean 50 cm (20 inch) square muslin squares
2 fresh bay leaves
3 sprigs fresh thyme
2 sprigs fresh oregano
2 cups (500 ml/16 fl oz) good-quality olive oil

1 Place the yoghurt in a bowl with 2 teaspoons salt and mix well. Put the muslin squares one on top of the other and place the yoghurt mixture in the centre. Gather up the corners of the muslin and tie securely with string, suspended over a bowl. Refrigerate and leave to drain for 3 days.
2 Once drained, the yoghurt will have become the texture and consistency of ricotta cheese. Remove from the cloth, and place in a bowl.
3 Roll tablespoons of mixture into balls and place on a large tray. You should have 18 balls. Cover and refrigerate for 3 hours, or until firm.
4 Place the balls in a clean, dry 1 litre glass jar with the bay leaves, fresh thyme and oregano sprigs. Fill the jar with the olive oil. Seal and refrigerate for up to 1 week. Return to room temperature for serving.

NOTE: This dish is traditionally served at breakfast or as an appetizer.

GREEK CHEESE TRIANGLES

Preparation time: 35 minutes
Total cooking time: 20 minutes
Makes 30

250 g (4 oz) Greek feta
180 g (6 oz) Gruyère cheese, grated
2 eggs, lightly beaten
white pepper, to taste
15 sheets filo pastry
½ cup (125 ml/4 fl oz) olive oil
125 g (4 oz) butter, melted

1 Preheat the oven to moderate 180°C (350°F/Gas 4). Place the feta in a bowl and mash with a fork. Add the Gruyère, egg and pepper and mix.
2 Cut the filo sheets in halves widthways. Keep the unused pastry covered with a damp tea towel to prevent it drying out. Place one half of one sheet lengthways on a work surface. Brush with the combined oil and butter, then fold into thirds lengthways. Brush with the oil and butter.
3 Place 1 tablespoon of the cheese mixture on the corner of the pastry strip. Fold this corner over the filling to edge of pastry to form a triangle. Continue to fold until the filling is enclosed and the end of pastry is reached. Repeat with the remaining pastry and filling.
4 Place the triangles on a lightly greased baking tray and brush them with the oil and butter mixture. Bake for 20 minutes, or until crisp.

NOTE: You can easily adapt these pastries to suit your personal taste. Try using ricotta instead of gruyère and adding your favourite fresh herbs, finely chopped. Flat-leaf parsley, mint or thyme are all suitable.

KIBBEH

Preparation time: 45 minutes +
    2 hours refrigeration
Total cooking time: 25 minutes
Makes 15

1⅓ cups (235 g/7½ oz) fine burghul
150 g (5 oz) lean lamb, chopped
1 onion, grated
2 tablespoons plain flour
1 teaspoon ground allspice

Filling
2 teaspoons olive oil
1 small onion, finely chopped
100 g (3½ oz) lean lamb mince
½ teaspoon ground allspice
½ teaspoon ground cinnamon
⅓ cup (80 ml/2¾ fl oz) beef stock
2 tablespoons pine nuts
2 tablespoons chopped fresh mint
oil, for deep-frying

1 Cover the burghul with boiling water and leave for 5 minutes. Drain in a colander, pressing well to remove the water. Spread on paper towels to absorb any moisture.
2 Process the burghul, lamb, onion, flour and allspice until a fine paste forms. Season well, then refrigerate for 1 hour.
3 For the filling, heat the oil in a frying pan, add the onion and cook over low heat for 3 minutes, or until soft. Add the mince, allspice and cinnamon, and cook, stirring, over high heat for 3 minutes. Add the stock and cook, partially covered, over low heat for 6 minutes, or until the mince is soft. Roughly chop the pine nuts and stir in with the mint. Season well with salt and cracked pepper, then transfer to a bowl and allow to cool.

4 Shape 2 tablespoons of the burghul mixture at a time into a sausage 6 cm (2½ inches) long. Dip your hands in cold water, and, with your index finger, make a long hole through the centre of each sausage and gently work your finger around to make a cavity for the filling. Fill each with 2 teaspoons of the filling and seal, moulding it into a torpedo shape. Smooth over any cracks with your fingers. Place on a foil-lined tray and refrigerate, uncovered, for 1 hour.
5 Fill a deep pan one third full of oil and heat until a cube of bread dropped into the oil browns in 15 seconds. Deep-fry the kibbeh in batches for 2–3 minutes, or until browned. Drain on paper towels. Serve hot.

ARTICHOKES IN AROMATIC VINAIGRETTE

Preparation time: 20 minutes + cooling
Total cooking time: 20 minutes
Serves 4

2 tablespoons lemon juice
4 large globe artichokes
2 cloves garlic, crushed
1 teaspoon finely chopped fresh oregano
½ teaspoon ground cumin
½ teaspoon ground coriander
pinch dried chilli flakes
3 teaspoons sherry vinegar
¼ cup (60 ml/2 fl oz) olive oil

1 Add the lemon juice to a large bowl of cold water. Trim the artichokes, cutting off the stalks to within 5 cm (2 inches) of the base of each artichoke and removing the tough outer leaves. Cut off the top quarter of the leaves from each. Slice each artichoke in half from top to base, or into quarters if large. Remove each small, furry choke with a teaspoon, then place each artichoke in the bowl of acidulated water to prevent it from discolouring while you prepare the rest.
2 Bring a large non-aluminium saucepan of water to the boil, add the artichokes and a teaspoon of salt and simmer for 20 minutes, or until tender. The cooking time will depend on the artichoke size. Test by pressing a skewer into the base. If cooked, the artichoke should be soft and give little resistance. Strain, then place the artichokes on their cut side to drain while cooling.
3 Combine the garlic, oregano, cumin, coriander and chilli flakes in a small bowl. Season with salt and pepper and blend in the vinegar. Beating constantly, slowly pour in the olive oil to form an emulsion. This step can be done in a small food processor.
4 Arrange the artichokes in rows on a serving platter. Pour the vinaigrette over the top and leave to cool completely.

BOREK
(TURKISH FILO PARCELS)

Preparation time: 1 hour
Total cooking time: 20 minutes
Makes 24

400 g (13 oz) feta
2 eggs, lightly beaten
¾ cup (25 g/¾ oz) chopped fresh flat-leaf
  parsley
375 g (12 oz) filo pastry
⅓ cup (80 ml/2¾ fl oz) good-quality olive
  oil

1 Preheat the oven to moderate 180°C
(350°F/Gas 4). Lightly grease a baking
tray. Crumble the feta into a large bowl
using a fork or your fingers. Mix in the
eggs and parsley and season with freshly
ground black pepper.
2 Cover the filo pastry with a damp tea
towel so it doesn't dry out. Remove one
sheet at a time. Brushing each sheet
lightly with olive oil, layer 4 sheets on top
of one another. Cut the pastry into four
7 cm (2¾ inch) strips.
3 Place 2 rounded teaspoons of the feta
mixture in one corner of each strip and
fold diagonally, creating a triangle pillow.
Place on the baking tray, seam-side-
down, and brush with olive oil. Repeat
with the remaining pastry and filling to
make 24 parcels. Bake for 20 minutes, or
until golden. Serve these as part of a
large meze plate.

NOTE: Fillings for borek are versatile and
can be adapted to include your favourite
cheeses such as haloumi, Gruyère,
Cheddar or mozzarella.

SAGANAKI HALOUMI
(FRIED HALOUMI CHEESE)

Preparation time: 5 minutes
Total cooking time: 2 minutes
Serves 6

400 g (13 oz) haloumi cheese
olive oil, for shallow-frying
2 tablespoons lemon juice

1 Pat the haloumi dry with paper towels
and cut into 1 cm (½ inch) slices.
2 Pour oil into a large frying pan to 5 mm
(¼ inch) depth and heat over medium
heat. Add the cheese and fry for 1 minute
each side, or until golden. Remove the
pan from the heat and pour the lemon
juice over the cheese. Season with ground
black pepper. Serve straight from the pan
or on a serving plate, as part of a meze
spread, with crusty bread to mop up the
lemon and olive oil mixture.

NOTE: Saganaki refers to the two-
handled frying pan in which this dish is
traditionally served.

CUCUMBER ROUNDS WITH
AVOCADO AND TURKEY

Preparation time: 20 minutes
Total cooking time: Nil
Makes 30

3 Lebanese cucumbers
100 g (3½ oz) sliced smoked turkey
½ avocado, mashed
1 clove garlic, crushed
2 tablespoons cranberry sauce
2 tablespoons sour cream
cranberry sauce, extra, to garnish
alfalfa sprouts or mustard cress, to
  garnish

1 Slice the cucumbers into 1.5 cm (⅝ inch)
rounds to make 30 pieces. Cut 30 rounds
from the turkey using a 3 cm (1¼ inch)
cutter.
2 Combine the avocado with the garlic,
cranberry sauce and sour cream. Spoon
1 teaspoon onto each cucumber round and
top with a round of turkey. Spoon a little
cranberry sauce on top and garnish with
alfalfa sprouts.

ANTIPASTO

ENTICING TO THE EYE, EMANATING A MOUTHWATERING SCENT AND CAPTIVATING THE PALATE, THESE SEDUCTIVE APPETIZERS ASSAULT THE SENSES, WHETHER EATEN ON THEIR OWN OR AS A TEMPTING INTRODUCTION TO A MEAL.

MARINATED ROASTED PEPPERS (CAPSICUMS)

Grill 1 large red pepper, 1 large yellow pepper, 1 large green pepper and, if available, 1 large purple pepper, until the skin blisters and blackens. Cover the peppers with a tea towel to cool slightly before peeling. Cut the peppers into thick strips and place into a bowl, add 2 crushed cloves of garlic, 2 tablespoons of balsamic vinegar, 2 tablespoons of shredded fresh basil and ¼ cup (60 ml/ 2 fl oz) of olive oil. Cover and refrigerate for 3 hours. Return to room temperature before serving. Serve on toasted bruschetta or focaccia.
Serves 4–6.

SWEET AND SOUR ONIONS

Carefully peel 3 medium (500 g/1 lb) red (Spanish) onions, keeping the ends intact so that the layers stay together. Cut the onions into eighths and place the pieces in a non-stick baking dish. Combine 2 tablespoons of wholegrain mustard, 2 tablespoons of honey, 2 tablespoons of red wine vinegar and 2 tablespoons of oil. Brush this mixture over the onions, cover the dish and bake in a preheated hot 220°C (425°F/Gas 7) oven for 20 minutes. Uncover and continue baking for another 15–20 minutes, or until the onions are soft and caramelised.
Serves 4–6.

GOLDEN FRIED GOAT'S CHEESE

Cut 250 g (8 oz) of goat's cheese into 5 mm (¼ inch) thick slices. Dust lightly with seasoned flour. Dip the slices into 2 lightly beaten eggs and gently toss to coat in a mixture of 1 cup (80 g/2⅔ oz) of fresh breadcrumbs, ½ cup (45 g/1½ oz) of grated pecorino cheese and 1 teaspoon of sweet paprika. Refrigerate for 1 hour. Deep-fry the crumbed goat's cheese in batches in hot oil for 2 minutes, or until the crust is crisp and golden. Serve with your favourite relish or a sweet dipping sauce. It is best to use the small logs of goat's cheese for this recipe.
Serves 4.

CHAR-GRILLED SPRING ONIONS AND ASPARAGUS

Cut 110 g (9¾ oz) of asparagus and 12 spring onions into 12 cm (5 inch) lengths. Brush the spring onions and asparagus lightly with macadamia nut oil and cook on a preheated char-grill or barbecue for 3 minutes, or until the vegetables are tender. Pour some balsamic vinegar over the top, sprinkle with pepper and then top with shavings of Parmesan cheese.
Serves 4–6.

MUSHROOMS IN LIME AND CHILLI

Brush 250 g (8 oz) of button mushrooms with oil; cook under a preheated grill, or on a barbecue grill, until tender. Combine 1 teaspoon chilli flakes, 1 tablespoon shredded lime rind, 1 crushed clove garlic, 1 tablespoon chopped fresh coriander, 1 teaspoon soft brown sugar, 2 tablespoons of lime juice and ¼ cup (60 ml/2 fl oz) of olive oil in a bowl. Toss the mushrooms in lime and chilli mixture and refrigerate for 1 hour before serving.
Serves 2–4.

CLOCKWISE, FROM TOP LEFT: Golden Fried Goat's Cheese; Marinated Roasted Peppers; Sweet and Sour Onions; Char-grilled Spring Onions and Asparagus; Mushrooms in Lime and Chilli

SESAME SHAPES

Preparation time: 35 minutes + standing
Total cooking time: 15–20 minutes
Makes about 30

1½ cups (185 g/6 oz) self-raising flour
4 tablespoons sesame seeds, toasted
2 teaspoons finely grated orange rind
2 eggs
2 teaspoons sesame oil
1 cup (250 ml/8 fl oz) milk
4 tablespoons orange juice
125 g (4 oz) sun-dried tomatoes, finely
    chopped

Filling
200 g (6½ oz) soft cream cheese
2 tablespoons chopped fresh coriander

1 Sift the flour and a pinch of salt into a
bowl, stir in the sesame seeds and orange
rind and make a well in the centre. With a
fork, gradually whisk in the combined
egg, sesame oil, milk and orange juice to
make a smooth lump-free batter. Set
aside for 15 minutes.
2 Heat a frying pan and brush lightly with
melted butter or oil. Pour ⅓ cup (80 ml/
2¾ fl oz) batter into the pan and cook over
medium heat for 3–4 minutes, or until
bubbles appear on the surface. Turn over
and cook the other side. Transfer to a
plate and cover with a tea towel while
cooking the remaining batter.
3 Use biscuit cutters to cut out various
shapes (you will be sandwiching 3 of each
shape together so make sure you have
the right number of each).
4 To make the filling, mix the cream
cheese and coriander and use to
sandwich together three pikelet shapes.
Decorate with sun-dried tomato.
in advance: Pikelets can be joined and cut
into shapes a day ahead. Store in an
airtight container in the refrigerator.

RED PEPPER (CAPSICUM) PIKELETS WITH PROSCIUTTO

Preparation time: 30 minutes + resting
Total cooking time: 25 minutes
Makes about 20

1 small red pepper (capsicum)
1 cup (125 g/4 oz) plain flour
½ teaspoon bicarbonate of soda
1¼ cups (315 ml/10 fl oz) buttermilk
1 egg
50 g (1¾ oz) butter, melted
130 g (4¼ oz) can corn kernels, drained
1 tablespoon finely chopped fresh chives,
    plus some for garnish
1 cup (250 ml/8 fl oz) crème fraîche or
    sour cream
5 slices prosciutto, cut into strips

1 Cut the red pepper into large flattish
pieces and remove the seeds and
membrane. Cook, skin-side-up, under a
hot grill until black and blistered. Place in
a plastic bag and leave to cool, then peel.
Chop the flesh finely.
2 Sift the flour, bicarbonate of soda and a
pinch of salt into a bowl and make a well
in the centre. Gradually add the combined
buttermilk, egg and melted butter and
mix until just combined and lump-free.
Stir in the pepper, corn and chives. Do not
overmix.
3 Heat a frying pan and brush with melted
butter or oil. Drop 2 teaspoons of batter
into the pan for each pikelet, leaving a
little room for spreading. Cook until
bubbles begin to form on the surface.
Turn over and cook the other side.
Transfer to a plate and cover with a tea
towel to keep warm while cooking the
remaining batter.
4 Top each pikelet with a teaspoon of
crème fraîche and a strip of prosciutto.
Garnish with fresh chives.

STEAMED PRAWN NORI ROLLS

Preparation time: 30 minutes +
    1 hour refrigeration
Total cooking time: 5 minutes
Makes 24

500 g (1 lb) peeled raw prawns
1½ tablespoons fish sauce
1 tablespoon sake (rice wine)
2 tablespoons chopped fresh coriander
1 large kaffir lime leaf, shredded
1 tablespoon lime juice
2 teaspoons sweet chilli sauce
1 egg white, lightly beaten
5 sheets nori (dried seaweed)

Dipping sauce
⅓ cup (80 ml/2¾ fl oz) sweet chilli sauce
1 tablespoon lime juice

1 Put the prawns, fish sauce, sake,
coriander, kaffir lime leaf, lime juice and
sweet chilli sauce into a food processor or
blender and process until smooth. Add
the egg white and pulse for a few
seconds, or until just combined.
2 Lay the nori sheets on a work surface
and spread prawn mixture over each,
leaving a 2 cm (¾ inch) border at one end.
Roll up tightly, cover and refrigerate for 1
hour. Trim the ends and with a very sharp
knife cut into 2 cm (¾ inch) lengths.
3 Place the nori rolls in a paper-lined
bamboo steamer, cover the steamer and
place over a wok of simmering water.
Steam for 5 minutes. Serve with the
dipping sauce.
4 Make the dipping sauce by combining
the sweet chilli sauce and lime juice in a
bowl.

BAKED PEPPERS (CAPSICUMS) WITH ANCHOVIES

Preparation time: 15 minutes
Total cooking time: 50 minutes
Serves 6

3 yellow peppers (capsicums)
3 red peppers (capsicums)
2 tablespoons extra virgin olive oil
12 anchovy fillets, halved lengthways
3 cloves garlic, thinly sliced
½ cup (25 g/¾ oz) fresh basil leaves
1 tablespoon baby capers, rinsed
extra virgin olive oil, for serving

1 Preheat the oven to moderate 180°C (350°F/Gas 4). Cut each pepper in half lengthways, leaving the stems intact. If the peppers are large, quarter them. Remove the seeds and membrane. Drizzle a little of the oil in a baking dish and place the peppers in, skin-side-down. Season with salt and pepper.
2 In each pepper, place a halved anchovy fillet, slivers of garlic and a torn basil leaf. Divide the capers among the peppers. Season with salt and pepper and drizzle with the remaining oil.
3 Cover the dish with foil and bake the peppers for 20 minutes. Remove the foil and cook for another 25–30 minutes, or until the peppers are tender. Drizzle with a little extra virgin olive oil. Scatter the remaining torn basil leaves over the peppers and serve warm or at room temperature.

SCALLOP POCKETS

Preparation time: 40 minutes
Total cooking time: 15 minutes
Makes 25

25 large scallops
1 tablespoon oil
5 cm (2 inch) piece fresh ginger, grated
4 spring onions, finely chopped
1 tablespoon Shaosing (Chinese) wine or dry sherry
2 teaspoons sesame oil
1 teaspoon cornflour
25 won ton or egg noodle wrappers
oil, for shallow frying
15 g (½ oz) garlic chives, blanched

1 Carefully slice or pull off any vein, membrane or hard white muscle from the scallops, leaving any roe attached.
2 Heat the oil in a pan, add the ginger and spring onion and cook over medium heat for 2 minutes, stirring occasionally. Increase the heat and, when the pan is very hot, add the scallops and stir-fry, tossing quickly, for 30 seconds. Remove the pan from the heat.
3 Blend the wine, sesame oil, cornflour and a little salt and pepper in a small bowl until it forms a smooth paste. Pour over the scallops, return to the heat and toss over high heat for 30 seconds or until the liquid has thickened. Cool completely.
4 Working with one wrapper at a time and keeping the rest covered, brush the edge of each lightly with water. Place a scallop in the centre, bring up the sides and pinch together to form a pouch with a frill at the top. Put on a paper-covered baking tray and repeat with the remaining wrappers and filling.
5 Heat 2 cm (¾ inch) oil in a pan to 180°C (350°F). The oil is hot enough when a cube of bread sizzles and turns golden brown in 15 seconds. Cook the scallop pouches, in batches if necessary, for 5 minutes, or until golden brown. Drain on paper towels. Tie a blanched garlic chive around each and serve immediately.

FALAFEL (DEEP-FRIED CHICKPEA BALLS)

Preparation time: 20 minutes + 48 hours soaking + 50 minutes standing
Total cooking time: 10 minutes
Makes 30

1 cup (150 g/5 oz) dried split broad beans (see Note)
1 cup (220 g/7 oz) dried chickpeas
1 onion, roughly chopped
6 cloves garlic, roughly chopped
2 teaspoons ground coriander
1 tablespoon ground cumin
½ cup (15 g/½ oz) chopped fresh flat-leaf parsley
¼ teaspoon chilli powder
½ teaspoon bicarbonate of soda
3 tablespoons chopped fresh coriander leaves
light oil, for deep-frying

1 Place the broad beans in a large bowl, cover well with water and soak for 48 hours. Drain, then rinse several times in fresh water.
2 Place the chickpeas in a large bowl, cover well with water and soak for 12 hours.
3 Drain the broad beans and chickpeas well, then process in a food processor with the onion and garlic until smooth.
4 Add the ground coriander, cumin, parsley, chilli powder, bicarbonate of soda and fresh coriander. Season, to taste, and mix until well combined. Transfer to a large bowl and set aside for 30 minutes.
5 Shape tablespoons of mixture into balls, flatten to 4 cm (1½ inch) rounds, place on a tray and refrigerate for 20 minutes.
6 Fill a deep, heavy-based saucepan one third full of oil and heat to 180°C (350°F), or until a cube of bread dropped in the oil browns in 15 seconds. Cook the felafel in batches for 1–2 minutes, or until golden. Drain on paper towels. Serve hot or cold with hummus, baba ghannouj and pitta bread.

OREGANO AND PROSCIUTTO PINWHEELS

Preparation time: 30 minutes + chilling
Total cooking time: 10 minutes
Makes about 40

1 red pepper (capsicum)
1 green pepper (capsicum)
1 yellow pepper (capsicum)
125 g (4 oz) cream cheese, softened
25 g (¾ oz) Parmesan, grated
2 spring onions, finely chopped
¼ cup (7 g/¼ oz) chopped fresh oregano
1 tablespoon bottled capers, drained and chopped
1 tablespoon pine nuts, chopped
12 thin slices prosciutto

1 Cut the peppers into quarters and remove the seeds and membrane. Cook, skin-side-up, under a hot grill until the skin blackens and blisters. Place in a plastic bag until cool, then peel.
2 Mix together the cream cheese, Parmesan, spring onion, oregano, capers and pine nuts.
3 Place the pepper pieces on the prosciutto slices and trim the prosciutto to the same size. Remove the pepper and spread some cheese mixture on the prosciutto. Top with the pepper and spread with a little more cheese mixture. Roll up tightly from the short end. Cover and refrigerate for 1 hour, or until firm. Slice into 1 cm (½ inch) rounds and serve on toothpicks.

CURRIED CHICKEN PIES

Preparation time: 45 minutes + chilling
Total cooking time: 50 minutes
Makes 24

3 cups (375 g/12 oz) plain flour
1 teaspoon ground cumin
1 teaspoon ground turmeric
200 g (6½ oz) butter, chopped
2 egg yolks, lightly beaten
50 g (1¾ oz) butter, extra
1 onion, chopped
350 g (12 oz) chicken tenderloins, trimmed and cut into small dice
1 tablespoon curry powder
1 teaspoon cumin seeds
1 tablespoon plain flour, extra
1 cup (250 ml/8 fl oz) chicken stock
2 tablespoons mango chutney (mango chopped)
3 tablespoons chopped fresh coriander
milk, for glazing

1 Sift the flour, cumin and turmeric into a bowl. Rub in the butter using just your fingertips, until the mixture resembles fine breadcrumbs. Make a well and add the egg yolks and 5–6 tablespoons water. Mix with a flat-bladed knife using a cutting action, until the mixture comes together. Lift onto a floured surface and gather into a ball. Wrap in plastic wrap and chill for 30 minutes.

2 Lightly grease two deep 12-hole patty tins. Roll out two-thirds of the pastry to 2 mm (⅛ inch) thick, and cut 8 cm (3 inch) rounds to fit the tins. Roll out the remaining pastry and cut 24 tops with a 5.5 cm (2¼ inch) cutter. Chill.
3 Heat the extra butter in a large pan and cook the onion until soft. Add the chicken and, when browned, stir in the curry powder and cumin seeds for 2 minutes. Add the extra flour and stir for 30 seconds. Remove from the heat and gradually stir in the stock. Return to the heat and stir until the sauce boils and thickens. Reduce the heat and simmer for 2–3 minutes, until reduced and very thick. Stir in the chutney and coriander leaves. Season and cool.
4 Preheat the oven to moderate 180°C (350°F/Gas 4). Divide the filling among the pies and brush the edges with water. Join the tops by pressing around the edges with the tip of a sharp knife. Slash each top to allow steam to escape. Brush with milk and bake for 30 minutes. Cool slightly before removing from tins. Serve warm.

BUNUELOS DE BACALAO (SALT COD FRITTERS)

Preparation time: 15 minutes +
  24 hours soaking
Total cooking time: 1 hour
Makes 35

500 g (1 lb) salt cod
1 large potato (200 g/6½ oz), unpeeled
2 tablespoons milk
3 tablespoons olive oil
1 small onion, finely chopped
2 cloves garlic, crushed
¼ cup (30 g/1 oz) self-raising flour
2 eggs, separated
1 tablespoon chopped fresh flat-leaf
  parsley
olive oil, extra, for deep-frying

1 Soak the cod in cold water for 24 hours,
changing the water regularly to remove
as much salt as possible. Cook the potato
in a pan of boiling water for 20 minutes, or
until soft. When cool, peel and mash with
the milk and 2 tablespoons of the olive oil.
2 Drain the cod, cut into large pieces and
place in a saucepan. Cover with water,
bring to the boil over high heat, then
reduce the heat to medium and cook for
10 minutes, or until soft and there is a froth
on the surface. Drain. When cool enough to
handle, remove the skin and any bones,
then mash well with a fork until flaky.
3 Heat the remaining oil in a small frying
pan and cook the onion over medium heat
for 5 minutes, or until softened and
starting to brown. Add the garlic and cook
for 1 minute. Remove from the heat.
4 Combine the potato, cod, onion, flour,
egg yolks and parsley in a bowl and
season. Whisk the egg whites until stiff,
then fold into the mixture. Fill a large
heavy-based saucepan one third full of
olive oil and heat to 190°C (375°F), or until
a cube of bread dropped into the oil
browns in 10 seconds. Drop heaped
tablespoons of mixture into the oil and
cook for 2 minutes, or until puffed and
golden. Drain and serve.

CURRY PUFFS

Preparation time: 20 minutes +
  30 minutes cooling + 30 minutes
  refrigeration
Total cooking time: 1 hour 25 minutes
Makes 24

1 large dried red chilli, chopped
1½ teaspoons coriander seeds
½ teaspoon fennel seeds
250 g (8 oz) potatoes, peeled
¼ cup (60 ml/2 fl oz) peanut oil
1 carrot, finely diced
¾ cup (115 g/4 oz) frozen peas, thawed
1 small onion, finely chopped
2 cloves garlic, crushed
2 tablespoons Malaysian curry powder
150 g (5 oz) lean beef mince
¼ cup (60 ml/2 fl oz) beef stock
6 sheets frozen ready-made puff pastry
2 egg yolks, lightly beaten
peanut oil, for deep-frying
raita, to serve

1 Finely grind the dried chilli, coriander
seeds and fennel seeds together, then set
aside.
2 Boil the potatoes for 15 minutes, or until
just tender but not fully cooked. Cool a
little; dice.
3 Heat a wok over high heat, add
1 tablespoon of the oil and swirl to coat.
Reduce the heat to medium and stir-fry
the carrot for 4–5 minutes, or until it
starts to soften. Add the peas and cook for
3 minutes. Transfer to a large, non-
metallic, heatproof bowl. Add 1 tablespoon
of oil to the wok and stir-fry the potato for
3–4 minutes, or until browned. Transfer to
the bowl with the peas.

4 Heat the remaining oil over high heat.
Cook the onion and garlic for 1 minute.
Stir in the ground spices and curry
powder for 30 seconds, or until fragrant.
Stir in the mince and cook until browned,
breaking up any lumps. Reduce the heat
to medium–low, pour in the stock and
simmer for 10 minutes. Transfer to the
bowl with the vegetables; stir well. Cool
for 30 minutes.
5 Meanwhile, separate the pastry sheets
with a knife and sit on a wire rack to thaw.
6 Cut out 24 pastry rounds with a 10 cm (4
inch) cutter. Place 1½–2 teaspoons of
filling on one side of a round, then fold
into a semicircle. Join the edges together,
using a little water if necessary. Seal the
edges with a fork. Repeat with the
remaining pastry rounds and filling.
Lightly brush one side of the puffs with
egg yolk, place on a tray and refrigerate
for 30 minutes.
7 Fill a wok one-third full of oil and heat
to 180°C (350°F), or until a cube of bread
dropped in the oil browns in 15 seconds.
Deep-fry the puffs four at a time for 3–5
minutes, or until browned and the filling
is cooked through. Serve with raita or
plain yoghurt.

BRUSCHETTA

CRUSTY BREAD—WHETHER IT'S AN ITALIAN LOAF, FRENCH STICK OR SOURDOUGH—LIGHTLY TOASTED AND TOPPED WITH COLOURFUL FRESH INGREDIENTS WILL SATISFY THE HUNGRIEST OF GUESTS.

SMOKED SALMON AND CAPERS

Cut 2 small French bread sticks into 1 cm (½ inch) slices and lightly grill until golden on both sides. Mix 250 g (8 oz) cream cheese with 2 tablespoons lemon juice and 15 g (½ oz) chopped chives. Spread over the toast and top with small slices of smoked salmon and a few baby capers. Garnish with sprigs of fresh dill before serving.
Makes about 24.

GRILLED PEPPERS (CAPSICUMS)

Cut 2 yellow, 2 green and 2 red peppers (capsicums) in half lengthways. Remove the seeds and membrane, place skin-side-up under a hot grill and cook until the skins have blackened. Cool in a plastic bag, then peel off the skins. Thinly slice the peppers and place in a large bowl. Add 1 small red onion, sliced into thin wedges, 1½ tablespoons olive oil, 1½ tablespoons balsamic vinegar and 2 crushed cloves of garlic. Slice 2 small sourdough bread sticks into 1 cm (½ inch) slices. Lightly grill until golden on both sides. Top with the pepper mixture.
Makes about 24.

ROCKET AND FETA

Cut a large French bread stick or an Italian loaf into 1 cm (½ inch) slices, brush with olive oil and grill until golden on both sides. Arrange rocket leaves over each piece, using about 90 g (3 oz) altogether. Toss 200 g (6½ oz) crumbled feta with 2 teaspoons finely grated orange rind and 2 tablespoons olive oil. Spoon 2 teaspoons of the mixture over the rocket on each bruschetta. Grill 6 slices prosciutto until crispy, then crumble over the bruschetta.
Makes about 30.

CAPRESSE

Mix 150 g (5 oz) finely diced bocconcini, with 3 tablespoons shredded fresh basil and 3 tablespoons warm extra virgin olive oil in a glass bowl. Season with salt and pepper, to taste. Cover and leave in a warm place for 1 hour to allow the flavours to develop. Cut a large French bread stick or an Italian loaf into 1 cm (½ inch) slices, brush with olive oil and grill until golden on both sides. Spread the bocconcini mixture over the toast. Makes about 30.

MUSHROOM AND PARSLEY

Cut a large French bread stick or Italian loaf into 1 cm (½ inch) slices, brush with olive oil and grill until golden on both sides. Heat 1 tablespoon of olive oil in a small frying pan, and fry 200 g (6½ oz) quartered small button mushrooms until just tender. Stir in 1 tablespoon lemon juice, 50 g (1¾ oz) crumbled goat's cheese, a tablespoon of chopped fresh flat-leaf parsley and season, to taste. Spread over the toast. Makes about 30.

TOMATO AND BASIL

Cut a large French bread stick or Italian loaf into 1 cm (½ inch) slices, brush with olive oil and grill until golden on both sides. Finely chop 4 ripe tomatoes and mix with ½ cup (30 g/1 oz) finely shredded fresh basil and 2 tablespoons extra virgin olive oil. Spread over the toast. Makes about 30.

PASTRAMI AND HERBS

Cut a large French bread stick or Italian loaf into 1 cm (½ inch) slices, brush with olive oil and grill until golden on both sides. Combine 200 ml (6½ fl oz) of crème fraîche with 1 teaspoon each of chopped fresh parsley, chives and basil. Spread 1 teaspoon over each slice of toast. Halve 30 slices of pastrami, fold in half again and place 2 pieces over the crème fraîche. Mix 2 chopped tomatoes with ½ finely chopped red onion and 2 teaspoons each of balsamic vinegar and olive oil. Spoon over the top and garnish with small fresh basil leaves. Makes about 30.

FROM LEFT: Smoked salmon and capers; Grilled peppers; Rocket and feta; Capresse; Mushroom and parsley; Tomato and basil; Pastrami and herbs

INARI SUSHI

Preparation time: 10 minutes +
   1 hour draining + cooling
Total cooking time: 15 minutes
Makes 6

1 cup (220 g/7 oz) Japanese short-grain
   rice
2 tablespoons white sesame seeds
2 tablespoons rice vinegar
1 tablespoon caster (superfine) sugar
1 teaspoon mirin
6 inari pouches

1 Wash the rice under cold running water
until the water runs clear, then drain
thoroughly. Leave the rice in the strainer
to drain for an hour. Put the rice in a
saucepan with 2 cups (500 ml/16 fl oz)
water and bring to the boil. Reduce the
heat and simmer for about 5 minutes, or
until all the water has been absorbed.
Reduce the heat to very low, cover and
cook for another 4–5 minutes. Remove
the pan from the heat and leave, covered,
for about 10 minutes.
2 Toast the sesame seeds in a dry frying
pan over medium heat for 3–4 minutes,
shaking the pan gently, until the seeds
are golden brown—watch them carefully
so they don't brown too quickly. Remove
the seeds from the pan at once to prevent
them burning.
3 To make the sushi dressing, combine
the rice vinegar, sugar, mirin and 1
teaspoon salt in a small bowl.
4 Spread the rice over the base of a non-
metallic dish or bowl, pour the sushi
dressing over the top and use a rice
paddle or spatula to mix the dressing
through the rice, separating the grains as
you do so. Fan the rice until it cools to
room temperature.
5 Gently separate the inari pockets and
open them up. Form the rice into balls and
place a ball of rice inside each pocket.
Sprinkle the rice with the toasted sesame
seeds and press the inari closed with your
fingers. Serve on a plate, cut-side down.

MUSHROOMS EN CROUTE

Preparation time: 40 minutes
Total cooking time: 20 minutes
Makes 48

8 slices white bread, crust removed
80 g (2¾ oz) butter, melted
1 tablespoon olive oil
1 clove garlic, crushed
½ small onion, finely chopped
375 g (12 oz) small button mushrooms,
   finely sliced
1 tablespoon dry sherry
⅓ cup (80 g/2¾ oz) sour cream
2 teaspoons cornflour
1 tablespoon finely chopped fresh parsley
1 teaspoon finely chopped fresh thyme
30 g (1 oz) Parmesan, grated

1 Preheat the oven to moderate 180°C
(350°F/Gas 4). Brush both sides of the
bread with the butter. Cut each slice in
half vertically, then each half into three
horizontally. Bake on a baking tray for
5–10 minutes, or until golden and crisp.
2 Heat the oil in a large frying pan, add
the garlic and onion and cook, stirring,
over low heat until the onion is soft. Add
the mushrooms and cook over medium
heat for 5 minutes, or until tender.
Season with salt and pepper.
3 Pour the sherry into the pan. Blend the
sour cream and cornflour, add to the
mushrooms and stir until the mixture
boils and thickens. Remove from the heat
and stir in the herbs. Allow to cool.
4 Spread the mushroom mixture onto
each croûte and sprinkle with the
Parmesan. Place on a baking tray and
bake for 5 minutes, or until heated
through. Serve decorated with small
sprigs of fresh herbs, if desired.

IN ADVANCE: Bake the bread up to 4 days
in advance and store in an airtight
container. Make the topping and
assemble just prior to serving.

PIZZETTA SQUARES

Preparation time: 20 minutes
Total cooking time: 40 minutes
Makes about 50

2 tablespoons oil
4 onions, finely sliced
2 sheets frozen puff pastry, thawed
⅓ cup (90 g/3 oz) sun-dried tomato pesto
10 anchovies, finely chopped
15 g (½ oz) fresh basil leaves, finely
   shredded

1 Preheat the oven to moderately hot
200°C (400°F/Gas 6). Heat the oil in a
large pan and cook the onion over
medium heat for 20 minutes, or until soft
and golden. Cool.
2 Lay each sheet of pastry on a lightly
greased oven tray, then spread the
tomato pesto evenly over the pastry.
Scatter the onion over the top.
3 Sprinkle the anchovies and basil over
the top and bake for 20 minutes, or until
the squares are puffed and golden. Cool,
then cut into squares. Serve warm or at
room temperature.

IN ADVANCE: Cook the onions 2 days
ahead and refrigerate. Bake no earlier
than 2 hours ahead.

CORNED BEEF, PARSNIP AND MINT PATTIES

Preparation time: 20 minutes
Total cooking time: 25 minutes
Makes 24

2 parsnips, chopped
1 cup (100 g/3½ oz) dry breadcrumbs
200 g (6½ oz) piece cooked corned beef, finely chopped
1 egg yolk
¼ small onion, finely chopped
20 g (¾ oz) fresh mint leaves, finely chopped
1 tablespoon lemon juice
3 teaspoons wholegrain mustard
2 tablespoons plain flour
1 egg
1 tablespoon milk
¼ cup (60 ml/2 fl oz) olive oil
½ cup (140 g/4½ oz) spicy tomato chutney
24 small fresh mint leaves, to garnish

1 Cook the parsnip in a large pan of boiling water for 10 minutes, or until tender. Drain and mash until smooth. Set aside to cool.
2 Mix the parsnip with ⅓ cup 35 g (1¼ oz) of the breadcrumbs, the corned beef, egg yolk, onion, mint, lemon juice, mustard and salt and freshly ground black pepper.
3 Shape into 24 patties, pressing firmly together. Dust with flour and shake off any excess. Dip into the combined egg and milk, then coat in the remaining breadcrumbs.
4 Heat the oil in a large frying pan over medium-low heat and cook the patties in batches for 2–3 minutes each side, or until golden brown and heated through. Drain on crumpled paper towels. Spoon 1 teaspoon of tomato chutney onto each patty and top with a mint leaf. Serve immediately.

IN ADVANCE: The patties can be prepared a day ahead. Keep covered in the refrigerator until ready to cook.

FRITTO MISTO DI MARE

Preparation time: 30 minutes
Total cooking time: 12 minutes
Makes about 50 pieces

Tartare sauce
1½ cups (375 ml/12 fl oz) mayonnaise
1 bottled gherkin, chopped
1 teaspoon bottled capers, drained and finely chopped
1 tablespoon chopped fresh chives
1 tablespoon chopped fresh parsley
¼ teaspoon Dijon mustard
¼ small onion, finely grated

Batter
1 cup (125 g/4 oz) self-raising flour
¼ cup (30 g/1 oz) cornflour
1 tablespoon oil

500 g (1 lb) fish fillets, bones removed
12 sardines
8 raw medium king prawns, peeled
8 scallops, cleaned and deveined
1 calamari hood, cut into rings
flour, for coating
oil, for deep-frying
lemon wedges, for serving

1 For the tartare sauce, combine all the ingredients in a small bowl and mix well.
2 To make the batter, sift the flour and cornflour and a little salt and pepper into a large bowl. Make a well in the centre. Combine the oil and 1 cup (250 ml/8 fl oz) water and gradually whisk into the flour until a smooth batter is formed.

3 Cut the fish fillets into 5 cm (2 inch) strips. To prepare the fresh sardines, remove the heads and split them open down the belly, then clean with salted water. Ease the backbone out with your fingers and cut the backbone at the tail end with sharp scissors.
4 Dry the prepared seafood on paper towels, then coat in the flour and shake off the excess.
5 Heat the oil in a large deep pan to 180°C (350°F). The oil is ready when a cube of bread dropped into the oil turns golden brown in 15 seconds. Coat a few pieces of seafood at a time with batter and gently lower into the hot oil with tongs or a slotted spoon. Cook for 2–3 minutes, or until crisp and golden brown. Drain on crumpled paper towels. Keep warm while cooking the remaining seafood. Serve with a bowl of tartare sauce and lemon wedges.

IN ADVANCE: The seafood for this dish can be prepared several hours ahead and kept covered in the refrigerator.

MINI LENTIL BURGERS WITH TOMATO RELISH

Preparation time: 40 minutes
Total cooking time: 55 minutes
Makes 32

1 cup (185 g/6 oz) brown lentils
1 bay leaf
1 onion, roughly chopped
1 clove garlic, crushed
1 small leek, finely sliced
1 small carrot, finely grated
1 cup (80 g/2¾ oz) fresh breadcrumbs
2 egg yolks
2 tablespoons chopped fresh coriander
2 tablespoons oil
8 slices bread, cut into 4 cm (1½ inch) squares
ready-made tomato relish, for serving

1 Place the lentils and bay leaf in a pan, cover with plenty of water, bring to the boil and simmer for 20–30 minutes, or until tender; drain well and discard the bay leaf.
2 Combine half the cooked lentils with the onion and garlic in a food processor until the mixture forms a smooth paste. Transfer to a bowl and mix with the remaining lentils, leek, carrot, breadcrumbs, egg yolks and coriander; season with salt and freshly ground black pepper. Form level tablespoons of the mixture into mini burgers.
3 Heat some of the oil in a non-stick frying pan and fry the mini burgers in batches until browned on both sides, adding more oil as necessary. Drain on paper towels and serve warm, on the bread squares (or toast), with a dollop of tomato relish on top. Garnish with fresh herbs.

PRAWN AND SCALLOP VOL-AU-VENTS

Preparation time: 25 minutes
Total cooking time: 20 minutes
Makes 36

1 cup (250 ml/8 fl oz) fish stock
1 cup (250 ml/8 fl oz) white wine
250 g (8 oz) scallops
250 g (8 oz) raw prawns, peeled
60 g (2 oz) butter
4 spring onions, finely chopped
1 bacon rasher, finely chopped
¼ cup (30 g/1 oz) plain flour
½ cup (125 ml/4 fl oz) cream
1 teaspoon lemon juice
½ cup (30 g/1 oz) finely chopped fresh parsley
36 small ready-made vol-au-vent cases

1 Heat the stock and wine in a pan until simmering. Add the scallops and prawns and cook gently for 2–3 minutes. Remove with a slotted spoon, cool and chop. Reserve 1 cup (250 ml/8 fl oz) of the cooking liquid. Refrigerate the seafood while making the sauce. Preheat the oven to warm 160°C (315°F/Gas 2–3).
2 Melt the butter in a pan, add the onion and bacon and cook over medium heat for about 3 minutes, until softened but not browned. Stir in the flour and cook for 2 minutes. Remove from the heat and gradually stir in the reserved liquid. Return to the heat and stir until the sauce boils and thickens. Stir in the cream, juice and parsley, reserving a little parsley. Season.
3 Heat the vol-au-vent cases in the oven for 5 minutes. Reheat the sauce, stir in the seafood and warm through. Divide among the cases, garnish with parsley and serve.

ZUCCHINI (COURGETTE) BOATS

Preparation time: 20 minutes
Total cooking time: 10 minutes
Makes 30

5 large zucchini (courgettes)
1 large tomato, finely chopped
2 spring onions, finely chopped
1 tablespoon chopped fresh parsley
2 slices salami, finely chopped
½ cup (60 g/2 oz) grated Cheddar

1 Cut each zucchini into three equal pieces, about 4 cm (1½ inches) long. Cut each piece in half lengthways.
2 Using a teaspoon, scoop a small hollow from each piece. Add the zucchini to a pan of simmering water for about 3 minutes, or until tender; drain. Refresh under cold water, then pat dry with paper towels.
3 Combine the tomato, onion, parsley, salami and Cheddar in a small bowl. Spoon the filling into the zucchini boats. Cook under a preheated grill until the Cheddar has melted and the boats are warmed through. Serve immediately.

PRAWN TOASTS

Preparation time: 50 minutes
Total cooking time: 8 minutes
Makes 25

Mayonnaise
½ cup (125 g/4 oz) whole-egg mayonnaise
1 teaspoon wasabi paste
2 teaspoons Japanese soy sauce

25 small raw prawns
1 loaf stale unsliced white bread
3 sheets nori (dried seaweed)
½ cup (80 g/2¾ oz) sesame seeds
3 eggs, lightly beaten
oil, for deep-frying

1 Mix the mayonnaise, wasabi paste and soy in a small bowl, then cover and refrigerate until ready to use.
2 Peel the prawns leaving the tails intact. Gently pull out the dark vein from each prawn back starting at the head end.
3 Cut the crust off the bread and cut the bread into twenty-five 3 cm (1¼ inch) cubes. With a sharp knife, make an incision in the top of the bread three-quarters of the way through. Gently ease a prawn into the cut in each bread cube, leaving the tail sticking out. Cut 25 strips from the nori measuring 1 cm (½ inch) x 15 cm (6 inch). Wrap a strip around the outside of each bread cube and secure with a toothpick.
4 Measure the sesame seeds into a bowl. Put the eggs in a small bowl and dip the bread in, draining off the excess. Coat the bread in the sesame seeds.
5 Fill a wok or a deep heavy-based saucepan one third full of oil and heat until a cube of bread browns in 15 seconds. Cook the prepared cubes in batches for 1–2 minutes, or until the bread is golden and the prawns cooked through. Drain on crumpled paper towels, remove the toothpicks and season with salt. Serve topped with a teaspoon of the mayonnaise.

LAMB ON POLENTA

Preparation time: 15 minutes
Total cooking time: 15 minutes
Makes 24

3 cups (750 ml/24 fl oz) chicken stock
¾ cup (110 g/3½ oz) instant polenta
2 tablespoons grated Parmesan
2 lamb fillets (150 g/5 oz)
oil, for frying
¼ small cucumber, thinly sliced
3 tablespoons natural yoghurt

1 Lightly grease a 20 x 30 cm (8 x 12 inch) shallow tray. Pour the stock into a saucepan and bring to the boil. Add the polenta and stir over medium heat for 5 minutes, or until thick. Remove from the heat. Stir in the Parmesan and salt and pepper, to taste. Spread into the tray; cool.
2 When cool, cut the polenta into rounds with a 4 cm (1½ inch) cutter. Trim the lamb of any excess fat and sinew.
3 Heat a little oil in a frying pan, add the lamb and cook until brown all over and cooked as desired, about 3 minutes each side for medium. Remove the lamb fillets from the pan and wipe the pan clean. Add more oil to the pan and fry the polenta rounds until lightly browned on both sides. Remove from the pan.
4 Cut the cucumber slices into quarters. Thinly slice the lamb and place on top of the polenta. Top with yoghurt and a piece of cucumber.

NOTE: For extra flavour, the lamb can be rolled in cracked black peppercorns prior to cooking.

RICE NOODLE ROLLS FILLED WITH PRAWNS

Preparation time: 20 minutes
Total cooking time: 20 minutes
Makes 8

500 g (1 lb) fresh rice noodle rolls, at room temperature
1 teaspoon roasted sesame oil
1 tablespoon peanut oil
1 tablespoon grated ginger
3 spring onions (scallions), thinly sliced
200 g (6½ oz) water chestnuts, chopped
500 g (1 lb) raw prawns (shrimp), peeled, deveined and chopped
1 tablespoon fish sauce
1 tablespoon soft brown sugar
1 tablespoon snipped garlic chives
2 tablespoons vegetable oil
⅓ cup (80 ml/2¾ fl oz) light soy sauce
1 teaspoon roasted sesame oil, extra
½ teaspoon white sugar
extra garlic chives, to garnish

1 Open out the rice noodle sheets and cut eight 15 cm (6 inch) squares. Heat the sesame and peanut oils in a wok, add the ginger and spring onions and cook over medium heat for 2 minutes. Add the water chestnuts and prawns and cook, stirring, for 5 minutes, or until the prawns turn pink. Stir in the fish sauce, sugar and chives. Remove from the wok and allow to cool slightly.
2 Spoon the mixture down the centre of each rice noodle sheet and roll over to enclose the filling.
3 Heat the vegetable oil in a clean, non-stick frying pan. Cook the noodle rolls in batches over medium heat until golden on both sides. Serve drizzled with the combined soy sauce, sugar, extra sesame oil and garnish with the extra garlic chives.

SEAFOOD BITES

IF YOU ARE MAKING A
SELECTION OF THESE DELICIOUS
PIECES AS PART OF A BUFFET,
THE QUANTITIES WE HAVE GIVEN
WILL BE ENOUGH TO SERVE
ABOUT 4 TO 6 PEOPLE.

SEARED SALMON

Remove the skin and bones from 600 g
(1¼ lb) salmon fillet, cut into 3 cm (1¼
inch) cubes and toss the cubes in a
mixture of 1 tablespoon cracked black
pepper and 1 teaspoon sea salt. Heat 2
tablespoons olive oil in a large frying pan
and brown the salmon over high heat.
Insert a toothpick in each piece and serve
with cocktail sauce.

TEMPURA OCTOPUS

Clean 500 g (1 lb) baby octopus. First,
remove the heads from the tentacles with
a sharp knife. Push out the beaks from
the centre of the tentacles, then cut the
tentacles into sets of two or three.
Measure 1 cup (125 g/4 oz) tempura flour
into a bowl, make a well in the centre and
quickly stir in ¾ cup (185 ml/6 fl oz) iced
water, until just combined—the mixture
should still be lumpy. Fill a large
saucepan one third full of oil and heat to
180°C (350°F), or until a cube of bread
dropped in the oil browns in 15 seconds.
Dip the octopus in the batter and deep-fry
until lightly golden and crisp. Drain well
on crumpled paper towels. Serve
immediately. Delicious with ginger and
almond sauce.

MUSSELS WITH TOMATO SALSA

Scrub 16–18 mussels with a stiff brush and pull out the hairy beards. Discard any broken mussels, or open ones that don't close when tapped on the bench. Rinse well. Place ¼ cup (60 ml/2 fl oz) each of water and white wine in saucepan and bring to the boil. Add the mussels, cover and cook over high heat for 3–5 minutes, until the mussels are open. Remove from the pan and discard any unopened mussels. Remove and discard one half of each mussel shell and loosen the mussels from the shells with a sharp knife. Combine ¼ small finely diced red onion in a bowl with 1 finely diced small ripe tomato, 1 finely chopped garlic clove, 2 teaspoons balsamic vinegar and 1 tablespoon each of extra virgin olive oil and chopped fresh basil. Season, to taste, and spoon over the mussels.

WRAPPED PRAWNS WITH JAZZY TARTARE

Peel 500 g (1 lb) cooked medium prawns, leaving the tails intact. Gently pull out the dark vein from each prawn back, starting at the head end. Place 16 long garlic chives in a small pan of boiling water until just wilted. Drain, then refresh in cold water. Wrap one of the chives around each prawn, like a candy cane. Refrigerate while preparing the jazzy tartare sauce. Combine ½ cup (125 g/4 oz) whole-egg mayonnaise in a bowl with 2 small finely chopped pickled gherkins, 1 finely chopped hard-boiled egg, 1 tablespoon chopped fresh parsley, 1 finely chopped spring onion, 1 tablespoon drained bottled capers and 3 teaspoons lemon juice, or to taste. Season with salt and freshly ground black pepper, to taste.

SEARED SCALLOPS WITH LIME

Remove 16 scallops from their shells and toss in a mixture of 1 tablespoon oil, ¼–½ teaspoon sesame oil, some salt and pepper and 1 tablespoon chopped fresh chives. Rinse and dry the shells. Place the scallops on a hot frying pan for 30 seconds each side, or until just cooked through, being careful not to overcook. Return the scallops to the shells and squeeze lime juice over the top. Sprinkle with chopped fresh chives and some toasted sesame seeds.

FROM LEFT: Seared salmon; Tempura octopus (top of tray); Mussels with tomato salsa; Wrapped prawns with jazzy tartare; Seared scallops with lime. Sauces in bowls (from left): Jazzy tartare; Cocktail sauce; Ginger and almond sauce

SPICY TORTILLA TRIANGLES

Preparation time: 20 minutes
Total cooking time: 5 minutes
Makes 24

2 x 23 cm (9 inch) round flour tortillas
¼ cup (60 ml/2 fl oz) oil

Topping
1 onion, finely chopped
2 cloves garlic, crushed
2 small red chillies, finely chopped
425 g (14 oz) can pinto beans, drained, mashed roughly
1 cup (250 ml/8 fl oz) thick and chunky bottled salsa
2 tablespoons chopped fresh coriander leaves
90 g (3 oz) Cheddar, grated

1 Cut the tortillas into quarters and cut each quarter into three triangles.
2 Heat 2 tablespoons of the oil in a frying pan. Add a few triangles to the pan, cook for 30 seconds on each side, or until crisp and golden brown. Remove from the pan and drain on paper towels. Repeat with the remaining triangles, adding extra oil as necessary.
3 For the topping, heat 1 tablespoon of oil in a medium pan, add the onion, garlic and chilli and stir over medium heat for 3 minutes, or until the onion is tender. Stir in the pinto beans, salsa and fresh coriander. Remove from the heat and leave to cool.
4 Spread the topping on the triangles, leaving a border around the edges, and sprinkle with Cheddar. Grill for 1 minute, or until the cheese has melted.

NOTES: Tortilla triangles can be cooked in the oven instead of fried and grilled. Place the triangles on a baking tray in a preheated moderate 180°C (350°F/Gas 4) oven for 5 minutes or until crisp. Add the topping and cook for another 3–5 minutes, or until the cheese has melted.

HERBED MUSSEL TARTS

Preparation time: 30 minutes
Total cooking time: 15 minutes
Makes 24

Filling
2 kg (4 lb) black mussels
90 g (3 oz) butter, softened
2 cloves garlic, crushed
2 tablespoons chopped fresh chives
2 tablespoons chopped fresh flat-leaf parsley

24 slices white bread
60 g (2 oz) butter, melted

1 Scrub the mussels with a stiff brush and pull out the hairy beards. Discard any broken mussels, or open ones that don't close when tapped. Rinse well. Bring 2 cups (500 ml/16 fl oz) water to the boil in a large pan, then add half the mussels. Cover and cook for 3–5 minutes, until just opened. Discard any unopened mussels. Repeat with the remaining mussels. Cover the mussels immediately with cold water and remove the flesh from the shells (if the mussels are very large, cut in half). Pat dry with paper towels. Beat the butter until smooth. Add the garlic, chives and parsley and season, to taste.
2 Preheat the oven to moderate 180°C (350°F/Gas 4). Flatten the bread slices with a rolling pin and, using an 8 cm (3 inch) biscuit cutter, cut a circle from each slice. Brush both sides of each circle with the melted butter, then press into two 12-hole round-based patty tins. Bake for 8 minutes, or until crisp and lightly golden.
3 Divide the mussels among the hot bread cases and carefully spread herb butter over the top. Bake for 5 minutes, or until the mussels are heated through. Serve at once.

MINI MEAT PIES

Preparation time: 20 minutes
Total cooking time: 25 minutes
Makes 24

6 sheets ready-rolled shortcrust pastry
2 small tomatoes, sliced
½ teaspoon dried oregano leaves

Filling
1 tablespoon oil
1 onion, chopped
2 cloves garlic, crushed
500 g (1 lb) beef mince
2 tablespoons plain flour
1½ cups (375 ml/12 fl oz) beef stock
⅓ cup (80 ml/2¾ fl oz) tomato sauce
2 teaspoons Worcestershire sauce
½ teaspoon dried mixed herbs

1 Preheat the oven to moderately hot 200°C (400°F/Gas 6). Cut the pastry into 48 circles (if making traditional pies, only 24 if making uncovered pies) using a 7 cm (2¾ inch) round cutter. Press 24 circles into two lightly greased 12-hole patty tins.
2 To make the filling, heat the oil in a heavy-based pan, add the onion and garlic and cook over medium heat for 2 minutes, or until the onion is soft. Add the mince and stir over high heat for 3 minutes, or until well browned and all the liquid has evaporated. Use a fork to break up any lumps of mince.
3 Add the flour, stir until combined, then cook over medium heat for 1 minute. Add the stock, sauces and herbs and stir over the heat until boiling. Reduce the heat to low and simmer for 5 minutes, or until the mixture has reduced and thickened; stir occasionally. Allow to cool.
4 Divide the filling among the pastry circles. Top each with two half slices of tomato and sprinkle with oregano. Bake for 25 minutes, or until the pastry is golden brown and crisp. For traditional pies, place the remaining pastry rounds over the tomato and oregano topping and seal the edges with beaten egg before baking. Serve hot.

TUNA TARTLETS WITH APPLE MOUSSELINE MAYONNAISE

Preparation time: 1 hour + curing + freezing
Total cooking time: 10–15 minutes
Makes about 48

375 g (12 oz) tuna, in one piece, skinned
24 hard-boiled quail eggs, halved lengthways, to garnish
45 g (1½ oz) fresh coriander leaves, to garnish

Cure
500 g (1 lb) rock salt
1½ cups (375 g/12 oz) sugar
½ teaspoon ground black peppercorns
1 teaspoon ground ginger

Filo tartlets
250 g (8 oz) filo pastry
250 g (8 oz) unsalted butter, melted

Apple mousseline mayonnaise
2 tablespoons smooth apple sauce
1 cup (250 ml/8 fl oz) whole egg mayonnaise
2 tablespoons cream, whipped

1 Choose a large flat glass dish for curing. Cut the tuna into 3 cm (1¼ inch) strips the length of the tuna, then cut the lengths to fit the dish.
2 Mix the cure ingredients and cover the base of the dish with a layer of the cure, then a layer of tuna. Continue layering, finishing with a layer of cure. Weigh down and refrigerate for 4 hours.
3 Remove the tuna from the cure. Wash the tuna under cold running water, then dry thoroughly. If not using right away, wrap in a lightly oiled cloth to prevent drying out. Refrigerate before slicing.

4 Preheat the oven to moderately hot 190°C (375°F/Gas 5). For the filo cups, layer 6 sheets of filo on top of one another, brushing each with butter. Keep the remainder under a damp cloth.
5 Cut 8 cm (3 inch) rounds of the layered filo with a cutter. Cut through with scissors if necessary. Line two 12-hole round-based patty tins with the rounds, butter-side-down. Press into the holes and prick with a fork. Arrange on baking trays and freeze for at least 10 minutes. (This can be done a day ahead.) While chilling, prepare the remaining filo rounds, but keep covered to prevent them drying out.
6 Bake the pastry cases for 4–5 minutes. Remove from the tins and cool on a wire rack. Repeat with the remaining filo rounds.
7 For the apple mousseline mayonnaise, fold the apple sauce into the mayonnaise, then fold in the cream. Taste and add salt and pepper if necessary.
8 Do not assemble until just before serving. Slice the tuna across the grain in paper-thin slices with a sharp knife. Spoon a teaspoonful of mayonnaise into each case. Top with a slice of tuna, half a quail egg and a coriander leaf. Serve at once.

NOTE: Cook quail eggs in boiling water for 5 minutes, then place in cold water to cool.

TORTILLA FLUTES

Preparation time: 25 minutes
Total cooking time: 15 minutes
Makes 24

¼ cup (60 ml/2 fl oz) olive oil
2 small onions, finely chopped
2 garlic cloves, crushed
½ teaspoon chilli powder
2 teaspoons ground cumin
1 kg (2 lb) cooked chicken, finely chopped
2 tablespoons finely chopped fresh coriander
24 soft flour or corn tortillas
oil, for shallow-frying
red or green chilli sauce, for serving
1 avocado, sliced, for serving

1 Heat the olive oil in a frying pan and fry the onion and garlic over medium heat for 2–3 minutes, or until the onion is just tender but not soft. Add the chilli powder and cumin and stir for 1 minute.
2 Add the chicken and mix well. Cook over medium heat until just heated through. Stir in the coriander and remove from the heat.
3 Soften the tortillas, one at a time, by heating in a dry heavy-based frying pan over high heat for about 30 seconds each side.
4 Lay a tortilla flat on a work surface and place a large spoonful of chicken mixture along the centre. Carefully roll up to form a flute.
5 Pour oil in a deep frying pan to 5 cm (2 inches) deep and heat the oil to 180°C (350°F). The oil is ready when a cube of bread dropped into the oil turns golden brown in 15 seconds. Holding the flute together with tongs (or fasten with toothpicks), cook one at a time until slightly crisp. Drain on crumpled paper towels. Serve with chilli sauce and avocado slices.

CRISPY CHICKEN AND FISH WRAPS WITH SWEET AND SOUR SAUCE

Preparation time: 30 minutes
Total cooking time: 4 minutes per batch
Makes 30

Sweet and sour sauce
½ cup (125 g/4 oz) sugar
½ cup (125 ml/4 fl oz) white vinegar
1 tablespoon tomato sauce
1 tablespoon cornflour

30 won ton wrappers
oil, for deep-frying

Filling
100 g (3½ oz) chicken, finely chopped
100 g (3½ oz) fish fillets, finely chopped
½ stalk celery, finely chopped
1 small spring onion, finely chopped
2 teaspoons light soy sauce

1 To make the sauce, combine the sugar, vinegar and tomato sauce with ¾ cup (185 ml/6 fl oz) water in a small saucepan. Blend the cornflour with 1 tablespoon of water in a small bowl. Add to the saucepan and stir over low heat until the mixture boils and thickens and the sugar has dissolved.
2 Combine the filling ingredients with ¼ teaspoon salt. Place 1 teaspoon of mixture onto each won ton wrapper. Brush the edges lightly with water. Fold to form a triangle. Dab water onto the left front corner of the triangle. Fold the two bottom corners across, one on top of the other, and press together lightly with your finger.
3 Fill a deep heavy-based pan one third full of oil. Heat the oil to 180°C (350°F). The oil is hot enough when a cube of bread dropped into the oil turns golden brown in 15 seconds. Deep-fry in batches until crisp and golden brown. Shake off the excess oil and drain on crumpled paper towel. Serve with the sauce.

TURKEY FILO PARCELS

Preparation time: 35 minutes
Total cooking time: 40 minutes
Makes 24

20 g (¾ oz) butter
200 g (6½ oz) button mushrooms, sliced
4 rashers bacon, diced
350 g (11 oz) cooked turkey, chopped
150 g (5 oz) ricotta
2 spring onions, sliced
3 tablespoons shredded fresh basil
24 sheets filo pastry
butter, melted, extra, for brushing
sesame seeds, for sprinkling

1 Melt the butter in a large saucepan and add the mushrooms and bacon. Cook over high heat for 5 minutes, or until the mushrooms are soft and there is no liquid left. Combine the turkey, ricotta, spring onion and basil in a bowl, add the mushroom mixture, then season, to taste.
2 Preheat the oven to moderate 180°C (350°F/Gas 4). Cover the pastry with a damp tea towel to prevent drying out. Working with 3 sheets at a time, brush each layer with melted butter. Cut into 3 strips. Place 1 tablespoon of filling at the end of each strip and fold the pastry over to form a triangle. Fold until you reach the end of the pastry. Repeat with the remaining pastry and filling. Place on a greased baking tray, brush with butter and sprinkle with sesame seeds. Bake for 30–35 minutes, or until golden.

SMOKED SALMON PIKELETS

Preparation time: 15 minutes + standing
Total cooking time: 10–15 minutes
Makes about 50

Pikelets
1 cup (125 g/4 oz) self-raising flour
2 eggs, lightly beaten
½ cup (125 ml/4 fl oz) milk
1 tablespoon sour cream

Topping
½ cup (125 g/4 oz) sour cream
2 tablespoons mayonnaise
2 teaspoons lemon juice
1 tablespoon finely chopped fresh chives
1 tablespoon finely chopped fresh mint
125 g (4 oz) sliced smoked salmon
strips of lemon peel, to decorate

1 Sift the flour into a bowl and make a well in the centre. Mix the beaten egg, milk and sour cream and pour into the well. Stir into the flour until the batter is smooth and free of lumps. Set aside for 10 minutes.
2 Heat a large frying pan, brush with oil or melted butter, then drop teaspoons of mixture into the pan. When bubbles appear on the surface, turn the pikelets over and cook the other side. Remove and set aside. Repeat until all the batter has been used.
3 For the topping, stir the sour cream, mayonnaise, lemon juice, chives and mint together until well combined. Spoon a small amount onto each pikelet. Top with a piece of smoked salmon and decorate with strips of lemon peel.

IN ADVANCE: The pikelets can be made a day ahead, or frozen in single layers for up to a month. The sour cream mixture for the topping can be prepared a day ahead. You can assemble the pikelets up to an hour before you are going to serve them.

ZUCCHINI (COURGETTE) PATTIES

Preparation time: 20 minutes
Total cooking time: 15 minutes
Makes 16

300 g (10 oz) zucchini (courgettes), grated
1 small onion, finely chopped
¼ cup (30 g/1 oz) self-raising flour
⅓ cup (35 g/1¼ oz) grated kefalotyri or Parmesan
1 tablespoon chopped fresh mint
2 teaspoons chopped fresh flat-leaf parsley
pinch of ground nutmeg
¼ cup (25 g/¾ oz) dry breadcrumbs
1 egg, lightly beaten
olive oil, for shallow-frying

1 Put the zucchini and onion in the centre of a clean tea towel, gather the corners together and twist as tightly as possible to remove all the juices. Combine the zucchini, onion, flour, cheese, mint, parsley, nutmeg, breadcrumbs and egg in a large bowl. Season well with salt and cracked black pepper, then mix with your hands to a stiff mixture that clumps together.
2 Heat the oil in a large frying pan over medium heat. When hot, drop level tablespoons of mixture into the pan and shallow-fry for 2–3 minutes, or until well browned all over. Drain well on crumpled paper towels and serve hot, with lemon wedges.

SUSHI CREPES

Preparation time: 1 hour + 1 hour draining
Total cooking time: 30 minutes
Makes about 40

4 eggs

Sushi
1 cup (220 g/7 oz) Japanese short-grain rice
2 tablespoons rice vinegar
1 tablespoon sugar
1 tablespoon mirin
a little wasabi paste
125 g (4 oz) sashimi grade tuna, cut into thin strips
1 small cucumber, peeled and cut into julienne strips
½ avocado, cut into julienne strips
3 tablespoons pickled ginger, cut into thin strips
Shoyu (Japanese soy sauce), for dipping

1 To make the crepes, gently whisk the eggs with 2 tablespoons cold water and a pinch of salt in a bowl until combined. Heat and lightly oil a small crepe pan or heavy-based frying pan, and pour enough of the egg mixture into the pan to lightly cover the base. Cook over low heat for 1 minute, being careful not to allow the crepe to brown. Turn the crepe over and cook for 1 minute. Transfer to a plate and repeat with the remaining mixture.
2 To make the sushi, wash the rice under cold running water until the water runs clear, then drain. Leave the rice in the strainer to drain thoroughly for 1 hour. Put the rice in a saucepan with 2 cups (500 ml/16 fl oz) water, bring to the boil, then reduce the heat and simmer for 5 minutes, or until small tunnels begin to appear in the rice. If using gas, cover and turn the heat to very low, and continue cooking for 7 minutes, or until all the liquid is absorbed. If using an electric stove-top, remove the pan from the heat, cover and leave the rice to steam for 10–12 minutes.

3 To make the sushi dressing, combine the rice vinegar, sugar, mirin and 1 teaspoon salt in a jug and stir until the sugar dissolves.
4 Spread the rice over the base of a non-metallic dish or bowl, pour the sushi dressing over the top and use a rice paddle or spatula to mix the dressing through the rice. Fan the rice until it cools to room temperature.
5 Place one egg crepe on a sushi mat. Spread 4 tablespoons of the sushi rice over a third of the crepe, using a spatula or the back of a spoon.
6 Spread a tiny amount of wasabi along the centre of the rice. Place some tuna, cucumber, avocado and ginger over the wasabi.
7 Using the sushi mat to help you, fold the crepe over to enclose the filling and roll up firmly in the mat. Trim the ends with a sharp knife and cut the crepe roll into 2 cm (¾ inch) rounds with a sharp knife. Serve with Shoyu for dipping.

NOTE: The crepes can be made ahead and stored in an airtight container in the refrigerator. Do not slice until serving or they may dry out.

CHICKEN TAMALES

Preparation time: 45 minutes
Total cooking time: 1 hour 15 minutes
Makes 12

Dough
100 g (3½ oz) butter, softened
1 clove garlic, crushed
1 teaspoon ground cumin
1½ cups (210 g/7 oz) masa harina
⅓ cup (80 ml/2¾ fl oz) cream
⅓ cup (80 ml/2¾ fl oz) chicken stock

Filling
1 corn cob
2 tablespoons oil
150 g (5 oz) chicken breast fillets
2 cloves garlic, crushed
1 red chilli, seeded and chopped
1 red onion, chopped
1 red pepper (capsicum), chopped
2 tomatoes, peeled and chopped

1 To make the dough, beat the butter with electric beaters until creamy. Add the garlic, cumin and 1 teaspoon salt and mix well. Add the masa harina and combined cream and stock alternately, beating until combined.
2 To make the filling, add the corn to a pan of boiling water and cook for 5–8 minutes, or until tender. Cool, then cut off the kernels with a sharp knife. Heat the oil in a frying pan and cook the chicken until golden. Remove, cool and shred finely. Add the garlic, chilli and onion to the pan and cook until soft. Add the red pepper and corn and stir for 3 minutes. Add the chicken, tomato and 1 teaspoon salt and simmer for 15 minutes, or until the liquid has reduced.
3 Bring a large pan of water to the boil and place a large bamboo steamer over it, making sure it doesn't touch the water.
4 Cut 12 pieces of baking paper 20 x 15 cm (8 x 6 inches). Spread a thick layer of dough over each piece, leaving a border at each end. Place filling in the centre, roll up and secure both ends with string. Cook in the steamer for 35 minutes, or until firm.

CRISPY CHEESE AND CURRY LENTIL BALLS

Preparation time: 15 minutes
Total cooking time: 20 minutes
Makes about 30

1 cup (250 g/4 oz) red lentils
4 spring onions, chopped
2 cloves garlic, crushed
1 teaspoon ground cumin
1 cup (80 g/2¾ oz) fresh breadcrumbs
1 cup (125 g/4 oz) grated Cheddar
1 large zucchini (courgette), grated
1 cup (150 g/5 oz) cornmeal (polenta)
oil, for deep-frying

1 Place the lentils in a pan and cover with water. Bring to the boil, reduce the heat, cover and simmer for 10 minutes, or until tender. Drain.
2 Combine half the lentils in a food processor or blender with the spring onion and garlic. Process until smooth. Transfer to a large bowl, then stir in the remaining lentils, cumin, breadcrumbs, cheese and zucchini until well combined. Roll level teaspoons of mixture into balls and toss lightly in cornmeal to coat.
3 Fill a heavy-based pan one third full of oil and heat the oil to 180°C (350°F). The oil is ready when a cube of bread dropped into the oil turns golden brown in 15 seconds. Cook small batches of the lentil balls in the oil for 1 minute each batch, or until golden brown, crisp and heated through. Carefully remove with tongs or a slotted spoon and drain on crumpled paper towels. Serve hot.

BABY SQUASH WITH RICE STUFFING

Preparation time: 20 minutes
Total cooking time: 10 minutes
Makes 24

24 baby yellow squash
1 tablespoon oil
2 teaspoons Thai red curry paste
1 spring onion, finely chopped
1 small red pepper (capsicum), finely chopped
1 cup (185 g/6 oz) cooked jasmine rice
1 tablespoon finely chopped fresh coriander
2 kaffir lime leaves, finely shredded
24 fresh coriander leaves, to garnish

1 Blanch or steam the squash for 5 minutes, or until just tender.
2 Cut a thin slice off the base of each squash to allow it to stand upright, then slice a thin piece off the top to make a lid. Set aside.
3 Using a melon baller, scoop out the flesh from the squash, leaving a thin shell. Discard the flesh.
4 Heat the oil in a wok, then add the curry paste, spring onion and red pepper and stir-fry for 2–3 minutes. Add the rice and stir-fry for another 2–3 minutes. Add the chopped coriander and kaffir lime leaves and toss to combine.
5 Remove from the heat and spoon 1 teaspoon of rice into each of the yellow squash. Garnish each with a coriander leaf and gently arrange the lids on top. Arrange on a platter and serve.

NOTE: For 1 cup (185 g/6 oz) jasmine rice, you will need to cook ⅓ cup (65 g/2¼ oz) of rice in boiling water for about 10 minutes.

IN ADVANCE: The filling and squash can be prepared a day ahead. Cover and store separately in the refrigerator. Assemble several hours before you are serving.

MUSSELS WITH CRISPY PROSCIUTTO

Preparation time: 20 minutes
Total cooking time: 15–20 minutes
Makes about 20

1 tablespoon oil
1 onion, finely chopped
6 thin slices prosciutto, chopped
4 cloves garlic, crushed
1.5 kg (3 lb) black mussels
60 g (2 oz) Parmesan, grated
60 g (2 oz) Cheddar, grated

1 Heat the oil in a small frying pan and add the onion, prosciutto, and garlic. Cook over medium heat for 5–8 minutes, until the prosciutto is crispy and the onion softened, then set aside.
2 Scrub the mussels with a stiff brush and pull out the hairy beards. Discard any broken mussels, or open ones that don't close when tapped on the bench. Add to a large pan of boiling water and cook for 5 minutes. Stir occasionally and discard any mussels that don't open. Remove the mussels from their shells, keeping half of each shell. Place 2 mussels on each half-shell and top each with a little of the prosciutto mixture.
3 Combine the Parmesan and Cheddar and sprinkle over the prosciutto. Cook under a preheated grill until the cheese has melted and the mussels are warmed through.

IN ADVANCE: The mussels can be scrubbed and beards removed several hours ahead of time.

INDIVIDUAL HERB TARTS

Preparation time: 20 minutes
Total cooking time: 35 minutes
Makes 18

18 slices white bread, crusts removed
40 g (1⅓ oz) butter, softened

Filling
2 eggs
2 tablespoons milk
½ cup (125 ml/4 fl oz) cream
2 teaspoons chopped fresh chives
1 teaspoon chopped fresh dill
1 teaspoon chopped fresh thyme
1 tablespoon chopped fresh parsley
2 tablespoons freshly grated Parmesan cheese

1 Preheat the oven to hot 210°C (415°C/Gas 6–7). Brush two 12-cup muffin or patty pan trays with melted butter or oil. Cut bread into rounds using a 7 cm (2¾ inch) plain biscuit cutter. Flatten out each round with a rolling pin.
2 Spread both sides of rounds with butter and gently press into muffin pan. Bake for 10 minutes or until lightly browned and crisp. Do not overcook.
3 To make Filling: Reduce the heat to moderate 180°C (350°F/Gas 4). Combine the eggs, milk, cream and herbs in a medium bowl and mix well. Pour the egg mixture into the bread cases and sprinkle with Parmesan cheese. Bake for 25 minutes or until the filling is lightly browned and set. Serve the tarts immediately.

THAI STUFFED MUSSELS

Preparation time: 45 minutes
Total cooking time: 45 minutes
Serves 6

2 kg (4 lb) black mussels
½ cup (125 ml/4 fl oz) white wine
3 garlic cloves, chopped
4 coriander (cilantro) roots
1 stem lemon grass
1 lime, sliced
2 small red onions, chopped
1 tablespoon peanut oil
1 cup (200 g/6½ oz) jasmine rice
½ cup (80 g/2¾ oz) roasted unsalted peanuts, chopped
2 teaspoons finely chopped ginger
1 tablespoon fish sauce
1 tablespoon tamarind purée
4 tablespoons coriander (cilantro) leaves, chopped
4 makrut (kaffir) lime leaves, shredded
shredded Vietnamese mint, to garnish

1 Scrub the mussels with a stiff brush and remove the beards. Rinse. Put the mussels in a large bamboo steamer and cover.
2 Put the wine, 1½ cups (375 ml/12 fl oz) water, 2 of the garlic cloves, the coriander roots, the green part of the lemon grass stem, the lime slices and one of the chopped onions in a wok. Bring to a simmer.
3 Sit the steamer over the wok and steam for about 5 minutes, or until the mussels open. Remove and discard the upper shell. Strain and reserve the cooking liquid.
4 Heat the oil in a wok over medium heat. Add the remaining onion and garlic, the finely chopped white part of the lemon grass stem and the rice, and stir-fry for 2–3 minutes, or until the onion is soft. Add 2 cups (500 ml/16 fl oz) of the reserved liquid and simmer for 20 minutes. Preheat the oven to 200°C (400°F/Gas 6).
5 Toss in the peanuts, ginger, fish sauce, tamarind, coriander and lime leaves. Spoon a little of the mixture onto each shell half, transfer to an ovenproof baking dish and bake for 10 minutes. Garnish and serve.

CALIFORNIA ROLLS

Preparation time: 25 minutes +
  1 hour draining + cooling
Total cooking time: 25 minutes
Makes 12

1 cup (220 g/7 oz) Japanese short-grain
  rice
1 tablespoon rice vinegar
2 generous pinches of caster (superfine)
  sugar
1 large egg
1 teaspoon sake
1 teaspoon oil
2 sheets of roasted nori, 20 x 18 cm
  (8 x 7 inches)
2 crabsticks, 40 g (1¼ oz) each, cut into
  strips
25 g (¾ oz) pickled daikon, cut into
  julienne strips
25 g (¾ oz) carrot, cut into julienne strips
25 g (¾ oz) cucumber, cut into julienne
  strips
Shoyu (Japanese soy sauce), to serve
wasabi paste, to serve
pickled ginger, to serve

1 Wash the rice under cold running water
until the water runs clear, then drain
thoroughly. Drain for an hour. Put the rice
into a saucepan and cover with 220 ml
(7 fl oz) cold water. Cover the pan and
bring the water to the boil. Reduce the
heat and simmer for 10 minutes. When
the rice is cooked, remove the pan from
the heat and leave, covered, for 10 minutes.
2 To make the sushi dressing, mix
together the vinegar, a pinch of the sugar
and a pinch of salt.

3 Spread the rice over the base of a non-
metallic dish or bowl, pour the sushi
dressing over the top and use a rice
paddle or spatula to mix the dressing
through the rice, separating the grains as
you do so. Fan the rice until it cools to
room temperature. Cover the pan with a
damp tea towel and set aside—do not
refrigerate.
4 To make the omelette, gently combine
the egg, sake, a pinch of sugar and a
pinch of salt. Heat the oil in a small frying
pan. Add the egg mixture and cook until
firm around the edges but still slightly
soft in the middle. Roll the omelette, then
tip it out of the pan. Cool, then slice into
strips.
5 Put a nori sheet on a sushi mat, shiny-
side down. Add half of the rice, leaving a 2
cm (¾ inch) gap at the edge furthest away
from you. Lay half of the fillings on the
rice in the following order: omelette,
crabstick, daikon, carrot, cucumber.
Starting with the end nearest to you,
tightly roll the mat and the nori. Repeat
this process with the remaining
ingredients.
6 Using a sharp knife, cut each roll into
six slices. After cutting each slice, rinse
the knife under cold running water to
prevent sticking. Serve with Shoyu,
wasabi and pickled ginger.

ASPARAGUS AND PROSCIUTTO ROLLS

Preparation time: 20 minutes
Total cooking time: 8 minutes
Makes 24

12 slices prosciutto
24 asparagus spears
100 g (3½ oz) butter, melted
60 g (2 oz) Parmesan, grated
fresh nutmeg, grated
1 lemon

1 Preheat the oven to moderate 180°C
(350°F/Gas 4). Cut each slice of prosciutto
in half. Cut off the base of each asparagus
stem so that the spear is about 9 cm
(3½ inches) long. Bring a pan of lightly
salted water to the boil, add the
asparagus and cook for 1 minute, or until
just tender.
2 Drain the asparagus and pat dry. Brush
with the melted butter, then roll the
spears in the grated Parmesan. Wrap
each asparagus spear in half a slice of
prosciutto.
3 Brush an ovenproof dish, large enough
to hold the asparagus in a single layer,
with melted butter. Place the asparagus
bundles in the dish. Sprinkle with any
remaining Parmesan, grated nutmeg and
cracked black pepper, to taste. Bake for
7 minutes. Squeeze a little fresh lemon
juice over the top and serve.

NOTE: Thinly sliced bacon can be
substituted for the prosciutto.
in advance: The rolls can be assembled
up to 6 hours ahead, covered and
refrigerated. Cook just before serving.

VEGETARIAN CALIFORNIA ROLLS

Preparation time: 35 minutes + 1 hour
    draining + 15 minutes standing
Total cooking time: 15 minutes
Makes 30

500 g (1 lb) Japanese short-grain rice
¼ cup (60 ml/2 fl oz) rice vinegar
1 tablespoon caster (superfine) sugar
5 sheets of roasted nori
1 large Lebanese (short) cucumber, cut
    lengthways into long batons
1 avocado, thinly sliced
1 tablespoon black sesame seeds,
    toasted
30 g (1 oz) pickled ginger slices
½ cup (125 g/4 oz) Japanese or whole-egg
    mayonnaise
3 teaspoons wasabi paste
2 teaspoons Shoyu (Japanese soy sauce)

1 Wash the rice under cold running water
until the water runs clear, then drain
thoroughly. Drain for an hour. Put the rice
and 3 cups (750 ml/24 fl oz) water in a
saucepan. Bring to the boil over low heat
and cook for 5 minutes, or until tunnels
form in the rice. Remove from the heat,
cover and leave for 15 minutes.
2 To make the sushi dressing, put the
vinegar, sugar and 1 teaspoon salt in a
small saucepan and stir over low heat
until the sugar and salt dissolve.
3 Spread the rice over the base of a non-
metallic dish or bowl, pour the sushi
dressing over the top and use a rice
paddle or spatula to mix the dressing
through the rice, separating the grains as
you do so. Fan the rice until it cools to
room temperature.

4 To assemble, lay a nori sheet, shiny-
side down, on a sushi mat and spread out
one-fifth of the rice, leaving a 2 cm (¾ inch)
border at one end. Arrange one fifth of
the cucumber, avocado, sesame seeds
and ginger lengthways over the rice, 3 cm
(1¼ inches) from the border. Spread on
some of the combined mayonnaise,
wasabi and Shoyu and roll to cover the
filling. Continue rolling tightly to join the
edge, then hold in place for a few
seconds. Trim the ends and cut into 2 cm
(½ inch) slices, wetting your knife in
vinegared water between each slice.
Repeat. Serve with any remaining wasabi
mayonnaise.

PAN-FRIED CHEESE SANDWICHES

Preparation time: 20 minutes
Total cooking time: 20 minutes
Makes about 40

20 thick slices white bread
2–3 tablespoons Dijon mustard
12 slices Cheddar
oil, for shallow-frying
plain flour, for dusting
3 eggs, lightly beaten
watercress, to garnish

1 Remove the crusts from the bread.
Spread the bread with mustard, place a
slice of cheese on top, then finish with
another bread slice.
2 Heat a little oil in a frying pan. Dust the
sandwiches lightly with flour and dip
quickly into the beaten egg.
3 Cook the sandwiches on both sides until
golden; drain on paper towels. Cut into
quarters and garnish with watercress.
Serve hot.

IN ADVANCE: Assemble the sandwiches
up to 4 hours in advance, but don't dust
with flour and dip in the egg until just
before frying.

CHEESES

EVERYONE LOVES CHEESE, AND THE CREATIVE TOUCHES ADDED TO THIS SELECTION OF POPULAR FRESH CHEESES DRESS THEM UP JUST ENOUGH TO TURN A NEARLY PERFECT NATURAL FOOD INTO A PERFECTLY DELECTABLE COURSE ON ITS OWN.

ASHED HERB GOAT'S CHEESE

Place 4 sprigs each of sage, rosemary, thyme and marjoram in a small pan. Cover and cook the herbs over medium heat for 20 minutes without removing the lid. Transfer blackened herbs to a food processor and finely chop. Remove four 100 g (3⅓ oz) goat's cheese logs or rounds from their packages and pat dry on paper towels. Coat the goat's cheese in the ashed herbs, cover with plastic wrap and refrigerate overnight.

MARINATED GRILLED GARLIC HALOUMI

Pat 500 g (1 lb) haloumi cheese dry on paper towels. Cut haloumi into thick slices and place in a shallow dish; add 2 finely sliced cloves of garlic, 2 tablespoons of chopped fresh basil, 1 teaspoon lime juice, 60 g (2 oz) sliced sun-dried tomatoes and 1 cup (250 ml/

8 fl oz) olive oil. Cover and leave to marinate overnight. Remove haloumi and tomatoes from marinade and arrange on top of slices of wood-fired bread; cook under a preheated grill on high until cheese is soft and golden brown. Drizzle with lime juice and sprinkle with freshly ground black pepper.

FETA CHEESE AND SUN-DRIED TOMATOES IN OIL

Pat dry 350 g (11¼ oz) feta cheese with paper towels. Cut into cubes. Sprinkle 1 tablespoon each cracked black pepper and dried oregano leaves and 1 teaspoon coriander seeds over base of a sterilised 3-cup (750 ml/24 fl oz) jar. Arrange the feta, 4 small fresh red chillies, several sprigs of rosemary and 125 g (4 oz) sun-dried tomatoes in a jar. Cover with olive oil, seal tightly and refrigerate. This will keep, refrigerated, for 1–2 months.

BAKED RICOTTA CHEESE

Drain 500 g (1 lb) ricotta cheese through muslin over a bowl for 3 hours. Mix the ricotta and 3 lightly beaten egg whites in a bowl. Spoon into a loaf tin and press down firmly. Drizzle with ½ cup (125 ml/4 fl oz) of olive oil and sprinkle with 1 tablespoon of sweet paprika, 1 teaspoon of ground cumin and freshly ground black pepper. Bake in a preheated moderate 180°C (350°F/Gas 4) oven for 40 minutes or until golden brown. Cool slightly, remove from the tin and spoon over pan juices. Serve sliced with wood-fired bread and an antipasto platter.

PESTO HERB SPREAD

Place 500 g (1 lb) cream cheese and 1 tablespoon of ready-made pesto into a food processor and process until smooth. Add 30 g (1 oz) of chopped fresh chives and 3 tablespoons of chopped fresh coriander and process until combined. Spoon mixture into a 20 cm (8 inch) round cake tin lined with plastic wrap. Cover and refrigerate for 3 hours or until firm. Remove from tin and coat with chopped smoked almonds. Serve with crackers, sun-dried tomatoes and olives.

ALMOND RICOTTA CREAM WITH FRESH FRUITS AND BERRIES

Combine 250 g (8 oz) ricotta cheese, 1 tablespoon of thick cream, 100 g (3⅓ oz) ground almonds, 200 g (6½ oz) of vanilla fromage frais, 4 tablespoons of caster sugar and 1 teaspoon of vanilla essence in a bowl. Spoon into a double layer of muslin, tie ends together and suspend over a bowl in a cool place overnight. Turn out onto a plate; serve with fresh fruits and berries.

CLOCKWISE, FROM TOP LEFT: Marinated Grilled Garlic Haloumi; Feta Cheese and Sun-dried Tomatoes in Oil; Ashed Herb Goat's Cheese; Pesto Herb Spread; Baked Ricotta Cheese; Almond Ricotta Cream with Fruits and Berries

PRAWN, NOODLE AND NORI PARCELS

Preparation time: 45 minutes
Total cooking time: 10 minutes
Makes 24

1 kg (2 lb) raw medium prawns
250 g (8 oz) dried somen noodles
2 sheets nori (dried seaweed)
½ cup (60 g/2 oz) plain flour
2 egg yolks
oil, for deep-frying

Dipping sauce
⅓ cup (80 ml/2¾ fl oz) Tonkatsu sauce or
   barbecue sauce
2 tablespoons lemon juice
1 tablespoon sake or mirin
1–2 teaspoons grated fresh ginger

1 Peel the prawns, leaving the tails intact.
Gently pull out the dark vein from each
prawn back, starting at the head end. Set
aside.
2 Using a sharp knife, cut the noodles to
the same length as the prawn bodies to
the base of the tail. Keep the noodles in
neat bundles and set aside. Cut the nori
into 2.5 cm (1 inch) wide strips.
3 Sift the flour into a large bowl and make
a well in the centre. Mix the egg yolks
with 3 tablespoons of water. Gradually
add to the flour, whisking to make a
smooth lump-free batter. Add another
tablespoon of water if the mixture is too
thick. Set aside.

4 Mix the dipping sauce ingredients in a
small bowl, adding the ginger according
to taste.
5 Dip a prawn in the batter, letting the
excess run off. Roll the prawn lengthways
in noodles to coat it with a single layer.
Secure the noodles by rolling a seaweed
strip around the centre of the prawn,
securing the seaweed with a little batter.
Repeat with the rest of the prawns.
6 Fill a deep, heavy-based pan one third
full of oil and heat to 180°C (350°F), or
until a cube of bread browns in 15
seconds. Deep-fry 2–3 coated prawns at a
time, for about 1–2 minutes, or until the
prawns are cooked. Drain on crumpled
paper towels and keep warm while
cooking the remainder. Serve warm with
the dipping sauce.

NOTE: Nori, Tonkatsu sauce and sake are
available at Asian speciality stores.

PARMESAN TUILE CONES

Preparation time: 40 minutes
Total cooking time: 30 minutes
Makes 36

150 g (5 oz) Parmesan, finely grated
pinch of paprika
150 g (5 oz) ricotta cheese
2 teaspoons lemon juice
1½ tablespoons milk
2 teaspoons fresh chopped chives, plus
   extra, cut into short lengths, to garnish
3 slices prosciutto
2 fresh figs, cut into small pieces

1 Preheat the oven to hot 220°C
(425°F/Gas 7). Line two baking trays with
baking paper. Using a 7 cm (2¾ inch)
cutter as a guide, draw circles on the
paper. Invert the paper onto the trays.
Place the cutter back over each round and
sprinkle with 3 teaspoons of Parmesan
combined with the paprika, spreading
evenly to the edges.
2 Bake only 3–4 at a time for 3 minutes, or
until melted and golden. Remove each
round from the tray, using a spatula, and
wrap around the end of a cream horn
mould to form a cone shape. Cool. If they
begin to harden too quickly, return to the
oven for 10 seconds to soften again.
3 Beat the ricotta cheese, lemon juice and
milk in a bowl until smooth. Stir in the
chopped chives and salt and cracked
black pepper, to taste.
4 Grill the prosciutto until crisp. Allow to
cool, then break into pieces about 2 cm
(¾ inch) long. Carefully spoon 2 teaspoons
of the cheese mixture into each
Parmesan tuile. Decorate the end of each
tuile with a piece of fig, prosciutto and
chives.

FLORENTINE SCONES WITH MORTADELLA AND ARTICHOKE

Preparation time: 30 minutes
Total cooking time: 15 minutes
Makes 60

100 g (3½ oz) English spinach leaves
20 g (¾ oz) butter
3 spring onions, finely sliced
1¼ cups (155 g/5 oz) self-raising flour
50 g (1¾ oz) Parmesan, grated
⅓ cup (80 ml/2¾ fl oz) milk, approximately
2 teaspoons milk, extra
200 g (6½ oz) artichokes in olive oil, drained
¼ cup (60 ml/2 fl oz) thick (double) cream
100 g (3½ oz) thinly sliced mortadella
1½ tablespoons finely chopped pistachio nuts

1 Preheat the oven to hot 220°C (425°F/Gas 7). Wash the spinach and cook, covered, in a saucepan over medium heat for 2 minutes, or until wilted. Drain and cool. Squeeze the spinach with your hands to remove as much liquid as possible, then chop finely.
2 Heat the butter in a small pan, add the onion and cook over medium heat for 2 minutes, or until very soft.

3 Sift the flour into a bowl and stir in the spinach, onion mixture and Parmesan. Make a well and use a flat-bladed knife to stir in enough milk to mix to a soft, sticky dough. Turn onto a lightly floured surface and knead lightly until just smooth. Roll out to about 1.5 cm (⅝ inch) thickness, then cut 30 rounds with a 4 cm (1½ inch) cutter. Lightly grease a baking tray and place the rounds on it so they are almost touching. Brush the tops lightly with the extra milk and bake on the middle shelf for 10–12 minutes, or until cooked and golden brown.
4 Meanwhile, chop the artichokes in a food processor until smooth. Add the cream and process quickly until combined. Do not overprocess or the mixture may curdle. Season with salt and pepper, to taste.
5 To assemble, split the scones horizontally in half, top each half with artichoke cream, then torn and folded pieces of mortadella. Sprinkle with pistachio nuts.

IN ADVANCE: The scones are best made on the day of serving. The artichoke cream can be prepared a day ahead and refrigerated.

SMOKED SALMON AND ROCKET ROLLS

Preparation time: 20 minutes
Total cooking time: Nil
Makes 36

200 g (6½ oz) ricotta cheese
¼ cup (60 g/2 oz) crème fraîche or sour cream
2 teaspoons wasabi paste
1 tablespoon lime juice
12 slices brown bread, crusts removed
300 g (10 oz) smoked salmon
100 g (3½ oz) baby rocket, trimmed
rocket leaves, extra, to garnish

1 Mix together the ricotta, crème fraîche, wasabi and lime juice.
2 Roll the bread out with a rolling pin to flatten.
3 Spread the ricotta over the bread, then top with the smoked salmon and rocket leaves, leaving a border. Roll up lengthways, wrap tightly in plastic wrap to hold the shape, then refrigerate for 30 minutes.
4 Unwrap, trim the ends and cut into 2 cm (¾ inch) slices. Garnish with rocket leaves.

RATATOUILLE TARTS

Preparation time: 40 minutes +
 30 minutes refrigeration +
 20 minutes standing
Total cooking time: 1 hour 10 minutes
Makes 12

3 cups (375 g/12 oz) plain flour
170 g (5½ oz) butter, chilled and chopped
1 eggplant (aubergine), about 500 g (1 lb)
¼ cup (60 ml/2 fl oz) oil
1 onion, chopped
2 cloves garlic, crushed
2 zucchini (courgettes), sliced
1 red pepper (capsicum), chopped
1 green pepper (capsicum), chopped
250 g (8 oz) cherry tomatoes, halved
1 tablespoon balsamic vinegar
1 cup (125 g/4 oz) grated Cheddar

1 Sift the flour into a bowl and rub in the butter with your fingertips until the mixture resembles fine breadcrumbs. Make a well and add ½ cup (125 ml/4 fl oz) chilled water. Mix with a flat-bladed knife, adding a little more water if necessary, until the dough just comes together. Gather into a ball and divide into 12 portions.
2 Grease 12 loose-based fluted flan tins measuring 8 cm (3 inches) across the base and 3 cm (1¼ inches) deep. Roll each portion of dough out on a sheet of baking paper to a circle a little larger than the tins. Lift into the tins, press into the sides, then trim away any excess pastry. Refrigerate for 30 minutes. Preheat the oven to moderately hot 200°C (400°F/Gas 6).
3 Put the tins on baking trays, prick the pastry bases all over with a fork and bake for 20–25 minutes, or until the pastry is fully cooked and lightly golden. Cool completely.

4 Meanwhile, to make the ratatouille filling, cut the eggplant into 2 cm (¾ inch) cubes, put into a colander and sprinkle with salt. After 20 minutes, rinse, drain and pat dry with paper towels.
5 Heat 2 tablespoons of the oil in a large frying pan. Cook batches of eggplant for 8–10 minutes, or until browned, adding more oil if necessary. Drain on paper towels. Heat the remaining oil, add the onion and cook over medium heat for 5 minutes, or until very soft. Add the garlic and cook for 1 minute, then add the zucchini and peppers and cook, stirring frequently, for 10 minutes, or until softened. Add the eggplant and tomatoes. Cook, stirring, for 2 minutes. Transfer to a bowl, stir in the vinegar, then cover and cool completely.
6 Reduce the oven to moderate 180°C (350°F/Gas 4). Divide the mixture among the tart shells with a slotted spoon, draining off any excess liquid. Sprinkle with the Cheddar and cook for 10–15 minutes, or until the cheese has melted and the tarts are warmed through.

MUSHROOMS WITH HERB NUT BUTTER

Preparation time: 20 minutes
Total cooking time: 20 minutes
Serves 4–6

12 large mushrooms
1 tablespoon olive oil
1 small onion, finely chopped
¼ cup (40 g/1⅓ oz) blanched almonds
1 clove garlic, peeled and chopped
1 tablespoon lemon juice
3 tablespoons parsley sprigs
3 teaspoons chopped fresh thyme or 1 teaspoon dried thyme
3 teaspoons chopped fresh rosemary or 1 teaspoon dried rosemary
1 tablespoon chopped fresh chives
½ teaspoon salt
¼ teaspoon black pepper
75 g (2½ oz) butter, chopped

1 Preheat oven to moderate 180°C (350°F/Gas 4). Brush a shallow baking dish with oil or melted butter. Remove stalks from mushrooms, chop stalks finely. Heat oil in a small pan, add onion. Cook over medium heat 2–3 minutes or until soft and golden. Add chopped stalks. Cook 2 minutes or until softened. Remove from heat.
2 Place the almonds, garlic, lemon juice, parsley, thyme, rosemary, chives, salt, pepper and butter in a food processor. Process for 20–30 seconds or until the mixture is smooth.
3 Place the mushroom caps in the baking dish. Spoon equal amounts of the onion and mushroom mixture into each cap and smooth the surface. Top each mushroom with the almond and herb mixture. Bake 10–15 minutes, or until mushrooms are cooked through and butter has melted.

NOTE: Mushrooms are best cooked just before serving. Assemble the caps up to two hours before serving and store, covered, on a flat tray, in the refrigerator.

CHICKEN ROLLS

Preparation time: 1 hour 15 minutes
Total cooking time: 1 hour 5 minutes
Makes about 40

60 g (2 oz) butter
1 large onion, chopped
2 cloves garlic, crushed
2 tablespoons plain flour
½ cup (125 ml/4 fl oz) chicken stock
½ cup (125 ml/4 fl oz) milk
1 large barbecued chicken, skin removed
    and flesh shredded
¼ cup (25 g/¾ oz) grated Parmesan
2 teaspoons fresh thyme leaves
¼ cup (25 g/¾ oz) dry breadcrumbs
2 eggs, lightly beaten
13 sheets filo pastry, cut into thirds
    crossways
140 g (4½ oz) butter, extra, melted

1 Melt the butter in a pan and add the onion. Cook over low heat for 12 minutes, or until soft, stirring occasionally. Increase the heat to medium–high and add the garlic. Cook, stirring, for 1 minute, then add the flour and cook for 1 minute. Remove from the heat and gradually stir in the stock and milk. Return to the heat and stir constantly until the sauce boils and thickens. Boil for 1 minute, then remove from the heat and add the chicken, Parmesan, thyme, breadcrumbs, salt and pepper. Cool, then stir in the eggs.
2 Preheat the oven to hot 220°C (425°F/ Gas 7). Lightly grease three baking trays.
3 Put one piece of filo pastry on the bench with the short end closest to you (cover the remaining pieces with a damp tea towel). Brush with the extra melted butter and place a level tablespoon of chicken mixture on the base end closest to you. Fold in the sides, brush along the length with butter and roll up tightly to form a roll 8 cm (3 inches) long. Put onto the baking tray and brush the top with some of the butter. Repeat with the remaining filo, butter and chicken mixture.
4 Bake for 15 minutes in the top half of the oven until well browned. Serve hot.

MEDITERRANEAN SQUARES

Preparation time: 15 minutes
Total cooking time: 15 minutes
Makes about 20 pieces

1 medium red (Spanish) onion
3 tablespoons pitted black olives
1 medium red pepper (capsicum)
1 medium green pepper (capsicum)
2 tablespoons fresh basil leaves
3 teaspoons balsamic vinegar
2 cloves garlic, crushed
¼ cup (60 ml/2 fl oz) oil
3 cloves garlic, crushed, extra
1 large 30 x 40 cm (12 x 16 inch) piece of
    focaccia
¾ cup (90 g/3 oz) Cheddar cheese, grated

1 Preheat the oven to moderate 180°C (350°F/Gas 4) and line an oven tray with foil. Slice the onion and olives. Cut the peppers in half, remove the seeds and membrane and cut the remaining flesh into fine strips. Finely shred the basil leaves.
2 Combine the onions, olives, peppers, basil, vinegar and garlic in a medium bowl. Mix well, then cover and set aside.
3 Combine oil and extra garlic in a small bowl. Using a serrated knife, split focaccia through the centre. Brush focaccia halves with combined oil and garlic. Arrange the combined olive and pepper filling evenly over the bottom half of the focaccia. Sprinkle with the cheese and top with the remaining piece of focaccia. Place on prepared oven tray; bake for 15 minutes or until cheese melts. Cut into squares and serve hot or at room temperature.

SEMI-DRIED TOMATOES

Preparation time: 10 minutes +
    overnight chilling
Total cooking time: 2 hours 30 minutes
Makes 64

16 Roma (egg) tomatoes
3 tablespoons fresh thyme, chopped
2 tablespoons olive oil

1 Preheat the oven to warm 160°C (315°F/Gas 2–3). Quarter the tomatoes lengthways and lay skin-side-down on a rack in a baking tray.
2 Sprinkle with 1 teaspoon each of salt and cracked black pepper and the thyme and bake for 2½ hours. Check occasionally to make sure the tomatoes don't burn. Toss in the oil and cool before packing into sterilized jars and sealing. Refrigerate for 24 hours before using. Return to room temperature before serving. Suitable for an antipasto plate.

NOTE: To sterilize storage jars, rinse them thoroughly with boiling water, invert and drain, then place in a very slow oven to dry thoroughly. Don't dry with a tea towel.

IN ADVANCE: Can be kept in an airtight container in the fridge for up to 7 days.

SANDWICHES

SANDWICHES DON'T HAVE TO BE UNGAINLY CHUNKS OF BREAD FILLED WITH SALMON PASTE OR CHEESE SPREAD. WELCOME TO THE SOPHISTICATED PARTY SANDWICH. IT COULD JUST BE THE STAR OF YOUR SHOW.

HAM AND CORN RELISH RIBBONS

Mix 1 cup (250 g/8 oz) sour cream with ½ cup (140 g/4½ oz) corn relish and spread on 8 slices of white bread. Top each with a slice of dark seed bread. Top that with sliced ham, then sandwich with a buttered slice of white bread. Remove the crusts and slice each sandwich into three. Makes 24 ribbon sandwiches.

VEGETABLE TRIANGLES

Cut 500 g (1 lb) butternut pumpkin into chunks, put in a baking dish, drizzle with oil and bake in a moderately hot 200°C (400°F/Gas 6) oven for 1 hour, or until tender. Cool, then mash. Spread 4 slices of soy and linseed bread with 1 tablespoon of tomato salsa. Top each with sliced marinated eggplant, coriander leaves and sliced spring onion. Spread 4 more slices of bread with the mashed pumpkin and place on top. Remove the crusts and cut into triangles.
Makes 16.

CHICKEN AND GUACAMOLE SQUARES

Mash 2 avocados with 1 tablespoon mayonnaise, 1 teaspoon chopped chilli, 1 tablespoon lemon juice, 1 small chopped tomato and ½ finely chopped red onion. Spread over 8 slices of wholemeal bread and top with 250 g (8 oz) sliced smoked chicken breast. Add trimmed snow pea (mangetout) sprouts. Sandwich with more bread, remove the crusts and cut into squares.
Makes 32.

TURKEY AND BRIE TRIANGLES

Trim the crusts from 8 slices bread. Spread 4 with cranberry sauce. Using 120 g (4 oz) turkey breast, 120 g (4 oz) sliced brie and 4 butter lettuce leaves, make into sandwiches. Cut into triangles.
Makes 16.

ROAST BEEF, PATE AND ROCKET FINGERS

Trim the crusts from 16 slices of bread. Spread 160 g (5½ oz) cracked pepper paté over half the bread. Make sandwiches using 250 g (8 oz) sliced rare roast beef, 160 g (5½ oz) semi-dried tomatoes and rocket leaves. Cut each into three fingers to serve.
Makes 24.

LEMON SANDWICHES WITH PRAWNS

Wash and dry 1½ thin-skinned lemons and slice finely. Make lemon sandwiches with 10 slices of multi-grain bread. Cut each sandwich into 8 triangles. Remove the crusts and serve with 500 g (1 lb) peeled and deveined cooked king prawns, leaving the tails intact.
Makes 40.

CHICKEN, ROCKET AND WALNUT SANDWICHES

Fry 250 g (8 oz) chicken breast fillets and 500 g (1 lb) chicken thigh fillets until cooked. Cool, then chop finely. Mix with 1 cup (250 g/8 oz) mayonnaise, some finely chopped celery and chopped walnuts. Season. Make into sandwiches with 20 slices bread, adding trimmed rocket to each. Remove the crusts and cut the sandwiches into fingers.
Makes 30.

CLOCKWISE, FROM BOTTOM LEFT: Chicken and guacamole squares; Vegetable triangles; Ham and corn relish ribbons; Turkey and brie triangles; Roast beef, pâté and rocket fingers; Chicken, rocket and walnut sandwiches; Lemon sandwiches with prawns

VEGETABLE PASTIES WITH RICH TOMATO SAUCE

Preparation time: 40 minutes
Total cooking time: 50 minutes
Makes 12

1 potato
1 carrot
1 parsnip
100 g (3⅓ oz) pumpkin
2 teaspoons oil
1 onion, finely chopped
½ cup (125 ml/4 fl oz) vegetable stock
⅓ cup (50 g/1⅔ oz) fresh or frozen peas
1 tablespoon finely chopped fresh parsley
3 sheets ready-rolled puff pastry
1 egg, lightly beaten

Tomato Sauce
1 tablespoon oil
1 small onion, chopped
1 clove garlic, crushed
2 tomatoes, peeled and chopped
¼ cup (60 ml/2 fl oz) good-quality red
   wine
¼ cup (60 ml/2 fl oz) vegetable stock
2 tablespoons tomato paste
½ teaspoon dried basil
½ teaspoon dried oregano

1 Preheat the oven to hot 210°C (415°F/
Gas 6–7). Brush an oven tray with melted
butter or oil. Peel and cut the potato,
carrot, parsnip and pumpkin into 1 cm
(½ inch) cubes. Heat the oil in a frying pan
and cook the onion over medium heat for
2 minutes, or until soft. Add potato,
carrot, parsnip, pumpkin and stock; bring
to the boil. Reduce heat and simmer for
10 minutes, stirring occasionally, until the
vegetables are soft and the liquid has
evaporated. Stir in the peas and parsley
and leave to cool.

2 Using a plate as a guide, cut four 12 cm
(5 inch) circles from each sheet of pastry.
Place 1 level tablespoon of mixture onto
each round, brush the edges of pastry
with water and fold the pastry over so the
edges meet. Twist the edges together
decoratively to seal. Brush with beaten
egg, place on prepared tray and bake for
25 minutes, until puffed and golden.
3 To make Tomato Sauce: Heat the oil in a
small pan and add the onion and garlic.
Cook over medium heat for 2 minutes, or
until soft. Add the tomatoes, wine and
stock and bring to boil. Reduce heat and
simmer for 15 minutes, stirring
occasionally. Remove from heat; cool.
Process tomato mixture in a food
processor until smooth. Return to pan,
add tomato paste, basil and oregano and
stir until hot. Serve hot or cold.

MANDARIN AND DUCK RICE PAPER ROLLS

Preparation time: 40 minutes
Total cooking time: Nil
Makes 24

1 whole Chinese roast duck
24 small rice paper wrappers
3 mandarins, peeled and segmented
1 cup (20 g/¾ oz) mint
60 g (2 oz) chives, cut into 3 cm (1¼ inch)
   lengths
2 tablespoons hoisin sauce
2 tablespoons fresh mandarin juice

1 Remove the flesh and skin from the
duck and shred into 1 x 3 cm (½ x 1¼ inch)
pieces, trying to keep some skin on each
piece of flesh.
2 Working with one wrapper at a time,
briefly soak each wrapper in cold water
until softened, then place on a dry tea
towel. Arrange 2–3 pieces of duck at the
end of the wrapper closest to you. Top
with 2 segments of mandarin, 3 mint
leaves and several lengths of chives. Fold
the end closest to you over the filling, fold
in the sides and firmly roll up the rice
paper.
3 Combine the hoisin sauce and mandarin
juice in a bowl and serve as a dipping
sauce with the rice paper rolls. Serve
immediately.

MEAT PATTIES WITH HALOUMI FILLING

Preparation time: 25 minutes + chilling
Total cooking time: 10 minutes
Makes 24

8 slices (125 g/4 oz) white bread, crusts
    removed
700 g (23 oz) lamb or beef mince
1 tablespoon chopped fresh flat-leaf
    parsley
3 tablespoons chopped fresh mint leaves
1 onion, grated
2 eggs, lightly beaten
140 g (4½ oz) haloumi cheese (see Note)
⅓ cup (40 g/1¼ oz) plain flour
olive oil, for shallow-frying

1 Put the bread in a bowl, cover with
water and then squeeze out as much
water as possible. Place the bread in a
bowl with the mince, parsley, mint, onion,
egg, pepper and ½ teaspoon salt. Knead
the mixture by hand for 2–3 minutes,
breaking up the mince and any large
pieces of bread with your fingers. The
mixture should be smooth and leave the
side of the bowl. Cover and refrigerate for
30 minutes.
2 Cut the haloumi into 24 rectangles,
3 x 1 x 1 cm (1¼ x ½ x ½ inch). Place the
flour in a shallow dish. Divide the mince
mixture into level tablespoon portions.
Roll a portion into a long shape and
flatten in the palm of your hand. Place the
cheese in the centre and top with another
portion of mince. Pinch the edges
together and roll into a torpedo 6 cm
(2½ inches) long. Repeat with the
remaining mince.
3 Heat 2 cm (¾ inch) oil in a deep heavy-
based frying pan to 180°C (350°F), or until
a cube of bread dropped into the oil
browns in 15 seconds. Toss the patties in
flour, shake off the excess and fry in
batches for 3–5 minutes, or until brown
and cooked through. Drain on crumpled
paper towels. Serve hot.

BOCCONCINI TOMATO SKEWERS

Preparation time: 20 minutes + chilling
Total cooking time: Nil
Makes 20

20 cherry bocconcini or ovolini, or 5 regular
    bocconcini, sliced into quarters
2 tablespoons olive oil
2 tablespoons chopped fresh parsley
1 tablespoon chopped fresh chives
20 small cherry tomatoes
40 small fresh basil leaves

1 Put the bocconcini in a bowl with the
oil, parsley, chives, ¼ teaspoon salt and
½ teaspoon ground black pepper. Cover
and refrigerate for at least 1 hour, or
preferably overnight.
2 Cut each cherry tomato in half and
thread one half on a skewer or toothpick,
followed by a basil leaf, then bocconcini,
another basil leaf and then another
tomato half. Repeat with more skewers
and the remaining ingredients and serve.

IN ADVANCE: These can be served
immediately, or covered and chilled for
up to 8 hours.

GRAVLAX

Preparation time: 10 minutes +
    24 hours chilling
Total cooking time: 5 minutes
Serves 12

¼ cup (60 g/2 oz) sugar
2 tablespoons sea salt
1 teaspoon crushed black peppercorns
2.5 kg (5 lb) salmon, filleted, skin on
1 tablespoon vodka or brandy
4 tablespoons very finely chopped fresh
    dill

Mustard sauce
1½ tablespoons cider vinegar
1 teaspoon caster sugar
½ cup (125 ml/4 fl oz) olive oil
2 teaspoons chopped fresh dill
2 tablespoons Dijon mustard

1 Combine the sugar, salt and
peppercorns in a small dish. Remove any
bones from the salmon with tweezers. Pat
dry with paper towels and lay a fillet skin-
side-down in a shallow tray or baking
dish. Sprinkle the fillet with half the
vodka, rub half the sugar mixture into the
flesh, then sprinkle with half the dill.
Sprinkle the remaining vodka over the
second salmon fillet and rub the
remaining sugar mixture into the flesh.
Lay it flesh-side-down on top of the other
fillet. Cover with plastic wrap, place a
heavy board on top and then weigh the
board down with 3 heavy cans or a foil-
covered brick. Refrigerate for 24 hours,
turning it over after 12 hours.
2 For the mustard sauce, whisk all the
ingredients together, then cover until
needed.
3 Uncover the salmon and lay both fillets
on a wooden board. Brush off all the dill
and seasoning with a stiff pastry brush.
Sprinkle with the remaining fresh dill and
press it onto the salmon flesh, shaking off
any excess. Serve whole on the serving
board, or thinly sliced on an angle
towards the tail, with the sauce.

MINI PIZZAS

IS THERE ANYONE WHO DOESN'T
LOVE PIZZA? MAKE THE BASIC
PIZZA BASES AS INSTRUCTED,
THEN TOP THEM OFF WITH ONE,
OR SEVERAL, OF THE
FOLLOWING IDEAS. THEN WATCH
THEM WALK OFF THE PLATE.

PIZZA BASES

Mix 7 g (¼ oz) dried yeast, ½ teaspoon
sugar and ¾ cup (185 ml/6 fl oz) warm
water, cover and set aside for 10 minutes,
or until frothy. Sift 2 cups (250 g/8 oz)
plain flour and ½ teaspoon salt into a
large bowl and make a well. Pour in the
yeast mixture and add 1 tablespoon olive
oil. Mix with a flat-bladed knife using a
cutting action until the mixture forms a
dough. Turn onto a lightly floured surface
and knead for 10 minutes, or until
smooth. Place in a lightly oiled bowl,
cover with plastic wrap and leave for
45 minutes, or until the dough has
doubled. Punch down the dough (give it
one firm punch with your fist to remove
the air) and knead for 8 minutes. Roll to 1
cm (½ inch) thick. Cut out 7 cm (2¾ inch)
rounds with a cutter. Place the rounds on
a lightly greased baking tray, top with one
of the following fillings and bake in a
moderately hot 200°C (400°F/Gas 6) oven
for 15 minutes.
Makes 25.

BEEF AND ROAST PEPPER
(CAPSICUM)

Press 1½ tablespoons cracked black
pepper onto a 250 g (8 oz) piece of rump
steak. Heat a large frying pan, cook the
steak for 5 minutes each side, then slice
into thin strips. Cut a red pepper in half
lengthways and remove the membrane
and seeds. Grill skin-side-up until the
skin is black and blistered. Place in a
plastic bag until cool, then peel away the
skin. Slice the flesh into thin strips. Mix
⅓ cup (90 g/3 oz) tomato paste (tomato
purée) with 2 teaspoons dried mixed
herbs and spread the mixture over the
pizza bases, leaving a small border.
Sprinkle with ½ cup (75 g/2½ oz) grated
mozzarella cheese, then top each one
with a few beef and pepper strips and
bake for 15 minutes, or until the bases are
crisp and golden. Mix ⅓ cup (90 g/3 oz)
sour cream with 2½ tablespoons seeded
mustard, spoon over the pizzas and
garnish with trimmed snow pea
(mangetout) sprouts.

SPINACH AND BOCCONCINI

Spread 1 teaspoon tomato relish over each base (you will need ½ cup/125 ml/ 4 fl oz relish). Divide 60 g (2 oz) shredded English spinach leaves, 25 slices Roma (egg) tomato and 180 g (6 oz) sliced bocconcini among the pizza bases, then bake for 15 minutes, or until the bases are crisp.

PRAWN AND MANGO

Spread 1 teaspoon mango chutney over each base—you will need ½ cup (140 g/ 5 oz) chutney. Sprinkle with fresh coriander leaves and top each pizza with a peeled cooked prawn. Bake for 15 minutes, then top with thin slices of pepper brie cheese and allow to melt.

BRIE AND PEAR

Put 50 g (1¾ oz) brie, 1 tablespoon each of chopped fresh coriander, basil and parsley and 1 tablespoon each of cream, water and olive oil in a food processor and mix until smooth. Season, to taste, with a little salt. Core 2 small pears and cut each one into 14 thin slices. Spread half the brie mixture over the pizza bases, top each with a slice of pear and cover with the remaining cheese mixture. Bake for 15 minutes, or until the bases are golden and crisp. Serve immediately.

SUN-DRIED TOMATO PESTO AND CHICKEN

Fry 2 chicken breast fillets for 5–8 minutes on each side, or until golden. Cool slightly and slice into thin strips. Using 100 g (3½ oz) sun-dried tomato pesto, spread 1 teaspoon pesto over each base, leaving a small border. Mix together 35 g (1¼ oz) grated mozzarella cheese and 25 g (¾ oz) grated Parmesan, sprinkle over the bases and top with a few chicken strips. Bake for 15 minutes, or until the bases are golden and crisp. Garnish with small fresh basil leaves.

FROM LEFT: Beef and roast pepper; Spinach and bocconcini; Prawn and mango; Brie and pear; Sun-dried tomato pesto and chicken

HERBED CHEESE CRACKERS

Preparation time: 40 minutes
Total cooking time: 8 minutes each tray
Makes 20

Biscuit pastry
1 cup (125 g/4 oz) plain flour
½ teaspoon baking powder
60 g (2 oz) butter
1 egg, lightly beaten
60 g (2 oz) Cheddar, grated
1 teaspoon chopped fresh chives
1 teaspoon chopped fresh parsley

Cheese filling
80 g (2¾ oz) cream cheese, softened
20 g (¾ oz) butter
1 tablespoon chopped fresh chives
1 tablespoon chopped fresh parsley
¼ teaspoon lemon pepper
90 g (3 oz) Cheddar, grated

1 Preheat the oven to moderately hot 190°C (375°F/Gas 5). Line two baking trays with baking paper.
2 To make the biscuit pastry, sift the flour and baking powder into a large bowl and add the chopped butter. Rub in with your fingertips, until the mixture resembles fine breadcrumbs.
3 Make a well in the centre and add the egg, cheese, herbs and 1 tablespoon iced water. Mix with a flat-bladed knife, using a cutting action until the mixture comes together in beads. Gently gather together and lift out onto a lightly floured surface. Press together into a ball.

4 Roll the pastry between sheets of baking paper to 3 mm (⅛ inch) thickness. Remove the top sheet of paper and cut the pastry into rounds, using a 5 cm (2 inch) cutter. Place the rounds onto the trays. Re-roll the remaining pastry and repeat cutting. Bake for about 8 minutes, or until lightly browned. Transfer to a wire rack to cool.
5 To make the filling, beat the cream cheese and butter in a small bowl with electric beaters until light and creamy. Add the herbs, pepper and cheese and beat until smooth. Spread half a teaspoon of filling on half of the biscuits and sandwich together with the remaining biscuits.

NOTE: You can use freshly chopped lemon thyme instead of parsley.

IN ADVANCE: The biscuits can be made 2 days ahead and stored in an airtight container, or frozen. The filling can be made a day ahead and stored, covered, in the refrigerator.

BAKED POLENTA WITH SPICY RELISH

Preparation time: 20 minutes + chilling
Total cooking time: 1 hour
Makes 48

600 ml (20 fl oz) milk
⅔ cup (100 g/3½ oz) polenta
25 g (¾ oz) butter, diced
1 tablespoon olive oil
1 tablespoon polenta, extra

Spicy relish
1 tablespoon oil
2 red onions, roughly chopped
500 g (1 lb) Roma (egg) tomatoes, chopped
1 large red chilli, finely chopped
¼ teaspoon Mexican chilli powder, or to taste
1 tablespoon soft brown sugar
1 tablespoon red wine vinegar

1 Lightly grease a 30 x 20 cm (12 x 8 inch) cake tin. Bring the milk to the boil in a pan. Reduce the heat to medium and whisk in the polenta, pouring it in a stream, until it thickens, then stir continuously with a wooden spoon for 20 minutes, or until it leaves the side of the pan. Remove from the heat and stir in the butter. Season, to taste.
2 Spread the polenta into the tin and smooth the top. Refrigerate for 2 hours, or until set.
3 To make the spicy tomato relish, heat the oil in a pan, add the onion and cook, stirring, over high heat, for 3 minutes. Add the tomato, chilli, chilli powder, sugar and vinegar. Simmer, stirring occasionally, for 20 minutes, or until thickened. Season with salt.
4 Preheat the oven to moderately hot 200°C (400°F/Gas 6). Turn the polenta out onto a board, cut into 5 cm (2 inch) squares, then into triangles. Place on a baking tray covered with paper, brush with olive oil and sprinkle with the extra polenta. Bake for 10 minutes, or until the polenta is golden and has a crust. Serve hot or warm with the warm relish.

TUNA PATTIES

Preparation time: 30 minutes +
   30 minutes chilling
Total cooking time: 40 minutes
Makes 8

3 floury potatoes, quartered
30 g (1 oz) butter
1 onion, finely chopped
1 clove garlic, crushed
1 red pepper (capsicum), finely chopped
415 g (13 oz) can tuna
1 egg, lightly beaten
2 tablespoons lemon juice
3 tablespoons chopped fresh parsley
¼ cup (30 g/1 oz) plain flour
1 cup (100 g/3½ oz) dry breadcrumbs
1 egg, lightly beaten, extra
2 tablespoons milk
oil, for shallow-frying

1 Steam or boil the potatoes for
8–10 minutes, or until tender (pierce with
the point of a small sharp knife—if the
potato comes away easily, it is ready).
Drain and return to the pan. Stir over
medium heat, then mash. Set aside to cool.
2 Melt the butter in a frying pan, add the
onion and garlic and stir over medium
heat for 5 minutes, or until soft. Add the
red pepper and cook, stirring, for 5 minutes,
or until soft.
3 Drain the tuna, transfer to a bowl and
flake with a fork. Mix in the potato, beaten
egg, onion mixture, lemon juice and parsley.
4 Place the flour on a shallow plate and
the breadcrumbs on another plate.
Combine the beaten egg and milk in a
shallow dish or bowl. Form the mixture
into 8 patties, coat lightly in flour, then in
the egg and milk. Finally, coat with the
breadcrumbs. Place on a plate or baking
tray. Reshape if necessary, then cover
and chill for 30 minutes.
5 Heat about 3 tablespoons of oil in a
heavy-based frying pan over medium
heat and cook the patties in batches for
2–3 minutes on each side, or until golden
brown. Drain and serve hot.

DEEP-FRIED CHICKEN BALLS

Preparation time: 20 minutes +
   30 minutes refrigeration
Total cooking time: 15 minutes
Makes about 30

50 g (1¾ oz) dried rice vermicelli
500 g (1 lb) minced (ground) chicken
3 garlic cloves, finely chopped
1 tablespoon chopped ginger
1 red chilli, seeded and finely chopped
1 egg, lightly beaten
2 spring onions (scallions), thinly sliced
4 tablespoons chopped coriander
   (cilantro) leaves
⅓ cup (40 g/1¼ oz) plain (all-purpose)
   flour
⅓ cup (60 g/2 oz) finely chopped water
   chestnuts
oil, for deep-frying
Dipping sauce
½ cup (125 ml/4 fl oz) sweet chilli sauce
½ cup (125 ml/4 fl oz) soy sauce
1 tablespoon Chinese rice wine

1 Cover the dried rice vermicelli with
boiling water and soak for 6–7 minutes.
Drain, then cut into short lengths.
2 Combine the chicken, garlic, ginger,
chilli, egg, spring onion, coriander, flour
and water chestnuts in a large bowl. Mix
in the vermicelli and season with salt.
Refrigerate for 30 minutes. Roll heaped
tablespoons of the mixture into balls.
3 Fill a wok or deep-fat fryer one-third
full of oil and heat to 180°C (350°F), or
until a cube of bread dropped into the oil
browns in 15 seconds. Deep-fry the balls
in batches for 2 minutes, or until golden
brown and cooked through. Drain on
paper towels.
4 To make the dipping sauce, combine
the sweet chilli sauce, soy sauce and rice
wine. Serve with the hot chicken balls.

CORNMEAL CHILLIES

Preparation time: 40 minutes + chilling
Total cooking time: 2–3 minutes each
   batch
Makes 24

2 x 330 g (11 oz) jars mild whole chillies
125 g (4 oz) Cheddar, grated
200 g (6½ oz) cream cheese, softened
⅔ cup (85 g/3 oz) plain flour
4 eggs, lightly beaten
1¼ cups (185 g/6 oz) cornmeal
1¼ cups (125 g/4 oz) dry breadcrumbs
oil, for deep-frying
sour cream, for serving

1 Select 24 large, uniform chillies. Drain
well and dry with paper towels. With a
sharp knife, cut a slit down the length of
one side of each chilli. Remove the seeds
and membrane.
2 Combine the Cheddar and cream cheese
and spoon some into each chilli. Put the
flour on a large plate and the beaten egg
in a small bowl. Combine the cornmeal
and breadcrumbs on a flat dish. Roll each
chilli in the flour, shake off the excess, dip
in the egg and roll in the crumb mixture
to coat thoroughly. Refrigerate for 1 hour.
Re-dip in egg and re-roll in breadcrumbs.
Refrigerate for another hour.
3 Fill a deep heavy-based pan one third
full of oil and heat the oil to 180°C (350°F).
The oil is ready when a cube of bread
dropped into the oil turns golden brown in
15 seconds. Deep-fry the chillies in small
batches until golden brown. Drain on
crumpled paper towels. Serve with sour
cream.

IN ADVANCE: These can be prepared up
to 3 hours ahead.

DUTCH-STYLE BEEF AND RICE CROQUETTES

Preparation time: 30 minutes +
  1 hour refrigeration + overnight chilling
Total cooking time: 1 hour 30 minutes
Makes 12

Béchamel sauce
20 g (¾ oz) butter
¼ cup (30 g/1 oz) plain (all-purpose) flour
⅔ cup (170 ml/5½ fl oz) milk
pinch of freshly grated nutmeg

10 g (¼ oz) butter
⅓ cup (75 g/2½ oz) arborio rice
1⅔ cups (410 ml/13 fl oz) chicken stock
2 tablespoons olive oil
1 onion, finely chopped
2 garlic cloves, crushed
500 g (1 lb) lean minced (ground) beef
100 ml (3½ fl oz) chicken stock, extra
1 tablespoon tomato paste (purée)
1 tablespoon Worcestershire sauce
50 g (1¾ oz) gingernut biscuits, crushed
  (see Note)
2 tablespoons chopped flat-leaf (Italian)
  parsley
¾ cup (75 g/2½ oz) dry breadcrumbs
oil, for deep-frying

1 To make the béchamel sauce, melt the butter in a small saucepan over medium heat. Stir in the flour and cook for 1 minute, or until foaming. Remove from the heat and gradually stir in the milk, beating well after each addition. After the last of the milk has been added, add the nutmeg and some salt and pepper. Return to the heat and stir constantly until the sauce boils and thickens. Set aside to cool.
2 Melt the butter in a saucepan. Add the rice and stir to coat. Gradually stir in the stock and continue stirring until it has come to the boil. Reduce the heat and simmer for about 20 minutes, or until the rice is very tender and all the stock has been absorbed.

3 Heat the oil in a large frying pan and cook the onion and garlic over low heat for about 5 minutes, or until softened but not browned. Add the beef and cook for 8 minutes, or until browned. Stir in the extra stock, tomato paste, Worcestershire sauce, crushed gingernut biscuits and parsley. Simmer, covered, for 20 minutes. If there is still some liquid left after this time, take the lid off and cook over high heat to reduce it.
4 Combine the béchamel, rice and beef and season well with salt and pepper. Cool slightly, then refrigerate for 1 hour.
5 Divide the mixture into twelve parts and roll each into a log approximately 7 cm (2¾ inches) long and 3 cm (1¼ inches) in diameter. The mixture will be soft, but manageable. Roll the logs in breadcrumbs to coat all over and place on a plate in a single layer. Cover with plastic wrap and refrigerate overnight.
6 Fill a deep-fat fryer or large saucepan one-third full of oil and heat to 180°C (350°F), or until a spoonful of the batter dropped into the oil browns in 15 seconds. Cook the croquettes, a few at a time, turning them with tongs to give an evenly golden brown surface. Drain on crumpled paper towels.

NOTE: If gingernut biscuits are unavailable, crush 50 g (1¾ oz) wheatmeal biscuits with ½ teaspoon ground ginger.

CROSTINI WITH PEPPER (CAPSICUM) ROULADE

Preparation time: 30 minutes + chilling
Total cooking time: 10 minutes
Makes about 20

2 red peppers (capsicums)
2 yellow peppers (capsicums)
8 English spinach leaves
1 tablespoon chopped fresh flat-leaf
  parsley
1 small French bread stick
2 tablespoons olive oil
shaved Parmesan, to garnish

1 Cut each pepper in half and remove the seeds and membrane. Cook skin-side-up under a hot grill until the skin is black and blistered. Place in a plastic bag and leave to cool. Peel.
2 Remove the stalks from the spinach and put the leaves in a bowl. Cover with boiling water and set aside for a couple of minutes until the leaves have wilted. Drain and cool. Squeeze out the excess water and spread the leaves out. Pat dry with paper towels.
3 Place two sheets of overlapping plastic wrap on a flat surface. Flatten out the red pepper to form a rectangle, overlapping the ends. Lay the spinach leaves over the pepper to make a second layer. Place the flattened yellow pepper on top to make a third layer, making sure there are no gaps, and overlapping the ends. Sprinkle with the parsley. Using the plastic wrap to assist, roll up the pepper tightly lengthways, sealing the ends. Wrap tightly in foil, twist the ends firmly and chill for 3 hours.
4 Preheat the oven to moderately hot 200°C (400°F/Gas 6). Cut the bread stick into 1 cm (½ inch) slices. Place on a baking tray, lightly brush with olive oil, sprinkle with salt and bake for 5–10 minutes, until golden.
5 Remove the plastic wrap, cut the roulade into 1.5 cm (⅝ inch) thick slices and place on the crostini. Drizzle with oil. Garnish with Parmesan.

COCKTAIL TARTLETS

Preparation time: 30 minutes + chilling
Total cooking time: 10 minutes
Makes about 30

1½ cups (185 g/6 oz) plain flour
100 g (3½ oz) chilled butter, chopped
30 g (1 oz) Parmesan, grated
1 egg, lightly beaten

Fillings
pesto, sun-dried tomato and black olives
olive tapenade, hard-boiled quail eggs
    and fresh flat-leaf parsley
cream cheese, shredded sliced smoked
    salmon, thinly sliced Lebanese
    cucumber, and chopped fresh chives

1 Sift the flour and ¼ teaspoon salt into a
large bowl, add the butter and rub into the
flour with your fingertips until the mixture
resembles fine breadcrumbs. Stir in the
Parmesan, then make a well in the
centre. Add the egg and a little water and
mix with a flat-bladed knife, using a
cutting action, until the mixture comes
together in beads. Gently gather together
and lift out onto a lightly floured surface.
Press together into a ball. Wrap in plastic
wrap and refrigerate for 30 minutes.
2 Preheat the oven to hot 210°C
(415°F/Gas 6–7). Lightly grease two
12-hole round-based patty tins. Roll the
pastry out very thinly and using an 8 cm
(3 inch) cutter, cut 30 rounds from the
pastry. Press the pastry into the tins and
prick lightly all over. Bake for 8–9 minutes,
or until golden. Allow to cool in the tins.
Remove and repeat with the remaining
pastry.
3 Fill the cooled shells with the different
fillings.

IN ADVANCE: The tartlet shells can be
made up to a few days ahead and stored
in an airtight container. If necessary,
re-crisp briefly in a moderate 180°C
(350°F/Gas 4) oven before use.

PARMESAN AND PESTO TOASTS

Preparation time: 30 minutes
Total cooking time: 5 minutes
Makes about 40

1 bread stick
16 large sun-dried tomatoes, cut into thin
    strips
150 g (4¾ oz) fresh Parmesan cheese,
    shaved thinly

Pesto
1 cup (50 g/1⅔ oz) firmly packed fresh
    basil leaves
2 tablespoons chopped fresh chives
4 tablespoons pine nuts
2–3 cloves garlic, peeled
¼ cup (60 ml/2 fl oz) olive oil

1 Freeze the bread stick until firm. Cut it
into very thin slices, using a sharp
serrated knife. Toast the slices under a
hot grill until they are golden brown on
both sides.
2 To make Pesto: Place the basil leaves,
chives, pine nuts, garlic and olive oil in a
food processor. Process for 20–30 seconds
or until smooth.
3 Spread the pesto mixture evenly over
the toasted slices. Top with strips of
tomato and shavings of Parmesan
cheese.

CORNBREAD WITH BEANS

Preparation time: 1 hour
Total cooking time: 30 minutes
Makes 24

1 large green chilli
1 large red chilli
1 cup (150 g/5 oz) cornmeal (polenta)
1 cup (125 g/4 oz) self-raising flour
½ cup (60 g/2 oz) grated Cheddar
1 egg, lightly beaten
¾ cup (185 ml/6 fl oz) milk
310 g (10 oz) can creamed corn
Tabasco sauce, for serving
fresh coriander leaves, to garnish

Topping
1 cup (230 g/7½ oz) refried beans
2 tablespoons sour cream
½ teaspoon ground cumin
½ teaspoon ground coriander
½ teaspoon paprika

1 Preheat the oven to moderately hot 200°C
(400°F/Gas 6). Grease a 20 x 30 cm (8 x 12
inch) shallow baking tin. Roast the chillies
by holding them with tongs (one at a time)
over a gas flame, until well blackened.
Alternatively, cut the chillies in half,
remove the seeds and membrane, flatten
out and grill skin-side-up until black and
blistered. Place in a plastic bag until cool,
then peel, cut in half and chop finely.
2 Combine the cornmeal, flour, Cheddar,
chilli flesh and 1 teaspoon salt in a bowl.
Make a well in the centre and add the egg,
milk and creamed corn. Stir until just
combined, being careful not to overbeat.
3 Pour into the tin and bake for 20 minutes,
or until lightly browned and firm to touch.
Turn onto a wire rack to cool.
4 For the topping, mix all the ingredients
in a small bowl until well combined.
5 Using a serrated knife, trim the edges of
the cornbread. Cut into 3 cm (1¼ inch)
squares. Place on a platter and top each
square with a teaspoon of topping.
Sprinkle each with a drop of Tabasco and
garnish with a coriander leaf.

OLIVES

ALL THESE RECIPES WILL KEEP IN THE FRIDGE FOR 3 MONTHS IF STORED IN PROPERLY STERILIZED JARS. WASH JARS AND LIDS THOROUGHLY IN BOILING WATER, RINSE IN BOILING WATER AND DRY IN A SLOW 150°C (300°F/GAS 2) OVEN FOR 30 MINUTES.

OLIVES WITH HERBS DE PROVENCE

Rinse and drain 500 g (1 lb) Niçoise or Ligurian olives. Put 1 crushed clove garlic, 2 teaspoons chopped fresh basil, 1 teaspoon each chopped fresh thyme, rosemary, marjoram, oregano and mint, 1 teaspoon fennel seeds, 2 tablespoons lemon juice and ½ cup (125 ml/4 fl oz) olive oil in a bowl and mix together. Layer the olives and marinade in a wide-necked, 3-cup (750 ml/24 fl oz) sterilized jar, adding extra olive oil to cover the olives. Seal and marinate in the refrigerator for at least 1 week before using. Serve at room temperature.

HONEY CITRUS OLIVES

Mix together the rind of 1 lemon, lime and orange, 2 tablespoons lime juice, 4 tablespoons lemon juice, 1 tablespoon orange juice, 1 tablespoon honey, 2 teaspoons wholegrain mustard, ½ cup (125 ml/4 fl oz) extra virgin olive oil, 2 thinly sliced cloves garlic, ¼ teaspoon dried oregano or 1 tablespoon chopped fresh oregano leaves and 6 thin slices of lemon and lime. Add 1½ cups (265 g/8½ oz) drained unpitted black olives, 1½ cups (265 g/8½ oz) drained unpitted green olives and 2 tablespoons chopped fresh parsley. Place in a wide-necked, 3-cup (750 ml/24 fl oz) sterilized jar, then seal and marinate in the refrigerator for at least 1 week before using. Serve at room temperature.

LEMON OLIVES WITH VERMOUTH

Combine 3 tablespoons dry vermouth, 1 tablespoon lemon juice, 2 teaspoons shredded lemon rind and 2 tablespoons extra virgin olive oil. Rinse 1 cup (170 g/ 5½ oz) of Spanish green or stuffed olives and pat dry. Add to the marinade and toss well. Cover and refrigerate overnight. Serve at room temperature.

DILL, GARLIC AND ORANGE OLIVES

Combine 500 g (1 lb) Kalamata olives with 3 tablespoons coarsely chopped fresh dill, 1 bruised clove garlic, 4 thin slices of orange cut into eighths and 2 torn bay leaves. Spoon into a 1-litre sterilized jar and pour in about 1¾ cups (440 ml/14 fl oz) olive oil or enough to cover the olives completely. Seal and marinate in the refrigerator for at least 2 days. Serve at room temperature.

CHILLI AND LEMON OLIVES

Combine 500 g (1 lb) cured black olives (olives with wrinkled skin) with 2 teaspoons finely grated lemon rind, 2 teaspoons chopped fresh oregano and 3 teaspoons dried chilli flakes. Transfer to a 3-cup (750 ml/24 fl oz) sterilized jar; cover with olive oil. Seal; chill for at least 2 days. Serve at room temperature.

SUN-DRIED TOMATO OLIVES

Rinse 500 g (1 lb) Spanish black olives; pat dry. Score or crack the olives. Layer in a 3-cup (750 ml/24 fl oz) sterilized jar, with 100 g (3½ oz) drained and chopped sun-dried tomatoes (reserve the oil), 2 crushed cloves garlic, 2 bay leaves, 3 teaspoons fresh thyme leaves and 2 teaspoons red wine vinegar. Pour over the reserved oil and 1 cup (250 ml/8 fl oz) extra virgin olive oil, or enough to cover. Seal and refrigerate overnight. Serve at room temperature.

MIXED OLIVE PICKLES

Combine 200 g (6½ oz) jumbo green olives, 4 gherkins, thickly sliced diagonally, 1 tablespoon capers, 2 brown pickling onions, quartered, 2 teaspoons mustard seeds and 1 tablespoon fresh dill sprigs in a bowl. Spoon into a 2-cup (500 ml/16 fl oz) sterilized jar and pour in ½ cup (125 ml/ 4 fl oz) tarragon vinegar. Top with about ½ cup (125 ml/4 fl oz) olive oil, or enough to cover completely. Seal and refrigerate for at least 2 days. Shake the jar occasionally. Serve at room temperature.

CLOCKWISE, FROM TOP LEFT: Olives with herbs de provence; Honey citrus olives; Lemon olives with vermouth; Dill, garlic and orange olives; Chilli and lemon olives; Sun-dried tomato olives; Mixed olive pickles

POLENTA (CORNMEAL) CHILLIES

Preparation time: 30 minutes +
  2 hours refrigeration
Total cooking time: 2–3 minutes each batch
Serves 6

330 g (10½ oz) jar mild, whole chillies
½ cup (60 g/2 oz) grated Cheddar cheese
100 g (3⅓ oz) soft cream cheese
⅓ cup (40 g/1⅓ oz) plain flour
2 eggs, lightly beaten
¾ cup (110 g/3⅔ oz) polenta (cornmeal)
¾ cup (75 g/2½ oz) dry breadcrumbs
oil, for deep-frying
sour cream, for serving (optional)

1 Select twelve large, similar-sized chillies from the jar. Drain well and dry with paper towels. With a sharp knife, cut a slit down the length of one side of each chilli. Remove all the seeds and membrane. Combine the grated Cheddar and cream cheeses; fill each chilli with the cheese mixture.
2 Place the flour onto a large plate and beaten eggs in a small bowl. Combine the polenta and breadcrumbs in a small plastic bag; transfer to a large plate. Roll each chilli in flour; shake off excess; dip in egg and roll in crumb mixture to coat chillies thoroughly. Refrigerate for 1 hour. Re-dip in egg and re-roll in the breadcrumbs. Return to the refrigerator for 1 hour.
3 Heat the oil in a medium pan. Test the oil by frying a small cube of bread; if it browns in 30 seconds, the oil is ready. Deep-fry the prepared chillies in small batches until golden; drain on paper towels.

NOTE: Delicious served with sour cream and your favourite salsa.

RISOTTO CAKES WITH PRESERVED LEMON MAYONNAISE

Preparation time: 30 minutes +
  2 hours 30 minutes standing
Total cooking time: 40 minutes
Makes 30

1 litre (32 fl oz) chicken stock
1 tablespoon olive oil
1 garlic clove, finely chopped
1 small onion, finely chopped
1 cup (220 g/7 oz) risotto rice
½ cup (125 ml/4 fl oz) dry white wine
4 marinated artichokes, drained and
  finely chopped
¼ cup (25 g/¾ oz) coarsely grated
  Parmesan cheese
1 teaspoon grated lemon zest
½ cup (60 g/2 oz) plain (all-purpose)
  flour, seasoned
2 eggs
1 cup (100 g/3½ oz) dry breadcrumbs
3 slices (50 g/1¾ oz) pancetta
oil, for pan-frying
15 pitted Kalamata olives, halved
flat-leaf (Italian) parsley, to garnish

Preserved lemon mayonnaise
⅓ cup (80 g/2¾ oz) whole-egg
  mayonnaise
2 teaspoons finely chopped preserved
  lemon

1 Pour the stock into a saucepan and bring to the boil. Reduce the heat, cover with a lid and keep at a low simmer.
2 Heat the oil in a large saucepan. Cook the garlic and onion over low heat for 4–5 minutes, or until the onion is softened but not browned. Stir in the rice until well coated. Add the wine and stir over medium heat until it has all been absorbed. Add ½ cup (125 ml/4 fl oz) of the hot stock, and stir constantly until nearly all the stock has been absorbed. Continue adding more liquid, ½ cup (125 ml/4 fl oz) at a time until all the liquid is absorbed and the rice is tender and creamy, this will take around 25–30 minutes.

3 Remove from the heat and stir in the artichokes, Parmesan and lemon zest. Spread the risotto out on a tray and allow it to cool for 2 hours.
4 Put the flour in one bowl, the eggs in another and the breadcrumbs in a third. Lightly beat the eggs. Using wet hands, roll the risotto into thirty 3 cm (1¼ inch) discs. First, coat them with flour, next dip them in egg and, finally, coat them in the breadcrumbs. Refrigerate for at least 30 minutes.
5 Cook the pancetta in a non-stick frying pan until crisp, then tear each slice into 10 pieces.
6 To make the preserved lemon mayonnaise, mix the preserved lemon into the mayonnaise.
7 Heat the oil in a frying pan and cook the risotto cakes in batches for 2–3 minutes on each side, or until golden and crisp. Drain on crumpled paper towels. Top each risotto cake with ½ teaspoon of the mayonnaise, a piece of pancetta, half an olive and a torn parsley leaf. Serve warm or hot.

NOTE: You can make the risotto 2 days ahead of time, then spread it out on a tray and keep covered in the fridge until needed.

KALAMARIA TOURSI (PICKLED SQUID)

Preparation time: 25 minutes +
 1 week maturing
Total cooking time: 5 minutes
Serves 4

1 kg (2 lb) small squid
4 fresh bay leaves
4 sprigs of fresh oregano
10 whole black peppercorns
2 teaspoons coriander seeds
1 small fresh red chilli, halved and
 seeded
2½ cups (625 ml/20 fl oz) good-quality
 white wine vinegar
2–3 tablespoons olive oil, to top up the jar

1 To prepare the squid, grasp each squid body in one hand and the head and tentacles in the other and pull apart to separate them. Cut the tentacles from the head by cutting below the eyes. Discard the head. Push out the beak and discard. Pull the quill from inside the body and discard. Under cold running water, pull away the skin (the flaps can be used). Cut into 7 mm (⅜ inch) rings.
2 Place 2 litres water and 1 bay leaf in a large saucepan. Bring to the boil and add the calamari and 1 teaspoon salt. Reduce the heat and simmer for 5 minutes. Drain and dry well.
3 Pack the squid rings into a clean, dry 2 cup (500 ml/16 fl oz) jar with a sealing lid. Add the oregano, peppercorns, coriander seeds, chilli and remaining bay leaves. Cover completely with the vinegar then gently pour in enough olive oil to cover by 2 cm (¾ inch). Seal and refrigerate for 1 week before opening. When you are ready to serve, remove from the marinade, place on a serving dish and garnish with lemon wedges and chopped fresh parsley.

SPRING ROLLS

Preparation time: 30 minutes +
 30 minutes soaking
Total cooking time: 25 minutes
Makes 20

4 dried Chinese mushrooms
80 g (2¾ oz) dried rice vermicelli
1 tablespoon peanut oil
2 garlic cloves, chopped
2 teaspoons grated ginger
250 g (8 oz) minced (ground) pork
250 g (8 oz) raw prawns (shrimp), peeled
 and finely chopped
1 tablespoon light soy sauce
1 tablespoon oyster sauce
1 tablespoon Chinese rice wine
1 carrot, grated
8 water chestnuts, finely chopped
4 spring onions (scallions), thinly sliced
200 g (6½ oz) Chinese cabbage (wom
 bok), finely shredded
1 tablespoon sweet chilli sauce
2 teaspoons cornflour (cornstarch)
20 large spring roll wrappers
oil, for deep-frying

1 Soak the dried mushrooms in boiling water for 30 minutes, then drain and squeeze. Remove and discard the stems and chop the caps. Put the vermicelli in a heatproof bowl, cover with boiling water and soak for 6–7 minutes, or until soft and transparent. Drain and cut into 5 cm (2 inch) lengths.
2 Heat the oil in a wok over high heat and swirl to coat. Add the garlic and ginger, and cook for 1 minute. Add the pork mince and cook for another 3 minutes, stirring to break up any lumps. Add the prawns and cook for 1 minute, or until they just turn pink. Stir in the soy sauce, oyster sauce, rice wine, carrot, water chestnuts, spring onion, Chinese cabbage and sweet chilli sauce and cook for 2 minutes, or until warmed through. Season to taste with salt and pepper. Stir in the mushrooms and vermicelli.

3 Combine the cornflour and 2 tablespoons water in a small bowl until smooth.
4 Lay the spring roll wrappers under a damp tea towel. Working with one at a time, place a wrapper on the work surface with one corner facing you. Place 2 tablespoons of the filling along the centre of each spring roll wrapper. Brush the edges with the cornflour paste and roll up firmly, tucking in the ends as you go, and sealing with the cornflour paste. Continue, covering the completed rolls with a damp tea towel to prevent them drying out.
5 Fill a wok one-third full of oil and heat to 180°C (350°F), or until a cube of bread dropped in the oil browns in 15 seconds. Cook the spring rolls in batches of 2–3 rolls, turning gently to brown evenly, for 2 minutes, or until golden. Drain on crumpled paper towels. Serve with light soy sauce or your favourite dipping sauce.

NOTE: If the rolls are too big, serve cut in half on the diagonal.

SIGARA BOREGI
(FRIED CIGAR PASTRIES)

Preparation time: 30 minutes
Total cooking time: 20 minutes
Makes 12

500 g (1 lb) English spinach
1 tablespoon olive oil
4 cloves garlic, crushed
200 g (6½ oz) French shallots, finely
  chopped
½ cup (75 g/2½ oz) crumbled feta cheese
1 egg, lightly beaten
3 tablespoons chopped fresh flat-leaf
  parsley
¼ teaspoon finely grated lemon rind
¼ teaspoon paprika
pinch of nutmeg
6 sheets filo pastry
125 g (4 oz) butter, melted
light olive oil, for deep-frying

1 Wash the spinach, leaving a substantial amount of water on the leaves. Place in a large saucepan, cover and briefly cook over low heat until just wilted. Tip the spinach into a colander and press out most of the excess liquid with a wooden spoon. When cool, squeeze dry.
2 Heat the olive oil in a frying pan, add the garlic and shallots and cook for 2 minutes, or until soft but not browned. Transfer to a bowl and add the crumbled feta cheese, egg, parsley, spinach and lemon rind. Season with the paprika, nutmeg and salt and pepper, and mix well.

3 Remove a sheet of filo and cover the rest with a damp tea towel to prevent them drying out. Brush the sheet with melted butter, then fold it in half lengthways. It should measure about 32 x 12 cm (13 x 5 inches). Cut it in half widthways. Brush with butter, place about 1 heaped tablespoon of filling at one end of each and spread it to within 1 cm (½ inch) of each side. Fold the sides over to cover the ends of the filling, continuing the folds right up the length of the pastry. Brush with melted butter, then roll up tightly. Brush the outside with butter and seal well. Cover with a damp tea towel while you prepare the rest.
4 Heat the light olive oil in a deep frying pan to 180°C (350°F), or until a cube of bread browns in 15 seconds. Deep-fry in small batches until golden. Serve warm or at room temperature.

MINI SPICY BURGERS

Preparation time: 30 minutes
Total cooking time: 15 minutes
Makes 24

6–8 rounds of naan bread
600 g (1¼ lb) lean beef mince
1 green chilli, chopped
1 tablespoon curry powder
3 cloves garlic, crushed
2 teaspoons finely chopped fresh ginger
1 tablespoon peanut oil
3 tablespoons thick natural yoghurt
3 tablespoons mango chutney
24 fresh mint leaves

1 Heat the oven to warm 160°C (315°F/ Gas 2–3). Using a 6 cm (2½ inch) round cutter, mark the naan bread into 48 rounds, then cut with scissors. Loosely wrap in foil and warm in the oven while you make the patties.
2 In a bowl, combine the beef mince, chopped chilli, curry powder, garlic and ginger. Season with salt and black pepper. With wet hands, form the meat into 24 patties, about 6 cm (2½ inches) in diameter.
3 Heat the oil in a large frying pan and cook the burgers in batches, for 2–3 minutes each side, or until done to your liking. Drain on crumpled paper towels.
4 Place 24 of the warm rounds of naan on a serving platter, top each with a beef patty, then some yoghurt, mango chutney and a mint leaf. Top with the remaining rounds of naan and serve immediately.

NOTE: Prepared naan bread can be bought at most supermarkets where you find pita bread and lavash bread. These can be substituted if naan is unavailable.

SESAME CHICKEN STICKS

Preparation time: 25 minutes +
  overnight marinating
Total cooking time: 25 minutes
Makes about 32

4 chicken breast fillets, cut into strips
¼ cup (60 ml/2 fl oz) teriyaki sauce
1 tablespoon chilli sauce
1 tablespoon natural yoghurt
2 teaspoons curry powder
2 cups (100 g/3½ oz) crushed cornflakes
¼ cup (40 g/1¼ oz) sesame seeds
35 g (1¼ oz) Parmesan, grated

Sweet and sour sauce
1 tablespoon cornflour
½ cup (125 ml/4 fl oz) white vinegar
½ cup (125 g/4 oz) caster sugar
¼ cup (60 ml/2 fl oz) tomato sauce
1 teaspoon chicken stock powder

1 Combine the chicken strips in a bowl
with the teriyaki sauce, chilli sauce,
yoghurt and curry powder. Mix well, cover
and refrigerate overnight.
2 Preheat the oven to moderately hot
190°C (375°F/Gas 5). Combine the
cornflakes, sesame seeds and Parmesan
in a shallow dish. Drain the excess
marinade from the chicken. Coat each
chicken strip in the crumb mixture.
3 Place the strips in a single layer on
a greased baking tray. Bake for
20–25 minutes, or until crisp and
golden. Serve hot with the sauce.
4 To prepare the sauce, blend the
cornflour with the vinegar and combine
with the remaining ingredients and 1 cup
(250 ml/8 fl oz) water in a small saucepan.
Stir over medium heat until the mixture
boils and thickens.

IN ADVANCE: Crumbed chicken strips can
be frozen in a single layer for 2 months.

OMELETTE ROLLS

Preparation time: 15 minutes
Total cooking time: 10 minutes
Makes 5

4 eggs
2 tablespoons water
2 teaspoons soy sauce
2 teaspoons peanut oil

1 Place the eggs, water and sauce in a
medium bowl. Beat with a wire whisk for
2 minutes.
2 Brush the base of a small non-stick pan
with oil. Heat pan on high. Pour one-fifth
of the egg mixture into the base of the
pan. Shake pan to spread mixture evenly
over the base. Heat for 20 seconds, or
until the egg has almost set. Remove pan
from heat. Using an egg slice or a large
flat-bladed knife, roll the omelette from
one end, forming a roll. Transfer to a
warm plate and cover with a tea towel.
3 Repeat the process with the remaining
egg mixture, using one-fifth of the egg
mixture to make each omelette.

NOTE: For extra flavour, before rolling
spread the omelettes with a pesto or olive
paste, or other filling of your choice. Roll
up tightly and cut into rounds for serving.

MARINATED BABY MUSHROOMS

Preparation time: 30 minutes
Total cooking time: Nil
Serves 6–8

500 g (1 lb) button mushrooms, halved
½ cup (125 ml/4 fl oz) olive oil
½ cup (125 ml/4 fl oz) white wine vinegar
3 cloves garlic, chopped
2 tablespoons chopped fresh parsley
2 teaspoons chopped chilli
1 teaspoon caster sugar
salt and pepper

1 Wipe the mushrooms with a damp cloth
and trim the stalks to the level of the cap.
Place the mushroom caps in a large bowl.
Combine the olive oil, vinegar, garlic,
parsley, chilli, sugar, salt and pepper in a
screw-top jar; shake well.
2 Pour the marinade over the mushrooms
and toss to combine. Cover with plastic
wrap and refrigerate for at least 1 hour.
Mushrooms can be marinated for up to
2 days, depending on how intense you
want the flavour. Turn mushrooms
occasionally as they marinate.
3 Serve mushrooms at room temperature
with other marinated vegetables as part
of an antipasto platter, if desired.

BEEF ROLLS

Preparation time: 30 minutes
Total cooking time: 30 minutes
Makes about 20

500 g (1 lb) beef fillet, 8 cm (3 inch) in
    diameter
3 tablespoons olive oil
1½ tablespoons horseradish cream
1½ tablespoons wholegrain mustard
1 zucchini (courgette), cut into fine strips
1 small carrot, cut into fine strips
1 small red pepper (capsicum), cut into
    fine strips
60 g (2 oz) snow peas (mangetout), cut
    into fine strips

1 Preheat the oven to moderately hot
200°C (400°F/Gas 6). Trim the beef of
excess fat and sinew and brush with a
little of the oil. Heat a heavy-based frying
pan over high heat and brown each side of
the beef fillet quickly, to seal in the juices.
Transfer to a baking dish and bake for
20 minutes. Remove and set aside to cool.
2 Slice the cooled beef very thinly.
Combine the horseradish cream and the
mustard, then spread a little over each
slice of beef.
3 Heat the remaining oil in a pan and cook
the zucchini, carrot, pepper and snow
peas quickly over high heat, and then
allow to cool. Place a small bunch of the
cooked vegetable strips on the end of
each beef slice and roll up. Arrange on a
platter and serve.

IN ADVANCE: The beef can be cooked and
the vegetables prepared up to 2 hours in
advance. Don't cook the vegetables or fill
the rolls any earlier than 30 minutes
before serving.

STARS AND STRIPES BARBECUED RIBS

Preparation time: 30 minutes +
    overnight marinating
Total cooking time: 15 minutes
Makes about 30

½ teaspoon dry mustard, or prepared
    English mustard
½ teaspoon ground sweet paprika
¼ teaspoon ground oregano
¼ teaspoon ground cumin
1½ tablespoons peanut oil
1 teaspoon Tabasco sauce
1 clove garlic, crushed
½ cup (125 ml/4 fl oz) tomato sauce
2 tablespoons tomato paste (tomato
    purée)
2 tablespoons soft brown sugar
1 tablespoon Worcestershire sauce
2 teaspoons brown vinegar
1.5 kg (3 lb) American-style pork spare
    ribs

1 For the sauce, combine the mustard,
paprika, oregano, cumin and oil in a pan.
Add the remaining ingredients, except the
ribs. Cook, stirring, over medium heat for
3 minutes, or until combined. Allow to
cool.
2 Coat the ribs with sauce and marinate
overnight. Cook on a hot barbecue grill,
turning frequently, until firm and well
done. Cut into individual ribs before
serving.

NOTE: Get very lean pork spare ribs as
fatty ones tend to flare up and burn. You
can use beef spare ribs if you prefer but
first simmer until tender, then drain.

HONEY VEAL TAGINE ON PAPPADUMS

Preparation time: 20 minutes
Total cooking time: 1 hour 10 minutes
Makes 24

2 tablespoons olive oil
650 g (1 lb 5 oz) whole piece leg veal, cut
    into small cubes
1 onion, chopped
2 cloves garlic, crushed
1 cinnamon stick
2 teaspoons ground cumin
1 teaspoon coriander seeds, crushed
¼ teaspoon ground cardamom
1¼ cups (315 ml/10 fl oz) chicken stock
24 small pappadums
3 pitted dates, thinly sliced
4 pitted prunes, finely chopped
3 teaspoons honey
½ cup (125 g/4 oz) Greek-style natural
    yoghurt
fresh coriander leaves, to garnish

1 Heat 1 tablespoon of the olive oil and
brown the veal in batches over high heat.
Transfer the veal and any juices to a bowl.
2 Heat the remaining oil in the same pan,
add the onion and garlic and stir over
medium heat for 5 minutes, or until the
onion is slightly softened. Add the spices
and cook for another minute, or until the
spices are aromatic. Return the veal to
the pan, pour in the stock and bring to the
boil. Reduce the heat and simmer,
covered, over low heat for 30 minutes.
3 Uncover and simmer for 30 minutes, or
until the mixture is thickened and the veal
is tender. Meanwhile, cook the
pappadums according to the
manufacturer's instructions.
4 Stir the dates, prunes and honey into
the veal mixture. To assemble, spoon the
veal tagine in the centre of the
pappadums, top each with 1 teaspoon of
yoghurt and sprinkle with coriander
leaves. Serve immediately.

PEPPER (CAPSICUM) AND BLACK OLIVE PIKELETS

Preparation time: 15 minutes +
20 minutes standing
Total cooking time: 15 minutes
Makes 16

2 medium red peppers (capsicums)
½ cup (125 ml/4 fl oz) milk
½ cup (60 g/2 oz) self-raising flour
½ teaspoon salt
¼ teaspoon black pepper
3 eggs, lightly beaten
2 tablespoons finely chopped black olives
1 tablespoon finely chopped basil
olive oil, for frying

1 Cut each red pepper in half, remove the seeds and flatten the halves. Cook under a preheated grill, skin-side up, for 10 minutes or until the skin blisters and turns black. Cover with a damp tea towel, set aside and allow to cool. Remove the skin and chop the flesh roughly.
2 Process the cooked red pepper with the milk in a food processor or blender.
3 Sift the flour with salt into a bowl. Add the black pepper and make a well in the centre. Add the eggs, and the red pepper and milk mixture. Stir until all the ingredients are combined and the mixture is free of lumps. Stir in the olives and basil. Set aside, covered with plastic wrap, for 20 minutes.
4 Brush the base of a small frying pan with oil. When the oil is hot, pour 1–2 tablespoons of batter into the pan and cook over medium-high heat until the underside is golden. Turn over and cook the other side. Repeat the process with the remaining mixture. Serve with goat's cheese and a sprinkling of fresh herbs.

SCOTCH QUAIL EGGS

Preparation time: 30 minutes
Total cooking time: 20 minutes
Makes 24 whole eggs or 48 halves

24 quail eggs
600 g (1¼ lb) chicken mince
2 teaspoons grated fresh ginger
2 tablespoons chopped fresh chives
2 teaspoons Dijon mustard
½ cup (60 g/2 oz) plain flour
2 eggs, lightly beaten
1 cup (100 g/3½ oz) dry breadcrumbs
oil, for deep-frying

1 Place the eggs in a pan and cover with water. Place over medium heat, stirring the eggs gently until the water boils (this centres the yolks). Cook for 5 minutes once boiling. Drain, place in a bowl of cold water and set aside to cool.
2 Mix the chicken mince, ginger, chives and mustard in a small bowl. Peel the eggs, and toss lightly in the flour.
3 Divide the chicken mixture into 24 even portions. Using damp hands, wrap each portion around an egg. Brush each wrapped egg with the beaten egg, and then roll in breadcrumbs, shaking off any excess.
4 Fill a deep heavy-based pan one third full of oil and heat the oil to 180°C (350°F). The oil is ready when a cube of bread dropped in the oil turns golden brown in 15 seconds. Deep-fry the coated eggs until golden brown, then drain on crumpled paper towels. Serve hot, either whole or cut in half.

IN ADVANCE: The eggs can be assembled up to 4 hours ahead and refrigerated, covered, until required. Deep-fry just before serving and garnish with fresh herb sprigs.

POTATO AND ROSEMARY PIZZETTAS

Preparation time: 25 minutes + standing
Total cooking time: 12–15 minutes
Makes 48

1 teaspoon dried yeast
½ teaspoon sugar
2½ cups (310 g/10 oz) plain flour
⅓ cup (80 ml/2¾ fl oz) olive oil
400 g (13 oz) pontiac potatoes, unpeeled
2 tablespoons olive oil, extra
1 tablespoon fresh rosemary leaves

1 Place the yeast, sugar and ⅓ cup (80 ml/2¾ fl oz) water in a small bowl, cover and leave in a warm place until foamy.
2 Sift the flour and ¼ teaspoon salt into a large bowl. Make a well in the centre and stir in the yeast mixture, the oil and ⅓ cup (80 ml/2¾ fl oz) water; mix to a soft dough. Turn out onto a lightly floured surface and knead for 5 minutes, or until the dough is smooth and elastic. Place the dough in an oiled bowl, cover and leave in a warm place for about 1 hour, or until the dough has doubled in size.
3 Preheat the oven to hot 220°C (425°F/Gas 7). Punch down the dough to expel the air. Turn out and knead for 1 minute, or until smooth. Divide into 48 portions and roll each portion to a 5 cm (2 inch) round. Place on lightly greased baking trays.
4 Cut the potatoes into slices. Cover each dough round with a slice of potato, leaving a 1 cm (½ inch) border. Brush the pizzettas with the extra olive oil and sprinkle with rosemary leaves and salt. Bake on the highest shelf in the oven for 12–15 minutes, or until the pastry is crisp and lightly browned. Serve immediately.

PURIS WITH CORIANDER RELISH

Preparation time: 40 minutes
Total cooking time: 10–15 minutes
Makes 32

¾ cup (90 g/3 oz) plain flour
¾ cup (110 g/3½ oz) wholemeal plain flour
1 teaspoon salt
1 tablespoon cracked black pepper
3 tablespoons oil or ghee
1 teaspoon kalonji (nigella) seeds
oil, for deep-frying

Coriander relish
60 g (2 oz) fresh coriander leaves
20 g (¾ oz) fresh mint leaves
½ small onion
1 green chilli
2 tablespoons lemon juice

1 Sift the flours and salt and pepper into a large bowl. Add the oil or ghee and rub it into the flour with your fingertips until it resembles fine breadcrumbs. Stir in the kalonji seeds. Make a well, add 3–4 tablespoons hot water and mix with a flat-bladed knife. It should be rough but hold together. Form into a ball.
2 Divide the dough into 4 and then each portion into 8 pieces, making 32 altogether. On a lightly floured surface, roll one piece at a time into a 6 cm (2½ inch) round. Keep the rest covered with a damp tea towel or plastic wrap. Don't worry about the cracked edges.
3 Heat 2.5 cm (1 inch) of oil in a wok or large heavy-based frying pan to 180°C (350°F). The oil is ready when a cube of bread dropped into the oil turns golden brown in 15 seconds. Fry 3 or 4 puris at a time, turning them halfway through. They will only take a few seconds to turn golden on each side. Remove from the oil and drain on crumpled paper towel while you fry the remainder.
4 For the coriander relish, process all the relish ingredients together in a food processor until smooth. Serve with the puris.

PRAWN CROUSTADE

Preparation time: 45 minutes
Total cooking time: 25 minutes
Serves 6

½ loaf unsliced white bread
½ cup (125 ml/4 fl oz) olive oil
1 clove garlic, crushed

Filling
500 g (1 lb) raw medium prawns
1½ cups (375 ml/12 fl oz) fish stock
2 slices lemon
50 g (1¾ oz) butter
6 spring onions, chopped
¼ cup (30 g/1 oz) plain flour
1 tablespoon lemon juice
½–1 teaspoon chopped fresh dill
¼ cup (60 ml/2 fl oz) cream

1 Preheat the oven to 210°C (415°F/Gas 6–7). Remove the crust from the bread and cut the bread into slices about 5 cm (2 inches) thick. Cut each slice diagonally to form triangles. Cut triangles 1 cm (½ inch) inside the others, leaving a base on each, then scoop out the centres to create cavities for the filling. Heat the oil and garlic in a small pan, brush all over the bread cases, then place on a baking tray and bake for 10 minutes, or until golden brown.
2 For the filling, peel the prawns and gently pull out the dark vein from each prawn back, starting at the head end. Roughly chop the prawns, place in a small pan and cover with stock. Add the lemon slices, simmer for 15 minutes, strain and reserve the liquid and prawns separately.
3 Melt the butter in a small pan, add the spring onion and stir over medium heat until soft. Stir in the flour and some pepper and cook for 2 minutes. Remove from the heat and gradually stir in the reserved prawn liquid. Return to the heat and stir constantly over medium heat for 5 minutes, or until the sauce boils and thickens. Add the lemon juice, dill, cream and reserved prawns, and stir until heated through.
4 Spoon the filling into the warm bread cases.

TOMATO AND ANCHOVY TOASTS

Preparation time: 10 minutes
Total cooking time: 5 minutes
Makes 16

16 x 1 cm (½ inch) thick slices Italian bread
3 cloves garlic, halved
8 ripe vine-ripened tomatoes
⅓ cup (80 ml/2¾ fl oz) extra virgin olive oil
2 x 45 g (1½ oz) cans anchovy fillets, drained and sliced lengthways

1 Toast the bread on both sides until golden. While warm, rub both sides of the toast with the cut garlic.
2 Cut the tomatoes in half and rub each side of the toast with them, so that the juice and seeds soak well into the toast but do not saturate it. Chop the remaining tomato and pile it on the toast.
3 Drizzle each toast with the oil and top with anchovy fillets. Sprinkle with salt and ground black pepper and serve.

THAI BEEF SALAD RICE PAPER ROLLS

Preparation time: 35 minutes +
  2 hours marinating
Total cooking time: 5 minutes
Makes 16

Dipping sauce
¼ cup (60 ml/2 fl oz) soy sauce
1 tablespoon rice vinegar
1 teaspoon sesame oil
1 tablespoon mirin
2 teaspoons finely julienned ginger

⅓ cup (80 ml/2¾ fl oz) kecap manis (see
  Notes)
⅓ cup (80 ml/2¾ fl oz) lime juice
1 tablespoon sesame oil
2 small red chillies, finely chopped
300 g (10 oz) piece of beef eye fillet
1 stem lemon grass, white part only,
  finely chopped
3 tablespoons finely chopped mint
3 tablespoons finely chopped coriander
  (cilantro) leaves
1½ tablespoons fish sauce
¼ cup (60 ml/2 fl oz) lime juice, extra
16 square (16 cm/6½ inch) rice paper
  wrappers (see Notes)

1 To make the dipping sauce, combine all
the ingredients in a small bowl. Set aside
until ready to serve.
2 Mix the kecap manis, lime juice,
sesame oil and half the chilli in a large
bowl. Add the beef and toss well to
ensure all the beef is coated. Cover with
plastic wrap and refrigerate for 2 hours.
3 Heat a barbecue or chargrill plate over
high heat and cook the beef for 2–3 minutes
on each side, or until cooked to your
liking. It should be cooked just until it is
quite pink in the middle so that it remains
tender. Cool, then slice into thin strips,
against the grain.

4 Combine the beef with the lemon grass,
mint, coriander, fish sauce, extra lime
juice and remaining chilli, then toss well.
5 Dip one rice paper wrapper at a time in
warm water for a few seconds until
softened. Drain, then place on a flat
surface. Put a tablespoon of the mixture
in the centre of the rice paper wrapper
and roll up, tucking in the edges. Repeat
with the remaining ingredients to make 16
rolls in total. Serve with the dipping
sauce.

NOTES: Kecap manis is also known as
sweet soy sauce. It is a thick dark sauce
used in Indonesian cooking as a
seasoning and condiment. If it is not
available, use soy sauce with a little soft
brown sugar.
 If square rice paper wrappers are not
available, use round wrappers of the
same diameter.

CRAB-STUFFED MUSHROOMS

Preparation time: 25 minutes
Total cooking time: 6 minutes
Makes 24

24 small cap mushrooms
30 g (1 oz) butter, softened
4 spring onions, chopped
200 g (6½ oz) can crab meat, drained
2 tablespoons lemon juice
½ teaspoon chilli powder
1 cup (250 g/8 oz) sour cream
25 g (¾ oz) Parmesan, grated
125 g (4 oz) Cheddar, grated
pinch of paprika

1 Preheat the oven to moderate 180°C
(350°F/Gas 4). Remove the mushroom
stalks and chop finely; set aside. Place
the mushroom caps on a baking tray.
2 Combine the butter, spring onion, crab,
lemon juice, chilli powder and freshly
ground pepper, to taste, in a bowl.
3 Mix in the mushroom stalks, sour
cream and Parmesan. Spoon even
amounts into the mushroom caps and
sprinkle with the combined Cheddar and
paprika.
4 Bake for 5–6 minutes, or until the
Cheddar has melted and the mushrooms
heated through. Serve warm.

MINI EGGS FLORENTINE

Preparation time: 20 minutes
Total cooking time: 25 minutes
Makes 24

8 slices white bread
1–2 tablespoons olive oil
12 quail eggs
2 teaspoons lemon juice
85 g (3 oz) butter, melted, cooled
2 teaspoons finely chopped fresh basil
20 g (¾ oz) butter, extra
50 g (1¾ oz) baby English spinach leaves

1 Preheat the oven to moderate 180°C (350°F/Gas 4). Cut 24 rounds from the bread with a 4 cm (1½ inch) cutter. Brush both sides of the rounds with the oil and bake for 10–15 minutes, or until golden brown.
2 Add the quail eggs to a small pan of cold water, bring to the boil, stirring gently (to centre the yolk) and simmer for 4 minutes. Drain, then soak in cold water until cool. Peel, then cut in half, remove the yolks and reserve the whites.
3 Process the quail egg yolks and lemon juice together in a food processor for 10 seconds. With the motor running, add the cooled melted butter in a thin stream. Add the chopped basil and process until combined.
4 Melt the extra butter in a pan, add the spinach leaves and toss until just wilted. Place a little on each bread round, top each with half a quail egg white and fill the cavity with basil mixture.

SPINACH AND OLIVE TURNOVERS

Preparation time: 1 hour 20 minutes +
    1 hour refrigeration
Total cooking time: 15 minutes
Makes 30

2 cups (250 g/8 oz) plain flour
200 g (6½ oz) butter, cut into small cubes
¾ cup (185 ml/6 fl oz) water
1 egg, lightly beaten, for glazing

Filling
60 g (2 oz) English spinach leaves
100 g (3⅓ oz) feta cheese
2 tablespoons chopped pitted black
    olives
2 teaspoons chopped fresh rosemary
1 clove garlic, crushed
2 tablespoons pistachio nuts, shelled
1 egg, lightly beaten

1 Sift the flour into a large bowl and stir in the cubed butter until just combined. Make a well in the centre of the flour, add almost all the water and mix to a slightly sticky dough with a knife, adding more water if necessary. Gather the dough together.
2 Turn the dough onto a well-floured surface, and lightly press together until almost smooth, taking care not to overwork the dough. Roll out to a neat 20 x 40 cm (8 x 16 inch) rectangle, trying to keep the corners fairly square. Fold the top third of the pastry down and fold the bottom third of the pastry up over it. Make a quarter turn to the right so that the edge of the top fold is on the right. Re-roll the pastry to a rectangle 20 x 40 cm (8 x 16 inches), and repeat the folding step. Wrap in plastic wrap and refrigerate for 30 minutes.

3 Repeat the previous step, giving a roll, fold and turn twice more. Refrigerate for another 30 minutes. The folding and rolling give the pastry its flaky characteristics. Roll out the pastry on a well-floured surface to a 3 mm (⅛ inch) thickness, and then cut out thirty 8 cm (3 inch) rounds.
4 Preheat the oven to moderate 180°C (350°F/Gas 4). Brush a large baking tray with melted butter or oil.
5 To make Filling: Wash and dry the spinach leaves thoroughly. Shred the spinach finely and place in a medium bowl. Crumble the feta cheese over the spinach; add the olives, rosemary and garlic. Spread the pistachio nuts on a baking tray and toast under a moderately hot grill for 1–2 minutes. Cool and chop finely. Add to spinach mixture with beaten egg and stir until well combined.
6 Place two teaspoonsful of mixture in the centre of each pastry round; fold in half and pinch edges to seal. Place on the prepared tray; brush lightly with beaten egg and bake for 15 minutes or until golden and crisp. Serve hot.

LAYERED SUSHI

Preparation time: 25 minutes + 1 hour
   draining + cooling + 1 hour refrigeration
Total cooking time: 35 minutes
Makes 36

2½ cups (550 g/1 lb 1¾ oz) Japanese
   short-grain rice
1 piece of kombu (optional)
100 ml (3½ fl oz) rice vinegar
1 tablespoon mirin
¼ cup (60 g/2 oz) caster (superfine) sugar
⅓ cup (90 g/3 oz) Japanese mayonnaise
   (see Note)
2 teaspoons wasabi paste
4 sheets of roasted nori
300 g (10 oz) smoked salmon
¼ cup (40 g/1¼ oz) pickled ginger slices
black sesame seeds, to garnish

1 Wash the rice under cold running water
until the water runs clear, then leave in
the strainer to drain for an hour. Put the
rice and kombu in a saucepan with 3 cups
(750 ml/24 fl oz) water if desired, and
bring to the boil. Cook for 5–10 minutes,
or until tunnels form on the surface of the
rice, then remove the kombu. Reduce the
heat to low, cover and cook the rice for
12–15 minutes, or until the rice is cooked
and all the water has been absorbed.
Remove from the heat, remove the lid
from the pan, cover the rice with a clean
tea towel and leave for 15 minutes.
2 To make the sushi dressing, combine
the vinegar, mirin, sugar and 1 teaspoon
salt in a small bowl and stir until the
sugar is dissolved.

3 Spread the rice over the base of a non-
metallic dish or bowl, pour the sushi
dressing over the top and use a rice
paddle or spatula to mix the dressing
through the rice, separating the grains—
the aim is to make the rice grains stick
together slightly. Fan the rice until it
cools to room temperature.
4 Combine the mayonnaise and wasabi in
a small bowl. Lay a sheet of nori, shiny-
side up, on top of a piece of baking paper
on a dry tray. Entirely cover the nori with
a cup of loosely packed rice. Spread with
a little wasabi mayonnaise, then top with
a layer of smoked salmon and some
slices of pickled ginger. Place another
sheet of nori on top and flatten lightly
with a rolling pin. Repeat the layering
twice, to form three layers, finishing with
a sheet of nori, and again flattening with
the rolling pin. Reserve the remaining
wasabi mayonnaise.
5 Cover and refrigerate for at least an
hour, then, using a very sharp knife
dipped in water, trim any filling
protruding from the edges and slice into 2
cm (¾ inch) squares. Garnish with wasabi
mayonnaise, pickled ginger and black
sesame seeds.

NOTE: Japanese mayonnaise typically
comes in easy-to-use squeeze bottles. If
you can't find it, use whole-egg
mayonnaise instead.

CORN AND POTATO FRITTERS

Preparation time: 15 minutes
Total cooking time: 20 minutes
Makes about 40

2 large potatoes
260 g (8 oz) can corn kernels, drained
4 eggs, lightly beaten
6 spring onions, chopped
½ cup (50 g/1¾ oz) dry breadcrumbs
1 teaspoon garam masala
3 tablespoons oil

Dipping sauce
⅔ cup (160 g/5½ oz) natural yoghurt
2 tablespoons chopped fresh mint leaves
2 teaspoons sweet chilli sauce

1 Peel and coarsely grate the potatoes.
Drain on paper towel and squeeze out the
excess moisture. Combine in a bowl with
the corn, eggs, spring onion, breadcrumbs
and garam masala. Mix well.
2 Heat 2 tablespoons of the oil in a heavy-
based frying pan. Cook heaped
tablespoons of mixture over medium heat
for 2 minutes each side, or until golden.
Drain on crumpled paper towel and keep
warm. Repeat until all the mixture is used,
adding extra oil to the pan if necessary.
3 For the dipping sauce, combine all the
ingredients in a bowl.

NORI CONES

Preparation time: 45 minutes +
  1 hour draining 15 minutes standing +
  5 minutes soaking
Total cooking time: 15 minutes
Makes 40

2 cups (440 g/14 oz) Japanese short-
  grain rice
2 tablespoons rice vinegar
2 tablespoons caster (superfine) sugar
10 g (¼ oz) sliced dried shiitake
  mushrooms
250 g (4 oz) choy sum (Chinese flowering
  cabbage), shredded and blanched
1 tablespoon pickled ginger, shredded
1 tablespoon sesame seeds, toasted
1 tablespoon kecap manis
½ teaspoon wasabi paste
2 teaspoons mirin
1 tablespoon Shoyu (Japanese soy sauce)
10 sheets of roasted nori
ready-made sushi dipping sauce, to serve

1 Wash the rice under cold running water
until the water runs clear, then drain.
Drain for an hour. Put in a saucepan with
2 cups (500 ml/16 fl oz) water. Bring to the
boil, then reduce the heat and simmer for
10 minutes. Remove from the heat, cover
and stand for 15 minutes.
2 To make the sushi dressing, put the
vinegar, sugar, ½ teaspoon salt and
2 tablespoons water in a saucepan and
stir over low heat until the sugar and salt
have dissolved.

3 Spread the rice over the base of a non-
metallic dish or bowl, pour the sushi
dressing over the top and use a rice
paddle or spatula to mix the dressing
through the rice, separating the grains as
you do so. Fan the rice until it cools.
4 Soak the mushrooms in boiling water
for 5 minutes. Drain, squeeze dry and
roughly chop.
5 Put the rice in a bowl and stir in the
choy sum, mushrooms, ginger, sesame
seeds and the combined kecap manis,
wasabi, mirin and Shoyu.
6 Lay the nori sheets shiny-side down and
cut each one into four squares. Brush the
joining edge with water and put 1
tablespoon of the mixture in the centre of
the square. Roll up on the diagonal to
form a cone and top up with 2 teaspoons
of filling. Repeat. Serve with the dipping
sauce.

DOLMADES

Preparation time: 40 minutes + 1 hour
  soaking
Total cooking time: 50 minutes
Makes about 35

250 g (8 oz) vine leaves in brine
¾ cup (185 ml/6 fl oz) olive oil
2 large onions, finely chopped
¾ cup (165 g/5½ oz) short-grain rice
6 spring onions, chopped
4 tablespoons coarsely chopped fresh dill
1 tablespoon finely chopped fresh mint
salt and freshly ground black pepper
1 tablespoon lemon juice

1 Rinse the vine leaves in cold water and
soak in warm water for 1 hour; drain. Heat
½ cup (125 ml/4 fl oz) of the oil in a small
heavy-based pan. Add the onions; cook
over low heat for 5 minutes. Remove from
the heat; set aside, covered, for 5 minutes.
Add the rice, spring onions, herbs, salt
and pepper to the pan and mix
thoroughly.
2 Lay out a vine leaf, vein-side up. Place
3 teaspoons of the rice mixture onto the
centre of the leaf. Fold the sides over the
mixture and then roll towards the tip of
the vine leaf. Repeat the process with the
remaining filling and leaves.
3 Place five vine leaves over the base of a
medium heavy-based pan. Arrange the
rolled dolmades in the pan in two layers
and drizzle with the remaining oil. Place a
heatproof plate on top of the dolmades
and cover the dolmades with water. Bring
to the boil, reduce the heat and simmer,
covered, for 45 minutes. Remove the
plate, drain the dolmades and drizzle with
lemon juice. Serve warm or cold.

NOTE: Fresh vine leaves can be used in
this recipe if they are available. Use small
leaves, blanched briefly in boiling water.

STUFFED MUSSELS

reparation time: 40 minutes + cooling
Total cooking time: 16 minutes
Makes 18

18 black mussels
2 teaspoons olive oil
2 spring onions, finely chopped
1 clove garlic, crushed
1 tablespoon tomato paste (tomato
    purée)
2 teaspoons lemon juice
3 tablespoons chopped fresh flat-leaf
    parsley
⅓ cup (35 g/1¼ oz) dry breadcrumbs
2 eggs, beaten
olive oil, for deep-frying

White sauce
40 g (1¼ oz) butter
¼ cup (30 g/1 oz) plain flour
⅓ cup (80 ml/2¾ fl oz) milk

1 Scrub the mussels and remove their beards. Discard any open ones that do not close when given a sharp tap. Bring 1 cup (250 ml/8 fl oz) water to the boil in a medium saucepan, add the mussels, cover and cook for 5 minutes, shaking occasionally. Strain the liquid into a jug until you have ⅓ cup (80 ml/2¾ fl oz). Discard any unopened mussels. Remove the mussels from their shells and discard half the shells. Finely chop the mussels.

2 Heat the oil in a pan, add the spring onion and cook for 1 minute. Add the garlic and cook for 1 minute. Stir in the mussels, tomato paste, lemon juice and 2 tablespoons of parsley. Season with salt and pepper and set aside to cool.
3 To make the white sauce, melt the butter in a pan over low heat, add the flour and cook for 1 minute, or until pale and foaming. Remove from the heat and gradually stir in the reserved mussel liquid, the milk and some pepper. Return to the heat and stir constantly until the sauce boils and thickens and leaves the side of the pan. Transfer to a bowl to cool.
4 Spoon the mussel mixture into the shells. Top with the sauce and smooth so it is heaped.
5 Combine the crumbs and remaining parsley. Dip the mussels in the egg, then the crumbs, pressing on to cover the top.
6 Fill a deep heavy-based pan one third full of oil and heat to 180°C (350°F), or until a cube of bread dropped into the oil browns in 15 seconds. Cook the mussels in batches for 2 minutes, or until brown. Remove with a slotted spoon and drain on crumpled paper towels. Serve hot.

KEFTEDES
(MEATBALLS)

Preparation time: 15 minutes +
    1 hour refrigeration
Total cooking time: 15 minutes
Serves 4

1 egg, lightly beaten
½ cup (40 g/1¼ oz) fresh breadcrumbs
1 brown onion, finely chopped
2 tablespoons chopped fresh flat-leaf
    parsley
3 tablespoons chopped fresh mint
500 g (1 lb) beef or lamb mince
2 tablespoons lemon juice
plain flour, for coating
vegetable oil, for shallow-frying
lemon wedges, for serving

1 In a large bowl, mix the egg, breadcrumbs, onion, herbs, mince and lemon juice until well combined. Season well, then with wet hands, shape the mixture into large walnut-sized balls and flatten slightly. Place on a tray, cover and refrigerate for 1 hour.
2 Roll the balls in flour, shaking off any excess. In a large frying pan, heat the oil until very hot. Fry the meatballs for 3–4 minutes on each side, or until crisp and brown, being careful not to overcrowd the pan. Drain on crumpled paper towels and serve with lemon wedges.

MINI QUICHES

MAKE THE PASTRY CASES AS DIRECTED, THEN FILL WITH ONE OF OUR QUICHE MIXTURES. MAKING TWO TRAYS OF QUICHES TAKES NO EXTRA TIME, AS THEY CAN BE BAKED SIDE BY SIDE.

PASTRY CASES

Preheat the oven to moderately hot 200°C (400°F/Gas 6). Grease two round-based shallow 12-hole patty tins. Lay 2 sheets of ready-rolled shortcrust pastry on a work surface and cut 12 rounds from each with an 8 cm (3 inch) cutter. Line the tins with pastry, fill with one of the following suggestions and bake as instructed. Remove from the tins while warm and cool on wire racks. Makes 24.

CARAMELIZED ONION AND BACON

Heat 2 teaspoons oil in a large pan. Add 1 large, finely chopped onion, cover and cook over medium-low heat for 30 minutes, or until golden (caramelized onion is slow-cooked to bring out the sweetness, so don't rush this step).

Transfer to a bowl to cool. Add 125 g (4 oz) finely chopped bacon to the pan and cook until crisp. Mix with the onion, add 3 teaspoons wholegrain mustard and season with pepper. Place a small amount in each pastry case. Beat 2 eggs with ½ cup (125 ml/4 fl oz) milk and pour over the onion and bacon. Bake for 15–20 minutes, or until puffed and golden.

GOAT'S CHEESE AND SEMI-DRIED TOMATO

Mix together 60 g (2 oz) crumbled goat's cheese and 60 g (2 oz) chopped semi-dried tomatoes and place a small amount in the bottom of each pastry case. Beat 2 eggs with ½ cup (125 ml/4 fl oz) milk and 3 tablespoons chopped fresh basil. Season and pour into the cases. Bake for 15–20 minutes, or until puffed and golden.

CURRIED APPLE AND ONION

Heat a little oil in a pan. Lightly brown a small thinly sliced onion, then add a small peeled and grated green apple. Add ¼ teaspoon curry powder and stir for 1 minute. Cool slightly. Spoon heaped teaspoons into the pastry cases. Mix ½ cup (125 ml/4 fl oz) milk, 2 lightly beaten eggs and 2 tablespoons cream in a jug and pour enough into each pastry case to cover the onion. Sprinkle with a little grated Cheddar—you'll need about 20 g (¾ oz) altogether. Bake for 15–20 minutes, or until puffed and golden.

CREAMY HERB

Mix together 2 beaten eggs, 2 tablespoons milk, ½ cup (125 ml/4 fl oz) cream, 2 teaspoons chopped fresh chives and 1 teaspoon each of chopped fresh dill, thyme and parsley. Pour into the pastry cases and sprinkle with grated Parmesan, using only about 2 tablespoons altogether. Bake for 15–20 minutes, or until puffed and golden.

SMOKED SALMON

Put 100 g (3½ oz) cream cheese, ¼ cup (60 ml/2 fl oz) cream and 2 eggs in a food processor and mix together, then add some cracked black pepper, to taste. Sprinkle a little finely chopped smoked salmon into the pastry case—you will need about 100 g (3½ oz) smoked salmon. Pour the cream cheese mixture over the top and bake for 15–20 minutes, or until puffed and golden.

CORN AND RED PEPPER (CAPSICUM)

Drain a 130 g (4 oz) can corn kernels and mix with ⅓ cup (40 g/1½ oz) grated Cheddar and half a finely chopped red pepper. Beat 2 eggs, ⅔ cup (170 ml/ 5½ fl oz) cream, 2 teaspoons Dijon mustard and a dash of Tabasco sauce in a jug and season with salt and pepper. Spoon the corn mixture into the pastry cases, dividing evenly among them, and top with the egg mixture until almost full. Bake for 15–20 minutes, or until puffed and golden.

QUICHES, FROM LEFT: Caramelized onion and bacon; Goat's cheese and semi-dried tomato; Curried apple and onion; Creamy herb; Smoked salmon; Corn and red pepper

CHEESY ZUCCHINI FLOWERS

Preparation time: 1 hour 20 minutes + standing
Total cooking time: 10 minutes
Makes 24

1½ cups (185 g/6 oz) plain flour
7 g (¼ oz) dry yeast or 15 g (½ oz) compressed fresh yeast
24 zucchini with flowers
50 g (1¾ oz) kefalotyri cheese or Parmesan
8 anchovy fillets in oil, drained
oil, for deep-frying

1 Sift the flour and 1¼ teaspoons salt into a bowl and make a well. Whisk the yeast and 1¼ cups (315 ml/10 fl oz) warm water in a bowl until dissolved and pour into the well. Gradually stir with the whisk to form a thick batter. Cover with plastic wrap and leave in a warm place for 1 hour, or until frothy. Do not stir.
2 Gently open the zucchini flowers and remove the centre stamens. Wash and drain. Cut the cheese into 1 cm (½ inch) cubes. Cut the anchovies into 1.5 cm (⅝ inch) pieces.
3 Put a cube of cheese and a piece of anchovy into the centre of each flower. Fold the petals around them. Fill a deep pan one third full of oil and heat to 180°C (350°F), or until a cube of bread dropped into the oil browns in 15 seconds. Dip the flowers into the batter, turning to coat and drain off the excess. Deep-fry in batches for 1–2 minutes, or until puffed and lightly brown. Drain on crumpled paper towel. Serve hot.

FRESH VEGETABLE SPRING ROLLS

Preparation time: 40 minutes
Total cooking time: Nil
Makes 12

1 cup (155 g/5 oz) grated carrot
100 g (3⅓ oz) snow peas (mange tout), sliced
1 cup (90 g/3 oz) bean sprouts, trimmed
30 g (1 oz) rice vermicelli, soaked, drained and cooled
2 tablespoons chopped fresh coriander
2 tablespoons chopped fresh mint
¼ cup (40 g/1⅓ oz) chopped, dry-roasted peanuts
12 rice paper rounds

Dipping Sauce
1 tablespoon caster sugar
¼ cup (60 ml/2 fl oz) warm water
2 tablespoons fish sauce (optional)
1 clove garlic, crushed
¼ cup (60 ml/2 fl oz) lime juice
1 small fresh chilli, finely sliced
1 tablespoon chopped fresh coriander

1 Combine the carrot, snow peas and bean sprouts in a large bowl. Chop the cooked vermicelli roughly and add to the vegetables with the coriander, mint and peanuts.
2 Dip each rice paper round into a bowl of warm water for about 1 minute, until softened. Carefully remove from the water and lay on a clean, flat surface. Place about 2 level tablespoons of vegetable mixture on the lower half of the rice paper; roll up gently but firmly into a spring roll shape. (The moist rice paper will adhere to itself on rolling.) Serve with Dipping Sauce.
3 To make Dipping Sauce: Place the sugar in a bowl; add water and stir until dissolved. Add the remaining ingredients and stir.

SPICY KOFTAS

Preparation time: 25 minutes
Total cooking time: 25 minutes
Makes 45

500 g (1 lb) lamb mince
1 small onion, finely chopped
1 clove garlic, crushed
1 teaspoon ground coriander
1 teaspoon ground cumin
¼ teaspoon ground cinnamon
½ teaspoon finely chopped red chilli
1 teaspoon tomato paste (tomato purée)
1 tablespoon chopped fresh mint
1 tablespoon chopped fresh coriander
oil, for frying

Yoghurt dip
1 small tomato, peeled, seeded and finely chopped
½ Lebanese cucumber, peeled and finely chopped
1 clove garlic, crushed
1 tablespoon chopped fresh mint
½ cup (125 g/4 oz) natural yoghurt

1 Combine the mince, onion, garlic, coriander, cumin, cinnamon, chilli, tomato paste and mint and coriander leaves in a large bowl and mix well with your hands. Season well, then roll into small balls (about 1½ teaspoons each).
2 Place a large heavy-based frying pan over moderate heat and heat a little oil. Cook the koftas in batches until well browned all over and cooked through. Drain on crumpled paper towels.
3 Mix together the dip ingredients and place in a small bowl.
4 Skewer each kofta with a cocktail stick and serve with the dip.
in advance: You can freeze the cooked koftas. When required, defrost, cover with foil and reheat in an ovenproof dish in a moderate 180°C (350°F/Gas 4) oven for 5–10 minutes. The dip can be made several hours ahead.

GRILLED SARDINES WITH CUCUMBER

Preparation time: 20 minutes +
  marinating
Total cooking time: 10 minutes
Makes 30

30 butterflied sardines, without heads
2 tablespoons olive oil
2 tablespoons vegetable oil
2 tablespoons lemon juice
2 cloves garlic, sliced
1 tablespoon fresh oregano leaves
1 Lebanese cucumber
¼ teaspoon sugar

1 Place half the sardines in a single layer in a non-metallic dish. Combine the olive and vegetable oils, lemon juice, garlic and oregano leaves and pour half over the sardines. Top with the remaining sardines and pour over the rest of the oil mixture. Cover with plastic wrap and marinate for 30 minutes in the refrigerator.
2 Meanwhile, using a wide vegetable peeler, peel strips lengthways off the cucumber, making four even sides and avoiding peeling off any cucumber with seeds. You should end up with about 15 slices of cucumber. Cut in half to make 30 strips the same length as the sardines.
3 Lay the cucumber strips flat around the sides and base of a colander and sprinkle with sugar and a little salt. Place over a bowl. Leave for 15 minutes to drain off any juices.
4 Preheat the grill. Wash the cucumber well and pat dry with paper towels. Place one strip of cucumber on the flesh side of each sardine and roll up like a pinwheel. Secure with toothpicks.
5 Place half the sardines under the grill and cook for 5 minutes, or until cooked through. Repeat with the remaining sardines. Serve warm, with tzatziki if desired.

MUSHROOMS IN BASIL PESTO ON SOURDOUGH

Preparation time: 20 minutes
Total cooking time: 20–25 minutes
Makes 24

Basil pesto
25 g (¾ oz) fresh basil leaves
30 g (1 oz) Parmesan, grated
2 tablespoons pine nuts, toasted
2 tablespoons olive oil

1 small clove garlic, crushed
2½ tablespoons olive oil
1 sourdough bread stick, cut into
  24 x 1 cm (½ inch) thick slices
500 g (1 lb) small flat mushrooms, thinly
  sliced
3 teaspoons balsamic vinegar
80 g (2¾ oz) thinly sliced prosciutto

1 For the basil pesto, finely chop the basil leaves, Parmesan and pine nuts in a food processor. Gradually add the olive oil in a thin stream, with the motor running, and process until smooth. Season with salt and pepper.
2 Combine the garlic with 2 tablespoons of the olive oil in a small bowl and brush it over both sides of the bread slices. Place on baking trays and cook both sides under a medium-hot grill until golden brown.
3 Heat the remaining ½ tablespoon of olive oil in a large frying pan. Add the mushrooms and cook over medium heat for 3–4 minutes, or until the mushrooms are heated through. Drain away any liquid. Add the pesto and the vinegar to the mushrooms, stir to combine, then cook over low heat for 1–2 minutes, or until heated through.
4 Preheat the oven to moderately hot 200°C (400°F/Gas 6). To assemble, top the toasts with mushroom, then torn and folded prosciutto. Bake on baking trays for 6 minutes, or until the prosciutto is crisp. Serve immediately.

MINI TORTILLAS WITH CHORIZO SALSA

Preparation time: 25 minutes
Total cooking time: 12–15 minutes
Makes about 30

4 x 20 cm (8 inch) round flour tortillas
2 tablespoons olive oil
250 g (8 oz) chorizo sausages
⅓ cup (90 g/3 oz) Greek-style natural
  yoghurt
20 g (¾ oz) finely chopped fresh coriander
1 ripe avocado
1 large tomato, seeded
¼ red onion
2 teaspoons balsamic vinegar
1 tablespoon virgin olive oil
30 small fresh coriander leaves, to
  garnish

1 Preheat the oven to moderate 180°C (350°F/Gas 4). Cut 7–8 circles from each tortilla with a 5.5 cm (2¼ inch) cutter, or cut into triangles. Heat 1 tablespoon of the oil in a large non-stick frying pan, add one third of the mini tortillas and cook in a single layer, turning once, until crisp and golden. Drain on crumpled paper towels. Repeat with the remaining oil and tortillas.
2 Chop the sausages into small cubes and bake on a baking tray for 10 minutes, or until cooked through. Cool; drain on crumpled paper towel.
3 Meanwhile, combine the yoghurt and chopped coriander in a small bowl; set aside.
4 Chop the avocado, tomato and onion into small cubes and combine in a bowl. Add the sausage, vinegar, oil and salt and pepper, to taste, and gently stir to combine.
5 To assemble, spoon the sausage onto tortillas and top with yoghurt and coriander leaves.

CHARRED PRAWNS WITH PEPPER (CAPSICUM) MAYONNAISE

Preparation time: 20 minutes +
  marinating
Total cooking time: 40 minutes
Makes 24

1 kg (2 lb) large raw prawns
4 cloves garlic, crushed
3 tablespoons lime juice
1 teaspoon ground cumin
3 tablespoons chopped fresh coriander
lime wedges, for serving

Pepper (capsicum) mayonnaise
1 small red pepper (capsicum)
6 cloves garlic, unpeeled
1 tablespoon olive oil
⅓ cup (90 g/3 oz) whole-egg mayonnaise
1 tablespoon lime juice

1 Peel and devein the prawns, leaving the tails intact. Combine the garlic, lime juice, cumin and coriander in a bowl, place the prawns in the marinade and mix well. Cover and refrigerate for at least 2 hours.

2 To make the pepper mayonnaise, preheat the oven to moderately hot 190°C (375°F/Gas 5). Cut the red pepper into quarters and remove the seeds and membrane. Place on a baking tray with the garlic and drizzle with the olive oil. Cook for 20–30 minutes, or until the skin blisters on the pepper and the garlic is soft but not burnt. Place in a plastic bag until cool, then peel the red pepper and garlic.
3 Combine the red pepper and garlic in a food processor with the mayonnaise until smooth. Transfer to a bowl and stir in the lime juice. Add salt, to taste.
4 Preheat a lightly oiled chargrill or heavy-based pan until it just starts to smoke. Drain the prawns, discarding the marinade and cook in batches for 2 minutes on each side, or until cooked. Serve the prawns with the mayonnaise and a wedge of lime.

GOAT'S CHEESE AND APPLE TARTS

Preparation time: 10 minutes
Total cooking time: 25 minutes
Makes 32

2 sheets frozen puff pastry
300 g (10 oz) goat's cheese, sliced
2 cooking apples
2 tablespoons extra virgin olive oil
1 tablespoon chopped fresh lemon thyme

1 Preheat the oven to hot 210°C (415°F/Gas 6–7). While the pastry is still frozen, cut each sheet into four squares and then each square into quarters. Place slightly apart on a lightly greased baking tray. Set aside for a few minutes to thaw and then lay the cheese over the centre of each square of pastry, leaving a small border.
2 Core the unpeeled apples and slice them thinly. Interleave several slices over the pastry, making sure the cheese is covered completely. Lightly brush the apples with oil and sprinkle with lemon thyme and a little salt and pepper, to taste.
3 Bake the tarts for 20–25 minutes, or until the pastry is cooked through and golden brown at the edges. The tarts are best served immediately.

IN ADVANCE: The pastry can be topped with cheese, covered and refrigerated overnight. Top with the apple just before cooking.

PRAWN CREPES

Preparation time: 40 minutes +
    20 minutes resting
Total cooking time: 20 minutes
Serves 4–6

5 eggs
1½ cups (375 ml/12 fl oz) water
2 tablespoons oil
½ cup (60 g/2 oz) cornflour
½ cup (60 g/2 oz) plain flour

Prawn Filling
500 g (1 lb) raw prawns
1 tablespoon oil
300 g (9⅔ oz) bamboo shoots, cut into
    matchsticks
1 cup (90 g/3 oz) bean sprouts, scraggly
    ends removed
½ cup (80 g/2⅔ oz) unsalted roasted
    peanuts, roughly chopped
½ lettuce, shredded
1 cup (30 g/1 oz) fresh coriander leaves

1 Beat the eggs, water and oil in a bowl
until combined. Whisk in the cornflour and
plain flour and beat until smooth. Cover and
allow the batter to rest for 20 minutes.
2 Brush a small nonstick frying pan or
crepe pan with oil, heat over low heat, add
2 tablespoons of the batter and swirl the
pan to ensure the base has a very thin
covering of batter; pour any excess batter
back into the bowl. Cook the crepe for
2 minutes or until lightly golden. Turn and
cook the other side for 2 minutes. Repeat
with remaining batter.
3 Filling: Peel and devein the prawns, and
cut them in half lengthways if large. Heat
the oil in a nonstick pan; add the prawns
and cook over medium heat for 3 minutes or
until they are bright pink. Arrange the
prawns, bamboo shoots, bean sprouts,
peanuts, lettuce and coriander on a platter.
4 On each crepe place a little shredded
lettuce, a few coriander leaves, prawns,
bamboo shoots bean sprouts and
peanuts; fold in the sides and roll up the
crepe to enclose the mixture.

BREAD BOWLS FILLED
WITH DHAL

Preparation time: 25 minutes
Total cooking time: 35 minutes
Makes 24

½ cup (125 g/4 oz) red lentils, rinsed and
    drained
1 cup (250 ml/8 fl oz) vegetable stock
24 slices white bread
60 g (2 oz) ghee or butter
½ teaspoon cumin seeds
½ teaspoon ground coriander
¼ teaspoon yellow mustard seeds
2 cloves garlic, crushed
½ teaspoon chopped red chilli
2 tablespoons chopped fresh coriander
    leaves

1 Preheat the oven to moderately hot
200°C (400°F/Gas 6). Combine the red
lentils and stock in a heavy-based pan.
Bring to the boil, reduce the heat and
simmer, covered, for 10 minutes, or until
tender. Stir occasionally and check that
the mixture is not catching on the bottom
of the pan. Remove from the heat.
2 Meanwhile, using an 8 cm (3 inch) cutter,
cut 24 rounds of bread. Roll each to 1 mm
(1/16 inch) thick with a rolling pin. Melt half
the ghee or butter, brush on both sides of
the bread, then push into two 12-hole mini
muffin tins to form little bowls. Bake for
12–15 minutes, or until firm and golden.
3 Heat the remaining ghee or butter in a
small frying pan and add the cumin,
ground coriander and mustard seeds.
Cook until the mustard seeds begin to
pop, then add the garlic and chilli. Cook
stirring, for 1 minute, or until fragrant.
Stir the spice mixture into the cooked
lentils, return to the heat and simmer
over very low heat, stirring frequently
until the dhal is thick and creamy.
Season, to taste, with salt and set aside to
cool a little before serving
4 Fill each bread bowl with 2–3 teaspoons
of warm dhal, scatter with the chopped
coriander and serve immediately.

JAPANESE RICE BALLS

Preparation time: 20 minutes + 1 hour
    draining + 20 minutes standing
Total cooking time: 25 minutes
Serves 4

1¼ cups (275 g/9 oz) Japanese short-
    grain rice
55 g (2 oz) smoked salmon, chopped
2 tablespoons finely chopped pickled
    ginger
2 spring onions (scallions), finely
    chopped
2 teaspoons black sesame seeds, toasted

1 Wash the rice under cold running water
until the water runs clear, then drain.
Drain for an hour. Put the rice in a
saucepan with 1⅓ cups (350 ml/11 fl oz)
water and bring to the boil. Reduce the
heat to very low, cover and cook for
15 minutes. Remove the pan from the heat
and stand, covered, for about 20 minutes.
2 Combine the salmon, ginger and spring
onion in a small bowl. Using wet hands,
form a small handful of rice into a ball,
push 2 teaspoons of the smoked salmon
mixture into the centre of the rice and
remould the ball around it. Repeat with
the remaining rice and salmon, keeping
your hands wet to prevent the rice from
becoming sticky. Sprinkle with the
sesame seeds.

PEARL BALLS

Preparation time: 25 minutes +
    1 hour standing + 30 minutes soaking
Total cooking time: 30 minutes
Serves 6

330 g (11 oz) glutinous or sweet rice
8 dried Chinese mushrooms
150 g (5 oz) peeled water chestnuts
450 g (14 oz) minced (ground) pork
1 small carrot, grated
2 spring onions (scallions), finely chopped
1½ tablespoons finely chopped ginger
2 tablespoons light soy sauce
1 tablespoon Chinese rice wine
1½ teaspoons roasted sesame oil
2½ tablespoons cornflour (cornstarch)
soy sauce, to serve

1 Put the rice in a bowl and, using your fingers as a rake, rinse under cold running water to remove any dust. Drain the rice in a colander, then place it in a bowl with enough cold water to cover. Set aside for 1 hour. Drain the rice and transfer it to a baking tray in an even layer.
2 Soak the dried mushrooms in boiling water for 30 minutes, drain and squeeze. Discard the stems and chop the caps.
3 Blanch the water chestnuts in a saucepan of boiling water for 1 minute, then refresh in cold water. Drain, pat dry and finely chop them.
4 Place the pork in a bowl, add the mushrooms, water chestnuts, carrot, spring onion, ginger, soy sauce, rice wine, sesame oil and cornflour. Stir vigorously.
5 Roll the mixture into 2 cm (¾ inch) balls, then roll each meatball in the glutinous rice so that it is completely coated. Lightly press the rice to make it stick to the meatball. Place the pearl balls well apart in three steamers lined with greaseproof paper punched with holes, or some damp cheesecloth. Cover and steam over simmering water in a wok, swapping the steamers halfway through, for 25 minutes. If the rice is still firm, continue to cook until it softens. Serve with the soy sauce.

CHICKEN FELAFEL WITH TABBOULI CONES

Preparation time: 30 minutes + standing
Total cooking time: 20 minutes
Makes 24

¼ cup (45 g/1½ oz) cracked wheat
    (burghul)
4 pieces Lavash bread 30 x 23 cm
    (12 x 9 inch)
2 spring onions, thinly sliced
1 large tomato, seeded, finely chopped
1 small Lebanese cucumber, finely
    chopped
15 g (½ oz) fresh flat-leaf parsley,
    chopped
1 tablespoon lemon juice
1 tablespoon virgin olive oil
1 tablespoon olive oil
1 onion, finely chopped
1 clove garlic, crushed
2 teaspoons ground coriander
1 teaspoon cumin seeds
½ teaspoon ground cinnamon
250 g (8 oz) chicken mince
300 g (10 oz) can chickpeas, rinsed,
    drained and mashed
10 g (¼ oz) fresh flat-leaf parsley, extra,
    chopped
10 g (¼ oz) fresh mint leaves, chopped
2 tablespoons plain flour
vegetable oil, for shallow-frying
¼ cup (60 g/2 oz) Greek-style natural
    yoghurt

1 Soak the cracked wheat in hot water for 20 minutes. Slice the bread into thirds widthways, then cut in half. Keep the bread covered with a damp cloth to prevent it drying out. Cut some baking paper the same size as the bread. Roll the paper up around the bottom half of the bread to form a cone and secure. Twist at the bottom. You will need 24 bread cones.

2 Drain the wheat in a fine mesh sieve, pressing out as much water as possible. Transfer to a bowl and mix with the onion, tomato, cucumber, parsley, lemon juice and virgin olive oil. Season.
3 Heat the olive oil in a pan, add the onion and garlic and cook, stirring over medium-low heat, for 5 minutes, or until the onion is soft. Add the spices and cook for another minute, or until the spices are aromatic.
4 Place the onion mixture, chicken mince, chickpeas, parsley and mint in a bowl, season with salt and pepper and mix until combined. Shape into 24 patties, pressing firmly together. Toss in the flour and shake off the excess.
5 Fill a deep, heavy-based pan one third full of oil and heat to 180°C (350°F), or until a cube of bread dropped into the oil turns golden brown in 15 seconds. Cook the felafels in batches for 3–4 minutes each side, or until golden and heated through. Drain on crumpled paper towels.
6 To assemble, place a felafel in each bread cone, top with tabbouli, then ½ teaspoon yoghurt.

IN ADVANCE: The salad is best made on the day of serving. The felafel can be prepared up to a day ahead and cooked just before serving.

BAGUETTE WITH EGG, DILL PESTO AND PROSCIUTTO

Preparation time: 20 minutes
Total cooking time: 25 minutes
Makes 30

8 thin slices prosciutto
45 g (1½ oz) fresh dill sprigs
75 g (2½ oz) pine nuts, toasted
60 g (2 oz) Parmesan, finely grated
2 cloves garlic, crushed
⅓ cup (80 ml/2¾ fl oz) virgin olive oil
1 French bread stick, sliced diagonally
2 teaspoons butter
7 eggs, lightly beaten
⅓ cup (80 ml/2¾ fl oz) milk
1 tablespoon light sour cream

1 Preheat the oven to moderately hot 200°C (400°F/Gas 6). Spread the prosciutto on a baking tray lined with baking paper. Bake for 5 minutes, or until sizzling and lightly crisp. Set aside.
2 Finely chop the dill, pine nuts, Parmesan and garlic together in a food processor. With the motor running, add the oil in a thin stream and process until smooth. Season.
3 Arrange the bread on baking trays and grill until golden on both sides. Spread with dill pesto.
4 Heat the butter in a large non-stick frying pan over low heat. Add the combined eggs and milk. As the egg begins to set, use a wooden spoon to scrape along the base with long strokes to bring the cooked egg to the surface in large lumps. Repeat several times over 10 minutes, or until the mixture is cooked but still creamy-looking. Remove from the heat and stir in the sour cream. Season with salt and pepper.
5 Divide the egg among the toasts and top with torn prosciutto. Serve immediately. in advance: Pesto can be made 3 days ahead and refrigerated. Use at room temperature.

BEEF SAMOSAS WITH MINT CHUTNEY DIP

Preparation time: 50 minutes
Total cooking time: 15 minutes
Makes about 20

2 tablespoons oil
1 onion, finely chopped
2 teaspoons finely chopped fresh ginger
400 g (13 oz) beef mince
1 tablespoon curry powder
1 tomato, peeled and chopped
1 potato, cubed
1 tablespoon finely chopped fresh mint
6 sheets ready-rolled puff pastry
1 egg yolk, lightly beaten
1 tablespoon cream

Mint chutney dip
20 g (¾ oz) fresh mint leaves
4 spring onions
1 red chilli, seeded
¼ teaspoon salt
1 tablespoon lemon juice
2 teaspoons caster sugar
¼ teaspoon garam masala

1 Heat the oil in a pan, add the onion and ginger and cook over medium heat for 3–5 minutes, or until the onion is soft.
2 Add the mince and curry powder and stir over high heat until the beef has browned. Add 1 teaspoon salt and the tomato and cook, covered, for 5 minutes. Add the potato and 3 tablespoons water and cook, stirring, for 5 minutes. Remove from the heat, then cool. Stir in the mint.

3 Preheat the oven to hot 210°C (415°F/Gas 6–7). Cut the pastry into 13 cm (5¼ inch) circles using a cutter or small plate as a guide, then cut in half. Form cones by folding each in half and pinching the sides together.
4 Spoon 2 teaspoons of the mince into each cone. Pinch the top edges together to seal. Place on a lightly greased baking tray. Beat the egg yolk with the cream and brush over the pastry. Bake for 10–15 minutes, or until puffed and golden brown. Serve with mint chutney dip.
5 To make the dip, roughly chop the mint leaves, spring onion and chilli and place in a food processor or blender with 3 tablespoons water and the remaining ingredients. Mix thoroughly and serve with the hot samosas.

IN ADVANCE: Prepare the samosas up to a day ahead and refrigerate. Cook just before serving. Dip can be made and refrigerated a day ahead.

TWISTS

QUICK AND SIMPLE, USING FROZEN READY-ROLLED PUFF PASTRY, TWISTS CAN BE MADE UP TO THREE DAYS IN ADVANCE AND STORED IN AN AIRTIGHT CONTAINER. CRISP IN THE OVEN IF THEY SOFTEN. ALL RECIPES CAN BE DOUBLED OR TREBLED.

THYME TWISTS

Lay 1 sheet of puff pastry on a work surface and, when thawed, brush lightly with beaten egg. Remove the hard stems from a bunch of fresh thyme and sprinkle the leaves over the pastry. Gently press onto the pastry and top with a second sheet of pastry. Cut the pastry into 2 cm (¾ inch) strips. Holding both ends, twist the strip in opposite directions twice. Place on a lightly greased baking tray and bake in a hot 210°C (415°F/Gas 6–7) oven for 10–15 minutes, or until puffed and golden. Makes 12.

CHEESE TWISTS

Lay 1 sheet of puff pastry on a work surface and, when thawed, brush lightly with beaten egg and cut into 1.5 cm (⅝ inch) strips. Holding both ends, twist the strip in opposite directions twice. Place on a lightly greased baking tray and sprinkle 3 tablespoons finely grated Parmesan over the flat part of the twists. Bake in a hot 210°C (415°F/Gas 6–7) oven for 10 minutes, or until puffed and golden. Makes 16.

SESAME AND POPPY SEED TWISTS

Lay 1 sheet of puff pastry on a work surface and, when thawed, brush lightly with beaten egg, then sprinkle with 1 tablespoon sesame or poppy seeds and gently press onto the pastry. Cut the pastry into 1.5 cm (⅝ inch) strips. Holding both ends, twist the strip in opposite directions twice. Bake on a lightly greased baking tray in a hot 210°C (415°F/Gas 6–7) oven for 10 minutes, or until puffed and golden. Makes 16.

PROSCIUTTO TWISTS

Lay 1 sheet of puff pastry on a work surface and, when thawed, brush lightly with beaten egg and cut into 1.5 cm (⅝ inch) strips. Holding both ends, twist the strips in opposite directions twice. Bake on a lightly greased baking tray in a hot 210°C (415°F/Gas 6–7) oven for 10 minutes, or until puffed and golden. Cut 8 slices of prosciutto in half lengthways. Wrap a slice around and down each twist. Makes 16.

ASPARAGUS SPEARS

Lay 1 sheet of puff pastry on a work surface and, when thawed, brush lightly with beaten egg and cut into 1.5 cm (⅝ inch) strips. Secure to one end of a blanched fresh asparagus spear (you will need 16). Wrap around and down the asparagus, brush the end of the pastry with egg and secure to the other end of the asparagus. Place on a lightly greased baking tray and bake in a hot 210°C (415°F/Gas 6–7) oven for 10–15 minutes, or until puffed and golden. Makes 16.

SUN-DRIED TOMATO PLAITS

Lay 1 sheet of puff pastry on a work surface and, when thawed, brush lightly with beaten egg and cut into 1 cm (½ inch) strips. Join 3 strips together at the top, by pressing. Plait them together, inserting slices of semi-dried tomato at intervals in the plait (you will need 40 g/1½ oz tomatoes for this). Place on a lightly greased baking tray and bake in a hot 210°C (415°F/Gas 6–7) oven for 10–15 minutes, or until puffed and golden. Makes 8.

FROM LEFT: Thyme twists; Cheese twists; Sesame and poppy seed twists; Prosciutto twists; Asparagus spears; Sun-dried tomato plaits

WHITEBAIT FRITTERS

Preparation time: 20 minutes + resting
Total cooking time: 15 minutes
Makes 12–15

¼ cup (30 g/1 oz) self-raising flour
¼ cup (30 g/1 oz) plain flour
½ teaspoon bicarbonate of soda
1 egg, lightly beaten
3 tablespoons dry white wine
2 teaspoons chopped fresh flat-leaf
   parsley
1 clove garlic, crushed
½ small onion, grated
200 g (6½ oz) Chinese or New Zealand
   whitebait
olive oil, for shallow-frying
lemon wedges, for serving

1 Sift the flours, bicarbonate of soda,
½ teaspoon salt and some freshly ground
black pepper into a bowl. Stir in the egg
and wine, whisk until smooth, then add
the parsley, garlic, onion and whitebait.
Cover and refrigerate for 20 minutes.
2 Heat about 2 cm (¾ inch) of the oil in a
deep frying pan to 180°C (350°F). The oil is
ready when a cube of bread dropped into
the oil turns golden brown in 15 seconds.
Drop in level tablespoons of batter and,
when the batter is puffed and bubbles
appear on the surface, carefully turn to
cook the other side.
3 Drain on paper towels and serve
immediately with lemon wedges.
note: The whitebait is very small and fine
and is available fresh or frozen. There is
no need to gut or scale them as they are
so small.

LAHM BI AJEEN
(LAMB FILO FINGERS)

Preparation time: 25 minutes
Total cooking time: 25 minutes
Makes 12

1 tablespoon olive oil
350 g (11 oz) lean lamb mince
1 small onion, finely chopped
2 cloves garlic crushed
1 tablespoon ground cumin
1 teaspoon ground ginger
1 teaspoon paprika
1 teaspoon ground cinnamon
pinch of saffron threads, soaked in a little
   warm water
1 teaspoon harissa (see Glossary page 15)
2 tablespoons chopped fresh coriander
2 tablespoons chopped fresh flat-leaf
   parsley
3 tablespoons pine nuts, toasted
1 egg
6 sheets filo pastry
60 g (2 oz) butter, melted
1 tablespoon sesame seeds

Yoghurt sauce
1 cup (250 g/8 oz) natural yoghurt
2 tablespoons chopped fresh mint
1 clove garlic, crushed

1 Preheat the oven to moderate 180°C
(350°F/Gas 4). Lightly grease a large
baking tray.
2 Heat the oil in a large frying pan, add
the lamb and cook for 5 minutes,
breaking up any lumps with the back of a
wooden spoon. Add the onion and garlic
and cook for 1 minute. Add the spices,
harissa, chopped coriander and parsley
and cook for 1 minute, stirring to combine.
Transfer to a sieve and drain to remove
the fat.

3 Place the mixture in a bowl and allow to
cool slightly. Mix in the pine nuts and egg.
4 Place a sheet of filo on the bench with
the shortest side facing you. Cover the
remaining sheets with a damp tea towel
to prevent them from drying out. Cut the
sheet of filo into four equal strips
lengthways. Brush one of the strips with
melted butter and place another on top.
Do the same with the other two pieces.
Place 1 tablespoon of the lamb mixture on
each at the short end of the filo and roll
each up, tucking in the ends to hold the
mixture in and form each into a cigar
shape. Repeat this process until you have
used up all the filo and meat mixture.
5 Place the lamb fingers on the baking
tray. Brush with any remaining melted
butter and sprinkle with sesame seeds.
Bake for 15 minutes, or until lightly
golden.
6 For the yoghurt sauce, stir all the
ingredients together in a small bowl.
Serve the filo fingers warm with the sauce
on the side.

PUMPKIN AND HAZELNUT PESTO BITES

Preparation time: 20 minutes
Total cooking time: 35 minutes
Makes 48

750 g (1½ lb) butternut pumpkin
3 tablespoons oil
35 g (1¼ oz) roasted hazelnuts
35 g (1¼ oz) rocket
3 tablespoons grated Parmesan

1 Preheat the oven to moderately hot 200°C (400°F/Gas 6). Peel the pumpkin and cut into 2 cm (¾ inch) slices, then cut into rough triangular shapes about 3 cm (1¼ inches) along the base. Toss with half the oil and some salt and cracked black pepper, until coated. Spread on a baking tray and bake for 35 minutes, or until cooked.
2 For the hazelnut pesto, process the hazelnuts, rocket, 1 tablespoon of the Parmesan and the remaining oil, until they form a paste. Season with salt and cracked black pepper.
3 Spoon a small amount of the hazelnut pesto onto each piece of pumpkin and sprinkle with the remaining Parmesan and black pepper if desired. Serve warm or cold.

IN ADVANCE: Pesto can be made several days ahead. Pour a film of oil over the surface to prevent discoloration. Tip the oil off before using the pesto.

FENNEL RISOTTO BALLS WITH CHEESY FILLING

Preparation time: 30 minutes + 1 hour refrigeration
Total cooking time: 50 minutes
Serves 4–6

1.5 litres (48 fl oz) vegetable stock
1 tablespoon oil
30 g (1 oz) butter
2 garlic cloves, crushed
1 onion, finely chopped
2 fennel bulbs, thinly sliced
1 tablespoon balsamic vinegar
½ cup (125 ml/4 fl oz) white wine
3 cups (660 g/1 lb 5 oz) risotto rice
½ cup (50 g/1¾ oz) freshly grated Parmesan cheese
½ cup (25 g/¾ oz) snipped chives
1 egg, lightly beaten
150 g (5 oz) sun-dried (sun-blushed) tomatoes, chopped
100 g (3½ oz) fresh mozzarella cheese, diced
½ cup (80 g/2¾ oz) frozen peas, thawed
½ cup (60 g/2 oz) plain (all-purpose) flour, seasoned
3 eggs, extra
2 cups (200 g/6½ oz) dry breadcrumbs
oil, for deep-frying

1 Pour the stock into a saucepan and bring to the boil. Reduce the heat, cover with a lid and keep at a low simmer.
2 Heat the oil and butter in a large saucepan and cook the garlic and onion over medium heat for 3 minutes, or until softened but not browned. Add the fennel and cook for 10 minutes, or until it starts to caramelize. Add the vinegar and wine, increase the heat and boil until the liquid evaporates. Stir in the rice until well coated.

3 Add ½ cup (125 ml/4 fl oz) hot stock, stirring constantly over medium heat until the liquid is absorbed. Continue adding more stock, ½ cup (125 ml/4 fl oz) at a time, stirring, for 20–25 minutes, or until all the stock is absorbed and the rice is tender and creamy.
4 Remove from the heat and stir in the Parmesan, chives, egg and tomato. Transfer to a bowl, cover and cool. Put the mozzarella and peas in a bowl and mash together. Season.
5 Put the flour in one bowl, the extra eggs in another and the breadcrumbs in a third. Lightly beat the eggs. With wet hands, shape the risotto into 14 even balls. Flatten each ball out, slightly indenting the centre. Put a heaped teaspoon of the pea mash into the indentation, then shape the rice around the filling to form a ball. Roll each ball in seasoned flour, then dip in the extra egg and roll in breadcrumbs. Place on a foil-covered tray and refrigerate for 30 minutes.
6 Fill a deep-fat fryer or large saucepan one-third full of oil and heat to 180°C (350°F), or until a cube of bread dropped into the oil browns in 15 seconds. Cook the risotto balls in batches for 5 minutes, or until golden and crisp and the cheese has melted inside. Drain on crumpled paper towels and season with salt. If the cheese has not melted by the end of the cooking time, cook the balls on a tray in a (180°C/350°F/Gas 4) oven for 5 minutes. Serve with a salad.

VEGETABLE FRITTATA WITH HUMMUS AND BLACK OLIVES

Preparation time: 30 minutes
Total cooking time: 35 minutes
Makes 30

Hummus
425 g (14 oz) can chickpeas, drained
2 cloves garlic, crushed
⅓ cup (80 ml/2¾ fl oz) lemon juice
2 tablespoons natural yoghurt

2 large red peppers (capsicums)
600 g (1¼ lb) orange sweet potato
500 g (1 lb) eggplant (aubergine)
3 tablespoons olive oil
2 leeks, finely sliced
2 cloves garlic, crushed
250 g (8 oz) zucchini (courgettes), thinly
    sliced
8 eggs, lightly beaten
2 tablespoons finely chopped fresh basil
125 g (4 oz) Parmesan, grated
60 g (2 oz) black olives, pitted and halved,
    to garnish

1 In a food processor, purée the chickpeas, garlic, lemon juice, yoghurt and black pepper.
2 Quarter the peppers, remove the seeds and membrane and cook, skin-side-up, under a hot grill until the skin is black and blistered. Cool in a plastic bag, then peel.
3 Cut the sweet potato into 1 cm (½ inch) thick slices and cook until just tender; drain.

4 Cut the eggplant into 1 cm (½ inch) slices. Heat 1 tablespoon oil in a 23 cm (9 inch) round, high-sided frying pan and stir the leek and garlic over medium heat for 1 minute, or until soft. Add the zucchini and cook for another 2 minutes. Remove from the pan and set aside.
5 Heat the remaining oil in the same frying pan and cook the eggplant slices, in batches, for 1 minute each side, or until golden. Line the base of the pan with half the eggplant and spread the leek over the top. Cover with the roasted peppers, remaining eggplant and sweet potato.
6 Combine the eggs, basil, Parmesan and some black pepper in a jug, pour over the vegetables and cook over low heat for 15 minutes, or until almost cooked. Place the frying pan under a preheated grill for 2–3 minutes, until the frittata is golden and cooked. Cool for 10 minutes before inverting onto a cutting board. Trim the edges and cut into 30 squares. Top with hummus and olives. Serve cold or at room temperature.

CHEESE AND SPINACH ROULADE BRUSCHETTA

Preparation time: 30 minutes
Total cooking time: 10 minutes
Makes about 24

1 French bread stick
2 tablespoons oil
500 g (1 lb) English spinach
90 g (3 oz) spreadable cream cheese
90 g (3 oz) goat's cheese
3 tablespoons canned pimiento, drained
    and finely chopped

1 Preheat the oven to moderately hot 200°C (400°F/Gas 6). Cut the bread into 24 thin slices and lightly brush both sides with oil. Bake in a single layer on a baking tray for 10 minutes, or until lightly browned, turning once. Remove and allow to cool.
2 Remove the stalks from the spinach and place the leaves in a bowl. Cover with boiling water and leave for a couple of minutes, or until the leaves have wilted. Drain and leave to cool. Squeeze out the excess liquid and drain on crumpled paper towels.
3 Lay the spinach leaves flat, overlapping, on a piece of plastic wrap, to form a 25 x 20 cm (10 x 8 inch) rectangle. Beat the cheeses together until soft and smooth. Spread the cheese mixture evenly and carefully over the spinach. Top the cheese evenly with pimiento. Using the plastic wrap as a guide, carefully roll up the spinach to enclose the cheese. Remove the plastic wrap and cut the log into thin slices using a sharp knife. Serve on the toast.

NOTE: Be sure to thoroughly drain the spinach and pimiento to avoid a watery result.

TAHINI AND CHILLI PALMIERS

Preparation time: 25 minutes + chilling
Total cooking time: 20 minutes
Makes 32

½ cup (135 g/4½ oz) tahini
1 fresh red chilli, seeded and finely chopped
½ teaspoon paprika
2 sheets ready-rolled puff pastry, thawed

1 Preheat the oven to moderately hot 200°C (400°F/Gas 6).
2 Put the tahini, chilli and paprika in a bowl, season with some salt and stir to combine. Spread half the paste evenly over each pastry sheet, making sure the paste goes all the way to the edges.
3 Take one pastry sheet and fold from opposite sides until the folds meet in the middle. Then fold one side over the other to resemble a closed book. Repeat with the remaining pastry sheet and tahini mixture. Refrigerate the pastry at this stage for at least 30 minutes, to firm it up and make it easier to work with.
4 Cut the pastry into 1 cm (½ inch) slices. Cover two baking trays with baking paper and place the palmiers on them, making sure that the palmiers are not too close to one another as they will spread during cooking.
5 Bake the palmiers for 10–12 minutes on one side, then flip them over and bake for another 5–6 minutes, or until golden and cooked through. They are delicious served at room temperature or cold.

NOTE: To freeze the palmiers, place the sliced, uncooked palmiers on a tray and freeze until firm, then seal in plastic bags. Allow to thaw on trays and cook as above. Cooked palmiers can be stored in an airtight container for up to 1 week. If the palmiers soften, recrisp in a moderate oven for 3–5 minutes, then cool on a wire rack. Tahini is a paste made from crushed sesame seeds and is available from most supermarkets and health food stores.

SMOKED SALMON ROLLS

Preparation time: 30 minutes + chilling
Total cooking time: 5 minutes
Makes 36

6 eggs
3 teaspoons cornflour
125 g (4 oz) spreadable cream cheese
2 tablespoons chopped pickled ginger
2 tablespoons chopped fresh chives
200 g (6½ oz) sliced smoked salmon, chopped
sprigs of fresh parsley, to garnish

1 Beat 1 egg in a bowl with 1 teaspoon water and half a teaspoon of cornflour. Season.
2 Heat a frying pan and brush it lightly with oil. Add the egg and cook over medium heat, drawing the outside edges of the mixture into the centre with a spatula, until the mixture is lightly set. Cool in the pan for 2 minutes, then carefully slide out onto a clean, flat surface with the uncooked side upwards. Set aside to cool. Repeat with the remaining eggs, beaten with water and cornflour, to make five more omelettes.
3 Place each omelette on a sheet of baking paper on a flat surface. Divide the cream cheese among the omelettes, spreading over each. Sprinkle with pickled ginger, chives and salmon. Season with black pepper. Roll each gently but firmly, using the paper to help pull the roll towards you. Chill, wrapped in plastic wrap, for at least 3 hours.
4 Using a sharp knife, cut the rolls into 2 cm (½ inch) slices, discarding the uneven ends. Garnish with parsley sprigs. in advance: Can be made a day ahead, covered and refrigerated. Serve at room temperature.

NOODLE NESTS WITH SMOKED SALMON TARTARE

Preparation time: 25 minutes
Total cooking time: 20 minutes
Makes 30

200 g (6½ oz) fresh flat egg noodles
olive oil, for brushing
200 g (6½ oz) smoked salmon, diced
1 tablespoon extra virgin olive oil
3 teaspoons white wine vinegar
½ cup (125 g/4 oz) whole-egg mayonnaise
1 clove garlic, crushed
1 tablespoon finely chopped fresh dill

1 Preheat the oven to moderately hot 200°C (400°F/Gas 6). Lightly grease three 12-hole mini-muffin tins. (You can use two 12-hole mini-muffin tins and cook the remaining 6 after the first batch is finished.) Use scissors or a sharp knife to cut the noodles into 10 cm (4 inch) lengths. Put the egg noodles in a heatproof bowl and pour boiling water over to cover. Soak for 5 minutes, then drain and pat dry with paper towels. Divide the noodles among 30 holes of the mini muffin tins, pressing down to form 'nests'. Brush lightly with olive oil and bake for 15 minutes.
2 Turn the noodles out onto a wire rack, then put the rack in the oven for 5 minutes, or until the noodles are crisp.
3 Stir together the salmon, extra virgin olive oil, vinegar, mayonnaise, garlic and fresh dill in a bowl. Spoon 1 heaped teaspoon into each noodle nest and garnish with fresh dill.

GOW GEES

Preparation time: 25 minutes +
 20 minutes soaking
Total cooking time: 15 minutes
Makes 20

4 dried shiitake mushrooms
220 g (7 oz) pork mince
100 g (3½ oz) finely chopped leek (white
 part only)
50 g (1¾ oz) pickled daikon radish,
 chopped
2 teaspoons light soy sauce
2 teaspoons sesame oil
2 teaspoons cornflour
½ teaspoon grated fresh ginger
20 round gow gee wrappers
oil, for deep-frying
Chinese black vinegar, to serve
light soy sauce, to serve

1 Soak the mushrooms in hot water for
20 minutes. Squeeze dry, discard the
stalks and finely chop the caps. Mix with
the mince, leek, daikon, soy sauce,
sesame oil, cornflour, ginger and ½
teaspoon salt in a non-metallic bowl.
2 Place 2 teaspoons of the filling in the
centre of a gow gee wrapper. Brush the
edges with water, then bring together to
form a half-moon shape. Crimp the edges
together.
3 Fill a wok one-third full of oil and heat
to 180°C (350°F), or until a cube of bread
browns in 15 seconds. Deep-fry the gow
gees in batches for 2–3 minutes, or until
golden and cooked. Drain on paper
towels. Serve with Chinese black vinegar
and light soy sauce for dipping.

GLAZED CHICKEN WINGS

Preparation time: 30 minutes +
 marinating
Total cooking time: 45 minutes
Makes about 40

2 kg (4 lb) chicken wings
½ cup (125 ml/4 fl oz) barbecue sauce
½ cup (160 g/5½ oz) apricot jam
2 tablespoons white vinegar
2 tablespoons soy sauce
2 tablespoons tomato sauce
1 tablespoon sesame oil
2 cloves garlic, crushed

1 Trim excess fat from the wings. Stir the
barbecue sauce, jam, vinegar, soy sauce,
tomato sauce, oil and garlic in a small
pan over low heat until just combined.
Cool slightly, pour over the chicken wings
and mix well. Cover and marinate in the
refrigerator for at least 2 hours.
2 Preheat the oven to moderate 180°C
(350°F/Gas 4). Drain the excess marinade
from the wings and reserve. Bake the
wings in a lightly greased baking dish for
45 minutes. To prevent sticking, you can
add a little water. Turn halfway through
the cooking time, brushing occasionally
with the reserved marinade.

POTATO BASKETS WITH CHEESE

Preparation time: 15 minutes
Total cooking time: 55 minutes
Makes about 40

20 small new potatoes
250 g (8 oz) ricotta cheese
35 g (1¼ oz) Cheddar, grated
25 g (¾ oz) Parmesan, shredded
oil, for spraying or brushing
15 g (½ oz) fresh chives, finely chopped, to
 garnish

1 Preheat the oven to moderately hot
200°C (400°F/Gas 6). Boil or steam the
potatoes for 10 minutes, or until just
tender when tested with a skewer (do not
overcook or the potatoes will fall apart
when you are preparing them). Drain well
and cool completely.
2 Meanwhile, in a small bowl combine the
ricotta, Cheddar and Parmesan. Season,
to taste, and set aside.
3 Cut the cooled potatoes in half and use a
melon baller to scoop out the flesh,
leaving a 5 mm (¼ inch) border. Discard
the flesh.
4 Lightly spray the potato halves
with oil and bake on baking trays for
30–45 minutes, or until crisp and golden.
Heat the grill to high.
5 Fill each potato shell with a teaspoon
of the cheese mixture and grill for
5–8 minutes, or until the tops are lightly
golden and the cheese has melted.
Arrange on a serving dish and garnish
each with chopped chives. Serve
immediately.

IN ADVANCE: The potatoes can be cooked
and filled in advance, then grilled just
before serving.

CHICKEN DRUMSTICKS WITH RANCH DRESSING

Preparation time: 25 minutes +
  marinating
Total cooking time: 10 minutes
Makes 32

32 small chicken drumsticks
1 tablespoon cracked black pepper
1 tablespoon garlic salt
1 tablespoon onion powder
olive oil, for deep-frying
1 cup (250 ml/8 fl oz) tomato sauce
1/3 cup (80 ml/2¾ fl oz) Worcestershire
  sauce
40 g (1¼ oz) butter, melted
1 tablespoon sugar
Tabasco sauce, to taste

Ranch dressing
1 cup (250 g/8 oz) whole egg mayonnaise
1 cup (250 g/8 oz) sour cream
1/3 cup (80 ml/2¾ fl oz) lemon juice
1/3 cup (20 g/¾ oz) chopped fresh chives

1 Remove the skin from the chicken and
use a cleaver or large knife to cut off the
knuckle. Wash the chicken thoroughly
and pat dry with paper towels. Combine
the pepper, garlic salt and onion powder
and rub some into each piece of chicken.
2 Fill a deep heavy-based pan one third
full of oil and heat the oil to 180°C (350°F).
The oil is ready when a cube of bread
dropped into the oil turns golden brown in
15 seconds. Cook the chicken in batches
for 2 minutes each batch, remove with
tongs or a slotted spoon and drain on
paper towels.

3 Transfer the chicken to a large non-
metal bowl or shallow dish. Combine the
sauces, butter, sugar and Tabasco, pour
over the chicken and stir to coat.
Refrigerate, covered, for several hours or
overnight. Prepare and heat the barbecue
1 hour before cooking.
4 Place the chicken on a hot lightly oiled
barbecue grill or flatplate and cook for
20–25 minutes, or until cooked through.
Turn and brush with the marinade during
cooking. Serve with the ranch dressing.
5 For the ranch dressing, mix together
the mayonnaise, sour cream, juice,
chives, and salt and pepper, to taste.

FRIED WHITEBAIT

Preparation time: 10 minutes + chilling
Total cooking time: 10 minutes
Serves 6–8

500 g (1 lb) whitebait
2 teaspoons sea salt
1/3 cup (40 g/1¼ oz) plain flour
¼ cup (30 g/1 oz) cornflour
2 teaspoons finely chopped fresh flat-
  leaf parsley
olive oil, for deep-frying
1 lemon, cut into wedges, for serving

1 Combine the whitebait and sea salt in a
bowl and mix well. Cover and refrigerate.
2 Combine the sifted flours and chopped
parsley in a bowl and season well with
cracked pepper. Fill a deep heavy-based
pan one third full of oil and heat to 180°C
(350°F), or until a cube of bread browns in
15 seconds. Toss a third of the whitebait
in the flour mixture, shake off the excess
and deep-fry for 1½ minutes, or until pale
and crisp. Remove with a slotted spoon
and drain well on crumpled paper towels.
Repeat with the remaining whitebait,
cooking in two batches.
3 Reheat the oil and fry the whitebait a
second time in three batches for 1 minute
each, or until lightly browned. Drain on
crumpled paper towels and serve hot with
lemon wedges.

SPICY SAUSAGE ROLL-UPS

Preparation time: 20 minutes
Total cooking time: 20 minutes
Makes about 25

2 sheets frozen shortcrust pastry
2 tablespoons French mustard
5 sticks cabanossi
1 egg yolk, beaten

1 Preheat the oven to hot 200°C
(400°F/Gas 6). Cut each pastry sheet in
half. Cut triangles with bases of 6 cm
(2½ inches). Place a small dob of mustard
at the base of each pastry piece. Cut the
cabanossi into 7 cm (2¾ inch) lengths and
place across the mustard on the pastry
triangles.
2 Dampen the tips of the triangles with a
little water. Working from the base, roll
each pastry triangle around the pieces of
cabanossi. Press lightly to secure the tip
to the rest of the pastry.
3 Place the roll-ups on a lightly greased
baking tray and brush with a mixture of
egg yolk and 2 teaspoons cold water.
Bake for 15–20 minutes, or until the roll-
ups are golden brown.
in advance: These can be made up to
2 days ahead, refrigerated, then gently
reheated in the oven when required.

MUSHROOMS WITH TWO SAUCES

Preparation time: 30 minutes +
   1 hour refrigeration
Total cooking time: 2 minutes each batch
Serves 8

750 g (1½ lb) button mushrooms
⅓ cup (40 g/1¼ oz) plain flour
1 cup (100 g/3½ oz) dry breadcrumbs
3 eggs
olive oil, for deep-frying

Sauces
1 small red pepper (capsicum)
2 egg yolks
1 teaspoon Dijon mustard
1 tablespoon lemon juice
1 cup (250 ml/8 fl oz) olive oil
1 small clove garlic, crushed
2 tablespoons natural yoghurt
2 teaspoons finely chopped fresh parsley

1 Wipe the mushrooms with paper towel
and remove the stems. Measure the
flour into a large plastic bag and the
breadcrumbs into a separate bag.
Lightly beat the eggs in a bowl.
2 Put the mushrooms in with the flour
and shake until evenly coated. Shake off
any excess flour, then dip half the
mushrooms in egg to coat well. Transfer
to the bag with the breadcrumbs and
shake to cover thoroughly. Place on a tray
covered with baking paper. Repeat with
the rest of the mushrooms, then
refrigerate them all for 1 hour.
3 Cut the red pepper into large flattish
pieces, discarding the membranes and
seeds. Cook, skin-side-up, under a hot
grill until the skin blackens and blisters.
Cool in a plastic bag, then peel. Process
in a food processor or blender to a
smooth paste.

4 Place the egg yolks, mustard and half
the lemon juice in a bowl. Beat together
for 1 minute with electric beaters. Add the
oil, a teaspoon at a time, beating
constantly until thick and creamy.
Continue beating until all the oil is added,
then add the remaining lemon juice. (If
you prefer, you can make the mayonnaise
in a blender.) Divide the mayonnaise
between two bowls. Into one, stir the
garlic, yoghurt and parsley and into the
other, the red pepper mixture.
5 Fill a heavy-based saucepan one third
full of oil and heat the oil to 180°C (350°F),
or until a cube of bread dropped into the
oil browns in 15 seconds. Gently lower
batches of the mushrooms into the oil and
cook for 1–2 minutes, or until golden
brown. Remove with a slotted spoon and
drain on paper towels.
6 To serve, arrange the mushrooms on
serving plates and spoon a little of each
sauce into each mushroom. If you prefer,
you can keep the sauces separate, filling
each mushroom with either one or the
other.

NOTE: Cook the mushrooms just before
serving. The sauces can be made up to
1 day ahead and refrigerated, covered.

CRAB AND LIME QUICHES

Preparation time: 15 minutes
Total cooking time: 20 minutes
Makes 18

2 sheets frozen puff pastry, thawed
2 eggs
¾ cup (185 ml/6 fl oz) coconut cream
finely grated rind of 1 small lime
2 teaspoons lime juice
200 g (6½ oz) can crab meat, drained
1 tablespoon chopped fresh chives

1 Preheat the oven to hot 210°C
(415°F/Gas 6–7). Using two 12-hole round-based patty tins, lightly grease 18 of the holes. Cut 18 rounds of pastry, using an 8 cm (3 inch) cutter.
2 Beat the eggs lightly in a small bowl and add the remaining ingredients. Season with salt and white pepper. Spoon about 1 tablespoon of filling into each pastry case.
3 Bake for 20 minutes, or until golden. The quiches will rise during cooking, then deflate slightly. Serve warm.

BEEF EN CROUTE WITH BEARNAISE

Preparation time: 20 minutes
Total cooking time: 30–35 minutes
Makes 40

500 g (1 lb) piece beef eye fillet, trimmed
2 teaspoons oil
60 g (2 oz) butter, melted
1 clove garlic, crushed
2 small bread sticks, cut into very thin slices
25 g (¾ oz) mustard cress, cut in short lengths

Béarnaise
200 g (6½ oz) butter, melted
⅓ cup (80 ml/2¾ fl oz) white wine vinegar
1 bay leaf
1 tablespoon chopped fresh tarragon
6 black peppercorns
3 fresh parsley stalks
2 egg yolks
2 teaspoons chopped fresh tarragon, extra

1 Preheat the oven to moderate 180°C (350°F/Gas 4). Tie the beef with string at even intervals; season. Heat the oil in a pan and fry the beef to brown all over. Transfer to a small baking dish and bake for 20–25 minutes for medium to medium-rare. Remove and set aside.
2 Combine the butter and garlic in a bowl and brush over both sides of the bread. Bake on baking trays for 10 minutes, or until just golden.

3 For the Béarnaise, melt the butter slowly over low heat, remove from the heat and leave for 2–3 minutes to allow the milky mixture to separate to the bottom. Pour off the butter, leaving the milky sediment behind; discard the sediment. Combine the vinegar, bay leaf, tarragon, peppercorns and parsley in a pan and simmer briefly until reduced to 1 tablespoon; strain. Beat the egg yolks and the reduced sauce in a heatproof bowl over a pan of simmering water until slightly thickened. Remove from the heat and drizzle in the butter a few drops at a time, beating continuously until thick. Stir in the extra tarragon and season, to taste. If the mixture becomes too thick (it should be the consistency of mayonnaise), stir in a little water. If the butter is added too quickly, the mixture will separate.
4 Cut the beef into very thin slices, drape on each crouton and top with Béarnaise. Place the mustard cress on the Béarnaise.

SESAME PRAWNS WITH TANGY MINT CHUTNEY

Preparation time: 20 minutes
Total cooking time: 20 minutes
Makes 24

1 kg (2 lb) raw king prawns (about 24)
¼ cup (30 g/1 oz) plain flour
1 egg, lightly beaten
⅔ cup (65 g/2¼ oz) dried breadcrumbs
½ cup (80 g/2¾ oz) sesame seeds
oil, for deep-frying

Tangy mint chutney
50 g (1¾ oz) fresh mint leaves
½ cup (140 g/4½ oz) fruit chutney
2 tablespoons lemon juice

1 Peel the prawns, leaving the tails intact. Carefully cut the prawns down the back, devein and flatten slightly.
2 Toss the prawns in the flour and shake off the excess. Dip the floured prawns in the beaten egg and coat with the combined breadcrumbs and sesame seeds.
3 Fill a deep, heavy-based pan one third full of oil and heat the oil to 180°C (350°F). The oil is ready when a cube of bread dropped into the oil turns golden brown in 15 seconds. Deep-fry the prawns, in batches, for about 2 minutes each batch, until golden brown. Remove from the oil with tongs or a slotted spoon. Drain on crumpled paper towel.
4 To make the tangy mint chutney, combine the mint, chutney and lemon juice in a blender or food processor for 15 seconds, or until smooth. Serve as a dip.

IN ADVANCE: The prawns can be crumbed a day ahead. Place in a single layer on a tray, cover and refrigerate. Alternatively, freeze in a single layer and when frozen, place in a plastic bag and seal. Thaw in a single layer on a baking tray in the refrigerator. Prepare the mint chutney close to serving time.

SCALLOP FRITTERS

Preparation time: 20 minutes
Total cooking time: 4–5 minutes per batch
Makes 40

250 g (8 oz) scallops
6 eggs
25 g (¾ oz) Parmesan, grated
3 cloves garlic, crushed
1 cup (125 g/4 oz) plain flour
2 tablespoons chopped fresh thyme
2 tablespoons chopped fresh oregano
oil, for shallow-frying
mayonnaise, for serving, optional

1 Clean and roughly chop the scallops. Lightly beat the eggs and combine with the Parmesan, garlic, flour and herbs. Stir in the scallops.
2 Heat 3 cm (1¼ inches) oil in a deep frying pan to 180°C (350°F). The oil is ready when a cube of bread browns in 15 seconds. Cook the fritters in batches. Using 1 tablespoon of batter for each fritter, pour into the oil and cook for 4–5 minutes, over moderate heat, until golden brown. Drain on crumpled paper towels and sprinkle lightly with salt. Can be served with mayonnaise for dipping.

CHILLI PRAWNS WITH SHREDDED COCONUT

Preparation time: 40 minutes + marinating
Total cooking time: 8–10 minutes
Makes about 48

1 cup (250 ml/8 fl oz) tomato sauce
3 cloves garlic, crushed
1 teaspoon ground chilli
¼ cup (60 ml/2 fl oz) lemon juice
2 teaspoons finely grated lemon rind
2 tablespoons soy sauce
2 tablespoons honey
1 tablespoon oil
2 kg (4 lb) raw king prawns, peeled and deveined
1 cup (60 g/2 oz) shredded coconut

1 In a large bowl, mix the tomato sauce, garlic, chilli, lemon juice, rind, soy sauce and honey. Add the prawns and marinate in the refrigerator for at least 2 hours. Drain. Reserve the marinade.
2 Heat the oil in a large frying pan. Add the prawns and coconut and cook until the prawns turn pink. Stir in the marinade and cook for 2 minutes, or until heated through. Stir in the coconut. Serve on a platter.

PESTO PALMIERS

Preparation time: 20 minutes
Total cooking time: 15–20 minutes per
    batch
Makes 60

1 cup (50 g/1¾ oz) fresh basil leaves
1 clove garlic, crushed
¼ cup (25 g/¾ oz) grated Parmesan
1 tablespoon pine nuts, toasted
2 tablespoons olive oil
4 sheets ready-rolled puff pastry, thawed

1 Preheat the oven to hot 220°C
(425°F/Gas 7). Roughly chop the basil
leaves in a food processor with the garlic,
Parmesan and pine nuts. With the motor
running, gradually add the oil in a thin
stream and process until smooth.
2 Spread each pastry sheet with a quarter
of the basil mixture. Roll up one side until
you reach the middle then repeat with the
other side. Place on a baking tray. Repeat
with the remaining pastry and basil
mixture. Freeze for 30 minutes.
3 Slice each roll into 1.5 cm (⅝ inch)
slices. Curl each slice into a semi-circle
and place on a lightly greased baking tray.
Allow room for the palmiers to expand
during cooking. Bake in batches for
15–20 minutes, or until golden brown.

NOTE: Palmiers are delicious bite-sized
specially shaped pastry snacks which
traditionally were sweet. They were made
by sprinkling sugar between the pastry
folds and then cutting into slices before
baking until crisp and golden. Sometimes
they were dusted with icing sugar and
served as a petit four with coffee. Other
savoury variations include spreading with
a prepared tapenade paste made with
olives, capers, anchovies, oil and garlic,
or with tahini, a sesame seed paste.
Another simple version is to sprinkle just
the grated Parmesan between the pastry
layers.

TAMALE BEEF AND BEAN PIES

Preparation time: 1 hour
Total cooking time: 50 minutes
Makes 30

1 tablespoon oil
1 small onion, finely chopped
250 g (8 oz) beef mince
1 clove garlic, crushed
¼ teaspoon chilli powder
200 g (6½ oz) canned crushed tomatoes
1½ cups (375 ml/12 fl oz) beef stock
300 g (10 oz) can red kidney beans,
    drained
2½ cups (360 g/11½ oz) masa harina
1 teaspoon baking powder
125 g (4 oz) butter, cut into cubes and
    chilled
125 g (4 oz) Cheddar, grated
sour cream, for serving

1 Heat the oil in a frying pan. Add the
onion and cook over low heat for 3–4
minutes, or until soft. Increase the heat,
add the mince and cook until browned all
over. Add the garlic, chilli, tomato and ½
cup (125 ml/4 fl oz) stock. Bring to the
boil, then reduce the heat and simmer for
35 minutes, or until the liquid has
evaporated to a thick sauce. Stir in the
beans and cool.
2 Lightly grease 30 holes in deep mini
muffin tins. Sift the masa harina, baking
powder and ½ teaspoon salt into a bowl.
Rub the butter into the flour with your
fingertips until it resembles fine
breadcrumbs. Make a well in the centre
and, with a flat-bladed knife, mix in the
remaining stock, then use your hands to
bring the mixture together into a ball.
Divide into thirds and roll two thirds
between 2 sheets of baking paper and cut
out rounds with a 7 cm (2¾ inch) cutter.
Line the muffin tins. Trim the edges and
reserve any leftover pastry.

3 Preheat the oven to moderately hot
200°C (400°F/Gas 6). Spoon the filling into
the pastry cases and sprinkle with the
Cheddar. Roll out the remaining pastry
and reserved pastry as above. Cut into 4
cm (1½ inch) rounds to cover the tops of
the pies. Brush the edges with water and
place over the filling. Trim the edges and
press the pastry together to seal. Bake
for 20–25 minutes, or until the pastry is
crisp and lightly browned. Serve with sour
cream.

CURRIED MINCE MEATBALLS

Preparation time: 40 minutes + chilling
Total cooking time: 40 minutes
Makes 25–30

2 tablespoons olive oil
1 large onion, finely chopped
1 clove garlic, finely chopped
45 g (1½ oz) butter
1 tablespoon curry powder
2 tablespoons plain flour
¾ cup (185 ml/6 fl oz) milk
1 tablespoon mango or tomato chutney
400 g (13 oz) minced, cooked, cold lamb, beef or chicken
¼ cup (30 g/1 oz) plain flour, extra, for coating
2 eggs
1¼ cups (125 g/4 oz) dry breadcrumbs
oil, for deep-frying
mango or tomato chutney, extra, for serving

1 Heat the oil in a medium saucepan, add the onion and cook over medium heat for about 5 minutes, or until soft and golden. Add the garlic and cook for 30 seconds. Add the butter to the pan and, when melted, stir in the curry powder until aromatic. Add the flour and cook for 1 minute, or until foaming. Remove from the heat and gradually stir in the milk. Return to the heat and stir constantly over medium heat until the sauce boils and thickens. Reduce the heat and simmer for 2 minutes. Add the chutney and ¼ teaspoon each of salt and black pepper. Remove from the heat and add the meat, stirring until the mixture is well combined. Cool, cover with plastic wrap and refrigerate for at least 1 hour.

2 Using wet hands, form tablespoons of the mixture into balls and place on greaseproof paper covered trays.
3 Place the extra flour on a plate. Beat the eggs in a shallow bowl. Put the breadcrumbs on a sheet of greaseproof paper. Lightly coat the balls in flour, shake off any excess, dip in egg and then coat with breadcrumbs. Cover and refrigerate on paper-covered trays for 1 hour, or overnight.
4 Fill a deep heavy-based pan one third full of oil and heat the oil to 180°C (350°F). The oil is ready when a cube of bread dropped into the oil turns golden brown in 15 seconds. Deep-fry the meatballs in batches for about 2 minutes each batch, or until golden brown all over. Remove from the oil with a slotted spoon and drain on crumpled paper towels. Serve with chutney.

NOTE: You can use any leftover roast meat. Mince it in a food processor or cut finely with a sharp knife.

IN ADVANCE: The meat mixture can be made up to 2 days ahead. The crumbed balls can be frozen for up to 2 months. Allow to thaw thoroughly before frying.

CARAMELIZED APPLES ON PUMPERNICKEL

Preparation time: 30 minutes
Total cooking time: 15 minutes
Makes about 24

2 golden delicious or pink lady apples
2 tablespoons lemon juice
½ cup (60 g/2 oz) icing sugar
30 g (1 oz) butter
175 g (6 oz) blue cheese, crumbled
30 g (1 oz) walnuts, finely chopped
1 stick celery, finely chopped
250 g (8 oz) pumpernickel rounds

1 Peel and core the apples and slice each into twelve wedges. Brush with lemon juice and sprinkle generously with icing sugar. Heat the butter in a frying pan and, when foaming, add a few wedges and cook until brown and beginning to caramelize. Cool on a sheet of baking paper. Repeat with the remaining apple wedges, adding more butter to the pan as needed.
2 Combine the cheese, walnuts and celery in a bowl and spoon a little onto each pumpernickel round. Top with an apple wedge.

NOTE: Granny Smith apples are not suitable.

IN ADVANCE: Prepare a few hours ahead and refrigerate, covered with plastic wrap.

STILTON, PEAR AND WATERCRESS SHORTBREADS

Preparation time: 20 minutes
Total cooking time: 20–25 minutes
Makes 20

125 g (4 oz) Stilton cheese
100 g (3½ oz) butter
2 cups (250 g/8 oz) plain flour
250 g (4 oz) walnuts, finely chopped
2 small ripe pears
½ cup (125 ml/4 fl oz) crème fraîche or light sour cream
watercress leaves, to garnish

1 Preheat the oven to moderate 180°C (350°F/Gas 4). In a small bowl, beat the cheese and butter with electric beaters for 2–3 minutes, until pale and creamy. Add the flour and walnuts and season with black pepper. Stir until the mixture forms a stiff paste, then turn out onto a lightly floured surface and gather together.
2 Press the mixture into a 30 x 20 cm (12 x 8 inch) shallow tin and score with a knife into 20 even pieces. Bake for 20–25 minutes, or until the shortbread begins to brown. While hot, cut into individual biscuits following the score lines. Cool in the tin.
3 Quarter, core and thinly slice the pears close to serving. To assemble, dot a small amount of crème fraîche in the centre of each biscuit to hold the pear in place. Top the biscuit with slices of pear. Spoon the remaining crème fraîche on top of the pear and garnish with watercress leaves.

IN ADVANCE: The shortbread biscuits can be made up to 3 days ahead and stored in an airtight container when cold. If you need to assemble the whole dish a while before serving, lightly brush all over the sliced pear with a little lemon juice to prevent the pear browning.

VEGETARIAN STICKY RICE POCKETS

Preparation time: 1 hour +
  10 minutes soaking
Total cooking time: 2 hours
Makes 20

20 dried bamboo leaves (see Note)
½ cup (125 ml/4 fl oz) oil
6 spring onions (scallions), chopped
400 g (13 oz) eggplant (aubergine), cut into 1 cm (½ inch) cubes
½ cup (90 g/3 oz) drained water chestnuts, chopped
1 tablespoon mushroom soy sauce
3 small red chillies, seeded and finely chopped
2 teaspoons sugar
3 tablespoons chopped coriander (cilantro)
4 cups (800 g/1 lb 10 oz) white glutinous rice, washed and well drained
2 tablespoons soy sauce
1 teaspoon ground white pepper

1 Soak the bamboo leaves in boiling water for 10 minutes, or until soft. Drain.
2 Heat half the oil in a wok and swirl to coat the side. Cook the spring onion and eggplant over high heat for 4–5 minutes, or until golden. Stir in the water chestnuts, soy sauce, chilli, sugar and coriander. Allow to cool.
3 Bring 3 cups (750 ml/24 fl oz) water to a simmer. Heat the remaining oil in a saucepan, add the rice and stir for 2 minutes, or until coated. Stir in ½ cup (125 ml/4 fl oz) of the hot water over low heat until it is all absorbed. Repeat until all the water has been added; this should take about 20 minutes. Add the soy sauce and season with white pepper.
4 Fold one end of a bamboo leaf on the diagonal to form a cone. Hold securely in one hand and spoon in 2 tablespoons of rice. Make an indent in the rice, add 1 tablespoon of the eggplant filling, then top with another tablespoon of rice. Fold the other end of the bamboo leaf over to enclose the filling, then secure with a toothpick. Tie tightly with kitchen string. Repeat with the remaining bamboo leaves, rice and filling.
5 Put the rice parcels in a single layer inside a double bamboo steamer. Cover with a lid and sit over a wok half filled with simmering water. Steam for 1½ hours, or until the rice is tender, adding more boiling water to the wok as needed. Serve hot.

NOTE: Bamboo leaves are used to wrap food prior to cooking, but they are not eaten.

SPICY PUMPKIN PUFFS

Preparation time: 20 minutes
Total cooking time: 50 minutes
Makes 20

1 tablespoon vegetable oil
1 onion, finely chopped
3 fresh or dried curry leaves
1 tablespoon brown mustard seeds
2 teaspoons mild Madras curry powder
½ teaspoon chilli powder
½ teaspoon ground turmeric
350 g (11 oz) pumpkin, diced
½ cup (80 g/2¾ oz) frozen peas
¾ cup (185 ml/6 fl oz) chicken stock
5 sheets ready-rolled puff pastry
1 egg, lightly beaten

1 Heat the oil in a frying pan and cook the onion for 2–3 minutes over moderate heat. Add the curry leaves and mustard seeds and fry for 1–2 minutes, or until the mustard seeds pop. Add the curry powder, chilli powder and turmeric to the pan and stir for about 30 seconds, or until combined.
2 Add the pumpkin to the pan and stir for 1–2 minutes, or until the pumpkin is well coated with spices. Add the peas and stock to the pan and simmer gently for 8–10 minutes, or until the pumpkin is tender and most of the liquid has evaporated. Remove from the heat and allow to cool completely.
3 Preheat the oven to hot 220°C (425°F/ Gas 7). Lightly brush two baking trays lightly with oil. Cut four 10 cm (4 inch) circles from each of the pastry sheets and spoon 1 tablespoon of the mixture into the centre of each. Brush the edges with the beaten egg and fold over to enclose the filling. Seal the edges by rolling and folding, or pressing with a fork. Place the puffs on the trays and lightly brush with the remaining beaten egg. Bake for 25–30 minutes, or until puffed and golden. in advance: Can be made 2 days ahead or frozen for up to 2 months.

CRUSTED TUNA CRISPS

Preparation time: 45 minutes + chilling
Total cooking time: 15 minutes
Makes 24

Wasabi cream
¼ cup (60 ml/2 fl oz) cream
2 tablespoons sour cream
1 tablespoon wasabi powder
½ tablespoon lemon juice
1 tablespoon rice wine vinegar
½ teaspoon sugar

12 round gow gee wrappers
oil, for deep-frying
500 g (1 lb) tuna steaks, 2.5 cm (1 inch) thick
½ cup (80 g/2¾ oz) sesame seeds

Salad
125 g (4 oz) watercress
1 Lebanese cucumber
3 radishes
1 teaspoon grated fresh ginger
3 teaspoons rice wine vinegar
1 tablespoon sesame oil
1 tablespoon peanut or corn oil

1 For the wasabi cream, whisk the cream until it thickens, then gently stir in the sour cream, wasabi powder, lemon juice, rice wine vinegar and sugar. Season with salt and pepper. Refrigerate for at least 30 minutes.
2 Cut each gow gee wrapper in half. Fill a deep heavy-based saucepan one third full of oil and heat the oil to 180°C (350°F). The oil is ready when a cube of bread dropped into the oil turns golden brown in 15 seconds. Fry batches of gow gee wrappers until slightly brown and crisp, about 30 seconds per side. Drain on crumpled paper towels.

3 Cut the tuna steaks into 4 cm (1½ inch) wide strips (about 2 or 3 pieces). Lightly brush with 2 teaspoons of oil, season with salt and pepper and toss in the sesame seeds. Refrigerate.
4 Divide the watercress into small sprigs. Use a vegetable peeler to slice the cucumber into thin strips. Rotate the cucumber and stop when you get to the seeds. Use the peeler to slice the radishes into thin pieces. Combine the cucumber, radish and watercress and set aside. Combine the ginger, rice wine vinegar, sesame and peanut oils in a small non-metallic bowl. Season; set aside.
5 Heat 1 tablespoon oil in a heavy-based pan over medium heat. Sear the tuna on all sides for 1 minute per side. The sesame seeds should be golden brown and the centre of the tuna pink. Slice the tuna crossways into 24 pieces.
6 When ready to serve, stir the ginger dressing, then toss through the watercress, cucumber and radish. Place a small pile of salad on the wrappers, followed by a piece of tuna and some wasabi cream. Serve at room temperature.

BOREK OF ASPARAGUS

Preparation time: 20 minutes
Total cooking time: 25 minutes
Makes 16

16 fresh asparagus spears
½ teaspoon salt
½ teaspoon black pepper
2 tablespoons finely grated lemon rind
2 sheets ready-rolled puff pastry
1 egg yolk
1 tablespoon sesame seeds

1 Preheat the oven to moderately hot
200°C (400°F/Gas 6).
2 Add the asparagus to a large pan of
lightly salted boiling water and simmer
for about 3 minutes, then drain and
refresh under cold running water. Trim
to 10 cm (4 inch) lengths.
3 Combine the salt, black pepper and
lemon rind in a shallow dish and roll each
asparagus spear in this mixture.
4 Cut the puff pastry sheets into 12 x 6 cm
(5 x 2½ inch) rectangles and place one
asparagus spear on each piece of pastry.
In a bowl, combine the egg yolk with
2 teaspoons water and brush some on the
sides and ends of the pastry. Roll the
pastry up like a parcel, enclosing the
sides so that the asparagus is completely
sealed in. Press the joins of the pastry
with a fork.
5 Place the parcels on lightly greased
baking trays. Brush with the remaining
egg and sprinkle with sesame seeds.
Bake for 15–20 minutes, or until golden.

GRILLED MUSHROOMS WITH SESAME SEEDS

Preparation time: 15 minutes
Total cooking time: 10 minutes
Makes 30–35

1 tablespoon sesame seeds
400 g (13 oz) medium, flat mushrooms or
   shiitake mushrooms
2 tablespoons teriyaki sauce
2 tablespoons mirin or sweet sherry
1 tablespoon sugar
1 tablespoon finely chopped chives
1 teaspoon sesame oil
10 chives, cut into short lengths

1 Preheat the oven to moderate 180°C
(350°/Gas 4). Sprinkle the sesame seeds
on a baking tray and bake for 10 minutes,
or until golden. Remove from the tray.
2 Wipe the mushrooms with a damp cloth
and discard the stalks. Put the
mushrooms in a shallow dish. Combine
the teriyaki sauce, mirin, sugar, chives
and sesame oil, pour over the
mushrooms and leave for 5 minutes.
3 Put the mushrooms on a greased
baking tray, brush with half the marinade
and grill under a preheated hot grill for
5 minutes. Turn the mushrooms over,
brush with the remaining marinade and
grill for another 5 minutes or until
browned. Garnish the mushrooms with
the roasted sesame seeds and chopped
chives.

COMBINATION DIM SIMS

Preparation time: 1 hour + chilling +
   standing
Total cooking time: 30 minutes
Makes about 30

6 dried Chinese mushrooms
200 g (6½ oz) lean pork mince
30 g (1 oz) pork fat, finely chopped
100 g (3½ oz) peeled raw prawns, finely
   chopped
2 spring onions, finely chopped
1 tablespoon sliced bamboo shoots, finely
   chopped
1 celery stick, finely chopped
3 teaspoons cornflour
2 teaspoons soy sauce
1 teaspoon caster sugar
30 won ton or egg noodle wrappers
chilli or soy sauce, for serving

1 Put the mushrooms in a small heatproof
bowl, cover with boiling water and leave
for 10 minutes. Drain, discard the stems,
and finely chop.
2 Mix the mushrooms, pork mince, pork
fat, prawns, spring onion, bamboo shoots
and celery in a bowl. Combine the
cornflour, soy, sugar and salt and pepper
into a smooth paste in another bowl. Stir
into the pork mixture, cover and
refrigerate for 1 hour.
3 Work with 1 wrapper at a time, keeping
the rest covered with a tea towel. Place 1
tablespoon of filling in the centre of each,
then moisten the edges with water and
gather the edges into the centre, pressing
together to seal. Set aside on a lightly
floured surface.
4 Line the base of a bamboo steamer with
a circle of baking paper. Arrange the dim
sims on the paper, spacing them well
(they will need to be cooked in batches).
Cover the steamer and cook over a pan of
simmering water for 8 minutes, or until
the filling is cooked. Serve with chilli or
soy sauce.

MEXICAN MEATBALLS

Preparation time: 30 minutes
Total cooking time: 35 minutes
Makes about 28

2 slices white bread, crusts removed
3 tablespoons milk
250 g (8 oz) veal or beef mince
250 g (8 oz) pork mince
1 small onion, grated
1 egg, lightly beaten
1 teaspoon cumin seeds
2 tablespoons chopped fresh coriander
1 litre beef stock
2 tablespoons tomato paste (tomato purée)
sprigs of fresh coriander, to garnish

Tomato chilli sauce
3–4 red serrano chillies (or to taste)
1 small onion, finely chopped
2 cloves garlic, crushed
400 g (13 oz) can chopped tomatoes
2 teaspoons sugar

1 Roughly tear the bread into a bowl and soak in the milk for about 2 minutes. Squeeze, then break the bread into small pieces. Combine with the minces, onion, egg, cumin and fresh coriander. Season. The mixture will be sloppy. Mix well with your hands, then roll into about 28 small balls.
2 Mix the stock and tomato paste in a large saucepan and bring to the boil. Add the meatballs and return to the boil, then reduce the heat and simmer over low heat for 20 minutes, or until cooked through. Remove the meatballs with a slotted spoon, place in a warm serving bowl. Garnish with coriander to serve. Strain and reserve the cooking liquid for another use, or freeze.
3 For the sauce, cut the chillies in half, discard the seeds, then finely chop. Heat a little oil in a pan and cook the onion over low heat for about 3 minutes, until soft and golden. Stir in the garlic and chilli for 1 minute. Stir in the tomato and sugar and simmer for 15 minutes. Cool slightly, then purée in a food processor. Season with salt and pepper and serve with the meatballs.

OLIVE OIL BISCUITS

Preparation time: 30 minutes + standing
Total cooking time: 1 hour 30 minutes
Makes about 45

7 g (¼ oz) dried yeast or 15 g (½ oz) fresh
1 teaspoon sugar
1½ cups (185 g/6 oz) plain flour
1½ cups (225 g/7 oz) plain wholemeal flour
1 teaspoon ground cinnamon
1½ tablespoons sesame seeds, toasted
½ cup (125 ml/4 fl oz) olive oil

Topping
4 ripe tomatoes, diced
160 g (5½ oz) feta, crumbled
⅓ cup (80 ml/2¾ fl oz) extra virgin olive oil
2 tablespoons red wine vinegar
1 teaspoon dried oregano

1 Mix the yeast, sugar, 2 tablespoons of the plain flour and ¼ cup (60 ml/2 fl oz) warm water in a bowl. Cover with plastic wrap and leave in a warm place for 10 minutes, or until frothy.
2 Sift the remaining flours and cinnamon into a large bowl, return the husks to the bowl and stir through the sesame seeds and ½ teaspoon salt. Pour in the oil and rub it in by lifting the flour mixture onto one hand and lightly rubbing the other hand over the top. Make a well in the centre and add the yeast mixture and about ¼ cup (60 ml/2 fl oz) warm water, or enough to mix to a soft but not sticky dough. Knead on a floured surface for about 2 minutes, or until smooth and elastic. Place in a lightly oiled bowl, turning the dough to coat in the oil. Cover loosely with plastic wrap and leave in a warm place for 45–60 minutes, or until doubled in bulk.
3 Preheat the oven to moderately hot 200°C (400°F/Gas 6). Lightly grease a baking tray. Punch down the dough to expel the air, divide it into three portions and roll each on a lightly floured surface into a long sausage shape about 30 cm (12 inches) long. Place the first roll on the baking tray. Cut through almost to the base of the roll at 2 cm (¾ inch) intervals with a serrated knife (about 15 portions). Repeat with the remaining rolls.
4 Cover with a tea towel and leave in a warm place for 30 minutes, or until well risen. Bake for 30 minutes, or until browned underneath and the rolls sound hollow when tapped. Reduce the oven temperature to very slow 120°C (250°F/Gas ½). Cool the rolls on the tray for 5 minutes. Transfer each roll to a cutting board and cut through the markings. Place cut-side-up on two baking trays. Bake for 30 minutes, or until the tops feel dry. Turn each biscuit and bake for another 30 minutes, or until completely dry and crisp. Cool. Store in an airtight container for up to 3 weeks.
5 Dunk each biscuit quickly into cold water and place on a tray. Top with the combined tomato and feta. Drizzle with the combined oil and vinegar and sprinkle with oregano. Season.

NOTE: To make another delicious topping, combine 1 sliced roasted pepper (capsicum), 10 pitted and quartered Kalamata olives and 2 tablespoons chopped flat-leaf parsley. Season. Combine 3 tablespoons of extra virgin olive oil and 1 tablespoon of red wine vinegar and drizzle over the top.

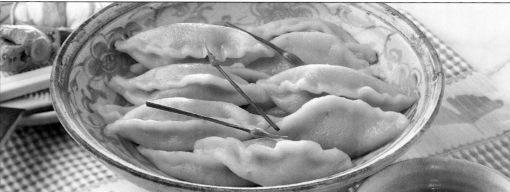

MARINATED CHILLI MUSHROOMS

Preparation time: 20 minutes +
  marinating
Total cooking time: Nil
Makes 20–25

750 g (1½ lb) button mushrooms
2 cups (500 ml/16 fl oz) light olive oil
2 tablespoons lemon juice
1 clove garlic, finely chopped
¼ teaspoon caster sugar
1 red chilli, finely chopped
1 green chilli, finely chopped
1 tablespoon chopped fresh coriander
1 tablespoon chopped fresh parsley

1 Wipe the mushrooms with a damp paper towel to remove any dirt and place in a bowl.
2 Mix together the oil, lemon juice, garlic, sugar and chilli. Pour over the mushrooms and mix well so that the mushrooms are evenly coated. Cover with plastic wrap and marinate for at least 30 minutes. Just before serving, add the herbs, season and mix well.

NOTE: If you prefer a stronger flavour, add the herbs before marinating.
in advance: The mushrooms can be marinated up to 1 week ahead and stored in the fridge.

SPINACH AND WATER CHESTNUT DUMPLINGS

Preparation time: 1 hour 30 minutes +
  cooling
Total cooking time: 50 minutes
Makes 30

Filling
1 tablespoon peanut oil
1 teaspoon sesame oil
1 clove garlic, crushed
2.5 cm (1 inch) piece fresh ginger, grated
2 tablespoons chopped fresh garlic
  chives
30 g (1 oz) water spinach, chopped into 1
  cm (½ inch) lengths
120 g (4 oz) can water chestnuts, drained,
  finely chopped
1 tablespoon soy sauce

Pastry
2 cups (350 g/11 oz) rice flour
⅔ cup (85 g/3 oz) tapioca starch
2 tablespoons arrowroot flour
1 tablespoon glutinous rice flour
Dipping sauce
½ teaspoon sesame oil
½ teaspoon peanut oil
1 tablespoon soy sauce
1 tablespoon lime juice
1 small red chilli, seeded and finely
  chopped

tapioca flour, for dusting

1 For the filling, heat the oils over medium-low heat in a wok. Add the garlic and ginger and cook, stirring, for 1 minute, or until fragrant but not brown. Add the chives, water spinach, water chestnuts and soy sauce and cook for 2 minutes. Remove from the pan and cool for about 5 minutes. Drain away any liquid.

2 Combine the pastry ingredients in a large pan with 2½ cups (600 ml/20 fl oz) water, stirring to remove any lumps. Stir over low heat for 10 minutes, or until thick. Cook stirring, for another 5 minutes, or until the liquid is opaque. Turn onto a work surface dusted liberally with tapioca flour and cool for 10 minutes. (You will need to use the tapioca flour to continually dust the surface and your hands while kneading.) With floured hands, knead the dough for 10 minutes. Divide into two, covering one half with plastic wrap.
3 Roll out the dough to 2 mm (⅛ inch) thick. Cut out 9 cm (3½ inch) rounds with a cutter. Place a heaped teaspoon of filling in the centre of each circle, dampen the edge, fold over and pleat to seal. This is very easy with a dumpling press. Place on a lightly floured board or tray and repeat with the remaining dough and filling. Do not re-roll any pastry scraps. Before steaming, lightly brush the dumplings with oil.
4 Half fill a wok or pan with water, cover and bring to the boil. Place the dumplings, leaving a gap between each, in a bamboo steamer lined with lightly oiled baking paper. Cover and steam for 10 minutes, or until the pastry is opaque. Repeat until all the dumplings are done, then serve with the dipping sauce on the side.
5 For the sauce, whisk all the ingredients together in a small bowl.
Note: Water spinach, also known as kangkung, is available at Asian greengrocers. Rice flour, tapioca starch, arrowroot flour and glutinous rice flour are available from large Asian food stores and some supermarkets.

SWEET POTATO CREPES WITH DUCK FILLING

Preparation time: 25–30 minutes +
   chilling
Total cooking time: 55 minutes
Makes 24

1 cup (125 g/4 oz) plain flour
½ teaspoon bicarbonate of soda
3 eggs, lightly beaten
1½ cups (375 ml/12 fl oz) milk
1 tablespoon light olive oil
2 teaspoons ground cumin
3 duck breast fillets (about 450 g/14 oz)
¼ cup (60 ml/2 fl oz) olive oil
2 tablespoons orange juice
1 tablespoon lime juice
1 teaspoon pomegranate molasses
¼ teaspoon finely grated orange rind
½ teaspoon sugar
pinch of ground cumin
60 g (2 oz) orange sweet potato, finely
   grated
2 tablespoons chopped fresh coriander
fresh coriander leaves, extra

1 Preheat the oven to moderately hot 200°C
(400°F/Gas 6). Sift the flour and soda into a
large bowl and make a well in the centre.
Gradually add the combined eggs, milk,
light olive oil and cumin, whisking to make
a smooth, lump-free batter. Cover and
refrigerate for 30 minutes.
2 Season the duck all over with salt and
pepper. Heat a non-stick frying pan,
brown the duck over medium-high heat,
then bake, skin-side up, on a wire rack in
a baking dish for 20 minutes, or until
tender. Rest the duck in a warm place for
at least 5 minutes.
3 Combine the olive oil, juices, molasses,
orange rind, sugar and cumin in a screw-
top jar and shake until well combined.
4 Discard the duck skin, then finely slice
the duck across the grain or shred into

thin pieces. Wrap in foil and keep warm in
the oven.
5 Press the sweet potato between sheets
of paper towel to extract as much
moisture as possible. Stir into the batter
with the coriander leaves. Spoon 1
tablespoon of batter into a non-stick or
greased crepe pan. Quickly spread with
the back of a spoon so the crepe
measures about 12 cm (5 inches) across.
Cook for 1 minute, or until lightly browned
underneath. Turn and brown on the other
side. Repeat to make 24 crepes. The
crepes can be stacked, wrapped loosely in
foil and kept warm in the oven.
6 To assemble, lay the crepes flat, and
pile even amounts of duck in one quarter
of each. Drizzle with pomegranate
dressing and top with the extra coriander
leaves. Fold the crepes in half to enclose
the filling, then into quarters. Serve.

NOTE: Pomegranate molasses is
available from gourmet speciality stores.

IN ADVANCE: The crepes and duck can
both be prepared a day ahead, covered
separately in the refrigerator, then
reheated in foil. The dressing can be
made a day ahead, refrigerated and
brought to room temperature
before serving.

MINI CROISSANTS

Preparation time: 30 minutes + chilling
Total cooking time: 40 minutes
Makes 30

40 g (1¼ oz) butter
3 onions, finely chopped
12 pitted black olives, finely sliced
2 tablespoons chopped fresh parsley
3 sheets frozen puff pastry, thawed
1 egg, beaten

1 Melt the butter in a frying pan and cook
the onions over medium-low heat for 20
minutes, or until golden and sweet
tasting. Remove from the heat and stir in
the olives, parsley, salt and cracked black
pepper, to taste. Allow to cool.
2 Cut each sheet of pastry in half, then
each half into 5 triangles with a base
(shortest side) of 8 cm (3 inches). You will
have a couple of odd shapes left at each
end. Place a little onion mixture at the
base of each triangle and roll up towards
the point, enclosing the filling. Curl the
ends around to form a croissant shape.
3 Place the croissants on a lightly
greased baking tray and refrigerate for
about 30 minutes. Preheat the oven to
moderately hot 200°C (400°F/Gas 6).
Brush each croissant with beaten egg,
then bake for 20 minutes, or until puffed
and golden.

IN ADVANCE: Croissants can be prepared
up to 6 hours ahead. Bake just before
serving.

TROUT CREPE CORNETS

Preparation time: 45 minutes + standing
Total cooking time: 15–20 minutes
Makes 20

¾ cup (90 g/3 oz) plain flour
1 egg, plus 1 egg yolk, lightly beaten
1 cup (250 ml/8 fl oz) milk
20 g (¾ oz) butter, melted
2 tablespoons chopped fresh chives

Filling
250 g (8 oz) smoked trout
125 g (4 oz) cream cheese, at room temp
¼ cup (60 g/2 oz) sour cream
¼ cup (60 ml/2 fl oz) cream

Tabasco sauce
2 teaspoons lemon juice
1 tablespoon chopped fresh chives
1 tablespoon drained capers, chopped
2 small gherkins, finely chopped
1 carrot, cut into julienne strips
1 celery stalk, cut into julienne strips
strips of fresh chives

1 Sift the flour into a bowl, make a well and gradually add the combined egg, yolk, milk and butter, mixing until smooth. Pour into a jug, cover and leave for 30 minutes.
2 Heat a crepe or frying pan measuring 20 cm (8 inch) across the base and brush lightly with melted butter. Pour enough batter into the pan to thinly cover the base. Sprinkle some chopped chives over the batter and cook for about 30 seconds. Turn the crepe over and cook the other side until lightly brown. Transfer to a plate.
3 Remove the skin from the trout. Lift the flesh from the bones, keeping it as intact as possible. Divide into twenty even-sized pieces. Mix together the cream cheese, sour cream, cream, a few drops of Tabasco, lemon juice, chopped chives, capers and gherkins.
4 Blanch the carrot and celery in boiling water for 1 minute, then refresh in cold water. Drain on crumpled paper towels.

TURKISH PIZZA

Preparation time: 25 minutes + rising
Total cooking time: 45 minutes
Makes 8

1 teaspoon dried yeast
½ teaspoon sugar
225 g (7 oz) plain flour
4 tablespoons olive oil
250 g (8 oz) onions, finely chopped
500 g (1 lb) lamb mince
2 cloves garlic
1 teaspoon ground cinnamon
1½ teaspoons ground cumin
½ teaspoon cayenne pepper
3 tablespoons tomato paste (tomato purée)
400 g (13 oz) can good-quality crushed tomatoes
⅓ cup (50 g/1¾ oz) pine nuts
3 tablespoons chopped fresh coriander
Greek-style natural yoghurt, for serving

1 Mix the yeast, sugar and ¼ cup (60 ml/ 2 fl oz) warm water in a bowl. Leave in a warm place for 20 minutes, or until bubbles appear on the surface. The mixture should be frothy and increased in volume.
2 Sift the flour and 1 teaspoon salt into a bowl, stir in the yeast mixture, 1 tablespoon oil and 100 ml (3 fl oz) warm water. Mix to form a soft dough, then turn onto a floured board and knead for 10 minutes, or until smooth. Place in an oiled bowl, cover and leave in a warm place for 1 hour, or until doubled in size.

3 Heat 2 tablespoons oil in a frying pan over low heat and cook the onion for 5 minutes, or until soft but not golden. Add the lamb and cook for 10 minutes, or until brown. Add the garlic and spices, tomato paste and tomato. Cook for 15 minutes, until quite dry. Add half the pine nuts and 2 tablespoons coriander. Season, then leave to cool. Preheat the oven to hot 210°C (415°F/Gas 6–7). Grease two baking trays.
4 Knock down the dough, then turn out onto a floured surface. Form into 8 portions and roll each into an 18 x 12 cm (7 x 5 inch) oval. Place on the trays. Divide the lamb among them and spread, leaving a small border. Sprinkle with pine nuts. Brush the edges with oil. Roll the uncovered dough over to cover the outer edges of the filling. Pinch the sides together at each end. Brush with oil. Bake for 15 minutes, or until golden. Sprinkle with coriander and serve with yoghurt.

SWEET ONION TARTS

Preparation time: 25 minutes + chilling
Total cooking time: 40 minutes
Makes 20

1 cup (125 g/4 oz) plain flour
75 g (2½ oz) butter, chopped
1 tablespoon bottled green peppercorns, drained
1 egg yolk
1 teaspoon Dijon mustard

Sweet onion filling
2 tablespoons olive oil
3 onions, sliced
1 clove garlic, sliced
2 teaspoons sugar
2 tablespoons balsamic vinegar
3 tablespoons raisins

1 tablespoon olive paste
75 g (2½ oz) feta cheese

1 Lightly grease 20 holes in two 12-hole round-based patty tins. Sift the flour and ¼ teaspoon salt into a bowl and add the butter. Rub in with your fingertips until the mixture resembles fine breadcrumbs. Make a well in the centre. Crush the peppercorns with the back of a knife and chop finely. Add to the flour with the egg yolk, mustard and up to 2 teaspoons water. Mix with a flat-bladed knife until the mixture comes together in beads. Turn onto a lightly floured surface and press together into a ball. Wrap in plastic wrap and refrigerate for 20 minutes.

2 Preheat the oven to moderately hot 200°C (400°F/Gas 6). Roll the dough out on a lightly floured surface to 2–3 mm (about 1/8 inch). Cut 20 rounds with an 8 cm (3 inch) cutter. Put in the patty tins and prick with a fork. Bake for 8–10 minutes, or until golden.
3 For the filling, heat the oil in a heavy-based pan. Add the onion and garlic and cook, covered, over low heat for 30 minutes, or until the onion is very soft and beginning to brown. Increase the heat to moderate, add the sugar and vinegar and cook, stirring, until most of the liquid has evaporated and the onion is glossy. Stir in the raisins.
4 Spread a little olive paste into the base of each pastry case. Spoon the onion mixture over it and crumble the feta cheese on top. Serve warm or at room temperature.

PARSNIP AND CHICKEN PATTIES WITH CRISPY LEEK

Preparation time: 15 minutes
Total cooking time: 25 minutes
Makes 24

1 large parsnip, chopped
500 g (1 lb) English spinach leaves
250 g (8 oz) chicken mince
4 spring onions, thinly sliced
1 egg yolk
½ cup (50 g/1¾ oz) dry breadcrumbs
1 tablespoon lemon juice
2 teaspoons chopped fresh thyme
2 tablespoons polenta
1 leek
¼ cup (60 ml/2 fl oz) light olive oil
½ cup (125 g/4 oz) light sour cream
50 g (1¾ oz) creamy blue cheese

1 Cook the parsnip in a pan of boiling water for 10 minutes, or until tender. Drain and mash smooth. Set aside to cool.
2 Trim the spinach, rinse and add to pan of boiling water. Boil for 1 minute, drain and rinse under cold water; drain thoroughly. Squeeze the spinach to remove as much liquid as possible; chop finely.
3 In a bowl, mix the parsnip, spinach, chicken, spring onion, egg yolk, breadcrumbs, lemon juice, thyme and salt and pepper. Shape into 24 patties, pressing firmly together. Dust with polenta and shake off any excess.
4 Remove the tough green portion of the leek and trim the base. Cut the leek widthways into 6 cm (2½ inch) lengths, then cut lengthways into thin strips. Heat the oil in a large frying pan over medium-high heat and cook the leek until golden brown; drain on crumpled paper towels. Add the patties to the pan and cook, in batches, for 3–4 minutes each side, or until golden and heated through. Drain.
5 Meanwhile, combine the sour cream and blue cheese in a small bowl and season with salt and pepper. To assemble, spoon 1 teaspoon of blue cheese mixture on top of each patty and top with crispy leek.

LAMB KORMA PIES

Preparation time: 30 minutes + chilling
Total cooking time: 1 hour 20 minutes
Makes 24

3 cups (375 g/12 oz) plain flour, sifted
2 tablespoons caraway seeds
180 g (6 oz) butter, chopped
1 tablespoon olive oil
1 small onion, finely chopped
1 clove garlic, crushed
2 tablespoons bottled mild curry paste
250 g (8 oz) lamb fillets, trimmed, finely diced
1 small potato, finely diced
¼ cup (40 g/1¼ oz) frozen baby peas
¼ cup (60 g/2 oz) natural yoghurt
1 egg, lightly beaten
2 tablespoons chopped fresh coriander

1 Combine the flour and caraway seeds in a large bowl. Rub in the butter using just your fingertips, until the mixture resembles fine breadcrumbs. Make a well, add 4 tablespoons water and mix with a flat-bladed knife, using a cutting action, until the mixture comes together in beads. Lift onto a floured surface and gather into a ball. Flatten slightly into a disc, wrap in plastic wrap and chill for 20 minutes.

2 Heat the oil in a heavy-based pan, add the onion and garlic and stir over medium heat for 3–4 minutes, or until the onion is soft. Add the curry paste and stir for 1 minute. Increase the heat to high and add the lamb, potato and peas, stirring for 5 minutes, or until the lamb is well browned all over. Add the yoghurt, bring to the boil, then reduce the heat and simmer, covered, for 30 minutes, or until the lamb is tender. Uncover and simmer for 10 minutes, or until the sauce thickens. Remove from the heat and allow to cool.
3 Preheat the oven to 180°C (350°F/Gas 5). Lightly grease two 12-hole mini muffin tins. Roll two-thirds of the dough between baking paper to 2 mm (⅛ inch) thick. Cut 24 rounds with a 7 cm (2¾ inch) cutter and ease into the tins. Spoon the lamb into the cases. Roll out the remaining pastry into a rectangle. Cut 24 strips 1 x 20 cm (½ x 8 inches) and twist onto the top of each pie. Brush with the egg and bake for 25–30 minutes, or until golden brown. Cool slightly before removing from the tins. Serve warm, sprinkled with fresh coriander.

CHEESY RISOTTO FRITTERS WITH BACON AND TOMATOES

Preparation time: 20 minutes + refrigeration
Total cooking time: 50 minutes
Makes 12

1.125 litres (36 fl oz) chicken stock
1 tablespoon olive oil
1 small onion, finely chopped
1½ cups (330 g/11 oz) risotto rice
½ cup (60 g/2 oz) freshly grated Cheddar cheese
½ cup (50 g/1¾ oz) freshly grated Parmesan cheese
2 tablespoons finely chopped parsley
3 spring onions (scallions), finely chopped
6 Roma (plum) tomatoes, halved
12 back bacon rashers
plain (all-purpose) flour, for dusting
¼ cup (60 ml/2 fl oz) olive oil, extra

1 Preheat the oven to 180°C (350°F/Gas 4). Pour the stock into a saucepan and bring to the boil. Reduce the heat, cover with a lid and keep at a low simmer.
2 Heat the oil in a large saucepan over medium heat. Cook the onion for 3 minutes, or until softened but not browned. Stir in the rice until well coated. Add ½ cup (125 ml/4 fl oz) of the hot stock to the rice, and stir constantly over medium heat until all the liquid is absorbed. Add more liquid, ½ cup (125 ml/4 fl oz) at a time until all the liquid is absorbed and the rice is tender and creamy, this will take around 25–30 minutes.
3 Remove the pan from the heat and stir in the cheeses, parsley and spring onion. Refrigerate until completely cooled.
4 Preheat the grill (broiler), then cook the bacon until crisp.
5 Lay the tomatoes, skin-side down, on a baking tray and grill (broil) for 3–4 minutes.
6 Using wet hands, shape the cold risotto mixture into 12 patties, then toss in flour. Heat the extra oil in a frying pan. Cook the patties in batches over medium heat for 3 minutes each side, or until golden. Drain well. Serve with the tomatoes and bacon.

FIRST COURSE

TOMATO AND BASIL CROUSTADES

Preparation time: 30 minutes
Total cooking time: 20 minutes
Serves 4

1 day-old unsliced white bread loaf
3 tablespoons olive oil
2 cloves garlic, crushed
3 tomatoes, diced
250 g (8 oz) bocconcini, cut into small
    chunks
1 tablespoon tiny capers, rinsed and dried
1 tablespoon extra virgin olive oil
2 teaspoons balsamic vinegar
4 tablespoons shredded fresh basil

1 Preheat the oven to moderate 180°C
(350°F/Gas 4). Remove the crusts from
the bread and cut the loaf into 4 even
pieces. Using a small serrated knife, cut a
square from the centre of each cube of
bread, leaving a border of about 1.5 cm
(⅝ inch) on each side. You should be left
with 4 'boxes'. Combine the oil and garlic
and brush all over the croustades. Place
them on a baking tray and bake for about
20 minutes, or until golden and crisp.
Check them occasionally to make sure
they don't burn.
2 Meanwhile, combine the tomato and
bocconcini with the tiny capers in a bowl.
In a jug, stir together the oil and balsamic
vinegar, then gently toss with the tomato
mixture. Season with salt and freshly
ground black pepper, then stir in the
basil. Spoon into the croustades, allowing
any excess to tumble over the sides.

NOTE: This recipe is a delicious first
course for serving in summer. Choose
very ripe tomatoes for maximum flavour.
You can substitute diced feta for the
bocconcini.

CHILLI PUFFS WITH CURRIED VEGETABLES

Preparation time: 35 minutes
Total cooking time: 1 hour 5 minutes
Makes 12

Choux Pastry
90 g (3 oz) butter
1¼ cups (315 ml/10 fl oz) water
1¼ cups (155 g/5 oz) plain flour, sifted
¼ teaspoon chilli powder
4 eggs, lightly beaten

Curried Vegetables
4 yellow squash
100 g (3⅓ oz) snow peas (mange tout)
1 carrot
50 g (1⅔ oz) butter, extra
2 medium onions, sliced
2 tablespoons mild curry paste
300 g (9⅔ oz) small oyster mushrooms
1 tablespoon lemon juice

1 Preheat the oven to hot 210°C
(415°F/Gas 6). Sprinkle two 32 x 28 cm
(13 x 11 inch) oven trays with water.
2 To make Choux Pastry: Combine the
butter and water in a medium pan. Stir
over low heat for 5 minutes, or until the
butter melts and the mixture comes to
the boil. Remove from heat; add the flour
and chilli powder all at once and stir with
a wooden spoon until just combined.
3 Return pan to heat and beat constantly
over low heat for 3 minutes or until the
mixture thickens and comes away from
the sides and base of pan. Transfer
mixture to large bowl. Using electric
beaters, beat the mixture on high speed
for 1 minute. Add eggs gradually, beating
until mixture is stiff and glossy. (This
stage could take up to 5 minutes.)

4 Place Choux Pastry mixture, in mounds
measuring about 2 tablespoons each,
onto the prepared trays, spacing them
about 10 cm (4 inches) apart. Sprinkle
with a little water. Bake for 20 minutes.
Reduce the heat to moderate 180°C
(350°F/Gas 4) and bake for 50 minutes
more, or until the puffs are crisp and well
browned. (Cut a small slit into each puff
halfway through cooking to allow excess
steam to escape and puff to dry out.)
Transfer the puffs to a wire rack to cool.
5 To make Curried Vegetables: Slice the
squash thinly. Cut the snow peas in half
diagonally. Cut the carrot into thin strips.
Heat the extra butter in a medium pan
and add onions. Cook over low heat for 5
minutes or until golden; stir in curry
paste. Add the mushrooms and prepared
vegetables and stir over high heat for 1
minute. Add the lemon juice, remove from
heat and stir. Cut the puffs in half, remove
any uncooked mixture from the centre
with a spoon. Fill with vegetables. Serve
immediately.

EGGPLANT AND ZUCCHINI POTS WITH PEPPER RELISH
(AUBERGINE AND COURGETTE POTS WITH CAPSICUM RELISH)

Preparation time: 30 minutes +
    20 minutes standing
Total cooking time: 1 hour 15 minutes
Makes 6

1 large eggplant (aubergine), cut into
    1 cm (½ inch) cubes
1 tablespoon salt
200 g (6½ oz) fresh ricotta cheese
1¼ cups (310 g/9¾ oz) sour cream
3 eggs
1 tablespoon cornflour
1 cup (135 g/4½ oz) grated zucchini
    (courgette)
½ teaspoon cracked black pepper

Pepper (Capsicum) Relish
¾ cup (185 ml/6 fl oz) brown vinegar
⅓ cup (90 g/3 oz) sugar
1 teaspoon yellow mustard seeds
1 green apple, peeled and chopped
1 pear, peeled and chopped
1 red pepper (capsicum), chopped
1 green pepper (capsicum), chopped

1 Preheat the oven to hot 210°C
(415°F/Gas 6–7). Brush six ½ -¾ cup
capacity ramekins with oil. Place the
eggplant in a colander, sprinkle with salt
and set aside for 20 minutes. Rinse under
cold water; drain well.
2 Using electric beaters, beat ricotta and
sour cream in a small bowl until light and
creamy. Add eggs and cornflour and beat
until smooth. Transfer to large bowl and
gently fold in the eggplant, zucchini and
black pepper.

3 Spoon the mixture evenly into prepared
ramekins. Arrange in a deep baking dish.
Fill dish two-thirds up the side of
ramekins with warm water; cover baking
dish loosely with foil. Bake for 40 minutes
or until a skewer comes out clean when
inserted into the centre of ramekins.
When ready to serve, top or accompany
with Pepper Relish.
4 To make Pepper Relish: Heat vinegar,
sugar and mustard seeds in a pan for 5
minutes or until sugar dissolves and
mixture boils. Add remaining ingredients.
Bring to boil, reduce heat and simmer,
uncovered, for 30 minutes.

QUAIL IN VINE LEAVES

Preparation time: 15 minutes
Total cooking time: 25 minutes
Serves 4

12 black grapes
1 tablespoon olive oil
1 clove garlic, crushed
4 large quail
8 fresh or preserved vine leaves
4 slices prosciutto
black grapes, extra, for garnish

1 Preheat the oven to moderate 180°C
(350°F/Gas 4). Cut each grape in half and
toss them all with the oil and crushed
garlic. Place 6 grape halves in the cavity
of each quail.
2 If you are using fresh vine leaves,
blanch them for 1 minute in boiling water,
then remove the central stem. If using
preserved vine leaves, wash them under
running water to remove any excess
preserving liquid.
3 Wrap each quail in a piece of prosciutto
and place each on top of a vine leaf. Place
another vine leaf over the top of each
quail and wrap into parcels, tying with
string to secure. Bake on a baking tray for
20–25 minutes, depending on the size of
the quail. Serve garnished with the whole
grapes.

NOTE: Vine leaves are available from
speciality food stores.

POLENTA

ORIGINS UNCLEAR—DATING
BACK TO ANCIENT ROME OR
DISCOVERED IN THE NEW
WORLD—AND ITS NAME USED
INTERCHANGEABLY WITH
CORNMEAL, THIS FLOUR-LIKE
STAPLE HAS FOUND A
NEW IDENTITY IN THE
CONTEMPORARY KITCHEN.

BASIC POLENTA

Bring 4 cups (1 litre) of water or stock to
the boil. Reduce heat and slowly whisk in
1 cup (150 g/4¾ oz) coarse polenta.
Continue whisking 5 minutes. Replace
whisk with a wooden spoon and stir until
spoon can stand and polenta comes away
from sides of pan. Stir in 2 tablespoons of
softened butter and season with salt and
pepper.

MEDITERRANEAN POLENTA FRITTATA

Make polenta as instructed in Basic
Polenta recipe. Transfer the mixture to a
bowl; add ½ cup (50 g/1⅔ oz) freshly
grated Parmesan cheese, 4 finely
chopped marinated artichoke hearts,
90 g (3 oz) chopped sun-dried tomatoes,
60 g (2 oz) pitted and chopped niçoise
olives, and 1 tablespoon fresh oregano
leaves. Spoon the mixture into a lightly
greased 30 cm (12 inch) springform
(spring-release) pan; spread the mixture
evenly over the pan and press down with
the back of a spoon. Set aside to cool.
Release the frittata from the tin, brush
lightly with oil and cook under a
preheated grill until just crisp and golden
brown. Cut into wedges and serve hot or
at room temperature.
Serves 6–8.

CHAR-GRILLED POLENTA

Make polenta as directed in the Basic Polenta recipe. Stir in ¼ cup (25 g/¾ oz) of freshly grated Parmesan cheese and 1 tablespoon of chopped fresh basil. Spread the mixture over a large pizza tray to form a 2 cm (¾ inch)-thick circle. Set aside to cool. Cut the polenta into wedges. Brush lightly with oil and cook on a preheated char-grill or barbecue for 3 minutes on each side, or until the wedges are crisp. Serve warm as a finger food.
Serves 4–6.

POLENTA WITH CHILLI JAM

Serve char-grilled wedges accompanied by a large spoonful of mascarpone cheese, some rocket leaves drizzled with balsamic vinegar, and home-made chilli jam (see page 745) or your favourite spicy tomato relish.
Serves 4–6.

POLENTA STICKS WITH ARTICHOKES, FETA AND PEPPERS (CAPSICUMS)

Make polenta as directed in the Basic Polenta recipe. Spread the mixture into a lightly greased 18 cm (7 inch) square pan. Set aside to cool. Cut polenta into 3 cm (1¼ inch)-wide sticks. Brush the sticks lightly with oil and cook under a preheated grill until they are crisp and golden. Serve polenta sticks with quartered marinated artichokes (with stems attached), a round of marinated feta cheese, and strips of roasted red and yellow pepper (capsicum). Serves 4–6.

POLENTA PIZZA

Make polenta as directed in the Basic Polenta recipe. Stir in ½ cup (50 g/1⅔ oz) of freshly grated Parmesan cheese. Spread the mixture over the base of a deep 30 cm (12 inch) pizza tray. Set aside to cool. Brush the polenta with oil and bake in a preheated moderately hot 200°C (400°F/Gas 6) oven for 10 minutes. Remove the polenta from the oven and spread 3 tablespoons of pesto sauce over the top, leaving a 1 cm (½ inch) border. Top with some sliced button mushrooms, halved cherry and teardrop tomatoes and 1 sliced green pepper (capsicum). Sprinkle with 125 g (4 oz) grated mozzarella cheese. Bake for 20 minutes or until the cheese is golden.
Serves 4.

CHIPOLATA SAUSAGES WITH HORSERADISH CREAM

Preparation time: 15 minutes
Total cooking time: 25 minutes
Makes 12

2 tablespoons virgin olive oil
2 red onions, cut into thin wedges
2 tablespoons dark brown sugar
3 teaspoons balsamic vinegar
100 g (3½ oz) spreadable cream cheese
1 tablespoon horseradish cream
12 chipolata sausages
12 par-baked mini bread rolls
100 g (3½ oz) rocket leaves, stalks removed

1 Preheat the oven to hot 220°C (425°F/Gas 7). Heat 1½ tablespoons olive oil in a small pan. Add the onion and 1½ tablespoons water, cover, and cook over medium heat for about 10 minutes, stirring occasionally, until the onion is soft and starting to brown. Stir in the sugar and vinegar and cook, uncovered, for 3 minutes, or until thick. Season and keep warm.
2 Meanwhile, in a small bowl, mix the cream cheese and horseradish cream until smooth.
3 Heat the remaining oil in a large frying pan and cook the sausages in batches over medium-low heat for 6–8 minutes, or until brown and cooked. Remove; drain on crumpled paper towels.
4 Meanwhile, heat the bread rolls according to the manufacturer's instructions. When hot, slice vertically, three-quarters of the way through, and spread with the horseradish mixture. Fill the rolls with rocket and a sausage, then onion. Serve.

NOTE: If you can't get chipolatas, you can use thin sausages and twist them through the centre.

VIETNAMESE PANCAKES IN LETTUCE PARCELS

Preparation time: 20 minutes + 45 minutes standing
Total cooking time: about 30 minutes
Makes 10

1 cup (175 g/5⅔ oz) rice flour
2 teaspoons cornflour
½ teaspoon curry powder (see note)
½ teaspoon ground turmeric
1 cup (250 ml/8 fl oz) coconut milk
½ cup (125 ml/4 fl oz) water
¼ cup (60 ml/2 fl oz) coconut cream
2 teaspoons oil
150 g (4¾ oz) pork ribs, boned and thinly sliced
300 g (9⅔ oz) raw prawns, peeled, deveined and the meat finely chopped
4 spring onions, chopped
150 g (4¾ oz) bean sprouts, scraggly ends removed
10 large lettuce leaves
1 cup (20 g/⅔ oz) fresh mint

Dipping Sauce
2 tablespoons fish sauce
2 tablespoons lime juice
1–2 teaspoons chopped fresh chilli
½ teaspoon sugar

1 Place the rice flour, cornflour, curry powder, turmeric, coconut milk, water and coconut cream in a food processor, and process for 30 seconds or until smooth. Cover and set aside for 45 minutes so the batter thickens.
2 Heat 1 teaspoon oil in a heavy-based frying pan; cook the pork in batches over moderately high heat for 1 to 2 minutes or until browned.

3 Stir the batter well. Heat the remaining oil and add 2 tablespoons batter to the pan, swirling it to form a small round pancake. Cook the pancake for 30 seconds or until it begins to crisp on the underside. Place 2 pieces of pork, 1 tablespoon prawn meat, 1 tablespoon spring onion and 1 tablespoon bean sprouts in the centre of the pancake. Cover the pan and cook for 1 to 2 minutes, or until the prawns become pink and the vegetables soften. (The base of the pancake will be very crisp, the top side will be set but soft.) Place the pancake on a platter and repeat with the remaining ingredients.
4 Place each cooked pancake inside a lettuce leaf and top with 2 mint leaves. Fold the lettuce to form a parcel. Serve with the Dipping Sauce.
5 To make Dipping Sauce: Combine the fish sauce, lime juice, chilli and sugar in a bowl and whisk until well blended.

NOTE: Use a mild Asian curry powder labelled 'for meat', available from Asian food stores. A standard supermarket curry powder is not suitable for this recipe.

VEGETABLE STRUDEL

Preparation time: 30 minutes
Total cooking time: 35 minutes
Serves 4–6

12 English spinach leaves
2 tablespoons olive oil
1 medium onion, finely sliced
1 medium red pepper (capsicum), cut into strips
1 medium green pepper (capsicum), cut into strips
2 medium zucchinis (courgettes), sliced
2 slender eggplants (aubergines), sliced
salt and pepper
6 sheets filo pastry
40 g (1⅓ oz) butter, melted
⅓ cup (20 g/⅔ oz) finely sliced fresh basil leaves
½ cup (60 g/2 oz) grated Cheddar cheese
2 tablespoons sesame seeds

1 Preheat oven to hot 210°C (415°F/Gas 6–7). Brush an oven tray with melted butter or oil. Wash the spinach leaves thoroughly and steam or microwave them until they are just softened. Squeeze out excess moisture and spread the leaves out to dry.
2 Heat the oil in a frying pan, add the onion and cook over medium heat for 3 minutes. Add the peppers, zucchinis and eggplants; cook, stirring, for another 5 minutes or until vegetables have softened. Season and then set aside to cool.
3 Brush 1 sheet of filo pastry with melted butter, top with a second sheet. Repeat with remaining pastry, brushing with butter between each layer. Place the spinach, cooled vegetable mixture, basil and cheese along one long side of pastry, about 5 cm (2 inches) in from the edge. Fold the sides over the filling, fold short end over and roll up tightly.
4 Place the strudel, seam-side down, on prepared tray. Brush with remaining melted butter and sprinkle with sesame seeds. Bake for 25 minutes, or until golden brown and crisp.

STUFFED PEPPERS (CAPSICUMS)

Preparation time: 25 minutes
Total cooking time: 1 hour 15 minutes
Serves 6

175 g (4½ oz) long-grain white rice
1¼ cups (315 ml/10 fl oz) chicken stock
6 medium-sized red, yellow or orange peppers (capsicums)
60 g (2 oz) pine nuts
⅓ cup (80 ml/2¾ fl oz) olive oil
1 large onion, chopped
½ cup (125 g/4 oz) tomato passata
60 g (2 oz) currants
2½ tablespoons chopped fresh flat-leaf parsley
2½ tablespoons chopped fresh mint leaves
½ teaspoon ground cinnamon

1 Put the rice and stock in a saucepan and bring to the boil over medium heat. Reduce the heat to medium-low, cover tightly and cook for 15 minutes, or until tender. Remove from the heat and set aside, covered.
2 Bring a large saucepan of water to the boil. Cut off the tops of the peppers, reserving the lids. Remove the seeds and membrane from the peppers and discard. Blanch the peppers in the boiling water (not the lids) for 2 minutes, then drain and leave upturned to dry on paper towels.
3 Preheat the oven to moderate 180°C (350°F/Gas 4). Toast the pine nuts in a small frying pan over low heat until golden brown, then remove from the pan and set aside. Increase the heat to medium and heat 2 tablespoons of oil. Add the onion and cook for 10 minutes or until soft, stirring occasionally.
4 Add the tomato passata, currants, parsley, mint, cinnamon, cooked rice and toasted pine nuts to the pan. Stir for 2 minutes, then season, to taste, with salt and pepper.
5 Stand the peppers in a baking dish in which they fit snugly. Divide the rice mixture among the pepper cavities. Replace the lids.
6 Pour 100 ml (3½ fl oz) boiling water into the dish and drizzle the remaining oil over the top of the peppers. Bake for 40 minutes, or until the peppers are just tender when tested with the point of a small knife. Serve warm or cold.

THAI FISH CAKES

Preparation time: 30 minutes
Total cooking time: 10 minutes
Serves 4–6

450 g (14 oz) skinless firm white fish
    fillets (eg. cod, hake, ling, redfish),
    chopped
¼ cup (45 g/1½ oz) rice flour or cornflour
1 tablespoon fish sauce
1 egg, lightly beaten
3 tablespoons fresh coriander leaves
3 teaspoons red curry paste
1–2 teaspoons chopped fresh red chillies,
    optional
100 g (3½ oz) green beans, very finely
    sliced
2 spring onions, finely chopped
½ cup (125 ml/4 fl oz) oil, for frying
sweet chilli sauce, or other dipping
    sauce, for serving

1 Process the fish in a food processor for
20 seconds, or until smooth. Add the rice
flour, fish sauce, egg, coriander leaves,
curry paste and chillies, if using. Process
for 10 seconds, or until well combined,
then transfer to a large bowl. Mix in the
green beans and spring onion.
2 With wet hands, form 2 tablespoons of
mixture at a time into flattish patties.
3 Heat the oil in a heavy-based frying pan
over medium heat. Cook 4 fish cakes at a
time until golden brown on both sides.
Drain on crumpled paper towels, then
serve with sweet chilli sauce. The sauce
can be garnished with a sprinkle of
chopped peanuts and finely diced
cucumber.

NOTES: Red curry paste is available from
most supermarkets, or from Asian
speciality stores.
    The fish cakes can be prepared up to
the end of Step 2 and stored, covered, in
the refrigerator for up to 4 hours. Cook
just before serving.

COCONUT-CRUSTED LAMB CUTLETS

Preparation time: 10 minutes +
    marinating
Total cooking time: 10 minutes
Makes 24

24 thin, lean lamb cutlets
1 large onion, grated
2 cloves garlic, crushed
2 teaspoons ground turmeric
1 tablespoon soft dark brown or palm
    sugar
⅔ cup (60 g/2 oz) desiccated coconut
2 teaspoons soy sauce
2 tablespoons lemon juice

1 Trim the meat of excess fat and sinew.
Combine all the remaining ingredients
in a bowl with 1 teaspoon of salt and
½ teaspoon of freshly ground black
pepper. Stir until the coconut is
thoroughly moistened.
2 Add the lamb cutlets and press the
coconut mixture onto the surface of each
one. Cover with plastic wrap and marinate
in the refrigerator for 2 hours.
3 Preheat and lightly oil the grill, then
grill the cutlets for 3–5 minutes on each
side, or until crisp and golden brown.

IN ADVANCE: This recipe can be prepared
a day or two ahead and refrigerated,
covered. Bring to room temperature
before grilling.

HERBED SCALLOP KEBABS

Preparation time: 1 hour + soaking
Total cooking time: 10 minutes
Makes 24

24 scallops
6 large spring onions, green part only
2 zucchini (courgettes)
2 carrots
20 g (¾ oz) butter, melted
2 teaspoons lemon juice
1 tablespoon white wine
2 teaspoons mixed dried herbs
¼ teaspoon onion powder

1 Soak 24 wooden skewers in cold water
for 30 minutes. Wash the scallops, slice
or pull off any vein, membrane or hard
white muscle, then pat dry with paper
towels. Cut the spring onions in half
lengthways, then into 8 cm (3 inch)
lengths. Line a baking tray with foil.
2 Using a vegetable peeler, slice the
zucchini and carrots lengthways into thin
ribbons. Plunge the vegetable strips into
a bowl of boiling water, leave for 1 minute,
then drain. Plunge into a bowl of iced
water and leave until cold. Drain and pat
dry with paper towels.
3 Roll each scallop in a strip of onion,
carrot and zucchini and secure with a
wooden skewer.
4 Combine the butter, juice and wine in a
small bowl. Brush over the scallops.
Sprinkle with the combined herbs and
onion powder. Place under a hot grill for
5–10 minutes, or chargrill or barbecue
until the scallops are tender and cooked
through.

IN ADVANCE: Scallops can be prepared
several hours ahead. Refrigerate,
covered, until needed.

TWO-CHEESE RICE FRITTERS

Preparation time: 30 minutes +
  1 hour 15 minutes refrigeration
Total cooking time: 30 minutes
Serves 6

3¼ cups (810 ml/26 fl oz) chicken stock
1 tablespoon olive oil
20 g (¾ oz) butter
1 small onion, finely chopped
1¼ cups (275 g/9 oz) short-grain rice
⅓ cup (35 g/1¼ oz) freshly grated
  Parmesan cheese
30 g (1 oz) fresh mozzarella cheese, cut
  into 1 cm (½ inch) cubes
35 g (1¼ oz) sun-dried tomatoes, chopped
oil, for deep-frying
70 g (2¼ oz) mixed salad leaves, to serve

1 Pour the chicken stock into a small saucepan and bring to the boil. Reduce the heat a little, cover the pan with a lid and keep at a low simmer until needed.
2 Heat the oil and butter in a large saucepan. Cook the onion until softened but not brown. Stir in the rice until well coated. Add a quarter of the stock to the pan. Stir for 5 minutes, or until all the liquid has been absorbed.
3 Repeat the process until all the stock has been added and the rice is almost tender, stirring constantly. Stir in the Parmesan. Remove from heat. Transfer to a bowl to cool, then refrigerate for 1 hour.

4 With wet hands, roll 2 tablespoonfuls of rice mixture into a ball. Make an indentation into the ball, and press in a cube of mozzarella and a couple of pieces of sun-dried tomato. Reshape the ball to completely encase the tomato, then flatten slightly into a disc. Refrigerate for 15 minutes.
5 Fill a deep-fat fryer or large pot one-third full of oil and heat to 180°C (350°F), or until a cube of bread dropped into the oil browns in 15 seconds. Gently lower the rice fritters a few at a time into the oil and cook for 1–2 minutes, or until golden brown. Remove with a slotted spoon, then drain on crumpled paper towels. To serve, arrange salad leaves on each plate and place three rice fritters on top.

NOTE: These fritters can be prepared up to 24 hours in advance. Store, uncooked, in the refrigerator and fry just before serving.

BAKED RICOTTA

Preparation time: 15 minutes +
  overnight draining
Total cooking time: 30 minutes
Serves 8–10

1 whole fresh ricotta (2 kg/4 lb)
¾ cup (185 ml/6 fl oz) olive oil
¾ cup (185 ml/6 fl oz) lemon juice
2 tablespoons thin strips of lemon rind
2 cloves garlic, crushed
6 tablespoons fresh basil leaves, finely
  shredded
50 g (1¾ oz) semi-dried tomatoes,
  roughly chopped

1 Remove any paper from the base of the ricotta and put the ricotta in a plastic colander. Place over a bowl, ensuring t he base of the colander is not touching the base of the bowl. Cover with plastic wrap and leave overnight in the refrigerator, to drain.
2 Preheat the oven to very hot 250°C (500°F/Gas 10). Line a baking tray with baking paper. Transfer the ricotta to the tray and brush with a little of the olive oil. Bake for 30 minutes, or until golden brown. Allow to cool slightly.
3 Mix the remaining olive oil, lemon juice and rind, garlic and basil in a bowl. Season, to taste, with salt and pepper. Place the whole ricotta on a platter, pour on the dressing and scatter with the semi-dried tomatoes. Serve with thin slices of Italian-style bread or bruschetta.

GOLDEN NUGGET SOUFFLES

Preparation time: 20 minutes
Total cooking time: 1 hour 40 minutes
Serves 4

4 golden nugget pumpkins
60 g (2 oz) butter
3 tablespoons plain flour
⅔ cup (170 ml/5½ fl oz) milk
3 eggs, separated
½ cup (65 g/2¼ oz) grated Gruyère cheese

1 Preheat oven to hot 210°C (415°F/Gas 6–7). Cut the tops from each pumpkin and scoop out all the seeds and fibre. Place the pumpkins in an ovenproof dish; cover the dish with foil; bake for 1 hour. Remove pumpkins from the dish; invert onto a wire rack to drain away any liquid.
2 Using a metal spoon, scoop most of the softened flesh from the pumpkins, leaving a little behind to support the skin. Mash the pumpkin flesh in a bowl. Let cool.
3 Melt the butter in a small pan; add the flour and stir for 1 minute, or until golden and bubbling. Add milk gradually, stirring until smooth between each addition. Stir constantly over medium heat until mixture thickens; cook for another minute, then remove from heat. Stir the egg yolks and cheese into the milk mixture; add the pumpkin and mix together until smooth and creamy. Season with salt and pepper.
4 Beat the egg whites with electric beaters until stiff peaks form; fold whites into pumpkin mixture with a metal spoon. Make sure the egg white is mixed in thoroughly so that no white streaks are visible but, at the same time, fold in gently and quickly, to retain the volume.
5 Spoon mixture into pumpkin shells, filling to just below the rim. Don't overfill or pumpkins will overflow while cooking. If there is any filling remaining, bake it in a small ramekin at the same time the pumpkins are baked. Place filled pumpkins in a baking dish; bake 20–25 minutes, or until puffed and golden. Serve immediately.

GRILLED TOMATOES WITH BRUSCHETTA

Preparation time: 15 minutes
Total cooking time: 35 minutes
Serves 4

1 loaf Italian bread
4 large ripe tomatoes
½ teaspoon dried marjoram leaves
salt and freshly ground black pepper
⅓ cup (80 ml/2¾ fl oz) olive oil
2 tablespoons red wine vinegar
1 teaspoon soft brown sugar
1 clove garlic, cut in half
½ cup (110 g/3⅔ oz) chopped, marinated artichokes
1 tablespoon finely chopped flat-leaf parsley

1 Cut bread into thick slices. Preheat grill. Cut the tomatoes in half; gently squeeze out seeds. Place tomatoes, cut side down, in a shallow, ovenproof dish. Place marjoram, salt and pepper, oil, vinegar and sugar in a small screw-top jar; shake well. Pour half over the tomatoes.
2 Cook the tomatoes under a hot grill for 30 minutes; turn halfway during cooking. Pour remaining oil mixture over the tomatoes. Remove from heat and keep warm.
3 Brush the bread slices liberally with some oil, on both sides, and toast until golden. Rub cut surface of garlic over bread. Place cooked tomatoes onto bread, top with artichokes and sprinkle with parsley.

EGGPLANT (AUBERGINE) SANDWICHES

Preparation time: 30 minutes +
    30 minutes standing
Total cooking time: 25–30 minutes
Serves 4

3 medium eggplants (aubergines)
olive oil, for frying
salt and cracked black pepper
ground cumin (optional)
2 red peppers (capsicums)
10–12 sun-dried tomatoes
200 g (6½ oz) ricotta or goats cheese
4 tablespoons small fresh basil leaves
fresh basil leaves, extra

1 Cut the eggplants lengthways into slices about 1 cm (½ inch) thick. Choose the eight largest slices and place on a tray or board. Refrigerate the remaining eggplant (see Note). Sprinkle the eight eggplant slices with salt and allow to stand for 30 minutes. Rinse well and pat dry with paper towels.
2 Heat a large frying pan over medium heat. Add enough oil to cover the base of the pan. When the oil is hot, add the eggplant slices, a few at a time. Cook for 2–3 minutes each side or until brown. Drain on paper towels. Season each slice with salt and pepper. Sprinkle with cumin, if desired.
3 Cut the peppers in half lengthways. Remove the seeds and membrane and then cut into large, flattish pieces. Grill until the skin blackens and blisters. Place on a cutting board, cover with a tea towel and allow to cool. Peel the peppers and cut the flesh into strips.
4 Cut the sun-dried tomatoes into strips. On each of four serving plates, place a slice of eggplant. Spread the slices with ricotta or goats cheese. Top with sun-dried tomatoes and peppers, reserving some for garnish. Sprinkle with basil leaves. Cover each with a second slice of eggplant. Decorate the top with strips of peppers and sun-dried tomatoes. Garnish with extra basil leaves.

FRESH OYSTERS WITH TARRAGON

Preparation time: 15 minutes +
   30 minutes marinating
Total cooking time: Nil
Serves 4

1 tablespoon chopped fresh tarragon
2 teaspoons very finely chopped spring
   onion
2 teaspoons white wine vinegar
1 tablespoon lemon juice
2 tablespoons extra virgin olive oil
24 fresh oysters

1 Whisk together the tarragon, spring onion, vinegar, lemon juice and olive oil in a bowl.
2 Remove the oysters from their shells, keeping the shells. Mix the oysters with the vinaigrette, cover and chill for 30 minutes. Rinse and refrigerate the oyster shells as well.
3 To serve, spoon the oysters back into their shells. Drizzle with any remaining vinaigrette.

GRILLED VEGETABLES WITH GARLIC MAYONNAISE

Preparation time: 30 minutes
Total cooking time: 15 minutes
Serves 8

2 medium eggplants (aubergines), cut
   into thin slices
salt
4 small leeks, halved lengthways
2 medium red peppers (capsicums), cut
   into eighths
4 small zucchinis (courgettes), halved
   lengthways
8 large flat mushrooms

Dressing
1 tablespoon balsamic vinegar
2 tablespoons Dijon mustard
2 teaspoons dried oregano leaves
1 cup (250 ml/8 fl oz) olive oil

Garlic Mayonnaise
2 egg yolks
1 tablespoon lemon juice
2 cloves garlic, crushed
1 cup (250 ml/8 fl oz) olive oil
1 tablespoon chopped fresh chives
1 tablespoon chopped fresh parsley
1 tablespoon water

1 Sprinkle eggplant slices with salt and allow to stand for 30 minutes. Rinse under cold water, then pat dry with paper towels.
2 Place eggplants, leeks, red peppers and zucchinis in a single layer on a flat grill tray; brush with dressing. Cook under preheated grill on high for 5 minutes, turning once; brush occasionally with dressing. Add mushrooms, cap-side up, to grill tray and brush with dressing. Continue cooking vegetables for 10 minutes or until tender, turning mushrooms once. Brush vegetables with dressing during cooking. Serve with Garlic Mayonnaise.
3 To make Dressing: Combine vinegar, mustard and oregano in bowl; gradually whisk in oil.
4 To make Garlic Mayonnaise: Place egg yolks, lemon juice and garlic in a food processor or blender, blend for 5 seconds until combined. With motor running, add oil slowly in a thin, steady stream until it is all added and mayonnaise is thick and creamy. Add chives, parsley and water and blend for 3 seconds until combined.

NOTE: Garlic mayonnaise can be made several days ahead and refrigerated. Do not worry if the dressing separates— simply brush on as required.

FRIED AND STEAMED SCALLOPS WITH GINGER

Preparation time: 10 minutes
Total cooking time: 10 minutes
Serves 4

12 scallops attached to the shell
¼ teaspoon ground white pepper
2 tablespoons soy sauce
2 tablespoons dry sherry
2 tablespoons oil
8 cm (3 inch) piece fresh ginger, shredded
1 spring onion, white part only, cut into long shreds

1 Sprinkle the scallops with the pepper. Mix together the soy sauce and sherry in a bowl.
2 Heat the oil in a large, heavy-based pan until very hot. Carefully add several shells, scallop-side-down, and cook for 30 seconds to sear. Turn face-up and place in a shallow dish. Repeat with the remaining scallops.
3 Sprinkle the scallops with sherry–soy mixture and scatter a few shreds of ginger and spring onion over them.
4 Fill a wok about one-third full with water and bring to a simmer. Put a steamer lined with baking paper in the wok and place 6 scallops on it. Cover the steamer tightly and steam the scallops for 1 minute. If they aren't cooked, they may need about 30 seconds more. Remove and set aside to keep warm. Repeat with the remaining scallops. Serve at once.

MINI PUMPKIN AND CURRY QUICHES

Preparation time: 30 minutes +
  30 minutes refrigeration
Total cooking time: 40 minutes
Makes 8

Cream Cheese Pastry
1½ cups (185 g/6 oz) plain flour
125 g (4 oz) cream cheese, chopped
125 g (4 oz) butter, chopped

Filling
1 tablespoon oil
2 onions, finely chopped
3 cloves garlic, crushed
1 teaspoon curry powder
3 eggs
½ cup (125 ml/4 oz) thick (double) cream
1 cup mashed, cooked pumpkin (about
  350 g/11¼ oz raw)
2 teaspoons cumin seeds

1 Preheat the oven to 210°C (415°F/Gas 6–7). To make the pastry, sift the flour into a large bowl and add the cream cheese and butter. Using your fingertips, rub the ingredients together for 2 minutes or until the mixture is smooth and comes together in a ball.
2 Turn dough onto a lightly floured surface, knead for 10 seconds or until smooth. Place, covered with plastic wrap, in the refrigerator for 30 minutes. Divide the pastry into 8 equal portions, roll out and line 8 deep, greased 10 cm (4 inch) flan tins. Bake for 15 minutes or until lightly browned. Remove from the oven. Reduce the heat to 180°C (350°F/Gas 4).
3 To make Filling: Heat oil in a small pan, add the onions and garlic and stir over low heat for 5 minutes or until soft. Add curry powder, stir for 1 minute. Spread over bases of pastry cases.
4 Combine eggs, cream and pumpkin in a large bowl, beat until combined. Pour over onion mixture, sprinkle with cumin seeds. Bake in 180°C (350°F/Gas 4) oven for 20 minutes, or until filling has set.

EGGPLANT (AUBERGINE) MARINATED IN CHERMOULA

Preparation time: 40 minutes +
  1 hour refrigeration
Total cooking time: 10 minutes
Serves 4

2 medium eggplants (aubergines)
salt
olive oil

Chermoula
2 cloves garlic, crushed
1 tablespoon ground cumin
1 teaspoon ground cinnamon
¼ teaspoon cayenne pepper
1 teaspoon allspice
¼ cup (60 ml/2 fl oz) lemon juice
3 tablespoons chopped fresh coriander
2 tablespoons chopped fresh mint
½ cup (125 ml/4 fl oz) olive oil

1 Cut eggplants into 1 cm (½ inch) thick slices and sprinkle with salt. Set aside for 30 minutes, then rinse and pat dry.
2 Brush the eggplant slices liberally with olive oil and cook under a preheated grill until golden brown on both sides. Drain on paper towels.
3 To make Chermoula: Combine all ingredients. Add eggplant and toss. Cover and refrigerate for 1 hour. Serve at room temperature.

ARTICHOKE FRITTATA

Preparation time: 20 minutes
Total cooking time: 25 minutes
Makes 8 wedges

30 g (1 oz) butter
2 small leeks, sliced
1 clove garlic, sliced
6 eggs
100 g (3½ oz) bottled marinated artichoke
   hearts, sliced
1 teaspoon chopped fresh tarragon
lemon juice, for drizzling

1 Heat the butter in a 20 cm (8 inch) non-stick frying pan, add the leek and garlic and cook until soft. Spread evenly over the bottom of the pan.
2 Lightly beat the eggs and season with salt and black pepper. Pour the eggs into the pan and arrange the artichoke slices on top. Sprinkle with the tarragon and cook over low heat until set (this will take about 10 minutes), shaking the pan occasionally to evenly distribute the egg.
3 Place under a hot grill to lightly brown. Cut into wedges and drizzle with a little lemon juice.

SCALLOPS AND VEGETABLES WITH BALSAMIC DRESSING

Preparation time: 30 minutes
Total cooking time: 8 minutes
Serves 4

16 large scallops, in shells
olive oil, for brushing
1 tablespoon olive oil
2 spring onions, finely chopped
2 bacon rashers, finely chopped
½ small red pepper (capsicum), seeded
   and finely diced
½ stick celery, finely diced
1 tablespoon finely chopped fresh parsley
100 g (3½ oz) mixed salad leaves
60 g (2 oz) snow pea (mangetout) sprouts,
   trimmed
1 spring onion, cut into thin shreds, to
   garnish

Balsamic dressing
⅓ cup (80 ml/2¾ fl oz) olive oil
1 tablespoon balsamic vinegar
½ teaspoon Dijon mustard
½ teaspoon honey

1 Slice or pull off any vein, membrane or hard white muscle from the scallops, leaving any roe attached. Gently pat dry with paper towels. Very lightly brush with olive oil and place on a large baking tray in their shells. Preheat the grill to hot.
2 Heat the oil in a heavy-based frying pan. Add the spring onion and bacon, cook for 2 minutes, then add the red pepper and celery. Cook and stir frequently for 3 minutes, or until the vegetables are softened. Add the parsley and season well with salt and black pepper.
3 Combine the balsamic dressing ingredients in a glass jar and shake well.
4 Grill the scallops for 1–2 minutes. Take care not to overcook. Arrange 4 shells around the outside of four large serving plates. Spoon some warm vegetable mixture over each scallop. Divide the mixed salad leaves and snow pea sprouts into 4 portions and place some in the centre of each plate. Garnish the salad with the spring onion shreds. Drizzle a little dressing over the scallops and the salad. Serve at once.

SATAYS & KEBABS

TO PREVENT THE WOODEN
SKEWERS USED FOR SATAYS
AND KEBABS BURNING BEFORE
THE MEAT IS COOKED, SOAK
THEM IN WATER FOR AT LEAST
30 MINUTES. THE ENDS CAN
ALSO BE WRAPPED IN FOIL.

CHICKEN SATAYS

Cut 500 g (1 lb) chicken tenderloins in half
lengthways. In a shallow non-metallic
dish, combine 1 tablespoon honey, ¼ cup
(60 ml/2 fl oz) soy sauce, 2 teaspoons
sesame oil, 1 teaspoon ground coriander,
1 teaspoon ground turmeric and ½
teaspoon chilli powder. Thread the
chicken lengthways onto soaked wooden
skewers and place the skewers in the
marinade. Cover and refrigerate for at
least 2 hours. To make Quick Satay
Sauce, cook a small finely chopped onion
in 1 tablespoon oil until softened and then
stir in ½ cup (125 g/4 oz) crunchy peanut
butter, 2 tablespoons soy sauce, ½ cup
(125 ml/4 fl oz) coconut cream and 2
tablespoons sweet chilli sauce. Cook
gently until smooth and heated through.
To cook the satays, place the skewers on
a preheated grill and cook for 5–7 minutes,
turning and basting with the marinade
frequently. Serve with warm Quick
Satay Sauce.
Makes 8 satays.

TERIYAKI STEAK KEBABS

Cut 750 g (1½ lb) lean rump steak into thin
strips, 15 cm (6 inches) long and thread
the slices onto skewers. Combine ½ cup
(125 ml/4 fl oz) soy sauce, ½ cup (125 ml/4
fl oz) sherry or sake, 1 crushed clove
garlic and 1 teaspoon each ground ginger
and sugar. Place the steak in a shallow
non-metallic dish and marinate it for at
least 1 hour in the refrigerator. Drain and
place the skewers on a preheated, oiled
grill tray or barbecue flatplate and cook
for 3–4 minutes each side.
Makes 24 kebabs.

KOFTA ON SKEWERS

Combine 750 g (1½ lb) minced beef, 1 small grated onion, ½ cup (30 g/1 oz) chopped fresh parsley, 2 tablespoons chopped fresh coriander leaves, ½ teaspoon each ground cumin, nutmeg and cardamom, and ½ teaspoon each dried oregano and mint. Let stand for 1 hour. With wet hands, form the mixture into 24 sausage shapes; thread 2 koftas onto each skewer between wedges of lime. Place the koftas under a hot grill or on a preheated barbecue flatplate and cook for 10–12 minutes, turning frequently. Makes 12 skewers.

MALAYSIAN LAMB SATAYS

Trim any fat or silver sinew from 500 g (1 lb) lamb fillets. Slice the meat across the grain into very thin strips (if you have time, leave the meat in the freezer for 30 minutes as this will make it easier to thinly slice.) In a food processor, combine 1 roughly chopped onion, 2 crushed cloves garlic, 2 cm (¾ inch) lemon grass (white part only), 2 slices fresh galangal, 1 teaspoon chopped fresh ginger, 1 teaspoon ground cumin, ½ teaspoon ground fennel, 1 tablespoon ground coriander, 1 teaspoon turmeric, 1 tablespoon soft brown sugar and 1 tablespoon lemon juice and process until a smooth paste is formed. Transfer the paste to a shallow non-metallic dish and add the lamb, stirring to coat well. Cover and refrigerate overnight. Thread the meat onto skewers and cook under a preheated grill for 3–4 minutes on each side, or until cooked. Brush regularly with the remaining marinade while cooking. Makes 8 satays.

CHILLI PORK KEBABS

Trim the fat and sinew from 500 g (1 lb) pork fillet and cut into small cubes. Combine 2 tablespoons sweet chilli sauce, 2 tablespoons tomato sauce, 2 tablespoons hoisin sauce, 2 crushed cloves garlic, 3 tablespoons lemon juice, 2 tablespoons honey and 2 teaspoons grated fresh ginger. Pour over the pork and stir well. Cover and refrigerate for several hours or overnight. Thread the pork onto skewers; cook on a lightly oiled grill or barbecue flatplate for 3–4 minutes each side, or until cooked. Brush with the remaining marinade while cooking. Serve with Quick Satay Sauce (opposite). Makes 8 kebabs.

NOODLE PANCAKES WITH PEKING DUCK

Preparation time: 20 minutes
Total cooking time: 15 minutes
Serves 4

½ Chinese roast duck
500 g (1 lb) fresh rice noodle sheets
1 teaspoon roasted sesame oil
¼ cup (40 g/1¼ oz) sesame seeds, toasted
2 tablespoons vegetable oil
50 g (1¾ oz) snow pea (mangetout) sprouts, to garnish

Sauce
¼ cup (60 ml/2 fl oz) hoisin sauce
1 tablespoon plum sauce

1 Remove the flesh and skin from the duck, trying to keep some of the skin on each piece.
2 Cut the noodle rolls into 5 cm (2 inch) slices, then halve them. Rinse them under cold water and separate them slightly with your hands. Drain and pat dry, then transfer to a bowl and mix in the sesame oil, sesame seeds and 1 tablespoon of the vegetable oil.
3 Lightly grease eight egg rings and place four of them in a large non-stick frying pan with a little of the oil. Press the noodle mixture firmly into the rings and cook the pancakes over medium heat until crisp and golden. Remove the egg rings and turn the pancakes over. Repeat with the remaining noodle mixture until you have eight noodle pancakes. Keep the pancakes warm.
4 To make the sauce, put the hoisin and plum sauces in a saucepan with 1 tablespoon water and bring to the boil.
5 To serve, place two noodle pancakes on top of one another on each plate, top with snow pea sprouts and barbecued duck and drizzle with the sauce.

POTTED PRAWNS

Preparation time: 12 minutes + overnight chilling
Total cooking time: 3 minutes
Makes 1⅓ cups (350 g/11 oz)

250 g (8 oz) small cooked prawns
100 g (3½ oz) butter
¼ teaspoon ground nutmeg
¼ teaspoon ground ginger
pinch of cayenne pepper

1 Peel the prawns and gently pull out the dark vein from each prawn back, starting at the head end. Chop the prawns very finely. Melt 60 g (2 oz) of the butter over low heat in a small saucepan. Add the prawns, nutmeg, ginger, cayenne pepper and salt and pepper, to taste.
2 Stir over low heat for 2 minutes, or until all the butter has been absorbed into the mixture. Spoon into a 1⅓ cup (350 ml/ 11 fl oz) capacity ramekin, press down, then smooth the surface.
3 Melt the remaining butter in a small pan and pour over the surface (leaving the white sediment behind in the pan) to cover completely. Refrigerate overnight to allow the flavours to develop. Bring back to room temperature and serve with toast.

SMOKED SALMON IN DILL DRESSING

Preparation time: 15 minutes
Total cooking time: Nil
Serves 4

400 g (13 oz) smoked salmon
2 tablespoons light olive oil
2 tablespoons oil
2 tablespoons lemon juice
3 teaspoons soft brown sugar
3 tablespoons chopped fresh dill

1 Arrange the smoked salmon slices in a single layer, on individual plates or a large platter.
2 Combine the oils, juice and sugar in a bowl and stir until the sugar dissolves. Season, to taste, then mix in 2 tablespoons of the dill.
3 Drizzle the dressing over the salmon. Using the back of a spoon, cover the salmon with the dressing. Sprinkle with the remaining dill and some cracked black pepper and serve with extra lemon wedges and slices of rye bread.

SALMON RILLETTES

Preparation time: 10 minutes +
  overnight chilling
Total cooking time: 10 minutes
Serves 4–6

200 g (6½ oz) salmon fillet
125 g (4 oz) unsalted butter, softened
100 g (3½ oz) smoked salmon, finely
  chopped
1 egg yolk, lightly beaten
1 tablespoon olive oil
1 teaspoon lemon juice
1 tablespoon chopped fresh dill

1 Remove the skin and any bones from
the salmon fillet. Melt 50 g (1¾ oz) of the
butter in a frying pan over low heat and
cook the salmon for 5 minutes, then turn
and cook for another 5 minutes. Remove
from the pan and cool slightly before
flaking into small pieces and combining
with the remaining softened butter and
smoked salmon, egg yolk, oil, lemon juice
and dill. Season with salt and pepper, to
taste.
2 Transfer to a serving dish and
refrigerate overnight. Serve with Melba
toasts.

CRUDITES WITH GARLIC SAUCE

Preparation time: 30 minutes
Total cooking time: 20 minutes
Serves 4–6

a selection of fresh vegetable sticks, for
  serving

Garlic Sauce
2 large old potatoes, peeled and cubed
4–5 cloves garlic, crushed
1 tablespoon white wine vinegar
freshly ground white pepper
lemon juice
salt
⅓ cup (80 ml/2¾ fl oz) olive oil

1 Cover and refrigerate the prepared
vegetables.
2 To make Garlic Sauce: Cook the potatoes
in a pan of boiling water until tender. Test
with a sharp knife or a fork. If the knife
comes away easily, the potato should be
ready to mash; alternatively, try to mash a
cube with the fork. Drain the potatoes well
and place in a bowl. Mash the potato until
smooth. Add the crushed garlic and
vinegar and mix well. Season with pepper,
a little lemon juice, and salt, to taste.
3 Add olive oil a few drops at a time,
beating well after each addition. Continue
adding the oil and beating until the
mixture is quite smooth and thick—this
process may take up to 5 minutes. Serve
the sauce warm with vegetable sticks and
crusty bread or toasted flatbread.

NOTE: This garlic sauce is often made
using almonds and soaked white bread
instead of potato. Substitute 4 tablespoons
of ground almonds and 90 g (3 oz) of stale
white bread that has been soaked in
water and squeezed dry. Blend in a food
processor, adding the oil in drops through
the feed tube while the motor is running.
The consistency should be that of a thick
mayonnaise. If mixture is too thick, add a
little more oil or lemon juice.

PRAWN COCKTAILS

Preparation time: 20 minutes
Total cooking time: Nil
Serves 4

¼ cup (60 g/2 oz) whole-egg mayonnaise
2 teaspoons tomato sauce
dash of Tabasco sauce
¼ teaspoon Worcestershire sauce
2 teaspoons thick (double) cream
¼ teaspoon lemon juice
24 cooked large prawns
4 lettuce leaves, shredded
lemon wedges, for serving

1 Mix the mayonnaise, sauces, cream and
juice together in a small bowl.
2 Peel the prawns, leaving the tails intact
on eight of them. Gently pull out the dark
vein from the back of each prawn, starting
at the head end.
3 Divide the lettuce among 4 glasses.
Arrange the prawns without the tails in
the glasses and drizzle with the sauce.
Hang 2 of the remaining prawns over the
edge of each glass and serve with lemon
wedges.

MARINATED EGGPLANT (AUBERGINE)

Preparation time: 15 minutes +
 salting + marinating
Total cooking time: 15 minutes
Serves 6–8

750 g (1½ lb) slender eggplant
 (aubergine)
¼ cup (60 ml/2 fl oz) olive oil
2 tablespoons balsamic vinegar
2 cloves garlic, crushed
1 anchovy fillet, finely chopped
2 tablespoons chopped fresh parsley

1 Cut the eggplant into thick diagonal
slices, place in a colander and sprinkle
well with salt. After 30 minutes, rinse and
pat dry.
2 Whisk the oil, vinegar, garlic and
anchovy until smooth. Season, to taste.
3 Heat a little oil in a frying pan and brown
the eggplant in batches. Transfer to a
bowl, toss with the dressing and parsley
and marinate for 4 hours. Serve at room
temperature.

CARPACCIO

Preparation time: 15 minutes + freezing
Total cooking time: Nil
Serves 8

400 g (13 oz) beef eye fillet
1 tablespoon extra virgin olive oil
rocket leaves, torn
60 g (2 oz) Parmesan, shaved
black olives, cut into slivers

1 Remove all the visible fat and sinew
from the beef, then freeze for 1–2 hours,
until firm but not solid. This makes the
meat easier to slice thinly.
2 Cut paper-thin slices of beef with a
large, sharp knife. Arrange on a serving
platter and allow to return to room
temperature.
3 Just before serving, drizzle with oil,
then scatter with rocket, Parmesan and
olives.

IN ADVANCE: The beef can be cut into
slices a few hours in advance, covered
and refrigerated. Drizzle with oil and
garnish with the other ingredients just
before serving.

FRESH SALMON TARTARE

Preparation time: 20 minutes
Total cooking time: Nil
Serves 4

400 g (13 oz) salmon fillet
2 spring onions, finely chopped
1 tablespoon tiny capers or finely
 chopped regular capers
1 tablespoon finely chopped gherkin
chopped fresh dill, to garnish
1 lemon, cut into wedges

1 Remove the skin and any connective
tissue or bones from the salmon. This
should leave you with about 70 g (2¼ oz)
of fish per person. Using a large, sharp
knife, finely chop the salmon until it has
the texture of mince. Mix in a bowl with
the spring onion, capers, gherkin and
some salt and freshly ground black
pepper. Refrigerate, covered, until just
before serving.
2 When ready to serve, roughly pile onto
individual plates and sprinkle with dill.
Grind some more black pepper over the
fish and serve with lemon wedges. Can be
served with slices of buttered rye bread.
Note: You can also use fresh tuna fillet.

BARBECUED QUAIL

Preparation time: 30 minutes +
   3 hours chilling
Total cooking time: 10 minutes
Serves 6

6 quails
1 cup (250 ml/8 fl oz) dry red wine
2 sticks celery, including tops, chopped
1 carrot, chopped
1 small onion, chopped
1 bay leaf, torn into small pieces
1 teaspoon allspice
1 teaspoon dried thyme
2 cloves garlic, crushed
2 tablespoons olive oil
2 tablespoons lemon juice
1 lemon, cut into wedges, for serving

1 To prepare the quails, use poultry shears to cut down either side of the backbone on each quail, then discard the backbone. Remove the innards, wash the insides of the quails and pat dry with paper towels. Place the quails breast-side-up on the bench, open them out flat and gently press to flatten. With the poultry shears, cut each quail in half through the breast, then cut each quail half in half again, into the thigh and drumstick piece and breast and wing piece.
2 In a non-metallic bowl, combine the wine, celery, carrot, onion, bay leaf and allspice. Add the quail and stir to coat. Cover and marinate in the refrigerator for 3 hours, or preferably overnight, stirring occasionally. Drain and sprinkle with thyme and some salt and pepper.
3 Whisk the garlic, oil and lemon juice together in a small bowl.
4 Heat a lightly oiled barbecue plate until hot or heat a grill to its highest setting. Reduce the heat to medium and cook the quail breast pieces for 4–5 minutes on each side and the drumstick pieces for 3 minutes on each side, or until tender and cooked through. Brush frequently with the lemon mixture during cooking. Serve hot, with lemon wedges.

SUPPLI

Preparation time: 25 minutes + cooling
Total cooking time: 45 minutes
Serves 6

1.5 litres (48 fl oz) chicken stock
60 g (2 oz) butter
1 small onion, finely chopped
400 g (13 oz) risotto rice
¾ cup (75 g/2½ oz) freshly grated
   Parmesan cheese
2 eggs, beaten
9 basil leaves, torn in half
150 g (5 oz) fresh mozzarella cheese, cut
   into 18 cubes (about 1.5 cm/5/8 inch
   square)
150 g (5 oz) dry breadcrumbs
oil, for deep-frying

1 Pour the stock into a saucepan and bring to the boil. Reduce the heat, cover with a lid and keep at a low simmer.
2 Melt the butter in a large saucepan. Cook the onion over low heat for 3–4 minutes, or until softened but not browned. Stir in the rice until well coated. Add ½ cup (125 ml) of the hot stock and stir constantly over medium heat until all the liquid is absorbed. Continue adding more liquid, ½ cup (125 ml) at a time until all the liquid is absorbed and the rice is tender and creamy, this will take around 25–30 minutes. When making suppli, it is not so essential to keep the rice al dente—if it is a little more glutinous, it will stick together better.
3 Remove the pan from the heat and stir in the Parmesan and eggs. Season with salt and freshly ground black pepper. Spread out on a large baking tray to cool completely.
4 Divide the rice into 18 portions. Take one portion in the palm of your hand and put a piece of basil and a cube of mozzarella in the centre. Fold the rice over to encase the cheese and at the same time mould the croquette into an egg shape. Roll the croquette in breadcrumbs and put on a baking tray while you make the rest.
5 Heat enough oil in a deep-fat fryer or large saucepan to fully cover the croquettes. Heat the oil to 180°C (350°F), or until a cube of bread dropped into the oil browns in 15 seconds. Deep-fry the suppli in batches, without crowding, for about 4 minutes, or until evenly golden brown. Drain on crumpled paper towels and serve at once, as they are or with a fresh tomato sauce.

PORK AND LETTUCE PARCELS

Preparation time: 1 hour
Total cooking time: 55 minutes
Serves 4–6

500 g (1 lb) pork loin
5 cm (2 inch) piece fresh ginger, thinly sliced
1 tablespoon fish sauce
20 spring onions (choose thin ones)
2 soft-leaf lettuces
1 Lebanese cucumber, thinly sliced
3 tablespoons fresh mint
3 tablespoons fresh coriander leaves
2 green chillies, seeded and very finely sliced, optional
2 teaspoons sugar
Lemon and Garlic Dipping Sauce (page 765), to serve

1 Place the pork, ginger and fish sauce in a large pan and cover with cold water. Bring to the boil, reduce the heat and simmer, covered, for about 45 minutes or until the pork is tender. Remove the pork and allow to cool; discard the liquid.
2 Trim both ends from all the spring onions so that you have long stems of equal length. Bring a large pot of water to the boil and blanch the spring onions 2 to 3 at a time for about 2 minutes, or until softened. Remove the spring onions from the hot water with tongs and place them in a bowl of iced water. Drain them and lay them flat and straight on a tray to be used later.
3 Separate the lettuce into leaves. If the leaves have a firm section at the base, trim this away (or making a neat parcel will be difficult).
4 When the pork is cool enough to handle, cut it into thin slices and finely shred each slice. Spread out a lettuce leaf, place about 1 tablespoon of the shredded pork in the centre of the leaf. Top with a few slices of cucumber, a few mint and coriander leaves, a little chilli, if using, and a light sprinkling of sugar. Fold a section of the lettuce over the filling, bring in the sides to meet each other and carefully roll up the parcel. Tie one of the spring onions around the parcel; trim off the excess or tie it into a bow. Repeat with the remaining ingredients. Arrange the parcels on a serving platter and serve with Lemon and Garlic Dipping Sauce.

CRAB CAKES WITH AVOCADO SALSA

Preparation time: 25 minutes + chilling
Total cooking time: about 15 minutes
Makes 20

2 eggs
340 g (11 oz) can crab meat, drained
2 spring onions, finely chopped
1 tablespoon mayonnaise
2 teaspoons sweet chilli sauce
1¼ cups (100 g/3 oz) fresh white breadcrumbs
oil, for shallow-frying

Avocado salsa
2 ripe Roma (egg) tomatoes, chopped
1 small red onion, finely chopped
1 large avocado, finely diced
3 tablespoons lime juice
2 tablespoons fresh chervil leaves
1 teaspoon caster sugar

1 Beat the eggs lightly in a bowl. Add the crab meat, spring onion, mayonnaise, sweet chilli sauce and breadcrumbs, and stir well. Season, then cover and refrigerate for 30 minutes.
2 To make the avocado salsa, combine all the ingredients in a bowl, season with salt and pepper, and toss gently to combine.
3 Using wet hands, form the crab mixture into 20 small flat cakes. Heat 3 cm (1¼ inches) oil in a large heavy-based pan and cook the crab cakes over medium heat for about 3 minutes each side, or until golden brown on both sides. Drain well on crumpled paper towels and serve immediately, with avocado salsa to spoon onto the top.

IN ADVANCE: The crab mixture can be made a day ahead, then covered and refrigerated. Prepare the salsa close to serving time.

SWEET AND SOUR SARDINES

Preparation time: 20 minutes +
  marinating
Total cooking time: 15–20 minutes
Serves 4

12 fresh butterflied sardines
plain flour, for dusting
olive oil, for frying
½ red onion, thinly sliced
1 clove garlic, crushed
2 bay leaves
1 tablespoon raisins
1 tablespoon pine nuts
½–1 teaspoon dried chilli flakes
1 teaspoon soft brown sugar
⅓ cup (80 ml/2¾ fl oz) balsamic vinegar
⅓ cup (80 ml/2¾ fl oz) red wine

1 Dust the sardines with the flour and
season well with salt and pepper.
2 Add enough olive oil to a large heavy-
based frying pan to come about 1 cm
(½ inch) up the side. Heat the oil over
medium heat and fry the sardines in
batches for about 5–10 minutes, until
crisp and golden. Drain well on crumpled
paper towels, then lay them in a non-
metallic dish.
3 Fry the onion in a little olive oil over
medium heat for about 5 minutes, until
tender but not brown. Add the garlic, bay
leaves, raisins, pine nuts and chilli flakes.
Stir well, then add the sugar, vinegar and
red wine, and bring everything to a simmer.
Pour this mixture over the sardines, cover
and marinate in the refrigerator until cool.
Serve at room temperature, perhaps on a
bed of snow pea (mangetout) sprouts or
mixed lettuce leaves.

VIETNAMESE DUCK RICE PAPER ROLLS

Preparation time: 20 minutes
Total cooking time: Nil
Serves 4

16 x 22 cm (9 inch) round rice paper
  wrappers
1 whole Chinese roast duck, meat
  removed from the bones and chopped
1 telegraph cucumber
150 g (5 oz) bean sprouts, tailed

Sauce
1 tablespoon hoisin sauce
2 teaspoons chilli sauce
1 tablespoon plum sauce

1 Half-fill a large bowl with warm water
and a second bowl with cold water. Dip
each wrapper into the warm water for
10 seconds and then into the cold water.
Drain on paper towels and stack on a
serving plate with a piece of baking paper
between each wrapper.
2 Remove any remaining bones from the
duck and shred the meat. Place in a
serving dish. Cut the cucumber in half
lengthways and scrape out the seeds.
Cut the cucumber flesh into 1 x 6 cm
(½ x 2½ inch) strips. Put in a serving dish.
Put the bean sprouts in a separate
serving dish. Combine the sauce
ingredients in a small dish.
3 Invite your guests to assemble their
rolls at the table. To assemble, spread a
little sauce onto the rice paper wrapper,
then arrange the filling ingredients on the
top half of the wrapper. Fold over the
bottom edge then roll up, tucking in the
sides.

SCALLOP CEVICHE

Preparation time: 20 minutes +
  marinating
Total cooking time: Nil
Makes 15

15 scallops on the half shell
1 teaspoon finely grated lime rind
2 cloves garlic, chopped
2 red chillies, seeded and chopped
¼ cup (60 ml/2 fl oz) lime juice
1 tablespoon chopped fresh parsley
1 tablespoon olive oil

1 Take the scallops off their half shells. If
the scallops need to be cut off the shells,
use a small, sharp paring knife to
carefully slice the attached part away
from the shell, being careful to leave as
little scallop meat on the shell as
possible. Remove the dark vein and white
muscle from the scallops, and wash the
shells.
2 In a bowl, mix together the lime rind,
garlic, chilli, lime juice, parsley and olive
oil and season with salt and freshly
ground black pepper. Place the scallops
in the dressing and stir to coat evenly.
Cover with plastic wrap and marinate in
the refrigerator for 2 hours to 'cook' the
scallop meat.
3 To serve, slide each of the scallops back
onto a half shell and spoon the dressing
over the top. Serve cold.

MARINATED LAMB CUTLETS WITH SALSA VERDE

Preparation time: 30 minutes +
    marinating
Total cooking time: 20–25 minutes
Makes 24

2 lemons
4 tablespoons virgin olive oil
1 tablespoon Dijon mustard
3 racks of 8 small lamb cutlets (about 1.1
    kg), trimmed of fat
40 g (1¼ oz) flat-leaf parsley
3 drained anchovy fillets, finely chopped
1 clove garlic, crushed
1 tablespoon olive oil
1½ tablespoons baby capers, rinsed and
    drained

1 Finely grate the rind of the lemons and squeeze the juice from the fruit. Combine 1 teaspoon of the rind and 2 tablespoons of the juice with half the virgin olive oil and the mustard in a large bowl. Add the lamb racks and turn to coat thoroughly. Cover and refrigerate for at least 3 hours, or overnight.
2 To make the salsa verde, mix the parsley, anchovies, garlic, 1 tablespoon of the remaining lemon juice and 1 teaspoon of the rind in a food processor until finely chopped. With the motor running, add the remaining virgin olive oil and process until smooth and thickened. Transfer to a bowl, cover and refrigerate for at least 2½ hours.

3 Preheat the oven to moderately hot 200°C (400°F/Gas 6). Drain the lamb and discard the marinade. Heat the olive oil in a large baking dish over medium-high heat, add the lamb racks and cook, turning occasionally, for 5 minutes, or until the lamb is browned all over. Transfer the dish to the oven and bake for 15–20 minutes, or until the lamb is tender. Set aside for at least 10 minutes before slicing between the bones. Arrange in a single layer on a plate, top with salsa verde and sprinkle with capers.
note: When you buy the racks of lamb, ask the butcher to cut through the bones at the base to make slicing into cutlets easier.

IN ADVANCE: Lamb can be prepared a day ahead, refrigerated, then brought to room temperature just before slicing and serving. Salsa verde can be made a day ahead and refrigerated until use.

CRISPY FRIED CRAB

Preparation time: 30 minutes +
    2 hours freezing + overnight marinating
Total cooking time: 15 minutes
Serves 4

1 x 1 kg (2 lb) live mud crab
1 egg, lightly beaten
1 red chilli, finely sliced
½ teaspoon crushed garlic
½ teaspoon salt
¼ teaspoon ground white pepper
oil, for deep-frying

Seasoning Mix
4 tablespoons plain flour
4 tablespoons rice flour
3 teaspoons caster sugar
1 teaspoon ground white pepper

1 Place the crab in the freezer for 2 hours or until it is absolutely immobile and dead (this is the most humane way to kill crab or lobster).
2 Scrub the crab clean of any mossy bits. Pull back the apron from the underbelly and snap off. Twist off the legs and claws. Pull the body apart and remove the feathery gills and internal organs. Using a cleaver, chop the body into 4 pieces. Crack the claws with a good hit with the back of the cleaver.
3 Combine the egg with the chilli, garlic, salt and pepper in a large bowl. Put the crab pieces in the mixture; cover and refrigerate overnight.
4 To make Seasoning Mix: Sift all the seasoning ingredients together on a large plate. Dip all the crab segments in the seasoning and dust off excess.
5 Heat the oil in a wok and deep-fry the claws for 7 to 8 minutes, the body portions for 3 to 4 minutes and the legs for 2 minutes. Drain on paper towels and serve.

NOTE: Eat the crab with your fingers. This dish should be served on its own, without rice.

TIMBALLO OF LEEKS, ZUCCHINI AND BASIL

Preparation time: 15 minutes
Total cooking time: 1 hour
Serves 4–6

pinch of saffron threads
½ cup (125 ml/4 fl oz) dry white wine
3 cups (750 ml/24 fl oz) chicken stock
50 g (1¾ oz) butter
1 onion, finely chopped
2 garlic cloves, crushed
1⅔ cups (360 g/12 oz) risotto rice
leaves from 2 thyme sprigs
½ cup (50 g/1¾ oz) freshly grated
    Parmesan cheese
2 tablespoons olive oil
2 leeks (white part only), thinly sliced
400 g (13 oz) thin zucchini (courgettes),
    thinly sliced on the diagonal
¼ teaspoon freshly grated nutmeg
10 basil leaves, shredded
75 g (2½ oz) thinly sliced prosciutto, cut
    into strips
⅓ cup (80 g/2¾ oz) sour cream

1 Soak the saffron in the wine. Pour the stock and ½ cup (125 ml/4 fl oz) water into a saucepan and bring to the boil. Reduce the heat, cover with a lid and keep at a low simmer.
2 Melt half the butter in a large saucepan wider than it is high. Add the onion and garlic and cook over low heat for about 5 minutes, or until softened but not browned. Add the rice and stir until well coated. Stir in the thyme and season well. Stir in the saffron-infused wine, then increase the heat and cook, stirring constantly, until it is absorbed. Stir ½ cup (125 ml/4 fl oz) of the stock into the rice, then reduce the heat and cook until it is absorbed. Continue adding more liquid, ½ cup (125 ml/4 fl oz) at a time until all the liquid is absorbed and the rice is tender and creamy. This will take around 25–30 minutes. Remove from the heat and stir in the remaining butter and the Parmesan.

3 Heat the oil in a frying pan and cook the leeks without browning over low heat for 5 minutes. Add the zucchini slices and cook for about 5 minutes, or until softened. Add the nutmeg and season well with salt and freshly ground black pepper. Stir in the basil, prosciutto and sour cream. Cook, stirring, for 2–3 minutes, or until the sauce thickens.
4 Preheat the oven to moderate 180°C (350°F/Gas 4) and grease a 1.5 litre (48 fl oz) pudding basin or rounded ovenproof bowl. Cut out a piece of greaseproof paper the size of the basin's base and line the base. Cover with half the rice mixture, pressing it down firmly. Spoon in two-thirds of the zucchini mixture, keeping the remaining one-third warm in the pan. Press in the last of the rice mixture. Cover with foil and transfer to the oven.
5 Bake for 20 minutes. Remove from the oven and rest for 5 minutes. Carefully unmould onto a serving plate. Serve the reserved zucchini on the side and serve at once.

NOTE: The prosciutto can be eliminated and the stock changed to vegetable if you'd prefer a vegetarian version.

NACHOS WITH GUACAMOLE

Preparation time: 20 minutes
Total cooking time: 3–5 minutes
Serves 4

440 g (14 oz) canned red kidney beans,
    rinsed and drained
4 tablespoons ready-made tomato salsa
250 g (8 oz) corn chips
2 cups (250 g/8 oz) grated Cheddar
    cheese
1½ cups (375 g/12 oz) ready-made tomato
    salsa, extra
4 tablespoons sour cream

Guacamole
1 large avocado
1 spring onion, finely chopped
1 small tomato, finely chopped
1 tablespoon lemon juice
freshly ground black pepper

1 Preheat oven to moderate 180°C (350°F/Gas 4). Combine kidney beans and salsa; divide mixture between four ovenproof serving plates. Cover with corn chips and grated cheese. Place in the oven for 3–5 minutes, until cheese has melted.
2 To assemble, spoon the extra salsa onto melted cheese; top with guacamole and sour cream.
3 To make Guacamole: Cut the avocado in half, discard the skin and stone. Mash the flesh lightly with a fork and combine with spring onion, tomato, lemon juice and pepper.

HERBED FISH TARTLETS

Preparation time: 40 minutes +
   15 minutes chilling
Total cooking time: 45 minutes
Makes 8

1¼ cups (155 g/5 oz) plain flour
90 g (3 oz) butter, chopped
1 tablespoon chopped fresh thyme
1 tablespoon chopped fresh dill
2 tablespoons chopped fresh parsley
90 g (3 oz) Cheddar, finely grated
3–4 tablespoons iced water

Filling
400 g (13 oz) skinless white fish fillets
   (eg. blue-eye, warehou, cod, jewfish)
2 spring onions, finely chopped
2 tablespoons chopped fresh parsley
60 g (2 oz) Cheddar, finely grated
2 eggs
½ cup (125 ml/4 fl oz) cream

1 Lightly grease eight 10 cm (4 inch) round fluted flan tins. Sift the flour into a large bowl. Rub the butter into the flour with your fingertips until it resembles fine breadcrumbs. Stir in the herbs and cheese. Make a well in the centre. Add almost all the water and mix with a flat-bladed knife, using a cutting action, until the mixture comes together in beads. Gather together and form into a ball, adding more water if necessary. Wrap in plastic and refrigerate for 15 minutes.

2 Preheat the oven to hot 210°C (415°F/Gas 6–7). Divide the pastry into 8 portions. Roll each on a lightly floured surface, large enough to fit the tins. Ease into the tins, pressing into the sides. Trim the edges with a sharp knife or rolling pin. Place the tins on a baking tray. Cover each piece of pastry with a sheet of crumpled baking paper. Spread a single layer of dried beads or uncooked rice evenly over the base. Bake for 10 minutes. Remove the paper and beans and bake for 10 minutes, or until lightly browned. Cool.

3 Place the fish in a frying pan and add water to cover. Bring to the boil, reduce the heat and simmer gently for 3 minutes. Remove from the pan with a slotted spoon and drain on crumpled paper towel. Allow to cool, then flake with a fork. Divide among the cases and sprinkle with the combined spring onion, parsley and cheese. In a jug, whisk together the eggs and cream, then pour over the fish. Bake for 25 minutes, or until set and golden brown. Serve immediately.

NOTE: Smoked fish can be used. You can make the recipe in a 23 cm (9 inch) flan tin. Cooking time may be longer but check after 25 minutes.

GRILLED RICE WITH DIPPING SAUCE

Preparation time: 30 minutes
Total cooking time: 15 minutes
Makes 6

Dipping sauce
½ cup (125 ml/4 fl oz) rice vinegar
½ cup (110 g/3½ oz) sugar
2 garlic cloves, crushed
2 bird's eye chillies, finely chopped

2 eggs
1 tablespoon fish sauce
½ teaspoon sugar
3 cups (650 g/1 lb 5 oz) cooked glutinous
   short-grain rice, well drained

1 Preheat the grill (broiler) to its highest setting. To make the dipping sauce, combine all the ingredients in a small bowl and stir until the sugar is dissolved.
2 Beat the eggs with the fish sauce, sugar and a pinch of black pepper.
3 Divide the cooked rice into six portions and form each one into three small balls. Press each ball to flatten. Thread three flat rounds onto each skewer.
4 Line a grill tray with foil and brush it lightly with oil. Dip each rice skewer into the egg mixture, shake off any excess and put it on the grill tray. Grill (broil) the rice until it is browned on one side, then turn it over and cook the other side. Serve with the dipping sauce.

EGGPLANT (AUBERGINE) SLICES IN BLACK BEAN SAUCE

Preparation time: 20 minutes
Total cooking time: 35 minutes
Serves 4

500 g (1 lb) medium eggplant (aubergine)
⅓ cup (80 ml/2¾ fl oz) oil
4 cloves garlic, finely chopped
4 cm (1½ inch) piece fresh ginger, grated
2 medium onions, finely chopped
⅓ cup (80 ml/2¾ fl oz) chicken stock
2 teaspoons canned black beans, rinsed well, roughly chopped
2 tablespoons oyster sauce
1 tablespoon soy sauce
2 teaspoons fish sauce
4 spring onions, sliced into long diagonal strips

1 Slice the eggplant into long slices and lightly brush each side with oil.
2 Heat a frying pan over moderately low heat; add the eggplant, 4 to 5 slices at a time, and cook until golden on both sides; remove from the pan. Do not hurry this process as cooking the eggplant slowly allows the natural sugars to caramelise and produces a wonderful flavour. If the eggplant begins to burn, reduce the heat and sprinkle it with a little water.
3 Increase the heat to moderately high and add any remaining oil, the garlic, ginger, onion and about 1 tablespoon of the chicken stock; cover and cook for 3 minutes. Add the remaining stock, black beans, oyster sauce, soy sauce and fish sauce. Bring to the boil and cook for 2 minutes. Return the eggplant to the pan and simmer for 2 minutes or until it is heated through. Scatter over the spring onion and serve.

NOTE: Always rinse black beans very well before using, as they are extremely salty. They will keep indefinitely if refrigerated after opening.

SUSHI HAND-ROLLS

Preparation time: 25 minutes + 1 hour draining + cooling
Total cooking time: 15 minutes
Serves 6

1 cup (220 g/7 oz) Japanese short-grain rice
2 tablespoons rice vinegar
generous pinch of caster (superfine) sugar
175 g (6 oz) sashimi grade fish, such as tuna or salmon
6 sheets of roasted nori, 20 x 18 cm (8 x 7 inches)
1 small avocado
1 tablespoon lemon juice
wasabi paste
60 g (2 oz) pickled daikon
85 g (3 oz) cucumber, cut into thin strips
Shoyu (Japanese soy sauce), to serve
pickled ginger, to serve

1 Wash the rice under cold running water until the water runs clear, then drain thoroughly. Drain for an hour. Put the rice into a saucepan and cover with 220 ml (7 fl oz) cold water. Cover the pan and bring the water to the boil, then reduce the heat and simmer for 10 minutes. When the rice is cooked, remove it from the heat and let it stand, covered, for 10 minutes.
2 To make the sushi dressing, mix together 1 tablespoon of the vinegar, the sugar and ¼ teaspoon salt.

3 Spread the rice over the base of a non-metallic dish or bowl, pour the sushi dressing over the top and use a rice paddle or spatula to mix the dressing through the rice, separating the grains as you do so. Fan the rice until it cools to room temperature. Cover with a damp tea towel and set it aside, but do not refrigerate.
4 Meanwhile, using a sharp knife, cut the fish into 16 paper-thin pieces, measuring 2 x 5 cm (¾ x 2 inches). Cut each sheet of nori in half. Thinly slice the avocado and sprinkle with a little lemon juice. Mix the remaining vinegar with ¼ cup (60 ml/2 fl oz) water in a small bowl. Use the vinegar water to stop the rice sticking to your fingers as you form the sushi. Taking 1 tablespoon of rice at a time, carefully mould the rice into oval shapes—you should end up with 12 ovals.
5 Holding a piece of nori seaweed in the palm of your hand, smear a little wasabi over it, put an oval of rice on top, then fill it with a piece of fish, avocado, daikon and cucumber. Wrap the nori around the ingredients in a cone shape, using a couple of grains of cooked rice to secure the rolls. Alternatively, put the ingredients on the table for guests to help themselves. Serve with Shoyu, extra wasabi and pickled ginger.

STUFFED ZUCCHINI/COURGETTES WITH YOGHURT SAUCE

Preparation time: 20 minutes
Total cooking time: 1 hour 10 minutes
Serves 4

4 zucchini (courgettes)
1½ cups (375 ml/12 fl oz) chicken stock

Filling
1 tablespoon olive oil
1 onion, finely chopped
1½ tablespoons pine nuts
125 g (4 oz) lamb mince
¼ cup (55 g/2 oz) short-grain rice
1 ripe tomato, seeded and chopped
2 tablespoons chopped fresh flat-leaf parsley
½ teaspoon ground allspice
½ teaspoon ground cinnamon

Yoghurt sauce
250 g (8 oz) thick natural yoghurt
1 teaspoon cornflour
1 clove garlic, crushed
1 teaspoon dried mint

1 Cut each zucchini in half lengthways. Scoop out the flesh from each piece, leaving a 2 mm (⅛ inch) border on each shell. This can be done with an apple corer, but be careful not to pierce the skins of the zucchini. Soak the zucchini in salted water for 10 minutes, then drain and pat dry.
2 For the filling, heat the oil in a frying pan, add the onion and cook over medium heat for 5 minutes, or until soft. Add the pine nuts and cook for 3–4 minutes, until golden. Cool slightly, then transfer to a large bowl. Add the remaining filling ingredients and combine well.

3 Spoon filling into each zucchini half and carefully place in a wide, heavy-based saucepan or casserole. Cover with the chicken stock then invert a dinner plate over the top. Gently simmer over low heat for 1 hour.
4 About 15 minutes before the zucchini is ready, make the sauce by warming the yoghurt in a saucepan over medium heat. Stir the cornflour into 1 tablespoon water in a small bowl until smooth, then add to the yoghurt and stir well. Bring to the boil and add the crushed garlic and mint. Season well, then reduce the heat and simmer for 8–10 minutes, stirring regularly.
5 Remove the zucchini from the casserole and serve the yoghurt sauce poured over the top. Serve hot with steamed rice.

SALMON SATAY WITH GINGER LIME MAYONNAISE

Preparation time: 30 minutes + chilling
Total cooking time: 4 minutes
Makes 24 skewers

500 g (1 lb) Atlantic salmon (or ocean trout) fillet
24 small wooden skewers
light olive oil

Ginger lime mayonnaise
1 cup (250 g/8 oz) whole egg mayonnaise
¼ cup (60 g/2 oz) natural yoghurt
1 teaspoon finely grated fresh ginger
1 teaspoon finely grated lime rind
2 teaspoons lime juice

1 Remove the skin from the salmon. Use kitchen tweezers to remove any bones from the fish, then wrap the fish in plastic wrap and freeze for 1 hour. Soak small wooden satay sticks in cold water for 30 minutes (this will prevent them burning during cooking).
2 Cut the salmon fillets into 5 cm (2 inch) strips. Thread the strips loosely onto the satay sticks and place them on an oiled tray. Brush all over with oil and season, to taste, with salt and freshly ground pepper. Grill in two batches for 2 minutes, taking care not to overcook. Serve with the ginger lime mayonnaise.
3 To make ginger lime mayonnaise, place the mayonnaise in a small bowl and stir until smooth. Add the yoghurt, ginger and lime rind and juice. Add salt and pepper, to taste, and stir until blended thoroughly. Chill for at least 1 hour.

IN ADVANCE: The skewers can be assembled up to 1 hour in advance and refrigerated. Cook just prior to serving. Make the mayonnaise up to 2 days ahead and store, covered, in the refrigerator. The prepared skewers can be frozen in a single layer for up to 2 months.

SPINACH RISOTTO CAKE

Preparation time: 30 minutes
Total cooking time: 35 minutes
Serves 6

250 g (8 oz) baby English spinach leaves
3 cups (750 ml/24 fl oz) chicken stock
100 g (3½ oz) butter
1 onion, finely chopped
1 garlic clove, finely chopped
1 cup (220 g/7 oz) arborio rice
155 ml (5 fl oz) dry white vermouth or
    white wine
¼ teaspoon freshly grated nutmeg
¼ cup (25 g/¾ oz) freshly grated
    Parmesan cheese, plus extra to serve

1 Cook the spinach in a small amount of salted water until just wilted. Refresh in cold water and squeeze dry. Finely chop and set aside.
2 Pour the stock into a saucepan and bring to the boil. Reduce the heat, cover with a lid and keep at a low simmer.
3 Melt 75 g (2½ oz) of the butter in a deep heavy-based frying pan and gently cook the onion and garlic until softened but not browned. Stir in the rice until well coated. Season.
4 Add the vermouth to the rice and cook, stirring, until all the liquid has been absorbed. Add ½ cup (125 ml/4 fl oz) of the hot stock and stir constantly over medium heat until all the liquid is absorbed. Continue adding more stock, ½ cup (125 ml/4 fl oz) at a time until a quarter of the stock is left, then mix in the chopped spinach. Continue to add the last of the stock. When making risotto cake, it is not so essential to keep the rice al dente—if it is a little more glutinous, it will stick together better. Make sure all the liquid is absorbed or the cake may break up when you unmould it.
5 Remove the pan from the heat and stir in the nutmeg, Parmesan cheese and the rest of the butter.
6 Smear a little butter into a mould such as a 1.25 litre (40 fl oz) cake tin. Spoon the risotto into the mould, pressing it down firmly. Leave to rest for 5 minutes, then unmould and put on a warm serving plate with some Parmesan sprinkled over the top.

SWEET BRAISED PUMPKIN

Preparation time: 20 minutes
Total cooking time: 15 minutes
Serves 4

750 g (1½ lb) pumpkin
1½ tablespoons oil
3 cloves garlic, finely chopped
4 cm (1½ inch) piece fresh ginger, grated
6 red Asian shallots, chopped
1 tablespoon soft brown sugar
½ cup (125 ml/4 fl oz) chicken stock
2 tablespoons fish sauce
1 tablespoon lime juice

1 Peel the pumpkin and cut it into large chunks.
2 Heat the oil in a heavy-based frying pan; add the garlic, ginger and shallots and cook over medium heat for 3 minutes, stirring regularly.
3 Add the pumpkin and sprinkle with the sugar. Cook for 7 to 8 minutes, turning the pieces regularly, until the pumpkin is golden and just tender.
4 Add the chicken stock and fish sauce, bring to the boil, then reduce the heat and simmer until all the liquid has evaporated, turning the pumpkin over regularly. Sprinkle with the lime juice, season to taste with salt and pepper, and serve. Delicious as an accompaniment to meat dishes such as curries, or on its own with plenty of steamed rice.

NOTE: The sweeter pumpkins, such as butternut and Japanese pumpkin, will produce a dish with a delicious flavour and soft texture.

SIMPLE PASTA, SPEEDY STIR-FRIES

PENNE WITH OLIVE AND PISTACHIO PESTO

Ready to eat in 20 minutes
Serves 4

500 g (1 lb) penne
125 g (4 oz) unsalted, shelled pistachio nuts
4 cloves garlic
1 tablespoon green peppercorns
2 tablespoons lemon juice
150 g (5 oz) pitted black olives
1½ cups (150 g/5 oz) freshly grated Parmesan plus extra, shaved, for serving
½ cup (125 ml/4 fl oz) light olive oil

1 Cook the penne in a large pan of rapidly boiling salted water until al dente. Drain and return to the pan.
2 While the penne is cooking, combine the pistachio nuts, garlic, peppercorns, lemon juice, black olives and Parmesan in a food processor for 30 seconds, or until roughly chopped.
3 While the motor is running, gradually pour in the olive oil in a thin stream. Blend until the mixture is smooth. Toss the pesto through the hot pasta and serve topped with extra Parmesan.

LINGUINE WITH ANCHOVIES, OLIVES AND CAPERS

Ready to eat in 30 minutes
Serves 4

500 g (1 lb) linguine
2 tablespoons olive oil
2 cloves garlic, crushed
2 very ripe tomatoes, peeled and chopped
3 tablespoons capers
½ cup (75 g/2½ oz) pitted black olives, finely chopped
¼ cup (55 g/2 oz) pitted green olives, finely chopped
¼ cup (60 ml/2 fl oz) dry white wine
3 tablespoons chopped fresh parsley or basil
90 g (3 oz) can anchovies, drained and chopped

1 Cook the linguine in a large pan of rapidly boiling salted water until al dente. Drain and return to the pan.
2 While the pasta is cooking, heat the oil in a large frying pan. Add the garlic and stir over low heat for 1 minute. Add the tomato, capers and olives and cook for 2 minutes.
3 Stir in the wine, parsley or basil, and freshly ground black pepper, to taste. Bring to the boil, reduce the heat and simmer for about 5 minutes. Remove from the heat. Add the anchovies and stir gently to combine.
4 Add to the warm pasta in the pan and toss well to distribute the sauce evenly. Note: For variation or on special occasions, you may like to serve this dish with the following topping. Heat a little olive oil in a small pan and add some fresh breadcrumbs and a crushed clove of garlic. Toss over the heat until crisp and golden and sprinkle over the top with freshly grated Parmesan.

PENNE WITH PROSCIUTTO

Preparation time: 15 minutes
Total cooking time: 25 minutes
Serves 4

2 teaspoons olive oil
6 thin slices prosciutto, chopped
1 onion, finely chopped
1 tablespoon chopped fresh rosemary
825 g (1 lb 11 oz) can Italian tomatoes
500 g (1 lb) penne or macaroni
grated Parmesan, for serving

1 Heat the oil in a heavy-based frying pan. Add the prosciutto and onion and cook, stirring occasionally, over low heat for 5 minutes, or until golden.
2 Add the rosemary and tomato and season to taste. Simmer for 10 minutes.
3 Meanwhile, cook the pasta in a large pan of rapidly boiling water until al dente. Drain. Divide the pasta among serving bowls and top with the sauce. Sprinkle with a little grated Parmesan to serve.

NOTE: Rosemary is a herb commonly used in Mediterranean cooking and lends a distinctive flavour to the dish. Fresh basil or parsley could be used but dried rosemary is not suitable.

BRANDIED CREAM AND SALMON FUSILLI

Ready to eat in 30 minutes
Serves 2

375 g (12 oz) fusilli
45 g (11/2 oz) butter
1 leek, finely sliced
1 large clove garlic, crushed
1/4 cup (60 ml/2 fl oz) brandy
1/2 teaspoon sambal oelek
2 tablespoons finely chopped fresh dill
1 tablespoon tomato paste (tomato purée, double concentrate)
1 cup (250 ml/8 fl oz) cream
250 g (8 oz) smoked salmon, thinly sliced
red caviar or lumpfish roe, to garnish, optional

1 Cook the fusilli in a large pan of rapidly boiling salted water until al dente. Drain.
2 Heat the butter in a large pan and cook the leek over medium heat for a few minutes, until soft. Add the garlic and cook for another minute. Add the brandy and cook for another minute. Stir in the sambal oelek, dill, tomato paste and cream. Simmer gently for 5 minutes, until the sauce reduces and thickens slightly.
3 Add the pasta and smoked salmon to the sauce. Toss to combine and season with freshly ground black pepper, to taste. Divide the mixture between two serving bowls. Garnish with a spoonful of caviar, if you like, and a sprig of dill. Serve immediately.

NOTE: Wash the leek thoroughly, as dirt and grit can sometimes be difficult to remove from the inner leaves.

PENNE WITH ROCKET

Ready to eat in 20 minutes
Serves 4

500 g (1 lb) penne
100 g (31/2 oz) butter
200 g (61/2 oz) rocket, roughly chopped
3 tomatoes, finely chopped
1/2 cup (45 g/11/2 oz) grated pecorino cheese
freshly grated Parmesan, for serving

1 Cook the penne in a large pan of rapidly boiling salted water until al dente. Drain and return to the pan. Place the pan over low heat. Add the butter, tossing it through until it melts and coats the pasta.
2 Add the rocket leaves to the pasta along with the tomato. Toss through to wilt the rocket. Stir in the pecorino cheese and season with salt and pepper, to taste. Serve sprinkled with freshly grated Parmesan.

SPAGHETTI WITH GARLIC AND CHILLI

Ready to eat in 20 minutes
Serves 4

500 g (1 lb) spaghetti
1/2 cup (125 ml/4 fl oz) extra virgin olive oil
3 cloves garlic, crushed
1 red chilli, finely chopped

1 Cook the spaghetti in a large pan of rapidly boiling salted water until al dente. Drain and return to the pan.
2 Just before the spaghetti is cooked, heat the olive oil in a small pan until warm. Add the garlic and red chilli and stir over low heat for 2 minutes. Add the flavoured oil to the pasta and toss to combine.

SPAGHETTI WITH CREAMY LEMON SAUCE

Ready to eat in 20 minutes
Serves 4

500 g (1 lb) spaghetti
1 cup (250 ml/8 fl oz) cream
¾ cup (185 ml/6 fl oz) chicken stock
1 tablespoon finely grated lemon rind
   plus some shredded, to garnish
2 tablespoons finely chopped fresh
   parsley
2 tablespoons chopped fresh chives

1 Cook the spaghetti in a large pan of rapidly boiling salted water until al dente. Drain and return to the pan.
2 While the spaghetti is cooking, combine the cream, chicken stock and lemon rind in a pan over medium heat. Bring to the boil, stirring occasionally. Reduce the heat and simmer gently for 10 minutes, or until the sauce is reduced and thickened slightly.
3 Add the sauce and herbs to the spaghetti and toss to combine. Serve immediately, garnished with finely shredded lemon rind.

ARTICHOKE, EGG AND SORREL PASTA

Ready to eat in 25 minutes
Serves 4

500 g (1 lb) conchiglie (shell pasta)
2 tablespoons oil
3 cloves garlic, crushed
315 g (10 oz) marinated artichoke hearts,
   halved
3 tablespoons chopped fresh parsley
160 g (51/2 oz) sorrel leaves, roughly
   chopped
4 hard-boiled eggs, chopped
fresh Parmesan shavings, for serving

1 Cook the conchiglie in a large pan of rapidly boiling salted water until al dente. Drain and keep warm.
2 While the pasta is cooking, heat the oil in a frying pan, add the garlic and cook over medium heat until golden. Add the artichoke hearts and chopped parsley and cook over low heat for 5 minutes, or until the artichoke hearts are heated through.
3 Transfer the pasta to a large bowl. Add the sorrel leaves, eggs and artichoke hearts and toss to combine. Serve immediately, topped with shavings of fresh Parmesan and cracked black pepper, to taste.

FARFALLE WITH PEAS, PROSCIUTTO AND MUSHROOMS

Ready to eat in 20 minutes
Serves 4

375 g (12 oz) farfalle
60 g (2 oz) butter
1 onion, chopped
200 g (6½ oz) mushrooms, thinly sliced
250 g (8 oz) frozen peas
3 slices of prosciutto, sliced
1 cup (250 ml/8 fl oz) cream
1 egg yolk
fresh Parmesan, optional, for serving

1 Cook the farfalle in a large pan of rapidly boiling salted water until al dente. Drain and return to the pan.
2 While the pasta is cooking, heat the butter in a pan, add the onion and mushrooms and stir over medium heat for 5 minutes or until tender.
3 Add the peas and prosciutto to the pan. Combine the cream and the yolk in a small jug and pour into the pan. Cover and simmer for 5 minutes or until heated through.
4 Mix the sauce through the pasta or serve the sauce over the top of the pasta. Can be topped with shaved or grated fresh Parmesan.

CREAM OF ONION PASTA

Ready to eat in 30 minutes
Serves 4

500 g (1 lb) fettucine or linguine
50 g (1¾ oz) butter
6 onions, thinly sliced
½ cup (125 ml/4 fl oz) beef stock
½ cup (125 ml/4 fl oz) cream
shavings of Parmesan cheese, for serving
spring onion, to garnish, optional

1 Cook the fettucine in a large pan of rapidly boiling salted water until al dente. Drain and return to the pan.
2 While the pasta is cooking, melt the butter, add the onion and cook over medium heat for 10 minutes, until soft. Stir in the stock and cream and simmer for 10 minutes. Season with salt and pepper, to taste.
3 Stir the sauce through the fettucine and serve with shavings of Parmesan. Garnish with chopped spring onion if you wish.

FUSILLI WITH VEGETABLES

Ready to eat in 30 minutes
Serves 4–6

500 g (1 lb) fusilli
3 tablespoons olive oil
6 yellow squash, sliced
3 zucchini (courgettes), sliced
2 cloves garlic, crushed
3 spring onions, chopped
1 red pepper (capsicum), cut into strips
⅓ cup (65 g/2¼ oz) corn kernels
4 tomatoes, chopped
2 tablespoons chopped fresh parsley

1 Cook the fusilli in a large pan of rapidly boiling salted water until al dente. Drain and return to the pan.
2 While the fusilli is cooking, heat 2 tablespoons of the oil in a wok or frying pan, add the squash and zucchini and stir-fry for 3 minutes, or until the vegetables are just tender. Add the garlic, spring onion, red pepper and corn kernels to the wok and stir-fry for another 2–3 minutes. Add the tomato and stir until combined.
3 Add the remaining olive oil and fresh parsley to the pasta and toss well. Serve the pasta topped with the vegetable mixture.

NOTE: This is a good recipe to use up any vegetables you have on hand. Mushrooms, broccoli, snow peas (mangetout) and asparagus are all suitable, and other fresh herbs such as chives or coriander can be added.

SPAGHETTI WITH HERBS

Ready to eat in 20 minutes
Serves 4

500 g (1 lb) spaghetti
50 g (13/4 oz) butter
½ cup (30 g/1 oz) shredded fresh basil
⅓ cup (10 g/¼ oz) chopped fresh oregano
⅓ cup (20 g/¾ oz) chopped fresh chives

1 Cook the spaghetti in a large pan of rapidly boiling salted water until al dente. Drain and return to the pan.
2 Add the butter to the pan, tossing it through until it melts and coats the strands of spaghetti. Add the basil, oregano and chives to the pan and toss the herbs through the buttery pasta until well distributed. Season, to taste, and serve immediately.

MAKING GNOCCHI

TODAY, OUR FAVOURITE
GNOCCHI ARE POTATO-BASED
BUT VARIATIONS CAN BE MADE
USING OTHER VEGETABLES
SUCH AS PUMPKIN OR PARSNIP,
OR TRADITIONAL SEMOLINA OR
CHEESE.

Gnocchi are little dumplings. No matter
what they are based on, the consistency of
the dough should be soft and light. When
cooking vegetables to be used for
gnocchi, ensure that the cooking process
doesn't result in soggy vegetables,
otherwise you will have to add more flour,
thus making the dough too heavy. Work
quickly so the dough doesn't become too
sticky or soft.

Gnocchi are best eaten as soon after
cooking as possible and you should have
any accompanying sauce ready before you
cook the dumplings.

TRADITIONAL POTATO GNOCCHI

When making potato gnocchi, it is
important to use floury potatoes,
preferably old boiling potatoes, because
they have a low moisture content.
Traditionally, the potatoes are prepared
by baking in their skins, thus keeping the
potato dry. However, as this is quite time-
consuming, most people prefer to steam
or boil them. If you do this, make sure you
don't overcook the potatoes or they will
break up and absorb too much moisture.
Also, drain them thoroughly.

Many recipes for potato gnocchi include eggs, to make the gnocchi easier to handle. However, eggs also require the addition of more flour to absorb the extra moisture, thus making the gnocchi a little tougher. Experiment to find which way you prefer to work. The traditional method follows. To make enough for 4–6 people, you will need 1 kg (2 lb) of floury old potatoes, unpeeled, and about 200 g (6½ oz) of plain flour.

1 Prick the unpeeled potatoes all over with a fork and bake in a moderately hot 200°C (400°F/Gas 6) oven for 1 hour, or until tender. Don't wrap in foil. When cool enough to handle but still hot, peel and mash in a bowl with a masher, or put through a ricer or food mill into a bowl.
2 Add three-quarters of the flour and gradually work it in with your hands. When a loose dough forms, transfer it to a lightly floured surface and knead gently. Work in the remaining flour as you knead, but only enough to give a soft, light dough that does not stick to your hands or the work surface, but is still damp to touch. Stop kneading at this stage. Lightly flour the work surface and dust the inside tines of a fork with flour. Take a portion of the dough, about one-fifth, and roll it with your hands on the floured surface to form a long, even rope the thickness of your ring finger. Cut it into 2 cm (¾ inch) pieces.

3 Put a piece on the tines of a fork and press down with your finger, flipping the gnocchi as you do so. It will be rounded into a concave shell shape, ridged on the outer surface. Form a good hollow in the centre, as this allows the gnocchi to cook evenly and hold the sauce more easily. Continue with the remaining dough.
4 Lower the gnocchi in batches, about 20 at a time, into a large pan of boiling salted water. The gnocchi are cooked when they all rise to the surface, after 2–3 minutes cooking. Remove each batch with a slotted spoon and keep them warm while cooking the remainder. Sauce, and serve. Potato gnocchi can be frozen, shaped but uncooked, for up to two months. They will need to be first frozen in a single layer, not touching, before being stored in airtight containers. When you are ready to use them, lower them gently, in batches, into boiling water straight from the freezer.

GNOCCHI ROMANA (SEMOLINA GNOCCHI WITH RICH CHEESE SAUCE)

Preparation time: 20 minutes +
    1 hour refrigeration
Total cooking time: 40 minutes
Serves 4

3 cups (750 ml/24 fl oz) milk
½ teaspoon ground nutmeg
⅔ cup (85 g/3 oz) semolina
1 egg, beaten
1½ cups (150 g/5 oz) freshly grated
    Parmesan
60 g (2 oz) butter, melted
½ cup (125 m/4 fl oz) cream
½ cup (75 g/2½ oz) freshly grated
    mozzarella cheese

1 Line a deep Swiss roll tin with baking paper. Combine the milk, half the nutmeg, and salt and freshly ground pepper, to taste, in a medium pan. Bring to the boil, reduce the heat and gradually stir in the semolina. Cook, stirring occasionally, for 5–10 minutes, or until the semolina is stiff.
2 Remove the pan from the heat, add the egg and 1 cup of the Parmesan. Stir to combine and then spread the mixture in the tin. Refrigerate for 1 hour, or until the mixture is firm.
3 Preheat the oven to moderate 180°C (350°F/Gas 4). Cut the semolina into rounds using a floured 4 cm (1½ inch) cutter and arrange in a greased shallow casserole dish.
4 Pour the melted butter over the top, followed by the cream. Combine the remaining grated Parmesan with the mozzarella cheese and sprinkle them on the rounds. Sprinkle with the remaining nutmeg. Bake for 20–25 minutes, or until the mixture is golden. You can serve garnished with a sprig of fresh herbs.
Note: Some claim that this traditional dish from Rome can be traced as far back as Imperial Roman times. A crisp garden salad is the ideal accompaniment for this lovely rich recipe.

PUMPKIN GNOCCHI WITH SAGE BUTTER

Preparation time: 45 minutes
Total cooking time: 1 hour 30 minutes
Serves 4

500 g (1 lb) pumpkin
1½ cups (185 g/6 oz) plain flour
1/2 cup (50 g/1¾ oz) freshly grated
    Parmesan
1 egg, beaten
100 g (3½ oz) butter
2 tablespoons chopped fresh sage

1 Preheat the oven to warm 160°C (315°F/Gas 2–3). Brush a baking tray with oil or melted butter. Cut the pumpkin into large pieces, leaving the skin on, and put on the tray. Bake for 1¼ hours, or until very tender. Cool slightly. Scrape the flesh from the skin, avoiding any tough or crispy parts. Transfer to a large bowl. Sift the flour into the bowl, add half the Parmesan, the egg and a little black pepper. After mixing thoroughly, turn onto a lightly floured surface and knead for 2 minutes, or until smooth.
2 Divide the dough in half. Using floured hands, roll each half into a sausage about 40 cm (16 inches) long. Cut into 16 equal pieces. Form each piece into an oval shape and press firmly with the floured prongs of a fork, to make an indentation.
3 Lower batches of gnocchi into a large pan of boiling salted water. Cook for about 2 minutes, or until the gnocchi rise to the surface. Drain with a slotted spoon and keep them warm.
4 To make the sage butter, melt the butter in a small pan, remove from the heat and stir in the chopped sage.
5 To serve, divide the gnocchi among four bowls, drizzle with sage butter and sprinkle with the remaining Parmesan.

POTATO GNOCCHI WITH TOMATO AND BASIL SAUCE

Preparation time: 1 hour
Total cooking time: 45–50 minutes
Serves 4–6

Tomato sauce
1 tablespoon oil
1 onion, chopped
1 celery stick, chopped
2 carrots, chopped
2 x 425 g (14 oz) cans crushed tomatoes
1 teaspoon sugar
½ cup (30 g/1 oz) fresh basil, chopped

Potato gnocchi
1 kg (2 lb) old potatoes
30 g (1 oz) butter
2 cups (250 g/8 oz) plain flour
2 eggs, beaten

freshly grated Parmesan, for serving

1 To make the tomato sauce, heat the oil in a large frying pan, add the onion, celery and carrot and cook for 5 minutes, stirring regularly. Add the tomato and sugar and season with salt and pepper, to taste. Bring to the boil, reduce the heat to very low and simmer for 20 minutes. Cool slightly and process, in batches, in a food processor until smooth. Add the basil; set aside.
2 To make the potato gnocchi, peel the potatoes, chop roughly and steam or boil until very tender. Drain thoroughly and mash until smooth. Using a wooden spoon, stir in the butter and flour, then beat in the eggs. Cool.
3 Turn onto a floured surface and divide into two. Roll each into a long sausage shape. Cut into short pieces and press each piece with the back of a fork.
4 Cook the gnocchi, in batches, in a large pan of boiling salted water for about 2 minutes, or until the gnocchi rise to the surface. Using a slotted spoon, drain the gnocchi, and transfer to serving bowls. Serve with the tomato sauce and freshly grated Parmesan. Garnish with herbs.

GNOCCHI WITH FONTINA SAUCE

Preparation time: 10 minutes
Total cooking time: 15 minutes
Serves 4

200 g (6½ oz) fontina cheese, finely
    chopped
½ cup (125 ml/4 fl oz) cream
80 g (2¾ oz) butter
2 tablespoons freshly grated Parmesan
400 g (13 oz) fresh potato gnocchi

1 Combine the fontina cheese, cream,
butter and Parmesan in a bowl over a pan
of simmering water. Heat, stirring
occasionally, for 6–8 minutes, or until the
cheese has melted and the sauce is
smooth and hot.
2 When the sauce is halfway through
cooking, lower the gnocchi, in batches,
into a large pan of boiling salted water
and cook for about 2 minutes, or until the
gnocchi rise to the surface.
3 Drain the gnocchi, using a slotted
spoon, and serve with sauce over the top.
Can be garnished with fresh oregano
leaves or other fresh herbs.

SPINACH AND RICOTTA GNOCCHI

Preparation time: 45 minutes +
    1 hour refrigeration
Total cooking time: 30 minutes
Serves 4–6

4 slices white bread
½ cup (125 ml/4 fl oz) milk
500 g (1 lb) frozen spinach, thawed
250 g (8 oz) ricotta cheese
2 eggs
½ cup (50 g/1¾ oz) freshly grated
    Parmesan, plus some shaved
    Parmesan, for serving
¼ cup (30 g/1 oz) plain flour

1 Remove the crust from the bread and
soak the bread in the milk, in a shallow
dish, for 10 minutes. Squeeze out all the
excess liquid. Then squeeze excess liquid
from the spinach.
2 Combine the bread in a bowl with the
spinach, ricotta cheese, eggs, Parmesan
and salt and pepper. Use a fork to mix
thoroughly. Cover and refrigerate for
1 hour.
3 Lightly dust your hands in flour. Roll
heaped teaspoonsful of the mixture into
dumplings. Lower batches of the gnocchi
into a large pan of boiling salted water.
Cook for about 2 minutes, or until the
gnocchi rise to the surface. Transfer to
serving plates. Drizzle with foaming
butter, if you wish, and serve with shaved
Parmesan.

POTATO GNOCCHI WITH TOMATO SAUCE

Preparation time: 35 minutes
Total cooking time: 45–50 minutes
Serves 4

500 g (1 lb) potatoes, peeled and chopped
2 cups (250 g/8 oz) plain flour, sifted
¼ cup (25 g/¾ oz) freshly grated
    Parmesan cheese
30 g (1 oz) butter or margarine, melted
salt and freshly ground black pepper
freshly grated Parmesan cheese, extra,
    for serving

Tomato Sauce
1 kg (2 lb) tomatoes, peeled and chopped
2 cloves garlic, crushed
¼ cupcup (125 ml/4 fl oz) red wine
3 tablespoons finely chopped fresh basil
salt and freshly ground black pepper

1 Cook the potatoes in a pan of boiling
water for 15–20 minutes, or until tender.
Drain thoroughly and mash until smooth.
Transfer to a bowl and allow to cool
slightly. Add the flour, Parmesan cheese,
butter, salt and pepper. Using a flat-
bladed knife, mix together in a cutting
motion, to form a firm dough. Knead
briefly on a lightly floured surface until
smooth. Do not over-handle the dough, or
the finished gnocchi will be tough.
2 Roll heaped teaspoonsful of dough into
oval shapes. Indent one side using the
back of a fork. Cook the gnocchi in
batches in a large pan of rapidly boiling
water for 3–5 minutes each batch. The
gnocchi will float on the surface when
cooked. Drain well and keep warm while
cooking the remaining gnocchi. Serve in
warmed bowls, with the Tomato Sauce.
Sprinkle with the extra grated Parmesan.
3 To make Tomato Sauce: In a pan,
combine the tomatoes, garlic, wine, basil,
salt and pepper. Bring to the boil. Reduce
the heat and simmer gently for 15–20
minutes, stirring occasionally, until the
sauce reduces and thickens slightly.

PENNE WITH CREAMY PESTO AND TOMATO

Preparation time: 5 minutes
Total cooking time: 20 minutes
Serves 4

375 g (12 oz) penne
2 teaspoons oil
200 g (61/2 oz) mushrooms, sliced
¾ cup (185 g/6 oz) sour cream
½ cup (125 g/4 oz) ready-made pesto
¼ cup (40 g/1⅓ oz) chopped sun-dried
  tomatoes
freshly ground black pepper

1 Add the pasta to a large pan of rapidly boiling water and cook until just tender; drain.
2 Return the pan to the heat, add the oil and heat. Add the mushrooms to the pan and cook for 4 minutes or until soft and golden. Stir in the sour cream, pesto, tomatoes and pepper. Mix well and cook for 2 minutes or until the sauce is heated through.
3 Return the pasta to the pan and mix well. Cook, stirring, for 1 minute or until heated through. Garnish with extra sliced tomatoes and shredded basil, if you like.

NOTE: Pesto can be bought in jars from supermarkets and delicatessens.

CALABRIAN SPAGHETTI

Ready to eat in 20 minutes
Serves 4

500 g (l lb) spaghetti
⅓ cup (80 ml/2¾ fl oz) olive oil
3 cloves garlic, crushed
50 g (1¾ oz) anchovy fillets, finely
  chopped
1 teaspoon finely chopped fresh red
  chillies
3 tablespoons chopped fresh parsley

1 Cook the spaghetti in a large pan of rapidly boiling salted water until al dente. Drain and return to the pan.
2 While the spaghetti is cooking, heat the olive oil in a small pan. Add the garlic, anchovy fillets and red chillies and cook over low heat for 5 minutes. Be careful not to burn the garlic or brown it too much as it will become bitter. Add the parsley to the garlic mixture and cook for a few more minutes. Season with salt and freshly ground black pepper, to taste.
3 Add the sauce to the pasta and toss through until well combined. Serve garnished with extra anchovies and sliced red chillies as well as a sprig of fresh herbs, if desired.

RICOTTA AND BASIL WITH TAGLIATELLE

Ready to eat in 25 minutes
Serves 4

500 g (1 lb) tagliatelle
1 cup (20 g/¾ oz) fresh flat-leaf parsley
1 cup (50 g/1¾ oz) fresh basil leaves
1 teaspoon olive oil
⅓ cup (50 g/1¾ oz) chopped sun-dried
  pepper (capsicum)
1 cup (250 g/8 oz) sour cream
250 g (8 oz) fresh ricotta cheese
¼ cup (25 g/¾ oz) freshly grated
  Parmesan

1 Cook the tagliatelle in a large pan of rapidly boiling salted water until al dente. Drain and return to the pan.
2 While the pasta is cooking, process the parsley and basil in a food processor or blender until just chopped.
3 Heat the oil in a pan. Add the sun-dried pepper and fry for 2–3 minutes. Stir in the sour cream, ricotta and Parmesan and stir over low heat for 4 minutes, or until heated through. Do not allow to boil.
4 Add the herbs and sauce to the pasta, toss to combine and serve.

FETTUCINE WITH SPINACH AND PROSCIUTTO

Ready to eat in 20 minutes
Serves 4–6

500 g (1 lb) spinach or plain fettucine
2 tablespoons olive oil
8 thin slices prosciutto, chopped
3 spring onions, chopped
500 g (1 lb) English spinach
1 tablespoon balsamic vinegar
½ teaspoon caster sugar
½ cup (50 g/1¾ oz) freshly grated
   Parmesan

1 Cook the pasta in a large pan of rapidly boiling salted water until just al dente. Drain and return to the pan.
2 While the pasta is cooking, heat the oil in a large heavy-based deep pan. Add the prosciutto and the spring onion and cook, stirring occasionally, over medium heat for 5 minutes or until crisp.
3 Trim the stalks from the spinach, roughly chop the leaves and add them to the pan. Stir in the vinegar and the sugar, cover and cook for 1 minute or until the spinach has softened. Add salt and pepper, to taste.
4 Add the sauce to the pasta and toss well to distribute sauce evenly. Sprinkle with Parmesan and serve immediately.

SPAGHETTI WITH PEAS AND ONIONS

Ready to eat in 25 minutes
Serves 4–6

500 g (1 lb) spaghetti or vermicelli
1 kg (2 lb) large bulb spring onions
1 tablespoon olive oil
4 bacon rashers, chopped
2 teaspoons plain flour
1 cup (250 ml/8 fl oz) chicken stock
½ cup (125 ml/4 fl oz) white wine
1 cup (155 g/5 oz) shelled fresh peas

1 Cook the pasta in a large pan of rapidly boiling salted water until al dente. Drain and return to the pan.
2 While the pasta is cooking, trim the outer skins and ends from the onions, leaving only a small section of the green stem attached.
3 Heat the oil in a large heavy-based pan. Add the bacon and onions and stir over low heat for 4 minutes or until golden. Sprinkle the flour lightly over the top and stir for 1 minute.
4 Add the combined stock and wine and stir until the mixture boils and thickens slightly. Add the peas and cook for 5 minutes or until the onions are tender. Add black pepper, to taste. Add the mixture to the pasta and toss gently. Garnish with sprigs of fresh herbs if you like.

PASTA POMODORO

Preparation time: 15 minutes
Total cooking time: 10–15 minutes
Serves 4

500 g (1 lb) pasta
1½ tablespoons olive oil
1 onion, very finely chopped
2 x 400 g (13 oz) cans Italian tomatoes,
   chopped
¼ cup (7 g/¼ oz) fresh basil leaves

1 Cook the pasta in a large pan of rapidly boiling salted water until al dente. Drain, return to the pan and keep warm.
2 Heat the oil in a large frying pan. Add the onion and cook over medium heat until softened. Stir in the chopped tomato and simmer for 5–6 minutes, or until the sauce has reduced slightly and thickened. Season with salt and freshly ground pepper. Stir in the basil leaves and cook for another minute. Pour the sauce over the warm pasta and gently toss through. Serve immediately. This is a sauce suitable for serving with freshly grated Parmesan.

NOTE: Traditionally, pomodoro is served with tagliatelle. We have shown it with fettucine.

PASTA NICOISE

Ready to eat in 25 minutes
Serves 4

500 g (1 lb) farfalle
350 g (11 oz) green beans
⅓ cup (80 ml/2¾ fl oz) olive oil
60 g (2 oz) sliced anchovy fillets
2 garlic cloves, finely sliced
250 g (8 oz) cherry tomatoes, halved
freshly grated Parmesan, for serving

1 Cook the farfalle in a large pan of rapidly boiling salted water until al dente. Drain and return to the pan.
2 While the pasta is cooking, place the beans in a heatproof bowl and cover with boiling water. Set aside for 5 minutes, drain and rinse under cold water.
3 Heat the olive oil in a frying pan and stir-fry the beans and anchovy fillets for 2–3 minutes. Add the garlic and cook for 1 minute. Add the cherry tomatoes and stir through.
4 Add the sauce to the pasta, toss well and warm through. Serve with freshly grated Parmesan.

RAVIOLI WITH PEAS AND ARTICHOKES

Ready to eat in 30 minutes
Serves 4

650 g (1 lb 5 oz) fresh cheese and spinach ravioli
1 tablespoon olive oil
8 marinated artichoke hearts, quartered
2 large cloves garlic, finely chopped
½ cup (125 ml/4 fl oz) dry white wine
½ cup (125 ml/4 fl oz) chicken stock
2 cups (310 g/10 oz) frozen peas
125 g (4 oz) thinly sliced prosciutto, chopped
¼ cup (7 g/¼ oz) chopped fresh flat-leaf parsley
1/2 teaspoon seasoned cracked pepper

1 Cook the ravioli in a large pan of rapidly boiling salted water until al dente. Drain.
2 While the ravioli is cooking, heat the olive oil in a pan and cook the artichoke hearts and garlic over medium heat for 2 minutes, stirring frequently. Add the wine and stock and stir until well mixed. Bring to the boil, reduce the heat slightly and simmer for 5 minutes. Add the peas (they don't need to be thawed first) and simmer for another 2 minutes.
3 Stir the prosciutto, parsley and pepper into the artichoke mixture. Serve the ravioli topped with the artichoke mixture. Note: You can buy marinated artichoke hearts in jars from supermarkets and delicatessens.

SPICY SAUSAGE AND FENNEL RIGATONI

Ready to eat in 25 minutes
Serves 4–6

500 g (1 lb) rigatoni
30 g (1 oz) butter
1 tablespoon oil
500 g (1 lb) chorizo sausage, thickly sliced diagonally
1 bulb fennel, thinly sliced
2 cloves garlic, crushed
⅓ cup (80 ml/2¾ fl oz) lime juice
400 g (13 oz) can red pimientos, sliced
100 g (3½ oz) small rocket leaves, chopped
shavings of fresh Parmesan, for serving

1 Cook the rigatoni in a large pan of rapidly boiling salted water until al dente. Drain and return to the pan.
2 While the rigatoni is cooking, heat the butter and oil in a large frying pan. Add the chorizo sausage slices and cook over medium heat until well browned. Add the fennel to the pan and cook, stirring occasionally, for 5 minutes.
3 Add the garlic to the pan and stir for 1 minute. Stir in the lime juice and pimientos, bring to the boil, reduce the heat and simmer for another 5 minutes.
4 Add the sausage mixture and rocket to the pasta and toss to combine. Serve topped with shavings of fresh Parmesan.

NOTE: Chorizo is a spicy dried sausage, heavily flavoured with garlic and chilli. It is similar to salami, which can be substituted if chorizo sausage is not available.

FARFALLE WITH PEAS

Ready to eat in 20 minutes
Serves 4

500 g (1 lb) farfalle
1½ cups (235 g/7½ oz) frozen baby peas
8 thin slices pancetta
60 g (2 oz) butter
2 tablespoons each shredded fresh basil
   and mint

1 Cook the farfalle in a large pan of rapidly boiling salted water until al dente. Drain and return to the pan.
2 While the pasta is cooking, steam, microwave or lightly boil the baby peas until just tender and drain. Chop the pancetta and cook in the butter over medium heat for 2 minutes. Toss the butter and pancetta mixture through the pasta with the peas, basil and mint. Season with cracked black pepper and serve.

SPAGHETTI WITH TOMATO SAUCE

Ready to eat in 30 minutes
Serves 4

500 g (1 lb) spaghetti
1 tablespoon olive oil
1 onion, finely chopped
2 cloves garlic, crushed
825 g (1 lb 11 oz) can crushed tomatoes
1 teaspoon dried oregano
2 tablespoons tomato paste (tomato
   purée, double concentrate)
2 teaspoons sugar
shavings fresh Parmesan, for serving

1 Cook the spaghetti in a large pan of rapidly boiling salted water until al dente. Drain.
2 Heat the oil in a pan, add the onion and cook for 3 minutes, until soft. Add the garlic and cook for another minute.
3 Add the tomato and bring to the boil. Add the oregano, tomato paste and sugar; reduce the heat and simmer for 15 minutes. Season with salt and pepper, to taste. Serve the pasta topped with the tomato sauce and shavings of fresh Parmesan.

PENNE WITH SUN-DRIED TOMATOES AND LEMON

Ready to eat in 25 minutes
Serves 4

250 g (8 oz) penne
¼ cup (60 ml/2 fl oz) olive oil
3 bacon rashers, chopped
1 onion, chopped
⅓ cup (80 ml/2¾ fl oz) lemon juice
1 tablespoon fresh thyme leaves
⅓ cup (50 g/1¾ oz) chopped sun-dried
   tomatoes
½ cup (80 g/2¾ oz) pine nuts, toasted

1 Cook the pasta in a large pan of rapidly boiling salted water until al dente. Drain.
2 While the pasta is cooking, heat the olive oil in a large pan, add the chopped bacon and onion and stir over medium heat for 4 minutes or until the bacon is brown and the onion has softened.
3 Add the pasta to the pan with the lemon juice, thyme leaves, sun-dried tomato and pine nuts. Stir over low heat for 2 minutes, or until heated through.

NOTE: You can use pancetta instead of bacon, if preferred.

RAVIOLI WITH HERBS

Preparation time: 15 minutes
Total cooking time: 4–6 minutes
Serves 6

2 tablespoons olive oil
1 clove garlic, halved
800 g (1 lb 10 oz) ricotta-filled ravioli
60 g (2 oz) butter, chopped
2 tablespoons chopped fresh parsley
⅓ cup (20 g/⅔ oz) chopped fresh basil
2 tablespoons chopped fresh chives

1 Combine oil and garlic in a small bowl; set aside. Add ravioli to a large pan of rapidly boiling water and cook until tender.
2 Drain ravioli well in a colander and return to pan. Add oil to pasta; discard garlic. Add butter and herbs to ravioli and toss well. As a variation, use fresh coriander instead of parsley. Season with salt and pepper. Sprinkle with Parmesan when serving, if you wish.

PASTA WITH PESTO AND PARMESAN

Ready to eat in 15 minutes
Serves 4

500 g (1 lb) linguine or taglierini
¼ cup (40 g/1¼ oz) pine nuts
2 firmly packed cups (100 g/3½ oz) fresh basil leaves
2 cloves garlic, chopped
¼ cup (25 g/¾ oz) freshly grated Parmesan plus shavings, to garnish
½ cup (125 ml/4 fl oz) extra virgin olive oil

1 Cook the pasta in a large pan of rapidly boiling salted water until al dente. Drain and return to the pan.
2 While the pasta is cooking, mix the pine nuts, fresh basil leaves, garlic and Parmesan in a food processor until finely chopped. With the motor running, add the extra virgin olive oil in a slow stream until a smooth paste is formed. Season with salt and freshly ground black pepper, to taste. Toss the pesto through the hot pasta until it is thoroughly distributed. Garnish with shavings of fresh Parmesan.

SPAGHETTI MEDITERRANEAN

Ready to eat in 30 minutes
Serves 4–6

500 g (1 lb) spaghetti
750 g (1 1/2 lb) tomatoes
½ cup (125 ml/4 fl oz) extra virgin olive oil
2 garlic cloves, crushed
4 spring onions, finely sliced
6 anchovy fillets, chopped
½ teaspoon grated lemon rind
1 tablespoon fresh thyme leaves
12 stuffed green olives, thinly sliced
shredded fresh basil, for serving

1 Cook the spaghetti in a large pan of rapidly boiling salted water until al dente. Drain and return to the pan.
2 While the pasta is cooking, score small crosses in the bases of the tomatoes. Add to a pan of boiling water for 1–2 minutes, drain and plunge into cold water. Peel down from the cross and discard the skin. Cut the tomatoes in half horizontally. Place a sieve over a small bowl and squeeze the tomato seeds and juice into it; discard the seeds. Chop the tomatoes roughly and set aside.
3 In a bowl, combine the olive oil, garlic, spring onion, anchovies, lemon rind, thyme leaves and stuffed green olives. Add the chopped tomato and tomato juice, mix well and season with salt and freshly ground black pepper, to taste. Add the sauce to the pasta, toss to combine and sprinkle with shredded fresh basil.

SPAGHETTI WITH MEATBALLS

Preparation time: 40 minutes
Total cooking time: 30 minutes
Serves 4

Meatballs
500 g (1 lb) beef mince
½ cup (40 g/1¼ oz) fresh breadcrumbs
1 onion, finely chopped
2 cloves garlic, crushed
2 teaspoons Worcestershire sauce
1 teaspoon dried oregano
¼ cup (30 g/1 oz) plain flour
2 tablespoons olive oil

Sauce
2 x 400 g (13 oz) cans chopped tomatoes
1 tablespoon olive oil
1 onion, finely chopped
2 cloves garlic, crushed
2 tablespoons tomato paste
½ cup (125 ml/4 fl oz) beef stock
2 teaspoons sugar

500 g (1 lb) spaghetti
grated Parmesan, to serve

1 Combine the mince, breadcrumbs, onion, garlic, Worcestershire sauce and oregano and season to taste. Use your hands to mix the ingredients well. Roll level tablespoons of the mixture into balls, dust lightly with the flour and shake off the excess. Heat the oil in a deep frying pan and cook the meatballs in batches, turning often, until browned all over. Drain well.

2 To make the sauce, purée the tomatoes in a food processor or blender. Heat the oil in the cleaned frying pan. Add the onion and cook over medium heat for a few minutes until soft and lightly golden. Add the garlic and cook for 1 minute more. Add the puréed tomatoes, tomato paste, stock and sugar to the pan and stir to combine. Bring the mixture to the boil, and add the meatballs. Reduce the heat and simmer for 15 minutes, turning the meatballs once. Season with salt and pepper.
3 Meanwhile, cook the spaghetti in a large pan of boiling water until just tender. Drain, divide among serving plates and top with the meatballs and sauce. Serve with grated Parmesan.

CHICKEN RAVIOLI WITH LIME BALSAMIC DRESSING

Ready to eat in 30 minutes
Serves 4

250 g (8 oz) chicken mince
1 egg, lightly beaten
1 teaspoon finely grated orange rind
½ cup (50 g/1¾ oz) freshly grated
  Parmesan
1 tablespoon finely shredded fresh basil
275 g (9 oz) won ton wrappers
2 tablespoons lime juice
2 tablespoons balsamic vinegar
½ teaspoon honey
1 tablespoon oil

1 Combine the chicken mince, egg, orange rind, Parmesan and basil in a bowl. Place a heaped tablespoon of chicken mixture in the centre of a won ton wrapper, lightly brush the edges with water and top with another wrapper. Press the edges together to seal. Repeat with remaining filling and wrappers. (This is a quick way to make ravioli.)
2 Cook the chicken ravioli in a large pan of rapidly boiling salted water for 5 minutes.
3 Meanwhile, combine the lime juice, balsamic vinegar, honey and oil in a small jug and whisk to combine. Drain the ravioli. Serve drizzled with the dressing and sprinkled with finely chopped fresh chives. Garnish with lime slices, if you like.

FETTUCINE CARBONARA

Preparation time: 10 minutes
Total cooking time: 25 minutes
Serves 4

500 g (1 lb) fettucine
3 eggs, lightly beaten
½ cup (125 ml/4 oz) cream
⅓ cup (35 g/1¼ oz) finely grated
　Parmesan
20 g (¾ oz) butter
250 g (8 oz) bacon, rind removed, cut into
　thin strips
2 cloves garlic, crushed
4 spring onions, finely chopped

1 Bring a large pan of water to the boil,
add the fettucine and cook for 10–12
minutes, or until just tender.
2 Whisk together the eggs, cream and
Parmesan and season generously.
3 Meanwhile, melt the butter in a frying
pan, add the bacon strips and cook for
5–8 minutes, or until lightly golden. Add
the garlic and spring onion and cook for
2–3 minutes more. Remove from the
heat.
4 Drain the pasta, and transfer to a large
serving bowl. While the pasta is still hot
pour in the egg mixture and toss well to
combine (the heat from the pasta should
be sufficient to cook the egg). Add the
bacon mixture and toss through the
pasta. Season to taste with cracked black
pepper and serve immediately.

PENNE WITH ROASTED PEPPERS (CAPSICUMS)

Ready to eat in 30 minutes
Serves 4

1 red pepper (capsicum)
1 green pepper (capsicum)
1 yellow or orange pepper (capsicum)
1 tablespoon olive oil
2 cloves garlic, crushed
6 anchovy fillets, finely chopped
1 teaspoon seasoned cracked pepper
⅓ cup (80 ml/2¾ fl oz) dry white wine
1 cup (250 ml/8 fl oz) vegetable stock
2 tablespoons tomato paste (tomato
　purée, double concentrate)
500 g (1 lb) penne
1 tablespoon chopped fresh parsley

1 Cut the peppers into large flat pieces
and discard the seeds and membrane.
Grill, skin-side up, for 8 minutes, or until
the skin is black and blistered. Remove
from the heat and cover with a damp tea
towel. When cool, peel the skin away and
cut the flesh into thin strips.
2 Heat the oil in a large pan, add the
garlic and anchovy fillets and cook over
low heat for 2–3 minutes. Add the strips of
pepper, seasoned pepper and wine. Bring
to the boil, reduce the heat and simmer
for 5 minutes. Stir in the stock and tomato
paste and simmer for 10 minutes.
3 While the sauce is cooking, cook the
penne in a large pan of rapidly boiling
water until al dente. Drain, add to the
pepper sauce and toss until well
combined. Stir in the fresh parsley and
serve immediately with crusty Italian
bread.

NOTE: If you can't find yellow peppers,
use an extra red one, as they are sweeter
than green.

SPAGHETTI PUTTANESCA

Ready to eat in 25 minutes
Serves 4–6

500 g (1 lb) spaghetti
2 tablespoons olive oil
3 cloves garlic, crushed
2 tablespoons chopped fresh parsley
¼–½ teaspoon chilli flakes or powder
2 x 425 g (14 oz) cans crushed tomatoes
1 tablespoon capers
3 anchovy fillets, chopped
3 tablespoons black olives
freshly grated Parmesan, for serving

1 Cook the spaghetti in a large pan of
rapidly boiling salted water until al dente.
Drain and return to the pan.
2 While the spaghetti is cooking, heat the
oil in a large heavy-based frying pan. Add
the garlic, parsley and chilli flakes and
cook, stirring constantly, for 1 minute,
over medium heat.
3 Add the crushed tomato to the pan,
bring to the boil, reduce the heat and
simmer for 5 minutes.
4 Add the capers, anchovies and olives
and cook, stirring, for 5 minutes. Season
with black pepper. Toss gently with the
pasta until the sauce is evenly distributed.
Serve with Parmesan.

PENNE WITH RICOTTA AND BASIL SAUCE

Preparation time: 20 minutes
Total cooking time: 15 minutes
Serves 4

2 bacon rashers
2 teaspoons olive oil
2–3 cloves garlic, crushed
1 onion, finely chopped
2 spring onions, finely chopped
250 g (8 oz) ricotta
325 g (11 oz) penne
½ cup (30 g/1 oz) finely chopped fresh basil
8 cherry tomatoes, halved

1 Remove the fat and rind from the bacon and chop roughly. Heat the oil in a pan, add the bacon, garlic, onion and spring onion and stir over medium heat for 5 minutes, or until cooked. Remove from the heat, stir in the ricotta and chopped basil and beat until smooth.
2 Meanwhile, cook the pasta in a large pan of rapidly boiling salted water for 10 minutes, or until al dente. Just prior to draining the pasta, add about a cup of the pasta water to the ricotta mixture to thin the sauce. Add more water if you prefer an even thinner sauce. Season well.
3 Drain the pasta and stir the sauce and tomato halves into the pasta.

GARLIC BUCATINI

Ready to eat in 15 minutes
Serves 4

500 g (1 lb) bucatini
⅓ cup (80 ml/2¾ fl oz) olive oil
8 garlic cloves, crushed
2 tablespoons chopped fresh parsley
freshly grated Parmesan, for serving

1 Cook the bucatini in a large pan of rapidly boiling water until al dente. Drain and return to the pan.
2 When the pasta is almost finished cooking, heat the olive oil over low heat in a frying pan and add the garlic. Cook for 1 minute before removing from the heat. Add the garlic oil and the parsley to the pasta and toss to distribute thoroughly. Serve with Parmesan.

NOTE: Olives or diced tomato can be added. Do not overcook the garlic or it will be bitter.

TOMATO MUSSELS ON SPAGHETTI

Ready to eat in 30 minutes
Serves 4

16 fresh black mussels
500 g (1 lb) spaghetti
4 tablespoons olive oil
1 large onion, finely chopped
2 cloves garlic, crushed
850 g (1 lb 12 oz) can crushed tomatoes
½ cup (125 ml/4 fl oz) white wine

1 Scrub the mussels thoroughly and remove the beards. Discard any open mussels.
2 Cook the spaghetti in a large pan of rapidly boiling salted water until al dente. Drain, return to the pan and toss with half the olive oil.
3 While the pasta is cooking, heat the remaining olive oil in a pan, add the onion and cook until soft, but not brown. Add the garlic and cook for another minute. Stir in the tomato and wine and bring to the boil. Reduce the heat and simmer gently.
4 Meanwhile, put the mussels in a large pan and just cover with water. Cook over high heat for a few minutes, until the mussels have opened. Shake the pan often and discard any mussels that have not opened after 5 minutes.
5 Add the mussels to the tomato sauce and stir to combine. Serve the pasta with mussels and sauce over the top. Garnish with sprigs of thyme, if desired.

COTELLI WITH SPRING VEGETABLES

Preparation time: 15 minutes
Total cooking time: 20 minutes
Serves 4

500 g (1 lb) cotelli
2 cups (310 g/10 oz) frozen peas
2 cups (310 g/10 oz) frozen broad beans,
   blanched and peeled
⅓ cup (80 ml/2¾ fl oz) olive oil
6 spring onions, cut into 3 cm
   (1¼ inch) pieces
2 cloves garlic, finely chopped
1 cup (250 ml/8 fl oz) chicken stock
12 thin fresh asparagus spears,
   cut into 5 cm (2 inch) lengths
1 lemon

1 Cook the pasta in a large saucepan of boiling water until al dente. Drain, then return to the pan. Meanwhile, place the peas in a saucepan of boiling water and cook them for 1–2 minutes, or until tender. Remove with a slotted spoon and plunge into cold water. Add the broad beans to the same saucepan of boiling water and cook for 1–2 minutes, then drain and plunge into cold water. Remove and slip the skins off.
2 Heat 2 tablespoons of the oil in a frying pan. Add the spring onion and garlic and cook over medium heat for 2 minutes, or until softened. Pour in the stock and cook for 5 minutes, or until slightly reduced. Add the asparagus and cook for 3–4 minutes, or until bright green and just tender. Stir in the peas and broad beans and cook for 2–3 minutes, or until heated through.
3 Toss the remaining oil through the pasta, then add the vegetable mixture, ½ teaspoon finely grated lemon rind and ¼ cup (60 ml/2 fl oz) lemon juice. Season to taste with salt and cracked black pepper and toss together well. Divide among four bowls and top with shaved Parmesan, if desired.

FETTUCINE WITH CHERRY TOMATOES, AVOCADO AND BACON

Preparation time: 15 minutes
Total cooking time: 25 minutes
Serves 4

4 cloves garlic, unpeeled
⅓ cup (80 ml/2¾ fl oz) olive oil
250 g (8 oz) cherry tomatoes
300 g (10 oz) short cut bacon
350 g (11 oz) fresh fettucine
1 tablespoon white wine vinegar
2 tablespoons roughly chopped fresh
   basil
2 ripe avocados, diced
whole fresh basil leaves, to garnish

1 Preheat the oven to moderately hot 200°C (400°F/Gas 6). Place the garlic at one end of a roasting tin and drizzle with 2 tablespoons of the olive oil. Place the tomatoes at the other end and season well. Bake for 10 minutes, then remove the garlic. Return the tomatoes to the oven for a further 5–10 minutes, or until soft.
2 Cook the bacon under a hot grill for 4–5 minutes each side, or until crisp and golden. Roughly chop. Meanwhile, cook the pasta in a large saucepan of boiling water until al dente. Drain well and transfer to a large bowl. Drizzle 1 table-spoon of the olive oil over the pasta and toss well. Season to taste with salt and freshly ground black pepper and keep warm.
3 Slit the skin of each garlic clove and squeeze the garlic out. Place in a screw-top jar with the vinegar, chopped basil and remaining oil and shake well to combine. Add the tomatoes and their juices, bacon and avocado to the fettucine, pour on the dressing and toss well. Garnish with the basil leaves and serve with a green salad and crusty bread.

FARMHOUSE PASTA

Preparation time: 10 minutes
Total cooking time: 15 minutes
Serves 4

375 g (12 oz) pasta
1 large potato, cut into small cubes
400 g (13 oz) broccoli
⅓ cup (80 ml/2¾ fl oz) olive oil
3 cloves garlic, crushed
1 small fresh red chilli, finely chopped
2 x 400 g (13 oz) cans diced tomatoes
¼ cup (30 g/1 oz) grated Pecorino cheese

1 Bring a large saucepan of salted water to the boil and cook the pasta and potato together for 8–10 minutes, or until the pasta is al dente. Drain and return to the saucepan. Meanwhile, trim the broccoli into florets and discard the stems. Place in a saucepan of boiling water and cook for 1–2 minutes, then drain and plunge into iced water. Drain and add to the cooked pasta and potato.
2 Heat the oil in a saucepan, add the garlic and chilli and cook for 30 seconds. Add the tomato and simmer for 5 minutes, or until slightly reduced and thickened. Season to taste with salt and cracked black pepper.
3 Pour the tomato mixture over the pasta, potato and broccoli. Toss well and stir over low heat until warmed through. Serve sprinkled with grated Pecorino cheese.

SWEET POTATO RAVIOLI

Preparation time: 20 minutes
Total cooking time: 50 minutes
Serves 4

500 g (1 lb) orange sweet potato, cut into
   large pieces
¼ cup (60 ml/2 fl oz) olive oil
150 g (5 oz) ricotta cheese
1 tablespoon chopped fresh basil
1 clove garlic, crushed
2 tablespoons grated Parmesan
2 x 250 g (8 oz) packets egg won ton
   wrappers
60 g (2 oz) butter
4 spring onions, sliced on the diagonal
2 cloves garlic, crushed, extra
300 ml (10 fl oz) cream
baby basil leaves, to serve

1 Preheat the oven to hot 220°C (425°F/
Gas 7). Place the sweet potato on a
baking tray and drizzle with oil. Bake for
40 minutes, or until tender.
2 Transfer the sweet potato to a bowl with
the ricotta, basil, garlic and Parmesan
and mash until smooth.
3 Cover the won ton wrappers with a
damp tea towel. Place 2 level teaspoons of
the sweet potato mixture into the centre
of one wrapper and brush the edges with
a little water. Top with another wrapper.
Place onto a baking tray lined with baking
paper and cover with a tea towel. Repeat
with the remaining ingredients to make 60
ravioli, placing a sheet of baking paper
between each layer.
4 Melt the butter in a frying pan. Add the
spring onion and garlic and cook over
medium heat for 1 minute. Add the cream,
bring to the boil, then reduce the heat and
simmer for 4–5 minutes, or until the cream
has reduced and thickened. Keep warm.
5 Bring a large saucepan of water to the
boil. Cook the ravioli in batches for
2–4 minutes, or until just tender. Drain
well. Ladle the hot sauce over the top of
the ravioli, garnish with the basil leaves
and serve immediately.

COTELLI WITH CAPERS, BOCCONCINI AND BASIL OIL

Preparation time: 10 minutes
Total cooking time: 20 minutes
Serves 4

½ cup (125 ml/4 fl oz) olive oil
125 g (4 oz) jar capers in brine, drained
500 g (1 lb) cotelli
2 tablespoons lemon juice
2 cups (100 g/3½ oz) firmly packed fresh
   basil
⅓ cup (35 g/1 oz) grated Parmesan
250 g (8 oz) cherry tomatoes, quartered
8 bocconcini, quartered
extra virgin olive oil, for serving

1 Heat half the olive oil in a pan, add the
capers and cook over high heat for 3–4
minutes, or until crisp and golden. Drain
on paper towels and set aside.
2 Cook the pasta in a large pan of rapidly
boiling salted water until al dente. Drain
and return to the pan to keep warm.
Meanwhile, mix the lemon juice, 1½ cups
(75 g/2½ oz) of the basil and the remaining
olive oil in a food processor until smooth.
Season.
3 Roughly tear the remaining basil leaves,
then toss through the warm pasta with
the basil mixture, 2 tablespoons of the
Parmesan and the cherry tomatoes.
Spoon into warmed bowls and top with
the bocconcini and capers. Drizzle with
extra virgin olive oil and garnish with the
remaining grated Parmesan. Serve
immediately.

BLUE CHEESE WITH WALNUT LASAGNETTE

Preparation time: 10 minutes
Total cooking time: 25 minutes
Serves 4

375 g (13 oz) lasagnette
100 g (1 cup) walnuts
40 g (1½ oz) butter
3 French shallots, finely chopped
1 tablespoon brandy or cognac
250 ml (1 cup) crème fraîche
200 g (7 oz) gorgonzola cheese, crumbled
70 g (2½ oz) baby English spinach leaves

1 Preheat the oven to 200°C (400°F/Gas 6).
Cook the pasta in a large saucepan of
boiling salted water until al dente. Drain,
return to the pan and keep warm.
2 Meanwhile, place the walnuts on a
baking tray and roast for 5 minutes, or
until golden and toasted. Cool, then
roughly chop.
3 Heat the butter in a large saucepan, add
the shallots and cook over medium heat
for 1–2 minutes, or until soft, taking care
not to brown. Add the brandy and simmer
for 1 minute, then stir in the crème
fraîche and gorgonzola. Cook for 3–4
minutes, or until the cheese has melted
and the sauce has thickened.
4 Stir in the spinach and toasted walnuts,
reserving 1 tablespoon for garnish. Heat
gently until the spinach has just wilted.
Season with salt and cracked black
pepper. Gently mix the sauce through the
pasta. Divide among serving plates and
sprinkle with the reserved walnuts.

NOTE The gorgonzola needs to be young
as this gives a sweeter, milder flavour to
the sauce.

PASTA PRONTO

Preparation time: 10 minutes
Total cooking time: 15 minutes
Serves 4

2 tablespoons extra virgin olive oil
4 garlic cloves, finely chopped
1 small red chilli, finely chopped
3 x 400 g (14 oz) cans crushed tomatoes
1 teaspoon sugar
80 ml (⅓ cup) dry white wine
3 tablespoons chopped herbs such as
    basil or parsley
400 g (14 oz) vermicelli (see note)
35 g (⅓ cup) shaved Parmesan cheese

1 Heat the oil in a large deep frying pan
and cook the garlic and chilli for 1 minute.
Add the tomato, sugar, wine, herbs and
440 ml (1¾ cups) water. Bring to the boil
and season.
2 Reduce the heat to medium and add the
pasta, breaking the strands if they are too
long. Cook for 10 minutes, or until the
pasta is cooked, stirring often to stop the
pasta from sticking. The pasta will
thicken the sauce as it cooks. Season to
taste and serve in bowls with shaved
Parmesan.

NOTE Vermicelli is a pasta similar to
spaghetti, but thinner. You can also use
spaghettini or angel hair pasta for this
recipe.

SPAGHETTINI WITH ASPARAGUS AND ROCKET

Preparation time: 10 minutes
Total cooking time: 20 minutes
Serves 4

100 ml extra virgin olive oil
16 thin asparagus spears, cut into 5 cm
    lengths
375 g spaghettini
120 g rocket, shredded
2 small fresh red chillies, finely chopped
2 teaspoons finely grated lemon rind
1 clove garlic, finely chopped
1 cup (100 g) grated Parmesan
2 tablespoons lemon juice

1 Bring a large saucepan of water to the
boil over medium heat. Add 1 tablespoon
of the oil and a pinch of salt to the water
and blanch the asparagus for 3–4
minutes. Remove the asparagus with a
slotted spoon, refresh under cold water,
drain and place in a bowl. Return the
water to a rapid boil and add the
spaghettini. Cook the pasta until al dente.
Drain and return to the pan.
2 Meanwhile, add the rocket, chilli, lemon
rind, garlic and ⅔ cup (65 g) of the
Parmesan to the asparagus and mix well.
Add to the pasta, pour on the lemon juice
and remaining olive oil and season with
salt and freshly ground black pepper. Stir
well to evenly coat the pasta with the
mixture. Divide among four pasta bowls,
top with the remaining Parmesan and
serve.

NOTE You can use other types of pasta
such as tagliatelle, macaroni or spiral-
shaped pasta.

LEMON THYME TUNA WITH TAGLIATELLE

Preparation time: 10 minutes
Total cooking time: 25 minutes
Serves 4

375 g tagliatelle
140 ml extra virgin olive oil
1 small fresh red chilli, seeded and finely
    chopped
¼ cup (50 g) drained capers
1½ tablespoons fresh lemon thyme leaf
    tips
500 g tuna steaks, trimmed and cut into
    3 cm cubes
¼ cup (60 ml) lemon juice
1 tablespoon grated lemon zest
½ cup (30 g) chopped fresh flat-leaf
    parsley

1 Cook the tagliatelle in a large saucepan
of rapidly boiling salted water until al
dente. Drain, then return to the pan.
2 Meanwhile, heat 1 tablespoon of the oil
in a large frying pan. Add the chilli and
capers and cook, stirring, for 1 minute, or
until the capers are crisp. Add the thyme
and cook for another minute. Transfer to
a bowl.
3 Heat another tablespoon of oil in the
pan. Add the tuna cubes and toss for 2–3
minutes, or until evenly browned on the
outside but still pink in the centre—check
with the point of a sharp knife. Remove
from the heat.
4 Add the tuna to the caper mixture along
with the lemon juice, lemon rind, parsley
and the remaining oil, stirring gently until
combined. Toss through the pasta, season
with freshly ground black pepper and
serve immediately.

SPAGHETTI NICOISE

Preparation time: 10 minutes
Total cooking time: 25 minutes
Serves 4

350 g spaghetti
8 quail eggs (or 4 hen eggs)
3 x 185 g cans tuna in oil
⅓ cup (50 g) pitted and halved Kalamata
    olives
100 g semi-dried tomatoes, halved
    lengthways
4 anchovy fillets, chopped into small
    pieces
1 teaspoon finely grated lemon zest
2 tablespoons lemon juice
3 tablespoons baby capers, drained
3 tablespoons chopped fresh flat-leaf
    parsley

1 Cook the pasta in a large saucepan of
rapidly boiling salted water until al dente.
Meanwhile, place the eggs in a saucepan
of cold water, bring to the boil and cook
for 4 minutes (10 minutes for hen eggs).
Drain, cool under cold water, then peel.
Cut the quail eggs into halves or the hen
eggs into quarters.
2 Empty the tuna and its oil into a large
bowl. Add the olives, tomato halves,
anchovies, lemon rind and juice, capers
and 2 tablespoons of the parsley. Drain
the pasta and rinse in a little cold water,
then toss gently through the tuna mixture.
Divide among serving bowls, garnish with
egg and the remaining chopped fresh
parsley, and serve.

PENNE WITH RUSTIC
LENTIL SAUCE

Preparation time: 15 minutes
Total cooking time: 20 minutes
Serves 4

1 litre vegetable or chicken stock
350 g (11 oz) penne
⅓ cup (80 ml/2¾ fl oz) virgin olive oil, plus
    extra for serving
1 onion, chopped
2 carrots, diced
3 celery stalks, diced
3 cloves garlic, crushed
1 tablespoon plus 1 teaspoon chopped
    fresh thyme
400 g (13 oz) can lentils, drained

1 Boil the chicken stock in a large
saucepan for 10 minutes, or until reduced
by half. Meanwhile, cook the pasta in a
large pan of rapidly boiling salted water
until al dente. Drain well and toss with
2 tablespoons of the olive oil.
2 Heat the remaining oil in a large, deep
frying pan, add the onion, carrot and
celery and cook over medium heat for
10 minutes, or until browned. Add two-
thirds of the crushed garlic and 1
tablespoon of the thyme and cook for a
further 1 minute. Add the stock, bring to
the boil and cook for 8 minutes, or until
tender. Stir in the lentils and heat
through.
3 Stir in the remaining garlic and thyme
and season well—the stock should be
slightly syrupy at this point. Combine the
pasta with the lentil sauce in a large bowl
and drizzle with virgin olive oil to serve.

PASTA WITH TOMATO AND
BASIL SAUCE

Preparation time: 15 minutes
Total cooking time: 15 minutes
Serves 4

500 g (1 lb 2 oz) penne rigate
80 ml (⅓ cup) extra virgin olive oil
4 garlic cloves, crushed
4 anchovy fillets, finely chopped
2 small red chillies, seeded and finely
    chopped
6 large, vine-ripened tomatoes, peeled,
    seeded and diced
80 ml (⅓ cup) white wine
1 tablespoon tomato paste (purée)
2 teaspoons sugar
2 tablespoons finely chopped flat-leaf
    (Italian) parsley
3 tablespoons shredded basil

1 Cook the pasta in a saucepan of boiling
salted water until al dente. Drain well.
2 Meanwhile, heat the oil in a frying pan
and cook the garlic for 30 seconds. Stir in
the anchovy and chilli and cook for a
further 30 seconds. Add the tomato and
cook for 2 minutes over high heat. Add the
wine, tomato paste and sugar and
simmer, covered, for 10 minutes, or until
thickened.
3 Toss the tomato sauce through the
pasta with the herbs. Season and serve
with grated Parmesan, if desired.

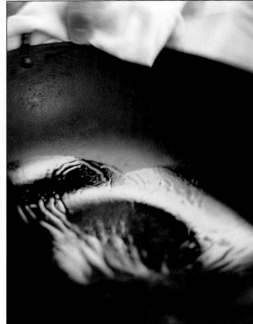

HOW TO STIR-FRY

WITH A SEARING HOT WOK, A DRIZZLE OF OIL AND SOME FRESH, COLOURFUL INGREDIENTS ALL CHOPPED UP AND READY TO GO, YOU'RE WELL ON YOUR WAY TO THE PERFECT STIR-FRY.

WHAT IS STIR-FRYING?

Stir-frying involves the quick cooking of small pieces of food over high heat using minimal oil. The characteristic action of stir-frying is to toss the food constantly with a shovel-like utensil called a 'wok charn'. The aim of stir-frying is for food to retain its flavour, colour, texture and nutritive value.

The marriage of the wok to cooking style is at its most perfect in the stir-fry. The wide, conical shape of the wok continually tips food back into the centre where the heat is at its most intense, thus searing food and cooking it in a few minutes, while imparting a delicious smoky flavour. The Chinese refer to the movement and rhythm associated with stir-frying as wok hei, which roughly translates as 'the breath of the wok'. It is hard to describe in English, but means that the food is at the perfect heat, is perfectly cooked and is ready to be eaten. It diminishes as the food cools, so stir-fries are best eaten piping hot from the wok.

HEALTH BENEFITS

Stir-frying is regarded as a healthy cooking method, with good reason. The rapid cooking time preserves many of the food's nutrients, particularly in vegetables, with most of their colour and vitamins retained.

Because properly seasoned woks develop a non-stick coating, very little oil is needed when stir-frying, and what little oil is used does not have time to be absorbed by the rapidly moving food.

STIR-FRYING PREPARATION

The key to successful stir-frying is to remember that once you begin, you must keep going. There is no time to interrupt cooking to chop an ingredient or mix together a sauce. All foods to be stir-fried should be prepared before you even heat the wok.

Stir-fry aficionados often set out all the ingredients in small bowls, placing them in the order that they will be added to the wok. This prevents food already in the wok from burning and ensures the quick and even cooking of all ingredients.

When preparing stir-fry ingredients, cut them into small, even pieces, so that they cook rapidly and evenly. The dish will also look more appealing and be easier to eat, which is particularly important if chopsticks are being used.

Meat or poultry fillets should be sliced into thin, uniform-sized slices across the grain. This helps to tenderise the meat by breaking up the fibres, thus allowing the meat to cook quickly and evenly so that it retains its juices and remains tender rather than becoming tough. Slicing is easier if the meat is frozen for 30 minutes beforehand. However, don't refreeze meat that has already been thawed or there is a risk of food poisoning.

Long vegetables, such as leafy vegetable stems, asparagus and green beans are also generally cut on the diagonal, as this increases their exposed surface area, thereby hastening the cooking time. If vegetables have been washed, they should be dried thoroughly so that they don't stew.

THE GOOD OIL

Choosing the right oil is important to both the method and flavour of stir-fries. The oil should have a high burning point due to the intensity of the heat required for successful stir-frying. It should also complement but not interfere with the main flavours. Oils with a high smoking point, which can withstand the high bursts of heat without turning bitter, include peanut, sunflower, safflower, canola and vegetable oil. These oils also have a comparatively bland flavour that makes them suitable for stir-frying, unlike the robust taste of olive oil, for example.

STEPS TO STIR-FRYING

The first step is to heat the wok over high heat before the oil is added. This enables the oil to be swirled around to coat the wok's entire surface before it has a chance to burn and taint the flavour of the food.

Any ginger or garlic will usually be added straight after the oil before the oil starts to smoke—this will prevent them from burning.

Add food that takes the longest to cook first, leaving the fastest-cooking additions, such as leafy green vegetables, bean sprouts or snow peas until last, Meat is often the first ingredient introduced to the wok. Only enough meat should be added that can fit in a single layer at one time. It should be left to cook briefly before starting to toss from the centre of the wok to the sides, so that it seals and doesn't stick to the bottom of the wok and tear when turned.

After the meat has been cooked, it is usually set aside while other ingredients such as vegetables or noodles are cooked, again using the method of tossing from the centre of the wok to the sides. The meat is then returned to the wok to be heated through and combined with the other ingredients, usually at the same time that any seasoning ingredients, such as soy sauce or fish sauce, are added. However, for 'wetter' dishes (those that have more sauce), the method is slightly different with the seasoning ingredients (often with some stock) added to the wok first and then reduced to a glossy consistency before returning the meat or other vegetables to the wok to coat with sauce.

The final addition of the flavourings helps unify the dish, bringing all the flavours together. There is another important reason why flavourings are added towards the end of the cooking time: if salty seasonings, such as soy sauce, are added earlier, the salt can draw out the liquid of other ingredients and make them go soggy.

HINTS AND TIPS

• If you are cooking meat that has been marinated, make sure that you drain the meat thoroughly before you cook it. It might be tempting to add the marinade for flavour, but if you add it too early, all you are doing is encouraging the meat to stew in its juices.
• When large quantities of meat, poultry or seafood are called for, cook it in batches to avoid stewing the food. Most recipes will specify if it needs to be cooked in batches, but some might not. When increasing a recipe to feed more people, keep in mind the batch rule.
• Combine the stir-fry sauce in advance— it saves hassle when you're in the middle of cooking.
• To maintain the heat of the wok, you may need to reheat the wok between batches. The aim is to ensure that the heat of the wok is intense enough to sear the food and seal in any juices and prevent stewing, even accounting for the temperature drop once the food is added.

CHICKEN, THAI BASIL AND CASHEW STIR-FRY

Preparation time: 15 minutes
Total cooking time: 15 minutes
Serves 4

750 g (1½ lb) chicken breast fillets, cut into strips
2 stems lemon grass, white part only, finely chopped
3 small fresh red chillies, seeded and chopped
4 cloves garlic, crushed
1 tablespoon finely chopped fresh ginger
2 fresh coriander roots, finely chopped
2 tablespoons vegetable oil
100 g (3½ oz) cashews
1½ tablespoons lime juice
2 tablespoons fish sauce
1½ tablespoons grated palm sugar
2 cups (60 g/2 oz) lightly packed fresh Thai basil
2 teaspoons cornflour

1 Place the chicken in a large bowl with the lemon grass, chilli, garlic, ginger and coriander root. Mix together well.
2 Heat a wok over medium heat, add 1 teaspoon of the oil and swirl to coat the side of the wok. Add the cashews and cook for 1 minute, or until lightly golden. Remove and drain on crumpled paper towels.
3 Heat the remaining oil in the wok, add the chicken in batches and stir-fry over medium heat for 4–5 minutes, or until browned. Return the chicken to the wok.
4 Stir in the lime juice, fish sauce, palm sugar and basil, and cook for 30–60 seconds, or until the basil just begins to wilt. Mix the cornflour with 1 tablespoon water, add to the wok and stir until the mixture thickens slightly. Stir in the cashews and serve with steamed rice.

PORK, ASPARAGUS AND BABY CORN STIR-FRY

Preparation time: 15 minutes + 10 minutes marinating
Total cooking time: 10 minutes
Serves 4

1 clove garlic, chopped
1 teaspoon grated fresh ginger
2 tablespoons soy sauce
¼ teaspoon ground white pepper
1 tablespoon Chinese rice wine
600 g (1¼ lb) pork loin fillet, thinly sliced across the grain
1 tablespoon peanut oil
1 teaspoon sesame oil
6 fresh shiitake mushrooms, thinly sliced
150 g (5 oz) baby corn
100 g (3½ oz) fresh asparagus, cut into 4 cm (1½ inch) lengths on the diagonal
2 tablespoons oyster sauce

1 Combine the garlic, ginger, soy sauce, pepper and wine in a non-metallic bowl. Add the pork and toss well. Marinate for at least 10 minutes.
2 Heat a wok over high heat, add half the oils and swirl to coat the side of the wok. Remove half the pork from the marinade (reserving the marinade) and stir-fry for 2 minutes, or until the pork changes colour. Remove from the wok. Reheat the wok, then repeat with the remaining oil and pork.
3 Add the mushrooms, corn and asparagus to the wok and stir-fry for 2 minutes. Return the pork and any juices to the wok and stir in the oyster sauce and reserved marinade. Cook, stirring, for another 2 minutes, or until it is heated through.

STIR-FRIED FISH WITH GINGER

Preparation time: 20 minutes
Total cooking time: 15 minutes
Serves 4

1 tablespoon peanut oil
1 small onion, thinly sliced
3 teaspoons ground coriander
600 g (1¼ lb) boneless white fish fillets (e.g. perch), cut into bite-sized strips
1 tablespoon julienned fresh ginger
1 teaspoon finely chopped and seeded fresh green chilli
2 tablespoons lime juice
2 tablespoons fresh coriander leaves

1 Heat a wok over high heat, add the oil and swirl to coat the side of the wok. Add the onion and stir-fry for 4 minutes, or until soft and golden. Add the ground coriander and cook for 1–2 minutes, or until fragrant.
2 Add the fish, ginger and chilli, and stir-fry for 5–7 minutes, or until the fish is cooked through, but be careful that the fish doesn't break up. Stir in the lime juice and season to taste with salt and pepper. Garnish with the coriander leaves and serve with steamed rice.

OYSTER SAUCE LAMB STIR-FRY

Preparation time: 10 minutes
Total cooking time: 10 minutes
Serves 4

1 tablespoon vegetable oil
750 g (1½ lb) lamb loin fillets, thinly sliced across the grain
4 cloves garlic, finely chopped
2 small fresh red chillies, thinly sliced
⅓ cup (80 ml/2¾ fl oz) oyster sauce
2½ tablespoons fish sauce
1½ teaspoons sugar
½ cup (25 g/¾ oz) chopped fresh mint
3 tablespoons whole fresh mint leaves

1 Heat a wok over high heat, add the oil and swirl to coat. Add the lamb and garlic in batches and stir-fry for 1–2 minutes each batch, or until the lamb is almost cooked. Return to the wok. Stir in the chilli, oyster sauce, fish sauce, sugar and the chopped mint leaves, and cook for another 1–2 minutes.
2 Remove from the heat, fold in the whole mint leaves and serve immediately with rice.

STIR-FRIED SCALLOPS WITH SUGAR SNAP PEAS

Preparation time: 20 minutes
Total cooking time: 5 minutes
Serves 4

2½ tablespoons oyster sauce
2 teaspoons soy sauce
½ teaspoon sesame oil
2 teaspoons sugar
2 tablespoons vegetable oil
2 large cloves garlic, crushed
3 teaspoons finely chopped fresh ginger
300 g (10 oz) sugar snap peas
500 g (1 lb) scallops, without roe, membrane removed
2 spring onions, cut into 2 cm (¾ inch) lengths

1 Combine the oyster and soy sauces, sesame oil and sugar in a small bowl and stir until the sugar dissolves.
2 Heat a wok over medium heat, add the oil and swirl to coat. Add the garlic and ginger and stir-fry for 30 seconds, or until fragrant. Add the peas and cook for 1 minute, then add the scallops and spring onion and cook for 1 minute, or until the spring onion is wilted. Stir in the sauce and heat for 1 minute, or until heated through and combined. Serve with rice.

SESAME PORK

Preparation time: 10 minutes
Total cooking time: 20 minutes
Serves 4

2 tablespoons hoisin sauce
2 tablespoons teriyaki sauce
2 teaspoons cornflour
¼ cup (60 ml) peanut oil
600 g (1¼ lb) pork loin fillet, thinly sliced across the grain
2 teaspoons sesame oil
8 spring onions, sliced on the diagonal
2 cloves garlic, crushed
2 teaspoons finely grated fresh ginger
2 carrots, julienned
200 g (6½ oz) snake beans, sliced
2 tablespoons sesame seeds, toasted

1 To make the stir-fry sauce, combine the hoisin and teriyaki sauces, cornflour and 1 tablespoon water in a small bowl. Set aside until needed.
2 Heat a wok to hot, add 1 tablespoon peanut oil and swirl. Add half the pork and stir-fry for 3 minutes, or until browned. Remove. Repeat.
3 Heat the remaining peanut oil and the sesame oil in the wok. Add the spring onion, garlic and ginger, and stir-fry for 1 minute.
4 Add the carrot and beans, and stir-fry for 3 minutes, or until almost cooked. Return the pork to the wok, add the stir-fry sauce and stir until the sauce thickens and everything is combined, the meat is tender and the vegetables are just cooked. Toss in the sesame seeds, then serve with steamed rice.

SCALLOPS WITH BLACK BEAN SAUCE

Preparation time: 15 minutes
Total cooking time: 10 minutes
Serves 4–6

600 g (1¼ lb) large fresh scallops, without roe
2 tablespoons cornflour
⅓ cup (80 ml/2¾ fl oz) peanut oil
3 spring onions, cut into 3 cm (1¼ inch) lengths
1 teaspoon finely chopped fresh ginger
2 cloves garlic, crushed
2 tablespoons Chinese rice wine
¼ cup (55 g/2 oz) black beans, rinsed and roughly chopped
1 tablespoon rice vinegar
1 tablespoon soy sauce
1 teaspoon soft brown sugar
½ teaspoon sesame oil

1 Remove and discard any veins, membrane or hard white muscle from the scallops. Toss them in the cornflour to coat, then shake off any excess.
2 Heat a wok over high heat, add 1 teaspoon peanut oil and swirl. Add the spring onion and stir-fry for 30 seconds; remove from the wok.
3 Add 1 tablespoon peanut oil to the hot wok, then add one-third of the scallops and stir-fry for 1–2 minutes, or until golden and well sealed—no liquid should be released. Remove from the wok. Repeat with the rest of the scallops.
4 Add the remaining peanut oil to the wok and swirl. Add the ginger, garlic, rice wine, black beans, vinegar, soy sauce and sugar, and stir-fry for 1 minute, or until the sauce thickens slightly.
5 Return the scallops to the wok and stir-fry for 1 minute, or until heated through and the sauce has thickened again. Stir in the spring onion and sesame oil. Serve with steamed rice.

SWORDFISH WITH BOK CHOY

Preparation time: 20 minutes
Total cooking time: 10 minutes
Serves 4

500 g (1 lb) swordfish steak, cut into bite-sized pieces
2 tablespoons freshly cracked black pepper
2 tablespoons hoisin sauce
2 tablespoons rice wine
1 tablespoon oyster sauce
1 tablespoon soy sauce
oil, for cooking
3 cloves garlic, thinly sliced
1 onion, sliced
1 kg (2 lb) baby bok choy, leaves separated
100 g (3½ oz) fresh shiitake mushrooms, sliced
1 tablespoon sesame seeds, toasted
1 teaspoon sesame oil

1 Dip the swordfish in cracked black pepper until coated, then shake off any excess.
2 Combine the hoisin sauce, rice wine, oyster sauce and soy sauce in a small bowl or jug.
3 Heat a wok over high heat, add 2 tablespoons of the oil and swirl it around to coat the side of the wok. Stir-fry the swordfish in batches for 1–2 minutes each batch, or until tender. Be careful not to overcook the fish or it will break up. Remove from the wok.
4 Reheat the wok, add 1 tablespoon of the oil, then stir-fry the garlic for 30 seconds, or until crisp and golden. Add the onion and stir-fry for 1–2 minutes, or until golden. Add the bok choy and mushrooms and cook briefly until the leaves wilt. Pour the sauce into the wok and stir until everything is coated in the sauce.
5 Return the swordfish to the wok and toss everything together. Serve sprinkled with sesame seeds and drizzled with the sesame oil.

PORK AND BROWN BEAN SAUCE NOODLES

Preparation time: 10 minutes
Total cooking time: 15 minutes
Serves 4–6

¼ cup (60 ml/12 fl oz) brown bean sauce
2 tablespoons hoisin sauce
¾ cup (185 ml/6 fl oz) chicken stock
1/2 teaspoon sugar
2 tablespoons peanut oil
3 cloves garlic, finely chopped
6 spring onions, sliced, white and green parts separated
650 g (1 lb 5 oz) pork mince
500 g (1 lb) fresh Shanghai noodles
1 telegraph cucumber, halved lengthways, seeded and sliced on the diagonal
1 cup (30 g/1 oz) fresh coriander leaves
1 cup (90 g/3 oz) bean sprouts, tailed
1 tablespoon lime juice

1 Combine the bean and hoisin sauces, stock and sugar and mix until smooth.
2 Heat a wok over high heat, add the oil and swirl. Add the garlic and spring onion (white part) and cook for 10–20 seconds. Add the pork and cook over high heat for 2–3 minutes, or until it has browned. Add the bean mixture, reduce the heat and simmer for 7–8 minutes.
3 Cook the noodles in a large saucepan of boiling water for 4–5 minutes, or until tender. Drain and rinse, then divide among bowls. Toss together the cucumber, coriander, sprouts, lime juice and remaining spring onion. Spoon the sauce over the noodles and top with the salad.

EASY BEEF STIR-FRY

Preparation time: 15 minutes
Total cooking time: 15 minutes
Serves 4

2 tablespoons oyster sauce
1 clove garlic, crushed
1 teaspoon grated fresh ginger
2 tablespoons light soy sauce
2 tablespoons rice wine
1 tablespoon honey
1 teaspoon sesame oil
2 teaspoons cornflour
2 tablespoons peanut oil
350 g (11 oz) lean beef fillet, thinly sliced
   across the grain
1 large onion, cut into thin wedges
1 large carrot, thinly sliced on the
   diagonal
1 red pepper (capsicum), cut into thin
   strips
100 g (3½ oz) snow peas (mangetout),
   sliced in half on the diagonal
150 g (5 oz) baby corn, sliced in half on
   the diagonal
200 g (61/2 oz) straw mushrooms,
   drained

1 To make the stir-fry sauce, combine the oyster sauce with the garlic, ginger, soy sauce, rice wine, honey, sesame oil and 1 tablespoon water in a small, non-metallic bowl or jug. Mix the cornflour with 1 tablespoon water in a separate small bowl until a paste forms. Set aside both bowls until needed.

2 Heat a wok over high heat, add 1 tablespoon of the peanut oil and swirl around to coat the side of the wok. Add the meat in batches and cook for 2–3 minutes, or until nicely browned. Remove the meat from the wok.
3 Heat the remaining peanut oil in the wok, add the onion, carrot and red pepper and cook, stirring, for 2–3 minutes, or until the vegetables are just tender. Add the snow peas, corn and straw mushrooms, cook for a further minute, then return all the meat to the wok. Pour the stir-fry sauce into the wok, then the cornflour paste and cook, stirring, for 1 minute, or until the sauce thickens and all the ingredients are combined. Season to taste with salt and freshly ground black pepper. Serve with thin egg noodles or steamed rice.

FIVE-SPICE PORK STIR-FRY

Preparation time: 20 minutes
Total cooking time: 20 minutes
Serves 4

375 g (12 oz) fresh thin egg noodles
1 tablespoon sesame oil
3 teaspoons grated fresh ginger
1½ teaspoons five-spice powder
2 teaspoons rice flour
500 g (1 lb) pork loin fillet, thinly sliced
   across the grain
2 tablespoons vegetable oil
2 cloves garlic, crushed
1 red pepper (capsicum), thinly sliced
300 g (10 oz) baby bok choy or wom bok
   (Chinese cabbage), chopped
6 spring onions, sliced on the diagonal
2 tablespoons Chinese rice wine
2 tablespoons hoisin sauce
1 tablespoon soy sauce

1 Cook the noodles in boiling water for 1 minute. Drain, rinse, then return to the saucepan. Stir in half the sesame oil.
2 Place the ginger, five-spice powder and rice flour in a bowl, season with salt and pepper, then mix well. Add the pork and toss to coat.
3 Heat a wok over high heat, add half the oil and swirl to coat. Add the pork in batches and stir-fry for 5 minutes, or until tender. Remove from the wok. Add the remaining oil, garlic, pepper, bok choy and spring onion, and stir-fry for 3 minutes, or until softened.
4 Return the pork to the wok and stir in the rice wine, hoisin sauce, soy sauce and the remaining sesame oil, and simmer for 2 minutes. Add the noodles and reheat gently before serving.

LAMB AND MINT STIR-FRY

Preparation time: 10 minutes
Total cooking time: 15 minutes
Serves 4

¼ cup (60 ml/2 fl oz) lime juice
2 tablespoons sweet chilli sauce
2 tablespoons fish sauce
2 tablespoons vegetable oil
750 g (1½ lb) lamb loin fillets, thinly sliced
   across the grain
2 cloves garlic, finely chopped
1 small red onion, cut into wedges
1 fresh bird's eye chilli, finely chopped
½ cup (10 g/¼ oz) fresh mint

1 To make the stir-fry sauce, combine the
lime juice, chilli sauce and fish sauce in a
small non-metallic bowl.
2 Heat a wok over high heat, add
1 tablespoon of the oil and swirl it around
to coat the side of the wok. Add the lamb
in batches and cook for 2 minutes each
batch, or until browned. Remove from the
wok.
3 Heat the remaining oil in the wok,
add the garlic and onion and stir-fry for
1 minute, then add the chilli and cook for
30 seconds. Return the lamb to the wok,
pour in the stir-fry sauce and cook for
2 minutes over high heat. Stir in the mint,
then serve with steamed jasmine rice.

TAMARI ROASTED ALMONDS WITH SPICY GREEN BEANS

Preparation time: 10 minutes
Total cooking time: 5 minutes
Serves 4–6

2 tablespoons sesame oil
1 long fresh red chilli, seeded and finely
   chopped
2 cm (¾ inch) piece fresh ginger, grated
2 cloves garlic, crushed
375 g (12 oz) green beans, cut into 5 cm
   (2 inch) lengths
½ cup (125 ml/4 fl oz) hoisin sauce
1 tablespoon soft brown sugar
2 tablespoons mirin
250 g (8 oz) tamari roasted almonds,
   roughly chopped (see Note)

1 Heat a wok over high heat, add the oil
and swirl to coat. Add the chilli, ginger
and garlic and stir-fry for 1 minute, or
until lightly browned. Add the beans,
hoisin sauce and sugar and stir-fry for
2 minutes. Stir in the mirin and cook for
1 minute, or until the beans are tender but
still crunchy.
2 Remove from the heat and stir in the
almonds just before serving. Serve on a
bed of rice.

NOTE: Tamari roasted almonds are
available from health-food stores. Tamari
is a naturally brewed, thick Japanese soy
sauce made with soy beans and rice.

TERIYAKI BEEF AND SOY BEAN STIR-FRY

Preparation time: 15 minutes
Total cooking time: 20 minutes
Serves 4

1 tablespoon mirin
2 tablespoons sake
2 tablespoons Japanese soy sauce
2 teaspoons sugar
400 g (13 oz) frozen soy beans (see Note)
1 tablespoon peanut oil
700 g (1 lb 7 oz) lean beef fillet, thinly
   sliced across the grain
6 spring onions, thinly sliced
2 cloves garlic, chopped
2 teaspoons finely chopped fresh ginger
50 g (1¾ oz) soy bean sprouts, tailed
1 red pepper (capsicum), thinly sliced

1 To make the stir-fry sauce, combine the
mirin, sake, Japanese soy sauce and
sugar in a small bowl or jug and set aside
until it is needed.
2 Cook the soy beans in a saucepan of
boiling water for 2 minutes. Drain.
3 Heat a large wok over high heat. Add
2 teaspoons of the peanut oil and swirl it
around to coat the side of the wok. Cook
the beef in three batches for 3–4 minutes
per batch, or until well browned. Remove
from the wok. Add the spring onion and
stir-fry for 30 seconds, or until it has
wilted.
4 Return the beef to the wok, add the
garlic, ginger, soy beans, soy bean
sprouts and pepper, and stir-fry for
2 minutes. Add the stir-fry sauce to the
wok and stir-fry until heated through.
Serve hot with steamed rice.

NOTE: Frozen soy beans are available in
packets, either in their pods or shelled.
They are available from Asian food stores.
This recipe uses the shelled variety.

CARAMEL PORK AND PUMPKIN STIR-FRY

Preparation time: 15 minutes
Total cooking time: 20 minutes
Serves 4

500 g (1 lb) pork fillet, thinly sliced across
  the grain
2 cloves garlic, crushed
2–3 tablespoons peanut oil
300 g (10 oz) butternut pumpkin, sliced
  into pieces about 2 x 4 cm (¾ x 1½ inch)
  and 5 mm (¼ inch) thick
⅓ cup (60 g/2 oz) soft brown sugar
¼ cup (60 ml/2 fl oz) fish sauce
¼ cup (60 ml/2 fl oz) rice vinegar
2 tablespoons chopped fresh coriander
  leaves

1 Place the pork in a bowl, add the
crushed garlic and about 2 teaspoons of
the peanut oil, then season with salt and
plenty of freshly ground pepper.
2 Heat a wok over high heat, add 1
tablespoon oil and swirl to coat the side of
the wok. Stir-fry the pork in two batches
for about 1 minute per batch, or until the
meat changes colour. Transfer the meat
to a plate.
3 Add the remaining oil to the wok and
stir-fry the pumpkin for about 4 minutes,
or until tender but not falling apart, then
remove and add to the plate with the pork.
4 Put the sugar, fish sauce, rice vinegar
and ½ cup (125 ml/4 fl oz) water in the
wok, stir thoroughly, then bring to the boil
and boil for about 10 minutes, or until
syrupy. Return the pork and pumpkin to
the wok and stir for 1 minute, or until well
coated with the syrup and heated through.
Stir in the coriander and serve
immediately with steamed rice and some
steamed Asian greens, if desired.

TEMPEH STIR-FRY

Preparation time: 15 minutes
Total cooking time: 15 minutes
Serves 4

1 teaspoon sesame oil
1 tablespoon peanut oil
2 cloves garlic, crushed
1 tablespoon grated fresh ginger
1 fresh red chilli, thinly sliced
4 spring onions, sliced on the diagonal
300 g (10 oz) tempeh, cut into 2 cm
  (¾ inch) cubes
500 g (1 lb) baby bok choy leaves
800 g (1 lb 10 oz) gai larn (Chinese
  broccoli), chopped
½ cup (125 ml/4 fl oz) vegetarian oyster
  sauce
2 tablespoons rice vinegar
2 tablespoons fresh coriander leaves
¼ cup (40 g/1¼ oz) toasted cashew nuts

1 Heat a wok over high heat, add the oils
and swirl to coat the side of the wok. Add
the garlic, ginger, chilli and spring onion
and cook for 1–2 minutes, or until the
onion is soft. Add the tempeh and cook for
5 minutes, or until golden. Remove from
the wok.
2 Add half the greens and 1 tablespoon
water to the wok and cook, covered, for
3–4 minutes, or until the greens have
wilted. Remove from the wok and repeat
with the remaining greens and a little
more water.
3 Return the greens and tempeh to the
wok, add the sauce and vinegar and warm
through. Top with the coriander and nuts.
Serve with rice.

CHICKEN AND SNOW PEA (MANGETOUT) STIR-FRY

Preparation time: 15 minutes
Total cooking time: 15 minutes
Serves 4

1 tablespoon red curry paste (see Notes)
2 tablespoons vegetable oil
2 tablespoons fish sauce
2 tablespoons lime juice
3 tablespoons chopped fresh coriander
  leaves
1 tablespoon grated fresh ginger
1 teaspoon caster sugar
1 teaspoon sesame oil
750 g (1½ lb) chicken thigh fillets, cut into
  strips
1 tablespoon vegetable oil, extra
10 spring onions, cut into 2 cm (¾ inch)
  lengths
100 g (3½ oz) snow peas (mangetout),
  trimmed

1 Whisk together the red curry paste, oil,
fish sauce, lime juice, coriander, ginger,
sugar and sesame oil in a large non-
metallic bowl. Add the chicken strips and
toss until they are evenly coated in the
sauce.
2 Heat a wok over high heat, add the extra
oil and swirl to coat the side of the wok.
Add the chicken in batches and stir-fry for
3–5 minutes each batch, or until browned
all over, then remove from the wok.
3 Add the spring onion and snow peas to
the wok and stir-fry for 2 minutes. Return
all the chicken and any juices to the wok
and stir-fry for a further 2–3 minutes, or
until the chicken is heated through and
everything is thoroughly combined.
Season to taste with salt and freshly
ground black pepper. Serve on a bed of
steamed jasmine rice.

CHICKEN STIR-FRY WITH SNOW PEA (MANGETOUT) SPROUTS

Preparation time: 15 minutes
Total cooking time: 15 minutes
Serves 4

2 tablespoons vegetable oil
1 onion, thinly sliced
3 kaffir lime leaves, shredded
3 chicken breast fillets, cut into 2 cm
 (¾ inch) cubes
1 red pepper (capsicum), sliced
¼ cup (60 ml/2 fl oz) lime juice
100 ml (3½ fl oz) soy sauce
100 g (3½ oz) snow pea (mangetout)
 sprouts
2 tablespoons chopped fresh coriander
 leaves

1 Heat a wok over medium heat, add the oil and swirl. Add the onion and lime leaves and stir-fry for 3–5 minutes, or until the onion begins to soften. Add the chicken and cook for 4 minutes, then add the pepper and stir-fry for 2–3 minutes.
2 Stir in the lime juice and soy sauce and cook for 1–2 minutes, or until the sauce reduces slightly. Toss in the sprouts and coriander and cook until the sprouts have wilted slightly. Serve with steamed jasmine rice and extra coriander and chilli, if desired.

WHEAT NOODLES AND FISH WITH BLACK BEANS

Preparation time: 10 minutes
Total cooking time: 15 minutes
Serves 4

270 g (9 oz) fresh wheat noodles
200 g (6½ oz) gai larn (Chinese broccoli),
 cut into 5 cm (2 inch) lengths
550 g (1 lb 2 oz) skinless snapper or cod
 fillets, cut into 4 cm (1½ inch) pieces
2 tablespoons light soy sauce
1½ tablespoons Chinese rice wine
1 teaspoon sugar
½ teaspoon sesame oil
2 teaspoons cornflour
1 tablespoon vegetable oil
5 cloves garlic, crushed
2 teaspoons finely chopped fresh ginger
2 spring onions, finely chopped
2 small fresh red chillies, finely chopped
2 tablespoons black beans, rinsed and
 roughly chopped
150 ml (5 fl oz) fish stock
spring onions, extra, sliced on the
 diagonal, to garnish

1 Cook the wheat noodles in a large saucepan of boiling water for 2 minutes, or until tender. Drain. Put the gai larn in a steamer and steam for 3–4 minutes, or until slightly wilted. Remove from the heat and keep warm.
2 Put the fish in a bowl. Combine the soy sauce, rice wine, sugar, sesame oil and cornflour. Pour over the fish and toss to coat well.
3 Heat a wok over high heat, add the vegetable oil and swirl to coat. Add the garlic, ginger, spring onion, chilli and black beans and stir-fry for 1 minute. Add the fish and marinade and cook for a further 2 minutes. Remove the fish with a slotted spoon and keep warm.
4 Add the stock to the wok, reduce the heat to low and bring to a slow simmer. Cook for 5 minutes, or until the sauce has slightly thickened. Return the fish to the wok, cover and continue to simmer gently for 2–3 minutes, or until just cooked.
5 To serve, divide the noodles among the serving dishes, top with the gai larn and spoon the fish and black bean sauce on top. Garnish with the extra spring onion.

SPICY LAMB AND EGGPLANT (AUBERGINE) STIR-FRY

Preparation time: 15 minutes
Total cooking time: 20 minutes
Serves 4

2 tablespoons vegetable oil
1 onion, finely chopped
500 g (1 lb) eggplant (aubergine), peeled and cut into batons
600 g (1¼ lb) lamb loin fillets, thinly sliced across the grain
2 cloves garlic, finely chopped
1 small fresh red chilli, seeded and finely chopped
1 tablespoon ground cumin
1 tablespoon ground coriander
2 teaspoons ground turmeric
1 teaspoon ground cinnamon
1 cup (250 ml/8 fl oz) coconut cream
1 tablespoon chopped fresh mint
2 tablespoons chopped fresh parsley
lemon wedges, to serve

1 Heat a wok over high heat, add 2 teaspoons of the oil and swirl to coat the side of the wok. Stir-fry the onion until soft and golden. Remove from the wok.
2 Heat 1 tablespoon of the oil in the wok and cook the eggplant in two batches over high heat until golden and cooked. Drain on crumpled paper towels.
3 Reheat the wok, then add 2 teaspoons of the oil. Stir-fry the lamb in two batches over high heat for about 2 minutes each batch, or until browned and just cooked.
4 Return all the lamb to the wok with the onion and eggplant. Add the garlic, chilli and spices, and cook for 1 minute. Pour in the coconut cream and bring to the boil.
5 Stir in the fresh mint and parsley and season with salt and freshly ground black pepper. Serve with lemon wedges.

SWEET CHILLI CHICKEN STIR-FRY

Preparation time: 10 minutes
Total cooking time: 10 minutes
Serves 4–6

375 g (12 oz) Hokkien noodles
4 chicken thigh fillets, cut into small pieces
1–2 tablespoons sweet chilli sauce
2 teaspoons fish sauce
1 tablespoon vegetable oil
100 g (3½ oz) baby sweet corn, halved lengthways
150 g (5 oz) sugar snap peas, topped and tailed
1 tablespoon lime juice

1 Put the noodles in a large bowl, cover with boiling water for 1 minute, then gently separate. Drain and rinse.
2 Combine the chicken, sweet chilli sauce and fish sauce in a bowl.
3 Heat a wok over high heat, add the oil and swirl to coat the side of the wok. Add the chicken and stir-fry for 3–5 minutes, or until cooked through. Add the corn and peas and stir-fry for 2 minutes. Stir in the noodles and lime juice, then serve.

TOFU, SNOW PEA (MANGETOUT) AND MUSHROOM STIR-FRY

Preparation time: 10 minutes
Total cooking time: 15 minutes
Serves 4

¼ cup (60 ml/2 fl oz) peanut oil
600 g (1¼ lb) firm tofu, drained, cut into 2 cm (¾ inch) cubes
2 teaspoons sambal oelek or chilli paste
2 cloves garlic, finely chopped
300 g (10 oz) snow peas (mangetout), trimmed
400 g (13 oz) fresh Asian mushrooms (e.g. shiitake, oyster or black fungus), sliced
¼ cup (60 ml/2 fl oz) kecap manis

1 Heat a wok over high heat, add 2 tablespoons of the peanut oil and swirl to coat the side of the wok. Add the tofu in two batches and stir-fry each batch for 2–3 minutes, or until lightly browned on all sides, then transfer to a plate.
2 Heat the remaining oil in the wok, add the sambal oelek, garlic, snow peas, mushrooms and 1 tablespoon water and stir-fry for 1–2 minutes, or until the vegetables are almost cooked but still crunchy.
3 Return the tofu to the wok, add the kecap manis and stir-fry for another minute, or until heated through. Serve immediately with steamed jasmine rice.

STIR-FRIED CAULIFLOWER AND SNAKE BEANS

Preparation time: 15 minutes
Total cooking time: 10 minutes
Serves 4

4 coriander roots, chopped, or
   1 tablespoon chopped leaves and stems
1 teaspoon soft brown sugar
½ teaspoon ground turmeric
2 cloves garlic, crushed
2 tablespoons fish sauce
400 g (12⅔ oz) cauliflower
6 spring onions
200 g (6½ oz) snake beans
2 tablespoons oil
4 cloves garlic, extra, sliced lengthways
20 leaves spinach, coarsely shredded
½ teaspoon cracked black pepper
½ cup (125 ml/4 fl oz) water
1 tablespoon lime juice

1 Using a mortar and pestle or a blender, blend the coriander, sugar, turmeric, crushed garlic and 1 tablespoon fish sauce to make a smooth paste.
2 Cut the cauliflower into florets. Cut the spring onions in half lengthways, then cut the white parts into short lengths, reserving some of the green tops for a garnish. Cut the snake beans into short lengths.

3 Heat half the oil in a large pan or wok, add the extra sliced garlic and stir-fry for 30 seconds or until just beginning to brown. Reserve some of the garlic for a garnish.
4 Add the spinach to the pan and stir-fry for another 30 seconds or until just wilted. Add the pepper and the remaining fish sauce and mix well. Arrange on a serving plate; keep warm.
5 Heat the remaining oil in the same pan; add the paste and cook over high heat for 1 minute or until aromatic. Add the cauliflower and stir-fry until well combined. Add the water, bring to the boil, reduce heat and simmer, covered, for 3 minutes. Add the beans, cover and cook for another 3 minutes. Add the spring onion and stir until just wilted. Spoon the vegetables over the spinach, drizzle with lime juice and sprinkle over the reserved fried garlic and spring onion.

ORANGE SWEET POTATO, SPINACH AND WATER CHESTNUT STIR-FRY

Preparation time: 15 minutes
Total cooking time: 20 minutes
Serves 4

500 g (1 lb) orange sweet potato, peeled
   and cut into 1.5 cm (⅝ inch) cubes
1 tablespoon vegetable oil
2 cloves garlic, crushed
2 teaspoons sambal oelek
227 g (7 oz) can water chestnuts, sliced
2 teaspoons grated palm sugar
390 g (13 oz) English spinach, stems
   removed
2 tablespoons soy sauce
2 tablespoons vegetable stock

1 Cook the sweet potato in a large saucepan of boiling water for 15 minutes, or until tender. Drain well.
2 Heat a wok over high heat, add the oil and swirl to coat the side of the wok. Stir-fry the garlic and sambal oelek for 1 minute, or until fragrant. Add the sweet potato and water chestnuts and stir-fry over medium–high heat for 2 minutes. Reduce the heat to medium, add the palm sugar and cook for a further 2 minutes, or until the sugar has melted. Add the spinach, soy sauce and stock and toss until the spinach has just wilted. Serve with steamed rice.

GINGER BEEF STIR-FRY

Preparation time: 20 minutes +
 15 minutes marinating
Total cooking time: 15 minutes
Serves 4

1 clove garlic, crushed
1 teaspoon grated fresh ginger
¼ cup (60 ml/2 fl oz) kecap manis
¼ cup (60 ml/2 fl oz) Chinese rice wine
1 teaspoon sugar
pinch of five-spice powder
500 g (1 lb) lean beef fillet, thinly sliced
½ teaspoon cornflour
¼ cup (60 ml/2 fl oz) peanut oil
1 red onion, sliced into thin wedges
1½ tablespoons julienned fresh ginger
400 g (13 oz) gai larn (Chinese broccoli),
 cut into 6 cm (2½ inch) lengths

1 Combine the garlic, grated ginger, kecap manis, rice wine, sugar and five-spice powder in a large non-metallic bowl. Add the beef, toss together, then cover and marinate in the fridge for at least 15 minutes.
2 Mix together the cornflour with 1 tablespoon water to form a paste.
3 Heat a wok over high heat, add 1 tablespoon of the oil and swirl to coat the side of the wok. Remove half the meat from the marinade with tongs or a slotted spoon, add to the wok and stir-fry for 2–3 minutes, or until browned and just cooked. Remove from the wok. Repeat with more oil and the remaining beef, reserving the marinade.
4 Add the remaining oil to the wok and stir-fry the onion for 2–3 minutes, or until it starts to soften, then add the julienned ginger and stir-fry for another minute. Stir in the gai larn and cook for 2–3 minutes, or until wilted and tender.
5 Return the beef to the wok, along with the reserved marinade and any meat juices. Add the cornflour paste and stir until combined. Continue to cook for 1–2 minutes, or until the sauce has thickened slightly and the meat is heated through. Serve with steamed rice or noodles.

VEGETABLE STIR-FRY

Preparation time: 15 minutes
Total cooking time: 5–10 minutes
Serves 4

1 tablespoon sesame seeds
2 spring onions
250 g (8 oz) broccoli
1 medium red pepper (capsicum)
1 medium yellow pepper (capsicum)
150 g (4¾ oz) button mushrooms
1 tablespoon oil
1 teaspoon sesame oil
1 clove garlic, crushed
2 teaspoons grated fresh ginger
¼ cup (45 g/1½ oz) black olives
1 tablespoon soy sauce
1 tablespoon honey
1 tablespoon sweet chilli sauce

1 Place the sesame seeds on an oven tray and cook under a hot grill until golden; set aside until needed. Finely slice the spring onions and cut the broccoli into small florets. Cut the peppers in half, remove and discard the seeds and membrane and cut the flesh into thin strips. Cut the mushrooms in half.
2 Heat the oils in a wok or large frying pan. Add the garlic, ginger and spring onions. Stir-fry over medium heat for 1 minute. Add the broccoli, peppers, mushrooms and olives. Stir-fry for another 2 minutes or until the vegetables are a bright colour and just tender.
3 Combine the soy sauce, honey and chilli sauce in a bowl and mix well. Pour the sauce over the vegetables and toss lightly to combine. Sprinkle with the sesame seeds and serve immediately.

VIETNAMESE CARAMEL PRAWNS

Preparation time: 20 minutes
Total cooking time: 10 minutes
Serves 4–6

¼ cup (45 g/1½ oz) grated light palm
 sugar
1.5 kg (3 lb) raw medium prawns, peeled
 and deveined
3 spring onions, finely chopped, white
 and greens separated
1 tablespoon vegetable oil
2 tablespoons fish sauce
1 tablespoon rice vinegar
1 tablespoon grated light palm sugar,
 extra
2 cloves garlic, finely chopped
large pinch of white pepper
1 tablespoon finely chopped fresh
 coriander leaves (optional)

1 Put the palm sugar and 1 tablespoon water in a small saucepan over high heat and stir until the sugar dissolves. Bring to the boil and swirl the pan occasionally (but don't stir) for 3–4 minutes, or until it is dark golden and there is the first smell of toffee. Using a long-handled spoon, gradually stir in ¼ cup (60 ml/2 fl oz) water until a thin caramel sauce forms. Remove from the heat.
2 Combine the prawns and the white part of the spring onion in a bowl.
3 Heat a wok over high heat, add the oil and swirl to coat. Add the prawns and stir-fry for 1 minute, or until the prawns turn pink, then add the caramel sauce, fish sauce, rice vinegar, extra palm sugar, garlic, spring onion greens and pepper and stir-fry for 2 minutes, or until the prawns are curled and glazed. Toss in the coriander, if using. Serve as part of a banquet.

SEAFOOD

KING PRAWNS WITH PEANUTS

Preparation time: 20 minutes + 1 hour
    marinating
Total cooking time: 3 minutes
Serves 4

1.25 kg (2½ lb) raw king prawns
4 spring onions, chopped
1 clove garlic, crushed
1 teaspoon grated fresh ginger
1 teaspoon sambal oelek
1 teaspoon ground coriander
½ teaspoon ground turmeric
1 teaspoon grated lemon rind
1 tablespoon lemon juice
⅔ cup (110 g/3⅔ oz) chopped unsalted
    roasted peanuts
2 tablespoons peanut oil

1 Peel and devein the prawns, leaving the
tails intact.
2 Combine the prawns with the spring
onion, garlic, ginger, sambal oelek,
coriander, turmeric, lemon rind, lemon
juice and peanuts. Cover and refrigerate
for 1 hour.
3 Heat the oil in a frying pan; add the
prawn mixture and stir-fry over high heat
for about 3 minutes or until the prawns
are cooked. Serve with rice.

CREOLE SHRIMP WITH RICE

Preparation time: 20 minutes
Total cooking time: 1 hour 10 minutes
Serves 4

40 g (1¼ oz) butter
1 tablespoon oil
1 large onion, finely chopped
200 g (6½ oz) smoked ham, diced
2 celery stalks, diced
1 large red capsicum (pepper) finely diced
3 garlic cloves, crushed
3 teaspoons sweet paprika
large pinch of cayenne pepper
1 teaspoon ground cumin
2 teaspoons finely chopped thyme
2 teaspoons finely chopped oregano
400 g (13 oz) tin chopped tomatoes
1 tablespoon tomato paste (purée)
1 bay leaf
½ teaspoon finely grated lemon zest
2 tablespoons Worcestershire sauce
24 large raw prawns (shrimp), peeled
    and deveined
3 tablespoons finely chopped flat-leaf
    (Italian) parsley
cooked long-grain rice, to serve
lemon wedges, to serve

1 Melt half the butter with the oil in a
large saucepan over medium heat. Add
the onion and ham and sauté for about
5 minutes, or until the onion is softened
but not browned. Add the celery and
capsicum and cook for 10 minutes longer.
Add the garlic, paprika, cayenne, cumin,
thyme and oregano, stir to combine and
cook for a further minute, or until
fragrant. Add the chopped tomatoes,
tomato paste, bay leaf, lemon zest,
Worcestershire sauce and 3 cups (750 ml/
24 fl oz) water to the pan and bring to the
boil. Reduce to a simmer and cook for
45 minutes, or until you have a thick and
chunky sauce.
2 Melt the remaining butter in a frying
pan over medium heat. When the butter is
sizzling, sauté the lightly seasoned
prawns in batches until just pink and
slightly curled, then add them to the
sauce in the saucepan and cook for a
further 2 minutes.
3 Remove the saucepan from the heat,
stir in the parsley and season to taste
with salt and freshly ground black
pepper. Serve on a bed of the hot rice
with lemon wedges, if desired.

FREEFORM PRAWN PIES

Preparation time: 30 minutes +
  15 minutes chilling
Total cooking time: 30 minutes
Serves 4

2 cups (250 g/8 oz) plain flour
125 g (4 oz) chilled butter, cubed
1 kg (2 lb) raw medium prawns
1 tablespoon oil
5 cm (2 inch) piece fresh ginger, grated
3 cloves garlic, crushed
⅓ cup (80 ml/2¾ fl oz) sweet chilli sauce
⅓ cup (80 ml/2¾ fl oz) lime juice
⅓ cup (80 ml/2¾ fl oz) thick (double) cream
25 g (¾ oz) chopped fresh coriander
1 egg yolk, lightly beaten, to glaze
strips of lime rind, to garnish

1 Sift the flour into a large bowl, add the butter and rub into the flour with your fingertips until the mixture resembles fine breadcrumbs. Make a well, add 3 tablespoons water and mix with a flat-bladed knife, using a cutting action, until the mixture comes together in beads. Gather the dough together and lift out onto a lightly floured surface. Press into a ball and flatten into a disc. (Alternatively, make in a food processor.) Wrap in plastic wrap and chill for 15 minutes.

2 Preheat the oven to moderately hot 200°C (400°F/Gas 6). Peel the prawns and gently pull out the dark vein from each prawn back, starting at the head end.
3 Heat the oil in a large frying pan and fry the ginger, garlic and prawns for 2–3 minutes. Remove the prawns and set aside. Add the chilli sauce, lime juice and cream to the pan and simmer over medium heat, until the sauce has reduced by about one third. Return the prawns to the pan and add the coriander; cool.
4 Grease 2 baking trays. Divide the pastry into 4 and roll out each portion, between sheets of baking paper, into a 20 cm (8 inch) circle. Divide the filling into 4 and place a portion in the centre of each pastry, leaving a wide border. Fold the edges loosely over the filling. Brush the pastry with egg yolk. Bake for 25 minutes, or until golden. Serve garnished with lime rind.

HONEY PRAWNS

Preparation time: 20 minutes
Total cooking time: 15 minutes
Serves 4

16 raw large prawns
cornflour, for dusting
oil, for deep-frying
3 egg whites, lightly beaten
2 tablespoons cornflour, extra
2 tablespoons vegetable oil, extra
¼ cup (90 g/3 oz) honey
2 tablespoons sesame seeds, toasted

1 Peel and devein the prawns, leaving the tails intact. Pat them dry and lightly dust with the cornflour, shaking off any excess. Fill a wok one-third full of oil and heat to 180°C (350°F), or until a cube of bread dropped in the oil browns in 15 seconds.
2 Beat the egg whites in a clean dry bowl until soft peaks form. Add the extra cornflour and some salt and gently whisk until combined and smooth. Using the tail as a handle, dip the prawns in the batter, then slowly lower them into the oil. Cook in batches for 3–4 minutes, or until crisp and golden and the prawns are cooked. Remove with a slotted spoon, then drain on crumpled paper towels and keep warm.
3 Heat the extra oil and honey in a saucepan over medium heat for 2–3 minutes, or until bubbling. Place the prawns on a serving plate and pour on the honey sauce. Sprinkle with the sesame seeds and serve immediately with steamed rice.

FRAGRANT LEMON GRASS RICE AND PRAWNS

Preparation time: 20 minutes
Total cooking time: 30 minutes
Serves 4

5 garlic cloves, peeled
4 cm (1½ inch) piece of ginger, chopped
3 coriander (cilantro) roots, washed thoroughly
2 long green chillies, seeded and chopped
1 onion, chopped
2 tablespoons lime juice
1 teaspoon grated palm sugar
¼ cup (60 ml/2 fl oz) oil
2 stems lemon grass (white part only), bruised
4 makrut (kaffir) lime leaves
750 g (1½ lb) raw prawns (shrimp), peeled and deveined
2 cups (400 g/13 oz) long-grain rice, washed and drained
1 cup (250 ml/8 fl oz) fish stock
100 g (3½ oz) snake beans, cut into 3 cm (1¼ inch) lengths
1 Lebanese (short) cucumber
2 tablespoons coriander (cilantro) leaves
2 tablespoons crisp fried shallots

1 In the small bowl of a food processor, put the garlic, ginger, coriander roots, green chillies and onion. Add 2–3 tablespoons of water, and blend to a smooth paste.
2 In a small bowl, combine the lime juice and palm sugar, stirring until the sugar is dissolved. Set aside.

3 In a heavy-based, deep frying pan with a tight-fitting lid, heat half the oil on medium heat. Add the prepared paste, lemon grass and lime leaves, and cook for 5 minutes, or until the mixture is soft and fragrant, taking care not to brown it. Add the prawns and cook for 2 minutes, or until pink. Remove with a slotted spoon and set aside.
4 Add the rice to the pan, stir for 1 minute to coat well, then pour in the fish stock and 2 cups (500 ml/16 fl oz) water, and stir again. Increase the heat to high and bring the mixture to the boil. Stir in the beans and lime juice mixture, then season well with salt. Cover with a lid and simmer over low heat for 15–20 minutes, or until most of the water has been absorbed. Meanwhile, cut the cucumber in half, lengthways, remove the seeds with a teaspoon and dice the flesh.
5 When most of the water has been absorbed by the rice, reduce the heat to very low, stir in the prawns, then replace the lid and cook for an additional 5 minutes, or until the rice is tender and the prawns are cooked through. Let the rice stand, covered, for 5 minutes before fluffing with a fork. Discard the lemon grass and lime leaves. Serve sprinkled with the diced cucumber, coriander leaves and crisp fried shallots.

CRYSTAL PRAWNS

Preparation time: 15 minutes +
1 hour marinating
Total cooking time: 10 minutes
Serves 4

12 large raw prawns
2 tablespoons Chinese rice wine
2 tablespoons light soy sauce
½ teaspoon sugar
2 cloves garlic, crushed
1 tablespoon finely chopped spring onion
2 teaspoons finely chopped fresh ginger
1 spring onion, thinly sliced on the diagonal
¼ teaspoon sesame oil

1 Peel and devein the prawns, leaving the tails intact. Put the rice wine, soy sauce, sugar, garlic, chopped spring onion, ginger and 1/4 teaspoon salt in a large heatproof ceramic pie plate that will fit into a large steamer. Stir to dissolve the sugar and salt. Add the prawns, tossing to coat the prawns with the marinade. Cover and refrigerate for 1 hour.
2 Set the plate with the prawns in the steamer and place over a wok of simmering water. Cover and steam for 8–10 minutes. Serve hot with the extra spring onion scattered over the prawns and drizzled with the sesame oil.

WARM PRAWN AND SCALLOP STIR-FRY

Preparation time: 30 minutes +
    10 minutes marinating
Total cooking time: 15 minutes
Serves 4

500 g (1 lb) raw small prawns
300 g (10 oz) scallops
2 teaspoons five-spice powder
1–2 small fresh red chillies, seeded and
    finely chopped
2–3 cloves garlic, crushed
2 tablespoons oil
2 teaspoons sesame oil
200 g (6½ oz) fresh asparagus, cut into
    short lengths
150 g (5 oz) snow peas (mangetout),
    trimmed
125 g (4 oz) rocket leaves, torn into pieces
2 tablespoons light soy sauce
2 tablespoons lemon juice
1 tablespoon mirin
1 tablespoon oil, extra
1 tablespoon honey
6 spring onions, chopped
1 tablespoon chopped fresh coriander
1 tablespoon sesame seeds, lightly
    toasted

1 Peel the prawns, leaving the tails intact.
Gently pull out the dark vein from each
prawn back, starting at the head end.
Slice or pull off any vein, membrane or
hard white muscle from the scallops,
leaving any roe attached.
2 Combine the five-spice powder, chilli,
garlic and oils in a large glass or ceramic
bowl. Add the prawns and scallops and
toss to coat. Cover and refrigerate for at
least 10 minutes.

3 Blanch the asparagus and snow peas
briefly in a pan of boiling water. Drain and
plunge into a bowl of iced water, then
drain again. Arrange the asparagus, snow
peas and rocket on 4 plates.
4 Put the soy sauce, lemon juice, mirin,
extra oil and honey in a small bowl. Stir
to combine.
5 Heat the wok, and stir-fry the prawns,
scallops and spring onion over high heat,
in batches, for 3–4 minutes, or until
cooked through. Remove from the wok
and set aside.
6 Add the sauce and coriander to the wok,
and bring to the boil. Cook over high heat
for 1–2 minutes. Return the seafood to
the wok and toss. Divide among the
serving plates and sprinkle with the
sesame seeds.

STUFFED PRAWN OMELETTES
(KAI YAK SAI)

Preparation time: 25 minutes
Total cooking time: 15 minutes
Makes 8

500 g (1 lb) raw prawns
1½ tablespoons vegetable oil
4 eggs, lightly beaten
2 tablespoons fish sauce
8 spring onions, chopped
6 fresh coriander roots, chopped
2 cloves garlic, chopped
1 small fresh red chilli, seeded and
    chopped, plus extra, to garnish
2 teaspoons lime juice
2 teaspoons grated palm sugar
3 tablespoons chopped fresh coriander
    leaves
fresh coriander sprigs, to garnish
sweet chilli sauce, to serve

1 Peel and devein the prawns, then chop
the prawn meat.
2 Heat a wok over high heat, add
2 teaspoons of the oil and swirl to coat.
Combine the egg with half the fish sauce.
Add 2 tablespoons of the mixture to the
wok and swirl to a 16 cm (6½ inch) round.
Cook for 1 minute, then gently lift out.
Repeat with the remaining egg mixture to
make 8 omelettes.
3 Heat the remaining oil in the wok. Add
the prawns, spring onion, coriander root,
garlic and chilli. Stir-fry for 3–4 minutes,
or until the prawns are cooked. Stir in the
lime juice, palm sugar, coriander and the
remaining fish sauce.
4 Divide the prawn mixture among the
omelettes and fold each into a small firm
parcel. Cut a slit in the top and garnish
with the chilli and coriander. Serve with
sweet chilli sauce.

CHILLI PRAWN AND SNAKE BEAN STIR-FRY

Preparation time: 35 minutes
Total cooking time: 15 minutes
Serves 4

300 g (9⅔ oz) medium raw prawns
250 g (8 oz) snake beans
2 tablespoons oil
2 medium onions, very finely sliced
5 cloves garlic, finely chopped
2 stems lemon grass (white part only), very finely sliced
3 red chillies, seeded and very finely sliced
2 teaspoons sugar
1 tablespoon fish sauce
1 tablespoon rice vinegar
chopped garlic chives, to garnish

1 Peel and devein the prawns. Top and tail the beans and cut them into 2 cm (¾ inch) pieces.
2 Heat the oil in a large heavy-based wok, add the onion, garlic, lemon grass and chilli and stir-fry over moderately high heat for 4 minutes, or until the onion is soft and golden.
3 Add the beans to the wok and stir-fry for 2 to 3 minutes or until they become bright green. Add the prawns and sugar and toss gently for 2 minutes. Add the fish sauce and vinegar, toss well and serve immediately, sprinkled with the garlic chives.

NOTE: The equivalent weight of green beans may be used if snake beans are unavailable.

KING PRAWNS WITH GARLIC BEAN SAUCE

Preparation time: 20 minutes +
    10 minutes marinating
Total cooking time: 10 minutes
Serves 4

1 kg (2 lb) raw medium prawns, peeled and deveined, with tails intact
2 egg whites
2 tablespoons cornflour
2 tablespoons rice vinegar
oil, for deep-frying, plus 1 tablespoon extra
125 g (4 oz) cellophane noodles, broken up into small pieces
4 cloves garlic, finely chopped
1 teaspoon finely chopped fresh ginger
2 teaspoons hoisin sauce
1 tablespoon bean sauce
1 tablespoon oyster sauce
6 spring onions, cut into 3 cm (1¼ inch) lengths on the diagonal
½ cup (15 g/½ oz) fresh coriander leaves
lemon wedges, to serve

1 Put the prawns in a large non-metallic bowl. Process the egg white, cornflour and 1 tablespoon rice vinegar in a food processor until smooth. Pour over the prawns, season with 1 teaspoon each of salt and pepper, and stir. Marinate for 10 minutes, then drain well.
2 Heat a wok over high heat, add the oil and heat to 190°C (375°F), or until a cube of bread dropped into the oil browns in 10 seconds. Add the noodles and cook for 10 seconds, or until puffed up. Drain on crumpled paper towels.
3 Remove all but ¼ cup (60 ml/2 fl oz) oil from the wok, add the drained prawns and cook for 2–3 minutes, or until the prawns change colour. Drain on paper towels. Remove all but 1 tablespoon of the oil from the wok.
4 Reheat the wok over medium heat. Add the garlic and ginger and stir-fry for 30 seconds, then add the hoisin sauce, bean sauce, oyster sauce and the remaining vinegar, and stir well for 1 minute. Add the prawns to the sauce and toss to coat, then add the spring onion and cook for 1–2 minutes, or until soft. Arrange the prawns on a bed of crispy noodles, garnish with the coriander and serve with some lemon wedges on the side.

SUGAR CANE PRAWNS

Preparation time: 30 minutes +
 15 minutes refrigeration
Total cooking time: 10 minutes
Makes 10

1 kg (2 lb) raw medium prawns, peeled,
 deveined and roughly chopped
2 tablespoons chopped fresh coriander
 leaves
2 tablespoons chopped fresh mint
1 stem lemon grass, finely chopped
1 small fresh red chilli, seeded and finely
 chopped
1 clove garlic, crushed
1½ tablespoons fish sauce
2 teaspoons lime juice
½ teaspoon sugar
10 pieces of sugar cane, each 10 cm
 (4 inches) long, 5 mm (¼ inch) wide
lime wedges, to serve

1 Put the prawns and other ingredients
(except the sugar cane and lime wedges)
and ¼ teaspoon salt in a food processor
and process until smooth.
2 Using wetted hands, roll 2 tablespoons
of the mixture into a ball, then mould
around the middle of a sugar cane
skewer, pressing firmly to secure onto
the skewer. Repeat with the remaining
mixture and sugar cane. Refrigerate the
skewers for 15 minutes.
3 Line a bamboo steamer with baking
paper. Place the skewers in a single layer
in the steamer. Cover and steam over a
wok of simmering water for 7–8 minutes,
or until cooked through. 4 Serve the
skewers with lime wedges or with a
dipping sauce made up of sweet chilli
sauce mixed with a little fish sauce.

PRAWN AND PEA NOODLE BASKETS

Preparation time: 40 minutes
Total cooking time: 20–25 minutes
Serves 4

700 g (1 lb 7 oz) raw medium prawns
oil, for deep-frying
200 g (6½ oz) fresh egg noodles
2 spring onions, chopped
1 clove garlic, crushed
½ teaspoon finely grated fresh ginger
½ teaspoon sesame oil
½ teaspoon fish sauce
100 g (3½ oz) green peas, cooked
3 canned water chestnuts, sliced
1 tablespoon chopped fresh mint
2 teaspoons chopped fresh chives
80 g (2¾ oz) snow pea (mangetout)
 sprouts
chive stalks or spring onion greens, to
 garnish

1 Peel the prawns and pull out the dark
vein from each prawn back, starting at the
head end.
2 Fill a deep-fryer or large heavy-based
pan one third full of oil and heat to 180°C
(350°F), or until a noodle dropped into the
oil browns in 8–10 seconds. Before the oil
is too hot, dip 2 wire baskets (see Note),
one slightly smaller than the other, in the
oil, then shake dry. The oil will prevent
the noodles sticking.
3 Separate the noodles; divide into 4
portions. Arrange the first portion inside
the large basket and press the smaller
basket inside to mould the noodles.
Holding the handles firmly together, ease
the baskets into the oil, keeping the
noodles under. Gently twist the top basket
to prevent sticking, tipping from side to
side, and cook the noodles to an even
golden brown. Remove from the baskets,
taking care, as the metal will be hot.
Drain on crumpled paper towels and keep
warm. Repeat with the other noodles.
4 Heat 2 tablespoons of oil in a wok. Stir-
fry the prawns, spring onion, garlic and
ginger over high heat for 2 minutes, or
until the prawns turn pink. Stir in the
sesame oil, fish sauce, peas and water
chestnuts. Remove from the heat and
season, to taste, with salt and pepper. Stir
in the mint, chives and snow pea sprouts.
5 Pile the prawn and pea mixture into the
noodle baskets, garnish and serve.

NOTE: Wire baskets, available at
kitchenware shops, come clipped
together. Otherwise, use a large and a
small metal Asian straining spoon.

PRAWN AND OKRA GUMBO

Preparation time: 35 minutes
Total cooking time: 3 hours
Serves 8

Prawn stock
1 kg (2 lb) raw prawns (shrimp)
1 tablespoon olive oil
1 onion, chopped
1 carrot, chopped
1 celery stalk, chopped
1 bay leaf
2 cloves
3 garlic cloves, bruised
a few parsley stalks
thyme sprig
½ teaspoon black peppercorns

2 tablespoons olive oil
500 g (1 lb) okra, thickly sliced
200 g (6½ oz) chorizo sausage, thickly
    sliced
250 g (8 oz) smoked ham, diced
¼ cup (60 ml/2 fl oz) olive oil, extra
¼ cup (30 g/1 oz) plain (all-purpose) flour
2 onions, chopped
2 celery stalks, diced
1 red capsicum (pepper), diced
6 garlic cloves, finely chopped
½ teaspoon cayenne pepper
2 teaspoons sweet paprika
2 teaspoons mustard powder
large pinch of ground allspice
400 g (13 oz) tomato passata
1 tablespoon tomato paste (purée)
2 teaspoons finely chopped thyme
2 teaspoons finely chopped oregano
2 bay leaves
2½ tablespoons Worcestershire sauce
500 g (1 lb) scallops without roe
12 oysters
3 tablespoons chopped flat-leaf (Italian)
    parsley
cooked long-grain rice, to serve

1 To make the stock, peel the prawns, reserving the shells. Gently pull out the dark vein from each prawn back, starting at the head end. Cover the prawn meat and refrigerate until ready to use. Heat the oil in a large saucepan, add the prawn shells and cook over high heat for about 8 minutes, or until bright orange. Add 2½ litres (80 fl oz) cold water and the remaining stock ingredients and bring to the boil. Reduce the heat to low and simmer for 30 minutes, skimming occasionally, then strain well and set aside—you should have about 2 litres (64 fl oz).
2 Meanwhile, heat the olive oil in a frying pan and sauté the okra over medium heat for 10 minutes, or until slightly softened, then remove the okra from the pan and set aside. Add the chorizo to the pan and cook for about 5 minutes, or until well browned, then set aside. Add the ham to the pan and cook for a few minutes, or until lightly browned.
3 Heat the extra olive oil in a large saucepan, add the flour and stir to combine. Cook, stirring regularly, over medium heat for 30 seconds, or until the roux turns a colour somewhere between milk and dark chocolate, but do not allow to burn.
4 Add the onion, celery, capsicum and garlic to the roux and cook for about 10 minutes, or until softened. Add the cayenne, paprika, mustard and allspice and stir for 1 minute. Add the tomato passata, tomato paste, prawn stock, thyme, oregano, bay leaves, Worcestershire sauce, chorizo and ham and bring to the boil. Reduce the heat to low and simmer for 1 hour, then add the okra and continue cooking for a further hour or until the gumbo is thick and glossy.
5 Add the prawns, scallops and oysters and cook for about 5–8 minutes, or until all the seafood is cooked through. Stir in the parsley and season to taste. Ladle over hot rice in individual bowls and accompany with lemon wedges if desired.

PRAWNS WITH SPICY TAMARIND SAUCE

Preparation time: 15 minutes
Total cooking time: 25 minutes
Serves 4

½ cup (80 g/2¾ oz) raw cashews
2 cloves garlic, finely chopped
1½ tablespoons fish sauce
1 tablespoon sambal oelek
1 tablespoon peanut oil
1 kg (2 lb) raw medium prawns, peeled
    and deveined, with tails intact
2 teaspoons tamarind purée
1½ tablespoons grated palm sugar
350 g (11 oz) choy sum, cut into 10 cm
    (4 inch) lengths

1 Preheat the oven to moderate 180°C (350°F/ Gas 4). Spread the cashews on a baking tray and bake for 5–8 minutes, or until lightly golden—watch carefully, as they will burn easily.
2 Put the garlic, fish sauce, sambal oelek and toasted cashews in a food processor and blend to a rough paste, adding 2–3 tablespoons of water, if needed, to combine the ingredients.
3 Heat a non-stick wok over high heat, add the oil and swirl to coat. Add the prawns, toss for 1–2 minutes, or until starting to turn pink. Remove from the wok. Add the cashew paste and stir-fry for 1 minute, or until it starts to brown slightly. Add the tamarind, sugar and about ⅓ cup (80 ml/2¾ fl oz) water, then bring to the boil, stirring well. Return the prawns to the wok and stir to coat. Cook for 2–3 minutes, or until the prawns are cooked through.
4 Place the choy sum in a paper-lined bamboo steamer and steam over a wok of simmering water for 3 minutes, or until tender. Serve with the prawns and steamed rice, if desired.

PIRI PIRI PRAWNS

Preparation time: 20 minutes +
    3 hours marinating
Total cooking time: 10 minutes
Serves 4

6 tablespoons oil
2 teaspoons dried chilli flakes, or 1–2 red
    bird's eye chillies, finely chopped
4 large cloves garlic, crushed
1 teaspoon salt
1 kg (2 lb) raw medium prawns
75 g (2½ oz) butter
¼ cup (60 ml/2 fl oz) lemon juice

1 Place the oil, chilli flakes, garlic and salt
in a large glass bowl and mix well. Peel
the prawns, leaving the tails intact. Gently
pull the dark vein from each prawn back,
starting at the head end. Stir into the chilli
mixture, cover and refrigerate for 3 hours,
stirring and turning occasionally.
2 Preheat the grill to very hot. Place the
prawns in a single layer on a baking tray
and brush with any of the remaining oil
and chilli mixture. Grill for about 5 minutes,
or until tender.
3 Meanwhile, melt the butter with the
lemon juice in a small pan and pour into a
serving jug. Serve the prawns hot,
drizzled with lemon butter.

GARLIC AND GINGER PRAWNS

Preparation time: 25 minutes
Total cooking time: 10 minutes
Serves 4

1 kg (2 lb) raw large prawns
2 tablespoons oil
3–4 cloves garlic, finely chopped
5 cm (2 inch) piece fresh ginger,
    julienned
2–3 small red chillies, seeded and finely
    chopped
6 fresh coriander roots, finely chopped
8 spring onions, cut diagonally into short
    lengths
½ red pepper (capsicum), thinly sliced
2 tablespoons lemon juice
½ cup (125 ml/4 fl oz) white wine
2 teaspoons grated palm sugar or brown
    sugar
2 teaspoons fish sauce
1 tablespoon fresh coriander leaves, to
    garnish

1 Peel the prawns, leaving the tails intact.
Gently cut a slit down the back of each
prawn and remove the dark vein from
each. Press each prawn out flat.
2 Heat a wok until very hot, add the oil
and swirl it around to coat the side. Stir-
fry half of the prawns, garlic, ginger, chilli
and coriander root for 1–2 minutes over
high heat, or until the prawns have just
turned pink, then remove from the wok.
Repeat with the remaining prawns, garlic,
ginger, chilli and coriander root. Remove
all of the prawns from the wok and set
aside.
3 Add the spring onion and pepper to the
wok. Cook over high heat for 2–3 minutes.
Add the combined lemon juice, wine and
palm sugar. Boil until the liquid has
reduced by two thirds.
4 Return the prawns to the wok and
sprinkle with the fish sauce, to taste.
Toss until the prawns are heated through.
Remove from the heat and serve
sprinkled with coriander leaves.

HONEYED PRAWN AND SCALLOP SKEWERS

Preparation time: 15 minutes +
    3 hours marinating
Total cooking time: 5 minutes
Makes 8

500 g (1 lb) raw medium prawns
250 g (8 oz) scallops

Marinade
¼ cup (60 ml/2 fl oz) honey
2 tablespoons soy sauce
¼ cup (60 ml/2 fl oz) bottled barbecue
    sauce
2 tablespoons sweet sherry

1 Soak 8 wooden skewers in water for
30 minutes, or until they sink. This will
ensure they don't burn during cooking.
2 Meanwhile, peel the prawns, leaving the
tails intact. Gently pull out the dark vein
from each prawn back, starting at the
head end.
3 Slice or pull off any vein, membrane or
hard white muscle from the scallops,
leaving any roe attached.
4 Thread the prawns and scallops
alternately onto the skewers (about
2 prawns and 3 scallops per skewer).
Place in a shallow non-metallic dish.
Combine the honey, soy sauce, barbecue
sauce and sherry in a jug and pour over
the skewers. Cover and marinate in the
refrigerator for 3 hours, or overnight.
5 Preheat the barbecue. Cook the
skewers on a lightly greased barbecue
flatplate, turning several times, for
5 minutes, or until cooked through. Brush
frequently with marinade while cooking.

NOTE: You can substitute cubes of firm-
fleshed fish for the prawns or scallops.

PRAWN RAVIOLI WITH BASIL BUTTER

Preparation time: 30 minutes +
  30 minutes chilling
Total cooking time: 20 minutes
Serves 4

500 g (1 lb) raw medium prawns
1 tablespoon chopped fresh chives
1 egg white, lightly beaten
1⅓ cups (350 ml/11 fl oz) cream
200 g (6½ oz) packet gow gee wrappers
1 egg, lightly beaten

Basil butter
90 g (3 oz) butter
1 clove garlic, crushed
15 g (½ oz) fresh basil leaves, finely
  shredded
40 g (1¼ oz) pine nuts

1 Peel the prawns and gently pull out the dark vein from each prawn back, starting at the head end. Put the prawns in a food processor with the chives and egg white and process until smooth. Season with salt and pepper. Add the cream, being careful not to overprocess or the mixture will curdle. Transfer to a bowl, cover and chill for 30 minutes.
2 Place 2–3 teaspoons of the prawn mixture in the centre of half the gow gee wrappers. Brush the edges with beaten egg, then cover with the remaining wrappers. Press the edges to seal. Add in batches to a large pan of boiling water and cook each batch for 4 minutes. Drain, taking care not to damage the ravioli, and divide among 4 warm serving plates.
3 For the basil butter, melt the butter gently in a pan, add the garlic and stir until fragrant. Add the shredded basil, pine nuts and a little freshly ground black pepper, and cook until the butter turns a nutty brown colour. Drizzle the butter over the pasta. Serve immediately.

NOTE: Buy the gow gee wrappers from Asian food speciality stores.

PRAWN JAMBALAYA

Preparation time: 20 minutes
Total cooking time: 1 hour 10 minutes
Serves 6

1 kg (2 lb) raw large prawns
1 small onion, chopped
2 sticks celery, chopped
1 cup (250 ml/8 fl oz) dry white wine
¼ cup (60 ml/2 fl oz) vegetable oil
200 g (6½ oz) chorizo or spicy sausage,
  chopped
1 onion, extra, chopped
1 red pepper (capsicum), chopped
425 g (14 oz) can crushed tomatoes
½ teaspoon cayenne pepper
½ teaspoon cracked black pepper
¼ teaspoon dried thyme
¼ teaspoon dried oregano
2 cups (400 g/13 oz) long-grain rice

1 Peel the prawns and pull out the dark vein from each prawn back, starting at the head end. Reserve the shells. Refrigerate the prawn meat. Put the heads, shells and tails in a pan with the small onion, 1 chopped stick celery, wine and 1 litre (32 fl oz) water. Bring to the boil, then reduce the heat and simmer for 20 minutes. Strain.
2 Heat the oil in a large heavy-based pan and cook the chopped sausage for 5 minutes, or until browned. Remove from the pan with a slotted spoon and set aside.
3 Add the extra onion, red pepper and remaining celery to the pan and cook, stirring occasionally, for 5 minutes. Add the tomato, cayenne, black pepper and dried herbs and bring to the boil. Reduce the heat and simmer, covered, for 10 minutes.
4 Return the sausage to the pan and add the rice and prawn stock. Bring back to the boil, reduce the heat and simmer, covered, for 25 minutes, until almost all the liquid has been absorbed and the rice is tender.
5 Add the prawns to the pan and stir through gently. Cover and cook for another 5 minutes. Serve immediately.

SPICED PRAWN PAKORAS

Preparation time: 20 minutes
Total cooking time: 10 minutes
Makes 16

¾ cup (85 g/3 oz) besan (chickpea flour)
½ teaspoon baking powder
¼ teaspoon ground turmeric
1 teaspoon ground coriander
½ teaspoon ground cumin
½ teaspoon chilli powder
oil, for deep-frying
1 tablespoon egg white
16 raw medium prawns, peeled and
  deveined, with tails intact

Dipping sauce
1 cup (250 g/8 oz) plain yoghurt
3 tablespoons chopped fresh coriander
  leaves
1 teaspoon ground cumin
garam masala, to sprinkle

1 Sift the besan, baking powder and spices into a large bowl and season with a little salt. Make a well in the centre, gradually add 1 cup (250 ml/ 8 fl oz) water and stir gently until mixed.
2 Fill a wok one-third full of oil and heat to 160°C (315°F), or until a cube of bread dropped in the oil browns in 30–35 seconds. Beat the egg white until firm peaks form, and fold into the batter. Using the tail as a handle, dip the prawns into the batter, then lower gently into the oil.
3 Cook about four prawns at a time, without overcrowding the wok. Cook for 2 minutes, until the batter is lightly golden; it won't become really crisp. Drain on paper towels.
4 To make the dipping sauce, combine the yoghurt, coriander and cumin. Sprinkle with the garam masala. Serve with the prawns.

PRAWNS WITH DILL MAYONNAISE

Preparation time: 15 minutes +
    2 hours marinating
Total cooking time: 10–15 minutes
Serves 4

Marinade
½ cup (125 ml/4 fl oz) olive oil
⅓ cup (80 ml/2¾ fl oz) lemon juice
2 tablespoons wholegrain mustard
2 tablespoons honey
2 tablespoons chopped fresh dill

20 raw large prawns

Dill mayonnaise
¾ cup (185 g/6 oz) whole-egg mayonnaise
2 tablespoons chopped fresh dill
1½ tablespoons lemon juice
1 gherkin, finely chopped
1 teaspoon drained bottled capers,
    chopped
1 clove garlic, crushed

1 For the marinade, combine the olive oil, lemon juice, mustard, honey and fresh dill in a bowl, pour over the unpeeled prawns and coat well. Cover and refrigerate for at least 2 hours, turning occasionally.
2 For the dill mayonnaise, whisk together the mayonnaise, dill, lemon juice, gherkin, capers and garlic in a small bowl, then cover and chill.
3 Lightly oil a heated chargrill pan or barbecue grill or hotplate. Add the drained prawns and cook in batches over high heat for 4 minutes, turning frequently until pink and cooked through. Serve with the dill mayonnaise.

COCONUT PRAWNS WITH CHILLI DRESSING

Preparation time: 35 minutes +
    30 minutes refrigeration
Total cooking time: 30 minutes
Serves 4 as an entrée

24 raw large prawns, peeled and
    deveined, with tails intact
plain flour, to coat
1 egg
1 tablespoon milk
1 cup (60 g/2 oz) shredded coconut
½ cup (25 g/¾ oz) chopped fresh
    coriander leaves
2½ tablespoons vegetable oil
300 g (10 oz) red Asian shallots, chopped
2 cloves garlic, finely chopped
2 teaspoons finely chopped fresh ginger
1 fresh red chilli, seeded and thinly sliced
1 teaspoon ground turmeric
270 ml (9 fl oz) coconut cream
2 kaffir lime leaves, thinly sliced
2 teaspoons lime juice
2 teaspoons palm sugar
3 teaspoons fish sauce
oil, for deep-frying
1 tablespoon chopped fresh coriander
    leaves, extra
150 g (5 oz) mixed lettuce leaves

1 Holding the prawns by their tails, coat them in flour, then dip them into the combined egg and milk and then in the combined coconut and coriander. Refrigerate for 30 minutes.
2 Heat the oil in a saucepan and cook the shallots, garlic, ginger, chilli and turmeric over medium heat for 3–5 minutes, or until fragrant. Add the coconut cream, lime leaves, lime juice, sugar and fish sauce. Bring to the boil, then reduce the heat and simmer for 2–3 minutes, or until thick. Keep warm.
3 Fill a wok one-third full of oil and heat to 170°C (325°F), or until a cube of bread dropped in the oil browns in 20 seconds. Gently lower the prawns into the wok and cook in batches for 3–5 minutes, or until golden. Drain on crumpled paper towels and season with salt.
4 Add the extra coriander to the dressing. Divide the lettuce among four bowls, top with the prawns and drizzle with the dressing.

PICKLED SEAFOOD

ENSURE GLASS STORAGE JARS
ARE CLEAN BY RINSING THEM
WITH BOILING WATER AND
DRYING IN A WARM OVEN. DON'T
USE A TEA TOWEL TO DRY THEM.

PICKLED MUSSELS/SARDINES

Scrub 1 kg (2 lb) black mussels. Remove the hairy beards. Discard any broken mussels or open ones that don't close when tapped on the bench. Place in a large saucepan, cover with water, cover and cook for 4–5 minutes, or until all the mussels have opened. Discard any that do not open. Cool slightly before removing the mussel meat from the shells. Toss the meat in flour, then shallow-fry batches in hot oil, until brown and crisp. Remove and arrange in a single layer in a large non-metallic dish. Combine 2 cups (500 ml/16 fl oz) white wine vinegar, 6 sliced spring onions, 1 finely chopped fresh chilli, 2 bay leaves and 2 teaspoons sugar in a saucepan. Stir over low heat until the sugar dissolves, then boil for 1 minute. Stir in 1 tablespoon chopped fresh mint. Pour over the mussels and refrigerate at least overnight, and up to 5 days, turning once. Serve at room temperature. Serves 4–6. To prepare 12 fresh sardines, gut them, rinse in water, toss in flour and follow the same method.

PICKLED PRAWNS

Peel and devein 40 cooked large prawns, leaving the tails intact. Thinly slice 1 fennel bulb. Put the prawns, fennel, 2 thinly sliced small red onions, and the rind of 2 oranges and 2 limes, cut into thin strips, in a non-metallic container and mix. Mix ⅔ cup (170 ml/5½ fl oz) lime juice, ⅓ cup (80 ml/2¾ fl oz) orange juice, 1 cup (250 ml/8 fl oz) olive oil, ½ cup (125 ml/4 fl oz) tarragon vinegar, 2 finely sliced bird's eye red chillies and 1 teaspoon each of salt and sugar. Pour over the prawn mixture. Cover and refrigerate for at least 2 days, and up to 5 days.
Serves 4–6.

PICKLED OCTOPUS

Clean 1 kg (2 lb) octopus and combine in a pan with 2 bay leaves and 12 black peppercorns. Cover and cook over medium–low heat, in its own liquid, for 1 hour, or until tender. Drain and cool. Put the peppercorns, bay leaves and cooled octopus in a 4 cup (1 litre) clean jar. Add 1 tablespoon fresh oregano leaves, 2 teaspoons fresh thyme and 1 thinly sliced garlic clove. Pour in 1 cup (250 ml/8 fl oz) red wine vinegar and enough olive oil to completely cover the octopus. Seal, then gently turn the jar upside down a couple of times. Refrigerate for at least 2 days, and up to 5 days. Return to room temperature to serve.
Serves 4–6.

ROLLMOPS

Wash 8 herrings. Place your knife behind the gill and fin and cut off the head. Cut along the belly, remove the gut and open the fish out flat. Pinch the bone at the tail end and carefully lift out, pulling the bone towards the head. Remove any small bones with tweezers. Place the butterflied fillets in a large non-metallic dish. Combine 4 cups (1 litre) water with 200 g (6½ oz) salt and stir over medium heat until the salt dissolves. Allow to cool before pouring over the fish. Cover and refrigerate overnight. Meanwhile, prepare the pickling vinegar then allow it to cool. Combine 4 cups (1 litre) white wine vinegar, 2 bay leaves, 1 tablespoon pickling spice (available from most supermarkets) and 5 black peppercorns. Rinse and dry the brined herring fillet and place skin-side-down on a wooden board. Place a thin slice of onion on the centre of each fillet and top with a slice of gherkin. Roll each fillet up from the head end and secure with a toothpick. Pack the rollmops into a 4 cup (1 litre) clean jar, pour the spiced vinegar over and seal. Refrigerate for at least 2 days, and up to 5 days, before serving. Serve with sour cream, onion and pumpernickel.
Serves 4–6.

FROM LEFT: Pickled mussels; Pickled sardines; Pickled prawns; Pickled octopus; Rollmops

RICE NOODLE ROLLS FILLED WITH PRAWNS

Preparation time: 30 minutes + cooling
Total cooking time: 20 minutes
Serves 4

Sauce
½ cup (140 g/4½ oz) sesame paste
⅓ cup (80 ml/2¾ fl oz) light soy sauce
¼ cup (60 ml/2 fl oz) lime juice
¼ cup (45 g/1½ oz) grated palm sugar
1 tablespoon sesame oil

2 tablespoons peanut oil
1 teaspoon sesame oil
4 cloves garlic, finely chopped
5 spring onions, thinly sliced
160 g (5½ oz) garlic chives, cut into 2 cm (¾ inch) lengths
160 g (5½ oz) water chestnuts, thinly sliced
¼ cup (40 g/1¼ oz) sesame seeds, lightly toasted
500 g (1 lb) fresh rice sheet noodles
800 g (1 lb 10 oz) raw small prawns, peeled and deveined
⅓ cup (50 g/1¾ oz) unsalted peanuts, crushed

1 To make the sauce, combine the sesame paste, soy sauce, lime juice, palm sugar and sesame oil in a bowl and stir until the sugar dissolves and the sauce is smooth. Add a tablespoon of water if it appears to be a little too thick.

2 Heat the peanut oil and sesame oil in a frying pan, add the garlic and cook for 1 minute. Add the spring onion and garlic chives and cook for 2 minutes, or until softened. Add the water chestnuts and sesame seeds. Remove from the heat and allow to cool.
3 Unroll the noodle sheets and cut into eight pieces, each 15 x 17 cm (6 x 6½ inches). Put 1 tablespoon of the chive mixture along one long end. Place four prawns, curled up, side-by-side, on top of the chive mixture and roll up the noodle sheet tightly, then carefully sit it on a plate that will fit in the steamer. Repeat with the remaining rolls and filling ingredients. Lay the rolls side-by-side in two layers, with a layer of baking paper in between the rolls to prevent them sticking together.
4 Place the plate in a steamer, cover and steam over a wok of simmering water for 10 minutes, or until the prawns turn opaque and are cooked.
5 Carefully lift the plate out of the steamer with a tea towel and drizzle some of the sauce over the top, and around the rolls, then sprinkle with the peanuts. Serve extra sauce on the side.

TAGLIATELLE WITH PRAWNS AND CREAM

Preparation time: 30 minutes
Total cooking time: 20 minutes
Serves 4

500 g (1 lb) raw medium prawns
500 g (1 lb) fresh tagliatelle
60 g (2 oz) butter
6 spring onions, finely chopped
¼ cup (60 ml/2 fl oz) brandy
1¼ cups (315 ml/10 fl oz) thick (double) cream
1 tablespoon chopped fresh thyme
½ cup (15 g/½ oz) finely chopped fresh flat-leaf parsley
grated Parmesan, for serving

1 Peel the prawns, leaving the tails intact. Gently pull out the dark vein from each prawn back, starting at the head end.
2 Cook the pasta in a large pan of boiling water until al dente. Drain thoroughly.
3 Meanwhile, melt the butter in a large heavy-based pan, add the spring onion and stir for 2 minutes. Add the prawns and stir for 2 minutes, or until the prawns just start to change colour. Remove the prawns from the pan and set aside.
4 Add the brandy to the pan and boil for 2 minutes, or until the brandy is reduced by half. Stir in the cream and add the thyme and half the parsley. Season with freshly ground black pepper. Simmer for 5 minutes, or until the sauce begins to thicken. Return the prawns to the sauce and cook for 2 minutes. Season well.
5 Toss the sauce through the pasta. If you prefer a thinner sauce, add a little hot water or milk. Sprinkle with the remaining fresh parsley and grated Parmesan.

NOTE: You can use sherry or white wine instead of brandy, if preferred.

PRAWN PULAO

Preparation time: 30 minutes
Total cooking time: 25 minutes
Serves 4

200 g (61/2 oz) basmati rice
300 g (10 oz) small prawns (shrimp)
¼ cup (60 ml/2 fl oz) oil
1 onion, finely chopped
3 cm (1¼ inch) piece of cinnamon
6 cardamom pods
5 cloves
4 Indian bay leaves (see Note)
1 stem lemon grass, finely chopped
4 garlic cloves, crushed
5 cm (2 inch) piece of ginger, grated
¼ teaspoon ground turmeric

1 Wash the rice in a sieve under cold running water until the water from the rice runs clear. Drain. Peel and devein the prawns, then wash thoroughly and pat dry with paper towels.
2 Heat the oil in a karhai (Indian wok) or heavy-based frying pan over low heat and fry the onion, cinnamon, cardamom, cloves, bay leaves and lemon grass until the onion is lightly browned. Stir in the garlic, ginger and turmeric. Add the prawns and stir until the prawns turn pinkish. Add the rice and fry over medium heat for 2 minutes. Add 2 cups (500 ml/ 16 fl oz) boiling water and some salt and bring to the boil. Reduce the heat and simmer for about 15 minutes. Remove from the heat, cover tightly with a lid and leave for 10 minutes. Lightly fluff up the rice before serving.

NOTE: Indian bay leaves are the dried leaves of the cassia tree. They look somewhat like European bay leaves but they have a cinnamon flavour. They are available from Indian grocery shops.

BARBECUED PRAWNS WITH SWEET CUCUMBER VINEGAR

Preparation time: 30 minutes
Total cooking time: 5 minutes
Serves 4

¼ cup (60 ml/2 fl oz) white wine vinegar
⅓ cup (90 g/3 oz) caster sugar
2 tablespoons lime juice
2 tablespoons fish sauce
1 long red chilli, seeded, thinly sliced
1 long green chilli, seeded, thinly sliced
2 spring onions, diagonally sliced
1 Lebanese cucumber, peeled, halved, seeded and thinly sliced
2 tablespoons chopped fresh coriander
24 raw prawns

1 Combine the white wine vinegar and caster sugar in a pan and bring to the boil. Stir, remove from the heat and cool. Stir in the lime juice, fish sauce, chilli, spring onion, cucumber and coriander.
2 Cook the unpeeled prawns on a chargrill or barbecue plate over medium heat for 1–2 minutes each side, or until pink and cooked through. Pour the sauce over the prawns.

NOTE: You can also use yabbies for this recipe. They will take a little longer to cook.

SPICY PRAWN MEXICANA

Preparation time: 20 minutes
Total cooking time: 15 minutes
Serves 4

500 g (1 lb) rigatoni
1 tablespoon oil
2 cloves garlic, crushed
2 red chillies, finely chopped
3 spring onions, sliced
750 g (1½ lb) raw prawns, peeled and deveined
300 g (10 oz) hot bottled salsa
1½ cups (375 ml/12 fl oz) cream
2 tablespoons chopped fresh parsley

1 Cook the rigatoni in a large pan of rapidly boiling salted water until al dente. Drain.
2 Heat the oil, add the garlic, chilli and spring onion and cook over medium heat for 2 minutes, or until the garlic is soft and golden.
3 Add the prawns and cook for 5 minutes, or until the prawns are browned. Stir in the salsa and cream and bring to the boil. Reduce the heat and simmer for 3–5 minutes, or until the sauce thickens slightly. Divide the pasta among four plates, top with sauce and garnish with parsley.

PRAWN TORTELLONI

Preparation time: 40 minutes
Total cooking time: 20–30 minutes
Serves 4

300 g (10 oz) raw prawns
20 g (¾ oz) butter
1 clove garlic, crushed
2 spring onions, chopped
125 g (4 oz) ricotta cheese
1 tablespoon chopped fresh basil
200 g (6½ oz) packet gow gee wrappers

Sauce
5 tablespoons olive oil
shells and heads of prawns
1 clove garlic, crushed
2 spring onions, including green part,
    chopped
1 dried chilli, crumbled
1 firm tomato, finely diced, or
    1 tablespoon diced sun-dried tomato

1 Shell the prawns, reserving the heads and shells to flavour the sauce. With a sharp knife, slit down the back of each prawn and discard the vein. Chop the prawns roughly.
2 Heat the butter and gently cook the garlic and spring onion until soft and golden. Allow to cool, mix with the prawns, ricotta and basil and season, to taste. Put a teaspoonful of the mixture on each gow gee wrapper, moisten the edges with water, fold over to form a semi-circle and press firmly to seal. Press the corners together to make a tortelloni shape. For a large circular shape, use more filling and cover with another circle of pasta.

3 To make the sauce, heat 3 tablespoons of the olive oil in a large frying pan. When hot, add the shells and heads of the prawns and toss over high heat until they turn red. Lower the heat and cook for a few minutes, pressing the heads to extract as much flavour as possible. Add ½ cup (125 ml/4 fl oz) of water, cover and cook over low heat for 5 minutes. Remove the shells and heads from the pan using a slotted spoon, pressing out as much of the flavoured oil as possible before discarding them.
4 In another pan, heat the remaining 2 tablespoons of olive oil, add the garlic, spring onion and dried chilli and stir over low heat until the garlic is pale golden. Add the prawn stock and diced tomato and heat through.
5 Bring a large pan of salted water to the boil. Drop the tortelloni into the boiling water and cook for 3–4 minutes. Drain, then add to the sauce and toss so the pasta is well coated.

NOTE: Tortelloni are large tortellini.

PRAWN SAFFRON RISOTTO

Preparation time: 20 minutes
Total cooking time: 40 minutes
Serves 4

¼ teaspoon saffron threads
500 g (1 lb) raw medium prawns
¼ cup (60 ml/2 fl oz) olive oil
2 cloves garlic, crushed
3 tablespoons chopped fresh parsley
¼ cup (60 ml/2 fl oz) dry sherry
¼ cup (60 ml/2 fl oz) white wine
1.5 litres (48 fl oz) fish stock
1 onion, chopped
2 cups (440 g/14 oz) arborio rice

1 Soak the saffron threads in a small bowl with 3 tablespoons hot water. Peel the prawns, leaving the tails intact. Gently pull out the dark vein from each prawn back, starting at the head end.
2 Heat half the olive oil in a medium pan. Add the garlic, parsley and prawns and season with salt and pepper. Cook for 2 minutes, then add the sherry, wine and saffron threads with their liquid. Remove the prawns with a slotted spoon and set aside. Simmer until the liquid has reduced by half. Pour in the fish stock and 1 cup (250 ml/8 fl oz) water, cover and leave to simmer.
3 In a separate large, heavy-based pan, heat the remaining oil. Add the onion and cook for 3 minutes, or until golden. Add the rice and stir over medium heat for 3 minutes.
4 Keep the pan of stock constantly at simmering point. Add ½ cup (125 ml/ 4 fl oz) hot stock to the rice mixture and stir constantly over low heat, with a wooden spoon, until all the liquid has been absorbed. Add ½ cup (125 ml/4 fl oz) stock and repeat the process until all the stock has been added and the rice is tender and creamy—this will take 25–30 minutes. Add the prawns and stir until heated through. Season, to taste, with salt and cracked black pepper and serve immediately.

SALT AND PEPPER PRAWNS

Preparation time: 20 minutes +
   30 minutes refrigeration
Total cooking time: 5 minutes
Serves 4–6

1 egg white
2 cloves garlic, crushed
1 kg (2 lb) raw medium prawns, peeled
   and deveined, with tails intact
1 tablespoon peanut oil
1 long fresh red chilli, sliced on the
   diagonal
½ cup (90 g/3 oz) rice flour
1 tablespoon ground Sichuan
   peppercorns
1 teaspoon ground white pepper
2 teaspoons ground sea salt
1 teaspoon caster sugar
peanut oil, for deep-frying

1 Put the egg white and garlic in a bowl
and mix together before adding the
prawns. Stir to coat the prawns, then
cover with plastic wrap and refrigerate for
30 minutes.
2 Meanwhile, heat the oil in a small frying
pan until hot, add the chilli and cook,
stirring, for 1 minute. Remove from the
pan and drain on paper towels. Put the
rice flour, Sichuan peppercorns, white
pepper, salt and sugar in a bowl and
combine well.
3 Fill a wok one-third full of oil and heat
to 180°C (350°F), or until a cube of bread
dropped into the oil browns in 15 seconds.
Coat each prawn in the flour, shaking off
any excess, and deep-fry in batches for
about 1 minute, or until lightly golden and
cooked through. Drain on crumpled paper
towels, season with salt and pepper and
serve.

PRAWNS IN CHINESE PANCAKES

Preparation time: 20 minutes +
   10 minutes marinating
Total cooking time: 15 minutes
Makes 24

⅓ cup (80 ml/2¾ fl oz) Chinese rice wine
2 tablespoons soy sauce
2 teaspoons sesame oil
24 raw medium prawns, peeled and deveined
2 tablespoons vegetable oil
4 cloves garlic, finely chopped
1 x 4 cm (½ x 1½ inch) piece fresh ginger,
   julienned
120–160 ml (4–5½ fl oz) Chinese plum sauce
2 teaspoons chilli sauce
2 spring onions, finely chopped
24 Chinese pancakes (see Note)
1 small Lebanese cucumber, peeled,
   seeded and cut into thin 5 cm (2 inch)
   long strips
12 garlic chives, cut into 5 cm (2 inch)
   lengths

1 Combine the rice wine, soy sauce and
sesame oil in a large non-metallic bowl. Add
the prawns and marinate for 10 minutes.
2 Heat a wok over high heat, add the
vegetable oil and swirl to coat the side of
the wok. Add the garlic and ginger and
stir-fry for 1–2 minutes. Use a slotted
spoon or tongs to remove the prawns
from the marinade and add them to the
wok, reserving the marinade. Stir-fry the
prawns for 2 minutes, or until they start
to turn pink, then add the plum sauce,
chilli sauce and the reserved marinade.
3 Stir-fry for 2–3 minutes, or until the
prawns are cooked, curled and slightly
glazed. Remove from the heat and stir in
the spring onion.
4 Heat the pancakes in a non-stick frying
pan over medium heat for 1 minute, or
until warm.
5 To assemble, put a prawn, a few slices
of cucumber and a few chive pieces on
each pancake, spoon on some sauce, then
fold over.

TEMPURA PRAWNS

Preparation time: 25 minutes
Total cooking time: 10 minutes
Serves 4

12 raw large prawns
oil, for deep-frying
1 egg
1 cup (250 ml/8 fl oz) iced water
1 cup (125 g/4 oz) tempura flour, sifted
2 ice cubes
1 sheet roasted nori, shredded

1 Peel and devein the prawns, keeping the
tails intact. Using a sharp knife, make
three or four diagonal cuts in the
underside of each prawn one-third of the
way through. Pat the prawns dry with
paper towels.
2 Fill a wok one-third full of oil and heat
to 180°C (350°F), or until a cube of bread
browns in 15 seconds. While the oil is
heating, put the egg in a large bowl and,
using chopsticks or a fork, break it up.
Add the iced water and mix well with
chopsticks. Add the sifted flour all at once
and mix with chopsticks until just
combined, then add the ice cubes—the
mixture should be lumpy. Dip the prawns
in the batter and deep-fry in batches, four
at a time, drizzling with some of the
remaining batter to give a spiky effect.
Cook for 1 minute, or until crisp.
3 Drain the prawns on crumpled paper
towels, sprinkle with the nori and serve
immediately.

BARBECUED PRAWNS WITH ROMESCO SAUCE

Preparation time: 30 minutes +
    30 minutes refrigeration + 15 minutes
    cooling
Total cooking time: 25 minutes
Serves 6–8

30 raw large prawns

Romesco sauce
4 cloves garlic, unpeeled
1 Roma tomato, halved and seeded
2 long fresh red chillies
¼ cup (35 g/1¼ oz) blanched almonds
60 g (2 oz) sun-dried peppers
    (capsicums) in oil
1 tablespoon olive oil
1 tablespoon red wine vinegar

1 Peel the prawns, leaving the tails intact. Gently pull out the dark vein from each prawn back, starting at the head end. Mix with ¼ teaspoon salt and refrigerate for 30 minutes.
2 For the Romesco sauce, preheat the oven to moderately hot 200°C (400°F/ Gas 6). Wrap the garlic in foil, place on a baking tray with the tomato and chillies and bake for 12 minutes. Spread the almonds on the tray and bake for another 3–5 minutes. Leave to cool for 15 minutes.
3 Transfer the almonds to a small blender or food processor and blend until finely ground. Squeeze the garlic and scrape the tomato flesh into the blender, discarding the skins. Split the chillies and remove the seeds. Scrape the flesh into the blender, discarding the skins. Pat the peppers dry with paper towels, then chop them and add to the blender with the oil, vinegar, some salt and 2 tablespoons water. Blend until smooth, adding more water, if necessary, to form a soft dipping consistency. Preheat a grill or lightly oiled barbecue.
4 Brush the prawns with a little oil and cook for 3 minutes, or until curled up and changed colour. Serve with the sauce.

PRAWN PURLOO

Preparation time: 20 minutes
Total cooking time: 55 minutes
Serves 4–6

1 tablespoon olive oil
3 streaky bacon rashers, chopped
1 onion, finely chopped
1 celery stalk, finely chopped
1 red capsicum (pepper), finely diced
1 bay leaf
1½ teaspoons finely chopped thyme
40 g (1¼ oz) butter
2 cups (400 g/13 oz) long-grain rice
3 cups (750 ml/24 fl oz) chicken stock
1½ tablespoons Worcestershire sauce
1 kg (2 lb) raw prawns (shrimp), peeled
    and deveined
2 tablespoons chopped flat-leaf (Italian)
    parsley
2 spring onions (scallions), finely
    chopped
Tabasco sauce, to serve
lemon wedges, to serve

1 Heat 1 teaspoon of the oil in a large, deep frying pan, add the bacon and cook for 5 minutes over medium heat, or until slightly crispy, then remove from the pan. Heat the remaining oil in the pan, then sauté the onion, celery, capsicum, bay leaf and thyme for about 5 minutes, or until softened and just starting to brown. Remove from the pan.

2 Add the butter to the pan and allow to melt. Add the rice and cook, stirring, for 4 minutes, or until the rice is lightly golden. Return the vegetables and bacon to the pan, stir to combine, then stir in 1 cup (250 ml/8 fl oz) of the stock and keep stirring for 3 minutes, or until the liquid has absorbed. Repeat with another cup of stock. Add the final cup of stock with the Worcestershire sauce, then cover. Reduce the heat to low and cook for about 15 minutes, then quickly stir in the prawns, re-cover and cook for a further 3 minutes, or until prawns are pink and curled.
3 Remove the pan from the heat, allow to sit for a couple of minutes, then stir in the parsley and spring onion and season to taste. Serve with Tabasco and lemon wedges.

NOTE: Purloo is a southern American term for pilaff. It is also known as perlieu, perlo, perlu and perloo.

GREEK PRAWN AND FETTA BAKE

Preparation time: 20 minutes
Total cooking time: 50 minutes
Serves 6–8

2 tablespoons extra virgin olive oil
1 red onion, chopped
3 garlic cloves, crushed
1 teaspoon ground cumin
3 tablespoons chopped oregano
2 tablespoons red wine vinegar
3 cups (660 g/1 lb 5½ oz) risotto rice
2 x 400 g (13 oz) tins chopped tomatoes
1½ tablespoons tomato paste (purée)
¼ cup (35 g/1¼ oz) currants
1 litre (32 fl oz) chicken stock
1 kg (2 lb) raw prawns (shrimp), peeled and deveined, tails intact
250 g (8 oz) fetta, crumbled

1 Preheat the oven to moderately hot 200°C (400°F/Gas 6). Lightly grease a 30 x 23 cm (12 x 9 inch) ovenproof dish.
2 Heat the oil in a large heavy-based frying pan, add the onion and cook over medium heat until softened but not browned. Add the garlic, cumin and 1 tablespoon of the oregano. Pour in the vinegar, cook for a further minute, then add the rice, stirring to coat. Add the tomatoes, tomato paste, currants and stock and season. Bring to the boil and pour into the ovenproof dish. Cover with foil and bake for 30 minutes, or until the rice is soft.
3 Add the prawns, poking them in under the rice, then sprinkle with fetta and the remaining oregano, and bake for a further 10 minutes. Serve with a salad.

CARAMELIZED PRAWNS

Preparation time: 25 minutes
Total cooking time: 15 minutes
Serves 4

500 g (1 lb) raw medium prawns
6 spring onions
4 tablespoons sugar
1 tablespoon oil
3 cloves garlic, finely chopped
1 tablespoon fish sauce
1 tablespoon lime juice
1 tablespoon soft brown sugar
½ teaspoon salt
¼ red pepper (capsicum), cut into fine strips

1 Remove the prawn heads but leave the tails, shells and legs intact. Make a small cut in the base of the prawns, three-quarters of the way along. Using a fine needle, lift out the dark veins. Rinse the prawns under running water and pat dry with paper towels.
2 Finely chop half the spring onions. Cut the rest into 4 cm (1½ inch) pieces and finely shred into thin strips.
3 For the caramel sauce, combine the sugar with 3 tablespoons of water in a small pan. Stir over low heat, without boiling, until the sugar has dissolved. Bring to the boil, reduce the heat and simmer gently, without stirring, for 5 minutes, or until the syrup turns dark golden. Take care not to burn it. Remove the pan from the heat and add 4 tablespoons of water—it will spit and sizzle, and the caramel will form hard lumps. Return the pan to low heat and stir until the lumps have dissolved.

4 Heat the oil in a heavy-based frying pan over medium heat. Add the garlic and chopped spring onion. Add the prawns in batches and cook for 3 minutes, tossing the prawns until they turn pink. Drizzle the caramel sauce and fish sauce over the top and continue to cook for 1 minute. Add the lime juice, sugar, salt and the remaining spring onion, then toss well. Serve immediately, garnished with the strips of red pepper.

NOTE: If the prawn shells are tender, they can be eaten. Supply finger bowls and napkins, so people can peel them if they prefer.

SEARED SCALLOPS WITH CHILLI BEAN PASTE

Preparation time: 20 minutes
Total cooking time: 15 minutes
Serves 4

500 g (1 lb) Hokkien noodles
¼ cup (60 ml/2 fl oz) peanut oil
20 scallops, without roe
1 large onion, cut into thin wedges
3 cloves garlic, crushed
1 tablespoon grated fresh ginger
1 tablespoon chilli bean paste
150 g (5 oz) choy sum, cut into 5 cm
   (2 inch) lengths
¼ cup (60 ml/2 fl oz) chicken stock
2 tablespoons light soy sauce
2 tablespoons kecap manis
½ cup (15 g/½ oz) fresh coriander leaves
1 cup (90 g/3 oz) bean sprouts, washed
1 large fresh red chilli, seeded and thinly
   sliced
1 teaspoon sesame oil
1 tablespoon Chinese rice wine

1 Put the noodles in a heatproof bowl, cover with boiling water and soak for 1 minute to separate. Drain, rinse, then drain again.
2 Heat a wok over high heat, add 2 tablespoons of the peanut oil and swirl to coat the side of the wok. Add the scallops in batches and sear for 20 seconds on each side, or until sealed. Remove, then wipe the wok clean. Add the remaining peanut oil to the wok and swirl to coat. Stir-fry the onion for 1–2 minutes, or until softened. Add the garlic and ginger and cook for 30 seconds. Stir in the chilli bean paste and cook for 1 minute, or until fragrant.
3 Add the choy sum to the wok with the noodles, stock, soy sauce and kecap manis. Stir-fry for 4 minutes, or until the choy sum has wilted and the noodles have absorbed most of the liquid. Return the scallops to the wok, add the coriander, bean sprouts, chilli, sesame oil and rice wine, tossing gently until combined.

SCALLOP TIMBALES WITH OYSTER CREAM SAUCE

Preparation time: 20 minutes
Total cooking time: 35 minutes
Serves 6

400 g (13 oz) scallops
200 g (6½ oz) skinless white fish fillets
   (eg. snapper, bream, pike, flathead)
2 egg whites
1 teaspoon grated lemon rind
¾ cup (185 ml/6 fl oz) cream

Oyster cream sauce
15 g (½ oz) butter
½ carrot, very finely diced
½ stick celery, very finely diced
2 spring onions, finely chopped
1 bay leaf
¼ cup (60 ml/2 fl oz) white wine
½ cup (125 ml/4 fl oz) fish stock
½ cup (125 ml/4 fl oz) cream
1 teaspoon butter
1 teaspoon flour
18 fresh oysters, removed from the shells
2 tablespoons sour cream
1 teaspoon chopped fresh dill

1 Slice or pull off any vein, membrane or hard white mussel from the scallops. Process the scallops and fish in a food processor until smooth. Add the egg whites, rind and salt and white pepper, and process until combined. Pour in the cream and process quickly until only just combined. Do not overprocess or the mixture will curdle. To test for seasoning, poach a small amount of mixture in simmering water.

2 Preheat the oven to warm 170°C (325°F/ Gas 3). Lightly oil six ½ cup (125 ml/4 fl oz) capacity timbales. Spoon the scallop mixture into each mould, tapping firmly on a work surface to remove any air bubbles, then cover the tops loosely with lightly greased foil. Place in a baking tray and add boiling water to come halfway up the sides of the moulds. Bake for 15–20 minutes, or until cooked through. A knife inserted into the centre of the scallop mixture should come out clean.
3 While the timbales are cooking, prepare the oyster cream sauce. Melt the butter in a small saucepan, add the vegetables and bay leaf and stir for 5 minutes, until softened but not brown. Add the wine and simmer for 1 minute. Add the fish stock and cream, bring to the boil, reduce the heat and simmer for 5 minutes. Blend the butter and flour into a paste, add to the pan and whisk until the sauce boils and thickens. Stir in the oysters and any of their juices, the sour cream, dill and salt and cracked black pepper, to taste.
4 Drain off any liquid and turn the moulds out onto serving plates. Spoon some of the sauce over each timbale.

SCALLOPS EN BROCHETTE

Preparation time: 15 minutes +
  30 minutes soaking skewers
Total cooking time: 10 minutes
Serves 6

36 scallops
8–10 slices prosciutto
8–10 spring onions
60 g (2 oz) butter, melted
1 clove garlic, crushed
2 tablespoons lime juice
lime slices or wedges, for serving

1 If using wooden skewers, soak them in cold water for 30 minutes to prevent them burning during cooking.
2 Slice or pull off any vein, membrane or hard white muscle from the scallops, leaving the roe attached. Cut each slice of prosciutto into 3 pieces (this may depend on the size of the scallop) and gently wrap a piece of prosciutto around each scallop. Cut the spring onions into short lengths. Thread them onto skewers, alternating 3 scallops and 3 pieces of spring onion on each skewer.
3 Place on a preheated grill or barbecue and cook for 3–5 minutes each side, or until the prosciutto is lightly browned and the scallops are just cooked through. Brush occasionally with the combined melted butter, garlic and lime juice. Serve with any remaining warm butter mixture and lime slices.

JAPANESE CRUMBED PRAWNS WITH PONZU

Preparation time: 15 minutes
Total cooking time: 10 minutes
Makes 18

18 raw large prawns
2 tablespoons cornflour
3 eggs
2 cups (120 g/4 oz) Japanese
  breadcrumbs (panko)
peanut oil, for deep-frying
⅓ cup (80 ml/2¾ fl oz) ponzu sauce (see
  Note)

1 Peel and devein the prawns, leaving the tails intact. Cut down the back of each prawn to form a butterfly, then place between two layers of plastic wrap and beat gently to form a cutlet.
2 Put the cornflour, eggs and breadcrumbs in separate bowls. Lightly beat the eggs. Dip each prawn first into the cornflour, then into the egg and finally into the breadcrumbs, ensuring that each cutlet is well covered in crumbs.
3 Fill a wok one-third full of oil, and heat it to 180°C (350°F), or until a cube of bread browns in 15 seconds. Cook six prawn cutlets at a time for about 1 minute each side, or until the crumbs are golden—be careful they don't burn. Serve immediately with ponzu sauce.

NOTE: If ponzu isn't available, mix ¼ cup (60 ml/ 2 fl oz) soy sauce with 1 tablespoon lemon juice.

SCALLOP AND SNOW PEA (MANGETOUT) SPROUT DUMPLINGS

Preparation time: 30 minutes +
  4 hours refrigeration
Total cooking time: 10 minutes
Makes 24

½ teaspoon baking soda
250 g (8 oz) snow pea (mangetout)
  sprouts, washed, dried and cut into
  1 cm (½ inch) pieces
250 g (8 oz) scallop meat, white part only
1 teaspoon finely grated fresh ginger
1½ tablespoons oyster sauce
1 teaspoon light soy sauce
1 teaspoon Chinese rice wine
½ teaspoon sesame oil
1½ teaspoons sugar
1 teaspoon cornflour
1 egg white
24 gow gee wrappers

1 Bring a saucepan of salted water to the boil, add the baking soda and the snow pea sprouts and blanch for 10 seconds. Drain and refresh under cold water. Drain thoroughly until dry.
2 Put the scallops in a food processor with the ginger, oyster sauce, soy sauce, Chinese rice wine, sesame oil, sugar, cornflour, egg white and ¼ teaspoon salt and blend until smooth and evenly mixed. Transfer to a bowl, cover and refrigerate for 4 hours. Add the snow pea sprouts, and mix thoroughly.
3 Place 2 teaspoons of the filling in the centre of each gow gee wrapper, wet the edges and gather together to cover the filling, then squeeze shut, making a round bundle. Break off any surplus dough. Line a double bamboo steamer with baking paper. Place the dumplings in the steamer in a single layer, seam-side-down. Cover and steam over a wok of simmering water for 8 minutes, or until cooked through.

CREAMY SCALLOPS

Preparation time: 30 minutes
Total cooking time: 20 minutes
Serves 4

500 g (1 lb) scallops
60 g (2 oz) butter
6 spring onions, white part only, chopped
¾ cup (185 ml/6 fl oz) dry white wine
2 tablespoons plain flour
1 egg yolk
½ cup (125 ml/4 fl oz) cream

1 Slice or pull off any vein, membrane or hard white muscle from the scallops, leaving any roe attached. Heat half the butter in a pan, add the spring onion and cook until soft. Add the scallops; fry until lightly coloured. Add the wine, salt and white pepper, and water to just cover. Bring to the boil, reduce the heat and cook over low heat for 2–3 minutes, until the scallops are tender.
2 Drain the scallops, reserving the cooking liquid, and divide the scallops among 4 shallow flameproof serving dishes. Keep warm.
3 Melt the remaining butter in a small pan over low heat. Stir in the flour for 2 minutes, or until pale and foaming. Remove from the heat and gradually pour in the strained reserved liquid. Return to the heat and stir constantly until the mixture boils and thickens. Reduce the heat and simmer for 2 minutes. Season, to taste.
4 Preheat a grill. Beat the egg yolk lightly with a fork in a bowl and pour on 2 tablespoons hot sauce, whisking constantly. Return the egg yolk mixture to the saucepan and stir until just heated through. Remove from the heat and add the cream very carefully. Pour the sauce over the scallops and grill until lightly browned.

LEMON GRASS AND LIME SCALLOP PASTA

Preparation time: 20 minutes
Total cooking time: 15 minutes
Serves 4

500 g (1 lb) spaghetti or chilli fettucine
1 tablespoon oil
1 onion, sliced
2 tablespoons finely chopped lemon grass
500 g (1 lb) scallops
1 cup (250 ml/8 fl oz) coconut milk
2 kaffir lime leaves, finely shredded
½ cup (15 g/½ oz) coriander leaves

1 Cook the pasta in rapidly boiling salted water until al dente. Drain.
2 Meanwhile, heat the oil in a large heavy-based frying pan, add the onion and lemon grass and cook over medium heat for 5 minutes, or until the onion is soft. Add the scallops in batches and cook until tender and lightly browned. Remove and keep warm.
3 Add the coconut milk and kaffir lime leaves to the pan and simmer for 5 minutes, or until the sauce thickens slightly.
4 Return the scallops to the pan and cook until heated through. Toss the pasta through the sauce with the coriander leaves. Season, to taste, with salt and pepper.

SCALLOPS WITH SOY, GINGER AND SPRING ONION

Preparation time: 5 minutes +
    10 minutes marinating
Total cooking time: 15 minutes
Serves 4–6

24 scallops in their shells
3 teaspoons light soy sauce
3 teaspoons Chinese rice wine
1 tablespoon chicken stock or water
3 spring onions, shredded
1½ tablespoons julienned fresh ginger
½–1 tablespoon light soy sauce
½ teaspoon sugar (optional)

1 To prepare the scallops, pull off the roe and any vein, membrane or hard white muscle. Remove the scallops from their shells. Rinse and dry the shells and set aside.
2 Combine the soy sauce and rice wine in a non-metallic bowl with the scallop meat, and marinate for 10 minutes.
3 Line a bamboo steamer with baking paper. Arrange six of the shells in a single layer on top, then return a scallop to each shell. Combine the marinade with the chicken stock, then drizzle some over the scallops. Sprinkle with some of the spring onion and ginger. Cover and steam over a wok of simmering water for 2–3 minutes, or until just cooked, being careful not to overcook them. Repeat with the remaining scallops.
4 Serve with some of the soy sauce (dissolve the sugar in the sauce, if using) drizzled over the top and the remainder for dipping, if desired.

STEAMED SCALLOPS

Preparation time: 20 minutes
Total cooking time: 10 minutes
Serves 4

1 small red pepper (capsicum)
90 g (3 oz) butter
1 tablespoon chopped fresh chives
2 teaspoons Dijon mustard
¼ teaspoon cracked black pepper
2 teaspoons lime juice
24 scallops on the shell
6 spring onions, cut into long thin strips

1 Cut the red pepper into quarters and remove the seeds and membrane. Cook, skin-side-up, under a hot grill until the skin blackens and blisters. Cool in a plastic bag, then peel. Purée the flesh until smooth.
2 Beat the butter in a small bowl until light, then beat in the chives, mustard, pepper, lime juice and red pepper purée. Set aside.
3 Remove the scallops and slice or pull off any vein, membrane or hard white mussel from each. Place a few strips of spring onion over each shell and top with the scallop. Place the scallops in a single layer in a bamboo or metal steamer. Place over a large pan of simmering water and steam in batches for 2–3 minutes. Transfer to a warmed serving platter while cooking the remaining scallops. Top with a dollop of butter. The butter will melt from the heat of the scallops. Serve.

MUSSELS MASALA

Preparation time: 40 minutes
Total cooking time: 20 minutes
Serves 6

Curry paste
1 teaspoon grated fresh ginger
1 stem lemon grass, white part only, finely chopped
3 cloves garlic, crushed
3 fresh green chillies, finely chopped
2 teaspoons garam masala
1 teaspoon ground cumin
2 tablespoons chopped fresh coriander stems
1 tablespoon tomato paste (tomato purée)
1/3 cup (80 ml/23/4 fl oz) lemon juice
1 tablespoon vegetable oil

1.5 kg (3 lb) black mussels
1 tablespoon ghee
1 large red onion, sliced
4 tablespoons chopped fresh coriander leaves

1 To make the curry paste, put the ginger, lemon grass, garlic, chilli, garam masala, cumin, coriander stems and tomato paste in a food processor or blender, and grind until smooth. With the motor running, gradually pour in the lemon juice and oil until the mixture forms a smooth paste.

2 Thoroughly scrub the mussels with a stiff brush to remove any grit or weed from the shell. Pull out the hairy beards. Discard any broken mussels or open ones that don't close when tapped lightly on the bench. Rinse well under cold running water.
3 Heat the ghee in a wok. Add the onion and cook for 5 minutes, or until it has softened. Stir in the curry paste and cook for 2 minutes, or until fragrant. Add 21/2 cups (625 ml/20 fl oz) water, bring to the boil, then reduce the heat and simmer. Add the mussels and cook for 5 minutes, or until they open. Remove the mussels from the wok as soon as they open, transfer to a plate and keep warm. Discard any mussels that do not open.
4 Continue to boil the liquid for 5 minutes, or until it has reduced and thickened slightly. Stir in the coriander.
5 Place the mussels in a serving bowl, then pour the sauce over them and serve with steamed rice to soak up the juices.

NOODLES WITH SEAFOOD AND DRIED SCALLOPS

Preparation time: 25 minutes +
    10 minutes soaking
Total cooking time: 40 minutes
Serves 4

4 dried scallops
12 prawns (shrimp)
200 g (6½ oz) squid tubes
400 g (13 oz) thin rice stick noodles
1 tablespoon oil
2 tablespoons shredded ginger
2 spring onions (scallions), thinly sliced
150 g (5 oz) Chinese cabbage (wom bok),
    finely shredded
1 cup (250 ml/8 fl oz) chicken stock
2 tablespoons light soy sauce
2 tablespoons Chinese rice wine
1 teaspoon roasted sesame oil

1 Put the dried scallops in a heatproof bowl with 1 tablespoon water and put them in a steamer. Cover and steam over simmering water in a wok for 30 minutes, or until they are completely tender. Remove the scallops and shred the meat.
2 Peel the prawns and cut them in half through the back, removing the vein.
3 Open up the squid tubes by cutting down one side, scrub off any soft jelly-like substance, then score the inside of the flesh with a fine crisscross pattern, making sure you do not cut all the way through. Cut the squid into 3 x 5 cm (1¼ x 2 inch) pieces.
4 Soak the noodles in hot water for 10 minutes, then drain.
5 Heat a wok over high heat, add the oil and heat until very hot. Stir-fry the ginger and spring onion for 1 minute, then add the prawns and squid and stir-fry until just opaque. Add the scallops and Chinese cabbage and toss together. Pour in the stock, soy sauce and rice wine and boil for 1 minute. Add the noodles and sesame oil, toss together and serve.

MUSSELS IN TWO SAUCES

Preparation time: 25 minutes
Total cooking time: 45 minutes
Serves 4

1.25 kg (2½ lb) black mussels
3 tablespoons olive oil
3 tablespoons grated mozzarella
2 tablespoons grated Parmesan

Tomato sauce
2 cloves garlic, crushed
½ cup (125 ml/4 fl oz) white wine
3 tablespoons tomato paste (tomato purée)

White sauce
25 g (3/4 oz) butter
¼ cup (30 g/1 oz) plain flour
1 cup (250 ml/8 fl oz) milk

1 Scrub the mussels with a stiff brush and pull out the hairy beards. Discard any broken mussels or open ones that don't close when tapped on the bench. Rinse well.
2 Heat half the oil in a large pan. Add the mussels and cook over high heat, shaking the pan, for 4–5 minutes until opened. Discard any unopened mussels. Strain the liquid and reserve. Allow the mussels to cool, then remove from their shells and discard the shells. Preheat the oven to moderately hot 190°C (375°F/Gas 5).
3 For the tomato sauce, heat the remaining oil in a pan. Add the garlic and fry over medium heat until golden. Add the wine and reserved mussel liquid, bring to the boil, reduce the heat and simmer gently for 4–5 minutes. Blend the tomato paste with 3 tablespoons water, then whisk into the simmering liquid. Simmer for another 10 minutes and season, to taste. Remove from the heat.
4 For the white sauce, melt the butter in a pan over low heat. Stir in the flour and cook for 1 minute, or until pale and foaming. Remove from the heat and gradually stir in the milk. Return to the heat and stir constantly until the sauce boils and thickens. Reduce the heat and simmer for 2 minutes. Season, to taste.
5 Combine the tomato sauce and mussels and spoon into four 1-cup (250 ml/8 fl oz) ovenproof ramekins. Carefully spoon the white sauce over the top and sprinkle with the combined cheeses. Bake for 20 minutes, or until the cheese has melted and the tops are golden brown. Serve with crusty bread.

SPAGHETTI WITH CREAMY GARLIC MUSSELS

Preparation time: 20 minutes
Total cooking time: 10–15 minutes
Serves 4

500 g (1 lb) spaghetti
1.5 kg (3 lb) fresh mussels
2 tablespoons olive oil
2 cloves garlic, crushed
½ cup (125 ml/4 fl oz) white wine
1 cup (250 ml/8 fl oz) cream
2 tablespoons chopped fresh basil

1 Cook the spaghetti in a large pan of rapidly boiling salted water until al dente. Drain.
2 While the spaghetti is cooking, remove the beards from the mussels and scrub away any grit. Discard any open mussels. Set aside. Heat the oil in a large pan. Add the garlic and stir over low heat for 30 seconds.
3 Add the wine and mussels. Simmer, covered, for 5 minutes. Remove the mussels, discarding any that don't open, and set aside.
4 Add the cream, basil and salt and pepper, to taste, to the pan. Simmer for 2 minutes, stirring occasionally. Serve the sauce and mussels over the spaghetti.

MUSSELS WITH LEMON GRASS, BASIL AND WINE

Preparation time: 30 minutes
Total cooking time: 15 minutes
Serves 4–6

1 kg (2 lb) small black mussels
1 tablespoon oil
1 onion, chopped
4 cloves garlic, chopped
2 stems lemon grass, white part only, sliced
1–2 fresh red chillies, seeded, chopped
1 cup (250 ml/8 fl oz) white wine or water
1 tablespoon fish sauce
1 cup (50 g/1¾ oz) fresh Thai basil leaves, roughly chopped

1 Scrub the mussels with a stiff brush and pull out the hairy beards. Discard any broken mussels, or open ones that don't close when tapped on the bench. Rinse well.
2 Heat the oil in a large pan. Add the onion, garlic, lemon grass and chilli, and cook for 4 minutes over low heat, stirring occasionally. Add the wine and fish sauce and continue to cook for 3 minutes.
3 Add the mussels to the pan and toss well. Cover, increase the heat and cook for 4–5 minutes, or until the mussels open. Discard any unopened mussels. Add the basil; toss and serve with rice.

MUSSELS SAGANAKI

Preparation time: 45 minutes
Total cooking time: 25 minutes
Serves 6

750 g (11/2 lb) black mussels
½ cup (125 ml/4 fl oz) dry white wine
3 sprigs of fresh thyme
1 bay leaf
1 tablespoon olive oil
1 large onion, finely chopped
1 clove garlic, finely chopped
420 g (14 oz) ripe tomatoes, peeled and very finely chopped
2 tablespoons tomato paste (tomato purée)
½ teaspoon sugar
1 tablespoon red wine vinegar
70 g (2¼ oz) Greek feta, crumbled
1 teaspoon fresh thyme leaves

1 Scrub the mussels with a stiff brush and pull out the hairy beards. Discard any broken mussels, or open ones that don't close when tapped on the bench. Rinse well.
2 Bring the wine, thyme and bay leaf to the boil in a large pan, add the mussels and cook for 4–5 minutes, or until just opened. Pour the mussel liquid through a strainer into a heatproof jug and reserve. Discard any unopened mussels. Remove the top half shell from each mussel and discard.
3 Heat the oil in a saucepan, add the onion and stir over medium heat for 3 minutes. Add the garlic and cook for 1 minute, or until turning golden. Pour in the reserved mussel liquid, increase the heat and bring to the boil, then boil for 2 minutes, or until almost dry. Add the tomato, tomato paste and sugar, then reduce the heat and simmer for 5 minutes. Add the vinegar and simmer for another 5 minutes.
4 Add the mussels to the saucepan and cook over medium heat for 1 minute, or until heated through. Spoon into a warm serving dish. Top with the crumbled feta and fresh thyme leaves. Serve hot.

STEAMED MUSSELS WITH LEMON GRASS AND GINGER

Preparation time: 15 minutes
Total cooking time: 10 minutes
Serves 4

2 kg (4 lb) black mussels
1 tablespoon fish sauce
2 cloves garlic, crushed
4 small red Asian shallots, thinly sliced
1 tablespoon finely shredded fresh ginger
2 bird's eye chillies, seeded and thinly sliced
2 stems lemon grass, white part only, bruised and cut into 5 cm (2 inch) lengths
4 fresh kaffir lime leaves
1 tablespoon lime juice
1 lime, cut into wedges (optional)

1 Scrub the mussels with a stiff brush and pull out the hairy beards. Discard any broken mussels or open ones that don't close when tapped on the bench. Rinse well.
2 Pour the fish sauce and ½ cup (125 ml/ 4 fl oz) water into a wok and bring to the boil. Add half the mussels and scatter with half the garlic, shallots, ginger, chilli, lemon grass and lime leaves. Cover and steam over high heat for 2–3 minutes, shaking the wok frequently, until the mussels have just opened. Remove the mussels with a slotted spoon, discarding any that have not opened. Repeat with the remaining mussels and aromatics (you do not need to add more water or fish stock to the wok at this stage). Transfer the mussels to a large serving bowl, leaving the cooking liquid in the wok.
3 Add the lime juice to the wok and season to taste with salt and pepper. Pour the liquid and all the aromatics over the mussels and serve with the lime wedges, if desired.

SCALLOPS PROVENCALE

Preparation time: 20 minutes
Total cooking time: 30 minutes
Serves 4 as a starter

600 g (1¼ lb) ripe tomatoes
3 tablespoons olive oil
1 onion, finely chopped
4 French shallots, finely chopped
¼ cup (60 ml/2 fl oz) dry white wine
60 g (2 oz) butter
20 fresh scallops, cleaned and dried, with shells
4 cloves garlic, crushed
2 tablespoons finely chopped fresh parsley
½ teaspoon fresh thyme leaves
2 tablespoons fresh breadcrumbs

1 Score a cross in the base of each tomato. Place the tomatoes in boiling water for 10 seconds, then plunge into cold water and peel. Cut each tomato in half and scoop out the seeds with a teaspoon and discard them. Finely dice the tomato flesh.
2 Heat 2 tablespoons of the oil in a frying pan over medium heat until hot, add the onion and shallots, then reduce the heat to low and cook slowly for 5 minutes, or until soft. Add the wine and simmer for several minutes until reduced slightly, then add the tomato. Season with salt and pepper and cook, stirring occasionally, for 20 minutes, or until thick and pulpy. Preheat the oven to moderate 180°F (350°F/Gas 4).
3 Heat the butter and remaining oil in a frying pan over high heat until foamy. Cook half the scallops for 1–2 minutes each side, or until lightly golden and cooked to your liking. Remove and repeat with the remaining scallops. Set aside.
4 Add the garlic to the hot scallop pan and stir for 1 minute. Remove from the heat and stir in the parsley, thyme and breadcrumbs.
5 To serve, warm the shells on a baking tray in the oven. Place a small amount of tomato mixture on each shell, top with a scallop and sprinkle with breadcrumb and parsley mixture.

STEAMED SHELLS IN WINE AND GARLIC

Preparation time: 25 minutes + 1 hour soaking
Total cooking time: 5 minutes
Serves 4

1 kg (2 lb) pipis
60 g (2 oz) butter, softened
2 cloves garlic, crushed
2 tablespoons chopped fresh dill
2 tablespoons chopped fresh chives
1 teaspoon chopped fresh thyme leaves
2 tablespoons toasted pine nuts
1/4 teaspoon cracked black pepper
1 small ripe tomato
½ cup (125 ml/4 fl oz) white wine
1 small onion, finely chopped

1 Soak the pipis for 1 hour to remove any sand. Discard any open pipis that do not close when tapped on the bench.
2 Beat the butter and garlic in a bowl with a wooden spoon until well combined and light in colour. Beat in the herbs, pine nuts and pepper.
3 Cut a cross in the base of the tomato. Place the tomato in a heatproof bowl and cover with boiling water. Leave for 30 seconds, plunge into cold water, then peel away from the cross. Remove the core and finely chop the flesh.
4 Place the wine, onion and ½ cup (125 ml/ 4 fl oz) water in a large saucepan and bring to the boil. Add the pipis, cover and cook over high heat, shaking the pan occasionally, for 3–5 minutes, or until the pipis have opened.
5 Add the herb and garlic butter and the tomato to the pan and stir well until the butter has melted. Spoon into serving bowls and serve immediately with lots of crusty bread to soak up the juices. Discard any unopened pipis.

SPAGHETTI MARINARA

Preparation time: 40 minutes
Total cooking time: 50 minutes
Serves 6

Tomato sauce
2 tablespoons olive oil
1 onion, finely chopped
1 carrot, sliced
2 cloves garlic, crushed
425 g (14 oz) can crushed tomatoes
½ cup (125 ml/4 fl oz) white wine
1 teaspoon sugar

20 black mussels
200 g (6½ oz) raw medium prawns
¼ cup (60 ml/2 fl oz) white wine
¼ cup (60 ml/2 fl oz) fish stock
1 clove garlic, crushed
375 g (12 oz) spaghetti
30 g (1 oz) butter
125 g (4 oz) calamari rings
125 g (4 oz) skinless fish fillets (eg. blue-
    eye, groper, striped marlin), cubed
½ cup (10 g/¼ oz) fresh parsley, chopped
200 g (6½ oz) can clams, drained

1 For the tomato sauce, heat the olive oil in a pan, add the onion and carrot and stir over medium heat for 10 minutes, or until the vegetables are lightly browned. Add the garlic, tomato, white wine and sugar, bring to the boil, reduce the heat and gently simmer for 30 minutes, stirring occasionally.
2 Scrub the mussels with a stiff brush and pull out the hairy beards. Discard any broken mussels, or open ones that don't close when tapped on the bench. Rinse well.

3 Peel the prawns and gently pull out the dark vein from each prawn back, starting at the head end.
4 Heat the wine together with the stock and garlic in a large pan. Add the unopened mussels. Cover the pan and shake it over high heat for 4–5 minutes. After 3 minutes, start removing any opened mussels and set them aside. After 5 minutes, discard any unopened mussels and reserve the liquid.
5 Cook the spaghetti in a large pan of rapidly boiling salted water until al dente. Drain and keep warm.
6 Meanwhile, melt the butter in a frying pan, add the calamari rings, fish and prawns in batches and stir-fry for 2 minutes, or until just cooked through. Remove from the heat and add the reserved liquid, mussels, calamari, fish, prawns, parsley and clams to the tomato sauce and stir gently until heated through. Gently combine the sauce with the pasta and serve at once.

SPAGHETTI VONGOLE
(SPAGHETTI WITH CLAM SAUCE)

Preparation time: 25 minutes + soaking
Total cooking time: 20–35 minutes
Serves 4

1 kg (2 lb) fresh small clams in shells or
    750 g (1½ lb) can clams in brine
1 tablespoon lemon juice
⅓ cup (80 ml/2¾ fl oz) olive oil
3 cloves garlic, crushed
2 x 425 g (14 oz) cans crushed tomatoes
250 g (8 oz) spaghetti
4 tablespoons chopped fresh parsley

1 If using fresh clams, clean thoroughly (see Note). Place in a large pan with the lemon juice. Cover the pan and shake over medium heat for 7–8 minutes until the shells open, discarding any that don't open. Remove the clam flesh from the shell of the opened clams and set aside; discard the empty shells. If using canned clams, drain, rinse well and set aside.
2 Heat the oil in a large pan. Add the garlic and cook over low heat for 5 minutes. Add the tomato and stir to combine. Bring to the boil and simmer, covered, for 20 minutes. Add freshly ground black pepper, to taste, and the clams, and stir until heated through.
3 While the sauce is cooking, cook the spaghetti in a large pan of rapidly boiling salted water until al dente. Drain and return to the pan. Gently stir in the sauce and the chopped parsley until combined. Serve immediately in a warm dish. Caperberries and a slice of lemon peel make an attractive garnish for special occasions.

NOTE: To clean the clams, any sand and grit needs to be drawn out of the shells. Combine 2 tablespoons each of salt and plain flour with enough water to make a paste. Add to a large bucket or bowl of cold water and soak the clams in this mixture overnight. Drain and scrub the shells well, then rinse thoroughly and drain again.

BARBECUED SQUID

Preparation time: 40 minutes +
  30 minutes chilling
Total cooking time: 10 minutes
Serves 6

500 g (1 lb) small squid (see Note)
¼ teaspoon salt

Picada dressing
2 tablespoons extra virgin olive oil
2 tablespoons finely chopped fresh
  flat-leaf parsley
1 clove garlic, crushed
¼ teaspoon cracked black pepper

1 To clean the squid, gently pull the tentacles away from the hood (the intestines should come away at the same time). Remove the intestines from the tentacles by cutting under the eyes, then remove the beak, if it remains in the centre of the tentacles, by using your fingers to push up the centre. Pull away the soft bone.
2 Rub the hoods under cold running water and the skin should come away easily. Wash the hoods and tentacles and drain well. Place in a bowl, add the salt and mix well. Cover and refrigerate for about 30 minutes.
3 Heat a lightly oiled barbecue hotplate or preheat a grill to its highest setting.
4 For the picada dressing, whisk together the olive oil, parsley, garlic, pepper and some salt in a small jug or bowl.
5 Cook the squid hoods in small batches on the barbecue hotplate, or under the grill, for about 2–3 minutes, or until the hoods are white and are tender. Barbecue or grill the squid tentacles, turning to brown them all over, for 1 minute, or until they curl up. Serve hot, drizzled with the picada dressing.

GREEK-STYLE CALAMARI

Preparation time: 30 minutes
Total cooking time: 35 minutes
Serves 4–6

Stuffing
1 tablespoon olive oil
2 spring onions, chopped
11/2 cups (280 g/9 oz) cold, cooked rice
60 g (2 oz) pine nuts
75 g (21/2 oz) currants
2 tablespoons chopped fresh parsley
2 teaspoons finely grated lemon rind
1 egg, lightly beaten

1 kg (2 lb) medium squid hoods

Sauce
4 large ripe tomatoes
1 tablespoon olive oil
1 onion, finely chopped
1 clove garlic, crushed
1/4 cup (60 ml/2 fl oz) good-quality red
  wine
1 tablespoon chopped fresh oregano

1 Preheat the oven to warm 160°C (315°F/ Gas 2–3). For the stuffing, mix the oil, spring onion, rice, pine nuts, currants, parsley and lemon rind in a bowl. Add enough egg to moisten all the ingredients.
2 Wash the squid hoods and pat dry inside and out with paper towels. Three-quarters fill each hood with the stuffing. Secure the ends with toothpicks or skewers. Place in a single layer in a casserole dish.
3 For the sauce, score a cross in the base of each tomato, put in a bowl of boiling water for 30 seconds, then plunge into cold water and peel away from the cross. Chop the flesh. Heat the oil in a pan. Add the onion and garlic and cook over low heat for 2 minutes, or until the onion is soft. Add the tomato, wine and oregano and bring to the boil. Reduce the heat, cover and cook over low heat for 10 minutes.
4 Pour the hot sauce over the squid, cover and bake for 20 minutes, or until the squid is tender. Remove the toothpicks before cutting into thick slices for serving. Spoon the sauce over just before serving.

NOTE: You will need to cook ½ cup (100 g/ 3½ oz) rice for this recipe.

SPAGHETTI WITH CHILLI CALAMARI

Preparation time: 20 minutes
Total cooking time: 20 minutes
Serves 4

500 g (1 lb) calamari, cleaned
500 g (1 lb) spaghetti
2 tablespoons olive oil
1 leek, chopped
2 cloves garlic, crushed
1–2 teaspoons chopped chilli
½ teaspoon cayenne pepper
425 g (14 oz) can crushed tomatoes
½ cup (125 ml/4 fl oz) fish stock
1 tablespoon chopped fresh basil
2 teaspoons chopped fresh sage
1 teaspoon chopped fresh marjoram

1 Pull the tentacles from the body of the calamari. Using your fingers, pull the quill from the pouch of the calamari. Pull the skin away from the flesh and discard. Use a sharp knife to slit the tubes up one side. Lay out flat and score one side in a diamond pattern. Cut each tube into four.
2 Cook the spaghetti in a large pan of rapidly boiling salted water until al dente. Drain and keep warm.
3 While the pasta is cooking, heat the oil in a large frying pan. Add the leek and cook for 2 minutes. Add the garlic and stir over low heat for 1 minute. Stir in the chilli and cayenne. Add the tomato, stock and herbs and bring to the boil. Reduce the heat and simmer for 5 minutes.
4 Add the calamari to the pan. Simmer for another 5–10 minutes, or until tender. Serve the chilli calamari over the spaghetti.

MARINATED TROUT AND CUCUMBER TARTS

Preparation time: 30 minutes + standing + freezing
Total cooking time: 10 minutes
Makes 20

Filling
300 g (10 oz) ocean trout fillet
¼ cup (60 ml/2 fl oz) lemon juice
2 tablespoons extra virgin olive oil
½ small Lebanese cucumber, finely chopped
2 spring onions, finely sliced
1 tablespoon chopped fresh dill or chervil
20 baby English spinach leaves

1 cup (125 g/4 oz) plain flour
2 tablespoons grated Parmesan
75 g (2½ oz) chilled butter, cubed
1 egg, lightly beaten

1 Remove the skin from the trout, then, using kitchen tweezers, remove the bones. Freeze the fish in plastic wrap for 1 hour. Whisk the lemon juice and oil in a bowl. Cut the fish into strips about 3 x 1 cm (1¼ x ½ inch) and add to the lemon juice marinade. Cover and set aside at room temperature for 20 minutes, or until the fish turns opaque (in summer, refrigerate— the process will take a little longer). Drain off most of the marinade, leaving just enough to moisten the fish. Add the cucumber, spring onion, dill or chervil, and season with salt and black pepper.

2 While the fish is marinating, sift the flour and a pinch of salt into a large bowl and add the Parmesan and butter. Rub in with your fingertips until the mixture resembles fine breadcrumbs. Make a well, add the egg and stir in with a flat-bladed knife until the mixture comes together in beads. Turn onto a lightly floured surface and gather into a ball. Wrap in plastic wrap and refrigerate for 30 minutes.
3 Preheat the oven to hot 210°C (415°F/Gas 6–7). Lightly grease two 12-hole round-based patty tins. Roll out the pastry to about 2 mm (⅛ inch) thick and cut 8 cm (3 inch) rounds to line 20 holes. Prick the pastry lightly with a fork and bake for 8–10 minutes, or until golden. Remove from the tins and set aside to cool. Place a spinach leaf in each tart case and top with 1 level tablespoon of filling. Serve at once.

IN ADVANCE: Prepare the tart cases up to 2 days ahead and store in an airtight container.

MARINATED CHILLI SQUID

Preparation time: 10 minutes +
    2–3 hours marinating
Total cooking time: 15 minutes
Serves 4

500 g (1 lb) squid hoods
1 tablespoon finely chopped fresh ginger
2–3 teaspoons finely chopped fresh red
    chilli
3 cloves garlic, finely chopped
¼ cup (60 ml/2 fl oz) oil
2 onions, thinly sliced
500 g (1 lb) baby bok choy, roughly
    chopped

1 Wash the squid well and pat dry with paper towels. Cut into 1 cm (½ inch) rings and place in a shallow glass or ceramic bowl. Combine the ginger, chilli, garlic and oil, pour over the rings and toss well. Cover and refrigerate for 2–3 hours.
2 Drain the rings and reserve the marinade. Heat the wok until very hot and stir-fry the rings over high heat in batches for 1–2 minutes. Remove from the wok as soon as the squid turns white. Do not overcook or the squid will be rubbery. Remove all the rings from the wok and set aside.
3 Heat the reserved marinade in the wok. Add the onion and cook over medium heat for 3–4 minutes, or until it is slightly softened. Add the bok choy and cook, covered, for 2 minutes, or until it has wilted slightly. Return the rings to the wok and toss until well combined. Season well with salt and pepper, to taste. Remove from the wok and serve immediately.

NOTE: Reheat the wok between cooking batches of rings—otherwise the flesh will be tough.

BALINESE CHILLI SQUID

Preparation time: 30 minutes
Total cooking time: 10 minutes
Serves 4

750 g (1½ lb) squid hoods
¼ cup (60 ml/2 fl oz) lime juice
3 tablespoons oil
1 large fresh red chilli, seeded and finely
    chopped
3 spring onions, sliced
1 tablespoon tamarind concentrate
1 stem lemon grass, white part only,
    finely sliced
1 cup (250 ml/8 fl oz) fish stock
1 tablespoon fresh Thai basil leaves,
    shredded

Spice paste
2 large fresh red chillies, seeded and
    chopped
2 cloves garlic, chopped
2 cm (¾ inch) piece fresh ginger, chopped
2 cm (¾ inch) piece fresh turmeric,
    chopped
3 spring onions, chopped
1 ripe tomato, peeled, seeded and
    chopped
2 teaspoons coriander seeds
1 teaspoon dried shrimp paste

1 Cut each squid hood in half lengthways and open out flat with the inside uppermost. Score a shallow lattice pattern all over the squid, taking care not to cut all the way through. Cut into 4 cm (1½ inch) pieces and mix in a bowl with the lime juice. Season well.
2 For the spice paste, combine the ingredients in a food processor until finely chopped.
3 Heat 2 tablespoons of the oil in a wok or large frying pan. Cook the squid, chilli and spring onion in batches for 2 minutes over medium heat, or until the squid begins to curl. Remove from the wok.
4 Heat the remaining oil in the wok and add the spice paste, tamarind concentrate and lemon grass. Stir over medium heat for 5 minutes, or until fragrant.
5 Return the squid to the wok and add the stock. Season, to taste, with pepper and add the basil. Bring to the boil, then reduce the heat and simmer for 2 minutes.

SQUID WITH GREEN PEPPERCORNS

Preparation time: 10 minutes +
    30 minutes marinating
Total cooking time: 5 minutes
Serves 4

600 g (1¼ lb) cleaned squid hoods,
    washed and dried
2 teaspoons chopped fresh coriander root
3 cloves garlic, crushed
⅓ cup (80 ml/2¾ fl oz) vegetable oil
25 g (¾ oz) Thai green peppercorns on
    the stalk, in brine, or lightly crushed
    fresh peppercorns
2 tablespoons Thai mushroom soy sauce
½ teaspoon grated palm sugar
⅔ cup (20 g/¾ oz) fresh Thai basil
green peppercorns, extra, to garnish

1 Cut the squid hoods in half lengthways. Clean and remove the quills. Score a diamond pattern on the inside of the squid. Cut into 4 cm (1½ inch) square pieces.
2 Put the coriander root, 1 clove garlic and 1 tablespoon oil in a food processor and process to form a smooth paste. Mix together the paste and squid pieces, cover and marinate in the fridge for 30 minutes.
3 Heat a wok over high heat, add the remaining oil and swirl to coat the side. Add the squid pieces and the remaining garlic and stir-fry for 1 minute. Add the peppercorns and stir-fry for a further 2 minutes, or until the calamari is just cooked—it will toughen if overcooked. Add the soy sauce and palm sugar, and stir until the sugar has dissolved. Serve immediately, garnished with Thai basil and green peppercorns.

CHILLI SALT AND PEPPER SQUID AND CELLOPHANE NOODLE SALAD

Preparation time: 30 minutes +
    10 minutes soaking + 15 minutes
    marinating
Total cooking time: 10 minutes
Serves 4

1 tablespoon dried shrimp
2 tablespoons Chinese rice wine
2 tablespoons light soy sauce
1 tablespoon Chinese black vinegar
2 teaspoons finely chopped fresh ginger
2 spring onions, thinly sliced
1 teaspoon chilli garlic sauce
1 teaspoon sesame oil
Salad
600 g (1¼ lb) cleaned squid hoods
½ cup (125 ml/4 fl oz) lemon juice
250 g (8 oz) cellophane noodles
1 small Lebanese cucumber, seeded and
    cut into batons
1 cup (90 g/3 oz) bean sprouts, tops and
    tails removed
2 tablespoons chopped fresh coriander
    leaves
1 tablespoon Sichuan peppercorns, dry-
    roasted
2 teaspoons sea salt
1 teaspoon ground white pepper
1 teaspoon freshly ground black pepper
¼ teaspoon chilli flakes
½ cup (60 g/2 oz) plain flour
¼ cup (45 g/1½ oz) rice flour
peanut oil, for deep-frying
2 egg whites, lightly beaten
fresh coriander leaves, extra, to garnish

1 Put the dried shrimp in a small heatproof bowl, cover with boiling water and soak for 10 minutes. Drain and finely chop. Return the shrimp to the bowl, cover with the rice wine and leave to soak until needed.

2 To make the dressing, put the soy sauce, black vinegar, ginger, spring onion, chilli garlic sauce and sesame oil in a small bowl. Mix together well, then set aside until needed.
3 Open out the squid hoods, then wash and thoroughly pat dry with paper towels. With the soft inside flesh facing upwards, score a shallow diamond pattern in the squid, taking care not to cut all the way through. Cut the squid into 2.5 x 4 cm (1 x 1½ inch) pieces. Put the pieces in a flat, non-metallic dish, then pour the lemon juice on top. Cover with plastic wrap and marinate in the refrigerator for 15 minutes.
4 Meanwhile, put the cellophane noodles in a heatproof bowl, cover with boiling water and soak for 3–4 minutes, or until softened. Drain and rinse under cold running water. Drain again, then transfer to a serving bowl. Add the cucumber, bean sprouts and chopped coriander to the bowl.
5 Combine the dry-roasted Sichuan peppercorns, sea salt, white pepper, black pepper and chilli flakes in a mortar and pestle or spice grinder and grind to a fine powder. Transfer to a bowl with the plain and rice flours and combine thoroughly. Drain the squid and pat dry with paper towels.

RICE-STUFFED SQUID

Preparation time: 30 minutes
Total cooking time: 1 hour
Serves 4

8 squid (about 600 g/1¼ lb)

Tomato sauce
1 garlic clove, thinly sliced
2 tablespoons extra virgin olive oil
2 x 400 g (13 oz) tins chopped tomatoes
100 ml (3½ fl oz) red wine
2 tablespoons chopped flat-leaf (Italian) parsley

Stuffing
100 ml (3½ fl oz) olive oil
1 small onion, finely chopped
1 small fennel bulb, finely chopped
2 garlic cloves, chopped
⅓ cup (75 g/2½ oz) risotto rice
large pinch of saffron threads
½ large red chilli, chopped
155 ml (5 fl oz) white wine
3 tablespoons chopped flat-leaf (Italian) parsley

1 Prepare the squid by pulling off the skin and wings. Pull out the quill (the transparent cartilage), the head and tentacles and scoop out the innards. Cut the heads off below the eyes, leaving just the tentacles. Discard the heads. Rinse the tentacles and bodies, making sure any sand is removed, then leave to drain in a colander for a few minutes. Finely chop the tentacles and set aside with the bodies (put them in the fridge if the kitchen is hot).

2 To make the sauce, gently fry the garlic in the extra virgin olive oil for 1 minute. Add the chopped tomatoes and simmer until some of the liquid has evaporated and the sauce is quite thick. Add the wine and parsley and cook until it has reduced and thickened. Set aside.

3 To make the stuffing, heat the oil in a large saucepan and gently cook the onion, fennel and garlic for about 10 minutes, or until softened but not browned. Add the rice, saffron, chilli and chopped squid tentacles and cook for a few minutes, stirring frequently until the tentacles are opaque. Season, then add the wine and 6 tablespoons of the tomato sauce.

4 Cook, stirring frequently, until the tomato and wine has reduced into the rice. Cook for about 5 minutes, or until the liquid has reduced, then add ½ cup (125 ml/4 fl oz) water and continue cooking until the rice is tender and all the liquid has been absorbed. You may need to add a little more water if the rice absorbs all the liquid and is not quite tender. Add 2 tablespoons of the parsley and set aside to cool for a few minutes.

5 Stuff the squid with the filling, using a teaspoon to push it down into the bottom of the tubes. Do not overfill the tubes—you need to be able to close them easily without any filling squeezing out. Seal the tops with cocktail sticks.

6 Put the remaining tomato sauce in a saucepan with 220 ml (7 fl oz) water. Cook for 2 minutes, then add the stuffed squid to the pan. Cover the saucepan and simmer gently for 30–45 minutes, or until the squid are soft and tender—the cooking time will depend on the size of the squid so test it and give it a little more time if you need to. Don't stir the squid too much when cooking or the filling will fall out. Shake the pan a little if you are worried about the squid sticking to the bottom. Remove the cocktail sticks and sprinkle with the remaining parsley just before serving. Serve with a salad.

GARLIC SQUID WITH PARMESAN

Preparation time: 30 minutes +
  10 minutes marinating
Total cooking time: 5 minutes
Serves 2–4

350 g (11 oz) squid hoods
4 cloves garlic, chopped
2 tablespoons olive oil
2 tablespoons finely chopped fresh parsley
1 large tomato
25 g (¾ oz) Parmesan, grated

1 Cut the squid hoods in half lengthways, wash and pat dry. Score a shallow lattice pattern all over the fleshy side of the squid, taking care not to cut right through. Lay them flat, with the fleshy side facing upwards, and cut into rectangles, about 6 x 2.5 cm (2½ x 1 inch).

2 Mix the garlic, oil, half the parsley, and salt and pepper, in a bowl. Add the squid and refrigerate for at least 10 minutes.

3 Score a cross in the base of the tomato. Place in a heatproof bowl, cover with boiling water for 30 seconds, then transfer to a bowl of cold water. Drain and peel away from the cross. Scoop out the seeds with a teaspoon, then chop the flesh.

4 Heat a lightly oiled chargrill pan or barbecue hotplate until very hot. Cook the squid in 2 batches, tossing regularly, until the squid curls and turns white. Add the chopped tomato and toss through to just heat.

5 Arrange the squid on a plate and scatter the grated Parmesan and remaining parsley over the top.

BABY SQUID STUFFED WITH PORK AND VERMICELLI NOODLES

Preparation time: 30 minutes +
    10 minutes soaking + cooling
Total cooking time: 35 minutes
Serves 6

12 baby squid tubes (about 100 g/3½ oz
    each)
75 g (2½ oz) dried rice vermicelli
2 tablespoons peanut oil
2 small red chillies, halved lengthways
    with the stem attached
2 garlic cloves, finely chopped
1½ tablespoons grated palm sugar
½ cup (80 g/2¾ oz) roughly chopped
    unsalted peanuts
750 g (1½ lb) minced (ground) pork
2 teaspoons yellow bean sauce (see Note)
½ cup (30 g/1 oz) finely chopped Thai basil
½ cup (25 g/¾ oz) finely chopped
    coriander (cilantro) leaves
cornflour (cornstarch), to dust
¼ cup (60 ml/2 fl oz) oil
lime wedges, to serve

1 To clean the squid, pull out the tentacles and remove the quill—the transparent cartilage. Pull the skin away from the tubes and discard. Rinse well under cold running water. Pat dry.
2 Put the vermicelli in a large heatproof bowl, cover with boiling water and soak for 7 minutes, or until softened. Drain and rinse under cold water. Cut into short lengths.

3 Heat the peanut oil and chilli in a wok over low heat for 2 minutes to infuse. Remove the chilli and increase the heat to high. Add the garlic, palm sugar and peanuts and stir-fry for 5 seconds. Add the pork and stir for 7 minutes, or until cooked through, stirring to break up any lumps. Stir in the vermicelli until well combined. Remove from the heat and stir in the yellow bean sauce. Allow to cool slightly, then stir in the herbs. Divide the filling into 12 even portions.
4 Fill each squid tube with a portion of filling, then lightly dust with cornflour.
5 Heat a clean wok over high heat, add the oil and swirl to coat. Cook the squid in batches, two at a time, and sear for 2 minutes on each side, or until golden and tender. Drain on paper towels and repeat with the remaining squid. Season with salt and serve with lime wedges.
Note: Yellow bean sauce here refers to the Southeast Asian version, which is made from salted and fermented yellow soy beans. It has a runnier consistency and is paler in colour than the Chinese variety.

TAGLIATELLE WITH OCTOPUS

Preparation time: 30 minutes
Total cooking time: 25 minutes
Serves 4

500 g (1 lb) mixed tagliatelle
1 kg (2 lb) baby octopus
2 tablespoons olive oil
1 onion, sliced
1 clove garlic, crushed
425 g (14 oz) can tomato purée (passata)
½ cup (125 ml/4 fl oz) dry white wine
1 tablespoon bottled chilli sauce
1 tablespoon chopped fresh basil

1 Cook the tagliatelle in a large pan of rapidly boiling salted water until al dente. Drain and return to the pan.
2 Clean the octopus by using a small sharp knife to remove the gut—either cut off the head entirely or slice open the head and remove the gut. Pick up the body and use your index finger to push the beak up. Remove the beak and discard. Clean the octopus thoroughly, pat dry and, if you prefer, cut in half. Set aside.
3 While the pasta is cooking, heat the oil in a large frying pan. Add the onion and garlic and stir over low heat until the onion is tender. Add the tomato purée, wine, chilli sauce, basil, and salt and pepper, to taste, to the pan. Bring to the boil, reduce the heat and simmer for 10 minutes.
4 Add the octopus to the pan and simmer for 5–10 minutes, or until tender. Serve over the pasta.

OCTOPUS IN RED WINE

Preparation time: 45 minutes
Total cooking time: 2 hours 20 minutes
Serves 4

1 kg (2 lb) baby octopus
2 tablespoons olive oil
180 g (6 oz) small brown pickling onions
⅓ cup (80 ml/2¾ fl oz) red wine vinegar
¾ cup (185 ml/6 fl oz) dry red wine
1 ripe tomato, grated
1 bay leaf
1 teaspoon dried oregano leaves

1 To prepare the octopus, use a small sharp knife and remove the heads from the tentacles. Remove the eyes by cutting a round of flesh from the base of the heads. To clean the heads, carefully slit them open and remove the gut. Rinse thoroughly. Cut the heads in half. Push out the beaks from the centre of the tentacles from the cut side. Cut the tentacles into sets of four or two, depending on the size of the octopus. Pull away the skin from the heads and tentacles if it comes away easily.
2 Place the octopus in a large pan and cook over high heat in their own liquid for 15–20 minutes, or until dry. Add the oil and the onions, and toss over heat until well coated. Add the vinegar, wine, tomato, bay leaf, oregano, 1 cup (250 ml/ 8 fl oz) water and ½ teaspoon cracked black pepper, and bring to the boil. Reduce the heat to low and simmer for 1½–2 hours, or until the flesh is tender. If not yet tender, add a little more water and continue cooking. The liquid remaining in the pan should just coat the octopus like a sauce.

NOTE: Young, small octopus are more tender than large ones. The octopus is closely related to squid and cuttlefish, so if you are unable to buy small octopus, you can use either of these.

CHARGRILLED BABY OCTOPUS

Preparation time: 15 minutes +
  3 hours marinating
Total cooking time: 5 minutes
Serves 4

1 kg (2 lb) baby octopus
¾ cup (185 ml/6 fl oz) red wine
2 tablespoons balsamic vinegar
2 tablespoons soy sauce
2 tablespoons hoisin sauce
1 clove garlic, crushed

1 Wash the octopus thoroughly and wipe dry with paper towel. Use a small sharp knife to cut off the heads. Discard the heads. If the octopus are large, cut the tentacles in half.
2 Put the octopus in a large bowl. Combine the wine, vinegar, sauces and garlic in a jug and pour over the octopus. Stir to coat thoroughly, then cover and marinate in the refrigerator for several hours, or overnight.
3 Heat the grill or barbecue hotplate to high. Drain the octopus, reserving the marinade. Cook the octopus, in batches, on a lightly greased hotplate for 3–5 minutes, until the octopus flesh turns white. Brush the reserved marinade over the octopus during cooking. Serve warm or cold.

OCTOPUS IN GARLIC ALMOND SAUCE

Preparation time: 25 minutes + cooling
Total cooking time: 50 minutes
Serves 4

1 kg (2 lb) baby octopus
½ small red pepper (capsicum), seeded
125 g (4 oz) flaked almonds
3 cloves garlic, crushed
⅓ cup (80 ml/2¾ fl oz) red wine vinegar
¾ cup (185 ml/6 fl oz) olive oil
2 tablespoons chopped fresh flat-leaf parsley

1 Using a small knife, carefully cut between the head and tentacles of the octopus and push the beak out and up through the centre of the tentacles with your finger. Cut the eyes from the head of the octopus by slicing off a small disc with a sharp knife. Discard the eye section. To clean the octopus head, carefully slit through one side and rinse out the gut. Drop the octopus into a large pan of boiling water and simmer for 20–40 minutes, depending on size, until tender. After 15 minutes cooking, start pricking them with a skewer to test for tenderness. When ready, remove from the heat and cool in the pan for 15 minutes.
2 For the sauce, heat the griller to high. Grill the red pepper skin-side-up until charred and blistered. Cool in a plastic bag, then peel and place in a food processor with the almonds and garlic, then purée. With the motor running, gradually pour in the vinegar followed by the oil. Stir in ½ cup (125 ml/4 fl oz) boiling water and parsley and season, to taste, with salt and black pepper.
3 To serve, cut the tentacles into pieces. Place in a serving bowl with the sauce and toss to coat. Serve warm, or chill and serve as a salad.

STIR-FRIED BABY OCTOPUS

Preparation time: 30 minutes +
   overnight marinating
Total cooking time: 10 minutes
Serves 4

500 g (1 lb) baby octopus
3 tablespoons chopped fresh coriander
2 cloves garlic, finely chopped
2 fresh red chillies, seeded and chopped
2 teaspoons grated fresh ginger
2 stems lemon grass, white part only,
   chopped
1 tablespoon vegetable oil
2 tablespoons lime juice
oil, for cooking
550 g (1 lb 2 oz) bok choy, leaves
   separated
400 g (13 oz) choy sum, leaves separated
2 cloves garlic, crushed, extra
1 teaspoon grated fresh ginger, extra

1 To prepare the baby octopus, remove
the head, cut off the eyes, and remove the
gut by slitting the head open. Grasp the
body firmly and push the beak out with
your index finger. Clean the octopus
thoroughly under cold running water and
pat dry with paper towels. Cut the head
into two or three pieces.
2 Combine the coriander, garlic, chilli,
ginger, lemon grass, oil and lime juice in
a large non-metallic bowl. Add the
octopus, cover with plastic wrap and
refrigerate for at least 2 hours, or
overnight, if time permits.
3 Heat a wok over high heat, add
1 tablespoon of the oil and swirl it around
to coat the side of the wok. Stir-fry the
vegetables with 1 tablespoon water.
Spread on a serving plate.
4 Reheat the wok, add 1 tablespoon of the
oil and stir-fry the extra garlic and ginger
for 30 seconds, or until fragrant. Add the
octopus and stir-fry over high heat for
7–8 minutes, or until cooked through.
Serve on a bed of the wilted greens.

LOBSTER MORNAY

Preparation time: 25 minutes +
   15 minutes standing
Total cooking time: 5–10 minutes
Serves 2

1 cooked medium lobster
1¼ cups (315 ml/10 fl oz) milk
1 slice of onion
1 bay leaf
6 black peppercorns
30 g (1 oz) butter
2 tablespoons plain flour
2 tablespoons cream
pinch of nutmeg
60 g (2 oz) Cheddar, grated
pinch of paprika, to garnish

1 Using a sharp knife, cut the lobster in
half lengthways through the shell. Lift the
meat from the tail and body. Remove the
cream-coloured vein and soft body matter
and discard. Cut the meat into 2 cm
(¾ inch) pieces, cover and refrigerate.
Wash the head and shell halves, then
drain and pat dry. Set aside.
2 Heat the milk, onion, bay leaf and
peppercorns in a small pan. Bring to the
boil. Remove from the heat, cover and
leave for 15 minutes. Strain.
3 Melt the butter in a large pan, stir in the
flour and cook for 1 minute, or until pale
and foaming. Remove from the heat and
gradually stir in the milk. Return to the
heat and stir constantly until the mixture
boils and thickens. Reduce the heat and
simmer for 1 minute. Stir in the cream.
Season with the nutmeg and salt and
pepper, to taste.
4 Fold the lobster meat through the
sauce. Stir over low heat until the lobster
is heated through. Spoon the mixture into
the shells and sprinkle with cheese. Heat
the grill and place the lobster under the
grill for 2 minutes, or until the cheese is
melted. Sprinkle with paprika. Can be
served with thick potato chips.

MARINATED OCTOPUS WITH SWEET CHILLI DRESSING

Preparation time: 30 minutes + 4 hours
   marinating
Total cooking time: 4 minutes
Serves 4–6

1 kg (2 lb) baby octopus
½ cup (125 ml/4 fl oz) olive oil
2 cloves garlic, crushed
2 tablespoons finely chopped fresh
   coriander
1 fresh red chilli, finely chopped
2 tablespoons lemon juice

Sweet chilli dressing
1 red chilli, finely chopped
¼ cup (60 ml/2 fl oz) lemon juice
2 tablespoons soft brown sugar
1 tablespoon fish sauce
2 tablespoons finely chopped fresh
   coriander
1 tablespoon sweet chilli sauce

1 To clean the octopus, use a small sharp
knife to cut off the head. Discard the head
and gut. Pick up the octopus body and
push up the beak with your index finger.
Remove and discard the beak. Clean the
octopus under running water and drain on
crumpled paper towels.
2 In a glass or ceramic bowl, combine the
oil, garlic, coriander, chilli and lemon
juice. Add the octopus, mix well, then
cover and refrigerate overnight, or for at
least 4 hours.
3 Drain the octopus on crumpled paper
towels. Heat the barbecue or grill plate to
very hot. Coat the plate with oil. Cook the
drained octopus, turning frequently, for
3–4 minutes, or until tender, basting with
marinade often to keep the octopus moist.
Do not overcook, or the octopus will
toughen. Serve either warm with
dressing, or cold as part of a salad.
4 For the dressing, combine all the
ingredients in a small screw top jar and
shake well.

BALMAIN BUGS WITH MANGO SAUCE

Preparation time: 10 minutes +
  1 hour freezing
Total cooking time: 5 minutes
Serves 4

8 large fresh Balmain bugs or 2 large raw
  lobster tails
1 large or 2 small mangoes
2–3 tablespoons sour cream
¼ cup (60 ml/2 fl oz) lemon or lime juice
1 teaspoon soft brown sugar
2–3 teaspoons Thai sweet chilli sauce
1 mango, extra, for serving

1 Immobilize the bugs in the freezer for
1 hour, before cooking. Lower the bugs
into a large pan of lightly salted boiling
water. Simmer, uncovered, for 4–5
minutes, or until the shells have changed
to orange-red. If using lobster, you will
need to cook for 8–10 minutes
2 Gently separate the heads from the
bodies. To remove the meat, cut down
each side of the shell on the soft
underside of the bugs. Using kitchen
scissors, starting at the head end and
working towards the tail, pull back the
flap and remove the meat from the shell.
Cut each piece of flesh in half lengthways,
or the lobster into slices.
3 For the mango sauce, roughly chop the
mango flesh and place in a food
processor. Add the sour cream, juice,
sugar and chilli sauce and mix for
20–30 seconds, or until smooth.
Refrigerate, covered, until required. If the
sauce is too thick, add a little extra cream
or juice.
4 Serve the bug meat on a bed of mixed
salad leaves, with extra slices of fresh
mango. Drizzle with sauce and serve with
the rest on the side.

NOTE: If fresh mango is unavailable for
the sauce, you can use canned mango
slices, or a 170 g (5½ oz) can of mango
purée.

BALMAIN BUGS WITH LIME AND CORIANDER BUTTER

Preparation time: 10 minutes +
  refrigeration
Total cooking time: 5–6 minutes
Serves 4–6

90 g (3 oz) butter, softened
2 teaspoons finely grated lime rind
2 tablespoons lime juice
3 tablespoons chopped fresh coriander
1 teaspoon cracked black pepper
1 kg (2 lb) raw Balmain bugs
3 cloves garlic, crushed
2 tablespoons oil

1 Mix the butter, lime rind and juice,
coriander and pepper in a bowl. Put in the
centre of a piece of foil and roll into a log
shape. Twist the ends tightly, then
refrigerate until firm.
2 Fill a large bowl with plenty of ice, some
water and a pinch of salt. Submerge the
live Balmain bugs for 20–30 minutes.
3 Heat the barbecue. Place the bugs,
garlic and oil on the barbecue plate and
toss for 5–6 minutes, or until the bugs
turn deep orange and the flesh turns
white and starts to come away from the
shell. Cut the butter into rounds and serve
on the hot bugs.

STUFFED CRABS

Preparation time: 30 minutes
Total cooking time: 25 minutes
Serves 6

6 cooked medium blue swimmer crabs
60 g (2 oz) butter
2 cloves garlic, finely chopped
½ red pepper (capsicum), finely chopped
½ small green pepper (capsicum), finely
  chopped
1 small onion, finely chopped
1 stick celery, finely chopped
½ fresh red chilli, chopped
¼ teaspoon celery salt
¼ teaspoon dried thyme
⅔ cup (170 ml/5½ fl oz) canned condensed
  seafood bisque
1 cup (80 g/2¾ oz) fine fresh
  breadcrumbs

1 Pull away the crab legs and claws, crack
open and extract the meat from the legs.
Reserve 2 front claws on each crab. Lift
the flap on the underside of each crab and
prise off the top shell. Remove the soft
organs and pull off the gills. Scrub the
crab back shells and set aside. Shred the
crab meat, picking out the shell
fragments.
2 Melt the butter in a pan and add the
chopped garlic, pepper, onion, celery and
chilli. Cook, stirring over medium heat, for
about 5 minutes.
3 Add the celery salt, thyme and bisque
and cook for 3 minutes. Add the crab
meat with half the breadcrumbs. Stir until
combined and season, to taste, with salt
and pepper if necessary.
4 Preheat the oven to moderately hot
200°C (400°F/Gas 6). Spoon the mixture
into the crab shells, smooth the tops and
press the remaining crumbs over the
surface. Bake the crabs on a baking tray
for about 15 minutes, or until heated
through and golden, adding the extra
claws close to the end of cooking, to
warm through.

LOBSTER THERMIDOR

Preparation time: 25 minutes
Total cooking time: 5–10 minutes
Serves 2

1 cooked medium lobster
80 g (2¾ oz) butter
4 spring onions, finely chopped
2 tablespoons plain flour
½ teaspoon dry mustard
2 tablespoons white wine or sherry
1 cup (250 ml/8 fl oz) milk
¼ cup (60 ml/2 fl oz) cream
1 tablespoon chopped fresh parsley
60 g (2 oz) Gruyère cheese, grated

1 Using a sharp knife, cut the lobster in half lengthways through the shell. Lift the meat from the tail and body. Remove the cream-coloured vein and soft body matter and discard. Cut the meat into 2 cm (¾ inch) pieces, cover and refrigerate. Wash the head and shell halves, then drain and pat dry.
2 In a frying pan, heat 60 g (2 oz) of the butter, add the spring onion and stir for 2 minutes. Stir in the flour and mustard and cook for 1 minute, or until pale and foaming. Remove from the heat and gradually stir in the wine and milk. Return to the heat and stir constantly until the mixture boils and thickens. Reduce the heat and simmer for 1 minute. Stir in the cream, parsley and lobster meat, then season with salt and pepper, to taste. Stir over low heat until the lobster is heated through.
3 Heat the grill. Spoon the mixture into the lobster shells, sprinkle with cheese and dot with the remaining butter. Place under the grill for 2 minutes, or until lightly browned. Serve with mixed salad leaves and lemon slices.

SOLE VERONIQUE

Preparation time: 45 minutes
Total cooking time: 20 minutes
Serves 4

12 sole fillets or 3 whole sole, filleted and
    skinned
1 cup (250 ml/8 fl oz) fish stock
¼ cup (60 ml/2 fl oz) white wine
1 French shallot, thinly sliced
1 bay leaf
6 black peppercorns
2 sprigs fresh parsley
3 teaspoons butter
3 teaspoons flour
½ cup (125 ml/4 fl oz) milk
¼ cup (60 ml/2 fl oz) cream
125 g (4 oz) seedless white grapes,
    peeled

1 Preheat the oven to moderate 180°C (350°F/ Gas 4). Roll the fillets into coils with the skin side on the inside. Secure the coils with toothpicks and place side-by-side in a well-greased shallow ovenproof dish.
2 Combine the stock, wine, shallot, bay leaf, peppercorns and parsley in a jug and pour over the fish. Cover with greased foil and bake for 15 minutes, or until the fish flakes when tested with a fork. Carefully lift the rolls out of the liquid with a slotted spoon and transfer to another dish. Cover and keep warm.
3 Pour the cooking liquid into a saucepan and boil for about 2 minutes, or until reduced by half, then strain through a fine strainer.
4 In a clean pan, melt the butter, add the flour and stir for 1 minute, or until pale and foaming. Remove from the heat and gradually stir in the combined milk, cream and reduced cooking liquid. Return to the heat and stir until the mixture boils and thickens. Season, to taste, add the grapes, then stir until heated through. Serve the sauce over the fish.

NOTE: You can substitute flounder for the sole.

VERMICELLI AND CRAB MEAT STIR-FRY

Preparation time: 20 minutes +
20 minutes soaking
Total cooking time: 15 minutes
Serves 4

200 g (6½ oz) dried mung bean vermicelli
2 tablespoons oil
10 red Asian shallots, very finely sliced
3 cloves garlic, finely chopped
2 stems lemon grass (white part only),
    very finely sliced
1 red pepper (capsicum), cut into thin 4
    cm (1½ inch) matchsticks
170 g (5½ oz) can crab meat, well drained
2 tablespoons fish sauce
2 tablespoons lime juice
2 teaspoons sugar
3 spring onions, cut into very fine
    diagonal slices

1 Soak the noodles in hot water for 20 minutes or until softened; drain. Using scissors, cut the noodles into short lengths for easy eating.
2 Heat the oil in a wok or heavy-based pan; add the shallots, garlic and lemon grass and stir-fry over high heat for 2 minutes. Add the red pepper and cook for 30 seconds, tossing well. Add the vermicelli and toss. Cover and steam for 1 minute, or until the vermicelli is heated through.
3 Add the crab meat, fish sauce, lime juice and sugar and toss well, using 2 wooden spoons. Season with salt and pepper to taste, sprinkle with the spring onion and serve.

CHILLI CRAB

Preparation time: 20 minutes
Total cooking time: 15 minutes
Serves 4

1 kg (2 lb) raw blue swimmer crabs
2 tablespoons peanut oil
2 cloves garlic, finely chopped
2 teaspoons finely chopped fresh ginger
2 fresh red chillies, seeded and sliced 2
    tablespoons hoisin sauce
½ cup (125 ml/4 fl oz) tomato sauce
¼ cup (60 ml/2 fl oz) sweet chilli sauce
1 tablespoon fish sauce
½ teaspoon sesame oil
4 spring onions, sliced
fresh coriander sprigs, to garnish

1 Pull back the apron and remove the top shell from the crabs. Remove the intestines and grey feathery gills. Segment each crab into 4 pieces. Use a cracker to crack the claws open; this will make it easier to eat later and will also allow the flavours to get into the crab meat.
2 Heat a wok over high heat, add the oil and swirl to coat. Add the garlic, ginger and chilli, and stir-fry for 1–2 minutes.
3 Add the crab pieces and stir-fry for about 6 minutes, or until they turn orange. Stir in the hoisin, tomato, sweet chilli and fish sauces, the sesame oil and ¼ cup (60 ml/2 fl oz) water. Bring to the boil, then reduce the heat and simmer, covered, for 6 minutes, or until the crab shell turns bright orange and the flesh turns white and flakes easily.
4 Sprinkle with the spring onion and serve on a platter, garnished with the coriander sprigs. Serve with steamed rice.

SALMON PIE

Preparation time: 25 minutes +
30 minutes refrigeration
Total cooking time: 1 hour
Serves 4–6

60 g (2 oz) butter
1 onion, finely chopped
200 g (6½ oz) button mushrooms, sliced
2 tablespoons lemon juice
200 g (6½ oz) cooked poached salmon
    fillet, broken into small pieces, or 220 g
    (7 oz) can red salmon
2 hard-boiled eggs, chopped
2 tablespoons chopped fresh dill
3 tablespoons chopped fresh parsley
1 cup (185 g/6 oz) cooked long-grain
    brown rice (see Note)
¼ cup (60 ml/2 fl oz) cream
375 g (12 oz) packet frozen puff pastry
1 egg, lightly beaten
sour cream, optional, for serving

1 Melt half the butter in a frying pan and cook the onion for 5 minutes until soft but not brown. Add the mushrooms and cook for 5 minutes. Stir in the juice, then remove from the pan.
2 Melt the remaining butter in the pan, add the salmon and stir for 2 minutes. Remove from the heat, cool slightly and add the egg, dill, parsley, and salt and pepper, to taste. Mix gently and set aside. Mix the rice and cream in a small bowl.

3 Roll out half the pastry to 15 x 25 cm (6 x 10 inches). Trim the pastry neatly, saving the trimmings, and put on a greased baking tray.
4 Layer the filling onto the pastry, leaving a 3 cm (1¼ inch) border. Put half the rice into the centre of the pastry, then the salmon and egg mixture, followed by the mushrooms, then the remaining rice. Brush the border with egg.
5 Roll out the other pastry half to 20 x 30 cm (8 x 12 inches) and place over the filling. Seal the edges. Make two slits in the top. Decorate with the trimmings and chill for 30 minutes.
6 Preheat the oven to hot 200°C (400°F/Gas 6). Brush the pie with egg and bake for 15 minutes. Reduce the oven to 180°C (350°F/Gas 4) and bake the pie for 25–30 minutes, or until crisp and golden. Serve with sour cream.

NOTE: You will need to cook about ½ cup (100 g/3½ oz) brown rice for this recipe.

INTERNATIONAL BARBECUED SHELL PLATTER

Preparation time: 40 minutes +
  1 hour freezing
Total cooking time: 30 minutes
Serves 6

6 raw Balmain bugs
30 g (1 oz) butter, melted
1 tablespoon oil
12 black mussels
12 scallops on their shells
12 oysters
18 raw large prawns, unpeeled

Salsa verde, for scallops
1 tablespoon finely chopped preserved
  lemon (see Note)
1 cup (20 g/¾ oz) fresh parsley leaves
1 tablespoon drained bottled capers
1 tablespoon lemon juice
3 tablespoons oil, approximately

Vinegar and shallot dressing,
  for mussels
¼ cup (60 ml/2 fl oz) white wine vinegar
4 French shallots, finely chopped
1 tablespoon chopped fresh chervil

Pickled ginger and wasabi sauce,
  for oysters
1 teaspoon soy sauce
¼ cup (60 ml/2 fl oz) mirin
2 tablespoons rice wine vinegar
¼ teaspoon wasabi paste
2 tablespoons finely sliced pickled ginger

Sweet balsamic dressing,
  for Balmain bugs
1 tablespoon olive oil
1 tablespoon honey
½ cup (125 ml/4 fl oz) balsamic vinegar

Thai coriander sauce, for prawns
½ cup (125 ml/4 fl oz) sweet chilli sauce
1 tablespoon lime juice
2 tablespoons chopped fresh coriander

1 Freeze the bugs for 1 hour to
immobilize. Cut each bug in half with a
sharp knife, then brush the flesh with the
combined butter and oil. Set aside while
you prepare the rest of the seafood.
2 Scrub the mussels with a stiff brush and
pull out the hairy beards. Discard any
broken mussels, or open ones that don't
close when tapped on the bench. Rinse
well.
3 Slice or pull off any vein, membrane or
hard white muscle from the scallops,
leaving any roe attached. Brush the
scallops with the combined butter and oil.
4 Remove the oysters from the shells,
then rinse the shells under cold water. Pat
the shells dry and return the oysters to
their shells. Cover and refrigerate all the
seafood while you make the dressings.
5 For the salsa verde, combine all the
ingredients in a food processor and
process in short bursts until roughly
chopped. Transfer to a bowl and add
enough oil to moisten the mixture. Season
with salt and pepper. Serve a small dollop
on each cooked scallop.
6 For the vinegar and shallot dressing,
whisk the vinegar, shallots and chervil in
a bowl until combined. Pour over the
cooked mussels.
7 For the pickled ginger and wasabi sauce,
whisk all the ingredients in a bowl until
combined. Spoon over the cooked oysters.
8 For the sweet balsamic dressing, heat
the oil in a pan, add the honey and vinegar
and bring to the boil, then boil until reduced
by half. Drizzle over the cooked bugs.
9 For the Thai coriander sauce, combine
all the ingredients in a jug or bowl and
drizzle over the cooked prawns.
10 Cook the seafood in batches on a
preheated barbecue grill and flatplate. If
necessary, do this in batches, depending
on the size of your barbecue. The Balmain
bugs will take the longest time to cook,
about 5 minutes—they are cooked when
the flesh turns white and starts to come
away from the shells. The mussels,
scallops, oysters and prawns all take
about 2–5 minutes to cook.

DEEP-FRIED SQUID

Preparation time: 30 minutes + 30
  minutes chilling
Total cooking time: 5 minutes
Serves 4

500 g (1 lb) small squid (about 20)
⅓ cup (40 g/1¼ oz) plain flour
oil, for deep-frying
lemon wedges, for serving

1 To clean the squid, gently pull the
tentacles away from the hood—the
intestines should come away with them.
Remove the intestines from the tentacles
by cutting under the eyes and remove the
beak if it remains in the centre of the
tentacles. Pull away the soft bone 'quill'
from the hood. Rub the hoods under
running water and the skin should come
away easily. Wash the hoods and
tentacles and drain well. Place in a bowl
and season well with salt. Cover and
refrigerate for about 30 minutes.
2 Combine the flour with a pinch each of
salt and cracked pepper in a shallow dish.
Fill a deep, heavy-based pan one third full
of oil and heat to 180°C (350°F), or until a
cube of bread browns in 15 seconds. Coat
the squid hoods in flour and deep-fry in
batches for about 30–60 seconds, or until
light brown and tender. Toss the tentacles
in the flour and deep-fry for 20–30 seconds,
or until lightly browned and tender.
Partially cover the deep-fryer while
cooking as the squid tends to splatter.
Drain on crumpled paper towels, then
transfer to a serving platter and sprinkle
with salt. Serve hot with lemon wedges.

THAI-STYLE FISH WITH SWEET CHILLI GLAZE

Preparation time: 30 minutes + 2 hours
  marinating
Total cooking time: 35 minutes
Serves 4–6

2 whole fish (eg. snapper, bream, murray
  cod, ocean perch, flathead, about 1 kg/
  2 lb each)
1 stem lemon grass, white part only,
  bruised with the side of a knife, cut into
  quarters
6 kaffir lime leaves, cut in half
25 g (¾ oz) fresh coriander leaves and
  stalks
½ cup (125 ml/4 fl oz) fish sauce
⅓ cup (80 ml/2¾ fl oz) lime juice
peanut oil, for deep-frying

Sweet chilli glaze
1 teaspoon oil
1 teaspoon shrimp paste
180 g (6 oz) grated palm sugar or brown
  sugar
1 stem lemon grass, white part only,
  bruised with the side of a knife, cut in half
5 cm (2 inch) piece fresh galangal, cut in
  half
4 small red chillies, finely sliced
2 teaspoons finely grated lime rind
⅓ cup (80 ml/2¾ fl oz) lime juice

1 Wash the fish and pat dry inside and out.
Make deep cuts in the thickest part of the
fish. Fill each cavity with half the lemon
grass, lime leaves and coriander. Secure
the openings with skewers. Place in a
shallow, non-metallic dish.

2 Combine the fish sauce and lime juice,
pour over the fish and marinate in the
refrigerator for about 2 hours, turning the
fish after an hour. Drain and pat dry with
crumpled paper towels.
3 For the glaze, heat the oil in a small pan
and fry the shrimp paste until fragrant.
Add the sugar, lemon grass, galangal, red
chilli, lime rind and juice, and ¾ cup (185
ml/6 fl oz) water. Stir over medium heat
until the sugar has dissolved, bring to the
boil, then reduce the heat and simmer for
10 minutes, or until slightly thickened.
Discard the galangal and lemon grass.
Keep warm.
4 Fill a wok one third full of oil and heat
to 180°C (350°F), or until a cube of bread
dropped into the oil browns in 15 seconds.
Cook each fish for 10 minutes, or until
crisp and golden, spooning hot oil over
the fish with a long-handled metal spoon.
Drain on crumpled paper towels. Serve
drizzled with the glaze.

SALMON AND PASTA FRITTATA

Preparation time: 25 minutes
Total cooking time: 35–40 minutes
Serves 6

150 g (5 oz) spaghettini (see Note)
300 g (10 oz) frozen broad beans
415 g (13 oz) can red salmon, drained
30 g (1 oz) butter
1 leek, white part only, thinly sliced
6 eggs, lightly beaten
½ cup (125 ml/4 fl oz) cream
¾ cup (185 ml/6 fl oz) milk

1 Add the pasta to a large pan of boiling
water and boil until al dente; drain. Put
the broad beans in a large bowl, cover
with boiling water and leave for 10 minutes.
Drain, then remove and discard the outer
skins. Remove and discard any skin and
bones from the salmon and roughly flake
the flesh.
2 Melt the butter in a saucepan, add the
leek and cook, stirring over medium heat
until soft, but not browned. In a large
bowl, mix the pasta, broad beans, leek,
salmon, eggs, cream and milk. Season, to
taste, with salt and cracked black pepper.
3 Pour the mixture into a lightly greased
heated frying pan 25 cm (10 inches) across
the base. Cover with foil or a lid and cook
over low heat for 25 minutes, or until
nearly set.
4 Meanwhile, heat the grill. Place the
frying pan under the grill (wrap the
handle with foil to protect it from the
heat) and grill until the top has set. Set
aside for 5 minutes. Gently ease the
frittata away from the edges of the pan,
then hold a large plate over the top and
turn the pan over to release the frittata
onto the plate or cut into wedges directly
from the pan. Serve with a leafy green
salad.

CRUNCHY FISH FILLETS

Preparation time: 10 minutes
Total cooking time: 6 minutes
Serves 4
O

½ cup (75 g/21/2 oz) cornmeal
4 firm white fish fillets (eg. snapper, perch, John dory, whiting, haddock, cod)
1/4 cup (60 ml/2 fl oz) oil
2/3 cup (170 g/51/2 oz) mayonnaise
2 tablespoons chopped fresh chives
1 tablespoon sweet chilli sauce

1 Place the cornmeal on a plate. Cut 4 shallow diagonal slashes in the skin side of each fish fillet, to prevent the fish curling during cooking.
2 Press the fillets into the cornmeal to coat thoroughly. Heat the oil in a frying pan over medium heat. Add the fish and cook skin-side-up for 3 minutes. Turn and cook for another 3 minutes, or until tender and the fish flakes easily when tested with a fork. Remove and drain on crumpled paper towels.
3 Combine the mayonnaise, chives and chilli sauce in a small bowl and serve with the fish.

CREOLE SEAFOOD STEW

Preparation time: 25 minutes
Total cooking time: 1 hour 10 minutes
Serves 4

400 g (13 oz) raw prawns (shrimp)
250 g (8 oz) squid tubes
1/4 cup (60 ml/2 fl oz) olive oil
1 large onion, chopped
4 back bacon rashers, chopped
1 small green capsicum (pepper), diced
1 green serrano chilli, chopped
3 garlic cloves, chopped
1 teaspoon paprika
1½ teaspoons dried thyme
2 teaspoons dried oregano
1/4 teaspoon cayenne pepper
1/4 cup (60 ml/2 fl oz) sherry
1/4 cup (30 g/1 oz) plain (all-purpose) flour
31/2 cups (875 ml/28 fl oz) chicken stock
400 g (13 oz) tin chopped tomatoes
1½ cups (300 g/10 oz) long-grain rice
1 bay leaf
250 g (8 oz) scallops

1 Peel and devein the prawns, keeping the tails intact. Cut the squid tubes into 5 mm (1/4 inch) rings. Refrigerate on a plate covered with plastic wrap until needed.
2 Heat the oil in large heavy-based saucepan, add the onion, bacon and capsicum and cook over high heat for 5 minutes, or until the bacon is cooked.
3 Add the chilli and garlic to the bacon mixture and cook for 1 minute. Add the herbs and spices and cook for 30 seconds, then pour in the sherry. Continue cooking until the sherry has evaporated, then reduce the heat to medium and stir in the flour. Cook for 3 minutes, or until the flour is cooked, then gradually pour in the stock. Slowly bring the mixture to the boil, then simmer for 3 minutes, or until the mixture has thickened.
4 Stir in the chopped tomatoes rice and bay leaf and simmer, covered, for 30–40 minutes, stirring reasonably often to prevent the mixture from catching on the base of the pan.
5 Add the prawns, squid rings and scallops, and cook for a further 8 minutes, stirring after 4 minutes, or until the seafood is cooked through and tender. Add a little water or extra stock with the seafood if the mixture seems too thick and gluggy. Remove the bay leaf. Ladle into deep bowls and serve immediately.

SALMON AND FENNEL FRITTATA

Preparation time: 35 minutes
Total cooking time: 1 hour 15 minutes
Serves 8

1½ tablespoons olive oil
1 onion, finely chopped
1 fennel bulb (about 280 g/9 oz), chopped
¼ cup (60 ml/2 fl oz) white wine
2 cups (60 g/2 oz) watercress sprigs
12 eggs
1¾ cups (440 ml/14 fl oz) cream
3 tablespoons chopped fresh dill
½ cup (50 g/1¾ oz) grated Parmesan
300 g (10 oz) smoked salmon, cut into strips

1 Preheat the oven to moderate 180°C (350°F/ Gas 4). Lightly grease a 22 cm (9 inch) springform tin and line the base and side with baking paper, making sure you have a tight seal all the way around the tin. Place the tin on a baking tray in case it leaks.
2 Heat the olive oil in a heavy-based saucepan and add the onion, fennel and a pinch of salt. Cook over low heat for 5 minutes, stirring occasionally. Add the white wine and cook for another 5 minutes, or until the vegetables are tender. Remove from the heat and leave to cool.
3 Finely chop half the watercress and divide the remainder into small sprigs. Beat the eggs lightly in a bowl, then add the cream, dill, grated Parmesan, chopped watercress, and onion and fennel mixture. Season, to taste, with salt and black pepper.
4 Pour half the egg mixture into the prepared tin, sprinkle with 200 g (6½ oz) smoked salmon and pour in the remaining egg mixture. Bake for 1 hour, or until the frittata is set in the centre and golden on the surface. Remove from the pan and peel off the baking paper from the side. Flip over onto a plate and remove the paper from the base. Flip over again onto a serving dish and arrange the remaining salmon and watercress on top. Cut into wedges and serve warm.

POACHED ATLANTIC SALMON

Preparation time: 50 minutes
Total cooking time: 1 hour
Serves 8–10

2 litres (64 fl oz) good-quality white wine
¼ cup (60 ml/2 fl oz) white wine vinegar
2 onions
10 whole cloves
4 carrots, chopped
1 lemon, cut in quarters
2 bay leaves
4 sprigs fresh parsley
1 teaspoon whole black peppercorns
2.5 kg (5 lb) Atlantic salmon, cleaned and scaled

Dill mayonnaise
1 egg, at room temperature
1 egg yolk, at room temperature, extra
1 tablespoon lemon juice
1 teaspoon white wine vinegar
11/2 cups (375 ml/12 fl oz) light olive oil
1–2 tablespoons chopped fresh dill

1 Put the wine, wine vinegar and 2.5 litres (80 fl oz) water in a large heavy-based pan.
2 Stud the onions with the cloves. Add to the pan with the carrot, lemon, bay leaves, parsley and peppercorns. Bring to the boil, reduce the heat and simmer for 30–35 minutes. Cool. Strain into a fish kettle that will hold the salmon.
3 Place the whole fish in the fish kettle and cover. Bring to the boil, reduce the heat and poach gently for 10–15 minutes, until the fish flakes when tested in the thickest part. Remove from the heat and cool the fish in the liquid.
4 Process the egg, extra yolk, juice and vinegar in a food processor for 10 seconds, or until blended. With the motor running, add the oil in a thin, steady stream, blending until all the oil is added and the mayonnaise is thick and creamy—it should be thick enough to form peaks. Transfer to a bowl and stir in the dill, and salt and pepper.
5 Remove the cold fish from the liquid, place on a work surface or serving platter and peel back the skin. Serve garnished with watercress and lemon slices. Serve with the mayonnaise.

NOTES: Ocean trout, snapper, sea bass or red emperor can also be used.
You can use a baking dish big enough to hold the fish and bake the fish in a moderate 180°C (350°F/Gas 4) oven for 20–30 minutes.

COULIBIAC

Preparation time: 20 minutes +
    30 minutes refrigeration
Total cooking time: 45 minutes
Serves 6

60 g (2 oz) butter
1 onion, finely chopped
200 g (6½ oz) button mushrooms, sliced
2 tablespoons lemon juice
225 g (7 oz) salmon fillet, skin and bones
    removed, cut into 1.5 cm (⅝ inch) chunks
2 hard-boiled eggs, chopped
2 tablespoons chopped dill
2 tablespoons chopped parsley
1 cup (185 g/6 oz) cooked, cold long-grain
    rice
¼ cup (60 ml/2 fl oz) thick (double/heavy)
    cream
370 g (12 oz) block puff pastry
1 egg, lightly beaten

1 Melt half the butter in a frying pan, add
the onion and cook over medium heat
until soft. Add the mushrooms and cook
for 5 minutes. Stir in the lemon juice and
transfer to a bowl.
2 Melt the remaining butter in a pan, then
add the salmon and cook for 2 minutes.
Transfer to a bowl, cool slightly and add
the egg, dill and parsley. Season, combine
gently and set aside. In a small bowl,
combine the rice and cream, and season
with salt and pepper.

3 Roll out half the pastry to an 18 x 30 cm
(7 x 12 inch) rectangle and put it on the
baking tray. Spread half the rice mixture
onto the pastry, leaving a 3 cm (1 inch)
border all around. Top with the salmon
mixture, then the mushrooms and, finally,
the remaining rice.
4 Roll out the remaining pastry to 20 x 32
cm (8 x 13 inch) and put it over the filling.
Press the pastry edges together, then
crimp to seal. Decorate with pastry cut-
outs, if you like, then refrigerate for 30
minutes. Preheat the oven to hot 210°C
(415°F/Gas 6–7).
5 Brush the pastry top with the beaten
egg and bake for 15 minutes. Reduce the
heat to moderate 180°C (350°F/Gas 4) and
bake for another 15–20 minutes.

FARFALLE WITH TUNA, MUSHROOMS AND CREAM

Preparation time: 10 minutes
Total cooking time: 15 minutes
Serves 4

60 g (2 oz) butter
1 tablespoon olive oil
1 onion, chopped
1 clove garlic, crushed
125 g (4 oz) button mushrooms, sliced
1 cup (250 ml/8 fl oz) cream
450 g (14 oz) can tuna in brine, drained
    and flaked
1 tablespoon lemon juice
1 tablespoon chopped fresh parsley
500 g (1 lb) farfalle

1 Heat the butter and olive oil in a large
frying pan. Add the onion and garlic to the
pan and stir over low heat for 3–5 minutes,
until the onion is soft.
2 Add the mushrooms to the pan and cook
for 2 minutes. Pour in the cream, bring to
the boil, then reduce the heat and simmer
until the sauce begins to thicken. Add the
tuna, lemon juice and parsley and stir
until heated through. Add salt and pepper,
to taste.
3 While the sauce is cooking, add the
farfalle to a large pan of rapidly boiling
water and cook until al dente. Drain
thoroughly, then return to the pan. Add
the sauce to the farfalle and toss to
combine. Serve immediately.

NOTES: You can use a can of salmon,
drained and flaked, instead of tuna.
 Farfalle, attractive pasta made into the
shape of a bow or butterfly, comes in
various sizes, as well as flavours other
than the plain, such as tomato or spinach.

COATINGS & BATTERS

EACH OF THESE MIXTURES WILL COAT FOUR MEDIUM FISH FILLETS (WE USED SNAPPER). THE EGG WHITE BATTER IS ENOUGH FOR SIX FILLETS. YOU CAN USE THE MIXTURES FOR OTHER SEAFOOD AS WELL.

To prepare for all the deep-fried recipes, fill a deep heavy-based saucepan one third full of oil and heat the oil to 180°C (350°F), or until a cube of bread dropped into the oil browns in 15 seconds. Fry the food in batches for even cooking.

BASIC BATTER

Sift 1 cup (125 g/4 oz) self-raising flour into a large bowl, then make a well in the centre. Beat an egg with 1 cup (250 ml/ 8 fl oz) milk and 1 tablespoon oil in a large jug. Gradually pour into the well, whisking to make a smooth batter. Cover and leave to stand for 10 minutes before using. The mixture should be the consistency of thick cream. Thin with a little extra milk if necessary. Pat the fish dry with paper towel, dust lightly with flour, then dip in the batter, in batches, allowing the excess to drain off. Lower the fish in batches into the oil and deep-fry until golden brown. Drain on crumpled paper towels.

EGG WHITE BATTER

Sift 1 cup (125 g/4 oz) self-raising flour into a large bowl, make a well in the centre and gradually whisk in 1 cup (250 ml/8 fl oz) water to make a smooth batter. Leave to stand for 5 minutes. Beat 2 egg whites in a small clean bowl with electric beaters until stiff peaks form, then fold into the batter in two batches. Use immediately. Pat the fish dry with paper towel, dust lightly with flour, then dip into the batter in batches, allowing the excess batter to drain off. Lower the fish in batches into the oil and deep-fry until golden brown. Drain well on crumpled paper towels.

BEER BATTER

Sift 1 cup (125 g/4 oz) plain flour into a large bowl, make a well in the centre and gradually whisk in 1 cup (250 ml/8 fl oz) chilled beer. Pat the fish dry with paper towel, dust with flour, then dip into the batter in batches, allowing the excess to drain off. Lower into the oil in batches and deep-fry until golden. Drain on crumpled paper towels. (Soda water can be used instead of beer.)

SESAME SEED COATING

Season some flour with pepper and salt in a shallow bowl. Put 1 cup (155 g/5 oz) sesame seeds in another. Lightly beat an egg in a separate bowl. Pat the fish dry with paper towel, dust lightly with the flour, then dip in the egg, allowing the excess to drain off. Coat in sesame seeds. Heat 3 cm (1¼ inches) oil in a heavy-based frying pan to 180°C (350°F), or until a cube of bread dropped into the oil browns in 15 seconds. Shallow-fry the fish in batches until golden, turning once. Drain on crumpled paper towels.

NORI AND CRUMB COATING

Place 1½ cups (90 g/3 oz) Japanese breadcrumbs in a bowl. Tear or cut a sheet of nori into small pieces and stir into the crumbs. Season some flour with a little salt and pepper in a shallow bowl. Lightly beat an egg in a separate bowl. Pat the fish fillet dry with paper towel and dust lightly with flour. Dip in the egg, allowing the excess to drain off, then coat in the nori. Deep-fry the fish in batches until golden, then drain on crumpled paper towels.

CHIVE AND LEMON COATING

Combine 1¼ cups (100 g/3½ oz) fresh breadcrumbs with 6 tablespoons finely chopped fresh chives and 1 teaspoon finely grated lemon rind. Season some flour with salt and pepper in a shallow bowl. Lightly beat an egg in a separate bowl. Pat the fillet dry with paper towel and dust lightly with the flour. Dip in the egg, allowing the excess to drain off, then coat in the breadcrumbs. Melt 30 g (1 oz) butter and 2 tablespoons oil in a large frying pan, add the fish in batches and cook over medium heat until golden brown. Turn and cook the other side, adding butter and oil as required.

CLOCKWISE, FROM TOP LEFT: Basic batter; Beer batter (with prawns); Nori and crumb coating (with calamari); Chive and lemon coating; Sesame seed coating; Egg white batter

BREAM WITH TOMATO CHEESE CRUST

Preparation time: 40 minutes
Total cooking time: 15 minutes
Serves 4

2 ripe tomatoes
1 small onion, finely chopped
1 tablespoon tomato paste (tomato purée)
½ teaspoon ground cumin
½ teaspoon ground coriander
Tabasco, to taste
¼ teaspoon ground pepper
1 tablespoon lemon juice
20 g (¾ oz) butter, melted
4 medium skinless bream fillets
90 g (3 oz) Cheddar, grated
½ cup (40 g/1¼ oz) fresh breadcrumbs
lemon wedges, for serving

1 Score a cross in the base of each tomato, place in a heatproof bowl and cover with boiling water. Leave for 30 seconds, then plunge briefly in cold water. Peel away from the cross. Cut each tomato in half, remove the core and scoop out the seeds with a teaspoon. Finely chop the tomato flesh.
2 Preheat the oven to moderate 180°C (350°F/ Gas 4). Lightly grease a baking tray. Put the tomato in a small bowl and mix with the onion, tomato paste, cumin, coriander and Tabasco.
3 Combine the pepper, lemon juice and butter in a small bowl. Put the bream fillets on the prepared tray. Brush each fillet with the pepper mixture and top with tomato. Sprinkle with the combined Cheddar and breadcrumbs and bake for 15 minutes, or until tender and the fish flakes easily when tested with a fork. Serve with lemon wedges.

NOTE: Instead of bream, you can use snapper, John dory or ocean perch.

PAELLA

Preparation time: 30 minutes + 2 hours soaking
Total cooking time: 45 minutes
Serves 4

12 raw medium prawns
12–16 black mussels
½ cup (125 ml/4 fl oz) white wine
1 small red onion, chopped
½ cup (125 ml/4 fl oz) olive oil
1 small chicken breast fillet, cut into bite-sized cubes
100 g (3½ oz) calamari rings
100 g (3½ oz) skinless white fish fillet (eg. cod, ling, mahi mahi, blue-eye, monkfish), cut into bite-sized cubes
½ small red onion, extra, finely chopped
1 rasher bacon, finely chopped
4 cloves garlic, crushed
1 small red pepper (capsicum), finely chopped
1 ripe tomato, peeled and chopped
90 g (3 oz) chorizo or pepperoni, thinly sliced
pinch of cayenne pepper
1 cup (200 g/6½ oz) long-grain rice
¼ teaspoon saffron threads
2 cups (500 ml/16 fl oz) chicken stock, heated
½ cup (80 g/2¾ oz) fresh or frozen peas
2 tablespoons finely chopped fresh parsley

1 Peel the prawns and pull out the dark vein from each prawn back, starting at the head end.
2 Scrub the mussels with a stiff brush and pull out the hairy beards. Discard any broken mussels, or open ones that don't close when tapped on the bench.

3 Heat the wine and onion in a large pan. Add the mussels, cover and gently shake the pan for 4–5 minutes over high heat. After 3 minutes, start removing opened mussels and set aside. At the end of 5 minutes, discard any unopened mussels. Reserve the cooking liquid.
4 Heat half the oil in a large frying pan. Pat the chicken dry with paper towels, then cook the chicken for 5 minutes, or until golden brown. Remove from the pan and set aside. Add the prawns, calamari and fish to the pan and cook for 1 minute. Remove from the pan; set aside.
5 Heat the remaining oil in the pan, add the extra onion, bacon, garlic and red pepper and cook for 5 minutes, or until the onion is soft. Add the tomato, chorizo and cayenne. Season, to taste. Stir in the reserved cooking liquid, then add the rice and mix well.
6 Blend the saffron with ½ cup (125 ml/ 4 fl oz) of stock, then add with the remaining stock to the rice and mix well. Bring slowly to the boil. Reduce the heat to low and simmer, uncovered, for 15 minutes, without stirring.
7 Place the peas, chicken, prawns, calamari and fish on top of the rice. Using a wooden spoon, push pieces into the rice, cover and cook over low heat for 10–15 minutes, or until the rice is tender and the seafood cooked. Add the mussels for the last 2 minutes to heat. If the rice is not quite cooked, add a little extra stock and cook for a few more minutes. Serve sprinkled with parsley.

CAJUN SWORDFISH

Preparation time: 15 minutes
Total cooking time: 10 minutes
Serves 4

1 tablespoon garlic powder
1 tablespoon onion powder
2 teaspoons white pepper
2 teaspoons cracked black pepper
2 teaspoons dried thyme
2 teaspoons dried oregano
1 teaspoon cayenne pepper
4 swordfish steaks
oil, for cooking
lime wedges, for serving
yoghurt, optional, for serving

1 Mix all the dried spices and herbs in a bowl.
2 Pat the swordfish steaks dry with paper towels, then coat both sides of each steak in the spice mixture, shaking off any excess.
3 Heat a barbecue hotplate and drizzle with a little oil. Cook the swordfish steaks for about 3–5 minutes each side, depending on the thickness of each steak. Serve with wedges of lime and yoghurt, if desired.

NOTE: You can use tuna, mahi mahi, kingfish or striped marlin instead of the swordfish.

STEAMED FISH

Preparation time: 15 minutes + 4 hours marinating
Total cooking time: 25 minutes
Serves 4

¼ cup (60 g/2 oz) white miso paste
1 tablespoon vegetable oil
2 cloves garlic, crushed
1½ tablespoons grated fresh ginger
2 tablespoons light soy sauce
2 tablespoons oyster sauce
1.5 kg (3 lb) large whole red snapper, cleaned and scaled
4 spring onions, sliced on the diagonal
fresh coriander leaves, to garnish

1 Combine the miso paste, oil, garlic, ginger, soy and oyster sauces in a food processor until smooth. If the fish is too big to fit into the steamer, cut off the head.
2 Make four deep diagonal slashes on both sides of the fish. Spoon half the paste over one side of the fish and rub well into the skin and slashes. Repeat on the other side with the remaining paste. Place on a plate, cover with plastic wrap and refrigerate for 2–4 hours.
3 Line a large bamboo steamer with baking paper. Place the fish in the steamer and sprinkle with the spring onion. Cover and steam over a wok of simmering water for 20–25 minutes, or until the fish is cooked. Replenish the boiling water, if necessary.
4 Remove the fish from the steamer, pour any juices collected in the baking paper over the top and garnish with coriander. Serve with steamed rice and stir-fried vegetables.

TUNA MORNAY

Preparation time: 20 minutes
Total cooking time: 25 minutes
Serves 4

60 g (2 oz) butter
2 tablespoons plain flour
2 cups (500 ml/16 fl oz) milk
½ teaspoon dry mustard
90 g (3 oz) Cheddar, grated
600 g (1¼ lb) canned tuna in brine, drained
2 tablespoons finely chopped fresh parsley
2 eggs, hard-boiled and chopped
⅓ cup (25 g/¾ oz) fresh breadcrumbs
paprika, for dusting

1 Preheat the oven to moderate 180°C (350°F/ Gas 4). Melt the butter in a small pan. Add the flour and stir over low heat for 1 minute, or until pale and foaming. Remove the pan from the heat and gradually stir in the milk. Return the pan to the heat and stir constantly until the sauce boils and thickens. Reduce the heat and simmer for 2 minutes. Remove from the heat and whisk in the mustard and 60 g (2 oz) of the Cheddar, until melted and smooth.
2 Flake the tuna with a fork and mix into the sauce, with the parsley and egg. Season with salt and pepper, to taste. Spoon into four 1 cup (250 ml/8 fl oz) capacity ovenproof ramekins. Mix the breadcrumbs and remaining Cheddar and sprinkle over the mornay. Dust very lightly with paprika. Bake for 15–20 minutes, or until golden brown.

NOTES: For an interesting crunch to your tuna mornay, substitute roughly crushed potato crisps for some or all of the breadcrumbs in the topping. Choose plain, or salt-and-vinegar flavoured crisps.
 Cans of salmon can be substituted for the tuna, using the same amount.

SALMON WITH LEMON CANNELLONI

Preparation time: 25 minutes
Total cooking time: 40 minutes
Serves 4–6

Filling
415 g (13 oz) can pink salmon
250 g (8 oz) ricotta cheese
1 tablespoon lemon juice
1 egg yolk, lightly beaten
2 tablespoons finely chopped onion

Sauce
125 g (4 oz) butter
⅔ cup (85 g/3 oz) plain flour
2¾ cups (685 ml/23 fl oz) milk
1 teaspoon finely grated lemon rind
¼ teaspoon ground nutmeg

16 cannelloni tubes
1–2 tablespoons chopped fresh dill, to
    garnish

1 Drain the salmon, reserving the liquid for the sauce. Remove and discard the skin and bones. Flake the salmon flesh and mix with the ricotta, lemon juice, egg yolk and onion in a bowl. Add a little salt and pepper, to taste.

2 For the sauce, melt the butter in a saucepan over low heat. Stir in the flour and cook for 1 minute, or until pale and foaming. Remove from the heat and gradually stir in the milk. Return to the heat and stir constantly until the sauce boils and thickens. Reduce the heat and simmer for 2 minutes. Add the reserved salmon liquid, lemon rind, nutmeg and salt and pepper, to taste. Set aside to cool.

3 Preheat the oven to moderate 180°C (350°F/ Gas 4). Fill the cannelloni tubes with filling, using a small spoon or piping bag. Spread one third of the sauce over the bottom of a shallow ovenproof dish, then sit the cannelloni tubes in the dish side-by-side. Pour the remaining sauce over the top, covering all the exposed pasta. Bake for about 30 minutes, until bubbly. Serve garnished with the dill.

RED EMPEROR POACHED IN COCONUT MILK

Preparation time: 20 minutes
Total cooking time: 30–40 minutes
Serves 4

1 litre (32 fl oz) coconut milk
2 teaspoons grated fresh ginger
3 small red chillies, finely chopped
1 tablespoon chopped coriander roots
    and stems
6 Asian shallots, finely chopped
6 kaffir lime leaves, shredded
2 stems lemon grass, white part only,
    sliced
2 teaspoons grated lime rind
2 cups (500 ml/16 fl oz) fish stock
⅓ cup (80 ml/2¾ fl oz) fish sauce
⅓ cup (80 ml/2¾ fl oz) lime juice, strained
4 x 250 g (8 oz) red emperor fillets, skin
    on
coriander leaves, to garnish
1 small red chilli, cut in long strips, to
    garnish
2 kaffir lime leaves, shredded, to garnish

1 Bring the coconut milk to the boil in a saucepan and boil for 3 minutes. Add the ginger, chilli, coriander roots and stems, shallots, kaffir lime leaves, lemon grass and lime rind and bring back to the boil. Add the fish stock and fish sauce and simmer for 15 minutes. Pass through a fine strainer and add the lime juice. Taste and add extra fish sauce if necessary.

2 Heat the sauce in a wide-based frying pan and when it comes to the boil add the fish, then reduce the heat and simmer very gently for 10–15 minutes, or until just cooked through.

3 Carefully transfer the fish to a serving platter. Serve with some of the liquid and a sprinkling of coriander, chilli and shreds of kaffir lime leaf.

NOTE: You can also use coral trout, snapper or murray cod.

OCEAN TROUT WITH LEEK AND CAPER SAUCE

Preparation time: 10 minutes
Total cooking time: 10 minutes
Serves 4

45 g (11/2 oz) butter, melted
4 thick skinless ocean trout fillets (about 150 g/ 5 oz each)

Leek and caper sauce
50 g (13/4 oz) butter
1 leek, white part only, chopped
1 cup (250 ml/8 fl oz) white wine
2 tablespoons bottled capers, drained
1 tablespoon chopped fresh flat-leaf parsley

1 Brush a baking tray with melted butter, put the trout on the tray and brush with melted butter. Grill under moderate heat, without turning, until the fish is just cooked and flakes easily when tested with a fork. Remove and cover loosely with foil to keep warm.
2 For the sauce, melt the butter in a small pan over low heat and cook the leek until soft, but not brown. Add the wine and simmer for 3–4 minutes. Stir in the capers and parsley and salt and pepper, to taste.
3 Spoon the hot sauce over the fish and serve immediately with steamed baby potatoes.

NOTE: You can use salmon fillets or cutlets or any thick white fish instead of trout.

ROSEMARY TUNA KEBABS

Preparation time: 20 minutes
Total cooking time: 20 minutes
Serves 4

3 tomatoes
1 tablespoon olive oil
2–3 small fresh red chillies, seeded and chopped
3–4 cloves garlic, crushed
1 red onion, finely chopped
¼ cup (60 ml/2 fl oz) white wine or water
2 x 300 g (10 oz) cans chickpeas
3 tablespoons chopped fresh oregano
4 tablespoons chopped fresh parsley
lemon wedges, for serving

Tuna kebabs
1 kg (2 lb) tuna fillet, cut into 4 cm (1½ inch) cubes
8 stalks of fresh rosemary, about 20 cm (8 inch) long, with leaves
cooking oil spray

1 Cut the tomatoes into halves or quarters and use a teaspoon to scrape out the seeds. Roughly chop the flesh.
2 Heat the oil in a large non-stick frying pan. Add the chilli, garlic and red onion and stir over medium heat for 5 minutes, or until softened. Add the chopped tomato and the white wine or water. Cook over low heat for 10 minutes, or until the mixture is soft and pulpy and most of the liquid has evaporated.
3 Stir in the rinsed chickpeas with the fresh oregano and parsley. Season with salt and pepper, to taste.
4 Heat a grill or barbecue plate. Thread the tuna onto the rosemary stalks, lightly spray with oil, then cook, turning, for 3 minutes. Do not overcook or the tuna will be dry and fall apart. Serve with the chickpeas and lemon wedges.

NOTE: Swordfish, striped marlin or salmon are also suitable for this recipe.

BARBECUED SARDINES

Preparation time: 25 minutes +
    2 hours marinating
Total cooking time: 6 minutes
Serves 4

8 large fresh sardines
8 sprigs fresh lemon thyme
3 tablespoons extra virgin olive oil
2 cloves garlic, crushed
1 teaspoon finely grated lemon rind
2 tablespoons lemon juice
1 teaspoon ground cumin
lemon wedges, for serving

1 Carefully slit the sardines from head to tail and remove the gut. Rinse, then pat dry inside and out with paper towels. Place a sprig of fresh lemon thyme in each fish cavity and arrange the fish in a shallow non-metallic dish.
2 Combine the olive oil, garlic, lemon rind, lemon juice and cumin in a small bowl and pour over the fish. Cover and refrigerate for 2 hours.
3 Cook on a preheated barbecue hotplate for 2–3 minutes each side, basting frequently with the marinade, or until the flesh flakes easily when tested with a fork. Alternatively, barbecue in a sardine cooking rack until tender. Serve with lemon wedges.

MARINADES & BASTES

ADD A LITTLE EXTRA ZEST TO YOUR CHARGRILLED SEAFOOD BY USING ONE OF THESE TANGY MARINADES OR SPICY BASTES.

SPICED YOGHURT MARINADE

(For firm-fleshed skinless fish fillets—snapper, bream, ocean perch, flake.) Combine 400 g (13 oz) natural yoghurt, 1 tablespoon each of grated fresh ginger, ground cumin, ground cinnamon, ground coriander and ground mace, add 1–2 tablespoons each of grated lime rind and juice and 2 tablespoons chopped fresh mint. Add 1 kg (2 lb) fish fillets, cover and refrigerate for 3 hours. Cook on a preheated barbecue hotplate until tender.
Serves 4–6.

SWEET AND SPICY BASTING SAUCE

(For yabbies, bugs and scampi.) Combine 1 cup (250 ml/8 fl oz) sweet chilli sauce, 2 crushed cloves garlic, 1–2 tablespoons lemon juice, 1 tablespoon peanut oil, 50 g (1¾ oz) melted butter and 2 tablespoons chopped fresh coriander in a large jug. Toss 1 kg (2 lb) yabby, bug or scampi meat in 1 tablespoon oil and cook in batches on a preheated barbecue hotplate, turning and basting frequently with the sauce. Serve with any leftover sauce.
Serves 4–6.

LIME AND PEPPERCORN MARINADE

(For prawns, fish steaks and cutlets—tuna, swordfish, blue-eye, salmon.) Stir-fry 1 cup (60 g/2 oz) Szechwan or black peppercorns in a wok until fragrant. Transfer to a mortar and pestle or spice grinder, add 4 chopped Asian shallots and crush together. Transfer to a shallow glass dish and add ⅓ cup (80 ml/2¾ fl oz) lime juice, 1 tablespoon salt, 1 teaspoon sesame oil and ¼ cup (60 ml/ 2 fl oz) peanut oil. Add 1 kg (2 lb) firm white fish fillets or 1 kg (2 lb) peeled, deveined prawns with tails intact. Cover; chill for 3 hours. Cook on a preheated barbecue hotplate in batches until the seafood is cooked through. If you are using tuna or salmon, don't overcook it or it will be dry.
Serves 4–6.

GARLIC MARINADE

Combine 6 crushed cloves garlic, 1 cup (250 ml/8 fl oz) extra virgin olive oil, 1 tablespoon lemon juice and chopped fresh dill in a shallow dish. Add 1 kg (2 lb) cubed firm white fish or 1 kg (2 lb) peeled, deveined prawns. Coat in the marinade, cover and chill overnight. Return to room temperature, thread onto skewers and cook on a hot barbecue grill or hotplate until cooked through.
Serves 4–6.

TEXAN BARBECUE BASTING SAUCE (FOR ALL SHELLFISH.)

Combine 1 cup (250 ml/8 fl oz) tomato sauce, 6 splashes of Tabasco, 3 chopped rehydrated chipotle chillies, 1 tablespoon each of vinegar and oil in a bowl. Use to baste while cooking 1 kg (2 lb) prawns, bugs or yabbies.
Serves 4–6.

THAI MARINADE

Combine ½ cup (125 ml/4 fl oz) fish sauce, 4 finely shredded kaffir lime leaves, 2–3 tablespoons grated palm sugar or brown sugar, juice and rind of 2 limes and 1 teaspoon sesame oil. Add 1 kg (2 lb) cleaned octopus and marinate overnight. Drain well. Cook over very high heat on a barbecue grill, turning frequently, for 3 minutes or until cooked.
Serves 4–6.

CLOCKWISE, FROM TOP LEFT: Spiced yoghurt marinade; Lime and peppercorn marinade; Thai marinade; Texan barbecue basting sauce; Garlic marinade; Sweet and spicy basting sauce

BRIK A L'OEUF

Preparation time: 30 minutes
Total cooking time: 15 minutes
Serves 2

6 sheets filo pastry
30 g (1 oz) butter, melted
1 small onion, finely chopped
200 g (6½ oz) can tuna in oil, drained
6 black olives, pitted and chopped
1 tablespoon finely chopped fresh parsley
2 eggs

1 Preheat the oven to moderately hot 200°C (400°F/Gas 6). Cut the filo pastry sheets in half widthways. Layer 4 sheets together with melted butter. Keep the remaining pastry covered with a damp tea towel. Combine the onion, tuna, olives and parsley in a bowl and spoon half the mixture onto one end of the buttered pastry, leaving a border. Make a well in the centre of the tuna mixture and break an egg into the well, being careful to leave it whole. Season with salt and freshly ground black pepper.
2 Layer 2 more sheets of filo together with melted butter and place on top of the tuna and egg. Fold in the pastry sides, then roll into a firm parcel, keeping the egg whole. Place on a lightly greased baking tray and brush with melted butter. Repeat with the remaining pastry, filling and egg.
3 Bake for 15 minutes, or until the pastry is golden brown. Serve warm.

NOTE: The yolk is still soft after 15 minutes. If you prefer a firmer egg, bake a little longer.

CAPONATA WITH TUNA

Preparation time: 25 minutes +
    1 hour standing + cooling
Total cooking time: 45 minutes
Serves 6

Caponata
500 g (1 lb) ripe tomatoes
750 g (1½ lb) eggplant (aubergine), cut
    into 1 cm (½ inch) cubes
½ cup (125 ml/4 fl oz) olive oil
1 onion, chopped
3 stalks celery, chopped
2 tablespoons capers
½ cup (125 g/4 oz) green olives, pitted
1 tablespoon sugar
½ cup (125 ml/4 fl oz) red wine vinegar

6 x 200 g (6½ oz) tuna steaks
olive oil, for brushing

1 Score a cross in the base of each tomato. Place the tomatoes into a bowl of boiling water for 10 seconds, then plunge into cold water and peel the skin away from the cross. Cut the tomato into 1 cm (½ inch) cubes.

2 Sprinkle the eggplant with salt and leave in a colander for 1 hour. Rinse under cold water and pat dry. Heat 2 tablespoons oil in a frying pan over medium heat and cook half the eggplant for 4–5 minutes, or until golden and soft. Remove from the pan and drain on crumpled paper towels. Repeat with 2 tablespoons oil and the remaining eggplant.
3 Heat the remaining olive oil in the same pan, add the onion and celery, and cook for 5–6 minutes, or until softened. Reduce the heat to low, add the tomato and simmer for 15 minutes, stirring occasionally. Stir in the capers, olives, sugar and vinegar, season and continue to simmer, stirring occasionally, for 10 minutes, or until slightly reduced. Stir in the eggplant. Remove from the heat and cool to room temperature.
4 Heat a chargrill plate and brush lightly with olive oil. Cook the tuna for 2–3 minutes each side, or to your liking. Serve with the caponata.

FISH ON EGGPLANT (AUBERGINE) WITH ROASTED RED PEPPER (CAPSICUM) AIOLI

Preparation time: 15–20 minutes +
    20 minutes standing
Total cooking time: 10 minutes
Serves 4

8 thick slices of large eggplant
    (aubergine)
1 large red pepper (capsicum)
2 tablespoons oil
4 x 200 g (6½ oz) white fish fillets (eg.
    snapper, monkfish, perch, cod), each
    cut diagonally into 6 pieces

Roasted red pepper (capsicum) aioli
2 cloves garlic, roughly chopped
1 egg yolk
2–3 teaspoons lemon juice
½ cup (125 ml/4 fl oz) olive oil
2 tablespoons chopped fresh parsley

1 Rub some salt into each cut side of the
eggplant, place on a plate and set aside
for 20 minutes. Rinse off the salt and pat
the eggplant dry with paper towels. Set
aside.
2 Cut the red pepper into large flattish
pieces. Cook, skin-side-up, under a hot
grill until the skin blackens and blisters.
Cool in a plastic bag, then peel and
discard the seeds and membrane. Slice
into strips. Reserve half for the aioli.

3 For the roasted red pepper aioli, mix
the garlic, egg yolk and juice in a food
processor or blender until smooth. With
the motor running, pour in half the olive
oil in a thin steady stream, blending until
the aioli thickens. Add the reserved red
pepper and blend until smooth. Transfer
to a bowl and season, to taste. Stir in the
parsley, cover and refrigerate.
4 Heat a grill to high. Brush the eggplant
with half the oil and grill on both sides
until brown and tender.
5 Heat the remaining oil in a frying pan
and cook the fish for 1–2 minutes each
side, or until the fish flakes when tested
in the thickest part. Do not overcook or
the fish will toughen.
6 To serve, place the eggplant on a plate
and top with some sliced roasted pepper.
Arrange 3 pieces of fish over the pepper
and spoon some aioli over the top.

PICKLED FRIED FISH

Preparation time: 15 minutes +
    24 hours marinating
Total cooking time: 15 minutes
Serves 4–6

½ cup (60 g/2 oz) plain flour
pinch of cayenne pepper
500 g (1 lb) firm white fish such as ling or
    blue eye, cut into 24 strips
½ cup (125 ml/4 fl oz) olive oil
250 g (8 oz) brown onions, thinly sliced
250 g (8 oz) carrots, thinly sliced
8 spring onions, diagonally sliced
12 cloves garlic, chopped
1 tablespoon chopped fresh thyme
2 bay leaves
2 cloves
8 juniper berries
1 teaspoon black peppercorns
1 cup (250 ml/8 fl oz) white wine vinegar
1 cup (250 ml/8 fl oz) white wine
2 tablespoons chopped fresh flat-leaf
    parsley

1 Season the flour with the cayenne
pepper and salt. Pat the fish dry with
paper towels, coat each piece in the flour
and shake off any excess.
2 Heat 2 tablespoons oil in a large frying
pan and cook the fish in batches until
golden brown. Don't overcook the fish or it
will break up when the marinade is poured
over it. Place the fish in a non-metallic dish.
3 Clean the frying pan, heat 3 tablespoons
oil and sauté the onion, carrot and spring
onion for 5 minutes, or until soft but not
brown. Add the garlic, herbs and spices,
wine vinegar, wine and 1 cup (250 ml/
8 fl oz) water. Simmer for 2 minutes, then
season with 1 teaspoon salt.
4 Pour the hot mixture over the fish and
leave to cool. Cover and refrigerate for at
least 24 hours.
5 Bring back to room temperature and
remove the fish and vegetables from the
liquid with a slotted spoon. Place on a dish,
combine the parsley with 2 tablespoons of
the liquid and pour over the fish.

CRAWFISH ETOUFFEE

Preparation time: 10 minutes
Total cooking time: 30 minutes
Serves 6

¼ cup (60 ml/2 fl oz) oil
¼ cup (30 g/1 oz) plain (all-purpose) flour
45 g (11/2 oz) unsalted butter
½/ onion, finely chopped
1 short celery stalk, finely chopped
1 red capsicum (pepper), cut into thin strips
½ green capsicum (pepper), cut into thin strips
1 teaspoon Cajun spices
1 teaspoon celery salt
½ teaspoon dried basil
1 red chilli, seeded and finely chopped
2 cups (500 ml/16 fl oz) fish stock
500 g (1 lb) lobster tail, cut into bite-sized pieces
3 spring onions (scallions), finely chopped

1 Start by making the roux. Heat the oil in a small, heavy-based saucepan, add the flour and stir to make a smooth paste. Cook over very low heat, stirring constantly, until it turns into a rich, dark, mahogany brown roux. Remove the pan from the heat.
2 Heat the butter in a large frying pan. Cook the onion, celery and capsicums for 5 minutes, then add the Cajun spices, celery salt, basil and chopped chilli.
3 Bring the stock to the boil in a separate saucepan, whisk in the roux and simmer over medium heat for 5 minutes. Add the cooked vegetables and simmer over medium heat for 15 minutes.
4 Add the lobster and spring onions and cook for 3–4 minutes, or until just tender. Season to taste with salt and freshly ground black pepper. Serve on a bed of steamed white rice.

SEAFOOD, FENNEL AND POTATO STEW

Preparation time: 25 minutes
Total cooking time: 30 minutes
Serves 6

18–20 black mussels
6 baby octopus
16 raw medium prawns
1 large fennel bulb
2 tablespoons olive oil
2 leeks, white part only, thinly sliced
2 cloves garlic, crushed
½ teaspoon paprika
2 tablespoons Pernod or Ricard (see Note)
⅔ cup (170 ml/5½ fl oz) dry white wine
¼ teaspoon saffron threads
¼ teaspoon fresh thyme leaves
500 g (1 lb) fish cutlets (eg. swordfish, kingfish, warehou, monkfish), cut into large chunks
400 g (13 oz) baby new potatoes
fennel greens, to garnish

1 Scrub the mussels with a stiff brush and pull out the hairy beards. Discard any broken mussels, or open ones that don't close when tapped on the bench. Rinse well.
2 Use a small sharp knife to cut off the octopus heads. Grasp the bodies and push the beaks out with your index finger; remove and discard. Slit the heads and remove the gut, then wash well.
3 Peel the prawns and pull out the dark vein from each prawn back, starting at the head end.

4 Trim off any discoloured parts and thinly slice the fennel. Heat the oil in a large pan over medium heat. Add the fennel, leek and garlic. Stir in the paprika, season lightly with salt and pepper and cook for 8 minutes, or until softened. Add the Pernod and wine and boil for 1 minute, or until reduced by a third.
5 Add the mussels to the pan, cover and cook, shaking the pan occasionally for 4–5 minutes, or until opened, discarding any unopened mussels. Remove from the pan and allow to cool. Remove the mussel meat from the shells and set aside.
6 Add the saffron and thyme to the pan and cook, stirring over medium heat, for 1–2 minutes. Season if necessary, with salt and pepper, then transfer to a large, flameproof casserole dish.
7 Stir the octopus, prawns, fish and potatoes into the stew. Cover and cook gently for 10 minutes, or until the potatoes and seafood are tender. Add the mussels, cover and heat through. Garnish with fennel greens and serve.

NOTES: Pernod and Ricard are aniseed-flavoured liqueurs and complement the fennel.
Choose very small potatoes for this recipe. Sometimes they are called chat potatoes. Otherwise, cut larger ones in half.

CUCUMBER AND WHITE FISH STIR-FRY

Preparation time: 20 minutes
Total cooking time: 20 minutes
Serves 4

½ cup (60 g/2 oz) plain flour
½ cup (60 g/2 oz) cornflour
½ teaspoon five-spice powder
750 g (1½ lb) firm white boneless fish fillets, such as ling, cut into 3 cm (1¼ inch) cubes
2 egg whites, lightly beaten
oil, for deep-frying
1 tablespoon vegetable oil
1 onion, cut into wedges
1 telegraph cucumber, halved, seeded and sliced on the diagonal
1 teaspoon cornflour, extra
¾ teaspoon sesame oil
1 tablespoon soy sauce
⅓ cup (80 ml/2¾ fl oz) rice vinegar
1½ tablespoons soft brown sugar
3 teaspoons fish sauce

1 Combine the plain flour, cornflour and five-spice powder in a shallow bowl, and season with salt and freshly ground black pepper. Dip the fish in the beaten egg white, drain off any excess, then toss gently in the flour mixture, shaking off any excess.
2 Fill a large saucepan one-third full of oil and heat to 180°C (350°F), or until a cube of bread dropped in the oil browns in 15 seconds. Cook the fish in batches for 6 minutes, or until golden brown. Drain on crumpled paper towels.
3 Heat a wok over high heat, add 1 tablespoon oil and swirl to coat the side of the wok. Add the onion and stir-fry for 1 minute, then add the cucumber and stir-fry for 30 seconds.
4 Blend the cornflour with 2 tablespoons water and add to the wok with the sesame oil, soy sauce, vinegar, sugar and fish sauce. Stir-fry for 3 minutes, or until the mixture boils and thickens. Add the fish and toss thoroughly to coat and heat through. Serve hot.

RED MULLET IN VINE LEAVES

Preparation time: 20 minutes +
    30 minutes draining
Total cooking time: 15 minutes
Serves 4 as a first course

4 large vine-ripened tomatoes
2 cloves garlic, crushed
4 anchovy fillets, chopped
4 tablespoons chopped fresh flat-leaf parsley
2 tablespoons chopped fresh basil
4 Kalamata olives, pitted and chopped
4 red mullet (about 250 g/8 oz each), cleaned and scaled
8 preserved vine leaves
1 tablespoon olive oil
1 tablespoon lemon juice
lemon wedges, to garnish

1 Score a cross in the base of each tomato. Place the tomatoes in a bowl of boiling water for 10 seconds, then plunge into cold water and peel each down from the cross. Scoop out the seeds with a teaspoon. Finely chop the flesh, then place the tomatoes in a sieve over a bowl and leave to drain for 30 minutes to remove excess moisture. Preheat the oven to moderate 180°C (350°F/Gas 4).
2 Discard the drained liquid, then place the tomatoes in the bowl and add the garlic, anchovies, parsley, basil and olives. Season with salt and pepper.
3 Season the fish well inside and out, then stuff each fish with ½ tablespoon of the tomato mixture.
4 Rinse the vine leaves well and pat dry. Place two vine leaves together slightly overlapping. Divide the remaining tomato mixture into 4 portions. Spread half of one portion over the vine leaves, place a fish on top and spread the other half of the filling portion on top of the fish. Fold the leaves over to form a parcel, leaving some of the fish head and tail exposed. Repeat to make three more parcels.
5 Mix the oil and lemon juice in a small bowl. Place the fish parcels in a non-metallic baking dish and brush all over with the lemon and oil (especially the tails, which burn easily). Bake for 15 minutes, then carefully lift onto serving plates and garnish with lemon wedges.

SEAFOOD RISOTTO

Preparation time: 20 minutes
Total cooking time: 35 minutes
Serves 4

185 g (6 oz) squid tubes
200 g (61/2 oz) prawns (shrimp)
16 scallops
1/3 cup (80 ml/2¾ fl oz) olive oil
2 garlic cloves, crushed
185 g (6 oz) firm white fish fillets, skinned and cut into bite-size pieces
1 litre (32 fl oz) fish stock
1 leek (white part only), thinly sliced
1½ cups (360 g/12 oz) risotto rice
½ cup (125 ml/4 fl oz) dry white wine
3 Roma (plum) tomatoes, chopped
20 g (¾ oz) butter
1½ tablespoons finely chopped parsley
1½ tablespoons finely chopped dill

1 Cut the squid tubes into thinner rings. Peel and devein the prawns. Clean the scallops.
2 Heat half the olive oil in a saucepan. Add the garlic and cook gently for 20 seconds. Add the squid and prawns and season. Increase the heat and cook until opaque. Remove the squid and prawns from the pan.
3 Add the fish and scallops to the pan and cook until they change colour. Remove from the pan and set aside. Pour the stock into a saucepan and bring to the boil. Reduce the heat, cover with a lid and keep at a low simmer.
4 Heat the remaining olive oil in the large wide saucepan. Add the leek and cook for about 4 minutes, or until softened but not browned. Stir in the rice until well coated. Pour in the wine, increase the heat and cook, stirring, until all the liquid is absorbed. Add ½ cup (125 ml/4 fl oz) of the hot stock and stir constantly over medium heat until all the liquid is absorbed. Continue adding more stock, ½ cup (125 ml/4 fl oz) at a time until all the liquid is absorbed, this will take around 25–30 minutes.
5 Add the tomato and cooked seafood and toss. Remove the pan from the heat and gently stir in the butter and herbs. Season with salt and freshly ground black pepper.

CREAMY SEAFOOD RAVIOLI

Preparation time: 45 minutes +
  30 minutes standing
Total cooking time: 15 minutes
Serves 4

Pasta
2 cups (250 g/8 oz) plain flour
3 eggs
1 tablespoon olive oil
1 egg yolk, extra

Filling
100 g (3½ oz) scallops
50 g (1¾ oz) butter, softened
3 cloves garlic, finely chopped
2 tablespoons chopped fresh flat-leaf parsley
100 g (3½ oz) raw prawn meat, finely chopped
Sauce
60 g (2 oz) butter
¼ cup (30 g/1 oz) plain flour
1½ cups (375 ml/12 fl oz) milk
300 ml (10 fl oz) cream
½ cup (125 ml/4 fl oz) white wine
50 g (13/4 oz) Parmesan, grated
2 tablespoons chopped fresh flat-leaf parsley

1 Sift the flour and a pinch of salt into a bowl and make a well. Whisk the eggs, oil and 1 tablespoon water in a jug, add gradually to the flour and mix to a firm dough. Gather into a ball. (This can also be done in a food processor.)
2 Knead on a lightly floured surface for 5 minutes, or until smooth and elastic. Place in a lightly oiled bowl, cover with plastic wrap and set aside for at least 30 minutes.

3 For the filling, slice or pull off any vein, membrane or hard white muscle from the scallops, leaving any roe attached. Chop finely. Stir together the butter, garlic, parsley, scallops and prawn meat in a bowl. Set aside.
4 Roll out a quarter of the pasta dough at a time on a lightly floured surface, or use a pasta machine, until very thin (each portion should be roughly 10 cm/4 inches wide when rolled). Place 1 teaspoon of filling at 5 cm (2 inch) intervals down one side of each strip. Whisk the extra egg yolk with 3 tablespoons water. Brush along one side of the dough and between the filling. Fold the dough over the filling to meet the other side. Repeat with the remaining filling and dough. Press the edges together firmly to seal.
5 Cut between the mounds with a knife or fluted pastry cutter. Cook batches in a large pan of rapidly boiling water for 6 minutes. Drain well and return to the pan to keep warm.
6 For the sauce, melt the butter in a pan over low heat. Stir in the flour and cook for 1 minute, or until pale and foaming. Remove from the heat and gradually stir in the combined milk, cream and white wine. Return to the heat and stir constantly until the sauce boils and thickens. Reduce the heat and simmer for 2 minutes. Add the grated Parmesan and chopped parsley and stir. Season, to taste. Remove from the heat, add to the ravioli in the pan and toss gently to coat.

CITRUS FISH WITH AVOCADO SALSA

Preparation time: 25 minutes +
    5 minutes marinating
Total cooking time: 10 minutes
Serves 4

4 firm fish cutlets (eg. snapper, salmon,
    jewfish, blue-eye), about 185 g (6 oz)
    each
3 teaspoons finely grated orange rind
3 teaspoons finely grated lemon rind
1 tablespoon lime juice
2 tablespoons olive oil

Avocado salsa
1 small fresh red chilli
1½ teaspoons ground cumin
1 large avocado, finely chopped
1 red onion, very finely chopped
2 teaspoons lemon juice
2 teaspoons olive oil

1 Place the fish in a shallow, non-metallic
dish. Combine the orange and lemon rind,
lime juice and olive oil in a small bowl and
season with freshly ground black pepper.
Pour over the fish and set aside to
marinate for about 5 minutes.
2 Lightly oil a preheated chargrill pan or
barbecue and cook the fish for
3–5 minutes on each side, or until lightly
browned and cooked through. The fish
will flake easily when tested with a fork.
3 For the avocado salsa, discard the
seeds from the chilli and finely chop the
flesh. Fry the cumin in a dry frying pan for
about 40 seconds, shaking the pan
constantly until fragrant. Combine the
cumin with the avocado, onion, chilli,
lemon juice and olive oil in a bowl.
4 Serve the fish steaks with the avocado
salsa. The fish is delicious served with
grilled halved cherry tomatoes, steamed
snow peas (mangetout) and steamed baby
potatoes.

TUNA STEAKS WITH TAPENADE

Preparation time: 15 minutes +
    10 minutes marinating
Total cooking time: 6 minutes
Serves 4

2 tablespoons tapenade (olive paste)
2 tablespoons olive oil
2 cloves garlic, finely chopped
2 teaspoons finely grated lemon rind
4 tuna steaks
spring onion, diagonally sliced, to garnish

1 Combine the tapenade, oil, garlic, lemon
rind and some black pepper. Spread over
both sides of the tuna and refrigerate for
10 minutes.
2 Place the tuna on a heated and lightly
oiled chargrill pan, barbecue grill or
flatplate and cook, turning once, for about
3 minutes each side. When cooked, the
steak should still be pink in the centre.
Sprinkle with the slices of spring onion.

NOTE: Instead of tuna, you can use
swordfish, kingfish, warehou or blue-eye.

TUNA WITH SORREL HOLLANDAISE

Preparation time: 15 minutes
Total cooking time: 10 minutes
Serves 4

4 tuna steaks (about 150 g/5 oz each)
2 tablespoons olive oil

Sorrel hollandaise
15 young fresh sorrel leaves, stems
    removed
150 g (5 oz) butter
3 egg yolks
1 tablespoon lemon juice

1 Brush the tuna with the oil. Heat a large
frying pan and cook the tuna for
2–3 minutes each side over medium heat,
or until cooked to your liking. Remove
from the pan, cover and keep warm.
2 For the sorrel hollandaise, place the
sorrel leaves in a bowl, cover with boiling
water, drain and rinse in cold water. Pat
the leaves dry with paper towels and chop
roughly. Melt the butter in a small pan.
Put the egg yolks in a food processor and
process for 20 seconds. With the motor
running, add the hot butter in a thin
steady stream and process until thick and
creamy. Add the lemon juice and sorrel,
and season, to taste, with salt and black
pepper. Process for another 20 seconds.
3 Put the warm tuna on individual plates,
spoon sorrel hollandaise over each and
serve.

NOTE: You can substitute swordfish, blue-
eye, salmon or striped marlin for the
tuna.

SALMON STEAKS WITH HERB SAUCE

Preparation time: 25 minutes
Total cooking time: 20 minutes
Serves 4

4 salmon steaks (250 g/8 oz each)
2 tablespoons oil

Herb sauce
1½ cups (375 ml/12 fl oz) fish stock
½ cup (125 ml/4 fl oz) good-quality white wine
3 tablespoons chopped fresh chives
3 tablespoons chopped fresh parsley
2 tablespoons chopped fresh basil
2 tablespoons chopped fresh tarragon
1 cup (250 ml/8 fl oz) cream
2 egg yolks

1 Pat the salmon steaks dry with paper towels.
2 For the herb sauce, combine the stock and wine in a saucepan and bring to the boil. Boil for 5 minutes or until the liquid has reduced by half. Transfer to a blender or food processor, add the chives, parsley, basil and tarragon and blend for 30 seconds. Return to the pan, then stir in the cream and bring to the boil. Reduce the heat to low and simmer for 5 minutes, or until the sauce has reduced by half. Place the egg yolks in a blender or food processor and blend until smooth. With the motor running, gradually drizzle in the hot herb mixture. Process until the sauce is smooth and creamy. Season, to taste.
3 Heat the oil in a frying pan, add the salmon steaks and cook over medium heat for 3 minutes each side, or until just cooked through (do not overcook). Serve hot with herb sauce.

DEEP-FRIED WHOLE FISH WITH TAMARIND SAUCE

Preparation time: 25 minutes
Total cooking time: 10 minutes
Serves 4

2 tablespoons tamarind pulp
2 tablespoons peanut oil
3 cloves garlic, crushed
2 tablespoons grated fresh galangal
2 tablespoons grated palm sugar
2 tablespoons fish sauce
2 tablespoons lime juice
750 g (1½ lb) whole snapper or bream, cleaned and scaled
cornflour, to dust
oil, for deep-frying
1 tablespoon crisp fried shallots
2 small fresh red chillies, seeded and finely shredded
2 tablespoons fresh coriander leaves

1 Put the tamarind pulp and 1/3 cup (80 ml/ 2¾ fl oz) boiling water in a bowl and set aside to cool. Mash the mixture with your fingertips to dissolve the pulp, then strain and reserve the liquid. Discard the pulp.

2 Heat the oil in a saucepan. Add the garlic and galangal and cook for 1 minute. Add the palm sugar, tamarind liquid, fish sauce and lime juice and stir over medium heat until the sugar has dissolved. Boil for 1–2 minutes, or until slightly thickened. Cover and keep hot.
3 Score the fish on both sides in a crisscross pattern 2 cm (3/4 inch) wide and 5 mm (1/4 inch) deep. Pat dry with paper towels. Lightly coat with the cornflour.
4 Fill a wok one-third full of oil and heat to 180°C (350°F), or until a cube of bread dropped in the oil browns in 15 seconds. Deep-fry the fish for 6–7 minutes, or until golden and cooked through—you may need to turn the fish halfway through cooking. Drain on crumpled paper towels and season to taste with salt and freshly ground black pepper.
5 Place the fish on a serving platter and pour the sauce over the top. Serve, sprinkled with the shallot flakes, chilli and coriander leaves.

PAN-FRIED FISH

Preparation time: 5 minutes
Total cooking time: 8 minutes
Serves 4

2–3 tablespoons plain flour
4 firm white fish cutlets (eg. blue-eye,
    jewfish, warehou, snapper)
olive oil, for shallow-frying

1 Sift the flour together with a little salt
and pepper onto a dinner plate. Pat the
fish dry with paper towels, then coat both
sides of the cutlets with seasoned flour,
shaking off any excess.
2 Heat about 3 mm (⅛ inch) oil in a large
frying pan until very hot. Put the fish into
the hot oil immediately and cook for
3 minutes on one side, then turn and cook
the other side for 2 minutes, or until the
coating is crisp and well browned. Reduce
the heat to low and cook for another
2–3 minutes, until the flesh flakes easily
when tested with a fork.
3 Remove the fish from the pan and drain
briefly on crumpled paper towels. If
cooking in batches, keep warm while
cooking the remaining cutlets. Serve
immediately.

NOTE: This method is good for any fish
cutlet, fillet or steak. However, the
cooking time will vary depending on the
thickness of the fish.

TROUT WITH ALMONDS

Preparation time: 25 minutes
Total cooking time: 10 minutes
Serves 2

2 rainbow trout, or baby salmon
plain flour, for coating
60 g (2 oz) butter
¼ cup (25 g/¾ oz) flaked almonds
2 tablespoons lemon juice
1 tablespoon finely chopped fresh parsley
lemon or lime wedges, for serving

1 Wash the fish and pat dry with paper
towels. Open the fish out skin-side-up.
Run a rolling pin along the backbone,
starting at the tail, pressing gently down.
Turn the fish over and use scissors to cut
through the backbone at each end of the
fish. Lift out the backbone. Remove any
remaining bones. Trim the fins with
scissors.
2 Coat the fish with flour. In a large frying
pan, heat half the butter and add the fish.
Cook for 4 minutes each side, or until
golden brown. Remove the fish and place
on heated serving plates. Cover with foil.
3 Heat the remaining butter, add the
flaked almonds and stir until light golden.
Add the juice, parsley, and salt and
freshly ground pepper. Stir until the
sauce is heated through. Pour over the
fish and serve with lemon or lime wedges.

SMOKED FISH WITH WHITE SAUCE

Preparation time: 15 minutes
Total cooking time: 8 minutes
Serves 6–8

White sauce
3 cups (750 ml/24 fl oz) milk
1 onion, halved
1 clove
1 bay leaf
60 g (2 oz) butter
⅓ cup (40 g/1¼ oz) plain flour
1–2 tablespoons chopped fresh chives or
    parsley

1 kg (2 lb) smoked cod or haddock fillets
1 cup (250 ml/8 fl oz) milk

1 For the white sauce, combine the milk in
a small pan with the onion, clove, bay leaf
and a pinch of white pepper. Heat slowly
to a simmer, then remove from the heat
and allow to stand for 3 minutes before
straining into a jug. Melt the butter in a
pan over low heat, stir in the flour and
cook for 1 minute, or until pale and
foaming. Remove from the heat and
gradually stir in the milk.
2 Return to the heat and stir constantly
until the sauce boils and thickens. Reduce
the heat and simmer for 2 minutes.
Remove from the heat and season, to
taste, with salt and pepper. Stir in the
chopped fresh chives or parsley.
3 Cut the fish fillets into serving-sized
pieces and place in a large frying pan.
Cover with the milk, combined with 1 cup
(250 ml/8 fl oz) water. Bring to the boil,
reduce the heat to low and gently cook
the fish until it flakes easily at the thickest
part when tested with a fork. Lift out of
the pan with a slotted egg slice. Drain
briefly on crumpled paper towel and place
on serving plates. Top with the white
sauce and garnish with snipped fresh
chives.

SALTED GRILLED FISH

Preparation time: 25 minutes
Total cooking time: 20 minutes
Serves 4

400 g (12⅔ oz) small whole bream,
    whiting or snapper, cleaned and scaled
    with eyes removed (see note)
½ lemon, cut into thin slices
5 cm (2 inch) piece fresh ginger
1 tablespoon mirin
2 tablespoons Japanese soy sauce
3 teaspoons salt

Garnishes
1 large carrot
¼ daikon
5 cm (2 inch) piece fresh ginger, very
    finely sliced

1 Rinse the fish under cold water and pat
dry with paper towels. Place the lemon
slices inside the fish. Finely grate the
ginger over a plate using the smallest
side of a metal grater or, alternatively,
use a Japanese wooden or ceramic ginger
grater. Use your hands to squeeze out as
much juice as possible from the pulp.
Reserve the juice and discard the dry
pulp.

2 Place the ginger juice, mirin and soy
sauce in a small bowl and mix to
combine. Lightly brush some of the
mixture over the fish and sprinkle both
sides of each fish with about 1/4 teaspoon
salt. Sprinkle a thicker coating of salt
onto the fins and tail (this will help stop
them burning).
3 Line a grill tray with aluminium foil and
place it on the level furthest away from
heat—if the fish is too close to the heat it
will cook too quickly and perhaps burn.
Cook the fish until golden brown on both
sides and the flesh flakes easily when
tested with a fork—this will take about 6
to 8 minutes, depending on the thickness
and variety of the fish.
4 Finely grate the carrot and daikon in
longish strips using the thick side of a
cheese grater. Arrange the strips on a
serving platter with the sliced ginger.
Place the fish on the platter, garnish with
some of the ginger slices, and serve
immediately with steamed rice.

NOTE: As the eyes of fish are unappealing
when cooked, ask the fishmonger to
remove them when scaling and cleaning.

LIGHT RED SEAFOOD CURRY
(CHU CHEE TA-LEH)

Preparation time: 20 minutes
Total cooking time: 20 minutes
Serves 4

2 x 270 ml (9 fl oz) cans coconut cream
    (do not shake)
3 tablespoons chu chee curry paste
500 g (1 lb) raw medium king prawns,
    peeled and deveined, with tails intact
500 g (1 lb) scallops, without roe
2–3 tablespoons fish sauce
2–3 tablespoons grated palm sugar
8 fresh kaffir lime leaves, finely shredded
2 small fresh red chillies, thinly sliced
    (optional)
1 cup (30 g/1 oz) fresh Thai basil

1 Open the cans of coconut cream and lift
off the thick cream from the top. You
should have about 1 cup (250 ml/8 fl oz).
Put the cream in a wok, bring to the boil,
then stir in the curry paste. Reduce the
heat and simmer for 10 minutes, or until
fragrant and the oil begins to separate
from the cream.
2 Stir in the seafood and remaining
coconut cream and cook for 5 minutes.
Add the fish sauce, sugar, lime leaves and
chilli and cook for 1 minute. Stir in half the
basil and use the rest for garnish.

NOTE: To make Tofu in a light red curry
(Chu chee tofu), use the curry paste below
and replace the seafood with 200 g (6½ oz)
fried tofu puffs, halved on the diagonal.
Cook as directed in the recipe above.

KEDGEREE

Preparation time: 10 minutes
Total cooking time: 15 minutes
Serves 4

600 g (1¼ lb) smoked cod fillets
3 slices lemon
1 bay leaf
4 eggs, hard-boiled
60 g (2 oz) butter
1 small onion, finely chopped
1–2 tablespoons mild curry paste
4 cups (740 g/24 fl oz) cooked long-grain rice
1 tablespoon finely chopped fresh parsley
⅔ cup (170 ml/5½ fl oz) cream

1 Put the cod in a deep frying pan with the lemon and bay leaf, cover with water and simmer for 6 minutes, or until cooked through. Remove the fish with a slotted spoon and break into flakes. Discard any bones.
2 Finely chop 2 eggs. Cut the other 2 eggs into quarters and set aside to use as garnish.
3 Melt the butter in a frying pan over medium heat. Add the onion and cook for 3 minutes, or until soft. Add the curry paste and cook for another 2 minutes. Add the rice and carefully stir through, cooking for 2–3 minutes, or until heated through. Add the parsley, fish, chopped egg and cream and stir until heated through.
4 Serve immediately with toast, garnishing each portion with egg quarters.

SEAFOOD QUICHE

Preparation time: 20 minutes +
    20 minutes chilling
Total cooking time: 1 hour
Serves 4–6

2 sheets ready-rolled shortcrust pastry
100 g (3½ oz) scallops
30 g (1 oz) butter
100 g (3½ oz) raw prawn meat
100 g (3½ oz) canned, fresh or frozen crab meat
90 g (3 oz) Cheddar, grated
3 eggs
1 tablespoon plain flour
½ cup (125 ml/4 fl oz) cream
½ cup (125 ml/4 fl oz) milk
1 small fennel bulb, finely sliced
1 tablespoon grated Parmesan

1 Lightly grease a 22 cm (9 inch) diameter loose-based flan tin. Place the 2 sheets of pastry slightly overlapping, on a work bench, and roll out until large enough to fit the prepared tin. Press the pastry into the base and side of the tin and trim off any excess with a sharp knife. Refrigerate for 20 minutes.
2 Slice off any vein or hard white muscle from the scallops, leaving any roe attached. Preheat the oven to 190°C (375°F/Gas 5).
3 Cover the pastry with baking paper, fill evenly with baking beads or uncooked rice and bake for 10 minutes. Remove the paper and rice and bake for another 10 minutes, or until lightly golden. Cool on a wire rack. If the pastry puffs up, press down lightly with a tea towel.
4 Melt the butter in a frying pan and fry the prawns and scallops for 2–3 minutes, or until cooked. Allow to cool, then arrange all the seafood over the base of the pastry shell. Sprinkle with the Cheddar.
5 Beat the eggs in a small jug, whisk in the flour, cream and milk, and season with salt and pepper. Pour over the filling. Sprinkle with fennel and Parmesan. Bake for 30–35 minutes, or until set and golden brown. Cool slightly before serving.

STEAMED TROUT WITH LIME BUTTER

Preparation time: 15 minutes
Total cooking time: 15 minutes
Serves 2

Lime butter
90 g (3 oz) butter, softened
1 teaspoon finely grated lime rind
1 tablespoon lime juice

2 small fresh rainbow trout, washed and dried
4 tablespoons lime juice
pinch of mixed dried herbs (thyme, rosemary, marjoram and oregano)

1 Put the butter in a small bowl and beat with a wooden spoon until smooth. Add the lime rind and juice and beat together thoroughly. Transfer to a serving bowl and set aside until needed.
2 Cut two 30 cm (12 inch) squares (depending on the size of the fish) of foil and grease lightly. Place a trout on each piece of foil and spoon 1 teaspoon of lime butter inside each fish. Sprinkle some lime juice over both the fish, then sprinkle with herbs (see Note below) and some black pepper. Wrap the foil around the trout to enclose. Place in a bamboo or metal steamer over a pan of simmering water and steam for about 15 minutes, or until the fish flakes easily when tested with a fork. Serve with the remaining lime butter. Lime wedges can also be served with the fish.

NOTES: This recipe is equally delicious made with baby salmon or ocean trout steaks or cutlets. Follow the same preparation and dollop the fish with the butter. Wrap firmly in foil and steam for 15 minutes.

   If fresh herbs are available, you can substitute, using twice the quantity of fresh herbs as dried.

SEAFOOD PLATTERS

PRESENTATION IS VITAL WHEN SERVING SEAFOOD PLATTERS. KEEP THE HOT AND COLD SEAFOOD SEPARATE. SERVE WITH WEDGES OF LEMON OR LIME AND THE SAUCES OF YOUR CHOICE.

PLANNING AND SERVING

We have suggested quantities of seafood required to assemble platters for 4 people. Most of the preparation can be done before your guests arrive. If it is a hot day, chill the platter you will be using for the cold seafood, or serve it on a bed of crushed ice. Serve the platters with bowls of tartare sauce, sour cream mixed with sweet chilli sauce, or soy sauce mixed with a little honey. And don't forget lime and lemon wedges, finger bowls and maybe wedges or chips.

COLD PLATTER

You will need 500 g (1 lb) cooked tiger prawns, 2 quartered cooked crabs, 12 oysters and 100 g (3½ oz) smoked salmon. If you are feeling extravagant, you could add 2 halved cooked lobsters.

HOT PLATTER

A hot platter can be very simple, using prepared, ready to cook, deep-fried calamari rings, battered fish and crumbed prawn cutlets, found in the freezer at the fishmongers or supermarket. They don't need thawing before cooking. Or, you can stun your guests by combining some of the easy dishes with your choice of the following recipes. For deep-frying, fill a deep heavy-based saucepan one third full of oil and heat to 180°C (350°F), or until a cube of bread browns in 15 seconds. Don't cook too many pieces at once or the oil temperature will lower and the batter will be soggy. Skim crumbs from the surface as you go.

PRAWNS AND SQUID

Combine 2 cups (120 g/4 oz) Japanese breadcrumbs and 1 tablespoon chopped fresh parsley. Lightly beat 2 eggs and stir in 1 teaspoon sesame oil and 1 crushed garlic clove. Season 1 cup (125 g/4 oz) plain flour. Peel, devein and butterfly 1 kg (2 lb) raw medium prawns and cut 4 squid hoods into calamari rings. Coat the prawns and rings in the seasoned flour. Dip, in batches, into the egg, then coat in the breadcrumbs, shaking off any excess. Lower batches of prawns into the oil and deep-fry until golden. Drain on paper towels. Repeat with the squid.

JAPANESE OYSTERS

Place 12 fresh oysters in a bamboo steamer, top with thin slivers of spring onion and a little grated fresh ginger. Drizzle with bottled teriyaki marinade. Cover and steam for 4 minutes, or until heated through.

CRISPY LEMON FISH STRIPS

Sift ½ cup (60 g/2 oz) plain flour into a bowl, make a well in the centre and whisk in ½ cup (125 ml/4 fl oz) soda water with the grated rind from 1 lemon. Cut 2 skinless snapper fillets into thin strips. Dust lightly with seasoned flour and dip, in batches, into the batter, allowing any excess to drip off. Carefully lower into the oil and deep-fry until golden brown. Drain thoroughly on crumpled paper towels.

PROSCIUTTO-WRAPPED SCALLOPS

Rinse 16 cleaned scallops (without roe) and pat dry. Cut 4 thin slices of prosciutto into quarters, each large enough to enclose a scallop. Wrap around the scallops and thread in pairs onto small wooden skewers. Grill under a preheated grill, or on a barbecue for 5 minutes, turning a couple of times during cooking.

FROM LEFT: Cold seafood platter; Hot seafood platter

POACHED FLOUNDER FILLETS WITH WINE AND OYSTER SAUCE

Preparation time: 10 minutes
Total cooking time: 15 minutes
Serves 4

2 teaspoons butter
1 French shallot, finely chopped
½ cup (125 ml/4 fl oz) sparkling wine
1 tablespoon white wine vinegar
½ cup (125 ml/4 fl oz) fish stock
1 teaspoon sugar
150 g (5 oz) unsalted butter, chopped, extra
2 teaspoons chopped fresh dill
2 bay leaves
whole black peppercorns
4 x 150 g (5 oz) flounder fillets
12 fresh oysters
lemon wedges, for serving

1 Melt the butter in a small saucepan and cook the shallot over medium heat for 1 minute, or until softened. Add the sparkling wine, vinegar and fish stock and bring to the boil. Reduce the heat and simmer until the liquid has reduced to 3 tablespoons. Stir in the sugar, then remove from the heat.
2 Whisk in the extra butter until it has melted and the sauce has thickened slightly. Add the chopped dill and salt and pepper, to taste. Keep warm while you cook the fish.
3 Put 2½ cups (600 ml/20 fl oz) water, the bay leaves and peppercorns in a frying pan large enough to fit the fillets. Bring to the boil, reduce the heat and add the fillets. Simmer for about 3 minutes, or until the fish flakes easily when tested with a fork.
4 Just before serving, place the oysters in the wine sauce to heat through. Serve the fish on serving plates with wine and oyster sauce spooned over the top and a wedge of lemon on the side.

PASTA SOUFFLE

Preparation time: 35 minutes
Total cooking time: 55 minutes
Serves 4

2 tablespoons freshly grated Parmesan
60 g (2 oz) butter
1 small onion, finely chopped
2 tablespoons plain flour
2 cups (500 ml/16 fl oz) milk
½ cup (125 ml/4 fl oz) chicken stock
3 eggs, separated
¾ cup (115 g/4 oz) small macaroni, cooked
210 g (7 oz) can salmon, drained and flaked
1 tablespoon chopped fresh parsley
grated rind of 1 lemon

1 Preheat the oven to hot 210°C (415°F/Gas 6–7). Brush a round 6-cup capacity (18 cm/ 7 inch) soufflé dish with oil. Coat the base and sides with Parmesan. Shake off excess.
2 To collar a soufflé dish, cut a piece of aluminium foil or greaseproof paper 5 cm (2 inches) longer than the circumference of the soufflé dish. Fold the foil in half lengthways. Wrap the foil around the outside of the souffle dish; it should extend 5 cm (2 inches) above the rim. Secure the foil with string.

3 Heat the butter in a large pan. Add the onion and cook over low heat until tender. Add the flour and stir for 2 minutes, or until the mixture is lightly golden. Remove from the heat. Gradually blend in the milk and stock, stirring until the mixture is smooth. Return to the heat. Stir constantly over medium heat until the mixture boils and thickens. Reduce the heat and simmer for 3 minutes. Add the egg yolks and whisk until smooth. Add the macaroni, salmon, parsley, lemon rind and salt and pepper, to taste. Stir until combined. Transfer the mixture to a large bowl.
4 Using electric beaters, beat the egg whites in a small dry mixing bowl until stiff peaks form. Using a metal spoon, fold gently into the salmon mixture. Spoon into the prepared dish. Bake for 40–45 minutes, or until well risen and browned. Serve immediately.

NOTE: Hot soufflés should be made just before you want to serve them as they will collapse very quickly after removal from the oven. The base mixture can be prepared, up to the end of Step 3, well in advance. Soften the mixture before folding in the beaten egg whites. Whites should be folded into the mixture just before cooking.

SALMON CUTLETS WITH FRUIT SALSA

Preparation time: 20 minutes + 2 hours marinating
Total cooking time: 10 minutes
Serves 4

4 salmon cutlets
11/2 tablespoons seasoned pepper
2 tablespoons lemon juice
½ cup (125 ml/4 fl oz) lime juice
1 tablespoon chopped fresh thyme

Fruit salsa
½ small pawpaw, cut into small cubes
½ small pineapple, cut into small cubes
3 spring onions, chopped
1 tablespoon chopped fresh coriander
2 tablespoons lime juice
3 teaspoons caster sugar

1 Sprinkle the salmon all over with the pepper and place in a shallow non-metal dish. Combine the juices and thyme in a jug and pour over the salmon. Cover and refrigerate for 2 hours.
2 For the fruit salsa, combine the pawpaw, pineapple, spring onion, coriander, lime juice and caster sugar in a bowl. Add salt, to taste.
3 Heat a little oil in a frying pan, add the salmon and brush with any remaining marinade. Cook for 3–5 minutes each side, turning once, until the outside is lightly browned and the flesh is just cooked on the inside. Serve with the fruit salsa.

NOTES: Ocean trout can also be used to make this recipe.
   Don't marinate the salmon for more than 2 hours or the citrus juices will begin to 'cook' the fish and turn the flesh opaque. If this should happen, halve the cooking time. The salsa should be made just before serving.

SMOKED COD FLAN

Preparation time: 30 minutes + 20 minutes chilling
Total cooking time: 55 minutes
Serves 6

Pastry
1 cup (125 g/4 oz) plain flour
60 g (2 oz) butter, chopped
1 egg, lightly beaten
1 tablespoon lemon juice

Filling
300 g (10 oz) smoked cod or haddock fillets
3 eggs, lightly beaten
½ cup (125 ml/4 fl oz) cream
60 g (2 oz) Cheddar, grated
1 tablespoon chopped fresh dill

1 Preheat the oven to hot 210°C (415°F/Gas 6–7). Lightly grease a 22 cm (9 inch) diameter loose-bottomed fluted flan tin.
2 Sift the flour into a large bowl and rub in the butter with your fingertips until it resembles fine breadcrumbs. Make a well in the centre and add the egg, lemon juice and up to 1–2 tablespoons of water. Mix with a flat-bladed knife until the mixture comes together in beads. Gently gather the dough together into a ball, flatten into a disc and wrap in plastic. Refrigerate for 20 minutes.

3 Roll the dough out, between 2 sheets of baking paper, until large enough to cover the base and side of the tin. Remove the top sheet of paper and put the pastry in the tin, pressing into the sides. Line with crumpled baking paper large enough to cover the base and sides and spread a layer of uncooked rice or baking beads over the top. Bake for 10 minutes. Remove from the oven and discard the paper and rice or beads. Bake for another 5 minutes, or until golden. Remove and cool slightly. Reduce the oven to moderate 180°C (350°F/Gas 4).
4 Put the cod in a frying pan and cover with water. Bring to the boil, reduce the heat and simmer for 10–15 minutes, or until the cod flakes easily when tested with a fork. Drain on crumpled paper towels, then allow to cool.
5 For the filling, flake the cod into small pieces, using a fork. Combine the eggs, cream, cheese and dill in a bowl, add the cod and mix well. Spoon into the pastry shell and bake for 40 minutes, or until set. Serve the flan hot or cold with wedges of lemon or lime and a green salad.

JOHN DORY WITH PRAWNS AND CREAMY DILL SAUCE

Preparation time: 15 minutes
Total cooking time: 20 minutes
Serves 4

12 raw large prawns
2½ cups (600 ml/20 fl oz) fish stock
30 g (1 oz) butter
1 clove garlic, finely chopped
2 tablespoons plain flour
2 tablespoons cream
4 x 200 g (6½ oz) John dory fillets
1 tablespoon chopped fresh chives
1 tablespoon chopped fresh dill

1 Peel the prawns and pull out the dark vein from each prawn back, starting at the head end.
2 Heat the stock in a saucepan and bring to the boil. Reduce the heat and simmer for 10 minutes, or until the liquid has reduced. You will need 1½ cups (375 ml/ 12 fl oz) fish stock.
3 Melt the butter in a small saucepan and add the garlic. Stir in the flour and cook for 1 minute, or until pale and foaming. Remove from the heat and gradually stir in the stock. Return to the heat and stir constantly until the sauce boils and thickens. Reduce the heat and simmer for 1 minute. Remove from the heat and stir in the cream. Season, to taste. Keep warm while you cook the fish and prawns.
4 Heat a little oil in a frying pan and cook the fish fillets over medium heat for 2 minutes each side, or until the fish flakes easily when tested with a fork. Transfer to serving plates.
5 Add the prawns to the same pan (add a little more oil to the pan if necessary) and cook for 2–3 minutes, or until the prawns turn pink and are cooked through.
6 To serve, stir the fresh chives and dill into the hot sauce, then arrange the prawns on top of the fillets and spoon sauce over the top. Each serving can be garnished with strips of fresh chives or sprigs of dill.

SPAGHETTI WITH SARDINES, FENNEL AND TOMATO

Preparation time: 30 minutes
Total cooking time: 45 minutes
Serves 4–6

3 Roma tomatoes, peeled, seeded and chopped
⅓ cup (80 ml/2¾ fl oz) olive oil
3 cloves garlic, crushed
1 cup (80 g/2¾ oz) fresh white breadcrumbs
1 red onion, thinly sliced
1 fennel bulb, quartered and thinly sliced
¼ cup (40 g/1¼ oz) raisins
¼ cup (40 g/1¼ oz) pine nuts, toasted
4 anchovy fillets, chopped
½ cup (125 ml/4 fl oz) white wine
1 tablespoon tomato paste (tomato purée)
4 tablespoons finely chopped fresh flat-leaf parsley
350 g (11 oz) butterflied sardine fillets
500 g (1 lb) spaghetti

1 Score a cross in the base of each tomato. Place the tomatoes in a bowl of boiling water for 10 seconds, then plunge into cold water and peel the skin away from the cross. Cut the tomatoes in half and scoop out the seeds with a teaspoon. Roughly chop the tomato flesh.
2 Heat 1 tablespoon of the oil in a large frying pan over medium heat. Add 1 clove of the garlic and the breadcrumbs and stir for about 5 minutes, until golden and crisp. Transfer to a plate.

3 Heat the remaining oil in the same pan and cook the onion, fennel and remaining garlic for 8 minutes, or until soft. Add the tomato, raisins, pine nuts and anchovies and cook for another 3 minutes. Add the wine, tomato paste and ½ cup (125 ml/ 4 fl oz) water. Simmer for 10 minutes, or until the mixture thickens slightly. Stir in the parsley and set aside.
4 Pat the sardines dry with paper towels. Cook the sardines in batches in a lightly greased frying pan over medium heat for 1 minute, or until cooked through. Take care not to overcook or they will break up. Set aside.
5 Cook the pasta in a large saucepan of rapidly boiling salted water until al dente. Drain and return to the pan.
6 Stir the sauce through the pasta until the pasta is well coated and the sauce evenly distributed. Add the sardines and half the breadcrumbs and toss gently. Sprinkle the remaining breadcrumbs over the top and serve immediately.

SEAFOOD MORNAY

Preparation time: 35 minutes
Total cooking time: 35 minutes
Serves 8–10

80 g (23/4 oz) butter
½ cup (60 g/2 oz) plain flour
½ cup (125 ml/4 fl oz) dry white wine
1 cup (250 ml/8 fl oz) thick (double) cream
1 cup (250 ml/8 fl oz) milk
125 g (4 oz) Cheddar, grated
2 tablespoons wholegrain mustard
1 tablespoon horseradish cream
6 spring onions, chopped
1 cup (80 g/2¾ oz) fresh breadcrumbs
1 kg (2 lb) skinless white fish fillets (eg. monkfish, coley, snapper, flathead), cut into cubes
450 g (14 oz) scallops, cleaned
400 g (13 oz) cooked peeled small prawns

Topping
3 cups (240 g/7½ oz) fresh breadcrumbs
3 tablespoons chopped fresh parsley
60 g (2 oz) butter, melted
125 g (4 oz) Cheddar, grated

1 Preheat the oven to moderate 180°C (350°F/ Gas 4). Lightly grease a 2 litre (64 fl oz) capacity ovenproof dish.
2 Melt 60 g (2 oz) of the butter in a pan over low heat. Stir in the flour until pale and foaming. Remove from the heat and gradually stir in the wine, cream and milk. Return to the heat and stir over high heat until the sauce boils and thickens. Season with salt and pepper, to taste. Add the Cheddar, mustard, horseradish, spring onion and breadcrumbs. Mix well and set aside.
3 Melt the remaining butter in a large pan and add the fish and scallops in batches. Stir over low heat until the seafood starts to change colour. Drain the seafood, add to the sauce with the prawns, then transfer to the greased dish.
4 For the topping, mix all the ingredients and spread over the seafood. Bake for 35 minutes, or until the top is golden and the sauce bubbling.

OMELETTE ARNOLD BENNETT

Preparation time: 10 minutes
Total cooking time: 10 minutes
Serves 2

100 g (3½ oz) smoked haddock or cod fillets
60 g (2 oz) butter
2 tablespoons cream
4 eggs, separated
¼ cup (60 ml/2 fl oz) cream, extra
60 g (2 oz) Parmesan or Gruyère cheese, grated

1 Place the haddock in a small frying pan and cover with water. Bring slowly to boil, then turn off the heat. Cover and leave for 10 minutes, then drain. Remove any skin and bones, then flake the flesh and set aside.
2 Wipe out the pan, return to the heat and melt half the butter. Add the cream and the flaked fish. Stir over medium heat for 2–3 minutes. Remove from the heat and allow to cool.
3 Beat the egg yolks and 1 tablespoon of the extra cream in a small bowl. Whisk the egg whites in a clean dry bowl until soft peaks form. Fold in the yolks, haddock mixture and half the grated cheese.
4 Melt the remaining butter in a non-stick frying pan. When hot, add the egg mixture. Cook until golden and set on the bottom. Do not fold.
5 Sprinkle with the remaining cheese and pour the remaining cream over the omelette. Sprinkle with salt and freshly ground black pepper, to taste. Brown quickly under a preheated grill. Slide onto a serving plate, then cut into wedges. Serve with lime wedges and mixed salad.

NOTE: Arnold Bennett was an English novelist who died in 1931. This dish was created for him at the Savoy Hotel. Traditionally, grated Parmesan cheese was used.

SKEWERED SWORDFISH

Preparation time: 15 minutes + 3 hours marinating
Total cooking: 10 minutes
Serves 6

Marinade
⅓ cup (80 ml/2¾ fl oz) lemon juice
2 tablespoons olive oil
1 small red onion, sliced thinly
1 teaspoon paprika
2 fresh bay leaves, crumpled
10 fresh sage leaves torn

1.5 kg (3 lb) swordfish, cut into 3 cm (1¼ inch) cubes

Lemon sauce
¼ cup (60 ml/2 fl oz) olive oil
¼ cup (60 ml/2 fl oz) lemon juice
3 tablespoons chopped fresh flat-leaf parsley

1 Combine the marinade ingredients with 1 teaspoon salt and some ground black pepper in a bowl. Add the fish, toss to coat with the marinade, then cover and refrigerate for 3 hours, turning the fish occasionally.
2 Thread the fish onto 6 metal skewers and cook over a hot grill for 5 minutes, turning and brushing with marinade several times.
3 Combine the lemon sauce ingredients in a jar, seal and shake several times. Serve over the fish.

NOTE: You can substitute any firm fish such as blue eye, hake, mahi mahi, or use prawns.

TUNA AND WHITE BEAN SALAD

Preparation time: 15 minutes
Total cooking time: Nil
Serves 4–6

750 g (1½ lb) canned tuna in oil
1 clove garlic, crushed
1–2 teaspoons fresh thyme leaves
1–2 teaspoons finely chopped fresh
    parsley
¼ cup (60 ml/2 fl oz) white wine vinegar
⅓ cup (80 ml/2¾ fl oz) extra virgin olive
    oil
400 g (13 oz) can cannellini beans,
    drained and rinsed
1 large red onion, coarsely chopped
3 hard-boiled eggs, cut into wedges
3 tomatoes, cut into wedges

1 Drain the tuna and flake into chunks.
Combine the garlic, thyme, parsley,
vinegar and olive oil in a bowl, and whisk
with a fork. Season, to taste, with salt and
black pepper.
2 Combine the beans and onion in a large
bowl, add the dressing and toss. Add the
tuna, toss gently, then add half the egg
wedges and half the tomato. Lightly
combine. Pile on a platter and garnish
with the remaining egg and tomato.

FISH WELLINGTON

Preparation time: 30 minutes
Total cooking time: 1 hour 15 minutes
Serves 6

40 g (1¼ oz) butter
3 onions, thinly sliced
2 x 300 g (10 oz) skinless fish fillets
    (eg. monkfish, flake, hake, ling,
    each 30 cm/12 inches long)
½ teaspoon sweet paprika
2 red peppers (capsicums)
1 large (320 g/11 oz) eggplant (aubergine),
    cut into 1 cm (½ inch) thick slices
375 g (12 oz) frozen block puff pastry,
    thawed
⅓ cup (35 g/1¼ oz) dry breadcrumbs
1 egg, lightly beaten
1 cup (250 g/8 oz) natural yoghurt
1–2 tablespoons chopped fresh dill

1 Melt the butter in a saucepan, add the
sliced onion and stir to coat. Cover and
cook over low heat, stirring occasionally,
for 15 minutes. Uncover and cook,
stirring, for 15 minutes, or until the onion
is very soft and lightly browned. Cool, then
season with salt and pepper, to taste.
2 Rub one side of each fillet with paprika.
Place one on top of the other, with the
paprika on the outside. If the fillets have a
thin and a thick end, sandwich together so
the thickness is even along the length
(thin ends on top of thick ends).

3 Cut the red peppers into quarters,
remove the seeds and membrane and
cook, skin-side-up, under a hot grill until
the skin blackens and blisters. Cool in a
plastic bag, then peel. Place the eggplant
on a greased baking tray and brush with
oil. Sprinkle with salt and pepper. Grill
until golden, then turn to brown the other
side.
4 Preheat the oven to hot 220°C
(425°F/Gas 7). Roll the pastry out on a
floured surface until large enough to
enclose the fish, about 35 x 25 cm (14 x 10
inches). The pastry size and shape will be
determined by the fish. Sprinkle the
breadcrumbs lengthways along the
centre of the pastry and place the fish
over the breadcrumbs. Top with the onion,
then an overlapping layer of red pepper,
followed by an overlapping layer of
eggplant.
5 Brush the pastry edges with egg. Fold
the pastry over, pinching firmly together
to seal. Use any trimmings to decorate.
Brush with egg, then bake for 30 minutes.
Cover loosely with foil if the pastry is
overbrowning. Slice to serve.
6 Stir the yoghurt and dill with a little salt
and pepper in a bowl. Serve with the
Wellington.

FISH PATTIES

Preparation time: 25 minutes +
 15 minutes chilling
Total cooking time: 10 minutes
Makes 8–10

750 g (1½ lb) skinless firm fish fillets (eg.
 flake, haddock, cod, pike), cut into
 cubes
1 cup (80 g/2¾ oz) stale white
 breadcrumbs
3 spring onions, chopped
¼ cup (60 ml/2 fl oz) lemon juice
2 teaspoons seasoned pepper
1 tablespoon chopped fresh dill
2 tablespoons chopped fresh parsley
90 g (3 oz) Cheddar, grated
1 egg
plain flour, for dusting

Herbed mayonnaise
½ cup (125 g/4 oz) good-quality
 mayonnaise
1 tablespoon chopped fresh parsley
1 tablespoon chopped fresh chives
2 teaspoons drained, bottled capers,
 chopped

1 Heat the barbecue. Process the fish in a
food processor for 20–30 seconds, until
smooth. Transfer to a large bowl.
2 Add the breadcrumbs, spring onion,
juice, pepper, herbs, cheese and egg to
the fish. Mix well, divide into 8–10 portions
and shape into round patties. Place on a
tray and refrigerate for 15 minutes, or
until firm.
3 Toss the patties in flour and shake off
any excess. Cook on a hot lightly greased
barbecue flatplate for 2–3 minutes each
side, until browned and cooked through.
4 For the herbed mayonnaise, combine
the mayonnaise, herbs and capers in a
small bowl and mix well.
5 Serve the hot patties with the herbed
mayonnaise and a salad.
serving.

FISH PIE

Preparation time: 10 minutes
Total cooking time: 45 minutes
Serves 4

2 large potatoes (500 g/1 lb), chopped
¼ cup (60 ml/2 fl oz) milk or cream
1 egg, lightly beaten
60 g (2 oz) butter
60 g (2 oz) Cheddar, grated
800 g (1 lb 10 oz) skinless white fish fillets
 (eg. ling, hake), cut into large chunks
1½ cups (375 ml/12 fl oz) milk
1 onion, finely chopped
1 clove garlic, crushed
2 tablespoons plain flour
2 tablespoons lemon juice
2 teaspoons lemon rind
1 tablespoon chopped fresh dill

1 Preheat the oven to 180°C (350°F/ Gas
4). Boil or steam the potatoes until tender
(pierce with the point of a small knife—if
the potato comes away easily, it is ready)
and mash well with the milk or cream,
egg and half the butter. Mix in half the
Cheddar, then set aside and keep warm.
2 Put the fish in a shallow frying pan and
cover with the milk. Bring to the boil, then
reduce the heat and simmer for 2–3 minutes,
or until the fish is cooked. Drain the fish well,
reserving the milk, and set aside.
3 Melt the rest of the butter in a pan and
cook the onion and garlic over medium
heat for 2 minutes. Stir in the flour and
cook for 1 minute, or until pale and
foaming. Remove from the heat and
gradually stir in the reserved milk. Return
to the heat and stir constantly until the
sauce boils and thickens. Reduce the heat
and simmer for 2 minutes. Add the lemon
juice, lemon rind and dill, and season with
plenty of salt and cracked black pepper.
4 Put the fish in a 1.5 litre (48 fl oz)
capacity ovenproof dish and gently mix in
the sauce. Spoon the mashed potato over
the fish and top with the remaining
Cheddar. Bake for 35 minutes, or until
golden brown.

SMOKED SALMON AND PASTA

Preparation time: 10 minutes
Total cooking time: 10 minutes
Serves 4

1 tablespoon olive oil
1 clove garlic, crushed
1½ cups (375 ml/12 fl oz) cream
3 tablespoons chopped fresh chives
¼ teaspoon mustard powder
200 g (6½ oz) smoked salmon, cut
 into strips
2 teaspoons lemon juice
500 g (1 lb) fettucine
3 tablespoons sun-dried tomatoes,
 chopped
2 tablespoons grated Parmesan, for
 serving

1 Heat the oil in a pan and cook the garlic
briefly over low heat. Add the cream,
chives and mustard powder. Season, to
taste, and bring to the boil. Reduce the
heat and stir until the sauce thickens.
2 Add the salmon and lemon juice and stir
until heated through. Meanwhile, add the
fettucine to a large pan of rapidly boiling
water and cook until al dente. Drain well
and return to the same pan. Toss the
sauce through the pasta. Top with the
tomato, Parmesan and extra chives.

NOTE: You can also use smoked trout.

STUFFED SARDINES

Preparation time: 25 minutes
Total cooking time: 15 minutes
Serves 4

½ cup (100 g/3½ oz) long-grain rice
2 tablespoons olive oil
2 tablespoons chopped dried apricots
2 tablespoons raisins
1 tablespoon flaked almonds, toasted
1 tablespoon chopped parsley
1 tablespoon chopped mint
grated zest of 1 orange
2 tablespoons freshly squeezed orange
    juice
1 teaspoon finely chopped preserved
    lemon zest
1 teaspoon ground cinnamon
½ teaspoon harissa
16 whole large sardines, butterflied
16 large vine leaves
1 cup (250 g/8 oz) thick natural yoghurt,
    to serve

1 Cook the rice in boiling water until it is tender. Drain and transfer to a bowl. Add 1 tablespoon of the olive oil, the dried apricots, raisins, almonds, parsley, mint, orange zest and juice, preserved lemon, cinnamon, harissa and the second tablespoon of oil. Season with salt and freshly ground black pepper, and mix together.
2 Divide the stuffing among the sardines, folding the two fillets of each fish together to enclose the rice mixture (save any extra stuffing to serve with the sardines). Wrap a vine leaf around each sardine and secure with a toothpick.
3 Preheat a chargrill pan or barbecue hotplate. Cook the sardines for 6 minutes, turning them over halfway through. Serve each one with a dollop of yoghurt and any extra rice.

CRUMBED FISH WITH WASABI CREAM

Preparation time: 25 minutes +
    15 minutes refrigeration
Total cooking time: 20 minutes
Serves 4

¾ cup (60 g/2 oz) fresh breadcrumbs
¾ cup (25 g/¾ oz) cornflakes
1 sheet nori, torn roughly
¼ teaspoon paprika
4 x 150 g (5 oz) pieces firm white fish
    fillets
plain flour, for dusting
1 egg white
1 tablespoon skim milk
1 spring onion, thinly sliced

Wasabi cream
½ cup (125 g/4 oz) low-fat natural yoghurt
1 teaspoon wasabi
1 tablespoon low-fat mayonnaise
1 teaspoon lime juice

1 Preheat the oven to moderate 180°C (350°F/Gas 4). Combine the crumbs, cornflakes, nori and paprika in a food processor and process until the nori is finely chopped.
2 Dust the fish lightly with plain flour, dip into the combined egg white and milk, then into the breadcrumb mixture. Press the crumb mixture on firmly, then refrigerate for 15 minutes.
3 Line a baking tray with non-stick baking paper and put the fish on the paper. Bake for 15–20 minutes, or until the fish flakes easily with a fork.
4 To make the wasabi cream, mix the ingredients thoroughly in a bowl. Serve with the fish and sprinkle with a little spring onion.

BAKED FISH WITH TOMATO AND ONION

Preparation time: 20 minutes
Total cooking time: 45 minutes
Serves 4

¼ cup (60 ml/2 fl oz) olive oil
2 onions, finely chopped
1 small stick celery, finely chopped
1 small carrot, finely chopped
2 cloves garlic, chopped
400 g (13 oz) can good-quality chopped
    tomatoes
2 tablespoons tomato passata
¼ teaspoon dried oregano
½ teaspoon sugar
50 g (2 oz) white bread, preferably one
    day old
500 g (1 lb 2 oz) white fish fillets or
    steaks, such as snapper or cod
3 tablespoons chopped fresh flat-leaf
    parsley
1 tablespoon fresh lemon juice

1 Preheat the oven to moderate 180°C (350°F/ Gas 4). Heat 2 tablespoons of the oil in a heavy-based frying pan. Add the onion, celery and carrot and cook over low heat for 10 minutes, or until soft. Add the garlic, cook for 2 minutes, then add the chopped tomato, passata, oregano and sugar. Simmer for about 10 minutes, stirring occasionally, until reduced and thickened. Season, to taste.
2 To make the breadcrumbs, chop the bread in a food processor for a few minutes, until fine crumbs form.
3 Arrange the fish in a single layer in a baking dish. Stir the chopped parsley and the lemon juice into the sauce. Season, to taste, and pour over the fish. Scatter the breadcrumbs all over the top and drizzle with the remaining oil. Bake for 20 minutes, or until the fish is just cooked.

TUNA WITH LIME AND CHILLI SAUCE

Preparation time: 15 minutes
Total cooking time: 5 minutes
Serves 4

½ cup (25 g/¾ oz) chopped and firmly packed fresh mint leaves
½ cup (25 g/¾ oz) chopped fresh coriander leaves
1 teaspoon grated lime rind
1 tablespoon lime juice
1 teaspoon grated fresh ginger
1 jalapeno chilli, seeded and finely chopped
1 cup (250 g/8 oz) low-fat natural yoghurt
4 tuna steaks

1 Mix together the mint, coriander, lime rind, lime juice, ginger and chilli. Fold in the yoghurt and season.
2 Cook the tuna in a lightly oiled chargrill pan for 2 minutes each side. Serve with the sauce.

NOTE: Jalapeno chillies are smooth and thick-fleshed and are available both red and green. They are quite fiery and you can use a less powerful variety of chilli if you prefer.

RISOTTO NERO (SQUID INK RISOTTO)

Preparation time: 20 minutes
Total cooking time: 35 minutes
Serves 6

3 squid
1 litre (32 fl oz) fish stock
100 g (3½ oz) butter
1 red onion, finely chopped
2 garlic cloves, crushed
1½ cups (360 g/12 oz) risotto rice
3 sachets of squid or cuttlefish ink or the ink sacs of the squid
155 ml (5 fl oz) white wine
2 teaspoons olive oil

1 Prepare the squid by pulling the heads and tentacles out of the bodies along with any innards. If there is an ink sac, carefully remove it and rinse it. Cut the heads off below the eyes, leaving just the tentacles. Discard the heads and set the tentacles aside. Rinse the tentacles and bodies, pulling out the transparent quills. Pull the skin off the tentacles and bodies. Finely chop the bodies and cut the tentacles in half.
2 Pour the stock into a saucepan and bring to the boil. Reduce the heat, cover with a lid and keep at a low simmer.
3 Heat the butter in a deep heavy-based frying pan and cook the onion until softened but not browned. Increase the heat and add the squid bodies. Cook for 3 minutes, or until opaque. Add the garlic and stir briefly. Stir in the rice until well coated.
4 Squeeze the ink from the sachets (or use the ink sacs) and add with the wine. Increase the heat and stir until absorbed.
5 Add ½ cup (125 ml/4 fl oz) of the hot stock and stir constantly over medium heat until all the liquid is absorbed. Continue adding more stock, ½ cup (125 ml/4 fl oz) at a time until all the liquid is absorbed and the rice is tender and creamy, this will take around 25 minutes.
6 Heat the olive oil in a frying pan and fry the squid tentacles quickly. Use to garnish the risotto.

STEAMED FISH IN BANANA LEAVES

Preparation time: 45 minutes
Total cooking time: 10 minutes
Makes 10

2 large banana leaves
350 g (11 oz) firm white fish fillets, cut into thin strips
1–2 tablespoons red curry paste (see Notes)
½ cup (125 ml/4 fl oz) coconut cream
1 cup (75 g/2½ oz) finely shredded cabbage
2 tablespoons fish sauce
2 tablespoons lime juice
1–2 tablespoons sweet chilli sauce
1 fresh red chilli, chopped (optional)

1 Cut the banana leaves into 10 cm (4 inch) squares and make a 3 cm (1¼ inch) cut towards the centre on each corner. Fold in the corners, then staple and/or tie around with a piece of string to form a cup. Trim the corners to neaten, if necessary.
2 Put the fish in a bowl with the curry paste and coconut cream and stir gently to mix. Place spoonfuls of the mixture in each banana leaf cup.
3 Line a large bamboo steamer with extra banana leaves or cabbage leaves and place the prepared cups in the basket. Top each piece of fish with shredded cabbage and a little fish sauce. Cover and steam over a wok of simmering water for about 7 minutes. Drizzle lime juice and sweet chilli sauce over the top and serve immediately, sprinkled with chilli.

NOTES: You can make your own curry paste or use a ready-made one.
   The fish can be cooked in foil cups instead of banana leaves.

TUNA SKEWERS WITH MOROCCAN SPICES AND CHERMOULA

Preparation time: 20 minutes +
  10 minutes marinating
Total cooking time: 5 minutes
Serves 4

800 g (1 lb 10 oz) tuna steaks, cut into
  3 cm (1¼ inch) cubes
2 tablespoons olive oil
½ teaspoon ground cumin
2 teaspoons finely grated lemon rind

Chermoula
½ teaspoon ground coriander
3 teaspoons ground cumin
2 teaspoons paprika
pinch of cayenne pepper
4 garlic cloves, crushed
½ cup (15 g/½ oz) chopped fresh flat-leaf
  parsley
½ cup (25 g/¾ oz) chopped fresh
  coriander
⅓ cup (80 ml/2¾ fl oz) lemon juice
½ cup (125 ml/4 fl oz) olive oil

1 If using wooden skewers, soak them for about 30 minutes to prevent them from burning during cooking.
2 Place the tuna in a shallow non-metallic dish. Combine the oil, cumin and lemon rind and pour over the tuna. Toss to coat, then cover and marinate in the refrigerator for 10 minutes.
3 Meanwhile, for the chermoula, place the coriander, cumin, paprika and cayenne pepper in a small frying pan and cook over medium heat for 30 seconds, or until fragrant. Combine with the remaining chermoula ingredients and set aside.
4 Thread the tuna onto the skewers. Lightly oil a chargrill or barbecue and cook the skewers for 1 minute on each side for rare or 2 minutes for medium. Serve the skewers on a bed of couscous with the chermoula drizzled over the tuna.

SALMON WITH DILL CREAM

Preparation time: 25 minutes
Total cooking time: 25 minutes
Serves 4

4 baby salmon
4 cloves garlic, peeled
2 lemons, sliced
8 fresh bay leaves
8 sprigs fresh flat-leaf parsley
8 sprigs fresh thyme
olive oil, for brushing

Dill cream
90 g (3 oz) butter
1 cup (250 ml/8 fl oz) fish stock
1½ teaspoons wholegrain mustard
1 cup (250 ml/8 fl oz) cream
2 tablespoons lemon juice
3 tablespoons chopped fresh dill

1 Preheat a barbecue or chargrill pan to hot. Wash the fish and pat dry inside and out with paper towels. Place a clove of garlic, a few slices of lemon and a bay leaf in the cavity of each fish. Bundle together 1 sprig of parsley and thyme and tie a bundle with string onto each fish, near the tail. Reserve the other sprigs. Brush both sides of the fish with a little of the olive oil.
2 For the dill cream, melt the butter in a pan and add the fish stock, mustard and cream. Bring to the boil, then reduce the heat and simmer for 15 minutes, or until the sauce is slightly thickened. Stir in the lemon juice and dill. Set aside and keep warm. Season, to taste, with salt and pepper.
3 While the dill cream is cooking, barbecue or chargrill the fish for 3–6 minutes on each side, turning carefully, or until cooked through. Discard the herbs. For serving, bundle together a fresh parsley sprig, a thyme sprig and a bay leaf, and tie a bundle near each fish tail. Serve warm with the dill cream.

NOTE: Rainbow trout is also a suitable fish for this recipe.

FRAGRANT SEAFOOD PASTA

Preparation time: 30 minutes
Total cooking time: 20 minutes
Serves 4

500 g (1 lb) conchiglie (shell pasta)
2–3 tablespoons light olive oil
4 spring onions, finely sliced
1 small chilli, finely chopped
500 g (1 lb) raw prawns, peeled and
  deveined, tails intact
250 g (8 oz) scallops, halved
¼ cup (15 g/½ oz) chopped fresh coriander
¼ cup (60 ml/2 fl oz) lime juice
2 tablespoons sweet chilli sauce
1 tablespoon fish sauce
1 tablespoon sesame oil
shredded lime rind, to garnish

1 Cook the conchiglie in a large pan of rapidly boiling salted water until al dente.
2 While the pasta is cooking, heat the oil in a pan and add the spring onion, chilli, prawns and scallops. Stir constantly over medium heat until the prawns turn pink and the scallops are lightly cooked. Remove from the heat immediately. Stir in the coriander, lime juice, chilli sauce and fish sauce.
3 Drain the pasta and return to the pan. Toss the sesame oil through, add the prawn mixture and mix gently to combine. Serve the pasta garnished with lime rind, if desired.

SPICY BAKED FISH WITH VEGETABLES

Preparation time: 15 minutes +
   30 minutes marinating
Total cooking time: 45 minutes
Serves 4

1 tablespoon cumin seeds
4 cloves garlic
1 small fresh red chilli
1 small bunch of coriander, leaves, stems
   and roots, roughly chopped
1 teaspoon salt
1 tablespoon lemon juice
5 tablespoons olive oil
1.5 kg (3 lb), or 2 x 750 g (1½ lb) whole
   fish, (eg. snapper, red emperor, ocean
   perch, monkfish), scaled and cleaned
2–3 ripe tomatoes
450 g (14 oz) new potatoes, sliced
100 g (3½ oz) pitted green olives, cut in
   halves

1 Toast the cumin seeds in a dry pan over medium heat for 2–3 minutes, or until fragrant. Grind the seeds to a fine powder in a mortar and pestle, or in a spice grinder.
2 Mix the ground cumin, garlic, chilli, coriander, salt and lemon juice in a food processor, to form a smooth paste. With the motor running, add 2 tablespoons of the olive oil, in a thin steady stream.
3 Rinse the fish and pat dry with paper towels. Make 3–4 diagonal slits on both sides of the fish, then rub the spice mixture over the fish. Cover with plastic wrap and marinate in the refrigerator for 30 minutes.
4 Preheat the oven to very hot 240°C (475°F/ Gas 9). Thickly slice the tomatoes and cut the slices in half. Place the fish in the centre of a large baking dish. Scatter the tomato, potato and green olives around the fish. Pour ¼ cup (60 ml/2 fl oz) water and the remaining olive oil over the fish and vegetables. Bake, basting often, for 40 minutes, or until the fish is cooked through. When cooked, the fish will flake easily when tested with a fork.

SEAFOOD FAJITAS

Preparation time: 30 minutes
Total cooking time: 20 minutes
Serves 4

250 g (8 oz) scallops
300 g (10 oz) raw medium prawns
250 g (8 oz) skinless white fish fillets
   (eg. flake, ling, blue-eye, groper)
3 ripe tomatoes, finely chopped
1 small red chilli, finely chopped
2 spring onions, finely sliced
⅓ cup (80 ml/2¾ fl oz) lime juice
1 clove garlic, crushed
1 ripe avocado, sliced
2 tablespoons lemon juice
4 flour tortillas
1 onion, thinly sliced
1 green pepper (capsicum), cut into thin
   strips

1 Slice or pull off any vein, membrane or white muscle from the scallops, leaving any roe attached.
2 Peel the prawns and gently pull out the dark vein from each prawn back, starting at the head end. Cut the white fish fillets into bite-sized pieces.
3 Preheat the oven to warm 160°C (315°F/ Gas 2–3). Combine the tomato, chilli and spring onion in a bowl and season, to taste, with salt and pepper.

4 Combine the scallops, prawns, fish, lime juice and garlic in a bowl, cover and refrigerate.
5 Slice the avocado and brush with the lemon juice, to prevent browning.
6 Wrap the flour tortillas in foil and heat in the oven for 10 minutes to soften.
7 Heat a lightly oiled chargrill or cast-iron pan to very hot, add the onion and green pepper and cook, turning occasionally, until soft and lightly brown. Push them all over to one side of the pan. Drain the seafood thoroughly and cook briefly until it is seared all over and cooked through.
8 To serve, wrap the seafood, green pepper, onion, sliced avocado and tomato mixture in the tortillas.

NOTE: From Tex-Mex cuisine, fajitas (pronounced fah-hee-tuhs) although originally made with meat, are now also made with marinated chicken or seafood, cooked on a sizzling cast-iron plate and wrapped in tortillas with salsa, avocado and other salad ingredients.

SALMON AND PASTA MORNAY

Preparation time: 15 minutes
Total cooking time: 10–15 minutes
Serves 4

400 g (13 oz) conchiglie (shell pasta)
30 g (1 oz) butter
6 spring onions, chopped
2 cloves garlic, crushed
1 tablespoon plain flour
1 cup (250 ml/8 fl oz) milk
1 cup (250 g/8 oz) sour cream
1 tablespoon lemon juice
425 g (14 oz) can salmon, drained and flaked
½ cup (30 g/1 oz) chopped fresh parsley

1 Cook the pasta in a large pan of rapidly boiling salted water until al dente. Drain and return to the pan.
2 While the pasta is cooking, melt the butter in a medium pan, add the onion and garlic and stir over low heat for 3 minutes, or until tender. Add the flour and stir for 1 minute. Combine the milk, sour cream and lemon juice in a jug. Add gradually to the onion mixture, stirring constantly. Stir over medium heat for 3 minutes, or until the mixture boils and thickens.
3 Add the salmon and parsley to the pan and stir for 1 minute, or until heated through. Add to the drained pasta and toss until well combined. Season with salt and pepper, to taste, before serving.
note: As a variation, use a can of drained and flaked tuna instead of salmon, or add 1 teaspoon of mustard to the sauce.

SEAFOOD BURRITOS

Preparation time: 45 minutes
Total cooking time: 40 minutes
Serves 4

250 g (8 oz) scallops
500 g (1 lb) raw medium prawns
500 g (1 lb) skinless salmon or ocean trout fillet
2 tablespoons oil
60 g (2 oz) butter
2 cloves garlic, crushed
3 small red chillies, seeded and finely chopped
4 large flour tortillas
2½ tablespoons plain flour
½ cup (125 ml/4 fl oz) cream
¾ cup (185 ml/6 fl oz) milk
½ cup (125 g/4 oz) sour cream
⅓ cup (35 g/1¼ oz) grated Parmesan
2 tablespoons chopped fresh parsley
125 g (4 oz) Cheddar, grated
chilli sauce, for serving

1 Slice or pull off any vein, membrane or white muscle from the scallops, leaving any roe attached. Peel the prawns and gently pull out the dark vein from each prawn back, starting at the head end. Cut the salmon into small pieces.
2 Preheat the oven to warm 160°C (315°F/ Gas 2–3). Heat the oil and half the butter in a frying pan. Add the garlic and chilli and cook for 1 minute. Add the scallops and cook for 2–3 minutes, then remove and drain on crumpled paper towels. Add the prawns and cook for 2–3 minutes; drain on paper towels. Add the salmon, cook for 3–4 minutes, then remove and drain on crumpled paper towels. Put all the seafood in a bowl.

3 Wrap the tortillas in foil and warm in the oven for 10 minutes. Melt the remaining butter in a pan over low heat, stir in the flour and cook for 1 minute, or until pale and foaming. Remove from the heat and gradually stir in the combined cream and milk. Return to the heat and stir constantly until the sauce boils and thickens. Stir in the sour cream (do not boil), Parmesan and parsley, pour over the seafood and mix well.
4 Fill each tortilla with some seafood and roll up to enclose. Place in a lightly greased ovenproof dish, sprinkle with the Cheddar and bake for 15–20 minutes, or until the tortillas are heated through and the cheese has melted. Serve with chilli sauce.

JAPANESE-STYLE SALMON PARCELS

Preparation time: 40 minutes
Total cooking time: 20 minutes
Serves 4

2 teaspoons sesame seeds
4 x 150 g (5 oz) salmon cutlets or fillets
2.5 cm (1 inch) piece fresh ginger
2 sticks celery
4 spring onions
¼ teaspoon dashi granules
¼ cup (60 ml/2 fl oz) mirin
2 tablespoons tamari

1 Cut baking paper into four squares large enough to enclose the salmon steaks. Preheat the oven to very hot 230°C (450°F/Gas 8). Stir the sesame seeds over low heat in a small pan until lightly browned, then remove from the pan.
2 Wash the salmon and pat dry with paper towels. Place a salmon cutlet in the centre of each paper square.
3 Cut the ginger into paper-thin slices. Slice the celery and spring onions into long thin strips. Arrange a bundle of the prepared strips and several slices of ginger on each salmon steak.
4 Combine the dashi granules, mirin and tamari in a small saucepan. Stir gently over low heat until the granules dissolve. Drizzle over each parcel, sprinkle with sesame seeds and carefully wrap the salmon, folding in the sides to seal in all the juices. Arrange the parcels in a bamboo steamer over a pan of simmering water and steam for about 15 minutes. (The paper will puff up when the fish is cooked.) Serve immediately with boiled rice.

NOTES: You can use ocean trout as a substitute for this recipe.
Dashi, mirin and tamari are all available from Japanese food stores.

BAKED SPICED FISH CUTLETS

Preparation time: 15 minutes
Total cooking time: 15–20 minutes
Serves 4

1 tablespoon oil
1 onion, very finely chopped
2 cloves garlic, finely chopped
5 cm (2 inch) piece fresh ginger, finely grated
1 teaspoon ground coriander
1 stem lemon grass, white part only, finely chopped
2 teaspoons tamarind purée
2 teaspoons finely grated lemon rind
4 small fish cutlets (eg. blue-eye, snapper, kingfish, jewfish), tail end
lime wedges, to garnish

1 Preheat the oven to warm 160°C (315°F/Gas 2–3). Line a baking dish or tray with foil and lightly oil, to prevent the fish from sticking.
2 Heat the oil in a frying pan, add the onion, garlic, ginger, coriander and lemon grass, and stir over medium heat for 5 minutes, or until aromatic.
3 Stir in the tamarind, rind and some black pepper. Remove from the heat. Allow to cool, then spread over the fish. Arrange in the dish, in a single layer. Bake for 10–15 minutes, or until the flesh flakes easily when tested with a fork. Don't overcook. Garnish with lime wedges.

RED MULLET IN CORN HUSKS

Preparation time: 10 minutes
Total cooking time: 5–6 minutes
Serves 6

6 small red mullet, cleaned and scaled
12 sprigs fresh lemon thyme
1 lemon, sliced
2 cloves garlic, sliced
12 large corn husks
olive oil
cracked black pepper

1 Wash the fish and pat dry inside and out with paper towels. Fill each fish cavity with thyme, lemon and garlic, then place each in a corn husk. Drizzle with oil and sprinkle with pepper, then top each fish with another husk. Tie each end of the husks with string to enclose.
2 Place on coals or on a barbecue and cook, turning once, for 6–8 minutes, or until the fish is cooked and flakes easily when tested with a fork.

NOTE: You can also use redfish to make this recipe.

STEAMED WHOLE FISH WITH CHILLI, GARLIC AND LIME
(PLA NOONG MAHAO)

Preparation time: 20 minutes
Total cooking time: 25 minutes
Serves 4–6

1–1.5 kg (2–3 lb) whole snapper, cleaned
1 lime, sliced
finely chopped fresh red chillies, to garnish
fresh coriander leaves, to garnish
lime wedges, to garnish

Sauce
2 teaspoons tamarind purée
5 long fresh red chillies, seeded and chopped
6 large cloves garlic, roughly chopped
6 fresh coriander roots and stalks
8 red Asian shallots, chopped
1½ tablespoons vegetable oil
2½ tablespoons lime juice
¾ cup (130 g/4½ oz) shaved palm sugar
¼ cup (60 ml/2 fl oz) fish sauce

1 Rinse the fish and pat dry with paper towels. Cut two diagonal slashes through the thickest part of the fish on both sides, to ensure even cooking. Place the lime slices in the fish cavity, then cover with plastic wrap and refrigerate until ready to use.

2 To make the sauce, combine the tamarind with 1/4 cup (60 ml/2 fl oz) water. Blend the chilli, garlic, coriander and shallots in a food processor until finely puréed—add a little water, if necessary.
3 Heat the oil in a saucepan. Add the paste and cook over medium heat for 5 minutes, or until fragrant. Stir in the tamarind mixture, lime juice and palm sugar. Reduce the heat and simmer for 10 minutes, or until thick. Stir in the fish sauce.
4 Line a bamboo steamer with baking paper. Place the fish on top. Cover and steam over a wok of simmering water for 6 minutes per 1 kg (2 lb) fish, or until the flesh flakes easily when tested with a fork.
5 Pour the sauce over the fish and garnish with the chilli, coriander and lime wedges. Serve with steamed rice.

CAJUN BLACKENED FISH

Preparation time: 10 minutes
Total cooking time: 5 minutes
Serves 4

3 teaspoons paprika
½ teaspoon cayenne pepper
3 teaspoons black pepper
1 teaspoon white pepper
1 teaspoon dried thyme
50 g (1¾ oz) butter
4 x 200 g (6½ oz) firm white fish fillets
2 cloves garlic, crushed
1 lemon, cut into wedges

1 Place the paprika, cayenne pepper, black pepper, white pepper and dried thyme in a bowl and mix well.
2 Melt the butter in a large frying pan over medium heat, then remove the pan from the heat. Brush both sides of the fillets with some of the melted butter, then spread the crushed garlic over the fish. Sprinkle each side of the fillets with the spice mixture.
3 Return the pan to medium heat and cook the fish for 1–2 minutes each side, or until cooked through (the fish will flake easily when tested with a fork). Spoon the pan juices over the fish and serve immediately with the lemon wedges on the side.

SUGGESTED FISH: Deep-sea perch, ling, ocean perch.

NOTE: For less heat, you can omit the cayenne and white peppers.

LEMONY HERB AND FISH RISOTTO

Preparation time: 20 minutes
Total cooking time: 30 minutes
Serves 4

60 g (2 oz) butter
400 g (13 oz) skinless white fish fillets
  (eg. coley, cod, blue-eye, ling), cut into
  3 cm (1¼ inch) cubes
1.25 litres (40 fl oz) fish stock
1 onion, finely chopped
1 clove garlic, crushed
1 teaspoon ground turmeric
1½ cups (330 g/11 oz) arborio rice
2 tablespoons lemon juice
1 tablespoon chopped fresh parsley
1 tablespoon chopped fresh chives
1 tablespoon chopped fresh dill

1 Melt half the butter in a pan. Add the fish in batches and fry over medium-high heat for 3 minutes, or until the fish is just cooked through. Remove from the pan and set aside.
2 Pour the fish stock into another pan, bring to the boil, cover and keep at simmering point.
3 To the first pan, add the remaining butter, onion and garlic and cook over medium heat for 3 minutes, or until the onion is tender. Add the turmeric and stir for 1 minute. Add the rice and stir to coat, then add ½ cup (125 ml/4 fl oz) of the fish stock and cook, stirring constantly, over low heat until all the stock has been absorbed. Continue adding ½ cup (125 ml/4 fl oz) of stock at a time until all the stock has been added and the rice is translucent, tender and creamy.
4 Stir in the lemon juice, parsley, chives and dill. Add the fish and stir gently. Serve, maybe garnished with slices of lemon or lime and fresh herb sprigs.

PAN-FRIED CRUSTED FISH CURRY

Preparation time: 30 minutes +
  15 minutes soaking
Total cooking time: 10 minutes
Serves 4

4 medium dried red chillies
100 g (3½ oz) Asian shallots
3 cloves garlic, chopped
2 stems lemon grass, white part only,
  finely sliced
4 fresh coriander roots
2 teaspoons lime rind
½ teaspoon drained, bottled green
  peppercorns, roughly chopped
½ cup (125 ml/4 fl oz) oil
4 thick skinless fish fillets (eg. blue-eye,
  snapper, ling, gemfish, about 200 g/
  6½ oz each)
½ cup (125 ml/4 fl oz) coconut milk
1 tablespoon fish sauce
4 kaffir lime leaves, finely shredded
2 tablespoons lime juice

1 Soak the red chillies in a bowl of boiling water for 15 minutes, or until softened. Drain and chop roughly.
2 Process the chillies, shallots, garlic, lemon grass, coriander roots, lime rind and peppercorns in a food processor, until a smooth paste forms. Add 1 tablespoon of the oil to help the processing, and regularly scrape down the sides of the bowl with a rubber spatula. Spread the paste lightly over one side of each fish fillet.
3 Heat the remaining oil in a large heavy-based pan. Cook the fish in a single layer, for 2–3 minutes on each side, until just cooked, turning over carefully with 2 egg slices so the fish doesn't break.
4 Stir together the coconut milk, fish sauce, kaffir lime leaves and lime juice in a small jug. Pour over the fish, reduce the heat and simmer for 3 minutes. Remove the fish from the pan, using an egg slice. Serve the fish drizzled with any pan juices.

PASTA WITH FRAGRANT LIME AND SMOKED TROUT

Ready to eat in 30 minutes
Serves 4

500 g (1 lb) spinach and white linguine
1 tablespoon extra virgin olive oil
3 cloves garlic, crushed
1 tablespoon grated lime rind
2 tablespoons poppy seeds
250 g (8 oz) smoked trout, skin and bones
  removed
400 g (13 oz) camembert cheese, chopped
2 tablespoons chopped fresh dill
lime wedges, for serving

1 Cook the linguine in rapidly boiling salted water until al dente. Drain.
2 Heat the olive oil in a large heavy-based frying pan. Add the garlic, cook over low heat for 3 minutes or until fragrant. Add the rind, poppy seeds and pasta to the pan and toss to coat.
3 Fold the trout, camembert and dill through the mixture and cook over low heat until the camembert begins to melt. Toss gently through the pasta and serve immediately with a squeeze of lime.

SMOKED SEAFOOD

THERE ARE TWO METHODS OF
SMOKING SEAFOOD. HOT
SMOKING CAN BE DONE AT
HOME, WHEREAS COLD IS
RESERVED FOR COMMERCIAL
PURPOSES. SMOKED FISH CAN
BE KEPT FOR 3–5 DAYS.

Cold smoking is the commercial method used to produce smoked salmon. The fish is smoked at a low temperature and not actually cooked.

Hot smoking is the method described here, using a kettle barbecue. This method is particularly suitable for whole trout and mackerel. The fish is simultaneously smoked and cooked on the hot barbecue.

BRINING

All fish for smoking must first be soaked in a brine solution (salted water), or salted by rubbing generous quantities of salt into the skin. This helps preservation and improves the flavour. To determine the strength of the brine solution, see if a potato will float. If it doesn't, keep adding and dissolving more salt until the potato floats. If it does, add the whole fish and leave it for 3 hours, or 2 hours if gutted. Fish fillets will only need 30 minutes. Next, clean the fish and gut, if necessary. If you don't have time to brine the fish, you can leave this step out, but the fish won't keep after smoking and you will have to eat it straight away. Ungutted fish are the most suitable to use for hot smoking, so ask your fishmonger for advice on types.

TYPE OF WOOD TO USE

The recommended smoking woodchips are hickory, oak, apple, red gum, or any hardwood, available from barbecue and related speciality stores. Resinous woods, including pine, should never be used as they tend to taint the fish with an antiseptic flavour. Adding some herbs such as thyme, rosemary or bay leaves will infuse aromatic flavours into the fish.

TO SMOKE WHOLE FISH

The first thing you will need if you want to smoke fish at home is a covered kettle barbecue or a smoke box. We have given a recipe for use with a kettle barbecue as these are more popular.

1 Place a cupful of smoking chips (apple, hickory or oak) in a non-reactive bowl, add ½ cup (125 ml/4 fl oz) white wine or water, and allow to stand for 1 hour. Drain well.
2 Meanwhile, light your coals and leave them until they turn white.
3 Fill the cavities of 4 whole rainbow trout with thin slices of lime and red onion. Tie a small bunch of fresh herbs around each tail. Suitable fresh herbs include bay leaves, sprigs of dill, lemon thyme and parsley.
4 Carefully lift the sides of the rack and scatter the chips over the coals.
5 Place the rainbow trout directly on the lightly greased rack or a double layer of foil. Spray lightly with olive oil, and season generously with sea salt and cracked black pepper. Cover and smoke for 7–15 minutes, or until the fish flakes easily when tested with the tip of a knife. The cooking time will vary, depending on the size of the fish.

TO SMOKE FISH FILLETS

Fish fillets or butterflied fish can be smoked in the same way, but the cooking time will depend on the size of the fillet. Oily fish, including salmon, mackerel, tailor or warehou, are best.

TO SMOKE MUSSELS

Mussels do not require soaking. Thoroughly scrub the mussels and pull out the hairy beards. Discard any that do not close when tapped on the bench. Put the mussels in a baking dish in the prepared barbecue. Cover and cook for 3–5 minutes.

BARBECUED FISH WITH ONIONS AND GINGER

Preparation time: 25 minutes +
  20 minutes marinating
Total cooking time: 25 minutes
Serves 4–6

1 kg (2 lb) small, firm, white-fleshed
  whole fish (eg. red emperor, bream,
  snapper), cleaned and scaled
2 teaspoons drained, bottled green
  peppercorns, finely crushed
2 teaspoons chopped red chillies
3 teaspoons fish sauce
3 tablespoons oil
2 onions, finely sliced
4 cm (1½ inch) piece fresh ginger, thinly
  sliced
3 cloves garlic, cut into very thin slivers
2 teaspoons sugar
4 spring onions, finely shredded

Lemon and garlic dipping sauce
¼ cup (60 ml/2 fl oz) lemon juice
2 tablespoons fish sauce
1 tablespoon sugar
2 small fresh red chillies, finely chopped
3 cloves garlic, chopped

1 Wash the fish and pat dry inside and out.
Cut 2 or 3 diagonal slashes into the
thickest part on both sides. In a food
processor, process the peppercorns,
chillies and fish sauce to a paste and brush
over the fish. Refrigerate for 20 minutes.
2 Heat a grill or barbecue hotplate until
very hot and brush with 1 tablespoon of
oil. Cook the fish for 8 minutes each side,
or until the flesh flakes easily. If grilling,
don't cook too close to the heat.
3 While the fish is cooking, heat the
remaining oil in a pan and stir the onion
over medium heat, until golden. Add the
ginger, garlic and sugar and cook for 3
minutes. Serve over the fish. Sprinkle
with spring onion.
4 Stir all the dipping sauce ingredients in
a bowl until the sugar has dissolved.
Serve with the fish.

CREAMY GARLIC SEAFOOD

Preparation time: 20 minutes
Total cooking time: 20 minutes
Serves 6

12 scallops, with roe
500 g (1 lb) skinless firm white fish fillets
6 raw slipper lobsters or crabs
500 g (1 lb) raw medium prawns,
  peeled and deveined
50 g (1¾ oz) butter
1 onion, finely chopped
5–6 large cloves garlic, finely chopped
½ cup (125 ml/4 fl oz) white wine
2 cups (500 ml/16 fl oz) cream
1½ tablespoons Dijon mustard
2 teaspoons lemon juice
2 tablespoons chopped fresh flat-leaf parsley

1 Slice or pull off any membrane or hard
muscle from the scallops. Cut the fish
into 2 cm (¾ inch) cubes. Cut the heads off
the slipper lobsters, then use scissors to
cut down around the sides of the tail so
you can flap open the shell. Remove the
flesh in one piece, then slice each piece in
half. Refrigerate all the seafood, covered,
until ready to use.
2 Melt the butter in a frying pan and cook
the onion and garlic over medium heat for
2 minutes, or until the onion is softened
(be careful not to burn the garlic).
3 Add the wine to the pan and cook for
4 minutes, or until reduced by half. Stir in
the cream, mustard and lemon juice and
simmer for 5–6 minutes, or until reduced
to almost half.
4 Add the prawns to the pan and cook for 1
minute, then add the slipper lobster meat
and cook for another minute, or until white.
Add the fish and cook for 2 minutes, or until
cooked through (the flesh will flake easily).
Finally, add the scallops and cook for 1
minute. If any of the seafood is still not
cooked, cook for another minute or so, but
be careful not to overcook as this will result
in tough flesh. Remove the frying pan from
the heat and toss the parsley through.
Season, to taste. Serve with salad and bread.

SALT COD WITH RED PEPPERS (CAPSICUMS)

Preparation time: 35 minutes +
  10 minutes cooling + 12 hours soaking
Total cooking time: 25 minutes
Serves 6

400 g (13 oz) dried salt cod or bacalao
1 red pepper (capsicum)
1 tablespoon olive oil
1 small onion, chopped
1 clove garlic, crushed
¼ teaspoon dried chilli flakes
1 teaspoon paprika
¼ cup (60 ml/2 fl oz) dry white wine
2 ripe tomatoes, finely chopped
1 tablespoon tomato paste (tomato purée)
1 tablespoon chopped fresh flat-leaf
  parsley

1 Soak the dried salt cod in plenty of water
for 8–12 hours, changing the water five or
six times. This will remove excess
saltiness. Add the cod to a pan of boiling
water and boil for 5 minutes. Drain and
leave for 10 minutes, or until cool enough
to handle. Remove the skin and flake the
fish into large pieces, removing any
bones. Place in a bowl.
2 Preheat the grill. Cut the red pepper
into quarters and grill, skin-side-up, until
the skin blackens and blisters. Place in a
plastic bag and leave to cool, then peel
away the skin. Slice thinly.
3 Heat the oil in a pan over medium heat,
add the onion and cook, stirring
occasionally, for 3 minutes, or until
transparent. Add the garlic, chilli flakes
and paprika and cook for 1 minute.
Increase the heat to high, add the white
wine and simmer for 30 seconds. Reduce
the heat, add the tomato and tomato
paste and cook, stirring occasionally, for
5 minutes, or until thick.
4 Add the cod, cover and simmer for
about 5 minutes. Gently stir in the sliced
pepper and parsley and taste before
seasoning with salt. Serve hot.

SWEET AND SOUR FISH KEBABS

Preparation time: 20 minutes +
    3 hours marinating
Total cooking time: 10 minutes
Makes 12 skewers

750 g (1½ lb) skinless thick fish fillets (eg.
    ling, cod, blue-eye, striped marlin)
225 g (7 oz) can pineapple pieces
1 large red pepper (capsicum)
3 teaspoons soy sauce
1½ tablespoons soft brown sugar
2 tablespoons white vinegar
2 tablespoons tomato sauce

1 Soak 12 wooden skewers in cold water
for 30 minutes, or until they sink. This is
to ensure they don't burn during cooking.
2 Meanwhile, cut the fish into 2.5 cm
(1 inch) cubes. Drain the pineapple,
reserving 2 tablespoons of liquid. Cut the
pepper into 2.5 cm (1 inch) pieces. Thread
the pepper, fish and pineapple alternately
onto skewers.
3 Place the kebabs in a shallow non-
metallic dish. Combine the soy sauce,
reserved pineapple juice, sugar, vinegar
and tomato sauce in a small bowl. Mix
well and pour over the kebabs. Cover and
refrigerate for 3 hours.
4 Preheat the barbecue. Barbecue the
kebabs on a lightly greased barbecue,
brushing frequently with the marinade,
for 2–3 minutes each side, or until just
cooked through. Serve immediately with
cooked noodles and a dressed green
salad.

NOTE: Do not marinate the kebabs for
more than 3 hours or the vinegar in the
marinade will start to 'cook' the fish. This
method of cooking the fish with acid,
vinegar or lemon/lime juice is used in
many recipes.

SARDINAS MURCIANA (MURCIA-STYLE SARDINES)

Preparation time: 20 minutes
Total cooking time: 30 minutes
Serves 6

1 kg (2 lb) ripe tomatoes
24 fresh large sardines, cleaned, with
    backbones, heads and tails removed
2 green peppers (capsicums), cored,
    seeded and cut into thin rings
2 onions, sliced into thin rings
2 potatoes, cut into 5 mm (¼ inch) slices
2 tablespoons chopped fresh flat-leaf
    parsley
3 cloves garlic, crushed
¼ teaspoon saffron threads, lightly
    toasted
2 tablespoons olive oil
chopped fresh flat-leaf parsley, extra, for
    serving, optional

1 Score a cross in the base of each tomato
and plunge in boiling water for 10 seconds.
Transfer to cold water and peel away
from the cross. Cut each tomato into thin
slices.
2 Preheat the oven to moderate 180°C
(350°F/ Gas 4). Oil a large shallow
earthenware or ceramic baking dish wide
enough to hold the length of the sardines.
Open out the sardines and lightly sprinkle
the insides with salt. Fold them back into
their original shape.

3 Cover the base of the prepared dish with
a third of the tomatoes. Layer half the
sardines on top. Follow with a layer of
half the peppers, then half the onion, then
half the potatoes. Sprinkle with half the
parsley and garlic and season with freshly
ground black pepper. Crumble half the
saffron over the top.
4 Layer the remaining sardines, a third of
the tomatoes and then the other
ingredients as before. Finish with the last
of the tomatoes. Season well with salt and
freshly ground black pepper. Drizzle the
oil over the surface and cover with foil.
Bake for 30 minutes, or until the potatoes
are cooked. Sprinkle with parsley. Spoon
off any excess liquid. Serve straight from
the dish.
NOTE: The bodies of the sardines should
be about 15 cm (6 inches) long.

SNAPPER PIES

Preparation time: 25 minutes
Total cooking time: 1 hour 10 minutes
Serves 4

2 tablespoons olive oil
4 onions, thinly sliced
1½ cups (375 ml/12 fl oz) fish stock
3½ cups (875 ml/28 fl oz) cream
1 kg (2 lb) skinless snapper fillets, cut
  into large pieces
2 sheets ready-rolled puff pastry, thawed
1 egg, lightly beaten

1 Preheat the oven to hot 220°C (425°F/
Gas 7). Heat the oil in a large deep-sided
frying pan, add the onion and stir over
medium heat for 20 minutes, or until the
onion is golden brown and slightly
caramelized.
2 Add the fish stock, bring to the boil and
cook for 10 minutes, or until the liquid is
nearly evaporated. Stir in the cream and
bring to the boil. Reduce the heat and
simmer for about 20 minutes, until the
liquid is reduced by half, or until it coats
the back of a spoon.
3 Divide half the sauce among four 2-cup
(500 ml/16 fl oz) capacity, deep ramekins.
Put some fish in each ramekin, then top
each with some of the remaining sauce.
4 Cut the pastry sheets into rounds
slightly larger than the tops of the
ramekins. Brush the edges of the pastry
with a little of the egg. Press onto the
ramekins. Brush lightly with the
remaining beaten egg. Bake for 30 minutes,
or until crisp, golden and puffed.

NOTE: You can substitute bream, sea
perch or garfish for the snapper fillets.

FISH WITH GARLIC BREADCRUMBS

Preparation time: 15 minutes
Total cooking time: 10–15 minutes
Serves 4

4 skinless white fish fillets (eg. John
  dory, ocean perch, snapper, bream,
  200 g/6½ oz each)
75 g (2½ oz) butter, melted
3 cloves garlic, crushed
2 cups (160 g/5½ oz) fresh white
  breadcrumbs
1 tablespoon finely chopped fresh parsley
lemon wedges, for serving

1 Preheat the oven to moderately hot
200°C (400°F/Gas 6). Brush an ovenproof
dish (large enough to hold the fish in a
single layer) with olive oil and arrange the
fish on the base.
2 Combine the butter and garlic in a bowl
and set aside. Mix the breadcrumbs and
parsley and scatter in a thick layer over
the fish. Drizzle with the garlic butter.
3 Bake for 10–15 minutes, or until the fish
is white and flakes easily and the crumbs
are golden brown. If the crumbs are not
golden but the fish is cooked, place under
a hot grill for a couple of minutes. Don't
take your eyes off it as it can burn very
quickly. Serve with lemon wedges.

GRILLED FISH WITH FENNEL AND LEMON

Preparation time: 10 minutes
Total cooking time: 10 minutes
Serves 4

4 whole red mullet or bream, scaled and
  gutted
1 lemon, thinly sliced
1 baby fennel bulb, thinly sliced
1½ tablespoons fennel seeds
¼ cup (60 ml/2 fl oz) lemon juice
⅓ cup (80 ml/2¾ fl oz) olive oil

1 Cut 3 diagonal slashes on both sides of
each fish. Place two or three slices of
lemon and some slices of fennel bulb in
the cavity of each fish. Place the fennel
seeds in a mortar and pestle and bruise
roughly. Sprinkle both sides of each fish
with the cracked fennel seeds and some
salt, making sure you rub well into the
flesh.
2 Mix the lemon juice and olive oil in a
bowl. Heat a chargrill or hotplate and
when very hot, add the fish. Drizzle a little
of the lemon and oil over each fish. After 5
minutes, turn carefully with tongs,
ensuring the filling doesn't fall out, and
drizzle with the oil mix. Gently flake a
piece of flesh gently with a fork to test
whether it is cooked through, then serve
with salad.

SEAFOOD SPAGHETTI PAPER PARCELS

Preparation time: 20 minutes
Total cooking time: 35 minutes
Makes 6

185 g (6 oz) thin spaghetti
4 ripe Roma (egg) tomatoes
1 tablespoon olive oil
4 spring onions, finely chopped
1 stick celery, finely chopped
⅓ cup (80 ml/2¾ fl oz) white wine
½ cup (125 ml/4 fl oz) tomato pasta sauce
4 gherkins, finely diced
2 tablespoons drained bottled capers, chopped
6 x 175 g (6 oz) pieces of skinless salmon fillet or ocean trout, boned
6 large dill sprigs
shredded rind of 2 lemons
30 g (1 oz) butter, cut into small cubes

1 Preheat the oven to moderate 180°C (350°F/ Gas 4). Cook the pasta in a large pan of boiling water until al dente. Drain in a colander and run under cold water to cool. Transfer to a bowl.
2 Score a cross in the base of each tomato. Place in a heatproof bowl and cover with boiling water. Leave for 30 seconds, transfer to cold water, drain and peel away from the cross. Halve each tomato, scoop out the seeds and chop the flesh.
3 Heat the oil in a frying pan, add the spring onion and celery and stir for 2 minutes. Add the tomato and wine and bring to the boil. Boil for 3 minutes to reduce. Reduce the heat and stir in the pasta sauce, gherkins and capers. Season well with salt and black pepper. Mix thoroughly through the pasta.
4 To assemble, cut six 30 cm (12 inch) square sheets (depending on the shape of your fish) of baking paper and brush the outside edges with oil. Divide the pasta among the sheets, using a fork to curl the pasta. Place a piece of salmon on top of each, then top with dill and lemon rind. Divide the butter among the parcels.
5 Fold into parcels, turning over twice at the top to seal. Tuck the ends under and bake on a baking tray for 20 minutes. To serve, cut or pull open the parcel and serve in the paper, or if you prefer, slide off the paper onto serving plates.

NOTE: The parcels can be assembled a few hours ahead and refrigerated until required. If you do this, allow a couple of extra minutes cooking.

BAKED SEA BASS WITH WILD RICE STUFFING

Preparation time: 20 minutes
Total cooking time: 1 hour 10 minutes
Serves 4

2 small fennel bulbs
⅓ cup (65 g/2¼ oz) wild rice
1 cup (250 ml/8 fl oz) fish stock
40 g (11/4 oz) butter
2 tablespoons olive oil
1 onion, chopped
1 garlic clove, crushed
grated zest of 1 lemon
2 kg (4 lb) sea bass, bass or any large white fish, gutted and scaled
extra virgin olive oil
1 lemon, quartered
2 teaspoons chopped oregano
lemon wedges, to serve

1 Preheat the oven to 190°C (375°F/Gas 5) and lightly grease a large, shallow ovenproof dish. Thinly slice the fennel, reserving and chopping the green fronds.
2 Put the wild rice and stock in a saucepan with ¼ cup (60 ml/2 fl oz) water and bring to the boil. Simmer for 30 minutes, or until tender, then drain.
3 Heat the butter and olive oil in a large frying pan and gently cook the fennel, onion and garlic for 12–15 minutes, or until softened but not browned. Add the lemon zest, then stir in the rice and season with salt and freshly ground black pepper.
4 Stuff the fish with a heaped tablespoon of the fennel mixture and a quarter of the reserved fronds. Brush with extra virgin olive oil, squeeze over some lemon juice and season well with salt and pepper.
5 Spoon the remainder of the cooked fennel and rice mixture into the ovenproof dish and sprinkle with half the oregano. Put the fish on top of the fennel. Sprinkle the remaining oregano and fennel fronds over the fish and loosely cover the dish with foil. Bake for 25 minutes, or until the fish is just cooked through. Serve with lemon wedges.

DILL FISH WITH LEMON BUTTER SAUCE

Preparation time: 10 minutes + 3 hours marinating
Total cooking time: 10 minutes
Serves 4

4 skinless fish fillets (eg. perch, snapper, jewfish, red mullet, ocean trout, John dory)
1½ tablespoons lemon pepper
1–2 tablespoons chopped fresh dill
⅓ cup (80 ml/2¾ fl oz) lemon juice

Lemon butter sauce
2 tablespoons lemon juice
½ cup (125 ml/4 fl oz) cream
40 g (1¼ oz) butter, chopped
2 tablespoons chopped fresh chives

1 Sprinkle the fish fillets with the lemon pepper and place in a shallow non-metallic dish. Mix the dill with the lemon juice, then pour over the fish, cover and refrigerate for several hours.
2 Heat the barbecue and cook the fish on a hot lightly greased barbecue flatplate for 2–3 minutes each side, or until the flesh flakes easily when tested with a fork.
3 For the lemon butter sauce, simmer the lemon juice in a small pan until reduced by half. Stir in the cream. Remove from the heat and whisk in the butter a little at a time until all the butter has melted. Stir in the chives.
4 Serve the fish with the lemon butter sauce poured over the top. The fish can be garnished with fresh dill sprigs and perhaps served with barbecued citrus slices and fresh bread.

FISH EN PAPILLOTE

Preparation time: 20 minutes
Total cooking time: 20 minutes
Serves 4

4 skinless fish fillets (eg. John dory, orange roughy, snapper, bream, 200 g/6½ oz each)
1 leek, white part only, cut into julienne strips
4 spring onions, julienned
30 g (1 oz) butter, softened
1 lemon, cut into 12 very thin slices
2–3 tablespoons lemon juice

1 Preheat the oven to moderate 180°C (350°F/ Gas 4). Place each fish fillet in the centre of a piece of baking paper large enough to enclose the fish.
2 Scatter with the leek and spring onion. Top each with a teaspoon of butter and 3 slices of lemon. Sprinkle with the extra lemon juice. Bring the paper together and fold over several times. Fold the ends under to form a parcel. Bake on a baking tray for 20 minutes (the steam will make the paper puff up). Check to see that the fish is cooked (it should be white and flake easily when tested with a fork) and then serve. You can serve as parcels or remove the fish from the parcels with a fish slice and serve on warm plates.

TROUT, FETTUCINE AND FENNEL FRITTATA

Preparation time: 20 minutes
Total cooking time: 1 hour
Serves 4

250 g (8 oz) whole smoked trout
200 g (6½ oz) dried fettucine
1 cup (250 ml/8 fl oz) milk
½ cup (125 ml/4 fl oz) cream
4 eggs
pinch of nutmeg
40 g (1¼ oz) finely sliced fennel, plus fennel greens for garnish
4 spring onions, sliced
⅔ cup (85 g/3 oz) grated Cheddar cheese

1 Preheat the oven to moderate 180°C (350°F/Gas 4). Lightly brush a 23 cm (9 inch) ovenproof frying pan or flan dish with oil. Remove and discard the skin and bones from the trout.
2 Cook the fettucine in a large pan of rapidly boiling salted water until al dente. Drain.
3 Combine the milk, cream, eggs and nutmeg in a large bowl and whisk until smooth. Season with salt and pepper, to taste. Add the trout, fettucine, fennel and spring onion and toss to distribute evenly. Pour into the prepared dish, sprinkle with the cheese and bake until set, about 1 hour. Garnish with 2–3 sprigs of fennel greens and serve.

FUSILLI WITH TUNA, CAPERS AND PARSLEY

Preparation time: 15 minutes
Total cooking time: 10 minutes
Serves 4

425 g (14 oz) can tuna in spring water, drained
2 tablespoons olive oil
2 cloves garlic, finely chopped
2 small red chillies, finely chopped
3 tablespoons drained bottled capers
½ cup (30 g/1 oz) chopped fresh parsley
¼ cup (60 ml/2 fl oz) lemon juice
375 g (12 oz) fusilli
½ cup (125 ml/4 fl oz) hot chicken stock

1 Place the drained tuna in a bowl and flake lightly with a fork. In a small bowl, combine the oil, garlic, chilli, capers, parsley and lemon juice. Pour over the tuna and mix lightly. Season well with salt and freshly ground black pepper.
2 Meanwhile, cook the pasta in a large pan of rapidly boiling salted water for 10 minutes, or until al dente. Drain. Toss the tuna mixture through the pasta, adding enough of the hot chicken stock to give a moist consistency. Serve immediately.

SEAFOOD LASAGNE

Preparation time: 15 minutes
Total cooking time: 45 minutes
Serves 4–6

250 g (8 oz) instant lasagne sheets
125 g (4 oz) scallops
500 g (1 lb) raw medium prawns
500 g (1 lb) skinless white fish fillets (eg. hake, snapper, flake, gemfish, ling)
125 g (4 oz) butter
1 leek, white part only, thinly sliced
⅔ cup (85 g/3 oz) plain flour
2 cups (500 ml/16 fl oz) milk
2 cups (500 ml/16 fl oz) dry white wine
125 g (4 oz) Cheddar, grated
½ cup (125 ml/4 fl oz) cream
60 g (2 oz) Parmesan, grated
2 tablespoons chopped fresh parsley

1 Preheat the oven to moderate 180°C (350°F/ Gas 4). Line a greased shallow ovenproof dish (about 30 cm/12 inches square) with lasagne sheets, gently breaking them to fill any gaps. Set aside.
2 Slice or pull off any vein, membrane or hard white muscle from the scallops, leaving any roe attached.
3 Peel the prawns and gently pull out the dark vein from each prawn back, starting at the head end. Chop the seafood into even-sized pieces.

4 Melt the butter in a large pan over low heat, add the leek and cook, stirring over medium heat for 1 minute, or until starting to soften. Stir in the flour and cook for 1 minute, or until pale and foaming. Remove from the heat and gradually stir in the combined milk and wine. Return to the heat and stir constantly over medium heat until the sauce boils and thickens. Reduce the heat and simmer for 2 minutes. Add the seafood and simmer for 1 minute. Remove from the heat and stir in the cheese and some salt and pepper.
5 Spoon half the seafood mixture over the lasagne sheets in the dish, then top with another layer of lasagne sheets. Spoon the remaining seafood mixture over the lasagne sheets, then cover with another layer of lasagne sheets.
6 Pour the cream over the top, then sprinkle with the combined Parmesan and parsley. Bake, uncovered, for 30 minutes, or until bubbling and golden brown.

FRESH TUNA AND GREEN BEAN STIR-FRY

Preparation time: 25 minutes
Total cooking time: 10 minutes
Serves 4

300 g (10 oz) small green beans
2 tablespoons oil
600 g (1¼ lb) fresh tuna, cut into small cubes
250 g (8 oz) small cherry tomatoes
16 small black olives
2–3 tablespoons lemon juice
2 cloves garlic, finely chopped
8 anchovy fillets, rinsed, dried and finely chopped
3 tablespoons small fresh basil leaves (or roughly torn basil leaves)

1 Trim the beans if necessary and cook in a small pan of boiling water for 2 minutes. Drain and refresh under cold water. Set aside.
2 Heat a wok until very hot, add the oil and swirl it around to coat the side. Stir-fry the tuna in batches for about 5 minutes, or until cooked on the outside but still pink on the inside.
3 Add the cherry tomatoes, olives and beans, and gently toss until heated through. Stir in the lemon juice, garlic and anchovies. Season with salt and black pepper, to taste. Serve scattered with the fresh basil leaves.

MARINATED SALMON STRIPS

Preparation time: 15 minutes + 1 hour marinating
Total cooking time: Nil
Serves 4

2 salmon fillets, each about 400 g (12⅔ oz), skinned
4 cm (1½ inch) piece fresh ginger, grated
2 cloves garlic, finely chopped, optional
3 spring onions, finely chopped
1 teaspoon sugar
1 teaspoon salt
2 tablespoons Japanese soy sauce
½ cup (125 ml/4 fl oz) sake
pickled ginger (page 767) and pickled cucumber, to garnish

1 Cut the salmon into thin strips, and arrange them in a single layer in a large deep dish.
2 Place the ginger, garlic, spring onion, sugar, salt, soy sauce and sake in a small bowl and stir to combine. Pour the marinade over the salmon, cover and refrigerate for 1 hour.
3 Arrange the salmon, strip by strip, on a serving plate. Garnish with the pickled ginger and cucumber, and serve chilled.

POACHED WHOLE SNAPPER

Preparation time: 15 minutes
Total cooking time: 40 minutes
Serves 4–6

10–15 cos lettuce leaves
1.25 kg (2½ lb) whole snapper, gutted and scaled
2 onions, thinly sliced
1 lemon, thinly sliced
⅔ cup (170 ml/5½ fl oz) fish stock
⅔ cup (170ml/5½ fl oz) white wine
12 whole black peppercorns
1 bay leaf
155 g (5 oz) unsalted butter, chopped
1 tablespoon lime juice

1 Preheat the oven to moderate 180°C (350°F/Gas 4). Place the lettuce in a large bowl, cover with boiling water to soften, then drain well and refresh in cold water.
2 Trim the fins off the fish with kitchen scissors. Fill the cavity of the fish with one of the sliced onions and the lemon. Wrap the fish completely in the lettuce leaves and place into a deep-sided baking dish.
3 Pour the stock and wine over the fish. Add the remaining onion, peppercorns and bay leaf to the dish, then dot the lettuce with 30 g (1 oz) of the butter. Cover tightly with foil and bake for 30 minutes, or until the flesh flakes in the thickest part when tested with a fork.
4 Remove the fish from the dish, transfer to a serving dish and keep warm. Strain the liquid into a saucepan, then boil for about 10 minutes, or until reduced by half. Remove from the heat and whisk in the remaining butter a little at a time, whisking constantly until the mixture has thickened slightly. Stir in the lime juice and season, to taste, with salt and pepper. Serve on the side.

NOTE: You can substitute red emperor, coral trout or murray cod for the snapper.

POACHED SNAPPER WITH FRESH TOMATO SAUCE

Preparation time: 20 minutes
Total cooking time: 45 minutes
Serves 4

1 kg (2 lb) whole snapper, gutted and
    scaled
4 ripe tomatoes
1 onion, finely chopped
4 spring onions, finely sliced
2 tablespoons chopped fresh parsley
1¼ cups (315 ml/10 fl oz) fish stock
60 g (2 oz) butter
1 tablespoon plain flour

1 Preheat the oven to moderately hot 190°C
(375°F/Gas 5). Wash the fish in cold water,
pat dry inside and out with paper towels.
2 Score a cross in the base of each
tomato. Place in a heatproof bowl and
cover with boiling water. Leave for 30
seconds, then transfer to cold water.
Peel, then cut each in half and remove the
core. Scrape out the seeds with a
teaspoon and roughly chop the flesh.
3 Lightly grease a baking dish, large
enough to hold the fish, with butter.
Spread half the tomato, onion and spring
onion over the base. Place the fish over
the top and cover with the remaining
vegetables. Sprinkle with half the parsley,
then pour in the stock. Dot the fish with
half the butter.
4 Bake for 30 minutes, or until the fish is
cooked and flakes easily when tested with
a fork.
5 Carefully lift the fish out of the dish, drain
well, place on a serving dish and keep
warm. Transfer the cooking liquid and
vegetables to a small pan. Taste and adjust
the seasoning. Bring to the boil and simmer
for 5 minutes, or until reduced by a quarter.
6 Make a paste with the remaining butter
and the flour in a small bowl. Gradually add
to the pan and simmer, whisking until the
sauce has thickened. Add salt and pepper,
to taste, and pour over the fish. Garnish
with the remaining chopped parsley.

FISH MEUNIERE

Preparation time: 5 minutes
Total cooking time: 10 minutes
Serves 4

4 thick white fish fillets (eg. blue-eye,
    warehou, cod, jewfish)
plain flour, for dusting
125 g (4 oz) butter
1–2 tablespoons lemon juice
1 tablespoon chopped fresh parsley

1 Dust the fish lightly with flour and shake
off any excess. Heat a little oil in a pan
and cook the fish for 5–8 minutes each
side, until lightly golden. Transfer to
serving plates. Wipe out the pan with
paper towel.
2 Heat the pan over high heat, add the
butter and swirl quickly to melt (the
butter will start to brown). Remove from
the heat, immediately add the lemon
juice, parsley and some cracked black
pepper, then pour over the fish. Serve
with extra lemon wedges.

NOTE: The cooking time will depend on
the thickness of the fish. This recipe, with
its simple sauce, is suitable for most
types and cuts of fish.

CREAMY SMOKED HADDOCK

Preparation time: 12 minutes
Total cooking time: 20 minutes
Serves 4

1 large onion, thinly sliced
500 g (1 lb) smoked haddock fillets
1⅔ cups (420 ml/13½ fl oz) milk
¼ teaspoon cracked black pepper
1½ teaspoons mustard powder
20 g (3/4 oz) butter, softened
2 teaspoons plain flour
1 spring onion, finely chopped

1 Spread the onion slices over the base of
a large pan. Cut the fish into 2 cm (¾ inch)
wide pieces and arrange over the top of
the onion.
2 Combine the milk, pepper and mustard
in a jug and pour over the fish. Bring
slowly to the boil, then reduce the heat to
low. Cover and simmer for 5 minutes.
Uncover and simmer for another 5 minutes.
3 Transfer the fish to a serving dish; keep
warm. Simmer the mixture in the pan for
another 5 minutes, to reduce, stirring
occasionally.
4 Mix the butter and flour to a smooth
paste. Whisk into the boiling milk mixture
a little at a time. Add the spring onion and
stir over low heat until the mixture boils
and thickens, then boil for 1–2 minutes.
Serve over the fish.

LEMON AND HERB RAINBOW TROUT

Preparation time: 20 minutes
Total cooking time: 15 minutes
Serves 4

3 tablespoons chopped fresh dill
2 tablespoons chopped fresh rosemary
4 tablespoons coarsely chopped fresh
   flat-leaf parsley
2 teaspoons fresh thyme leaves
1½ tablespoons crushed green
   peppercorns
⅓ cup (80 ml/2¾ fl oz) lemon juice
1 lemon
4 whole fresh rainbow trout
⅓ cup (80 ml/2¾ fl oz) dry white wine
1 lime, sliced, to garnish

Horseradish cream
1 tablespoon horseradish cream
½ cup (125 g/4 oz) sour cream
2 tablespoons cream

Lemon sauce
150 g (5 oz) butter
2 egg yolks
3–4 tablespoons lemon juice

1 Prepare and heat the barbecue. Cut
8 sheets of foil large enough to wrap the
fish. Place 4 on top of the others, so you'll
have double thickness, and lightly grease
the top ones.
2 Mix the herbs, peppercorns, juice and
salt and pepper, to taste, in a bowl. Cut
the lemon into slices and put some in
each fish cavity. Wipe any slime off the
fish with paper towel. Spoon the herb
mixture into the fish cavities.

3 Place each fish on the foil and sprinkle
each with 1 tablespoon of wine. Fold the
foil to form parcels. Cook on the barbecue
for 10–15 minutes, or until the fish is just
cooked through. (Test for doneness. The
fish will flake easily when tested with a
fork.) Leave the wrapped fish for 5 minutes,
then serve with horseradish cream and
lemon sauce.
4 For the horseradish cream, mix the
creams in a bowl and season with salt and
pepper, to taste.
5 For the lemon sauce, melt the butter in
a small saucepan over low heat, without
stirring. Skim the foam off the surface
and pour off the clear yellow liquid,
leaving the milky sediment behind.
Discard the sediment. Blend the egg yolks
in a food processor for 20 seconds. With
the motor running, add the butter slowly
in a thin, steady stream. Continue
processing until all the butter has been
added and the mixture is thick and
creamy. Add the juice and season with
salt and pepper. Garnish the fish with
lime slices and perhaps some strips of
chives.

NOTE: If small trout are unavailable,
choose baby salmon or Atlantic salmon
steaks. They have a similar oily flesh and
flavour to the trout. Place the salmon on a
bed of the lemon slices and spread the
herb mixture over the top, or cut a slit
through the centre of the steak and fill
with the lemon and herb mixture. Cook as
above.

GLAZED GRILLED FISH FILLETS

Preparation time: 10 minutes +
   1 hour marinating
Total cooking time: 8 minutes
Serves 4

2 tablespoons olive oil
2 tablespoons lemon juice
2 tablespoons fruit chutney
1 tablespoon honey
1 tablespoon chopped fresh coriander
2 cloves garlic, crushed
4 firm-fleshed white fish fillets (eg.
   snapper, flounder, John dory, bream,
   leatherjacket)

1 Combine the olive oil, lemon juice, fruit
chutney, honey, fresh coriander and garlic
in a small bowl.
2 Place the fish fillets in a flat non-
metallic dish and pour the oil mixture
over the fish. Cover and refrigerate for
1 hour.
3 Preheat the grill to high and place the
fish fillets on a lightly oiled grill tray. Cook
the fish fillets, brushing with the
remaining marinade occasionally, for
about 4–6 minutes each side, or until the
flesh flakes easily when tested with a
fork.

FISH BALL CURRY

Preparation time: 20 minutes
Total cooking time: 20 minutes
Serves 6

1 large onion, chopped
1 teaspoon sambal oelek
1 tablespoon finely chopped fresh ginger
1 stem lemon grass, white part only, finely chopped
3 tablespoons chopped fresh coriander roots
½ teaspoon ground cardamom
1 tablespoon tomato paste (tomato purée)
1 tablespoon vegetable oil
1 tablespoon fish sauce
2 cups (500 ml/16 fl oz) coconut milk
24 fish balls (if frozen, thawed) (see Note)
2 teaspoons lime juice
3 tablespoons chopped fresh coriander
fresh coriander, extra, to garnish

1 Put the onion, sambal oelek, ginger, lemon grass, coriander, cardamom and tomato paste in a food processor, and process to a smooth paste.
2 Heat a wok over medium heat, add the oil and swirl to coat. Add the paste and cook, stirring, over medium heat for 4 minutes, or until fragrant.
3 Stir in the fish sauce, coconut milk and 1 cup (250 ml/8 fl oz) water. Bring to the boil and boil for 5 minutes, then reduce the heat and simmer for a further 5 minutes, or until the sauce has reduced and thickened slightly.
4 Add the fish balls and lime juice and cook for 2 minutes. Do not overcook or the fish balls will be tough and rubbery. Stir in the coriander and garnish with extra coriander. Serve with rice.

NOTE: Fish balls are available from the refrigerated section of large supermarkets.

SPAGHETTINI WITH ROASTED SALMON AND GARLIC

Preparation time: 10 minutes
Total cooking time: 20 minutes
Serves 4–6

4 small fillets fresh baby salmon, about 100 g (3½ oz) each
4–5 tablespoons extra virgin olive oil
8–10 cloves garlic, peeled
300 g (10 oz) dry spaghettini
50 g (1¾ oz) thinly sliced fennel
1½ teaspoons finely grated lime rind
2 tablespoons lime juice
4 sprigs fennel fronds, to garnish

1 Preheat the oven to hot 220°C (425°F/Gas 7) and oil a ceramic baking dish. Brush the salmon fillets with 2 tablespoons of the olive oil, salt lightly and position in a single layer in the dish.
2 Slice the garlic cloves lengthways and spread them all over the salmon fillets. Brush lightly with olive oil. Bake for 10–15 minutes, or until the salmon is cooked through.
3 Meanwhile, cook the spaghettini in a large pan of rapidly boiling salted water until al dente. Drain and stir through enough extra virgin olive oil to make it glisten. Toss the fennel and lime rind through the pasta and arrange on warmed serving plates.
4 Top each serving with a salmon fillet then spoon the pan juices over them, with any stray slices of garlic. Drizzle with lime juice. Garnish with fennel fronds and serve accompanied by a plain tomato salad.

STUFFED FISH

Preparation time: 30–40 minutes
Total cooking time: 45 minutes
Serves 4

1 kg (2 lb) whole fish (eg. snapper, murray cod, sea bass), scaled and cleaned
¼ cup (60 ml/2 fl oz) lemon juice
30 g (1 oz) butter, chopped

Stuffing
2 tablespoons olive oil
1 small onion, finely chopped
3 tablespoons chopped celery leaves
2 tablespoons chopped fresh parsley
1 cup (80 g/2¾ oz) fresh breadcrumbs
1½ tablespoons lemon juice
1 egg, lightly beaten

1 Preheat the oven to moderate 180°C (350°F/ Gas 4). Pat the fish dry and sprinkle with salt and the lemon juice. Set aside.
2 For the stuffing, heat the oil in a pan, add the onion and cook over medium heat for 2 minutes, or until softened. Add the celery leaves and parsley and cook, stirring, for another 2 minutes. Spoon into a bowl, add the breadcrumbs, lemon juice and salt, to taste, then mix well. Cool slightly, then stir in the egg.
3 Place the stuffing in the fish cavity and secure the opening with skewers. Place the fish in a large greased baking dish and dot with butter. Bake for 30–35 minutes, or until the fish is cooked and flakes easily when tested with a fork. The thickness of the fish will determine the cooking time. Transfer to a serving dish. Can be garnished with lemon slices and fresh dill sprigs.

ARROZ CON MARISCOS
(RICE WITH SHELLFISH)

Preparation time: 30 minutes
Total cooking time: 1 hour 10 minutes
Serves 4

1 large garlic clove, peeled
1 onion, quartered
2 firm tomatoes
1 red capsicum (pepper), seeded and
   quartered
¼ cup (60 ml/2 fl oz) olive oil
55 g (2 oz) bacon, chopped
1⅓ cups (265 g/8 oz) long-grain rice
2½ cups (625 ml/20 fl oz) hot fish stock or
   water
2 tinned and drained, or fresh, poblanos
   chillies, finely shredded
16 raw prawns (shrimp), peeled and
   deveined, tails intact
250 g (8 oz) firm fish, such as snapper,
   skinned and cut into chunks
2 tablespoons chopped coriander
   (cilantro) leaves
1 lime, cut into 4 wedges

1 Dry-roast the garlic, onion, tomatoes
and capsicum in a heavy-based frying pan
over low heat, turning now and then, for
about 45 minutes, or until the ingredients
are browned all over,
2 When cool enough to handle, peel the
tomato and capsicum, and roughly chop
the flesh. Put the flesh in a food
processor with the garlic and onion, and
blend to a purée. Alternatively, finely chop
the ingredients by hand.

3 Heat the olive oil in a deep frying pan.
Add the bacon and cook until crisp. Add
the rice and cook for 1 minute, stirring the
grains to make sure they are completely
coated in oil.
4 Add the puréed tomato mixture and
cook for 3 minutes. Add the stock and
1 teaspoon salt. Bring to the boil and stir
once. Reduce the heat to low and cover
with a lid. Cook gently for 15 minutes.
5 Add the chillies, prawns and fish to the
frying pan, and cook for another 5
minutes. Add a little hot water to the rice
if it is becoming too dry. When ready,
taste to check the seasoning, adding more
salt if necessary.
6 Sprinkle the coriander over the top of
the dish and serve with the lime wedges.

NOTE: This is the Mexican version of
paella. It includes firm-fleshed fish and a
unique, delicious flavour derived from
roasting the base ingredients before
adding them to the sauce.

SARDINES WITH CHARGRILLED VEGETABLES

Preparation time: 25 minutes
Total cooking time: 35 minutes
Serves 4

2 large red peppers (capsicums)
4 finger eggplants (aubergines), cut into
   quarters lengthways

Dressing
1 tablespoon olive oil
1 tablespoon balsamic vinegar
½ teaspoon soft brown sugar
1 clove garlic, crushed
1 tablespoon chopped fresh chives
16 fresh sardines, butterflied (about
   300 g/10 oz)
1 slice white bread, crusts removed
2 tablespoons fresh parsley
1 clove garlic, crushed
1 teaspoon grated lemon rind

1 Preheat the oven to moderate 180°C
(350°F/ Gas 4). Lightly grease a large
baking dish with oil. Preheat the grill and
line with foil.
2 Quarter and seed the peppers and grill
until the skin is blistered and blackened.
Cool in a plastic bag, peel and slice thickly
lengthways. Lightly brush the eggplant
with oil and grill each side for 3–5 minutes,
until softened.
3 Combine the oil, vinegar, sugar, garlic
and chives in a jar and shake well. Put the
peppers and eggplant in a bowl, pour the
dressing over, toss well and set aside.
4 Place the sardines on a baking tray in a
single layer, well spaced. Finely chop the
bread, parsley, garlic and lemon rind
together in a food processor. Sprinkle
over each sardine. Bake for 10–15
minutes, until cooked through. Serve the
pepper and eggplant topped with the
sardines.

CIOPPINO

Preparation time: 30 minutes + 30
  minutes soaking
Total cooking time: 1 hour
Serves 4

2 dried Chinese mushrooms
1 kg (2 lb) skinless white fish fillets
  (eg. hake, snapper, ocean perch, red
  mullet)
375 g (12 oz) raw large prawns
1 raw lobster tail (about 400 g/13 oz)
12–15 black mussels
¼ cup (60 ml/2 fl oz) olive oil
1 large onion, finely chopped
1 green pepper (capsicum), finely
  chopped
2–3 cloves garlic, crushed
425 g (14 oz) can crushed tomatoes
1 cup (250 ml/8 fl oz) white wine
1 cup (250 ml/8 fl oz) tomato juice
1 cup (250 ml/8 fl oz) fish stock
1 bay leaf
2 sprigs of fresh parsley
2 teaspoons chopped fresh basil
1 tablespoon chopped fresh parsley, extra

1 Place the mushrooms in a small bowl,
cover with boiling water and soak for 20
minutes. Cut the fish into bite-size pieces,
removing bones.
2 Peel the prawns, leaving the tails intact.
Gently pull out the dark vein from each
prawn back, starting at the head end.

3 Starting at the end where the head was,
cut down the sides of the lobster shell on
the underside of the lobster with kitchen
scissors. Pull back the flap, remove the
meat from the shell and cut into small
pieces.
4 Scrub the mussels with a stiff brush
and pull out the hairy beards. Discard any
broken mussels, or open ones that don't
close when tapped on the bench. Rinse
well.
5 Drain the mushrooms, squeeze dry and
chop finely. Heat the oil in a heavy-based
pan, add the onion, pepper and garlic and
stir over medium heat for about 5
minutes, or until the onion is soft. Add the
mushrooms, tomato, wine, tomato juice,
stock, bay leaf, parsley sprigs and basil.
Bring to the boil, reduce the heat, then
cover and simmer for 30 minutes.
6 Layer the fish and prawns in a large
pan. Add the sauce, then cover and leave
on low heat for 10 minutes, or until the
prawns are pink and the fish is cooked.
Add the lobster and mussels and simmer
for another 4–5 minutes. Season. Discard
any unopened mussels. Sprinkle with
parsley.

WHOLE RED MULLET IN TOMATO AND OLIVE SAUCE

Preparation time: 15 minutes
Total cooking time: 35 minutes
Serves 4

8 small whole red mullet
  (about 1 kg/2 lb), cleaned and scaled
2 tablespoons chopped fresh parsley, for
  serving

Tomato and olive sauce
1½ tablespoons olive oil
1 large onion, sliced
2 cloves garlic, finely chopped
2 x 400 g (13 oz) cans crushed tomatoes
1½ tablespoons red wine vinegar
2 tablespoons tomato paste (tomato
  purée)
1 tablespoon sugar
¼ cup (60 ml/2 fl oz) white wine
¾ cup (185 ml/6 fl oz) fish stock
1 tablespoon chopped fresh oregano
1 tablespoon chopped fresh basil
100 g (3½ oz) black olives

1 Pat the fish dry inside and out with
paper towels. Refrigerate until ready to
use.
2 Heat the oil in a large deep frying pan
large enough to fit the fish in one layer.
Cook the onion and garlic over medium
heat for 5 minutes, or until softened. Add
the remaining sauce ingredients and
bring to the boil. Reduce the heat and
simmer for 15 minutes, or until the sauce
is pulpy and thickened slightly.
3 Add the fish, in a single layer, and cover
the pan. Simmer for another 10–12 minutes,
or until the fish flakes easily when tested
in the thickest part with a fork. As red
mullet is a soft-fleshed fish, there is no
need to turn it over during cooking (it will
fall apart). Serve garnished with parsley if
you wish.

THAI GINGER FISH WITH CORIANDER BUTTER

Preparation time: 15 minutes + 30
  minutes refrigeration
Total cooking time: 10 minutes
Serves 4

60 g (2 oz) butter, at room temperature
1 tablespoon finely chopped fresh
  coriander leaves
2 tablespoons lime juice
1 tablespoon vegetable oil
1 tablespoon grated palm sugar
4 fresh long red chillies, seeded and
  chopped
2 stems lemon grass, trimmed
4 x 200 g (6½ oz) firm white fish fillets
  (e.g. blue-eye or john dory)
1 lime, thinly sliced
1 tablespoon finely shredded fresh ginger

1 Thoroughly mix the butter and chopped
coriander together and roll it into a log.
Wrap the log in plastic wrap and chill in
the refrigerator for at least 30 minutes, or
until required.
2 Combine the lime juice, oil, palm sugar
and chilli in a small non-metallic bowl
and stir until the sugar has dissolved. Cut
the lemon grass into halves.
3 Lay a piece of lemon grass in the centre
of a sheet of foil large enough to fully
enclose one fish fillet. Place a fish fillet
on top and smear the surface with the
lime juice mixture. Top with some lime
slices and ginger shreds, then wrap into a
secure parcel. Repeat with the remaining
ingredients to make four parcels.
4 Line a bamboo steamer with baking
paper. Lay the fish parcels on top. Cover
and steam over a wok of simmering water
for 8–10 minutes, or until the fish flakes
easily when tested with a fork.
5 To serve, place the parcels on individual
serving plates and serve open with slices
of coriander butter, steamed rice and
some steamed green vegetables.

FRIED FISH WITH MILD CURRY AND CORIANDER

Preparation time: 15 minutes
Total cooking time: 10 minutes
Serves 4

2 tablespoons ghee or oil
4 firm white fish fillets, 125 g (4 oz) each
1 medium onion, finely chopped
1 teaspoon finely chopped garlic
1 teaspoon ground coriander
2 teaspoons ground cumin
½ teaspoon ground turmeric
½ teaspoon chilli flakes
1 tablespoon tomato paste (tomato purée,
  double concentrate)
½ cup (125 ml/4 fl oz) water
chopped coriander leaves, to serve

1 Melt the ghee in a large pan and cook
the fish over medium heat for 1 minute on
each side. Transfer the fish to a plate.
2 Add the onion and garlic to the pan and
cook until soft and golden. Add the
coriander, cumin, turmeric and chilli and
stir-fry for 30 seconds.
3 Add the tomato paste and water and
simmer for 2 minutes. Add the fish and
cook for 1 minute on each side. Sprinkle
with coriander and serve with rice.

DRY FISH CURRY

Preparation time: 20 minutes
Total cooking time: 25 minutes
Serves 6

1 kg (2 lb) firm white fish fillets, such as
  sea perch
2 tablespoons fish sauce
2 cups (310 g/93/4 oz) roughly chopped
  onion
4 cloves garlic, crushed
2 teaspoons finely chopped fresh ginger
2 teaspoons turmeric
1 red chilli, seeded and finely chopped
1 teaspoon salt
3 tablespoons oil
2 tablespoons chopped fresh coriander
  leaves
lemon wedges, to serve

1 Cut the fish into 4 cm (1½ inch) cubes.
Place the fish pieces in a shallow dish and
pour over the fish sauce.
2 Place the onion, garlic, ginger, turmeric,
chilli and salt into a food processor and
process until a paste is formed.
3 Heat the oil in a deep-sided frying pan;
carefully add the spicy paste (at this stage
it will splutter), stir it into the oil, lower
the heat and cook gently for about 10
minutes. If the mixture starts to burn, add
a little water. When the paste is cooked it
should be a golden brown colour and have
oil around the edges.
4 Remove the fish pieces from the fish
sauce and add them to the pan, stirring to
cover them with the spicy paste. Raise the
heat to medium and cook for about 5
minutes until the fish is cooked through,
turning it so it cooks evenly. Transfer the
fish to a warm serving dish. If the
remaining sauce is very liquid, reduce it
over high heat until it thickens, then
spoon it over the fish. Scatter the
coriander over the fish and serve with rice
and lemon wedges.

SALMON WITH LEEK AND CAMEMBERT

Preparation time: 10 minutes
Total cooking time: 15 minutes
Serves 4

500 g (1 lb) skinless salmon fillet
¼ cup (60 g/2 oz) wholegrain mustard
1 tablespoon lime juice
2 tablespoons oil
1 leek, white part only, julienned
2 tablespoons tamari
2 teaspoons fish sauce
1 tablespoon honey
75 g (2½ oz) snow pea (mangetout) sprouts
2 tablespoons fresh coriander leaves
100 g (3½ oz) Camembert, sliced
fresh coriander leaves, extra, to garnish
lime wedges, for serving

1 Cut the salmon into thick strips and place in a glass or ceramic bowl with the mustard and lime juice. Toss to coat the salmon.
2 Heat a wok until very hot, add the oil and swirl it around to coat the side. Add the salmon in batches and stir-fry over high heat until it turns soft pink and is slightly browned on the outside. Remove from the wok.
3 Add 1 tablespoon water to the wok, then add the leek and stir-fry until it is golden brown. Return the salmon to the wok, along with the tamari, fish sauce and honey. Cook until the salmon is heated through.
4 Remove the wok from the heat and toss the snow pea sprouts and coriander leaves through the salmon. Serve topped with the Camembert and extra coriander, and lime wedges on the side.

NOTES: Tamari is a thick Japanese-style soy sauce made from soy beans. Ocean trout fillets can also be used to make this recipe.

SEAFOOD CREPES

Preparation time: 25 minutes +
   1 hour standing
Total cooking time: 30 minutes
Serves 6

⅔ cup (85 g/3 oz) plain flour
1 cup (250 ml/8 fl oz) milk
1 egg
15 g (½ oz) butter, melted
1 teaspoon sugar

Seafood filling
300 g (10 oz) raw prawns
60 g (2 oz) unsalted butter
4 spring onions, finely chopped, white and green chopped separately
1 teaspoon Cajun spice mix (see Note)
½ teaspoon sweet paprika
1 large tomato, chopped
½ cup (125 ml/4 fl oz) dry white wine
170 g (5½ oz) canned crab meat, drained, flaked
½ cup (125 ml/4 fl oz) cream
1 tablespoon plain flour
24 fresh oysters
2 tablespoons grated Cheddar

1 Sift the flour into a large bowl and make a well in the centre. Combine the milk, egg, butter and sugar in a bowl. Gradually add to the flour and whisk to make a smooth batter. Cover and stand for 1 hour.
2 For the filling, peel the prawns and gently pull out the dark vein from each prawn back, starting at the head end. Chop the prawns. Melt the butter in a pan, add the white parts of the spring onion and cook, stirring over medium heat for 2 minutes. Add the Cajun spice mix, paprika and tomato, and cook, stirring, for 3–4 minutes. Add the wine and cook, stirring until the sauce has thickened.

3 Stir the prawns and crab meat into the sauce and simmer for 2–3 minutes. Blend the cream and flour together in a small bowl and add to the pan. Cook, stirring, until the mixture boils and thickens. Add the oysters and green onion tops. Remove from the heat and set aside.
4 Preheat the oven to moderate 180°C (350°F/ Gas 4). Rub a crepe pan or small (16 cm/ 6½ inch) non-stick pan with paper towel dipped in butter or oil, then heat over moderate heat. Pour in a small quantity of the batter and tip the pan so the batter spreads to cover the base. Cook until bubbles form on the surface, then turn and cook the other side until light golden. Remove from the pan. Repeat the process until all the batter is used. Stack the cooked crepes on top of each other and cover with a clean cloth.
5 Spoon some seafood mixture into each crepe and roll up to enclose. Arrange in a single layer in a lightly greased ovenproof dish. Sprinkle with the cheese and bake for 10 minutes, or until heated through. Can be served with lemon or lime wedges or slices and garnished with watercress sprigs.

NOTE: Cajun spice mix is available in some supermarkets and speciality food stores.

LEMON GRASS, CORIANDER AND FISH BAKE

Preparation time: 15 minutes
Total cooking time: 40 minutes
Serves 4

4 fish cutlets (eg. blue-eye, mahi mahi, snapper, jewfish, about 200 g/6½ oz each)
plain flour, seasoned with salt and ground pepper
2–3 tablespoons peanut oil
2 onions, sliced
2 stems lemon grass, white part only, finely chopped
4 kaffir lime leaves, finely shredded
1 teaspoon ground cumin
1 teaspoon ground coriander
1 teaspoon finely chopped red chilli
¾ cup (185 ml/6 fl oz) chicken stock
1½ cups (375 ml/12 fl oz) coconut milk
3 tablespoons chopped fresh coriander
2 teaspoons fish sauce

1 Preheat the oven to moderate 180°C (350°F/ Gas 4). Toss the fish lightly in the flour. Heat half the oil in a large heavy-based frying pan and cook the fish, in batches if necessary, over medium heat until lightly browned on both sides. Transfer to a shallow ovenproof dish.
2 Heat the remaining oil in the pan. Add the onion and lemon grass and cook, stirring, for 5 minutes, or until the onion softens. Add the lime leaves, cumin, coriander and chilli and stir for about 2 minutes, or until fragrant.
3 Add the stock and coconut milk to the pan and bring to the boil. Pour over the fish, then cover and bake for 30 minutes, or until the fish is tender.
4 Transfer the fish to a serving plate. Stir the chopped coriander and the fish sauce into the remaining sauce, and season, to taste, with salt and freshly ground pepper. Pour over the fish.

FISH ROLLS

Preparation time: 45 minutes
Total cooking time: 25 minutes
Makes 12

500 g (1 lb) black mussels
300 g (10 oz) skinless salmon or ocean trout fillet
300 g (10 oz) raw medium prawns
300 g (10 oz) skinless firm white fish fillets (eg. cod, flake, ling, snapper)
1 egg white
½ cup (125 ml/4 fl oz) cream
1 tablespoon chopped fresh dill
1 tablespoon chopped fresh chives
80 g (2¾ oz) butter
1 tablespoon lime juice
1 teaspoon thin strips lime rind
1 tablespoon chopped fresh parsley
2 tablespoons drained bottled baby capers

1 Clean the mussels with a stiff brush and pull out the hairy beards. Discard any broken mussels or open ones that don't close when tapped on the bench. Heat 1 cup (250 ml/8 fl oz) water in a saucepan, add the mussels, cover and cook for 4–5 minutes, or until open. Discard any unopened mussels. Remove the meat from the shells, chop roughly, cover and chill until required. Finely chop the salmon, cover and chill.

2 Peel the prawns and gently pull out the dark vein from each prawn back, starting at the head end. Put the prawns, fish and the egg white in a food processor and mix until smooth. Add the cream and process until just combined. Transfer to a large bowl and stir in the mussels, salmon, dill, chives and salt and pepper. To test for seasoning, fry a small amount in a pan. Divide into 12 portions. Place each portion on a sheet of plastic wrap and roll into a log shape. Wrap again in squares of foil, twisting the ends firmly to seal and form a firm log shape. Add the rolls to a pan of simmering water and simmer for 5–8 minutes, or until firm. Remove from the pan and cut the ends off the rolls. Lightly pan-fry or barbecue. Serve on warm plates.
3 Heat the same pan over medium heat, add the butter and swirl until melted. Add the lime juice, rind, parsley and capers, then spoon over the rolls. Can be garnished with extra rind strips.

FISH WITH RICE STUFFING

Preparation time: 20 minutes
Total cooking time: 12–15 minutes
Serves 4

8 large garfish or whiting, scaled and
    cleaned
2 teaspoons oil
1 small onion, finely chopped
1 clove garlic, crushed
1 tomato, finely chopped
1 tablespoon tomato paste (tomato purée)
1/4 green pepper (capsicum), finely
chopped
3/4 cup (140 g/41/2 oz) cold cooked rice
2 teaspoons soy sauce

1 Wash the fish thoroughly and pat dry
inside and out with paper towels.
2 Heat the oil in a pan, add the onion and
garlic and stir over medium heat for 2–3
minutes. Add the tomato, tomato paste,
green pepper, rice and soy sauce and stir
over medium heat for 2 minutes. Transfer
to a bowl and cool slightly.
3 Heat the grill to high. Fill the cavity of
each fish with the stuffing and secure with
toothpicks. Grill on a greased baking tray
for 3–4 minutes each side, or until the fish
is cooked and flakes easily. Remove the
toothpicks before serving.

NOTE: You will need to cook 1/4 cup (55 g/
2 oz) raw white rice for this recipe.

BAKED FISH WITH NOODLE FILLING

Preparation time: 20 minutes +
    10 minutes soaking
Total cooking time: 50 minutes
Serves 10–12

2 kg (4 lb) ocean trout or 1 whole salmon,
    boned and butterflied (see Note)
100 g (31/2 oz) rice stick noodles
1 tablespoon peanut oil
6 red Asian shallots, chopped
2 red chillies, chopped
2 tablespoons grated ginger
200 g (61/2 oz) water chestnuts, chopped
200 g (61/2 oz) bamboo shoots, chopped
6 spring onions (scallions), sliced
2 tablespoons chopped coriander
    (cilantro) root
3 tablespoons chopped coriander
    (cilantro) leaves
2 tablespoons fish sauce
2 tablespoons grated palm sugar

Lime butter sauce
4 makrut (kaffir) lime leaves, finely
    shredded
2 tablespoons lime juice
125 g (4 oz) butter

1 Preheat the oven to 180°C (350°F/Gas 4).
Pat the fish dry and use tweezers to
remove any remaining small bones.
2 Soak the noodles in boiling water for 10
minutes. Drain well, pat dry and cut into
short lengths.
3 Heat the oil in a frying pan and cook the
shallots, chillies and ginger over medium
heat for about 5 minutes, or until the
shallots are golden. Transfer to a bowl.
Add the noodles, water chestnuts,
bamboo shoots, spring onions, coriander
root and leaves, fish sauce and palm
sugar to the bowl and mix well.
4 Open the salmon or trout fillet out flat
and spread the noodle filling over the
centre. Fold the fish over to enclose the
filling and secure with string every 5 cm
(2 inches) along the fish. Place onto a
baking tray lined with foil and bake for
30–40 minutes, or until tender.
5 To make the sauce, place the lime
leaves, lime juice and butter in a
saucepan and cook over medium heat
until the butter turns nutty brown. Cut the
salmon into slices, discarding the string,
then serve topped with the sauce.

NOTE: A fish that has been butterflied has
been carefully slit through the middle,
along the bones, but not all the way
through. The effect is of having a hinge on
one side of the fish. Another term for this
is 'pocket boning'. Ask your fishmonger to
do this for you.

SKATE WITH BLACK BUTTER

Preparation time: 20 minutes
Total cooking time: 25 minutes
Serves 4

185 g (6 oz) unsalted butter, chopped
1 kg (2 lb) small skate wings
2½ cups (600 ml/20 fl oz) fish stock
1/3 cup (80 ml/2¾ fl oz) vinegar
2 tablespoons vinegar, extra
1 tablespoon chopped fresh parsley
2 tablespoons drained bottled capers

1 To clarify the butter, melt it in a pan over low heat, without stirring. Remove from the heat and cool slightly. Skim the foamy mixture from the surface. Pour off the clear yellow liquid and reserve. Discard the milky sediment left behind in the pan.
2 Pat the skate with paper towels. Cut fillets from either side of the cartilage with a sharp knife, cutting close to the cartilage. Place on a board skin-side-down, slide the knife between the skin and flesh and, using a sawing motion, cut along the length of the wing. Cut into equal-sized pieces.
3 Place the stock and vinegar in a large pan and bring to the boil. Add the skate and poach for 8 minutes. Drain well and pat dry with paper towels. Melt a little butter in a frying pan and cook the skate for 1–2 minutes each side, or until tender. Place on a serving dish and keep warm.
4 Heat the clarified butter in a pan until brown and foaming, but not black. Sprinkle the extra vinegar over the skate, then pour the butter over. Sprinkle with the parsley and capers. Serve hot.

SWEET AND SOUR FISH WITH HOKKIEN NOODLES

Preparation time: 20 minutes
Total cooking time: 20 minutes
Serves 4

425 g (14 oz) Hokkien noodles
1 tablespoon peanut oil
1 clove garlic, crushed
2 teaspoons grated fresh ginger
1 onion, cut into thin wedges
1 carrot, halved lengthways and thinly sliced
½ red pepper (capsicum), cut into thin strips
½ green pepper (capsicum), cut into thin strips
1 celery stick, thinly sliced
½ cup (60 g/2 oz) plain flour
¼ cup (45 g/1½ oz) rice flour
1 teaspoon caster sugar
½ teaspoon ground white pepper
500 g (1 lb) firm white fish fillets, cut into 3 cm (1¼ inch) cubes
1 egg, beaten with 1 tablespoon water
oil, to deep-fry
2 spring onions, sliced on the diagonal

Sauce
¼ cup (60 ml/2 fl oz) rice vinegar
1 tablespoon cornflour
¼ cup (60 ml/2 fl oz) tomato sauce
2 tablespoons sugar
2 teaspoons light soy sauce
1 tablespoon dry sherry
¼ cup (60 ml/2 fl oz) pineapple juice
2 tablespoons vegetable stock

1 Put the noodles in a heatproof bowl, cover with boiling water and soak for 1 minute. Separate gently, then drain.
2 To make the sauce, combine the vinegar and cornflour in a small jug, then stir in the rest of the ingredients and ¾ cup (185 ml/6 fl oz) water until combined.
3 Heat a wok over medium heat, add the oil and swirl to coat. Cook the garlic and ginger for 30 seconds. Add the onion, carrot, red and green pepper and celery and stir-fry for 3–4 minutes. Add the sauce to the wok, increase the heat to high and stir-fry for 1–2 minutes, or until thickened. Remove the wok from the heat.
4 Combine the flours, sugar and white pepper in a medium bowl. Dip the fish in the egg, then the flour mix, shaking off any excess. Fill a clean wok one-third full of oil and heat to 180°C (350°F), or until a cube of bread dropped in the oil browns in 15 seconds. Deep-fry the fish in batches for 3 minutes, or until cooked and golden. Drain on paper towels and keep warm.
5 Return the wok with the sauce to medium heat, add the noodles and toss for 3–4 minutes, or until heated through. Gently toss in the fish, top with the spring onion and serve.

SALMON IN NORI WITH NOODLES

Preparation time: 30 minutes
Total cooking time: 10 minutes
Serves 4

2 spring onions, cut into long thin strips
4 salmon cutlets, cut from the centre of the fish
1 sheet nori (dried seaweed)
2 teaspoons oil
250 g (8 oz) somen noodles

Dressing
½–¾ teaspoon wasabi paste
2 tablespoons rice wine vinegar
2 tablespoons mirin
1 tablespoon lime juice
2 teaspoons soft brown sugar
1 tablespoon oil
2 teaspoons soy sauce
2 teaspoons black sesame seeds

1 Put the spring onion in a bowl of cold water. Remove the skin and bones from the salmon, keeping the cutlets in one piece. Cut the nori into strips, the same width as the salmon, and wrap a strip tightly around each cutlet to form a neat circle. Seal the edges with a little water. Season with salt and pepper.
2 Heat a little oil in a frying pan and cook the salmon for 2–3 minutes each side, or until cooked to your liking (ideally, it should be a little pink in the centre).
3 While the salmon is cooking, prepare the dressing and noodles. Combine the dressing ingredients in a jug and mix well.
4 Place the noodles in a large bowl, cover with boiling water and stand for 5 minutes, or until softened. Drain well. Divide the noodles among serving plates, top with salmon and drizzle with the dressing. Drain the spring onion and serve over the top.

YELLOW FISH CURRY

Preparation time: 10 minutes
Total cooking time: 15 minutes
Serves 4

150 ml (5 fl oz) vegetable stock
1 tablespoon Thai yellow curry paste
1 tablespoon tamarind purée
1 tablespoon grated palm sugar
1½ tablespoons fish sauce
150 g (5 oz) green beans, trimmed and cut into 4 cm (1½ inch) lengths
1 cup (140 g/4½ oz) sliced bamboo shoots
400 ml (13 fl oz) coconut cream
400 g (13 oz) white fish fillets (e.g. ling, snapper), cut into cubes
1 tablespoon lime juice
lime wedges, to serve
fresh coriander leaves, to garnish

1 Pour the stock into a non-stick wok and bring to the boil. Add the curry paste and cook, stirring, for 3–4 minutes, or until fragrant. Stir in the combined tamarind purée, palm sugar and 1 tablespoon of the fish sauce. Add the beans and bamboo shoots, and cook over medium heat for 3–5 minutes, or until the beans are almost tender.
2 Add the coconut cream and bring to the boil, then reduce the heat, add the fish and simmer for 3–5 minutes, or until the fish is just cooked. Stir in the lime juice and remaining fish sauce. Garnish with the lime wedges and fresh coriander leaves. Serve with rice.

BLACKENED FISH

Preparation time: 5 minutes
Total cooking time: 6–8 minutes
Serves 6

6 large white fish fillets (eg. blue-eye, snapper, ling, warehou, mahi mahi), 2 cm (3/4 inch) thick
125 g (4 oz) unsalted butter, melted
2 tablespoons Cajun spices
2 teaspoons sweet paprika
lemon wedges or halves, for serving

1 Brush each fish fillet liberally with the butter.
2 Combine the Cajun spices and paprika, then sprinkle thickly over the fish. Use your fingers to rub the spice mix evenly over the fillets.
3 Heat a large frying pan over high heat. Place two fillets in the pan and cook for 1–2 minutes. Turn and cook for another few minutes, until the fish is cooked and flakes easily. The surface should be well charred on each side. Add extra butter if necessary. Cook the remaining fillets.
4 Serve drizzled with any remaining melted butter. The lemon can be served lightly charred.

CHICKEN, TURKEY AND DUCK

CHICKEN AND VEAL LOAF WITH MUSHROOMS AND SOUR CREAM

Preparation time: 20 minutes
Total cooking time: 1 hour
Serves 6

100 g (3½ oz) pappardelle
¼ cup (20 g/¾ oz) fresh breadcrumbs
1 tablespoon white wine
375 g (12 oz) chicken mince
375 g (12 oz) veal mince
2 cloves garlic, crushed
100 g (3½ oz) button mushrooms, finely chopped
2 eggs, beaten
pinch of nutmeg
pinch of cayenne pepper
¼ cup (60 ml/2 fl oz) sour cream
4 spring onions, finely chopped
2 tablespoons chopped fresh parsley

1 Grease a 6-cup capacity loaf tin. Cook the pappardelle in a large pan of rapidly boiling salted water until al dente. Drain.
2 Preheat the oven to moderately hot 200°C (400°F/Gas 6).
3 Soak the breadcrumbs in the wine. Mix the crumbs in a bowl with the chicken and veal minces, garlic, mushrooms, eggs, nutmeg, cayenne pepper, and salt and freshly ground black pepper, to taste. Mix in the sour cream, spring onion and parsley.
4 Place half the mince mixture into the prepared tin with your hands. Form a deep trough along the entire length. Fill the trough with the pappardelle. Press the remaining mince mixture over the top. Bake for 50–60 minutes, draining the excess fat and juice from the tin twice during cooking. Cool slightly before slicing.

NOTE: Mushrooms can be chopped in a food processor. Don't prepare too far in advance or they will discolour and darken the loaf.

CHICKEN AND LEEK PIE

Preparation time: 20 minutes
Total cooking time: 40 minutes
Serves 4

50 g (1¾ oz) butter
2 large leeks, white part only, finely sliced
4 spring onions, sliced
1 clove garlic, crushed
¼ cup (30 g/1 oz) plain flour
1½ cups (375 ml/12 fl oz) chicken stock
½ cup (125 ml/4 fl oz) cream
2 cups (280 g/9 oz) chopped cooked chicken
2 sheets frozen puff pastry, thawed
¼ cup (60 ml/2 fl oz) milk

1 Melt the butter in a saucepan and add the leek, spring onion and garlic. Cook over low heat for 6 minutes, or until the leek is soft but not browned. Stir in the flour and cook for 1 minute, or until pale and foaming. Remove from the heat and gradually stir in the stock. Return to the heat and stir constantly until the sauce boils and thickens. Stir in the cream and chicken, then spoon into a shallow 20 cm (8 inch) pie dish and set aside to cool. Preheat the oven to moderately hot 200°C (400°F/Gas 6).
2 Brush around the rim of the pie dish with a little milk. Put 1 sheet of pastry on top and seal around the edge firmly. Trim off any overhanging pastry with a sharp knife and decorate the edge with the back of a fork. Cut the other sheet into 1 cm (½ inch) strips and roll each strip up loosely like a snail. Arrange the spirals on top of the pie, starting from the middle and leaving a gap between each one. The spirals may not cover the whole pie. Make a few small holes between the spirals to let out any steam, and brush the top of the pie lightly with milk. Bake for 25–30 minutes, or until the top is crisp and golden. Make sure the spirals look well cooked and are not raw in the middle.

DEEP-FRIED CHICKEN WITH SEAWEED

Preparation time: 25 minutes + 15 minutes marinating
Total cooking time: 20 minutes
Serves 4

400 g (12⅔ oz) chicken breast fillets
¼ cup (60 ml/2 fl oz) Japanese soy sauce
¼ cup (60 ml/2 fl oz) mirin
4 cm (1½ inch) piece fresh ginger, very finely grated
1 sheet nori, finely chopped or crumbled into very small pieces
⅓ cup (40 g/1⅓ oz) cornflour
oil, for deep-frying
pickled ginger (page 766) and thin cucumber slices, to serve

1 Carefully trim any sinew from the chicken. Cut the chicken into bite-sized pieces and discard any thin ends so that the pieces will be even in size. Place the chicken pieces in a bowl.
2 Combine the soy sauce, mirin and ginger in a small jug and pour the mixture over the chicken; toss until the chicken pieces are evenly coated with the marinade. Set aside for 15 minutes, then drain off any excess marinade.
3 Mix the nori with the cornflour. Using your fingertips, lightly coat each piece of chicken in the cornflour mixture.
4 Heat the oil in a pan until moderately hot; add the chicken, 6 to 7 pieces at a time, and fry until golden, turning regularly. Drain on paper towels. Serve with steamed rice, pickled ginger and sliced cucumber. Garnish with extra strips of nori, if desired.

CHICKEN BALLOTTINE

Preparation time: 40 minutes
Total cooking time: 1 hour 45 minutes +
   refrigeration
Serves 8

1.6 kg (3¼ lb) chicken
2 red peppers (capsicums)
1 kg (2 lb) silverbeet
30 g (1 oz) butter
1 onion, finely chopped
1 clove garlic, crushed
½ cup (50 g/1¾ oz) grated Parmesan
1 cup (80 g/2¾ oz) fresh breadcrumbs
1 tablespoon chopped fresh oregano
200 g (6½ oz) ricotta

1 To bone the chicken, cut through the skin on the centre back with a sharp knife. Separate the flesh from the bone down one side to the breast, being careful not to pierce the skin. Follow along the bones closely with the knife, gradually easing the meat from the thigh, drumstick and wing. Cut through the thigh bone where it meets the drumstick and cut off the wing tip. Repeat on the other side, then lift the rib cage away, leaving the flesh in one piece and the drumsticks still attached to the flesh. Scrape all the meat from the drumstick and wings, discarding the bones. Turn the wing and drumstick flesh inside the chicken and lay the chicken out flat, skin-side-down. Refrigerate.
2 Preheat the oven to moderate 180°C (350°F/Gas 4). Cut the peppers into large flattish pieces, discarding the membranes and seeds. Cook skin-side-up under a hot grill until the skins blister and blacken. Cool in a plastic bag, then peel.

3 Discard the stalks from the silverbeet and finely shred the leaves. Melt the butter in a large frying pan and cook the onion and garlic over medium heat for 5 minutes, or until soft. Add the silverbeet and stir until wilted and all the moisture has evaporated. Cool. In a food processor, process the silverbeet and onion mixture with the Parmesan, breadcrumbs, oregano and half the ricotta. Season with salt and cracked pepper.
4 Spread the silverbeet mixture over the chicken and lay the pepper pieces over the top. Form the remaining ricotta into a roll and place across the width of the chicken. Fold the sides of the chicken in over the filling so they overlap slightly. Tuck the ends in neatly. Secure with toothpicks, then tie with string at 3 cm (1¼ inch) intervals.
5 Grease a large piece of foil and place the chicken in the centre. Roll the chicken up securely in the foil, sealing the ends well. Bake on a baking tray for 1¼–1½ hours, or until the juices run clear when a skewer is inserted in the centre of the meat. Cool, then refrigerate until cold before removing the foil, toothpicks and string. Cut into 1 cm (½ inch) slices to serve.

NOTE: You can ask the butcher or chicken specialist to bone the chicken.

CHICKEN AND ASPARAGUS GRATIN

Preparation time: 10 minutes
Total cooking time: 30 minutes
Serves 6

4 cups (540 g/1 lb 2 oz) chopped cooked
   chicken
425 g (14 oz) can asparagus spears,
   drained
420 g (14 oz) can creamy chicken and
   corn soup, or cream of mushroom soup
½ cup (125 g/4 oz) sour cream
2 spring onions, sliced diagonally
1 red pepper (capsicum), thinly sliced
1 cup (125 g/4 oz) grated Cheddar
½ cup (50 g/1¾ oz) grated Parmesan
½ teaspoon sweet paprika

1 Preheat the oven to moderate 180°C (350°F/Gas 4). Cover the base of a large, shallow ovenproof dish with the chicken and top with half the asparagus spears.
2 Combine the soup, sour cream, spring onion and red pepper in a bowl. Season, to taste, and pour over the chicken.
3 Arrange the remaining asparagus spears on top of the chicken and cover with the combined cheeses. Sprinkle with paprika and bake for 30 minutes, or until golden brown and bubbling. Serve immediately.

CHICKEN AND MUSHROOM RICE PAPER PARCELS

Preparation time: 15 minutes + 2 hours
    marinating + 20 minutes soaking +
    15 minutes cooling
Total cooking time: 20 minutes
Makes 24

1–2 tablespoons Chinese barbecue sauce
1 tablespoon Chinese rice wine
2 teaspoons hoisin sauce
2 teaspoons light soy sauce
½ teaspoon sesame oil
pinch of five-spice powder
pinch of white pepper
2 teaspoons grated fresh ginger
2 spring onions, finely chopped, white
    and green parts separated
400 g (13 oz) chicken breast fillet, thinly
    sliced
4 dried shiitake mushrooms
¼ cup (60 ml/2 fl oz) vegetable oil, plus
    extra, for deep-frying
125 g (4 oz) canned bamboo shoots,
    rinsed, drained and julienned
12 snow peas (mangetout), shredded
2 cloves garlic, finely chopped
24 square Chinese rice paper wrappers
hoisin sauce, for dipping (optional)

1 Combine the Chinese barbecue sauce,
rice wine, hoisin sauce, soy sauce,
sesame oil, five-spice powder, white
pepper, 1 teaspoon of the ginger and the
white part of the spring onion in a non-
metallic bowl, then add the chicken.
Cover and refrigerate for at least 2 hours.
2 Meanwhile, put the shiitake mushrooms
in a bowl, cover with boiling water and
soak for 20 minutes. Squeeze the
mushrooms dry, discard the stalks and
thinly slice the caps.

3 Heat a wok over high heat, add
1 tablespoon of the oil and swirl to coat.
Add the mushrooms, bamboo shoots and
snow peas and stir-fry for 1–2 minutes.
Add another tablespoon of oil, the garlic
and remaining ginger, and stir-fry for
30 seconds. Transfer to a non-metallic
bowl. Heat another tablespoon of the oil
in the wok, add the drained chicken and
stir-fry for 2–3 minutes, or until the
chicken is cooked. Transfer to the bowl
with the vegetables. Add the green part of
the spring onions to the bowl. Mix well.
Cool for 15 minutes.
4 Take a rice paper wrapper and place it
diagonally on the work surface, so the
bottom corner of a diamond is closest to
you. Using 1 tablespoon of the chicken
mixture, roll a sausage shape and lay it
vertically in the middle of the wrapper.
Fold up the wrapper like an envelope,
tucking in the edges. Repeat with the
remaining wrappers and filling.
5 Fill a wok one-third full of oil and heat
to 180°C (350°F), or until a cube of bread
browns in 15 seconds. Gently lower
4–6 of the 'envelopes' into the wok at a
time, and deep-fry for 1–2 minutes,
turning halfway through to ensure both
sides are evenly browned and crisp, and
that the filling is cooked through. Drain
well on crumpled paper towels and serve
immediately, with some hoisin sauce for
dipping, if desired.

SAFFRON CHICKEN AND RICE

Preparation time: 20 minutes
Total cooking time: 40 minutes
Serves 4

½ teaspoon saffron threads, chopped
¼ cup (60 ml/2 fl oz) olive oil
4 chicken thighs and 4 drumsticks
1 large red onion, finely chopped
1 large green capsicum (pepper), two-
    thirds diced and one-third julienned
3 teaspoons sweet paprika
400 g (13 oz) tin chopped tomatoes
1¼ cups (250 g/8 oz) long-grain rice
3¼ cups (810 ml/26 fl oz) hot chicken
    stock

1 Soak the saffron threads in ¼ cup
(60 ml/2 fl oz) warm water. Heat
2 tablespoons of the oil in a large heavy-
based saucepan or deep frying pan with a
lid over high heat. Season the chicken
pieces with salt and freshly ground black
pepper and brown in batches. Remove the
chicken from the pan and drain on
crumpled paper towels.
2 Reduce the heat to medium and add the
remaining oil. Add the onion and diced
capsicum, and cook gently for 5 minutes,
or until the onion is softened but not
browned. Stir in the paprika and cook for
about 30 seconds. Add the tomato and
simmer for 1–3 minutes, or until the
mixture thickens. Add the rice and cook
until lightly golden.
3 Add the saffron water with the stock.
Return the chicken to the pan and stir to
combine. Season with salt and pepper.
Bring to the boil, cover, reduce the heat to
medium and simmer for 20 minutes, or
until all the liquid has been absorbed and
the chicken is tender. Stir in the julienned
capsicum, then allow it to stand, covered,
for several minutes before serving.

BAKED LEMON CHICKENS

Preparation time: 30 minutes +
    1 hour marinating
Total cooking time: 40 minutes
Serves 4

4 baby chickens, about 500 g (1 lb) each
2 medium onions, chopped
1 spring onion, chopped
2 red chillies, chopped
2 cloves garlic, crushed
¼ cup (60 ml/2 fl oz) peanut oil
¼ cup (60 ml/2 fl oz) lemon juice

1 Cut the chickens in half along the breast and backbone. Press down on each half to flatten it slightly.
2 Combine the onion, spring onion, chilli, garlic, oil and lemon juice in a food processor and process until smooth. Spoon the mixture over the chickens; cover and marinate for 1 hour or overnight in the refrigerator.
3 Preheat the oven to moderate 180°C (350°F/Gas 4). Using tongs, remove the chickens from the marinade, reserving the marinade. Place the chickens in a baking dish in a single layer. Bake for 40 minutes, or until cooked and browned, brushing occasionally with the marinade. Serve with rice or noodles, and a vegetable dish.

CHICKEN MEZZELUNE WITH CREAM SAUCE

Preparation time: 45 minutes
Total cooking time: 15 minutes
Serves 4–6 as a first course

250 g (8 oz) packet gow gee wrappers

Chicken and ham filling
250 g (8 oz) chicken breast fillet
1 egg, beaten
90 g (3 oz) cooked ham or prosciutto
2 teaspoons finely snipped chives
2 teaspoons chopped fresh marjoram

Cream sauce
30 g (1 oz) butter
2 spring onions, finely chopped
2 tablespoons white wine
1½ cups (375 ml/12 fl oz) cream

1 To make the filling, remove any excess fat and sinew from the chicken breast. Cut the flesh into pieces and chop in a food processor. Add the egg, ½ teaspoon of salt and a pinch of white pepper and process until finely chopped. Transfer to a bowl. Chop the ham or prosciutto finely and stir into the chicken with the herbs.
2 Lay the gow gee wrappers on a work surface, six at a time, and put a teaspoonful of chicken filling in the centre of each. Brush the edges with cold water, fold in half to form a half moon shape (mezzelune), and press the edges together firmly to seal. Place on a tea towel and continue with the remaining circles.

3 If making your own pasta, roll the dough as thinly as possible on a lightly floured surface, or use a pasta machine and pass the dough through 5 or 6 settings. Cut into circles with an 8 cm (3 inch) cutter, fill and seal as above.
4 To make the cream sauce, heat the butter in a small pan, add the spring onion and cook for 2–3 minutes. Add the wine and cream and simmer until reduced. Season, to taste.
5 Cook the mezzelune in batches, in rapidly boiling salted water. Don't crowd the pan. Simmer for 2–3 minutes, until the chicken is cooked. Don't overcook or the chicken will be dry. Drain.
6 Serve the sauce immediately with the mezzelune. Garnish, if you like.

CHICKEN WITH PEPPERS AND OLIVES

Preparation time: 30 minutes
Total cooking time: 1 hour 10 minutes
Serves 4

6 ripe tomatoes
1.5 kg (3 lb) chicken, cut into 8 portions
3 tablespoons olive oil
2 large red onions, sliced into 5 mm (¼ inch) slices
2 cloves garlic, crushed
3 red peppers (capsicums), seeded, white pith removed, cut into 1 cm (½ inch) strips
60 g (2 oz) thickly sliced prosciutto, finely chopped
1 tablespoon chopped fresh thyme
2 teaspoons sweet paprika
8 pitted black olives
8 pitted green olives

1 Score a cross in the base of each tomato. Place in a bowl of boiling water for 10 seconds, then plunge into cold water and peel away from the cross. Cut each tomato in half and scoop out the seeds with a teaspoon. Finely chop the flesh.
2 Pat dry the chicken with paper towel and season well with salt and pepper. Heat the oil in a heavy-based frying pan and cook the chicken a few pieces at a time skin-side-down, over moderate heat for 4–5 minutes, until golden. Turn the chicken over and cook for another 2–3 minutes. Transfer to a plate.
3 Add the onion, garlic, pepper, prosciutto and thyme to the frying pan. Cook over medium heat, stirring frequently for 8–10 minutes, until the vegetables have softened but not browned.
4 Add the tomato and paprika, increase the heat and cook for 10–12 minutes, or until the sauce has thickened and reduced. Return the chicken to the pan and coat with the sauce. Cover the pan and reduce the heat to low. Simmer the chicken for 25–30 minutes, or until tender. Add the olives and adjust the seasoning, if necessary, before serving.

CHICKEN AND SUGAR PEA PARCELS

Preparation time: 40 minutes
Total cooking time: 30 minutes
Makes 8

200 g (6½ oz) sugar snap peas
1 tablespoon oil
6 chicken thigh fillets, cut into 1 cm (½ inch) thick strips
40 g (1¼ oz) butter
2 tablespoons plain flour
¾ cup (185 ml/6 fl oz) chicken stock
⅔ cup (170 ml/5½ fl oz) dry white wine
1 tablespoon wholegrain mustard
150 g (5 oz) feta cheese, cut into 1 cm (½ inch) cubes
⅓ cup (50 g/1¾ oz) sliced sun-dried tomatoes, finely chopped
24 sheets filo pastry
60 g (2 oz) butter, extra, melted
sesame and sunflower seeds

1 Preheat the oven to hot 210°C (415°F/Gas 6–7). Top and tail the sugar snap peas, then plunge into boiling water for 1 minute, or until bright in colour but still crunchy. Drain well.
2 Heat the oil in a heavy-based pan. Cook the chicken quickly, in small batches, over medium heat until well browned. Drain on paper towels.
3 Melt the butter in a pan and add the flour. Stir over low heat for 2 minutes, or until the flour mixture is light golden and bubbling. Add the stock, wine and mustard, stirring until the mixture is smooth. Stir constantly over medium heat until the mixture boils and thickens. Stir in the chicken, sugar snap peas, feta and tomato and mix gently. Remove from the heat and allow to cool. Divide the mixture evenly into eight portions.
4 Brush three sheets of the pastry with the melted butter. Place the sheets on top of each other. Place one portion of the mixture at one short end of the pastry. Roll and fold the pastry, enclosing the filling to form a parcel. Brush with a little more butter and place seam-side down on a greased baking tray. Repeat with the remaining pastry, butter and filling. Brush the tops with butter. Sprinkle with the sesame and sunflower seeds. Bake for 20 minutes, or until golden brown and heated through.

CHICKEN AND ALMOND PILAFF

Preparation time: 15 minutes + 1 hour
  marinating + 30 minutes soaking
Total cooking time: 45 minutes
Serves 4–6

Baharat
1½ tablespoons coriander seeds
3 tablespoons black peppercorns
1½ tablespoons cassia bark
1½ tablespoons cloves
2 tablespoons cumin seeds
1 teaspoon cardamom seeds
2 whole nutmeg
3 tablespoons paprika

700 g (1 lb 6½ oz) chicken thigh fillets,
  trimmed, cut into 3 cm (1¼ inch) wide
  strips
2 cups (400 g/13 oz) basmati rice
3 cups (750 ml/24 fl oz) chicken stock
2 tablespoons ghee
1 large onion, chopped
1 garlic clove, finely chopped
1 teaspoon ground turmeric
400 g (13 oz) tin chopped tomatoes
1 cinnamon stick
4 cardamom pods, bruised
4 cloves
½ teaspoon finely grated lemon zest
3 tablespoons fresh coriander (cilantro)
  leaves, chopped
2 teaspoons lemon juice
⅓ cup (40 g/1¼ oz) slivered almonds,
  toasted

1 To make the baharat, grind the
coriander seeds, peppercorns, cassia
bark, cloves, cumin seeds and cardamom
seeds to a powder in a mortar and pestle
or spice grinder—you may need to do this
in batches. Grate the nutmeg on the fine
side of the grater and add to spice
mixture with the paprika. Stir together.

2 Combine the chicken and 1 tablespoon
of the baharat in a large bowl, cover with
plastic wrap and refrigerate for 1 hour.
Meanwhile, put the rice in a large bowl,
cover with cold water and soak for at
least 30 minutes. Rinse under cold
running water until the water runs clear,
then drain and set aside.
3 Bring the stock to the boil in a
saucepan. Reduce the heat, cover and
keep at a low simmer. Meanwhile, heat
the ghee in a large, heavy-based
saucepan over medium heat. Add the
onion and garlic and cook for 5 minutes,
or until soft and golden. Add the chicken
and turmeric and cook for 5 minutes, or
until browned. Add the rice and cook,
stirring, for 2 minutes.
4 Add the tomato, simmering chicken
stock, cinnamon stick, cardamom pods,
cloves, lemon zest and 1 teaspoon salt.
Stir well and bring to the boil, then reduce
the heat to low and cover the saucepan
with a tight-fitting lid. Simmer for 20
minutes, or until the stock is absorbed
and the rice is cooked. Remove from the
heat and allow to stand, covered, for
10 minutes.
5 Stir in the fresh coriander, lemon juice
and almonds. Season to taste.

NOTE: Baharat is an aromatic spice blend
used in Arabic cuisine to add depth of
flavour to dishes such as soups, fish
curries and tomato sauces. Leftover
baharat can be stored in an airtight jar for
up to 3 months in a cool, dry place. It can
be used in Middle Eastern casseroles and
stews, rubbed on fish that is to be grilled,
pan-fried or barbecued, or used with salt
to dry marinate lamb roasts, cutlets or
chops.

CHICKEN AND MUSHROOM RISOTTO

Preparation time: 15 minutes
Total cooking time: 45 minutes
Serves 4

1.25 litres (40 fl oz) vegetable or chicken stock
2 tablespoons olive oil
300 g (10 oz) chicken breast fillets, cut
  into 1.5 cm (⅝ inch) wide strips
250 g (8 oz) small button mushrooms, halved
pinch of nutmeg
2 garlic cloves, crushed
20 g (¾ oz) butter
1 small onion, finely chopped
1⅔ cups (360 g/12 oz) arborio rice
⅔ cup (170 ml/5½ fl oz) dry white wine
¼ cup (60 g/2 oz) sour cream
½ cup (50 g/1¾ oz) grated Parmesan cheese
3 tablespoons chopped parsley

1 Bring the stock to the boil over high heat,
then reduce the heat and keep at a
simmer. Heat the oil in a large saucepan.
Cook the chicken pieces over high heat for
3–4 minutes, or until golden brown. Add
the mushrooms and cook for 1–2 minutes
more, or until starting to brown. Stir in the
nutmeg and garlic, and season with salt
and freshly ground black pepper. Cook for
30 seconds, then remove from the pan.
2 Melt the butter in the same pan
and cook the onion over low heat for
5–6 minutes. Add the rice, stir to coat,
then stir in the wine. Once the wine is
absorbed, reduce the heat and add ½ cup
(125 ml/4 fl oz) of the stock, stirring
constantly over medium heat until all the
liquid is absorbed. Continue adding more
liquid, ½ cup (125 ml/4 fl oz) at a time,
until all the stock has been used and the
rice is creamy. This will take about 20–25
minutes. Stir in the mushrooms and the
chicken with the last of the chicken stock.
3 Remove the pan from the heat and stir
in the sour cream, Parmesan and parsley.
Season with salt and freshly ground black
pepper, then serve, with a little extra
Parmesan, if desired.

CHICKEN CHOW MEIN

Preparation time: 15 minutes +
    1 hour standing
Total cooking time: 40 minutes
Serves 4

250 g (8 oz) fresh thin egg noodles
2 teaspoons sesame oil
½ cup (125 ml/4 fl oz) peanut oil
1 tablespoon Chinese rice wine
1½ tablespoons light soy sauce
3 teaspoons cornflour
400 g (13 oz) chicken breast fillets, cut
    into thin strips
1 clove garlic, crushed
1 tablespoon finely chopped fresh ginger
100 g (3½ oz) sugar snap peas, trimmed
250 g (8 oz) wom bok (Chinese cabbage),
    finely shredded
4 spring onions, cut into 2 cm (¾ inch)
    lengths
100 ml (3½ fl oz) chicken stock
1½ tablespoons oyster sauce
100 g (3½ oz) bean sprouts, tailed
1 small fresh red chilli, seeded and
    julienned, to garnish (optional)

1 Cook the noodles in a saucepan of
boiling water for 1 minute, or until tender.
Drain well. Add the sesame oil and
1 tablespoon of the peanut oil and toss
well. Place on a baking tray and spread
out in a thin layer. Leave in a dry place for
at least 1 hour.
2 Meanwhile, combine the rice wine,
1 tablespoon of the soy sauce and
1 teaspoon of the cornflour in a large
non-metallic bowl. Add the chicken and
toss well. Cover with plastic wrap and
marinate for 10 minutes.

3 Heat 1 tablespoon of the peanut oil in a
small non-stick frying pan over high heat.
Add one quarter of the noodles, shaping
into a pancake. Reduce the heat to
medium and cook for 4 minutes on each
side, or until crisp and golden. Drain on
crumpled paper towels and keep warm.
Repeat with 3 tablespoons of the oil and
the remaining noodles to make four
noodle cakes in total.
4 Heat a wok over high heat, add the
remaining peanut oil and swirl to coat the
side of the wok. Stir-fry the garlic and
ginger for 30 seconds. Add the chicken
and stir-fry for 3–4 minutes, or until
golden and tender. Add the sugar snap
peas, shredded wom bok and spring onion
and stir-fry for 2 minutes, or until the
cabbage has wilted. Stir in the chicken
stock, oyster sauce and bean sprouts and
bring to the boil.
5 Combine the remaining cornflour with
1–2 teaspoons cold water. Stir it into the
wok with the remaining soy sauce and
cook for 1–2 minutes, or until the sauce
thickens.
6 To assemble, place a noodle cake on
each serving plate, then spoon the
chicken and vegetable mixture on top.
Serve immediately, garnished with chilli,
if desired.

CHICKEN ADOBO

Preparation time: 20 minutes +
    2 hours marinating
Total cooking time: 50 minutes
Serves 6

6 cloves garlic, crushed
1 cup (250 ml/8 fl oz) cider vinegar
1½ cups (375 ml/12 fl oz) chicken stock
1 bay leaf
1 teaspoon coriander seeds
1 teaspoon black peppercorns
1 teaspoon annatto seeds (see note)
3 tablespoons soy sauce
1.5 kg (3¼ lb) chicken pieces
2 tablespoons oil

1 Combine the garlic, vinegar, chicken
stock, bay leaf, coriander seeds, black
peppercorns, annatto seeds and soy
sauce in a large bowl. Add the chicken,
cover and leave to marinate in the
refrigerator for 2 hours.
2 Transfer the chicken mixture to a large
heavy-based pan and bring to the boil.
Reduce the heat, cover and simmer for
30 minutes. Remove the lid from the pan
and continue cooking for 10 minutes, or
until the chicken is tender. Remove the
chicken from the pan and set aside. Bring
the liquid to the boil again and cook over
high heat for 10 minutes, or until the
liquid has reduced by half.
3 Heat the oil in a wok or large frying pan,
add the chicken in batches and cook over
medium heat for 5 minutes, or until crisp
and brown. Pour the reduced vinegar
mixture over the chicken pieces and serve
with rice.

NOTE: If annatto seeds are unavailable,
substitute ¼ teaspoon paprika combined
with a generous pinch of turmeric. The
annatto seeds can be left in the dish, but
are too hard to eat.

SPAGHETTI WITH CHICKEN MEATBALLS

Preparation time: 45 minutes + chilling
Total cooking time: 1 hour 30 minutes
Serves 4–6

500 g (1 lb) chicken mince
60 g (2 oz) freshly grated Parmesan
2 cups (160 g/5½ oz) fresh white
    breadcrumbs
2 cloves garlic, crushed
1 egg
1 tablespoon chopped fresh flat-leaf
    parsley
1 tablespoon chopped fresh sage
3 tablespoons vegetable oil
500 g (1 lb) spaghetti
2 tablespoons chopped fresh oregano,
    to serve

Tomato sauce
1 tablespoon olive oil
1 onion, finely chopped
2 kg (4 lb) very ripe tomatoes, chopped
2 bay leaves
1 cup (30 g/1 oz) fresh basil leaves,
    loosely packed
1 teaspoon coarsely ground black pepper

1 In a large bowl, mix the chicken mince,
Parmesan, breadcrumbs, garlic, egg and
herbs. Season, to taste, with salt and
freshly ground black pepper. Shape
tablespoonsful of the mixture into small
balls and chill for about 30 minutes, to firm.

2 Heat the oil in a shallow pan and fry the
balls, in batches, until golden brown. Turn
them often by gently shaking the pan.
Drain on paper towels.
3 To make the tomato sauce, heat the oil
in a large pan, add the onion and fry for
about 1–2 minutes, until softened. Add the
tomato and bay leaves, cover and bring to
the boil, stirring occasionally. Reduce the
heat to low, partially cover and cook for
50–60 minutes.
4 Add the meatballs to the sauce, along
with the basil leaves and freshly ground
black pepper and simmer, uncovered, for
10–15 minutes.
5 While the sauce is simmering, cook the
spaghetti in a large pan of rapidly boiling
salted water until al dente. Drain and
return to the pan. Add some sauce to the
pasta and toss to distribute. Serve the
pasta in individual bowls with sauce and
meatballs, sprinkled with chopped fresh
oregano and perhaps some extra
Parmesan.

CORONATION CHICKEN

Preparation time: 15 minutes
Total cooking time: 10 minutes
Serves 4–6

500 g (1 lb) cooked chicken
1 tablespoon oil
1 onion, finely chopped
2 teaspoons curry powder
1 tablespoon tomato paste (tomato purée)
2 tablespoons red wine
1½ tablespoons fruit chutney
½ cup (125 g/4 oz) whole-egg mayonnaise
2 sticks celery, sliced
3 spring onions, finely sliced

1 Remove all the skin and any fat from
the chicken and cut the flesh into bite-
sized pieces. Heat the oil in a saucepan
and add the onion. Cover and cook,
stirring occasionally, over low heat for
5–10 minutes, or until soft, but not
browned. Add the curry powder and stir
until fragrant. Add the tomato paste and
red wine and stir for 1 minute. Set aside to
cool, then mix in a bowl with the chutney
and mayonnaise.
2 Put the chicken, celery and 2 of the
spring onions into a large bowl. Add the
mayonnaise mixture and toss lightly to
coat. Spoon into a serving bowl and
sprinkle with finely sliced spring onion.

NOTE: Coronation chicken is often
accompanied by apricots. The addition of
sliced celery is not traditional in this salad
but it gives a nice crunchy texture.

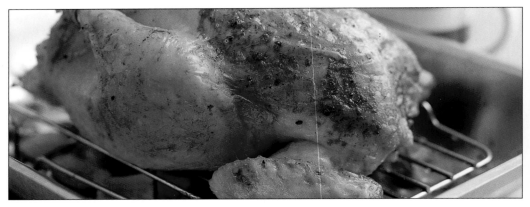

ROAST CHICKEN STUFFED WITH WILD RICE

Preparation time: 30 minutes + cooling
Total cooking time: 1 hour 45 minutes
Serves 6

50 g (1¾ oz) wild rice
200 g (6½ oz) basmati rice
¼ cup (60 ml/2 fl oz) orange juice
100 g (3½ oz) dried cranberries
½ teaspoon ground cinnamon
100 g (3½ oz) roasted, roughly chopped
    macadamias
50 g (1¾ oz) shelled pistachios
2 teaspoons chopped fresh rosemary
1 large orange, zested
20 g (¾ oz) butter, melted
40 g (1¼ oz) butter, extra, softened
1 cup (250 ml/8 fl oz) chicken stock
1.6–2 kg (3¼ lb–4 lb) chicken
1 large onion, cut into large chunks
1 carrot, cut into large chunks
2 celery stalks, cut into large chunks
1 tablespoon plain (all-purpose) flour

1 Add the wild rice to a saucepan of cold, salted water. Bring to the boil and simmer for 10 minutes, then add the basmati rice and cook for 15 minutes. At the same time, bring the orange juice to the boil in a small saucepan and add the cranberries. Turn off the heat and soak for 15 minutes. Drain the rice under cold water, then cool. Transfer to a bowl and add the cranberries, cinnamon, macadamias, pistachios, rosemary and orange zest. Season, then stir in the melted butter. Cool completely.
2 Pat the inside of the chicken dry with paper towels. Using clean hands, fill the cavity of the chicken with the cold stuffing.

3 Truss the chicken. To do this, use a 90 cm (36 inch) piece of kitchen string, tie both chicken legs together, twisting the string around a couple of times. Run the string around the thighs and under the wings on both sides of the bird, then pull it tightly and tie a firm knot at the neck. Trim off any excess string. Any excess skin at the neck of the bird can be tucked under the wings.
4 Preheat the oven to moderately hot 200°C (400°F/Gas 6). Spread the remaining butter over the skin of the chicken, then season well with sea salt and pepper. Place the chicken with the breast-side up on a roasting rack.
5 Spread the vegetables in the base of a sturdy roasting tin. Place the chicken, on its rack, over the vegetables and roast for 45 minutes. Baste the chicken, then return to the oven and roast for another 30 minutes, or until the chicken is cooked. Test by piercing through the lower part of the thigh with a skewer. If the juices run clear, it is cooked, but if not, return it to the oven for another 10–15 minutes. Cover loosely with foil if browning too quickly. Leave the chicken to rest while you prepare the gravy.
6 Remove the vegetables from the roasting tin with a slotted spoon and discard. Spoon all but 3 tablespoons of the fat from the roasting tin, then place the tin on the stove-top. Stir in the flour and cook for 1 minute, until it starts to brown. Scrape the crusty bits from the base. Add the remaining chicken stock and cook for 3–4 minutes. Add any juices from the chicken. Strain the gravy through a sieve. Serve the chicken with the gravy.

CHICKEN AND PUMPKIN STEW

Preparation time: 20 minutes
Total cooking time: 50 minutes
Serves 6

½ cup (110 g/3⅔ oz) short-grain rice
2 tablespoons oil
1 kg (2 lb) chicken pieces
3 cloves garlic, crushed
3 tablespoons finely chopped lemon
    grass (white part only)
2 teaspoons grated fresh turmeric or
    1 teaspoon ground turmeric
2 tablespoons grated fresh galangal
6 kaffir lime leaves, finely shredded
6 spring onions, chopped
4 cups (1 litre) chicken stock
500 g (1 lb) pumpkin, cubed
1 small green pawpaw, peeled and
    chopped
125 g (4 oz) snake beans, cut into short
    lengths

1 Preheat the oven to moderate 180°C (350°F/Gas 4). Spread the rice on a baking tray and roast it for 15 minutes or until golden. Remove the rice from the oven, allow it to cool slightly and then process it in a food processor until finely ground.
2 Heat the oil in a large pan; add the chicken pieces in batches and cook for 5 minutes, or until brown. Drain on paper towels.
3 Add the garlic, lemon grass, turmeric, galangal, lime leaves and spring onion to the pan; cook over medium heat for 3 minutes or until the spring onion is golden. Return the chicken to the pan; add the stock, cover and simmer for 20 minutes.
4 Add the pumpkin and pawpaw, and simmer, covered, for 10 minutes. Add the beans and simmer, covered, for another 10 minutes, or until the chicken is tender. Stir in the ground rice, bring to the boil, reduce heat and simmer, uncovered, for 5 minutes or until the mixture thickens slightly.

CHICKEN POT PIES WITH HERB SCONES

Preparation time: 25 minutes
Total cooking time: 35 minutes
Serves 6

60 g (2 oz) butter
1 onion, chopped
⅓ cup (40 g/1¼ oz) plain flour
2⅔ cups (670 ml/22 fl oz) milk
1 cup (125 g/4 oz) grated Cheddar
2 teaspoons wholegrain mustard
2½ cups (450 g/14 oz) chopped cooked chicken
2 cups (200 g/6½ oz) frozen vegetables

topping
2 cups (250 g/8 oz) self-raising flour
15 g (½ oz) butter
1 cup (250 ml/8 fl oz) milk
2 tablespoons chopped fresh parsley
1 tablespoon milk, extra

1 Preheat the oven to 210°C (415°F/Gas 6–7). Lightly grease six 1 cup (250 ml/8 fl oz) individual dishes with oil or melted butter. Heat the butter in a large heavy-based pan. Add the onion and cook over medium heat until soft. Add the flour and stir over the heat for 1 minute, or until lightly golden and bubbling. Gradually add the milk, stirring constantly over the heat until the sauce boils and thickens. Remove from heat. Stir in the Cheddar, mustard, chicken and vegetables. Spoon the mixture into the prepared dishes.
2 To make the topping, place the flour in a bowl. Using your fingertips, rub the butter into the flour for 2 minutes, or until the mixture is fine and crumbly. Make a well in the centre. Stir in the milk and parsley with a flat-bladed knife. Using a cutting action, stir until the mixture is soft and sticky. Turn onto a floured surface.
3 Gather the dough into a smooth ball and pat out to a 2.5 cm (1 inch) thickness. Cut rounds from the pastry with a 4.5 cm (1¾ inch) cutter. Place three rounds on top of each chicken pot. Brush the tops with the extra milk. Bake for 25 minutes, or until the scones are browned and cooked.

CHICKEN WITH PILAFF

Preparation time: 20 minutes
Total cooking time: 1 hour 10 minutes
Serves 4

2½ cups (600 ml/20 fl oz) chicken stock
1 tablespoon peanut oil
1 onion, finely chopped
2 garlic cloves, crushed
2 tablespoons finely chopped lemon grass
1 red capsicum (pepper), finely chopped
1½ cups (300 g/10 oz) basmati rice
1.4 kg (2 lb 13 oz) whole chicken
⅓ cup (80 ml/2¾ fl oz) coconut milk
2 tablespoons sweet chilli sauce
2 tablespoons lime juice
1 cup (50 g/1¾ oz) roughly chopped coriander (cilantro) leaves
2 teaspoons soft brown sugar

1 Pour the stock into a saucepan, bring to the boil, then remove from the heat. Preheat the oven to moderately hot 200°C (400°F/Gas 6).
2 Heat the oil in a large, 3 cm (1¼ inch) deep flameproof casserole dish over medium heat. Add the onion, garlic, lemon grass and capsicum and cook, stirring, for 5 minutes, or until soft. Stir in the rice, mixing well to combine. Remove the dish from the heat. Add the hot stock and mix well.
3 Wash the chicken and pat dry inside and out with paper towels. Tie the legs together with string and tuck the wings under.
4 Combine the coconut milk, chilli sauce, lime juice, coriander and sugar in a bowl. Put the chicken on a rack over the rice. Brush half the coconut mixture over the chicken and bake for 15 minutes. Reduce the temperature to moderate 180°C (350°F/Gas 4) and stir 1 cup (250 ml/ 8 fl oz) water into the rice mixture. Cover the chicken tightly with lightly greased foil and bake for a further 30 minutes.
5 Remove the chicken and rack. Stir the rice, adding extra water if the rice is a little dry. Return the rack and chicken to the dish. Brush with the remaining coconut mixture. Bake, uncovered, for 15 minutes, or until the chicken is cooked and lightly browned and the juices run clear when a skewer is inserted into the thigh. Remove the chicken and stir the rice. Serve the pilaff with pieces of chicken.

NONYA CHICKEN AND LIME CURRY

Preparation time: 30 minutes
Total cooking time: 1 hour
Serves 4

Spice Paste
1 large onion, roughly chopped
6 red chillies, seeded and finely chopped
4 cloves garlic, crushed
1 teaspoon finely chopped lemon grass (white part only)
2 teaspoons finely chopped fresh galangal
1 teaspoon ground turmeric

3 tablespoons oil
1 x 1.3 kg (2¾ lb) chicken, cut into 8 pieces and skin removed
1 cup (250 ml/8 fl oz) coconut milk
2 limes, cut in half
5 lime leaves, stems removed and finely shredded
1 teaspoon salt
fresh coriander leaves, to garnish
2 limes, extra, cut in half, to serve

1 To make Spice Paste: Place the onion, chilli, garlic, lemon grass, galangal and turmeric in a food processor and process for a few minutes until a thick rough paste is formed.
2 Heat the oil in a large heavy-based pan and add the Spice Paste. Cook over low heat for about 10 minutes, or until the paste is fragrant.
3 Add the chicken and stir-fry for 2 minutes, making sure that the chicken is covered with the paste. Add the coconut milk, lime halves and shredded leaves; cover and simmer for about 50 minutes, or until the chicken is tender. For the last 10 minutes of cooking remove the lid and allow the cooking liquid to reduce until it is thick and creamy. Add the salt, garnish with the coriander leaves and serve with the lime halves and steamed rice.

CHICKEN WITH PINEAPPLE AND CASHEWS

Preparation time: 35 minutes
Total cooking time: 20 minutes
Serves 4

2 tablespoons shredded coconut
½ cup (80 g/2⅔ oz) raw cashews
2 tablespoons oil
1 large onion, cut into large chunks
4 cloves garlic, finely chopped
2 teaspoons chopped red chilli
350 g (11¼ oz) chicken thigh fillets, chopped
½ red pepper (capsicum), chopped
½ green pepper (capsicum), chopped
2 tablespoons oyster sauce
1 tablespoon fish sauce
1 teaspoon sugar
2 cups (320 g/10¼ oz) chopped fresh pineapple
3 spring onions, chopped

1 Preheat the oven to slow 150°C (300°F/Gas 2). Spread the coconut on an oven tray and toast in the oven for 10 minutes or until dark golden, shaking the tray occasionally. Remove the coconut from the tray immediately, to prevent burning, and set aside.
2 Increase the heat to moderate 180°C (350°F/Gas 4). Roast the cashews on an oven tray in the oven for about 15 minutes, until deep golden. Remove the cashews from the tray and set aside to cool.
3 Heat the oil in a wok or large, deep frying pan; add the onion, garlic and chilli and stir-fry over medium heat for 2 minutes, then remove from the pan. Increase the heat to high; add the chicken and red and green pepper, in 2 batches, and stir-fry until the chicken is light brown. Return the onion mixture to the wok; add the oyster sauce, fish sauce, sugar and pineapple and toss for 2 minutes. Toss the cashews through.
4 Arrange the chicken mixture on a serving plate, scatter the toasted coconut and spring onion over the top, and serve.

CHICKEN AND MACARONI BAKE

Preparation time: 20 minutes
Total cooking time: 55 minutes
Serves 6

4 chicken breast fillets
2 cups (310 g/10 oz) macaroni elbows
¼ cup (60 ml/2 fl oz) olive oil
1 onion, chopped
1 carrot, chopped
3 bacon rashers, chopped
2 zucchini, chopped
440 g (14 oz) can tomato soup
⅓ cup (90 g/3 oz) sour cream
1½ cups (185 g/6 oz) grated Cheddar cheese

1 Trim the chicken of excess fat and sinew. Preheat the oven to moderate 180°C (350°F/Gas 4). Cook the macaroni in a large pan of rapidly boiling salted water until al dente; drain.
2 Slice the chicken breasts into long strips and then cut into cubes. Heat the oil in a heavy-based pan. Cook the chicken quickly over high heat until browned but not cooked through; drain on paper towels. Add the onion, carrot and bacon to the pan. Stir over medium heat for 10 minutes. Add the zucchini and soup, bring to the boil and simmer for 5 minutes. Remove from the heat.
3 Combine the pasta, chicken, tomato mixture and sour cream. Season with salt and pepper, to taste. Spread into a shallow ovenproof dish and top with cheese. Bake for 20 minutes, or until golden and cooked through.

CHICKEN PIE

Preparation time: 30 minutes
Total cooking time: 1 hour 10 minutes
Serves 6

1 kg (2 lb) boneless skinless chicken
   breasts
2 cups (500 ml/16 fl oz) chicken stock
60 g (2 oz) butter
2 spring onions, trimmed and finely
   chopped
½ cup (60 g/2½ oz) plain flour
½ cup (125 ml/4 fl oz) milk
8 sheets filo pastry (40 x 30 cm/
   16 x 12 inches)
60 g (2 oz) butter, extra, melted
200 g (7 oz) feta, crumbled
1 tablespoon chopped fresh dill
1 tablespoon chopped fresh chives
¼ teaspoon ground nutmeg
1 egg, lightly beaten

1 Cut the chicken into bite-sized pieces.
Pour the stock into a saucepan and bring
to the boil over high heat. Reduce the heat
to low, add the chicken and poach gently
for 10–15 minutes, or until the chicken is
cooked through. Drain, reserving the
stock. Add water to the stock to bring the
quantity up to 2 cups (500 ml/16 fl oz).
Preheat the oven to moderate 180°C
(350°F/Gas 4).
2 Melt the butter in a saucepan over low
heat, add the spring onion and cook,
stirring, for 5 minutes. Add the flour and
stir for 30 seconds. Remove the pan from
the heat and gradually add the chicken
stock and milk, stirring after each
addition. Return to the heat and gently
bring to the boil, stirring. Simmer for a
few minutes, or until the sauce thickens.
Remove from the heat.

3 Line a baking dish measuring 25 x 18 x
4 cm (10 x 7 x 1½ inches) with 4 sheets of
filo pastry, brushing one side of each
sheet with melted butter as you go. Place
the buttered side down. The filo will
overlap the edges of the dish. Cover the
unused filo with a damp tea towel to
prevent it drying out.
4 Stir the chicken, feta, dill, chives,
nutmeg and egg into the sauce. Season,
to taste, with salt and freshly ground
black pepper. Pile the mixture
on top of the filo pastry in the dish. Fold
the overlapping filo over the filling and
cover the top of the pie with the remaining
4 sheets of filo, brushing each sheet with
melted butter as you go. Scrunch the
edges of the filo so they fit in the dish.
Brush the top with butter. Bake for
45–50 minutes, or until the pastry is
golden brown and crisp.

NOTE: If you prefer, you can use puff
pastry instead of filo. If you do so, bake in
a hot 220°C (425°F/Gas 7) oven for
15 minutes, then reduce the temperature
to moderate 180°C (350°F/Gas 4) and cook
for another 30 minutes, or until the pastry
is golden.

SATAY CHICKEN STIR-FRY

Preparation time: 10 minutes
Total cooking time: 20 minutes
Serves 4

1½ tablespoons peanut oil
6 spring onions, cut into 3 cm (1¼ inch)
   lengths
800 g (1 lb 10 oz) chicken breast fillets,
   thinly sliced on the diagonal
1–1½ tablespoons Thai red curry paste
   (see page 762)
⅓ cup (90 g/3 oz) crunchy peanut butter
270 ml (9 fl oz) coconut milk
2 teaspoons soft brown sugar
1½ tablespoons lime juice

1 Heat a wok over high heat, add
1 teaspoon of the peanut oil and swirl to
coat. Add the spring onion and stir-fry for
30 seconds, or until softened slightly.
Remove from the wok.
2 Add a little extra peanut oil to the wok
as needed and stir-fry the chicken in
three batches for about 1 minute per
batch, or until the meat just changes
colour. Remove from the wok.
3 Add a little more oil to the wok, add the
curry paste and stir-fry for 1 minute, or
until fragrant. Add the peanut butter,
coconut milk, sugar and 1 cup (250 ml/
8 fl oz) water and stir well. Bring to the
boil and boil for 3–4 minutes, or until
thickened and the oil starts to separate—
reduce the heat slightly if the sauce spits
at you. Return the chicken and the spring
onion to the wok, stir well and cook for
2 minutes, or until heated through. Stir in
the lime juice, season and serve.

STEAMED CHICKEN AND SAUSAGE RICE

Preparation time: 30 minutes +
 30 minutes soaking
Total cooking time: 50 minutes
Serves 4

4 dried Chinese mushrooms
250 g (8 oz) skinless chicken thigh fillet
1 teaspoon Chinese rice wine
2 teaspoons cornflour (cornstarch)
3 Chinese sausages (lap cheong)
200 g (6½ oz) long-grain rice
1 spring onion (scallion), chopped

Sauce
2 tablespoons light soy sauce
1 tablespoon Chinese rice wine
½ teaspoon caster (superfine) sugar
½ garlic clove, chopped (optional)
½ teaspoon chopped ginger
½ teaspoon roasted sesame oil

1 Soak the dried mushrooms in boiling water for 30 minutes, then drain and squeeze out any excess water. Remove and discard the stems and shred the caps.
2 Cut the chicken into bite-sized pieces and combine with the rice wine, cornflour and a pinch of salt.

3 Put the sausages on a plate in a steamer. Cover and steam over simmering water in a wok for 10 minutes, then thinly slice on the diagonal.
4 Put the rice in a bowl and, using your fingers as a rake, rinse under cold running water to remove any dust. Drain in a colander. Place in a large clay pot or casserole dish or four individual clay pots and add enough water so that there is 2 cm (¾ inch) of water above the surface of the rice. Bring the water slowly to the boil, stir, then place the chicken pieces and mushrooms on top of the rice, with the sausage slices on top of them. Cook, covered, over very low heat for about 15 minutes, or until the rice is cooked.
5 To make the sauce, combine the soy sauce, rice wine, sugar, garlic, ginger and sesame oil in a small saucepan and heat until nearly boiling. Pour the sauce over the chicken and sausage and garnish with the spring onion.

LEMON AND GINGER CHICKEN STIR-FRY

Preparation time: 25 minutes +
 20 minutes marinating
Total cooking time: 15 minutes
Serves 4

1 teaspoon grated lemon rind
⅓ cup (80 ml/2¾ fl oz) lemon juice
1 small fresh red chilli, finely chopped
1 clove garlic, crushed
1 tablespoon grated fresh ginger
2 tablespoons chopped fresh coriander leaves
700 g (1 lb 7 oz) chicken breast fillets, sliced
1 tablespoon sesame seeds
2 tablespoons vegetable oil
150 g (5 oz) snow peas (mangetout), halved lengthways
150 g (5 oz) baby corn, quartered
2 tablespoons soy sauce
200 g (6½ oz) bean sprouts, tailed

1 Combine the lemon rind and juice, chilli, garlic, ginger and coriander in a large non-metallic bowl. Add the chicken, toss well, then cover with plastic wrap and marinate in the fridge for 20 minutes.
2 Heat a wok over high heat, add the sesame seeds and stir-fry for 30 seconds, or until light brown. Remove from the wok.
3 Heat 1 tablespoon oil in the wok and swirl to coat. Drain the chicken and stir-fry in batches for 5 minutes, or until lightly browned. Remove from the wok.
4 Heat the remaining oil, then add the snow peas, baby corn and soy sauce, and stir-fry for 2 minutes. Return the chicken to the wok, add the bean sprouts and stir-fry for 1 minute. Sprinkle the sesame seeds over the top and serve with rice or noodles.

CHICKEN AND ORANGE CASSEROLE

Preparation time: 50 minutes
Total cooking time: 1 hour 30 minutes
Serves 4–6

2 small chickens
1 tablespoon olive oil
2 thick slices bacon, rind removed and
   thinly sliced
50 g (1¾ oz) butter
16 small pickling onions, peeled, ends left
   intact
2–3 cloves garlic, crushed
3 teaspoons grated fresh ginger
2 teaspoons grated orange rind
2 teaspoons ground cumin
2 teaspoons ground coriander
2 tablespoons honey
1 cup (250 ml/8 fl oz) fresh orange juice
1 cup (250 ml/8 fl oz) white wine
½ cup (125 ml/4 fl oz) chicken or
   vegetable stock
1 bunch baby carrots
1 large parsnip, peeled
fresh coriander and orange zest, to serve

1 Using a sharp knife or a pair of kitchen scissors, cut each chicken into 8 pieces, discarding the backbone. Remove any excess fat and discard (remove the skin as well, if preferred).
2 Heat about a teaspoon of the oil in a large, deep, heavy-based pan. Add the bacon and cook over medium heat for 2–3 minutes or until just crisp. Remove from the pan and set aside to drain on paper towels. Add the remaining oil and half the butter to the pan. Cook the onions over medium heat until dark golden brown. Shake the pan occasionally to ensure even cooking and browning. Remove from the pan and set aside.

3 Add the chicken pieces to the pan and brown in small batches over medium heat. Remove from the pan and drain on paper towels.
4 Add the remaining butter to the pan. Stir in the garlic, ginger, orange rind, cumin, coriander and honey, and cook, stirring, for 1 minute. Add the orange juice, wine and stock to the pan. Bring to the boil, then reduce the heat and simmer for 1 minute. Return the chicken pieces to the pan, cover and leave to simmer over low heat for 40 minutes.
5 Return the onions and bacon to the pan and simmer, covered, for a further 15 minutes. Remove the lid and leave to simmer for a further 15 minutes.
6 Trim the carrots, leaving a little green stalk, and wash well or peel if necessary. Cut the parsnip into small batons. Add the carrots and parsnip to the pan. Cover and cook for 5–10 minutes, or until the carrots and parsnip are just tender. Do not overcook the carrots or they will lose their bright colouring. When you are ready to serve, arrange 2–3 chicken pieces on each plate. Arrange a couple of carrots and a few parsnip batons with the chicken and spoon a little sauce over the top. Garnish with the coriander leaves and orange zest.

STIR-FRIED SESAME, CHICKEN AND LEEK

Preparation time: 15 minutes
Total cooking time: 20 minutes
Serves 4–6

2 tablespoons sesame seeds
1 tablespoon vegetable oil
2 teaspoons sesame oil
800 g (1 lb 10 oz) chicken tenderloins,
   sliced on the diagonal
1 leek, julienned
2 cloves garlic, crushed
2 tablespoons soy sauce
1 tablespoon mirin
1 teaspoon sugar

1 Heat the wok over high heat, add the sesame seeds and fry until golden. Remove from the wok.
2 Reheat the wok over high heat, add the oils and swirl to coat the side. Stir-fry the chicken strips in three batches, tossing constantly, for 3–5 minutes each batch, or until just cooked. Reheat the wok before each addition. Return the chicken to the wok.
3 Add the julienned leek and the garlic and cook for 1–2 minutes, or until the leek is soft and golden. Check that the chicken is cooked through; if it is not cooked, reduce the heat and cook, covered, for 2 minutes, or until it is completely cooked.
4 Add the soy sauce, mirin, sugar and toasted sesame seeds to the wok, and toss well to combine. Season, and serve immediately.

ROAST CHICKEN STUFFED WITH PINE NUTS AND RICE

Preparation time: 30 minutes
Total cooking time: 2 hours 30 minutes
Serves 4–6

Stuffing
60 g (2 oz) clarified butter (see Note)
   or ghee, melted
1 onion, chopped
1 teaspoon ground allspice
⅓ cup (65 g/2¼ oz) long-grain rice
¼ cup (30 g/1 oz) walnuts, chopped
⅓ cup (50 g/1¾ oz) pine nuts
⅓ cup (55 g/2 oz) sultanas
½ cup (125 ml/4 fl oz) chicken stock

1.6 kg (3½ lb) chicken
⅔ cup (170 ml/5½ fl oz) chicken stock

1 Preheat the oven to moderate 180°C (350°F/Gas 4). Pour half the butter into a large frying pan, then add the onion and cook for 5 minutes over medium heat until softened but not browned. Stir in the allspice.
2 Add the rice and nuts to the pan and cook for 3–4 minutes. Add the sultanas, stock and ¼ cup (60 ml/2 fl oz) water. Bring to the boil, then reduce the heat and simmer for 8–10 minutes, or until all the water is absorbed. Allow to cool.
3 Thoroughly rinse the cavity of the chicken with cold water, then pat dry inside and out with paper towels.
4 When the stuffing is cool, spoon the stuffing into the cavity. Tie the legs together and tuck the wing tips under. Put in a deep ovenproof dish, then rub ½ teaspoon salt and ¼ teaspoon freshly ground black pepper into the skin using your fingertips.
5 Pour the rest of the butter over the chicken, then add the stock to the pan. Roast for 2 hours 10 minutes, basting every 20–25 minutes with juices from the pan, until the chicken is tender and the juices run clear when the thigh is pierced with a skewer. Rest the chicken for 15 minutes before carving. Serve with the stuffing.

ANDHRA-STYLE CHICKEN PULAO

Preparation time: 30 minutes +
   10 minutes standing
Total cooking time: 1 hour
Serves 8

1.5 kg (3 lb) chicken or chicken pieces
1 kg (2 lb) basmati rice
3 onions, sliced
½ teaspoon salt
100 ml (3½ fl oz) oil
175 g (6 oz) ghee
4 cm (1½ inch) piece of cinnamon stick
2 cardamom pods
3 cloves
2 star anise
2 stalks of curry leaves
2 cm (¾ inch) piece of ginger, grated
6 garlic cloves, crushed
4–6 green chillies, slit lengthways
400 ml (13 fl oz) buttermilk
4 ripe tomatoes, diced
200 ml (6½ fl oz) coconut milk
1 litre (32 fl oz) chicken stock
1 lemon, cut into wedges

1 If using a whole chicken, cut it into 16 pieces by removing both legs and cutting between the joint of the drumstick and thigh. Cut each of these in half through the bone with a cleaver or poultry shears (make sure there are no bone shards). Cut down either side of the backbone and remove the backbone. Turn the chicken over and cut through the cartilage down the centre of the breastbone. Cut each breast into three pieces and cut off the wings. Trim off the wing tips. Trim off any excess fat or skin from the pieces of chicken.
2 Wash the rice in a sieve under cold, running water until the water from the rice runs clear. Drain well. Put the sliced onion in a sieve, sprinkle with the salt and leave for 10 minutes to drain off any liquid that oozes out. Rinse and then pat dry.

3 Heat the oil and ghee over medium heat in a large, ovenproof 'degchi' (thick-based pot), or heavy casserole dish. Add the cinnamon, cardamom and cloves and heat until they begin to crackle. Reduce the heat to low and add the star anise and the curry leaves from one stem. Add the sliced onion and cook until golden brown. Add the ginger and garlic and cook until golden. Add the chicken, increase the heat to medium and fry until the pieces are browned on all sides. Add the slit chillies, the remaining curry leaves, the buttermilk and some salt. Cook for 12 minutes, or until the chicken is cooked through and the liquid is reduced by half. Add the diced tomato and the coconut milk. Cook until the tomato is tender, then pour in the stock and bring up to the boil.
4 Preheat the oven to 220°C (425°F/Gas 7). Add the drained rice to the chicken and stir it in well. Check the seasoning, adjust if necessary, and cook for 10 minutes, or until nearly all the liquid is absorbed.
5 Remove the pot from the heat, cover it with a clean wet cloth, then a tight-fitting lid, and put it in the oven for 15 minutes, or until the rice is cooked through. Serve hot with lemon wedges.

CHICKEN CACCIATORA

Preparation time: 15 minutes
Total cooking time: 1 hour
Serves 4

¼ cup (60 ml/2 fl oz) olive oil
1 large onion, finely chopped
3 cloves garlic, crushed
150 g (5 oz) pancetta, finely chopped
125 g (4 oz) button mushrooms, thickly sliced
1 large chicken (at least 1.6 kg/3¼ lb), cut
   into 8 pieces
⅓ cup (80 ml/2¾ fl oz) dry vermouth or
   dry white wine
2 x 400 g (13 oz) cans chopped good-
   quality tomatoes
¼ teaspoon soft brown sugar
¼ teaspoon cayenne pepper
1 sprig of fresh oregano
1 sprig of fresh thyme
1 bay leaf

1 Heat half the olive oil in a large
heatproof casserole dish. Add the onion
and garlic and cook for 6–8 minutes over
low heat, stirring, until the onion is
golden. Add the pancetta and mushrooms,
increase the heat and cook, stirring, for
4–5 minutes. Transfer to a bowl.
2 Add the remaining oil to the casserole
dish and brown the chicken pieces, a few at
a time, over medium heat. Season with salt
and black pepper as they brown. Spoon off
the excess fat and return all the chicken to
the casserole dish. Increase the heat, add
the vermouth to the dish and cook until the
liquid has almost evaporated.
3 Add the chopped tomato, brown sugar,
cayenne pepper, oregano, thyme and bay
leaf, and stir in ⅓ cup (80 ml/2¾ fl oz) water
to the dish. Bring to the boil, then stir in
the reserved onion mixture. Reduce the
heat, cover and simmer for 25 minutes, or
until the chicken is tender.
4 If the liquid is too thin, remove the
chicken from the casserole dish, increase
the heat and boil until the liquid has
thickened. Discard the sprigs of herbs
and adjust the seasoning.

MOROCCAN CHICKEN FILO PIE

Preparation time: 40 minutes
Total cooking time: 40 minutes
Serves 4–6

1 tablespoon olive oil
1 red onion, chopped
2–3 cloves garlic, crushed
2 teaspoons grated fresh ginger
1 teaspoon ground turmeric
1 teaspoon ground cumin
1 teaspoon ground coriander
500 g (1 lb) cooked chicken, shredded
60 g (2 oz) slivered almonds, toasted
1 cup (50 g/1¾ oz) chopped fresh
   coriander
⅓ cup (20 g/¾ oz) chopped fresh parsley
1 teaspoon grated lemon rind
2 tablespoons stock or water
1 egg, lightly beaten
9 sheets filo pastry
50 g (1¾ oz) butter, melted
1 teaspoon caster sugar
¼ teaspoon ground cinnamon

1 Heat the oil in a large heavy-based
frying pan and cook the onion, garlic and
ginger, stirring, for 5 minutes, or until the
onion is soft. Stir in the turmeric, cumin
and coriander and cook, stirring, for
1–2 minutes. Remove from the heat and
stir in the chicken, almonds, coriander,
parsley and lemon rind. Leave to cool for
5 minutes, then stir in the stock or water
and the beaten egg.

2 Preheat the oven to moderate 180°C
(350°F/Gas 4). Grease a baking tray. Cut
6 sheets of filo into approximately 30 cm
(12 inch) squares, retaining the extra
strips. Cut each of the remaining sheets
into 3 equal strips. Cover with a damp
cloth. Brush 1 square with the melted
butter and place on the baking tray. Lay
another square at an angle on top and
brush with melted butter. Repeat with the
other squares to form a rough 8-pointed
star. Spoon the chicken mixture into the
centre, leaving a 5 cm (2 inch) border.
3 Turn the pastry edge in over the filling,
leaving the centre open. Brush the pastry
strips with melted butter and lightly
scrunch and lay them over the top of the
pie. Sprinkle with the combined caster
sugar and cinnamon. Bake for 25
minutes, or until the pastry is cooked and
golden brown.

CLAY POT CHICKEN AND VEGETABLES

Preparation time: 20 minutes +
    30 minutes marinating
Total cooking time: 25 minutes
Serves 4

500 g (1 lb) chicken thigh fillets
1 tablespoon soy sauce
1 tablespoon dry sherry
6 dried Chinese mushrooms
2 small leeks
250 g (8 oz) orange sweet potato
2 tablespoons peanut oil
5 cm (2 inch) piece fresh ginger, shredded
½ cup (125 ml/4 fl oz) chicken stock
1 teaspoon sesame oil
3 teaspoons cornflour

1 Wash the chicken under cold water and pat it dry with paper towels. Cut the chicken into small pieces. Place it in a dish with the soy sauce and sherry, cover and marinate for 30 minutes in the refrigerator.
2 Cover the mushrooms with hot water and soak for 20 minutes. Drain and squeeze to remove excess liquid. Remove the stems and chop the caps into shreds. Wash the leeks thoroughly to remove all grit. Cut the leeks and sweet potato into thin slices.
3 Drain the chicken, reserving the marinade. Heat half the oil in a wok or heavy-based frying pan, swirling it gently to coat the base and sides. Add half the chicken pieces and stir-fry briefly until seared on all sides. Transfer the chicken to a flameproof clay pot or casserole. Stir-fry the remaining chicken and add it to the clay pot.
4 Heat the remaining oil in the wok; add the leek and ginger and stir-fry for 1 minute. Add the mushrooms, remaining marinade, stock and sesame oil and cook for 2 minutes. Transfer to the clay pot with the sweet potato and cook, covered, on the top of the stove over very low heat for about 20 minutes.
5 Dissolve the cornflour in a little water and add it to the pot. Cook, stirring, until the mixture boils and thickens. Serve the chicken and vegetables at once.

CHICKEN AND HAM PIE

Preparation time: 40 minutes
Total cooking time: 1 hour
Serves 6

Pastry
3 cups (375 g/12 oz) plain flour
180 g (6 oz) butter, chopped
⅓ cup (80 ml/2¾ fl oz) iced water

filling
1 kg (2 lb) chicken mince
½ teaspoon dried thyme
½ teaspoon dried sage
2 eggs, lightly beaten
3 spring onions, finely chopped
2 teaspoons finely grated lemon rind
1 teaspoon French mustard
⅓ cup (80 ml/2¾ fl oz) cream
100 g (3½ oz) sliced leg ham, finely
    chopped
1 egg, lightly beaten, extra

1 Preheat the oven to moderate 180°C (350°F/Gas 4). Process the flour and butter in a food processor for 20 seconds, or until the mixture is fine and crumbly. Add almost all the water and process for 20 seconds, or until mixture comes together. Add more water if needed. Turn onto a lightly floured surface and press together until smooth. Roll out two-thirds of the pastry and line a 20 cm (8 inch) springform tin, bringing the pastry up 2 cm (¾ inch) higher than the sides. Cover with plastic wrap. Set the pastry trimmings aside.

2 To make the filling, place the chicken, thyme, sage, eggs, spring onion, lemon rind, mustard and cream in a large bowl and stir with a wooden spoon until well combined. Place half the chicken mixture into the pastry-lined tin and smooth the surface. Top with the chopped ham, then the remaining chicken mixture.
3 Brush around the inside edge of the pastry with the egg. Roll out the remaining pastry and lay over the top of the mixture. Press the edges of the pastry together. Trim the pastry edges with a sharp knife.
4 Turn the pastry edges down. Use your index finger to make indentations around the inside edge. Decorate the top of the pie with pastry trimmings. Brush the top of the pie with beaten egg and bake for 1 hour, or until golden brown. Serve the pie warm or at room temperature.

CHICKEN CHASSEUR

Preparation time: 20 minutes
Total cooking time: 1 hour 30 minutes
Serves 4

1 kg (2 lb) chicken thigh fillets
2 tablespoons oil
1 clove garlic, crushed
1 large onion, sliced
100 g (3½ oz) button mushrooms, sliced
1 teaspoon fresh thyme leaves
400 g (13 oz) can chopped tomatoes
¼ cup (60 ml/2 fl oz) chicken stock
¼ cup (60 ml/2 fl oz) white wine
1 tablespoon tomato paste

1 Preheat the oven to moderate 180°C (350°F/Gas 4). Trim the chicken of excess fat and sinew. Heat the oil in a heavy-based frying pan and brown the chicken in batches over medium heat. Drain on paper towels, then transfer to a casserole dish.
2 Add the garlic, onion and sliced mushrooms to the pan and cook over medium heat for 5 minutes, or until soft. Add to the chicken with the thyme and tomatoes.
3 Combine the stock, wine and tomato paste and pour over the chicken. Bake, covered, for 1¼ hours, or until the chicken is tender.

COQ AU VIN

Preparation time: 20 minutes
Total cooking time: 1 hour
Serves 6

2 fresh thyme sprigs
4 fresh parsley sprigs
2 bay leaves
2 kg (4 lb) chicken pieces
plain flour, seasoned with salt and freshly ground pepper
¼ cup (60 ml/2 fl oz) oil
4 thick bacon rashers, sliced
12 pickling onions
2 cloves garlic, crushed
2 tablespoons brandy
1½ cups (375 ml/12 fl oz) red wine
1½ cups (375 ml/12 fl oz) chicken stock
¼ cup (60 g/2 oz) tomato paste
250 g (8 oz) button mushrooms
fresh herbs, for sprinkling

1 To make the bouquet garni, wrap the thyme, parsley and bay leaves in a small square of muslin and tie well with string, or tie them between two 5 cm (2 inch) lengths of celery.
2 Toss the chicken in flour to coat, shaking off any excess. In a heavy-based pan, heat 2 tablespoons of oil and brown the chicken in batches over medium heat. Drain on paper towels.
3 Wipe the pan clean with paper towels and heat the remaining oil. Add the bacon, onions and garlic and cook, stirring, until the onions are browned. Add the chicken, brandy, wine, stock, bouquet garni and tomato paste. Bring to the boil, reduce the heat and simmer, covered, for 30 minutes.
4 Stir in the mushrooms and simmer, uncovered, for 10 minutes, or until the chicken is tender and the sauce has thickened. Remove the bouquet garni, sprinkle with fresh herbs and serve with crusty French bread.

BRANDY CHICKEN FETTUCINE

Preparation time: 40 minutes
Total cooking time: 40 minutes
Serves 4–6

10 g (¼ oz) porcini mushrooms
2 tablespoons olive oil
2 cloves garlic, crushed
200 g (6½ oz) button mushrooms, sliced
125 g (4 oz) prosciutto, chopped
375 g (12 oz) fettucine
¼ cup (60 ml/2 fl oz) brandy
1 cup (250 ml/8 fl oz) cream
1 barbecued chicken, shredded
1 cup (155 g/5 oz) frozen peas
⅓ cup (20 g/¾ oz) finely chopped fresh parsley

1 Put the porcini mushrooms in a bowl and cover with boiling water. Set aside for 10 minutes, then drain, squeeze dry and chop.
2 Heat the oil in a large, heavy-based pan. Add the crushed garlic and cook, stirring, for 1 minute over low heat. Add the button and porcini mushrooms, along with the prosciutto, and cook over low heat, stirring often, for 5 minutes.
3 Meanwhile, cook the pasta in a large pan of rapidly boiling salted water until al dente. Drain and return to the pan.
4 Add the brandy and cream to the mushroom mixture. Cook, stirring, over low heat for 2 minutes. Add the chicken, peas and parsley. Cook, stirring, for 4–5 minutes, until heated through. Add the chicken mixture to the hot pasta and mix through.

NOTE: Cut the slices of prosciutto separately, otherwise they stick together. Use bacon slices instead, if preferred. If porcini mushrooms are not available, use 30 g (1 oz) of dried Chinese mushrooms.

HONEY CHICKEN

Preparation time: 15 minutes
Total cooking time: 25 minutes
Serves 4

500 g (1 lb) chicken thigh fillets, cut into cubes
1 egg white, lightly beaten
⅓ cup (40 g/1¼ oz) cornflour
⅓ cup (80 ml/2¾ fl oz) vegetable oil
2 onions, thinly sliced
1 green pepper (capsicum), cubed
2 carrots, cut into batons
100 g (3½ oz) snow peas (mangetout), sliced
¼ cup (90 g/3 oz) honey
2 tablespoons toasted almonds

1 Dip the chicken cubes into the egg white, then lightly dust with the cornflour, shaking off any excess.
2 Heat a wok over high heat, add 1½ tablespoons of the oil and swirl it around to coat the side of the wok. Add the chicken in two batches and stir-fry each batch for 4–5 minutes, or until the chicken is golden brown and just cooked. Remove the chicken from the wok and drain on crumpled paper towels.
3 Reheat the wok over high heat, add 1 tablespoon of the oil and stir-fry the sliced onion for 3–4 minutes, or until slightly softened. Add the green pepper and carrot, and cook, tossing constantly, for 3–4 minutes, or until tender. Stir in the sliced snow peas and cook for 2 minutes.
4 Ensure that the wok is still very hot, then pour in the honey and toss with the vegetables until well coated. Return all the chicken to the wok and toss thoroughly until it is heated through and well coated in the honey. Remove the wok from the heat and season well with salt and freshly ground black pepper. Serve immediately, sprinkled with the toasted almonds. Serve with steamed white rice.

THAI STUFFED CHICKEN WINGS
(PEEK GAI YUD SAI)

Preparation time: 30 minutes + cooling time
Total cooking time: 20 minutes
Makes 12

12 large chicken wings
20 g (¾ oz) dried rice vermicelli
1 tablespoon grated palm sugar
2 tablespoons fish sauce
200 g (6½ oz) pork mince
2 spring onions, chopped
3 cloves garlic, chopped
1 small fresh red chilli, chopped
3 tablespoons chopped fresh coriander leaves
peanut oil, for deep-frying
rice flour, well seasoned, to coat
sweet chilli sauce, to serve

1 Using a small, sharp knife, with each chicken wing, start at the fatter end of the wing and scrape down the bone, pushing the flesh and skin as you go until you reach the connecting joint. Twist and pull the exposed bone from its socket and discard the bone. Take care not to pierce the skin.
2 Soak the vermicelli in a bowl of boiling water for 6–7 minutes. Drain well. Cut into 2 cm (¾ inch) pieces with a pair of scissors. Set aside. Put the palm sugar and fish sauce in a small bowl and stir until the sugar has dissolved.

3 Combine the pork mince, spring onion, garlic, chilli and the fish sauce mixture in a food processor until well mixed. Transfer to a bowl, then stir in the coriander and noodles.
4 Divide the pork mixture into 12 balls. Stuff each boned-out section of chicken wing with a ball of mixture and firmly secure the opening with a toothpick.
5 Put the chicken wings in a bamboo or metal steamer over a wok of simmering water—ensure the base of the steamer doesn't touch the water. Cover with a lid and steam for 8 minutes. Remove the wings from the steamer, then set aside to firm and cool.
6 Fill a dry, clean wok one-third full of oil and heat to 200°C (400°F), or until a cube of bread dropped in the oil browns in 5 seconds. Coat the wings in the seasoned flour. Deep-fry in small batches for 3 minutes each batch, or until the wings are golden brown. Drain on crumpled paper towels. Remove the toothpicks and serve the wings with the sweet chilli sauce.

BUTTER CHICKEN

Preparation time: 30 minutes +
  4 hours marinating
Total cooking time: 30 minutes
Serves 4

1 kg (2 lb) chicken thigh fillets
1 teaspoon salt
¼ cup (60 ml/2 fl oz) lemon juice
1 cup (8 fl oz) yoghurt
1 medium onion, chopped
2 cloves garlic, crushed
3 cm (1¼ inch) piece fresh ginger, grated
1 green chilli, chopped
2 teaspoons garam masala
2 teaspoons yellow food colouring
1 teaspoon red food colouring
½ cup (125 ml/4 fl oz) tomato purée
  (passata)
½ cup (125 ml/4 fl oz) water
2 cm (¾ inch) piece fresh ginger, extra,
  finely grated
1 cup (250 ml/8 fl oz) cream
1 teaspoon garam masala, extra
2 teaspoons sugar
¼ teaspoon chilli powder
1 tablespoon lemon juice
1 teaspoon ground cumin
100 g (3⅓ oz) butter

1 Cut the chicken into strips 2 cm (¾ inch) thick. Sprinkle with the salt and lemon juice.
2 Place the yoghurt, onion, garlic, ginger, chilli and garam masala in a food processor and process until smooth.
3 Combine the food colourings in a small bowl, brush over the chicken and turn to coat. Add the yoghurt mixture and toss to combine. Cover and refrigerate for 4 hours. Remove the chicken from the marinade and allow to drain for 5 minutes.
4 Preheat the oven to hot 220°C (425°F/Gas 7). Bake the chicken in a shallow baking dish for 15 minutes, or until tender. Drain off any excess juice, cover loosely with foil and keep warm.
5 Combine the tomato purée and water in a large jug. Add the ginger, cream, extra garam masala, sugar, chilli powder, lemon juice and cumin and stir to combine.
6 Melt the butter in a large pan over medium heat. Stir in the tomato mixture and bring to the boil. Cook for 2 minutes, then reduce the heat and add the chicken pieces. Stir to coat the chicken in the sauce and simmer for 2 minutes longer or until heated through. Serve with rice.

CHICKEN AND BROCCOLI BAKE

Preparation time: 20 minutes
Total cooking time: 1 hour
Serves 6

30 g (1 oz) butter
4 chicken breast fillets, cut into cubes
6 spring onions, sliced
2 cloves garlic, crushed
2 tablespoons plain flour
1½ cups (375 ml/12 fl oz) chicken stock
2 teaspoons Dijon mustard
280 g (9 oz) broccoli, cut into florets
1 kg (2 lb) potatoes, cut into quarters
2 tablespoons milk
60 g (2 oz) butter, extra
2 eggs
⅓ cup (30 g/1 oz) flaked toasted almonds
snipped fresh chives, to garnish

1 Preheat the oven to moderate 180°C (350°F/Gas 4). Heat half the butter in a large frying pan, and cook the chicken in batches until browned and cooked through. Remove from the pan. In the same pan melt the remaining butter and cook the spring onion and garlic for 2 minutes. Stir in the flour and mix well. Pour in the stock and cook, stirring, until the mixture boils and thickens. Add the mustard and then stir in the chicken. Season well.
2 Meanwhile, steam or microwave the broccoli until just tender, taking care not to overcook it. Refresh the broccoli in iced water and drain well.
3 Boil the potato in plenty of salted water for 15–20 minutes, or until tender. Drain and mash well with the milk, extra butter and eggs. Put the broccoli in a 2.5 litre ovenproof dish and pour in the chicken mixture. Pipe or spoon the mashed potato over the top. Sprinkle with the almonds and bake for 25 minutes, or until the top is browned and cooked through. Scatter the chives over the top before serving.

CHICKEN AND APPLE CURRY

Preparation time: 20 minutes
Total cooking time: 1 hour 5 minutes
Serves 4–6

1 kg (2 lb) chicken wings
¼ cup (60 ml/2 fl oz) oil
1 large onion, sliced
1 tablespoon curry powder
1 large carrot, chopped
1 celery stick, sliced
400 ml (13 fl oz) can coconut cream
1 cup (250 ml/8 fl oz) chicken stock
2 green apples, chopped
1 tablespoon finely chopped fresh
  coriander
¼ cup (30 g/1 oz) sultanas
½ cup (80 g/2¾ oz) roasted peanuts

1 Pat the chicken wings dry with paper towels. Tuck the wing tips to the underside.
2 Heat 2 tablespoons of the oil in a large heavy-based pan and add the chicken in small batches. Cook quickly over medium heat for 5 minutes, or until well browned on both sides. Drain on paper towels.
3 Heat the remaining oil in the pan. Add the onion and curry powder and cook, stirring, over medium heat for 3 minutes, or until soft.
4 Return the chicken to the pan. Add the carrot, celery, coconut cream and stock, and bring to the boil. Reduce the heat and simmer. Cook, covered, for 30 minutes. Add the apple, coriander and sultanas, and cook for a further 20 minutes, or until the chicken is tender, stirring occasionally. Serve sprinkled with the peanuts.

SPICY ROAST CHICKEN

Preparation time: 20 minutes
Total cooking time: 40 minutes
Serves 4–6

1.6 kg (3½ lb) chicken
3 teaspoons chopped red chillies
3 cloves garlic
2 teaspoons peppercorns, crushed
2 teaspoons soft brown sugar
2 tablespoons soy sauce
2 teaspoons ground turmeric
1 tablespoon lime juice
30 g (1 oz) butter, chopped

1 Preheat the oven to moderate 180°C (350°F/Gas 4).
2 Using a large cleaver, cut the chicken in half by cutting down the backbone and along the breastbone. To prevent the wings from burning, tuck them underneath. Place the chicken, skin-side-up, on a rack in a baking dish and bake for 30 minutes.
3 Meanwhile, combine the chilli, garlic, peppercorns and sugar in a food processor or mortar and pestle and process briefly, or pound, until smooth. Add the soy sauce, turmeric and lime juice, and process in short bursts, or stir if using a mortar and pestle, until combined.
4 Brush the spice mixture over the chicken, dot it with the butter pieces and bake it for another 25 to 30 minutes, or until cooked through and rich red. Serve warm or at room temperature.

ORIENTAL CHICKEN PASTA

Preparation time: 25 minutes
Total cooking time: 10 minutes
Serves 4

1 barbecued chicken
1 onion
1 carrot
150 g (5 oz) tagliatelle
1 tablespoon oil
1 clove garlic, crushed
2 teaspoons curry powder
2 teaspoons bottled crushed chilli
1 large red pepper (capsicum), thinly
  sliced
150 g (5 oz) snow peas (mangetout),
  halved
3 spring onions, sliced
2 teaspoons sesame oil
¼ cup (60 ml/2 fl oz) soy sauce

1 Remove the chicken meat from the bones and discard the bones. Slice the chicken into thin strips. Cut the onion into thin wedges and the carrot into long strips.
2 Cook the tagliatelle in a large pan of rapidly boiling salted water until al dente. Drain well.
3 Heat the oil in a wok or heavy-based pan, swirling gently to coat the base and sides. Add the onion, carrot, garlic, curry powder and chilli. Stir until aromatic and the garlic is soft. Add the pasta and the remaining ingredients. Stir-fry over medium heat for 4 minutes, or until heated through. Add salt, to taste.

STEAMED CHICKEN BREAST WITH ASIAN GREENS AND SOY MUSHROOM SAUCE

Preparation time: 10 minutes +
  20 minutes soaking + 1 hour marinating
Total cooking time: 20 minutes
Serves 4

10 g (¼ oz) dried shiitake mushrooms
2 tablespoons light soy sauce
2 tablespoons Chinese rice wine
½ teaspoon sesame oil
1 tablespoon thinly sliced fresh ginger
4 x 200 g (6½ oz) chicken breast fillets,
  trimmed
450 g (14 oz) bok choy, ends removed and
  cut lengthways into quarters
½ cup (125 ml/4 fl oz) chicken stock
1 tablespoon cornflour

1 Soak the dried mushrooms in ¼ cup
(60 ml/2 fl oz) boiling water for 20 minutes.
Drain, reserving the soaking liquid. Discard
the stalks and slice the caps thinly.
2 Combine the soy sauce, rice wine, sesame
oil and ginger in a non-metallic dish. Add
the chicken and turn to coat. Cover and
marinate in the refrigerator for 1 hour.
3 Line a bamboo steamer with baking
paper. Place the chicken on top, reserving
the marinade. Cover and steam over a
wok of simmering water for 6 minutes,
then turn the chicken over and steam for
a further 6 minutes. Place the bok choy
on top of the chicken and steam for a
further 2–3 minutes.
4 Meanwhile, put the reserved marinade,
mushrooms and their soaking liquid in a
small saucepan and bring to the boil. Add
enough stock to the cornflour in a small
bowl to make a smooth paste. Add the
cornflour paste and remaining stock to
the pan and stir for 2 minutes over
medium heat, or until the sauce thickens.
5 Place some bok choy and a chicken
fillet on each serving plate, then pour on
some sauce. Serve with rice.

HAINANESE CHICKEN RICE

Preparation time: 50 minutes +
  10 minutes resting
Total cooking time: 1 hour 30 minutes
Serves 6

2 kg (4 lb) whole chicken
6 spring onions (scallions)
a few thick slices of ginger
4 garlic cloves, bruised
1 teaspoon vegetable oil
1 teaspoon sesame oil

Rice
5 red Asian shallots, finely chopped
2 garlic cloves, crushed
1 tablespoon very finely chopped ginger
1½ cups (300 g/10 oz) jasmine rice
½ cup (100 g/3½ oz) long-grain glutinous
  rice
3 Roma (plum) tomatoes, cut into thin
  wedges
3 Lebanese (short) cucumbers, sliced
  diagonally
sprigs of coriander (cilantro), to garnish
Sauce
2 small red chillies, seeded and chopped
4 garlic cloves, roughly chopped
1½ tablespoons finely chopped ginger
3 coriander (cilantro) roots, chopped
2 tablespoons dark soy sauce
2 tablespoons lime juice
2 tablespoons sugar
pinch of ground white pepper

1 Remove any excess fat from around the
cavity of the chicken and reserve it. Rinse
and salt the inside of the chicken and rinse
again. Insert the spring onions, ginger
slices and garlic into the chicken cavity then
place, breast-side down in a large saucepan
and cover with cold water. Add 1 teaspoon
of salt and bring to the boil over high heat,
skimming the surface as required. Reduce
the heat to low and simmer gently for 15
minutes, then carefully turn over without
piercing the skin and cook for another 15
minutes, or until the thigh juices run clear
when pierced.
2 Carefully lift the chicken out of the

saucepan, draining any liquid from the
cavity into the rest of the stock. Reserve
1 litre (32 fl oz) of the stock. Plunge the
chicken into iced water for 5 minutes to
stop the cooking process and to firm the
skin. Rub the entire surface with the
combined vegetable and sesame oils and
allow to cool while you make the rice.
3 To make the rice, cook the reserved
chicken fat over medium heat for about
8 minutes, or until you have about
2 tablespoons of liquid fat, then discard
the solids. (If you prefer, use vegetable oil
instead.) Add the shallots and cook for a
few minutes, or until lightly golden, then
add the garlic and ginger and stir until
fragrant. Add both the rices and cook for
5 minutes, or until lightly golden, then
pour in the reserved chicken stock and
1 teaspoon salt and bring to the boil. Cover
and reduce the heat to low and cook for
about 20 minutes, or until tender and the
liquid has evaporated. Cool, covered, for
10 minutes, then fluff with a fork.
4 Meanwhile, to make the sauce, pound
the chillies, garlic, ginger and coriander
roots into a paste using a mortar and
pestle. Stir in the rest of the ingredients
and season to taste.
5 Cut the chicken up. Divide the rice into
six slightly wetted Chinese soup bowls
and press down firmly, then turn out onto
serving plates. Serve the pieces of
chicken on a platter with the tomato,
cucumber and coriander and pour the
dipping sauce into a small bowl or
individual sauce dishes and let your
guests help themselves.

TAGLIATELLE WITH CHICKEN LIVERS AND CREAM

Preparation time: 20 minutes
Total cooking time: 15 minutes
Serves 4

375 g (12 oz) tagliatelle
300 g (10 oz) chicken livers
2 tablespoons olive oil
1 onion, finely chopped
1 clove garlic, crushed
1 cup (250 ml/8 fl oz) cream
1 tablespoon snipped fresh chives
1 teaspoon seeded mustard
2 eggs, beaten
freshly grated Parmesan and some
   snipped chives, for serving

1 Cook the tagliatelle in a large pan of rapidly boiling salted water until al dente. Drain and return to the pan.
2 While the pasta is cooking, trim the chicken livers and slice. Heat the oil in a large frying pan. Add the onion and garlic and stir over low heat until the onion is tender.
3 Add the chicken livers to the pan and cook gently for 2–3 minutes. Remove from the heat and stir in the cream, chives, mustard, and salt and pepper, to taste. Return to the heat and bring to the boil. Add the beaten eggs and stir quickly to combine. Remove from the heat.
4 Add the sauce to the hot pasta and toss well to combine. Serve sprinkled with Parmesan and snipped chives.

CHICKEN GUMBO

Preparation time: 15 minutes
Total cooking time: 2 hours 30 minutes
Serves 4–6

⅓ cup (80 ml/2¾ fl oz) vegetable oil
¼ cup (30 g/1 oz) plain (all-purpose) flour
600 g (1¼ lb) chicken thigh fillets
60 g (2 oz) unsalted butter
100 g (3½ oz) smoked ham, diced
150 g (5 oz) chorizo, thinly sliced
2 onions, chopped
2 garlic cloves, finely chopped
2 celery stalks, thinly sliced
1 red capsicum (pepper), finely chopped
450 g (14 oz) tomatoes, peeled, seeded
   and chopped
2 cups (500 ml/16 fl oz) chicken stock
1 bay leaf
2 teaspoons thyme
Tabasco sauce, to taste
350 g (11 oz) okra, cut into 1 cm (½ inch)
   slices
2 spring onions (scallions), sliced
2 tablespoons chopped fresh parsley, to
   garnish

1 Heat 3 tablespoons of the oil in a small, heavy-based saucepan, add the flour and stir to make a smooth paste. Stir over very low heat for 1 hour, or until the roux turns very dark brown, but is not burnt. This requires a great deal of patience and stirring but provides the gumbo with its dark look and rich flavour—when it is done, the roux should be the colour of dark chocolate. Remove from the heat.
2 Pat dry the chicken thigh fillets with paper towels, cut into quarters and lightly season with salt and pepper. Heat the remaining oil and half the butter in a heavy-based frying pan over medium heat. Cook the chicken for about 5 minutes, or until golden brown. Remove the chicken with a slotted spoon. Add the ham and chorizo and cook for another 4–5 minutes, or until lightly golden. Remove, leaving as much rendered fat in the pan as possible.

3 Add the remaining butter to the same pan and cook the onion, garlic, celery and capsicum over medium heat for 5–6 minutes, or until the vegetables have softened but not browned. Transfer the vegetables to a heavy-based, flameproof casserole dish. Add the tomato and the roux to the vegetables and stir well. Gradually stir the stock into the pan. Add the herbs and season with the Tabasco. Bring to the boil, stirring constantly.
4 Reduce the heat, add the chicken, ham and chorizo to the casserole dish and simmer, uncovered, for 1 hour. Add the okra and cook for another hour. Skim the surface as the gumbo cooks because a lot of oil will come out of the chorizo. The gumbo should thicken considerably in the last 20 minutes as the okra softens. Remove the bay leaf and serve. Garnish with spring onion and parsley, if desired. Serve with rice.

NOTE: Gumbo is a speciality of Cajun cuisine and is a cross between a soup and a stew. Traditionally, gumbo is often served in deep bowls, each containing a few tablespoons of cooked rice in the bottom.

BAKED CHICKEN AND ARTICHOKE PANCAKES

Preparation time: 30 minutes
Total cooking time: 1 hour
Serves 4

1 teaspoon baking powder
1⅓ cups (165 g/5½ oz) plain flour
¼ teaspoon salt
2 eggs
300 ml (10 fl oz) milk
90 g (3 oz) butter
2½ cups (600 ml/20 fl oz) chicken stock
2 egg yolks
1 cup (250 ml/8 fl oz) cream
1 teaspoon lemon juice
300 g (10 oz) cooked chicken, chopped
   roughly
350 g (11 oz) artichoke hearts, drained
   and sliced
2 teaspoons chopped fresh thyme
2 teaspoons chopped fresh parsley
100 g (3½ oz) grated Parmesan

1 Sift the baking powder, 1 cup (125 g/4 oz) flour and salt into a large bowl and make a well in the centre. Whisk the eggs and milk in a jug and pour into the well, whisking until just smooth. Heat a frying pan and brush lightly with melted butter. Add ¼ cup (60 ml/2 fl oz) batter and cook over medium heat until the underside is brown. Turn over and cook the other side. Transfer to a plate and cover with a tea towel while cooking the remaining batter.

2 Melt the butter in a pan and stir in the remaining flour. Cook for 2 minutes, then remove from the heat. Slowly whisk in the chicken stock until smooth. Whisk in the combined egg yolks and cream. Return to the heat and bring slowly to the boil, stirring constantly. Boil for 30 seconds to thicken the sauce, then remove from the heat and stir in the lemon juice. Season with salt and freshly ground black pepper.
3 Preheat the oven to moderately hot 200°C (400°F/Gas 6). Grease a 3 litre ovenproof dish with melted butter. Line the base with 2 pancakes, slightly overlapping. Spoon half of the chicken, artichokes and herbs evenly over the pancakes. Pour a third of the sauce over the top and layer with another two pancakes. Repeat, finishing with a layer of 3 pancakes. Spread the remaining sauce over the top, sprinkle with the Parmesan and bake for 30–35 minutes, or until golden brown.

CHICKEN, CHILLI JAM AND NOODLE STIR-FRY

Preparation time: 15 minutes +
   20 minutes soaking
Total cooking time: 10 minutes
Serves 4

250 g (8 oz) flat rice stick noodles
   (1 cm/½ inch wide)
400 g (13 oz) chicken breast fillet
1 onion
1 red capsicum (pepper)
1 tablespoon peanut oil
2 tablespoons chilli jam
2 teaspoons fish sauce
2 tablespoons light soy sauce
90 g (3 oz) bean sprouts, tailed
100 g (3½ oz) unsalted cashew nuts
1 cup (30 g/1 oz) loosely packed basil,
   plus extra, to garnish

1 Put the noodles in a large heatproof bowl, cover with warm water and soak for about 20 minutes, or until soft. Drain well.
2 Meanwhile, cut the chicken breast fillets into 5 mm (¼ inch) slices against the grain. Slice the onion into thin wedges. Thinly slice the capsicum.
3 Heat a wok over high heat, add the peanut oil and swirl to coat the side. Cook the onion for 1–2 minutes, or until lightly golden. Add the chicken slices and cook for a further 3–5 minutes, or until browned and almost cooked through. Stir in the chilli jam, then add the capsicum and cook for another minute.
4 Add the fish sauce, soy sauce, bean sprouts, cashew nuts, basil and the noodles to the wok and toss until warmed through and well combined. Garnish with the extra basil and serve immediately.

TANGY ORANGE AND GINGER CHICKEN

Preparation time: 15 minutes
Total cooking time: 20 minutes
Serves 4

¼ cup (60 ml/12 fl oz) vegetable oil
10 chicken thigh fillets, cut into small
   pieces
3 teaspoons grated fresh ginger
1 teaspoon grated orange rind
½ cup (125 ml/4 fl oz) chicken stock
2 teaspoons honey
1 bunch (550 g/1 lb 2 oz) bok choy,
   trimmed and halved
toasted sesame seeds, to garnish

1 Heat a wok over high heat, add the oil
and swirl to coat the side of the wok. Add
the chicken in batches and stir-fry each
batch for 3–4 minutes, or until golden.
2 Return all the chicken to the wok, add
the ginger and orange rind, and cook for
20 seconds, or until fragrant. Add the
stock and the honey and stir to combine.
Increase the heat and cook for
3–4 minutes, or until the sauce has
thickened slightly. Add the bok choy and
cook until slightly wilted. Season well,
then sprinkle with toasted sesame seeds
and serve with steamed rice.

MUSTARD CHICKEN AND ASPARAGUS QUICHE

Preparation time: 25 minutes +
   40 minutes refrigeration
Total cooking time: 1 hour 20 minutes
Serves 8

2 cups (250 g/8 oz) plain flour
100 g (3½ oz) cold butter, chopped
1 egg yolk

Filling
150 g (5 oz) asparagus, chopped
25 g (¾ oz) butter
1 onion, chopped
¼ cup (60 g/2 oz) wholegrain mustard
200 g (6½ oz) soft cream cheese
½ cup (125 ml/4 fl oz) cream
3 eggs, lightly beaten
200 g (6½ oz) cooked chicken, chopped
½ teaspoon black pepper

1 Process the flour and butter until crumbly.
Add the egg yolk and ¼ cup (60 ml/2 fl oz) of
water. Process in short bursts until the
mixture comes together. Add a little extra
water if needed. Turn onto a floured surface
and gather into a ball. Cover with plastic
wrap and chill for 30 minutes. Grease a deep
loose-based flan tin measuring 19 cm
(7½ inches) across the base.

2 Roll out the pastry and line the tin. Trim
off any excess with a sharp knife. Place
the flan tin on a baking tray and chill for
10 minutes. Preheat the oven to
moderately hot 200°C (400°F/Gas 6).
Cover the pastry with baking paper and fill
evenly with baking beads. Bake for
10 minutes. Remove the paper and beads
and bake for about 10 minutes, or until the
pastry is lightly browned and dry. Cool.
Reduce the oven to moderate 180°C
(350°F/Gas 4).
3 To make the filling, boil or steam the
asparagus until tender. Drain and pat dry
with paper towels. Heat the butter in a
pan and cook the onion until translucent.
Remove from the heat and add the
mustard and cream cheese, stirring until
the cheese has melted. Cool. Add the
cream, eggs, chicken and asparagus and
mix well.
4 Spoon the filling into the pastry shell
and sprinkle with the pepper. Bake for
50 minutes to 1 hour, or until puffed and
set. Cool for at least 15 minutes before
cutting.

CHICKEN CURRY

Preparation time: 30 minutes
Total cooking time: 55 minutes
Serves 4

1.5 kg (3¼ lb) chicken pieces, such as
    thighs, drumsticks and wings
2 tablespoons oil
4 cloves garlic, finely chopped
5 cm (2 inch) piece fresh ginger, finely
    chopped
2 stems lemon grass (white part only),
    finely chopped
2 teaspoons chilli flakes
2 tablespoons curry powder
2 medium brown onions, chopped
2 teaspoons sugar
1 teaspoon salt
1½ cups (375 ml/12 fl oz) coconut milk
½ cup (125 ml/4 fl oz) water

Garnishes
garlic chives, thickly chopped
fresh coriander leaves
unsalted roasted peanuts

1 Using a large heavy knife or cleaver,
chop each piece of chicken into 2 pieces,
chopping straight through the bone. Wash
the chicken and pat dry with paper towels.
2 Heat the oil in a large pan; add the
garlic, ginger, lemon grass, chilli and
curry powder, and cook over medium heat
for 3 minutes, stirring regularly. Add the
chicken, onion, sugar and salt, and toss
gently. Cover and cook for 8 minutes, until
the onion has softened, and then toss well
to coat the chicken pieces evenly with the
curry mixture. Cover and cook for
15 minutes over low heat—the chicken
will braise gently, producing its own
liquid.
3 Add the coconut milk and water to the
pan and bring it to the boil, stirring
occasionally. Reduce the heat and
simmer, uncovered, for 30 minutes or
until chicken is very tender. Serve
garnished with the chives, coriander and
peanuts.

CHICKEN BIRYANI

Preparation time: 20 minutes +
    10 minutes standing
Total cooking time: 1 hour
Serves 8

4 cups (800 g/1 lb 10 oz) basmati rice
3 onions, sliced
½ cup (125 ml/4 fl oz) oil
180 g (6 oz) ghee or unsalted butter
4 cm (1½ inch) piece of cinnamon stick
2 cardamom pods
3 cloves
2 star anise
2 stalks of curry leaves
2 cm (¾ inch) piece of fresh ginger, grated
6 garlic cloves, crushed
1.3 kg (2 lb 10 oz) chicken pieces
4–6 green chillies, slit lengthways
2 cups (500 ml/16 fl oz) buttermilk
4 ripe tomatoes, diced
¾ cup (185 ml/6 fl oz) coconut milk
1 litre (32 fl oz) chicken stock
1 lemon, cut into wedges

1 Wash the rice in a sieve under cold,
running water until the water runs clear.
Drain well. Put the onion in a sieve,
sprinkle with ½ teaspoon of salt and leave
for 10 minutes to drain off any liquid that
oozes out. Rinse and pat dry.
2 Heat the oil and ghee over medium heat
in a large, heavy-based ovenproof
casserole. Add the cinnamon, cardamom
and cloves, and heat until they begin to
crackle. Reduce the heat to low and add the
star anise and the curry leaves from one
stalk. Stir in the sliced onion and cook for a
few minutes until golden brown. Toss in the
ginger and garlic, and cook until golden.

3 Mix in the chicken, increase the heat a
little and fry until the pieces are browned
on all sides. Add the chillies, the
remaining curry leaves, buttermilk and
some salt. Cook for 12 minutes, or until
the chicken is cooked through and the
liquid is reduced by half. Stir in the
tomato and coconut milk. Cook until the
tomato is tender, then pour in the stock
and bring to the boil.
4 Preheat the oven to hot 220°C
(425°F/Gas 7). Add the drained rice to the
chicken and stir well. Season, then cook
for 10 minutes, or until most of the liquid
is absorbed.
5 Remove the pot from the heat, cover
with a clean wet cloth, then a tight-fitting
lid, and put the pot in the oven for 15
minutes, or until the rice is cooked. Serve
hot with lemon wedges.

FETTUCINE WITH CHICKEN AND MUSHROOM SAUCE

Preparation time: 20 minutes
Total cooking time: 20 minutes
Serves 4

400 g (13 oz) fettucine
2 large chicken breast fillets
1 tablespoon olive oil
30 g (1 oz) butter
2 bacon rashers, chopped
2 cloves garlic, crushed
250 g (8 oz) button mushrooms, sliced
⅓ cup (80 ml/2¾ fl oz) white wine
⅔ cup (170 ml/5½ fl oz) cream
4 spring onions, chopped
1 tablespoon plain flour
2 tablespoons water
⅓ cup (35 g/1¼ oz) freshly grated
    Parmesan, for serving

1 Cook the fettucine in a large pan of rapidly boiling salted water until al dente. Drain and return to the pan.
2 Trim the chicken of excess fat and cut into thin strips. Heat the oil and butter in a heavy-based frying pan, add the chicken and cook over medium heat for 3 minutes, or until browned. Add the bacon, garlic and mushrooms and cook for 2 minutes, stirring occasionally.
3 Add the wine and cook until the liquid has reduced by half. Add the cream and spring onion and bring to the boil. Blend the flour with the water until smooth, add to the pan and stir until the mixture boils and thickens. Reduce the heat and simmer for 2 minutes. Season with salt and pepper, to taste.
4 Add the sauce to the pasta and stir over low heat until combined. Sprinkle with Parmesan. Serve immediately with a green salad and perhaps some hot herb bread.

RICE WITH CHICKEN AND SEAFOOD

Preparation time: 30 minutes
Total cooking time: 40 minutes
Serves 4–6

500 g (1 lb) medium raw prawns
500 g (1 lb) mussels
200 g (6½ oz) squid hoods
¼ teaspoon saffron threads
4 large tomatoes
3 tablespoons oil
2 chorizo sausages, thickly sliced
500 g (1 lb) chicken pieces
300 g (9⅔ oz) pork fillet, thickly sliced
4 cloves garlic, crushed
2 red (Spanish) onions, chopped
¼ teaspoon ground turmeric
2 cups (440 g/14 oz) short-grain rice
1.25 litres chicken stock
125 g (4 oz) green beans, cut into 4 cm
    (1½ inch) lengths
1 red pepper (capsicum), cut into thin
    strips
1 cup (155 g/5 oz) peas

1 Peel and devein the prawns, leaving the tails intact. Scrub the mussels thoroughly and remove the beards. Cut the squid hoods into ½ cm (¼ inch) thick slices. Soak the saffron threads in 2 tablespoons boiling water for 15 minutes.
2 Score a cross in the base of each tomato, place in a heatproof bowl, cover with boiling water and leave for 2 minutes. Plunge into cold water and then peel the skin away from the cross. Cut the tomatoes in half horizontally, scoop out the seeds with a teaspoon and chop the flesh.

3 Heat 1 tablespoon oil in a large, heavy-based pan; add the chorizo slices and cook over medium heat for 5 minutes, or until browned. Drain on paper towels. Add the chicken pieces to the pan and cook for 5 minutes, or until golden, turning once. Drain on paper towels. Add the pork to the pan and cook for 3 minutes, or until browned, turning once. Drain on paper towels.
4 Heat the remaining oil in the pan; add the garlic, onion, saffron and soaking liquid and turmeric, and cook over medium heat for 3 minutes or until the onion is golden. Add the tomatoes and cook for 3 minutes or until soft. Add the rice and stir for 5 minutes, or until the rice is translucent. Stir in the stock and bring to the boil; cover and simmer for 10 minutes.
5 Add the chicken pieces to the pan, cover and continue cooking for 20 minutes. Add the pork, prawns, mussels, squid, chorizo and vegetables; cover and cook for 10 minutes or until the liquid is absorbed.

SPAGHETTI WITH CHICKEN BOLOGNESE

Preparation time: 20 minutes
Total cooking time: 15 minutes
Serves 4

2 tablespoons olive oil
2 leeks, thinly sliced
1 red pepper (capsicum), diced
2 cloves garlic, crushed
500 g (1 lb) chicken mince
2 cups (500 g/1 lb) tomato pasta sauce
1 tablespoon chopped fresh thyme
1 tablespoon chopped fresh rosemary
2 tablespoons seeded and chopped black
   olives
400 g (13 oz) spaghetti
125 g (4 oz) feta cheese, crumbled

1 Heat the oil in a large, heavy-based pan. Add the leek, pepper and garlic and cook over medium-high heat for 2 minutes, or until lightly browned.
2 Add the chicken mince and cook over high heat for 3 minutes, or until browned and any liquid has evaporated. Stir occasionally and break up any lumps as the mince cooks.
3 Add the tomato pasta sauce, thyme and rosemary and bring to the boil. Reduce the heat and simmer for 5 minutes, or until the sauce has reduced and thickened. Add the olives and stir to combine. Season, to taste.
4 Cook the spaghetti in a large pan of rapidly boiling salted water until al dente. Drain. Place the spaghetti on individual serving plates or pile into a large deep serving dish and pour the Chicken Bolognese over the top. (The sauce can be mixed through the pasta.) Sprinkle with feta and serve immediately.

CHICKEN AND BACON GOUGERE

Preparation time: 40 minutes
Total cooking time: 50 minutes
Serves 6

60 g (2 oz) butter
1–2 cloves garlic, crushed
1 red onion, chopped
3 slices bacon, chopped
¼ cup (30 g/1 oz) plain flour
1½ cups (375 ml/12 fl oz) milk
½ cup (125 ml/4 fl oz) cream
2 teaspoons wholegrain mustard
250 g (8 oz) cooked chicken, chopped
½ cup (30 g/1 oz) chopped fresh parsley

Choux Pastry
60 g (2 oz) butter, chopped
½ cup (60 g/2 oz) plain flour
2 eggs, lightly beaten
⅓ cup (35 g/1¼ oz) grated Parmesan

1 Melt the butter in a frying pan and cook the garlic, onion and bacon for 5–7 minutes, stirring occasionally, until cooked but not browned. Stir in the flour and cook for 1 minute. Gradually add the milk and stir until thickened. Simmer for 2 minutes, then add the cream and mustard. Remove from the heat and fold in the chopped chicken and parsley. Season with pepper.
2 To make the pastry, place the butter and ½ cup (125 ml/4 fl oz) water in a pan. Stir until melted. Bring to the boil. Add the flour and beat for 2 minutes, or until the mixture leaves the side of the pan. Cool for 5 minutes. Gradually mix in the egg with an electric beater, until thick and glossy. Add the Parmesan.
3 Preheat the oven to hot 210°C (415°F/Gas 6–7). Grease a deep 23 cm (9 inch) ovenproof dish, pour in the filling and spoon heaped tablespoons of choux around the outside. Bake for 10 minutes, then reduce the oven to 180°C (350°F/Gas 4) and bake for 20 minutes, or until the choux is puffed and golden. Sprinkle with grated Parmesan.

CHICKEN RAVIOLI WITH BUTTERED SAGE SAUCE

Preparation time: 15 minutes
Total cooking time: 10 minutes
Serves 4

500 g (1 lb) fresh or dried chicken-filled
   ravioli or agnolotti
60 g (2 oz) butter
4 spring onions, chopped
2 tablespoons fresh sage, chopped
½ cup (50 g/1¾ oz) freshly grated
   Parmesan, for serving
fresh sage leaves, extra, for garnish

1 Cook the ravioli in a large pan of rapidly boiling salted water until al dente. Drain and return to the pan.
2 While the ravioli is cooking, melt the butter in a heavy-based pan. Add the spring onion and sage and stir for 2 minutes. Add salt and pepper, to taste.
3 Add the sauce to the pasta and toss well. Pour into warmed serving bowls and sprinkle with Parmesan. Serve immediately, garnished with fresh sage leaves.

MEXICAN CHICKEN BAKE

Preparation time: 15 minutes
Total cooking time: 1 hour
Serves 4

¾ cup (165 g/5½ oz) short-grain rice
1 tablespoon oil
600 g (1¼ lb) boneless, skinless chicken
    thigh fillets, unrolled
400 g (13 oz) spicy taco sauce
300 g (10 oz) tin red kidney beans,
    drained and rinsed
3½ tablespoons chopped coriander
    (cilantro) leaves
2 cups (250 g/8 oz) grated Cheddar cheese
½ cup (125 g/4 oz) sour cream

1 Preheat the oven to moderate 180°C
(350°F/Gas 4). Lightly grease a 7 cm
(2¾ inch) deep, 21 cm (8½ inch) round
ceramic casserole dish. Bring a large
saucepan of water to the boil, add the rice
and cook for 10–12 minutes, stirring
occasionally. Drain.
2 Heat the oil in a large frying pan over
medium heat. Add the chicken thighs and
sauté for 3 minutes, then turn over. Pour
in the spicy taco sauce, stir well and then
cook for a further 3 minutes.
3 To assemble the Mexican chicken bake,
combine the beans, rice and 1½
tablespoons of the coriander in a large
bowl and toss together. Lightly press the
mixture into the bottom of the prepared
casserole dish. Spread half the cheese
over the rice mixture. Arrange the
chicken thighs and sauce on top in a star
shape, sprinkle with 1½ tablespoons of the
coriander, then sprinkle with the rest of
the Cheddar cheese. Cover with foil.
4 Bake for 35–40 minutes, or until the
mixture is bubbling and the cheese is
melted and slightly browned—remove the
foil for the last 5 minutes of cooking. Cut
into four servings with a knife and scoop
out each serving carefully, trying to keep
the layers intact. Serve sprinkled with the
remaining coriander and a dollop of sour
cream.

CHICKEN CORIANDER PIE

Preparation time: 40 minutes
Total cooking time: 45 minutes
Serves 4

50 g (1¾ oz) butter
2 onions, chopped
100 g (3½ oz) button mushrooms, sliced
250 g (8 oz) cooked chicken, roughly
    chopped
4 hard-boiled eggs
1 tablespoon plain flour
280 ml (9 fl oz) chicken stock
1 egg yolk
¼ cup (15 g/½ oz) chopped fresh coriander
250 g (8 oz) block or packet puff pastry
1 egg, lightly beaten, to glaze

1 Melt half of the butter in a large pan.
Add the onion and mushrooms and sauté
for about 5 minutes, or until soft, then stir
in the chicken. Spoon half of the mixture
into a 20 cm (8 inch) round, straight-sided
pie dish. Slice the eggs and lay over the
chicken. Top with the remaining mixture.
2 Preheat the oven to moderately hot
200°C (400°F/Gas 6). Melt the remaining
butter in a pan, add the flour and cook for
1 minute. Gradually add the stock and
cook for 4 minutes, stirring constantly,
then remove from the heat. Stir in the egg
yolk and coriander, and season with salt
and ground black pepper. Allow the
mixture to cool before pouring over the
chicken filling.
3 Roll out the pastry into a square larger
than the pie dish. Dampen the dish rim
with water and lay the pastry over,
pressing down firmly to seal. Trim the
edges and roll out the leftover pastry into
a long strip. Slice it into 3 equal lengths
and make a plait. Brush the top of the pie
with beaten egg and place the plait
around the edge. Brush again with beaten
egg. Make a few slits in the centre and
bake for 35 minutes, or until golden.

CONCHIGLIE WITH CHICKEN AND RICOTTA

Preparation time: 15 minutes
Total cooking time: 1 hour 10 minutes
Serves 4

500 g (1 lb) conchiglie (shell pasta)
2 tablespoons olive oil
1 onion, chopped
1 clove garlic, crushed
60 g (2 oz) prosciutto, sliced
125 g (4 oz) mushrooms, chopped
250 g (8 oz) chicken mince
2 tablespoons tomato paste (tomato
    purée, double concentrate)
425 g (14 oz) can crushed tomatoes
½ cup (125 ml/4 fl oz) dry white wine
1 teaspoon dried oregano
250 g (8 oz) ricotta cheese
1 cup (150 g/5 oz) grated mozzarella cheese
1 teaspoon snipped fresh chives
1 tablespoon chopped fresh parsley
3 tablespoons freshly grated Parmesan

1 Cook the conchiglie in a large pan of
rapidly boiling salted water until al dente.
Drain well.
2 Heat the oil in a large frying pan. Add
the onion and garlic and stir over low heat
until the onion is tender. Add the
prosciutto and stir for 1 minute. Add the
mushrooms and cook for 2 minutes. Add
the chicken mince and brown well,
breaking up with a fork as it cooks.
3 Stir in the tomato paste, tomato, wine,
oregano and salt and pepper, to taste.
Bring to the boil, reduce the heat and
simmer for 20 minutes.
4 Preheat the oven to moderate 180°C
(350°F/Gas 4). Combine the ricotta,
mozzarella, chives, parsley and half the
Parmesan. Spoon a little of the mixture
into each shell. Spoon some of the
chicken sauce into the base of a casserole
dish. Arrange the conghiglie on top.
Spoon the remaining sauce over the top.
Sprinkle with the remaining Parmesan.
Bake for 25–30 minutes, or until golden.

CHICKEN MARYLANDS WITH REDCURRANT SAUCE

Preparation time: 25 minutes + 2 hours
  marinating
Total cooking time: 30 minutes
Serves 4

4 chicken marylands (drumstick and
  thigh)
½ cup (125 ml/4 fl oz) red wine
1 tablespoon finely chopped fresh thyme
1 tablespoon finely chopped fresh
  rosemary
1 tablespoon olive oil
½ cup (160 g/5½ oz) redcurrant jelly

1 Trim the chicken of excess fat and
sinew. Place the chicken in a shallow
non-metal dish. Combine the wine, thyme
and rosemary in a small jug and pour over
the chicken. Refrigerate, covered, for
2 hours or overnight, turning the chicken
occasionally.
2 Preheat the oven to moderately hot
200°C (400°F/Gas 6). Drain the chicken
and reserve the marinade. Place the
chicken in a baking dish and brush with
the oil. Bake for 30 minutes, or until
tender, turning occasionally.
3 Combine the reserved marinade and
redcurrant jelly in a small pan. Stir over
medium heat until smooth, then bring to
the boil. Reduce the heat and simmer,
uncovered, for 15 minutes. Pour over the
chicken and serve with rosemary and
some berries.

OMELETTE RICE

Preparation time: 15 minutes
Total cooking time: 25 minutes
Serves 4

20 g (¾ oz) butter
1 onion, finely chopped
2 garlic cloves, crushed
2 teaspoons very finely chopped ginger
250 g (8 oz) chicken thigh fillets, cut into
  dice
½ cup (125 g/4 oz) tomato sauce
⅓ cup (50 g/1¾ oz) cooked peas
3 cups (255 g/7 oz) cooked Japanese
  short-grain rice, rinsed well
Japanese mayonnaise, to serve (see
  Notes)
tomato sauce, to serve (optional)

Omelettes
8 eggs
1 tablespoon Shoyu (Japanese soy sauce)
1 tablespoon mirin

1 Melt the butter in a large frying pan, add
the onion and cook over medium heat for
about 8–10 minutes, or until golden. Add
the garlic, ginger and chicken and cook,
stirring, for 1 minute, or until the chicken
starts to change colour, then add the
tomato sauce and peas and mix well. Add
the rice and mix again until the rice is
evenly pink from the tomato sauce.
Continue cooking, stirring occasionally,
for about 5 minutes until the chicken is
cooked and the rice is completely heated
through. Season to taste, then cover and
set aside while you make the omelettes.

2 Put all the omelette ingredients in a
bowl and lightly beat. Spray a non-stick
frying pan with a little cooking oil spray.
Heat over medium heat, then pour one-
quarter of the egg mixture in. Using
chopsticks or a soft spatula, gently drag
the outside edges of the egg into the
centre until it just starts to set, then leave
to cook for 1 minute. Spoon one-quarter
(about 1 cup) of the rice mixture along the
centre line of the egg, then very carefully
fold two sides towards the centre, over
the rice so you have a rectangular
omelette. Put a serving plate over the top
and very carefully invert the omelette
onto the plate so the seam is underneath.
Repeat with the remaining mixture to
make four omelettes.
3 If desired, squeeze a little mayonnaise
and tomato sauce over the top—you'll get
the best result if you use a squeeze
bottle. Serve immediately, accompanied
by a green salad.

NOTES: Japanese mayonnaise typically
comes in easy-to-use squeeze bottles. If
you can't find it, use whole-egg
mayonnaise instead.
  Try experimenting with other filling
ingredients such as mushrooms, ham,
corn or cheese.
  Another simpler version of Omelette
rice is to make the omelettes, then serve
them over the rice or to break them up
and mix through the rice mixture.

CHICKEN WITH LEMON, PARSLEY AND ORECCHIETTE

Preparation time: 10 minutes
Total cooking time: 20 minutes
Serves 4

375 g (12 oz) orecchiette
1 tablespoon oil
60 g (2 oz) butter
4 small chicken breast fillets
⅓ cup (80 ml/2¾ fl oz) lemon juice
⅓ cup (20 g/¾ oz) finely chopped fresh
   parsley plus some extra, to garnish
lemon slices, to garnish

1 Cook the pasta in a large pan of rapidly boiling salted water until al dente. Drain.
2 While the pasta is cooking, heat the oil and half the butter in a large, heavy-based pan. Add the chicken fillets and cook for 2 minutes each side; set aside. Add the lemon juice, parsley and the remaining butter to the pan. Stir to combine and return the fillets to the pan. Cook over low heat for 3–4 minutes, turning once, or until cooked through. Season, to taste, with salt and freshly ground black pepper.
3 Serve the pasta topped with a chicken fillet and sauce. Garnish with lemon slices and sprinkle with some chopped fresh parsley.

BEGGARS' CHICKEN

Preparation time: 40 minutes +
   30 minutes refrigerating
Total cooking time: 1 hour 35 minutes
Serves 4

4 x 400 g (13 oz) baby chickens
2 tablespoons olive oil
1 tablespoon soy sauce
2 tablespoons orange juice
1 tablespoon soft brown sugar
6 cups (750 g/1½ lb) plain flour
1 kg (2 lb) cooking salt
4 thin strips orange rind
4 star anise

1 Remove the giblets and any large fat deposits from the chickens. Pat the chickens dry with paper towels. Place the chickens in a shallow, non-metal dish. Whisk the oil, soy sauce, orange juice and sugar in a bowl until combined. Brush the mixture all over the chickens, inside and out. Cover and refrigerate for 30 minutes. Preheat the oven to 240°C (475°F/Gas 9).
2 Sift the flour into a large mixing bowl and add the salt. Make a well in the centre and add 2½ cups (600 ml/20 fl oz) water all at once. Mix the water into the flour and salt gradually, using your hands to make a firm dough. Turn onto a floured surface and press the dough together until smooth.
3 Divide the dough into four portions. Roll each portion out large enough to cover one of the chickens. Place a strip of orange rind and a star anise into the cavity of each chicken. Wrap each chicken securely with a greased sheet of foil then place, breast-side down, in the centre of a sheet of dough.
4 Wrap the dough over the chickens to enclose. Press firmly, ensuring there are no gaps or openings. Place breast-side up in a large, shallow baking dish. Bake for 1 hour 35 minutes, or until the casing is crisp and well browned. Crack the casing with a hammer or meat mallet and discard. Serve the chicken with baked vegetables.

TAMARIND CHICKEN

Preparation time: 15 minutes +
   2 hours marinating
Total cooking time: 30 minutes
Serves 4

4 chicken thighs
4 chicken drumsticks
⅓ cup (80 ml/2¾ fl oz) tamarind
   concentrate
2 teaspoons ground coriander
1 teaspoon ground turmeric
2 cloves garlic, crushed
2 tablespoons peanut oil
2 red chillies, finely chopped
6 spring onions, finely chopped
oil, for deep-frying

1 Remove the skin from the chicken pieces. Place the chicken in a large pan with enough water to cover it. Cover and simmer for 15 minutes, or until cooked through. Drain and cool.
2 Combine the tamarind, coriander, turmeric and garlic. Add the tamarind mixture to the chicken and toss well to coat. Cover and marinate in the refrigerator for at least 2 hours, or preferably overnight.
3 Heat the peanut oil in a frying pan; add the chilli and spring onion, and stir-fry over low heat for 3 minutes. Set aside.
4 Heat the oil for deep-frying in a large pan; cook the chicken in 3 batches over medium heat for 5 minutes, or until the chicken is golden brown and heated through. Drain the chicken on paper towels, and keep it warm while frying the remaining chicken. Serve the chicken pieces with a spoonful of the chilli mixture on the side.

FRIED CRISPY CHICKEN

Preparation time: 20 minutes +
 30 minutes marinating
Total cooking time: 30 minutes
Serves 4

4 chicken marylands (quarters) or
 8 drumsticks
4 cloves garlic, chopped
3 coriander roots, finely chopped
2 teaspoons ground turmeric
1 teaspoon freshly ground pepper
1 teaspoon salt
1 teaspoon caster sugar
2 tablespoons chilli sauce
oil, for deep-frying

1 Boil the chicken in water for 15 minutes,
or until cooked through. Cool.
2 Place the garlic, coriander root,
turmeric, pepper, salt, sugar and chilli
sauce in a mortar and pestle or food
processor and pound or process into a
smooth paste. Brush over the chicken,
cover and refrigerate for 30 minutes.
3 Heat the oil in a heavy-based pan, add
the chicken and cook until dark brown,
turning frequently. Drain on paper towels.
Serve hot or cold with chilli sauce, if
desired.

THAI STICKY RICE WITH BARBECUED CHICKEN

Preparation time: 30 minutes +
 6 hours marinating
Total cooking time: 1 hour
Serves 4–6

2 kg (4 lb) whole chicken, cut into
 8–10 pieces
8 garlic cloves, chopped
6 coriander (cilantro) roots, chopped
½ cup (15 g/½ oz) coriander (cilantro)
 leaves, chopped
1 tablespoon finely chopped ginger
1 teaspoon ground white pepper
¼ cup (60 ml/2 fl oz) fish sauce
¼ cup (60 ml/2 fl oz) lime juice
¼ cup (60 ml/2 fl oz) whisky (optional)
3 cups (600 g/1¼ lb) long-grain glutinous
 rice
cucumber slices, to serve

Sauce
6 coriander (cilantro) roots, chopped
4 garlic cloves, chopped
2 bird's eye chillies, deseeded and chopped
¾ cup (185 ml/6 fl oz) vinegar
4 tablespoons grated palm sugar or soft
 brown sugar

1 Put the chicken in a non-metallic bowl.
Combine the garlic, coriander roots and
leaves, ginger, white pepper and a pinch
of salt and pound to a paste using a
mortar and pestle. Mix in the fish sauce,
lime juice and whisky, then pour over the
chicken and mix well. Marinate for at
least 6 hours in the refrigerator. At the
same time, soak the rice for at least
3 hours in cold water.

2 To make the sauce, pound the coriander
root, garlic, chillies and a pinch of salt to a
paste using a mortar and pestle. Combine
the vinegar, sugar and ¾ cup (185 ml/6 fl
oz) water and stir until the sugar has
dissolved. Bring to the boil, then add the
paste and cook for 8–10 minutes, or until
reduced by half. Set aside until ready to
serve.
3 Drain the rice well, then line a bamboo
steamer with muslin or banana leaves,
spread the rice over and cover with a
tight-fitting lid. Steam over a wok or large
saucepan of boiling water for 40 minutes,
or until the rice is translucent, sticky and
tender. If steam is escaping, wrap some
foil over the top of the steamer. Keep
covered until ready to serve.
4 Meanwhile, heat a barbecue to medium
heat, then cook the chicken, turning
regularly for about 25 minutes, or until
tender and cooked through. The breast
pieces may only take about 15 minutes so
take them off first and keep warm.
5 Serve the chicken, rice, dipping sauce
and cucumber on separate plates in the
centre of the table and allow your guests
to help themselves.

RICE WITH CHICKEN AND MUSHROOMS

Preparation time: 15 minutes +
   15 minutes soaking
Total cooking time: 40 minutes
Serves 4–6

500 g (1 lb) short-grain rice
2½ cups (600 ml/20 fl oz) water
8 dried shiitake mushrooms
2 tablespoons Japanese soy sauce
2 tablespoons sake
2 teaspoons sugar
600 g (1¼ lb) chicken breast fillets, cut
   into strips
200 g (6½ oz) frozen peas
2 eggs, lightly beaten

1 Wash the rice thoroughly in a sieve under running water until the water runs clear. Place the rice in a heavy-based pan with the water and bring it to the boil. Reduce the heat to very low, cover and cook for 15 minutes. Remove the pan from the heat and leave, with the lid on, for 20 minutes.
2 Soak the mushrooms in hot water for about 15 minutes, or until soft. Drain well and slice into thin strips, discarding the hard stem.
3 Combine the soy sauce, sake and sugar in a frying pan. Cook over low heat stirring until the sugar dissolves. Add the mushrooms, chicken and peas. Cover and cook for 5 minutes until the chicken is cooked. Set aside and cover to keep warm.
4 Heat a non-stick pan; pour in the eggs and cook over medium heat, swirling the pan gently until the egg sets. Turn the omelette over and cook the other side. Remove the omelette from the pan and cut it into thin strips.
5 Arrange the rice in individual serving bowls, spoon over the chicken mixture with a little of the soy liquid and scatter over the egg strips. Serve immediately.

ROASTED ROSEMARY CHICKEN

Preparation time: 15 minutes +
   10 minutes standing
Total cooking time: 1 hour
Serves 4

1.5–1.8 kg (3 lb–3lb 10 oz) chicken
6 large sprigs fresh rosemary
4 cloves garlic
3 tablespoons olive oil

1 Preheat the oven to hot 220°C (425°F/Gas 7). Wipe the chicken inside and out and pat dry with paper towels. Season the chicken cavity and place 4 rosemary sprigs and the garlic cloves inside.
2 Rub the outside of the chicken with 1 tablespoon of the oil, season and place the chicken on its side in a roasting tin. Put the remaining rosemary sprigs in the tin and drizzle the remaining oil around the tin.
3 Place the tin on the middle shelf in the oven. After 20 minutes, turn the chicken onto the other side, baste with the juices and cook for another 20 minutes. Turn the chicken breast-side-up, baste again and cook for another 15 minutes, or until the juices between the body and thigh run clear when pierced with a knife. Transfer the chicken to a warm serving dish and set aside for at least 10 minutes before carving.
4 Meanwhile, pour most of the fat from the roasting tin and return the tin to the stovetop over high heat. Add 2 tablespoons water and, using a wooden spoon, scrape the base of the pan to loosen the residue. Check the seasoning and pour over the chicken to serve.

CHILLI CHICKEN PIE

Preparation time: 45 minutes
Total cooking time: 1 hour 20 minutes
Serves 4–6

2 tablespoons olive oil
1 onion, chopped
750 g (1½ lb) chicken breast fillets,
   chopped
3 cloves garlic, crushed
1 teaspoon chilli powder
2 teaspoons cumin seeds
1 tablespoon plain flour
2 x 410 g (13 oz) cans chopped tomatoes
1 tablespoon soft brown sugar
1 red capsicum, thinly sliced
375 g (12 oz) can red kidney beans, rinsed
   and drained
15 sheets filo pastry
100 g (3½ oz) butter, melted

1 Heat half the oil in a large frying pan and cook the onion until softened and golden. Remove from the pan, add the remaining oil and brown the chicken over high heat.
2 Stir in the garlic, chilli powder and cumin seeds and cook for 1 minute. Return the onion to the pan, stir in the flour and cook for 30 seconds. Stir in the chopped tomatoes.
3 Add the sugar and capsicum and simmer over low heat for 40 minutes, or until reduced and thickened. Increase the heat and, stirring constantly to prevent burning, add the kidney beans. Allow to cool, then spoon into a 20 x 28 cm (8 x 11 inch) casserole dish. Preheat the oven to moderate 180°C (350°F/Gas 4).
4 Cut the filo sheets in half, brush with the melted butter and scrunch up. Place on top of the filling, to cover it completely. Brush with the remaining butter and bake for 25–30 minutes, or until golden.

CRISPY-SKIN CHICKEN WITH FIVE-SPICE DIPPING SALT

Preparation time: 10 minutes + 5 hours 15
  minutes standing
Total cooking time: 50 minutes
Serves 4–6

1.6 kg (3¼ lb) chicken
3 star anise
2 cinnamon sticks
1 piece dried tangerine or orange peel
1 x 2 cm (½ x ¾ inch) piece fresh ginger,
  lightly smashed
½ cup (125 ml/4 fl oz) dark soy sauce
¼ cup (60 ml/2 fl oz) light soy sauce
⅓ cup (80 ml/2¾ fl oz) Chinese rice wine
¼ cup (60 g/2 oz) sugar
2 litres (64 fl oz) oil, for deep-frying
coriander sprigs, to garnish

Glaze
¼ cup (90 g/3 oz) honey
2 tablespoons dark soy sauce
2 tablespoons Chinese black vinegar
Dipping salt
1 tablespoon fine salt
1 teaspoon five-spice powder
½ teaspoon Sichuan peppercorns
1 teaspoon sugar (optional)

1 Rinse the chicken, pat dry with paper towels and remove any excess fat from the cavity. In a saucepan or pot just large enough to hold the chicken, combine the star anise, cinnamon sticks, tangerine peel, ginger, dark soy sauce, light soy sauce, Chinese rice wine and sugar with 2 litres (64 fl oz) water. Bring to the boil, then reduce to a simmer.
2 Carefully lower the chicken into the simmering liquid and, if necessary, add enough water to just cover the chicken. Simmer for 30 minutes, then remove the pan from the heat and allow the chicken to rest in the liquid for a further 10 minutes. Remove the chicken from the liquid, being careful not to break the skin, and put it on a wire rack over a plate or baking tray for 3 hours in the refrigerator—do not cover the chicken or the skin won't dry properly. After 3 hours, the skin should be very dry and feel like parchment.
3 To make the glaze, put the ingredients in a small wok or saucepan with ¾ cup (185 ml/6 fl oz) water. Bring to the boil, then brush the mixture over the chicken using a pastry brush, making sure that you coat all of the skin thoroughly. Leave the chicken to dry on the rack in the fridge for another 2 hours.
4 Meanwhile, to make the five-spice salt, heat a small wok or saucepan over low heat and add the salt, five-spice powder, peppercorns and sugar (if desired). Dry-fry for 3–4 minutes, or until the peppercorns turn black and smell fragrant. Sift the peppercorns out of the mixture and discard them. Divide the five-spice salt between two small dishes ready for serving.
5 Just before serving, heat the oil in a large wok over medium heat to 180°C (350°F), or until a piece of bread dropped in the oil browns in 15 seconds. Carefully lower the chicken into the oil and deep-fry on one side until it is a rich, dark brown colour and very crisp. Very carefully turn the chicken over and brown the other side. Extra caution is needed when turning the chicken in the wok as it may be heavy and awkward. When browned all over, carefully remove the chicken with a large sieve and drain well on crumpled paper towels. Sprinkle the skin with a little of the spice salt and allow the chicken to rest for 5 minutes.
6 To serve, use a cleaver or large kitchen knife to chop the chicken in half lengthways, then into pieces small enough that they can be picked up with chopsticks. Place the pieces on a platter, garnish with coriander sprigs and serve immediately with the five-spice salt.

CHICKEN STEW

Preparation time: 30 minutes
Total cooking time: 50 minutes
Serves 4

1 x 1.6 kg (3½ lb) chicken
6 cloves garlic, finely chopped
4 spring onions, chopped
1 teaspoon Korean chilli powder
2 tablespoons Japanese soy sauce
2 tablespoons sesame oil
1 tablespoon rice vinegar
2 zucchini (courgettes), thickly sliced

1 Using a cleaver or large cook's knife, cut the chicken into quarters, then into small eating pieces, chopping straight through the bone.
2 Combine the chicken, garlic, spring onion, chilli powder, soy sauce, sesame oil, vinegar and zucchini in a heavy-based pan or flameproof casserole dish. Toss the chicken well to coat it in the sauce. Cover and cook over a low heat for 45 to 50 minutes or until the chicken is very tender. The chicken should come off the bone easily, so it can be eaten with chopsticks.

CHICKEN AND SPINACH LASAGNE

Preparation time: 30 minutes
Total cooking time: 1 hour 10 minutes
Serves 8

500 g (1 lb) English spinach
1 kg (2 lb) chicken mince
1 clove garlic, crushed
3 bacon rashers, chopped
425 g (14 oz) can crushed tomatoes
½ cup (125 g/4 oz) tomato paste (tomato
   purée, double concentrate)
½ cup (125 ml/4 fl oz) tomato sauce
½ cup (125 ml/4 fl oz) chicken stock
12 instant lasagne sheets
1 cup (125 g/4 oz) grated Cheddar cheese

Cheese sauce
60 g (2 oz) butter
⅓ cup (40 g/1¼ oz) plain flour
2½ cups (600 ml/20 fl oz) milk
1 cup (125 g/4 oz) grated Cheddar cheese

1 Preheat the oven to moderate 180°C
(350°F/Gas 4). Remove and discard the
stalks from the spinach leaves. Plunge
the leaves in a pan of boiling water for
2 minutes, or until tender. Remove,
plunge immediately into a bowl of iced
water and then drain.
2 Heat a little oil in a heavy-based frying
pan. Add the mince, garlic and bacon.
Cook over medium heat for 5 minutes, or
until browned. Stir in the tomato, tomato
paste, sauce and stock and bring to the
boil. Reduce the heat and simmer,
partially covered, for 10 minutes, or until
the sauce is slightly thickened. Season
with salt and pepper, to taste.

3 To make the cheese sauce, melt the
butter in a medium pan, add the flour and
stir over low heat for 1 minute, or until the
mixture is lightly golden and smooth.
Remove from the heat and gradually stir
in the milk. Return to the heat and stir
constantly over medium heat for
4 minutes, or until the sauce boils and
thickens. Remove from the heat and stir
in the cheese.
4 To assemble the lasagne, brush a deep,
3-litre, ovenproof dish with melted butter
or oil. Spread one-quarter of the chicken
mixture over the base. Top with 4 sheets
of lasagne. Spread with one-third of the
cheese sauce, then another layer of the
chicken filling. Top with all of the spinach,
a layer of lasagne, a layer of cheese sauce
and the remaining chicken filling. Spread
evenly with the remaining cheese sauce
and sprinkle with the grated cheese. Bake
for 50 minutes, or until cooked through
and golden brown.

CHICKEN BRAISED WITH GINGER AND STAR ANISE

Preparation time: 10 minutes
Total cooking time: 30 minutes
Serves 4

1 teaspoon Sichuan peppercorns
2 tablespoons peanut oil
2 x 3 cm (¾ x 1¼ inch) piece fresh ginger,
   cut into julienne strips
2 cloves garlic, chopped
1 kg (2 lb) chicken thigh fillets, cut in half
⅓ cup (80 ml/2¾ fl oz) Chinese rice wine
1 tablespoon honey
¼ cup (60 ml/2 fl oz) light soy sauce
1 star anise

1 Heat a wok over medium heat, add the
peppercorns and cook, stirring often, for
2–4 minutes, or until fragrant. Remove
and lightly crush with the back of a knife.
2 Reheat the wok, add the oil and swirl to
coat. Add the ginger and garlic and cook
over low heat for 1–2 minutes, or until
lightly golden. Add the chicken, increase
the heat to medium and cook for
3 minutes, or until browned all over.
3 Add the remaining ingredients, reduce
the heat and simmer, covered, for
20 minutes, or until the chicken is tender.
Serve with rice.

CHICKEN CURRY BAGS

Preparation time: 30 minutes +
  30 minutes standing
Total cooking time: 1 hour
Makes 10

1 cup (125 g/4 oz) plain flour
1 egg
1 egg yolk
1¼ cups (315 ml/10 fl oz) milk
50 g (1¾ oz) butter, melted
½ cup (60 g/2 oz) finely grated Cheddar

Chicken Filling
1 large, cooked chicken breast
60 g (2 oz) butter
1 red onion, chopped
1–2 teaspoons curry powder
2 tablespoons plain flour
1¼ cups (315 ml/10 fl oz) milk
¼ cup (60 ml/2 fl oz) cream
¼ cup (15 g/½ oz) chopped fresh parsley
2 hard-boiled eggs, chopped

1 Mix the flour, egg, egg yolk and half the milk in a food processor for 10 seconds. Add the remaining milk and 1 tablespoon of the melted butter and process until smooth. Transfer to a jug, cover and set aside for 30 minutes.
2 To make the chicken filling, chop the cooked chicken breast into small cubes. Melt the butter in a pan, add the onion and cook over medium heat until softened. Add the curry powder and flour and cook for 1–2 minutes. Gradually add the milk, stirring until smooth. Cook for 2–3 minutes, or until the sauce has boiled and thickened. Remove from the heat and add the cream, chicken, parsley and egg. Cover and set aside.

3 Heat a small crepe pan and brush lightly with melted butter. Pour about ¼ cup (60 ml/2 fl oz) batter into the pan, swirling the pan to cover the base. Pour the excess batter back into the jug, adding a little more milk to the batter if it is too thick. Cook for about 30 seconds, then turn over and cook until lightly brown. Remove to a plate while cooking the remaining batter.
4 Preheat the oven to moderate 180°C (350°F/Gas 4). Place 3 tablespoons of the chicken filling in the centre of each crepe, then gather up into a bag. Tie loosely with a strip of foil, kitchen string or a couple of chives. Brush a large baking dish with melted butter, then brush each bag with melted butter and sprinkle with a little cheese. Bake for 10–15 minutes, or until the bags are heated and golden.

PESTO CHICKEN PASTA

Preparation time: 20 minutes
Total cooking time: 20 minutes
Serves 4

250 g (8 oz) fusilli or penne
1 small barbecued chicken
1 cup (125 g/4 oz) walnuts
4 bacon rashers
250 g (8 oz) cherry tomatoes, halved
60 g (2 oz) pitted and sliced olives
½ cup (125 g/4 oz) bottled pesto sauce
½ cup (30 g/1 oz) finely shredded fresh
  basil
shavings of Parmesan, for serving

1 Cook the pasta in a large pan of rapidly boiling salted water until al dente. Drain.
2 While the pasta is cooking, discard the skin of the chicken. Remove the meat from the chicken, cut or shred it into bite-sized pieces and put in a large bowl.
3 Toast the walnuts for 2–3 minutes under a hot grill, allow to cool and then chop roughly.
4 Remove the rind from the bacon rashers and grill the bacon for 3–4 minutes, or until crisp. Allow to cool and then chop into small pieces. Add the nuts, bacon, cherry tomatoes and olives to the chicken.
5 Add the pasta to the chicken mixture, along with the pesto sauce and the fresh basil. Toss until thoroughly mixed. Serve at room temperature, with Parmesan shavings.

CHICKEN OMELETTE WITH COCONUT GRAVY

Preparation time: 20 minutes
Total cooking time: 25 minutes
Serves 4

½ barbecued chicken
1 large tomato, finely chopped
1 tablespoon chopped fresh dill
8 eggs
2 spring onions, chopped

Coconut Gravy
1⅔ cups (410 ml/13 fl oz) coconut milk
½ teaspoon ground turmeric
2 cm (¾ inch) piece fresh ginger, grated
1 cinnamon stick
1 tablespoon lemon juice

1 Remove the bones from the chicken and shred the meat. Combine the chicken meat, tomato and dill in a bowl. Whisk the eggs and spring onion together in a large jug.
2 Cook a quarter of the egg mixture in a lightly greased 25 cm (10 inch) nonstick frying pan. When the omelette is cooked, place a quarter of the chicken mixture in the centre, and fold in the 4 edges to form a parcel. Carefully transfer the omelette to a plate and repeat with remaining mixture. Serve with Coconut Gravy.
3 To make Coconut Gravy: Place all the ingredients in a small pan and simmer for 15 minutes, or until the gravy thickens slightly.

CHICKEN CUTLETS WITH CORN RELISH

Preparation time: 20 minutes
Total cooking time: 25 minutes
Serves 4

8 chicken thigh cutlets, skin on (1 kg)
1 tablespoon olive oil
1 small clove garlic, crushed
¼ teaspoon ground turmeric
½ teaspoon salt

Corn Relish
1 cup (200 g/6½ oz) frozen corn kernels
1 tablespoon olive oil
1 red chilli, seeded and chopped
1 small green capsicum, finely chopped
1 onion, finely chopped
⅓ cup (80 ml/2¾ fl oz) white vinegar
¼ cup (60 g/2 oz) sugar
1 teaspoon wholegrain mustard
3 teaspoons cornflour
1 teaspoon paprika
1 teaspoon finely chopped fresh coriander leaves
1 tablespoon olive oil, extra

1 Preheat a barbecue grill or flatplate to high. Trim the chicken of excess fat and sinew. Prick the skin of the chicken cutlets with the point of a knife. Place the cutlets in a large frying pan of boiling water. Reduce the heat and simmer for 5 minutes. Remove from the pan, then drain and allow to cool.

2 Place the olive oil, garlic, turmeric and salt in a bowl and whisk to combine. Rub the mixture over the skin side of the chicken cutlets. Set aside.
3 To make the corn relish, cook the corn in a pan of boiling water for 2–3 minutes, or until tender, then drain. Heat the oil in a pan. Add the chilli, capsicum and onion. Cook over medium heat until tender. Add the corn, vinegar, sugar and mustard, and cook, stirring, for a further 5 minutes. Mix the cornflour with ½ cup (125 ml/4 fl oz) water. Pour into the corn mixture. Bring to the boil, then reduce the heat and stir until thickened. Stir in the paprika, coriander and extra oil. Remove from the heat and cool.
4 Lightly grease the hot barbecue grill or flatplate. Cook the cutlets, skin-side up for 2 minutes, then turn and cook for 4 minutes. Continue cooking for another 5–10 minutes, turning frequently, until the chicken is well browned and cooked through. Serve with the corn relish.

BAKED CHICKEN AND LEEK RISOTTO

Preparation time: 10 minutes
Total cooking time: 40 minutes
Serves 4–6

60 g (2 oz) butter
1 leek, thinly sliced
2 chicken breast fillets, cut into 2 cm (¾ inch) cubes
2 cups (440 g/14 oz) arborio rice
¼ cup (60 ml/2 fl oz) white wine
1.25 litres (40 fl oz) chicken stock
⅓ cup (35 g/1¼ oz) freshly grated Parmesan cheese, plus extra, to garnish
2 tablespoons thyme, plus extra, to garnish

1 Preheat the oven to slow 150°C (300°F/Gas 2) and place a 5 litre (160 fl oz) ovenproof dish with a lid in the oven to warm. Heat the butter in a saucepan over medium heat, add the leek and cook for 2 minutes, or until softened but not browned.
2 Add the chicken and cook, stirring, for 2–3 minutes, or until it colours. Add the rice and stir so that it is well coated with butter. Cook for 1 minute.
3 Add the wine and stock and bring to the boil. Pour the mixture into the warm ovenproof dish and cover. Place in the oven and cook for 30 minutes, stirring halfway through. Remove from the oven and stir through the Parmesan and thyme leaves. Season with salt and freshly ground black pepper. Sprinkle with extra thyme and Parmesan and serve.

CHICKEN KAPITAN

Preparation time: 35 minutes
Total cooking time: 30 minutes
Serves 4–6

30 g (1 oz) small dried shrimp
4 tablespoons oil
4–8 red chillies, seeded and finely chopped
4 cloves garlic, finely chopped
3 stems lemon grass (white part only), finely chopped
2 teaspoons ground turmeric
10 candlenuts
2 large onions, chopped
¼ teaspoon salt
500 g (1 lb) chicken thigh fillets, chopped
1 cup (250 ml/8 fl oz) coconut milk
1 cup (250 ml/8 fl oz) water
½ cup (125 ml/4 fl oz) coconut cream
2 tablespoons lime juice

1 Put the shrimp in a clean frying pan and dry-fry over low heat, shaking the pan regularly, for 3 minutes, or until the shrimp are dark orange and are giving off a strong aroma. Transfer the shrimp to a mortar and pestle and pound until finely ground. Alternatively, process in a food processor. Set aside.
2 Place half the oil with the chilli, garlic, lemon grass, turmeric and candlenuts in a food processor and process in short bursts until very finely chopped, regularly scraping down the sides of the bowl with a rubber spatula.

3 Heat the remaining oil in a wok or frying pan; add the onion and salt and cook over low heat for 8 minutes, or until golden, stirring regularly. Take care not to let the onion burn. Add the spice mixture and nearly all the ground shrimp meat, setting a little aside to use as a garnish. Stir for 5 minutes. If the mixture begins to stick to the bottom of the pan, add 2 tablespoons coconut milk to the mixture. It is important to cook the mixture thoroughly as it is this which develops the flavours.
4 Add the chicken to the wok and stir well. Cook for 5 minutes, or until the chicken begins to brown. Stir in the remaining coconut milk and water, and bring to the boil. Reduce the heat and simmer for 7 minutes, or until the chicken is cooked and the sauce is thick. Add the coconut cream and bring the mixture back to the boil, stirring constantly. Add the lime juice and serve immediately, sprinkled lightly with the reserved ground shrimp meat. Serve with steamed rice.

RAVIOLI WITH CHICKEN FILLING

Preparation time: 1 hour +
    30 minutes standing
Total cooking time: 35 minutes
Serves 4

Pasta
2 cups (250 g/8 oz) plain flour
3 eggs
1 tablespoon olive oil
1 egg yolk, extra

Filling
125 g (4 oz) chicken mince
75 g (2½ oz) ricotta or cottage cheese
60 g (2 oz) chicken livers, trimmed and
    chopped
30 g (1 oz) prosciutto, chopped
1 slice salami, chopped
2 tablespoons freshly grated Parmesan
1 egg, beaten
1 tablespoon chopped fresh parsley
1 clove garlic, crushed
¼ teaspoon mixed spice

Tomato sauce
2 tablespoons olive oil
1 onion, finely chopped
2 cloves garlic, crushed
2 x 425 g (14 oz) cans tomatoes, crushed
3 tablespoons chopped fresh basil
½ teaspoon mixed dried herbs
herb sprigs, optional

1 To make the pasta, sift the flour and a pinch of salt into a large bowl and make a well in the centre. Whisk together the eggs, oil and 1 tablespoon of water, add gradually to the flour and combine until the mixture forms a ball. Knead on a floured surface for 5 minutes, or until smooth and elastic. Transfer to an oiled bowl, cover with plastic wrap and set aside for 30 minutes.

2 To make the filling, mix all the filling ingredients with salt and pepper, to taste, in a food processor until finely chopped.
3 To make the tomato sauce, heat the oil in a pan, add the onion and garlic and stir over low heat until the onion is tender. Increase the heat, add the tomato, basil, herbs and salt and pepper, to taste. Bring to the boil, reduce the heat and simmer for 15 minutes. Remove from the heat.
4 Roll out half the pasta dough until 1 mm (½ 5 inch) thick. Cut with a knife or fluted pastry wheel into 10 cm (4 inch) wide strips. Place teaspoons of filling at 5 cm (2 inch) intervals down one side of each strip. Whisk the extra egg yolk with 3 tablespoons of water and brush along one side of the dough and between the filling. Fold the dough over the filling to meet the other side. Repeat with remaining filling and dough. Press the edges of the dough together firmly to seal. Cut between the mounds with a knife or a fluted pastry wheel. Cook, in batches, in a large pan of rapidly boiling salted water for 10 minutes. Reheat the sauce in a large pan. Add the ravioli and stir until heated through. Garnish and serve.

CHICKEN MINCE WITH HERBS AND SPICES

Preparation time: 30 minutes
Total cooking time: 20 minutes
Serves 4–6

¼ cup (55 g/1¾ oz) short-grain rice
1 kg (2 lb) chicken thigh fillets
2 tablespoons peanut oil
4 cloves garlic, crushed
2 tablespoons grated fresh galangal
2 small red chillies
4 spring onions, finely chopped
¼ cup (60 ml/2 fl oz) fish sauce
1 tablespoon shrimp paste
3 tablespoons chopped fresh Vietnamese
    mint
2 tablespoons chopped fresh basil
4 tablespoons lime juice

1 Preheat the oven to moderate 180°C (350°F/Gas 4). Spread the rice on an oven tray and roast it for 15 minutes or until golden. Cool slightly, then transfer the rice to a food processor and process until finely ground. Set aside.
2 Place the chicken fillets in a food processor and process until finely minced.
3 Heat the oil in a wok or frying pan; add the garlic, galangal, chilli and spring onion and cook over medium heat for 3 minutes. Add the minced chicken to the wok and stir for 5 minutes, or until the mince is browned, breaking up any large lumps with a wooden spoon. Stir in the fish sauce and shrimp paste and bring to the boil, then reduce the heat and simmer for 5 minutes.
4 Remove the wok from the heat, stir in the rice, mint, basil and lime juice, and mix to combine.

KUNG PAO CHICKEN

Preparation time: 15 minutes +
   30 minutes marinating
Total cooking time: 15 minutes
Serves 4

1 egg white
2 teaspoons cornflour
½ teaspoon sesame oil
2 teaspoons Chinese rice wine
1½ tablespoons soy sauce
600 g (1¼ lb) chicken thigh fillets, cut into
   2 cm (¾ inch) cubes
¼ cup (60 ml/2 fl oz) chicken stock
2 teaspoons Chinese black vinegar
1 teaspoon soft brown sugar
2 tablespoons vegetable oil
3 long dried red chillies, cut in half
   lengthways
3 cloves garlic, finely chopped
2 teaspoons finely grated fresh ginger
2 spring onions, thinly sliced on the diagonal
⅓ cup (50 g/1¾ oz) shelled unsalted raw
   peanuts, roughly crushed

1 Lightly whisk together the egg white,
cornflour, sesame oil, Chinese rice wine
and 2 teaspoons of the soy sauce in a
large non-metallic bowl. Add the chicken
and coat it in the marinade. Cover with
plastic wrap and marinate in the fridge for
30 minutes.
2 To make the stir-fry sauce, combine the
stock, vinegar, sugar and the remaining
soy sauce in a small jug or bowl.
3 Heat a wok over high heat, add
1 tablespoon of the vegetable oil and swirl
to coat the wok. Stir-fry the chicken in
batches for 3 minutes, or until browned.
Remove from the wok.
4 Heat the remaining oil in the wok, then
add the chilli and cook for 15 seconds, or
until it starts to change colour. Add the
garlic, ginger, spring onion and peanuts,
and stir-fry for 1 minute. Return the
chicken to the wok, along with the stir-fry
sauce, and stir-fry for 3 minutes, or until
heated through and the sauce thickens
slightly. Serve immediately.

THAI GREEN CHICKEN CURRY
(GAENG KHIAO WANG GAI)

Preparation time: 15 minutes
Total cooking time: 30 minutes
Serves 4

Curry paste
1 tablespoon shrimp paste
1 teaspoon coriander seeds, toasted
½ teaspoon cumin seeds, toasted
¼ teaspoon white peppercorns
5 fresh coriander roots
3 tablespoons chopped fresh galangal
10 long fresh green chillies, chopped
1 stem lemon grass, white part only,
   chopped
6 red Asian shallots
3 cloves garlic
1 teaspoon grated kaffir lime or lime rind
2 tablespoons peanut oil

1 cup (250 ml/8 fl oz) coconut cream
500 g (1 lb) chicken thigh fillets, thinly
   sliced
125 g (4 oz) snake beans, sliced
2 cups (500 ml/16 fl oz) coconut milk
150 g (5 oz) broccoli, cut into small florets
1 tablespoon grated palm sugar
2–3 tablespoons fish sauce
5 tablespoons fresh coriander leaves,
   plus extra, to garnish

1 To make the curry paste, preheat the grill
to high, wrap the shrimp paste in foil, and
put under the hot grill for 5 minutes. Cool,
remove the foil, then put in a food
processor.
2 Put the coriander seeds, cumin seeds
and peppercorns in a mortar and pestle
and grind into a fine powder. Transfer to
the food processor with ¼ teaspoon salt
and the remaining paste ingredients.
Blend until smooth.
3 Put the coconut cream in a wok over
high heat, bring to the boil, then simmer
for 10 minutes, or until the oil starts to
separate from the cream.
4 Reduce the heat to medium. Stir in half
the curry paste and cook for 2–3 minutes,
or until fragrant. Add the chicken and
cook for 3–4 minutes. Stir in the beans,
coconut milk and broccoli. Bring to the
boil, then reduce the heat and simmer for
4–5 minutes, or until cooked. Stir in the
sugar, fish sauce and coriander leaves.
Garnish with coriander and serve with
rice.

NOTE: Store the remainder of the curry
paste in an airtight container in the fridge
for up to 2 weeks.

CREAMY CHICKEN, SAGE AND TARRAGON PIE

Preparation time: 25 minutes
Total cooking time: 1 hour 10 minutes
Serves 4–6

1.5 kg (3 lb) chicken thigh fillets
2 tablespoons olive oil
2 slices bacon, finely chopped
1 onion, roughly chopped
4 fresh sage leaves, chopped
1 tablespoon chopped fresh tarragon
45 g (1½ oz) butter, melted
2 tablespoons plain flour
½ cup (125 ml/4 fl oz) milk
220 g (7 oz) can creamed corn
2 sheets ready-rolled puff pastry
1 egg, lightly beaten

1 Preheat the oven to hot 210°C (415°F/Gas 6–7). Brush a 23 cm (9 inch) pie dish with butter. Cut the chicken into bite-sized pieces. Heat the oil in a large frying pan. Add the chicken, bacon and onion, and cook over medium heat for 5 minutes, or until browned. Add the sage, tarragon, 1 cup (250 ml/8 fl oz) water, salt and pepper. Bring to the boil, then reduce the heat and simmer, covered, for 25 minutes, or until the chicken is tender. Drain, reserving the juices.
2 Melt the butter in a heavy-based pan. Add the flour and stir over low heat for 1 minute. Remove from the heat and gradually add the milk and reserved juice, stirring until smooth. Return to the heat and stir over medium heat until thickenened. Stir in the chicken mixture and corn. Spoon into the dish.
3 Brush a sheet of pastry with egg and top with a second sheet. Brush the rim of the pie dish with egg and place the pastry over the filling. Trim any excess.
4 Decorate the pie with pastry. Brush with egg and make a few slits in the top. Bake for 15 minutes, then reduce the heat to 180°C (350°F/Gas 4) and bake for 10–15 minutes, or until crisp and golden. Leave for 5 minutes.

CHICKEN IN MUSHROOM AND PAPRIKA SAUCE

Preparation time: 25 minutes
Total cooking time: 20 minutes
Serves 4

4 chicken breast fillets
¼ cup (30 g/1 oz) plain flour
30 g (1 oz) butter
1 tablespoon oil
1 onion, finely chopped
2 cloves garlic, crushed
250 g (8 oz) button mushrooms, thinly sliced
1 tablespoon sweet paprika
1 tablespoon tomato paste
½ cup (125 ml/4 fl oz) chicken stock
⅓ cup (80 g/2¾ oz) sour cream
2 tablespoons finely chopped fresh parsley

1 Trim the chicken of excess fat and sinew, and cut into bite-sized pieces. Coat the chicken pieces with the flour by shaking together in a plastic bag. Heat half the butter and oil in a large frying pan, add the chicken in small batches and cook over medium heat for 5 minutes, or until browned. Drain on paper towels.
2 Heat the remaining butter and oil in the same pan. Add the onion and garlic and cook over medium heat for 2 minutes, or until the onion has softened. Add the mushrooms and cook for 1–2 minutes, or until tender. Remove from the heat. Add the paprika and cooked chicken, and stir to combine.
3 Combine the tomato paste with the stock in a small bowl. Add to the pan and stir until well combined with the chicken mixture. Season to taste. Return to the heat and bring to the boil. Reduce the heat and simmer, covered, for 5 minutes, or until the chicken is cooked through. Stir in the sour cream and warm through, but do not boil. Serve sprinkled with the parsley.

FRIED CHICKEN PIECES

Preparation time: 10 minutes
Total cooking time: 30 minutes
Serves 4

1½ kg (3 lb) chicken pieces
2 teaspoons salt
1 teaspoon fresh ground black pepper
1 teaspoon five spice powder
oil, for deep-frying
1 tablespoon fish sauce
1 tablespoon lime juice
red chopped chilli, to serve

1 Place the chicken pieces in a medium pan, cover with cold water and bring to the boil. Skim any scum from the surface. Add the salt, pepper and five spice powder and simmer for 15 minutes or until the chicken is tender. Drain the chicken and pat it dry with paper towels.
2 Heat the oil in a deep pan; add the chicken pieces, about 3 at a time, and fry until golden and very crisp. Drain on paper towels.
3 Place the chicken on a serving plate, and sprinkle over the fish sauce, lime juice and chilli.

CHICKEN WITH FORTY CLOVES OF GARLIC

Preparation time: 20 minutes
Total cooking time: 1 hour 45 minutes
Serves 4

10 g (¼ oz) butter
1 tablespoon olive oil
1 large (No. 20) free-range chicken
40 cloves garlic, unpeeled (see Note)
2 tablespoons chopped fresh rosemary
2 sprigs fresh thyme
275 ml (9 fl oz) dry white wine
150 ml (5 fl oz) chicken stock
225 g (7 oz) plain flour

1 Preheat the oven to 180°C (350°F/Gas 4). You will need a 4.5 litre lidded casserole dish.
2 Melt the butter and oil in the casserole and brown the chicken over medium heat until golden all over. Remove the chicken and add the garlic cloves, rosemary and thyme and cook together for 1 minute. Return the chicken to the dish and add the wine and chicken stock. Bring to a simmer, basting the chicken with the sauce.
3 Place the flour in a bowl and add up to 150 ml (5 fl oz) water to form a firm pliable paste. Divide into four and roll into cylinder shapes. Place around the rim of the casserole. Replace the lid, pressing down well to form a seal. Bake for 1¼ hours. Remove the lid by cracking the paste. Return the chicken to the oven to brown for 15 minutes, then transfer to a plate. Reduce the juices to 1 cup (250 ml/ 8 fl oz) over medium heat. Carve the chicken, pierce the garlic skins and squeeze the garlic flesh onto the chicken. Serve with the jus.

NOTE: Don't be alarmed by the amount of garlic in this recipe. The garlic becomes soft and creamy when cooked in this way.

TERIYAKI CHICKEN

Preparation time: 15 minutes
Total cooking time: 40 minutes
Serves 6

½ cup (125 ml/4 fl oz) Japanese soy sauce
2 tablespoons mirin
1 tablespoon sugar
2 tablespoons oil
12 chicken drumsticks

1 Place the soy sauce, mirin and sugar in a small pan and stir over low heat until the sugar dissolves. Bring to the boil, reduce the heat and simmer, uncovered, for 2 minutes.
2 Heat the oil in a large heavy-based frying pan; add the chicken drumsticks in batches and cook over high heat until browned on both sides.
3 Return all the chicken to the pan, add the sauce, cover and cook for 20 minutes or until the chicken is tender. Serve with rice.

CHICKEN WITH PRESERVED LEMON AND OLIVES

Preparation time: 10 minutes
Total cooking time: 1 hour
Serves 4

¼ cup (60 ml/2¾ fl oz) olive oil
1.6 kg (3¼ lb) free-range chicken
1 onion, chopped
2 cloves garlic, chopped
2½ cups (600 ml/20 fl oz) chicken stock
½ teaspoon ground ginger
1½ teaspoons ground cinnamon
pinch saffron threads
100 g (3½ oz) green olives
¼ preserved lemon, pulp removed, rind washed and cut into slivers
2 bay leaves
2 chicken livers
3 tablespoons chopped fresh coriander leaves

1 Preheat the oven to moderate 180°C (350°F/Gas 4). Heat 2 tablespoons oil in a large frying pan, add the chicken and brown on all sides. Place in a deep baking dish.
2 Heat the remaining oil, add the onion and garlic and cook over medium heat for 3–4 minutes, or until softened. Add the stock, ginger, cinnamon, saffron, olives, lemon and bay leaves and pour around the chicken. Bake for 45 minutes, adding a little more water or stock if the sauce gets too dry.
3 Remove the chicken from the dish, cover with foil and leave to rest. Pour the contents of the baking dish into a frying pan, add the chicken livers and mash into the sauce as they cook. Cook for 5–6 minutes, or until the sauce has reduced and thickened. Add the chopped coriander. Cut the chicken into four pieces and serve with the sauce.

CRISP-SKINNED CHICKEN

Preparation time: 20 minutes +
20 minutes refrigeration
Total cooking time: 25 minutes
Serves 4

1 x 1.3 kg (2¾ lb) chicken
1 tablespoon honey
1 star anise
1 strip dried mandarin or tangerine peel
1 teaspoon salt
oil, for deep-frying
2 lemons, cut into wedges

Five Spice Salt
2 tablespoons salt
1 teaspoon white peppercorns
½ teaspoon five spice powder
½ teaspoon ground white pepper

1 Wash the chicken in cold water. Place the chicken in a large pan and cover with cold water. Add the honey, star anise, peel and salt and bring to the boil. Reduce heat to low and simmer for 15 minutes. Turn off the heat and leave the chicken, covered, for a further 15 minutes. Transfer chicken to a plate and cool.
2 Cut the chicken in half lengthways. Place it on paper towels, uncovered, in the refrigerator for 20 minutes.
3 Heat the oil in a wok. It is hot enough to use when a piece of bread turns brown in it in 30 seconds. Very gently lower in half the chicken, skin-side-down. Cook for 6 minutes, turn and cook another 6 minutes, making sure all the skin comes in contact with the oil. Drain on paper towels. Repeat with the second chicken half.
4 To make Five Spice Salt: Place the salt and peppercorns in a small pan and dry-fry until the mixture smells fragrant and the salt is slightly browned. Crush the mixture with a mortar and pestle. Mix with the five spice powder and white pepper and place in a tiny, shallow dish.
5 Chop the chicken Chinese-style. Sprinkle over the Five Spice Salt and serve with lemon wedges.

GARLIC CHICKEN

Preparation time: 20 minutes
Total cooking time: 35 minutes
Serves 6

1 kg (2 lb) chicken thigh fillets
1 tablespoon paprika
2 tablespoons olive oil
8 cloves garlic, unpeeled
¼ cup (60 ml/2 fl oz) brandy
½ cup (125 ml/4 fl oz) chicken stock
1 bay leaf
2 tablespoons chopped fresh flat-leaf parsley

1 Trim any excess fat from the chicken and cut the thighs into thirds. Combine the paprika with some salt and pepper in a bowl, add the chicken and toss to coat.
2 Heat half the oil in a large frying pan over high heat and cook the garlic for 1–2 minutes, until brown. Remove from the pan. Cook the chicken in batches for 5 minutes each batch, or until brown. Return all the chicken to the pan, add the brandy, boil for 30 seconds, then add the stock and bay leaf. Reduce the heat, cover and simmer over low heat for 10 minutes.
3 Meanwhile, place the garlic pulp in a mortar and pestle or small bowl. Add the parsley and pound or mix with a fork to form a paste. Stir into the chicken, cover and cook for 10 minutes, or until tender. Serve hot.

CHICKEN AND WATERCRESS STRUDEL

Preparation time: 30 minutes
Total cooking time: 50 minutes
Serves 6

¾ cup (60 g/2 oz) fresh white breadcrumbs
1–2 teaspoons sesame seeds
1 bunch (60 g/2 oz) watercress
4 chicken breast fillets
25 g (¾ oz) butter
3 tablespoons Dijon mustard
1 cup (250 ml/8 fl oz) thick cream
15 sheets filo pastry
100 g (3½ oz) butter, melted

1 Preheat the oven to moderately hot 190°C (375°F/Gas 5) and bake the breadcrumbs and sesame seeds, on separate trays, until golden. Steam the watercress for 3–5 minutes, or until just wilted, and squeeze out any water.
2 Slice the chicken into thin strips. Heat the butter in a pan and stir-fry the chicken until just cooked. Remove from the pan and season to taste. Stir the mustard and cream into the pan and simmer gently until reduced to about ½ cup (125 ml/4 fl oz). Remove from the heat and stir in the chicken and watercress.
3 Brush a sheet of filo with melted butter and sprinkle with toasted breadcrumbs. Lay another filo sheet on top, brush with butter and sprinkle with breadcrumbs. Repeat with the remaining filo and breadcrumbs and place on a baking tray.
4 Place the chicken filling along the centre of the filo pastry. Fold the sides over and roll into a parcel, with the join underneath. Brush with the remaining butter and sprinkle with the toasted sesame seeds. Bake for 30 minutes, or until golden. Cool slightly before serving.

BALTI CHICKEN

Preparation time: 10 minutes
Total cooking time: 50 minutes
Serves 4

1 kg (2 lb) chicken thigh fillets
2 tablespoons ghee or oil
2 cloves garlic, crushed
1 cinnamon stick
½ teaspoon cardamom seeds
1 tablespoon garam masala
1 teaspoon sesame seeds
1 teaspoon poppy seeds
½ teaspoon fennel seeds
2 medium onions, finely sliced
3 tablespoons Balti Curry Paste
   (see page 725)
1 cup (250 ml/8 fl oz) chicken stock
1 cup (250 ml/8 fl oz) cream
1 tablespoon fresh coriander leaves

1 Cut the chicken into 3 cm (1¼ inch) cubes.
2 Heat the ghee in a balti pan or wok; stir-fry the garlic, cinnamon stick, cardamom seeds and garam masala over medium heat for 1 minute. Add the sesame, poppy and fennel seeds, and fry for a further 30 seconds. Reduce the heat, add the onion and cook for 10 minutes or until the onion is soft and golden brown.
3 Add the masala paste and chicken and cook, stirring occasionally, for 5 minutes.
4 Reduce the heat and add the stock. Cover and simmer for 20 minutes. Add the cream and cook for a further 10 minutes, stirring occasionally.
5 Stir in the coriander leaves, and season with salt and pepper to taste. Serve with roti or naan bread.

ROAST DUCK WITH OLIVES

Preparation time: 30 minutes
Total cooking time: 1 hour 30 minutes
Serves 4

Sauce
1 tablespoon olive oil
1 onion, chopped
1 garlic clove, crushed
2 ripe Roma tomatoes, peeled and
   chopped
1 cup (250 ml/8 fl oz) Riesling
2 teaspoons fresh thyme leaves
1 bay leaf
24 Niçoise olives, pitted

Stuffing
⅓ cup (60 g/2 oz) medium-grain rice,
   cooked
1 garlic clove, crushed
100 g (4 oz) frozen chopped spinach,
   defrosted
2 duck's livers (about 100 g/3½ oz),
   chopped
1 egg, lightly beaten
1 teaspoon fresh thyme leaves
1.8 kg (4 lb) duck
2 bay leaves

1 Preheat the oven to moderately hot 200°C (400°F/Gas 6). For the sauce, heat the oil in a frying pan, add the onion and cook for 5 minutes, or until transparent. Add the garlic, tomato, wine, herbs and some seasoning. Cook for 5 minutes, then add the olives before removing from the heat.

2 For the stuffing, thoroughly mix all the ingredients in a bowl and season well. Before stuffing the duck, rinse out the cavity with cold water and pat dry inside and out with paper towels. Put the bay leaves in the cavity, then spoon in the stuffing.
3 Tuck the wings under the duck, then close the flaps of fat over the parson's nose and secure with a skewer or toothpick. Place in a deep baking dish and rub 1 teaspoon salt into the skin. Prick the skin all over with a skewer.
4 Roast on the top shelf for 35–40 minutes, then carefully pour off the excess fat. Roast for another 35–40 minutes. To check that the duck is cooked, gently pull away one leg from the side. The flesh should be pale brown with no blood in the juices. Remove, then carve, serving a spoonful of the stuffing next to the duck and topping with the sauce.

SAFFRON YOGHURT CHICKEN

Preparation time: 30 minutes
Total cooking time: 1 hour 15 minutes
Serves 4–6

1 x 1.5 kg (3 lb) chicken
½ teaspoon saffron threads
2 tablespoons hot milk
3 cloves garlic, crushed
3 cm (1¼ inch) piece fresh ginger, finely grated
½ teaspoon ground turmeric
½ teaspoon ground cumin
¼ teaspoon ground cardamom
¼ teaspoon ground cloves
¼ teaspoon ground cinnamon
¼ teaspoon ground mace
4 tablespoons yoghurt
1 tablespoon ghee or oil

1 Preheat the oven to moderate 180°C (350°F/Gas 4).
2 Wash the chicken and pat dry. Remove any excess fat from inside the cavity.
3 Soak the saffron threads in the hot milk for 10 minutes, then squeeze the saffron to release the flavour and colour into the milk.
4 Transfer the saffron milk to a larger bowl; add the remaining ingredients and mix to combine.
5 Carefully lift the skin on the breast side of the chicken by working your fingers between the skin and the flesh. Pat half the spice mixture over the flesh. Rub the remaining spice mixture over the skin.
6 Place the chicken on a wire rack in a baking dish. Pour 1 cup (250 ml/8 fl oz) water into the dish; this will keep the chicken moist while it cooks. Roast the chicken for 1¼ hours or until browned and tender. Transfer the chicken to a serving dish, cover loosely with foil and allow to stand for 5 minutes before carving.

ARROZ CON POLLO (RICE WITH CHICKEN)

Preparation time: 25 minutes
Total cooking time: 1 hour 15 minutes
Serves 6

2 kg (4 lb) whole chicken or chicken pieces
2 tablespoons olive oil
100 g (3½ oz) chorizo sausage, finely diced
1 large onion, finely chopped
1 green capsicum (pepper), diced
3 teaspoons sweet paprika
1 long red chilli, seeded and finely chopped
3 garlic cloves, crushed
2 cups (440 g/14 oz) paella rice
pinch of saffron threads
1 litre (32 fl oz) hot chicken stock
4 very ripe tomatoes, peeled, seeded and chopped
2½ tablespoons tomato paste (purée)
⅓ cup (80 ml/2¾ fl oz) sherry
⅔ cup (100 g/3½ oz) frozen peas
3 tablespoons finely chopped flat-leaf (Italian) parsley
⅓ cup (55 g/2 oz) stuffed green olives (optional)

1 Cut the chicken into eight pieces, pat dry with paper towels, then season with salt and pepper. Heat a little oil in the base of a large heavy-based saucepan or flameproof casserole dish, then cook the chicken in batches over medium heat for about 10 minutes, or until well browned all over. Remove from the pan and set aside

2 Add the chorizo to the pan and cook, stirring, for 1 minute, then remove with a slotted spoon and add to the chicken. Drain off any excess fat, if necessary, leaving 2 tablespoons in the pan. Add the onion and capsicum and cook for 5 minutes, or until softened and starting to brown. Add the paprika, chilli and garlic and stir for a further minute, or until fragrant. Add the rice and saffron and stir to coat well. Stir in the hot chicken stock until well combined, then add the tomatoes, tomato paste and sherry.
3 Return the chicken and chorizo to the pan, stirring well to combine. Allow the liquid to come to the boil, then reduce the heat to low and cover. Simmer, stirring occasionally, for about 25 minutes, or until most of the liquid has been absorbed, then stir in the peas, re-cover and cook for a further 10 minutes, or until the rice is tender and the chicken is cooked through—the liquid should be almost completely absorbed. Stir in the parsley and olives, if desired, and season to taste with salt and freshly ground black pepper. Serve immediately.

CHICKEN WITH MUSHROOMS

Preparation time: 15 minutes +
   30 minutes marinating + 20 minutes
   soaking + 10 minutes cooling
Total cooking time: 25 minutes
Serves 4–6

750 g (1½ lb) chicken breast fillets, cut
   into bite-sized pieces
3 spring onions, 1 finely chopped, the
   others cut into 2 cm (¾ inch) lengths
1 tablespoon very finely chopped fresh
   ginger
1 tablespoon finely chopped garlic
1½ tablespoons light soy sauce
1 tablespoon oyster sauce
1 tablespoon Chinese rice wine
2 teaspoons cornflour
¼ teaspoon sugar
2–3 drops of sesame oil
pinch of white pepper
5 dried shiitake mushrooms
¼ cup (40 g/1¼ oz) water chestnuts, thinly
   sliced into discs
spring onion, extra, thinly sliced on the
   diagonal, to garnish

1 Put the chicken, finely chopped spring
onion, ginger, garlic, soy sauce, oyster
sauce, rice wine, cornflour, sugar,
sesame oil and white pepper in a bowl
and mix well with your hands until the
mixture is evenly combined. Refrigerate
for 30 minutes.

2 Meanwhile, soak the dried mushrooms
in hot water for 20 minutes, or until soft.
Squeeze dry, discard the stalks and cut
the caps into quarters.
3 Add the mushrooms, water chestnuts
and spring onion lengths to the chicken
mixture, mix well, then put in a 1 litre
(32 fl oz) ceramic bowl that will fit in a
large steamer. Cover with a round of foil
or baking paper. Place the bowl in the
steamer basket, cover and steam over a
wok of simmering water for 20–25 minutes,
or until the chicken is just cooked
through. If you like, you can stir the
chicken halfway through cooking to check
that it is cooking evenly.
4 Remove the bowl from the steamer and
allow to cool for 10 minutes. Hold a
serving platter on top of the bowl and
invert the bowl so that the bowl is upside-
down. Carefully remove the bowl. Garnish
with finely sliced spring onion and serve
immediately with boiled rice or as part of
an Asian banquet.

CHICKEN WITH WALNUTS AND STRAW MUSHROOMS

Preparation time: 20 minutes
Total cooking time: 15 minutes
Serves 4

375 g (12 oz) chicken breast fillets or
   tenderloins, cut into thin strips
½ teaspoon five-spice powder
2 teaspoons cornflour
2 tablespoons soy sauce
2 tablespoons oyster sauce
2 teaspoons soft brown sugar
1 teaspoon sesame oil
oil, for cooking
75 g (2½ oz) walnuts
6 spring onions, sliced
150 g (5 oz) snake beans or green beans,
   chopped
425 g (14 oz) can straw mushrooms, rinsed
227 g (7 oz) can sliced bamboo shoots,
   drained and rinsed

1 Dry the chicken strips with paper towels
and sprinkle with the five-spice powder.
Mix the cornflour with the soy sauce in a
bowl until smooth. Add ½ cup (125 ml/
4 fl oz) water along with the oyster sauce,
brown sugar and sesame oil.
2 Heat a wok over high heat, add
1 tablespoon of the oil and swirl it around
to coat the side. Stir-fry the walnuts for
30 seconds, or until lightly browned.
Drain on paper towels.
3 Reheat the wok and add 1 tablespoon of
the oil. Stir-fry the chicken in batches
over high heat for 2–3 minutes, or until
just cooked through. Remove all the
chicken from the wok.
4 Add the spring onion, snake beans,
straw mushrooms and bamboo shoots to
the wok, and stir-fry for 2 minutes.
Remove from the wok. Add the soy sauce
mixture to the wok and heat for 1 minute,
or until slightly thickened. Return the
chicken and vegetables to the wok and
toss to coat with the sauce. Season well.
Serve at once, sprinkled with the walnuts.

LOW-FAT CHICKEN PIES

Preparation time: 50 minutes +
30 minutes refrigeration
Total cooking time: 1 hour
Serves 4

300 g (10 oz) chicken breast fillets
1 bay leaf
2 cups (500 ml/16 fl oz) chicken stock
2 large potatoes, chopped
250 g (8 oz) orange sweet potato, chopped
2 celery sticks, chopped
2 carrots, chopped
1 onion, chopped
1 parsnip, chopped
1 clove garlic, crushed
1 tablespoon cornflour
1 cup (250 ml/8 fl oz) skim milk
1 cup (155 g/5 oz) frozen peas, thawed
1 tablespoon chopped fresh chives
1 tablespoon chopped fresh parsley
1½ cups (185 g/6 oz) self-raising flour
20 g (¾ oz) butter
⅓ cup (80 ml/2¾ fl oz) milk
1 egg, lightly beaten
½ teaspoon sesame seeds

1 Combine the chicken, bay leaf and stock in a large, deep non-stick frying pan and simmer over low heat for about 10 minutes, until the chicken is cooked through. Remove the chicken, set aside and, when cool, cut into small pieces. Add the chopped potato, orange sweet potato, celery and carrot to the pan and simmer, covered, for about 10 minutes, or until just tender. Remove the vegetables from the pan with a slotted spoon.
2 Add the onion, parsnip and garlic to the pan and simmer, uncovered, for about 10 minutes, or until very soft. Discard the bay leaf. Purée the mixture in a food processor until smooth.

3 Stir the cornflour into 2 tablespoons of the skim milk until it forms a smooth paste. Stir the cornflour mixture into the puréed mixture with the remaining milk and then return to the pan. Stir over low heat until the mixture boils and thickens. Preheat the oven to moderately hot 200°C (400°F/Gas 6).
4 Combine the puréed mixture with the remaining vegetables, chicken, chives and parsley. Season with salt and pepper. Spoon into four 1¾ cup (440 ml/14 fl oz) ovenproof dishes.
5 To make the pastry, sift the flour into a large bowl, rub in the butter with your fingertips, then make a well in the centre. Combine the milk with ⅓ cup (80 ml/2¾ fl oz) water and add enough to the dry ingredients to make a soft dough. Turn out onto a lightly floured surface and knead until just smooth. Cut the dough into four portions and roll each out so that it is l cm (½ inch) larger than the top of the dish. Brush the edge of the dough with some of the egg and fit it over the top of each dish, pressing the edge firmly to seal.
6 Brush the pastry lightly with beaten egg and sprinkle with the sesame seeds. Bake for about 30 minutes, or until the tops are golden and the filling is heated through.

CHICKEN IN TANGY LIME MARMALADE SAUCE

Preparation time: 25 minutes
Total cooking time: 20 minutes
Serves 4

500 g (1 lb) chicken thigh fillets, cut into strips
5 cm (2 inch) piece ginger, cut into paper-thin slices
4 spring onions, thinly sliced
oil, for cooking
1 red capsicum, thinly sliced
1 tablespoon mirin
1 tablespoon lime marmalade
2 teaspoons grated lime rind
2 tablespoons lime juice

1 Put the chicken, ginger, spring onion and some ground black pepper in a dish. Toss well to combine.
2 Heat a wok until very hot, add 1 tablespoon of the oil and swirl it around to coat the side. Stir-fry the chicken mixture in three batches over high heat for about 3 minutes, or until it is golden brown and cooked through. Reheat the wok in between each batch, adding more oil when necessary. Remove all the chicken from the wok and set aside.
3 Reheat the wok, add the capsicum and stir-fry for 30 seconds. Add the mirin, marmalade, lime rind and juice, and season with salt and freshly ground black pepper. Cover and steam for 1 minute. Add the chicken and cook, uncovered, for 2 minutes, or until heated through.

CHICKEN JAMBALAYA

Preparation time: 30 minutes +
   10 minutes standing
Total cooking time: 1 hour 5 minutes
Serves 4–6

1 teaspoon paprika
¾ teaspoon dried basil
¾ teaspoon dried thyme
¾ teaspoon garlic powder
¾ teaspoon onion powder
½ teaspoon ground white pepper
½ teaspoon dried oregano
¼ teaspoon cayenne pepper
500 g (1 lb) chicken thigh fillets, cut into
   4 pieces
2 tablespoons oil
250 g (8 oz) chorizo, cut into 1 cm (½ inch)
   slices
1 large onion, chopped
2 celery stalks, sliced
1 large green capsicum (pepper), cut into
   rough 2 cm (¾ inch) pieces
4 garlic cloves, crushed
2 teaspoons thyme
400 g (13 oz) tin chopped tomatoes
2 bay leaves
¼ teaspoon Tabasco sauce
1 cup (200 g/6½ oz) long-grain white rice
3½ cups (875 ml/28 fl oz) hot chicken
   stock
450 g (14 oz) raw prawns (shrimp), peeled
   and deveined, tails intact (optional)
5 spring onions (scallions), thinly sliced
3 tablespoons chopped parsley

1 Put the paprika, basil, thyme, garlic powder, onion powder, white pepper, oregano, cayenne, ¾ teaspoon salt and ½ teaspoon freshly ground black pepper in a bowl. Add the chicken thigh pieces and mix to coat the chicken well.

2 Heat the oil in a wide, heavy-based frying pan over medium heat and cook the chorizo for 5–6 minutes, or until lightly browned. Remove with a slotted spoon, leaving as much oil in the pan as possible. Add the chicken to the pan in batches and cook over medium heat for 6–8 minutes, or until lightly browned, adding a little more oil if necessary. Remove from the pan with a slotted spoon, leaving as much fat in the pan as possible.

3 Add the onion, celery, capsicum, garlic and thyme to the pan and cook over medium heat for 6–8 minutes, stirring often with a wooden spoon to lift any sediment from the base of the pan. When the vegetables begin to brown, add the tomato, bay leaves and Tabasco and simmer for 2–3 minutes.

4 Return the chorizo and chicken to the pan. Add the rice, stir briefly, then pour in the stock. Don't stir at this point. Reduce the heat and simmer, uncovered, for 25–30 minutes, or until all the liquid has been absorbed and the rice is tender. Remove from the heat and add the prawns, if using them. Cover and leave for 10 minutes, then fluff the rice with a fork, season well and stir in the spring onion and parsley.

CHICKEN WITH OYSTER SAUCE AND BASIL

Preparation time: 20 minutes
Total cooking time: 10 minutes
Serves 4

¼ cup (60 ml/2 fl oz) oyster sauce
2 tablespoons fish sauce
1 tablespoon grated palm sugar
1 tablespoon oil
2–3 cloves garlic, crushed
1 tablespoon grated fresh ginger
1–2 red chillies, seeded and finely
   chopped
4 spring onions, finely chopped
375 g (12 oz) chicken breast fillets, cut
   into thin strips
250 g (8 oz) broccoli, cut into florets
230 g (7½ oz) can water chestnuts,
   drained
230 g (7½ oz) can sliced bamboo shoots,
   rinsed
20 fresh basil leaves, shredded

1 Put ¼ cup (60 ml/2 fl oz) water in a small jug with the oyster sauce, fish sauce and palm sugar. Mix well.

2 Heat a wok until very hot, add the oil and swirl it around to coat the side. Stir-fry the garlic, ginger, chilli and spring onion for 1 minute over medium heat. Increase the heat to medium-high, add the chicken and stir-fry for 2–3 minutes, or until it is just cooked. Remove from the wok.

3 Reheat the wok and add the broccoli, water chestnuts and bamboo shoots. Stir-fry for 2–3 minutes, tossing constantly. Add the sauce and bring to the boil, tossing constantly. Return the chicken to the wok and toss until it is heated through. Stir in the basil and serve at once.

TURKEY BUFFE WITH RICE AND FRUIT STUFFING

Preparation time: 1 hour
Total cooking time: 2 hours 10 minutes
Serves 6–8

2.8 kg (5 lb 10 oz) turkey buffe

Stuffing
1½ cups (280 g/9 oz) cooked long-grain rice
¼ cup (40 g/1¼ oz) pine nuts, toasted
180 g (6 oz) dried apricots, chopped
250 g (8 oz) chopped pitted prunes
4 spring onions, sliced
1 tablespoon finely grated orange rind
⅓ cup (80 ml/2¾ fl oz) orange juice
1 egg, lightly beaten

Glaze
½ cup (125 ml/4 fl oz) orange juice
15 g (½ oz) butter
2 teaspoons soft brown sugar

1 Bone the turkey breast and remove the bone from the wings.
2 To make the stuffing, combine the rice, pine nuts, apricots, prunes, spring onion, orange rind, juice, ½ teaspoon salt and some white pepper. Mix well and stir in the egg.
3 Lay the turkey flat and spread the stuffing along the centre. Fold the breast inwards and sew the turkey together using a trussing needle and kitchen string. Tuck in the skin at the neck and press the wings in towards the breast. Sew or tie securely with string, or secure well with skewers. Preheat the oven to 180°C (350°F/Gas 4).
4 To make the glaze, stir the orange juice, butter and sugar together in a small pan. Bring to the boil and stir until the sugar is dissolved. Allow to cool.
5 Put the turkey on a rack in a baking dish. Bake for 1¾–2 hours, basting with the glaze. (If the turkey is overbrowning, loosely cover it with foil.) When cooked, remove from the oven and cover and set aside for 20 minutes before removing the string or skewers. Slice and serve with the remaining glaze.

TURKEY EMPANADAS

Preparation time: 40 minutes
Total cooking time: 25 minutes
Makes 18

1 tablespoon oil
1 onion, finely chopped
1 clove garlic, crushed
2 teaspoons paprika
1 teaspoon ground cumin
½ teaspoon ground cinnamon
2 tablespoons sherry
400 g (13 oz) can crushed tomatoes
400 g (13 oz) cooked turkey, finely chopped
½ cup (110 g/3½ oz) pitted green olives, chopped
3 hard-boiled eggs, chopped
1 tablespoon chopped fresh parsley
4½ sheets ready-rolled shortcrust pastry
oil, for deep-frying

1 Heat the tablespoon of oil in a frying pan, add the onion and garlic. Cook over medium heat for 2 minutes, then add the paprika, cumin and cinnamon, and stir until fragrant. Add the sherry, tomato and turkey. Boil for about 10 minutes, or until thickened. Remove from the heat and stir in the olives, eggs and parsley. Season, to taste, then transfer to a bowl and allow to cool.
2 Cut eighteen 12 cm (5 inch) rounds from the pastry. Place 1½ tablespoons of the mixture on one half of each round, brush the edge with water and fold the pastry over to enclose the filling. Press the edges with a fork to seal.
3 Fill a deep heavy-based saucepan one third full of oil and heat to 180°C (350°F), or until a cube of bread browns in 15 seconds. Deep-fry the empanadas in batches for 2–3 minutes on each side, or until golden brown. Remove from the oil with a slotted spoon, then drain on crumpled paper towels.

TURKEY SAN CHOY BAU

Preparation time: 15 minutes +
   15 minutes soaking
Total cooking time: 5 minutes
Serves 4

8 small iceberg lettuce leaves
5 dried Chinese mushrooms
100 g (3½ oz) canned baby corn
1 teaspoon sesame oil
2 teaspoons oil
2 cloves garlic, crushed
1 tablespoon grated fresh ginger
300 g (10 oz) cooked turkey, finely chopped
½ cup (90 g/3 oz) water chestnuts, finely chopped
100 g (3½ oz) bean sprouts
2 spring onions, chopped
1 tablespoon chopped fresh coriander
1 teaspoon sugar
1 tablespoon oyster sauce
1 tablespoon soy sauce

1 Soak the lettuce leaves in cold water while preparing the filling. Soak the Chinese mushrooms in a bowl of boiling water for 15 minutes, or until soft. Drain, discard the stems and finely chop the mushrooms. Thinly slice the baby corn.
2 Heat the oils in a pan, add the garlic, ginger and corn, and toss over medium heat until fragrant. Add the mushrooms, turkey, water chestnuts, bean sprouts, spring onion, coriander, sugar and oyster and soy sauces. Toss well to heat through.
3 Drain the lettuce and pat dry with paper towels. Spoon some turkey filling into each lettuce cup and serve.

ROAST TURKEY BREAST WITH PARSLEY CRUST

Preparation time: 10 minutes
Total cooking itme: 45 minutes
Serves 8

Parsley crust
60 g (2 oz) butter
4 spring onions, finely chopped
2 garlic cloves, crushed
2 cups (160 g/5½ oz) fresh white
  breadcrumbs
2 tablespoons finely chopped fresh
  parsley
1 kg (2 lb) turkey breast supreme
1 egg, lightly beaten
raspberry and redcurrant sauce (see
  page 69) or beetroot relish (see page
  70), for serving

1 To make the parsley crust, melt the butter in a small frying pan over medium heat. Add the spring onion and garlic and stir until softened. Add the breadcrumbs and parsley and stir until combined. Cool.
2 Preheat the oven to moderate 180°C (350°F/Gas 4). Place the turkey in a deep baking dish and pat the turkey dry with paper towels. Brush with egg.
3 Press the parsley crust firmly onto the turkey. Bake for 45 minutes, or until the crust is lightly golden. Serve sliced, with raspberry and redcurrant sauce, or beetroot relish, or your favourite accompaniment.

NOTE: The parsley crust can be made a day in advance. Turkey breast supreme is a boneless breast of the turkey with the skin on. It is available from chicken shops and supermarkets.

THAI DUCK AND PINEAPPLE CURRY

Preparation time: 10 minutes
Total cooking time: 15 minutes
Serves 4–6

1 tablespoon peanut oil
8 spring onions, sliced on the diagonal
  into 3 cm (1¼ inch) lengths
2 cloves garlic, crushed
2–4 tablespoons Thai red curry paste
  (see page 762)
750 g (1½ lb) Chinese roast duck, chopped
400 ml (13 fl oz) coconut milk
450 g (14 oz) can pineapple pieces in
  syrup, drained
3 fresh kaffir lime leaves
3 tablespoons chopped fresh coriander
2 tablespoons chopped fresh mint

1 Heat a wok until very hot, add the oil and swirl. Add the spring onion, garlic and red curry paste, and stir-fry for 1 minute, or until fragrant.
2 Add the duck pieces, coconut milk, pineapple pieces, kaffir lime leaves, and half the fresh coriander and mint. Bring to the boil, then reduce the heat and simmer for 10 minutes, or until the duck is heated through and the sauce has thickened slightly. Stir in the remaining fresh coriander and mint, and serve with jasmine rice.

CHINESE ROAST DUCK WITH RICE NOODLES

Preparation time: 25 minutes
Total cooking time: 15 minutes
Serves 4

1.5 kg (3 lb) Chinese roast duck
500 g (1 lb) fresh flat rice noodles
  (1 cm/½ inch) wide)
3½ tablespoons peanut oil
3 small slender eggplants (aubergines),
  cut into 1 cm (½ inch) thick slices
1 tablespoon thinly sliced fresh ginger
2 small fresh red chillies, finely chopped
4 spring onions, thinly sliced on the
  diagonal
3 tablespoons torn fresh basil
¼ cup (60 ml/2 fl oz) Chinese barbecue
  sauce

1 Remove the crispy skin and meat from the duck, discarding the carcass and fat. Thinly slice the meat and skin and place it in a bowl—there should be at least 350 g (11 oz) of meat.
2 Put the noodles in a heatproof bowl, cover with boiling water and soak briefly. Gently separate the noodles. Rinse under cold water and drain well.
3 Heat a wok over high heat, add 2½ tablespoons of the peanut oil and swirl to coat the side of the wok. Add the eggplant and stir-fry for 3–4 minutes, or until softened. Transfer to a bowl.
4 Heat the remaining oil in the wok over high heat. Cook the ginger, chilli and spring onion for 30 seconds, stirring constantly. Return the eggplant to the wok along with the duck, basil and barbecue sauce, and gently toss together for 1–2 minutes, or until heated through. Add the noodles and stir-fry for 1–2 minutes, or until well combined and heated through, taking care not to break up the noodles. Serve immediately.

DUCK WITH PEARS

Preparation time: 20 minutes
Total cooking time: 1 hour 40 minutes
Serves 4

2 tablespoons olive oil
4 duck breasts
2 red onions, finely diced
1 carrot, finely diced
2 teaspoons fresh thyme
1 cup (250 ml/8 fl oz) chicken stock
2 ripe tomatoes, peeled, deseeded and diced
4 green, firm pears, peeled, halved and cored (leaving the stems intact)
1 cinnamon stick
60 g (2 oz) blanched almonds, toasted, chopped
1 clove garlic
100 ml (3 fl oz) brandy

1 Heat the oil in a heavy-based frying pan and cook the duck, skin-side-down first, over medium heat until brown all over. Remove and set aside, reserving 4 tablespoons of the cooking fat.
2 Return 2 tablespoons of the fat to the pan. Add the onion, carrot and thyme and cook over medium heat for 5 minutes, or until the onion has softened. Add the stock and tomato and bring to the boil. Reduce the heat and simmer for 30 minutes, with the lid slightly askew, or until the sauce has thickened and reduced. Cool slightly, then purée in a food processor until smooth. Return to the pan with the duck. Simmer gently over low heat for 30–40 minutes, or until the duck is tender.

3 While the duck is cooking, place the pears in a saucepan with the cinnamon and just cover with cold water. Bring to the boil, reduce the heat and simmer gently for 5 minutes or until the pears are tender but still firm to the bite. Remove the pears, cover to keep warm and add ½ cup (125 ml/4 fl oz) of the pear poaching liquid to the tomato sauce.
4 Remove the duck from the sauce and keep warm. Grind the almonds, garlic and brandy together in a mortar and pestle or blender to make a smooth paste. Add to the tomato sauce, season, to taste and cook for another 10 minutes.
5 Arrange the duck pieces on a serving plate and pour the sauce over the top. Arrange the warmed pears around the duck and serve.

NOTE: The sauce adds an interesting finish to this Spanish dish, which is traditionally made with goose.

KHORESHE FESENJAN
(DUCK BREAST WITH WALNUT AND POMEGRANATE SAUCE)

Preparation time: 15 minutes +
   5 minutes resting
Total cooking time: 25 minutes
Serves 4

4 large duck breasts
1 onion, finely chopped
1 cup (250 ml/4 fl oz) fresh pomegranate juice (see Note)
2 tablespoons lemon juice
2 tablespoons soft brown sugar
1 teaspoon ground cinnamon
1½ cups (185 g/6 oz) chopped walnuts
pomegranate seeds, to garnish, optional

1 Preheat the oven to moderate 180°C (350°F/Gas 4). Score each duck breast 2 or 3 times on the skin side with a sharp knife. Cook in a non-stick frying pan over high heat, skin-side-down, for 6 minutes, or until crisp and it has rendered most of its fat. Place in a baking dish.
2 Remove all but 1 tablespoon of fat from the pan. Add the onion to the pan and cook over medium heat for 2–3 minutes, or until golden. Add the pomegranate and lemon juice, sugar, cinnamon and 1 cup (125 g/4 oz) walnuts and cook for 1 minute. Pour over the duck breasts and bake for 15 minutes.
3 Rest the duck for 5 minutes. Skim any excess fat from the sauce. Slice the duck and serve with a little sauce. Garnish with the pomegranate seeds and the remaining walnuts.

NOTE: If fresh pomegranate juice isn't available, combine ¼ cup (60 ml/2 fl oz) pomegranate concentrate with ¾ cup (185 ml/6 fl oz) water.

BRAISED DUCK WITH MUSHROOMS

Preparation time: 20 minutes +
   20 minutes soaking
Total cooking time: 1 hour 10 minutes
Serves 6

1 cup (15 g/½ oz) dried Chinese mushrooms
1 x 1.5 kg (3 lb) duck
2 teaspoons oil
2 tablespoons soy sauce
2 tablespoons Chinese rice wine
2 teaspoons sugar
2 wide strips fresh orange peel
125 g (4 oz) watercress

1 Soak the mushrooms in hot water for 20 minutes. Drain well and slice.
2 Using a large heavy knife or cleaver, chop the duck into small pieces, cutting through the bone. Arrange the pieces on a rack and pour boiling water over them—the water will plump up the skin and help keep the duck succulent. Drain and pat dry with paper towels.
3 Brush the base of a heavy-based frying pan with the oil; add the duck in 2 or 3 batches and cook over medium heat for about 8 minutes, turning regularly, until browned. (The darker the browning at this stage, the better the colour when finished.) Between each batch, wipe out the pan with crumpled paper towels to remove excess oil.

4 Wipe the pan with paper towels again and return all the duck to the pan. Add the mushrooms, soy sauce, wine, sugar and orange peel. Bring the mixture to the boil; reduce the heat, cover and simmer gently for 35 minutes or until the duck is tender.
5 Carefully skim off any surface oil. Season with salt and pepper to taste, and stand for 10 minutes, covered, before serving. Remove the duck from the sauce and discard the orange peel. Pick off small sprigs of the watercress and arrange them on one side of a large serving platter. Carefully place the duck segments on the other side of the plate—try not to place the duck on the watercress as it will become soggy. Carefully spoon a little of the sauce over the duck and serve.

NOTE: Braising the duck over low heat produces tender, melt-in-the-mouth meat and a delicious sauce. If the heat is too high, the duck will dry out and lose its flavour.

DUCK WITH WILD RICE

Preparation time: 15 minutes
Total cooking time: 1 hour
Serves 4

Dressing
⅓ cup (80 ml/2¾ fl oz) olive oil
2 tablespoons orange juice
2 teaspoons walnut oil
1 teaspoon grated orange zest
1 tablespoon chopped preserved ginger

½ cup (95 g/3 oz) wild rice
2 teaspoons oil
50 g (1¾ oz) pecans, roughly chopped
½ teaspoon ground cinnamon
⅓ cup (65 g/2¼ oz) long-grain white rice
2 tablespoons finely chopped parsley
4 spring onions (scallions), thinly sliced
2 duck breasts
zest of 1 orange

1 To make the dressing, thoroughly mix the ingredients together. Season with salt and freshly ground black pepper. Set aside.
2 Put the wild rice in a saucepan with 300 ml (9½ fl oz) water. Bring to the boil, then cook, covered, for 30 minutes, or until tender. Drain away any excess water.
3 Meanwhile, heat the oil in a large frying pan. Add the pecans and cook, stirring, until golden. Add the cinnamon and a pinch of salt, and cook for 1 minute.
4 Bring a large saucepan of water to the boil. Add the white rice and cook, stirring occasionally, for 12 minutes, or until tender. Drain and mix with the wild rice and pecans in a large, shallow bowl. Add the parsley and spring onion. Add half the dressing and toss well.
5 Put the duck, skin-side down, in a cold frying pan, then heat the pan over high heat. Cook for 5 minutes, or until crisp, then turn over and cook for another 5 minutes. Tip out any excess fat and add the remaining dressing and the orange zest, and cook until bubbling. Transfer the duck to a serving dish and slice on the diagonal. Serve with the rice, drizzled with any juices.

BEEF, LAMB AND PORK

BRAISED BEEF WITH SPINACH AND LEEKS

Preparation time: 15 minutes +
  2 hours marinating
Total cooking time: 25 minutes
Serves 4

400 g (12⅔ oz) beef fillet
2 tablespoons light soy sauce
2 tablespoons fish sauce
3 tablespoons oil
4 coriander roots, finely chopped
¼ cup (15 g/½ oz) chopped fresh coriander
  leaves and stems
2 teaspoons cracked black peppercorns
2 cloves garlic, crushed
1 tablespoon soft brown sugar
½ cup (125 ml/4 fl oz) water
1 leek, sliced
20 spinach leaves, stalks removed
¼ cup (60 ml/2 fl oz) lime juice

1 Slice the beef into 2.5 cm (1 inch) thick steaks. Place the soy sauce, fish sauce, 1 tablespoon oil, coriander, peppercorns, garlic and sugar in a food processor and process until smooth. Pour the marinade over the beef; cover and refrigerate for at least 2 hours, or overnight.
2 Drain the beef, reserving the marinade. Heat 1 tablespoon oil in a wok or large frying pan. Add the steaks and brown well on each side. Add the marinade and water, reduce the heat and simmer for 8 minutes. Remove the meat and keep warm. Simmer the sauce for 10 minutes; set aside. Slice the beef into bite-sized pieces.
3 Heat the remaining oil in a wok or pan; add the leek and stir-fry for 2 minutes over medium heat. Add the spinach and cook for 30 seconds.
4 Arrange the leek and spinach on a serving plate with the meat. Pour the sauce over the meat and drizzle over the lime juice. Serve garnished with chilli slices, if you wish.

TURKISH RAVIOLI

Preparation time: 1 hour
Total cooking time: 30 minutes
Serves 4–6

Filling
1 tablespoon oil
1 small onion, finely grated
1 red chilli, finely chopped
1 teaspoon ground cinnamon
1 teaspoon ground cloves
500 g (1 lb) finely minced lamb
2 teaspoons grated lemon rind
2 teaspoons chopped fresh dill
3 tablespoons chopped fresh flat-leaf
  parsley

Sauce
1 cup (250 ml/8 fl oz) chicken stock
2 cups (500 ml/16 fl oz) natural yoghurt
4 cloves garlic, crushed

1¾ cups (215 g/7 oz) plain flour
⅓ cup (50 g/1¾ oz) plain wholemeal flour
½ cup (125 ml/4 fl oz) water
1 egg
1 egg yolk
½ cup fresh mint leaves, finely chopped

1 To make the filling, heat the oil in a large frying pan, add the onion, chilli and spices and cook over medium heat for 5 minutes, or until the onion is golden. Add the mince and cook over high heat until the meat is browned, stirring constantly to break up any lumps. Remove from the heat, stir in the lemon rind and chopped herbs. Set aside to cool.
2 To make the sauce, bring the chicken stock to the boil in a pan and cook until the stock is reduced by half. Remove from the heat, and whisk the stock with the yoghurt and garlic. Season, to taste, with salt and pepper.

3 Combine the flours, water, egg and yolk in a food processor until the mixture comes together to form a smooth dough. Turn the dough out onto a lightly floured surface. If the dough is too sticky you may need to add a little extra flour. (It is much easier to add more flour to a wet dough than add more egg to a dry dough.)
4 Divide the dough into quarters, open the rollers on your pasta machine to the widest setting, sprinkle the rollers generously with flour and roll the dough through the machine. Fold the dough into three, so that the width of the pasta remains the same and the length should now be one-third of what it was.
5 Pass the dough through the rollers again, and repeat the folding and rolling process, turning the dough right on a 90 degree angle each time. Repeat this at least ten times, dusting the machine and dough lightly with flour if you need to. When the pasta is smooth, set the rollers in a groove closer, pass the pasta through and keep setting the rollers closer until the pasta is 1 mm (¹⁄₁₆ inch) thick. Cover and set aside. Repeat with the remaining dough.
6 Cut the dough into 12 cm (5 inch) squares and place 1 tablespoon of the filling on the centre of each square, brush the edges lightly with water and fold each square into a triangle. Press the edges together to seal and place the ravioli in a single layer on a lightly floured baking tray. Keep them covered while making the rest of the ravioli.
7 Cook the ravioli, in batches, in a large pan of rapidly boiling salted water for 3 minutes, or until al dente. Drain and toss through the sauce. Garnish with chopped mint.

BEEF WELLINGTON

Preparation time: 25 minutes
Total cooking time: 1 hour 30 minutes
Serves 6–8

1.2 kg (2 lb 6½ oz) beef fillet or rib-eye in
    1 piece
1 tablespoon oil
125 g (4 oz) pâté
60 g (2 oz) button mushrooms, sliced
375 g (12 oz) block puff pastry, thawed
1 egg, lightly beaten
1 sheet ready-rolled puff pastry, thawed

1 Preheat the oven to hot 210°C
(415°F/Gas 6–7). Trim the meat of any
excess fat and sinew. Fold the thinner
part of the tail end under and tie the meat
securely with kitchen string at regular
intervals to form an even shape.
2 Rub the meat with freshly ground black
pepper. Heat the oil over high heat in a
large frying pan. Add the meat and brown
well all over. Remove from the heat and
allow to cool. Remove the string.
3 Spread the pâté over the top and sides
of the beef. Cover with the mushrooms,
pressing them onto the pâté. Roll the
block pastry out on a lightly floured
surface to a rectangle large enough to
completely enclose the beef.
4 Place the beef on the pastry, brush the
edges with egg, and fold over to enclose
the meat completely, brushing the edges
of the pastry with the beaten egg to seal,
and folding in the ends. Invert onto a
greased baking tray so the seam is
underneath. Cut leaf shapes from the
sheet of puff pastry and use to decorate
the Wellington. Use the egg to stick the
shapes on. Cut a few slits in the top to
allow the steam to escape. Brush the top
and sides of the pastry with egg, and cook
for 45 minutes for rare, 1 hour for
medium or 1½ hours for well done. Leave
in a warm place for 10 minutes before
cutting into slices for serving.

SHAKING BEEF

Preparation time: 10 minutes +
    1 hour marinating
Total cooking time: 10 minutes
Serves 4

1½ tablespoons fish sauce
1½ tablespoons light soy sauce
1½ teaspoons caster sugar
6 cloves garlic, crushed
3 spring onions, white part only, finely
    chopped
¼ cup (60 ml/2 fl oz) vegetable oil
750 g (1½ lb) lean beef fillet, cut into 2 cm
    (¾ inch) cubes
2 teaspoons rice vinegar
2 teaspoons lime juice
1 teaspoon light soy sauce, extra
100 g (3½ oz) mignonette lettuce or green
    oak lettuce leaves, washed, trimmed
    and dried

1 Combine the fish sauce, soy sauce, sugar,
garlic, spring onion, 1 teaspoon of the oil,
¾ teaspoon freshly ground black pepper
and ½ teaspoon salt in a large non-metallic
bowl. Add the beef, cover with plastic wrap
and marinate in the fridge for at least
1 hour, or overnight if time permits.
2 To make the dressing, combine the rice
vinegar, lime juice, extra soy sauce,
3 teaspoons of the oil and 2 teaspoons
water in a small non-metallic bowl or jug.
3 Place the lettuce leaves on a serving
plate, then pour on the dressing.
4 Heat a wok over high heat, add
1 tablespoon of the oil and swirl to coat the
side of the wok. Add half the beef in one
layer, allowing it to sit without stirring for
1 minute, so that a brown crust forms on the
bottom. Stir-fry the beef briefly, or use the
handle to shake the wok vigorously, tossing
the beef around in the heat, for
3–4 minutes for medium–rare, or until
cooked to your liking. Remove the beef from
the wok, then repeat with the remaining oil
and beef.
5 Arrange the beef over the lettuce leaves
and serve immediately with steamed rice.

THAI STIR-FRIED
NOODLES WITH BEEF
(PHAD SI-IEW)

Preparation time: 20 minutes
Total cooking time: 20 minutes
Serves 4–6

500 g (1 lb) fresh rice sheet noodles, cut
    lengthways into 2 cm (¾ inch) strips
2 tablespoons peanut oil
2 eggs, lightly beaten
500 g (1 lb) lean beef fillet, thinly sliced
    across the grain
¼ cup (60 ml/2 fl oz) kecap manis
1½ tablespoons soy sauce
1½ tablespoons fish sauce
300 g (10 oz) gai larn (Chinese broccoli),
    cut into 5 cm (2 inch) lengths
¼ teaspoon ground white pepper

1 Cover the noodles with boiling water and
gently separate the strips. Drain.
2 Heat a wok over high heat, add
1 tablespoon oil and swirl to coat. Add the
egg, swirl to coat and cook over medium
heat for 1–2 minutes, or until set. Remove
and slice.
3 Reheat the wok over high heat, add the
remaining oil and cook the beef in
batches for 3 minutes, or until browned.
Remove.
4 Reduce the heat to medium, add the
noodles and cook for 2 minutes. Combine
the kecap manis, soy and fish sauces. Add
to the wok with the gai larn and white
pepper, then stir-fry for 2 minutes. Return
the egg and beef to the wok and cook for
3 minutes.

ROAST BEEF WITH YORKSHIRE PUDDINGS

Preparation time: 15 minutes +
  1 hour refrigeration
Total cooking time: 1 hour 40 minutes
Serves 6

2 kg (4 lb) piece roasting beef (Scotch
  fillet, rump or sirloin)
2 cloves garlic, crushed

Yorkshire puddings
¾ cup (90 g/3 oz) plain flour
½ cup (125 ml/4 fl oz) milk
2 eggs

Red wine gravy
2 tablespoons plain flour
⅓ cup (80 ml/2¾ fl oz) red wine
2½ cups (600 ml/20 fl oz) beef stock

1 Preheat the oven to very hot 240°C
(475°F/Gas 9). Rub the piece of beef with
the crushed garlic and some freshly
cracked black pepper and drizzle with oil.
Bake on a rack in a baking dish for
20 minutes.
2 Meanwhile, for the Yorkshire puddings,
sift the flour and ½ teaspoon salt into a
large bowl, then make a well in the centre
and whisk in the milk. In a separate bowl,
whisk the eggs together until fluffy, then
add to the batter and mix well. Add ½ cup
(125 ml/4 fl oz) water and whisk until
large bubbles form on the surface. Cover
the bowl with plastic wrap and refrigerate
for 1 hour.
3 Reduce the oven to moderate 180°C
(350°F/Gas 4) and continue to roast the
meat for 1 hour for a rare result, or longer
for well done. Cover loosely with foil and
leave in a warm place while making the
Yorkshire puddings.

4 Increase the oven to hot 220°C
(425°F/Gas 7). Pour off all the pan juices
into a jug and spoon ½ teaspoon of the
juices into twelve ⅓ cup (80 ml/2¾ fl oz)
patty or muffin tins. (Reserve the
remaining juice for the gravy.) Heat the
muffin tins in the oven until the fat is
almost smoking. Whisk the batter again
until bubbles form on the surface. Pour
into each muffin tin to three-quarters full.
Bake for 20 minutes, or until puffed and
lightly golden. Make the gravy while the
Yorkshire puddings are baking.
5 To make the gravy, heat 2 tablespoons
of the reserved pan juices in the baking
dish on the stove over low heat. Add the
flour and stir well, scraping the dish to
incorporate all the sediment. Cook over
medium heat for 1–2 minutes, stirring
constantly, until the flour is well
browned. Remove from the heat and
gradually stir in the wine and stock.
Return to the heat, stirring constantly,
until the gravy boils and thickens.
Simmer for 3 minutes, then season, to
taste, with salt and freshly ground black
pepper. Strain, if desired.
6 Serve the beef with the hot Yorkshire
puddings and red wine gravy.

NOTE: Cooking times vary, but generally,
for every 500 g (1 lb) beef, allow 20 minutes
for rare, 30 minutes for medium, and
35 minutes for well done.

STIR-FRIED BEEF AND SNOW PEAS (MANGETOUT)

Preparation time: 10 minutes
Total cooking time: 10 minutes
Serves 4

2 tablespoons soy sauce
½ teaspoon grated fresh ginger
400 g (13 oz) lean beef fillet, thinly sliced
  across the grain
2 tablespoons peanut oil
200 g (6½ oz) snow peas (mangetout),
  topped and tailed
1 small red pepper (capsicum), sliced
1½ teaspoons cornflour
½ cup (125 ml/4 fl oz) beef stock
1 teaspoon soy sauce, extra
¼ teaspoon sesame oil

1 Combine the soy sauce and ginger in a
large non-metallic bowl, add the beef and
toss well.
2 Heat a wok over high heat, add the oil
and swirl to coat the side of the wok. Add
the beef in two batches and stir-fry for
2 minutes each batch, or until the meat is
golden. Return all the beef to the wok and
add the snow peas and red pepper. Stir-
fry for a further 2 minutes.
3 Dissolve the cornflour in the stock. Add
to the wok with the remaining stock, extra
soy sauce and the sesame oil. Stir until
the sauce boils and thickens. Serve with
steamed rice.

MADRAS CURRY

Preparation time: 20 minutes
Total cooking time: 1 hour 30 minutes
Serves 4

1 kg (2 lb) skirt or chuck steak
¼ cup (25 g/¾ oz) ground coriander
6 teaspoons ground cumin
1 teaspoon brown mustard seeds
½ teaspoon cracked black peppercorns
1 teaspoon chilli powder
1 teaspoon ground turmeric
1 teaspoon salt
2 teaspoons crushed garlic
2 teaspoons grated fresh ginger
2–3 tablespoons white vinegar
1 tablespoon oil or ghee
1 medium onion, chopped
¼ cup (60 g/2 oz) tomato paste (tomato
    purée, double concentrate)
1 cup (250 ml/8 fl oz) beef stock

1 Trim the excess fat and sinew from the meat, and cut it into 2.5 cm (1 inch) cubes.
2 Place the coriander, cumin, mustard seeds, peppercorns, chilli powder, turmeric, salt, garlic and ginger in a small bowl; stir to combine. Add the vinegar and mix to a smooth paste.
3 Heat the oil in a large pan; add the onion and cook over medium heat until just soft. Add the spice paste and stir for 1 minute. Add the meat and cook, stirring, until it is coated with the spice paste. Add the tomato paste and stock. Simmer, covered, for 1 hour 30 minutes, or until the meat is tender.

SURF 'N' TURF

Preparation time: 20 minutes
Total cooking time: 15–20 minutes
Serves 4

30 g (1 oz) butter
1 spring onion, finely chopped
1 clove garlic, crushed
1 tablespoon plain flour
1 cup milk
2 tablespoons cream
1 tablespoon lemon juice
2 teaspoons Dijon mustard
1 large or 2 small raw lobster tails
2 tablespoons oil
170 g (5½ oz) fresh or frozen crab meat
4 beef eye fillets (200 g/6½ oz each)

1 Melt the butter in a pan, add the onion and garlic and stir over medium heat for 1 minute, or until the onion has softened. Stir in the flour and cook for 1 minute, or until pale and foaming. Remove from the heat and gradually stir in the milk. Return to the heat and stir constantly until the sauce boils and thickens. Reduce the heat and simmer for 2 minutes. Remove from the heat and stir in the cream, lemon juice and mustard; keep warm.
2 Starting at the end where the head was, cut down each side of the lobster shell on the underside with kitchen scissors. Pull back the flap and remove the meat from the shell. Heat half the oil in a frying pan, add the lobster meat and cook over medium heat for 3 minutes each side until just cooked through. Remove and keep warm. Add the crab to the pan and stir until heated through. Remove and keep warm. Wipe the pan clean.
3 Heat the remaining oil in the pan, add the steaks and cook over high heat for 2 minutes each side to seal, turning once. For rare steaks, cook each side 1 more minute. For medium and well-done steaks, reduce the heat to medium and continue cooking for 2–3 minutes each side for medium or 4–6 minutes each side for well done. Serve, the steaks on plates. Top with crab followed by slices of lobster. Pour the sauce over the top.

LEMON GRASS BEEF

Preparation time: 15 minutes +
    10 minutes marinating
Total cooking time: 25 minutes
Serves 4

3 cloves garlic, finely chopped
1 tablespoon grated fresh ginger
4 stems lemon grass (white part only),
    finely chopped
2½ tablespoons vegetable oil
600 g (1¼ lb) lean beef fillet, thinly sliced
    across the grain
1 tablespoon lime juice
1–2 tablespoons fish sauce
2 tablespoons kecap manis
1 large red onion, cut into small wedges
200 g (6½ oz) green beans, sliced on the
    diagonal into 5 cm (2 inch) lengths

1 Combine the garlic, ginger, lemon grass and 2 teaspoons of the oil in a large non-metallic bowl. Add the beef, toss well until it is coated in the marinade, then cover with plastic wrap and marinate in the fridge for at least 10 minutes.
2 To make the stir-fry sauce, combine the lime juice, fish sauce and kecap manis in a small bowl or jug and set aside until needed.
3 Heat a wok over high heat, add 1 tablespoon oil and swirl to coat the side of the wok. Stir-fry the beef in batches for 2–3 minutes, or until browned. Remove from the wok.
4 Reheat the wok over high heat, heat the remaining oil, then add the onion and stir-fry for 2 minutes. Add the beans and cook for another 2 minutes, then return the beef to the wok. Pour in the stir-fry sauce and cook until heated through. Serve with steamed rice.

LAMB AND ARTICHOKE FRICASSEE

Preparation time: 50 minutes
Total cooking time: 1 hour 50 minutes
Serves 8

6 fresh globe artichokes
¼ cup (60 ml/2 fl oz) lemon juice
2 large, ripe tomatoes
⅓ cup (80 ml/2¾ fl oz) olive oil
2 kg (4 lb) diced lamb
750 g (1½ lb) brown onions, thinly sliced
1 tablespoon plain flour
2 cloves garlic, crushed
¾ cup (185 m/l6 fl oz) white wine
1⅓ cups (350 ml/11 fl oz) chicken stock
1 bouquet garni
chopped fresh flat-leaf parsley, to garnish
lemon wedges, for serving

1 To prepare the globe artichokes, bring a large saucepan of water to the boil and add the lemon juice. Trim the stems from the artichokes and remove the tough outer leaves. Cut off the hard tips of the remaining leaves using scissors. Blanch the artichokes for 5 minutes. Remove and turn upside-down to drain. When cool enough to handle, use a small spoon to remove the choke from the centre of each. Scrape the bases well to remove all the membrane. Cut the artichokes into quarters and set aside.
2 Score a cross in the base of each tomato and place in a bowl of boiling water for 10 seconds. Plunge into cold water and peel away from the cross. Cut each tomato in half and scoop out the seeds with a teaspoon. Chop the tomatoes.

3 Heat half the oil in a deep heatproof casserole and fry batches of the lamb until golden. Add the remaining oil and cook the onion for about 8 minutes, until soft and caramelized. Add the flour and cook for 1 minute. Add the garlic, tomato, wine and chicken stock. Return the lamb to the pan add the bouquet garni and simmer, covered, for 1 hour.
4 Place the artichokes in the casserole and simmer, uncovered, for another 15 minutes. Remove the meat and artichokes with a slotted spoon and place in a serving dish. Keep warm. Discard the bouquet garni. Cook the sauce over high heat until it thickens. Pour the sauce over the lamb and garnish with parsley. Serve with lemon wedges.

NOTE: If fresh artichokes are not available, you can use 1 cup (270 g/9 oz) marinated artichokes. Drain them well and pat dry with paper towels.

CINNAMON BEEF NOODLES

Preparation time: 15 minutes
Total cooking time: 1 hour 40 minutes
Serves 6

1 teaspoon oil
10 spring onions (scallions), cut into 4 cm (1½ inch) lengths, lightly crushed
10 garlic cloves, thinly sliced
6 slices of ginger
1½ teaspoons chilli bean paste (toban jiang)
2 cassia or cinnamon sticks (see Note)
2 star anise
½ cup (125 ml/4 fl oz) light soy sauce
1 kg (2 lb) chuck steak, trimmed and cut into 4 cm (1½ inch) cubes
250 g (8 oz) rice stick noodles
250 g (8 oz) baby spinach
3 tablespoons finely chopped spring onion (scallions)

1 Heat a wok over medium heat, add the oil and heat until hot. Stir-fry the spring onion, garlic, ginger, chilli bean paste, cassia and star anise for 10 seconds, or until fragrant. Transfer to a clay pot, casserole dish or saucepan. Add the soy sauce and 2.25 litres (72 fl oz) water. Bring to the boil, add the beef, then return to the boil. Reduce the heat and simmer, covered, for 1½ hours, or until the beef is very tender. Skim the surface occasionally to remove any impurities and fat. Remove and discard the ginger and cassia.
2 Meanwhile, soak the noodles in hot water for 10 minutes, then drain and divide among six soup bowls.
3 Add the spinach to the beef and bring to the boil. Spoon the beef mixture over the noodles and sprinkle with the spring onion.

NOTE: In China cassia bark is more often used than cinnamon to make this recipe. The bark of the cassia tree is similar to cinnamon, but the flavour is more woody.

STEAK IN ROASTED SESAME SEED MARINADE

Preparation time: 25 minutes +
   30 minutes marinating
Total cooking time: 12 minutes
Serves 4

2 tablespoons white Japanese sesame
   seeds
1 clove garlic, crushed
3 cm (1¼ inch) piece fresh ginger, grated
2 tablespoons Japanese soy sauce
1 tablespoon sake
1 teaspoon caster sugar
500 g (1 lb) scotch fillet, cut into 4 steaks
3 spring onions, to garnish
1 tablespoon oil

Dipping Sauce
4 cm (1½ inch) piece fresh ginger
½ teaspoon shichimi togarashi
½ cup (125 ml/4 fl oz) Japanese soy sauce
2 teaspoons dashi granules
2 tablespoons water

1 Roast the sesame seeds in a dry frying
pan over moderately low heat for
2 minutes, shaking the pan constantly,
until the seeds begin to pop. Crush the
roasted seeds in a mortar and pestle.
2 Place the crushed sesame seeds, garlic,
ginger, soy sauce, sake and sugar in a
bowl and whisk until the sugar has
dissolved. Place the steaks in a shallow
dish; spoon the marinade over the top and
marinate for 30 minutes.

3 To make Dipping Sauce: Cut the ginger
lengthways into very fine strips about
4 cm (1½ inches) long. Place the ginger,
shichimi togarashi, soy sauce, dashi and
water in a small bowl and whisk lightly
until well combined.
4 Cut the spring onions lengthways into
very fine strips about 4 cm (1½ inches)
long. Place the strips in a bowl of iced
water and leave until they are crisp and
curled; drain.
5 Lightly brush the oil over the steaks and
then grill or fry them for about 4 to 6
minutes on each side—don't overcook or
the steaks will become very tough. Set
the steaks aside for 5 minutes before
cutting them into diagonal slices. Arrange
the slices on serving plates and then
drizzle over a little of the Dipping Sauce.
Garnish with the spring onion curls and
serve with steamed rice and the
remaining Dipping Sauce.

STANDING RIB ROAST WITH PATE

Preparation time: 30 minutes
Total cooking time: 2 hours 20 minutes
Serves 6

1 rasher bacon, chopped
1 onion, finely chopped
125 g (4 oz) mushrooms, finely chopped
½ cup (50 g/1¾ oz) dry breadcrumbs
125 g (4 oz) pâté
2 tablespoons chopped fresh parsley
1 teaspoon chopped fresh oregano
1 egg, lightly beaten
4 kg (8 lb) standing rib roast (6 chops)

1 Preheat the oven to very hot 240°C
(475°F/Gas 9). Place the bacon in a dry
frying pan, and cook gently over medium
heat until it begins to soften and release its
fat. Add the onion and mushroom and
cook, stirring, for 3 minutes. Transfer to a
bowl and mix in the breadcrumbs, pâté,
parsley, oregano and egg. Season, to taste,
with salt and freshly ground black pepper.
2 Cut a slit in the meat, between the rib
bones and the meat, to form a pocket.
Spoon the pâté mixture into the pocket.
Secure the meat firmly with string.
3 Place the meat in a baking dish fat-
side-up (the bones form a natural rack).
Bake for 15 minutes, then reduce the heat
to moderate 180°C (350°F/Gas 4). Bake for
another 1½ hours for rare, or up to
2 hours for medium, or until cooked
according to taste. Work out the cooking
time based on 15–20 minutes per 500 g
(1 lb) of meat. This will achieve a roast
that is well done on the outside and rare
inside.
4 Allow the meat to rest for 15 minutes
before carving. Remove the string and cut
the meat into thick slices, allowing 1 bone
per person. Delicious served with gravy
(see page 742) and roast vegetables.
note: You can use any firm-textured pâté,
such as peppercorn or Grand Marnier.
Discard the jelly from the top of the pâté.

JAPANESE BEEF AND VEGETABLE HOTPOT

Preparation time: 1 hour
Total cooking time: 15 minutes
Serves 6

500 g (1 lb) scotch fillet, partially frozen
3 small white onions
5 spring onions
1 large carrot
400 g (12⅔ oz) small button mushrooms
½ small Chinese cabbage
2 cups (180 g/5¾ oz) bean sprouts
225 g (7¼ oz) can bamboo shoots, drained
100 g (3⅓ oz) firm tofu
100 g (3⅓ oz) fresh shirataki noodles
6 eggs
¼ cup (60 ml/2 fl oz) oil

Sauce

⅓ cup (80 ml/2¾ fl oz) Japanese soy
   sauce
¼ cup (60 ml/2 fl oz) beef stock
¼ cup (60 ml/2 fl oz) sake
¼ cup (60 ml/2 fl oz) mirin
2 tablespoons caster sugar

1 Using an extremely sharp knife, slice the partially frozen fillet as thinly as possible, then arrange the slices on a large tray or platter, leaving room for the vegetables, tofu and noodles. Cover the fillet slices and refrigerate the platter while preparing the remaining ingredients.
2 Cut each of the white onions into 6 wedges. Slice the firm section of the spring onions into 4 cm (1½ inch) lengths and discard the dark green tops. Cut the carrot into 4 cm (1½ inch) long thin matchsticks. Trim the stalks and cut the mushrooms in half. Cut the cabbage into bite-sized pieces, discarding any tough parts. Trim the scraggly ends from the bean sprouts. Trim the bamboo shoots into evenly sized pieces, similar to the other vegetables. Cut the tofu into 2 cm (¾ inch) cubes. Arrange the vegetables and tofu on the platter with the meat.

3 Cook the noodles for about 3 minutes or until just soft; do not overcook them or they will fall apart. Drain thoroughly and, if you like, use scissors to cut the cooked noodles into shorter lengths that can be picked up easily with chopsticks. Arrange the noodles on the platter with the meat and vegetables.
4 To make Sauce: Place the soy sauce, beef stock, sake, mirin and sugar in a small bowl and mix until the sugar dissolves.
5 Set the table with individual place settings, each with a serving bowl, a bowl of rice (see note), a bowl to break an egg into, chopsticks and napkins. Place an electric frying pan on the table so it is within easy reach of each diner.
6 When all the diners are seated, heat the frying pan and brush it lightly with oil. When the pan is very hot, take about a third of each of the vegetables and cook them quickly for about 2 minutes, tossing constantly. Push the vegetables to the side of the pan. Add about a third of the meat in one layer and sear the slices for 30 seconds on each side, taking care not to overcook them. Drizzle a little of the Sauce over the meat. Add some of the noodles and tofu to the pan and gently toss with the other ingredients.
7 Each diner breaks an egg into a bowl and whisks it with chopsticks. Mouthfuls of Sukiyaki are then selected from the hot pan, dipped into the egg and eaten. When the diners are ready for more, the pan is reheated and the cooking process repeated.

TAGLIATELLE WITH VEAL, WINE AND CREAM

Preparation time: 15 minutes
Total cooking time: 20 minutes
Serves 4

500 g (1 lb) veal scaloppine or escalopes,
   cut into thin strips
plain flour, seasoned with salt and
   pepper
60 g (2 oz) butter
1 onion, sliced
½ cup (125 ml/4 fl oz) dry white wine
3–4 tablespoons beef stock or chicken
   stock
⅔ cup (170 ml/5½ fl oz) cream
600 g (1¼ lb) fresh plain or spinach
   tagliatelle (or a mixture of both)
freshly grated Parmesan

1 Coat the veal strips with the seasoned flour. Melt the butter in a pan. Add the veal strips and fry quickly until browned. Remove with a slotted spoon and set aside.
2 Add the onion slices to the pan and stir until soft and golden, about 8–10 minutes. Pour in the wine and cook rapidly to reduce the liquid. Add the stock and cream and season with salt and pepper, to taste. Reduce the sauce again, and add the veal towards the end.
3 Meanwhile, cook the tagliatelle in a large pan of rapidly boiling salted water until al dente. Drain and transfer to a warm serving dish.
4 Stir 1 tablespoon of Parmesan through the sauce. Pour the sauce over the pasta. Serve with a sprinkle of Parmesan. Some chopped herbs can be used as an extra garnish and will add flavour.

NOTE: This dish is lovely served with a mixed salad. If you prefer a lighter sauce, you can omit the cream. The flavour is just as delicious.

BAKED VEAL WITH SPICY CHICKEN STUFFING

Preparation time: 15 minutes
Total cooking time: 1 hour 40 minutes
Serves 6

1.8 kg (3 lb 10 oz) shoulder of veal, boned and butterflied (ask your butcher to do this)
1 tablespoon olive oil

Spicy stuffing
2 teaspoons olive oil
6 spring onions, finely chopped
500 g (1 lb) chicken mince
1 cup (80 g/2¾ oz) fresh wholemeal breadcrumbs
1 teaspoon grated fresh ginger
2 red chillies, seeded and chopped
2 eggs, lightly beaten
⅓ cup (40 g/1¼ oz) chopped pecans
½ teaspoon ground black pepper
¼ teaspoon paprika
½ teaspoon ground coriander

1 Preheat the oven to moderate 180°C (350°F/Gas 4). Trim the veal of excess fat and sinew. Place the veal flesh-side-up on a board.
2 For the spicy stuffing, heat the oil in a large heavy-based frying pan, add the onion and chicken mince and cook over medium heat for 4 minutes, or until brown. Use a fork to break up any lumps.

3 Remove from the heat and add the remaining stuffing ingredients. Stir to combine. Place in a food processor and process until fairly smooth. Spread the stuffing over the flattened veal, then roll up and tie securely with kitchen string. Brush well with the tablespoon of olive oil and season with salt and pepper. Place on a rack in a baking dish. Pour 1½ cups (375 ml/12 fl oz) water into the baking dish.
4 Bake for 1½ hours for medium, or until cooked to your liking. Add extra water to the pan as necessary and skim fat from the surface. Remove the veal from the dish, cover and set aside for 10 minutes before removing the string and carving.
5 Drain any excess fat from the pan juices and boil the juices on the stovetop for 2–5 minutes, or until reduced by about half. Strain, then season, to taste, and serve with the sliced veal.

BARBECUED BEEF

Preparation time: 15 minutes +
    30 minutes freezing + 2 hours
    marinating
Total cooking time: 15 minutes
Serves 4–6

500 g (1 lb) scotch fillet or sirloin steak
¼ cup (40 g/1⅓ oz) white sesame seeds
½ cup (125 ml/4 fl oz) soy sauce
2 cloves garlic, finely chopped
3 spring onions, finely chopped
1 tablespoon sesame oil
1 tablespoon oil

1 Freeze the steak for 30 minutes.
2 Toast the sesame seeds in a dry pan over medium heat for 3 to 4 minutes, shaking the pan gently, until the seeds are golden brown; remove from the pan at once to prevent burning. Crush the seeds in a food mill or with a mortar and pestle.
3 Slice the steak into thin strips, cutting across the natural grain of the meat.
4 Combine the steak, soy sauce, garlic, spring onions and half the sesame seeds, mixing well. Marinate for 2 hours.
5 Combine the oils and brush them onto a cast-iron grill-plate, heavy-based frying pan or barbecue plate. Heat to very hot and cook the meat in 3 batches, searing each side for about 1 minute (don't overcook the steak or it will become chewy). Re-brush the grill with oil and allow it to reheat to very hot between batches. Sprinkle the extra crushed sesame seeds over the steak and serve with Kim Chi

CHILLI BEEF

Preparation time: 10 minutes + 20
minutes marinating
Total cooking time: 10 minutes
Serves 4

¼ cup (60 ml/2 fl oz) kecap manis
2½ teaspoons sambal oelek
2 cloves garlic, crushed
½ teaspoon ground coriander
1 tablespoon grated palm sugar
1 teaspoon sesame oil
400 g (13 oz) lean beef fillet, thinly sliced
   across the grain
1 tablespoon peanut oil
2 tablespoons chopped roasted peanuts
3 tablespoons chopped fresh coriander
   leaves

1 Combine the kecap manis, sambal
oelek, garlic, ground coriander, palm
sugar, sesame oil and 2 tablespoons
water in a large bowl. Add the beef and
toss well. Cover with plastic wrap and
marinate in the fridge for 20 minutes.
2 Heat a wok over high heat, add the
peanut oil and swirl around to coat the
side of the wok. Add the meat in batches
and cook each batch for 2–3 minutes, or
until browned.
3 Arrange the beef on a serving platter,
sprinkle with the chopped peanuts and
fresh coriander, and serve with steamed
rice.

BEEF FONDUE WITH RICE PAPER WRAPPERS AND SALAD

Preparation time: 20 minutes
Total cooking time: about 30 minutes
Serves 4

1 red (Spanish) onion, finely sliced
¾ cup (185 ml/6 fl oz) rice vinegar
3 red chillies, finely chopped
2 tablespoons fish sauce
2 tablespoons lime juice
6 cloves garlic, finely chopped
2 tablespoons sugar
500 g (1 lb) beef fillet
½ teaspoon freshly ground black pepper
4 cups (1 litre) water
410 g (13 oz) can chopped tomatoes
12 rice paper wrappers (plus a few extras
   to allow for breakages)
75 g (2½ oz) lettuce leaves, shredded
½ cup (10 g/⅓ oz) fresh mint
1 small Lebanese cucumber, sliced

1 Place the onion and 3 tablespoons of the
vinegar in a small bowl; mix to combine
and set aside. To make a dipping sauce,
place the chilli, fish sauce, lime juice, half
the garlic and half the sugar in a small
bowl; mix to combine and set aside for the
flavours to mingle. Cut the beef into thin
slices, season well with the pepper and
set aside.
2 Place the water in a large pan and bring
it to the boil. Add the tomato and the
remaining garlic, sugar and vinegar, and
simmer for 20 minutes.

3 Using a pastry brush, brush both sides
of each rice paper wrapper liberally with
water. Allow to stand for 2 minutes or
until they become soft and pliable. Stack
the wrappers on a plate. Sprinkle over a
little extra water and cover the plate with
plastic wrap to keep the wrappers moist
until needed.
4 Place the tomato mixture in a food
processor and process until smooth.
Return the tomato stock to the pan and
reheat to simmering point. Add the beef in
batches to the simmering stock, and cook
it quickly, just until it changes colour,
then place it in a serving bowl.
5 To serve, place the rice paper wrappers,
lettuce, mint and cucumber on a serving
platter in separate piles. Each diner takes
a wrapper, places a few slices of beef on
it along with a little of the lettuce,
cucumber, mint and the marinated onion,
then rolls it up and dips it in the dipping
sauce to eat.

SIMMERED BEEF IN COCONUT GRAVY

Preparation time: 30 minutes
Total cooking time: 2 hours 40 minutes
Serves 4–6

2 kg (4 lb) piece blade steak
2 tablespoons oil
3 tablespoons Ceylon curry powder
3 cloves garlic, crushed
2 tablespoons grated fresh ginger
3 tablespoons chopped fresh lemon
  grass (white part only)
2 medium onions, chopped
3 tablespoons tamarind concentrate
3 tablespoons vinegar
2 cups (500 ml/16 fl oz) beef stock
2 cups (500 ml/16 fl oz) coconut milk

1 Trim the meat of all fat and sinew and tie with string so that the meat holds its shape.
2 Heat the oil in a large heavy-based pan; add the meat and cook over high heat until it browns. Remove meat from pan and set aside.
3 Reduce the heat to medium; add the curry powder, garlic, ginger, lemon grass and onion, and cook for 5 minutes or until the oil begins to separate from the spices.
4 Return the meat to the pan; add the tamarind, vinegar, stock and coconut milk, and bring to the boil; reduce heat, cover and simmer for 1¾ hours, or until the meat is tender.
5 Remove the meat from the pan and keep it warm. Bring the liquid to the boil and cook it, uncovered, for 10 minutes or until a thick gravy forms. Slice the meat and serve topped with the gravy.

NOTE: If Ceylon curry powder is not available, ask for a curry powder blend made for meat at an Asian food shop.

CANNELLONI

Preparation time: 45 minutes
Total cooking time: 1 hour 10 minutes
Serves 6

Beef and spinach filling
1 tablespoon olive oil
1 onion, chopped
1 clove garlic, crushed
500 g (1 lb) beef mince
250 g (8 oz) packet frozen spinach, thawed
3 tablespoons tomato paste (tomato
  purée, double concentrate)
½ cup (125 g/4 oz) ricotta cheese
1 egg
½ teaspoon ground oregano

Béchamel sauce
1 cup (250 ml/8 fl oz) milk
1 sprig of fresh parsley
5 peppercorns
30 g (1 oz) butter
1 tablespoon plain flour
½ cup (125 ml/4 fl oz) cream

Tomato sauce
425 g (14 oz) can tomato purée
2 tablespoons chopped fresh basil
1 clove garlic, crushed
½ teaspoon sugar

12–15 instant cannelloni tubes
1 cup (150 g/5 oz) freshly grated
  mozzarella cheese
½ cup (50 g/1¾ oz) freshly grated Parmesan

1 Preheat the oven to moderate 180°C (350°F/Gas 4). Lightly oil a large shallow ovenproof dish. Set aside.
2 To make the beef and spinach filling, heat the oil in a frying pan, add the onion and garlic and stir over low heat until the onion is tender. Add the mince and brown well, breaking up with a fork as it cooks. Add the spinach and tomato paste. Stir for 1 minute and then remove from the heat. In a small bowl, mix the ricotta, egg, oregano and salt and pepper, to taste. Stir the mixture through the mince until combined. Set aside.

3 To make the béchamel sauce, combine the milk, parsley and peppercorns in a small pan. Bring to the boil. Remove from the heat and allow to stand for 10 minutes. Strain, discarding the flavourings. Melt the butter in a small pan over low heat, add the flour and stir for 1 minute, or until smooth. Remove from the heat and gradually stir in the strained milk. Return to the heat and stir constantly over medium heat until the sauce boils and begins to thicken. Reduce the heat, simmer for another minute, then stir in the cream and salt and pepper, to taste.
4 To make the tomato sauce, stir all the ingredients in a pan until combined. Bring to the boil, reduce the heat and simmer for 5 minutes. Season, to taste, with salt and pepper.
5 Spoon the beef and spinach filling into a piping bag and fill the cannelloni tubes or fill using a teaspoon.
6 Spoon a little of the tomato sauce in the base of the casserole dish. Arrange the cannelloni on top. Pour the béchamel sauce over the cannelloni, followed by the remaining tomato sauce. Sprinkle the combined cheeses over the top. Bake, uncovered, for 35–40 minutes, or until golden.

NOTE: Serve with a mixed green salad or steam some vegetables such as broccoli or beans, if desired.

PERSIAN LAYERED LAMB POLO

Preparation time: 20 minutes
Total cooking time: 1 hour 35 minutes
Serves 4

120 g (4 oz) butter
1 onion, finely chopped
800 g (1 lb 10 oz) lean lamb fillet, cut into
    2 cm (¾ inch) chunks
½ teaspoon ground turmeric
½ teaspoon ground cinnamon
¼ cup (85 g/3 oz) prunes, pitted
½ cup (80 g) dried apricots, halved
2 cups (100 g/3½ oz) English spinach
    leaves, washed and blanched
2 cups (400 g/13 oz) basmati rice

1 In a large heavy-based saucepan, melt half the butter over medium heat, add the onion and cook for 5 minutes, or until golden. Add the lamb and brown on all sides. Add the turmeric and cinnamon and a little salt and pepper. Add the prunes and apricots, then pour in enough water to cover the meat. Cover with a lid and simmer, stirring occasionally, over low heat for 1¼ hours, or until the mixture is thick and the meat is tender. Add a little more water if the mixture looks like it is drying out.

2 Meanwhile, pour 1 litre (32 fl oz) water into a large saucepan and add 1 teaspoon salt. Bring to the boil, then add the rice and stir until the water returns to the boil. Boil for 5 minutes, then drain the rice in a colander. Add half the remaining butter to the saucepan with ¼ cup (60 ml/2 fl oz) water and bring to the boil. Swirl to coat the base and sides of pan, then spread half the rice over the base of the pan and smooth the surface with a wooden spoon. Spoon the remaining rice over the top and make a mound. Make a tunnel in the mound with the handle of a wooden spoon to the bottom of the pan and pour the remaining butter into the hole. Cover the pan with greaseproof paper, then secure the lid tightly. Cook over medium-low heat for 10 minutes, then reduce the heat to low and cook for another 10 minutes. The rice should be fluffy.

3 In large, heavy-based casserole dish with a lid, arrange half the rice, top with spinach and meat and cover with another layer of rice. You may need to drizzle with 2 tablespoons water if the rice is dry. Cover tightly and steam over low heat for 20 minutes, or until the rice is tender and has absorbed some of the sauce.

SPICED BEEF AND ONIONS

Preparation time: 15 minutes
Total cooking time: 1 hour 30 minutes
Serves 4

1 kg (2 lb) chuck steak
¼ cup (60 ml/2 fl oz) olive oil
750 g (1½ lb) whole baby onions
3 cloves garlic, cut in half lengthways
½ cup (125 ml/4 fl oz) red wine
1 cinnamon stick
4 whole cloves
1 bay leaf
1 tablespoon red wine vinegar
2 tablespoons tomato paste (tomato
    purée)
2 tablespoons currants

1 Trim the meat of excess fat and sinew, then cut into bite-sized cubes. Heat the oil over medium heat in a large heavy-based saucepan. Add the onions and stir for 5 minutes, or until golden. Remove from the pan and drain on paper towels.
2 Add the meat all at once to the pan and stir over high heat for 10 minutes, or until the meat is well browned and almost all the liquid has been absorbed.
3 Add the garlic, wine, spices, bay leaf, vinegar, tomato paste, ¼ teaspoon cracked black pepper, some salt and 1½ cups (375 ml/12 fl oz) water to the pan and bring to the boil. Reduce the heat, cover and simmer for 1 hour, stirring occasionally.
4 Return the onions to the saucepan, add the currants and stir gently. Simmer, covered, for 15 minutes. Discard the cinnamon before serving. Serve with rice, bread or potatoes.

NOTE: For a richer flavour, use 1½ cups (375 ml/12 fl oz) beef or veal stock instead of water in this recipe, or 1 cup (250 ml/8 fl oz) each of wine and water.

TAMARIND BEEF

Preparation time: 20 minutes
Total cooking time: 2 hours
Serves 4

2 tablespoons vegetable oil
1 kg (2 lb) chuck steak, cut into 4 cm
   (1½ inch) cubes
2 red onions, sliced
3 cloves garlic, finely chopped
1 tablespoon julienned fresh ginger
2 teaspoons ground coriander
2 teaspoons ground cumin
½ teaspoon ground fenugreek
½ teaspoon chilli powder
½ teaspoon ground cloves
1 cinnamon stick
½ cup (125 g/4 oz) tamarind purée
6 fresh curry leaves
1 cup (250 ml/8 fl oz) coconut cream
100 g (3½ oz) green beans, halved
fresh coriander sprigs, to garnish

1 Heat a non-stick wok over high heat, add the oil and swirl to coat the side of the wok. Add the beef in batches and cook over high heat for 2–3 minutes, or until browned. Remove from the wok.
2 Add the onion and cook over medium heat for 2–3 minutes, or until softened, then add the garlic and ginger, and cook for a further 2 minutes. Add the coriander, cumin, fenugreek, chilli powder, cloves and cinnamon stick, and cook for 2 minutes.
3 Return the meat to the wok and stir thoroughly until it is coated with the spices. Add the tamarind purée, curry leaves and 1 litre (32 fl oz) water. Bring to the boil, then reduce the heat to very low and simmer, covered, for 1½ hours, or until the beef is tender. Stir occasionally to prevent the meat from sticking to the wok. Pour in the coconut cream and cook, uncovered, for a further 5–10 minutes, then add the beans and cook for 5 minutes, or until tender but still crisp. Garnish with the coriander sprigs and serve with rice.

STIR-FRIED CHILLI BEEF WITH SPAGHETTINI

Preparation time: 40 minutes
Total cooking time: 20 minutes
Serves 4

500 g (1 lb) spaghettini
3 tablespoons peanut oil
1 onion, sliced
1 clove garlic, crushed
½ teaspoon finely chopped fresh ginger
¼ teaspoon chilli flakes
400 g (13 oz) lean beef (rump or scotch
   fillet), cut into thin strips
1½ teaspoons soy sauce
few drops sesame oil
155 g (5 oz) bean sprouts, trimmed
1 heaped tablespoon chopped fresh
   coriander

1 Cook the spaghettini in a large pan of rapidly boiling salted water until al dente. Drain, return to the pan and cover with cold water. Drain again and return to the pan. Stir 1 tablespoon of peanut oil through the pasta and set aside.
2 Heat 1 tablespoon of peanut oil in a large frying pan or wok and cook the onion, without browning, until softened. Stir in the garlic, ginger and chilli flakes. Add the beef and stir-fry over high heat until browned.
3 Stir in the soy sauce, sesame oil, bean sprouts and coriander. Taste for salt, pepper and chilli, adjust if necessary, and continue stirring until all the ingredients have heated through. Remove from the pan or wok. Add some peanut oil to the wok or pan and add the pasta, tossing it briefly over high heat to heat it through. Serve the spaghettini topped with the beef.

NOTE: As with all stir-fries, this dish requires quick, attentive cooking over high heat. Although it's tempting to take short cuts, rinsing the spaghettini in cold water is necessary to stop the cooking process and give the correct texture and flavour to the pasta.

RICE STICK NOODLES WITH KECAP BEEF

Preparation time: 15 minutes +
   10 minutes soaking
Total cooking time: 10 minutes
Serves 4

250 g (8 oz) narrow, dried rice stick
   noodles
¼ cup (60 ml/2 fl oz) peanut oil
300 g (10 oz) rump steak, sliced
2 garlic cloves, finely chopped
1 stem lemon grass, white part only,
   finely chopped
3 spring onions (scallions), sliced
200 g (6½ oz) sugar snap peas
1 bunch broccolini, roughly chopped
¼ cup (60 ml/2 fl oz) kecap manis
2 tablespoons soy sauce
1 tablespoon fish sauce
2 tablespoons snipped garlic chives (see
   Note)

1 Pour boiling water over the noodles and allow them to stand for 10 minutes or until tender and pliable. Drain.
2 Heat half the oil in a wok, add the meat, garlic and lemon grass in batches and stir-fry over high heat until the meat is browned. Add the spring onions, snap peas and broccolini and stir-fry for a few minutes, or until bright green and tender, but still slightly crisp. Remove from the wok and keep warm.
3 Add the remaining oil to the wok and then the noodles. Stir-fry for 1 minute. Stir in the kecap manis, soy sauce and fish sauce to coat the noodles.
4 Return the meat and the vegetables to the wok, along with any juices, and toss together until heated through. Stir in the chives and serve.

NOTE: Garlic chives (also known as Chinese chives) have a stronger flavour than regular chives, and they look wider and flatter. If you can't find them, use regular chives instead.

RIGATONI WITH KIDNEY BEANS AND ITALIAN SAUSAGE

Preparation time: 25 minutes
Total cooking time: 30 minutes
Serves 4–6

1 tablespoon olive oil
1 large onion, chopped
2 cloves garlic, crushed
4 Italian sausages, chopped
825 g (1 lb 11 oz) can crushed tomatoes
425 g (14 oz) can kidney or borlotti beans, drained
2 tablespoons chopped fresh basil
1 tablespoon chopped fresh sage
1 tablespoon chopped fresh parsley
500 g (1 lb) rigatoni
freshly grated Parmesan, for serving

1 Heat the oil in a heavy-based pan. Add the onion, garlic and sausage to the pan and cook, stirring occasionally, over medium heat for 5 minutes.
2 Add the tomato, beans, basil, sage, parsley and salt and pepper, to taste. Reduce the heat and simmer for 20 minutes.
3 While the sauce is cooking, add the pasta to a large pan of rapidly boiling salted water and cook until al dente. Drain. Divide the pasta among serving bowls and top with the sauce. Sprinkle with Parmesan and serve immediately.
note: Dried beans can be used. Soak them overnight in water, drain and transfer to a pan. Cover well with water, bring to the boil and cook for 20 minutes, or until tender. Giant conchiglie (shell pasta) can be used instead of rigatoni as they hold the sauce well.

BEEF WITH MANDARIN

Preparation time: 15 minutes +
    15 minutes standing
Total cooking time: 5 minutes
Serves 4

350 g (11¼ oz) rib eye steak, finely sliced
2 teaspoons soy sauce
2 teaspoons dry sherry
1 teaspoon chopped fresh ginger
1 teaspoon sesame oil
1 tablespoon peanut oil
¼ teaspoon ground white pepper
2 teaspoons finely chopped dried mandarin or tangerine peel
2 teaspoons soy sauce, extra
1½ teaspoons caster sugar
1½ teaspoons cornflour
⅓ cup (80 ml/2¾ fl oz) beef stock

1 Place the beef in a bowl. Mix the soy sauce, sherry, ginger and sesame oil together; stir through the meat to coat it. Set aside for 15 minutes.
2 Heat the peanut oil in a wok or heavy-based frying pan, swirling gently to coat the base and sides. Add the beef and stir-fry over high heat for 2 minutes, until meat changes colour.
3 Add the pepper, peel, extra soy sauce and sugar; stir-fry briefly.
4 Dissolve the cornflour in a little of the stock; add the remaining stock. Add the cornflour mixture to the wok and stir until the sauce boils and thickens. Serve with rice.

BAKED CANNELLONI MILANESE

Preparation time: 40 minutes
Total cooking time: 1 hour 50 minutes
Serves 4

500 g (1 lb) pork and veal mince
½ cup (50 g/1¾ oz) dry breadcrumbs
1 cup (100 g/3½ oz) freshly grated Parmesan
2 eggs, beaten
1 teaspoon dried oregano
12–15 cannelloni tubes
375 g (12 oz) fresh ricotta cheese
½ cup (60 g/2 oz) freshly grated Cheddar cheese

Tomato sauce
425 ml (14 fl oz) can tomato purée (passata)
425 g (14 oz) can crushed tomatoes
2 cloves garlic, crushed
3 tablespoons chopped fresh basil

1 Preheat the oven to moderate 180°C (350°F/Gas 4). Lightly brush a rectangular casserole dish with melted butter or oil.
2 In a bowl, combine the pork and veal mince, breadcrumbs, half the Parmesan, egg, oregano and salt and pepper, to taste. Use a teaspoon to stuff the cannelloni tubes with the mince mixture. Set aside.
3 To make the tomato sauce, bring the tomato purée, tomato and garlic to the boil in a medium pan. Reduce the heat and simmer for 15 minutes. Add the basil and pepper, to taste, and stir well.
4 Spoon half the tomato sauce over the base of the prepared dish. Arrange the stuffed cannelloni tubes on top. Cover with the remaining sauce. Spread with ricotta cheese. Sprinkle with the combined remaining Parmesan and Cheddar cheeses. Bake, covered with foil, for 1 hour. Uncover and bake for another 15 minutes, or until golden. Cut into squares for serving.

BEEF FILLET IN COCONUT

Preparation time: 15 minutes +
   1 hour marinating
Total cooking time: 10 minutes
Serves 4

500 g (1 lb) beef eye fillet
2 cloves garlic, crushed
2 teaspoons finely grated lemon rind
1 teaspoon grated fresh ginger
2 teaspoons ground coriander
½ teaspoon ground turmeric
2 teaspoons grated palm sugar or soft
   brown sugar
3 tablespoons peanut oil
½ cup (45 g/1½ oz) desiccated coconut
3 spring onions, cut into thin strips
½ cup (125 ml/4 fl oz) coconut milk

1 Cut the beef into thin slices. Mix together the garlic, lemon rind, ginger, coriander, turmeric, palm sugar and 2 tablespoons oil, add the beef and toss well to coat. Cover and chill for 1 hour.
2 Heat the remaining oil in a wok or frying pan; add the beef and stir-fry in batches until well browned. Add the coconut and spring onion and stir-fry for 1 minute more. Return all the meat to the pan; add the coconut milk and stir until heated through. Serve with rice.

MEXICAN BEEF CHILLI WITH BEANS AND RICE

Preparation time: 20 minutes + soaking
Total cooking time: 2 hours
Serves 4–6

2 cups (400 g/13 oz) long-grain rice
2 tablespoons olive oil
600 g (1¼ lb) chuck steak, cut into 2 cm
   (¾ inch) cubes
1 red onion, chopped
3 garlic cloves, crushed
1 long green chilli, finely chopped
2½ teaspoons ground cumin
2 teaspoons ground coriander
1 teaspoon chilli powder
3 teaspoons dried oregano
400 g (13 oz) tin chopped tomatoes
2 tablespoons tomato paste (purée)
3 cups (750 ml/24 fl oz) beef stock
400 g (13 oz) tin kidney beans, drained
   and rinsed
2 tablespoons fresh oregano, chopped
sour cream, to serve
burritos, to serve

1 Put the rice in a heatproof bowl, add enough boiling water to cover it and leave it to soak until cool.
2 Meanwhile, heat 1 tablespoon of the oil in a large, heavy-based saucepan. Cook the beef in two batches until browned, then remove from the pan.

3 Heat the remaining oil in the pan and cook the onion for 2 minutes, or until softened but not browned. Add the garlic and chilli and cook for a further minute, then add the cumin, ground coriander, chilli powder and dried oregano, and cook for a further 30 seconds. Return the beef to the pan and add the chopped tomatoes, tomato paste and 1 cup (250 ml/8 fl oz) of the stock. Bring to the boil, then reduce the heat and simmer, covered, for 1½ hours, or until the beef is tender.
4 Drain the rice and stir it into the beef mixture along with the kidney beans and remaining stock. Bring the mixture to the boil, then reduce the heat and simmer, covered, for 20 minutes, or until the rice is tender and all the liquid has been absorbed. Stir in the fresh oregano and serve with warmed burritos and a dollop of sour cream. Let your guests assemble their own burritos at the table.

PEPPERED BEEF FILLET WITH BEARNAISE SAUCE

Preparation time: 30 minutes
Total cooking time: 45 minutes
Serves 6

1 kg (2 lb) beef eye fillet
1 tablespoon oil
2 cloves garlic, crushed
1 tablespoon cracked black peppercorns
2 teaspoons crushed coriander seeds

Béarnaise sauce
3 spring onions, chopped
½ cup (125 ml/4 fl oz) dry white wine
2 tablespoons tarragon vinegar
1 tablespoon chopped fresh tarragon
125 g (4 oz) butter
4 egg yolks
1 tablespoon lemon juice

1 Preheat the oven to hot 210°C (415°F/Gas 6–7). Trim the fillet, removing any excess fat. Tie at regular intervals with kitchen string. Combine the oil and garlic, brush over the fillet, then roll the fillet in the combined peppercorns and coriander seeds.
2 Place the meat on a rack in a baking dish. Bake for 10 minutes, then reduce the oven to moderate 180°C (350°F/Gas 4) and cook for another 15–20 minutes for a rare result, or until cooked according to taste. Cover and leave for 10–15 minutes.
3 For the béarnaise sauce, put the spring onion, wine, vinegar and tarragon in a small saucepan. Boil the mixture rapidly until only 2 tablespoons of the liquid is left. Strain and set aside. Melt the butter in a small pan.
4 Place the wine mixture in a food processor with the egg yolks, and process for 30 seconds. With the motor running, add the hot butter in a thin stream, leaving the milky white sediment behind in the saucepan. Process until thickened. Add the lemon juice, to taste, and season with salt and white pepper.
5 Serve the beef with the béarnaise sauce, and some broccoli and potatoes.

OSSO BUCCO ALLA MILANESE

Preparation time: 30 minutes
Total cooking time: 1 hour 40 minutes
Serves 4

12 pieces veal shank, about 4 cm (1½ inch) thick
plain (all-purpose) flour, seasoned, for dusting
¼ cup (60 ml/2 fl oz) olive oil
60 g (2 oz) butter
1 garlic clove, finely chopped
1 onion, finely chopped
1 celery stalk, finely chopped
1 cup (250 ml/8 fl oz) dry white wine
1 bay leaf or lemon leaf
pinch of ground allspice
pinch of ground cinnamon

Gremolata
2 teaspoons grated lemon zest
2 tablespoons finely chopped flat-leaf (Italian) parsley
1 garlic clove, finely chopped

1 Dust each piece of veal shank with seasoned flour. Heat the oil, butter, garlic, onion and celery in a heavy-based frying pan or saucepan that is big enough to hold the shanks in a single layer (but don't add the shanks yet). Cook for about 5 minutes over low heat until softened but not browned. Add the shanks to the pan and cook for 12–15 minutes, or until well browned all over. Arrange the shanks in the pan, standing them up in a single layer. Pour in the wine and add the bay leaf, allspice and cinnamon. Bring to the boil and cover the pan. Turn the heat down to low.

2 Cook at a low simmer for 15 minutes, then add ½ cup (125 ml/4 fl oz) warm water. Continue cooking, covered, for 45–60 minutes (the timing will depend on the age of the veal) or until the meat is tender and you can cut it with a fork. Check the volume of liquid once or twice during cooking time and add more warm water as needed.
3 To make the gremolata, mix together the lemon zest, parsley and garlic.
4 Transfer the veal shanks to a plate and keep warm. Discard the bay leaf. Increase the heat under the pan and stir for 1–2 minutes until the sauce has thickened, scraping up any bits off the bottom of the pan as you stir. Season to taste with salt and freshly ground black pepper and return the veal shanks to the sauce. Heat everything through, then stir in half the gremolata. Serve sprinkled with the remaining gremolata.

RAVIOLI WITH MASCARPONE AND PANCETTA

Preparation time: 10 minutes
Total cooking time: 20 minutes
Serves 4

500 g (1 lb) fresh spinach ravioli
2 teaspoons vegetable oil
90 g (3 oz) pancetta, finely chopped
½ cup (125 ml/4 fl oz) chicken stock
185 g (6 oz) mascarpone
½ cup (80 g/2¾ oz) finely sliced sun-dried tomatoes
2 tablespoons finely shredded fresh basil
½ teaspoon cracked black pepper

1 Cook the ravioli in a large pan of rapidly boiling salted water until al dente.
2 While the pasta is cooking, heat the oil in a frying pan and cook the pancetta for 2–3 minutes. Stir in the stock, mascarpone and sun-dried tomatoes.
3 Bring to the boil, reduce the heat and simmer for 5 minutes, until the sauce reduces and thickens. Stir in the basil and pepper.
4 Drain the ravioli and add to the pan with the sauce. Toss together gently to combine. Serve immediately.

VEAL FOYOT

Preparation time: 25 minutes
Total cooking time: 1 hour 35 minutes
Serves 6

50 g (1¾ oz) butter
1 onion, chopped
¾ cup (185 ml/6 fl oz) white wine
¾ cup (185 ml/6 fl oz) beef stock
1.4–1.5 kg (2 lb 13 oz–3 lb) nut of veal
1 cup (80 g/2¾ oz) fresh breadcrumbs
125 g (4 oz) Gruyère cheese, grated

1 Preheat the oven to moderate 180°C (350°F/Gas 4). Melt half the butter in a saucepan and fry the onion until soft. Add the wine and stock, bring to the boil and boil for 2 minutes. Add ¼ teaspoon each of salt and white pepper. Remove from the heat and allow to cool.
2 Place the veal in a baking dish and rub with salt and white pepper. Pour the onion and wine mixture into the baking dish with the veal.
3 Mix the breadcrumbs and cheese, and press firmly on the veal to form a thick coating. (This will help stop the veal drying out.) Melt the remaining butter and pour over the cheese crust.
4 Roast the veal for 1¼–1½ hours, checking every 30 minutes and being careful not to disturb the crust. If the crust is browning too quickly, cover lightly with foil. Leave for 10 minutes before carving into 1 cm (½ inch) slices. Spoon pan juices over the top.

NOTE: Nut of veal is a piece from the leg.

HERBED RACK OF VEAL

Preparation time: 45 minutes
Total cooking time: 1 hour 40 minutes
Serves 4–6

1.2 kg (2 lb 6½ oz) rack of veal (8 cutlets)
1 cup (80 g/2¾ oz) fresh breadcrumbs
½ cup (50 g/1¾ oz) dry breadcrumbs
1 tablespoon chopped fresh parsley
1 tablespoon chopped fresh basil
2 egg whites, lightly beaten
2 cloves garlic, crushed
1 tablespoon oil
30 g (1 oz) butter, melted

Lemon sauce
⅓ cup (80 ml/2¾ fl oz) dry white wine
2 tablespoons lemon juice
2 teaspoons sugar
½ cup (125 ml/4 fl oz) cream
60 g (2 oz) chilled butter, cubed
1 tablespoon chopped fresh parsley

1 Preheat the oven to warm 160°C (315°F/Gas 2–3). Trim the veal of excess fat. Combine all the breadcrumbs, parsley and basil in a bowl. Add the combined egg whites, garlic, oil and butter, and mix well. Add a little water if the mixture is too dry. Press the mixture firmly over the meat and place in a baking dish, crust-side-up. Bake for 1¼ hours for a medium result, or 1½ hours for well done.
2 Remove the meat from the pan and leave in a warm place for 10 minutes. Drain off all except 2 tablespoons of pan juices.
3 For the lemon sauce, put the baking dish with the reserved pan juices on the stove. Add ½ cup (125 ml/4 fl oz) water with the wine, lemon juice, sugar and cream. Bring to the boil, then reduce the heat. Simmer for 5–7 minutes, or until the mixture is reduced by about ½ cup (125 ml/4 fl oz). Remove from the heat and whisk in the butter, 1 cube at a time, then strain and stir in the parsley. Cut the veal rack into cutlets and serve with the lemon sauce and some steamed baby squash.

MEATBALLS STROGANOFF

Preparation time: 40 minutes
Total cooking time: 20–25 minutes
Serves 4

500 g (1 lb) macaroni
750 g (1½ lb) lean beef mince
2 cloves garlic, crushed
2–3 tablespoons plain flour
1 teaspoon sweet paprika
2 tablespoons oil
50 g (1¾ oz) butter
1 large onion, thinly sliced
250 g (8 oz) small button mushrooms, halved
2 tablespoons tomato paste (tomato purée, double concentrate)
2–3 teaspoons Dijon mustard
¼ cup (60 ml/2 fl oz) white wine
½ cup (125 ml/4 fl oz) beef stock
¾ cup (185 g/6 oz) sour cream
3 tablespoons finely chopped fresh parsley

1 Cook the macaroni in a large pan of rapidly boiling water until al dente. Drain; keep warm.
2 Combine the beef mince, garlic and some salt and cracked pepper in a bowl. Use your hands to mix well. Roll 2 heaped teaspoons of the mince into balls. Combine the flour, paprika and some freshly ground black pepper on a clean surface or sheet of greaseproof paper. Dust the meatballs in the seasoned flour.
3 Heat the oil and half the butter in a frying pan. When foaming, cook the meatballs over medium heat, in batches, until brown. Remove from the pan and drain on paper towels.
4 Melt the remaining butter in the pan, add the onion and cook until soft. Stir in the mushrooms and cook until the mushrooms are tender. Pour in the combined tomato paste, mustard, wine and stock. Return the meatballs to the pan and gently reheat. Bring the mixture to the boil, reduce the heat and simmer for 5 minutes, stirring occasionally. Season to taste. Stir the sour cream through until smooth. Sprinkle with a little parsley and serve with the pasta.

CHILLI PLUM BEEF

Preparation time: 15 minutes
Total cooking time: 15 minutes
Serves 4

2 tablespoons vegetable oil
600 g (1¼ lb) lean beef fillet, thinly sliced across the grain
1 large red onion, cut into wedges
1 red pepper (capsicum), thinly sliced
1½ tablespoons chilli garlic sauce
½ cup (125 ml/4 fl oz) good-quality plum sauce
1 tablespoon light soy sauce
2 teaspoons rice vinegar
good pinch of finely ground white pepper
4 spring onions, sliced on the diagonal

1 Heat a wok over high heat, add 1 tablespoon of the oil and swirl to coat the side of the wok. Stir-fry the beef in two batches for 2–3 minutes, each batch, or until browned and just cooked. Remove from the wok.
2 Heat the remaining oil in the wok, add the onion and stir-fry for 1 minute before adding the red pepper and continuing to stir-fry for 2–3 minutes, or until just tender. Add the chilli garlic sauce and stir for 1 minute, then return the meat to the wok and add the plum sauce, soy sauce, vinegar, white pepper and most of the spring onion.
3 Toss everything together for 1 minute, or until the meat is reheated. Sprinkle with the remaining spring onion, then serve with steamed rice or noodles.

CHINESE BEEF AND ASPARAGUS WITH OYSTER SAUCE

Preparation time: 10 minutes + 15 minutes marinating
Total cooking time: 10 minutes
Serves 4

1 tablespoon light soy sauce
½ teaspoon sesame oil
1 tablespoon Chinese rice wine
500 g (1 lb) lean beef fillet, thinly sliced across the grain
2½ tablespoons vegetable oil
200 g (6½ oz) fresh thin asparagus, cut into thirds on the diagonal
3 cloves garlic, crushed
2 teaspoons julienned fresh ginger
¼ cup (60 ml/2 fl oz) chicken stock
2–3 tablespoons oyster sauce

1 Combine the soy sauce, sesame oil and 2 teaspoons of the rice wine in a large non-metallic bowl. Add the beef, cover with plastic wrap and marinate in the fridge for at least 15 minutes.
2 Heat a wok over high heat, add 1 tablespoon of the vegetable oil and swirl to coat the side of the wok. Add the asparagus and stir-fry for 1–2 minutes. Remove from the wok.
3 Heat another tablespoon of oil in the wok over high heat, then add the beef in two batches, stir-frying each batch for 1–2 minutes, or until cooked through. Remove the meat from the wok and add to the asparagus.
4 Add the remaining oil to wok, add the garlic and ginger before the oil becomes too hot and stir-fry for 1 minute, or until fragrant. Pour the stock, oyster sauce and remaining rice wine into the wok, bring to the boil and boil rapidly for 1–2 minutes, or until the sauce is slightly reduced. Return the beef and asparagus to the wok and stir-fry for a further minute, or until heated through and coated in the sauce. Serve immediately with steamed rice.

PASTITSIO
(MEAT AND PASTA BAKE)

Preparation time: 40 minutes + standing
Total cooking time: 1 hour 30 minutes
Serves 6

150 g (5 oz) elbow macaroni
40 g (1¼ oz) butter
¼ teaspoon ground nutmeg
60 g (2 oz) kefalotyri or Parmesan, grated
1 egg , lightly beaten

Meat sauce
2 tablespoons oil
1 onion, finely chopped
2 cloves garlic, crushed
500 g (1 lb) beef mince
½ cup (125 ml/4 fl oz) red wine
1 cup (250 ml/8 fl oz) beef stock
3 tablespoons tomato paste (tomato
   purée)
1 teaspoon chopped fresh oregano

Béchamel sauce
40 g (1¼ oz) butter
1½ tablespoons plain flour
pinch of nutmeg
1½ cups (375 ml/12 fl oz) milk
1 egg, lightly beaten

1 Preheat the oven to moderate 180°C (350°F/Gas 4). Lightly grease a 1.5 litre ovenproof dish. Cook the macaroni in a large saucepan of boiling salted water for 10 minutes, or until al dente. Drain and return to the pan. Melt the butter in a small saucepan until golden, then pour it over the macaroni. Stir in the nutmeg and half the cheese and season, to taste. Leave until cool, then mix in the egg and set aside.

2 For the meat sauce, heat the oil in a large frying pan, add the onion and garlic and cook over medium heat for 6 minutes, or until the onion is soft. Increase the heat, add the beef and cook, stirring, for 5 minutes or until the meat is browned. Add the wine and cook over high heat for 1 minute, or until evaporated. Add the stock, tomato paste, oregano, salt and pepper. Reduce the heat, cover and simmer for 20 minutes.
3 Meanwhile, to make the béchamel sauce, melt the butter in a small saucepan over low heat. Stir in the flour and cook for 1 minute, or until pale and foaming. Remove from the heat and gradually stir in the milk. Return to the heat and stir constantly until the sauce boils and thickens. Reduce the heat and simmer for 2 minutes. Add the nutmeg and some salt and pepper. Allow to cool a little before stirring in the beaten egg. Stir 3 tablespoons of the béchamel into the meat sauce.
4 Spread half the meat sauce in the dish, then layer half the pasta over it. Layer with the remaining meat sauce and then the remaining pasta. Press down firmly with the back of a spoon. Spread the béchamel sauce over the pasta and sprinkle the remaining cheese on top. Bake for 45–50 minutes, or until golden. Let it stand for 15 minutes before serving.

NOTE: Tubular bucatini, which is available in varying thicknesses, can be used as a substitute for the elbow macaroni. Choose one that is a little thicker than spaghetti.

COTTAGE PIE

Preparation time: 30 minutes
Total cooking time: 1 hour 30 minutes
Serves 6–8

2 tablespoons olive oil
2 onions, chopped
2 carrots, diced
1 celery stick, diced
1 kg (2 lb) beef mince
2 tablespoons plain flour
1½ cups (375 ml/12 fl oz) beef stock
1 tablespoon soy sauce
1 tablespoon Worcestershire sauce
2 tablespoons tomato sauce
1 tablespoon tomato paste
2 bay leaves
2 teaspoons chopped fresh flat-leaf
   parsley

Topping
800 g (1 lb 10 oz) potatoes, diced
400 g (13 oz) parsnips, diced
30 g (1 oz) butter
½ cup (125 ml/4 fl oz) milk

1 Heat the oil in a large frying pan over medium heat and cook the onion, carrot and celery, stirring occasionally, for 5 minutes, or until softened and lightly coloured. Add the mince and cook for 7 minutes, then stir in the flour and cook for 2 minutes. Add the stock, soy sauce, Worcestershire sauce, tomato sauce, tomato paste and bay leaves and simmer over low heat for 30 minutes, stirring occasionally. Leave to cool. Remove the bay leaves and stir in the parsley.
2 To make the topping, boil the potato and parsnip in salted water for 15–20 minutes, or until cooked through. Drain, return to the pan and mash with the butter and enough of the milk to make a firm mash.
3 Preheat the oven to 180°C (350°F/ Gas 4) and lightly grease a 2.5 litre ovenproof dish. Spoon the filling into the dish and spread the topping over it. Fluff with a fork. Bake for 25 minutes, or until golden.

PARMESAN AND ROSEMARY CRUSTED VEAL CHOPS

Preparation time: 15 minutes
Total cooking time: 15 minutes
Serves 4

4 veal chops
150 g (5 oz) fresh white breadcrumbs
75 g (2½ oz) grated Parmesan
1 tablespoon fresh rosemary, finely chopped
2 eggs, lightly beaten, seasoned
3 tablespoons olive oil
60 g (2 oz) butter
4 cloves garlic

1 Trim the chops of excess fat and sinew and flatten to 1 cm (½ inch) thickness. Pat the meat dry with paper towels. Combine the breadcrumbs, Parmesan and rosemary in a shallow bowl.
2 Dip each chop in the beaten egg, draining off the excess. Press both sides of the chops firmly in the crumbs.
3 Heat the oil and butter in a heavy-based frying pan over low heat, add the garlic and cook until golden. Discard the garlic.
4 Increase the heat to medium, add the chops to the pan and cook for 4–5 minutes on each side, depending on the thickness of the chops, until golden and crisp. Transfer to a warm serving dish and season with salt and pepper.

CELLOPHANE NOODLES WITH LAMB AND PEANUTS

Preparation time: 20 minutes +
   20 minutes soaking + 1 hour marinating
Total cooking time: 15 minutes
Serves 4

6 dried shiitake mushrooms
100 g (3½ oz) cellophane noodles
¼ cup (60 ml/2 fl oz) soy sauce
2 teaspoons sugar
1½ tablespoons sesame oil
5 cloves garlic, finely chopped
300 g (10 oz) lamb loin fillets, thinly sliced across the grain
¼ cup (60 ml/2 fl oz) peanut oil
2 small fresh red chillies, finely chopped
1 large carrot, julienned
2 small zucchini (courgettes), julienned
175 g (6 oz) baby English spinach leaves
5 spring onions, thinly sliced on the diagonal
1/3 cup (50 g/1¾ oz) unsalted peanuts, crushed
3 tablespoons chopped fresh coriander leaves
ground white pepper, to taste

1 Soak the mushrooms in boiling water for 20 minutes, or until soft. Squeeze dry, discard the stalks and thinly slice the caps. Meanwhile, soak the noodles in boiling water for 3–4 minutes, or until they are soft. Drain, then cut into 8 cm (3 inch) lengths with scissors.
2 Combine the soy sauce, sugar, 1 tablespoon sesame oil and half the garlic in a large non-metallic bowl. Add the lamb and toss well. Cover and marinate in the fridge for 1 hour.
3 Heat a large wok over high heat, add 1 tablespoon of the peanut oil and 1 teaspoon of the sesame oil and swirl to coat. Stir-fry the lamb in two batches (adding another teaspoon sesame oil and tablespoon peanut oil with each batch) for about 2 minutes, or until browned. Remove from the wok.
4 Wipe the wok clean, then return to high heat. Add the remaining peanut oil and swirl to coat. Stir-fry the chilli and remaining garlic for 30 seconds. Add the carrot and zucchini and cook for 2 minutes. Add the spinach, spring onion and mushrooms and cook for 1 minute. Return the lamb and any juices to the wok and stir-fry for 1–2 minutes, or until heated through. Add the noodles with half the crushed peanuts and coriander, season with white pepper and toss together until well combined. Garnish with the remaining peanuts and fresh coriander.

CORIANDER BEEF

Preparation time: 15 minutes +
  1–2 hours marinating
Total cooking time: 15 minutes
Serves 4

4 cloves garlic, finely chopped
1 tablespoon finely chopped fresh ginger
½ cup (25 g/¾ oz) chopped fresh
  coriander roots, stems and leaves
¼ cup (60 ml/2 fl oz) vegetable oil
500 g (1 lb) lean beef fillet, thinly sliced
  across the grain
oil, extra, for cooking
2 red onions, thinly sliced
½ red pepper (capsicum), thinly sliced
½ green pepper (capsicum), thinly sliced
1 tablespoon lime juice
½ cup (25 g/¾ oz) chopped fresh
  coriander leaves, extra

1 Combine the garlic, ginger, coriander
and oil in a large non-metallic bowl. Add
the beef, cover and refrigerate for
1–2 hours.
2 Heat a wok over high heat, add the meat
in three batches and stir-fry each batch
over high heat for 2–3 minutes, or until
the meat is just cooked. Remove all the
meat from the wok and keep it in a warm
place.
3 Heat 1 tablespoon oil in the wok, add the
onion and cook over medium–high heat
for 3–4 minutes, or until slightly softened.
Add the red and green pepper, and cook,
tossing constantly, for 3–4 minutes, or
until the pepper is slightly softened.
4 Return all the meat to the wok with the
lime juice and extra coriander. Toss well,
then remove from the heat and season
well with salt and pepper. Serve
immediately.

STIR-FRIED BEEF WITH SNAKE BEANS AND BASIL

Preparation time: 10 minutes +
  2 hours marinating
Total cooking time: 10 minutes
Serves 4

3 fresh bird's eye chillies, seeded and
  finely chopped
3 cloves garlic, crushed
2 tablespoons fish sauce
1 teaspoon grated palm sugar
2 tablespoons peanut or vegetable oil
400 g (13 oz) lean beef fillet, thinly sliced
  across the grain
150 g (5 oz) snake beans, sliced into 3 cm
  (1¼ inch) lengths
1 cup (30 g/1 oz) loosely packed fresh
  Thai basil
thinly sliced fresh bird's eye chilli, to
  garnish

1 Combine the chilli, garlic, fish sauce,
palm sugar and 1 tablespoon of the oil in
a large non-metallic bowl. Add the beef,
toss well, then cover and marinate in the
fridge for 2 hours.
2 Heat a wok to hot, add 2 teaspoons of
the oil and swirl to coat. Stir-fry the beef
in two batches over high heat for 2 minutes
each batch, or until just browned. Remove
from the wok.
3 Heat the remaining oil in the wok, then
add the snake beans and ¼ cup (60 ml/
2 fl oz) water and cook over high heat for
3–4 minutes, tossing regularly until
tender. Return the beef to the wok with
the basil. Cook for a further 1–2 minutes,
or until warmed through. Garnish with
chilli, then serve.

BEEF AND SPINACH STIR-FRY

Preparation time: 20 minutes +
  2 hours marinating
Total cooking time: 15 minutes
Serves 4

¼ cup (60 ml/2 fl oz) sweet chilli sauce
2 tablespoons soy sauce
1 clove garlic, crushed
2 teaspoons grated fresh ginger
1 tablespoon dry sherry
500 g (1 lb) lean beef fillet, thinly sliced
  across the grain
2 tablespoons vegetable oil
2 onions, cut into wedges
500 g (1 lb) English spinach leaves,
  shredded

1 Combine the sweet chilli sauce, soy
sauce, garlic, ginger and sherry in a large
non-metallic bowl. Add the beef, toss well
until it is coated in the marinade, then
cover with plastic wrap and refrigerate for
at least 2 hours, or overnight if time
permits.
2 Remove the meat from the marinade
with tongs or a slotted spoon. Heat a wok
over high heat, add 1 tablespoon of the oil
and swirl it around to coat the side of the
wok. Add the meat in batches and stir-fry
over high heat for 2–3 minutes each
batch, or until it is well browned, adding a
little more oil when necessary. Remove
from the wok.
3 Reheat the wok over high heat, add
another tablespoon of the oil and stir-fry
the onion wedges for 3–4 minutes, or until
tender and lightly browned. Return all the
meat to the wok and mix together.
4 Just before serving, toss the English
spinach leaves through the beef mixture
until the spinach is just wilted. Serve
immediately with steamed jasmine rice.

MEATBALLS AND PASTA

Preparation time: 40 minutes
Total cooking time: 55 minutes
Serves 4

⅔ cup (100 g/3½ oz) macaroni
500 g (1 lb) beef mince
1 onion, finely chopped
1 cup (80 g/2¾ oz) fresh breadcrumbs
2 tablespoons freshly grated Parmesan
1 tablespoon chopped fresh basil
1 egg, beaten
2 tablespoons olive oil
1 cup (150 g/5 oz) freshly grated
  mozzarella cheese

Sauce
1 onion, sliced
1 clove garlic, crushed
1 pepper (capsicum), seeded and sliced
125 g (4 oz) mushrooms, sliced
¼ cup (60 ml/2 fl oz) tomato paste
  (tomato purée, double concentrate)
½ cup (125 ml/4 fl oz) red wine

1 Cook the macaroni in a large pan of rapidly boiling salted water until al dente. Drain thoroughly and set aside.
2 In a bowl, combine the mince, onion, half the breadcrumbs, Parmesan, basil and egg. Form heaped teaspoonsful into small balls.
3 Heat the oil in a frying pan. Add the meatballs and cook until well browned. Drain on paper towels. Transfer to an ovenproof dish. Preheat the oven to moderate 180°C (350°F/Gas 4).
4 To make the sauce, add the onion and garlic to the same pan and stir over low heat until the onion is tender. Add the pepper and mushrooms and cook for 2 minutes. Stir in the tomato paste and then the wine and 1 cup (250 ml/8 fl oz) of water. Bring to the boil, stirring continuously. Mix in the macaroni and salt and pepper, to taste. Pour over the top of the meatballs.
5 Bake, uncovered, for 30–35 minutes. Sprinkle with combined mozzarella cheese and remaining breadcrumbs. Bake for another 10 minutes, or until golden.

SWEET AND SOUR LIVER

Preparation time: 10 minutes
Total cooking time: 10 minutes
Serves 4

40 g (1¼ oz) butter
⅓ cup (80 ml/2¾ fl oz) olive oil
600 g (1¼ lb) calves' livers, cut into long
  thin slices
1 cup (80 g/2¾ oz) fresh white
  breadcrumbs
1 tablespoon sugar
2 cloves garlic, crushed
¼ cup (60 ml/2 fl oz) red wine vinegar
1 tablespoon chopped fresh flat-leaf
  parsley

1 Heat the butter and half the oil in a heavy-based frying pan over medium heat. Coat the liver in breadcrumbs, pressing them on firmly with your hands. Shake off the excess and place in the pan when the butter begins to foam. Cook on each side for 1 minute, or until the crust is brown and crisp. Remove from the pan and keep warm.
2 Add the remaining oil to the frying pan and cook the sugar and garlic over low heat until golden. Add the vinegar and cook for 30 seconds, or until almost evaporated. Add the parsley and pour over the liver. Serve hot or at room temperature.

SPICY DRY-FRIED BEEF

Preparation time: 15 minutes +
  2 hours marinating
Total cooking time: 10 minutes
Serves 4

1 tablespoon light soy sauce
½ teaspoon sesame oil
1 tablespoon Chinese rice wine
400 g (13 oz) lean beef fillet, thinly sliced
  across the grain, then shredded
2–3 tablespoons peanut oil
2 cloves garlic, finely chopped
1 teaspoon grated fresh ginger
3 spring onions, finely chopped

Sauce
1½ tablespoons brown bean sauce
1 tablespoon chilli bean paste
½ teaspoon caster sugar
½ teaspoon chilli oil
¼ teaspoon sea salt

1 Combine the soy sauce, sesame oil, 2 teaspoons of the rice wine and ½ teaspoon salt in a large non-metallic bowl. Add the beef, cover with plastic wrap and marinate in the fridge for at least 2 hours.
2 Combine all the ingredients in a small non-metallic bowl or jug.
3 Heat a wok over high heat, add 1 tablespoon of the peanut oil and swirl to coat the side of the wok. Add the beef in two batches, using your hands to break up any clumps. Stir-fry each batch for 1 minute, or until the beef is browned. Remove, place on crumpled paper towels and drain off any liquid from the meat.
4 Clean and dry the wok, then heat over high heat, add the remaining oil and swirl to coat. Add the garlic and ginger and stir-fry for 30 seconds, or until fragrant. Return the beef to the wok and cook for 2 minutes, or until it is dry. Add the remaining rice wine and stir-fry for 30 seconds, or until all the wine is absorbed. Add the bean sauce mixture and stir well, until the beef is well coated. Remove from the heat, stir in the spring onion and serve.

ASIAN PEPPERED BEEF

Preparation time: 10 minutes +
  2 hours marinating
Total cooking time: 15 minutes
Serves 4

2 onions, thinly sliced
2 cloves garlic, finely chopped
2 teaspoons finely chopped fresh ginger
2 tablespoons Chinese rice wine
1 tablespoon soy sauce
1 tablespoon oyster sauce
2 teaspoons sugar
1 teaspoon sesame oil
1 teaspoon Sichuan peppercorns, crushed
1 tablespoon black peppercorns, crushed
600 g (1¼ lb) lean beef fillet, thinly sliced
  across the grain
2 spring onions, cut into 2.5 cm (¾ inch)
  lengths
2 tablespoons vegetable oil

1 Combine the onion, garlic, ginger, rice
wine, soy sauce, oyster sauce, sugar,
sesame oil and peppercorns in a non-
metallic bowl. Add the beef, cover and
marinate in the refrigerator for at least
2 hours.
2 Drain the beef, discarding any excess
liquid, then stir in the spring onion.
3 Heat a wok over high heat, add half the
oil and swirl to coat. Add half the beef and
stir-fry for 6 minutes, or until seared and
cooked to your liking. Repeat with the
remaining oil and beef. Serve with
steamed rice.

PASTICCIO

Preparation time: 1 hour
Total cooking time: 1 hour 50 minutes
Serves 6

2 cups (250 g/8 oz) plain flour
125 g (4 oz) cold butter, chopped
¼ cup (60 g/2 oz) caster sugar
1 egg yolk

Filling
2 tablespoons olive oil
1 onion, chopped
2 cloves garlic, finely chopped
500 g (1 lb) beef mince
150 g (5 oz) chicken livers
2 tomatoes, chopped
½ cup (125 ml/4 fl oz) red wine
½ cup (125 ml/4 fl oz) rich beef stock
1 tablespoon chopped fresh oregano
¼ teaspoon nutmeg
½ cup (50 g/1¾ oz) freshly grated
  Parmesan

Béchamel sauce
60 g (2 oz) butter
2 tablespoons plain flour
1½ cups (375 ml/12 fl oz) cold milk

150 g (5 oz) bucatini

1 Put the flour, butter, sugar and egg yolk
in a food processor with 1 tablespoon of
water. Process lightly until the mixture
forms a ball, adding more water if
necessary. Lightly knead the dough on a
floured surface until smooth. Wrap in
plastic wrap and refrigerate.
2 To make the filling, heat the oil in a
heavy-based pan and cook the onion and
garlic until softened and lightly golden.
Increase the heat, add the mince and cook
until browned, breaking up any lumps
with a fork. Add the livers, tomato, red
wine, stock, oregano and nutmeg, then
season well with salt and pepper. Cook
the sauce over high heat until it boils, then
reduce to a simmer and cook, covered, for
40 minutes; cool. Stir in the Parmesan.

3 To make the béchamel sauce, heat the
butter in a medium pan over low heat.
Add the flour and stir for 1 minute, or until
the mixture is golden and smooth.
Remove from the heat and gradually stir
in the milk. Return to the heat and stir
constantly until the sauce boils and
begins to thicken. Simmer for another
minute. Add salt and pepper, to taste.
4 Cook the bucatini in a pan of rapidly
boiling salted water until al dente. Drain
and cool. Brush a 23 cm (9 inch) deep pie
dish with melted butter or oil and preheat
the oven to warm 160°C (315°F/Gas 2–3).
Divide the pastry into two and roll out one
piece to fit the base of the prepared dish,
overlapping the sides. Spoon about half of
the meat mixture into the dish, top with
the bucatini and slowly spoon the
béchamel sauce over the top, allowing it
to seep down and coat the bucatini. Top
with the remaining meat. Roll out the
remaining pastry and cover the pie. Trim
the edges and pinch lightly to seal. Bake
for 50–55 minutes, or until dark golden
brown and crisp. Set aside for 15 minutes
before cutting.

CLASSIC LASAGNE

Preparation time: 40 minutes
Total cooking time: 1 hour 40 minutes
Serves 8

2 tablespoons oil
30 g (1 oz) butter
1 large onion, finely chopped
1 carrot, finely chopped
1 celery stick, finely chopped
500 g (1 lb) beef mince
150 g (5 oz) chicken livers, finely chopped
1 cup (250 ml/8 fl oz) tomato purée
1 cup (250 ml/8 fl oz) red wine
2 tablespoons chopped fresh parsley
375 g (12 oz) fresh lasagne sheets

Béchamel sauce
60 g (2 oz) butter
⅓ cup (40 g/1¼ oz) plain flour
2¼ cups (560 ml/18 fl oz) milk
½ teaspoon nutmeg
1 cup (100 g/3½ oz) freshly grated
   Parmesan

1 Heat the oil and butter in a heavy-based pan and cook the onion, carrot and celery over medium heat until softened, stirring constantly. Increase the heat, add the mince and brown well, breaking up any lumps with a fork. Add the chicken livers and cook until they change colour. Add the tomato purée, wine, parsley, and salt and pepper, to taste. Bring to the boil, reduce the heat and simmer for 45 minutes; set aside.

2 To make the béchamel sauce, melt the butter in a medium pan over low heat. Add the flour and stir for 1 minute. Remove from the heat and gradually stir in the milk. Return to the heat and stir constantly until the sauce boils and begins to thicken. Simmer for another minute. Add the nutmeg and salt, pepper, to taste. Place a piece of plastic wrap on the surface of the sauce to prevent a skin forming; set aside.

3 Cut the lasagne sheets to fit snugly into a deep, rectangular ovenproof dish. Sometimes the sheets require precooking, so follow the instructions from the manufacturer and drain well before use.

4 To assemble, preheat the oven to moderate 180°C (350°F/Gas 4). Brush the ovenproof dish generously with melted butter or oil. Spread a thin layer of the meat sauce over the base and follow with a thin layer of béchamel. If béchamel has cooled and become too thick, warm it gently to make spreading easier. Lay lasagne sheets on top, gently pressing to push out any air. Continue the layers, finishing with the béchamel. Sprinkle with Parmesan and bake for 35–40 minutes, or until golden brown. Set aside 15 minutes before cutting.

NOTE: A packet of instant lasagne can be used instead of fresh. Follow the manufacturer's instructions. If you prefer, you can leave out the chicken livers and increase the amount of mince.

RIGATONI WITH SALAMI AND FRESH HERBS

Preparation time: 35 minutes
Total cooking time: 40 minutes
Serves 4

20 g (¾ oz) butter
1 tablespoon olive oil
1 onion, thinly sliced
1 carrot, cut into julienne strips
1 bay leaf
75 g (2½ oz) bacon rashers, chopped
200 g (6½ oz) spicy Italian salami, skinned
   and sliced
400 g (13 oz) can peeled egg (Roma)
   tomatoes
½ cup (125 ml/4 fl oz) beef or chicken
   stock
400 g (13 oz) rigatoni
1 tablespoon fresh oregano or marjoram
   leaves

1 Heat the butter and oil in a frying pan and cook the onion and carrot with the bay leaf until the onion is transparent and softened. Add the chopped bacon and sliced salami and cook, stirring often, until brown.

2 Squeeze half the tomatoes dry over the sink, pulp the flesh with your hand and add to the pan. Add the rest whole and break up loosely with the spoon while stirring. Season well with salt and pepper, to taste, and simmer for 30 minutes over low heat, gradually adding the stock as the sauce reduces.

3 Cook the rigatoni in a large pan of rapidly boiling salted water until al dente. Drain and transfer to a warm serving dish. Add the oregano or marjoram and sauce, and toss together lightly before serving.

NOTE: Use good-quality salami to ensure the success of this sauce. The use of fresh herbs is also important to produce the best flavour.

FRUITY LAMB PILAFF

Preparation time: 20 minutes +
   30 minutes soaking
Total cooking time: 2 hours
Serves 4–6

2 cups (400 g/13 oz) basmati rice
600 g (1¼ lb) lamb fillets, cubed
½ teaspoon cayenne pepper
1 teaspoon ground coriander
1 teaspoon ground cumin
1 tablespoon olive oil
40 g (1¼ oz) butter
2 onions, sliced
1 bay leaf
1 cinnamon stick
1 teaspoon ground allspice
¼ teaspoon ground cloves
2 tablespoons tomato paste (purée)
3½ cups (875 ml/28 fl oz) beef stock
3 tablespoons finely chopped parsley
⅓ cup (50 g/1¾ oz) pine nuts, toasted
⅓ cup (40 g/1¼ oz) raisins
50 g (1¾ oz) dried apricots, halved
2 tablespoons mint
⅓ cup (80 g/2¾ oz) thick natural yoghurt,
   to serve

1 Soak the rice in boiling water for 30 minutes.
2 Toss the lamb in the cayenne, coriander and cumin. Heat the oil in a large saucepan over medium heat and cook the lamb in batches until browned all over. Remove from the pan.

3 Melt the butter in the same pan and cook the onion over medium heat for 5 minutes, or until soft. Add the bay leaf, cinnamon, allspice and cloves and cook for 30 seconds, then add the tomato paste. Cook for 1 minute, then return the lamb to the pan. Add 2 cups (500 ml/16 fl oz) of the stock, bring to the boil, then reduce the heat and cover with a lid. Simmer for 1½ hours, or until the liquid has been absorbed and the lamb is tender.
4 Drain the rice and add it to the lamb mixture along with the remaining stock and the parsley, pine nuts, raisins and apricots. Bring to the boil, then reduce the heat and simmer, covered, for 20 minutes, or until the liquid has been absorbed and the rice is tender. Stir in the mint and serve with yoghurt.

SHEPHERD'S PIE

Preparation time: 30 minutes
Total cooking time: 1 hour 15 minutes
Serves 6

750 g (1½ lb) lean cooked roast lamb
25 g (¾ oz) butter
2 onions, finely chopped
¼ cup (30 g/1 oz) plain flour
½ teaspoon dry mustard
1½ cups (375 ml/12 fl oz) chicken stock
2 tablespoons Worcestershire sauce

Potato topping
4 large potatoes
½ cup (125 ml/4 fl oz) hot milk
30 g (1 oz) butter

1 Brush a 2 litre (64 fl oz) casserole with melted butter or oil. Preheat the oven to hot 210°C (415°F/Gas 6–7). Trim the meat of excess fat, then mince or finely chop. Melt the butter in a large pan, add the onion and stir over medium heat for 5–10 minutes, until golden.
2 Add the flour and mustard to the pan and cook for 1 minute, or until pale and foaming. Remove from the heat and gradually stir in the stock. Return to the heat and stir constantly until the sauce boils and thickens. Reduce the heat and simmer for 2 minutes.
3 Add the meat and Worcestershire sauce to the pan and stir. Season, to taste. Remove from the heat and spoon into the casserole dish.
4 For the potato topping, steam or boil the potatoes for 10–15 minutes, or until just tender (pierce with the point of a small sharp knife—if the potato comes away easily, it's ready). Drain and mash well. Add the milk, butter, and salt and pepper, to taste, to the mashed potato and mix until smooth and creamy. Spread evenly over the meat and rough up the surface with the back of a spoon. Bake for 40–45 minutes, or until the meat is heated through and the topping is golden.

ROAST LAMB WITH LEMON AND POTATOES

Preparation time: 20 minutes
Total cooking time: 3 hours
Serves 6

2.5–3 kg (5–6 lb) leg of lamb
2 cloves garlic
½ cup (125 ml/4 fl oz) lemon juice
3 tablespoons dried oregano
1 brown onion, sliced
2 sticks celery, sliced
40 g (1¾ oz) butter, softened
1 kg (2 lb) potatoes, quartered

1 Preheat the oven to moderate 180°C (350°F/Gas 4). Cut small slits in the lamb and cut the garlic into slivers. Insert the garlic into the slits. Rub the entire surface with half the lemon juice, sprinkle with salt, pepper and half the oregano. Place in a baking dish and bake for 1 hour.
2 Drain the fat from the pan and add the onion, celery and 1 cup (250 ml/8 fl oz) hot water. Spread the butter on the lamb, reduce the oven to warm 160°C (315°F/Gas 2–3) and cook for 1 hour. Turn during cooking to brown evenly.
3 Add the potatoes to the pan, sprinkle with the remaining oregano and lemon juice and some salt and pepper. Bake for another hour, adding more water if required and turning the potatoes halfway through cooking. Cut the lamb into chunks. Skim any excess fat from the pan and serve the juices with the potatoes and lamb.

LAMB WITH HOKKIEN NOODLES AND SOUR SAUCE

Preparation time: 25 minutes
Total cooking time: 15 minutes
Serves 4–6

450 g (14 oz) Hokkien noodles
½ cup (125 ml/4 fl oz) chicken stock
15 g (½ oz) palm sugar, grated
1 tablespoon lime juice
2 tablespoons vegetable oil
375 g (12 oz) lamb loin fillets, thinly sliced across the grain
75 g (2½ oz) red Asian shallots, thinly sliced
3 cloves garlic, crushed
2 teaspoons finely chopped fresh ginger
1 small fresh red chilli, seeded and chopped
1½ tablespoons Thai red curry paste (see page 762)
125 g (4 oz) snow peas (mangetout), trimmed and cut in half on the diagonal
1 small carrot, julienned
small whole fresh basil leaves, to garnish

1 Cover the noodles with boiling water and soak for 1 minute. Drain well.
2 To make the stir-fry sauce, combine the stock, palm sugar and lime juice in a small non-metallic bowl or jug and stir until the sugar has dissolved. Set aside until needed.
3 Heat a wok over high heat, add 1 tablespoon of the oil and swirl to coat the side of the wok. Stir-fry the lamb in batches over high heat for 2–3 minutes each batch, or until it just starts to brown. Remove from the wok.
4 Heat the remaining oil in the wok, then add the shallots, garlic, ginger and chilli and stir-fry for 1–2 minutes. Stir in the curry paste and cook for 1 minute. Add the snow peas and carrot and return the lamb to the wok. Cook, tossing often, for 1–2 minutes, or until thoroughly combined.
5 Pour in the stir-fry sauce, toss together well and cook for 2–3 minutes. Add the noodles and cook for 1 minute, or until heated through. Divide among serving bowls and garnish with the basil.

PARSEE LAMB WITH CUMIN, EGGS AND TAGLIATELLE

Preparation time: 40 minutes
Total cooking time: 1 hour 15 minutes
Serves 4

20 g (¾ oz) butter
1 large onion, finely chopped
2 cloves garlic, crushed
1 teaspoon finely chopped fresh ginger
¾ teaspoon each of chilli flakes, turmeric, garam masala and ground cumin
600 g (1¼ lb) minced lamb
2 large very ripe tomatoes, chopped
½ teaspoon sugar
1 tablespoon lemon juice
3 tablespoons finely chopped fresh coriander
1 small red chilli, finely chopped, optional
350 g (11 oz) tagliatelle
1 tablespoon vegetable oil
3 hard-boiled eggs, chopped

1 Heat the butter in a frying pan and add the onion, garlic and ginger. Fry over low heat until the onion is soft but not browned. Stir in the chilli flakes, turmeric, garam masala and cumin.
2 Add the mince, increase the heat and cook until the meat is well browned, stirring occasionally. Stir in the tomato, sugar, a good pinch of salt and 1 cup (250 ml/8 fl oz) of water. Reduce the heat and simmer, covered, for 50–60 minutes, or until the sauce thickens and darkens. Increase the heat and add the lemon juice, 2 tablespoons of the chopped coriander and the red chilli. Check the seasoning, add salt if required and cook, uncovered, for 2–3 minutes.
3 Cook the tagliatelle in a large pan of rapidly boiling salted water until al dente. Drain, return to the pan and stir in the oil. Transfer to warmed serving dishes and spoon the lamb mixture on top. Sprinkle with hard-boiled eggs and the remaining fresh coriander before serving.

ROAST LEG OF LAMB WITH GARLIC AND ROSEMARY

Preparation time: 20 minutes
Total cooking time: 1 hour 30 minutes
Serves 6

2 kg (4 lb) leg of lamb
2 cloves garlic, cut into thin slivers
2 tablespoons fresh rosemary sprigs
2 teaspoons oil

1 Preheat the oven to moderate 180°C (350°F/Gas 4). Using a small sharp knife, cut small slits all over the lamb. Insert the slivers of garlic and sprigs of rosemary into the slits.
2 Brush the lamb with the oil and sprinkle with salt and black pepper. Place on a rack in a baking dish. Add ½ cup (125 ml/4 fl oz) water to the dish. Bake for about 1 hour 30 minutes for medium, or until cooked as desired, basting often with the pan juices. Keep warm and leave for 10–15 minutes before carving. Serve with mint sauce

LAMB BRAISE WITH EGGPLANT CREAM

Preparation time: 30 minutes
Total cooking time: 1 hour 45 minutes
Serves 6–8

2 tablespoons olive oil
1 kg (2 lb) lamb, cut into 2 cm (¾ inch) cubes
1 large onion, chopped
1 bay leaf
small pinch of ground cloves
2 cloves garlic, crushed
2 tablespoons tomato paste (tomato purée)
400 g (13 oz) can good-quality chopped tomatoes
1 cup (30 g/1 oz) chopped flat-leaf parsley
3 cups (750 ml/24 fl oz) beef stock
125 g (4 oz) vine-ripened tomatoes, chopped
chopped fresh flat-leaf parsley, to garnish

Eggplant cream
1 kg (2 lb) eggplants (aubergines)
60 g (2 oz) butter
2½ tablespoons plain flour
1¼ cups (315 ml/10 fl oz) cream
2/3 cup (60 g/2 oz) grated kasseri cheese (see Note)
large pinch of ground nutmeg

1 Preheat the oven to moderately hot 200°C (400°F/Gas 6). Heat the olive oil in large deep saucepan over high heat and cook the lamb in three batches for 4–5 minutes, or until well browned. Remove the lamb from the pan with a slotted spoon and set aside.
2 Add the onion to the pan, cook for 5 minutes, or until golden, then add the bay leaf, cloves, garlic, tomato paste, tomato, parsley, stock and lamb and stir well. Bring to the boil, then reduce the heat to low, cover and simmer, stirring occasionally for 1½ hours, or until the lamb is very tender and the sauce is thick. Season.

3 Meanwhile, pierce the eggplants a few times with a fork and, using a long-handled fork, roast them over an open flame (either a gas stovetop or a barbecue) for about 5 minutes, turning occasionally, until blackened and blistered all over. This will give them a good smoky flavour. Place the eggplants in a baking tray and bake for about 30 minutes, or until the eggplants are shrivelled and the flesh is very soft. Transfer to a colander and leave to cool.
4 When cool, peel the eggplants, ensuring all the skin is removed and discarded. Chop the flesh and set aside. Melt the butter in a saucepan over medium heat and add the flour. Stir for 2 minutes, or until it has a toasty aroma and darkens slightly. Gradually pour in the cream, whisking until smooth then add the eggplant and combine. Add the cheese and nutmeg and stir until the cheese has melted. Season.
5 Spread the eggplant cream on a serving plate then place the lamb braise in the centre and sprinkle with the chopped tomato and parsley. Serve immediately.

NOTE: Kasseri cheese, available at specialist delicatessens, is a sheep or goat's milk cheese, often used on top of lamb stews.

SHISH KEBABS WITH PEPPERS (CAPSICUMS) AND HERBS

Preparation time: 20 minutes +
   4 hours marinating
Total cooking time: 5 minutes
Serves 4

1 kg (2 lb) boneless leg of lamb
1 red pepper (capsicum)
1 green pepper (capsicum)
3 red onions
olive oil, for brushing

Marinade
1 onion, thinly sliced
2 cloves garlic, crushed
¼ cup (60 ml/2 fl oz) lemon juice
⅓ cup (80 ml/2¾ fl oz) olive oil
1 tablespoon chopped fresh thyme
1 tablespoon paprika
½ teaspoon chilli flakes
2 teaspoons ground cumin
½ cup (15 g/½ oz) chopped fresh flat-leaf
   parsley
⅓ cup (20 g/¾ oz) chopped fresh mint

1 Trim the sinew and most of the fat from the lamb and cut the meat into 3 cm (1¼ inch) cubes.
2 Mix all the ingredients for the marinade in a large bowl. Season well, add the meat and mix well. Cover and refrigerate for 4–6 hours, or overnight.
3 Cut the peppers into 3 cm (1¼ inch) squares. Cut each red onion into 6 wedges.
4 Remove the lamb from the marinade and reserve the liquid. Thread the meat onto long skewers, alternating with onion and pepper pieces. Grill the skewers for 5–6 minutes, brushing frequently with the marinade for the first couple of minutes. Serve immediately. These are delicious served with bread or pilaf.

LAMB HOTPOT WITH RICE NOODLES

Preparation time: 20 minutes +
   2 hours marinating
Total cooking time: 2 hours
Serves 4

2 garlic cloves, crushed
2 teaspoons grated ginger
1 teaspoon five-spice powder
¼ teaspoon ground white pepper
2 tablespoons Chinese rice wine
1 teaspoon sugar
1 kg (2 lb) boneless lamb shoulder,
   trimmed and cut into 3 cm (1¼ inch)
   pieces
30 g (1 oz) dried Chinese mushrooms
1 tablespoon peanut oil
1 large onion, cut into wedges
2 cm (¾ inch) piece of ginger, julienned
1 teaspoon Sichuan peppercorns, crushed
2 tablespoons sweet bean paste
1 teaspoon black peppercorns, ground
   and toasted
2 cups (500 ml/16 fl oz) chicken stock
¼ cup (60 ml/2 fl oz) oyster sauce
2 star anise
¼ cup (60 ml/2 fl oz) Chinese rice wine,
   extra
80 g (2¾ oz) tin sliced bamboo shoots,
   drained
100 g (3½ oz) tin water chestnuts, drained
   and sliced
400 g (13 oz) fresh rice noodles, cut into 2
   cm (¾ inch) wide strips
1 spring onion (scallion), sliced on the
   diagonal

1 Combine the garlic, grated ginger, five-spice powder, white pepper, rice wine, sugar and 1 teaspoon salt in a large bowl. Add the lamb and toss to coat. Cover and marinate for 2 hours.
2 Meanwhile, soak the dried mushrooms in boiling water for 30 minutes, then drain and squeeze out any excess water. Remove and discard the stems and chop the caps.
3 Heat a wok over high heat, add the oil and swirl to coat. Stir-fry the onion, julienned ginger and Sichuan peppercorns for 2 minutes. Add the lamb in batches and cook for 2–3 minutes, or until starting to brown. Return all the lamb to the wok. Stir in the bean paste and ground peppercorns and cook for 3 minutes. Transfer to a 2 litre (64 fl oz) flameproof clay pot or casserole dish. Stir in the stock, oyster sauce, star anise and extra rice wine and simmer, covered, over low heat for 1½ hours, or until the lamb is tender. Stir in the bamboo shoots and water chestnuts and cook for 20 minutes. Add the mushrooms.
4 Cover the noodles with boiling water and gently separate. Drain and rinse, then add to the hotpot, stirring for 1–2 minutes, or until heated through. Sprinkle with spring onion.

SPICED ROAST LEG OF LAMB

Preparation time: 35 minutes
Total cooking time: 2 hours
Serves 6

2 kg (4½ lb) leg of lamb
1 tablespoon lemon juice
freshly ground black pepper
1 whole head garlic, unpeeled
2 tablespoons ghee or oil
1½ tablespoons ground coriander
2 teaspoons ground cumin
2 cinnamon sticks
2 cloves
4 bay leaves
1 teaspoon chilli powder
4 cardamom pods, lightly crushed
1½ cups (375 ml/12 fl oz) water
½ cup (125 g/4 oz) yoghurt

1 Preheat the oven to moderate 180°C (350°F/Gas 4).
2 Trim the excess fat from the lamb. Rub it all over with lemon juice and pepper, and place it in a roasting pan with the whole garlic and ghee. Bake for about 50 minutes, or until the garlic cloves are soft.
3 Squeeze the soft cooked garlic pulp from the skins. Spread the garlic pulp evenly over the lamb and sprinkle over the coriander and cumin. Add the cinnamon sticks, cloves, bay leaves, chilli powder and cardamom pods to the pan.
4 Roast the lamb for a further 50 minutes, or until cooked, basting it occasionally with the pan juices. Remove the lamb and set aside for 10 to 15 minutes before carving.
5 Add the water to the baking pan and stir to combine the juices. Place the pan on the stove top; cook over high heat until the liquid reduces and thickens. Remove the whole spices, and season with salt and pepper to taste. Stir in the yoghurt and heat through. Spoon the sauce over the carved roast.

MADRAS LAMB PULAO

Preparation time: 15 minutes
Total cooking time: 35 minutes
Serves 4

¼ cup (60 ml/2 fl oz) oil
2 onions, thinly sliced
1 cup (250 g/8 oz) thick natural yoghurt
¼ cup (60 g/2 oz) good-quality Madras curry paste
2 cups (400 g/13 oz) basmati rice, rinsed well
8 large French-trimmed lamb cutlets
4 tablespoons chopped mint
½ cup (60 g/2 oz) slivered almonds, lightly toasted

1 Heat 2 tablespoons of the oil in a large saucepan, add the onion and cook over medium heat for 4–5 minutes, or until soft. Remove half with a slotted spoon, set aside and keep warm. Add 200 g (6½ oz) of the yoghurt and 2 tablespoons of the curry paste to the pan. Cook, stirring, for 2 minutes. Stir in the rice until well coated. Pour in 2 cups (500 ml/16 fl oz) water, bring to the boil, then reduce the heat a little and cook for 15–20 minutes, or until all the water has been absorbed and the rice is tender.
2 Meanwhile, smear the cutlets with the remaining curry paste and marinate for at least 5 minutes. Heat the remaining oil in a frying pan over high heat, then cook the cutlets for 3–4 minutes on each side, or until cooked to your liking. Remove from the heat, cover with foil and allow to rest. Combine the remaining yoghurt with 1 tablespoon of the mint.
3 To serve, stir the remaining mint through the rice, season, then divide among four serving plates. Top with the remaining onions, the lamb and the almonds. Serve with a dollop of the minted yoghurt on the side.

BRAISED LAMB SHANKS WITH HARICOT BEANS

Preparation time: 10 minutes + overnight soaking
Total cooking time: 2 hours 15 minutes
Serves 4

2 cups (400 g/13 oz) dried haricot beans
4 tablespoons oil
4 lamb shanks, trimmed
2 tablespoons butter
2 cloves garlic, crushed
2 brown onions, finely chopped
1½ tablespoons thyme leaves
2 tablespoons tomato paste (tomato purée)
2 x 400 g (13 oz) cans good-quality crushed tomatoes
1 tablespoon paprika
1 dried jalapeño chilli, roughly chopped
1 cup (30 g/1 oz) roughly chopped fresh flat-leaf parsley

1 Put the haricot beans in a bowl, cover well with water and soak overnight.
2 Heat 3 tablespoons of the oil in a large heavy-based frying pan over medium heat and brown the shanks on all sides. Remove and set aside. Drain the fat from the pan.
3 Heat the butter and the remaining oil in the pan and cook the garlic and onion over medium heat for 3–4 minutes, or until softened. Add the thyme, tomato paste, tomato and paprika and simmer for 5 minutes. Add the lamb shanks and 2 cups (500 ml/16 fl oz) hot water. Season well and bring to the boil. Cover the pan, reduce the heat and simmer gently for 30 minutes.
4 Drain the beans and add to the pan with the jalapeño chilli and another 2 cups (500 ml/16 fl oz) of hot water. Bring to the boil again, cover and simmer for another 1–1½ hours or until both the beans and the meat are tender, adding more water, ½ cup (125 ml/4 fl oz) at a time, if necessary. Check the seasoning, adjust if necessary, and stir in half the parsley. Serve hot sprinkled with the remaining parsley.

MINTED RACKS OF LAMB

Preparation time: 15 minutes
Total cooking time: 45 minutes
Serves 4

4 x 4-cutlet racks of lamb
1 cup (300 g/10 oz) mint jelly
2 tablespoons white wine
3 tablespoons finely chopped fresh
  chives

1 Preheat the oven to moderately hot
200°C (400°F/Gas 6). Trim any excess fat
from the lamb, leaving a thin layer of fat,
and clean any meat or sinew from the
ends of the bones using a small sharp
knife. Cover the bones with foil. Place on
a rack in a baking dish.
2 Mix the mint jelly and white wine
together in a small pan over high heat.
Bring to the boil and boil for 4 minutes,
or until the mixture is reduced and
thickened. Cool slightly, add the chives,
then brush over the racks of lamb. Bake
for 15–20 minutes for rare, or 35 minutes
if you prefer medium-rare, brushing with
glaze every 10 minutes. Remove the foil
and leave the lamb to stand for 5 minutes
before serving with vegetables.

BALTI LAMB

Preparation time: 15 minutes
Total cooking time: 1 hour 25 minutes
Serves 4

1 kg (2 lb) lamb leg steaks, cut into 3 cm
  (1¼ inch) cubes
5 tablespoons Balti curry paste (see page
  758)
2 tablespoons ghee or vegetable oil
1 large onion, finely chopped
3 cloves garlic, crushed
1 tablespoon garam masala
2 tablespoons chopped fresh coriander
  leaves
fresh coriander leaves, extra, to garnish

1 Put the lamb, 1 tablespoon of the curry
paste and 1 litre (32 fl oz) boiling water in
a wok and mix together. Bring to the boil
over high heat, then reduce the heat to
very low and cook, covered, for
40–50 minutes, or until the meat is
almost cooked through. Drain, reserving
the sauce. Wipe the wok clean.
2 Heat the ghee in the clean wok over
medium heat. Add the onion and cook for
5–7 minutes, or until it is soft and golden
brown. Add the garlic and garam masala
and cook for a further 2–3 minutes.
Increase the heat, add the remaining
curry paste and return the lamb to the
wok. Cook for 5 minutes, or until the meat
has browned. Slowly add the reserved
sauce and simmer over low heat, stirring
occasionally, for 15 minutes.
3 Add the chopped coriander leaves and
1 cup (250 ml/8 fl oz) water and simmer
for 15 minutes, or until the meat is tender
and the sauce has thickened slightly.
Season to taste with salt and freshly
ground black pepper. Garnish with the
extra coriander leaves and serve with
poppadoms and steamed rice.

RACK OF LAMB WITH HERB CRUST

Preparation time: 25 minutes
Total cooking time: 25 minutes
Serves 4

2 x 6-chop racks of lamb trimmed and
  bones cleaned (ask your butcher to do
  this)
1 tablespoon oil
1 cup (80 g/2¾ oz) fresh breadcrumbs
3 cloves garlic
3 tablespoons finely chopped fresh flat-
  leaf parsley
½ tablespoon fresh thyme leaves
½ teaspoon finely grated lemon rind
60 g (2 oz) butter, softened
1 cup (250 ml/8 fl oz) beef stock
1 clove garlic, extra, finely chopped
1 sprig of fresh thyme

1 Preheat the oven to very hot 250°C
(500°F/Gas 10). Score the fat on racks in a
diamond pattern. Rub the rack with a
little of the oil and season with salt and
pepper.
2 Heat the oil in a frying pan over high
heat, add the lamb and brown for
4–5 minutes. Remove and set aside. Do
not wash the pan as you will need it later.
3 In a large bowl, mix the breadcrumbs,
garlic, parsley, thyme and lemon rind.
Season, then mix in the butter to form a
paste.
4 Firmly press a layer of breadcrumb
mixture over the fat on the racks, leaving
the bones and base clean. Bake in a
baking dish for 12 minutes for medium-
rare. Rest the lamb while you make the
jus.
5 To make a jus, add the beef stock, extra
garlic and thyme sprig to the roasting pan
juices, scraping the pan. Return this liquid
to the original frying pan and simmer over
high heat for 5–8 minutes, until the sauce
is reduced. Strain and serve on the side.

TURKISH LAMB PILAFF

Preparation time: 20 minutes +
  1 hour standing
Total cooking time: 35 minutes
Serves 4

1 large eggplant (aubergine), cut into
  small cubes
½ cup (125 ml/4 fl oz) olive oil
1 large onion, finely chopped
1 teaspoon ground cinnamon
2 teaspoons ground cumin
1 teaspoon ground coriander
1½ cups (300 g/10 oz) long-grain rice
2 cups (500 ml/16 fl oz) stock
500 g (1 lb) minced (ground) lamb
½ teaspoon ground allspice
2 tablespoons olive oil, extra
2 tomatoes, cut into wedges
¼ cup (35 g/1¼ oz) pistachios, toasted
2 tablespoons currants
chopped coriander (cilantro) leaves, to
  garnish

1 Put the eggplant in a colander, sprinkle
generously with salt and leave for 1 hour.
Rinse well and squeeze dry in a clean tea
towel. Heat 2 tablespoons of the oil in a
large, deep frying pan with a lid, add the
eggplant and cook over medium heat for
8–10 minutes, or until golden brown and
cooked through. Drain on crumpled paper
towels.

2 Heat the remaining oil in the same pan,
add the onion and cook for 4–5 minutes,
or until softened but not browned. Stir in
half of each the cinnamon, cumin and
coriander and cook for a minute, or until
fragrant. Stir in the rice, mixing well to
combine. Pour in the stock, season and
bring to the boil. Reduce the heat to low,
cover with a tight-fitting lid and simmer
for 15 minutes, or until the stock has been
absorbed and the rice is cooked. Add
more water if the pilaff starts to dry out.
3 Meanwhile, put the lamb in a bowl with
the allspice and the remaining cumin,
cinnamon and coriander. Season with salt
and freshly ground black pepper, and mix
well. Roll into small balls, the size of
macadamia nuts. Heat the extra oil in a
clean frying pan and cook the meatballs
in batches over medium heat for
5 minutes each batch, or until lightly
browned and cooked through. Drain on
crumpled paper towels.
4 Add the tomato wedges to the empty
pan and cook, turning, for 3–5 minutes, or
until lightly golden. Remove from the pan.
5 Stir the cooked eggplant, pistachios,
currants and meatballs through the rice
(this should be quite dry by now). Serve
the pilaff surrounded by the cooked
tomato and garnished with the coriander
leaves.

ABBACCHIO

(Roman lamb)
Preparation time: 15 minutes
Total cooking time: 1 hour 20 minutes
Serves 4–6

¼ cup (60 ml/2 fl oz) olive oil
1 kg (2 lb) spring lamb, cut into 2 cm
  (¾ inch) cubes
2 cloves garlic, crushed
6 fresh sage leaves
1 sprig fresh rosemary
1 tablespoon flour
½ cup (125 ml/4 fl oz) white wine vinegar
6 anchovy fillets

1 Heat the oil in a heavy-based frying pan
and cook the meat in batches over
medium heat for 3–4 minutes, until
browned on all sides.
2 Return all the meat to the pan and add
the garlic, sage and rosemary. Season
with salt and pepper, combine well and
cook for 1 minute.
3 Dust the meat with the flour using a fine
sieve, then cook for another minute. Add
the vinegar and simmer for 30 seconds,
then add 1 cup (250 ml/8 fl oz) water.
Bring to a gentle simmer, lower the heat
and cover, leaving the lid partially askew.
Cook for 50–60 minutes, or until the meat
is tender, stirring occasionally and adding
a little more water if necessary.
4 When the lamb is almost cooked, mash
the anchovies in a mortar and pestle with
1 tablespoon of the cooking liquid, until a
paste is formed. Add to the lamb and
cook, uncovered, for another 2 minutes.
Delicious served with Rosemary potatoes.

SATAY LAMB

Preparation time: 10 minutes
Total cooking time: 15 minutes
Serves 4

¼ cup (60 ml/2 fl oz) peanut oil
750 g (1½ lb) lamb loin fillets, thinly sliced across the grain
2 teaspoons ground cumin
1 teaspoon ground turmeric
1 red pepper (capsicum), sliced
¼ cup (60 ml/2 fl oz) sweet chilli sauce
¼ cup (60 g/2 oz) crunchy peanut butter
1 cup (250 ml/8 fl oz) coconut milk
2 teaspoons soft brown sugar
1–2 tablespoons lemon juice, to taste
4 tablespoons chopped fresh coriander leaves
¼ cup (40 g/1¼ oz) unsalted peanuts, roasted, chopped, to serve

1 Heat a wok over high heat, add 1 tablespoon oil and swirl. Add half the lamb and stir-fry for 3 minutes, or until browned. Remove. Repeat with 1 tablespoon oil and the remaining lamb.
2 Reheat the wok, add the remaining oil and cumin, turmeric and pepper, and stir-fry for 2 minutes, or until the pepper is tender.
3 Return the lamb to the wok. Stir in the chilli sauce, peanut butter, coconut milk and sugar. Bring to the boil, then reduce the heat and simmer for 5 minutes, or until the meat is tender and the sauce has thickened slightly. Remove from the heat and add the lemon juice. Stir in the coriander and sprinkle with the peanuts. Serve.

STUFFED LEG OF LAMB

Preparation time: 25 minutes
Total cooking time: 2 hours 15 minutes
Serves 6–8

Stuffing
1 thick slice white country-style bread, crusts removed
70 g (2¼ oz) chicken livers, trimmed
60 g (2 oz) tocino or streaky bacon
1 tablespoon dry sherry
1 clove garlic, crushed
1 tablespoon chopped fresh flat-leaf parsley
½ tablespoon chopped fresh chives
1 teaspoon finely chopped fresh rosemary
1 tablespoon capers, finely chopped
1 large leg of lamb (about 3 kg/6 lb), boned (see Note)
1 teaspoon sweet paprika
1 tablespoon plain flour
4 whole cloves garlic, peeled
2 tablespoons olive oil
1½ cups (375 ml/12 fl oz) dry white wine
1 tablespoon lard
½ cup (125 ml/4 fl oz) chicken or vegetable stock

1 To make the stuffing, break the bread into pieces and process with the chicken livers and tocino until medium-fine. Place in a bowl with the sherry, garlic, parsley, chives, rosemary and capers. Season well with salt and freshly ground black pepper and mix well.

2 Preheat the oven to hot 210°C (415°F/Gas 6–7). Lay the lamb out flat and place the filling down the centre. Roll the meat up to encase the filling. Tie up tightly with kitchen twine. Combine the paprika and flour with ¼ teaspoon salt and rub all over the surface of the lamb. Put the garlic in a row in the centre of a baking dish and pour the oil over the top. Place the lamb on the garlic and pour the wine over the top. Spread the lard over the surface.
3 Bake for 20 minutes, then reduce the heat to warm 170°C (325°F/Gas 3). Baste, then bake for another 1 hour 45 minutes, basting frequently, until the lamb is well cooked. Transfer to a carving tray and keep warm. Spoon off excess oil from the pan juices then transfer the contents of the baking dish to a small saucepan; there will be about ½ cup (125 ml/4 fl oz). Add the stock and cook over high heat until slightly thickened. Taste for seasoning. Slice the lamb and arrange on a warm serving platter. Pour the sauce over the lamb and serve warm.

NOTE: Have your butcher bone the lamb and flatten out the meat to form a rough rectangle.

MOUSSAKA

Preparation time: 20 minutes +
  30 minutes standing
Total cooking time: 2 hours
Serves 6

1.5 kg (3 lb) eggplants (aubergines), cut
  into 5 mm (¼ inch) slices
½ cup (125 ml/4 fl oz) olive oil
2 onions, finely chopped
2 large cloves garlic, crushed
½ teaspoon ground allspice
1 teaspoon ground cinnamon
750 g (1½ lb) lamb mince
2 large ripe tomatoes, peeled and
  chopped
2 tablespoons tomato paste (tomato
  purée)
½ cup (125 ml/4 fl oz) white wine
3 tablespoons chopped fresh flat-leaf
  parsley

Cheese sauce
60 g (2 oz) butter
½ cup (60 g/2 oz) plain flour
2½ cups (625 ml/20 fl oz) milk
pinch of ground nutmeg
⅓ cup (35 g/1¼ oz) finely grated kefalotyri
  or Parmesan
2 eggs, lightly beaten

1 Lay the eggplant on a tray, sprinkle with
salt and leave to stand for 30 minutes.
Rinse under water and pat dry. Preheat
the oven to moderate 180°C (350°F/Gas 4).
2 Heat 2 tablespoons olive oil in a frying
pan, add the eggplant in batches and cook
for 1–2 minutes each side, or until golden
and soft. Add a little more oil when
needed.

3 Heat 1 tablespoon olive oil in a large
saucepan, add the onion and cook over
medium heat for 5 minutes. Add the
garlic, allspice and cinnamon and cook
for 30 seconds. Add the mince and cook
for 5 minutes, or until browned, breaking
up any lumps with the back of a spoon.
Add the tomato, tomato paste and wine,
and simmer over low heat for 30 minutes,
or until the liquid has evaporated. Stir in
the chopped parsley and season, to taste.
4 For the cheese sauce, melt the butter in
a saucepan over low heat. Stir in the flour
and cook for 1 minute, or until pale and
foaming. Remove the saucepan from the
heat and gradually stir in the milk and
nutmeg. Return the saucepan to the heat
and stir constantly until the sauce boils
and thickens. Reduce the heat and
simmer for 2 minutes. Stir in 1 tablespoon
of the cheese until well combined. Stir in
the egg just before using.
5 Line the base of a 3 litre ovenproof dish
measuring 25 x 30 cm (10 x 12 inches) with
a third of the eggplant. Spoon half the
meat sauce over it and cover with another
layer of eggplant. Spoon the remaining
meat sauce over the top and cover with
the remaining eggplant. Spread the
cheese sauce over the top and sprinkle
with the remaining cheese. Bake for 1
hour. Leave to stand for 10 minutes
before slicing.

NOTE: You can substitute an equal
quantity of sliced, shallow-fried zucchini
or potatoes, or any combination of these
vegetables for the eggplant (aubergine).

LIVER WITH OREGANO

Preparation time: 15 minutes
Total cooking time: 10 minutes
Serves 6–8

500 g (1 lb) lamb's liver
¼ cup (30 g/1 oz) plain flour
½ teaspoon paprika
2 tablespoons olive oil
2 tablespoons lemon juice
1 teaspoon dried or chopped fresh
  oregano

1 Trim off any fatty deposits from the
liver. Pat the liver dry with paper towels,
cut into 2 cm (¾ inch) slices and cut the
larger slices in half or into thirds.
2 In a shallow dish, combine the flour,
paprika and ½ teaspoon each of salt and
cracked black pepper. Heat the oil in a
frying pan over medium heat. Toss a third
of the liver in the flour, shake off the
excess and fry for 1 minute on each side,
or until browned, but still pink inside.
Drain on crumpled paper towels and
place on warm plate. Repeat with the
remaining liver. Cover with foil to keep it
warm.
3 Remove the pan from the heat and pour
in the lemon juice — it should bubble in
the hot pan. When the bubbles subside,
pour the pan juices over the liver and
sprinkle with oregano. Serve hot.

LAMB BIRYANI

Preparation time: 30 minutes + overnight
  marinating + 10 minutes standing
Total cooking time: 1 hour 40 minutes
Serves 6

1 kg (2 lb) boneless lamb leg or shoulder,
  cut into 3 cm (1¼ inch) cubes
7 cm (2¾ inch) piece of ginger, grated
2 garlic cloves, crushed
2 tablespoons garam masala
½ teaspoon chilli powder
½ teaspoon ground turmeric
4 green chillies, finely chopped
3 tablespoons chopped mint
4 tablespoons chopped coriander
  (cilantro) leaves
2½ cups (500 g/1 lb) basmati rice
4 onions, thinly sliced
¼ teaspoon salt
½ cup (125 ml/4 fl oz) oil
125 g (4 oz) unsalted butter, melted
250 g (8 oz) thick natural yoghurt
½ teaspoon saffron threads, soaked in
  2 tablespoons hot milk
¼ cup (60 ml/2 fl oz) lemon juice

Sealing dough
1⅓ cups (200 g/6½ oz) wholemeal flour
1 teaspoon salt

1 Mix the lamb in a bowl with the ginger,
garlic, garam masala, chilli powder,
turmeric, chilli, mint and coriander. Cover
and refrigerate overnight.
2 Wash the rice in a sieve under cold,
running water until the water from the
rice runs clear. Put the sliced onion in a
sieve, sprinkle with the salt and leave for
10 minutes to drain off any liquid that
oozes out. Rinse and pat dry.

3 Heat the oil and butter in a large, heavy-
based saucepan, add the onion and fry for
about 10 minutes, or until golden brown.
Drain through a sieve, reserving the oil
and butter.
4 Remove the lamb from the marinade,
reserving the marinade, and fry in
batches in a little of the oil and butter
until the lamb is well browned all over.
Transfer to a heavy casserole dish and
add the onion, any remaining marinade
and the yoghurt and cook over low heat
for 30–40 minutes, or until the lamb is
tender.
5 In a separate saucepan, boil enough
water to cover the rice. Add the rice to the
pan. Return the water to the boil, cook the
rice for 5 minutes, then drain and spread
the rice over the meat. Pour 2
tablespoons of the leftover oil and ghee
over the rice and drizzle with the lemon
juice and saffron and milk mixture.
6 Preheat the oven to hot 220°C
(425°F/Gas 7). Make a dough by mixing
the flour and salt with a little water. Roll
the dough into a sausage shape and use
to seal the lid onto the rim of the pot or
casserole, pressing it along the rim
where the lid meets the pot. Put the pot
over high heat for 5 minutes to bring the
contents to the boil, then transfer it to the
oven for 40 minutes. Remove the pot and
break the seal of dough.

CURRIED BEEF SAUSAGES

Preparation time: 20 minutes
Total cooking time: 45 minutes
Serves 6–8

1 onion, chopped
2 cloves garlic
1 teaspoon chopped fresh ginger
2 teaspoons curry powder
1 teaspoon chilli powder
1½ teaspoons paprika
3 teaspoons poppy seeds
2 tablespoons oil
1.25 kg (2 lb 8 oz) medium-size good-
  quality beef sausages
6 tomatoes, skinned, quartered and
  seeded
2 tablespoons mango chutney
1⅔ cups (420 ml/13 fl oz) coconut milk

1 Place the onion, garlic, ginger, curry
powder, chilli powder, paprika and poppy
seeds in a food processor, and process
until smooth.
2 Heat 1 tablespoon of the oil in a
saucepan and cook for 6–8 minutes, or
until browned. Remove and wipe out the
pan with paper towels. Leave the
sausages to cool and slice into 1 cm
(½ inch) thick pieces.
3 Heat the remaining oil in the pan, add
the spice paste and cook, stirring, for 2
minutes, or until fragrant. Mix in the
tomato, mango chutney, coconut milk and
sausages, and simmer, covered, for 20
minutes, stirring occasionally.

GASCONNADE

Preparation time: 25 minutes
Total cooking time: 1 hour 30 minutes
Serves 6

1 large leg of lamb, about 2.5 kg (5 lb), partially boned (see Note)
1 carrot, coarsely chopped
1 stick celery, coarsely chopped
1 large onion, coarsely chopped
1 bay leaf
1 bouquet garni (see page 173)
2 cloves garlic, crushed
6 anchovy fillets, mashed
½ tablespoon finely chopped fresh parsley
½ tablespoon finely chopped fresh thyme
½ tablespoon finely chopped fresh rosemary
3 tablespoons olive oil
25 cloves garlic, unpeeled

1 Preheat the oven to hot 220°C (425°F/Gas 7). Place the removed lamb bone in a stockpot with the carrot, celery, onion, bay leaf and bouquet garni, and add just enough cold water to cover. Bring to the boil and simmer uncovered for 1 hour. Strain and if necessary simmer until reduced to 2 cups (500 ml/16 fl oz).

2 Meanwhile, combine the crushed garlic, anchovies, chopped herbs and olive oil in a small bowl with some freshly ground black pepper. Rub the cavity of the lamb with most of the herb mixture. Roll the meat up and tie securely with kitchen string. Rub the lamb with the remaining herb mixture and place in a baking dish. Bake for 15 minutes, then reduce the temperature to moderate 180°C (350°F/Gas 4). Continue baking for about 45 minutes (for medium-rare), basting with the pan juices occasionally, until cooked to your liking.

3 Bring a saucepan of water to the boil and add the garlic cloves. Boil for 5 minutes. Drain and rinse under cold water. Peel the garlic and purée the pulp. Put it in the saucepan with the 2 cups (500 ml/16 fl oz) of stock and bring to the boil. Simmer for 10 minutes. Transfer the lamb to a carving tray and keep warm. Spoon off the fat from the pan juices. Add the garlic stock and place the dish over high heat. Bring to the boil and cook until reduced by half. Adjust the seasoning. Serve the lamb sliced, accompanied by the sauce.

NOTE: Ask your butcher to partially bone the leg of lamb, leaving the shank bone in place. Take home the removed bone to use when making the stock.

LAMB DOPIAZA

Preparation time: 20 minutes
Total cooking time: 2 hours
Serves 4–6

1 kg (2 lb) onions
5 cloves garlic
5 cm (2 inch) piece fresh ginger, grated
2 red chillies
1 teaspoon paprika
4 tablespoons chopped fresh coriander leaves
2 tablespoons ground coriander
2 teaspoons black cumin seeds
4 tablespoons yoghurt
4 tablespoons ghee or oil
1 kg (2 lb) diced lamb
6 cardamom pods, lightly crushed
1 teaspoon garam masala

1 Slice half the onions and set aside; roughly chop the remaining onions.
2 Place the chopped onion, garlic, ginger, chilli, paprika, fresh and ground coriander, cumin seeds and yoghurt in a food processor and process until a smooth paste is formed.
3 Heat the ghee in a large pan; add the sliced onion and cook over medium heat for 10 minutes or until golden brown. Remove the onion from the pan using a slotted spoon and drain on paper towels.
4 Add the lamb to the pan in batches and cook over high heat until browned. Remove from the pan and cover loosely with foil.
5 Add the onion paste to the pan; cook for 5 minutes, or until the ghee starts to separate from the onion. Reduce the heat to low, return the meat to the pan with the cardamom, cover and cook for 1 hour or until the meat is tender.
6 Add the fried onion and sprinkle the garam masala over the lamb; cover and continue cooking for 15 minutes. Serve with rice and naan bread.

LAMB DUMPLINGS IN YOGHURT SAUCE

Preparation time: 40 minutes +
    30 minutes standing
Total cooking time: 35 minutes
Serves 4–6

250 g (8 oz) plain flour
60 g (2 oz) clarified butter, melted, for
    baking
40 g (1¼ oz) clarified butter, extra, for
    serving
2 cloves garlic, crushed, for serving
1 tablespoon dried mint, for serving

Filling
20 g (¾ oz) clarified butter
1 small onion, finely chopped
2 tablespoons pine nuts
250 g (8 oz) lamb mince
pinch of ground allspice

Yoghurt sauce
3 cups (750 g/1½ lb) natural yoghurt
2 teaspoons cornflour
1 egg white, lightly beaten

1 For the dough, sift the flour and 1
teaspoon salt into a bowl and add ¾ cup
(185 ml/6 fl oz) water a little at a time and
combine until the mixture comes
together in a ball. Cover and allow to rest
for 30 minutes.
2 For the filling, melt the clarified butter
in a deep heavy-based frying pan and
cook the onion over medium heat for
5 minutes, or until soft. Add the pine nuts
and allow them to brown, stirring
constantly. Increase the heat to high and
add the mince and allspice, stirring until
the meat changes colour. Season, to
taste, and allow to cool.

3 Preheat the oven to moderate 180°C
(350°/Gas 4). Lightly grease two baking
trays.
4 Roll out the dough on a floured board,
to about 5 mm (¼ inch) thick and cut into
rounds using a 5 cm (2 inch) cutter. Place
a teaspoon of filling in the centre of each
round and fold the pastry over into a
crescent. Press the edges together firmly
and then wrap the crescent around one
finger and press the two ends together to
make a hat shape. Place on the baking
trays and brush lightly with the clarified
butter. Bake for 10 minutes, or until
lightly browned. The pastries do not have
to be completely cooked.
5 Place the yoghurt in a large, heavy-
based saucepan and stir until smooth.
Combine the cornflour with 1½ cups
(375 ml/12 fl oz) of water, stir until
smooth, then add to the yoghurt with the
egg white and 2 teaspoons salt. Cook over
medium heat, stirring constantly until the
mixture thickens. Add the dumplings to
the pan, stir very gently, then cook,
uncovered, over low heat for 10 minutes,
stirring occasionally and being careful not
to boil the sauce.
6 Just before serving, melt the extra
clarified butter in a small frying pan and
fry the garlic gently for a few seconds.
Stir in the mint and remove from the
heat. Pour over the dumplings and serve
with rice.

LEMON AND CORIANDER BAKED LAMB

Preparation time: 15 minutes
Total cooking time: 1 hour 20 minutes
Serves 4–6

1.8 kg (3 lb 10 oz) leg of lamb
2 cloves garlic, sliced
3 large strips lemon rind, cut into 1 cm
    pieces
½ cup (25 g/¾ oz) chopped fresh
    coriander
3 tablespoons chopped fresh flat-leaf
    parsley
2 tablespoons olive oil

1 Preheat the oven to moderate 180°C
(350°F/Gas 4). Trim the lamb of excess fat
and sinew. Using a sharp knife, make
deep cuts in the flesh and place a slice of
garlic and a piece of lemon rind into each
cut.
2 Combine the coriander, parsley, oil and
1 teaspoon ground black pepper. Coat the
lamb with the herb mixture and place on a
rack in a baking dish. Pour 1 cup (250 ml/
8 fl oz) water into the dish and bake for
1 hour 20 minutes, or until the lamb is
cooked to your liking. Add extra water to
the pan while cooking if the lamb starts to
dry out. Serve the lamb in slices with pan
juices and vegetables in season.

MEATLOAF

Preparation time: 25 minutes
Total cooking time: 1 hour 15 minutes
Serves 6

125 g (4 oz) bacon, trimmed and chopped
500 g (1 lb) beef mince
500 g (1 lb) pork mince
1 onion, coarsely grated
2 cloves garlic, crushed
2 cups (160 g/5½ oz) fresh breadcrumbs
2 teaspoons fresh thyme leaves
1 egg, lightly beaten
1 tablespoon red wine vinegar
2 teaspoons soft brown sugar

1 Preheat the oven to moderate 180°C (350°F/Gas 4). Lightly grease a loaf tin then line with a single sheet of baking paper, leaving the paper to overhang on the long sides of the tin.
2 Heat a non-stick frying pan, add the chopped bacon, and cook, stirring, until crispy. Drain on paper towels.
3 Place the mince, onion, garlic, breadcrumbs, thyme, egg, vinegar, sugar and bacon in a bowl. Season and combine, using your hands. Don't overmix or the meatloaf will become too dense when cooked.
4 Spoon the mixture into the loaf tin and press down gently. Smooth the top and cook in the oven for 1 hour 10 minutes, or until browned and cooked through. Test if it is cooked by pushing a metal skewer or sharp knife into the centre, leaving it for 3 seconds, and then pulling it out and holding it against your wrist. If it is really hot, it is cooked through; if not, cook a little longer. Leave for 5 minutes and pour the cooking juices into a jug. Lift out the meatloaf using the overhanging baking paper. Cut into slices with a serrated knife and drizzle with the cooking juices. Serve with tomato sauce, peas, corn and potatoes.

MOROCCAN LAMB AND ROASTED PEPPER (CAPSICUM) WITH FUSILLI

Preparation time: 25 minutes +
  overnight marinating
Total cooking time: 25 minutes
Serves 4–6

500 g (1 lb) lamb fillets
3 teaspoons ground cumin
1 tablespoon ground coriander
2 teaspoons ground allspice
1 teaspoon ground cinnamon
½ teaspoon ground cayenne pepper
4 cloves garlic, crushed
⅓ cup 80 ml (2¾ fl oz) olive oil
½ cup (125 ml/4 fl oz) lemon juice
2 red peppers (capsicums)
400 g (13 oz) fusilli
¼ cup (60 ml/2 fl oz) extra virgin olive oil
2 teaspoons harissa
150 g (5 oz) rocket

1 Cut the fillets in half if they are very long. Mix the cumin, coriander, allspice, cinnamon, cayenne, garlic, olive oil and half the lemon juice in a bowl. Add the lamb, stir to coat and marinate, covered, in the refrigerator overnight.
2 Cut the peppers into large pieces and discard the seeds and membrane. Put skin-side-up, under a hot grill and cook for 8 minutes, or until the skin is black and blistered. Remove from the heat and cover with a damp tea towel. When cool, peel away the skin and slice thinly.
3 Cook the fusilli in a large pan of rapidly boiling salted water until al dente. Drain; keep warm.
4 Drain the lamb, heat 1 tablespoon of the extra virgin olive oil in a large frying pan and cook the lamb over high heat until done to your liking. Remove from the pan; cover with foil.
5 Heat 1 teaspoon of the oil in the frying pan and cook the harissa over medium heat for a few seconds. Be careful as the mixture may spit. Remove and place in a small screw top jar with the remaining oil and lemon juice and shake the jar until well combined. Season, to taste.
6 Thinly slice the lamb fillets and toss with the warm pasta, sliced pepper and rocket. Toss the harissa dressing through the pasta. Serve warm.

GARLIC LAMB WITH WILTED MUSHROOMS AND NOODLES

Preparation time: 30 minutes
Total cooking time: 20 minutes
Serves 4

8 red Asian shallots, very thinly sliced
4 cloves garlic, finely chopped
1½ tablespoons vegetable oil
1 teaspoon soft brown sugar
1 teaspoon freshly ground black pepper
350 g (11 oz) lamb loin fillets, thinly sliced across the grain
300 g (10 oz) fresh egg noodles
oil, extra, for cooking
200 g (6½ oz) button mushrooms, sliced
150 g (5 oz) small oyster mushrooms
2 tablespoons teriyaki sauce
75 g (2½ oz) fresh garlic chives, cut into short pieces

1 Combine the shallots, garlic, oil, sugar, 1 teaspoon salt and the freshly ground black pepper in a large non-metallic bowl. Add the lamb and toss until well coated.
2 Cook the noodles in boiling water for 1 minute, or until separated. Drain and rinse.
3 Heat a wok over high heat, add 1 tablespoon of the extra oil and swirl to coat. Stir-fry the lamb in three batches, searing the meat and tossing constantly until browned. Reheat the wok in between each batch, adding a little more oil when needed. Remove the meat from the wok.
4 Add the button mushrooms to the wok with about 2 teaspoons of water, and stir-fry for 1 minute. Add the oyster mushrooms and teriyaki sauce, and toss. Cover and steam for 10 seconds.
5 Return all the lamb and any juices to the wok with the noodles and chives. Toss well to heat through. Serve immediately.

MIDDLE EASTERN RICE-STUFFED LAMB

Preparation time: 20 minutes +
    20 minutes soaking + 25 minutes cooling
Total cooking time: 1 hour 40 minutes
Serves 6

⅓ cup (60 g/2 oz) dried figs
1 tablespoon olive oil
1 onion, finely chopped
2 garlic cloves, crushed
1 teaspoon ground cinnamon
¼ teaspoon ground allspice
1 tablespoon red wine vinegar
⅓ cup (65 g/2¼ oz) long-grain rice
2 tablespoons currants
2 tablespoons pistachios or pine nuts, toasted
3½ cups (875 ml/28 fl oz) chicken stock
2 tablespoons finely chopped flat-leaf (Italian) parsley
1 egg, lightly beaten
1.5 kg (3 lb) leg of lamb, deboned and butterflied
¼ cup (60 ml/2 fl oz) olive oil, extra
2 tablespoons lemon juice
2–3 teaspoons finely chopped oregano
1 tablespoon sumac
1 cup (250 ml/8 fl oz) white wine

1 Preheat the oven to moderately hot 200°C (400°F/Gas 6). Soak the dried figs in warm water for 20 minutes. Drain and chop the figs coarsely.
2 To make the stuffing, heat the olive oil in a frying pan, then cook the onion for 3 minutes, or until softened but not browned. Add the garlic, cinnamon and allspice and cook for 30 seconds before adding the vinegar. Cook over high heat until all the vinegar has been absorbed. Reduce the heat to medium, then add rice, soaked figs, currants and pistachios and stir to coat. Pour in 1 cup (250 ml/8 fl oz) chicken stock, bring to the boil, then reduce the heat to low and cook, covered, for 20 minutes, or until the stock has been absorbed and the rice is tender. Season well and stir in the parsley. Set aside for 25 minutes to cool.

3 When the stuffing has cooled, mix the beaten egg into it with a metal spoon until it binds together. Open out the lamb leg on a work surface and spread the stuffing over the exposed surface, then roll up and tie with string. Combine the extra olive oil with the lemon juice, oregano and sumac, then pour onto the lamb, rubbing to cover evenly. Season with salt and freshly ground black pepper. Place in a roasting tin and roast for 10 minutes.
4 Remove the lamb from the oven and reduce the heat to moderate 180°C (350°F/Gas 4). Pour the remaining stock and white wine into the roasting tin and bake for a further 1 hour, or until cooked to desired level of doneness. Add extra stock or water if liquid is evaporating too quickly. Remove the lamb and set aside on a serving plate to rest.
5 Meanwhile, to make the sauce, put the roasting tin on top of stove and simmer over medium heat for 3 minutes, or until the liquid has reduced and thickened slightly. Serve the lamb with the stuffing, sauce and a green salad or steamed vegetables.

PASTA WITH LAMB AND VEGETABLES

Preparation time: 20 minutes
Total cooking time: 20 minutes
Serves 4

2 tablespoons oil
1 large onion, chopped
2 cloves garlic, crushed
500 g (1 lb) minced lamb
125 g (4 oz) small mushroom caps, halved
1 red pepper (capsicum), seeded and chopped
150 g (5 oz) shelled broad beans
440 g (14 oz) can crushed tomatoes
2 tablespoons tomato paste (tomato purée, double concentrate)
500 g (1 lb) penne
125 g (4 oz) feta cheese
2 tablespoons shredded fresh basil

1 Heat the oil in a heavy-based pan over medium heat. Add the onion and garlic and stir-fry for 2 minutes or until lightly browned. Add the mince and stir-fry over high heat for 4 minutes or until the meat is well browned and all the liquid has evaporated. Use a fork to break up any lumps as the mince cooks.
2 Add the mushrooms, red pepper, broad beans, undrained tomato and tomato paste to the pan. Bring to the boil, reduce the heat and simmer, covered, for 10 minutes or until the vegetables are tender. Stir occasionally.
3 While the sauce is cooking, cook the pasta in a large pan of rapidly boiling salted water until al dente. Drain. Spoon into serving bowls, top with the lamb and vegetable sauce, crumble cheese over the top and sprinkle with basil.

NOTE: The sauce can be made up to two days ahead. Refrigerate, covered with plastic wrap. Reheat the sauce and cook the pasta just before serving. Unsuitable for freezing.

TANDOORI LAMB WITH MINT PULAO

Preparation time: 30 minutes + overnight marinating
Total cooking time: 1 hour 30 minutes
Serves 4–6

2 kg (4 lb) leg of lamb, butterflied
1 teaspoon chilli powder
2½ tablespoons lime juice
200 g (6½ oz) thick natural yoghurt
1 onion, finely chopped
4 garlic cloves, crushed
1 tablespoon grated fresh ginger
1 teaspoon cayenne pepper
1 tablespoon ground cumin
1 tablespoon ground coriander
1 teaspoon turmeric
1 teaspoon ground cinnamon
1 teaspoon sea salt

Mint pulao
1 tablespoon olive oil
1 onion, finely chopped
2 cups (400 g/13 oz) basmati rice
3½ cups (875 ml/28 fl oz) hot chicken stock
½ cup (25 g/¾ oz) chopped mint

1 Sprinkle the lamb with the chilli powder and half the lime juice.
2 To make the marinade, combine the yoghurt, onion, garlic, ginger, cayenne pepper, cumin, coriander, turmeric, cinnamon, sea salt and the remaining lime juice. Put the lamb in a large non-metallic dish and cover it with the marinade. Turn to coat well. Cover and refrigerate overnight.

3 Preheat the oven to moderately hot 200°C (400°F/Gas 6). Bring the meat to room temperature, then roll up and tie at intervals with string. Roast for about 1½ hours for medium–well done, or until cooked to your liking, basting regularly with the marinade.
Rest for 15 minutes. Remove the string and carve into slices.
4 Meanwhile, to make the pulao, heat the oil in a large saucepan and add the onion. Cook for 5–6 minutes over medium heat, or until soft. Add the rice and cook for 2 minutes, then add the stock and bring to the boil. Reduce the heat, cover with a lid and simmer for 15 minutes, or until all the liquid has been absorbed and the rice is tender. Stir in the mint and season to taste with salt and pepper. Serve with the lamb.

SPRING ONION LAMB

Preparation time: 10 minutes +
    10 minutes marinating
Total cooking time: 10 minutes
Serves 4

1 tablespoon Chinese rice wine
¼ cup (60 ml/2 fl oz) soy sauce
½ teaspoon white pepper
600 g (1¼ lb) lean lamb loin fillets, thinly
    sliced across the grain
1 tablespoon Chinese black vinegar
1 teaspoon sesame oil
2 tablespoons vegetable oil
750 g (1½ lb) choy sum, cut into 10 cm
    (4 inch) lengths
3 cloves garlic, crushed
6 spring onions, cut into 10 cm (4 inch)
    lengths

1 Combine the rice wine, 1 tablespoon of
the soy sauce, the white pepper and
½ teaspoon salt in a large non-metallic
bowl. Add the lamb and toss together well.
Cover with plastic wrap, and marinate in
the refrigerator for at least 10 minutes.
2 To make the stir-fry sauce, combine the
black vinegar, sesame oil and 1 tablespoon
of the soy sauce in a small, non-metallic
bowl or jug. Set aside until needed.

3 Heat a wok over high heat, add 2
teaspoons of the oil and swirl to coat the
side of the wok. Add the choy sum, stir-fry
briefly, then add 1 clove of the crushed
garlic and the remaining soy sauce. Cook
for 3 minutes, or until cooked, but still
crisp. Take the wok off the heat, then
remove the greens from the wok and keep
in a warm place.
4 Wipe the wok clean with paper towels,
then reheat the wok over high heat. Add 1
tablespoon of the oil and swirl it around to
coat the side of the wok. Add the lamb in
two batches and stir-fry each batch over
high heat for 1–2 minutes, or until nicely
browned. Remove from the wok.
5 Add a little more oil to the wok, if
necessary. Add the spring onion and
remaining garlic and stir-fry for 1–2
minutes. Pour the stir-fry sauce into the
wok and stir for 1 minute, or until
combined. Return the lamb to the wok
and continue to stir-fry for another
minute, or until combined and heated
through. Serve immediately with the
greens.

SPICY SAUSAGE PILAFF

Preparation time: 20 minutes
Total cooking time: 40 minutes
Serves 4–6

30 g (1 oz) butter
1 large onion, thinly sliced
2 garlic cloves, crushed
300 g (10 oz) chorizo sausage, thinly
    sliced
2 cups (400 g/13 oz) long-grain rice
1 bay leaf
1 litre (32 fl oz) chicken stock
1 cup (155 g/5 oz) frozen peas
½ cup (80 g/2¾ oz) sun-dried capsicums
    (peppers) in oil, drained and thinly
    sliced
4 spring onions (scallions), thinly sliced
shaved Parmesan cheese, to serve

1 Melt the butter in a large, deep frying
pan over medium heat. Add the onion and
garlic and cook, stirring, for 5 minutes, or
until the onion is softened but not
browned. Add the chorizo and cook,
stirring, for 2 minutes. Stir in the rice and
bay leaf, mixing well to combine.
2 Pour in the stock and bring to the boil.
Continue boiling until tunnels appear in
the rice, stir quickly, then cover and
reduce the heat to low. Cook for 20 minutes.
Sprinkle the peas and capsicum strips
over the top of the rice. Cover, remove
from the heat and leave for a further 10
minutes. Sprinkle with the spring onion
and fluff the mixture with a fork. Serve
topped with the shaved Parmesan.

SWEET KECAP PORK

Preparation time: 20 minutes
Total cooking time: 1 hour 10 minutes
Serves 4

500 g (1 lb) diced pork
¼ teaspoon each salt and pepper
2 tablespoons oil
1 large onion, finely chopped
3 cloves garlic, finely chopped
5 cm (2 inch) piece fresh ginger, grated
3 red chillies, finely chopped
2 tablespoons kecap manis
1 cup (250 ml/8 fl oz) coconut milk
2 teaspoons lime juice

1 Mix together the pork, salt, pepper and oil. Heat a wok or heavy-based pan and cook the pork in several batches over medium heat, until well browned. Remove all the meat from the wok and set aside.
2 Reduce the heat to low; add the onion, garlic, ginger and chilli and cook for 10 minutes, stirring occasionally, until the onion is very soft and golden.
3 Add the pork, kecap manis and coconut milk, and cook over low heat for 1 hour, stirring occasionally. Stir in the lime juice and serve with plenty of steamed rice and fresh chopped chilli.

PORK AND VEAL RAVIOLI WITH CHEESY SAUCE

Preparation time: 1 hour
Total cooking time: 15 minutes
Serves 4

Dough
2 cups (250 g/8 oz) plain flour
2 eggs, lightly beaten
2 tablespoons oil

Filling
1 tablespoon oil
4 spring onions, finely chopped
3 cloves garlic, crushed
250 g (8 oz) pork and veal mince
1 egg, lightly beaten

Sauce
60 g (2 oz) butter
1 cup (220 g/7 oz) mascarpone cheese
⅓ cup (35 g/1¼ oz) freshly grated
   Parmesan
2 tablespoons chopped fresh sage

1 To make the dough, combine the flour, beaten eggs and oil with ⅓ cup (80 ml/2¾ fl oz) of water in a food processor, for 5 seconds, or until the mixture comes together in a ball. Cover with plastic wrap and refrigerate for 15 minutes. If you don't have a food processor, combine the ingredients in a large bowl, using your fingertips.

2 To make the filling, heat the oil in a heavy-based pan, add the spring onion and garlic and stir-fry over medium heat for 2 minutes. Add the mince and stir-fry over high heat for 4 minutes, or until well browned and all the liquid has evaporated. Use a fork to break up any lumps as the mince cooks. Allow to cool and stir in the egg.
3 Roll half the dough out very thinly on a lightly floured surface. Use a large sharp knife to cut the dough into 6 cm (2½ inch) squares. Brush half the squares very lightly with water and place a teaspoon of filling on each. Place another square over each and press down firmly to seal the filling inside. Place in a single layer on well-floured oven trays. Repeat with the remaining dough and filling.
4 To make the sauce, melt the butter in a medium pan, add the mascarpone cheese and stir over medium heat until melted. Add the Parmesan and sage and gently heat while stirring, for 1 minute.
5 Cook the ravioli in a large pan of rapidly boiling water for 5 minutes, or until tender. Drain and serve with the sauce.

PORK AND HOKKIEN NOODLE STIR-FRY

Preparation time: 15 minutes + 10 minutes
  marinating
Total cooking time: 15 minutes
Serves 4

⅓ cup (80 ml/2¾ fl oz) soy sauce
¼ cup (60 ml/2 fl oz) mirin
2 teaspoons grated fresh ginger
2 cloves garlic, crushed
1½ tablespoons soft brown sugar
350 g (11 oz) pork loin fillet, thinly sliced
  across the grain
500 g (1 lb) Hokkien noodles
2 tablespoons peanut oil
1 onion, cut into thin wedges
1 red pepper (capsicum), cut into thin strips
2 carrots, thinly sliced on the diagonal
4 spring onions, thinly sliced on the diagonal
200 g (6½ oz) fresh shiitake mushrooms,
  sliced

1 Combine the soy sauce, mirin, ginger,
garlic and sugar in a large non-metallic
bowl. Add the pork and toss to coat. Cover
with plastic wrap and marinate in the
refrigerator for at least 10 minutes.
2 Put the noodles in a heatproof bowl,
cover with boiling water and soak for 1
minute to separate and soften. Drain well,
then rinse under running water.
3 Heat a large wok over high heat, add 1
tablespoon of the oil and swirl it around to
coat the side of the wok. Lift the pork out of
the marinade with tongs or a slotted spoon,
reserving the marinade. Stir-fry the pork in
batches for 3 minutes each batch, or until
nicely browned. Remove from the wok.
4 Reheat the wok over high heat, add the
remaining oil and swirl to coat. Add the
onion, pepper and carrot, and stir-fry for
2–3 minutes, or until just tender. Add the
spring onion and shiitake mushrooms and
cook for another 2 minutes. Return the
pork to the wok along with the noodles
and the reserved marinade. Toss together
thoroughly until combined and heated
through, then serve.

RIGATONI WITH CHORIZO AND TOMATO

Preparation time: 15 minutes
Total cooking time: 20–25 minutes
Serves 4

2 tablespoons olive oil
1 onion, sliced
250 g (8 oz) chorizo sausage, sliced
425 g (14 oz) can crushed tomatoes
½ cup (125 ml/4 fl oz) dry white wine
½–1 teaspoon chopped chilli, optional
375 g (12 oz) rigatoni
2 tablespoons chopped fresh parsley
2 tablespoons freshly grated Parmesan

1 Heat the oil in a frying pan. Add the
onion and stir over low heat until tender.
2 Add the sausage to the pan and cook,
turning frequently, for 2–3 minutes. Add
the tomato, wine, chilli and salt and
pepper, to taste, and stir. Bring to the
boil, reduce the heat and simmer for
15–20 minutes.
3 While the sauce is cooking, cook the
rigatoni in a large pan of rapidly boiling
salted water until al dente. Drain and
return to the pan. Add the sauce to the
hot pasta. Toss well to combine. Serve
sprinkled with the combined fresh
parsley and grated Parmesan.

RIGATONI WITH SAUSAGE AND PARMESAN

Preparation time: 15 minutes
Total cooking time: 15 minutes
Serves 4

2 tablespoons olive oil
1 onion, sliced
1 clove garlic, crushed
500 g (1 lb) Italian pork sausage, cut into
  chunks
60 g (2 oz) mushrooms, sliced
½ cup (125 ml/4 fl oz) dry white wine
500 g (1 lb) rigatoni
1 cup (250 ml/8 fl oz) cream
2 eggs
½ cup (50 g/1¾ oz) freshly grated
  Parmesan
2 tablespoons chopped fresh parsley

1 Heat the oil in a large frying pan. Add
the onion and garlic and stir over low heat
until the onion is tender. Add the sausage
and mushroom and cook until the
sausage is cooked through. Stir in the
wine and bring to the boil. Reduce the
heat and simmer until the liquid is
reduced by half.
2 While the sauce is cooking, cook the
rigatoni in a large pan of rapidly boiling
salted water until al dente. Drain and
return to the pan.
3 In a large jug, whisk together the
cream, eggs, half the Parmesan, the
parsley and salt and pepper, to taste. Add
to the rigatoni with the sausage mixture
and toss. Serve sprinkled with the
remaining Parmesan.

NOTE: You can freeze leftover wine for
use in recipes such as this one. You can
use salami instead of Italian pork
sausage.

PEA AND HAM RISOTTO

Preparation time: 25 minutes
Total cooking time: 45 minutes
Serves 4

1 tablespoon olive oil
1 celery stick, chopped
2 tablespoons chopped fresh flat-leaf
  parsley
75 g (2½ oz) sliced ham, coarsely chopped
1⅔ cups (250 g/8 oz) frozen green peas
½ cup (125 ml/4 fl oz) dry white wine
3 cups (750 ml/24 fl oz) chicken stock
60 g (2 oz) butter
1 onion, chopped
2 cups (440 g/14 oz) arborio rice
⅓ cup (35 g/1¼ oz) grated Parmesan
shaved Parmesan, for serving

1 Heat the oil in a frying pan, add the celery, parsley and some freshly ground black pepper and cook, stirring, over medium heat for 2–3 minutes to soften the celery. Add the ham and stir well. Add the peas and half the wine, bring to the boil, then reduce the heat and simmer, uncovered, until almost all the liquid has evaporated. Set aside.
2 Put the stock, remaining wine and 3 cups (750 ml/24 fl oz) water in a separate pan and keep at simmering point.
3 Melt the butter in a large heavy-based saucepan. Add the onion and stir until softened. Add the rice and stir well. Gradually stir in the hot stock mixture, ½ cup (125 ml/4 oz) at a time, making sure the liquid has been absorbed before adding more. Stir constantly over low heat with a wooden spoon, until all the stock has been absorbed and the rice is creamy and tender (this will take about 25–30 minutes altogether). Season, to taste.
4 Add the pea mixture and grated Parmesan to the rice and serve with Parmesan shavings and black pepper.

PORK, PUMPKIN AND CASHEW STIR-FRY

Preparation time: 20 minutes
Total cooking time: 20 minutes
Serves 4

2–3 tablespoons vegetable oil
½ cup (80 g/2¾ oz) cashews
750 g (1½ lb) pork loin fillet, thinly sliced
  across the grain
500 g (1 lb) pumpkin, cut into cubes
1 tablespoon grated fresh ginger
⅓ cup (80 ml/2¾ fl oz) chicken stock
¼ cup (60 ml/2 fl oz) dry sherry
1½ tablespoons soy sauce
½ teaspoon cornflour
500 g (1 lb) baby bok choy, chopped
1–2 tablespoons fresh coriander leaves

1 Heat a wok over high heat, add 1 tablespoon of the oil and swirl to coat. Stir-fry the cashews for 1–2 minutes, or until browned. Drain.
2 Reheat the wok, add a little extra oil and swirl to coat. Stir-fry the pork in batches for 5 minutes, or until lightly browned. Remove. Add 1 tablespoon oil and stir-fry the pumpkin and ginger for 3 minutes, or until lightly browned. Add the stock, sherry and soy sauce, and simmer for 3 minutes, or until the pumpkin is tender.
3 Blend the cornflour with 1 teaspoon water, add to the wok and stir until the mixture boils and thickens. Return the pork and cashews to the wok, and add the bok choy and coriander. Stir until the bok choy has just wilted. Serve.

PASTA PIE

Preparation time: 20 minutes
Total cooking time: 1 hour
Serves 4

250 g (8 oz) macaroni
1 tablespoon olive oil
1 onion, sliced
125 g (4 oz) pancetta, chopped
125 g (4 oz) ham, chopped
4 eggs
1 cup (250 ml/8 fl oz) milk
1 cup (250 ml/8 fl oz) cream
2 tablespoons snipped fresh chives
1 cup (125 g/4 oz) grated Cheddar cheese
125 g (4 oz) bocconcini (approximately 4),
  chopped

1 Preheat the oven to moderate 180°C (350°F/Gas 4). Cook the macaroni in a large pan of rapidly boiling salted water until al dente. Drain. Spread evenly over the base of a 5 cm (2 inch) deep casserole dish.
2 Heat the oil in a large pan, add the onion and stir over low heat until just tender. Stir in the pancetta and cook for 2 minutes. Add the ham to the mixture and stir well. Remove from the heat and allow to cool.
3 In a bowl, whisk together the eggs, milk, cream, chives and salt and pepper, to taste. Mix in the Cheddar cheese, bocconcini and pancetta mixture, stirring thoroughly. Spread evenly over the top of the macaroni. Bake for 35–40 minutes, or until the mixture is set.

SWEET AND SOUR PORK

Preparation time: 20 minutes +
    30 minutes marinating + 30 minutes
    cooling
Total cooking time: 30 minutes
Serves 4–6

1 tablespoon light soy sauce
3 teaspoons Chinese rice wine
pinch of white pepper
500 g (1 lb) pork loin, cut into 1.5 cm
    (⅝ inch) cubes
½ cup (60 g/2 oz) plain flour
½ cup (60 g/2 oz) cornflour
1 teaspoon bicarbonate of soda
oil, for deep-frying
Sauce
2 teaspoons vegetable oil
1 teaspoon very finely chopped fresh
    ginger
1 clove garlic, crushed
1 small onion, cut into thin wedges
1 small carrot, thinly sliced on the
    diagonal
1 small green pepper (capsicum), cut into
    thin strips about 5 cm (2 inches) long
½ cup (100 g/3½ oz) canned pineapple
    chunks, well drained with ⅓ cup (80
    ml/2¾ fl oz) juice reserved
¼ cup (60 g/2 oz) sliced bamboo shoots
¼ cup (60 ml/2 fl oz) tomato sauce
1½ tablespoons rice vinegar
1½ tablespoons sugar
1 tablespoon light soy sauce
2 teaspoons cornflour combined with ½
    cup (125 ml/4 fl oz) water

1 Combine the soy sauce, rice wine and
white pepper in a non-metallic bowl, add
the pork and marinate for 30 minutes.
2 Combine the plain flour, cornflour,
bicarbonate of soda and 1 teaspoon salt,
then gradually mix in 145 ml (5 fl oz) cold
water until you have a thick, sticky batter.
Add the pork cubes and mix well with
your hands.

3 Fill a wok one-third full of the oils and
heat to 180°C (350°F), or until a cube of
bread browns in 15 seconds. Using your
fingers to separate the pork pieces, drop
individual pieces into the oil and cook in
small batches for 1½ minutes, or until
golden—you may need to carefully loosen
the pieces from the bottom of the wok
once they have been cooking for about
1 minute, then they should float to the top.
Drain well in a single layer on crumpled
paper towels and allow to cool to room
temperature. Remove the wok from the
heat but reserve the oil in the wok.
4 To make the sauce, heat a second wok
until very hot, add the oil and swirl to
coat. Add the ginger, garlic and onion and
stir-fry for 1 minute. Add the carrot and
stir-fry for 2 minutes, then add the green
pepper and cook for 1 minute, or until the
vegetables are tender but still a little
crunchy. Add the pineapple chunks and
the bamboo shoots, toss well and cook
for 1 minute, or until heated through.
Remove from the wok. Combine the
tomato sauce, rice vinegar, sugar, soy
sauce, cornflour mixture and the
reserved pineapple juice, and pour
it into the wok. Cook over high heat for
2–3 minutes or until the sauce boils and
thickens, then return the vegetables to
the wok. Stir well, then remove from the
heat.
5 Reheat the deep-frying oil to 180°C
(350°F). Re-fry the pork in two batches
for 1–2 minutes or until crisp, golden and
heated through. Drain on paper towels,
then quickly combine with the sauce.
Serve immediately with rice or as part of
a banquet—it will go soggy if it sits for too
long.

PENNE WITH PROSCIUTTO

Preparation time: 15 minutes
Total cooking time: 25 minutes
Serves 4

1 tablespoon olive oil
6 thin slices prosciutto, chopped
1 onion, finely chopped
1 tablespoon chopped fresh rosemary
825 g (1 lb 11 oz) can crushed tomatoes
500 g (1 lb) penne or macaroni
½ cup (50 g/1¾ oz) freshly grated
    Parmesan

1 Heat the oil in a heavy-based frying pan.
Add the prosciutto and onion and cook,
stirring occasionally, over low heat for
5 minutes, or until golden.
2 Add the rosemary, tomato and salt and
pepper, to taste. Simmer for 10 minutes.
3 While the sauce is cooking, add the
pasta to a large pan of rapidly boiling
salted water and cook until al dente.
Drain. Divide the pasta among serving
bowls and top with the sauce. Sprinkle
with grated Parmesan.

NOTE: Rosemary, commonly used in
Mediterranean cookery, adds a distinctive
flavour to this dish.

PORK AND NOODLE BALLS WITH SWEET CHILLI SAUCE

Preparation time: 30 minutes
Total cooking time: 20 minutes
Makes 30

Dipping sauce
⅓ cup (80 ml/2¾ fl oz) sweet chilli sauce
2 teaspoons mirin
2 teaspoons finely chopped fresh ginger
½ cup (125 ml/4 fl oz) Japanese soy sauce

250 g (8 oz) Hokkien noodles
300 g (10 oz) pork mince
6 spring onions, finely chopped
2 cloves garlic, crushed
4 tablespoons finely chopped fresh coriander leaves
1 tablespoon fish sauce
2 tablespoons oyster sauce
1½ tablespoons lime juice
peanut oil, for deep-frying

1 To make the dipping sauce, combine the sweet chilli sauce, mirin, ginger and Japanese soy sauce in a bowl.
2 Place the noodles in a bowl and cover with boiling water. Soak for 1 minute, or until tender. Drain very well and pat dry with paper towels. Cut the noodles into 5 cm (2 inch) lengths, then transfer to a large bowl. Add the pork mince, spring onion, garlic, coriander leaves, fish sauce, oyster sauce and lime juice and combine the mixture well using your hands, making sure the pork is evenly distributed.
3 Using a tablespoon of mixture at a time, roll each spoonful into a ball to make 30 in total, shaping and pressing each ball firmly with your hands to ensure they remain intact.
4 Fill a wok one-third full of oil and heat to 170°C (325°F), or until a cube of bread browns in 20 seconds. Deep-fry the pork balls in batches for 2–3 minutes, or until golden and cooked through. Drain on crumpled paper towels. Serve hot with the dipping sauce.

SPICY MEAT PAELLA

Preparation time: 25 minutes +
  15 minutes standing
Total cooking time: 35 minutes
Serves 4

3 ripe tomatoes
8 lamb cutlets, trimmed of excess fat
1 tablespoon olive oil
200 g (6½ oz) pork fillet, cut into 3 cm (1¼ inch) pieces
1 red capsicum (pepper), cut into strips
250 g (8 oz) green beans, trimmed
125 g (4 oz) chorizo sausage, thinly sliced
1 tablespoon paprika
1 teaspoon chilli flakes
1⅓ cups (295 g/10 oz) paella rice
¼ teaspoon saffron threads, soaked in ¼ cup (60 ml/2 fl oz) hot water
2 cups (500 ml/16 fl oz) hot chicken stock
1 tablespoon rosemary

1 Score a cross in the base of each tomato, put in a heatproof bowl and cover with boiling water. Leave for 30 seconds, then transfer to a bowl of cold water. Peel the skin away from the cross and finely chop the flesh.
2 Rub ½ teaspoon each of salt and freshly ground black pepper over the lamb cutlets.
3 Heat the oil in a paella pan or large, deep heavy-based frying with a lid. Add the lamb cutlets and cook over medium heat for 2–3 minutes, or until browned on both sides. Remove and set aside. Add the pork to the pan and cook, stirring, for 2–3 minutes, or until browned all over. Remove and set aside.

4 Add the capsicum and beans to the pan and cook, stirring, for 2–3 minutes, or until just soft. Increase the heat to high and add the chorizo, paprika and chilli flakes, and cook, stirring, for 30 seconds, or until fragrant.
5 Add the rice and stir to coat in the oil and spices. Add the chopped tomatoes and stir over high heat for 1 minute, or until bubbling. Return the pork to the frying pan with any accumulated juices and stir together.
6 Pour in the saffron and its liquid, the hot chicken stock and ½ teaspoon each of salt and pepper. Arrange the lamb cutlets on top of the rice mixture and sprinkle with the rosemary. Bring to the boil, then reduce the heat to medium and simmer gently. Check the heat frequently during cooking so the paella maintains a constant gentle simmer. Cook, covered, for 20 minutes without stirring. Shake the pan occasionally during cooking to keep the rice from sticking to the base. The rice should not be soft, it should still have a slight bite. Remove the pan from the heat, cover loosely with foil and leave to rest for 5–10 minutes, then serve.

COLD MEATS

WHILE ITALY IS FAMOUS FOR ITS PASTA, COLD MEATS AND SALAMIS ARE ALSO CLOSE TO THE ITALIAN COOK'S HEART. EACH REGION IS PASSIONATELY ADAMANT ABOUT THE SUPERIORITY OF ITS OWN SPECIALITY.

Pancetta is the Italian version of bacon. The rind is removed and the meat is seasoned with salt and pepper and spices which include nutmeg, juniper, cloves, cinnamon, depending on the person who is packing it. It is cured for two weeks, then tightly rolled and packed in a case similar to that used for salami. The flavour is less salty than prosciutto, though it can be eaten raw as you would prosciutto. It is prized for the flavour it imparts to cooked dishes where it has no real substitute for its savoury sweet taste.

Prosciutto is the salt- and air-dried hind leg of a pig. The salt removes the moisture from the meat and the slow process of air-curing produces a soft delicate flavour. Prosciutto can be cured for up 18 months and the most prized are judged against genuine Italian Parma ham. Sliced prosciutto should be consumed as soon as possible after cutting as it gradually loses its flavour. Remove it from the refrigerator 1 hour before you plan to serve it. Parma ham gets its unique flavour from the pigs being fed the whey left over from cheese-making. Traditionally served with melon or figs on an antipasto platter.

Mortadella from Bologna takes its name from the mortar used to grind the pork. Flavoured with peppercorns, stuffed olives, pistachios and garlic and flecked with strips of fat, it can measure up to 40 cm (16 inches) in diameter. Mortadella is chopped and used on pizzas, in sandwiches or in tortellini.

Salami A cured dry sausage made from minced pork and seasoned with garlic, herbs and spices. Thought to have originated in Salamis in Cyprus, most Italian salamis take their names from the towns in which they are produced. Distinctive types of salami are also made in Denmark, Spain, Hungary, Austria and Germany.

Cacciatore is made from pork and beef, garlic and spices, and can be mild or hot. Milano salami is a mildly-flavoured Italian salami made with lean pork, beef and pork fat. It has a fine texture and is seasoned with garlic, pepper and wine.

Finocchiona toscana is a salami made from pork and seasoned with fennel seeds that are distributed throughout the salami. Mild or hot.

Pepperoni is a dried Italian sausage made from ground pork and beef, highly seasoned with pepper. It is used as a topping for pizzas and in pasta sauces.

Coppa is made from the pork shoulder that has been cured. It is fattier than prosciutto and is sold rolled and cased like salami. Coppa is frequently served as a part of an antipasto platter.

Speck is the fatty top part of a leg of bacon, usually smoked and salted. It is available in small pieces. Austrian in origin, it can be sliced for a cold snack or chopped into small cubes to use to add flavour to cooked dishes.

Chorizo is a coarsely-textured Spanish sausage that comes in many varieties, although it is always made from pork and seasoned with pimiento. It is sliced, fried and used in pasta sauces or, as it is best known, in paella.

CLOCKWISE, FROM TOP LEFT: Prosciutto on the bone, pancetta, prosciutto slices off the bone, Milano, Finocchiona Toscana, Coppa, Cacciatore, Speck, Chorizo, Pepperoni, Mortadella

CLASSIC JAMBALAYA

Preparation time: 30 minutes
Total cooking time: 55 minutes
Serves 4–6

2 tablespoons olive oil
1 large red onion, finely chopped
1 garlic clove, crushed
2 back bacon rashers, finely chopped
1½ cups (300 g/10 oz) long-grain white
   rice
1 red capsicum (pepper), diced
150 g (5 oz) ham, chopped
400 g (13 oz) tin chopped tomatoes
400 g (13 oz) tomato passata
1 teaspoon Worcestershire sauce
dash of Tabasco sauce
½ teaspoon dried thyme
½ cup (30 g/1 oz) chopped parsley
150 g (5 oz) cooked, peeled, small prawns
   (shrimp)
4 spring onions (scallions), thinly sliced

1 Heat the oil in a large saucepan over
medium heat. Add the onion, garlic and
bacon and cook, stirring, for 5 minutes, or
until the onion is softened but not
browned. Stir in the rice and cook for a
further 5 minutes, or until lightly golden.
2 Add the capsicum, ham, chopped
tomatoes, tomato passata,
Worcestershire and Tabasco sauces and
thyme and stir until well combined.
Bring the mixture to the boil, then reduce
the heat to low. Cook, covered, for
30–40 minutes, or until the rice is tender.
3 Stir in the parsley and prawns and
season with salt and freshly ground black
pepper. Sprinkle with the spring onion,
then serve.

PORK AND CHIVE DUMPLINGS

Preparation time: 45 minutes +
   3 hours marinating
Total cooking time: 15 minutes
Makes 24

1 teaspoon vegetable oil
2 cloves garlic, crushed
2 teaspoons finely grated fresh ginger
250 g (8 oz) garlic chives, cut into 1 cm
   (½ inch) lengths
200 g (6½ oz) pork mince
2 tablespoons oyster sauce
3 teaspoons Chinese rice wine
2 teaspoons light soy sauce
½ teaspoon sesame oil
1 teaspoon cornflour
24 round gow gee wrappers

1 Heat a wok over high heat, add the
vegetable oil and swirl to coat the side of
the wok. Add the garlic, ginger and garlic
chives, then stir-fry for 1 minute, or until
fragrant and the chives have wilted
slightly. Remove from the heat and allow
to cool.
2 Meanwhile, put the pork mince, oyster
sauce, rice wine, soy sauce, sesame oil
and cornflour in a non-metallic bowl and
mix well. Cover and refrigerate for
3 hours. Add the vegetable mixture once
it has cooled, mix it into the pork until
well combined and return to the fridge for
the remainder of the 3 hours.
3 Put 2 teaspoons of the mixture in the
centre of a gow gee wrapper. Moisten the
edges with water, then fold the sides
together to form a semicircle. Pinch the
edges together at 5 mm (¼ inch) intervals
to form a ruffled edge. Repeat with the
remaining filling and wrappers. Line a
double bamboo steamer with baking
paper. Put half the dumplings in a single
layer in each steamer basket. Cover and
steam over a wok of simmering water for
12 minutes, or until cooked through.

CHILLI SPARE RIBS

Preparation time: 20 minutes
Total cooking time: 1 hour
Serves 4

750 g (1½ lb) pork spare ribs
1 tablespoon peanut oil
2 teaspoons finely chopped garlic
¼ cup (60 ml/2 fl oz) dry sherry
1 tablespoon chilli bean paste or sambal
   oelek
2 cups (500 ml/16 fl oz) water
2 teaspoons hoisin sauce
3 teaspoons caster sugar
1 tablespoon soy sauce, preferably dark

1 Place the pork in a large pan with water
to cover. Bring to the boil, reduce heat,
simmer for 5 minutes; drain well.
2 Place all the remaining ingredients and
the pork ribs in a wok or deep, heavy-
based pan. Cover and simmer for
45 minutes. Drain, reserving 1 cup
(250 ml/8 fl oz) of liquid. Heat a clean wok
or heavy-based frying pan and sear the
pork pieces to brown them.
3 Add the reserved cooking liquid and
cook over medium heat until it forms a
glazed coating for the pork.
4 Chop the pork pieces into 3 cm (1¼ inch)
pieces and serve with the sauce poured
over them.

PORK WITH SAGE AND CAPERS

Preparation time: 25 minutes
Total cooking time 1 hour 15 minutes
Serves 4

¼ cup (60 ml/2 fl oz) extra virgin olive oil
25 g (¾ oz) unsalted butter
1 onion, finely chopped
100 g (3½ oz) fresh white breadcrumbs
2 teaspoons chopped fresh sage
1 tablespoon chopped fresh flat-leaf
  parsley
2 teaspoons grated lemon zest
2½ tablespoons salted baby capers,
  rinsed and drained
1 egg
2 large pork fillets (about 500 g/1 lb each)
8 large thin slices of streaky bacon or
  prosciutto
2 teaspoons plain flour
100 ml (3½ fl oz) dry vermouth
1¼ cups (315 ml/10 fl oz) chicken or
  vegetable stock
8 whole sage leaves, extra, to garnish

1 Preheat the oven to warm 170°C
(325°F/Gas 3). Heat 1 tablespoon of the oil
and the butter in a frying pan, add the
onion and cook for 5 minutes, or until
lightly golden.
2 Place the breadcrumbs, chopped sage,
parsley, lemon zest, ½ tablespoon capers
and the cooked onion in a bowl. Add the
egg and season well.

3 Split each pork fillet in half lengthways
and open out. Spread the stuffing down
the length of one and cover with the other
fillet.
4 Stretch the bacon or prosciutto with the
back of a knife and wrap each piece
slightly overlapping around the pork to
form a neat parcel. Tie with string at
intervals.
5 Place the pork in a baking dish and
drizzle with 1 tablespoon oil. Bake for
1 hour. To test if the meat is cooked,
insert a skewer in the thickest part. The
juices should run clear. Remove the meat
from the tin, cover with foil and leave to
rest. Place the baking dish on the
stovetop, add the flour and stir in well.
Add the vermouth and allow to bubble for
1 minute. Add the stock and stir while
cooking to remove all the lumps. Simmer
for 5 minutes. Add the remaining capers
to the sauce.
6 In a small saucepan, heat the remaining
oil and when very hot, fry the whole sage
leaves until crisp. Drain on crumpled
paper towels.
7 Slice the pork into 1 cm (½ inch) slices.
Spoon a little sauce over the pork and
serve each portion with fried sage leaves
on top.

BASIL TORTELLINI WITH BACON AND TOMATO SAUCE

Preparation time: 15 minutes
Total cooking time: 25 minutes
Serves 4

500 g (1 lb) fresh or dried basil tortellini
1 tablespoon olive oil
4 bacon rashers, chopped
2 cloves garlic, crushed
1 medium onion, chopped
1 teaspoon chopped fresh chillies
425 g (14 oz) can tomatoes
½ cup (125 ml/4 fl oz) cream
2 tablespoons chopped fresh basil

1 Cook the pasta in a large pan of rapidly
boiling salted water until al dente. Drain
and return to the pan.
2 While the pasta is cooking, heat the oil
in a medium heavy-based pan. Add the
bacon, garlic and onion and cook for
5 minutes over medium heat, stirring
regularly.
3 Add the chilli and undrained, chopped
tomato. Reduce the heat and simmer for
10 minutes. Add the cream and basil and
cook for 1 minute. Add the sauce to the
pasta and toss well. Serve immediately.

STICKY RICE AND PORK POCKETS

Preparation time: 15 minutes + 1 hour
    soaking + 30 minutes marinating
Total cooking time: 45 minutes
Makes 8

3 cups (600 g/1¼ lb) glutinous white rice
4 large lotus leaves
4 dried shiitake mushrooms
2 tablespoons dried shrimp
350 g (11 oz) pork leg or loin fillet, cut into
    2 cm (¾ inch) cubes
2 teaspoons thinly sliced fresh ginger
1½ tablespoons soy sauce
1½ tablespoons cornflour
1 tablespoon oyster sauce
2 teaspoons sugar
1 teaspoon sesame oil
2 tablespoons vegetable oil
1 clove garlic, finely chopped
2 lap choong sausages, thinly sliced
2 spring onions, thinly sliced

1 Wash the rice in cold water, drain well
and put in a saucepan with 2½ cups (600
ml/20 fl oz) water. Bring to the boil over
high heat, then reduce the heat to low,
cover with a tightly fitting lid and simmer
for 20 minutes. Allow to cool until needed.
2 Cut the lotus leaves in half. Put the lotus
leaves in a large bowl, cover with boiling
water and soak for 1 hour. Pat the leaves
dry with paper towels. At the same time,
put the dried mushrooms and dried
shrimp in separate bowls, cover each with
boiling water and soak for 20 minutes.
Drain well. Remove the stalks from the
mushrooms and finely chop the caps.
3 Meanwhile, put the pork in a food
processor and briefly pulse until coarsely
ground. Transfer to a bowl with the
ginger, 1 tablespoon of the soy sauce and
2 teaspoons of the cornflour, and toss
together well. Marinate for 20–30 minutes.

4 Combine the oyster sauce, sugar,
sesame oil and remaining soy sauce in a
bowl and stir well.
5 Heat a wok over high heat. Add the
vegetable oil and swirl to coat. When hot,
add the pork mixture and stir-fry for
2–3 minutes. Add the chopped
mushrooms, soaked shrimp, garlic,
sausage and spring onion. Stir-fry for
2 minutes. Add the soy and oyster sauce
mixture and toss well. Combine the
remaining cornflour with 220 ml (7 fl oz)
water, gradually add to the wok and stir
for a further minute, or until the pork
mixture has thickened.
6 With wet hands, roll and shape the
cooked rice into 16 balls. Fold one end of
a lotus leaf piece on the diagonal to form
a cone. Hold securely in one hand and
spoon in a ball of rice. Make an indent in
the centre of the rice, spoon one-eighth of
the pork mixture into the middle of the
rice, then top with another rice ball. Fold
the other end of the lotus leaf over to
enclose the filling, then secure with a
toothpick. Tie tightly with kitchen string.
The parcels should be triangular. Repeat
with the remaining lotus leaves, rice balls
and filling.
7 Place the rice parcels in a single layer
in a double bamboo steamer. Cover with
the steamer lid, and steam over a wok of
simmering water for 15 minutes. Reverse
the steamers and steam for a further 15
minutes, adding more hot water to the
wok as necessary. Serve immediately.

HASH HAM CAKE

Preparation time: 30 minutes +
    1 hour refrigeration
Total cooking time: 50 minutes
Serves 4–6

500 g (1 lb) floury potatoes, such as
    russet or King Edward, peeled and
    quartered
200 g (6½ oz) ham, finely chopped
4 spring onions, finely chopped
1 small gherkin, finely chopped
2 tablespoons chopped fresh parsley
1 egg, lightly beaten
50 g (1¾ oz) butter

1 Boil or steam the potato for 10–15 minutes,
until tender (pierce with the point of a
small knife—if the potato comes away
easily, it is ready). Drain well, then put the
potato in a large bowl and mash.
2 Mix in the ham, spring onion, gherkin,
parsley, egg and some freshly ground
black pepper. Spread on a plate, cover
and refrigerate for at least 1 hour, or
overnight, to firm.
3 Heat 30 g (1 oz) of the butter in a 20 cm
(8 inch) heavy-based frying pan. Add the
potato, spread evenly into the pan and
smooth the surface with the back of a
spoon. Cook over moderate heat for
15 minutes, then slide out onto a plate.
Add the remaining butter to the pan,
carefully flip the cake back into the pan
and cook for another 15–20 minutes, or
until the outside forms a brown crust. Cut
into wedges for serving.

NOTE: Floury potatoes have a low moisture
and sugar content and lots of starch. This
makes them very suitable for mashing as
well as baking. If you are not sure, ask your
greengrocer which variety is most suitable
for your needs. When you buy potatoes,
they should be firm, not wrinkled, cracked,
sprouting or green. Store away from light in
a cool, well-ventilated place. Leave the dirt
on unwashed potatoes during storage as it
helps to protect them.

ITALIAN OMELETTE

Preparation time: 20 minutes
Total cooking time: 15 minutes
Serves 4

2 tablespoons olive oil
1 onion, finely chopped
125 g (4 oz) ham, sliced
6 eggs
¼ cup (60 ml/2 fl oz) milk
2 cups cooked fusilli or spiral pasta
   (150 g/5 oz uncooked)
3 tablespoons grated Parmesan
2 tablespoons chopped fresh parsley
1 tablespoon chopped fresh basil
½ cup (60 g/2 oz) freshly grated Cheddar
   cheese

1 Heat half the oil in a frying pan. Add the onion and stir over low heat until softened. Add the sliced ham to the pan and stir for 1 minute. Transfer to a plate and set aside.
2 In a bowl, whisk the eggs, milk and salt and pepper, to taste. Stir in the pasta, Parmesan, herbs and onion mixture.
3 Heat the remaining oil in the same pan. Pour the egg mixture into the pan. Sprinkle with cheese. Cook over medium heat until the mixture begins to set around the edges. Place under a hot grill to complete the cooking. Cut into wedges for serving.

NOTE: This omelette goes well with a crisp green or mixed salad.

BARBECUED ASIAN PORK RIBS WITH SPRING ONION RICE

Preparation time: 15 minutes + overnight
   marinating
Total cooking time: 40 minutes
Serves 4

1 kg (2 lb) American-style pork ribs, cut
   into sections of 4–5 ribs
¼ cup (60 ml/2 fl oz) hoisin sauce
¼ cup (60 ml/2 fl oz) soy sauce
1 tablespoon Chinese rice wine
2 garlic cloves, chopped
2 tablespoons oil
3 spring onions (scallions), finely
   chopped
1 tablespoon grated ginger
1¼ cups (250 g/8 oz) long-grain rice
600 g (1¼ lb) baby bok choy (pak choi),
   leaves separated

1 Put the ribs in a non-metallic bowl. Combine the hoisin sauce, soy sauce, rice wine, garlic, 1 tablespoon of the oil, 2 tablespoons of the spring onion and half the ginger. Pour onto the ribs and mix to coat. Marinate for at least 10 minutes, or overnight in the refrigerator, if time permits.
2 Bring a large saucepan of water to the boil. Add the rice and cook for 12 minutes, stirring occasionally. Drain well.

3 Heat the remaining oil in a small saucepan over medium–low heat. When the oil is warm but not smoking, remove the pan from the heat and add the remaining spring onion and ginger. Season with ¼ teaspoon salt, stirring quickly to combine. Stir this mixture through the rice.
4 Preheat a chargrill pan or barbecue plate and brush with oil. Remove the ribs from the marinade with tongs and reserve the marinade. Cook the ribs, in batches, if necessary, for 8–10 minutes on each side, or until cooked through, occasionally basting with the marinade.
5 About 5 minutes before the ribs are cooked, pour the reserved marinade into a small saucepan. If there is not much liquid, add ⅓ cup (80 ml/2¾ fl oz) water. Boil for 2 minutes, then add the bok choy, stirring to coat. Cook, covered, for 1–2 minutes, or until just wilted. Serve the ribs with the rice and bok choy, and drizzle with the marinade.

BARBECUED PORK AND BROCCOLI STIR-FRY

Preparation time: 25 minutes
Total cooking time: 10 minutes
Serves 4–6

1 tablespoon vegetable oil
1 large onion, thinly sliced
2 carrots, julienned
200 g (6½ oz) broccoli, cut into bite-sized florets
6 spring onions, sliced on the diagonal
1 tablespoon finely chopped fresh ginger
3 cloves garlic, finely chopped
400 g (13 oz) Chinese barbecued pork, thinly sliced
2 tablespoons soy sauce
2 tablespoons mirin
2 cups (180 g/6 oz) bean sprouts, tailed

1 Heat a wok over high heat, add the oil and swirl it around to coat the side of the wok. Reduce the heat to medium, add the onion and stir-fry for 3–4 minutes, or until slightly softened.
2 Add the carrot, broccoli, spring onion, ginger and garlic, and cook for 4–5 minutes, tossing constantly until thoroughly combined.
3 Increase the heat to high and add the pork. Toss constantly until the pork is well mixed with the vegetables and is heated through.
4 Pour in the soy sauce and mirin, and toss until the ingredients are well coated. The wok should be hot enough that the sauce reduces a little to form a glaze-like consistency. Toss in the bean sprouts, then season to taste with salt and freshly ground black pepper. Serve immediately with rice noodles, if desired.

PORK WITH SPINACH

Preparation time: 20 minutes
Total cooking time: 15 minutes
Serves 4

1 tablespoon white sesame seeds
400 g (12⅔ oz) spinach
2 cloves garlic, very finely sliced
3 spring onions, chopped
½ teaspoon cayenne pepper
300 g (9⅔ oz) pork loin, cut into thick strips
2 tablespoons oil
2 teaspoons sesame oil
2 tablespoons Japanese soy sauce
2 teaspoons sugar

1 Toast the sesame seeds in a dry pan over medium heat for 3 to 4 minutes, shaking the pan gently, until the seeds are golden brown; remove from the pan at once to prevent burning.
2 Trim the ends from the spinach, roughly chop the leaves and wash to remove all grit.
3 Combine the garlic, spring onion, cayenne pepper and pork, mixing well. Heat the oils in a heavy-based frying pan and stir-fry the pork quickly in 3 batches over very high heat until golden. Remove the meat and set aside.
4 Add the soy sauce, sugar and spinach, and toss lightly. Cover and cook for 2 minutes or until the spinach is just soft. Return the pork to the pan, add the sesame seeds, toss well and serve immediately.

PORK AND PRAWN VERMICELLI

Preparation time: 25 minutes + 10 minutes soaking
Total cooking time: 10 minutes
Serves 4

100 g (3½ oz) dried rice vermicelli
2 tablespoons peanut oil
200 g (6½ oz) lean minced (ground) pork
100 g (3½ oz) red Asian shallots, finely chopped
2 garlic cloves, finely chopped
2 small red chillies, finely chopped
100 g (3½ oz) Chinese celery or celery, finely chopped
12 raw prawns (shrimp), peeled and deveined
1 makrut (kaffir) lime leaf, shredded
1½ tablespoons fish sauce
1 tablespoon sugar
2½ tablespoons lime juice
2 tablespoons mint
3 tablespoons Thai basil
4 tablespoons coriander (cilantro) leaves

1 Put the vermicelli in a large heatproof bowl, cover with boiling water and soak for 6–7 minutes, or until tender. Drain well and set aside.
2 Heat a wok until very hot, add 1 tablespoon of the oil and swirl to coat. Add the pork and stir-fry for 1–2 minutes, or until slightly brown, stirring to break up any lumps. Drain and transfer to a plate lined with paper towel.
3 Heat the remaining oil in the wok over high heat and stir-fry the shallots, garlic, chilli and celery for 1 minute. Add the prawns, lime leaf, fish sauce, sugar and lime juice and continue to stir-fry for 1 minute, or until the prawns start to turn pink.
4 Add the vermicelli and pork to the wok and stir-fry for 1–2 minutes, or until well combined and heated through. Divide among the serving dishes, then toss in the mint, basil and coriander. Serve immediately.

RAISED PORK PIE

Preparation time: 20 minutes + 2 hours 15
  minutes refrigeration + overnight
  setting
Total cooking time: 1 hour 5 minutes
Serves 6

1.2 kg (2 lb 6½ oz) minced pork
⅔ cup (90 g/3 oz) pistachio nuts, chopped
2 green apples, peeled and finely
  chopped
6 fresh sage leaves, finely chopped
4 cups (500 g/1 lb) plain flour
150 g (5 oz) butter
2 eggs, lightly beaten
1 egg yolk
1 cup (250 ml/8 fl oz) vegetable stock
⅔ cup (170 ml/5½ fl oz) unsweetened
  apple juice
2 teaspoons powdered gelatine

1 Preheat the oven to moderately hot
200°C (400°F/Gas 6). Put the pork,
pistachio nuts, apple and sage leaves in a
bowl, mix well and season. Fry a small
piece of the mixture, taste and adjust the
seasoning, to taste. Cover the mixture and
refrigerate.
2 Wrap a piece of plastic wrap around a
6 cm (2½ inch) high, 20 cm (8 inch)
diameter straight-sided tin, then turn the
tin over and grease the plastic on the
outside base and side of the tin.
3 Put the flour and 1 teaspoon salt in a
bowl and make a well in the centre. Put
the butter in a saucepan with ¾ cup
(185 ml/6 fl oz) water. Bring to the boil
and add to the flour, with the beaten eggs.
Mix with a wooden spoon until combined,
then turn out onto a lightly floured work
surface and bring the mixture together,
adding another 1–2 tablespoons boiling
water if necessary to form a smooth
dough. Wrap in plastic wrap and
refrigerate for 10 minutes.

4 Wrap a third of the pastry in plastic
wrap—do not refrigerate. Roll the
remaining pastry into a circle large
enough to just cover the outside of the tin.
Lift onto a rolling pin and place over the
tin, pressing to the shape of the tin and
working quickly before the pastry sets.
Refrigerate for about 2 hours, until the
pastry hardens, then carefully pull out the
tin and remove the plastic wrap. Put the
pastry on a lightly greased baking tray.
Attach a paper collar made of 2 layers of
greased baking paper around the outside
of the pastry so it fits snugly and supports
the pastry. Secure it with a paper clip at
the top and bottom. Fill the pastry with
the pork mixture, then roll out the
remaining pastry to form a lid. Brush the
rim of the base with a little water and
press the lid on to attach. Pinch to seal.
Cut a small hole in the top of the pie to fit
a funnel.
5 Bake for 40 minutes and check the
pastry top. If it is still pale, bake for
another 10 minutes, then remove the
paper. Brush with egg yolk mixed with
1 tablespoon water and bake for another
15 minutes, or until the sides are brown.
Cool completely.
6 Bring the vegetable stock and half the
apple juice to the boil in a saucepan, then
remove from the heat. Sprinkle the
gelatine over the surface of the remaining
apple juice in a jug, leave to go spongy,
then pour into the stock and mix well until
the gelatine dissolves. Place a small
funnel (large icing nozzles work well) in
the hole of the pie, pour in a little of the
gelatine mixture, leave to settle and then
pour in a little more until the pie is full. It
is important to fill the pie completely to
ensure there are no gaps when the
gelatine mixture sets. You may not need
to use all the liquid. Refrigerate for
several hours, or overnight, until the
gelatine has set completely. Serve cold.

CURRIED NOODLES WITH PORK

Preparation time: 20 minutes
Total cooking time: 10 minutes
Serves 4

125 g (4 oz) dried rice stick noodles
1 medium onion
2 tablespoons oil
2 teaspoons mild curry powder
½ teaspoon salt
½ cup (80 g/2⅔ oz) frozen peas
¼ cup (60 ml/2 fl oz) coconut milk or
  vegetable stock
2 teaspoons soy sauce
125 g (4 oz) Chinese barbecued pork or
  roast pork, thinly sliced

1 Place the rice noodles in a bowl, cover
with hot water, and leave to soak for
20 minutes. Drain well in a colander. Cut
the onion into eighths and separate the
layers.
2 Heat the oil in a wok; add the onion and
cook over high heat for 1 minute. Add the
curry powder, salt and noodles; toss to
coat.
3 Add the peas, coconut milk and soy
sauce, tossing a few times to combine.
Cover the wok tightly, reduce heat to very
low and cook for 3 minutes. Gently stir the
sliced pork through and heat for a further
minute. Serve either as a course on its
own or as a snack.

PORK SAUSAGES WITH WHITE BEANS

Preparation time: 25 minutes +
  overnight soaking
Total cooking time: 1 hour 40 minutes
Serves 4

350 g (11 oz) dried white haricot beans
150 g (5 oz) tocino, speck or pancetta,
  unsliced
½ leek, thinly sliced
2 whole cloves garlic
1 bay leaf
1 small red chilli, split and seeds
  removed
1 small onion
2 cloves
1 sprig of fresh rosemary
3 sprigs of fresh thyme
1 sprig of fresh parsley
3 tablespoons olive oil
8 pork sausages
½ onion, finely chopped
1 green pepper (capsicum), finely
  chopped
½ teaspoon paprika
½ cup (125 ml/4 fl oz) puréed tomato
1 teaspoon cider vinegar

1 Soak the beans overnight in plenty of
cold water. Drain and rinse the beans
under cold water. Put them in a large
saucepan with the tocino, leek, garlic, bay
leaf and chilli. Stud the onion with the
cloves and add to the saucepan. Tie the
rosemary, thyme and parsley together
and add to the saucepan. Pour in 3 cups
(750 ml/24 fl oz) cold water and bring to
the boil. Add 1 tablespoon oil, reduce the
heat and simmer, covered, for about 1
hour, until the beans are tender. When
necessary, add a little more boiling water
to keep the beans covered.

2 Prick each sausage 5 or 6 times and
twist tightly in opposite directions in the
middle to give 2 short fat sausages joined
in the middle. Put in a single layer in a
large frying pan and add enough cold
water to reach halfway up their sides.
Bring to the boil and simmer, turning two
or three times, until all the water has
evaporated and the sausages brown
lightly in the little fat that is left in the
pan. Remove from the pan and cut the
short sausages apart. Add the remaining
2 tablespoons oil, the chopped onion and
green pepper to the pan and fry over
medium heat for 5–6 minutes. Stir in the
paprika, cook for 30 seconds then add the
puréed tomato. Season, to taste. Cook,
stirring, for 1 minute.
3 Remove the tocino, herb sprigs and any
loose large pieces of onion from the bean
mixture. Leave in any loose leaves from
the herbs, and any small pieces of onion.
Add the sausages and sauce to the pan
and stir the vinegar through. Bring to the
boil. Adjust the seasoning.

NOTE: This dish improves if cooked in
advance and left for up to 2 days before
serving.

ROAST LEG OF PORK

Preparation time: 30 minutes
Total cooking time: 3 hours 25 minutes
Serves 6–8

4 kg (8 lb) leg of pork
oil and salt, to rub on pork

Gravy
1 tablespoon brandy or Calvados
2 tablespoons plain flour
1½ cups (375 ml/12 fl oz) chicken stock
½ cup (125 ml/4 fl oz) unsweetened apple
  juice

1 Preheat the oven to very hot 250°C
(500°F/Gas 10). Score the pork rind with a
sharp knife at 2 cm (¾ inch) intervals. Rub
in oil and salt to ensure a crisp crackling.
Place the pork, with the rind uppermost, on
a rack in a large baking dish.
2 Add a little water to the dish. Bake for
30 minutes, or until the rind begins to
crackle and bubble. Reduce the heat to
moderate 180°C (350°F/Gas 4) and
continue to bake for 2 hours 40 minutes
(20 minutes per 500 g/1 lb). The pork is
cooked if the juices run clear when the
flesh is pierced with a fork. Do not cover
or the crackling will soften. Leave in a
warm place for 10 minutes before carving.
3 For the gravy, drain off all but
2 tablespoons of the juices from the
baking dish. Place the dish on top of the
stove over moderate heat, add the brandy
and stir quickly to lift the sticky juices
from the bottom of the pan. Cook for 1
minute. Remove from the heat, stir in the
flour and mix well. Return the pan to the
heat and cook for 2 minutes, stirring
constantly. Remove from the heat,
gradually stir in the stock and apple juice,
then return to the heat and cook, stirring
constantly, until the gravy boils and
thickens. Season, to taste, with salt and
pepper. Slice the pork and serve with the
crackling, gravy and apple sauce

HAM, CHEESE AND ONION QUICKBREAD

Preparation time: 25 minutes
Total cooking time: 1 hour 5 minutes
Serves 6–8

1 tablespoon oil
3 onions, thinly sliced into rings
2 teaspoons soft brown sugar
200 g (6½ oz) sliced ham, finely chopped
3 cups (375 g/12 oz) self-raising flour
100 g (3½ oz) butter, chilled
¾ cup (90 g/3 oz) grated Cheddar
½ cup (125 ml/4 fl oz) milk

1 Heat half of the oil in a large, heavy-based frying pan. Add the onion and cook over medium heat for 10 minutes, stirring occasionally. Add the sugar and continue to cook for 10–15 minutes, or until the onion is golden brown. Set aside to cool.
2 Heat the remaining oil in a small frying pan, add the ham and cook over moderately high heat until golden brown. Drain on crumpled paper towels and add to the onion. Allow to cool slightly.
3 Preheat the oven to hot 210°C (415°F/Gas 6–7). Lightly grease a baking tray. Sift the flour into a large bowl and rub in the butter with your fingertips until the mixture resembles fine breadcrumbs.
4 Add three-quarters of the onion mixture and ½ cup (60 g/2 oz) of the Cheddar to the flour and mix well. Make a well in the centre and add the milk and about ½ cup (125 ml/4 fl oz) of water (add enough water to bring the dough together). Using a flat-bladed knife, mix to a soft dough. Gently gather together into a ball.
5 Lay the dough on the tray and press out to form a 22 cm (8¾ inch) circle. Using a sharp knife, mark the dough into quarters, cutting two-thirds of the way through. Sprinkle with the rest of the onion mixture and the remaining Cheddar. Bake for 15 minutes, then reduce the oven temperature to moderate 180°C (350°F/Gas 4). Cover the top loosely with foil if it starts getting too brown.

FRIED PORK CURRY

Preparation time: 30 minutes
Total cooking time: 2 hours
Serves 6

2 cups (310 g/9¾ oz) roughly chopped onion
15 cloves garlic, crushed
4 tablespoons finely chopped fresh ginger
3 tablespoons peanut oil
1 tablespoon sesame oil
1½ teaspoons chilli powder
1 teaspoon ground turmeric
1.5 kg (3 lb) boneless pork, cut into 3 cm (1¼ inch) cubes
1 tablespoon vinegar
1 cup (250 ml/8 fl oz) water or stock
2 tablespoons fresh coriander leaves

1 Place the onion, garlic and ginger in a food processor and process until a thick rough paste is formed.
2 Heat the peanut oil and sesame oil in a large pan; add the paste and cook it over medium heat for about 15 minutes until it becomes a golden brown colour and has oil around the edges. Add the chilli powder, turmeric and pork, and stir well for a few minutes until the pork is well coated with the mixture.
3 Add the vinegar and water, cover and simmer gently for 1½ hours or until the meat is tender. If necessary reduce the liquid by removing the lid and allowing the sauce to evaporate. Season with salt to taste (the dish will need more if you use water instead of stock) and scatter over the coriander. Serve with rice.

SPARERIBS WITH SESAME SEEDS

Preparation time: 30 minutes
Total cooking time: 1 hour
Serves 4–6

1 tablespoon white sesame seeds
1 kg (2 lb) pork spareribs, cut into 3 cm (1¼ inch) pieces
2 tablespoons oil
2 spring onions, finely chopped
4 cm (1½ inch) piece fresh ginger, grated
3 cloves garlic, finely chopped
2 tablespoons caster sugar
2 tablespoons sake
1 tablespoon soy sauce
2 teaspoons sesame oil
1¼ cups (315 ml/10 fl oz) hot water
2 teaspoons cornflour

1 Toast the sesame seeds in a dry pan over medium heat for 3 to 4 minutes, shaking the pan gently, until the seeds are golden brown. Remove the seeds from the pan immediately, to prevent them burning. Crush the seeds in a food mill or with a mortar and pestle.
2 Trim the pork of excess fat. Heat the oil in a heavy-based frying pan. Brown the spareribs over high heat, turning regularly, until dark golden brown. Drain any excess oil from the pan. Add half the sesame seeds, spring onion, ginger, garlic, sugar, sake, soy sauce, sesame oil and water; stir well to evenly coat the ribs. Bring to the boil over medium heat, then cover and simmer 45 to 50 minutes, stirring occasionally.
3 Combine the cornflour with a little cold water and mix to a smooth paste. Add to the pan, stirring constantly, until the mixture boils and thickens. Sprinkle with the remaining sesame seeds.

NOTE: Make sure the rib pieces can be held easily with chopsticks—if necessary, cut them into smaller pieces.

RUOTE WITH LEMON, OLIVES AND BACON

Ready to eat in 25 minutes
Serves 4

500 g (1 lb) ruote
6 bacon rashers
1 cup (125 g/4 oz) black olives, sliced
⅓ cup (80 ml/2¾ fl oz) lemon juice
2 teaspoons finely grated lemon rind
⅓ cup (80 ml/2¾ fl oz) olive oil
⅓ cup (20 g/¾ oz) chopped fresh parsley

1 Cook the ruote in a large pan of rapidly boiling salted water until al dente. Drain and return to the pan.
2 While the pasta is cooking, discard the bacon rind and cut the bacon into thin strips. Cook in a frying pan until lightly browned.
3 In a bowl, combine the black olives, lemon juice, lemon rind, olive oil, chopped parsley and the bacon. Gently toss the olive and bacon mixture through the pasta until it is evenly distributed. Serve with freshly ground black pepper, to taste.

NOTE: Ruote is a very attractive pasta resembling wagon wheels. Small chunks of sauce are trapped between the spokes.

SPICED LAMB RICE

Preparation time: 30 minutes
Total cooking time: 2 hours
Serves 6 as a side dish

3 lamb shanks (about 1 kg/2 lb)
1 large onion, sliced
10 whole cloves
1 cinnamon stick
5 cardamom pods
3 tablespoons ghee or oil
1 teaspoon crushed garlic
2 onions, thinly sliced, extra
¼ teaspoon ground cinnamon
¼ teaspoon ground cloves
¼ teaspoon freshly grated nutmeg
3 cups (600 g/1¼ lb) long-grain rice
¼ teaspoon saffron threads
currants and shelled pistachios, to garnish

1 Put the lamb in a large pan with the onion, cloves, cinnamon stick, cardamom pods, 2 litres (64 fl oz) water and 1½ teaspoons salt. Bring to the boil. Simmer for 1–1½ hours, or until the meat is tender, occasionally skimming any scum off the surface. Remove the shanks from the cooking liquid, then cool slightly. Strain the remaining liquid into a large measuring jug—you need 1.25 litres (40 fl oz); if necessary, add some water.

2 Heat the ghee in a small pan, cook the garlic and extra onion gently until well reduced and just golden. Add the ground spices and ¼ teaspoon freshly ground black pepper.
3 Remove the meat from the shanks and cut into cubes. Put in a bowl with the onion and spice mixture.
4 Wash and drain the rice. Put half of it in a large saucepan with a well-fitting lid and cover with the onion and lamb mixture. Put the remaining rice on top. Cook the saffron threads in a dry frying pan over a low heat until dry and crisp, stirring constantly. Cool. Put the strands in a bowl and crush with the back of a spoon. Add ¼ cup (60 ml/2 fl oz) water and dissolve. Gently pour the reserved cooking liquid and dissolved saffron into the saucepan with the rice and lamb mixture and bring to the boil. Cover, reduce the heat to very low and cook for 20 minutes. Remove the lid, then lightly fluff up the rice. Serve garnished with currants and pistachios.

PORK WITH APPLE AND PRUNE STUFFING

Preparation time: 35 minutes
Total cooking time: 2 hours
Serves 8

1 green apple, chopped
⅓ cup (90 g/3 oz) pitted prunes, chopped
2 tablespoons port
1 tablespoon chopped fresh parsley
2 kg (4 lb) piece boned pork loin
olive oil and salt, to rub on pork
gravy with wine (see page 68), for serving

1 Preheat the oven to very hot 240°C (475°F/Gas 9). To make the stuffing, combine the apple, prunes, port and parsley. Lay the pork loin on a board with the rind underneath. Spread the stuffing over the meat side of the loin, roll up and secure with skewers or string at regular intervals. If some of the filling falls out while tying, carefully push it back in. Score the pork rind with a sharp knife at 1 cm (½ inch) intervals (if the butcher hasn't already done so) and rub generously with oil and salt.
2 Place on a rack in a baking dish. Bake for 15 minutes, then reduce the heat to moderate 180°C (350°F/Gas 4) and bake for 1½–2 hours, or until the pork is cooked through. The juices will run clear when a skewer is inserted into the thickest part of the meat. Cover and stand for 15 minutes before removing the skewers or string and carving. Reserve any pan juices for making the gravy.
note: If the rind fails to crackle, carefully remove it from the meat, cutting between the fat layer and the meat. Scrape off any excess fat and put the rind on a piece of foil. Place under a moderate grill, and grill until the rind has crackled. Alternatively, place between several sheets of paper towel and microwave on high in 1 minute bursts, for about 2–3 minutes altogether (depending on the thickness of the rind).

STEAMED PORK AND WATER CHESTNUT DUMPLINGS

Preparation time: 25 minutes + 30 minutes resting
Total cooking time: 10 minutes
Makes 24

Dough
1 cup (125 g/4 oz) plain flour
½ cup (60 g/2 oz) tapioca flour
30 g (1 oz) lard

250 g (8 oz) pork mince
50 g (1¾ oz) water chestnuts, chopped
2 spring onions, chopped
1 teaspoon chopped fresh ginger
2 teaspoons soy sauce
1 teaspoon rice wine
½ teaspoon sugar
½ teaspoon cornflour
1 egg
¼ teaspoon sesame oil

1 To make the dough, put the flours and lard in a food processor. Process for several seconds until combined. With the motor running, slowly add ¾ cup (185 ml/6 fl oz) boiling water to the food processor to form a sticky, thick dough. Place the dough onto a lightly floured surface and knead for a couple of minutes. Roll into a ball, wrap in plastic wrap and set aside for 30 minutes.

2 To make the filling, put the pork mince, water chestnuts, spring onion, ginger, soy sauce, rice wine, sugar, cornflour, egg, sesame oil and ½ teaspoon salt in a food processor. Process for several seconds to evenly combine the mixture. Transfer to a bowl.
3 Divide the dough into four equal pieces. Roll each piece into a log about 10 cm (4 inches) long and 2 cm (¾ inch) in diameter. Cut each log into six pieces, each about 1.5 cm (⅝ inch) wide, then cover with a damp cloth.
4 Place each dough round on a lightly oiled surface and flatten with the oiled flat side of a cleaver to form a very thin, small disc about 10–12 cm (4–5 inches) in diameter.
5 Place 2 teaspoons of the filling into the centre of the dough balls and bring the edges together, pressing firmly and pulling upwards, twisting in one direction, pulling off any excess dough and making sure the dough is not too thick on top.
6 Line a large bamboo steamer with baking paper and place the dumplings in a single layer in the steamer. Cover and steam over a wok of simmering water for 6 minutes, or until cooked through. Serve hot.

GRILLED PORK

Preparation time: 10 minutes +
    4 hours marinating
Total cooking time: 15 minutes
Serves 4

1 kg (2 lb) pork chops
8 cloves garlic, crushed
2 tablespoons fish sauce
1 tablespoon soy sauce
2 tablespoons oyster sauce
½ teaspoon ground black pepper
2 tablespoons finely chopped spring
    onion

1 Place the pork chops in a large glass
bowl and add the garlic, fish sauce, soy
sauce, oyster sauce and black pepper.
Stir well so that all the meat is covered
with the marinade; cover and marinate for
4 hours in the refrigerator.
2 Preheat the grill to hot; grill the pork on
all sides until browned and cooked
through. If the meat starts to burn, move
it further away from the grill element.
Alternatively you can cook the meat on a
hot barbecue grill.
3 Arrange the pork on a serving platter
and scatter over the spring onion.

HOT PORK CURRY WITH PUMPKIN

Preparation time: 20 minutes
Total cooking time: 25 minutes
Serves 4

1 tablespoon oil
1–2 tablespoons Red Curry Paste (page
    762) or ready-made paste
500 g (1 lb) lean pork, cut into thick strips
    or chunks
1 cup (250 ml/8 fl oz) coconut milk
½ cup (125 ml/4 fl oz) water
350 g (11¼ oz) butternut pumpkin, cut into
    small chunks
6 kaffir lime leaves
¼ cup (60 ml/2 fl oz) coconut cream
1 tablespoon fish sauce
1 teaspoon soft brown sugar
2 red chillies, thinly sliced

1 Heat the oil in a wok or heavy-based
pan; add the curry paste and stir for
1 minute. Add the pork and stir-fry over
moderately high heat until golden brown.
2 Add the coconut milk, water, pumpkin
and lime leaves, reduce the heat and
simmer for 20 minutes, or until the pork
is tender.
3 Add the coconut cream, fish sauce and
sugar to the wok and stir to combine.
Scatter the chilli over the top. Garnish
with sprigs of basil, if you like, and serve
with steamed rice.

CHICKPEAS WITH CHORIZO SAUSAGE

Preparation time: 15 minutes +
    overnight soaking
Total cooking time: 1 hour 10 minutes
Serves 6

¾ cup (165 g/5½ oz) dried chickpeas
1 bay leaf
4 cloves
1 cinnamon stick
1 litre chicken stock
2 tablespoons olive oil
1 onion, finely chopped
1 clove garlic, crushed
pinch of dried thyme
375 g (12 oz) chorizo sausages, chopped
1 tablespoon chopped fresh flat-leaf
    parsley

1 Put the chickpeas in a large bowl, cover
well with water and soak overnight. Drain
well, then combine in a large saucepan
with the bay leaf, cloves, cinnamon stick
and stock. Cover well with water, bring to
the boil, then reduce the heat and simmer
for 1 hour, or until the chickpeas are
tender. If they need more time, add a little
more water. There should be just a little
liquid left in the saucepan. Drain and
remove the bay leaf, cloves and cinnamon
stick.
2 Heat the oil in a large frying pan, add
the onion and cook over medium heat for
3 minutes, or until translucent. Add the
garlic and thyme and cook, stirring, for
1 minute. Increase the heat to medium-
high, add the chorizo sausage and cook
for 3 minutes.
3 Add the chickpeas to the frying pan, mix
well, then stir over medium heat until
they are heated through. Remove from
the heat and mix in the parsley. Taste
before seasoning, to taste, with salt and
freshly ground black pepper. This dish is
equally delicious served hot or at room
temperature.

FRIED PORK AND NOODLES

Preparation time: 25 minutes
Total cooking time: 15 minutes
Serves 4

1 sheet nori
1 tablespoon oil
150 g (4¾ oz) pork loin, cut into small strips
5 spring onions, cut into short lengths
1 medium carrot, cut into thin strips
200 g (6½ oz) Chinese cabbage, shredded
500 g (1 lb) Hokkien noodles, gently pulled apart to separate
2 tablespoons water
2 tablespoons Japanese soy sauce
1 tablespoon Worcestershire sauce
1 tablespoon mirin
2 teaspoons caster sugar
1 cup (90 g/3 oz) bean sprouts, scraggly ends removed

1 Toast the nori by holding it over low heat and moving it back and forward for about 15 seconds; cut it into fine shreds.
2 Heat the oil in a large deep pan or wok; add the pork, spring onion and carrot and stir-fry over medium heat for 1 to 2 minutes, or until the pork just changes colour. Take care not to overcook the mixture or the pork will toughen and the vegetables will become limp.
3 Add the cabbage, noodles, water, soy sauce, Worcestershire sauce, mirin and sugar to the pan; cover and cook for 1 minute. Add the bean sprouts and toss to coat the vegetables and noodles with the sauce. Serve immediately, sprinkled with the shredded nori.

PORK WITH PLUM SAUCE AND CHOY SUM

Preparation time: 10 minutes
Total cooking time: 25 minutes
Serves 4

600 g (1¼ lb) choy sum, cut into 6 cm (2½ inch) lengths
¼ cup (60 ml/2 fl oz) plum sauce
2 tablespoons Chinese rice wine
1½ tablespoons soy sauce
1 teaspoon sesame oil
½ cup (125 ml/4 fl oz) peanut oil
1 large onion, sliced
3 cloves garlic, finely chopped
2 teaspoons finely chopped fresh ginger
500 g (1 lb) pork loin fillet, thinly sliced across the grain
2 tablespoons cornflour, seasoned with salt and pepper

1 Bring a large saucepan of lightly salted water to the boil, add the choy sum and cook for 2–3 minutes, or until the stems are crisp but still tender. Plunge into iced water, then drain.
2 To make the stir-fry sauce, combine the plum sauce, rice wine, soy sauce and sesame oil in a small non-metallic bowl. Set aside until needed.
3 Heat a wok over high heat, add 1 tablespoon of the peanut oil and swirl to coat the side of the wok. Add the onion, garlic and ginger and stir-fry over medium heat for 3 minutes, or until softened. Remove from the wok.
4 Toss the pork in the seasoned cornflour to coat, shaking off any excess. Reheat the wok over high heat, add the remaining peanut oil and swirl to coat the side. Add the pork in batches and cook for 3 minutes each batch, or until golden on both sides. Remove.
5 Drain the oil from the wok and return the meat and any juices to the wok. Pour the stir-fry sauce into the wok. Cook over high heat for 2–3 minutes, then add the choy sum and return the onion mixture. Cook, stirring, for a further 2 minutes.

PORK, PAPRIKA AND POPPY SEEDS WITH PASTA

Preparation time: 15 minutes
Total cooking time: 15–20 minutes
Serves 4

500 g (1 lb) pappardelle
20 g (¾ oz) butter
1½ tablespoons vegetable oil
1 onion, thinly sliced
1 clove garlic, crushed
2 teaspoons sweet paprika
pinch of cayenne pepper
500 g (1 lb) lean pork (fillet or leg steaks), thinly sliced
1 tablespoon finely chopped fresh parsley
1 tablespoon port or other dry fortified wine
1 tablespoon tomato paste (tomato purée, double concentrate)
300 g (10 oz) sour cream
150 g (5 oz) button mushrooms, sliced
2 teaspoons poppy seeds
2 tablespoons chopped fresh parsley

1 Cook the pappardelle in a large pan of rapidly boiling salted water until al dente. Drain and return to the pan.
2 Heat the butter and ½ tablespoon of oil in a frying pan and gently fry the sliced onion for 6–8 minutes, or until soft. Add the garlic, paprika, cayenne pepper, pork and parsley and season, to taste, with freshly ground pepper. Sauté quickly over high heat until the pork is cooked. Add the port, bring to the boil and stir briefly, for about 10 seconds. Add the tomato paste and sour cream and stir until combined. Stir in the mushrooms and adjust the seasoning. Reduce the heat to low.
3 Stir the remaining oil and the poppy seeds through the warm pasta. Serve the pork spooned over the pasta. Garnish with fresh parsley just before serving.

PORK SCHNITZEL CURRY

Preparation time: 25 minutes
Total cooking time: 30 minutes
Serves 4

1 tablespoon oil
1 onion, cut into thin wedges
2 large carrots, cut into 2 cm (¾ inch) cubes
1 large potato, cut into 2 cm (¾ inch) cubes
60 g (2 oz) Japanese curry paste block, broken into small pieces (see Note)
plain (all-purpose) flour, for coating
4 x 120 g (4 oz) pork schnitzels, pounded to 5 mm (¼ inch) thickness
2 eggs, lightly beaten
150 g (5 oz) Japanese breadcrumbs (panko)
oil, for deep-frying
pickled ginger, pickled daikon and umeboshi (baby pickled plums), to serve

1 Heat the oil in a saucepan, add the onion, carrot and potato, and cook over medium heat for 10 minutes, or until starting to brown. Add 2 cups (500 ml/ 16 fl oz) water and the curry paste, and stir until the curry paste dissolves and the sauce becomes smooth. Reduce the heat and simmer for 10 minutes, or until the vegetables are cooked through. Season.

2 Season the flour well with salt and pepper. Dip each schnitzel into the flour, shake off any excess, then dip into the beaten egg, allowing any excess to drip off. Coat with the Japanese breadcrumbs by pressing each side of the schnitzel firmly into the crumbs on a plate.
3 Fill a deep-fat fryer or heavy-based saucepan one-third full of oil and heat to 180°C (350°F), or until a cube of bread dropped into the oil browns in 15 seconds. Cook the schnitzels, one at a time, turning once or twice, for 5 minutes, or until golden brown all over and cooked through. Drain on crumpled paper towels.
4 Slice each schnitzel into 5–6 pieces and arrange, keeping the original shape, over cooked rice. Ladle the curry sauce over the schnitzels. Serve with the pickles on the side.

NOTE: Japanese curry comes in a solid block or in powder form and is available in Asian supermarkets. You can buy Japanese curry of varying heat, from mild to very hot, whichever is most suitable to your taste.

CORIANDER PORK WITH FRESH PINEAPPLE

Preparation time: 25 minutes
Total cooking time: 10–12 minutes
Serves 4

400 g (12⅔ oz) pork loin or fillet
¼ medium pineapple
1 tablespoon oil
4 cloves garlic, chopped
4 spring onions, chopped
1 tablespoon fish sauce
1 tablespoon lime juice
½ cup (15 g/½ oz) fresh coriander leaves
¼ cup (15 g/½ oz) chopped fresh mint

1 Partially freeze the pork until it is just firm, then slice it thinly. Trim the skin from the pineapple and cut the flesh into bite-sized pieces.
2 Heat the oil in a wok or heavy-based frying pan. Add the garlic and spring onion and cook for 1 minute. Remove from the wok.
3 Heat the wok to very hot; add the pork in 2 or 3 batches and stir-fry each batch for 3 minutes or until the meat is just cooked. Return the meat, garlic and spring onion to the wok and then add the pineapple pieces, fish sauce and lime juice. Toss well. Just before serving, sprinkle over the coriander leaves and mint and toss lightly. Serve with rice.

PORK WITH RICE NOODLE CAKE AND CUCUMBER SALAD

Preparation time: 40 minutes +
  5 minutes soaking
Total cooking time: 25 minutes
Serves 4

500 g (1 lb) thin fresh rice noodles, at
  room temperature
2 Lebanese (short) cucumbers, halved
  lengthways and thinly sliced
2 tablespoons chopped coriander
  (cilantro) leaves
1 tablespoon lime juice
1 tablespoon fish sauce
2 teaspoons caster (superfine) sugar
¼ cup (60 ml/2 fl oz) oil
1 red capsicum (pepper), thinly sliced
3 garlic cloves, finely chopped
1 tablespoon white vinegar
¼ cup (60 ml/2 fl oz) black bean sauce
⅓ cup (80 ml/2¾ fl oz) chicken stock
1 tablespoon soft brown sugar
300 g (10 oz) Chinese barbecued pork
  (char siu), sliced

1 Pour boiling water over the noodles and
leave for 5 minutes, or until softened.
Drain, then separate by pulling apart
slightly.
2 To make the cucumber salad, toss the
cucumber, coriander, lime juice, fish
sauce and sugar together in a large bowl.

3 Heat 1 tablespoon of the oil in a large
non-stick frying pan. Place four deep
10 cm (4 inch) rings in the frying pan. Fill
as firmly as possible with the noodles and
press down with the back of a spoon.
Cook over medium heat for 10 minutes, or
until crisp, pressing the noodles down
occasionally. Turn over and repeat on the
other side, adding another tablespoon of
the oil if necessary. Cover and keep
warm.
4 Meanwhile, heat 1 tablespoon of the
remaining oil in a wok, add the capsicum
and stir-fry over high heat for 2 minutes,
or until the capsicum has softened
slightly. Add the garlic to the wok and
toss for 1 minute, or until softened, then
add the vinegar, black bean sauce, stock
and sugar. Stir until the sugar has
dissolved, then simmer for 2 minutes, or
until the sauce thickens slightly. Add the
Chinese barbecued pork and stir to coat
with the sauce.
5 To serve, place a noodle cake on each
plate and top with some of the pork
mixture. Arrange the cucumber salad
around the noodle cake and then serve.

THAI PORK AND MUSHROOM STIR-FRY WITH PEPPER (PAHT HEHT)

Preparation time: 20 minutes +
  20 minutes soaking
Total cooking time: 5 minutes
Serves 4

15 g (½ oz) dried black fungus
1 tablespoon peanut oil
350 g (11 oz) pork loin fillet, thinly sliced
  across the grain
4 cloves garlic, thinly sliced
3 red Asian shallots, thinly sliced
1 carrot, thinly sliced on the diagonal
6 spring onions, cut into 2.5 cm (1 inch)
  lengths
2 tablespoons fish sauce
2 tablespoons oyster sauce
1 teaspoon ground white pepper

1 Soak the black fungus in a bowl of
boiling water for 20 minutes. Rinse, then
cut into slices.
2 Heat a wok over medium heat, add the
oil and swirl to coat. Add the pork, garlic
and shallots and stir-fry for 30 seconds.
Add the carrot and spring onion and stir-
fry for 2–3 minutes, or until the pork is
cooked.
3 Add the fish and oyster sauces and
ground white pepper and stir-fry for a
further 1 minute. Serve hot with rice.

BARBECUE TIME

BEST-EVER BURGER WITH BARBECUE SAUCE

Preparation time: 20 minutes +
30 minutes refrigeration
Total cooking time: 25 minutes
Serves 6

750 g (1½ lb) beef mince
250 g (8 oz) sausage mince
1 small onion, finely chopped
1 tablespoon Worcestershire sauce
2 tablespoons tomato sauce
1 cup (90 g/3 oz) fresh breadcrumbs
1 egg, lightly beaten
2 large onions, extra, thinly sliced
6 wholemeal rolls
6 small lettuce leaves
1 large tomato, sliced

Barbecue Sauce
2 teaspoons oil
1 small onion, finely chopped
3 teaspoons brown vinegar
1 tablespoon soft brown sugar
4 tablespoons tomato sauce
2 teaspoons Worcestershire sauce
2 teaspoons soy sauce

1 Place the beef and sausage mince in a large bowl. Add the onion, sauces, breadcrumbs and egg. Mix thoroughly with your hands. Divide the mixture into six equal portions and shape into patties. Refrigerate the patties for at least 30 minutes.
2 Place the patties on a hot, lightly oiled barbecue grill or flatplate. Barbecue over the hottest part of the fire for 8 minutes each side. Mean-while, fry the extra onions on an oiled flatplate until golden.
3 To make the barbecue sauce, heat the oil in a small pan. Cook the onion for 5 minutes or until soft. Add the vinegar, sugar and sauces and stir until the sauce comes to the boil. Reduce the heat and simmer for 3 minutes. Allow to cool.
4 Split the rolls in half and fill each one with a lettuce leaf, patty, tomato slice and fried onions. Top with a generous quantity of barbecue sauce.

LAMB PITTA

Preparation time: 20 minutes +
15 minutes marinating
Total cooking time: 5 minutes
Serves 4

400 g (13 oz) lamb leg steaks
2 teaspoons finely grated lemon rind
3 teaspoons finely chopped fresh
oregano
2 cloves garlic, finely chopped
2 tablespoons olive oil
1 red onion, thinly sliced
4 small pitta breads
½ cup (125 g/4 oz) hummus
½ cup (125 g /4 oz) plain yoghurt
1 small Lebanese cucumber, thinly sliced
1 small red chilli, seeds removed, finely
chopped
snow pea sprouts

1 Trim the lamb of excess fat and cut into thin strips. Mix together the lemon rind, oregano, garlic, olive oil and some cracked black pepper in a non-metallic bowl. Add the lamb and refrigerate for 15 minutes.
2 Cook the lamb and onion on a very hot, lightly oiled barbecue flatplate for 2–3 minutes, turning to brown the meat quickly and soften the onion. Remove from the plate and keep warm. Place the pitta breads on the flatplate and warm both sides.
3 Spread each round of bread with a little of the hummus and yoghurt. Add the barbecued lamb and onion and scatter with the cucumber, chilli and a few snow pea sprouts.

TUNA WITH MEDITERRANEAN VEGETABLES

Preparation time: 15 minutes +
30 minutes marinating
Total cooking time: 20 minutes
Serves 4

¾ cup (185 ml/6 fl oz) olive oil
3 cloves garlic, crushed
2 tablespoons sweet chilli sauce
1 red capsicum, cut into bite-sized pieces
1 yellow capsicum, cut into bite-sized
pieces
2 large zucchini, thickly sliced
2 slender eggplant, thickly sliced
olive oil, extra, for brushing
4 tuna steaks

Lemon and Caper Mayonnaise
1 egg yolk
1 teaspoon grated lemon rind
2 tablespoons lemon juice
1 small clove garlic, chopped
¾ cup (185 ml/6 fl oz) olive oil
1 tablespoon baby capers

1 Combine the olive oil, garlic and sweet chilli sauce in a large bowl. Add the capsicum, zucchini and eggplant, toss well, then marinate for 30 minutes.
2 For the mayonnaise, process the egg yolk, rind, lemon juice and garlic together in a food processor until smooth. With the motor running, gradually add the oil in a thin steady stream until the mixture thickens and is a creamy consistency. Stir in the capers and ½ teaspoon salt. Set aside.
3 Cook the drained vegetables on a hot, lightly oiled barbecue grill or flatplate for 4–5 minutes each side, or until cooked through. Keep warm.
4 Brush the tuna steaks with the extra oil and barbecue for 2–3 minutes each side, or until just cooked (tuna should be rare in the centre). Serve the vegetables and tuna steaks with the lemon and caper mayonnaise.

TANGY BEEF RIBS

Preparation time: 20 minutes +
    3 hours marinating
Total cooking time: 15–20 minutes
Serves 4

1 kg (2 lb) beef ribs
½ cup (125 ml/4 fl oz) tomato sauce
2 tablespoons Worcestershire sauce
2 tablespoons soft brown sugar
1 teaspoon paprika
¼ teaspoon chilli powder
1 clove garlic, crushed

1 Chop the ribs into individual serving pieces, if necessary. Bring a large pan of water to the boil. Cook the ribs in boiling water for 5 minutes and then drain.
2 Combine the tomato sauce, Worcestershire sauce, sugar, paprika, chilli powder and garlic in large non-metallic bowl and mix together well. Add the ribs, cover and marinate in the fridge for at least several hours or overnight if time permits.
3 Cook the ribs on a hot, lightly oiled barbecue grill or flatplate, brushing frequently with the marinade, for 10–15 minutes, or until the ribs are well browned and cooked through. Serve with slices of grilled fresh pineapple.

HINT: If time is short, toss the ribs in the marinade and leave at room temperature, covered, for up to 2 hours. The meat will absorb the flavours of the marinade more quickly at room temperature. (This principle applies to all marinades.)

KIDNEY KEBABS

Preparation time: 15 minutes +
    20 minutes marinating
Total cooking time: 5–10 minutes
Serves 4

200 g (6½ oz) lamb kidneys
3 cloves garlic, finely chopped
2 bay leaves, torn into small pieces
3 tablespoons olive oil
300 g (10 oz) chicken breast fillets
150 g (5 oz) double-smoked ham
2 small onions
2 tablespoons dry sherry

1 Soak 8 bamboo skewers in water to prevent scorching. Trim the kidneys of any sinew or fat and cut into bite-sized pieces. Combine the garlic, bay leaves and olive oil. Add the kidneys, cover and marinate in the refrigerator for about 20 minutes.
2 Cut the chicken and ham into bite-sized pieces and cut the onions into small wedges.
3 Drain the kidneys, keeping the marinade. Thread the pieces of onion, kidney, chicken and ham alternately onto the skewers.
4 Cook the kebabs on a hot, lightly oiled barbecue grill or flatplate for about 5–10 minutes, brushing lightly with the marinade and sherry as they cook and turning them regularly. Cook until golden brown.

HONEY-GLAZED CHICKEN BREASTS

Preparation time: 6 minutes +
    20 minutes marinating
Total cooking time: 10 minutes
Serves 6

6 chicken breast fillets
50 g (1¾ oz) butter, softened
3 tablespoons honey
3 tablespoons barbecue sauce
2 teaspoons wholegrain mustard

1 Trim the chicken of excess fat and sinew and remove the skin. Use a sharp knife to make three or four diagonal slashes across one side of each chicken breast.
2 Mix together the butter, honey, barbecue sauce and mustard. Spread half of the marinade thickly over the slashed side of the chicken and cover. Set the remaining marinade aside. Leave the chicken at room temperature for 20 minutes.
3 Place the chicken breasts, slashed-side-up, on a hot, lightly oiled barbecue flatplate or grill. Cook for 2–3 minutes each side or until tender. Brush with the reserved marinade several times during cooking.

LOBSTER TAILS WITH AVOCADO SAUCE

Preparation time: 15 minutes +
   3 hours marinating
Total cooking time: 10 minutes
Serves 4

3 tablespoons dry white wine
1 tablespoon honey
1 teaspoon sambal oelek
1 clove garlic, crushed
1 tablespoon olive oil
4 raw lobster tails

Avocado Sauce
1 ripe avocado, mashed
3 teaspoons lemon juice
2 tablespoons sour cream
1 small tomato, chopped finely

1 Mix together the wine, honey, sambal oelek, garlic and oil. Cut along the soft shell on the underside of the lobster. Gently pull the shell apart and ease out the flesh.
2 Put the lobster in a shallow, non-metallic dish. Add the marinade and toss to coat. Cover and refrigerate for at least 3 hours.
3 Cook the lobster on a hot, lightly oiled barbecue grill or flatplate for 5–10 minutes, turning frequently. Brush with the marinade until cooked through. Slice into medallions.
4 To make the sauce, mix together the avocado, juice and sour cream. Add the tomato and season well.

SPICY SEAFOOD SKEWERS

Preparation time: 40 minutes
Total cooking time: 15 minutes
Serves 4

Spice Paste
2 large red chillies, seeded and chopped
1 clove garlic, chopped
2 spring onions, finely chopped
1 teaspoon grated fresh ginger
1 tablespoon grated fresh turmeric
1 small tomato, peeled and seeded
½ teaspoon coriander seeds
2 tablespoons chopped roasted peanuts
½ teaspoon dried shrimp paste
2 teaspoons vegetable oil
1 tablespoon tamarind concentrate
1 tablespoon finely chopped lemon grass

350 g (11 oz) skinned boneless snapper fillet
350 g (11 oz) raw prawns, peeled and deveined
1 egg, lightly beaten
2 cups (120 g/4 oz) flaked coconut
4 kaffir lime leaves, shredded
2 tablespoons brown sugar
¾ cup (185 g/6 oz) whole egg mayonnaise
3 teaspoons grated lime rind
1 tablespoon chopped fresh coriander

1 Soak 6 thick wooden skewers in water for 30 minutes.
2 To make the paste, coarsely grind the chilli, garlic, spring onion, ginger, turmeric, tomato, coriander, peanuts and shrimp paste in a food processor. Heat the oil in a frying pan and cook the chilli mixture, tamarind and lemon grass for 5 minutes over medium heat, stirring frequently, until golden. Cool.
3 Finely mince the fish and prawns in a food processor. Add the egg, coconut, kaffir lime leaves, sugar and spice paste. Season well with salt and pepper. Process.
4 Using wet hands, shape ¼ cup of mixture around each skewer, then cook on a hot, lightly oiled barbecue flatplate or grill for 8–10 minutes, turning, until golden. Mix the mayonnaise, lime rind and coriander in a bowl and serve with the skewers.

VEAL STEAKS WITH CAPER BUTTER

Preparation time: 10 minutes
Total cooking time: 6 minutes
Serves 4

50 g (1¾ oz) butter, softened
2 tablespoons dry white wine
2 tablespoons capers, finely chopped
2 teaspoons finely grated lemon rind
8 small veal steaks, about 500 g (1 lb)

1 Mix together the butter, white wine, capers, lemon rind and some salt and black pepper with a wooden spoon. Cover and refrigerate until required.
2 Cook the veal steaks on a hot, lightly oiled barbecue flatplate or grill for 2–3 minutes on each side. Remove, place on warm plates and top with the caper butter. Serve immediately.

PRAWNS WITH MANGO SALSA

Preparation time: 25 minutes +
    1 hour marinating
Total cooking time: 5 minutes
Serves 4–6

1 kg (2 lb) raw prawns
⅓ cup (80 ml/2¾ fl oz) lemon juice
⅓ cup (80 ml/2¾ fl oz) olive oil
¼ cup (15 g/½ oz) chopped fresh dill
450 g (14 oz) mango, cubed
1 onion, finely diced
1 red chilli, seeded and finely chopped
1 tablespoon grated lemon rind

1 Peel and devein the raw prawns, keeping the tails intact.
2 Combine the lemon juice, olive oil, dill and a teaspoon of salt in a shallow, non-metallic dish, add the prawns and toss. Cover and refrigerate for 1 hour.
3 Drain the prawns, reserving the marinade, and cook on a very hot, lightly oiled barbecue flatplate for 3 minutes, or until they change colour.
4 Put the reserved marinade in a pan on the stovetop or barbecue and boil for 5 minutes. Mix with the prawns.
5 Mix together the mango, onion, chilli, lemon rind and some salt and pepper. Add the prawns and toss together gently.

CHILLI BEEF BURGERS

Preparation time: 25 minutes +
    2 hours marinating
Total cooking time: 10 minutes
Makes 18 burgers

1 kg (2 lb) beef mince
3 onions, grated
3 tablespoons chopped fresh parsley
1½ cups (150 g/5 oz) dry breadcrumbs
1 egg, lightly beaten
1 tablespoon milk
1 tablespoon malt vinegar
1 tablespoon tomato paste
2 tablespoons soy sauce
1 tablespoon chilli sauce
3 tablespoons dried oregano

Mustard butter
125 g (4 oz) butter, softened
2 tablespoons sour cream
2 tablespoons German mustard

1 Mix together the beef, onion, parsley, breacrumbs, egg, milk, vinegar, tomato paste, sauces and oregano. Refrigerate, covered with plastic wrap, for 2 hours.
2 To make the mustard butter, beat the butter, sour cream and mustard in a small bowl for 2 minutes or until well combined. Leave for 20 minutes to let the flavours develop.
3 Divide the burger mixture into 18 portions and shape each one into a burger. Cook on a hot, lightly oiled barbecue grill or flatplate for 4 minutes on each side. Serve immediately with the mustard butter.

THAI CHILLI GARLIC QUAIL

Preparation time: 15 minutes +
    2 hours marinating
Total cooking time: 20 minutes
Serves 6

6 quails
1 small red chilli, finely chopped
2 tablespoons chopped fresh coriander
    leaves and stems
4 cloves garlic, crushed
2 teaspoons soft brown sugar
2 teaspoons Thai red curry paste
1 tablespoon grated fresh ginger
2 teaspoons light soy sauce
2 teaspoons chilli sauce
2 teaspoons oil
lime wedges, to serve

1 Using poultry shears or kitchen scissors, cut each quail down either side of the backbone and then open out flat. Cut each one in half through the breastbone.
2 Using a mortar and pestle or blender, blend the chilli, coriander leaves and stems, garlic, brown sugar, paste, ginger, soy sauce, chilli sauce and oil, until smooth.
3 Brush the mixture all over the quails. Place them in a shallow, non-metallic dish, cover and refrigerate for at least 2 hours.
4 Cook the quails on a hot, lightly oiled barbecue grill or flatplate for 15–20 minutes, turning once, until browned and cooked through. Serve with lime wedges.

SALMON WITH CHILLI-CORN SALSA

Preparation time: 25 minutes
Total cooking time: 5 minutes
Serves 4

1 tablespoon olive oil
½ teaspoon ground cumin
½ teaspoon paprika
4 salmon cutlets
4 limes, cut into quarters, to serve

Chilli-Corn Salsa
2 corn cobs
4 spring onions, finely sliced
1 small clove garlic, crushed
½ red capsicum, finely diced
1 teaspoon diced red jalapeno chilli
1 teaspoon diced green jalapeno chilli
1 teaspoon ground cumin
2 tablespoons extra virgin olive oil
2 tablespoons lime juice
1 tablespoon finely chopped fresh parsley

1 Mix the oil, cumin and paprika.
2 To make the salsa, cook the corn cobs until tender in boiling water. Transfer to iced water to cool. Cut off the kernels and mix with the spring onion, garlic, capsicum, chilli, cumin, extra virgin olive oil, lime juice and parsley. Season to taste.
3 Brush the salmon with the spicy oil and cook on a hot, lightly oiled barbecue grill for 2 minutes on each side for rare, or a few extra minutes for well done. Take care not to overcook. Serve with the salsa and lime quarters.

PORK SAUSAGE BURGERS WITH MUSTARD CREAM

Preparation time: 20 minutes
Total cooking time: 10 minutes
Serves 6

1 kg (2 lb) pork mince
1 small onion, finely chopped
1 cup (90 g/3 oz) fresh breadcrumbs
2 cloves garlic, crushed
1 egg, lightly beaten
1 teaspoon dried sage
6 bread sticks

Mustard Cream
½ cup (125 g/4 oz) sour cream
1 tablespoon wholegrain mustard
2 teaspoons lemon juice

1 Mix together the mince, onion, breadcrumbs, garlic, egg and sage with your hands. Divide into six portions and shape into sausages.
2 Cook the sausages on a hot, lightly oiled barbecue flatplate or grill for 5–10 minutes, turning occasionally.
3 To make the mustard cream, put the sour cream, mustard and juice in a small bowl and stir together. Sandwich the sausage burgers in the bread sticks and serve with the mustard cream.

BRUNCH BURGER WITH THE WORKS

Preparation time: 40 minutes
Total cooking time: 15 minutes
Serves 6

750 g (1½ lb) lean beef mince
1 onion, finely chopped
1 egg
½ cup (40 g/1¼ oz) fresh breadcrumbs
2 tablespoons tomato paste
1 tablespoon Worcestershire sauce
2 tablespoons chopped fresh parsley
3 large onions
30 g (1 oz) butter
6 slices Cheddar cheese
6 eggs, extra
6 rashers bacon
6 large hamburger buns, lightly toasted
shredded lettuce
2 tomatoes, thinly sliced
6 large slices beetroot, drained
6 pineapple rings, drained
tomato sauce

1 Mix together the mince, onion, egg, breadcrumbs, tomato paste, Worcestershire sauce and parsley with your hands. Season well. Divide into six portions and shape into burgers. Cover and set aside.
2 Slice the onions into thin rings. Heat the butter on a barbecue flatplate. Cook the onions, turning often, until well browned. Move the onions to the outer edge of the flatplate to keep warm. Brush the barbecue grill or flatplate liberally with oil.
3 Cook the burgers for 3–4 minutes each side or until browned and cooked through. Move to the cooler part of the barbecue or transfer to plate and keep warm. Place a slice of cheese on each burger.
4 Heat a small amount of butter in a large frying pan. Fry the eggs and bacon until the eggs are cooked through and the bacon is golden and crisp. Fill the hamburger buns with lettuce, tomato, beetroot and pineapple topped with a burger. Pile the onions, egg, bacon and tomato sauce on top of the burger.

SMOKED CHICKEN FILLETS

Preparation time: 5 minutes
Total cooking time: 25 minutes
Serves 4

4 chicken breast fillets
1 tablespoon olive oil
seasoned pepper, to taste
hickory or mesquite chips, for smoking

1 Prepare a covered barbecue for indirect cooking at moderate heat (normal fire), see page 7. Trim the chicken of excess fat and sinew. Brush with oil and sprinkle with the seasoned pepper.
2 Spoon a pile of smoking chips (about 25) over the coals in each charcoal rail.
3 Cover the barbecue and cook the chicken for 15 minutes. Test with a sharp knife. If the juices do not run clear, cook for another 5–10 minutes until cooked through.

FILLET OF BEEF WITH MUSTARD COATING

Preparation time: 1 hour + 1 hour standing
Total cooking time: 40 minutes
Serves 8

2 kg (4 lb) scotch fillet of beef
3 tablespoons brandy
4 tablespoons wholegrain mustard
3 tablespoons cream
¾ teaspoon coarsely ground black
   pepper

1 Prepare a covered barbecue for indirect cooking at moderate heat (normal fire), see page 7. Trim the meat of excess fat and sinew and tie securely with string at regular intervals to retain its shape. Brush all over with the brandy and leave for 1 hour.
2 Mix together the mustard, cream and pepper and spread evenly over the fillet.
3 Place the meat on a large greased sheet of foil. Pinch the corners securely to form a tray to hold in the juices. Cover the barbecue and cook for 30–40 minutes for medium-rare meat. Leave for 10–15 minutes before carving into thick slices. If you like, stir a tablespoon of mustard into the pan juices to make a gravy.

FILLET STEAK WITH ONION MARMALADE

Preparation time: 20 minutes
Total cooking time: 1 hour
Serves 4

4 thick rib-eye steaks
30 g (1 oz) butter
2 red onions, thinly sliced
2 tablespoons soft brown sugar
1 tablespoon balsamic vinegar

1 Trim any fat from the steaks, then sprinkle liberally with freshly ground black pepper. Cover and refrigerate until ready to cook.
2 To make the onion marmalade, heat the butter in a heavy-based pan. Add the onion and cook, stirring often, for 10 minutes over low heat, or until the onion is soft but not brown. Stir in the brown sugar and balsamic vinegar and continue to cook for about 30 minutes, stirring frequently. The mixture will become thick and glossy.
3 Place the steaks on a hot, lightly oiled barbecue grill or flatplate and cook for 3 minutes each side to seal, turning once only. For rare steaks, cook a further minute. For medium, cook for another few minutes and for well done, about 5 minutes. Serve at once with the onion marmalade.

SAUSAGE MARINADES

THE FOLLOWING RECIPES MAKE ENOUGH MARINADE FOR ABOUT 12 SAUSAGES. LEAVE TO MARINATE FOR AT LEAST A FEW HOURS, AND OVERNIGHT IF TIME PERMITS. SOME OF THE MARINADES ARE ALSO SUITABLE TO USE AS BASTES—SIMPLY BRUSH OVER THE SAUSAGES DURING COOKING TO ADD EXTRA FLAVOUR.

There are many flavoured sausages available today that need no enhancement, just barbecue and serve with a salad, bread or vegetables. But for creative cooks, who want their traditional beef or pork sausages to take pride of place on the barbecue menu, a simple marinade or baste can change an ordinary sausage into something extra special.

Marinades add flavour to meat or vegetables and, when they have an acid ingredient such as lemon juice, wine or vinegar, they also work to tenderise the meat. Leave the sausages in the marinade for several hours (or preferably overnight) to give them time to absorb the flavours of the marinade. The longer you leave them, the more intense the flavours will be when the sausages are cooked.

A baste is similar to a marinade, but is brushed over the food while it cooks. The result is a lovely, subtle flavour. Basting will also keep sausages moist while they cook.

To use the following marinades as bastes, brush the mixture over the sausages while they are cooking, rather than marinating the sausages first.

FRESH HERB MARINADE

Mix the following ingredients thoroughly in a bowl: ¼ cup (60 ml/2 fl oz) olive oil, 2–3 tablespoons lemon juice or balsamic vinegar, 1–2 crushed cloves garlic, 3 teaspoons soft brown sugar, some salt and freshly ground black pepper and 4 tablespoons of chopped fresh mixed herbs (use any combination you have handy—chives, lemon thyme, rosemary, parsley, basil, coriander, mint, oregano or marjoram). Prick the sausages all over and marinate, covered in a non-metallic dish, for at least 3 hours or overnight in the refrigerator. Turn the sausages occasionally. Use with any type of sausage. This mixture is also suitable for use as a baste.

HONEY AND CHILLI MARINADE

Mix the following ingredients thoroughly in a bowl: ¼ cup (60 ml/2 fl oz) soy sauce, 1 tablespoon grated fresh ginger, 2 teaspoons grated lemon rind, ¼ cup (90 g/3 oz) honey, 1–2 crushed cloves garlic, 1 tablespoon sherry or rice wine and 3 tablespoons sweet chilli sauce. Prick the sausages all over and marinate, covered in a non-metallic dish, for at least 3 hours or overnight in the refrigerator. Turn the sausages occasionally. This marinade goes well with any kind of sausage. It is also suitable for basting.

APRICOT AND ONION MARINADE

Mix the following ingredients thoroughly in a bowl: ⅓ cup (80 ml/2¾ fl oz) apricot nectar, 3 tablespoons lime marmalade, 2 crushed cloves garlic, 2 tablespoons olive oil, 1–2 tablespoons French onion soup mix, 1 tablespoon chopped fresh chives, a dash of Worcestershire sauce. Prick the sausages all over and marinate, covered, for at least 3 hours or overnight in the refrigerator. Turn the sausages occasionally. This mixture is also suitable for use as a baste.

SPICY TANDOORI MARINADE

Mix the following ingredients thoroughly in a bowl: 1 tablespoon oil, 2 teaspoons each of ground cumin, coriander and paprika, 3 teaspoons turmeric, 2 teaspoons each of fresh grated ginger and tamarind sauce, 2 crushed cloves garlic, ½–1 teaspoon chilli powder, ½ teaspoon salt, 3 tablespoons tomato sauce and 200 g (6½ oz) plain yoghurt. Prick the sausages all over and marinate, covered, for at least 3 hours or overnight in the refrigerator. Turn the sausages occasionally. Use for lamb or chicken sausages. This mixture is also suitable for basting.

PLUM AND CORIANDER MARINADE

Mix the following ingredients thoroughly in a bowl: ¼ cup (60 ml/2 fl oz) plum sauce, 1–2 crushed cloves garlic, 1 tablespoon each of Worcestershire and soy sauce, 2 tablespoons each of lime juice and chopped fresh coriander and ¼ cup (60 ml/2 fl oz) tomato sauce. Prick the sausages all over and marinate, covered, for at least 3 hours or overnight in the refrigerator. Turn the sausages occasionally. This mixture is also suitable for basting.

Clockwise, from top left: Fresh Herb Marinade; Honey and Chilli Marinade; Spicy Tandoori Marinade; Plum and Coriander Marinade; Apricot and Onion Marinade

TOFU KEBABS WITH MISO PESTO

Preparation time: 30 minutes +
  1 hour marinating
Total cooking time: 10 minutes
Serves 4

1 large red capsicum, cubed
12 button mushrooms, halved
6 pickling onions, quartered
3 zucchini, cut into chunks
450 g (14 oz) firm tofu, cubed
½ cup (125 ml/4 fl oz) light olive oil
3 tablespoons light soy sauce
2 cloves garlic, crushed
2 teaspoons grated fresh ginger
Miso pesto
½ cup (90 g/3 oz) unsalted roasted
  peanuts
2 cups (60 g/2 oz) firmly packed fresh
  coriander leaves
2 tablespoons white miso paste
2 cloves garlic
100 ml (3½ oz) olive oil

1 If using wooden skewers, soak them in
water for 30 minutes to prevent
scorching. Thread the vegetables and tofu
alternately onto 12 skewers, then place in
a large non-metallic dish.
2 Mix together the olive oil, soy sauce,
garlic and ginger, then pour half over the
kebabs. Cover and leave to marinate for
1 hour.
3 To make the miso pesto, finely chop the
peanuts, coriander leaves, miso paste and
garlic in a food processor. Slowly add the
olive oil while the machine is still running
and blend to a smooth paste.
4 Cook the kebabs on a hot, lightly oiled
barbecue flatplate or grill, turning and
brushing with the remaining marinade,
for 4–6 minutes, or until the edges are
slightly brown. Serve with the miso pesto.

CHICKEN BURGERS WITH TARRAGON MAYONNAISE

Preparation time: 25 minutes
Total cooking time: 15 minutes
Serves 6

1 kg (2 lb) chicken mince
1 small onion, finely chopped
2 teaspoons finely grated lemon rind
2 tablespoons sour cream
1 cup (90 g/3 oz) fresh breadcrumbs
6 onion bread rolls

Tarragon Mayonnaise
1 egg yolk
1 tablespoon tarragon vinegar
½ teaspoon French mustard
1 cup (250 ml/8 fl oz) olive oil

1 Mix together the mince, onion, rind,
sour cream and breadcrumbs with your
hands. Divide into six portions and shape
into burgers.
2 To make the mayonnaise, put the yolk,
half the vinegar and the mustard in a
small bowl. Whisk for 1 minute until light
and creamy. Add the oil about 1 teaspoon
at a time, whisking constantly until the
mixture thickens. Increase the flow of oil
to a thin stream and continue whisking
until it has all been incorporated. Stir in
the remaining vinegar and season well
with salt and white pepper.
3 Cook the burgers on a hot, lightly oiled
barbecue flatplate or grill for 7 minutes
each side, turning once. Serve on a roll
with the mayonnaise.

HERB BURGERS

Preparation time: 20 minutes
Total cooking time: 20 minutes
Makes 8 burgers

750 g (1½ lb) beef or lamb mince
2 tablespoons chopped fresh basil
1 tablespoon chopped fresh chives
1 tablespoon chopped fresh rosemary
1 tablespoon chopped fresh thyme
2 tablespoons lemon juice
1 cup (90 g/3 oz) fresh breadcrumbs
1 egg
2 long crusty bread sticks
lettuce leaves
2 tomatoes, sliced
tomato sauce

1 Combine the mince with the herbs, juice,
breadcrumbs, egg and season well with
salt and pepper. Mix well with your hands.
Divide the mixture into eight portions and
shape into thick rectangular patties.
2 Place the burgers on a hot, lightly oiled
barbecue grill or flatplate. Cook for
5–10 minutes each side until well browned
and just cooked through.
3 Cut the bread sticks in half and
sandwich with the burgers, lettuce,
tomato and tomato sauce.

LAMB CHOPS WITH CITRUS POCKETS

Preparation time: 25 minutes
Total cooking time: 15 minutes
Serves 4

4 lamb chump chops, about 250 g (8 oz) each
2 tablespoons lemon juice

Citrus Filling
3 spring onions, finely chopped
1 celery stick, finely chopped
2 teaspoons grated fresh ginger
¾ cup (60 g/2 oz) fresh breadcrumbs
2 tablespoons orange juice
2 teaspoons finely grated orange rind
1 teaspoon chopped fresh rosemary

1 Cut a deep, long pocket in the side of each lamb chop.
2 Mix together all the filling ingredients and spoon into the pockets in the lamb.
3 Cook on a hot, lightly oiled barbecue flatplate or grill, turning once, for 15 minutes, or until the lamb is cooked through but still pink in the centre. Drizzle with the lemon juice.

CHICKEN TIKKA KEBABS

Preparation time: 10 minutes +
  2 hours marinating
Total cooking time: 10 minutes
Serves 4

10 chicken thigh fillets, cubed
1 red onion, cut into wedges
3 tablespoons tikka paste
½ cup (125 ml/4 fl oz) coconut milk
2 tablespoons lemon juice

1 Soak 8 skewers in water to prevent scorching. Thread 2 pieces of chicken and a wedge of onion alternately along each skewer. Place the skewers in a shallow, non-metallic dish.
2 Combine the tikka paste, coconut milk and lemon juice in a jar with a lid. Season and shake well to combine. Pour the mixture over the skewers and marinate for at least 2 hours, or overnight if time permits.
3 Cook the skewers on a hot, lightly oiled barbecue grill or flatplate for 4 minutes on each side, or until the chicken is cooked through. Put any leftover marinade in a small pan and bring to the boil. Serve as a sauce with the tikka kebabs.

MARINATED GRILLED VEGETABLES

Preparation time: 30 minutes +
  1 hour marinating
Total cooking time: 5 minutes
Serves 6

3 small slender eggplants
2 small red capsicums
3 zucchini
6 mushrooms

Marinade
3 tablespoons olive oil
3 tablespoons lemon juice
3 tablespoons shredded basil leaves
1 clove garlic, crushed

1 Cut the eggplant into diagonal slices. Place on a tray in a single layer, sprinkle with salt and leave for 15 minutes. Rinse thoroughly and pat dry with paper towels. Trim the capsicum, remove the seeds and membrane and cut into long, wide pieces. Cut the zucchini into diagonal slices. Trim each mushroom stalk so that it is level with the cap. Place all the vegetables in a large, shallow non-metallic dish.
2 To make the marinade, put the oil, juice, basil and garlic in a small screw-top jar. Shake vigorously to combine. Pour over the vegetables and toss well. Store, covered with plastic wrap, in the fridge for 1 hour, stirring occasionally.
3 Cook the vegetables on a hot, lightly oiled barbecue grill or flatplate. Cook each vegetable piece over the hottest part of the fire for 2 minutes on each side, brushing frequently with any remaining marinade.

MUSTARD BURGERS WITH TOMATO AND ONION SALSA

Preparation time: 20 minutes
Total cooking time: 10 minutes
Makes 8 burgers

1 kg (2 lb) beef mince
3 tablespoons wholegrain mustard
2 teaspoons Dijon mustard
1 teaspoon beef stock powder
1 cup (90 g/3 oz) fresh breadcrumbs (see NOTE)
1 egg
1 teaspoon black pepper
¼ red capsicum, chopped
Tomato and Onion Salsa
1 small red onion, diced
4 tomatoes, diced
2 tablespoons red wine vinegar
1½ teaspoons caster sugar
2 teaspoons lemon juice

1 Mix together the beef mince, mustards, stock powder, breadcrumbs, egg, pepper and capsicum with your hands. Divide into eight portions and shape into burgers.
2 Cook the burgers on a hot, lightly oiled barbecue grill or flatplate for 2–3 minutes each side.
3 To make the tomato and onion salsa, put all the ingredients in a bowl and mix together well.

CHICKEN WITH FRUIT SALSA

Preparation time: 25 minutes +
    3 hours marinating
Total cooking time: 20 minutes
Serves 4

4 chicken breast fillets
¾ cup (185 ml/6 fl oz) white wine
3 tablespoons olive oil
2 teaspoons grated fresh ginger
1 clove garlic, crushed

Fruit salsa
220 g (7 oz) can pineapple slices, drained
1 small mango, peeled
2 small kiwi fruit, peeled
150 g (5 oz) watermelon, peeled, seeds removed
1 tablespoon finely chopped fresh mint

1 Put the chicken in a shallow non-metallic dish. Combine the wine, oil, ginger and garlic and pour over the chicken. Refrigerate, covered with plastic wrap, for at least 3 hours, turning occasionally.
2 To make the fruit salsa, chop the fruit finely and combine with the mint in a small serving bowl.
3 Cook the chicken fillets on a hot, lightly oiled barbecue grill or flatplate for 5–10 minutes each side, or until well browned.

DRUMSTICKS IN TOMATO AND MANGO CHUTNEY

Preparation time: 10 minutes +
    2 hours marinating
Total cooking time: 20 minutes
Serves 4

8 chicken drumsticks, scored
1 tablespoon mustard powder
2 tablespoons tomato sauce
1 tablespoon sweet mango chutney
1 teaspoon Worcestershire sauce
1 tablespoon Dijon mustard
¼ cup (30 g/1 oz) raisins
1 tablespoon oil

1 Toss the chicken in the mustard powder and season.
2 Combine the tomato sauce, chutney, Worcestershire sauce, mustard, raisins and oil. Spoon over the chicken and toss well. Marinate for at least 2 hours, turning once.
3 Cook the chicken on a hot, lightly oiled barbecue flatplate for about 20 minutes, or until cooked through.

SWEET AND SOUR PORK KEBABS

Preparation time: 30 minutes +
   3 hours marinating
Total cooking time: 20 minutes
Serves 6

1 kg (2 lb) pork fillets, cubed
1 large red capsicum, cubed
1 large green capsicum, cubed
425 g (14 oz) can pineapple pieces,
   drained, juice reserved
1 cup (250 ml/8 fl oz) orange juice
3 tablespoons white vinegar
2 tablespoons soft brown sugar
2 teaspoons chilli garlic sauce
2 teaspoons cornflour

1 Soak wooden skewers in water for
30 minutes to prevent scorching. Thread
pieces of meat alternately with pieces of
capsicum and pineapple onto the
skewers. Mix the pineapple juice with the
orange juice, vinegar, sugar and sauce.
Place the kebabs in a shallow non-
metallic dish and pour half the marinade
over them. Cover and refrigerate for at
least 3 hours, turning occasionally.
2 Put the remaining marinade in a small
pan. Mix the cornflour with a tablespoon
of the marinade until smooth, then add to
the pan. Stir over medium heat until the
mixture boils and thickens. Transfer to a
bowl, cover the surface with plastic wrap
and leave to cool.
3 Cook the kebabs on a hot, lightly oiled
barbecue flatplate or grill for 15 minutes,
turning occasionally, until tender. Serve
with the sauce.

GARLIC CALAMARI WITH PARMESAN

Preparation time: 30 minutes +
   10 minutes marinating
Total cooking time: 5 minutes
Serves 2–4 (see NOTE)

350 g (11 oz) calamari tubes, cleaned
4 cloves garlic, chopped
2 tablespoons olive oil
2 tablespoons finely chopped fresh
   parsley
1 large tomato, peeled, seeded and finely
   chopped
¼ cup (25 g/¾ oz) grated Parmesan

1 Cut the calamari tubes in half
lengthways, wash and pat dry. Lay them
flat, with the soft, fleshy side facing
upwards, and cut into rectangular pieces,
about 6 x 2.5 cm (2½ x 1 inch). Finely
honeycomb by scoring the fleshy side with
diagonal strips, one way and then the
other, to create a diamond pattern.
2 Mix the garlic, oil, half the parsley, salt
and pepper in a bowl. Add the calamari
and refrigerate for at least 10 minutes.
3 Cook on a very hot, lightly oiled
barbecue flatplate in 2 batches, tossing
regularly, until they just turn white (take
care never to overcook calamari or it can
become tough). Add the chopped tomato
and toss through to just heat.
4 Arrange the calamari on a plate and
scatter with the Parmesan and remaining
parsley.

MEDITERRANEAN CHICKEN SKEWERS

Preparation time: 20 minutes +
   2 hours marinating
Total cooking time: 10 minutes
Makes 8 skewers

32 chicken tenderloins
24 cherry tomatoes
6 cap mushrooms, cut into quarters
2 cloves garlic, crushed
rind of 1 lemon, grated
2 tablespoons lemon juice
2 tablespoons olive oil
1 tablespoon fresh oregano leaves,
   chopped

1 Soak 8 wooden skewers in water to
prevent scorching. Thread a piece of
chicken onto each skewer, followed by a
tomato, then a piece of mushroom.
Repeat three times for each skewer. Put
the skewers in a shallow, non-metallic
dish.
2 Combine the garlic, lemon rind, lemon
juice, olive oil and chopped oregano, pour
over the skewers and toss well. Marinate
for at least 2 hours, or overnight if time
permits.
3 Cook the skewers on a hot, lightly oiled
barbecue grill or flatplate for 4 minutes
on each side, basting occasionally, until
the chicken is cooked and the tomatoes
have shrivelled slightly.

TERIYAKI FISH WITH MANGO SALSA

Preparation time: 30 minutes +
   30 minutes marinating
Total cooking time: 10 minutes
Serves 4

750 g (1½ lb) swordfish fillets, cut into
   cubes

Marinade
½ cup (125 ml/4 fl oz) teriyaki sauce
¼ cup (60 ml/2 fl oz) pineapple juice
2 tablespoons honey
1 tablespoon grated fresh ginger
2 cloves garlic, crushed
1 teaspoon sesame oil

Salsa
1 red onion, chopped
2 teaspoons sugar
2 tablespoons lime juice
1 firm mango, diced
1 cup (150 g/5 oz) diced pineapple
1 kiwi fruit, diced
2 small red chillies, seeded and finely
   chopped
2 tablespoons finely chopped fresh
   coriander leaves

1 Soak 8 wooden skewers in water to
prevent scorching. Place the cubes of fish
in a non-metallic bowl. Combine the
marinade ingredients, pour over the fish
and stir to coat. Cover and refrigerate for
30 minutes.
2 Thread the fish onto the skewers,
keeping the marinade.
3 To make the salsa, put the onion in a
bowl and sprinkle with sugar. Add the
other ingredients and mix together gently.
4 Cook the skewers on a hot, lightly oiled
barbecue flatplate or grill for 6–8 minutes,
turning often and basting with the
reserved marinade. Serve with the salsa.

SALMON AND PRAWN KEBABS WITH CHINESE SPICES

Preparation time: 15 minutes +
   2 hours marinating
Total cooking time: 20 minutes
Serves 6

4 x 200 g (6½ oz) salmon fillets
36 raw prawns, peeled, deveined, tails
   intact
5 cm (2 inch) piece fresh ginger, finely
   shredded
⅔ cup (170 ml/5½ fl oz) Chinese rice wine
¾ cup (185 ml/6 fl oz) kecap manis
½ teaspoon five-spice powder
200 g (6½ oz) fresh egg noodles
600 g (1¼ lb) baby bok choy, leaves
   separated

1 Remove the skin and bones from the
salmon and cut it into bite-sized cubes
(you should have about 36). Thread three
cubes of salmon alternately with three
prawns onto each skewer. Lay the
skewers in a non-metallic dish.
2 Mix together the ginger, rice wine,
kecap manis and five-spice powder. Pour
over the skewers, then cover and
marinate for at least 2 hours. Turn over a
few times to ensure even coating.
3 Drain, reserving the marinade. Cook the
skewers in batches on a hot, lightly oiled
barbecue flatplate or grill for 4–5 minutes
each side, or until they are cooked
through.
4 Meanwhile, place the noodles in a bowl
and cover with boiling water. Leave for
5 minutes, or until tender, then drain and
keep warm. Place the reserved marinade
in a saucepan and bring to the boil.
Reduce the heat, simmer and stir in the
bok choy leaves. Cook, covered, for
2 minutes, or until just wilted.
5 Top the noodles with the bok choy, then
the kebabs. Spoon on the heated
marinade, season and serve.

CITRUS CHICKEN DRUMSTICKS

Preparation time: 20 minutes +
   3 hours marinating
Total cooking time: 20 minutes
Serves 4

8 chicken drumsticks
4 tablespoons orange juice
4 tablespoons lemon juice
1 teaspoon grated orange rind
1 teaspoon grated lemon rind
1 teaspoon sesame oil
1 tablespoon olive oil
1 spring onion, finely chopped

1 Score the thickest part of the chicken so
that it cooks evenly. Place in a shallow
non-metallic dish.
2 Combine the juices, rinds, oils and
spring onion and pour over the chicken.
Cover and leave in the fridge for at least
3 hours, turning occasionally. Drain the
chicken, reserving the marinade.
3 Cook the drumsticks on a hot, lightly
oiled barbecue grill or flatplate for
15–20 minutes, or until tender. Brush
occasionally with the reserved marinade.
Serve immediately.

STEAK IN RED WINE

Preparation time: 10 minutes +
   3 hours marinating
Total cooking time: 10 minutes
Serves 4

750 g (1½ lb) rump steak
1 cup (250 ml/8 fl oz) good red wine
2 teaspoons garlic salt
1 tablespoon dried oregano leaves
cracked black pepper

1 Trim the steak of any fat. Mix together
the wine, salt, oregano and pepper. Put
the steak in a shallow, non-metallic dish
and add the marinade. Toss well, cover
and refrigerate for at least 3 hours.
2 Cook the steak on a hot, lightly oiled
barbecue flatplate or grill for 3–4 minutes
on each side, brushing frequently with the
marinade.

LAMB CHOPS WITH PINEAPPLE SALSA

Preparation time: 20 minutes
Total cooking time: 10 minutes
Serves 6

12 lamb loin chops
2 tablespoons oil
1 teaspoon cracked black pepper

Pineapple Salsa
½ ripe pineapple (or 400 g/13 oz drained
   canned pineapple)
1 large red onion, finely chopped
1 fresh red chilli, seeded and diced
1 tablespoon cider or rice vinegar
1 teaspoon sugar
2 tablespoons chopped fresh mint

1 Trim the meat of excess fat and sinew.
Brush the chops with oil and season with
pepper.
2 To make the salsa, peel the pineapple,
remove the core and eyes and dice the
flesh. Toss with the onion, chilli, vinegar,
sugar, salt, pepper and mint and mix well.
3 Cook the lamb chops on a hot, lightly
greased barbecue flatplate or grill for
2–3 minutes each side, turning once, until
just tender. Serve with the pineapple
salsa.

SPICY BURGERS WITH AVOCADO SALSA

Preparation time: 25 minutes
Total cooking time: 10 minutes
Serves 6

1 kg (2 lb) beef mince
1 small onion, finely chopped
3 teaspoons chopped chilli
1 teaspoon ground cumin
2 tablespoons tomato paste
2 tablespoons chopped fresh coriander
6 bread rolls

Avocado Salsa
1 avocado
2 tablespoons lime juice
1 small tomato, chopped
125 g (4 oz) can corn kernels, drained

1 With your hands, mix together the
mince, onion, chilli, cumin, tomato paste
and coriander. Divide into six portions and
shape into burgers.
2 Cook on a hot, lightly oiled grill or
flatplate for 4–5 minutes each side.
3 To make the salsa, dice the avocado and
toss with lime juice. Add the tomato and
corn and toss lightly. Sandwich the
burgers in the bread rolls and serve with
the salsa.

CHEESEBURGER WITH CAPSICUM SALSA

Preparation time: 25 minutes +
　1 hour standing
Total cooking time: 20 minutes
Serves 6

1 kg (2 lb) beef mince
1 small onion, finely chopped
2 tablespoons chopped fresh parsley
1 teaspoon dried oregano
1 tablespoon tomato paste
70 g (2½ oz) Cheddar cheese
6 bread rolls

Capsicum Salsa
2 red capsicums
1 ripe tomato, finely chopped
1 small red onion, finely chopped
1 tablespoon olive oil
2 teaspoons red wine vinegar

1 Mix together the mince, onion, herbs and tomato paste with your hands. Divide into six portions and shape into patties. Cut the cheese into small squares. Make a cavity in the top of each patty with your thumb. Place a piece of cheese in the cavity and smooth the mince over to enclose the cheese completely.
2 To make the salsa, quarter the capsicums, remove the seeds and membranes and cook on a hot, lightly oiled barbecue grill, skin-side-down, until the skin blackens and blisters. Place in a plastic bag and leave to cool. Peel away the skin and dice the flesh. Combine with the tomato, onion, olive oil and vinegar and leave for at least 1 hour to let the flavours develop. Serve at room temperature.
3 Cook the patties on a hot, lightly oiled barbecue grill or flatplate for 4–5 minutes each side, turning once. Serve in rolls with salad leaves and the capsicum salsa.

FILLET STEAK WITH FLAVOURED BUTTERS

Preparation time: 30 minutes
Total cooking time: 15 minutes
Serves 4

4 fillet steaks

Capsicum Butter
1 small red capsicum
125 g (4 oz) butter
2 teaspoons chopped fresh oregano
2 teaspoons chopped chives

Garlic Butter
125 g (4 oz) butter
3 cloves garlic, crushed
2 spring onions, finely chopped

1 Cut a pocket in each steak.
2 For the capsicum butter, cut the capsicum into large pieces and place, skin-side-up, under a hot grill until the skin blisters and blackens. Put in a plastic bag until cool. Peel away the skin and dice the flesh. Beat the butter until creamy. Add the capsicum and herbs, season and beat until smooth.
3 For the garlic butter, beat the butter until creamy, add the garlic and spring onions and beat until smooth.
4 Push capsicum butter into the pockets in two of the steaks and garlic butter into the other two.
5 Cook on a hot, lightly oiled barbecue grill or flatplate for 4–5 minutes each side, turning once. Brush frequently with any remaining flavoured butter while cooking.

SALMON WITH GREMOLATA AND POTATO GRIDDLE CAKES

Preparation time: 25 minutes
Total cooking time: 15 minutes
Serves 4

Gremolata
30 g (1 oz) fresh parsley, finely chopped
grated rind of 1 lemon
grated rind of 1 orange
2 cloves garlic, crushed

Potato Griddle Cakes
250 g (8 oz) potatoes
250 g (8 oz) sweet potatoes, peeled
⅓ cup (20 g/¾ oz) chopped fresh chives
2 tablespoons plain flour
1 egg, lightly beaten
4 salmon fillets, about 200 g (6½ oz) each
2–3 teaspoons baby capers, drained

1 For the gremolata, mix the parsley, lemon and orange rind and garlic.
2 To make the potato griddle cake, coarsely grate the peeled potatoes and sweet potatoes and squeeze to remove any excess moisture. Mix with the chives, flour, egg and salt and pepper. Preheat a barbecue flatplate and drizzle with olive oil. Use a heaped tablespoon of mixture to make each patty, flattening slightly. Cook, turning once, for 5 minutes, or until golden.
3 Cook the salmon on the lightly oiled hot plate for 2–3 minutes each side, or until just tender. Serve with the gremolata, griddle cakes and

SPICY CHICKEN WITH CHILLI GARLIC DIP

Preparation time: 20 minutes +
    1 hour marinating
Total cooking time: 25 minutes
Serves 4–6

6 cloves garlic
1 teaspoon black peppercorns
3 coriander roots and stems, roughly
    chopped
¼ teaspoon salt
12 chicken thigh fillets

Chilli Garlic Dip
4–5 dried red chillies
2 large cloves garlic, chopped
3 tablespoons sugar
4 tablespoons cider or rice vinegar
pinch of salt
3 tablespoons boiling water

1 Put the garlic, peppercorns, coriander and salt in a food processor and process for 20–30 seconds or until a smooth paste forms, or grind in a mortar and pestle. Put the chicken in a shallow, non-metallic dish and spread the paste over the chicken. Cover and leave in the fridge for 1 hour.
2 To make the dip, soak the chillies in hot water for 20 minutes. Drain the chillies and chop finely. Place in a mortar with the garlic and sugar and grind to a smooth paste. Place in a small pan, add the vinegar, salt and water and bring to the boil. Reduce the heat, simmer for 2–3 minutes and cool.
3 Cook the chicken on a hot, lightly oiled barbecue grill or flatplate for 5–10 minutes each side, turning once. Serve with the dip.

BACON-WRAPPED CHICKEN

Preparation time: 15 minutes
Total cooking time: 10 minutes
Serves 6

2 tablespoons olive oil
2 tablespoons lime juice
¼ teaspoon ground coriander
6 chicken breast fillets
4 tablespoons fruit chutney
3 tablespoons chopped pecan nuts
6 slices bacon

1 Mix together the oil, lime juice, coriander and salt and pepper. Using a sharp knife, cut a pocket in the thickest section of each fillet. Mix together the chutney and nuts. Spoon 1 tablespoon of the chutney mixture into each chicken breast pocket.
2 Turn the tapered ends of the fillets to the underside. Wrap a bacon slice around each fillet to enclose the filling and secure with a toothpick.
3 Put the chicken parcels on a hot, lightly oiled barbecue grill or flatplate and cook for 5 minutes on each side, or until cooked through, turning once. Brush with the lime juice mixture several times during cooking and drizzle with any leftover lime juice mixture to serve.

T-BONE STEAK WITH SWEET ONIONS

Preparation time: 10 minutes
Total cooking time: 20 minutes
Serves 4

4 tablespoons oil
6 onions, sliced into rings
3 tablespoons barbecue sauce
4 T-bone steaks

1 Heat 2 tablespoons of the oil on a hot barbecue flatplate or grill. Add the onions and barbecue sauce and cook, stirring regularly, for 10 minutes, or until the onions are very soft and brown. Push to one side of the hot plate to keep warm.
2 Brush the T-bone steaks with the remaining oil and add to the hot plate. Cook over high heat, turning once or twice, until tender and cooked to your liking. Arrange the steaks on warm plates, spoon over some of the sweet caramelised onions, and serve.

MARINADES & BUTTERS FOR MEAT

SOAK BEEF, LAMB OR PORK IN THE FOLLOWING TANGY MARINADES FOR A FEW HOURS, OR OVERNIGHT, TO TENDERISE AND FLAVOUR, OR BRUSH WITH THE BASTES WHILE THE MEAT IS COOKING. THE BUTTERS NEED TO BE PREPARED A FEW HOURS IN ADVANCE TO GIVE THEM TIME TO FIRM UP AGAIN IN THE FRIDGE BEFORE SLICING.

ASIAN MARINADE

Mix together 2 crushed cloves garlic, 3 tablespoons each of soy sauce, sweet chilli sauce and teriyaki marinade, 1 tablespoon lemon juice and 1 teaspoon each of sesame oil and peanut oil. Place in a shallow, non-metallic dish, add the meat and toss well to coat. Marinate in the fridge overnight before cooking on the barbecue.
Makes 1 cup (250 ml/8 fl oz)

TANDOORI MARINADE

Combine 1 cup (250 g/8 oz) yoghurt, 1 tablespoon each of grated onion and ginger, 2 crushed cloves garlic and 1 teaspoon each of brown sugar, ground turmeric, cumin, chilli and coriander. Place in a shallow, non-metallic dish, add the meat and toss well to coat. Marinate in the fridge overnight before cooking on the barbecue.
Makes 1 cup (250 ml/8 fl oz)

ROSEMARY MUSTARD BUTTER

Beat 125 g (4 oz) butter until light and creamy, add 3 tablespoons wholegrain mustard,1 tablespoon chopped fresh rosemary and 1 teaspoon each of lemon juice, lemon rind and honey. Mix together until well combined. Spoon the butter down the middle of a piece of plastic wrap, fold up the edges over the butter and roll the mixture into a log shape. Refrigerate until firm. Slice the butter into rounds and serve on top of barbecued lamb or beef.
Serves 6

ORANGE BUTTER

Beat 125 g (4 oz) butter until light and creamy, add 1 tablespoon chopped fresh mint and 1 teaspoon each of orange marmalade and Dijon mustard and mix until smooth. Roll the butter out between 2 pieces of baking paper and refrigerate until firm. Using small cookie cutters, cut out shapes from the butter and chill until ready to use. Delicious with barbecued lamb or beef.
Serves 6

CAJUN SPICE MIX

Place 2 tablespoons each of freshly ground black pepper, sweet paprika and white pepper into a bowl, add 1 tablespoon each of onion powder and garlic powder, 2 teaspoons dried oregano leaves and 1 teaspoon each of dried thyme leaves and cayenne pepper. Place in a shallow dish, add the meat and toss well to coat. Marinate in the fridge for at least 3 hours before cooking on the barbecue.
Makes ⅓ cup (80 g/2¾ oz)

SUN-DRIED TOMATO AND BASIL BUTTER

Beat 125 g (4 oz) butter until light and creamy, then add 30 g (1 oz) finely chopped sun-dried tomatoes, 1 tablespoon finely shredded fresh basil and 20 g (¾ oz) finely grated Parmesan and mix together well. Spoon the butter into small pots and swirl the surface with a flat-bladed knife. Serve in small slices on top of barbecued meats.
Serves 6

From left: Asian Marinade; Tandoori Marinade; Cajun Spice Mix; Rosemary Mustard Butter; Orange Butter; Sun-dried Tomato and Basil Butter

PERSIAN CHICKEN SKEWERS

Preparation time: 10 minutes +
  overnight marinating
Total cooking time: 10 minutes
Serves 4

2 teaspoons ground cardamom
½ teaspoon ground turmeric
1 teaspoon ground allspice
4 cloves garlic, crushed
3 tablespoons lemon juice
3 tablespoons olive oil
4 large chicken thigh fillets, excess fat
  removed
lemon wedges, to serve
plain yoghurt, to serve

1 Soak 8 wooden skewers in water to
prevent scorching. To make the
marinade, whisk together the cardamom,
turmeric, allspice, garlic, lemon juice and
oil. Season with salt and ground black
pepper.
2 Cut each chicken thigh fillet into
3–4 cm cubes. Toss the cubes in the spice
marinade. Thread the chicken onto
skewers and place on a tray. Cover and
refrigerate overnight.
3 Cook the skewers on a hot, lightly oiled
barbecue grill or flatplate for 4 minutes
on each side, or until the chicken is
cooked through. Serve with lemon
wedges and plain yoghurt.

PIRI-PIRI CHICKEN

Preparation time: 5 minutes +
  1 hour marinating
Total cooking time: 1 hour
Serves 4

6 bird's eye chillies, with seeds left in,
  finely chopped
1 teaspoon coarse salt
½ cup (125 ml/4 fl oz) olive oil
¾ cup (185 ml/6 fl oz) cider vinegar
1 clove garlic, crushed
4 chicken Maryland pieces
lemon wedges, to serve

1 Combine the chilli, salt, olive oil, vinegar
and garlic in a screw-top jar. Seal and
shake well to combine.
2 Place the chicken pieces in a shallow,
non-metallic dish and pour on the
marinade. Cover and marinate for at least
1 hour.
3 Cook the chicken on a hot, lightly oiled
barbecue grill or flatplate, basting
regularly with the marinade, for
50–60 minutes, or until the chicken is
cooked through and the skin begins to
crisp. Serve with lemon wedges.

MUSHROOM AND EGGPLANT SKEWERS

Preparation time: 20 minutes +
15 minutes marinating

Total cooking time: 30 minutes
Serves 4

12 long fresh rosemary sprigs
18 Swiss brown mushrooms, halved
1 small eggplant, cubed
3 tablespoons olive oil
2 tablespoons balsamic vinegar
2 cloves garlic, crushed
1 teaspoon sugar

Tomato sauce
5 tomatoes
1 tablespoon olive oil
1 small onion, finely chopped
1 clove garlic, crushed
1 tablespoon tomato paste
2 teaspoons sugar
2 teaspoons balsamic vinegar
1 tablespoon chopped fresh flat-leaf parsley

1 Remove the leaves from the lower part of
the rosemary sprigs. Reserve a tablespoon
of the leaves. Put the mushrooms and
eggplant in a large non-metallic bowl. Pour
on the combined oil, vinegar, garlic and
sugar and toss. Marinate for 15 minutes.
2 To make the tomato sauce, score a
cross in the base of each tomato. Put in a
bowl of boiling water for 30 seconds, then
plunge into cold water. Peel the skin away
from the cross. Cut in half and scoop out
the seeds with a teaspoon. Dice the flesh.
3 Heat the oil in a saucepan. Cook the onion
and garlic over medium heat for 2–3 minutes.
Reduce the heat, add the tomato, tomato
paste, sugar, vinegar and parsley and
simmer for 10 minutes, or until thick.
4 Thread alternating mushroom halves
and eggplant cubes onto the rosemary
sprigs. Cook on a hot, lightly oiled
barbecue grill or flatplate for 7–8 minutes, or
until the eggplant is tender, turning
occasionally. Serve with the sauce.

GINGER-ORANGE PORK

Preparation time: 15 minutes +
   3 hours marinating
Total cooking time: 20 minutes
Serves 6

6 pork butterfly steaks
1 cup (250 ml/8 fl oz) ginger wine
½ cup (150 g/5 oz) orange marmalade
2 tablespoons oil
1 tablespoon grated fresh ginger

1 Trim the pork steak of excess fat and sinew. Mix together the wine, marmalade, oil and ginger. Place the steaks in a shallow non-metallic dish and add the marinade. Store, covered with plastic wrap, in the fridge for at least 3 hours, turning occasionally. Drain, reserving the marinade.
2 Cook the pork on a hot, lightly oiled barbecue flatplate or grill for 5 minutes each side or until tender, turning once.
3 While the meat is cooking, place the reserved marinade in a small pan. Bring to the boil, reduce the heat and simmer for 5 minutes, or until the marinade has reduced and thickened slightly. Pour over the pork.

CHICKEN FAJITAS

Preparation time: 35 minutes +
   3 hours marinating
Total cooking time: 10 minutes
Serves 4

4 chicken breast fillets
2 tablespoons olive oil
3 tablespoons lime juice
2 cloves garlic, crushed
1 teaspoon ground cumin
¼ cup (15 g/¼ oz) chopped fresh
   coriander leaves
8 flour tortillas
1 tablespoon olive oil, extra
2 onions, sliced
2 green capsicums, cut into thin strips
1 cup (125 g/4 oz) grated Cheddar cheese
1 large avocado, sliced
1 cup (250 g/8 oz) bottled tomato salsa

1 Cut the chicken into thin strips and place in a shallow, non-metallic dish. Combine the oil, lime juice, garlic, cumin and coriander and pour over the chicken. Store, covered, in the fridge for at least 3 hours.
2 Wrap the tortillas in foil and place on a cooler part of the barbecue for 10 minutes to warm through. Heat the oil on a flatplate. Cook the onion and capsicum for 5 minutes or until soft. Push over to a cooler part of the plate to keep warm.
3 Place the chicken and marinade on the flatplate and cook for 5 minutes, or until just tender. Transfer the chicken, vegetables and wrapped tortillas to a serving platter. Make up individual fajitas by placing the chicken, cooked onion and capsicum, grated cheese and avocado over the flat tortillas. Top with the salsa and roll up.

PORK AND TOMATO BURGERS

Preparation time: 20 minutes +
   15 minutes refrigeration
Total cooking time: 15 minutes
Serves 4

350 g (11 oz) pork and veal mince
100 g (3½ oz) sun-dried tomatoes,
   chopped
3 spring onions, finely chopped
2 tablespoons chopped fresh basil
1 red capsicum, seeded and sliced
1 tablespoon balsamic vinegar

1 Mix together the mince, sun-dried tomato, spring onion and basil. Season well and knead for 2 minutes, or until a little sticky. Form into four burgers and refrigerate for 15 minutes.
2 Mix the capsicum with a little olive oil. Cook on a hot, lightly oiled barbecue grill or flatplate, tossing well and drizzling with the balsamic vinegar, until just softened. Set aside.
3 Wipe the barbecue clean and reheat. Brush the burgers with a little olive oil and cook for 4–5 minutes each side, or until browned and cooked through. Serve with the chargrilled capsicum.

VEGETABLE AND TOFU KEBABS

Preparation time: 40 minutes +
 30 minutes marinating
Total cooking time: 30 minutes
Serves 4

500 g (1 lb) firm tofu, cubed
1 red capsicum, cubed
3 zucchini, thickly sliced
4 small onions, cut into quarters
300 g (10 oz) button mushrooms, quartered
½ cup (125 ml/4 fl oz) tamari
½ cup (125 ml/4 fl oz) sesame oil
2.5 cm (1 inch) fresh ginger, peeled, grated
½ cup (180 g/6 oz) honey
1 tablespoon sesame oil, extra
1 small onion, finely chopped
1 clove garlic, crushed
2 teaspoons chilli paste
1 cup (250 g/8 oz) smooth peanut butter
1 cup (250 ml/8 fl oz) coconut milk
1 tablespoon soft brown sugar
1 tablespoon tamari
1 tablespoon lemon juice
3 tablespoons peanuts, roasted and chopped
3 tablespoons sesame seeds, toasted

1 Preheat the oven to 220°C (425°F/
Gas 7). Soak 12 bamboo skewers in water.
Thread the tofu, capsicum, zucchini,
onions and mushrooms onto the skewers.
Arrange in a shallow, non-metallic dish.
2 Combine the tamari, oil, ginger and
honey and pour over the kebabs. Leave
for 30 minutes.
3 To make the peanut sauce, heat the
extra oil in a large frying pan over
medium heat and cook the onion, garlic
and chilli paste for 1–2 minutes, or until
the onion is soft. Reduce the heat, add the
peanut butter, coconut milk, sugar, tamari
and lemon juice and stir. Bring to the boil,
then simmer for 10 minutes, or until just
thick. Stir in the peanuts. If the sauce is too
thick, add water.
4 Cook the kebabs for 10–15 minutes on a
hot, lightly oiled barbecue grill, basting with
the marinade and turning occasionally.

PEPPER STEAKS WITH HORSERADISH SAUCE

Preparation time: 15 minutes
Total cooking time: 15 minutes
Serves 4

4 sirloin steaks
3 tablespoons seasoned cracked pepper

Horseradish Sauce
2 tablespoons brandy
3 tablespoons beef stock
4 tablespoons cream
1 tablespoon horseradish cream
½ teaspoon sugar

1 Coat the steaks on both sides with
pepper, pressing it into the meat. Cook on
a hot, lightly oiled barbecue grill or
flatplate for 5–10 minutes, until cooked to
your taste.
2 To make the sauce, put the brandy and
stock in a pan. Bring to the boil, then
reduce the heat. Stir in the cream,
horseradish and sugar and heat through.
Serve with the steaks.

CRISPY CHICKEN WINGS

Preparation time: 10 minutes +
 2 hours marinating
Total cooking time: 15 minutes
Serves 6

12 chicken wings
3 tablespoons soy sauce
3 tablespoons hoisin sauce
½ cup (125 g/4 oz) tomato sauce
2 tablespoons honey
1 tablespoon brown sugar
1 tablespoon cider vinegar
2 cloves garlic, crushed
¼ teaspoon Chinese five-spice powder
2 teaspoons sesame oil

1 Tuck the chicken wing tips to the
underside and place in a non-metallic
bowl.
2 Mix together all the remaining
ingredients and pour over the wings,
tossing to coat. Cover and leave in the
fridge for at least 2 hours, turning
occasionally. Drain, reserving the
marinade.
3 Cook the wings on a hot, lightly oiled
barbecue grill or flatplate for 5 minutes,
or until cooked through, brushing with the
reserved marinade several times.

SCALLOPS WITH GREEN PEPPERCORNS

Preparation time: 20 minutes +
    20 minutes marinating
Total cooking time: 5 minutes
Serves 4

¼ cup (60 ml/2 fl oz) olive oil
2 teaspoons green peppercorns, chopped
2 teaspoons finely grated lime rind
1 teaspoon finely grated fresh ginger
500 g (1 lb) scallops with corals, deveined
salad leaves and pickled ginger, to serve

1 Combine the oil, peppercorns, rind and fresh ginger. Add the scallops and refrigerate for 20 minutes.
2 Cook the scallops on a very hot, lightly oiled barbecue flatplate, in batches, stirring gently, for about 2 minutes, or until they become lightly golden brown.
3 Serve the scallops on salad leaves and topped with ginger strips.

LAMB SHANKS

Preparation time: 5 minutes +
    overnight marinating
Total cooking time: 45 minutes
Serves 6

2 cloves garlic, halved
⅓ cup (80 ml/2¾ fl oz) olive oil
6 lamb shanks

1 Combine the garlic and oil in a small bowl, cover and marinate at room temperature overnight. Prepare the covered barbecue for indirect cooking at moderate heat (normal fire). Place a drip tray under the top grill. Trim the shanks of excess fat and sinew.
2 Brush the garlic oil generously over the shanks and sprinkle with salt and pepper.
3 Place the shanks on the top grill of the barbecue, cover and roast for 35–45 minutes or until the meat is tender when pierced with a fork.

GINGER-CHILLI DRUMSTICKS WITH CUCUMBER YOGHURT

Preparation time: 10 minutes +
    3 hours marinating
Total cooking time: 20 minutes
Serves 6

1 tablespoon grated fresh ginger
1 tablespoon brown sugar
1 teaspoon bottled crushed red chilli peppers
¼ teaspoon ground turmeric
1 teaspoon lemon juice
1 teaspoon finely grated lemon rind
1 cup (250 g/8 oz) plain yoghurt
12 chicken drumsticks

Cucumber Yoghurt
1 cup (250 g/8 oz) plain yoghurt
½ teaspoon bottled crushed red chlili peppers
1 cucumber, finely chopped
½ teaspoon sugar

1 Mix together the ginger, brown sugar, crushed chilli pepper, turmeric, lemon juice and lemon rind. Stir in the yoghurt. Add the chicken, stirring well to coat. Cover and refrigerate for at least 3 hours, stirring occasionally. Drain, reserving the marinade.
2 Cook the drumsticks on a hot, lightly oiled barbecue grill or flatplate for 15–20 minutes, or until tender. Brush occasionally with the reserved marinade.
3 To make the cucumber yoghurt, mix together the yoghurt, crushed chilli pepper, cucumber, sugar and salt and serve with the drumsticks.

MARINADES & GLAZES FOR CHICKEN

CHICKEN SHOULD BE LEFT
TO MARINATE FOR AT LEAST
2 HOURS AND OVERNIGHT IF YOU
HAVE THE TIME. A GOOD TIP IS
TO PUT CHICKEN PIECES IN A
PLASTIC BAG WITH THE
MARINADE AND THEN FREEZE
FOR FUTURE USE. WHEN YOU
BRING THE CHICKEN OUT TO
DEFROST, IT CAN BE
MARINATING AT THE SAME
TIME.

LIME AND GINGER GLAZE

Put ½ cup (160 g/5½ oz) lime marmalade,
¼ cup (60 ml/2 fl oz) lime juice,
2 tablespoons sherry, 2 table-spoons soft
brown sugar and 2 teaspoons finely
grated fresh ginger in a pan. Stir over low
heat until liquid. Pour over 1 kg (2 lb)
chicken wings and toss well to combine.
Cover and refrigerate for 2 hours or
overnight. Cook on a hot barbecue for
10 minutes, or until cooked through.

HONEY SOY MARINADE

Put ¼ cup (90 g/3 oz) honey, ¼ cup (60
ml/2 fl oz) soy sauce, 1 crushed garlic
clove, 2 tablespoons sake and ½ teaspoon
Chinese five-spice powder in a pan. Pour
over 500 g (1 lb) chicken thigh fillets and
toss well. Cover and refrigerate for
2 hours or overnight. Cook on a hot
barbecue for 10 minutes, or until cooked
through.

REDCURRANT GLAZE

Put 340 g (11 oz) redcurrant jelly,
2 tablespoons lemon juice, 2 tablespoons
brandy and 1 teaspoon chopped fresh
thyme in a pan and stir over low heat until
it becomes liquid. Pour over 500 g (1 lb)
chicken breast fillets and toss well to
combine. Cover and refrigerate for
2 hours or overnight. Cook on a hot
barbecue for 8 minutes, turning once, or
until cooked through.

TANDOORI MARINADE

Soak 8 bamboo skewers in water for
30 minutes to prevent scorching. Combine
2 tablespoons tandoori paste, 1 cup
(250 g/8 oz) plain yoghurt and 1 tablespoon
lime juice. Cut 500 g (1 lb) tenderloins in
half lengthways and thread onto skewers.
Pour over the marinade and toss well to
combine. Cover and refrigerate for
1–2 hours. Cook on a hot barbecue,
basting with the marinade, for
5–10 minutes, or until cooked through.

MEXICAN MARINADE

Combine 440 g (14 oz) bottled taco sauce,
2 tablespoons lime juice and 2 tablespoons
chopped fresh coriander leaves. Pour the
marinade over 1 kg (2 lb) scored chicken
drumsticks and toss well to combine.
Cover and refrigerate for 2 hours or
overnight. Cook on a hot barbecue for
30 minutes, or until cooked through.

THAI MARINADE

Combine 2 tablespoons fish sauce,
2 tablespoons lime juice, 1 crushed garlic
clove, 1 finely chopped lemon grass stem,
2 teaspoons soft brown sugar, ½ cup
(125 ml/4 fl oz) coconut cream and 2
tablespoons chopped fresh coriander
leaves. Pour the marinade over 1 kg (2 lb)
chicken drumettes and toss well to
combine. Cover and refrigerate for
2 hours or overnight. Cook on a hot
barbecue for 30 minutes, or until cooked
through.

This page, from top: Tandoori Marinade; Mexican Marinade; Thai Marinade Opposite, from top: Lime and Ginger Glaze; Honey Soy
Marinade; Redcurrant Glaze

VEGETARIAN

PULAO

Preparation time: 20 minutes
Total cooking time: 15 minutes
Serves 6

500 g (1 lb) basmati rice
1 teaspoon cumin seeds
4 tablespoons ghee or oil
2 tablespoons chopped almonds
2 tablespoons raisins or sultanas
2 onions, thinly sliced
2 cinnamon sticks
5 cardamom pods
1 teaspoon sugar
1 tablespoon ginger juice
15 saffron threads, soaked in
   1 tablespoon warm milk
2 Indian bay leaves (cassia leaves)
1 cup (250 ml/8 fl oz) coconut milk
2 tablespoons fresh or frozen peas
rosewater (optional)

1 Wash the rice in a sieve under cold, running water until the water from the rice runs clear. Drain the rice and put in a saucepan, cover with water and soak for 30 minutes. Drain.
2 Place a small frying pan over low heat and dry-fry the cumin seeds until aromatic.
3 Heat the ghee or oil in a karhai (Indian wok) or heavy-based frying pan and fry the almonds and raisins until browned. Remove from the pan, fry the onion in the same ghee until dark golden brown, then remove from the pan.

4 Add the rice, roasted cumin seeds, cinnamon, cardamom, sugar, ginger juice, saffron and salt to the pan and fry for 2 minutes, or until aromatic.
5 Add the bay leaves and coconut milk to the pan, then add enough water to come about 5 cm (2 inches) above the rice. Bring to the boil, cover and cook over medium heat for 8 minutes, or until most of the water has evaporated.
6 Add the peas to the pan and stir well. Reduce the heat to very low and cook until the rice is cooked through. Stir in the fried almonds, raisins and onion, reserving some for garnishing. Drizzle with a few drops of rosewater if you would like a more perfumed dish. Garnish with the reserved almonds, raisins and onion, then serve.

BONDAS

Preparation time: 30 minutes
Total cooking time: 25 minutes
Makes 24

2 teaspoons vegetable oil
1 teaspoon brown mustard seeds
1 onion, finely chopped
2 teaspoons grated fresh ginger
4 curry leaves
3 small green chillies, finely chopped
1.2 kg (2 lb 6½ oz) potatoes, diced and cooked
pinch of ground turmeric
2 tablespoons lemon juice
⅓ cup (20 g/¾ oz) chopped fresh coriander
oil, for deep-frying

Batter
1 cup (110 g/3½ o) besan (chickpea flour)
¼ cup (30 g/1 oz) self-raising flour
¼ cup (45 g/1½ oz) rice flour
¼ teaspoon ground turmeric
1 teaspoon chilli powder

1 Heat a wok over medium heat, add the oil and swirl to coat. Add the mustard seeds and stir for 30 seconds, or until fragrant. Add the onion, ginger, curry leaves and chilli and cook for 2 minutes. Add the potato, turmeric and 2 teaspoons of water and stir for 2 minutes, or until the mixture is dry. Remove from the heat and cool. Stir in the lemon juice and coriander leaves, then season to taste. Using a heaped tablespoon, shape into 24 balls.
2 To make the batter, sift the flours, turmeric, chilli powder and ¼ teaspoon salt into a bowl. Make a well in the centre of the dry ingredients. Gradually whisk in 1⅓ cups (350 ml/11 fl oz) water to make a smooth batter.
3 Fill a clean wok one-third full of oil and heat to 180°C (350°F), or until a cube of bread dropped into the oil browns in 15 seconds. Dip the balls into the batter, then cook in the hot oil, in batches, for 1–2 minutes, or until golden. Drain on crumpled paper towels and season with salt. Serve hot.

STEAMED VEGETABLE ROLLS

Preparation time: 20 minutes +
   25 minutes soaking
Total cooking time: 20 minutes
Serves 4–6

Dipping sauce
¼ cup (60 ml/2 fl oz) hot chilli sauce
2 tablespoons hoisin sauce
1 tablespoon light soy sauce
1 tablespoon crushed, unsalted peanuts

20 g (¾ oz) dried shiitake mushrooms
250 g (8 oz) wom bok (Chinese cabbage),
   shredded
1 large carrot, grated
4 spring onions, sliced
¼ cup (60 g/2 oz) bamboo shoots,
   julienned
2 cloves garlic, crushed
2 tablespoons water chestnuts, finely
   chopped
2 tablespoons chopped fresh coriander
   leaves
1½ tablespoons fish sauce
1 tablespoon soy sauce
1 teaspoon grated fresh ginger
2 bean curd sheets

1 To make the dipping sauce, combine all
the ingredients in a bowl. Set aside until
ready to serve the vegetable rolls.
2 Soak the mushrooms in hot water for
20 minutes, then drain, remove the stalks
and finely shred the caps. Squeeze out
any excess moisture. Combine the caps
with the rest of the filling ingredients
except the bean curd sheets.

3 If the bean curd sheets are large, cut
them in half. Soak them in warm water for
30 seconds, then remove from the water
one at a time and squeeze out the water.
4 Lay a bean curd sheet on a workbench.
Divide the filling into portions for the
number of bean curd sheets. Form the
filling into logs about 27 cm (11 inches)
long. Lay the log along the long side of
the sheet and gently but firmly roll the log
up, tucking in the sides as you go. Repeat
with the remaining sheets and mixture.
5 Line a bamboo steamer with baking
paper and place the rolls, seam-side-
down, in a single layer in the steamer.
Cover and steam over a wok of simmering
water for 20 minutes, then remove and
set aside to cool. When firm, slice the log
into 1.5 cm (⅝ inch) pieces. Serve with the
dipping sauce.

CAMEMBERT AND POTATO TERRINE

Preparation time: 1 hour +
   overnight refrigeration
Total cooking time: 55 minutes
Serves 8–10

6 new potatoes, unpeeled
3 green apples
125 g (4 oz) butter
3 tablespoons olive oil
200 g (6½ oz) Camembert, chilled and
   very thinly sliced
2 tablespoons chopped fresh parsley

1 Par-boil the potatoes in lightly salted
water for about 15 minutes. Drain and
cool, then peel and cut into slices 1 cm
(½ inch) thick.
2 Core and slice the apples into 5 mm
(¼ inch) thick rounds.
3 Heat half the butter and half the oil in a
large frying pan and cook the potato until
just golden. Drain on crumpled paper
towels. Heat the remaining butter and oil.
Lightly fry the sliced apple until golden,
then remove and drain on crumpled
paper towels. Preheat the oven to
moderate 180°C (350°F/Gas 4).
4 Line a 25 x 11 cm (10 x 4½ inch) terrine
with baking paper. Arrange a layer of
potato in the base of the terrine. Add a
layer of apple, then Camembert. Sprinkle
with parsley and season with salt and
pepper, to taste. Build up the layers,
finishing with potato.
5 Oil a piece of foil and cover the terrine,
sealing well. Place the terrine in a baking
dish and half fill the dish with boiling
water. Bake for 20 minutes. Remove from
the water-filled baking dish. Cover with
foil, then put a piece of heavy cardboard,
cut to fit, on top of the terrine. Put
weights or food cans on top of the
cardboard to compress the terrine.
Refrigerate overnight. Turn out and slice,
to serve.

FUSILLI WITH SAGE AND GARLIC

Preparation time: 5 minutes
Total cooking time: 15 minutes
Serves 4

500 g (1 lb) fusilli
60 g (2 oz) butter
2 cloves garlic, crushed
½ cup (10 g/¼ oz) fresh sage leaves
2 tablespoons cream
freshly grated Parmesan, for serving

1 Cook the fusilli in a large pan of rapidly boiling salted water until al dente. Drain and return to the pan.
2 While the pasta is cooking, melt the butter in a frying pan. Add the garlic and fresh sage leaves. Cook over low heat for 4 minutes, stirring frequently.
3 Stir in the cream and season with some salt and freshly ground black pepper, to taste. Stir the sauce through the drained pasta until thoroughly coated. Top each serving with freshly grated Parmesan.

LENTIL BHUJA CASSEROLE

Preparation time: 40 minutes + overnight soaking + 30 minutes refrigeration
Total cooking time: 1 hour 10 minutes
Serves 4–6

2 cups (370 g/11¾ oz) green lentils
1 large onion
1 large potato
1 teaspoon ground cumin
1 teaspoon ground coriander
1 teaspoon ground turmeric
¾ cup (90 g/3 oz) plain flour
oil, for shallow frying
2 tablespoons oil, extra
2 cloves garlic, crushed
1 tablespoon grated fresh ginger
1 cup (250 ml/8 fl oz) tomato purée (passata)
2 cups (500 ml/16 fl oz) vegetable stock
1 cup (250 ml/8 fl oz) cream
200 g (6½ oz) green beans, topped and tailed
2 carrots, sliced

1 Cover the lentils with cold water and soak overnight. Drain well.
2 Grate the onion and potato and drain the excess liquid. Combine the lentils, onion, potato, cumin, coriander, turmeric and flour in a bowl, and mix well. Roll the mixture into walnut-sized balls and place them on a foil-lined tray. Cover and refrigerate for 30 minutes.
3 Heat the oil, about 2 cm (¾ inch) deep, in a frying pan; add the lentil balls in small batches and fry over high heat for 5 minutes or until golden brown. Drain on paper towels.
4 Heat the extra oil in a large pan; add the garlic and ginger, and cook, stirring, over medium heat for 1 minute. Stir in the tomato purée, stock and cream. Bring to the boil, reduce the heat and simmer, uncovered, for 10 minutes. Add the lentil balls, beans and carrot, cover and simmer for 35 minutes, stirring occasionally. Serve with pitta bread.

CREAMY OMELETTE

Preparation time: 5 minutes
Total cooking time: 5 minutes
Serves 2

3 eggs
¼ cup (60 ml/2 fl oz) cream
salt and pepper
20 g (⅔ oz) butter

1 Place the eggs, cream, salt and pepper in a medium bowl. Beat with a wire whisk for 2 minutes.
2 Heat the butter in a small non-stick pan over medium heat. When the butter is foaming, add mixture to the pan all at once. Stir with a wooden spoon for 15 seconds.
3 Cook until the mixture is almost set, tilting the pan and lifting the edges of the omelette occasionally to allow the uncooked egg to flow underneath. When the mixture has almost set, fold the omelette in half using an egg slice or a flat-bladed knife. The centre of the omelette should be moist and creamy. Alternatively, instead of folding the omelette, complete the cooking process by covering the pan with a lid for about 2 minutes. Sprinkle with fresh herbs and serve with sliced avocado, if desired.

SUN-DRIED TOMATO SAUCE ON TAGLIATELLE

Preparation time: 20 minutes
Total cooking time: 20 minutes
Serves 4

500 g (1 lb) tagliatelle
2 tablespoons olive oil
1 onion, chopped
½ cup (80 g/2¾ oz) thinly sliced sun-dried tomatoes
2 cloves garlic, crushed
425 g (14 oz) can chopped tomatoes
1 cup (125 g/4 oz) pitted black olives
⅓ cup (20 g/¾ oz) chopped fresh basil
freshly grated Parmesan, for serving

1 Cook the tagliatelle in a large pan of rapidly boiling salted water until al dente. Drain and return to the pan.
2 Meanwhile, heat the oil in a large frying pan. Add the onion and cook for 3 minutes, stirring occasionally, until soft. Add the sliced sun-dried tomato along with the crushed garlic and cook for another minute.
3 Add the chopped tomato, olives and basil to the pan and season with freshly ground black pepper. Bring to the boil, reduce the heat, and simmer for 10 minutes.
4 Add the sauce to the hot pasta and gently toss through. Serve immediately, topped with some Parmesan.

NOTE: Sun-dried tomatoes are available either dry or loosely packed, or in jars with olive or canola oil. The tomatoes in oil need only to be drained, but the dry tomatoes must be soaked in boiling water for 5 minutes to rehydrate and soften before using.

CHEESE AND MUSHROOM PIES

Preparation time: 40 minutes
Total cooking time: 30 minutes
Makes 6

40 g (1⅓ oz) butter
2 cloves garlic, crushed
500 g (1 lb) button mushrooms, sliced
1 small red pepper (capsicum), finely chopped
⅔ cup (160 g/5¼ oz) sour cream
3 teaspoons seeded mustard
½ cup (65 g/2¼ oz) finely grated Gruyère or Cheddar cheese
6 sheets ready-rolled puff pastry
½ cup (65 g/2¼ oz) finely grated Gruyère or Cheddar cheese, extra
1 egg, lightly beaten

1 Preheat the oven to moderately hot 190°C (375°F/Gas 5). Lightly grease two oven trays with melted butter or oil. Heat the butter in a large pan. Add the garlic and mushrooms, cook over medium heat, stirring occasionally, until mushrooms are tender and liquid has evaporated. Remove from heat and cool. Stir in red pepper.
2 Combine the sour cream, mustard and cheese in a small bowl and mix well. Cut twelve circles with a 14 cm (5½ inch) diameter from pastry. Spread cream mixture over six of the circles, leaving a 1 cm (½ inch) border. Top each with mushroom mixture.
3 Sprinkle each with two teaspoons of extra grated cheese. Brush around the outer edges with beaten egg; place reserved pastry rounds on top of the filling, sealing the edges with a fork. Brush the tops of the pastry with egg. Sprinkle the remaining cheese over the pastry. Place the pies on oven trays and bake for 20 minutes or until lightly browned and puffed.

VEGETABLE TEMPURA PATTIES

Preparation time: 25 minutes
Total cooking time: 15 minutes
Serves 4

Wasabi mayonnaise
½ cup (125 g/4 oz) whole-egg mayonnaise
2 teaspoons wasabi paste
1 teaspoon Japanese soy sauce
1 teaspoon sake

1 small zucchini (courgette), grated
1 small potato, julienned
½ carrot, julienned
½ onion, thinly sliced
100 g (3½ oz) orange sweet potato, grated
4 spring onions, green part included, cut into 2 cm (¾ inch) lengths
4 nori sheets, shredded
2 cups (250 g/8 oz) tempura flour, sifted
2 cups (500 ml/16 fl oz) chilled soda water
oil, for deep-frying
2 tablespoons shredded pickled ginger

1 To make the wasabi mayonnaise, combine all the ingredients in a small bowl. Set aside until ready to serve.
2 To make the patties, put the zucchini, potato, carrot, onion, orange sweet potato, spring onion and nori in a bowl. Toss.
3 Sift the tempura flour into a large bowl and make a well in the centre. Add the soda water and loosely mix together with chopsticks or a fork until just combined— the batter should still be lumpy. Add the vegetables and quickly fold through until just combined.
4 Fill a wok one-third full of oil and heat to 180°C (350°F), or until a cube of bread dropped into the oil browns in 15 seconds. Gently drop ¼ cup (60 ml/2 fl oz) of the vegetable mixture into the oil, making sure that the patty is not too compact, and cook for 1–2 minutes, or until golden and crisp. Drain on crumpled paper towels and season with sea salt. Repeat with the remaining mixture to make 11 more patties. Serve immediately, topped with the wasabi mayonnaise and the pickled ginger.

TOFU WITH CARROT AND GINGER SAUCE

Preparation time: 25 minutes +
  overnight refrigeration
Total cooking time: 30 minutes
Serves 6

2 x 300 g (10 oz) packets firm tofu,
  drained
½ cup (125 ml/4 fl oz) orange juice
1 tablespoon soft brown sugar
1 tablespoon soy sauce
2 tablespoons chopped fresh coriander
  leaves
2 cloves garlic, crushed
1 teaspoon grated fresh ginger
2–3 tablespoons oil
1 kg (2 lb) baby bok choy, quartered
  lengthways

Carrot and ginger sauce
300 g (10 oz) carrots, chopped
2 teaspoons grated fresh ginger
⅔ cup (170 ml/5½ fl oz) orange juice
½ cup (125 ml/4 fl oz) vegetable stock

1 Slice each block of tofu into six
lengthways. Place in a single layer in a flat
non-metallic dish. Mix the juice, sugar,
soy sauce, coriander, garlic and ginger in
a jug, then pour over the tofu. Cover and
refrigerate overnight, turning once.
2 Drain the tofu, reserving the marinade.
Heat the oil in a large frying pan and cook
the tofu in batches over high heat for
2–3 minutes each side, or until golden.
Remove and keep warm. Put the
marinade in a saucepan and bring to the
boil over medium heat. Reduce the heat
and gently simmer for 1 minute. Remove
from the heat and keep warm.

3 Heat a wok, add the bok choy and
1 tablespoon water and cook, covered,
over medium heat for 2–3 minutes, or
until tender. Remove and keep warm.
4 Put all the sauce ingredients in a
saucepan, bring to the boil, then reduce
the heat and simmer, covered, for
5–6 minutes, or until the carrot is tender.
Transfer to a food processor and blend
until smooth.
5 To serve, divide the bok choy among six
plates. Top with some of the carrot and
ginger sauce, then the warm tofu and
drizzle with a little of the marinade before
serving.

ALMOND SESAME SOYA BURGERS

Preparation time: 20 minutes
Total cooking time: 3 hours 40 minutes +
  overnight soaking
Makes 10

1 cup (60 g/2 oz) dried soya beans
125 g (4 oz) smoked almonds
1 onion, chopped
1 carrot, grated
1 tablespoon tamari
3 tablespoons rolled oats
1 egg, lightly beaten
3 tablespoons chickpea (besan) flour
1 teaspoon ground cumin
1 teaspoon ground coriander
3 tablespoons sesame seeds
oil, for shallow-frying

1 Soak the soya beans in cold water
overnight; rinse and drain well.
2 Place the soya beans in a large heavy-
based pan, cover with water and bring to
the boil. Reduce the heat and simmer for
3 hours or until the beans are tender.
Rinse and drain.
3 Place the soya beans, almonds, onion,
carrot and tamari into a food processor
and process for 2 minutes or until roughly
chopped. Transfer the mixture to a bowl;
add oats, egg, chickpea flour, cumin,
coriander and sesame seeds; stir to
combine.
4 Shape mixture into 10 even-sized
patties. Heat the oil in a large frying pan
and cook the patties over medium heat
for 5 minutes on each side, or until golden
and heated through. Burgers are
delicious served with a tangy plum and
yoghurt sauce, or with a salad and maybe
a toasted bun.

NOTE: Canned soya beans may be used
instead of dried ones if you are short of
time (use 2½ cups/160 g/5¼ oz). Tamari is
a rich soy sauce which, unlike regular soy
sauce, is brewed without wheat.

HARVEST PIE

Preparation time: 40 minutes +
  refrigeration
Total cooking time: 1 hour
Serves 6

175 g (5⅔ oz) butter
2 cups (250 g/8 oz) plain flour
¼ cup (60 ml/2 fl oz) iced water
1 tablespoon oil
1 onion, finely chopped
1 small red pepper (capsicum), chopped
1 small green pepper (capsicum), chopped
150 g (4¾ oz) pumpkin, chopped
1 small potato, chopped
100 g (3⅓ oz) broccoli, cut into small
  florets
1 carrot, chopped
¼ cup (30 g/1 oz) plain flour
1 cup (250 ml/8 fl oz) milk
2 egg yolks
½ cup (60 g/2 oz) grated Cheddar cheese
1 egg, lightly beaten, for glazing

1 Preheat the oven to moderate 180°C
(350°F/Gas 4). Chop 125 g (4 oz) of the
butter. Sift the flour into a large bowl and
add the chopped butter. Using your
fingertips, rub the butter into the flour
until it is fine and crumbly. Add almost all
the water and use a knife to mix to a firm
dough, adding more water if necessary.
Turn onto a lightly floured surface and
press together until smooth.
2 Divide the dough in half, roll out one
portion and line a deep 21 cm (8½ inch)
fluted flan tin. Refrigerate for 20 minutes.
Roll the remaining pastry out to a 25 cm
(10 inch) diameter circle. Cut into strips
and lay half of them on a sheet of baking
paper, leaving a 1 cm (½ inch) gap
between each strip. Interweave the
remaining strips to form a lattice pattern.
Cover with plastic wrap and refrigerate,
keeping flat, until firm.

3 Cut a sheet of greaseproof paper to
cover the pastry-lined tin. Spread a layer
of dried beans or rice over the paper.
Bake for 10 minutes, remove from oven
and discard paper and beans or rice.
Bake for another 10 minutes or until
lightly golden; allow to cool.
4 Heat the oil in a frying pan. Add the
onion and cook for 2 minutes or until soft.
Add the peppers and cook, stirring, for
another 3 minutes. Steam or boil
remaining vegetables until just tender;
drain and cool. Mix the onion, peppers
and the other vegetables in a large bowl.
5 Heat the remaining butter in a small
pan. Add the flour and cook, stirring, for
2 minutes. Add the milk gradually,
stirring until smooth between each
addition. Stir constantly over medium
heat until the mixture boils and thickens.
Boil for 1 minute and then remove from
the heat. Add the egg yolks and cheese
and stir until smooth. Pour the sauce over
the vegetables and stir to combine. Pour
the mixture into the pastry case and
brush the edges with egg. Using baking
paper to lift, invert the pastry lattice over
the vegetables, trim the edges and brush
with a little beaten egg, sealing to the
cooked pastry. Brush the top with egg and
bake for 30 minutes or until golden
brown.

CREAMY ASPARAGUS LINGUINE

Preparation time: 15 minutes
Total cooking time: 15 minutes
Serves 4

200 g (6½ oz) fresh full-fat ricotta cheese
1 cup (250 ml/8 fl oz) cream
¾ cup (75 g/2½ oz) freshly grated
  Parmesan
freshly ground nutmeg, to taste
500 g (1 lb) linguine
500 g (1 lb) fresh asparagus spears, cut
  into short lengths
½ cup (45 g/1½ oz) toasted flaked
  almonds, for serving

1 Put the ricotta in a bowl and stir until
smooth. Stir in the cream, Parmesan and
nutmeg and season with salt and freshly
ground black pepper, to taste.
2 Cook the linguine in a large pan of
rapidly boiling salted water until not quite
tender. Add the asparagus to the pan and
cook for another 3 minutes.
3 Drain the pasta and asparagus,
reserving 2 tablespoons of the cooking
water. Return the pasta and asparagus to
the pan.
4 Add the reserved cooking water to the
ricotta mixture, stirring well to combine.
Spoon the mixture over the pasta and toss
gently. Serve sprinkled with the toasted
almonds.

NOTE: To toast flaked almonds, you can
heat them under a moderately hot grill
for about 2 minutes. Stir them
occasionally and be careful to avoid
burning them.

CARAMELIZED ONION AND BLUE CHEESE RISSONI

Preparation time: 20 minutes
Total cooking time: 35 minutes
Serves 4

500 g (1 lb) rissoni
30 g (1 oz) butter
3 tablespoons olive oil
4 onions, sliced
185 g (6 oz) blue cheese
100 g (3½ oz) mascarpone
2 cups (130 g/4½ oz) shredded English
  spinach leaves

1 Cook the rissoni in rapidly boiling salted water until al dente. Drain well and return to the pan.
2 While the pasta is cooking, heat the butter and the olive oil in a large heavy-based frying pan. Add the sliced onion and cook over low heat for about 20–30 minutes, until golden brown and caramelized. Remove from the pan with a slotted spoon and drain on paper towels.
3 Mix the blue cheese, mascarpone and onion in a bowl.
4 Add the cheese and onion mixture, as well as the spinach, to the rissoni and toss through. Season, to taste, with salt and freshly ground black pepper before serving.

VEGETABLE KORMA

Preparation time: 20 minutes
Total cooking time: 50 minutes
Serves 4–6

2 tablespoons oil
2 tablespoons ready-made green masala
  paste
1 teaspoon chilli powder
1 tablespoon grated fresh ginger
1 medium onion, chopped
300 g (9⅔ oz) cauliflower, cut into florets
300 g (9⅔ oz) pumpkin, cut into large
  pieces
3 slender eggplants (aubergines), cut
  into large pieces
2 carrots, cut into large pieces
3 tomatoes, peeled, seeded and chopped
1½ cups (375 ml/12 fl oz) vegetable stock
125 g (4 oz) green beans, chopped

1 Heat the oil in a large heavy-based pan; add the masala paste and cook over medium heat for 2 minutes or until the oil begins to separate from the paste.
2 Add the chilli powder, ginger and onion, and cook for 3 minutes or until the onion softens.
3 Add the cauliflower, pumpkin, eggplant and carrot and stir to coat in the paste mixture. Stir in the tomatoes and stock and bring to the boil, then reduce the heat and simmer, uncovered, for 30 minutes.
4 Add the beans and cook for 10 minutes or until the vegetables are tender. Serve with rice.

TOFU WITH CHILLI JAM AND CASHEWS

Preparation time: 20 minutes
Total cooking time: 30 minutes
Serves 4

⅓ cup (80 ml/2¾ fl oz) peanut oil
12 red Asian shallots, chopped
8 cloves garlic, chopped
8 fresh long red chillies, chopped
2 red peppers (capsicums), chopped
1 tablespoon tamarind purée
1 tablespoon soy sauce
100 g (3½ oz) palm sugar, grated
2 tablespoons kecap manis
1 tablespoon peanut oil
6 spring onions, cut into 3 cm (1¼ inch)
  lengths
750 g (1½ lb) silken firm tofu, cut into
  3 cm (1¼ inch) cubes
¾ cup (25 g/¾ oz) fresh Thai basil
⅔ cup (100 g/3½ oz) roasted salted
  cashews

1 To make the chilli jam, heat half the oil in a frying pan. Add the shallots and garlic and cook over medium heat for 2 minutes. Transfer to a food processor, add the chilli and red pepper and process until smooth. Heat the remaining oil in the pan, add the shallot mixture and cook over medium heat for 2 minutes. Stir in the tamarind, soy sauce and sugar and cook for 20 minutes.
2 To make the stir-fry sauce, combine 2–3 tablespoons of the chilli jam with the kecap manis in a small bowl or jug.
3 Heat the oil in a non-stick wok over high heat and swirl to coat the side of the wok. Add the spring onion and cook for 30 seconds. Remove. Add the tofu, stir-fry for 1 minute, then add the stir-fry sauce. Cook for 3 minutes, or until the tofu is coated and heated through. Return the spring onion to the wok, add the basil and cashews and cook until the basil has wilted.

LENTIL AND BURGHUL FRITTERS WITH YOGHURT SAUCE

Preparation time: 20 minutes +
    1 hour 30 minutes standing
Total cooking time: 1 hour
Makes 35

¾ cup (140 g/4½ oz) brown lentils, rinsed
½ cup (90 g/3 oz) burghul
⅓ cup (80 ml/2¾ fl oz) olive oil
1 onion, finely chopped
2 cloves garlic, finely chopped
3 teaspoons ground cumin
2 teaspoons ground coriander
3 tablespoons finely chopped fresh mint
4 eggs, lightly beaten
½ cup (60 g/2 oz) plain flour
1 teaspoon sea salt

Yoghurt sauce
1 small Lebanese cucumber, peeled
1 cup (250 g/8 oz) Greek-style natural
    yoghurt
1–2 cloves garlic, crushed

1 Place the lentils in a saucepan with
2½ cups (625 ml/20 fl oz) water. Bring to
the boil over high heat, then reduce the
heat and simmer for 30 minutes, or until
tender. Remove from the heat and top up
with enough water to just cover the
lentils. Pour in the burghul, cover and
leave to stand for 1½ hours, or until the
burghul has expanded.

2 For the yoghurt sauce, halve the
cucumber lengthways, remove the seeds
with a teaspoon and discard. Grate the
flesh and mix in a bowl with the yoghurt
and garlic.
3 Heat half the oil in a large frying pan
over medium heat, add the onion and
garlic and cook for 5 minutes, or until
soft. Stir in the cumin and coriander. Add
the onion mixture, mint, eggs, flour and
sea salt to the lentil mixture and mix well.
The mixture should hold together enough
to drop spoonfuls into the frying pan. If
the mixture is too wet, add flour to bind.
4 Heat the remaining oil over medium
heat in the cleaned frying pan. Drop
heaped tablespoons of mixture into the
pan (the fritters should be about 5 cm/
2 inches in diameter) and cook for
3 minutes each side, or until browned.
Drain on crumpled paper towels, season
with salt and serve with the yoghurt
sauce.

SNOW PEAS (MANGE TOUT) WITH RED PEPPER (CAPSICUM)

Preparation time: 15–20 minutes
Total cooking time: 7 minutes
Serves 4

1 large onion, peeled
185 g (6 oz) snow peas (mange tout)
1 tablespoon oil
1 tablespoon grated fresh ginger
1 red pepper (capsicum), cut into strips
1 small clove garlic, crushed
1 tablespoon oyster sauce (optional)
1 teaspoon sugar
pinch salt
1 tablespoon water

1 Cut the onion in half and slice thinly in
rings. Remove ends and threads from the
snow peas.
2 Heat the oil in a frying pan or wok. Add
the onion, ginger and red pepper and stir-
fry over high heat 4–5 minutes or until the
vegetables are just tender. Add the garlic
and snow peas and stir-fry for 2 minutes,
or until the snow peas become bright
green.
3 Add the oyster sauce, sugar, salt and
water to the pan and mix through. Serve
immediately.

MUSHROOMS

A VALUABLE SOURCE OF VITAMINS AND FIBRE, THESE CULTIVATED FUNGI ARE ADAPTABLE VEGETABLES, FITTING IN PERFECTLY WITH BOTH LIGHT MODERN DISHES AND HEAVIER RUSTIC FARE, WITH A FLAVOUR ALL THEIR OWN.

PESTO-FILLED MUSHROOMS

Place 2 cups (60 g/2 oz) of fresh basil leaves, 3 crushed cloves of garlic, ½ cup (80 g/2⅔ oz) of toasted pine nuts and ½ cup (50 g/1⅔ oz) of grated Parmesan cheese in a food processor and process until smooth. Gradually add ⅓ cup (80 ml/2¾ fl oz) of olive oil and process until all the ingredients are well combined. Remove the stalks from 14 small mushrooms (small enough for finger food) and brush the mushrooms lightly with macadamia nut oil. Cook, fan-side down, on a preheated char-grill or barbecue until the mushrooms are lightly browned. Turn the mushrooms over and spoon a level tablespoonful of the prepared pesto on the top of each mushroom. Serve immediately. Makes 14 filled mushrooms.

GOLDEN MUSHROOM TART

Preheat oven to moderately hot 200°C (400°F/Gas 6). Place a sheet of puff pastry on a non-stick baking tray. Heat 2 tablespoons of oil in a frying pan, add 2 thinly sliced onions and 1 tablespoon of red wine vinegar. Cook 10 minutes or until onions have caramelised. Remove from pan, cool slightly on paper towels. Add 60 g (2 oz) butter and 350 g (11¼ oz) assorted mushrooms to pan; cook for 5 minutes or until tender. Drain off any excess liquid and cool on paper towels. Season, to taste, with salt and pepper. Cook puff pastry for 10 minutes, then very carefully and quickly spread onions over puff pastry base, leaving a 2 cm (¾ inch) border. Top with mushrooms and sprinkle with fresh marjoram leaves and ¼ cup (25 g/¾ oz) grated Parmesan. Cook for another 10 minutes or until golden. Serves 4.

MUSHROOM YOGHURT DIP

Heat 1 tablespoon of oil in a frying pan, add 2 crushed cloves of garlic and 4 finely chopped spring onions. Cook for 3 minutes. Add 220 g (7 oz) of chopped button mushrooms and cook for 5 minutes or until golden. Remove from heat and drain off any excess liquid. Transfer mixture to a bowl, stir in 200 g (6½ oz) thick natural yoghurt, 1 teaspoon ground cumin and 2 tablespoons of chopped fresh lemon thyme. Use as a dip with crudités, grissini sticks, corn chips or sliced French bread.

MARINATED MUSHROOMS

Place 1 cup (250 ml/8 fl oz) apple cider vinegar, ½ cup (125 ml/4 fl oz) orange juice, 1 tablespoon coriander seeds, 2 sprigs rosemary and 1 bay leaf in a pan, bring to boil. Add 500 g (1 lb) button mushrooms and simmer for 3 minutes. Remove and spoon into a sterilized jar. Boil liquid until reduced by half. Discard rosemary sprigs and bay leaf and replace with fresh ones. Stir in ⅓ cup (80 ml/ 2¾ fl oz) of olive oil. Pour liquid over mushrooms and seal with a layer of olive oil. Will keep, refrigerated, for one month.

WILD MUSHROOM STUFFING

Heat 60 g (2 oz) butter in a frying pan, add 1 finely chopped onion and cook for 3 minutes or until golden. Add 220 g (7 oz) of mixed mushrooms (oyster, Swiss brown, enoki, button) and cook for 5 minutes. Transfer the mixture to a bowl, add 2 cups (60 g/2 oz) of croutons, 3 tablespoons of chopped fresh herbs, ½ cup (95 g/3¼ oz) cooked brown rice, ¼ cup (60 ml/2 fl oz) milk and 1 lightly beaten egg; mix well. Use the mixture to stuff cooked potatoes, eggplants (aubergines) and peppers (capsicums), or fill omelettes and crepes.

CLOCKWISE, FROM TOP LEFT: Marinated Mushrooms; Mushroom Yoghurt Dip; Pesto-filled Mushrooms; Golden Mushroom Tart; Wild Mushroom Stuffing

BLUE CHEESE AND BROCCOLI WITH RIGATONI

Preparation time: 15 minutes
Total cooking time: 15 minutes
Serves 4

500 g (1 lb) rigatoni
500 g (1 lb) broccoli
1 tablespoon vegetable oil
1 onion, sliced
½ cup (125 ml/4 fl oz) dry white wine
1 cup (250 ml/8 fl oz) cream
½ teaspoon spicy paprika
150 g (5 oz) blue Brie, chopped into small
    pieces
2 tablespoons flaked almonds, toasted

1 Cook the rigatoni in a large pan of
rapidly boiling salted water until al dente.
Drain and return to the pan.
2 Cut the broccoli into florets, steam or
microwave them for 2–3 minutes, until
tender, and drain well.
3 Heat the oil in a large pan and fry the
onion until soft. Add the wine and cream
and simmer for 4–5 minutes, until
reduced and thickened slightly. Stir in the
paprika and cheese, and season with salt
and pepper, to taste.
4 Add the broccoli and sauce to the pasta
and gently toss over low heat until well
mixed and heated through. Serve
sprinkled with the toasted, flaked
almonds.

NOTE: You can use a stronger blue
cheese, such as gorgonzola, if you like.

LEMON AND HERB RISOTTO WITH FRIED MUSHROOMS

Preparation time: 30 minutes
Total cooking time: 50 minutes
Serves 4

1 litre (32 fl oz) vegetable stock
pinch of saffron threads
2 tablespoons olive oil
2 leeks (white part only), thinly sliced
2 garlic cloves, crushed
2 cups (440 g/14 oz) risotto rice
2–3 teaspoons finely grated lemon zest
2–3 tablespoons lemon juice
2 tablespoons chopped flat-leaf (Italian)
    parsley
2 tablespoons snipped chives
2 tablespoons chopped oregano
¾ cup (75 g/2½ oz) freshly grated
    Parmesan cheese
100 g (3½ oz) mascarpone cheese
30 g (1 oz) butter
1 tablespoon virgin olive oil
200 g (6½ oz) small flat mushrooms, cut
    into thick slices
1 tablespoon balsamic vinegar

1 Pour the stock into a saucepan and add
the saffron threads. Bring to the boil, then
reduce the heat, cover and keep at a low
simmer.
2 Heat the olive oil in a large saucepan
over medium heat. Add the leek, cook for
5 minutes, then add the garlic and cook
for a further 5 minutes, or until golden.
Add the rice and stir until well coated.
Add half the lemon zest and half the juice,
then add ½ cup (125 ml/4 fl oz) of the hot
stock. Stir constantly over medium heat
until all the liquid has been absorbed.
Continue adding more liquid, ½ cup
(125 ml/4 fl oz) at a time until all the liquid
is absorbed and the rice is tender and
creamy; this will take around 25–30 minutes.
(You may not need to use all the stock, or
you may need a little extra—every risotto
will be slightly different.

3 Remove the pan from the heat. Stir in
the herbs, Parmesan, mascarpone and
the remaining lemon zest and lemon
juice, then cover and keep warm.
4 To cook the mushrooms, melt the
butter and virgin olive oil in a large frying
pan, add the mushroom slices and
vinegar and cook, stirring, over high heat
for 5–7 minutes, or until the mushrooms
are tender and all the liquid has been
absorbed.
5 Serve the risotto in large bowls topped
with the mushrooms. Garnish with sprigs
of fresh herbs, if desired.

ROCKET, BASIL AND LEEK QUICHE

Preparation time: 30 minutes +
  refrigeration
Total cooking time: 1 hour 10 minutes
Makes one 23 cm (9 inch) quiche

150 g (4¾ oz) rocket, stalks removed
1½ cups (185 g/6 oz) plain flour
125 g (4 oz) butter, chopped
1–2 tablespoons water
1 tablespoon oil
1 large leek, white part only, thinly sliced
2 cloves garlic, crushed
2 eggs
½ cup (125 ml/4 fl oz) milk
½ cup (125 ml/4 fl oz) cream

1 Preheat oven to hot 210°C (415°F/
Gas 6–7). Wash the rocket and shake off
excess water; finely slice rocket leaves.
2 Sift the flour into a bowl. Using your
fingertips, rub the butter into the flour for
2 minutes, or until the mixture is fine and
crumbly. Add water and mix to a soft dough.
Turn onto a lightly floured surface and knead
for 10 seconds or until smooth. Refrigerate,
covered in plastic wrap, for 30 minutes.
3 Roll the pastry, between 2 sheets of
plastic wrap, to cover the base and side of
a shallow 23 cm (9 inch) flan tin. Cover the
pastry-lined tin with a sheet of baking
paper. Spread dried beans or rice over the
paper. Bake for 10 minutes and then
remove from the oven and discard the
beans or rice. Return pastry to the oven for
5 minutes or until lightly golden. Reduce
heat to moderate 180°C (350°F/Gas 4).
4 Heat the oil in a frying pan, add the leek
and garlic and stir over low heat for
5 minutes or until the leek is soft. Add the
rocket and stir over heat for 1 minute.
Remove from heat and allow to cool.
Spread over base of pastry shell. Combine
eggs, milk and cream in a bowl; whisk
until smooth. Pour into pastry shell. Bake
at 180°C (350°F/Gas 4) for 50 minutes, or
until set and golden. Serve topped with
basil leaves and shaved Parmesan cheese.

CORN PANCAKES
(TOD MAN KAOPOT)

Preparation time: 15 minutes +
  1 hour refrigeration
Total cooking time: 25 minutes
Makes 12

6 fresh corn cobs or 325 g (11 oz) can corn
  kernels, drained
4 spring onions, finely chopped
1 clove garlic, crushed
1 teaspoon Asian curry powder
2 tablespoons self-raising flour
1 teaspoon soy sauce
1 egg
oil, for deep-frying
sweet chilli sauce, to serve (optional)

1 If using fresh corn, remove the kernels
with a sharp knife. Combine the corn,
spring onion, garlic, curry powder, flour,
soy sauce and egg, mashing lightly with a
potato masher. Cover with plastic wrap
and chill for 1 hour.
2 Fill a wok one-third full of oil and heat
to 180°C (350°F), or until a cube of bread
browns in 15 seconds. Drop tablespoons
of the corn mixture into the wok—avoid
overcrowding. Cook for 2–3 minutes, on
each side, or until golden brown—turn
carefully to prevent the pancakes
breaking. Remove from the wok and drain
on crumpled paper towels. Repeat with
the remaining mixture. Serve with sweet
chilli sauce, if desired.

THAI COCONUT VEGETABLES

Preparation time: 15–20 minutes
Total cooking time: 15 minutes
Serves 4–6

1 tablespoon oil
2 small onions, peeled, cut in wedges
1 teaspoon ground cumin
150 g (4¾ oz) cauliflower florets
1 medium red pepper (capsicum),
  chopped
2 celery sticks, sliced diagonally
1½ cups (185 g/6 oz) grated pumpkin
1 cup (250 ml/8 fl oz) coconut milk
1 cup (250 ml/8 fl oz) vegetable stock
1 tablespoon sweet chilli sauce
150 g (4¾ oz) green beans
1 tablespoon finely chopped fresh
  coriander

1 Heat oil in a frying pan or wok. Add
onion and cumin and stir-fry over medium
heat for 2 minutes, or until the onion is
golden.
2 Add cauliflower and stir-fry over high
heat for 2 minutes. Add red pepper, celery
and pumpkin and stir-fry over high heat
for 2 minutes, or until vegetables have
begun to soften.
3 Add coconut milk, stock and chilli sauce
and bring to boil. Reduce heat and cook,
uncovered, for 8 minutes, or until the
vegetables are almost tender. Trim tops
and tails from beans and cut beans in
half. Add to pan with coriander, cook
another 2 minutes or until beans are just
tender. Serve with steamed rice.

BLUE CHEESE AND ONION FLAN

Preparation time: 40 minutes +
  30 minutes refrigeration
Total cooking time: 1 hour 40 minutes
Serves 8

2 tablespoons olive oil
1 kg (2 lb) red onions, very thinly sliced
1 teaspoon soft brown sugar
1½ cups (185 g/6 oz) plain flour
100 g (3½ oz) cold butter, cubed
¾ cup (185 ml/6 fl oz) cream
3 eggs
100 g (3½ oz) blue cheese, crumbled
1 teaspoon chopped fresh thyme leaves

1 Heat the oil in a heavy-based frying pan over low heat and cook the onion and sugar, stirring, for 45 minutes until caramelized.
2 Sift the flour into a large bowl and rub in the butter with your fingertips until the mixture resembles fine breadcrumbs. Make a well in the centre and add 3–4 tablespoons cold water. Mix with a flat-bladed knife, using a cutting action until the mixture comes together in beads. Gently gather together and lift onto a lightly floured work surface. Press into a ball, wrap in plastic wrap and refrigerate for 30 minutes.
3 Preheat the oven to 180°C (350°F/Gas 4). Roll out the pastry on a lightly floured surface to fit a lightly greased 22 cm (8¾ inch) round loose-based flan tin. Invert the pastry over the tin and press in with a small ball of pastry, allowing excess to hang over the side. Trim any excess pastry, then chill for 10 minutes. Line the pastry shell with baking paper and fill with baking beads or uncooked rice. Bake on a baking tray for 10 minutes. Remove the beads and paper, then bake for 10 minutes, or until lightly golden and dry.
4 Cool, then gently spread the onion over the base of the pastry. Whisk the cream in a bowl with the eggs, blue cheese, thyme and some pepper. Pour over the onion and bake for 35 minutes, or until firm.

CARROT PESTO BAKE

Preparation time: 45 minutes +
  30 minutes standing
Total cooking time: 55 minutes
Serves 4

50 g (1⅔ oz) butter
½ cup (60 g/2 oz) plain flour
3 cups (750 ml/24 fl oz) milk
⅔ cup (160 g/5¼ oz) light sour cream
1 teaspoon cracked black pepper
100 g (3⅓ oz) Cheddar cheese, grated
4 eggs, lightly beaten
2 tablespoons ready-made pesto
750 g (1½ lb) carrots, peeled and grated
250 g (8 oz) instant lasagne sheets
50 g (1⅔ oz) Cheddar cheese, grated, extra

1 Brush a 30 x 20 cm (12 x 8 inch) ovenproof baking dish with melted butter or oil. Heat the butter in a large pan; add the flour. Stir over low heat until mixture is lightly golden and bubbling. Add combined milk, sour cream and pepper gradually to pan, stirring until mixture is smooth between each addition. Stir constantly over medium heat for 5 minutes, or until the mixture boils and thickens. Boil for another minute; remove from heat. Stir in cheese; cool slightly. Gradually add beaten eggs, stirring constantly.
2 Pour a third of the sauce into another bowl to make the topping and set aside. Add the pesto and grated carrot to the remaining sauce, stirring to combine.
3 Preheat the oven to slow 150°C (300°F/Gas 2). Beginning with one-third of the carrot mixture, alternate layers of carrot mixture with sheets of lasagne in prepared dish. Use three layers of each, finishing with lasagne sheets. Spread reserved sauce evenly over the top. Sprinkle with extra cheese. Set aside for 15 minutes before cooking to allow the pasta to soften. Bake for 40 minutes or until sauce has set and is golden.
4 Remove from the oven; cover and set aside for 15 minutes prior to serving—this will ensure that it will slice easily. Serve.

DEEP-FRIED SPICED TOFU

Preparation time: 10 minutes
Total cooking time: 10 minutes
Serves 4

375 g (12 oz) firm tofu
½ cup (90 g/3 oz) rice flour
2 teaspoons ground coriander
1 teaspoon ground cardamom
1 clove garlic, crushed
½ cup (125 ml/4 fl oz) water
oil, for deep-frying

1 Drain the tofu and cut it into 1 cm (½ inch) thick slices.
2 Combine the flour, coriander, cardamom and garlic in a bowl; add the water and stir until smooth.
3 Heat the oil in a large pan. Dip the tofu slices into the spice mixture and coat thickly. Place the tofu slices into the oil, 3 at a time, and cook over medium heat for about 2 minutes, or until crisp and golden brown. Drain on paper towels.

NOTE: Serve the tofu with stir-fried vegetables and any sauce of your choice; for example, peanut, chilli or soy sauce—the tofu soaks up the flavours.

CHILLI AND CORIANDER FRITTATA

Preparation time: 25 minutes
Total cooking time: 30 minutes
Serves 6

3 medium potatoes, peeled and cut into
   small cubes
2 medium banana chillies
2 tablespoons olive oil
1 medium onion, finely chopped
1 small red chilli, finely chopped
1 tablespoon coriander leaves
5 eggs, lightly beaten

1 Cook potatoes in a large pan of boiling
water until just tender; drain well.
Remove seeds from banana chillies and
slice the flesh. Heat half the oil in a non-
stick frying pan. Cook the banana chillies
over medium heat for 2 minutes or until
softened. Remove from pan and set aside.
Heat the remaining oil in pan. Add the
onion and small red chilli and cook over
medium heat for 3 minutes or until soft.
2 Add the potato and toss to combine.
Remove from pan and set aside. Return
half the banana chillies to the pan and
sprinkle with coriander leaves. Layer half
the potato mixture, remaining banana
chillies, and remaining potato mixture.
3 Pour the eggs into the pan, swirling to
distribute evenly. Cook over medium-low
heat for 8 minutes until the eggs are
almost cooked through, then place under
a hot grill for 5 minutes to cook the top.
Invert the frittata onto a plate and cut into
wedges. Serve hot or cold, garnished with
fresh herbs.

GOAT'S CHEESE GALETTE

Preparation time: 20 minutes +
   refrigeration
Total cooking time: 1 hour 15 minutes
Serves 6

Pastry
1 cup (125 g/4 oz) plain flour
¼ cup (60 ml/2 fl oz) olive oil
3–4 tablespoons chilled water

Filling
1 tablespoon olive oil
2 onions, thinly sliced
1 teaspoon fresh thyme leaves
125 g (4 oz) ricotta
100 g (3½ oz) goat's cheese
2 tablespoons pitted Niçoise olives
1 egg, lightly beaten
¼ cup (60 ml/2 fl oz) cream

1 For the pastry, sift the flour and a pinch
of salt into a large bowl and make a well.
Add the olive oil and mix with a flat-
bladed knife until crumbly. Gradually add
the water until the mixture comes
together. Remove and pat together to
form a disc. Refrigerate for 30 minutes.
2 For the filling, heat the olive oil in a
frying pan. Add the onion, cover and cook
over low heat for 30 minutes. Season and
stir in half the thyme. Cool slightly.
3 Preheat the oven to moderate 180°C
(350°F/Gas 4). Lightly flour the work
bench and roll out the pastry to a 30 cm
(12 inch) circle. Evenly spread the onion
over the pastry leaving a 2 cm (¾ inch)
border. Sprinkle the ricotta and the goat's
cheese evenly over the onion. Place the
olives over the cheeses, then sprinkle
with the remaining thyme. Fold the pastry
border in to the edge of the filling, gently
pleating as you go.
4 Combine the egg and cream in a small
jug, then carefully pour over the filling.
Bake on a heated baking tray on the lower
half of the oven for 45 minutes, or until
the pastry is golden. Serve warm or at
room temperature.

DRY POTATO AND PEA CURRY

Preparation time: 15 minutes
Total cooking time: 20–25 minutes
Serves 4

750 g (1½ lb) potatoes
2 teaspoons brown mustard seeds
2 tablespoons ghee or oil
2 medium onions, sliced
2 cloves garlic, crushed
2 teaspoons grated fresh ginger
1 teaspoon ground turmeric
½ teaspoon chilli powder
1 teaspoon ground cumin
1 teaspoon garam masala
½ cup (125 ml/4 fl oz) water
⅔ cup (100 g/3⅓ oz) peas
2 tablespoons chopped fresh mint

1 Peel the potatoes and cut them into
small cubes.
2 Place the mustard seeds in a large dry
pan and cook over medium heat until the
seeds start to pop. Add the ghee, onion,
garlic and ginger, and cook, stirring, until
the onion is soft.
3 Add the turmeric, chilli powder, cumin,
garam masala and potato; stir until the
potato is coated. Add the water, cover and
simmer for about 15 to 20 minutes, or
until the potato is just tender, stirring
occasionally.
4 Add the peas and stir until combined;
season with salt and pepper to taste.
Simmer, covered, for a further 3 to 5 minutes,
or until the potato is cooked through and
the liquid is absorbed. Stir in the mint and
serve with rice.

EGGPLANT (AUBERGINE), TOMATO AND GOAT'S CHEESE STACKS

Preparation time: 15 minutes
Total cooking time: 10 minutes
Serves 4

½ cup (125 ml/4 fl oz) olive oil
2 large cloves garlic, crushed
2 small eggplants (aubergines)
2 ripe tomatoes
150 g (5 oz) goat's cheese
8 large fresh basil leaves
small rocket leaves, to garnish
extra virgin olive oil, to drizzle

Dressing
135 g (4½ oz) sun-dried tomatoes in oil
1 clove garlic, crushed
1 tablespoon white wine vinegar
¼ cup (60 g/2 oz) whole-egg mayonnaise

1 Mix the oil and garlic in a bowl and set aside. Cut each eggplant into six 1 cm (½ inch) slices and each tomato into four 1 cm (½ inch) slices. Use a sharp knife to cut the cheese into eight 1 cm (½ inch) slices.
2 Brush both sides of the eggplant slices using half the oil. Heat a frying pan and cook the eggplant in batches over high heat for 3–4 minutes each side, or until golden. Remove and keep warm. Brush both sides of the tomatoes using the remaining oil and cook for 1 minute each side, or until sealed and warmed through.
3 For the dressing, drain the sun-dried tomatoes, reserving 1 tablespoon oil. Blend the tomatoes, oil and garlic in a food processor until smooth. Add the vinegar and process until combined. Stir in the mayonnaise and season, to taste.
4 Place an eggplant slice on each plate. Top each with a slice of tomato, then a basil leaf and a slice of cheese. Repeat with the remaining ingredients to give two layers, finishing with a third piece of eggplant. Add a dollop of dressing and arrange the rocket around each stack. Drizzle with a little of the extra virgin olive oil.

MEXICAN POLENTA (CORNMEAL) PANCAKES WITH AVOCADO

Preparation time: 30 minutes +
  20 minutes refrigeration
Total cooking time: 20 minutes
Serves 4–6

⅓ cup (50 g/1⅔ oz) yellow polenta
  (cornmeal)
½ cup (60 g/2 oz) plain flour
¼ teaspoon baking powder
¼ teaspoon salt
1 teaspoon sugar
1 cup (250 ml/8 fl oz) buttermilk
2 eggs
30 g (1 oz) butter, melted
vegetable oil
⅔ cup (160 g/5¼ oz) sour cream, for serving

Avocado Filling
1 large ripe avocado
8 spring onions, finely chopped
2 ripe tomatoes, seeded and finely chopped
1 teaspoon chilli sauce, or to taste
2 teaspoons lemon juice
¼–½ teaspoon salt
pepper

1 Sift polenta, flour, baking powder, salt and sugar into a bowl. Make a well in the centre. Place buttermilk, eggs and butter in a jug; beat to combine. Add to dry ingredients. Beat until liquid is incorporated and batter is free of lumps. Set aside, covered with plastic wrap, 20 minutes.

2 To make Avocado Filling: Cut the avocado in half lengthways, remove the seed and place the flesh in a bowl. Mash the avocado flesh with a fork. Add half the spring onions. Stir in the tomatoes, chilli sauce, lemon juice, salt and pepper. Mix well and chill for 20 minutes.
3 Brush a small frying pan with oil. When hot, pour in enough batter to thinly cover base of pan. Cook over medium heat until the underside is golden. Turn pancake over and cook the other side. Transfer to a plate; cover with a tea towel and keep warm. Repeat the process with remaining batter, greasing the pan when necessary. Spoon some avocado filling on one half of each pancake and fold the other half over. Serve with sour cream sprinkled with remaining spring onion.

MIXED VEGETABLES WITH TAMARIND

Preparation time: 25 minutes
Total cooking time: 30 minutes
Serves 4

250 g (8 oz) pumpkin
200 g (6½ oz) potatoes
100 g (3⅓ oz) beans
200 g (6½ oz) cabbage
100 g (3⅓ oz) English spinach leaves
2 cups (500 ml/16 fl oz) vegetable stock
½ cup (125 ml/4 fl oz) tamarind
   concentrate
2 cinnamon sticks
2 bay leaves
4 cloves garlic, finely chopped
10 red Asian shallots, very finely sliced
5 cm (2 inch) piece fresh ginger, grated
200 g (6½ oz) baby corn

1 Roughly chop the pumpkin. Cut the potatoes into thick slices. Top and tail the beans and cut them into short lengths. Shred the cabbage and spinach leaves.
2 Place the stock, tamarind, cinnamon, bay leaves, garlic, shallots and ginger in a large pan, and bring to the boil.
3 Add the pumpkin and potato and simmer for 5 minutes. Add the corn and beans and cook for another 5 minutes.
4 Add the cabbage and spinach and cook until just tender. Serve as an accompaniment to a main meal.

RIGATONI WITH PUMPKIN SAUCE

Preparation time: 15 minutes
Total cooking time: 25 minutes
Serves 6

500 g (1 lb) rigatoni or large penne
1 kg (2 lb) pumpkin
2 leeks
30 g (1 oz) butter
½ teaspoon ground nutmeg
1¼ cups (315 ml/10 fl oz) cream
3 tablespoons pine nuts, toasted

1 Cook the pasta in a large pan of rapidly boiling salted water until al dente. Drain and return to the pan.
2 Peel the pumpkin, remove and discard the seeds and cut the pumpkin into small cubes. Wash the leeks thoroughly to remove all traces of grit and then slice very finely. Heat the butter in a large pan over low heat. Add the sliced leek, cover the pan and cook, stirring occasionally, for 5 minutes.
3 Add the pumpkin and nutmeg, cover and cook for 8 minutes. Add the cream and 3 tablespoons of water to the pumpkin and bring the sauce to the boil. Cook, stirring occasionally, for 8 minutes, or until the pumpkin is tender.
4 Divide the pasta among serving bowls and top with sauce. Sprinkle with pine nuts and serve immediately.
note: Butternut or jap pumpkin will give the sweetest flavour to this sauce. To toast pine nuts, stir over low heat in a non-stick frying pan until lightly golden. Alternatively, spread on a baking tray and grill. Be sure to check frequently as they brown quickly.

CHILLI POLENTA CAKE

Preparation time: 25 minutes
Total cooking time: 25–30 minutes
Makes one 20 cm (8 inch) cake

1⅓ cups (165 g/5½ oz) plain flour
1½ teaspoons baking powder
1 teaspoon salt
1¼ cups (185 g/6 oz) polenta (cornmeal)
1 cup (125 g/4 oz) grated Cheddar cheese
1 cup (250 g/8 oz) natural yoghurt
½ cup (125 ml/4 fl oz) milk
2 eggs
½ cup (80 g/2⅔ oz) chopped red pepper
   (capsicum)
2 teaspoons chopped fresh chilli
60 g (2 oz) unsalted butter

1 Preheat oven to moderately hot 200°C (400°F/Gas 6). Sift flour, baking powder and salt into a large bowl. Mix in polenta and cheese. In a separate bowl, whisk yoghurt, milk, eggs, red pepper and chilli. Heat a 20 cm (8 inch) ovenproof frying pan, then melt butter. Stir butter into yoghurt mixture, then pour all liquid ingredients into dry ingredients. Mix well.
2 Pour into hot pan; cook in the oven for 25–30 minutes or until a skewer comes out clean.

MIXED VEGETABLES IN MILD CURRY SAUCE

Preparation time: 20 minutes
Total cooking time: 25 minutes
Serves 4

250 g (8 oz) peeled pumpkin
2 medium orange sweet potatoes
125 g (4 oz) yellow squash
125 g (4 oz) green beans
125 g (4 oz) cabbage
6 teaspoons oil
1 large onion, finely sliced
1 clove garlic, crushed
½ cup (100 g/3⅓ oz) peeled and chopped tomato
1 red chilli, chopped
3 strips lemon rind
4 kaffir lime leaves, dried or fresh
2 teaspoons grated palm sugar or soft brown sugar
1 teaspoon salt
1 tablespoon fish sauce
1⅔ cups (410 ml/13 fl oz) coconut milk
1 cup (250 ml/8 fl oz) chicken stock
2 teaspoons lemon juice

1 Cut the pumpkin into small wedges and the sweet potato into 2 cm (¾ inch) pieces. Quarter the squash; top and tail the beans, halving them if long; and cut the cabbage into 1 cm (½ inch) wide shreds.
2 Heat the oil in a medium pan; add the onion and garlic and cook over medium heat until soft and slightly golden.
3 Add the tomato, chilli, lemon rind, lime leaves, sugar, salt, fish sauce, coconut milk, stock and lemon juice; cook for 5 minutes until the flavour has intensified.
4 Add the sweet potato and pumpkin to the sauce and cook for 8 minutes. Add the beans, cabbage and squash and cook for 6 minutes. Serve with steamed rice.
Note: The sauce can be prepared a few hours ahead and reheated. Cook the vegetables just before serving.

CHINESE-STYLE STIR-FRIED VEGETABLES

Preparation time: 15 minutes
Total cooking time: 7 minutes
Serves 4

300 g (9⅔ oz) baby bok choy
100 g (3⅓ oz) snake beans
2 spring onions
150 g (4¾ oz) broccoli
1 medium red pepper (capsicum)
2 tablespoons oil
2 cloves garlic, crushed
2 teaspoons grated fresh ginger
1 tablespoon sesame oil
2 teaspoons soy sauce

1 Wash and trim the thick stalks from the bok choy, and then cut the leaves into wide strips. Slice the snake beans into 5 cm (2 inch) lengths and the spring onions diagonally. Cut the broccoli into small florets and the red pepper into diamonds about 2.5 cm (1 inch) wide.
2 Heat the oil in a large heavy-based frying pan or wok. Add the garlic and ginger and cook over medium heat for 30 seconds, stirring constantly. Add the beans, spring onions and broccoli, then stir-fry for 3 minutes.
3 Add the red peppers and stir-fry for another 2 minutes. Add the bok choy and stir-fry for 1 minute. Stir in the sesame oil and the soy sauce and toss until well combined with the vegetables. Transfer to a serving dish and serve immediately. Serve with steamed rice.

BAKED FETTUCINE

Preparation time: 20 minutes
Total cooking time: 25 minutes
Serves 4

500 g (1 lb) spinach fettucine
60 g (2 oz) butter or margarine
1 onion, finely chopped
300 g (9⅔ oz) sour cream
1 cup (250 ml/8 fl oz) cream
¼ teaspoon ground nutmeg
½ cup (50 g/1⅔ oz) freshly grated Parmesan cheese
salt and freshly ground black pepper, to taste
1 cup (150 g/4¾ oz) freshly grated mozzarella cheese

1 Preheat the oven to moderate 180°C (350°F/Gas 4). Add the fettucine to a large pan of rapidly boiling water and cook until just tender. Drain well and set aside. While the pasta is cooking, melt the butter in a large pan. Add the chopped onion and stir constantly over low heat until the onion is tender. Add the drained fettucine to the pan.
2 Add the sour cream to the pan and toss well, using a spoon and a fork. Simmer, stirring, until the pasta is well coated.
3 Add the cream, nutmeg, half of the Parmesan cheese, salt and pepper; stir. Pour into a greased casserole dish. Sprinkle with combined mozzarella and remaining Parmesan cheese. Bake for 15 minutes or until the cheese is softened and golden.

NOTE: You can vary this recipe by using plain fettucine or adding chopped fresh herbs such as basil, parsley or thyme. Grated carrot can be stirred in as well. If you like garlic, stir in a crushed clove or two just before the onion has finished cooking.

ROAST VEGETABLE TART

Preparation time: 30 minutes +
    30 minutes refrigeration
Total cooking time: 1 hour 50 minutes
Serves 4–6

1 eggplant (aubergine), cut into thick slices
350 g (11 oz) pumpkin, cut into large pieces
2 zucchini (courgettes), cut into thick slices
1–2 tablespoons olive oil
1 large red pepper (capsicum), chopped
1 teaspoon olive oil, extra
1 red onion, sliced
1 tablespoon Korma curry paste
natural yoghurt, for serving

Pastry
1½ cups (185 g/6 oz) plain flour
125 g (4 oz) butter, chilled and chopped
⅔ cup (100 g/3½ oz) roasted cashews,
    finely chopped
1 teaspoon cumin seeds
2–3 tablespoons chilled water

1 Preheat the oven to moderately hot
200°C (400°F/Gas 6). Put the eggplant,
pumpkin and zucchini on a lined baking
tray, then brush with oil and bake for
30 minutes. Remove from the oven, turn
and add the pepper. Bake for another
30 minutes, then allow to cool.
2 To make the pastry, sift the flour into a
large bowl and rub in the butter with your
fingertips until the mixture resembles
fine breadcrumbs. Stir in the cashews
and cumin seeds. Make a well in the
centre and add the water. Mix with a flat-
bladed knife, using a cutting action, until
the mixture comes together in small
beads. Gently gather together and lift out
onto a lightly floured work surface. Press
together into a ball and flatten slightly
into a disc, wrap in plastic wrap and
refrigerate for 30 minutes. Roll out
between two sheets of baking paper to a
circle about 35 cm (14 inch) in diameter.

3 Heat the extra oil in a frying pan and
cook the onion for 2–3 minutes, or until
soft. Add the curry paste and cook,
stirring, for 1 minute, or until fragrant and
well combined. Allow to cool. Reduce the
oven temperature to moderate 180°C
(350°F/Gas 4).
4 Lift onto a lightly greased baking tray
and spread the onion mixture over the
pastry, leaving a 6 cm (2½ inch) border all
around. Arrange the other vegetables
over the onion, piling them slightly higher
in the centre. Working your way around,
fold the edge of the pastry in pleats over
the vegetables. Bake for 45 minutes, or
until the pastry is lightly golden and
cooked. Serve immediately with a dollop
of yoghurt.

EGGPLANT (AUBERGINE)
AND TOMATO BAKE

Preparation time: 20 minutes +
    20 minutes standing
Total cooking time: 1 hour 15 minutes
Serves 6

2 large eggplants (aubergines)
¼ cup (60 ml/2 fl oz) olive oil
2 large onions, chopped
1 teaspoon ground cumin
1 cup (250 ml/8 fl oz) good-quality white
    wine
800 g (1 lb 10 oz) canned tomatoes,
    crushed
2 cloves garlic, crushed
2 red chillies, finely chopped (optional)
½ cup (75 g/2½ oz) currants
3 tablespoons chopped fresh coriander

1 Preheat the oven to hot 210°C
(415°F/Gas 6–7). Cut the eggplants into
2 cm (¾ inch) thick rounds. Place on a
tray and sprinkle generously with salt. Set
aside for 20 minutes.
2 Heat 2 tablespoons of oil in a large pan.
Add the onions and cook over medium
heat for 5 minutes or until softened. Add
the cumin and stir for 1 minute. Add the
wine. Bring to boil; reduce heat and
simmer for 10 minutes, or until the
mixture has reduced by three-quarters.
Add the tomatoes. Bring to the boil;
reduce the heat and cook for 10 minutes.
Add the garlic, chillies and currants.
Simmer for 5 minutes; remove from the
heat. Rinse the eggplant slices and
squeeze them dry using paper towels.
Heat the remaining oil in a large frying
pan. Fry the eggplant slices over medium
heat for 3–4 minutes. Drain on paper
towels.
3 Layer the eggplant slices and tomato
mixture in a large ovenproof dish,
sprinkle fresh coriander between each
layer. Finish with a layer of eggplant.
Bake for 30 minutes. Serve with pasta.

CONCHIGLIE WITH CHICKPEAS

Preparation time: 15 minutes
Total cooking time: 20 minutes
Serves 4

500 g (1 lb) conchiglie (pasta shells)
2 tablespoons extra virgin olive oil
1 red (Spanish) onion, finely sliced
2–3 cloves garlic, crushed
425 g (14 oz) can chickpeas
½ cup (75 g/2½ oz) sun-dried tomatoes, drained and thinly sliced
1 teaspoon finely grated lemon rind
1 teaspoon chopped fresh red chilli
2 tablespoons lemon juice
1 tablespoon chopped fresh oregano leaves
1 tablespoon finely chopped fresh parsley
fresh Parmesan shavings, for serving

1 Cook the conchiglie in a large pan of rapidly boiling salted water until al dente. Drain and return to the pan.
2 While the pasta is cooking, heat the oil in a frying pan, add the onion and cook until soft and lightly golden.
3 Add the garlic to the pan and cook for another minute. Add the rinsed and drained chickpeas, sun-dried tomato, lemon rind and chopped chilli and cook over high heat until heated through. Stir in the lemon juice along with the chopped fresh herbs.
4 Toss the chickpea mixture through the pasta. Season with salt and pepper, to taste, and serve immediately, scattered with Parmesan shavings.

ASIAN MUSHROOM RISOTTO

Preparation time: 20 minutes +
    30 minutes soaking
Total cooking time: 45 minutes
Serves 4

10 g (¾ oz) dried Chinese mushrooms
2 cups (500 ml/16 fl oz) vegetable stock
2 tablespoons soy sauce
⅓ cup (80 ml/2¾ fl oz) mirin
150 g (5 oz) Swiss brown mushrooms
150 g (5 oz) oyster mushrooms
100 g (3⅓ oz) fresh shiitake mushrooms
150 g (5 oz) shimeji mushrooms
40 g (1¼ oz) butter
1 tablespoon olive oil
1 onion, finely chopped
3 garlic cloves, crushed
1 tablespoon finely chopped ginger
2 cups (440 g/14 oz) arborio rice
100 g (3½ oz) enoki mushrooms, trimmed
2 tablespoons snipped chives
shaved Parmesan, to garnish (optional)

1 Put the Chinese mushrooms in a bowl, cover with 2½ cups (625 ml/20 fl oz) boiling water and soak for 30 minutes, then drain, reserving the liquid. Remove and discard the stems and thinly slice the caps.
2 Heat the vegetable stock, soy sauce, mirin, reserved mushroom liquid and 1 cup (250 ml/8 fl oz) water in a large saucepan, bring to the boil, then reduce the heat and keep at a low simmer, skimming off any scum that forms on the surface.
3 Trim and slice the Swiss brown, oyster and shiitake mushrooms, discarding any woody ends. Trim the shimeji and pull apart into small clumps. Melt 1 tablespoon of the butter in a large saucepan over medium heat, add all the mushrooms except the Chinese and enoki and cook, stirring, for 3 minutes, or until wilted, then remove from the pan.
4 Heat the oil and remaining butter in the same saucepan over medium heat, add the chopped onion and cook, stirring, for 4–5 minutes, or until the onion is soft and just starting to brown. Add the garlic and ginger and stir well until fragrant. Add the rice and stir for 1 minute, or until it is well coated in the oil mixture.
5 Gradually add ½ cup (125 ml/4 fl oz) of the hot stock to the rice. Stir constantly over medium heat until nearly all the liquid has been absorbed. Continue adding more stock, ½ cup (125 ml/4 fl oz) at a time, stirring constantly for 20–25 minutes, or until all of the stock has been absorbed and the rice is tender.
6 Add all the mushrooms and stir well. Season to taste with salt and pepper. Garnish with the chives and shaved Parmesan and serve.

SWEET GARLIC EGGPLANT (AUBERGINE)

Preparation time: 5 minutes
Total cooking time: 15 minutes
Serves 4

3 medium eggplants (aubergines)
7 tablespoons oil
1½ teaspoons finely chopped garlic
6 teaspoons caster sugar
6 teaspoons soy sauce
6 teaspoons cider vinegar
1 tablespoon dry sherry

1 Cut the eggplants in half lengthways and then slice into wedges about 3 cm (1¼ inches) wide. Cut the wedges into pieces about 3 cm (1¼ inches) long.
2 Heat 3 tablespoons oil in a wok or heavy-based frying pan, swirling gently to coat the base and sides. Add half the eggplant and stir-fry over high heat for 5 minutes, or until browned and all the oil is absorbed. Transfer to a plate. Repeat the cooking procedure with another 3 tablespoons oil and the remaining eggplant.
3 Heat the remaining oil in the wok, swirling gently to coat the base and sides. Add the garlic and cook slowly until just golden. Add the sugar, soy sauce, vinegar and sherry. Bring to the boil, stirring. Add the eggplant and simmer for 3 minutes to allow it to absorb the sauce. Serve with white rice.

NOTE: This dish can be cooked up to 2 days ahead and refrigerated until required. Serve it at room temperature.

BORLOTTI BEAN MOUSSAKA

Preparation time: 45 minutes +
    overnight soaking
Total cooking time: 2¼ – 2½ hours
Serves 6

250 g (8 oz) dried borlotti beans
2 large eggplants (aubergines), sliced
⅓ cup (80 ml/2¾ fl oz) olive oil
1 clove garlic, crushed
1 onion, chopped
125 g (4 oz) button mushrooms, sliced
2 x 440 g (14 oz) cans peeled tomatoes, chopped
1 cup (250 ml/8 fl oz) red wine
1 tablespoon tomato paste
1 tablespoon chopped fresh oregano

Topping
1 cup (250 g/8 oz) natural yoghurt
4 eggs, lightly beaten
2 cups (500 ml/16 fl oz) milk
¼ teaspoon ground paprika
½ cup (50 g/1⅔ oz) freshly grated Parmesan cheese
½ cup (40 g/1⅓ oz) fresh breadcrumbs

1 Soak the borlotti beans in cold water overnight; rinse and drain well.
2 Place the borlotti beans into a large heavy-based pan, cover with water and bring to the boil. Reduce heat and simmer for 1½ hours or until tender; drain.
3 Meanwhile, sprinkle the eggplant slices with salt and set aside for 30 minutes. Rinse and pat dry. Brush the eggplant slices with a little of the oil and cook under a preheated grill for 3 minutes on each side or until golden. Drain on paper towels.

4 Preheat the oven to moderately hot 200°C (400°F/Gas 6). Heat the remaining oil in a large heavy-based pan; add the garlic and onion and cook over medium heat for 3 minutes or until the onion is golden. Add mushrooms and cook for 3 minutes or until browned. Stir in the tomatoes, wine, tomato paste and oregano; bring to the boil; reduce heat and simmer for 40 minutes or until sauce has thickened.
5 To assemble Moussaka: Spoon the borlotti beans into a large, ovenproof dish, top with tomato sauce and eggplant slices.
6 To make Topping: Place the yoghurt, eggs, milk and paprika into a jug and whisk to combine. Pour over the eggplant and set aside for 10 minutes. Combine the Parmesan and breadcrumbs in a bowl. Sprinkle over the moussaka. Bake for 45–60 minutes or until the moussaka is heated through and top is golden.

PENNE ALLA NAPOLITANA

Preparation time: 20 minutes
Total cooking time: 25 minutes
Serves 4–6

2 tablespoons olive oil
1 onion, finely chopped
2–3 cloves garlic, finely chopped
1 small carrot, finely diced
1 celery stick, finely diced
2 x 400 g (13 oz) cans peeled, chopped
   tomatoes, or 1 kg (2 lb) ripe tomatoes,
   peeled and chopped
1 tablespoon tomato paste (tomato purée)
¼ cup (15 g/½ oz) shredded fresh basil
   leaves
500 g (1 lb) penne
Parmesan, for serving

1 Heat the oil in a large frying pan, add the
onion and garlic and cook for 2 minutes,
or until golden. Add the carrot and celery
and cook for another 2 minutes.
2 Add the tomato and tomato paste.
Simmer for 20 minutes, or until the sauce
thickens, stirring occasionally. Stir in the
shredded basil and season, to taste, with
salt and freshly ground black pepper.
3 While the sauce is cooking, cook the
pasta in a large saucepan of rapidly
boiling salted water until al dente. Drain
well and return to the pan. Add the sauce
to the pasta and mix well. This dish is
delicious served with freshly grated or
shaved Parmesan.

COUSCOUS VEGETABLE LOAF

Preparation time: 20 minutes +
   overnight refrigeration
Total cooking time: 15 minutes
Serves 6–8

1 litre (32 fl oz) vegetable stock
500 g (1 lb) couscous
30 g (1 oz) butter
3 tablespoons olive oil
2 cloves garlic, crushed
1 onion, finely chopped
1 tablespoon ground coriander
1 teaspoon ground cinnamon
1 teaspoon garam marsala
250 g (8 oz) cherry tomatoes, quartered
1 zucchini (courgette), finely chopped
130 g (4½ oz) can corn kernels, drained
8 large fresh basil leaves
150 g (5 oz) sun-dried peppers
   (capsicums) in oil
1 cup (60 g/2 oz) chopped fresh basil, extra

Dressing
⅓ cup (80 ml/2¾ fl oz) orange juice
1 tablespoon lemon juice
3 tablespoons chopped fresh flat-leaf
   parsley
1 teaspoon honey
1 teaspoon ground cumin

1 Bring the stock to the boil in a
saucepan. Place the couscous and butter
in a large bowl, cover with the stock and
set aside for 10 minutes.
2 Meanwhile, heat 1 tablespoon of the oil
in a large frying pan and cook the garlic
and onion over low heat for 5 minutes, or
until the onion is soft. Add the spices and
cook for 1 minute, or until fragrant.
Remove from the pan.
3 Add the remaining oil to the pan and fry
the tomatoes, zucchini and corn over high
heat in batches until soft.
4 Line a 3 litre (96 fl oz) loaf tin with
plastic wrap, allowing it to overhang the
side. Arrange basil leaves over the base
to form two flowers. Drain the peppers,
reserving 2 tablespoons oil, then roughly
chop. Add the onion, fried vegetables,
sun-dried peppers and extra basil to the
couscous and mix. Press into the tin and
fold the plastic wrap over to cover. Weigh
down with cans of food and refrigerate
overnight.
5 For the dressing, place all the
ingredients and the pepper oil in a jar
with a lid and shake well.
6 Turn out the loaf, slice and serve with
dressing.

GREEN PILAFF WITH CASHEWS

Preparation time: 15 minutes
Total cooking time: 1 hour 10 minutes
Serves 6

200 g (6½ oz) baby English spinach leaves
⅔ cup (100 g/3½ oz) cashew nuts, chopped
2 tablespoons olive oil
6 spring onions (scallions), chopped
2 garlic cloves, finely chopped
1 teaspoon fennel seeds
1½ cups (300 g/10 oz) long-grain brown rice
2 tablespoons lemon juice
2½ cups (600 ml/20 fl oz) vegetable stock
3 tablespoons chopped mint
3 tablespoons chopped flat-leaf (Italian) parsley

1 Preheat the oven to moderate 180°C (350°F/Gas 4). Shred the English spinach into 1 cm (½ inch) pieces.
2 Put the cashew nuts on a baking tray and roast for 5–10 minutes, or until golden brown—watch them carefully so they don't burn.
3 Heat the oil in a large, deep frying pan and cook the spring onion over medium heat for 2 minutes, or until softened. Add the garlic and fennel seeds and cook for 1 minute, or until fragrant. Stir in the rice, mixing well to combine. Increase the heat to high, add the lemon juice, stock and 1 teaspoon salt and bring to the boil. Reduce the heat to low, cover with a tight-fitting lid and cook, without lifting the lid, for 45 minutes, or until the stock has been absorbed and the rice is cooked. Remove from the heat and sprinkle with the spinach and herbs. Stand, covered, for 8 minutes, then fork the spinach and herbs through the rice. Season. Serve sprinkled with cashews.

LEEK, ZUCCHINI (COURGETTE) AND CHEESE FRITTATA

Preparation time: 20 minutes
Total cooking time: 40 minutes
Serves 4

2 tablespoons olive oil
3 leeks, thinly sliced
2 medium zucchinis (courgettes), cut into matchstick pieces
1 clove garlic, crushed
salt and pepper
5 eggs, lightly beaten
4 tablespoons freshly grated Parmesan cheese
4 tablespoons Swiss cheese, cut into small cubes

1 Heat 1 tablespoon olive oil in small pan; add the leeks and cook, stirring, over low heat until slightly softened. Cover and cook the leeks for 10 minutes. Add the zucchinis and garlic; cook for another 10 minutes. Transfer to a bowl. Allow to cool; add salt, pepper, egg and cheeses.
2 Heat remaining oil in pan; add egg mixture and smooth surface. Cook over low heat for 15 minutes or until the frittata is almost set.
3 Cook under a preheated hot grill for 3–5 minutes or until the top is set and golden. Allow the frittata to stand for 5 minutes before cutting into wedges for serving. Serve with a fresh green salad for lunch or a light meal.

PUMPKIN AND PINE NUT TAGLIATELLE

Preparation time: 25 minutes
Total cooking time: 25 minutes
Serves 4

30 g (1 oz) butter
1 large onion, chopped
2 cloves garlic, crushed
1½ cups (375 ml/12 fl oz) vegetable stock
750 g (1½ lb) butternut pumpkin, peeled and chopped into small pieces
¼ teaspoon ground nutmeg
½ teaspoon freshly ground black pepper
1 cup (250 ml/8 fl oz) cream
500 g (1 lb) fresh tagliatelle
½ cup (80 g/2¾ oz) pine nuts, toasted
2 tablespoons chopped fresh chives
freshly grated Parmesan, for serving

1 Melt the butter in a large pan. Add the onion and cook for 3 minutes, or until soft and golden. Add the garlic and cook for another minute. Stir in the vegetable stock and add the pumpkin. Bring to the boil, reduce the heat slightly and cook until the pumpkin is tender.
2 Reduce the heat to very low and season with the nutmeg and pepper. Stir in the cream until just warmed through; do not boil. Transfer to a food processor and process for about 30 seconds, until the mixture forms a smooth sauce.
3 Meanwhile, cook the tagliatelle in a large pan of rapidly boiling salted water until al dente. Drain and return to the pan.
4 Return the sauce to the pan and gently reheat. Add to the pasta with the pine nuts and toss well. Serve sprinkled with chives and offer Parmesan in a separate bowl. Pictured garnished with bay leaves.

NOTE: To toast pine nuts, stir over low heat in a non-stick frying pan until lightly golden.

VEGETABLE PIE

Preparation time: 25 minutes +
  30 minutes refrigeration
Total cooking time: 1 hour 10 minutes
Serves 6

Pastry
1 cup (125 g/4 oz) plain flour
60 g (2 oz) butter, chilled and chopped
1 egg yolk
2 teaspoons poppy seeds

30 g (1 oz) butter
2 tablespoons oil
1 onion, cut into thin wedges
1 leek, sliced
3 potatoes, cut into large chunks
300 g (10 oz) orange sweet potato
  (kumera), cut into large chunks
300 g (10 oz) pumpkin, cut into large chunks
200 g (6½ oz) swede, cut into large chunks
1 cup (250 ml/8 fl oz) vegetable stock
1 red pepper (capsicum), cut into large
  pieces
200 g (6½ oz) broccoli, cut into large florets
2 zucchini (courgettes), cut into large
  pieces
1 cup (125 g/4 oz) grated vintage
  peppercorn Cheddar

1 Preheat the oven to moderately hot
200°C (400°F/Gas 6). For the pastry, sift
the flour into a large bowl and rub in the
butter with your fingertips until the
mixture resembles fine breadcrumbs.
Make a well and add the egg yolk, poppy
seeds and 1–2 tablespoons iced water and
mix with a flat-bladed knife, using a
cutting action, until the mixture comes
together in beads. Gently gather together
and lift out onto a lightly floured work
surface. Press into a ball, flatten slightly
into a disc, then wrap in plastic wrap and
refrigerate for 30 minutes.

2 Roll the dough between two sheets of
baking paper, then remove the top sheet
and invert the pastry into a 23 cm (9 inch)
pie plate. Use a small ball of pastry to
press the pastry in, allowing excess to
hang over the sides. Trim any excess
pastry. Prick the base with a fork and
bake for 15–20 minutes, or until dry and
golden.
3 Meanwhile, for the filling, heat the
butter and oil in a large saucepan, add
the onion and leek and cook over medium
heat for 5 minutes, or until soft and
golden. Add the potato, sweet potato,
pumpkin and swede and cook, stirring
occasionally, until the vegetables start to
soften. Add the stock and cook for
30 minutes.
4 Add the remaining vegetables and cook,
partially covered, for 20 minutes, or until
the vegetables are soft—some may break
up slightly. Season and cool a little.
Spoon into the pie shell, sprinkle with
cheese and cook under a medium grill for
5 minutes, or until the cheese is golden.

TOMATO AND BOCCONCINI FLAN

Preparation time: 30 minutes +
  refrigeration
Total cooking time: 50 minutes
Serves 6

1½ cups (185 g/6 oz) plain flour
100 g (3⅓ oz) butter, chopped
1 egg
2 tablespoons cold water
5–6 egg (Roma) tomatoes
salt
1 tablespoon olive oil
8 bocconcini (220 g/7 oz), sliced
6 spring onions, chopped
2 tablespoons chopped fresh rosemary
salt and pepper, to taste

1 Combine flour and butter in a food
processor; process 10 seconds or until fine
and crumbly. Combine egg and water in a
small bowl. With motor constantly running,
gradually add to flour mixture; process
until mixture just comes together. Turn out
onto a lightly floured surface; knead to
form a smooth dough. Refrigerate, covered
with plastic wrap, for 20 minutes.
2 Preheat oven to hot 210°C (415°F/Gas
6–7). On a floured board, roll pastry to fit
a 23 cm (9 inch) round, loose-bottomed
flan tin. Ease pastry into tin; trim edges.
Cut a sheet of baking paper to cover
pastry-lined tin. Place over pastry then
spread a layer of dried beans or rice
evenly over paper. Bake 15 minutes, then
remove paper and beans or rice. Bake
another 10 minutes or until pastry case is
lightly golden; cool. Reduce oven to
moderate 180°C (350°F/Gas 4).
3 Cut the tomatoes in half; sprinkle with
salt and drizzle with oil. Place in a baking
dish, cut-side up; bake for 15 minutes.
Arrange the tomatoes, cut-side up, over
the pastry. Place the bocconcini slices and
spring onion between tomatoes; scatter
with rosemary and salt and pepper. Bake
for 10 minutes. Remove from oven and
cool for 10 minutes before serving.

MUSHROOM MOUSSAKA

Preparation time: 20 minutes
Total cooking time: 1 hour
Serves 4–6

1 eggplant (aubergine), about 250 g (4 oz),
    cut into 1 cm (½ inch) slices
1 large potato, cut into 1 cm (½ inch) slices
30 g (1 oz) butter
1 onion, finely chopped
2 cloves garlic, finely chopped
500 g (1 lb) flat mushrooms, sliced
400 g (13 oz) can chopped tomatoes
½ teaspoon sugar
40 g (1¼ oz) butter, extra
⅓ cup (40 g/1¼ oz) plain flour
2 cups (500 ml/16 fl oz) milk
1 egg, lightly beaten
40 g (1¼ oz) grated Parmesan

1 Preheat the oven to hot 220°C (425°F/
Gas 7). Line a baking tray with foil and
brush with oil. Put the eggplant and potato
in a single layer on the tray, sprinkle with
salt and pepper and bake for 20 minutes.
Meanwhile, melt the butter in a large
frying pan over medium heat. Add the
onion and cook, stirring, for 3–4 minutes,
or until soft. Add the garlic and cook for
1 minute, or until fragrant. Increase the
heat to high, add the mushrooms and stir
continuously for 2–3 minutes, or until soft.
Add the tomato, reduce the heat and
simmer rapidly for 8 minutes, or until
reduced. Stir in the sugar.

2 Melt the extra butter in a large saucepan
over low heat. Add the flour and cook for
1 minute, or until pale and foaming. Remove
from the heat and gradually stir in the milk.
Return to the heat and stir constantly until
the mixture boils and thickens. Reduce the
heat and simmer for 2 minutes. Remove
from the heat and, when the bubbles
subside, stir in the egg and Parmesan.
3 Reduce the oven temperature to
moderate 180°C (350°F/Gas 4). Grease a
shallow 1.5 litre (48 fl oz) ovenproof dish.
Spread half the mushroom mixture over
the base of the dish. Cover with potato
and top with half the remaining
mushrooms, then the eggplant. Finish
with the remaining mushrooms, pour on
the sauce and smooth the top with the
back of a spoon. Bake for 30–35 minutes,
or until the edges begin to bubble.
Remove from the oven and leave for
10 minutes before serving.

CRUNCHY STUFFED TOFU PUFFS

Preparation time: 30 minutes
Total cooking time: 5 minutes
Makes 24

12 deep-fried tofu puffs
1 cup (90 g/3 oz) bean sprouts, scraggly
    ends removed
¼ cup (40 g/1⅓ oz) unsalted roasted
    peanuts, chopped
1 carrot, grated
1 tablespoon chopped fresh coriander
    leaves

Chilli Sauce
2 small red chillies, finely chopped
2 cloves garlic, crushed
2 teaspoons soft brown sugar
1 tablespoon soy sauce
1 tablespoon vinegar
½ cup (125 ml/4 fl oz) boiling water

1 Cut the tofu puffs in half. Cut a small slit
in each half and open it up carefully to
form a pocket.
2 Place the bean sprouts, peanuts, carrot
and coriander in a bowl, and toss until
well mixed. Fill each pocket with a portion
of the mixture. Serve drizzled with a little
Chilli Sauce, and offer the rest of the
sauce for dipping.
3 To make Chilli Sauce: Combine all the
ingredients in a small pan, bring to the
boil, reduce heat and simmer for 5
minutes or until the sauce thickens
slightly.

NOTE: Tofu puffs are cubes of tofu which
have been deep-fried and are puffed and
golden. They are available from Asian
food shops.

FENNEL, TOMATO AND WHITE BEAN STEW

Preparation time: 25 minutes
Total cooking time: 1 hour 15 minutes
Serves 4–6

5 tomatoes, peeled seeded and chopped
2 leeks, washed and sliced
2 cloves garlic, finely chopped
1 large fennel bulb, washed, halved,
    cored and sliced
3 tablespoons extra virgin olive oil
¼ cup (60 ml/2 fl oz) Pernod
2 fresh bay leaves
5 sprigs fresh thyme
salt and freshly ground black pepper
500 g (1 lb) Desiree potatoes, peeled and
    cut into large chunks
400 g (12⅔ oz) canned cannellini beans,
    rinsed and drained
1 cup (250 ml/8 fl oz) vegetable stock
1 cup (250 ml/8 fl oz) white wine
½ cup (125 g/4 oz) ready-made pesto, for
    serving

1 Preheat the oven to moderate 180°C (350°F/Gas 4). In a large ovenproof dish combine the first nine ingredients. Mix well. (This should preferably be done well ahead of time to allow the flavours to develop.)
2 Cover the dish and bake for 30 minutes. Remove from the oven; add the potatoes, beans, stock and wine. Mix well and cover. Bake for another 35–45 minutes or until the potatoes are cooked through. Remove the bay leaves and thyme and discard them. Serve in warmed bowls, with a spoonful of pesto.

VEGETABLE TART WITH SALSA VERDE

Preparation time: 30 minutes +
    30 minutes refrigeration
Total cooking time: 50 minutes
Serves 6

Pastry
1¾ cups (215 g/7 oz) plain flour
120 g (4 oz) butter, chilled and cubed
¼ cup (60 ml/2 fl oz) cream

Salsa verde
1 clove garlic
2 cups (40 g/1¼ oz) fresh flat-leaf parsley
    leaves
⅓ cup (80 ml/2¾ fl oz) extra virgin olive oil
3 tablespoons chopped fresh dill
1½ tablespoons Dijon mustard
1 tablespoon red wine vinegar
1 tablespoon drained bottled baby capers

Filling
1 large all-purpose potato (eg. desiree,
    pontiac), cubed
1 tablespoon olive oil
2 cloves garlic, crushed
1 red pepper (capsicum), chopped
1 red onion, sliced into rings
2 zucchini (courgettes), sliced
2 tablespoons chopped fresh dill
1 tablespoon chopped fresh thyme
1 tablespoon drained bottled baby capers
150 g (5 oz) marinated artichoke hearts,
    drained
⅔ cup (30 g/1 oz) baby English spinach
    leaves

1 Sift the flour and ½ teaspoon salt into a large bowl and rub in the butter with your fingertips until the mixture resembles fine breadcrumbs. Add the cream and 1–2 tablespoons iced water and mix with a flat-bladed knife until the mixture comes together in small beads. Gather into a ball and turn out onto a lightly floured work surface. Flatten into a disc, cover with plastic wrap, and refrigerate for 30 minutes.

2 Preheat the oven to moderately hot 200°C (400°F/Gas 6). Lightly grease a 27 cm (11 inch) shallow fluted flan tin with a removable base.
3 Roll the dough out between 2 sheets of baking paper until large enough to line the flan tin. Remove the paper and carefully lift the pastry into the flan tin, pressing it gently into the fluted sides. Roll the rolling pin over the tin, cutting off any excess. Line the pastry with crumpled baking paper large enough to cover the base and side. Fill with baking beads or uncooked rice. Place the flan tin on a baking tray and bake for 15–20 minutes. Remove the beads and paper, reduce the oven to moderate 180°C (350°F/Gas 4) and bake for another 20 minutes, or until the pastry case is dry and golden.
4 For the salsa verde, blend all the ingredients together in a food processor until almost smooth.
5 For the filling, boil, steam or microwave the potato until just tender (the point of a sharp knife will come away easily when the potato is ready), but do not overcook. Drain.
6 Heat the oil in a large frying pan and add the garlic, pepper and onion. Cook over medium-high heat for 3 minutes, stirring frequently. Add the zucchini, dill, thyme and capers and cook for another 3 minutes, stirring often. Add the potato and artichokes, reduce the heat to low and cook for another 3–4 minutes, or until the potato and artichokes are heated through. Season, to taste.
7 To assemble the tart, spread ¼ cup (60 ml/2 fl oz) of the salsa verde over the base of the pastry case. Spoon the vegetable mixture into the case and drizzle with half the remaining salsa verde. Pile the spinach in the centre, drizzle with the remaining salsa verde and serve immediately.

SOUR CREAM TOMATO PIZZA

Preparation time: 30 minutes + 1 hour 30
  minutes standing
Total cooking time: 40 minutes
Serves 4

1 teaspoon dried yeast
1 teaspoon caster sugar
⅔ cup (170 ml/5½ fl oz) warm water
2 cups (250 g/8 oz) plain flour
pinch salt
½ cup (125 ml/4 fl oz) olive oil

Topping
½ cup (125 g/4 oz) sour cream
90 g (3 oz) ricotta cheese
2 tablespoons chopped fresh herbs
  (basil, lemon thyme, sage)
2 tablespoons oil
2 medium onions, thinly sliced
5 ripe tomatoes, sliced
2 cloves garlic, thinly sliced
45 g (1½ oz) marinated Niçoise olives
10 sprigs fresh lemon thyme
freshly cracked black pepper

1 Preheat oven to moderately hot 200°C
(400°F/Gas 6). To make base, place yeast,
sugar and warm water into a bowl and
mix to dissolve the sugar. Set aside in a
warm draught-free area for 5 minutes or
until the mixture is foamy.

2 Place flour and salt into a food processor,
add the olive oil and the yeast mixture with
the motor running and process until it
forms a rough dough. Turn out onto a
lightly floured surface and knead until
smooth. Place into a lightly oiled bowl,
cover and allow to rest in a warm area for
1½ hours or until doubled in volume. Punch
down dough and remove from bowl. Knead
and roll out to a 30 cm (12 inch) circle, or
four 14 cm (about 5½ inch) circles and place
on a non-stick baking tray.
3 Combine sour cream, ricotta and herbs.
Spread over base, leaving a 1 cm (½ inch)
border.
4 Heat oil in a frying pan, add onions and
cook for 10 minutes or until onions are
caramelised. Cool slightly, spoon over
ricotta mixture, top with sliced tomatoes
and garlic, olives, lemon thyme and black
pepper. Bake 15–30 minutes, depending
on size, until base is crisp and golden.

ROAST CAPSICUM RICE TARTS

Preparation time: 45 minutes + cooling
Total cooking time: 1 hour 5 minutes
Serves 6

1 litre (32 fl oz) vegetable stock
20 g (¾ oz) butter
½ cup (95 g/3 oz) wild rice
⅔ cup (140 g/4½ oz) short-grain brown rice
1 egg, lightly beaten with 1 egg yolk
½ cup (50 g/1¾ oz) freshly grated
  Parmesan cheese
2 green capsicums (peppers)
2 red capsicums (peppers)
2 yellow capsicums (peppers)
150 g (5 oz) Camembert cheese, thinly sliced
2 tablespoons oregano

1 Grease six 10 cm (4 inch) loose-based
fluted flan tins. Pour the stock into a saucepan
and bring to the boil. Reduce the heat,
cover with a lid and keep at a low simmer.
2 Melt the butter in a large saucepan over
low heat, then stir in the rice until well
coated. Add ½ cup (125 ml/4 fl oz) of the
hot stock to the rice, stirring well.
Increase the heat to medium and add the
remaining stock 1 cup (250 ml/8 fl oz) at a
time, stirring, until it has been absorbed.
This will take about 30 minutes. Remove
from the heat and cool. Add the eggs and
Parmesan and season to taste.
3 Divide the rice mixture among the
prepared flan tins and press it around the
base and sides. Allow to cool completely.
Preheat the oven to 200°C (400°F/Gas 6).
4 Cut the capsicums in half lengthways.
Remove the seeds and membrane and
then cut into large, flattish pieces. Grill or
hold over a gas flame until the skin
blackens and blisters. Cover with a tea
towel and allow to cool. Peel the skin off
and cut the flesh into smaller pieces.
5 Put the Camembert slices in the bottom
of the lined tins and divide the capsicum
evenly among the tarts. Bake for 30
minutes. Sprinkle the oregano leaves
over the top and serve hot.

PASTA WITH GREEN OLIVE PASTE AND THREE CHEESES

Preparation time: 10 minutes
Total cooking time: 20 minutes
Serves 4

400 g (13 oz) mafalda or pappardelle
2 tablespoons olive oil
2 cloves garlic, crushed
½ cup (125 g/4 oz) green olive paste
4 tablespoons cream
½ cup (50 g/1¾ oz) freshly grated
  Parmesan
½ cup (60 g/2 oz) grated Cheddar cheese
½ cup (50 g/1¾ oz) grated Jarlsberg
  cheese

1 Preheat the oven to moderately hot
200°C (400°F/Gas 6). Lightly brush a deep
ovenproof dish with oil.
2 Cook the pasta in a large pan of rapidly
boiling salted water until al dente. Drain
and return to the pan.
3 Toss the olive oil, garlic and green olive
paste through the pasta and then mix in
the cream. Season with black pepper.
Transfer to the prepared dish.
4 Sprinkle the top with the cheeses. Bake,
uncovered, for 20 minutes, or until the top
is crisp and cheeses have melted.

FILO RICE PIE

Preparation time: 45 minutes
Total cooking time: 1 hour 45 minutes
Serves 8

2 large red capsicums (peppers)
1 cup (250 ml/8 fl oz) dry white wine
1 litre (32 fl oz) vegetable stock
2 tablespoons oil
1 garlic clove, crushed
1 leek (white part only), sliced
1 fennel bulb, thinly sliced
2 cups (440 g/14 oz) arborio rice
⅔ cup (65 g/2¼ oz) freshly grated
  Parmesan cheese
10 sheets filo pastry
¼ cup (60 ml/2 fl oz) olive oil
500 g (1 lb) English spinach leaves,
  blanched
250 g (8 oz) fetta cheese, sliced
1 tablespoon sesame seeds

1 Cut the capsicums in half lengthways.
Remove the seeds and membrane and
then cut into large, flattish pieces. Grill or
hold over a gas flame until the skin
blackens and blisters. Put on a cutting
board, cover with a tea towel and allow to
cool. Peel the skin off and cut the flesh
into small pieces.
2 Pour the wine and stock into a large
saucepan and bring to the boil. Reduce
the heat, cover with a lid and keep at a
low simmer.
3 Heat the oil and garlic in a large
saucepan. Add the leek and fennel and
cook over medium heat for 5 minutes, or
until lightly browned. Add the rice and stir
for 3 minutes, or until well coated.

4 Add 1 cup (250 ml/8 fl oz) of the stock to
the rice and stir constantly until the liquid
is absorbed. Continue adding stock, ½ cup
(125 ml/4 fl oz) at a time, stirring
constantly until all the stock has been
used and the rice is tender. Remove from
the heat, stir in the Parmesan and
season. Cool slightly. Preheat the oven to
moderate 180°C (350°F/Gas 4).
5 Brush each sheet of filo with olive oil
and fold in half lengthways. Arrange like
overlapping spokes on a wheel, in a 23 cm
(9 inch) springform tin, with one side of
each pastry sheet hanging over the side
of tin.
6 Spoon half the rice mixture over the
pastry and top with half the red
capsicums, half the spinach and half the
fetta cheese. Repeat with the remaining
ingredients.
7 Fold the overhanging edge of the pastry
over the filling, then brush lightly with oil
and sprinkle with sesame seeds. Bake for
50 minutes, or until the pastry is crisp
and golden and the pie is heated through.

CAULIFLOWER AND PASTA BAKE WITH CROUTON TOPPING

Preparation time: 25 minutes
Total cooking time: 1 hour
Serves 6

150 g (4¾ oz) short pasta (such as penne)
600 g (1¼ lb) cauliflower, cut into florets
2 tablespoons olive oil
2 red (Spanish) onions, chopped
2 cloves garlic, finely chopped
80 g (2⅔ oz) butter
4 tablespoons plain flour
4 cups (1 litre) milk
2 cups (200 g/6½ oz) freshly grated
  Parmesan cheese
½ cup (30 g/1 oz) firmly packed shredded
  fresh basil
5 slices of day-old bread, crusts removed
50 g (1⅔ oz) butter, melted

1 Preheat the oven to moderate 180°C (350°F/Gas 4). Cook the pasta in rapidly boiling water until tender; drain. Steam the cauliflower until just tender. Heat the olive oil in a frying pan. Fry the onions and garlic over medium heat until the onions are soft. Combine in a bowl with the cauliflower.
2 Melt the butter in a large pan. Blend in the flour and cook, stirring constantly, for 1 minute. Gradually whisk in the milk. Stir constantly until the mixture boils and thickens. Remove from the heat and stir through 1¼ cups (125 g/4 oz) of the grated Parmesan cheese and the basil. Add the cauliflower, pasta and onions to the sauce; mix thoroughly.
3 Spoon the cauliflower mixture into a large ovenproof dish. Cut the bread into large cubes. Toss the cubes in melted butter and then scatter them over the cauliflower mixture. Sprinkle with the remaining Parmesan cheese. Bake for 35–40 minutes until the top is golden.

BUDDHIST VEGETARIAN NOODLES

Preparation time: 25 minutes +
  20 minutes soaking
Total cooking time: 15 minutes
Serves 4

15 g (½ oz) dried shiitake mushrooms
400 g (13 oz) fresh flat egg noodles
2–3 tablespoons peanut or sunflower oil
1 small carrot, julienned
150 g (5 oz) fresh baby corn, quartered
  lengthways
227 g (7 oz) can bamboo shoots, drained
  and julienned
150 g (5 oz) snow peas (mangetout),
  julienned
½ small red pepper (capsicum), julienned
1 small green pepper (capsicum),
  julienned
1 cup (90 g/3 oz) bean sprouts, topped
  and tailed
40 g (1¼ oz) wom bok (Chinese cabbage),
  finely shredded
1 tablespoon julienned fresh ginger
2 tablespoons vegetarian oyster sauce
1 tablespoon mushroom soy sauce
1 tablespoon light soy sauce
1 tablespoon Chinese rice wine
1 teaspoon sesame oil
ground white pepper, to taste
fresh coriander leaves, to garnish

1 Cover the mushrooms in boiling water and soak for 20 minutes. Drain. Discard the woody stalks and thinly slice the caps.
2 Meanwhile, cook the noodles in a large saucepan of boiling water for 1 minute, stirring to separate. Drain. Rinse under cold, running water and drain again.

3 Heat a wok over high heat, add 1 tablespoon of the peanut oil and swirl to coat the side of the wok. Stir-fry the carrot and corn for 1–2 minutes, then add the bamboo shoots and stir-fry for a further 1–2 minutes, or until just cooked but still crisp. Remove the vegetables from the wok.
4 Reheat the wok (add 2 teaspoons peanut oil if necessary) and add the snow peas and red and green peppers. Stir-fry for 1–2 minutes, or until just cooked but still crisp. Add to the carrot and corn mixture. Reheat the wok (add another 2 teaspoons peanut oil if needed), then add the bean sprouts, wom bok and mushrooms and stir-fry for 30 seconds, or until wilted. Add the ginger and stir-fry for a further 1–2 minutes. Remove from the wok and add to the other vegetables.
5 Heat the remaining oil in the wok, and quickly stir-fry the noodles for 1–2 minutes, or until heated through, taking care not to let them break up. Stir in the vegetarian oyster sauce, mushroom soy sauce, light soy sauce and rice wine and stir thoroughly. Return all the vegetables to the wok and stir gently for 1–2 minutes, or until well combined with the noodles. Drizzle with the sesame oil, season with white pepper and garnish with the coriander leaves. Serve immediately.

NOTE: Garlic, onions, spring onions and chillies have been omitted from this recipe because traditional Chinese vegetarians do not eat them.

WILD RICE, THYME AND MIXED MUSHROOM PILAFF

Preparation time: 20 minutes +
　5 minutes standing
Total cooking time: 45 minutes
Serves 4

⅔ cup (100 g/3½ oz) wild rice
1½ cups (375 ml/12 fl oz) vegetable stock
60 g (2 oz) butter
1 large onion, finely chopped
2 garlic cloves, crushed
1⅓ cups (265 g/8 oz) long-grain rice
300 g (10 oz) mixed mushrooms, sliced
　(e.g. button, field, Swiss brown)
1½ tablespoons chopped thyme
1 fresh bay leaf
2 tablespoons chopped flat-leaf (Italian)
　parsley
toasted pine nuts, to serve

1 Rinse the wild rice and cook in a saucepan of plenty of boiling water for 25 minutes—it will only be partially cooked after this time. Drain.
2 When the rice is nearly done, pour the stock into a large saucepan with 1½ cups (375 ml/12 fl oz) water and bring to the boil. Reduce the heat to a simmer.
3 Meanwhile, melt the butter in a large heavy-based frying pan, add the onion and garlic and cook until the onion is softened but not browned. Add the white rice and stir until the rice grains are coated with butter, then stir in the mushrooms.
4 Add the wild rice, stock, thyme and bay leaf. Bring to the boil while stirring, then reduce the heat, cover tightly with a lid and simmer for 15 minutes, or until the rice is tender and the stock has been absorbed.
5 Leave to stand for 5 minutes. Remove the bay leaf. Season, add the parsley and fluff up the rice with a fork. Sprinkle with pine nuts and serve.

SPICY CHICKPEA AND VEGETABLE CASSEROLE

Preparation time: 25 minutes +
　overnight soaking
Total cooking time: 1 hour 30 minutes
Serves 4

1½ cups (330 g/10½ oz) dried chickpeas
2 tablespoons oil
1 large onion, chopped
1 clove garlic, crushed
3 teaspoons ground cumin
½ teaspoon chilli powder
½ teaspoon allspice
425 g (13½ oz) canned peeled tomatoes,
　crushed
1½ cups (375 ml/12 fl oz) vegetable stock
300 g (9⅔ oz) pumpkin, cut into large cubes
150 g (4¾ oz) green beans, topped and
　tailed
200 g (6½ oz) button squash, quartered
2 tablespoons tomato paste
1 teaspoon dried oregano

1 Place the chickpeas in a large bowl; cover with cold water and soak overnight; drain.
2 Heat the oil in a large pan; add the onions and garlic and stir-fry for 2 minutes or until tender. Add the cumin, chilli powder and allspice; stir-fry for 1 minute. Add the chickpeas, tomatoes and stock to the pan. Bring to the boil; reduce heat and simmer, covered, for 1 hour, stirring occasionally.
3 Add the pumpkin, beans, squash, tomato paste and oregano. Stir to combine. Simmer, covered, for another 15 minutes. Remove the lid from the pan and simmer, uncovered, for another 10 minutes to reduce and thicken sauce slightly.

NOTE: A quick way to soak chickpeas is to place them in a large pan and cover with cold water. Bring to the boil; remove from heat and soak for two hours. If you are in a hurry, substitute canned chickpeas. Drain and rinse thoroughly before use.

SPINACH AND RICOTTA SHELLS

Preparation time: 20 minutes
Total cooking time: 15 minutes
Serves 4

20 giant conchiglie (shell pasta)
1 tablespoon oil
2 bacon rashers, finely chopped
1 onion, finely chopped
500 g (1 lb) English spinach, chopped
750 g (1½ lb) ricotta cheese
⅓ cup (35 g/1¼ oz) freshly grated
　Parmesan
1 cup (250 g/8 oz) bottled tomato pasta
　sauce

1 Cook the conchiglie in a large pan of rapidly boiling salted water until al dente; drain.
2 Heat the oil in a pan, add the bacon and onion and stir over medium heat for 3 minutes, or until lightly browned. Add the spinach and stir over low heat until wilted. Add the ricotta cheese and stir until combined.
3 Spoon the mixture into the pasta shells and sprinkle with Parmesan. Put the shells on a cold, lightly oiled grill tray. Cook under medium-high heat for 3 minutes, or until lightly browned and heated through.
4 Put the tomato pasta sauce in a small pan and stir over high heat for 1 minute, or until heated through. Spoon the sauce onto serving plates and top with the shells.

LENTIL AND CHICKPEA BURGERS WITH CORIANDER GARLIC CREAM

Preparation time: 30 minutes +
    refrigeration
Total cooking time: approximately
    30 minutes
Makes 10 burgers

1 cup (250 g/8 oz) red lentils
1 tablespoon oil
2 onions, sliced
1 tablespoon tandoori mix powder
425 g (13½ oz) canned chickpeas, drained
1 tablespoon grated fresh ginger
1 egg
3 tablespoons chopped fresh parsley
2 tablespoons chopped fresh coriander
2¼ cups (180 g/5¾ oz) stale breadcrumbs
flour, for dusting

Coriander Garlic Cream
½ cup (125 g/4 oz) sour cream
½ cup (125 ml/4 fl oz) cream
1 clove garlic, crushed
2 tablespoons chopped fresh coriander
2 tablespoons chopped fresh parsley

1 Prepare and heat barbecue. Bring a large pan of water to the boil. Add the lentils to the boiling water and simmer, uncovered, for 10 minutes or until the lentils are tender. Drain well. Heat the oil in a pan and cook the onions until tender. Add tandoori mix and stir until fragrant. Cool the mixture slightly.

2 Place the chickpeas, half the lentils, ginger, egg and onion mixture in a food processor. Process for 20 seconds or until smooth. Transfer to a bowl. Stir in the remaining lentils, parsley, coriander and breadcrumbs, combine well. Divide the mixture into 10 portions.
3 Shape the portions into round patties. (If the mixture is too soft, refrigerate for 15 minutes or until firm.) Toss the patties in flour and shake off excess. Place the patties on a lightly greased barbecue grill or flatplate. Cook for 3–4 minutes on each side or until browned, turning once. Serve with Coriander Garlic Cream.
4 To make Coriander Garlic Cream: Combine the sour cream, cream, garlic and herbs in a bowl and mix well.

NOTE: The patties can be prepared up to 2 days ahead and stored, covered, in the refrigerator. If you prefer, you can cook the patties in a frying pan brushed lightly with oil. The Coriander Garlic Cream can be made up to 3 days in advance. Place in a covered container and store in the refrigerator.

PEA, EGG AND RICOTTA CURRY

Preparation time: 15 minutes
Total cooking time: 30 minutes
Serves 4

4 hard-boiled eggs
½ teaspoon ground turmeric
3 tablespoons ghee or oil
1 bay leaf
2 small onions, finely chopped
1 teaspoon finely chopped garlic
1½ teaspoons ground coriander
1½ teaspoons garam masala
½ teaspoon chilli powder, optional
½ cup (125 g/4 oz) chopped, canned,
    peeled tomatoes
1 tablespoon tomato paste (tomato purée,
    double concentrate)
½ cup (125 ml/4 fl oz) water
125 g (4 oz) baked ricotta, cut in 1 cm
    (½ inch) cubes
¼ teaspoon salt
1 tablespoon yoghurt
½ cup (80 g/2⅔ oz) frozen peas
2 tablespoons finely chopped fresh
    coriander leaves

1 Peel the eggs and coat them with the turmeric.
2 Melt the ghee in a large pan and cook the eggs over moderate heat for 2 minutes until they are light brown, stirring constantly. Set aside.
3 Add the bay leaf, onion and garlic to the pan and cook over moderately high heat, stirring frequently, until the mixture is well reduced and pale gold. Lower the heat if the mixture is browning too quickly. Add the coriander, garam masala and chilli powder, if using, and cook until fragrant.
4 Add the tomato, tomato paste and water; cover and simmer for 5 minutes. Return the eggs to the pan with the ricotta, salt, yoghurt and peas, and cook for 5 minutes. Remove the bay leaf, sprinkle with coriander and serve immediately.

HUNGARIAN CASSEROLE

Preparation time: 30 minutes
Total cooking time: 30 minutes
Serves 4–6

4 large potatoes
1 tablespoon olive oil
30 g (1 oz) butter
1 medium onion, chopped
1 red and 1 green pepper (capsicum),
    roughly chopped
440 g (14 oz) can chopped tomatoes
1 cup (250 ml/8 fl oz) vegetable stock
2 teaspoons caraway seeds
2 teaspoons paprika
salt and freshly ground black pepper

Crispy Croutons
1 cup (250 ml/8 fl oz) oil
4 slices white bread, crusts removed and
    cut into small cubes

1 Peel the potatoes; cut into large chunks.
Heat the oil and butter in a large heavy-
based pan; cook the potatoes over
medium heat, turning regularly, until
crisp on the edges.
2 Add the onion and red and green
peppers; cook for 5 minutes. Add
tomatoes with juice, vegetable stock,
caraway seeds and paprika. Season to
taste with salt and pepper. Simmer,
uncovered, for 10 minutes or until
potatoes are tender. Serve with Crispy
Croutons.
3 To make Croutons: Heat oil in a frying
pan over medium heat. Cook croutons,
turning often, for 2 minutes or until
golden brown and crisp. Drain on kitchen
paper.

SANTA FE PIZZETTA

Preparation time: 15 minutes
Total cooking time: 15 minutes
Serves 6

6 ready-made small pizza bases
¾ cup (185 g/6 oz) ready-made spicy
    tomato salsa
4 spring onions, sliced
1 red pepper (capsicum), sliced
440 g (14 oz) canned red kidney beans,
    drained and washed
2 tablespoons chopped fresh basil
½ cup (75 g/2½ oz) grated mozzarella
    cheese
¼ cup (30 g/1 oz) grated Cheddar cheese
½ cup (125 g/4 oz) sour cream
125 g (4 oz) corn chips

Guacamole
1 clove garlic, crushed
1 small red (Spanish) onion, finely
    chopped
1 large avocado, mashed
1 teaspoon lemon juice
1 tablespoon ready-made tomato salsa
2 tablespoons sour cream

1 Preheat oven to moderately hot 200°C
(400°F/Gas 6). Spread the pizza bases
with the spicy tomato salsa.
2 Top with spring onions, red pepper,
kidney beans and basil.
3 Sprinkle with grated mozzarella and
Cheddar cheese. Bake for 15 minutes or
until the pizza bases are crisp and the
cheese is golden brown. Serve topped
with corn chips, guacamole and sour
cream.
4 To make Guacamole: Place the garlic,
onion, avocado, lemon juice, salsa and
sour cream in a bowl and stir to combine.

VEGETARIAN PHAD THAI

Preparation time: 20 minutes +
    20 minutes soaking
Total cooking time: 5 minutes
Serves 4

400 g (13 oz) flat rice stick noodles
¼ cup (60 ml/2 fl oz) soy sauce
2 tablespoons lime juice
1 tablespoon soft brown sugar
2 teaspoons sambal oelek
2 tablespoons peanut oil
2 eggs, lightly beaten
1 onion, cut into thin wedges
2 cloves garlic, crushed
1 small red pepper (capsicum), cut into
    thin strips
6 spring onions, thinly sliced on the diagonal
100 g (3½ oz) fried tofu puffs, cut into
    5 mm (¼ inch) wide strips
½ cup (25 g/¾ oz) chopped fresh
    coriander leaves
1 cup (90 g/3 oz) bean sprouts, tailed
¼ cup (40 g/1¼ oz) chopped roasted
    unsalted peanuts

1 Soak the noodles in warm water for
15–20 minutes, or until tender. Drain, then
set aside.
2 To make the stir-fry sauce, combine the
soy sauce, lime juice, sugar and sambal
oelek in a small bowl or jug.
3 Heat a wok over high heat and add
enough peanut oil to coat the bottom and
side. Add the egg and swirl to form a thin
omelette. Cook for 30 seconds, or until
just set. Remove from the wok, roll up,
then thinly slice.
4 Heat the remaining oil in the wok. Add
the onion, garlic and pepper and cook
over high heat for 2–3 minutes, or until
the onion softens. Add the noodles,
tossing well. Stir in the slices of omelette,
the spring onion, tofu and half of the
coriander. Pour in the stir-fry sauce, then
toss to coat the noodles. Sprinkle with the
bean sprouts and top with roasted
peanuts and the remaining coriander.
Serve immediately.

PUMPKIN TARTS

Preparation time: 20 minutes + 30
  minutes refrigeration
Total cooking time: 35 minutes
Serves 6

2 cups (250 g/8 oz) plain flour
125 g (4 oz) butter, chilled and cubed
1.2 kg (2 lb 6½ oz) pumpkin, cut into 6 cm
  (2½ inch) pieces
6 tablespoons sour cream or cream
  cheese
sweet chilli sauce, for serving

1 Sift the flour and a pinch of salt into a
large bowl and rub in the chopped butter
with your fingertips until the mixture
resembles fine breadcrumbs. Make a well
in the centre, add ⅓ cup (80 ml/2¾ fl oz)
iced water and mix with a flat-bladed
knife, using a cutting action until the
mixture comes together in beads. Gently
gather the dough together and lift out
onto a lightly floured work surface. Press
into a ball, then flatten slightly into a disc,
wrap in plastic wrap and refrigerate for
30 minutes.
2 Preheat the oven to moderately hot
200°C (400°F/Gas 6). Divide the pastry
into six portions, roll each one out and fit
into a 10 cm (4 inch) pie dish. Trim the
edges and prick the bases all over. Bake
on a baking tray for 15 minutes, or until
lightly golden, pressing down any pastry
that puffs up. Cool, then remove from the
tins.
3 Meanwhile, steam the pumpkin for
about 15 minutes, or until tender.
4 Place a tablespoon of sour cream in the
middle of each pastry case and pile
pumpkin pieces on top. Season with salt
and cracked black pepper and drizzle with
sweet chilli sauce, to taste. Return to the
oven for a couple of minutes to heat
through. Serve immediately.

TEX MEX CHILLI BEANS

Preparation time: 20 minutes
Total cooking time: 25 minutes
Serves 4

1 tablespoon oil
2 cloves garlic, crushed
2 small fresh red chillies, finely chopped
1 onion, finely chopped
1 green pepper (capsicum), chopped
440 g (14 oz) canned red kidney beans,
  drained and rinsed
440 g (14 oz) canned peeled tomatoes
½ cup (125 g/4 oz) ready-made tomato
  salsa
1 teaspoon soft brown sugar

1 Heat the oil, garlic, chillies and onion in
a heavy-based pan and cook over medium
heat for 3 minutes or until onion is
golden.
2 Add the green pepper, kidney beans,
undrained, crushed tomatoes, salsa and
sugar. Bring to the boil, reduce heat and
simmer, uncovered, for 15 minutes or
until the sauce thickens. Chilli Beans can
be served with sour cream, guacamole
and corn chips.

NOTE: It is said that red kidney beans
originated in Mexico approximately 5000
years ago. Red kidney beans contain
dietary fibre, iron, potassium, and several
B vitamins. Canned chickpeas, drained
and rinsed, may be substituted for kidney
beans in this recipe if you prefer.

PUMPKIN AND HERB
RAVIOLI

Preparation time: 40 minutes +
  30 minutes resting
Total cooking time: 1 hour 15 minutes
Serves 6

500 g (1 lb) pumpkin, cut into chunks
1¾ cups (215 g/7 oz) plain flour
3 eggs, lightly beaten
¼ teaspoon ground nutmeg
15 sage leaves
15 fresh flat-leaf parsley leaves
125 g (4 oz) butter, melted
60 g (2 oz) freshly grated Parmesan

1 Preheat the oven to moderate 180°C
(350°F/Gas 4). Bake the pumpkin on a
baking tray for 1 hour, or until tender.
Allow to cool before removing the skin.
2 Process the flour and eggs in a food
processor for 30 seconds, or until the
mixture forms a dough. Transfer to a
lightly floured surface and knead for
3 minutes, until the dough is very smooth
and elastic. Cover with a clean cloth and
set aside for 30 minutes.
3 Transfer the pumpkin to a bowl with the
nutmeg and mash with a fork. Roll out half
the dough to a rectangle about 1 mm (¹⁄₂₅
inch) thick. Roll out the remaining half to a
rectangle slightly larger than the first.
4 On the first rectangle of dough, put heaped
teaspoonsful of pumpkin filling at intervals,
in straight rows, about 5 cm
(2 inches) apart. Flatten each pumpkin
mound slightly and place one whole sage or
parsley leaf on top of each spoonful of filling.
5 Brush lightly between the mounds of
filling with water. Place the second sheet
of dough on top, press down gently
between pumpkin mounds to seal. Cut
into squares with a knife or fluted cutter.
Cook the ravioli, in batches, in a large pan
of rapidly boiling salted water for 4 minutes,
or until al dente. Don't crowd the pan.
Drain well and serve sprinkled with salt
and pepper, to taste, and tossed with
melted butter and Parmesan.

BROWN RICE AND PUY LENTILS WITH PINE NUTS AND SPINACH

Preparation time: 15 minutes
Total cooking time: 40 minutes
Serves 6–8

1 cup (200 g/6½ oz) brown rice
100 ml (3½ fl oz) extra virgin olive oil
1 red onion, diced
2 garlic cloves, crushed
1 carrot, diced
2 celery stalks, diced
1 cup (185 g/6 oz) Puy lentils
2 tomatoes, seeded and diced
3 tablespoons chopped coriander (cilantro)
3 tablespoons chopped mint
2 tablespoons balsamic vinegar
1 tablespoon lemon juice
2 tablespoons pine nuts, toasted
2 cups (90 g/3 oz) baby English spinach leaves, washed

1 Bring a large saucepan of water to the boil. Add 1 teaspoon salt and the rice, and cook for 20 minutes, or until tender. Drain and refresh under cold water.

2 Heat 2 tablespoons of the oil in a saucepan and add the onion, garlic, carrot and celery. Cook over low heat for 5 minutes, or until softened, then add the puy lentils and 1½ cups (375 ml/12 fl oz) water. Bring to the boil and simmer for 15 minutes, or until tender. Drain well, but do not rinse. Combine with the rice, tomato, coriander and mint in a large bowl.

3 Whisk the remaining oil with the balsamic vinegar and lemon juice, and season well with salt and freshly ground black pepper. Pour over the salad, add the pine nuts and the spinach, and toss well to combine.

ROASTED VEGETABLE LASAGNE

Preparation time: 50 minutes
Total cooking time: 1 hour
Serves 6

Marinade
½ cup (125 ml/4 fl oz) olive oil
2 tablespoons red wine vinegar
1 tablespoon finely chopped capers
1 tablespoon finely chopped parsley
1 clove garlic, finely chopped
1 teaspoon tomato paste
salt and pepper

1 red pepper (capsicum)
1 large eggplant (aubergine), sliced lengthways, salted, rinsed and well-drained
2 large zucchinis (courgettes), sliced thinly lengthways
400 g (12⅔ oz) sweet potato, peeled and sliced thinly lengthways
6 egg (Roma) tomatoes, quartered
375 g (12 oz) fresh lasagne sheets
⅓ cup (90 g/3 oz) good-quality pesto
300 g (9⅔ oz) bocconcini, finely sliced
olive oil
1 cup (100 g/3⅓ oz) freshly grated Parmesan cheese

1 Preheat the oven to moderately hot 200°C (400°F/Gas 6). Combine marinade ingredients in a bowl and whisk thoroughly.

2 Cut red pepper in half lengthways. Remove seeds and membrane and cut into large, flattish pieces. Grill until skin blackens and blisters. Place on a cutting board, cover with a tea towel; allow to cool. Peel, discard skin and cut flesh into thick strips. Place red pepper and remaining vegetables in large baking dish; coat with half the marinade. Bake for 15 minutes, turn and coat again with remaining marinade. Cook for another 15 minutes.

3 Cut the pasta into 24 sheets, each 10 x 16 cm (about 4 x 6½ inches). Make 6 individual stacks in the following order: pasta, zucchini and sweet potato, 2 teaspoons pesto and bocconcini slices, pasta, eggplant and red pepper, pasta, tomatoes, 2 teaspoons pesto and bocconcini slices, pasta. Transfer the stacks to greased baking dish. Brush the tops with olive oil and sprinkle with grated Parmesan cheese. Bake for 15–20 minutes or until heated through and tender.

GOLDEN FRIED EGGPLANT (AUBERGINE) AND CABBAGE

Preparation time: 20 minutes
Total cooking time: 5 minutes
Serves 4

2 tablespoons oil
3 spring onions, chopped
3 cloves garlic, chopped
1 tablespoon soft brown sugar
2 medium eggplants (aubergines), cut into wedges
2 teaspoons Golden Mountain sauce
¼ Chinese cabbage, shredded
2 tablespoons lime juice
2 teaspoons fish sauce (optional)
1 chilli, finely sliced

1 Heat oil in a wok or large frying pan. Add onions and garlic and stir for 1 minute over medium heat.
2 Add the sugar and eggplant wedges to the wok and stir-fry for 3 minutes, or until the eggplant is golden brown.
3 Add the Golden Mountain sauce, cabbage and lime juice to the wok. Toss, then cover and steam for 30 seconds or until the cabbage softens slightly. Add the fish sauce and stir through. Serve immediately sprinkled with sliced chilli.

NOTE: Thai eggplants are purple or have purple and white stripes, and come in a range of sizes. Some may be as small as a tiny pea, others the size of a golf ball or shaped like a small zucchini (courgette). Any of these may be used for this recipe, but make sure to alter the cooking time to suit the size of the eggplant. Golden Mountain sauce is an essential ingredient in Thai cooking. Buy it at Asian food stores.

OMELETTE STRIPS IN FRESH TOMATO SAUCE

Preparation time: 25 minutes
Total cooking time: 12 minutes
Serves 2

Tomato Sauce
3 ripe tomatoes, peeled and roughly chopped
½ teaspoon salt
½ teaspoon pepper
1 teaspoon sugar
2 tablespoons shredded fresh basil

4 eggs
2 teaspoons soy sauce
¼ teaspoon white pepper
1 tablespoon water
light olive oil

1 To make Tomato Sauce: Cook the tomatoes in a small pan with salt, pepper and sugar for 5 minutes or until the liquid has reduced and thickened. Add the basil.
2 Using a wire whisk, beat the eggs in a medium mixing bowl with the soy sauce, pepper and water.
3 Heat a lightly oiled small frying pan. Pour in sufficient egg mixture to cover the base. Cook for a few seconds and then tip onto a plate. Brush the pan with more oil and repeat the process to make 3 thin omelettes.
4 Place the omelettes on top of each other and roll into a cylinder shape. Using a sharp knife, cut into fine strips.
5 Reheat the sauce. Add the egg strips and warm gently, stirring until covered with tomato. If desired, serve with extra fresh shredded basil and cracked pepper.

NOTE: Serve omelette strips accompanied by a salad or as a side dish with roast chicken. They can also be used in soups, added to stir-fries or served over salads.

EGGPLANT (AUBERGINE) WITH TEMPEH (MAKUA PAD TEMPEH)

Preparation time: 20 minutes + 20 minutes soaking
Total cooking time: 10 minutes
Serves 6

2 small dried red chillies
8 black peppercorns
2 cloves garlic
2 tablespoons chopped fresh coriander stems and leaves
⅓ cup (80 ml/2¾ fl oz) vegetable oil
100 g (3½ oz) tempeh, thinly sliced
250 g (8 oz) slender eggplants (aubergines), cut into 2 cm (¾ inch) chunks
1 tablespoon soy sauce
1 tablespoon fish sauce
1 teaspoon grated palm sugar
1 tablespoon lime juice

1 Soak the chillies in a bowl of boiling water for 20 minutes. Drain, remove the seeds and finely chop the flesh.
2 Put the peppercorns, garlic and coriander in a food processor and process to a smooth paste —add a little water if needed.
3 Heat a wok over high heat, add the oil and swirl to coat. Add the paste and chilli and stir-fry for 10 seconds. Add the tempeh and stir-fry for a further 2 minutes, or until golden brown. Remove the tempeh.
4 Add the eggplant to the wok and stir-fry for 6 minutes, or until golden brown. Add the sauces, palm sugar, lime juice and tempeh and cook, stirring, for a further 30 seconds. Serve immediately with rice.

FUSILLI WITH GREEN SAUCE

Preparation time: 10 minutes
Total cooking time: 15 minutes
Serves 6

500 g (1 lb) fusilli or spiral pasta
1 onion
2 zucchini (courgettes)
5–6 large silverbeet leaves
2 anchovies, optional
2 tablespoons olive oil
1 tablespoon capers
50 g (1¾ oz) butter
¼ cup (60 ml/2 fl oz) white wine

1 Cook the pasta in a large pan of rapidly boiling salted water until al dente. Drain and return to the pan.
2 While the pasta is cooking, chop the onion very finely and grate the zucchini into fine pieces. Remove and discard the stalks from the silverbeet and chop or shred the leaves into small pieces. Roughly chop the anchovies, if using. Heat the olive oil and butter in a large heavy-based pan. Add the onion and zucchini and stir with a wooden spoon for 3 minutes over medium heat.
3 Add the anchovies, capers, wine and salt and pepper, to taste, to the pan and cook, stirring, for 2 minutes. Add the prepared silverbeet to the pan and cook for 1–2 minutes, or until the silverbeet has softened. Add the green sauce to the warm pasta and toss until well distributed through the sauce.

NOTE: If you prefer, you can use 500 g (1 lb) of English spinach instead of silverbeet. Cut the ends off and shred the leaves into small pieces.

BAKED CREAMY CHEESY PASTA

Preparation time: 10–15 minutes
Total cooking time: 35–40 minutes
Serves 4

500 g (1 lb) fusilli
2½ cups (600 ml/20 fl oz) cream
3 eggs
250 g (8 oz) feta, crumbled
2 tablespoons plain flour
2 teaspoons ground nutmeg
1 cup (125 g/4 oz) grated Cheddar or mozzarella cheese

1 Cook the fusilli in a large pan of rapidly boiling salted water until al dente. Drain, reserving 1 cup (250 ml/8 fl oz) of the cooking water. Set the pasta aside to cool a little.
2 Preheat the oven to moderate 180°C (350°F/Gas 4) and brush a 7-cup capacity ovenproof dish with olive oil.
3 Whisk the cream, eggs and reserved water in a large bowl until thoroughly combined. Stir in the crumbled feta, flour, ground nutmeg and salt and pepper, to taste.
4 Transfer the cooled pasta to the prepared dish. Pour the cream mixture over the top and sprinkle with the grated cheese. Bake for 30–35 minutes, or until the mixture is just set and the top is lightly golden.

FRITTATA DI ASPARAGI ALLA MENTA
(ASPARAGUS AND MINT FRITTATA)

Preparation time: 10 minutes
Total cooking time: 20 minutes
Serves 4

6 eggs
⅓ cup (35 g/1½ oz) grated Pecorino or Parmesan
¼ cup (5 g/¼ oz) fresh mint leaves, finely shredded
200 g (6½ oz) baby asparagus spears
2 tablespoons extra virgin olive oil

1 Put the eggs in a large bowl, beat well, then stir in the cheese and mint and set aside.
2 Trim the woody part off the asparagus, then cut the asparagus on the diagonal into 5 cm (2 inch) pieces. Heat the oil in a 20 cm (8 inch) frying pan that has a heatproof handle. Add the asparagus and cook for 4–5 minutes, until tender and bright green. Season with salt and pepper, then reduce the heat to low.
3 Pour the egg mixture over the asparagus and cook for 8–10 minutes. During cooking, use a spatula to gently pull the sides of the frittata away from the sides of the pan and tip the pan slightly so the egg runs underneath the frittata.
4 When the mixture is nearly set but still slightly runny on top, place the pan under a low grill for 1–2 minutes, until the top is set and just browned. Serve warm or at room temperature.

CHARGRILLED VEGETABLE TERRINE

Preparation time: 30 minutes +
 overnight refrigeration
Total cooking time: Nil
Serves 8

350 g (11 oz) ricotta
2 cloves garlic, crushed
8 large slices chargrilled eggplant
 (aubergine), drained
10 slices chargrilled red pepper
 (capsicum), drained
8 slices chargrilled zucchini (courgettes),
 drained
45 g (1½ oz) rocket leaves
3 marinated artichokes, drained and
 sliced
85 g (3 oz) semi-dried tomatoes, drained
 and chopped
100 g (3½ oz) marinated mushrooms,
 drained and halved

1 Line a 23.5 x 13 x 6.5 cm (9 x 5 x 2½ inch)
loaf tin with plastic wrap, leaving a
generous amount hanging over the sides.
Place the ricotta and garlic in a bowl and
beat until smooth. Season well and
set aside.
2 Line the base of the tin with half the
eggplant, cutting and fitting to cover the
base. Top with a layer of half the red
pepper, then all the zucchini slices.
Spread evenly with the ricotta mixture
and press down firmly. Place the rocket
leaves on top of the ricotta. Arrange
the artichoke, tomato and mushrooms
in three rows lengthways on top of
the ricotta.
3 Top with another layer of red pepper
and finish with the remaining eggplant.
Cover securely with the overlapping
plastic wrap. Put a piece of cardboard on
top and weigh it down with small food
cans. Refrigerate overnight.
4 To serve, peel back the plastic wrap and
turn the terrine out onto a plate. Remove
the plastic wrap and cut into thick slices.

TOMATO AND OLIVE FLAN

Preparation time: 30 minutes +
 30 minutes refrigeration
Total cooking time: 30–35 minutes
Makes one 20 cm (8 inch) flan

Pastry
2 cups (250 g/8 oz) plain flour
90 g (3 oz) butter, chopped
1 egg yolk
1 tablespoon water

Filling
2 tablespoons olive oil
1–2 tablespoons French mustard
15 g (½ oz) butter
6 small tomatoes, peeled and chopped
3 large onions, thinly sliced
1 teaspoon sugar
2 tablespoons shredded fresh basil
1 cup (125 g/4 oz) pitted olives, sliced
1 cup (220 g/7 oz) grated Gruyère cheese

1 Preheat oven to hot 210°C (415°F/
Gas 6–7). Brush a 20 cm (8 inch) deep flan
tin with melted butter or oil. Coat the base
and sides of tin evenly with flour and
shake off any excess.
2 To make Pastry: Place flour and butter
in a food processor; process for 30 seconds
or until mixture reaches a fine crumbly
texture. Add combined egg yolk and water
and process for 30 seconds or until
mixture comes together. Gather together
on a lightly floured surface. Store,
covered with plastic wrap, in the
refrigerator for 30 minutes.

3 To make Filling: Mix together the oil and
French mustard to make a smooth paste.
4 Roll the pastry out to fit the prepared
flan tin. Cover pastry with a large sheet of
baking paper. Spread a layer of dried
beans evenly over the paper. Bake for
15 minutes, remove from oven, discard
paper and beans and leave pastry to cool.
Spread the mustard and oil mixture over
the pastry base. Heat the butter in a
medium pan and cook the tomatoes and
onions until soft. Remove from heat.
Drain off excess liquid. Spoon the tomato
mixture over the pastry base. Mix
together the sugar, basil and olives and
sprinkle over the tomato mixture. Top
with cheese. Bake flan for 20 minutes or
until the pastry is crisp and the cheese
browned.

CRESPELLE RIPIENE
(STUFFED CREPES)

Preparation time: 25 minutes +
    30 minutes resting
Total cooking time: 1 hour 10 minutes
Makes about 12

Crepes
1¹/3 cups (165 g/5½ oz) plain flour
2 cups (500 ml/16 fl oz) milk
3 eggs, lightly beaten
30 g (1 oz) butter, melted

Tomato sauce
2 tablespoons oil
1 clove garlic, crushed
400 g (13 oz) can crushed good-quality
    tomatoes
3 tablespoons chopped fresh flat-leaf
    parsley

Cheese filling
400 g (13 oz) ricotta, crumbled
100 g (3½ oz) mozzarella, grated
¼ cup (25 g/¾ oz) freshly grated
    Parmesan
pinch of freshly grated nutmeg
3 tablespoons chopped fresh flat-leaf
    parsley

2 tablespoons extra virgin olive oil, to
    drizzle
¼ cup (25 g/¾ oz) freshly grated
    Parmesan

1 For the crepes, sift the flour and ½
teaspoon salt into a bowl. Make a well in
the flour and add the milk gradually,
stirring constantly until the mixture is
smooth. Add the eggs, one at a time,
beating well until smooth. Cover and set
aside for 30 minutes.

2 Meanwhile, to make the tomato sauce,
heat the oil in a heavy-based frying pan
and add the garlic. Cook for 30 seconds
over low heat until just golden, then add
the tomatoes and ½ cup (125 ml/4 fl oz)
water and season well. Simmer over low
heat for 30 minutes, or until the sauce
has reduced and thickened. Stir in the
parsley.
3 Heat a crepe or non-stick frying pan and
brush lightly with melted butter. Pour ¼
cup (60 ml/2 fl oz) of batter into the pan,
swirling quickly to thinly cover the base.
Cook for 1 minute, or until the underside
is golden. Turn and cook the other side
until golden. Transfer to a plate and
continue with the remaining batter,
stacking the crepes as you go.
4 Preheat the oven to moderately hot
200°C (400°F/Gas 6) and lightly grease a
shallow baking dish with butter or oil.
5 For the filling, mix all the ingredients
and season well.
6 To assemble, spread 1 heaped
tablespoon of filling over each crepe,
leaving a 1 cm (½ inch) border. Fold the
crepe in half and then in quarters. Place
in the baking dish, so that they overlap
but are not crowded. Spoon the tomato
sauce over the crepes, sprinkle with
Parmesan and drizzle with the oil. Bake
for 20 minutes, or until heated.

NOTE: The crepes can be made up to
3 days in advance but must be
refrigerated with greaseproof paper to
separate them.

MUSHROOM RAVIOLI

Preparation time: 30 minutes
Total cooking time: 15 minutes
Serves 4

½ cup (70 g/2¼ oz) hazelnut kernels,
    toasted and skinned
90 g (3 oz) unsalted butter
150 g (5 oz) mushrooms
1 tablespoon olive oil
200 g (6½ oz) packet won ton wrappers

1 Chop the hazelnuts in a food processor.
Heat the butter in a pan over medium
heat until it sizzles and turns nutty brown.
Remove from the heat, stir in the chopped
hazelnuts and season with salt and
pepper, to taste.
2 Wipe the mushrooms with paper towel.
Chop the stems and caps finely. Heat the
oil in a pan, add the mushrooms and stir
until soft. Add salt and pepper, and cook
until the liquid has evaporated. Allow to cool.
3 Lay 12 won ton wrappers on a work
surface and put a small teaspoonful of the
mushroom filling on six of them. Brush the
edges of the wrappers with water and
place another wrapper on top. Press firmly
to seal. If desired, trim the edges with a
pasta cutter. Lay the ravioli on a tray lined
with a clean tea towel and cover with
another tea towel. Repeat with 12 more
squares. Filling and sealing a few at a time
prevents the ravioli from drying out.
4 When all the ravioli are made, cook in
batches in a large pan of rapidly boiling
salted water. Don't crowd the pan. Very
thin pasta will be done in about 2 minutes
after the water returns to the boil, so lift
out with a slotted spoon and drain in a
colander while the next batch is cooking.
Serve with the hazelnut sauce.

NOTE: If you can't get toasted and
skinned hazelnuts from your health food
store, spread the nuts on a baking tray
and roast in a moderate oven for 10–12
minutes. Cool, then rub in a tea towel to
remove as many of the skins as possible.

BROWN RICE TART WITH FRESH TOMATO FILLING

Preparation time: 25 minutes + cooling
Total cooking time: 2 hours 25 minutes
Serves 6

Rice crust
1 cup (200 g/6½ oz) brown rice
½ cup (60 g/2 oz) grated Cheddar cheese
1 egg, lightly beaten

Fresh tomato filling
6 Roma (plum) tomatoes, halved
6 garlic cloves, unpeeled
1 tablespoon olive oil
8 lemon thyme sprigs
50 g (1¾ oz) goat's cheese, crumbled
3 eggs, lightly beaten
¼ cup (60 ml/2 fl oz) milk

1 To make the rice crust, cook the rice in plenty of boiling water for 35–40 minutes, or until tender, then drain and set aside to cool. Preheat the oven to moderately hot 200°C (400°F/Gas 6). Put the rice, cheese and egg into a bowl and mix together thoroughly. Spread the mixture over the base and sides of a lightly greased 25 cm (10 inch) flan tin or quiche dish and bake for 15 minutes.
2 To make the filling, put the tomatoes, cut-side up, and garlic on a non-stick baking tray, brush lightly with oil and sprinkle with a little freshly ground black pepper. Bake for 30 minutes. Remove from the oven and allow to cool slightly. When cool enough to handle, remove the skins from the garlic.
3 Reduce the oven temperature to moderate 180°C (350°F/Gas 4). Arrange the tomato halves, garlic, lemon thyme and goat's cheese over the rice crust.
4 Put the beaten eggs and milk in a bowl and whisk well. Pour over the tomatoes, then bake the tart for 1 hour, or until set. Cool slightly, then serve.

RED VEGETABLE CURRY

Preparation time: 25 minutes
Total cooking time: 25–30 minutes
Serves 4

1 tablespoon oil
1 medium onion, chopped
1–2 tablespoons red curry paste
1½ cups (375 ml/12 fl oz) coconut milk
1 cup (250 ml/8 fl oz) water
2 medium potatoes, chopped
220 g (7 oz) cauliflower florets
6 fresh kaffir lime leaves
155 g (5 oz) snake beans, cut into short pieces
½ red pepper (capsicum), cut into strips
10 fresh baby corn, cut in half lengthways
1 tablespoon green peppercorns, roughly chopped
¼ cup (20 g/⅔ oz) fresh basil leaves, roughly chopped
2 tablespoons fish sauce (optional)
1 tablespoon lime juice
2 teaspoons soft brown sugar
½ cup (15 g/½ oz) fresh coriander leaves

1 Heat the oil in a large wok or frying pan. Cook the onions and curry paste for 4 minutes over medium heat, stirring.
2 Add the coconut milk and water, bring to the boil and simmer, uncovered, for 5 minutes. Add the potatoes, cauliflower and lime leaves and simmer for 7 minutes. Add the snake beans, red pepper strips, corn and peppercorns; cook for 5 minutes or until the vegetables are tender.
3 Add the basil, sauce, juice and sugar. Sprinkle with coriander leaves. Serve with steamed rice.

NOTE: If fresh baby corn are not available use canned baby corn and add just before serving.

SWEET AND SOUR NOODLES AND VEGETABLES

Preparation time: 15 minutes
Total cooking time: 15 minutes
Serves 4–6

200 g (6½ oz) thin fresh egg noodles
4 fresh baby corn
¼ cup (60 ml/2 fl oz) oil
1 green pepper (capsicum), sliced
1 red pepper (capsicum), sliced
2 celery sticks, sliced diagonally
1 carrot, sliced diagonally
250 g (8 oz) button mushrooms, sliced
3 teaspoons cornflour
2 tablespoons brown vinegar
1 teaspoon chopped fresh chilli
2 teaspoons tomato paste
2 vegetable stock cubes, crumbled
1 teaspoon sesame oil
450 g (14⅓ oz) canned pineapple pieces
3 spring onions, sliced diagonally

1 Add the noodles to a large pan of boiling water and cook for 3 minutes; drain well. Slice the corn diagonally. Heat the oil in a wok; add the green and red peppers, celery, carrot and mushrooms. Stir over high heat for 5 minutes.
2 Add corn and noodles. Reduce heat to low; cook 2 minutes. Blend cornflour with vinegar in a small bowl until smooth. Add chilli, tomato paste, stock cubes, oil and undrained pineapple pieces to the bowl and stir to combine.
3 Pour pineapple mixture over ingredients in the wok. Stir over medium heat for 5 minutes or until the mixture boils and sauce thickens. Add the spring onions; serve immediately.

CHEESY BUCKWHEAT AND BEAN PASTA

Ready to eat in 30 minutes
Serves 4

500 g (1 lb) buckwheat fusilli
1 tablespoon oil
2 cloves garlic, crushed
1 onion, chopped
300 g (10 oz) bottled pasta sauce
⅓ cup (80 ml/2¾ fl oz) orange juice
400 g (13 oz) can kidney beans, drained
1 cup (125 g/4 oz) grated Cheddar cheese
    plus extra, for serving
3 tablespoons chopped fresh herbs

1 Cook the fusilli in a large pan of rapidly boiling salted water until al dente. Drain and return to the pan.
2 While the pasta is cooking, heat the oil in a frying pan. Add the garlic and onion and cook over medium heat for 3 minutes, or until the onion is golden but not brown.
3 Add the pasta sauce, orange juice and kidney beans. Bring to the boil, reduce the heat and simmer for 5 minutes, or until the sauce is heated through.
4 Add the sauce to the pasta with the Cheddar cheese and fresh herbs. Stir until the cheese melts and serve immediately. Top with extra grated Cheddar cheese.

POLENTA SQUARES WITH MUSHROOM RAGU

Preparation time: 25 minutes +
    refrigeration
Total cooking time: 25 minutes
Serves 4

2 cups (500 ml/16 fl oz) vegetable stock
    or water
1 cup (150 g/5 oz) polenta
20 g (¾ oz) butter
¾ cup (75 g/2½ oz) grated Parmesan
5 g (¼ oz) dried porcini mushrooms
200 g (6½ oz) Swiss brown mushrooms
300 g (10 oz) field mushrooms
½ cup (125 ml/4 fl oz) olive oil
1 onion, finely chopped
3 cloves garlic, finely chopped
1 fresh bay leaf
2 teaspoons finely chopped fresh thyme
2 teaspoons finely chopped fresh
    oregano
½ cup (15 g/½ oz) finely chopped fresh
    flat-leaf parsley
1 tablespoon balsamic vinegar
¼ cup (25 g/¾ oz) grated Parmesan, extra

1 Grease a 20 cm (8 inch) square shallow cake tin. Place the stock and a pinch of salt in a large saucepan and bring to the boil. Add the polenta in a steady stream, stirring constantly. Reduce the heat and simmer, stirring frequently, for 15–20 minutes. Remove from the heat and stir in the butter and Parmesan. Spread the mixture into the tin and refrigerate for 20 minutes.
2 Soak the porcini mushrooms in ½ cup (125 ml/4 fl oz) boiling water for 10 minutes, or until softened, then drain, reserving ⅓ cup (80 ml/2¾ fl oz) liquid.

3 Wipe the other mushrooms with a damp cloth. Thickly slice the Swiss brown mushrooms, and coarsely chop the field mushrooms. Heat ⅓ cup (80 ml/2¾ fl oz) oil in a large frying pan, add the mushrooms, including the porcini mushrooms, cook for 4–5 minutes, then remove from the pan. Heat the remaining oil in the pan and cook the onion and garlic over medium heat for 2–3 minutes, or until transparent.
4 Add the reserved soaking liquid, bay leaf, thyme and oregano to the pan, season and cook for 2 minutes. Return the mushrooms to the pan, add the parsley and vinegar and cook over medium heat for 1 minute, or until nearly dry. Remove the bay leaf and check the seasoning.
5 Sprinkle the extra Parmesan over the polenta and heat under a medium grill for 10 minutes, or until lightly browned and the cheese has melted. Cut into four 10 cm (4 inch) squares.
6 Place a polenta square in the centre of each serving plate and top with the mushroom mixture. Garnish with black pepper.

SPICY PENNE WITH PEPPERS (CAPSICUMS)

Preparation time: 30 minutes
Total cooking time: 12 minutes
Serves 4

1 large red pepper (capsicum)
1 large green pepper (capsicum)
1 large yellow pepper (capsicum)
500 g (1 lb) penne
1/3 cup (80 ml/2¾ fl oz) olive oil
2 tablespoons sweet chilli sauce
1 tablespoon red wine vinegar
1/3 cup (20 g/¾ oz) chopped fresh
   coriander
250 g (8 oz) cherry tomatoes, halved
freshly grated Parmesan, for serving

1 Cut the peppers into large flat pieces, and discard the seeds and membrane. Cook skin-side-up under a hot grill for 8 minutes, or until the skin is black and blistered. Remove from the heat and cover with a damp tea towel. When cool, peel away the skin and cut the pepper flesh into thin strips.
2 Meanwhile, cook the penne in a large pan of rapidly boiling salted water until al dente. Drain and return to the pan.
3 While the penne is cooking, whisk together the oil, chilli sauce and red wine vinegar, and season with salt and pepper, to taste.
4 Add the oil mixture, fresh coriander, peppers and cherry tomatoes to the pasta. Serve sprinkled with Parmesan.

NOTE: This dish can be served warm as a main meal, or at room temperature as a salad. It makes an excellent accompaniment to chicken or barbecued meat.

CHILLED SOBA NOODLES

Preparation time: 25 minutes
Total cooking time: 15 minutes
Serves 4

250 g (8 oz) dried soba (buckwheat)
   noodles
4 cm (1½ inch) piece fresh ginger
1 medium carrot
4 spring onions, outside layer removed

Dipping Sauce
1½ cups (375 ml/12 fl oz) water
3 tablespoons dashi granules
½ cup (125 ml/4 fl oz) Japanese soy sauce
1/3 cup (80 ml/2¾ fl oz) mirin
Garnishes
1 sheet nori
pickled ginger (page 766)
thinly sliced pickled daikon

1 Add the noodles to a large pan of boiling water. When the water returns to the boil, pour in 1 cup (250 ml/8 fl oz) cold water. Bring the water back to the boil and cook the noodles for about 2 to 3 minutes or until just tender—take care not to overcook them. Drain the noodles in a colander and then cool them under cold running water. Drain thoroughly and set aside.
2 Cut the ginger and carrot into fine matchsticks about 4 cm (1½ inches) long. Slice the spring onions very finely. Bring a small pan of water to the boil, then add the ginger, carrot and spring onion. Blanch for about 30 seconds, drain and place in a bowl of iced water to cool. Drain again when the vegetables are cool.
3 To make Dipping Sauce: Combine the water, dashi granules, soy sauce, mirin and a good pinch each of salt and pepper in a small pan. Bring the sauce to the boil, then cool completely. When ready to serve, pour the sauce into 4 small, wide dipping bowls.
4 Gently toss the cooled noodles and vegetables to combine. Arrange in 4 individual serving bowls, and sit the serving bowls onto plates.
5 Toast the nori by holding it over low heat and moving it back and forward for about 15 seconds. Cut it into thin strips with scissors, and scatter the strips over the noodles. Place a little pickled ginger and shredded daikon on the side of each plate. Serve the noodles with the Dipping Sauce. The noodles should be dipped into the sauce before being eaten.

SWISS ONION TART

Preparation time: 30 minutes
Total cooking time: 1 hour 10 minutes
Serves 4

2 sheets frozen shortcrust pastry
2 tablespoons oil
3 medium onions, sliced
½ cup (125 g/4 oz) sour cream
2 eggs
½ cup (65 g/2¼ oz) finely grated Gruyère
   cheese
cayenne pepper

1 Preheat the oven to hot 210°C
(415°F/Gas 6–7). Thaw the pastry and fit
the sheets, overlapping where necessary,
into a 20 cm (8 inch) fluted flan tin; trim
edges. Cut a sheet of baking paper large
enough to cover the pastry-lined tin.
Spread a layer of dried beans or rice
evenly over the paper. Bake the pastry
shell for 10 minutes, then remove from
oven. Discard the paper and beans or
rice. Return the pastry-lined tin to the
oven for another 5 minutes or until the
pastry is lightly golden. Reduce the oven
temperature to moderate 180°C
(350°F/Gas 4).
2 Heat the oil in a pan and add the onions.
Cook over low heat, stirring often, for
15 minutes or until onion is lightly
browned and very tender. Spread over
pastry base.
3 Whisk the sour cream and eggs in a
medium bowl until smooth. Add the
cheese and stir until combined. Place the
flan tin on a baking tray. Pour the egg
mixture over the onion and sprinkle
lightly with cayenne pepper. Bake for
40 minutes or until the filling is set. Serve
warm or cold.

LINGUINE WITH RED PEPPER (CAPSICUM) SAUCE

Preparation time: 20 minutes
Total cooking time: 30 minutes
Serves 6

3 red peppers (capsicums)
3 tablespoons olive oil
1 large onion, sliced
2 cloves garlic, crushed
¼–½ teaspoon chilli powder or flakes
½ cup (125 ml/4 oz) cream
2 tablespoons chopped fresh oregano
500 g (1 lb) linguine or spaghetti (plain or
   spinach)

1 Cut the red peppers into large flat
pieces and discard the seeds and
membrane. Place skin-side up, under a
hot grill and cook for 8 minutes, or until
black and blistered. Remove from the
heat, cover with a damp tea towel and,
when cool, peel away the skin and cut the
flesh into thin strips.
2 Heat the oil in a large heavy-based pan.
Add the onion and stir over low heat for
8 minutes, or until soft. Add the pepper
strips, garlic, chilli and cream and cook
for 2 minutes, stirring occasionally. Add
the oregano and salt and pepper, to taste.
3 About 15 minutes before the sauce is
cooked, cook the pasta in a large pan of
rapidly boiling salted water until al dente.
Drain and return to the pan. Add the
sauce to the hot pasta and toss until well
combined.

NOTE: If necessary, you can substitute
dried oregano. Use about one-third of the
quantity as dried herbs have a much
stronger flavour. For a stronger red
pepper flavour, just omit the cream.

PASTA AND SPINACH TIMBALES

Preparation time: 25 minutes
Total cooking time: 45 minutes + resting
Serves 6

30 g (1 oz) butter
1 tablespoon olive oil
1 onion, chopped
500 g (1 lb) English spinach, steamed and
   well-drained
8 eggs, beaten
1 cup (250 ml/8 fl oz) cream
100 g (3½ oz) spaghetti or tagliolini,
   cooked
½ cup (60 g/2 oz) grated Cheddar cheese
½ cup (50 g/1¾ oz) freshly grated
   Parmesan

1 Preheat the oven to moderate 180°C
(350°F/Gas 4). Brush six 1-cup capacity
dariole moulds with melted butter or oil.
Line the bases with baking paper. Heat
the butter and oil together in a frying pan.
Add the onion and stir over low heat until
the onion is tender. Add the well-drained
spinach and cook for 1 minute. Remove
from the heat and allow to cool. Whisk in
the eggs and cream. Stir in the spaghetti
or tagliolini, grated cheeses, and salt and
freshly ground pepper, to taste; stir well.
Spoon into the prepared moulds.
2 Place the moulds in a baking dish. Pour
boiling water into the baking dish to come
halfway up the sides of the moulds. Bake
for 30–35 minutes or until set. Halfway
through cooking, you may need to cover
the top with a sheet of foil to prevent
excess browning. Near the end of cooking
time, test the timbales with the point of a
knife. When cooked, the knife should
come out clean.
3 Allow the timbales to rest for 15 minutes
before turning them out. Run the point of
a knife around the edge of each mould.
Invert onto serving plates.

CHILLI SATAY NOODLES

Preparation time: 10 minutes
Total cooking time: 10 minutes
Serves 4–6

500 g (1 lb) thin fresh egg noodles
1 tablespoon oil
1 teaspoon sesame oil
4 tablespoons peanuts, shelled, peeled
2 small red chillies
4 slender eggplants (aubergines), sliced
200 g (6½ oz) sugar snap peas
100 g (3⅓ oz) bean sprouts
3 tablespoons crunchy peanut butter
1 tablespoon hoi sin sauce
⅓ cup (80 ml/2¾ fl oz) coconut milk
2 tablespoons lime juice
1 tablespoon Thai sweet chilli sauce

1 Add the noodles to a large pan of boiling water and cook for 3 minutes. Heat the oils in a wok or pan. Add the peanuts and toss over high heat for 1 minute or until golden. Add the chillies, eggplants and sugar snap peas and cook over high heat for 2 minutes. Reduce the heat to medium and add noodles and sprouts; toss for 1 minute or until combined.
2 Blend the peanut butter, hoi sin sauce, coconut milk, lime juice and chilli sauce until almost smooth. Add to the noodles. Toss over medium heat until the noodles are coated and the sauce is heated.

ZUCCHINI (COURGETTE) OMELETTE

Preparation time: 5 minutes
Total cooking time: 15 minutes
Serves 4

80 g (2¾ oz) butter
400 g (13 oz) zucchini (courgettes), sliced
1 tablespoon finely chopped fresh basil
pinch of ground nutmeg
8 eggs, lightly beaten

1 Melt half the butter in a non-stick 23 cm (9 inch) frying pan. Add the zucchini and cook over moderate heat for about 8 minutes, until lightly golden. Stir in the basil and nutmeg, season with salt and pepper and cook for 30 seconds. Transfer to a bowl and keep warm.
2 Wipe out the pan, return it to the heat and melt the remaining butter. Lightly season the eggs and pour into the pan. Stir gently over high heat. Stop stirring when the mixture begins to set in uniform, fluffy small clumps. Reduce the heat and lift the edges with a fork to prevent it catching. Shake the pan from side to side to prevent the omelette sticking. When it is almost set but still runny on the surface, spread the zucchini down the centre. Using a spatula, fold the omelette over and slide onto a serving plate.

IDIYAPPAM

Preparation time: 10 minutes +
  30 minutes soaking
Total cooking time: 20 minutes
Serves 4

225 g (7 oz) rice sticks or dried rice
  vermicelli
⅓ cup (80 ml/2¾ fl oz) oil
50 g (1¾ oz) cashew nuts
½ onion, chopped
3 eggs
150 g (5 oz) fresh or frozen peas
10 curry leaves
2 carrots, grated
2 leeks (white part only), finely shredded
1 red capsicum (pepper), diced
2 tablespoons tomato ketchup
1 tablespoon soy sauce

1 Soak the rice sticks in cold water for about 30 minutes, then drain and put them in a saucepan of boiling water. Remove from the heat and leave in the pan for 3 minutes. Drain and refresh in cold water.
2 Heat 1 tablespoon of the oil in a frying pan and fry the cashews until golden. Remove, add the onion to the pan, fry until dark golden, then drain on paper towels. Cook the eggs in boiling water for 10 minutes to hard-boil, then cool them immediately in cold water. When cold, peel them and cut into wedges. Cook the peas in boiling water until tender.
3 Heat the remaining oil in a frying pan and briefly fry the curry leaves. Add the carrot, leek and red capsicum and stir for 1 minute. Add the ketchup, soy sauce, 1 teaspoon salt and rice sticks and mix, stirring constantly to prevent the rice sticks from sticking to the pan. Serve on a platter and garnish with the peas, cashews, fried onion and egg wedges.

SPINACH RAVIOLI WITH SUN-DRIED TOMATO SAUCE

Preparation time: 20 minutes
Total cooking time: 15 minutes
Serves 4

¾ cup (155 g/5 oz) firmly packed, chopped, cooked English spinach
250 g (8 oz) ricotta cheese, well drained
2 tablespoons freshly grated Parmesan
1 tablespoon chopped fresh chives
1 egg, lightly beaten
200 g (6½ oz) packet gow gee wrappers

Sauce
⅓ cup (80 ml/2¾ fl oz) extra virgin olive oil
3 tablespoons pine nuts
100 g (3½ oz) sun-dried tomatoes, sliced

1 Combine the spinach, ricotta and Parmesan, chives and half the beaten egg in a medium bowl. Mix well and season with salt and pepper, to taste. Place 1½ teaspoons of the mixture into the centre of a gow gee wrapper. Brush the edge of the wrapper lightly with some of the remaining beaten egg, then cover with another wrapper, until they are all used. Press the edges firmly to seal. Using a 7 cm (2¾ inch) plain scone cutter, cut the ravioli into circles.
2 Cook the ravioli, in batches, in a large pan of rapidly boiling salted water for 4 minutes, or until al dente. Don't crowd the pan. Keep each batch warm while cooking the remainder. Carefully drain the ravioli, add to the sauce and toss very gently.
3 To make the sauce, combine the ingredients in a large pan and heat slowly until warm.

NORI-WRAPPED FRIED MUSHROOMS

Preparation time: 30 minutes
Total cooking time: 15 minutes
Serves 4

⅓ cup (80 ml/2¾ fl oz) Japanese soy sauce
100 ml (3½ fl oz) mirin
2 teaspoons grated fresh ginger
2 teaspoons sugar
3 nori sheets, toasted
12 open-cup mushrooms, stalks removed
400 g (13 oz) orange sweet potato
oil, for deep-frying
225 ml (7 fl oz) chilled soda water
1 egg, lightly beaten
1 cup (125 g/4 oz) tempura flour
2 tablespoons wasabi powder

1 To make the sauce, put the soy sauce, mirin, ginger, sugar and 1 tablespoon water in a saucepan and cook, stirring constantly, over medium heat until the sugar has dissolved. Cover and keep warm.
2 Cut the nori sheets into twelve 4 cm (1½ inch) wide strips with scissors. Wrap a strip around each mushroom, dampening the end to help it stick. Cut the orange sweet potato into ribbon strips with a vegetable peeler.
3 Fill a wok one-third full of oil and heat to 190°C (375°F), or until a cube of bread dropped into the oil browns in 10 seconds. Cook the sweet potato in batches for about 30–60 seconds, or until golden and crispy. Drain on crumpled paper towels, season and keep warm.
4 Put the soda water and egg in a large bowl and whisk well. Add the tempura flour and wasabi powder and loosely mix in with chopsticks or a fork until just combined—the batter should still be lumpy. Coat the mushrooms in the batter and cook in batches for 1–2 minutes, or until golden and crisp, turning once. Drain on crumpled paper towels and season with salt. Serve immediately with the sweet potato ribbons and the sauce.

CURRY-FLAVOURED NOODLES

Preparation time: 25 minutes
Total cooking time: 10 minutes
Serves 4

250 g (8 oz) thick fresh noodles
¼ cup (60 ml/2 fl oz) oil
2 cloves garlic, sliced
1 onion, finely sliced
1 red pepper (capsicum), cut into long, thin strips
1 small cucumber, unpeeled, cut into thin 4 cm (1½ inch) strips
2 teaspoons mild curry powder
½ cup (125 ml/4 fl oz) vegetable stock
2 teaspoons dry sherry
1 tablespoon soy sauce
½ teaspoon sugar
3 spring onions, sliced diagonally

1 Add the noodles to a large pan of boiling water and cook until just tender; drain.
2 Heat the oil in a wok or pan. Add the garlic, onion and red pepper and stir over medium heat for 3 minutes. Add the cucumber and curry powder and stir over medium heat for another 3 minutes.
3 Add the combined stock, sherry, soy sauce and sugar, stir until the mixture boils. Add the noodles and spring onions, stir over low heat for 3 minutes or until ingredients are well combined and heated through.

STUFFED PUMPKINS

Preparation time: 25 minutes
Total cooking time: 50 minutes
Makes 4

4 medium golden nugget pumpkins
¼ cup (60 ml/2 fl oz) water
½ cup (95 g/3¼ oz) cooked rice
2 teaspoons curry paste
1 tablespoon finely chopped fresh
   coriander
1 green apple, finely chopped
1 small zucchini (courgette), finely
   chopped
1 small carrot, finely chopped
60 g (2 oz) button mushrooms, thinly
   sliced
155 g (5 oz) asparagus spears, chopped
2 teaspoons currants
¼ teaspoon garam masala
60 g (2 oz) butter, melted

1 Preheat oven to hot 210°C (415°F/
Gas 6–7). Cut top off each pumpkin; set
aside. Scoop out seeds and discard.
Arrange pumpkins in medium ovenproof
dish; replace tops. Add water to dish and
cover firmly with foil; bake for 30 minutes.
Remove from oven; remove pumpkins;
drain water and brush dish with melted
butter or oil.
2 Combine rice, curry paste, coriander,
apple, zucchini, carrot, mushrooms,
asparagus, currants, garam masala and
butter in a medium bowl; mix well. Spoon
rice and vegetable mixture into the
pumpkin cavities. Top with lids. Return to
prepared dish and cover with foil. Bake
pumpkins for 20 minutes or until just
cooked.

TORTELLINI WITH MUSHROOM SAUCE

Preparation time: 40 minutes + 30
   minutes resting
Total cooking time: 35–40 minutes
Serves 4

Pasta
2 cups (250 g/9 oz) plain flour
pinch salt
3 eggs
1 tablespoon olive oil
¼ cup (60 ml/2 fl oz) water

Filling
125 g (4 oz) packet frozen spinach,
   thawed, excess liquid removed
½ cup 125 g (4 oz) ricotta cheese
2 tablespoons freshly grated Parmesan
   cheese
1 egg, beaten
salt and freshly ground black pepper

Sauce
1 tablespoon olive oil
1 clove garlic, crushed
125 g (4 oz) mushrooms, sliced
1 cup (250 ml/8 fl oz) cream
3 tablespoons freshly grated Parmesan
   cheese
salt and freshly ground black pepper

1 To make Pasta: Sift the flour and salt
onto a board. Make a well in the centre of
the flour. In a jug, whisk together eggs, oil
and 1 tablespoon of the water. Add the
egg mixture gradually to the flour,
working in with your hands until the
mixture forms a ball. Add extra water if
necessary. Knead on a lightly floured
surface for 5 minutes or until dough is
smooth and elastic. Place the dough in a
lightly oiled bowl. Cover with plastic wrap
and set aside for 30 minutes.

2 To make Filling: In a bowl, combine the
drained spinach, ricotta and Parmesan
cheeses, egg, salt and pepper. Set aside.
3 To make Sauce: Heat the oil in a frying
pan. Add the garlic and stir over low heat
for 30 seconds. Add the mushrooms and
cook for 3 minutes. Pour in the cream and
set aside.
4 Roll the dough out on a lightly floured
surface until it is very thin. Using a
floured cutter, cut into 5 cm (2 inch)
rounds. Spoon about ½ teaspoon of filling
in the centre of each round. Brush a little
water around the edge of each round.
Fold the rounds in half to form a semi-
circle. Press the edges together firmly.
Wrap each semi-circle around your
forefinger to form a ring. Press the ends
of the dough together firmly.
5 Cook the tortellini in batches in a large
pan of rapidly boiling water for about 8
minutes each batch, until just tender.
Drain well and return to the pan. Keep
warm.
6 Return sauce to medium heat. Bring to
the boil. Reduce heat and simmer for
3 minutes. Add the Parmesan cheese, salt
and pepper and stir well. Add the sauce to
the tortellini and toss until well
combined. Divide the tortellini and sauce
between individual warmed serving
bowls.

MEXICAN TOMATO BAKE

Preparation time: 25 minutes
Total cooking time: 30 minutes
Serves 4–6

2 tablespoons oil
2 red (Spanish) onions, chopped
2 cloves garlic, crushed
6 ripe tomatoes, peeled and chopped
1 green pepper (capsicum), seeded and
    chopped
1 tablespoon red wine vinegar
1 teaspoon sugar
½ teaspoon ground chilli powder
375 g (12 oz) canned corn kernels,
    drained
125 g (4 oz) plain corn chips
1¼ cups (155 g/5 oz) grated Cheddar
    cheese
1 cup (250 g/8 oz) sour cream

1 Preheat oven to warm 160°C (315°F/
Gas 2–3). Heat oil in a medium pan. Add
onions and garlic; cook over medium heat
for 3 minutes. Add tomatoes, pepper,
vinegar, sugar and chilli. Cook,
uncovered, for 6–7 minutes or until
tomatoes are soft and liquid has
evaporated. Stir in corn kernels over heat
for 3 minutes.
2 Arrange layers of corn chips, sauce and
cheese in a casserole dish, finishing with
cheese layer.
3 Spread with sour cream. Bake,
uncovered, for 15 minutes. Sprinkle with
chopped chives.

OLIVE AND MOZZARELLA
SPAGHETTI

Preparation time: 20 minutes
Total cooking time: 15 minutes
Serves 4

500 g (1 lb) spaghetti
50 g (1¾ oz) butter
2 cloves garlic, crushed
½ cup (70 g/2¼ oz) pitted black olives,
    halved
3 tablespoons olive oil
⅓ cup (20 g/¾ oz) chopped fresh parsley
150 g (5 oz) mozzarella cheese, cut into
    small cubes

1 Cook the spaghetti in a large pan of
rapidly boiling salted water until al dente.
Drain and return to the pan.
2 While the spaghetti is cooking, heat the
butter in a small pan until it begins to
turn nutty brown. Add the crushed garlic
and cook over low heat for 1 minute.
3 Add to the pasta with the black olives,
olive oil, fresh parsley and mozzarella
cheese. Toss until well combined.

FENNEL FRITTERS

Preparation time: 15 minutes
Total cooking time: 20 minutes
Serves 4

1 kg (2 lb) fennel bulbs
⅓ cup (30 g/1 oz) grated Pecorino
1 cup (80 g/2¾ oz) fresh breadcrumbs
½ cup (60 g/2 oz) plain flour
3 eggs, lightly beaten
olive oil, for shallow-frying
lemon wedges, for serving

1 Remove the tough outer leaves from the
fennel, then trim the base and small
stalks. Slice the fennel lengthways into
5 mm (¼ inch) widths and blanch in
boiling salted water for 3 minutes, or until
tender. Drain and pat dry. Leave to cool.
2 Mix together the cheese and
breadcrumbs and season with salt and
pepper.
3 Coat the fennel in flour, shake off the
excess and dip in beaten egg. Coat in the
crumb and cheese mix. Heat the oil in
large heavy-based frying pan until the oil
beings to sizzle. Fry the fennel in batches,
being careful not to overcrowd the pan,
for 2–3 minutes per side, until golden
brown and crisp. Drain on paper towels,
season and serve immediately with the
lemon wedges.

NOTE: Use the rounder, male fennel
bulbs, rather than the flatter female
bulbs, as they have more flavour.

FETTUCINE BOSCAIOLA (FETTUCINE WITH MUSHROOM AND TOMATO SAUCE)

Preparation time: 20 minutes
Total cooking time: 25 minutes
Serves 6

500 g (1 lb) button mushrooms
1 large onion
2 tablespoons olive oil
2 cloves garlic, finely chopped
2 x 425 g (14 oz) cans tomatoes, roughly
  chopped
500 g (1 lb) fettucine
2 tablespoons chopped fresh parsley

1 Carefully wipe the mushrooms with a damp paper towel and then slice finely, including the stems.
2 Chop the onion roughly. Heat the oil in a heavy-based frying pan and cook the onion and garlic over medium heat, stirring occasionally, for about 6 minutes, or until the vegetables are light golden. Add the tomato including the juice, along with the mushrooms, to the pan and bring the mixture to the boil. Reduce the heat, cover the pan and simmer for 15 minutes.
3 While the sauce is cooking, cook the fettucine in a large pan of rapidly boiling salted water until al dente. Drain and return to the pan.
4 Stir the parsley into the sauce and season well with salt and pepper, to taste. Toss the sauce through the pasta.

NOTE: If you would like a creamy sauce, add ½ cup (125 ml/4 fl oz) of cream when adding the parsley (do not reboil or it may curdle).

SWEET AND SOUR TOFU

Preparation time: 15 minutes
Total cooking time: 20 minutes
Serves 4

⅓ cup (80 ml/2¾ fl oz) rice vinegar
2 tablespoons light soy sauce
1½ tablespoons caster sugar
2 tablespoons tomato sauce
1½ cups (375 ml/12 fl oz) chicken or
  vegetable stock
600 g (1¼ lb) firm tofu
3–4 tablespoons vegetable oil
1 large carrot, julienned
2 cups (180 g/6 oz) bean sprouts or soy
  bean sprouts, tailed
1 cup (95 g/3 oz) sliced button
  mushrooms
6–8 spring onions, sliced on the diagonal
100 g (3½ oz) snow peas (mangetout), cut
  in half on the diagonal
1 tablespoon cornflour dissolved in
  2 tablespoons water

1 Combine the vinegar, soy sauce, sugar, tomato sauce and stock in a small bowl.
2 Cut the tofu in half horizontally, then cut into 16 triangles in total. Heat a wok over high heat, add 2 tablespoons of the oil and swirl to coat. Add the tofu in batches and stir-fry over medium heat for 2 minutes on each side, or until crisp and golden. Drain on paper towels and set aside. Keep warm.
3 Wipe the wok clean, then reheat it over high heat. Add the remaining oil and swirl to coat. Add the carrot, bean sprouts, mushrooms, spring onion and snow peas and stir-fry for 1 minute. Add the sauce and stir for a further 1 minute. Add the cornflour paste and cook until the sauce thickens. Divide the tofu among the serving bowls and spoon some sauce over the top. Serve with steamed rice on the side.

VEGETABLE COUSCOUS

Preparation time: 40 minutes
Total cooking time: 30 minutes
Serves 4–6

3 tablespoons olive oil
2 small onions, thinly sliced
1 teaspoon turmeric
½ teaspoon chilli powder
2 teaspoons grated fresh ginger
1 cinnamon stick
2 carrots, thickly sliced
2 parsnips, thickly sliced
1½ cups (375 ml/12 fl oz) vegetable stock
315 g (10 oz) pumpkin, cut into small cubes
250 g (8 oz) cauliflower, cut into florets
2 zucchini (courgettes), cut into thick slices
425 g (13½ oz) can chickpeas, drained
pinch of saffron threads
2 tablespoons chopped fresh coriander
2 tablespoons chopped fresh flat-leaf
  parsley
1¼ cups (230 g/7½ oz) instant couscous
1 cup (250 ml/8 oz) boiling water
30 g (1 oz) butter

1 Heat 2 tablespoons of the oil in a large saucepan. Add the onion and cook over medium heat for 5 minutes, or until the onion is soft, stirring occasionally. Add the turmeric, chilli powder and ginger and cook, stirring, for another minute.
2 Add the cinnamon stick, carrot, parsnip and stock to the pan and stir to combine. Cover and bring to the boil. Reduce the heat and simmer for 5 minutes, or until the vegetables are almost tender.
3 Add the pumpkin, cauliflower and zucchini and simmer for another 10 minutes. Stir in the chickpeas, saffron, coriander and parsley and simmer, uncovered, for 5 minutes. Remove the cinnamon stick.
4 Place the couscous in a bowl and add the boiling water. Cover, allow to stand for 5 minutes, then add the remaining oil and butter and fluff with a fork. Place a bed of couscous on each serving plate and top with the vegetables.

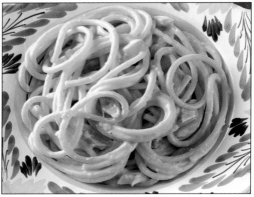

BUTTERNUT PUMPKIN FILLED WITH PASTA AND LEEKS

Preparation time: 30 minutes
Total cooking time: 1 hour
Serves 2 as a light meal, or 4 as an
    accompaniment

1 medium butternut pumpkin
20 g (¾ oz) butter
1 leek, thinly sliced
½ cup (125 ml/4 fl oz) cream
pinch of nutmeg
60 g (2 oz) cooked linguine or stellini
¼ cup (60 ml/2 fl oz) olive oil

1 Preheat the oven to moderate 180°C
(350°F/Gas 4). Cleanly cut a quarter off
the top end of the butternut pumpkin
(where the stalk attaches), to make a lid.
Level off the other end so that it stands
evenly. Scrape out the seeds and sinew
from the pumpkin and discard. Hollow out
the centre to make room for filling.
Sprinkle salt and pepper over the cut
surfaces and then transfer the pumpkin
to a small baking dish.
2 Melt the butter in a small frying pan and
gently cook the leek until softened. Add
the cream and nutmeg and cook over low
heat for 4–5 minutes, or until thickened.
Season with salt and white pepper, to
taste, and stir in the pasta.
3 Fill the butternut pumpkin with the
pasta mixture, place the lid on top and
drizzle with the olive oil. Bake for 1 hour,
or until tender. Test by inserting a skewer
through the thickest part of the vegetable.
note: Choose a butternut which is round
and fat, not one with a long stem of flesh.

BUCATINI WITH GORGONZOLA SAUCE

Preparation time: 10 minutes
Total cooking time: 20 minutes
Serves 6

375 g (12 oz) bucatini or spaghetti
200 g (6½ oz) gorgonzola cheese
20 g (¾ oz) butter
1 celery stick, chopped
1¼ cups (315 ml/10 fl oz) cream
250 g (8 oz) fresh ricotta cheese, beaten
    until smooth

1 Cook the pasta in a large pan of rapidly
boiling salted water until al dente. Drain
and return to the pan.
2 While the pasta is cooking, chop the
gorgonzola cheese into small cubes.
3 Heat the butter in a medium pan, add
the celery and stir for 2 minutes. Add the
cream, ricotta and gorgonzola and
season, to taste, with freshly ground
black pepper.
4 Bring to the boil over low heat, stirring
constantly, and then simmer for 1 minute.
Add the sauce to the warm pasta and toss
well.

TOFU AND VEGETABLES

Preparation time: 25–30 minutes
Total cooking time: 20 minutes
Serves 4–6

125 g (4 oz) rice vermicelli
¾ cup (185 ml/6 fl oz) oil
1 tablespoon soy sauce
1 tablespoon sherry
1 tablespoon oyster sauce (optional)
½ cup (125 ml/4 fl oz) vegetable stock
2 teaspoons cornflour
2 teaspoons water
1 tablespoon oil, extra
1 clove garlic, crushed
1 teaspoon grated fresh ginger
375 g (12 oz) firm tofu, cut into small
    cubes
2 medium carrots, cut into matchsticks
250 g (8 oz) snow peas (mange tout),
    trimmed
4 spring onions, finely sliced
425 g (13½ oz) canned straw mushrooms,
    drained

1 Break the vermicelli into short lengths.
Heat half the oil in a wok. Cook the
vermicelli in batches in the wok over
medium heat until crisp, adding more oil
when necessary. Drain on paper towels.
2 Combine the soy sauce, sherry, oyster
sauce and stock in a small bowl. Blend
the cornflour with the water in a small
bowl.
3 Heat the wok; add the extra oil and the
garlic and ginger and cook over high heat
for 1 minute. Add the tofu and stir-fry for
3 minutes. Remove the tofu from the wok.
Add the carrots and snow peas to the wok
and stir-fry for 1 minute. Add the
combined sauces and vegetable stock;
cover and cook for another 3 minutes, or
until the vegetables are just cooked.
4 Return the tofu to the wok. Add the
spring onions, mushrooms and blended
cornflour. Stir until the sauce has
thickened, then remove from the heat.
Serve with the crisp vermicelli.

FETTUCINE WITH SNOW PEAS (MANGETOUT) AND WALNUTS

Preparation time: 30 minutes
Total cooking time: 15 minutes
Serves 4

500 g (1 lb) fettucine or linguine
½ cup (60 g/2 oz) chopped walnuts
30 g (1 oz) butter
1 large onion, chopped
4 bacon rashers, chopped, optional
1 clove garlic, crushed
¾ cup (185 ml/6 fl oz) dry white wine
1 cup (250 ml/8 fl oz) cream
250 g (8 oz) snow peas (mangetout), cut
  into pieces

1 Cook the fettucine in a large pan of rapidly boiling salted water until al dente. Drain and return to the pan.
2 While the pasta is cooking, scatter the walnuts on a foil-lined grill tray. Cook under a moderately hot grill for 2 minutes, or until lightly toasted. Stir after 1 minute, and be careful they don't burn. Set aside to cool.
3 Melt the butter in a large pan. Add the onion and bacon and cook until the onion is soft and the bacon lightly browned. Add the garlic and cook for another minute.
4 Pour in the white wine and cream, bring to the boil and reduce the heat. Simmer for 4 minutes, add the snow peas and simmer for another minute. Toss the sauce and walnuts through the pasta. Season with salt and pepper, to taste.

NOTE: Don't be tempted to save time by not toasting the nuts. Raw nuts may be bitter and stale in flavour, particularly if they are old, or have been kept in the refrigerator.

TOFU IN BLACK BEAN SAUCE

Preparation time: 20 minutes
Total cooking time: 15 minutes
Serves 4

⅓ cup (80 ml/2¾ fl oz) vegetable stock
2 teaspoons cornflour
2 teaspoons Chinese rice wine
1 teaspoon sesame oil
1 tablespoon soy sauce
2 tablespoons peanut oil
450 g (14 oz) firm tofu, cut into 2 cm
  (¾ inch) cubes
2 cloves garlic, very finely chopped
2 teaspoons finely chopped fresh ginger
3 tablespoons black beans, rinsed and
  very finely chopped
4 spring onions, sliced on the diagonal
  (white and green parts)
1 red pepper (capsicum), cut into 2 cm (¾
  inch) chunks
300 g (10 oz) baby bok choy, chopped
  crossways into 2 cm (¾ inch) pieces

1 Combine the vegetable stock, cornflour, Chinese rice wine, sesame oil, soy sauce, ½ teaspoon salt and freshly ground black pepper in a small bowl.
2 Heat a wok over medium heat, add the peanut oil and swirl to coat. Add the tofu and stir-fry in two batches for 3 minutes each batch, or until lightly browned. Remove with a slotted spoon and drain on paper towels. Discard any bits of tofu stuck to the wok or floating in the oil.
3 Add the garlic and ginger and stir-fry for 30 seconds. Toss in the black beans and spring onion and stir-fry for 30 seconds. Add the pepper and stir-fry for 1 minute. Add the bok choy and stir-fry for a further 2 minutes. Return the tofu to the wok and stir gently. Pour in the sauce and stir gently for 2–3 minutes, or until the sauce has thickened slightly. Serve immediately with steamed rice.

FETTUCINE WITH ZUCCHINI (COURGETTES) AND CRISP-FRIED BASIL

Preparation time: 15 minutes
Total cooking time: 15 minutes
Serves 6

1 cup (250 ml/8 fl oz) olive oil
a handful of fresh basil leaves
500 g (1 lb) fettucine or tagliatelle
60 g (2 oz) butter
2 cloves garlic, crushed
500 g (1 lb) zucchini (courgettes), grated
¾ cup (75 g/2½ oz) freshly grated
  Parmesan

1 To crisp-fry the basil leaves, heat the oil in a small pan, add 2 leaves at a time and cook for 1 minute, or until crisp. Remove with a slotted spoon and drain on paper towels. Repeat with the remaining basil leaves.
2 Cook the pasta in a large pan of rapidly boiling salted water until al dente. Drain and return to the pan.
3 While the pasta is cooking, heat the butter in a deep heavy-based pan over low heat until the butter is foaming. Add the garlic and cook for 1 minute. Add the zucchini and cook, stirring occasionally, for 1–2 minutes or until softened. Add to the hot pasta. Add the Parmesan and toss well. Serve the pasta garnished with the crisp basil leaves.

NOTE: The basil leaves can be fried up to 2 hours in advance. Store in an airtight container after cooling.

VEGETABLE OMELETTE WITH PITTA BREAD

Preparation time: 50 minutes
Total cooking time: 20 minutes
Serves 4

4 baby beetroot, peeled and grated
2½ teaspoons grated fresh ginger
2 cloves garlic, crushed
1 teaspoon rice vinegar
1 teaspoon sesame oil
4–5 teaspoons soy sauce
2 spring onions, finely chopped
few drops Tabasco sauce
3 tablespoons peanut oil
1 onion, thinly sliced
1 red pepper (capsicum), cut in thin strips
1 medium carrot, peeled and grated
4 baby bok choy leaves, shredded
1 tablespoon sweet chilli sauce
3 eggs, lightly beaten
1 tablespoon cornflour
8 round pitta breads

1 Place the beetroot, ½ teaspoon of ginger, half the garlic, rice vinegar, sesame oil, 1 teaspoon of soy sauce, spring onions and Tabasco sauce in a medium bowl. Mix until well combined.
2 Heat half the peanut oil in a wok or frying pan. Add the onion and remaining garlic and cook over medium heat for 1 minute. Stir in the red pepper, carrot, bok choy, remaining ginger and chilli sauce. Cook for another 1–2 minutes, or until just tender. Remove from the heat and transfer the mixture to a large bowl; allow to cool slightly. Combine the eggs, cornflour and soy sauce in a bowl. Add to cooled vegetable mixture and stir well.
3 Heat remaining oil in a frying pan. Spoon a quarter of the egg and vegetable mixture into pan to make a thick circle. Cook for 1–2 minutes each side. Repeat.
4 Lightly toast the pitta breads. Drain the excess liquid from the beetroot mixture. Place four pitta breads on individual serving plates. On each pitta bread, place a vegetable omelette and some of the beetroot mixture.

RED PEPPER (CAPSICUM) GNOCCHI WITH GOAT'S CHEESE

Preparation time: 1 hour
Total cooking time: 40 minutes
Serves 6–8

1 large red pepper (capsicum)
500 g (1 lb) kumera (orange sweet potato), chopped
500 g (1 lb) old potatoes, chopped
1 tablespoon sambal oelek
1 tablespoon grated orange rind
2¾ cups (340 g/11 oz) plain flour
2 eggs, lightly beaten
2 cups (500 ml/16 fl oz) bottled pasta sauce
100 g (3½ oz) goat's cheese
2 tablespoons finely shredded fresh basil leaves

1 Cut the red pepper in half and discard the seeds and membrane. Put, skin-side-up, under a hot grill and cook for 8 minutes, or until the skin is black and blistered. Remove from the heat and cover with a damp tea towel. When cool, peel away the skin. Process the pepper in a food processor to form a smooth purée.
2 Steam or boil the kumera and potato in a large pan until very soft. Drain thoroughly, transfer to a large bowl and mash until smooth. Allow to cool slightly.
3 Add the pepper purée, sambal oelek, orange rind, flour and eggs, and mix to form a soft dough. Using floured hands, roll heaped teaspoonsful of the dough into oval shapes. Indent one side using lightly floured prongs on the back of a fork.
4 Lower batches of gnocchi into a large pan of boiling salted water. Cook for about 2 minutes, or until the gnocchi rise to the surface. Remove the gnocchi with a slotted spoon and divide among warmed serving plates. Top with the warmed pasta sauce. Crumble the goat's cheese and sprinkle over the top with the shredded basil.

PEPPERED STIR-FRIED SNAKE BEANS

Preparation time: 20 minutes
Total cooking time: 8 minutes
Serves 4

1 tablespoon drained, canned green peppercorns
½ cup (15 g/½ oz) fresh coriander leaves and chopped stems
1 tablespoon oil
2 cloves garlic, chopped
220 g (7 oz) snake beans, cut into 4 cm (1½ inch) lengths
155 g/5 oz asparagus, cut into 4 cm (1½ inch) lengths
1 teaspoon soft brown sugar
2 teaspoons water
1 tablespoon fish sauce (optional)
1 teaspoon chopped fresh red or green chillies (optional)

1 Finely crush the peppercorns. Chop the coriander leaves and mix in a bowl with the stems and peppercorns.
2 Heat oil in a wok or frying pan. Add peppercorn mixture, garlic, beans, asparagus and sugar; stir-fry for 30 seconds over medium heat.
3 Add the water, cover and steam for 2 minutes or until the vegetables are just tender. Season with fish sauce; sprinkle with chillies and serve immediately.

NOTE: Snake beans have a delicious crisp texture. However, if they are not available, green beans may be substituted.

POTATO NOODLES WITH VEGETABLES

Preparation time: 25 minutes +
    10 minutes soaking
Total cooking time: 25 minutes
Serves 4

300 g (9⅔ oz) dried potato starch noodles
4 tablespoons dried black fungus
¼ cup (60 ml/2 fl oz) sesame oil
2 tablespoons vegetable oil
3 cloves garlic, finely chopped
4 cm (1½ inch) piece fresh ginger, grated
2 spring onions, finely chopped
2 carrots, cut into 4 cm (1½ inch)
    matchsticks
2 spring onions, extra, cut into 4 cm
    (1½ inch) pieces
500 g (1 lb) baby bok choy or 250 g (8 oz)
    spinach, roughly chopped
¼ cup (60 ml/2 fl oz) Japanese soy sauce
2 tablespoons mirin
1 teaspoon sugar
2 tablespoons sesame and seaweed sprinkle

1 Cook the noodles in a large pot of boiling water for about 5 minutes, or until they are translucent. Drain and rinse thoroughly under cold running water until the noodles are cold (this will also remove any excess starch). Use scissors to roughly chop the noodles into shorter lengths—this will make them easy to eat with chopsticks. Pour hot water over the black fungus and soak for about 10 minutes.
2 Heat 1 tablespoon of the sesame oil with the vegetable oil in a large heavy-based pan or wok. Cook the garlic, ginger and spring onion for 3 minutes over medium heat, stirring regularly. Add the carrots and stir-fry for 1 minute. Add the drained cooled noodles, extra spring onion, bok choy, remaining sesame oil, soy sauce, mirin and sugar. Toss well to coat the noodles with the sauce. Cover and cook over low heat for 2 minutes. Add the fungus, then cover and cook for 2 minutes further. Scatter over the sesame and seaweed sprinkle and serve immediately.

FETA AND OLIVE HERB PIE

Preparation time: 40 minutes +
    rising of pastry
Total cooking time: 45 minutes
Serves 4–6

2 teaspoons sugar
2 teaspoons (7 g/¼ oz) dried yeast
2 tablespoons olive oil
½ cup (60 g/2 oz) plain flour
1 cup (125 g/4 oz) self-raising flour
1 onion, sliced
½ cup (15 g/½ oz) fresh flat-leaf parsley,
    chopped
1 sprig fresh rosemary, chopped
3 sprigs fresh thyme, chopped
5 fresh basil leaves, torn
¼ cup (40 g/1¼ oz) pine nuts, toasted
1 clove garlic, crushed
175 g (5¾ oz) feta cheese, crumbled
¼ cup (35 g/1¼ oz) pitted olives, chopped

1 Dissolve half the sugar in ½ cup (125 ml/4 fl oz) warm water and sprinkle the yeast over the top. Leave for 10 minutes, or until frothy (if it doesn't foam, the yeast is dead and you will need to start again), then mix with half the oil. Sift the flours and ½ teaspoon salt into a large bowl. Make a well in the centre and pour in the yeast mixture. Mix well and knead on a floured board until smooth. Cut in half, then roll each half into a 20 cm (8 inch) circle. Place one on a lightly greased baking tray, the other on a baking paper-covered baking tray. Cover the circles with a cloth and put in a warm place for 10–15 minutes, or until doubled in size.

2 Preheat the oven to moderately hot 200°C (400°F/Gas 6). Heat the remaining oil in a frying pan and cook the onion for 10 minutes, or until golden brown. Sprinkle with the remaining sugar and cook until caramelized. Transfer to a bowl and mix with the herbs, pine nuts, garlic, feta cheese and olives. Spread the mixture over the pastry on the greased tray. Brush the edge with water and put the second pastry circle on top, using the paper to help lift it over. Press the edges together to seal and pinch together to form a pattern. Cut a few slits in the top to allow steam to escape. Bake for 30–35 minutes, or until crisp and golden brown. Serve warm, cut into wedges.

SPANISH PIZZA

Preparation time: 30 minutes + standing
Total cooking time: 35 minutes
Serves 4–6

Base
7 g (¼ oz) sachet dried yeast
1 teaspoon caster sugar
2¼ cups (280 g/9 oz) plain flour
1 cup (250 ml/8 fl oz) warm water

Topping
10 English spinach leaves, shredded
1 tablespoon olive oil
2 cloves garlic, crushed
2 onions, chopped
440 g (14 oz) canned tomatoes, drained
   and crushed
¼ teaspoon ground pepper
12 pitted black olives, chopped

1 Preheat the oven to hot 210°C (415°F/
Gas 6–7). Brush a 30 x 25 cm (12 x 10 inch)
Swiss roll tin with melted butter or oil.
2 To make the Base: Combine the yeast,
sugar and flour in a large bowl. Gradually
add the warm water and blend until
smooth. Knead the dough on a lightly
floured surface until smooth and elastic.
Place in a lightly oiled basin, cover with a
tea towel and leave to rise in a warm
position for 15 minutes or until the dough
has almost doubled in size.
3 Put the spinach in a large pan, cover
and cook on low heat for 3 minutes. Drain
the spinach and cool. Squeeze out the
excess moisture and set spinach aside.
4 Heat the oil in a pan and add the garlic
and onions. Cook over low heat for
5–6 minutes. Add the tomatoes and
pepper and simmer gently for 5 minutes.
5 Punch the dough down, remove from
the bowl and knead on a lightly floured
board for 2–3 minutes. Roll the dough out
and fit it in the tin. Spread with spinach,
top with the tomato mixture and sprinkle
the olives on top.
6 Bake for 25–30 minutes. Cut into small
squares or fingers and serve hot or cold.

TAGLIATELLE WITH ASPARAGUS AND FRESH HERBS

Preparation time: 15 minutes
Total cooking time: 15 minutes
Serves 6

500 g (1 lb) tagliatelle
155 g (5 oz) asparagus spears
40 g (1¼ oz) butter
1 tablespoon chopped fresh parsley
1 tablespoon chopped fresh basil
1¼ cups (315 ml/10 fl oz) cream
½ cup (50 g/1¾ oz) freshly grated
   Parmesan

1 Cook the pasta in a large pan of rapidly
boiling salted water until al dente. Drain
and return to the pan.
2 While the pasta is cooking, cut the
asparagus spears into short pieces. Heat
the butter in a medium pan, add the
asparagus and stir over medium heat for
2 minutes or until just tender. Add the
parsley and basil, cream, and salt and
pepper, to taste. Cook for 2 minutes.
3 Add the grated Parmesan to the pan
and stir well. When thoroughly mixed, add
to the warm pasta in the pan and toss
gently to distribute ingredients evenly. If
serving as a first course, this dish will be
sufficient for eight.

VEGETARIAN RICE NOODLES

Preparation time: 25 minutes + 20
   minutes soaking
Total cooking time: 5 minutes
Serves 4–6

8 dried Chinese mushrooms
100 g (3⅓ oz) fried tofu
250 g (8 oz) dried rice vermicelli
2 tablespoons oil
3 cloves garlic, chopped
4 cm (1½ inch) piece fresh ginger, grated
1 medium carrot, cut into thin shreds
100 g (3⅓ oz) green beans, cut into short
   lengths
½ red pepper (capsicum), cut into fine
   strips
2 tablespoons Golden Mountain sauce
1 tablespoon fish sauce
2 teaspoons soft brown sugar
100 g (3⅓ oz) bean sprouts, scraggly ends
   removed
1 cup (75 g/2½ oz) finely shredded
   cabbage
bean sprouts, extra, to garnish
sweet chilli sauce, to serve

1 Soak the mushrooms in hot water for
20 minutes, then drain and slice. Cut the
tofu into small cubes.
2 Put the vermicelli in a heatproof bowl,
cover with boiling water and soak for
5 minutes until soft. Drain.
3 Heat a wok or large heavy-based frying
pan. Add the oil and, when very hot, add
the garlic, ginger and tofu; stir-fry for
1 minute. Add the carrot, beans, red
pepper and mushrooms and stir-fry for
2 minutes. Add the Golden Mountain
sauce, fish sauce and sugar; toss well,
cover and steam for 1 minute.
4 Add the vermicelli, bean sprouts and
three-quarters of the cabbage and toss
together. Cover and steam for 30 seconds.
Arrange the vermicelli on a serving
platter, garnish with the extra bean
sprouts and remaining cabbage and serve
with sweet chilli sauce.

TORTELLINI WITH EGGPLANT (AUBERGINE)

Preparation time: 10 minutes
Total cooking time: 20 minutes
Serves 4

500 g (1 lb) fresh cheese and spinach
    tortellini
¼ cup (60 ml/2 fl oz) oil
2 cloves garlic, crushed
1 red pepper (capsicum), cut into small
    squares
500 g (1 lb) eggplant (aubergine), cut into
    small cubes
425 g (14 oz) can crushed tomatoes
1 cup (250 ml/8 fl oz) vegetable stock
½ cup (125 ml/4 fl oz) chopped fresh basil

1 Cook the tortellini in a large pan of
rapidly boiling salted water until al dente.
Drain and return to the pan.
2 While the pasta is cooking, heat the oil
in a large pan, add the garlic and red
pepper and stir over medium heat for 1
minute.
3 Add the cubed eggplant to the pan and
stir gently over medium heat for 5 minutes,
or until lightly browned.
4 Add the undrained tomato and
vegetable stock to the pan. Stir and bring
to the boil. Reduce the heat to low, cover
the pan and cook for 10 minutes, or until
the vegetables are tender. Add the basil
and pasta and stir until mixed through.
note: Cut the eggplant just before using.
It turns brown when exposed to the air.

GIANT CONCHIGLIE WITH RICOTTA AND ROCKET

Preparation time: 50 minutes
Total cooking time: 1 hour
Serves 6

40 giant conchiglie (shell pasta)

Filling
500 g (1 lb) ricotta cheese
1 cup (100 g/3½ oz) grated Parmesan
150 g (5 oz) rocket, finely shredded
1 egg, lightly beaten
180 g (6 oz) marinated artichokes, finely
    chopped
½ cup (80 g/2¾ oz) sun-dried tomatoes,
    finely chopped
½ cup (95 g/3 oz) sun-dried pepper
    (capsicum), finely chopped

Cheese sauce
60 g (2 oz) butter
30 g (1 oz) plain flour
3 cups (750 ml/24 fl oz) milk
100 g (3½ oz) Gruyère cheese, grated
2 tablespoons chopped fresh basil

600 ml (20 fl oz) bottled pasta sauce
2 tablespoons fresh oregano leaves,
    chopped
2 tablespoons fresh basil leaves, finely
    shredded

1 Cook the giant conchiglie in a large pan
of rapidly boiling salted water until al
dente. Drain and arrange the shells on 2
non-stick baking trays to prevent them
sticking together. Cover lightly with
plastic wrap.
2 To make the filling, mix all the
ingredients in a large bowl. Spoon the
filling into the shells, taking care not to
overfill them or they will split.

3 To make the cheese sauce, melt the
butter in a small pan over low heat. Add
the flour and stir for 1 minute, or until
golden and smooth. Remove from the
heat and gradually stir in the milk. Return
to the heat and stir constantly until the
sauce boils and begins to thicken.
Simmer for another minute. Remove from
the heat and stir in the Gruyère cheese
with the basil and salt and pepper, to
taste.
4 Preheat the oven to moderate 180°C
(350°F/Gas 4). Spread 1 cup of the cheese
sauce over the base of a 3-litre capacity
ovenproof dish. Arrange the filled
conchiglie over the sauce, top with the
remaining sauce and bake for 30 minutes,
or until the sauce is golden.
5 Place the bottled pasta sauce and
oregano in a pan and cook over medium
heat for 5 minutes, or until heated
through. To serve, divide the sauce among
the warmed serving plates, top with the
conchiglie and sprinkle with the shredded
fresh basil leaves.

BRAISED VEGETABLES WITH CASHEWS

Preparation time: 15 minutes
Total cooking time: 10 minutes
Serves 4

1 tablespoon peanut oil
2 cloves garlic, crushed
2 teaspoons grated fresh ginger
300 g (10 oz) choy sum, cut into 10 cm (4 inch) lengths
150 g (5 oz) baby corn, sliced in half on the diagonal
¾ cup (185 ml/6 fl oz) chicken or vegetable stock
200 g (6½ oz) sliced bamboo shoots
150 g (5 oz) oyster mushrooms, sliced in half
2 teaspoons cornflour
2 tablespoons oyster sauce
2 teaspoons sesame oil
1 cup (90 g/3 oz) bean sprouts, tailed
75 g (2½ oz) roasted unsalted cashews

1 Heat a wok over medium heat, add the oil and swirl to coat. Add the garlic and ginger and stir-fry for 1 minute. Increase the heat to high, add the choy sum and baby corn and stir-fry for another minute.
2 Add the stock and cook for 3–4 minutes, or until the choy sum stems are just tender. Add the bamboo shoots and mushrooms, and cook for 1 minute.
3 Combine the cornflour and 1 tablespoon water in a small bowl and mix into a paste. Stir into the vegetables, along with the oyster sauce. Cook for 1–2 minutes, or until the sauce is slightly thickened. Stir in the sesame oil and bean sprouts and serve immediately on a bed of steamed rice sprinkled with the roasted cashews.

FETTUCINE WITH CREAMY MUSHROOM AND BEAN SAUCE

Preparation time: 20 minutes
Total cooking time: 20 minutes
Serves 4

280 g (9 oz) fettucine
250 g (8 oz) green beans
2 tablespoons oil
1 onion, chopped
2 cloves garlic, crushed
250 g (8 oz) mushrooms, thinly sliced
½ cup (125 ml/4 fl oz) white wine
1¼ cups (315 ml/10 fl oz) cream
½ cup (125 ml/4 fl oz) vegetable stock
1 egg
3 tablespoons chopped fresh basil
⅔ cup (100 g/3½ oz) pine nuts, toasted
¼ cup (35 g/1¼ oz) sun-dried tomatoes, cut into thin strips
50 g (1¾ oz) shaved Parmesan

1 Cook the fettucine in a large pan of rapidly boiling salted water until al dente. Drain, return to the pan and keep warm.
2 Trim the tops and tails of the beans and cut into long thin strips. Heat the oil in a large heavy-based frying pan. Add the onion and garlic and cook over medium heat for 3 minutes or until softened. Add the sliced mushrooms and cook, stirring, for 1 minute. Add the wine, cream and stock. Bring to the boil, reduce the heat and simmer for 10 minutes.
3 Lightly beat the egg in a small bowl. Stirring constantly, add a little cooking liquid. Pour the mixture slowly into the pan, stirring constantly for 30 seconds. Keep the heat low because if the mixture boils, it will curdle. Add the beans, basil, pine nuts and tomato and stir until heated through. Season, to taste, with salt and pepper. Serve the sauce over the pasta. Garnish with shavings of Parmesan, as well as sprigs of fresh herbs if you like.

SWEET VEGETABLE CURRY

Preparation time: 20 minutes
Total cooking time: 40 minutes
Serves 4

2 medium carrots
1 medium parsnip
1 medium potato
2 tablespoons oil
2 medium onions, chopped
1 teaspoon ground cardamom
¼ teaspoon ground cloves
1½ teaspoons cumin seeds
1 teaspoon ground coriander
1 teaspoon ground turmeric
1 teaspoon brown mustard seeds
½ teaspoon chilli powder
2 teaspoons grated fresh ginger
1⅓ cups (350 ml/11 fl oz) vegetable stock
¾ cup (185 ml/6 fl oz) apricot nectar
2 tablespoons fruit chutney
1 medium green pepper (capsicum), cut into 2 cm (¾ inch) squares
200 g (6½ oz) small button mushrooms
300 g (9⅔ oz) cauliflower, cut into small florets
¼ cup (45 g/1½ oz) ground almonds

1 Cut the carrots, parsnip and potato into 2 cm (¾ inch) pieces.
2 Heat the oil in a large heavy-based pan; add the onion and cook over medium heat for 4 minutes, or until just soft. Add the cardamom, cloves, cumin seeds, coriander, turmeric, mustard seeds, chilli powder and ginger, and cook, stirring, for 1 minute or until aromatic.
3 Add the carrot, parsnip, potato, stock, nectar and chutney. Cook, covered, over medium heat for 25 minutes, stirring occasionally.
4 Stir in the green pepper, mushrooms and cauliflower. Simmer for 10 minutes more or until the vegetables are tender. Stir in the ground almonds and serve with rice.

MUSHROOMS WITH BEAN PUREE, PUY LENTILS AND RED WINE SAUCE

Preparation time: 30 minutes
Total cooking time: 50 minutes
Serves 4

4 large flat field mushrooms
1 tablespoon olive oil
1 red onion, cut into thin wedges
3 cloves garlic, crushed
1 cup (200 g/6½ oz) puy green lentils
¾ cup (185 ml/6 fl oz) red wine
1¾ cups (440 ml/14 fl oz) vegetable stock
1 tablespoon finely chopped fresh flat-leaf parsley
30 g (1 oz) butter

Bean purée

1 large potato, cut into chunks
2 tablespoons extra virgin olive oil
400 g (13 oz) can cannellini beans, drained and rinsed
2 large cloves garlic, crushed
1 tablespoon vegetable stock

Red wine sauce

⅔ cup (170 ml/5½ fl oz) red wine
2 tablespoons tomato paste (tomato purée)
1½ cups (375 ml/12 fl oz) vegetable stock
1 tablespoon soft brown sugar

1 Wipe the mushrooms and finely chop the mushroom stalks. Heat the oil in a large saucepan, add the onion and cook over medium heat for 2–3 minutes, or until soft. Add 1 clove of the garlic and the mushroom stalks and cook for 1 minute. Stir in the lentils, red wine and vegetable stock and bring to the boil. Reduce the heat and simmer, covered, for 20–25 minutes, stirring occasionally, or until the liquid is reduced and the lentils are cooked. If the mixture is too wet, uncover and boil until slightly thick. Stir in the parsley. Keep warm.

2 For the bean purée, bring a small saucepan of water to the boil over high heat and cook the potato for 4–5 minutes, or until tender (pierce with the point of a sharp knife—if the knife comes away easily, the potato is cooked). Drain and mash with a potato masher or fork until smooth. Stir in half the extra virgin olive oil and set aside. Combine the cannellini beans and garlic in a food processor. Add the stock and remaining oil and process until smooth. Transfer to a bowl and fold the mashed potato through. Keep warm.

3 Melt the butter in a deep frying pan. Add the remaining garlic and the flat mushrooms and cook in batches over medium heat for 3–4 minutes each side, or until the mushrooms are tender. Set aside and keep warm.

4 For the sauce, add the red wine to the same frying pan, then scrape the bottom to release any sediment. Add the combined tomato paste, stock and sugar and bring to the boil. Cook for about 10 minutes, or until reduced and thick.

5 Place the mushrooms on individual serving plates and top with warm bean purée. Spoon some lentil mixture over the top and drizzle with the red wine sauce. Season and serve.

NOTE: The mushrooms will shrivel if kept warm in the oven.

BRIAMI (POTATO AND ZUCCHINI/COURGETTE CASSEROLE)

Preparation time: 20 minutes
Total cooking time: 1 hour 45 minutes
Serves 4–6

1 large red pepper (capsicum)
¼ cup (60 ml/2 fl oz) olive oil
2 onions, sliced
2 cloves garlic, crushed
400 g (13 oz) zucchini (courgettes), thickly sliced
400 g (13 oz) small waxy potatoes (pontiac, kipfler, desiree), unpeeled, cut into 1 cm (½ inch) slices
1 kg (2 lb) ripe tomatoes, peeled and roughly chopped
1 teaspoon dried oregano
2 tablespoons chopped fresh flat-leaf parsley
2 tablespoons chopped fresh dill
½ teaspoon ground cinnamon

1 Preheat the oven to moderate 180°C (350°F/Gas 4). Remove the seeds and membrane from the red pepper and cut the flesh into squares.

2 Heat 2 tablespoons of the olive oil in a heavy-based frying pan over medium heat. Add the onion and cook, stirring frequently, for 10 minutes. Add the garlic and cook for another 2 minutes. Place all the other ingredients in a large bowl and season generously with salt and pepper. Add the softened onion and garlic and toss everything together. Transfer to a large baking dish and drizzle the remaining oil over the vegetables.

3 Cover and bake for 1–1½ hours, or until the vegetables are tender, stirring every 30 minutes. Insert the point of a small knife into the potatoes. When the knife comes away easily, the potato is cooked.

NOTE: This vegetable casserole dish is delicious served warm with grilled meat, chicken or fish, or it can be served at room temperature as part of a meze selection.

GNOCCHI WITH TOMATO AND FRESH BASIL

Preparation time: 10 minutes
Total cooking time: 15 minutes
Serves 4

1 tablespoon olive oil
1 onion, finely chopped
2 cloves garlic, crushed
410 g (13 oz) can tomatoes
2 tablespoons tomato paste (tomato purée, double concentrate)
1 cup (250 ml/8 fl oz) cream
¼ cup (40 g/1¼ oz) chopped sun-dried tomatoes
375 g (12 oz) fresh potato gnocchi
1 tablespoon finely chopped fresh basil
60 g (2 oz) pepato cheese, grated

1 Heat the oil in a pan and cook the onion for 2 minutes, or until soft. Add the garlic and cook for another minute. Stir in the tomato and tomato paste, increase the heat and cook for about 5 minutes.
2 Reduce the heat, add the cream and sun-dried tomatoes and stir through. Simmer gently for another 3 minutes.
3 Meanwhile, lower batches of the fresh potato gnocchi into a large pan of boiling salted water. Cook for about 2 minutes, or until the gnocchi rise to the surface. Drain, using a slotted spoon, and add to the sauce with the fresh basil. Season with salt and freshly ground black pepper. Transfer to an ovenproof dish and sprinkle with the pepato cheese. Cook under a hot grill for 5 minutes, until bubbling. Garnish with fresh herbs, if you like.

NOTE: Pepato cheese is quite a pungent pepper cheese. Use a milder cheese if you prefer.

PASTA VEGETABLE BAKE

Preparation time: 20 minutes
Total cooking time: 45–50 minutes
Serves 4

1 tablespoon olive oil
1 large onion, finely chopped
1 clove garlic, crushed
3 medium zucchinis (courgettes), sliced
100 g (3⅓ oz) button mushrooms, sliced
2 cups (500 g/1 lb) ready-made tomato pasta sauce
1 cup (155 g/5 oz) frozen peas
salt and pepper
1½ cups (135 g/4½ oz) dried pasta (penne or spiralli)
4 tablespoons freshly grated Parmesan cheese

1 Preheat the oven to slow 150°C (300°F/Gas 2). Heat the oil in a frying pan. Add the onion and garlic to pan, cook over low heat for 4 minutes or until the onions are soft. Add zucchinis and mushrooms, cook for 3 minutes. Add the sauce and peas, cook for 3 minutes. Season with salt and pepper. Remove from heat and set aside.
2 Add pasta to a large pan of rapidly boiling water and cook for 10–12 minutes or until just tender. Drain; add to the vegetables in the pan.
3 Spoon the mixture into a casserole dish. Sprinkle with Parmesan cheese and bake, covered, for 20–30 minutes.

NOTE: Chopped fresh herbs can be added to this dish and the combination of vegetables varied, according to taste or availability.

OKRA WITH CORIANDER AND TOMATO SAUCE

Preparation time: 5 minutes
Total cooking time: 15 minutes
Serves 4–6

¼ cup (60 ml/2 fl oz) olive oil
1 onion, chopped
2 cloves garlic, crushed
500 g (1 lb) fresh okra (see Note)
400 g (13 oz) can chopped good-quality tomatoes
2 teaspoons sugar
¼ cup (60 ml/2 fl oz) lemon juice
60 g (2 oz) fresh coriander, finely chopped

1 Heat the oil in a large frying pan, add the onion and cook over medium heat for 5 minutes, or until transparent and golden. Add the garlic and cook for another minute.
2 Add the okra to the pan and cook, stirring, for 4–5 minutes, then add the tomato, sugar and lemon juice, and simmer, stirring occasionally, for 3–4 minutes, or until softened. Stir in the coriander, remove from the heat and serve.

NOTE: If fresh okra is not available, you can use an 800 g (1 lb 10 oz) can instead. Rinse and drain the okra before adding with the coriander.

DHAL

Preparation time: 15 minutes
Total cooking time: 1 hour
Serves 4–6

200 g (6½ oz) red lentils
4 cups (1 litre) water
4 cm (11½ inch) piece fresh ginger, cut
  into 3 slices
½ teaspoon ground turmeric
½ teaspoon salt
3 tablespoons ghee or oil
2 cloves garlic, crushed
1 medium onion, finely chopped
pinch of asafoetida, optional
1 teaspoon cumin seeds
1 teaspoon ground coriander
¼ teaspoon chilli powder
1 tablespoon chopped fresh coriander
  leaves

1 Place the lentils and water in a medium
pan, and bring to the boil. Reduce heat to
low, add the ginger and turmeric, and
simmer, covered, for 1 hour or until the
lentils are tender. Stir every 5 minutes
during the last 30 minutes to prevent the
lentils sticking to the pan. Remove the
ginger and stir in the salt.
2 Heat the ghee in a frying pan; add the
garlic and onion, and cook over medium
heat for 3 minutes or until the onion is
golden. Add the asafoetida, if using,
cumin seeds, coriander and chilli powder,
and cook for 2 minutes.
3 Add the onion mixture to the lentils and
stir gently to combine. Serve sprinkled
with fresh coriander.

TORTILLA

Preparation time: 25 minutes
Total cooking time: 20 minutes
Serves 6–8

500 g (1 lb) potatoes, cut into 1 cm
  (½ inch) slices
¼ cup (60 ml/2 fl oz) olive oil
1 brown onion, thinly sliced
4 cloves garlic, thinly sliced
2 tablespoons finely chopped fresh
  flatleaf parsley
6 eggs

1 Place the potato slices in a large pan,
cover with cold water and bring to the boil
over high heat. Boil for 5 minutes, then
drain and set aside.
2 Heat the oil in a deep-sided non-stick
frying pan over medium heat. Add the
onion and garlic and cook for 5 minutes,
or until the onion softens.
3 Add the potato and parsley to the pan
and stir to combine. Cook over medium
heat for 5 mintues, gently pressing down
into the pan.
4 Whisk the eggs with 1 teaspoon each of
salt and freshly ground black pepper and
pour evenly over the potato. Cover and
cook for about 20 minutes, on
low–medium heat until the eggs are just
set. Slide onto a serving plate or serve
directly from the pan.

ORIENTAL FRICELLI

Ready to eat in 30 minutes
Serves 4–6

500 g (1 lb) multicoloured fricelli
2 tablespoons peanut oil
1 teaspoon sesame oil
2 garlic cloves, crushed
1 tablespoon grated fresh ginger
½ Chinese cabbage, finely shredded
1 red pepper (capsicum), thinly sliced
200 g (6½ oz) sugar snap peas
3 tablespoons soy sauce
3 tablespoons sweet chilli sauce
2 tablespoons chopped fresh coriander
chopped peanuts or cashews, to garnish

1 Cook the fricelli in a large pan of rapidly
boiling salted water until al dente. Drain
and keep warm.
2 While the fricelli is cooking, heat the
oils in a pan, add the garlic and ginger
and cook over medium heat for 1 minute.
3 Add the cabbage, red pepper and peas
to the wok and stir-fry for 3 minutes over
high heat. Stir in the sauces and
coriander and cook for 3 minutes, or until
heated through. Add the fricelli to the wok
and toss to combine. Serve sprinkled with
chopped peanuts or cashews.

STEAMED TOFU WITH SOY

Preparation time: 15 minutes +
  30 minutes marinating
Total cooking time: 10 minutes
Serves 4

2 tablespoons soy sauce
2 tablespoons kecap manis
1 teaspoon sesame oil
500 g (1 lb) firm tofu, drained
1½ teaspoons julienned fresh ginger
3 spring onions, thinly sliced on the
  diagonal
1 cup (50 g/1¾ oz) chopped fresh
  coriander leaves
1–2 tablespoons crisp fried shallots

1 Combine the soy sauce, kecap manis
and oil in a bowl. Cut the tofu in half
widthways, then into triangles. Place on a
heatproof plate and pour the sauce over
the top. Marinate for 30 minutes, turning
the tofu once.
2 Sprinkle the ginger over the tofu. Place
the plate on a wire rack over a wok of
simmering water. Cover and steam for
3–4 minutes. Sprinkle with the spring
onion and coriander, then cover and
steam for 3 minutes. Sprinkle with the
crisp fried shallots.

VEGETABLES IN BEAN CURD

Preparation time: 15 minutes
  + 30 minutes soaking + cooling
  + 30 minutes refrigeration
Total cooking time: 10 minutes
Makes 6

4 large dried shiitake mushrooms
2 tablespoons peanut oil
1 teaspoon grated fresh ginger
2 spring onions, thinly sliced
1 small carrot, julienned
100 g (3½ oz) bamboo shoots, julienned
50 g (1¾ oz) firm tofu, finely chopped
1 tablespoon light soy sauce
½ teaspoon sugar
2 teaspoons cornflour
6 bean curd sheets each 20 x 25 cm
  (8 x 10 inches)
extra peanut oil, for deep-frying

1 Soak the mushrooms in hot water for
20 minutes. Squeeze dry, discard the
stalks and finely chop the caps.
2 To make the filling, heat a wok over high
heat, add the oil and swirl to coat. Add the
mushrooms, ginger, spring onion, carrot,
bamboo shoots and tofu, and stir-fry over
medium–high heat for 1 minute. Add the
soy sauce, sugar and ½ teaspoon salt and
cook for a further minute, tossing all the
ingredients together. Transfer to a
colander sitting over a bowl: drain and cool.
3 Combine the cornflour with 1 tablespoon
water to form a paste. Soak the bean curd
sheets in lukewarm water for 10–15
seconds to soften, then drain well and pat
dry with paper towels. Lay a sheet on a
work surface and brush the edges with the
cornflour paste. Place 2 tablespoons of filling
at one end of the sheet, then fold the edges
over towards the centre and roll up to form
a neat rectangular parcel. Repeat to make
six large rolls. Refrigerate for 30 minutes.
4 Fill a wok one-third full of peanut oil
and heat to 180°C (350°F). Deep-fry the
rolls in batches for 2–3 minutes each. Drain
on paper towels and serve immediately.

MANY MUSHROOM NOODLES

Preparation time: 30 minutes + 20
  minutes soaking
Total cooking time: 15 minutes
Serves 4–6

25 g (¾ oz) dried shiitake mushrooms
500 g (1 lb) thin Hokkien noodles, separated
1 tablespoon vegetable oil
½ teaspoon sesame oil
1 tablespoon finely chopped fresh ginger
4 cloves garlic, crushed
100 g (3½ oz) fresh shiitake mushrooms,
  trimmed, sliced
150 g (5 oz) oyster mushrooms, sliced
150 g (5 oz) shimeji mushrooms, trimmed
1½ teaspoons dashi granules dissolved in
  ¾ cup (185 ml/6 fl oz) water
¼ cup (60 ml/2 fl oz) soy sauce
¼ cup (60 ml/2 fl oz) mirin
25 g (¾ oz) butter
2 tablespoons lemon juice
100 g (3½ oz) enoki mushrooms, trimmed
1 tablespoon chopped fresh chives

1 Soak the dried mushrooms in 1½ cups
(375 ml/12 fl oz) boiling water for 20 minutes,
or until soft. Drain, reserving the liquid.
Discard the woody stalks and slice the caps.
Cover the noodles with boiling water for
1 minute, then drain and rinse.
2 Heat a wok over high heat, add the oils
and swirl to coat the side of the wok. Add
the ginger, garlic, fresh shiitake, oyster
and shimeji mushrooms, and stir-fry for
1–2 minutes, or until the mushrooms have
wilted. Remove from the wok.
3 Combine the dashi, soy, mirin, ¼ teaspoon
white pepper and ¾ cup (185 ml/6 fl oz)
reserved liquid, add to the wok and cook for
3 minutes. Add the butter, lemon juice and 1
teaspoon salt and cook for 1 minute, or until
the sauce thickens. Return the mushrooms
to the wok, cook for 2 minutes, then stir in
the enoki and shiitake mushrooms.
4 Add the noodles and stir for 3 minutes,
or until heated through. Sprinkle with the
chives and serve immediately.

EGGHOPPERS WITH EGGPLANT (AUBERGINE) SAMBOL

Preparation time: 40 minutes + 1 hour 30
   minutes standing
Total cooking time: 2 hours 45 minutes
Makes 12–15

7 g (¼ oz) dried yeast
½ cup (125 ml/4 fl oz) warm water
1 teaspoon caster sugar
1½ cups (330 g/10½ oz) short-grain rice
1½ cups (265 g/8½ oz) rice flour
2 teaspoons salt
4½ cups (1.125 litres) coconut milk
12–15 eggs

Eggplant Sambol
2 eggplants (aubergines), cut into 2 cm
   (¾ inch) cubes
¼ cup (60 ml/2 fl oz) oil
2 spring onions, finely chopped
1 teaspoon soft brown sugar
2 red chillies, finely chopped
2 green chillies, finely chopped
2 tablespoons chopped fresh coriander
   leaves
1 tablespoon lemon juice

1 Preheat the oven to moderate 180°C
(350°F/Gas 4). Place the yeast, warm
water and sugar in a small bowl. Put the
bowl in a warm, draught-free area for 10
minutes, or until foaming.
2 Spread the rice on an oven tray and toast
in the oven for about 15 minutes, until
golden. Cool slightly, transfer to a food
processor and process until finely ground.

3 Combine the ground rice, rice flour and
salt in a large bowl. Gradually whisk in the
yeast mixture and coconut milk and mix to
a smooth batter. Cover and set aside in a
warm, draught-free area for 1 hour.
4 Lightly grease a 23 cm (9 inch) nonstick
frying pan. Pour ⅓ cup (80 ml/2¾ fl oz)
batter into the pan or enough to thinly
coat the base of the pan; swirl the pan to
cover the base. Crack 1 egg into the
centre of the pan, and cook over low heat
for 5 to 10 minutes—time will vary
depending on the pan you use. When the
edges are crisp and golden and the
egghopper is cooked, gently remove it
from the pan by sliding it out over the side
of the pan. Cover the egghopper and keep
it warm while cooking the remainder.
Serve the egghoppers with Eggplant
Sambol.
5 To make Eggplant Sambol: Sprinkle the
eggplant with salt and leave for 20
minutes; rinse and thoroughly pat dry.
Heat the oil in a large frying pan; add the
eggplant, and cook over high heat for 10
minutes or until golden brown. Remove
the eggplant from the pan and toss
through the onion, sugar, chilli, coriander
and lemon juice.

ZITI WITH ROASTED TOMATOES AND OVOLINI

Ready to eat in 30 minutes
Serves 4

200 g (6½ oz) yellow teardrop tomatoes
200 g (6½ oz) red cherry tomatoes
500 g (1 lb) ziti
200 g (6½ oz) ovolini cheese
100 g (3½ oz) capers
3 tablespoons fresh marjoram leaves
3 tablespoons fresh lemon thyme leaves
2 tablespoons extra virgin olive oil
3 tablespoons balsamic vinegar

1 Preheat the oven to moderately hot
200°C (400°F/Gas 6). Cut all the tomatoes
in half and bake, cut-side-up, on an oven
tray for 15 minutes.
2 While the tomatoes are baking, cook the
ziti in a large pan of rapidly boiling salted
water until al dente. Drain and return to
the pan.
3 Add the tomatoes and remaining
ingredients to the drained pasta and toss
thoroughly. Serve immediately.

NOTE: Use smaller quantities of fresh
herbs if you prefer. Ovolini is a type of
small fresh cheese available from
speciality shops and some supermarkets.
Use bocconcini cut into small pieces, if
ovolini is unavailable.

GORGONZOLA AND TOASTED WALNUTS ON LINGUINE

Ready to eat in 25 minutes
Serves 4

¾ cup (75 g/2½ oz) walnut halves
500 g (1 lb) linguine
75 g (2½ oz) butter
150 g (5 oz) gorgonzola cheese, chopped
  or crumbled
2 tablespoons cream
1 cup (155 g/5 oz) shelled fresh peas

1 Preheat the oven to moderate 180°C (350°F/Gas 4). Lay the walnuts on an oven tray in a single layer and bake for about 5 minutes, until lightly toasted. Set the walnuts aside to cool.
2 Cook the linguine in a large pan of rapidly boiling water until al dente. Drain and return to the pan.
3 While the pasta is cooking, melt the butter in a small pan over low heat and add the gorgonzola, cream and peas. Stir gently for 5 minutes, or until the sauce has thickened. Season, to taste, with salt and pepper. Add the sauce and the walnuts to the pasta and toss until well combined. Serve immediately, sprinkled with freshly ground black pepper.

NOTE: You can use frozen peas if you prefer. Don't bother to thaw them, just add them as directed in the recipe. Use a milder blue cheese such as Castello in place of the gorgonzola, if you don't like really strong blue cheese.

CRISPY FRIED MUSHROOM CREPES

Preparation time: 25 minutes +
  20 minutes standing
Total cooking time: 35 minutes
Makes 12

¾ cup (90 g/3 oz) plain flour
pinch salt
3 eggs, lightly beaten
¾ cup (185 ml/6 fl oz) milk
1 tablespoon light olive oil
2 tablespoons finely chopped fresh chives
2 cups (160 g/5¼ oz) fresh breadcrumbs
oil, for frying

Mushroom Filling
1 tablespoon olive oil
1 medium onion, finely chopped
400 g (12⅔ oz) mushrooms, finely
  chopped
1 tablespoon cream
¼ teaspoon salt and ½ teaspoon pepper
2 tablespoons freshly grated Parmesan
  cheese

1 Sift the flour and salt into a medium bowl; make a well in the centre. Add the combined eggs and milk gradually. Beat until all the liquid is incorporated and the batter is free of lumps. Add the oil and chives. Set aside, covered with plastic wrap, for 20 minutes. Place ⅓ cup batter in a jug and set aside. Pour 2–3 tablespoons of remaining batter into a lightly greased small crepe pan; swirl evenly over the base. Cook over medium heat for 1 minute, or until the underside is golden. Turn crepe over and cook the other side. Transfer to a plate, cover with a tea towel and keep warm. Repeat the process with the remaining batter, greasing the pan when necessary.

2 To make Mushroom Filling: Heat the oil in a frying pan and cook the onion over medium heat until soft. Add the mushrooms and cook for 2–3 minutes. Stir in the cream, salt, pepper and cheese; cool.
3 Place crepes, one at a time, on a plate. Place 1 tablespoonful of mushroom mixture on one half of each crepe, spreading evenly and leaving a 1 cm (½ inch) border. Brush the edges of the crepe lightly with some reserved batter. Fold the uncovered half of the crepe over top of mushroom mixture. Repeat the process until all the crepes are filled. Spread a little reserved batter over each crepe with a pastry brush and sprinkle with breadcrumbs. Brush the top with more batter, mixing it with the breadcrumbs.
4 Cover the base of a large frying pan with the oil and heat. Add filled crepes and cook until golden on one side, then turn and cook the other side. Transfer to paper towels to drain.

NOTE: For best results, use stale bread to make the breadcrumbs for this recipe. Serve the crepes plain or with a tomato sauce, or a ready-made Italian pasta sauce.

EGGPLANT (AUBERGINE) WITH CHILLI BEAN PASTE

Preparation time: 20 minutes
Total cooking time: 15 minutes
Serves 4–6

½ cup (125 ml/4 fl oz) vegetable stock
¼ cup (60 ml/2 fl oz) Chinese rice wine
2 tablespoons rice vinegar
1 tablespoon tomato paste (tomato purée)
2 teaspoons soft brown sugar
2 tablespoons soy sauce
¼ cup (60 ml/2 fl oz) peanut oil
800 g (1 lb 10 oz) eggplant (aubergine), cut into 2 cm (¾ inch) cubes
4 spring onions, chopped
3 cloves garlic, crushed
1 tablespoon finely chopped fresh ginger
1 tablespoon chilli bean paste
1 teaspoon cornflour mixed with 1 tablespoon water into a paste

1 Combine the stock, rice wine, rice vinegar, tomato paste, sugar and soy sauce in a bowl.
2 Heat a wok over high heat, add half the oil and swirl to coat. Stir-fry the eggplant in batches for 3 minutes each batch, or until brown. Remove.
3 Heat the remaining oil in the wok. Stir-fry the spring onion, garlic, ginger and bean paste for 30 seconds. Pour in the sauce and stir-fry for 1 minute. Add the cornflour paste and bring to the boil. Return the eggplant to the wok and stir-fry for 2–3 minutes, or until heated through.

CHEESE TORTELLINI WITH NUTTY HERB SAUCE

Preparation time: 15 minutes
Total cooking time: 15 minutes
Serves 4–6

500 g (1 lb) ricotta-filled fresh or dried tortellini or ravioli
100 g (3⅓ oz) walnuts
60 g (2 oz) butter
⅔ cup (100 g/3⅓ oz) pine nuts
2 tablespoons chopped fresh parsley
2 teaspoons fresh thyme
salt and pepper
¼ cup (60 g/2 oz) fresh ricotta cheese
¼ cup (60 ml/2 fl oz) cream

1 Add the pasta to a large pan of rapidly boiling water and cook until just tender. Drain and return to the pan.
2 Chop walnuts into small pieces. While pasta is cooking, heat butter in a heavy-based pan over medium heat until foaming. Add walnuts and pine nuts and stir for 5 minutes or until golden brown. Add the parsley, thyme, salt and pepper.
3 Beat the ricotta with the cream. Add the sauce to the pasta and toss well to combine. Top with a dollop of ricotta cream. Serve immediately.
note: For the best flavour, use fresh herbs wherever possible when making pasta sauces.

WINTER VEGETABLE CASSEROLE

Preparation time: 15 minutes
Total cooking time: 40 minutes
Serves 4

2 medium potatoes
1 medium parsnip
200 g (6½ oz) pumpkin
30 g (1 oz) butter
1 tablespoon flour
1½ cups (375 ml/12 fl oz) milk
½ teaspoon ground nutmeg
salt and freshly ground black pepper, to taste

Crumble Topping
1 cup (80 g/2⅔ oz) fresh breadcrumbs
100 g (3⅓ oz) roasted cashew nuts, roughly chopped
30 g (1 oz) butter

1 Peel potatoes, parsnip and pumpkin; cut the pumpkin into large bite-sized pieces and potato and parsnip into smaller pieces. Cook vegetables in a large pan of boiling water for 8 minutes or until just tender. Drain and then arrange cooked vegetables in base of a large, deep ovenproof dish.
2 Melt butter in a pan over low heat. Add flour and cook, stirring constantly, for 1 minute. Remove from the heat and gradually stir in milk. Return pan to heat, bring mixture to the boil, stirring constantly, until thickened; boil for another minute. Add the nutmeg and salt and pepper; pour sauce over the vegetables. Preheat the oven to moderate 180°C (350°F/Gas 4).
3 To make Crumble Topping: Combine the breadcrumbs and cashews. Sprinkle them over the vegetables. Dot the crumble topping with butter; bake for 30 minutes or until golden. Garnish with cress, if desired.

WORLD CUISINE

CARCIOFI ALLA ROMANA (ROMAN-STYLE ARTICHOKES)

Preparation time: 25 minutes
Total cooking time: 1 hour 30 minutes
Serves 4 as an entrée or as part of an
    antipasto platter

4 globe artichokes
3 tablespoons lemon juice
1 tablespoon toasted fresh breadcrumbs
1 large clove garlic, crushed
3 tablespoons finely chopped fresh
    parsley
3 tablespoons finely chopped fresh mint
1½ tablespoons olive oil
¼ cup (60 ml/2 fl oz) dry white wine

1 Preheat the oven to moderately hot
190°C (375°F/Gas 5). Add the lemon juice
to a large bowl of cold water. Remove the
tough outer leaves from the artichokes
and trim the stalks to 5 cm (2 inches)
long. Peel the stalks with a potato peeler.
Slice off the top quarter of each artichoke
with a sharp knife to give a level surface.
Gently open out the leaves and scrape out
the hairy choke, using a teaspoon or a
small sharp knife. Drop each artichoke
into the lemon water as you go.
2 Combine the breadcrumbs, garlic,
parsley, mint and olive oil in a bowl and
season well. Fill the centre of each
artichoke with the mixture, pressing it in
well. Close the leaves as tightly as
possible to prevent the filling from falling
out.
3 Arrange the artichokes with the stalks
up in a deep ovenproof casserole just
large enough to fit them so they are
tightly packed. Sprinkle with salt and pour
in the wine. Cover with a lid, or a double
sheet of kitchen foil secured tightly at the
edges. Bake for about 1½ hours, until very
tender. Serve hot as a first course or side
vegetable, or at room temperature as an
antipasto.

POTATO AND CORIANDER SAMOSAS

Preparation time: 1 hour
Total cooking time: 45 minutes
Makes about 24

50 g (1¾ oz) butter
2 teaspoons grated fresh ginger
2 teaspoons cumin seeds
1 teaspoon Madras curry powder
½ teaspoon garam masala
500 g (1 lb) waxy potatoes, finely diced
30 g (1 oz) sultanas
80 g (2¾ oz) frozen baby peas
15 g (½ oz) fresh coriander leaves
3 spring onions, sliced
1 egg, lightly beaten
oil, for deep-frying
thick natural yoghurt, for serving

Samosa pastry
3¾ cups (465 g/15 oz) plain flour, sifted
1 teaspoon baking powder
110 g (3½ oz) butter, melted
½ cup (125 g/4 oz) thick natural yoghurt

1 Heat the butter in a large non-stick
frying pan, add the ginger, cumin seeds,
curry powder and garam masala and stir
over medium heat for 1 minute. Add the
potato and 3 tablespoons water and cook
over low heat for 15–20 minutes, or until
the potato is tender. Toss the sultanas,
peas, coriander leaves and spring onion
with the potato, remove from the heat and
set aside to cool.
2 To make the samosa pastry, sift the
flour, baking powder and 1½ teaspoons
salt into a large bowl. Make a well in the
centre, add the butter, yoghurt and ¾ cup
(185 ml/6 fl oz) of water. Using a flat-
bladed knife, bring the dough together.
Turn out onto a lightly floured surface and
bring together to form a smooth ball.
Divide the dough into four to make it
easier to work with. Roll one piece out
until very thin. Cover the rest until you are
ready to use it.

3 Using a 12 cm (5 inch) diameter bowl or
plate as a guide, cut out six circles. Place
a generous tablespoon of potato filling in
the centre of each circle, brush the edges
of the pastry with egg and fold over to
form a semi-circle. Make repeated folds
on the rounded edge by folding a little
piece of the pastry over as you move
around the edge. Continue with the
remaining pastry and filling.
4 Fill a deep heavy-based pan one third
full of oil and heat the oil to 180°C (350°F).
The oil is ready when a cube of bread
dropped into the oil turns golden brown in
15 seconds. It is important not to have the
oil too hot or the samosas will burn. Add
the samosas two or three at a time and
cook until golden. If they rise to the
surface as they puff up, you may need to
use a large, long-handled slotted spoon
to hold them in the oil to cook the other
side. Drain on crumpled paper towels.
Serve with yoghurt.

NOTE: The samosa pastry becomes very
tough if overworked. Use lightly floured
hands when working the dough to prevent
it sticking.

FLATBREAD WITH ZA'ATAR

Preparation time: 35 minutes +
  2 hours 50 minutes standing
Total cooking time: 30 minutes
Makes 10

2 x 7 g (¾ oz) sachets dried yeast
1 teaspoon sugar
3¼ cups (400 g/13 oz) plain flour
½ cup (125 ml/4 fl oz) olive oil
4 tablespoons za'atar
1 tablespoon sea salt flakes

1 Place the yeast and sugar in a small bowl with ¼ cup (60 ml/2 fl oz) warm water and stir until dissolved. Leave in a warm place for 10 minutes, or until bubbles appear on the surface. The mixture should be frothy and slightly increased in volume. If your yeast doesn't foam it is dead and you will have to start again.
2 Sift the flour and ½ teaspoon salt into a large bowl. Make a well and pour in the yeast mixture and 1¼ cups (315 ml/10 fl oz) warm water. Gradually combine to form a dough, then knead on a floured surface for 10–15 minutes, until smooth and elastic, gradually adding 1 tablespoon olive oil as you knead. Cover and set aside in a warm place for 1 hour, or until risen.
3 Punch down the dough with your fist and then knead again. Set aside and leave to rise for 30 minutes. Knead briefly and divide into 10 portions. Roll each portion until smooth and round. Roll each into a circle about 5 mm (¼ inch) thick. Set aside covered with a tea towel for another 20 minutes.
4 Preheat the oven to hot 220°C (425°F/Gas 7). Grease two baking trays. Place the rolls on the trays and gently press the surface with your fingers to create a dimpled effect. Brush with the remaining oil and sprinkle with za'atar and salt. Bake for 12–15 minutes. Serve warm.

ARANCINI
(FRIED STUFFED RICE BALLS)

Preparation time: 30 minutes +
  30 minutes cooling + 30 minutes
  refrigeration
Total cooking time: 45 minutes
Makes 12

2¼ cups (500 g/1 lb) short-grain white rice
¼ teaspoon saffron threads
2 eggs, beaten
1 cup (100 g/3½ oz) freshly grated Parmesan
plain flour, for coating
2 eggs, beaten, extra
1 cup (100 g/3½ oz) dry breadcrumbs
oil, for deep-frying

Filling
1 tablespoon olive oil
1 small onion, finely chopped
150 g (5 oz) pork and veal mince or beef
  mince
⅔ cup (170 ml/5½ fl oz) white wine
1 tablespoon tomato paste (tomato purée)
2 teaspoons fresh thyme leaves

1 Bring 1 litre water to the boil in a large saucepan and add the rice and saffron threads. Bring slowly back to the boil, then reduce the heat and simmer. Cover and cook over low heat for 20 minutes, or until tender. Transfer to a large bowl and cool to room temperature. Stir in the egg and grated Parmesan.
2 For the filling, heat the oil in a small frying pan over medium heat. Add the onion and cook for 2–3 minutes, or until soft. Add the mince and cook for 2 minutes, or until it changes colour, pressing out any lumps. Add the wine and tomato paste. Reduce the heat and simmer for 3–4 minutes, or until the wine has evaporated. Stir in the thyme and set aside to cool.
3 With wet hands, divide the rice mixture into 12 balls. Flatten each slightly, make an indent in the centre of each and place 2 heaped teaspoons of the filling into each ball. Close the rice around the filling.
4 Roll each ball in the flour, dip in the extra egg, then roll in the breadcrumbs. Refrigerate for 30 minutes.
5 Fill a deep heavy-based saucepan one third full of oil and heat to 180°C (350°F), or until a cube of bread dropped into the oil browns in 15 seconds. Deep-fry the balls in four batches for 2–3 minutes each, or until golden brown. Drain on crumpled paper towels. Serve warm or at room temperature.

HUEVOS A LA FLAMENCA
(SPANISH BAKED EGGS)

Preparation time: 20 minutes
Total cooking time: 50 minutes
Serves 4

500 g (1 lb) ripe tomatoes
400 g (13 oz) potatoes, cut into 2 cm
   (¾ inch cubes)
3 tablespoons olive oil
1 red pepper (capsicum), cut into strips
1 onion, chopped
100 g (3½ oz) serrano ham (or thickly
   sliced soft, pale prosciutto)
150 g (5 oz) thin green asparagus, trimmed

100 g (3½ oz) fresh or frozen green peas
100 g (3½ oz) baby green beans, sliced
2 tablespoons tomato paste (tomato purée)
4 eggs
100 g (3½ oz) chorizo, thinly sliced
2 tablespoons chopped fresh flat-leaf
   parsley

1 Score a cross in the base of each
tomato. Place in a bowl of boiling water
for 10 seconds, then plunge into cold
water and peel away from the cross.
Coarsely chop the tomatoes.
2 Heat the oil in a large frying pan and
saute the potato over medium heat for
8 minutes, or until golden. Remove with a
slotted spoon. Lower the heat and add the
red pepper and onion to the pan. Slice two
of the ham slices into pieces similar in
size to the red pepper and add to the pan.

Fry for 6 minutes, or until the onion is
soft.
3 Reserve four asparagus spears. Add the
rest to the pan with the peas, beans,
tomato and tomato paste. Stir in ½ cup
(125 ml/4 fl oz) water and season well with
salt and ground black pepper. Return the
potato to the pan. Cover and cook over low
heat for 10 minutes, stirring occasionally.
4 Preheat the oven to moderate 180°C
(350°F/Gas 4). Grease a large oval
ovenproof dish (see margin). Transfer the
vegetables to the dish, without any excess
liquid. Using the back of a spoon, make 4
evenly-spaced deep indentations and
break an egg into each. Top with the
reserved asparagus and the chorizo. Slice
the remaining ham into large pieces and
distribute on top. Sprinkle with parsley.
Bake for 20 minutes, or until the egg
whites are just set. Serve warm.

HYDERABADI FISH

Preparation time: 20 minutes
Total cooking time: 40 minutes
Serves 4

3 tablespoons desiccated coconut
2 tablespoons cumin seeds
3 tablespoons sesame seeds
1 tablespoon fenugreek seeds
2 medium onions, finely chopped
3 tablespoons oil
500 g (1 lb) firm white fish fillets, cut into
   5 cm (2 inch) pieces
1 tablespoon ground coriander
1 teaspoon ground ginger
1 teaspoon chilli powder
1 teaspoon ground turmeric
1 tomato, chopped
1 tablespoon tamarind concentrate
¼ cup (60 ml/2 fl oz) water

1 Dry-fry the coconut, cumin, sesame
seeds, fenugreek seeds and onion in a
frying pan for 10 minutes or until fragrant.
2 Transfer the mixture to a mortar and
pestle or food processor; process until a
paste is formed.
3 Heat the oil in a large deep frying pan;
add the fish and cook over medium heat
for 5 minutes.
4 Add the coconut mixture and the
remaining ingredients and stir gently to
combine. Cover and simmer for
5 to 10 minutes or until the fish is tender.
Serve with rice.

THAI RICE CRACKERS WITH DIPS

Preparation time: 40 minutes + cooling
Total cooking time: 2 hours
Serves 8–10 as a starter

370 g (12 oz) long-grain or jasmine rice
2 cups (500 ml/16 fl oz) oil

chilli jam
3 tablespoons dried shrimp
2 cups (500 ml/16 fl oz) oil
2 cups (220 g/7 oz) sliced red Asian
　shallots
35 garlic cloves, thinly sliced
4–5 long red chillies, seeded and finely
　chopped
½ cup (90 g/3 oz) grated light palm sugar
3 tablespoons tamarind syrup
2 tablespoons fish sauce

Tamarind and pork dip
2 teaspoons shrimp paste
3 garlic cloves, roughly chopped
1 small red chilli, roughly chopped
2 teaspoons grated ginger
1 tablespoon finely chopped spring onion
　(scallion)
1–2 tablespoons tamarind concentrate
100 g (3½ oz) lean minced (ground) pork
100 g (3½ oz) raw prawn (shrimp) meat
4 tablespoons finely chopped coriander
　(cilantro)
1 tablespoon peanut oil
½ cup (125 ml/4 fl oz) coconut milk
1 tablespoon fish sauce
1 tablespoon grated light palm sugar
1 tablespoon lime juice
2 tablespoons chopped coriander
　(cilantro) leaves

1 Wash the rice several times in cold water until the water runs clear. Put the rice and 3 cups (750 ml/24 fl oz) water in a saucepan over high heat. When the water boils, reduce the heat to low, cover with a tight-fitting lid and cook for 15 minutes, or until the rice is cooked. Allow the rice to cool.
2 Preheat the oven to very slow 140°C (275°F/Gas 1) and lightly grease a flat baking tray with oil. Spread the cooked rice over the bottom of the tray in a thin layer. Use wet hands to prevent the rice from sticking and spread the rice to a thickness of about two or three grains. Use a knife to score a grid in the rice forming 4 cm (1½ inch) squares.
3 Put the tray of rice in the oven and bake for 1 hour, or until the rice is completely dry. When cool enough to handle, break the rice along the scored lines and store in an airtight container.
4 To cook the rice squares, heat the vegetable oil in a wok or deep-fat fryer over high heat to 180°C (350°F), or until a cube of bread dropped in the oil browns in 15 seconds. When hot, add several of the rice squares at a time and cook for 1–2 minutes, or until golden. Remove and drain on paper towels. Serve immediately with the Chilli jam and Tamarind and pork dip.

5 To make the chilli jam, soak the dried shrimp in hot water for 5 minutes, drain well, then dry and roughly chop. Heat the oil in a saucepan over medium–high heat, add the shallots and garlic and cook for 10 minutes, stirring constantly, until the shallots and garlic turn golden. Add the shrimp and chillies and cook for 5 minutes, stirring constantly. Remove from the heat. Drain and reserve the oil. Put the fried mixture in a food processor and blend, gradually adding ¼ cup (60 ml/ 2 fl oz) of the reserved cooking oil to form a paste. Put the mixture in a saucepan over medium heat and when it begins to simmer add the palm sugar, tamarind syrup and fish sauce. Cook for 5 minutes, stirring frequently, until it thickens. Cool before serving.
6 To make the tamarind and pork dip, wrap the shrimp paste in foil and put under a hot grill (broiler) for 2–3 minutes. Put the garlic, chilli, ginger, spring onion, shrimp paste and tamarind concentrate with 1 teaspoon salt in a small food processor and combine to form a smooth paste.
7 Combine the pork, prawn meat and coriander in a bowl. Heat the peanut oil in a frying pan over medium heat and add the tamarind paste mixture. Cook for 2–3 minutes, or until fragrant. Add the pork and prawn mixture, stir well and cook for an additional 2–3 minutes, or until browned, stirring constantly.
8 Pour in the coconut milk and cook over medium heat for 5 minutes, or until the liquid is absorbed and the meat is cooked through, stirring constantly to prevent the mixture from sticking to the bottom of the pan. Remove the pan from the heat, then stir in the fish sauce, sugar, lime juice and coriander leaves. Best served warm.

ZARZUELA DE PESCADO
(CATALAN FISH STEW)

Preparation time: 30 minutes
Total cooking time: 35 minutes
Serves 6–8

300 g (10 oz) red mullet fillets
400 g (13 oz) firm white fish fillets
300 g (10 oz) cleaned calamari
1.5 litres fish stock
⅓ cup (80 ml/2¾ fl oz) olive oil
1 onion, chopped
6 cloves garlic, chopped
1 small fresh red chilli, chopped
1 teaspoon paprika
pinch of saffron threads
150 ml (5 fl oz) white wine
400 g (13 oz) can crushed good-quality
    tomatoes
16 raw medium prawns, peeled and
    deveined, tails intact
2 tablespoons brandy
24 black mussels, cleaned
1 tablespoon chopped fresh parsley

Picada
2 tablespoons olive oil
2 slices day-old bread, cubed
2 cloves garlic
5 blanched almonds, toasted
2 tablespoons fresh flat-leaf parsley, to
    garnish

1 Cut the fish and calamari into 4 cm
(1½ inch) even-sized pieces. Pour the
stock into a large saucepan, bring to the
boil and boil for 15–20 minutes, or until
reduced by half.

2 For the picada, heat the oil in a frying
pan, add the bread and stir for 2–3 minutes,
or until golden, adding the garlic for the
last minute. Process the bread, garlic,
almonds and parsley in a food processor
and add enough of the stock to make a
smooth paste.
3 Heat 2 tablespoons of the oil in a large
saucepan, add the onion, garlic, chilli and
paprika, and cook, stirring, for 1 minute.
Add the saffron, wine, tomato and stock.
Bring to the boil, then reduce the heat
and simmer.
4 Heat the remaining oil in a frying pan
over medium heat and fry the fish and
calamari for 3–5 minutes. Remove. Add
the prawns, cook for 1 minute and then
pour in the brandy. Ignite the brandy and
let the flames burn down. Remove from
the pan.
5 Add the mussels to the stock and
simmer, covered, for 2–3 minutes, or
until opened. Discard any that do not
open. Add all the seafood and the picada,
stirring until the sauce has thickened and
the seafood has cooked. Season, to taste.
Serve garnished with parsley.

ROGAN JOSH

Preparation time: 25 minutes
Total cooking time: 1 to 1½ hours
Serves 4–6

1 kg (2 lb) lamb
1 tablespoon ghee or oil
2 medium onions, chopped
½ cup (125 g/4 oz) yoghurt
1 teaspoon chilli powder
1 tablespoon ground coriander
2 teaspoons ground cumin
1 teaspoon ground cardamom
½ teaspoon ground cloves
1 teaspoon ground turmeric
3 cloves garlic, crushed
1 tablespoon grated fresh ginger
1 teaspoon salt
410 g (13 oz) can chopped tomatoes
¼ cup (30 g/1 oz) slivered almonds
3 teaspoons garam masala
chopped coriander leaves, to garnish

1 Cut the lamb into 2.5 cm (1 inch) cubes.
2 Heat the ghee in a large pan; add the
onion and cook, stirring, until soft. Add
the yoghurt, chilli powder, coriander,
cumin, cardamom, cloves, turmeric,
garlic and ginger. Combine well. Add the
salt and undrained tomatoes, and
simmer, uncovered, for 5 minutes.
3 Add the lamb and stir until coated.
Cover and cook over low heat for 1 to
1½ hours, or until the lamb is tender,
stirring occasionally. Uncover and
simmer until the liquid is thick.
4 Meanwhile toast the almonds in a dry
pan over medium heat for 3 to 4 minutes,
shaking the pan gently, until the nuts are
golden brown; remove from the pan at
once to prevent burning.
5 Sprinkle the lamb with the garam
masala and mix through. Serve with the
almonds sprinkled over and garnished
with coriander leaves.

ANTS CLIMBING TREES

Preparation time: 15 minutes + 15 minutes
   marinating + 5 minutes soaking
Total cooking time: 15 minutes
Serves 4

1 teaspoon cornflour
1½ tablespoons light soy sauce
2 tablespoons Chinese rice wine
1 teaspoon sesame oil
200 g (6½ oz) pork mince
150 g (5 oz) cellophane noodles
2 tablespoons vegetable oil
4 spring onions, finely chopped
1 clove garlic, crushed
1 tablespoon finely chopped fresh ginger
2 teaspoons chilli bean sauce
¾ cup (185 ml/6 fl oz) chicken stock
½ teaspoon sugar
2 spring onions, green part only, extra,
   thinly sliced on the diagonal

1 Combine the cornflour, 1 tablespoon each of the soy sauce and rice wine and ½ teaspoon of the sesame oil in a large non-metallic bowl. Add the mince and use a fork or your fingers to combine the ingredients and break up any lumps. Cover with plastic wrap and marinate in the fridge for 10–15 minutes.
2 Meanwhile, put the noodles in a heatproof bowl, cover with boiling water and soak for 3–4 minutes. Rinse and drain well.
3 Heat a wok over high heat, add the oil and swirl to coat the side of the wok. Cook the spring onion, garlic, ginger and chilli bean sauce for 10 seconds, then add the mince mixture and cook for 2 minutes, stirring to break up any lumps. Stir in the stock, sugar, ½ teaspoon salt and the remaining soy sauce, rice wine and sesame oil.
4 Add the noodles to the wok and toss to combine. Bring to a boil, then reduce the heat to low and simmer, stirring occasionally, for 7–8 minutes, or until the liquid is almost completely absorbed. Garnish with the extra spring onion and serve.

SOUTHERN RED BEANS AND RICE

Preparation time: 20 minutes +
   overnight soaking
Total cooking time: 3 hours 10 minutes
Serves 4

1 cup (210 g/7 oz) dried red kidney beans
2 tablespoons oil
1 onion, finely chopped
1 green capsicum (pepper), chopped
3 celery stalks, finely chopped
2 garlic cloves, crushed
225 g (7 oz) andouille or other spicy
   sausage, cut into pieces (see Note)
2 ham hocks
2 bay leaves
1 cup (200 g/6½ oz) long-grain rice
spring onions (scallions), thinly sliced, to
   garnish

1 Soak the red kidney beans overnight in cold water. Drain and put into a saucepan with enough cold water to cover the beans. Bring to the boil, then reduce the heat to a simmer.
2 Heat the oil in a frying pan and sauté the onion, capsicum, celery and garlic until the onion is softened but not browned. Add the sausage and cook until it begins to brown around the edges.
3 Add the sautéed vegetables and sausage to the saucepan with the beans, then add the ham and bay leaves. Bring to the boil, then reduce to a simmer and cook for 2½–3 hours, adding more water if necessary—the beans should be saucy but not too wet. When the beans are almost cooked, boil the rice in a separate saucepan until it is tender.
4 Top the cooked rice with the red kidney beans. Tear some meat off the ham hocks and add to each serving plate. Garnish with the sliced spring onions.

NOTES: Andouille is the name of the smoked pork sausage used in Louisiana cooking.

MAO PAHT KING

Preparation time: 20 minutes
Total cooking time: 10 minutes
Serves 4

2–3 tablespoons peanut oil
1 clove garlic, crushed
400 g (13 oz) pork loin fillet, thinly sliced
   across the grain
2 tablespoons julienned fresh ginger,
   plus extra, to garnish
3 red Asian shallots, thinly sliced
1 small red pepper (capsicum), cut into
   thin strips
4 spring onions, cut into 4 cm (1½ inch)
   lengths
100 g (3½ oz) snow peas (mangetout), cut
   in half on the diagonal
2 tablespoons soy sauce
2 tablespoons fish sauce
2 tablespoons grated palm sugar
2 tablespoons lime juice
2 tablespoons chopped fresh coriander
   leaves

1 Heat a wok over high heat. Add 1 tablespoon of the oil and swirl to coat the side of the wok. Add the garlic and cook for 30 seconds. Cook the pork in batches and stir-fry each batch for 1–2 minutes, or until lightly browned. Remove from the wok.
2 Heat the remaining oil in the wok, add the ginger and shallots and stir-fry for 1 minute, or until the shallots are tender. Add the pepper, spring onion and snow peas. Stir-fry for a further 1 minute, then return the pork to the wok.
3 Combine the soy sauce, fish sauce, palm sugar and lime juice, then add to the wok. Stir in the coriander and stir for 1 minute until combined and the pork is heated through. Garnish with ginger and serve with rice.

FAR EASTERN PANTRY

Pickled ginger/red ginger: used in Japanese cooking. It has a sweet/salty sharp taste. Available in brine or sweet vinegars, in various shades of red to pale orange.

Tamarind: an essential flavour in many Asian dishes. It is available as a rich brown liquid or compressed blocks of pulp that must be soaked, kneaded and seeds removed before use.

Shrimp paste (blachan): made from shrimps that have been dried, salted and pounded to form a paste. It is sold in a block or in jars. Store in an airtight container.

Wasabi paste: also known as Japanese horseradish. An extremely hot paste made from the knobbly green root of the wasabi, native to Japan. Also comes in powdered form.

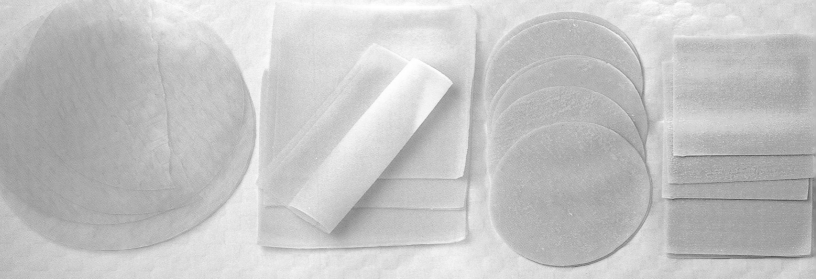

Rice paper: edible paper-thin dry rounds made from rice flour, water and salt. Only available in dry form. Must be moistened before use to make them pliable.

Spring roll wrappers: square or round and made from wheat flour and water dough. Also called egg roll wrappers.

Gow gee wrappers: rounds of dough made from wheat flour and water.

Won ton wrappers: thin squares of wheat flour and egg dough.

Asian basil: three varieties of aromatic basil are used in Asian cooking, all with their own distinct flavour, but fresh sweet basil is a good all-purpose one.

Cha plu: sometimes referred to as betel leaves. Sold in bunches at Asian shops. Traditionally used in Thai cuisine as a wrapping for snacks.

Water spinach: grown extensively throughout Asia. Not related to the spinach family, though English spinach can be used in its place. Requires only minimal cooking.

Vietnamese mint: also called laksa leaf and Cambodian mint, this trailing herb has a flavour more akin to coriander than its namesake.

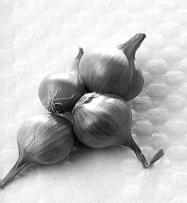   

Asian/golden shallots: small mild members of the onion family. Coppery brown and about the size of a large walnut. Prepare as onions.

Galangal: pinkish in colour with a distinctive peppery flavour. Available fresh (peel and slice as you would fresh ginger) or sliced, dried (must be soaked in hot water before use).

Daikon: a large elongated Asian carrot-shaped radish with quite a sweet flavour. Similar in taste and texture to ordinary radish. Also available pickled in jars.

Kampyo: thinly shaved dried strips of gourd, soaked until pliable and used as a filling in sushi or to tie wrapped food.

Bean curd skins: the skin that forms on heated soya bean milk and is then dried. Brush with water to soften. Comes in large sheets to cut to size. Use to wrap food before deep-frying, steaming or braising.

Star anise: dried star-shaped seed pod of a tree native to China. Adds aniseed taste to simmered meat and poultry. Available whole or ground.

Shiitake mushrooms: have a rich smoky flavour and are available fresh and dried. The dried variety must be soaked in boiling water for at least 20 minutes to soften before use.

Tempura flour: Available in packets in Asian grocery stores. Made up with iced water. Plain flour can be substituted but the batter won't be quite as light.

VEGETABLE DUMPLINGS

Preparation time: 40 minutes +
  20 minutes soaking
Total cooking time: 20 minutes
Makes 24

8 dried shiitake mushrooms
1 tablespoon vegetable oil
2 teaspoons finely chopped fresh ginger
2 garlic cloves, crushed
pinch of white pepper
100 g (3½ oz) garlic chives, chopped
100 g (3½ oz) water spinach, cut into 1 cm
  (½ inch) lengths
¼ cup (60 ml/2 fl oz) chicken stock
2 tablespoons oyster sauce
1 tablespoon cornflour
1 teaspoon soy sauce
1 teaspoon Chinese rice wine
¼ cup (45 g/1½ oz) water chestnuts,
  chopped
chilli sauce, to serve

Wrappers
200 g (6½ oz) wheat starch (see Note)
1 teaspoon cornflour
oil, for kneading

1 Soak the mushrooms in hot water for
20 minutes. Squeeze dry, discard the
stalks and finely chop the caps.
2 Heat a wok over high heat, add the oil
and swirl. Add the ginger, garlic, white
pepper and a pinch of salt and cook for
30 seconds. Add the chives and water
spinach and cook for 1 minute.
3 Combine the stock, oyster sauce,
cornflour, soy sauce and rice wine and
add to the spinach mixture along with the
water chestnuts and mushrooms. Cook
for 1–2 minutes, or until the mixture
thickens, them remove from the heat and
cool completely.

4 To make the wrappers, combine the
wheat starch and cornflour in a bowl.
Make a well in the centre and add ¾ cup
(185 ml/6 fl oz) boiling water, a little at a
time, while bringing the mixture together
with your hands. When it is combined,
immediately knead it, using lightly oiled
hands until the dough forms a shiny ball.
5 Keeping the dough covered with a cloth
while you work, pick walnut-sized pieces
from the dough and, using well-oiled
hands, squash them between the palms
of your hands. Roll the pieces out as
thinly as possible into rounds no larger
than 10 cm (4 inches) diameter. Place
1 tablespoon of the filling in the centre of
the round. Pinch the edges of the wrapper
together to enclose the filling and form a
tight ball.
6 Line a bamboo steamer with baking
paper. Place the dumplings in a single
layer in the steamer, leaving a gap
between each one. Cover with a lid and
steam each batch over a wok of
simmering water for 7–8 minutes. Serve
with chilli sauce.

NOTE: Wheat starch is a very fine white
powder similar to cornflour in texture. It
is available at Asian food stores.

GAMBAS AL AJILLO (GARLIC PRAWNS)

Preparation time: 20 minutes
Total cooking time: 15 minutes
Serves 4

1.25 kg (2½ lb) raw medium prawns
80 g (2¾ oz) butter, melted
¾ cup (185 ml/6 fl oz) olive oil
8 cloves garlic, crushed
2 spring onions, thinly sliced

1 Preheat the oven to very hot 250°C
(500°F/Gas 10). Peel the prawns, leaving
the tails intact. Pull out the vein from
each back, starting at the head end. Cut a
slit down the back of each prawn.
2 Combine the butter and oil and divide
among four 500 ml (16 fl oz) cast iron
pots. Divide half the crushed garlic among
the pots.
3 Place the pots on a baking tray and heat
in the oven for 10 minutes, or until the
mixture is bubbling. Remove and divide
the prawns and remaining garlic among
the pots. Return to the oven for 5 minutes,
or until the prawns are cooked. Stir in the
spring onion. Season, to taste. Serve with
bread to mop up the juices.

NOTE: Garlic prawns can also be made in
a cast iron frying pan in the oven or on the
stovetop.

IMAM BAYILDI
(BAKED EGGPLANT/AUBERGINE)

Preparation time: 15 minutes
Total cooking time: 1 hour
Serves 4–6

¾ cup (185 ml/6 fl oz) olive oil
1 kg (2 lb) elongated eggplants
   (aubergines), cut in half lengthways
3 onions, thinly sliced
3 cloves garlic, finely chopped
400 g (13 oz) Roma tomatoes, peeled and
   chopped, or a 400 g (13 oz) can good-
   quality chopped tomatoes
2 teaspoons dried oregano
4 tablespoons chopped fresh flat-leaf
   parsley
¼ cup (35 g/1¼ oz) currants
¼ teaspoon ground cinnamon
2 tablespoons lemon juice
pinch of sugar
½ cup (125 ml/4 fl oz) tomato juice

1 Preheat the oven to moderate 180°
(350°F/Gas 4). Heat half the olive oil in a
large heavy-based frying pan and cook
the eggplants on all sides for about
8–10 minutes, until the cut sides are
golden. Remove from the pan and scoop
out some of the flesh, leaving the skins
intact and some flesh lining the skins.
Finely chop the scooped-out flesh and set
aside.
2 Heat the remaining olive oil in the same
frying pan and cook the onion over medium
heat for 8–10 minutes, until transparent.
Add the garlic and cook for another
minute. Add the tomato, oregano, parsley,
currants, cinnamon, reserved eggplant
flesh and salt and pepper, to taste.
3 Place the eggplant shells in a large
ovenproof dish and fill each with tomato
mixture.
4 Mix the lemon juice, sugar, tomato juice
and some salt and pour over the eggplant.
Cover and bake for 30 minutes, then
uncover and cook for another 10 minutes.
To serve, place on a serving platter and
lightly drizzle with any remaining juice.

GYOZA

Preparation time: 50 minutes +
   30 minutes standing
Total cooking time: 25 minutes
Makes 40

150 g (5 oz) wom bok (Chinese cabbage),
   very finely shredded
225 g (7 oz) pork mince
2 cloves garlic, finely chopped
2 teaspoons finely chopped fresh ginger
2 spring onions, finely chopped
2 teaspoons cornflour
1 tablespoon light soy sauce
2 teaspoons Chinese rice wine
2 teaspoons sesame oil
40 round Shanghai dumpling wrappers
   (flour and water)
2 tablespoons vegetable oil
½ cup (125 ml/4 fl oz) chicken stock

1 Put the wom bok and ½ teaspoon salt in
a colander, then sit in a large bowl and
toss to combine. Leave for 30 minutes to
drain. Stir occasionally. This process will
draw the liquid out of the wom bok and
prevent the filling from going soggy.
2 Put the pork mince, garlic, ginger,
spring onion, cornflour, soy sauce, rice
wine and sesame oil in a bowl and mix
with your hands.

3 Rinse the wom bok under cold running
water. Press dry between layers of paper
towels. Add to the pork mixture and
combine well.
4 Place a teaspoon of mixture in the
centre of a wrapper, brushing the inside
edge of the wrapper with a little water.
Bring the two edges of the wrapper
together to form a semicircle. Using your
thumb and index finger, create a pleat,
pressing firmly as you do and gently
tapping the gyoza on a work surface to
form a flat bottom. Repeat with the
remaining wrappers and filling.
5 Heat a quarter of the oil in a wok over
medium–high heat. Cook ten of the gyozas
for 2 minutes, flat-side-down. Reduce the
heat and add a quarter of the stock,
shaking the wok to unstick the gyoza.
Cover and steam for 4 minutes, or until
the liquid has evaporated. Remove and
keep warm. Repeat with the remaining
oil, gyoza and stock. Serve with soy sauce
or Chinese black vinegar, if desired.

MALAYSIAN SPICED FISH AND RICE

Preparation time: 20 minutes
Total cooking time: 30 minutes
Serves 4–6

6 garlic cloves
4 cm (1½ inch) piece of ginger, chopped
1½ tablespoons coriander seeds
1 teaspoon cumin seeds
1 cinnamon stick
3 cloves
1½ teaspoons ground turmeric
¼ teaspoon cayenne pepper
750 g (1½ lb) thick fish fillet (e.g. blue eye cod or snapper), cut into 5 cm (2 inch) pieces
2½ tablespoons peanut oil
2 small red chillies, thinly sliced
1 large onion, sliced
2 cups (400 g/13 oz) long-grain rice, washed and drained
1 cup (250 ml/8 fl oz) coconut milk
½ cup (125 ml/4 fl oz) good-quality fish stock
3 large ripe tomatoes, peeled, seeded and finely diced
1 teaspoon grated lime zest
¼ cup (60 ml/2 fl oz) lime juice
3 tablespoons coriander (cilantro) leaves, chopped
3 tablespoons crisp fried shallots

1 In the small bowl of a food processor, blend the garlic and ginger with 1 tablespoon water to form a smooth paste.
2 Dry-fry the coriander seeds, cumin seeds, cinnamon and cloves for 2 minutes until the seeds start to brown and pop. Transfer to a spice grinder or mortar and pestle and grind to a fine powder. Mix them together with the turmeric and cayenne pepper and spread out on a plate.

3 Lightly coat the pieces of fish with the spices, then shake any excess spices back onto the plate and reserve for later.
4 Heat 2 teaspoons of the oil in a deep, non-stick frying pan with a lid, over high heat, add the pieces of fish in batches and brown on either side for 1 minute. Add more oil if required. Remove the fish with a slotted spoon and set aside.
5 Reduce the heat to medium and add the remaining oil. Add the chilli and onion and stir for 3 minutes, or until the onion is soft. Stir in the garlic and ginger purée and cook for 1 minute, or until the mixture starts to brown slightly and begins to catch on the base of the pan. Sprinkle in the reserved spices and stir for 30 seconds. Add the rice and coat with the mixture.
6 Increase the heat to high and quickly pour in the coconut milk and bring to the boil. Add the fish stock and 1 cup (250 ml/8 fl oz) water and bring to the boil again.
7 When nearly all the water has evaporated, reduce the heat to a low simmer, add 2 of the diced tomatoes, the lime zest and juice, half the coriander leaves and the fish, including any juices. Season with salt, stirring through gently to avoid breaking up the fish. Cover the pan with the lid and cook for 20 minutes, or until the rice is cooked. Gently stir the rice halfway through cooking.
8 Let the rice stand for 5 minutes before fluffing with a fork. To serve, spoon out the rice and arrange pieces of fish on top, then scatter the crisp fried shallots, remaining diced tomato and coriander on top.

INDONESIAN RENDANG

Preparation time: 15 minutes
Total cooking time: 2 hours 30 minutes
Serves 6

1.5 kg (3 lb) chuck steak
2 medium onions, roughly chopped
4 teaspoons crushed garlic
1⅔ cups (410 ml/13 fl oz) coconut milk
2 teaspoons ground coriander
½ teaspoon ground fennel
2 teaspoons ground cumin
¼ teaspoon ground cloves
4 red chillies, chopped
1 stem lemon grass (white part only) or 4 strips lemon rind
1 tablespoon lemon juice
2 teaspoons grated palm sugar or soft brown sugar

1 Trim the meat of any fat and sinew, and cut it evenly into small (about 3 cm/ 1¼ inch) cubes.
2 Place the onion and garlic in a food processor and process until smooth, adding water if necessary.
3 Place the coconut milk in a large pan and bring it to the boil, then reduce the heat to moderate and cook, stirring occasionally, until the milk has reduced by half and the oil has separated out. Do not allow the milk to brown.
4 Add the coriander, fennel, cumin and cloves, and stir for 1 minute. Add the meat and cook for 2 minutes until it changes colour. Add the onion mixture, chilli, lemon grass, lemon juice and sugar. Cook, over moderate heat for about 2 hours, or until the liquid is reduced and the mixture is quite thick. Stir frequently to prevent catching on the bottom of the pan.
5 Continue cooking until the oil from the coconut milk begins to emerge again, letting the curry develop colour and flavour. The dish needs constant attention at this stage to prevent it from burning. The curry is cooked when it is brown and dry.

SPANISH-STYLE BEEF KEBABS

Preparation time: 15 minutes +
  marinating
Total cooking time: 5 minutes
Makes 18–20

1 kg (2 lb) rump steak
3 cloves garlic, chopped
1 tablespoon chopped fresh flat-leaf
  parsley
⅓ cup (80 ml/2¾ fl oz) lemon juice
½ teaspoon black pepper
18–20 small wooden skewers

Paprika dressing
2 teaspoons paprika
large pinch of cayenne pepper
½ teaspoon salt
2 tablespoons red wine vinegar
⅓ cup (80 ml/2¾ fl oz) olive oil

1 Trim the excess fat from the rump steak
and cut into 2 cm (¾ inch) pieces.
Combine the steak, garlic, parsley, lemon
juice and pepper in a bowl, cover with
plastic wrap and marinate for 2 hours in
the refrigerator. Meanwhile, soak the
skewers in water for about 1 hour to
ensure they don't burn during cooking.
2 To make the paprika dressing, whisk
the paprika, cayenne pepper, salt, vinegar
and oil together until well blended.
3 Preheat a lightly oiled barbecue
hotplate or grill. Thread the pieces of
marinated meat onto the skewers, then
cook the kebabs, turning occasionally for
about 4–5 minutes, or until cooked
through. Drizzle with the paprika dressing
and serve hot with wedges of lemon.

THAI MUSAMAN BEEF CURRY
(GAENG MUSAMAN NUER)

Preparation time: 30 minutes + cooling
Total cooking time: 2 hours
Serves 4

1 tablespoon tamarind pulp
2 tablespoons vegetable oil
750 g (1½ lb) lean stewing beef, cubed
2 cups (500 ml/16 fl oz) coconut milk
4 cardamom pods, bruised
2 cups (500 ml/16 fl oz) coconut cream
2 tablespoons Musaman curry paste (see
  Sauces)
2 tablespoons fish sauce
8 pickling onions
8 baby potatoes
2 tablespoons grated palm sugar
½ cup (80 g/2¾ oz) unsalted peanuts,
  roasted and ground

1 Put the tamarind pulp and ½ cup
(125 ml/4 fl oz) boiling water in a bowl and
set aside to cool. Mash the pulp with your
fingertips to dissolve the pulp, then strain
and reserve the liquid—discard the pulp.
2 Heat a non-stick wok over high heat,
add the oil and swirl to coat. Add the beef
in batches and cook over high heat for
5 minutes each batch, or until browned all
over. Reduce the heat, add the coconut
milk and cardamom pods, and simmer for
1 hour, or until the beef is tender. Remove
the beef from the wok, then strain the
cooking liquid into a bowl.
3 Heat the coconut cream in the wok and
stir in the curry paste. Cook for 10 minutes,
or until the oil starts to separate from the
cream.
4 Add the fish sauce, onions, potatoes,
beef mixture, palm sugar, peanuts,
tamarind water and the reserved cooking
liquid. Simmer for 25–30 minutes, or until
thickened and the meat is tender.

POULPE PROVENCAL
(OCTOPUS BRAISED IN TOMATO AND WINE)

Preparation time: 25 minutes
Total cooking time: 1 hour 30 minutes
Serves 6

500 g (1 lb) ripe tomatoes
1 kg (2 lb) baby octopus
¼ cup (60 ml/2 fl oz) olive oil
1 large brown onion, chopped
2 cloves garlic
1⅓ cups (350 ml/11 fl oz) dry white wine
¼ teaspoon saffron threads
2 sprigs fresh thyme
2 tablespoons chopped flat-leaf parsley

1 Score a cross in the base of each tomato.
Place the tomatoes in a bowl of boiling
water for 10 seconds, then plunge into cold
water and peel the skin away from the
cross. Cut each tomato in half and scoop out
the seeds with a teaspoon. Chop the flesh.
2 To clean each octopus, use a small sharp
knife and cut each head from the tentacles.
Remove the eyes by cutting a round of flesh
from the base of each head. To clean the
heads, carefully slit them open and remove
the gut. Rinse thoroughly. Cut the heads in
half. Push out the beaks from the centre of
the tentacles from the cut side. Cut the
tentacles into sets of four or two,
depending on the size of the octopus.
3 Blanch all the octopus in boiling water
for 2 minutes then drain and allow to cool
slightly. Pat dry with paper towels.
4 Heat the olive oil in heavy-based frying
pan and cook the onion for 7–8 minutes
over medium heat until lightly golden.
Add the octopus and garlic to the pan and
cook for another 2–3 minutes. Add the
tomato, wine, saffron and thyme. Add just
enough water to cover the octopus.
5 Simmer, covered, for 1 hour. Uncover
and cook for another 15 minutes, or until
the octopus is tender and the sauce has
thickened. Season, to taste. Serve hot or
at room temperature, sprinkle with
chopped parsley.

SUSHI & SASHIMI

ONLY THE FRESHEST INGREDIENTS ARE USED BY THE JAPANESE TO PREPARE THESE TRADITIONAL DISHES. THEY ARE BEAUTIFULLY PRESENTED TO APPEAL TO THE EYE AS WELL AS THE TASTE BUDS.

WHAT'S THE DIFFERENCE?

Japanese sashimi is very thin slices of raw fish or other seafood, prepared in various delicate ways and usually served as an appetizer with dipping sauces. Sushi consists of cold vinegar-flavoured rice topped with sashimi and a limitless variety of ingredients, including omelette or vegetables. Alternatively, for sushi the rice can be rolled, with fillings in the centre, in precooked nori (seaweed). Sushi is served as a main meal with pickled ginger, soy and wasabi. For making sushi, you will need a bamboo mat. They are not expensive and are available at Asian grocery stores. There isn't really a successful substitute.

TUNA/SALMON NORI ROLLS

You will need a bamboo mat, 5 sheets of nori, each cut in half lengthways, 4 cups (800 g/1 lb 10 oz) cooked sushi rice, wasabi and 200 g (6½ oz) sashimi tuna or salmon, cut into thin strips. Place a piece of nori on the mat, shiny-side-down, and spread 4 tablespoons rice over it, leaving a 2 cm (¾ inch) border along one end. Make a slight indentation along the centre to hold the fish in place, then dab a small amount of wasabi along the ridge. Top with the fish. Roll the mat over to enclose the filling, pressing gently to form a firm roll. Slice the roll in half and then each half into three.
Makes 60.

HAND ROLLS

You will need 10 sheets of nori, each cut in half diagonally, 2 cups (400 g/13 oz) cooked sushi rice, wasabi, 20 peeled, deveined raw small prawns, 1 thinly sliced avocado and 1 cup (125 g/4 oz) tempura flour. Prepare the tempura batter, following the instructions on the flour packet. Dip the prawns in the batter and deep-fry in hot oil, in batches, until crisp and golden. Drain on crumpled paper towel. Hold a sheet of nori shiny-side-down, flat in your hand, place 2 tablespoons rice on the left-hand side and spread over half of the nori sheet. Dab with wasabi. Place a prawn on the rice with a slice of avocado, then roll the nori to form a cone, enclosing the smaller end. Repeat to use all the remaining ingredients.
Makes 20.

PRAWN AND TUNA NIGIRI

You will need 10 peeled, butterflied cooked prawns, 250 g (8 oz) sashimi tuna, wasabi and 2 cups (400 g/13 oz) cooked sushi rice. Trim the tuna into a rectangle, removing any connective tissue or blood. Cut thin slices, wiping the knife after each slice. Form a tablespoon of sushi rice into an oval the same length and width as the fish. Place one of the tuna slices flat on your hand, then spread a small dab of wasabi over the centre. Place the rice on the fish and cup your palm. Press the rice onto the fish, firmly pushing with a slight upward motion to make a neat shape. Turn over and repeat the shaping process, finishing with the fish on top. Repeat until you have used the remaining cooked sushi rice and prawns.
Makes 16–20.

SASHIMI SALMON, CUCUMBER AND CHIVE ROLLS

Cut a 200 g (6½ oz) fillet of salmon into paper-thin slices, on an angle. Cut 1 small Lebanese cucumber in half and discard the seeds. Cut the flesh into long thin strips. Place a salmon slice on a board, top with strips of cucumber, roll up and tie with trimmed chives. Serve with ginger, shoyu and wasabi.
Makes 25.

NOTE: Shoyu is Japanese-style soy sauce, a much lighter and sweeter sauce than the Chinese one. It should be refrigerated after opening.

FROM LEFT: Tuna and salmon nori rolls; Hand rolls; Prawn and tuna nigiri; Sashimi salmon, cucumber and chive rolls

SUSHI & SASHIMI

MAKING SUSHI RICE

Rinse 2½ cups (550 g/1 lb 2 oz) white short-grain rice under cold running water until the water runs clear; drain in the strainer for 1 hour. Transfer to a large saucepan with 3 cups (750 ml/24 fl oz) water, bring to the boil and cook for 5–10 minutes, without stirring, or until tunnels form on the surface. Reduce the heat to low, cover and cook for 12–15 minutes, or until tender. Remove from the heat, place a tea towel over the rice; leave for 15 minutes. Combine 5 tablespoons rice vinegar, 1 tablespoon mirin, 2 teaspoons salt and 2 tablespoons sugar in a bowl and stir until the sugar dissolves. Spread the rice over a flat non-metallic tray, top with the dressing and stir to mix through. Spread out and cool to body temperature. If the rice gets too cold, it will turn hard and be difficult to work with. Spread a damp tea towel over the rice and keep it covered as you work. To prevent rice sticking to your hands, dip your fingers in a bowl of warm water with a few drops of rice vinegar added. Makes 6 cups (1.2 kg/2 lb 6½ oz).

SASHIMI

Preparing sashimi is relatively simple. You will need a good, very sharp knife. There are four ways of cutting fish for sashimi, all used for different types of fish. The simplest is the straight down cut, about 2 cm (¾ inch) wide. For a cubed cut, the straight pieces are cut into cubes. There is also an angled cut and a paper-thin slice used for white fish.

CALIFORNIA ROLLS

To make these, you will need 4 sheets of nori, 3 cups (600 g/1¼ lb) cooked sushi rice, 10 g (¼ oz) flying fish roe, 1 sliced avocado, 10 cooked peeled, deveined prawns, each halved lengthways, or 2 crab sticks, and 2 tablespoons Japanese mayonnaise (kyuupi). Place 1 sheet of nori on a bamboo mat, shiny-side-down. Spread 2–3 tablespoons of rice in the middle of the nori, leaving a 2 cm (¾ inch) border along the end nearest you. Make a slight indentation along the centre of the rice to hold the filling in, then spread a small line of mayonnaise along the ridge.

Spread about 1 tablespoon of flying fish roe over the centre of the rice and top with some prawn and avocado. Roll the mat over to enclose the filling, then roll the mat, pressing gently to form a firm roll. Slice the roll in half and then each half into three.
Makes 24.

INSIDE-OUT ROLLS

These have the rice on the outside. Use 8 sheets of nori and 6 cups (1.2 kg/2 lb 6½ oz) cooked sushi rice. Place a sheet of nori on a bamboo mat and spread 1 cm (½ inch) rice over the top, leaving a 1 cm (1½ inch) border. Cover with a sheet of plastic wrap, slightly larger than the nori. In one quick motion, turn the whole thing over, then place it back on the mat, so the plastic is under the rice and the nori on top. Spread a little wasabi on the nori, along the short end, 4 cm (1½ inches) from the edge. Lay strips of cucumber, avocado

and fresh crab on top of the wasabi, then roll from this end, using the plastic as a guide. Rewrap in plastic, then roll up in the mat. Remove the plastic and roll in flying fish roe or sesame seeds. Cut in half, trim the ends, and cut each half into three. Serve with shoyu.
Makes 48.

CHIRASHI-ZUSHI

A Japanese sushi meal in a bowl, chirashi means scattered, and that is how it is prepared. A bed of cooked sushi rice is placed in the bottom of a lacquered bowl, then vegetables and seafood are scattered over the top. The seafood can be raw or cooked, but usually the fish will be sashimi. Chirashi-zushi is accompanied by pickled ginger, wasabi, and soy sauce. To make chirashi-zushi, you will need 4 cups (800 g/1 lb 10 oz) cooked sushi rice, 3 tablespoons each of toasted white sesame seeds, shredded

pickled daikon and shredded nori. Soak 6 dried shiitake mushrooms in boiling water for 10 minutes, then drain. Cut the mushrooms into thin strips and combine in a saucepan with 3 tablespoons soy sauce, 1 cup (250 ml/8 fl oz) dashi stock and 1 tablespoon mirin, and simmer for 10 minutes, then drain. Spread the sushi rice into a large bowl or four individual bowls. Top with the sesame seeds, pickled daikon, nori and mushrooms. Over the top, decoratively arrange 1 thinly sliced cucumber, 16 blanched snow peas (mangetout), 100 g (3½ oz) each of sashimi tuna and salmon and 16 cooked, peeled, deveined and butterflied prawns.
Serves 4–6.

FROM LEFT: Sashimi tuna (top) and salmon; California rolls; Inside-out rolls; Chirashi-zushi

SINGAPORE NOODLES

Preparation time: 30 minutes +
   30 minutes marinating
Total cooking time: 10 minutes
Serves 4–6

2 cloves garlic, crushed
2 teaspoons grated fresh ginger
¼ cup (60 ml/2 fl oz) oyster sauce
¼ cup (60 ml/2 fl oz) soy sauce
250 g (8 oz) chicken breast fillets, thinly
   sliced
400 g (13 oz) dried rice vermicelli
2 tablespoons vegetable oil
2 celery sticks, julienned
1 large carrot, julienned
3 spring onions, sliced on the diagonal
1½ tablespoons Asian curry powder
½ teaspoon sesame oil
65 g (2¼ oz) bean sprouts, tailed

1 Combine the garlic, ginger, 1 tablespoon
oyster sauce and 2 teaspoons soy sauce
in a large non-metallic bowl. Add the
chicken, toss well, cover with plastic wrap
and marinate in the fridge for 30 minutes.
2 Soak the noodles in boiling water for
6–7 minutes, or until soft. Drain.
3 Heat a wok over high heat, add the oil
and swirl to coat. Stir-fry the chicken until
browned. Add the celery, carrot and half
the spring onion, and stir-fry for
2–3 minutes, or until slightly softened.
Add the curry powder and stir-fry for
2 minutes, or until fragrant.
4 Toss in the noodles, stir in the
remaining ingredients, then serve.

PANZANELLA

Preparation time: 30 minutes +
   15 minutes standing
Total cooking time: 5 minutes
Serves 6–8

1 small red onion, thinly sliced
250 g (8 oz) stale bread such as ciabatta,
   crusts removed
4 ripe tomatoes
6 anchovy fillets, finely chopped
1 small clove garlic, crushed
1 tablespoon baby capers, chopped
2 tablespoons red wine vinegar
½ cup (125 ml/4 fl oz) extra virgin olive oil
2 small Lebanese cucumbers, peeled and
   sliced
1 cup (30 g/1 oz) fresh basil leaves, torn

1 In a small bowl, cover the onion with
cold water and leave for 5 minutes.
Squeeze the rings in your hand, closing
tightly and letting go and repeating that
process about five times. This removes
the acid from the onion. Repeat the whole
process twice more, using fresh water
each time.
2 Tear the bread into rough 3 cm (1¼ inch)
squares and toast lightly under a grill for
4 minutes, or until bread is crisp but not
browned. Allow to cool. Set aside.
3 Score a cross in the base of each
tomato and soak in boiling water for
10 seconds. Plunge into cold water and
peel away from the cross. Cut each
tomato in half and scoop out the seeds
with a teaspoon. Roughly chop two of the
tomatoes and purée the other two.
4 Combine the anchovies, garlic and
capers in a screw top jar. Add the vinegar
and olive oil, screw the lid on tightly and
shake well. Season, then transfer to a
large bowl and add the bread, onion,
puréed and chopped tomato, cucumber
and basil. Toss well and season, to taste.
Leave to stand for at least 15 minutes
to allow the flavours to develop. Serve at
room temperature.

FRIKKADELS

Preparation time: 30 minutes
Total cooking time: 40 minutes
Makes 26

½ cup (45 g/1½ oz) desiccated coconut
500 g (1 lb) minced beef
1 clove garlic, crushed
1 medium onion, finely chopped
1 teaspoon ground cumin
¼ teaspoon ground cinnamon
½ teaspoon finely grated lime rind
1 tablespoon chopped fresh dill
1 egg, lightly beaten
1 cup (100 g/3⅓ oz) dry breadcrumbs
oil, for deep-frying
Yoghurt and Mint Raita (page 769), to
   serve

1 Spread the coconut on an oven tray and
toast it in a slow 150°C (300°F/Gas 2) oven
for 10 minutes or until it is dark golden,
shaking the tray occasionally.
2 Place the coconut, minced beef, garlic,
onion, cumin, cinnamon, lime rind and dill
in a large bowl and mix to combine.
Season with salt and pepper to taste.
3 Shape tablespoons of the mixture into
balls; dip the meatballs in the egg and
toss to coat in the breadcrumbs.
4 Heat the oil in a wok or deep-sided
frying pan; add the meatballs in batches
and deep-fry over moderately high heat
for 5 minutes or until they become deep
golden brown and cooked through. Drain
on paper towels. Serve with Yoghurt and
Mint Raita.

CHICKEN NOODLE LARB IN BANANA LEAF CONES

Preparation time: 25 minutes
Total cooking time: 15 minutes
Makes 12

50 g (1¾ oz) dried rice vermicelli
vegetable oil, for deep-frying
1 tablespoon peanut oil
500 g (1 lb) minced (ground) chicken
⅓ cup (80 ml/2¾ fl oz) fish sauce
½ cup (125 ml/4 fl oz) lime juice
1 tablespoon grated light palm sugar
6 red Asian shallots, thinly sliced
4 spring onions (scallions), chopped
2 small red chillies, finely chopped
½ cup (10 g/¼ oz) mint, finely shredded
½ cup (15 g/½ oz) Thai basil, finely shredded
12 banana leaves, cut into 15 cm (6 inch) squares

1 Separate the vermicelli and break it into shorter lengths. Fill a wok or deep-fat fryer one-third full of oil and heat to 180°C (350°F), or until a cube of bread dropped into the oil browns in 15 seconds. Cook the vermicelli in batches until puffed and crisp. Drain on crumpled paper towels.
2 Heat the peanut oil in a wok, add the chicken and cook over medium heat until the meat is tender and cooked. Add the fish sauce, lime juice and palm sugar and stir until the sugar dissolves. Remove the wok from the heat and set aside. When cool, stir in the shallots, spring onions, chillies, mint and basil. Drain off any excess liquid.
3 Shape the banana leaves into cones and secure them with toothpicks. Fold the noodles through the salad and then spoon the mixture into the cones. Don't eat the banana leaves—they are merely a container for the filling. Serve with small forks.

NOTE: You can use pork or beef instead of the chicken, though in Thailand, where larb originates, chicken is almost always used. For the best results, finely chop the meat yourself.

GEFILTE FISH

Preparation time: 5 minutes
Total cooking time: 1 hour 35 minutes
Serves 4

1 kg (2 lb) firm white fish fillets (eg. cod, redfish, pike, haddock), with skin and bones
2 sticks celery, chopped
2 onions, chopped
2 carrots, sliced
1 tablespoon chopped fresh parsley
2 tablespoons ground almonds
2 eggs, beaten
matzo meal (see Notes)

1 Remove the skin and bones from the fish and place the skin and bones in a large pan with the celery, half the onion and half the carrot. Add 3 cups (750 ml/ 24 fl oz) water, bring to the boil and simmer for 20 minutes. Strain the stock.
2 Chop the fish roughly and combine in a food processor with the remaining onion and parsley. Process until fine, add the ground almonds, eggs, a little salt and pepper and sufficient matzo meal to bind. The amount of matzo meal will vary according to the texture of the fish. Roll the mixture into 8 balls with floured hands.
3 Simmer the remaining sliced carrot in the fish stock for 10 minutes, then remove. Add the fish balls to the stock, cover and simmer gently for 1 hour. Remove the fish balls with a slotted spoon and place on a serving plate. Top each with a slice of carrot.
4 Strain the fish stock and spoon a little over each fish ball.

NOTES: Matzo meal is finely crushed unleavened crispbreads that are made from flour and water. It is available in some supermarkets.

The remaining stock can be chilled until set to a jelly. Chop the jelly and use to garnish the fish balls if you like.

MONGOLIAN LAMB

Preparation time: 25 minutes + marinating
Total cooking time: 15 minutes
Serves 4–6

2 cloves garlic, crushed
2 teaspoons finely grated fresh ginger
¼ cup (60 ml/2 fl oz) Chinese rice wine
¼ cup (60 ml/2 fl oz) soy sauce
2 tablespoons hoisin sauce
1 teaspoon sesame oil
1 kg (2 lb) lamb loin fillets, thinly sliced across the grain
⅓ cup (80 ml/2¾ fl oz) peanut oil
6 spring onions, cut into 3 cm (1¼ inch) lengths
2 teaspoons chilli sauce
1½ tablespoons hoisin sauce, extra

1 Combine the garlic, ginger, Chinese rice wine, soy sauce, hoisin sauce and sesame oil in a large non-metallic bowl. Add the lamb and toss until well coated. Cover with plastic wrap and marinate in the refrigerator overnight, tossing occasionally.
2 Heat a wok over high heat, add 1 tablespoon of the peanut oil and swirl to coat the wok. Add the spring onion and stir-fry for 1 minute, or until lightly golden. Remove, reserving the oil in the wok.
3 Lift the lamb out of the marinade with tongs, reserving the marinade. Add the meat in four batches and stir-fry for 1–2 minutes per batch, or until browned but not completely cooked through, adding more oil and making sure the wok is very hot before cooking each batch. Return all the meat and any juices to the wok with the spring onion and stir-fry for 1 minute, or until meat is cooked through.
4 Remove the meat and spring onion from the wok with a slotted spoon and place in a serving bowl, retaining the liquid in the wok. Add any reserved marinade to the wok along with the chilli sauce and extra hoisin sauce, then boil for 3–4 minutes, or until the sauce thickens and becomes slightly syrupy. Spoon the sauce over the lamb, toss well, then serve with steamed rice.

NASI GORENG
(FRIED RICE)

Preparation time: 35 minutes
Total cooking time: 30 minutes
Serves 4

2 eggs
¼ teaspoon salt
⅓ cup (80 ml/2¾ fl oz) oil
3 cloves garlic, finely chopped
1 onion, finely chopped
2 red chillies, seeded and very finely
    chopped
1 teaspoon shrimp paste
1 teaspoon coriander seeds
½ teaspoon sugar
400 g (12⅔ oz) raw prawns, peeled and
    deveined
200 g (6½ oz) rump steak, finely sliced
1 cup (200 g/6½ oz) long-grain rice,
    cooked and cooled
2 teaspoons kecap manis
1 tablespoon soy sauce
4 spring onions, finely chopped
½ lettuce, finely shredded
1 cucumber, thinly sliced
3 tablespoons crisp fried onion

1 Beat the eggs and salt until foamy. Heat
a frying pan and lightly brush with a little
of the oil; pour about one-quarter of the
egg mixture into the pan and cook for 1 to
2 minutes over medium heat until the
omelette sets. Turn the omelette over and
cook the other side for 30 seconds.
Remove the omelette from the pan and
repeat with the remaining egg mixture.
When the omelettes are cold, gently roll
them up and cut them into fine strips; set
aside.

2 Combine the garlic, onion, chilli, shrimp
paste, coriander and sugar in a food
processor or mortar and pestle, and
process or pound until a paste is formed.
3 Heat 1 to 2 tablespoons of the oil in a
wok or large deep frying pan; add the
paste and cook over high heat for 1
minute or until fragrant. Add the prawns
and steak and stir-fry for 2 to 3 minutes,
or until they change colour.
4 Add the remaining oil and the cold rice
to the wok. Stir-fry, breaking up any
lumps, until the rice is heated through.
Add the kecap manis, soy sauce and
spring onion and stir-fry for another
minute.
5 Arrange the lettuce around the outside
of a large platter. Place the rice in the
centre, and garnish with the omelette
strips, cucumber slices and fried onion.
Serve immediately.

PASTA-FILLED VEGETABLES

Preparation time: 40 minutes
Total cooking time: 45 minutes
Serves 6

150 g (5 oz) rissoni
1 tablespoon olive oil
1 onion, finely chopped
1 clove garlic, crushed
3 rindless bacon rashers, finely chopped
1 cup (150 g/5 oz) freshly grated
    mozzarella cheese
½ cup (50 g/1¾ oz) freshly grated
    Parmesan
2 tablespoons chopped fresh parsley
4 large red peppers (capsicums), halved
    lengthways, seeds removed
425 g (14 oz) can crushed tomatoes
½ cup (125 ml/4 fl oz) dry white wine
1 tablespoon tomato paste (tomato purée,
    double concentrate)
½ teaspoon ground oregano
2 tablespoons shredded fresh basil

1 Cook the rissoni in a large pan of boiling
salted water until al dente. Drain.
2 Preheat the oven to moderate 180°C
(350°F/Gas 4). Lightly oil a large shallow
ovenproof dish.
3 Heat the oil in a pan. Add the onion and
garlic and stir over low heat until the
onion is tender. Add the bacon and stir
until crisp. Transfer to a large bowl and
combine with the rissoni, cheeses and
parsley. Spoon the mixture into the
pepper halves and arrange in the dish.
4 In a bowl, combine the tomato, wine,
tomato paste, oregano and salt and
pepper, to taste. Spoon over the rissoni
mixture. Sprinkle with basil. Bake for
35–40 minutes.

NASI LEMAK

Preparation time: 40 minutes +
    15 minutes standing
Total cooking time: 2 hours 40 minutes
Serves 4

Rendang
2 onions, roughly chopped
2 garlic cloves, crushed
400 ml (13 fl oz) tin coconut milk
2 teaspoons ground coriander
½ teaspoon ground fennel
2 teaspoons ground cumin
¼ teaspoon ground cloves
1.5 kg (3 lb) chuck steak, cut into cubes
4–6 small red chillies, chopped
1 tablespoon lemon juice
1 stem lemon grass (white part only),
    bruised and cut lengthways
2 teaspoons grated palm sugar

Coconut rice
1½ cups (300 g/10 oz) long-grain rice
2 red Asian shallots
2 slices ginger
pinch of fenugreek seeds
2 pandanus leaves, knotted
400 ml (13 fl oz) tin coconut milk

Sambal ikan bilis
¼ cup (60 ml/2 fl oz) oil
5 red Asian shallots, sliced
2 garlic cloves, crushed
1 stem lemon grass (white part only),
    thinly sliced
½ teaspoon shrimp paste
2 tablespoons chilli paste
100 g (3½ oz) ikan bilis, soaked and
    washed (see Notes)
1 teaspoon sugar
2 tablespoons lime juice

1 To make the rendang, process the onion, garlic and 1 tablespoon of water to form a smooth paste. Pour the coconut milk into a wok and bring to the boil, then reduce the heat to medium and cook, stirring occasionally, for 15 minutes, or until the milk is reduced by half and the oil has separated. Do not allow the milk to brown. Add the coriander, fennel, cumin and cloves to the pan and stir for 1 minute. Add the meat and cook for 2 minutes, or until it browns. Add the chilli, lemon juice, lemon grass, sugar and prepared onion mixture. Cook, covered, over medium heat for about 2 hours, or until the liquid is reduced and thickened. Stir often.
2 Uncover and continue cooking until the oil separates again. Take care not to burn the sauce. The curry is cooked when it is brown and dry.
3 Meanwhile, to make the coconut rice, put the rice, shallots, ginger, fenugreek, pandanus leaves and 1 teaspoon salt in a saucepan. Pour enough coconut milk over the rice so there is 2 cm (¾ inch) of liquid above the surface of the rice. Cover and cook until dry, then remove the pandanus leaf, sprinkle the rest of the coconut milk over the rice, then fluff up the grains. Stand for 15 minutes, until the coconut milk is absorbed.
4 To make the sambal, heat the oil in a wok, add the shallots, garlic, lemon grass, shrimp paste and chilli paste, and stir-fry until fragrant. Add the ikan bilis and stir-fry for a few more minutes. Mix in the sugar and lime juice. Serve with the rendang and rice.

NOTES: Ikan bilis are dried anchovies. In Malaysia, Nasi lemak is traditionally served for breakfast.

CHINESE VEGETABLES

Preparation time: 10 minutes
Total cooking time: 5 minutes
Serves 4

500 g (1 lb) Chinese green vegetables
    (see Note)
2 teaspoons peanut oil
½ teaspoon finely chopped garlic
1 tablespoon oyster sauce
½ teaspoon caster sugar
2 tablespoons water
1 teaspoon sesame oil

1 Bring a large pan of water to the boil.
2 Wash Chinese greens. Remove any tough leaves and trim stems. Chop greens into 3 equal portions.
3 Add the greens to the pan of boiling water. Cook for 1 to 2 minutes, or until just tender but still crisp. Use tongs to remove greens from the pan, drain well and place on a heated serving platter.
4 Heat the peanut oil in a small pan and cook the garlic briefly. Add the oyster sauce, sugar, water and sesame oil and bring to the boil. Pour over the greens and toss to coat. Serve immediately.

NOTE: Use choy sum, bok choy or Chinese broccoli (gai larn), or a combination of any two.

CRISPY NOODLES
(MEE GROB)

Preparation time: 30 minutes +
   20 minutes soaking
Total cooking time: 15 minutes
Serves 4–6

4 dried shiitake mushrooms
oil, for deep-frying
100 g (3½ oz) dried rice vermicelli
100 g (3½ oz) fried tofu puffs, julienned
4 cloves garlic, crushed
1 onion, chopped
1 chicken breast fillet, thinly sliced
8 green beans, sliced on the diagonal
6 spring onions, thinly sliced on the
   diagonal
8 raw medium prawns, peeled and
   deveined, with tails intact
30 g (1 oz) bean sprouts, tailed
fresh coriander leaves, to garnish

Sauce
¼ cup (60 ml/2 fl oz) white vinegar
¼ cup (60 ml/2 fl oz) fish sauce
5 tablespoons sugar
1 tablespoon soy sauce
1 tablespoon sweet chilli sauce

1 Soak the mushrooms in boiling water
for 20 minutes. Squeeze dry, discard the
stems and thinly slice the caps.
2 Fill a wok one-third full of oil and heat
to 180°C (350°F), or until a cube of bread
dropped into the oil browns in 15 seconds.
Cook the noodles in small batches for
5 seconds, or until puffed and crispy.
Drain well on crumpled paper towels.

3 Add the tofu to the wok in batches and
deep-fry for 1 minute, or until crisp. Drain.
Carefully remove all but 2 tablespoons of oil.
4 Reheat the wok until very hot. Add the
garlic and onion, and stir-fry for 1 minute.
Add the chicken, mushrooms, beans and
half the spring onion. Stir-fry for 2 minutes,
or until the chicken has almost cooked
through. Add the prawns and stir-fry for a
further 2 minutes, or until they just turn
pink.
5 Combine all the sauce ingredients in a
bowl, then add to the wok. Stir-fry for
2 minutes, or until the chicken and
prawns are tender and the sauce is
syrupy.
6 Remove from the heat and stir in the
noodles, tofu and bean sprouts. Garnish
with the coriander and remaining sliced
spring onion.

GAENG NUER FUG TONG

Preparation time: 20 minutes
Total cooking time: 1 hour 30 minutes
Serves 6

2 tablespoons vegetable oil
750 g (1½ lb) blade steak, thinly sliced
4 tablespoons Musaman curry paste (see
   Sauces)
2 cloves garlic, finely chopped
1 onion, sliced lengthways
6 curry leaves, torn
3 cups (750 ml/24 fl oz) coconut milk
3 cups (450 g/14 oz) roughly diced
   butternut pumpkin
2 tablespoons chopped unsalted peanuts
1 tablespoon palm sugar
2 tablespoons tamarind purée
2 tablespoons fish sauce
curry leaves, to garnish

1 Heat a non-stick wok over high heat.
Add the oil and swirl it around to coat the
side of the wok. Add the meat in batches
and cook for 5 minutes, or until browned.
Remove the meat from the wok.
2 Add the curry paste, garlic, onion and
curry leaves to the wok, and stir to coat.
Return the meat to the wok and cook,
stirring, over medium heat for 2 minutes.
3 Pour the coconut milk into the wok,
then reduce the heat and simmer for 45
minutes. Add the diced pumpkin and
simmer for a further 25–30 minutes, or
until the meat and vegetables are tender
and the sauce has thickened.
4 Stir in the peanuts, palm sugar,
tamarind purée and fish sauce, and
simmer for 1 minute. Garnish with curry
leaves. Serve with rice.

NOTE: Use a non-stick or stainless steel
wok because the acidity of the tamarind
may cause the seasoning surface of a
carbon-steel wok to lift off.

SAN CHOY BAU

Preparation time: 25 minutes
Total cooking time: 10 minutes
Makes 12 small or 4 large

¼ cup (60 ml/2 fl oz) oyster sauce
2 teaspoons soy sauce
¼ cup (60 ml/2 fl oz) sherry
1 teaspoon sugar
1½ tablespoons vegetable oil
¼ teaspoon sesame oil
3 cloves garlic, crushed
3 teaspoons grated fresh ginger
6 spring onions, sliced on the diagonal
500 g (1 lb) pork mince
100 g (3½ oz) bamboo shoots, finely
  chopped
100 g (3½ oz) water chestnuts, drained
  and finely chopped
1 tablespoon pine nuts, toasted
12 small or 4 large whole lettuce leaves
  (e.g. iceberg), trimmed
oyster sauce, to serve (optional)

1 To make the stir-fry sauce, combine the oyster and soy sauces, sherry and sugar in a small bowl or jug and stir until the sugar dissolves.
2 Heat a wok over high heat, add the vegetable and sesame oils and swirl to coat. Add the garlic, ginger and half the spring onion and stir-fry for 1 minute. Add the mince and cook for 3–4 minutes, or until just cooked, breaking up any lumps.
3 Add the bamboo shoots, water chestnuts and remaining spring onion, then pour in the stir-fry sauce. Cook for 2–3 minutes, or until the liquid thickens a little. Stir in the pine nuts.
4 Divide among the lettuce cups to make either 12 small portions or four very large ones. Drizzle with oyster sauce, if desired, then serve.

KIBBEH BIL SANIEH
(LAYERED LAMB AND BURGHUL)

Preparation time: 30 minutes +
  30 minutes soaking +
  10 minutes cooling
Total cooking time: 50 minutes
Serves 4–6

2 cups (350 g/11 oz) burghul
400 g (13 oz) lamb mince
1 large onion, finely chopped
1 tablespoon ground cumin
1 teaspoon ground allspice
olive oil, for brushing

Filling
1 tablespoon olive oil, plus extra for
  brushing
1 onion, finely chopped
1 teaspoon ground cinnamon
1 tablespoon ground cumin
500 g (1 lb) lamb mince
½ cup (80 g/2¾ oz) raisins
100 g (3½ oz) pine nuts, toasted

1 Soak the burghul in cold water for 30 minutes, drain and squeeze out excess water. Place the mince, onion, cumin, allspice and some salt and pepper in a food processor, and process until combined. Add the burghul and process to a paste. Refrigerate until needed. Preheat the oven to moderate 180°C (350°F/Gas 4). Lightly grease a 20 x 30 cm (8 x 12 inch) baking dish.

2 For the filling, heat the oil in a large frying pan over medium heat and cook the onion for 5 minutes, or until softened. Add the cinnamon and cumin and stir for 1 minute, or until fragrant. Add the mince, stirring to break up any lumps, and cook for 5 minutes, or until the meat is brown. Stir in the raisins and nuts and season, to taste.
3 Press half the burghul mixture into the base of the tin, smoothing the surface with wet hands. Spread the filling over the top, then cover with the remaining burghul, again smoothing the top.
4 Score a diamond pattern in the top of the mixture with a sharp knife and brush lightly with olive oil. Bake for 35–40 minutes, or until the top is brown and crisp. Cool for 10 minutes before cutting into diamond shapes. Serve with yoghurt and salad.

RICE

AS THE STAPLE OF ALL ASIAN CUISINES, THIS GRAIN IS OF HUGE IMPORTANCE—IN THAILAND AN INVITATION TO A MEAL IS 'KIN KHAO', LITERALLY 'COME AND EAT RICE'. ALMOST ALL THE RICE EATEN IS WHITE RATHER THAN BROWN.

COOKING METHODS

One cup (200 g/6½ oz) rice makes 3 cups (550 g/1 lb 1⅔ oz) cooked rice. Allow 1½–2 cups (280–370 g/9–11¾ oz) cooked rice per person.

RAPID BOILING

Bring a large pan of water to a fast boil. The quantity of water should be 6 times the quantity of rice. Add the rice and cook, uncovered, for 12–15 minutes, or until the swollen grains are soft and opaque. Drain.

STEAMING

The most common method of cooking rice throughout Asia, it is easy to obtain good results if the water to rice ratio is correct. A quick and easy method is to place the quantity of rice required in a large pan and add enough water to reach the first joint of your index finger when the tip is on the top of the rice. For a more accurate measure, add 2 cups (500 ml/ 16 fl oz) water for the first cup (200 g/6½ oz) long-grain rice and 1½ cups (375 ml/ 12 fl oz) water for each additional cup of rice. For short- or medium-grain rice, add 1½ cups (375 ml/12 fl oz) water for the first cup (200 g/6½ oz) rice and 1 cup (250 ml/ 8 fl oz) for each additional cup of rice. Absorption: Wash rice in a sieve until the water runs clear; place in a large pan with the water, bring to the boil and boil for 1 minute. Cover with a tight-fitting lid, then reduce the heat to as low as possible and cook for 10–15 minutes, or until all the water has been absorbed. Steam tunnels will form holes on the surface. Turn off the heat and leave the pan, covered, for at least 10 minutes. Fluff the rice with a fork. Electric rice cooker: This appliance steams rice in the same way as the absorption method and is ideal for making large quantities. Wash rice in a sieve until the water runs clear, drain and add to the rice cooker with water. Follow the manufacturer's instructions for cooking times.

Long-Grain: Cultivated throughout Southeast Asia, this long slender grain is the favoured rice of the Chinese. When cooked the grains separate easily, are non-starchy and are perfect for dishes such as fried rice. Long-grain rice is the most readily available and widely used rice in the Western world.

Jasmine: Originating in Thailand, this variety of long-grain rice is now popular throughout Southeast Asia. A lightly fragrant rice which goes well with all kinds of Asian dishes.

Basmati: This aromatic, narrow, long-grain rice is grown in the foothills of the Himalayas from Bangladesh to India. It is traditionally used for biryani and pilau dishes which incorporate the delicate flavour and colour of saffron and utilise the firm texture of the cooked basmati rice.

Short-grain: These small oval grains, which are high in starch, are preferred by the Japanese and Koreans. Best cooked by the absorption method, this rice is sticky and the grains adhere together, making it easier to eat with chopsticks and to prepare sushi.

Glutinous: White glutinous: This is the staple rice of the Laotians and northern Thais who use it as an accompaniment to savoury dishes. However its main use is for leaf-wrapped snacks or Asian desserts. The grains are short and turn translucent when cooked. Ill-named because it contains no gluten, it has a high starch content and is commonly called 'sticky rice' or 'sweet rice'.

Black glutinous: When the layer of bran is left on the rice, it is an unusual dark colour and has a nutty flavour. It combines well with palm sugar, coconut milk and sesame seeds and is a popular dessert rice in Burma, Thailand, Indonesia and the Philippines. For best results, the rice should be soaked overnight.

Clockwise from top left: Long-grain rice; jasmine rice; white glutinous rice; basmati rice; short-grain rice (cooked); black glutinous rice; short-grain rice

LAMB KORMA

Preparation time: 30 minutes + 1 hour
   marinating
Total cooking time: 1 hour
Serves 4–6

2 kg (4 lb) leg of lamb, boned
1 medium onion, chopped
2 teaspoons grated fresh ginger
3 cloves garlic
1 tablespoon coriander seeds
2 teaspoons ground cumin
1 teaspoon cardamom pods
½ teaspoon salt
large pinch cayenne pepper
2 tablespoons ghee or oil
1 medium onion, extra, sliced
2 tablespoons tomato paste (tomato
   purée, double concentrate)
½ cup (125 g/4 oz) yoghurt

1 Remove all excess fat, skin and sinew
from the lamb. Cut the meat into 3 cm
(1¼ inch) cubes and place it in a large bowl.
2 Place the onion, ginger, garlic,
coriander seeds, cumin, cardamom pods,
salt and cayenne pepper in a food
processor and process until the mixture
forms a smooth paste. Add the spice
mixture to the lamb and mix well to coat.
Set aside for 1 hour.
3 Heat the ghee in a large pan; add the
extra onion and cook, stirring, over
moderately low heat until the onion is
soft. Add the lamb mixture and cook for 8
to 10 minutes, stirring constantly, until
the lamb cubes are browned all over. Add
the tomato paste and 2 tablespoons of the
yoghurt, and stir until combined. Simmer,
uncovered, until the liquid has been
absorbed.
4 Add the remaining yoghurt, 2 tablespoons
at a time, stirring until the mixture is
nearly dry between each addition.
5 Cover the pan and simmer over low heat
for 30 minutes, or until the meat is
tender, stirring occasionally. Add a little
water if the mixture becomes too dry.
Serve with rice.

COCIDO MADRILENO
(MADRILENO MEAT AND VEGETABLES)

Preparation time: 25 minutes +
   overnight soaking
Total cooking time: 2 hours 45 minutes
Serves 6–8

1 cup (220 g/7 oz) dried chickpeas
1 kg (2 lb) chicken, trussed
500 g (1 lb) beef brisket, in one piece
250 g (8 oz) piece smoke-cured bacon
125 g (4 oz) tocino, streaky bacon or
   speck
1 pig's trotter
200 g (6½ oz) chorizo
1 onion, studded with 2 cloves
1 bay leaf
1 morcilla blood sausage (optional)
250 g (8 oz) green beans, sliced
   lengthways
250 g (8 oz) green cabbage, cut into
   sections through the heart
300 g (10 oz) silverbeet (Swiss chard)
   leaves, rinsed, stalks removed
4 small potatoes
2 leeks, cut into 10 cm (4 inch) lengths
pinch of saffron threads
75 g (2½ oz) dried rice vermicelli

1 Soak the chickpeas in cold water
overnight. Drain and rinse. Tie loosely in a
muslin bag.
2 Put 3 litres of cold water in a very large
deep saucepan. Add the chicken, beef,
bacon and tocino and bring to the boil.
Add the chickpeas, pig's trotter and
chorizo, return to the boil, then add the
onion, bay leaf and ½ teaspoon salt.
Simmer, partially covered, for 2½ hours.

3 After 2 hours, bring a saucepan of water
to the boil, add the morcilla and gently
boil for 5 minutes. Drain and set aside. Tie
the green beans loosely in a muslin bag.
Pour 1 litre of water into a large saucepan
and bring to the boil. Add the beans,
cabbage, silverbeet, potatoes, leek and
saffron with 1 teaspoon of salt. Return to
the boil and simmer for 30 minutes.
4 Strain the stock from both the meat and
vegetable pans and combine in a large
saucepan. Bring to the boil, adjust the
seasoning and add the vermicelli. Simmer
for 6–7 minutes. Release the chickpeas
and pile them in the centre of a large
warm platter. Discard the tocino, then
slice the meats and sausages. Arrange in
groups around the chickpeas at one end
of the platter. Release the beans. Arrange
the vegetables in groups around the other
end. Spoon a little of the simmering broth
(minus the vermicelli) over the meat, then
pour the rest into a soup tureen. Serve at
once. It is traditional to serve the two
dishes together, although the broth is
eaten first.

PEKING DUCK WITH MANDARIN PANCAKES

Preparation time: 1 hour +
    5 hours standing
Total cooking time: 1 hour 15 minutes
Serves 4 as a main course or 6 with
    other dishes

1 x 1.7 kg (3¾ lb) duck
3 litres boiling water
1 tablespoon honey
½ cup (125 ml/4 fl oz) hot water
1 Lebanese cucumber
12 spring onions
2 tablespoons hoisin sauce

Mandarin Pancakes
2½ cups (310 g/9¾ oz) plain flour
2 teaspoons caster sugar
1 cup (250 ml/8 fl oz) boiling water
1 tablespoon sesame oil

1 Wash the duck and remove the neck and any large pieces of fat from inside the carcass. Hold the duck over the sink and very carefully and slowly pour the boiling water over it, rotating the duck so the water scalds all the skin. You may need another kettle of boiling water at this stage.
2 Put the duck on a rack placed in a baking dish. Mix the honey and hot water together and brush 2 coats of this glaze over the duck, making sure it is entirely covered. Dry the duck, preferably by hanging in a cool, airy place for about 4 hours. Alternatively, you could use an electric fan on a cool setting, positioned a metre or so away. The skin is sufficiently dry when it feels papery.
3 Remove the seeds from the cucumber and slice the flesh into matchsticks. Cut an 8 cm (3 inch) section from the white end of each spring onion; make fine parallel cuts from the top of the section towards the white end. Place the spring onion pieces in iced water; they will open into 'brushes'.

4 Preheat the oven to hot 210°C (415°F/Gas 6–7). Roast the duck on the rack in the baking dish for 30 minutes. Turn the duck over carefully without tearing the skin; roast it for another 30 minutes. Remove the duck from the oven and let it stand for a minute or two, then place it on a warm dish.
5 To make Mandarin Pancakes: Place the flour and sugar in a medium bowl and pour over the boiling water. Stir the mixture a few times and leave until lukewarm. Knead the mixture on a lightly floured surface to make a smooth dough. Cover and set aside for 30 minutes.
6 Take 2 level tablespoons of dough; roll each one into a ball. Roll out to circles 8 cm (3 inches) in diameter. Lightly brush one of the circles with sesame oil and place the other circle on top. Re-roll to make a thin pancake about 15 cm (6 inches) in diameter. Repeat with the remaining dough and oil to make about 10 'double' pancakes.
7 Heat a frying pan and cook the pancakes one at a time. When small bubbles appear on the surface, turn the pancake over and cook the second side, pressing the surface with a clean tea towel. The pancake should puff up when done. Transfer the pancake to a plate. When cool enough to handle, peel the 2 halves of the double pancake apart. Stack them on a plate and cover them at once to prevent them drying out.
8 To serve: Finely slice the duck. Place the pancakes and duck on separate serving plates. Arrange the cucumber sticks and spring onion brushes on another serving plate. Place the hoisin sauce in a small dish. Each diner helps themselves to a pancake, spreads a little sauce on it and adds a couple of pieces of cucumber, a spring onion brush and finally a piece of duck. The pancake is then folded over into a neat envelope shape for eating.

CHORIZO EN SIDRA
(CHORIZO IN CIDER)

Preparation time: 5 minutes
Total cooking time: 15 minutes
Serves 4

3 teaspoons olive oil
1 small onion, finely chopped
1½ teaspoons paprika
½ cup (125 ml/4 fl oz) dry alcoholic apple
    cider
¼ cup (60 ml/2 fl oz) chicken stock
1 bay leaf
280 g (9 oz) chorizo, sliced diagonally
2 teaspoons sherry vinegar, or to taste
2 teaspoons chopped fresh flat-leaf
    parsley

1 Heat the oil in a saucepan over low heat, add the onion and cook for 3 minutes, stirring occasionally, or until soft. Add the paprika and cook for 1 minute.
2 Increase the heat to medium, add the apple cider, stock and bay leaf to the pan and bring to the boil. Reduce the heat and simmer for 5 minutes. Add the sliced chorizo and simmer for 5 minutes, or until the sauce has reduced slightly. Stir in the sherry vinegar and parsley. Serve hot.

BISTEEYA
(MOROCCAN CHICKEN PIE)

Preparation time: 30 minutes
Total cooking time: 1 hour 20 minutes
Serves 6–8

200 g (6½ oz) butter
1.5 kg (3 lb) chicken, cut into 4 portions
1 large onion, finely chopped
3 teaspoons ground cinnamon
1 teaspoon ground ginger
2 teaspoons ground cumin
¼ teaspoon cayenne pepper
½ teaspoon ground turmeric
½ teaspoon saffron threads soaked in
  2 tablespoons warm water
½ cup (125 ml/4 fl oz) chicken stock
4 eggs, lightly beaten
½ cup (25 g/¾ oz) chopped fresh
  coriander
3 tablespoons chopped fresh flat-leaf
  parsley
⅓ cup (50 g/1¾ oz) chopped almonds
3 tablespoons icing sugar, plus extra, for
  dusting
375 g (12 oz) filo pastry

1 Preheat the oven to moderate 180°C
(350°F/Gas 4). Grease a 30 cm (12 inch)
pizza tray.
2 Melt 40 g (1¼ oz) of the butter in a large
frying pan, add the chicken, onion,
2 teaspoons of the cinnamon, all the other
spices and the chicken stock. Season with
salt and pepper, cover and simmer for
30 minutes, or until the chicken is cooked
through.
3 Remove the chicken from the sauce.
When cool enough to handle, remove the
meat from the bones, discard the skin
and bones and shred the meat into thin
strips.

4 Bring the liquid in the pan to a simmer
and add the eggs. Cook the mixture,
stirring constantly, until the eggs are
cooked and the mixture is quite dry. Add
the chicken, chopped coriander and
parsley, season well with salt and pepper
and mix. Remove from the heat.
5 Bake the almonds on a baking tray until
golden brown. Cool slightly, then blend in
a food processor or spice grinder with the
icing sugar and remaining cinnamon until
they resemble coarse crumbs.
6 Melt the remaining butter. Place a
sheet of filo on the pizza tray and brush
with melted butter. Place another sheet
on top in a pinwheel effect and brush with
butter. Continue brushing and layering
until you have used 8 sheets. Place the
chicken mixture on top and sprinkle with
the almond mixture.
7 Fold the overlapping filo over the top of
the filling. Place a sheet of filo over the
top and brush with butter continue to
layer buttered filo over the top in the
same pinwheel effect until you have used
8 sheets. Tuck the overhanging edges
over the pie to form a neat round parcel.
Brush well with the remaining butter.
Bake the pie for 40–45 minutes until
cooked through and golden. Dust with
icing sugar before serving.

MALAYSIAN COCONUT
CHICKEN

Preparation time: 25 minutes
Total cooking time: 45–60 minutes
Serves 4–6

1 x 1.6 kg (3½ lb) chicken
1 tablespoon oil
2 onions, sliced
3 cloves garlic, crushed
2 red chillies, seeded and chopped
½ cup (45 g/1½ oz) desiccated coconut
2 teaspoons ground turmeric
2 teaspoons ground coriander
2 teaspoons ground cumin
2 stems lemon grass (white part only),
  chopped
8 curry leaves
2 cups (500 ml/16 fl oz) coconut milk

1 Cut the chicken into 8 to 10 pieces.
2 Heat the oil in a large pan and cook the
onion until soft. Add the garlic, chilli,
coconut and turmeric. Stir mixture for
1 minute. Add the coriander, cumin,
lemon grass, curry leaves and coconut
milk. Stir until well combined.
3 Add the chicken pieces and stir until
well coated with the sauce. Simmer,
uncovered, for 45 to 60 minutes, or until
the chicken is tender and the sauce has
thickened. Serve with vermicelli noodles.

CHICKEN AND PEANUT PANANG CURRY

Preparation time: 25 minutes
Total cooking time: 30–40 minutes
Serves 4

1 tablespoon oil
1 large red (Spanish) onion, chopped
1–2 tablespoons ready-made Panang curry paste
1 cup (250 ml/8 fl oz) coconut milk
500 g (1 lb) chicken thigh fillets, cut into bite-sized pieces
4 kaffir lime leaves
¼ cup (60 ml/2 fl oz) coconut cream
1 tablespoon fish sauce
1 tablespoon lime juice
2 teaspoons soft brown sugar
½ cup (80 g/2⅔ oz) unsalted roasted peanuts, chopped
½ cup (15 g/½ oz) Thai basil leaves
½ cup (80 g/2⅔ oz) chopped fresh pineapple
1 cucumber, sliced
chilli sauce for serving, optional

1 Heat the oil in a wok or large frying pan; add the onion and curry paste and stir over medium heat for 2 minutes. Add the coconut milk and bring to the boil.
2 Add the chicken and lime leaves to the wok; reduce the heat and cook for 15 minutes. Remove the chicken with a wire mesh strainer or slotted spoon. Simmer the sauce for 5 minutes or until it is reduced and quite thick.
3 Return the chicken to the wok. Add the coconut cream, fish sauce, lime juice and sugar and cook for 5 minutes. Stir in the peanuts, basil and pineapple. Serve with sliced cucumber on the side, some chilli sauce, if desired, as well as steamed rice.

NOTE: Panang curry paste is based on ground nuts (usually peanuts). Panang curry originated in Malaysia but is now also found in Thai and Indonesian cuisines.

PSARI TAHINA (BAKED FISH WITH TAHINI SAUCE)

Preparation time: 30 minutes
Total cooking time: 30 minutes
Serves 4

1 kg (2 lb) whole white-fleshed fish (snapper, bream or barramundi), scaled and cleaned
3 cloves garlic, crushed
2 teaspoons harissa
2 tablespoons olive oil
1 lemon, thinly sliced
1 onion, thinly sliced
2 large firm, ripe tomatoes, sliced
4 sprigs fresh thyme

Tahini sauce
2 teaspoons olive oil
1 clove garlic, crushed
3 tablespoons light tahini
2½ tablespoons lemon juice
1½ tablespoons chopped fresh coriander

1 Preheat the oven to moderately hot 200°C (400°F/Gas 6). Lightly grease a large baking dish. Make 3 diagonal cuts on each side of the fish through the thickest part of the flesh to ensure even cooking. Combine the garlic, harissa and olive oil in a small dish. Place 2 teaspoons in the fish cavity and spread the remainder over both sides of the fish rubbing it into the slits. Place 2 lemon slices in the cavity of the fish.

2 Arrange the onion in a layer on the baking dish. Top with the tomato, thyme and remaining lemon slices. Place the fish on top and bake, uncovered, for about 25–30 minutes, or until the fish flesh is opaque.
3 Meanwhile, to make the tahini sauce, heat the olive oil in a small saucepan over low heat. Add the garlic and cook over medium heat for 30 seconds, then add the tahini, lemon juice and ½ cup (125 ml/4 fl oz) water and stir until combined. Add more water, if necessary, to make a smooth, but fairly thick sauce. Cook for 2 minutes, then remove from the heat and stir in the coriander. Season.
4 Transfer the onion and tomato to a serving dish. Place the fish on top and season with salt. Pour some of the sauce on the fish and the rest in a serving dish on the side.

GOAN SPICED MUSSELS

Preparation time: 20 minutes
Total cooking time: 20 minutes
Serves 4

1 kg (2 lb) black mussels
3 tablespoons ghee or oil
5 cloves garlic, crushed
5 cm (2 inch) piece fresh ginger, grated
2 medium onions, finely chopped
3 red chillies, finely chopped
2 teaspoons ground cumin
2 teaspoons ground coriander
4 tomatoes, peeled, seeded and chopped
2 cups (500 ml/16 fl oz) fish stock
1 cup (50 g/1⅔ oz) chopped fresh
   coriander leaves
2 tablespoons lemon juice

1 Remove the beards from the mussels and scrub them under cold water to remove any excess grit. Discard any which are already open.
2 Heat the ghee in a wok, add the garlic, ginger and onion and cook over medium heat for 5 minutes, or until the onion is soft and golden. Add the chilli, cumin, coriander and tomato, and cook for 5 minutes.
3 Add the mussels and fish stock and bring to the boil. Reduce the heat and simmer for 5 minutes. Discard any mussels that have not opened after this time.
4 Remove the wok from the heat, stir through the chopped coriander and lemon juice, and serve with rice.

SMOKED FIVE SPICE CHICKEN

Preparation time: 30 minutes +
   4 hours marinating
Total cooking time: 35 minutes
Serves 6

1 x 1.7 kg (3¾ lb) chicken
¼ cup (60 ml/2 fl oz) soy sauce
1 tablespoon finely grated ginger
2 medium pieces dried mandarin or
   tangerine peel
1 star anise
¼ teaspoon five spice powder
3 tablespoons soft brown sugar

1 Wash the chicken in cold water. Pat it dry with paper towels. Discard any large pieces of fat from inside the chicken.
2 Place the chicken in a large non-metallic bowl with the soy sauce and ginger. Cover and marinate for at least 4 hours or leave overnight in the refrigerator, turning occasionally.
3 Place a small rack in the base of a pan large enough to hold the chicken. Add water to the level of the rack. Place the chicken on the rack. Bring water to the boil, cover tightly, reduce heat and steam for 15 minutes. Turn off the heat and allow the chicken to stand, covered, for another 15 minutes. Transfer the chicken to a bowl.

4 Wash the pan and line it with 3 or 4 large pieces of aluminium foil. Pound the dried peel and star anise in a mortar and pestle until the pieces are the size of coarse breadcrumbs, or process in a food processor. Add the five spice powder and sugar. Spread the spice mixture over the foil.
5 Replace the rack in the pan and place the chicken on it. Place the pan over medium heat and, when the spice mixture starts smoking, cover tightly. Reduce the heat to low; smoke the chicken for 20 minutes. Test if the chicken is cooked by piercing the thigh with a skewer; the juices should run clear. Remove the chicken from the pan and chop it Chinese-style. It is important to remember that the heat produced in this final step is very intense. When the chicken is removed from the pan, leave the pan on the stove to cool before handling it.

GREEK LIMA BEAN CASSEROLE

Preparation time: 20 minutes +
   overnight soaking
Total cooking time: 2 hours
Serves 6–8

1 cup (185 g/6 oz) dried lima beans
¼ cup (60 ml/2 fl oz) olive oil
1 large onion, halved and sliced
1 clove garlic, chopped
1 small carrot, chopped
1 small stick celery, chopped
400 g (13 oz) can good-quality crushed
   tomatoes
1 tablespoon tomato paste (tomato purée)
2 teaspoons chopped fresh dill
extra virgin olive oil, for serving

1 Cover the lima beans with plenty of cold water and leave to soak overnight. Drain well.
2 Bring a large pan of water to the boil, add the beans and return to the boil, then reduce the heat to medium and cook, partially covered, for 45–60 minutes, or until the beans are tender but not mushy. Drain. Preheat the oven to moderate 180°C (350°F/Gas 4).
3 Heat the oil in a 2.5 litre heatproof casserole dish over medium heat. Add the onion, garlic, carrot and celery, and cook for 5 minutes, or until the onion is translucent. Add the crushed tomato, tomato paste and ½ cup (125 ml/4 fl oz) water. Bring to the boil, then reduce the heat and simmer for 3 minutes.
4 Add the lima beans and dill to the casserole dish, then season, to taste. Bring back to the boil, then cover and bake for 50 minutes, or until the sauce is thick and the lima beans are soft. Serve hot or at room temperature, drizzled with the oil.

QUAIL MASALA

Preparation time: 30 minutes + overnight
   marinating + cooling
Total cooking time: 50 minutes
Serves 6

6 x 150 g (5 oz) quails

Marinade
⅔ cup (100 g/3½ oz) blanched almonds
3 garlic cloves, crushed
3 cm (1¼ inch) piece of ginger, grated
½ onion, finely chopped
½ teaspoon chilli powder
½ teaspoon ground cloves
½ teaspoon ground cinnamon
1 teaspoon ground cumin
1 teaspoon garam masala
2 tablespoons mint, finely chopped
200 g (6½ oz) thick natural yoghurt
1 teaspoon jaggery or soft brown sugar

Rice Stuffing
60 g (2 oz) basmati rice
1 teaspoon amchoor powder (see Notes)
⅓ cup (50 g/1¾ oz) chopped pine nuts
1½ tablespoons lemon juice

2 young banana leaves
¼ cup (60 ml/2 fl oz) lemon juice
cucumber slices
mango or green mango slices
mint leaves

1 Clean the quails by rinsing them well and wiping them dry. Prick the flesh all over so the marinade will penetrate the meat.
2 To make the marinade, grind the almonds in a food processor or finely chop them with a knife, then mix them with the remaining marinade ingredients. Coat the quails evenly with the marinade, then cover and marinate for 4 hours, or overnight, in the fridge.

3 To make the rice stuffing, preheat the oven to moderately hot 200°C (400°F/Gas 6). Cook the rice in boiling water for 15 minutes, or until just tender. Drain well and allow to cool. Combine the rice, amchoor powder, pine nuts and lemon juice and season with salt. Just before cooking, fill the quails with the rice stuffing and brush some marinade on the quails. If you are making the stuffing in advance, make sure you refrigerate it until you are ready to use it.
4 Cut the banana leaves into neat pieces big enough to wrap a quail. Soften the leaves by dipping them into a pan of very hot water. Wipe them dry as they become pliant. If you can't get banana leaves, use foil. Brush with oil.
5 Wrap each quail individually in a piece of banana leaf, drizzling with any excess marinade. Tie firmly with a piece of kitchen string. Place the parcels, with the seam-side up, on a rack above a baking tray and bake for 25–30 minutes. Check to see if the quails are cooked by opening one—the flesh should be slightly pink but the juices should run clear when the flesh is pierced. If necessary, cook the quails for another 5 minutes. Open the packets completely for 3 minutes at the end of cooking, to brown the quail slightly. Sprinkle a dash of lemon juice over each quail. Serve in the packets with some sliced cucumber, sliced mango and mint leaves.

NOTES: Amchoor powder is a fine beige powder made by drying green mangoes.
   Quail is an exotic dish, even in India. Many of the royal households traditionally used quail in many different ways. Tender young chicken or poussin can be successfully used instead.

QUESADILLAS

USE FLOUR TORTILLAS FROM THE BREAD SECTION OF YOUR SUPERMARKET TO MAKE THESE MEXICAN SNACKS. AND STUN YOUR GUESTS WITH YOUR AUTHENTIC PRONUNCIATION... 'KAY-SAH-DEE-YAH'.

GUACAMOLE ROLLS

Mix a 450 g (14 oz) can of refried beans with 90 g (3 oz) grated Cheddar. Cut 7 flour tortillas into rounds, using an 8 cm (3 inch) cutter. Wrap in foil and cook in a moderate 180°F (350°F/Gas 4) oven for 2–3 minutes, until warmed through. To make the guacamole, mash 2 avocados and mix with 1 small chopped red onion, 1 tablespoon mayonnaise, 1 chopped red chilli, 1 tablespoon lime juice and 1 tablespoon chopped fresh coriander. Spread a little bean mixture over the base of each tortilla and roll up like a horn. Place, seam-side-down, on a baking tray and bake for another 5 minutes, or until crisp. Spoon a teaspoon of guacamole into the open end and serve.
Makes 42.

CHEESE QUESADILLAS

Roast 2 jalapeno chillies by holding with tongs over a flame until blackened and blistered. You can also roast chillies under a hot grill. Put in a plastic bag and when cool, you will find the skin peels away easily. Finely chop the chilli flesh and mix with 250 g (8 oz) grated Cheddar and 75 g (2½ oz) grated mozzarella cheese. Spread evenly over 3 flour tortillas, then top with another 3 tortillas. Cut out rounds with a 6 cm (2½ inch) cutter, then fry in a little oil for 1–2 minutes, or until golden brown on each side. Serve with home-made salsa.
Makes about 25–30.

TACO CHICKEN QUESADILLAS

In a large frying pan, heat 1 tablespoon oil, add 1 finely chopped red onion and 1 finely diced red pepper (capsicum). Cook until the onion has softened. Add 2 crushed cloves garlic, ¼ teaspoon paprika, 1 teaspoon ground cumin and 1 teaspoon ground coriander and cook for 2 minutes. Add 400 g (13 oz) chicken mince and cook for 5–8 minutes, until brown, breaking up any lumps. Add a 400 g (13 oz) can chopped tomatoes and simmer for 20 minutes, or until thick. Cut 7 flour tortillas into rounds with an 8 cm (3 inch) cutter. Place a teaspoon of the mixture on one half of each round. Sprinkle with 220 g (7 oz) grated Cheddar. Bake in a

moderate 180°C (350°F/Gas 4) oven for 1 minute, or until the cheese has melted. Fold over and hold for a few seconds to stick. Garnish with sliced spring onion. Makes 42.

CORN, TOMATO AND BEAN QUESADILLAS

Combine 1 finely chopped red onion, 2 chopped tomatoes, a 310 g (10 oz) can drained and rinsed corn kernels and 1 diced red pepper (capsicum). Drain and rinse a 425 g (14 oz) can pinto beans and mash with a fork. Place 3 flour tortillas on a work surface, spread the pinto beans evenly over the tortillas, top with the corn and tomato mixture and sprinkle with 90 g (3 oz) grated Cheddar. Top with 3 more flour tortillas. Heat 2 teaspoons oil in a 25 cm (10 inch) frying pan and cook the stacks for 3–4 minutes each side, until golden brown. Remove from the pan and cut into 12 triangles. Makes 36.

CHILLI BEEF QUESADILLAS

Heat 1 tablespoon oil in a frying pan and cook 1 chopped onion and 2 crushed cloves garlic for 2–3 minutes. Add 400 g (13 oz) beef mince and cook for 5–7 minutes until brown, breaking up any lumps. Stir in a 325 g (11 oz) bottle of Mexican black bean salsa. Bring to the boil, reduce the heat and simmer for 3–4 minutes, or until the mixture reduces and thickens. Season. Place 3 flour tortillas on a work surface and sprinkle with 125 g (4 oz) grated Cheddar. Spoon the mince evenly over the cheese, then top with another 3 tortillas. Heat 2 teaspoons oil in a 25 cm (10 inch) frying pan and cook the stacks for 3–4 minutes each side, or until golden brown. Remove from the pan, trim off the sides and cut into 5 cm (2 inch) squares. Makes about 36.

CHIPOLTE VEGETABLE QUESADILLAS

Heat 1 tablespoon oil in a large frying pan, add 2 cloves of garlic and 1 finely chopped onion and cook until golden. Remove from the pan. Heat 2 tablespoons oil in the pan and cook 200 g (6½ oz) diced slender eggplant and 1 diced red pepper (capsicum) until golden. Return the onion and stir in a 400 g (13 oz) can chopped tomatoes, 2 canned chipolte chillies and 2 tablespoons tomato paste. Simmer for 15 minutes, or until thick. Stir through 2 tablespoons chopped fresh coriander. Cut 7 flour tortillas into rounds using a 8 cm (3 inch) cutter. Sprinkle half the rounds with 220 g (7 oz) grated Cheddar and place a teaspoon of filling on top. Seal with another tortilla round. Heat a large frying pan with a little oil. Fry on both sides until golden and serve with a dollop of sour cream, tomato slice and a coriander leaf. Makes 50.

FROM LEFT: Guacamole rolls; Cheese quesadillas; Taco chicken quesadillas; Corn, tomato and bean quesadillas; Chilli beef quesadillas

BHEL PURI

Preparation time: 40 minutes
Total cooking time: 25 minutes
Serves 6

Mint chutney
1⅔ cups (50 g/1¾ oz) coriander (cilantro)
2½ cups (50 g/1¾ oz) mint
6 garlic cloves, chopped
3 red chillies, chopped
½ red onion, chopped
¼ cup (60 ml/2 fl oz) lemon juice

Tamarind chutney
60 g (2 oz) fennel seeds
1¾ cups (440 ml/14 fl oz) tamarind purée
100 g (3½ oz) fresh ginger, sliced
300 g (10 oz) jaggery or soft brown sugar
1 teaspoon chilli powder
1 tablespoon ground cumin
1 tablespoon chaat masala (see Notes)
1 teaspoon black salt (see Notes)

3 potatoes, peeled
1 tomato
120 g (4 oz) puffed rice (see Notes)
60 g (2 oz) sev noodles (see Notes)
1 green unripe mango, sliced into thin
   slivers
1 onion, finely chopped
4 tablespoons finely chopped coriander
   (cilantro) or mint leaves
1 teaspoon chaat masala (see Notes)
12 crushed puri crisps (see Notes)
coriander (cilantro) leaves

1 To make the mint chutney, blend the ingredients together in a food processor or mortar and pestle. Transfer to a saucepan and bring to the boil. Remove from the heat, leave to cool, then season with salt.

2 To make the tamarind chutney, place a small frying pan over low heat and dry-fry the fennel seeds until fragrant. Mix together the tamarind, ginger and sugar with 1 cup (250 ml/8 fl oz) water in a saucepan. Cook over low heat until the tamarind blends into the mixture and the sugar completely dissolves.
3 Strain out the ginger and cook the remaining mixture to a thick pulp. Add the fennel seeds, chilli powder, cumin, chaat masala and black salt. Season with salt and reduce, stirring occasionally, over medium heat until thickened to a dropping consistency (it will fall in sheets off the spoon). Leave to cool.
4 To make the bhel puri, cook the potatoes in boiling water for 10 minutes, or until tender, then cut into small cubes. Score a cross in the top of the tomato. Plunge into boiling water for 20 seconds, then drain and peel. Roughly chop the tomato, discarding the core and seeds and reserving any juices.
5 Put the puffed rice, noodles, mango, onion, chopped coriander, chaat masala and puri crisps in a large bowl and toss them together. When well mixed, stir in a little of each chutney. Vary the chutney amounts depending on the flavour you want to achieve. The tamarind chutney has a tart flavour and the mint chutney is hot. Serve in small bowls and garnish with coriander leaves.

NOTES: Black salt, puffed rice, sev noodles, chaat masala and puri crisps are all available at Indian grocery stores.
   Bhel puri is India's most famous chaat (snack), and is sold by street vendors who make up a mixture to suit your tastes.

PAD THAI
(THAI FRIED NOODLES)

Preparation time: 25 minutes
Total cooking time: 10–15 minutes
Serves 4

200 g (6½ oz) raw prawns
250 g (8 oz) dried rice stick noodles
2 tablespoons oil
3 cloves garlic, chopped
2 teaspoons chopped red chilli
150 g (4¾ oz) pork, thinly sliced
½ cup (60 g/2 oz) garlic chives, chopped
2 tablespoons fish sauce
2 tablespoons lime juice
2 teaspoons soft brown sugar
2 eggs, beaten
1 cup (90 g/3 oz) bean sprouts
sprigs of fresh coriander
¼ cup (40 g/1⅓ oz) unsalted roasted
   peanuts, chopped
crisp fried onion, soft brown sugar and
   unsalted roasted peanuts, to serve

1 Peel and devein the prawns, and finely chop the meat. Set aside.
2 Soak the noodles in warm water for 10 minutes or until they are soft. Drain and set aside.
3 Heat the oil in a wok or large frying pan. When the oil is very hot, add the garlic, chilli and pork, and stir constantly for 2 minutes. Add the prawn meat and cook, stirring constantly, for 3 minutes. Add the garlic chives and drained noodles; cover and cook for another minute.
4 Add the fish sauce, lime juice, sugar and eggs to the wok. Toss well with tongs or 2 wooden spoons until heated through.
5 Sprinkle over the bean sprouts, coriander and peanuts. This dish is traditionally served with crisp fried onion, soft brown sugar and chopped peanuts on the side.

THAI WATER SPINACH IN FLAMES
(PAHK BOONG FAI DAENG)

Preparation time: 10 minutes
Total cooking time: 2 minutes
Serves 4

4 cloves garlic, crushed
2 fresh green chillies, thinly sliced
1 tablespoon black bean sauce
2 tablespoons fish sauce
2 teaspoons sugar
2 tablespoons vegetable oil
500 g (1 lb) water spinach, cut into 3 cm (1¼ inch) lengths

1 Combine the garlic, chilli, black bean sauce, fish sauce and sugar in a bowl.
2 Heat a wok over high heat, add the oil and swirl to coat. Add the spinach and stir-fry for 1 minute, or until wilted slightly. Add the sauce and stir-fry for 30 seconds, or until the spinach leaves are well coated. Serve immediately.

BOMBAY CURRY

Preparation time: 20 minutes
Total cooking time: 1 hour 15 minutes
    to 1 hour 45 minutes
Serves 4–6

1 tablespoon ghee or oil
2 medium onions, chopped
2 cloves garlic, crushed
2 green chillies, chopped
1 tablespoon grated fresh ginger
1½ teaspoons ground turmeric
1 teaspoon ground cumin
1 tablespoon ground coriander
½–1 teaspoon chilli powder
1 kg (2 lb) beef or lamb, cut into bite-sized cubes
1 teaspoon salt
410 g (13 oz) can crushed tomatoes
1 cup (250 ml/8 fl oz) coconut milk
fresh coriander leaves, to garnish

1 Heat the ghee in a large pan; add the onion and cook over medium heat, stirring, until just soft. Add the garlic, chilli, ginger, turmeric, cumin, coriander and chilli powder. Stir until just heated through.
2 Add the meat and cook, stirring, over high heat until the meat is well coated with the spice mixture and browned all over. Stir in the salt and undrained tomatoes and simmer, covered, for 1 to 1½ hours, or until the meat is tender.
3 Add the coconut milk and stir; simmer, uncovered, for another 5 minutes or until the sauce has thickened slightly. Serve garnished with coriander leaves, if desired.

NOTE: Raw, unsalted cashew nuts make a delicious garnish for this dish. Scatter them on top of the curry before serving.

VIETNAMESE-STYLE BEEF AND BAMBOO SHOOTS

Preparation time: 10 minutes
Total cooking time: 10 minutes
Serves 4

¼ cup (60 ml/2 fl oz) vegetable oil
400 g (13 oz) lean beef fillet, thinly sliced across the grain
227 g (7 oz) can sliced bamboo shoots, drained and rinsed
3 cloves garlic, crushed with ¼ teaspoon salt
2 tablespoons fish sauce
8 spring onions, cut into 4 cm (1½ inch) lengths on the diagonal
¼ cup (40 g/1¼ oz) sesame seeds, lightly toasted

1 Heat a wok over high heat, add 2 tablespoons of the oil and swirl to coat the side of the wok. Add the beef in two batches and stir-fry each batch for 1 minute, or until it starts to turn pink. Remove from the wok.
2 Add an extra tablespoon of oil to the wok, if necessary, then stir-fry the bamboo shoots for 3 minutes, or until starting to brown. Add the garlic, fish sauce and ¼ teaspoon salt and stir-fry for 2–3 minutes. Add the spring onion and stir-fry for a further 1 minute, or until starting to wilt. Return the beef to the wok, stir quickly and cook for 1 minute, or until heated through. Remove from the heat, toss in the sesame seeds and serve with rice.

RICE WITH FIVE THINGS

Preparation time: 25 minutes +
    1 hour 20 minutes resting
Total cooking time: 25 minutes
Serves 6

2 cups (440 g/14 oz) Japanese short-
    grain rice
5 dried shiitake mushrooms
20 g (¾ oz) deep-fried tofu
100 g (3½ oz) Konnyaku (see Notes)
1 small carrot
70 g (2¼ oz) bamboo shoot
4 chicken thigh fillets (about 500 g/1 lb)
1 teaspoon dashi granules dissolved in
    2 cups (500 ml/16 fl oz hot water
2 tablespoons mirin
⅓ cup (80 ml/2¾ fl oz) Shoyu (Japanese
    soy sauce)
3 tablespoons chopped mitsuba (optional)
    (see Note)

1 Wash the rice under cold running water
until the water runs clear, then soak for
1 hour. Drain.
2 Soak the mushrooms in 1½ cups (375 ml/
12 fl oz) hot water for 30 minutes, then
drain, reserving the liquid. Discard the
stems and thinly slice the caps. Put the
tofu in a heatproof bowl and cover with
boiling water for a few minutes then drain
and squeeze gently between paper towel
to remove excess oil.
3 Cut the konnyaku, carrot, bamboo shoot
and tofu into 3 cm (1¼ inch) long, 5 mm (¼
inch) wide strips and place in a bowl with
the mushrooms. Cut the chicken into bite-
sized pieces and add to the bowl. Combine
the dashi, mushroom liquid, mirin, Shoyu
and 1 teaspoon salt, then pour over the
chicken and vegetables and allow to sit
for about 20 minutes.

4 Drain the rice and spread over the base
of a large saucepan. Pour the chicken and
vegetable mixture over but do not stir.
Place over high heat and bring to the boil
then cover, reduce the heat to low and
cook for 15 minutes. Turn off the heat but
leave the pan on the stove and rest for
another 10 minutes before stirring to
combine all the ingredients well. Stir
through the mitsuba if desired, then
serve.

NOTES: This dish was traditionally only
made with rice and 5 vegetables;
however, now it often contains other
ingredients for extra flavour.
    Konnyaku is a chewy, brownish grey,
speckled, gelatinous paste and is made
from the starchy root of the Konjac or
Devil's tongue plant. It is usually formed
into blocks or thin strings (commonly
known as shirataki noodles).
    Mitsuba is a herb resembling flat-leaf
(Italian) parsley; its flavour is a cross
between parsley and cucumber with a
slightly peppery bite. Both konnyaku and
mitsuba are available at Japanese
specialist stores or Asian supermarkets.

SRI LANKAN LENTILS

Preparation time: 15 minutes
Total cooking time: 1 hour
Serves 4

2 tablespoons oil
2 medium onions, finely sliced
2 small red chillies, finely chopped
2 teaspoons dried shrimp
1 teaspoon ground turmeric
2 cups (500 g/1 lb) red lentils
4 curry leaves
2 cups (500 ml/16 fl oz) coconut milk
1 cup (250 ml/8 fl oz) vegetable stock
1 cinnamon stick
10 cm (4 inch) piece lemon grass

1 Heat the oil in a medium pan; add the
onion and cook over medium heat for 10
minutes, or until the onion is a deep
golden brown. Remove half the onion and
set aside to use as a garnish.
2 Add the chilli, dried shrimp and
turmeric, and cook for 2 minutes. Stir in
the lentils, curry leaves, coconut milk,
stock, cinnamon stick and lemon grass;
bring to the boil, reduce heat and simmer,
uncovered, for 45 minutes. Remove the
cinnamon stick and lemon grass and
garnish with the reserved onion.

INDONESIAN-STYLE FRIED NOODLES
(BAHMI GORENG)

Preparation time: 25 minutes
Total cooking time: 20 minutes
Serves 4

400 g (13 oz) fresh flat egg noodles
   (5 mm/¼ inch wide)
2 tomatoes
2 tablespoons peanut oil
4 red Asian shallots, thinly sliced
2 cloves garlic, chopped
1 small fresh red chilli, finely diced
100 g (3½ oz) pork loin fillet, thinly sliced
   across the grain
300 g (10 oz) chicken breast fillet, thinly
   sliced
200 g (6½ oz) small raw prawns, peeled
   and deveined, with tails intact
2 wom bok (Chinese cabbage) leaves,
   shredded
2 carrots, halved lengthways and thinly
   sliced
100 g (3½ oz) snake beans, cut into 3 cm
   (1¼ inch) lengths
¼ cup (60 ml/2 fl oz) kecap manis
1 tablespoon light soy sauce
4 spring onions, sliced on the diagonal
1 tablespoon crisp fried onion
fresh flat-leaf parsley, to garnish

1 Cook the noodles in a saucepan of boiling water for 1 minute, or until tender. Drain, then rinse under cold water.
2 Score a cross in the base of each tomato. Put the tomatoes in a bowl of boiling water for 30 seconds, then plunge into cold water and peel the skin away from the cross. Cut the tomatoes in half crossways, scoop out the seeds with a teaspoon, then chop the flesh.
3 Heat a wok over high heat, add the peanut oil and swirl to coat. Add the red Asian shallots and stir-fry for 1 minute. Add the garlic, chilli and pork and stir-fry for 2 minutes, then add the chicken and cook for a further 2 minutes. Add the prawns and stir-fry for a further 2 minutes, or until they are pink and cooked.
4 Stir in the wom bok, carrot and beans and cook for 3 minutes, then add the cooked noodles and stir-fry for another 4 minutes, or until everything is heated through.
5 Add the kecap manis, soy sauce, spring onion and tomato. Toss for 2 minutes. Season, then garnish with crisp fried onion and parsley. Serve.

CASSOULET

Preparation time: 20 minutes + overnight
   soaking
Total cooking time: 4 hours
Serves 6

500 g (1 lb) dried haricot beans
1.5 litres beef stock
2 tablespoons oil
500 g (1 lb) pork spareribs, trimmed
250 g (8 oz) diced lamb
250 g (8 oz) garlic or spiced sausage
125 g (4 oz) piece bacon, cut into cubes
2 onions, chopped
2 carrots, chopped
2 cloves garlic, crushed
1 bay leaf
1 sprig fresh parsley
1 sprig fresh thyme
6 black peppercorns
2 cups (160 g/5½ oz) fresh breadcrumbs
60 g (2 oz) butter, chilled and grated

1 Soak the beans overnight in water.
2 Drain the beans and place in a large saucepan with the stock. Bring slowly to the boil, then reduce the heat and simmer for 1 hour, or until tender. Drain the beans, reserving the liquid.
3 Heat the oil in a frying pan. Brown the pork, lamb, sausage and bacon in several batches. Remove and drain on paper towels. Add the onion, carrot and garlic to the pan, and brown well.
4 Preheat the oven to warm 160°C (315°F/Gas 2–3). Layer the meats, beans and vegetables in a large casserole dish. Tie the herbs and peppercorns together in a small piece of muslin, and add to the dish. Pour over the liquid from the beans, cover and bake for 2 hours.
5 Remove and discard the herb bag. Combine the breadcrumbs and butter, and sprinkle over the top of the casserole. Return to the oven for 30 minutes, or until the crust is golden and crisp.

CAMBODIAN FRAGRANT STEAMED FISH
(AMOK TREI)

Preparation time: 15 minutes +
  30 minutes refrigeration + standing
Total cooking time: 30 minutes
Serves 4

Spice paste
1 stem lemon grass, white part only,
  chopped
1 coriander root, washed
2 fresh kaffir lime leaves, finely shredded
3 cloves garlic, crushed
4 red Asian shallots, chopped
2 teaspoons fish sauce

550 g (1 lb 1¾ oz) boneless white fish
  fillets (e.g. ling or barramundi)
400 ml (13 fl oz) can coconut milk (do not
  shake)
1½–2 tablespoons ready-made red curry
  paste
3 teaspoons fish sauce
1 teaspoon grated palm sugar
4 fresh kaffir lime leaves, finely
  shredded
4 large gai larn (Chinese broccoli) or
  English spinach leaves, washed and
  sliced into 5 cm (2 inch) strips
1 fresh red chilli, finely shredded

1 To make the spice paste, put the
ingredients in a food processor and pulse
briefly until a very fine paste forms. Set
aside until required.
2 Cut the fish fillets into 2 cm (¾ inch)
strips, then put half in the food processor
and pulse briefly until roughly chopped,
but not minced.

3 Spoon off the thick coconut cream from
the top of the coconut milk—there should
be ½ cup (125 ml/4 fl oz). Combine ¾ cup
(185 ml/6 fl oz) of the remaining coconut
milk, the spice paste, red curry paste, fish
sauce, palm sugar and half the kaffir lime
leaves in a large non-metallic bowl. Stir
in one direction until thoroughly mixed.
Add all the fish, then mix with a wooden
spoon, stirring in one direction for
1–2 minutes, or until the fish is just
incorporated—take care not to overmix,
or the mixture will split when cooked.
Refrigerate for 30 minutes.
4 Fill a wok one-third full with water,
bring to the boil then reduce to a simmer.
Line a 1.25 litre (40 fl oz) deep, heatproof
soup bowl or pudding basin with gai larn,
then spoon the fish mixture into the bowl.
Cover the fish with the reserved coconut
cream, then scatter with chilli and the
remaining kaffir lime leaves. Put the bowl
in a bamboo steamer, then put on the
steamer lid and steam over the wok for
30 minutes, or until cooked. To test if the
fish is cooked, insert a clean skewer into
the centre—it should come out clean.
Remove the steamer from the heat and
stand for 5–10 minutes, then serve in the
bowl, garnished with coriander, if
desired.

ALMEJAS A LA MARINERA
(CLAMS IN WHITE WINE)

Preparation time: 10 minutes +
  1 hour soaking
Total cooking time: 20 minutes
Serves 4

1 kg (2 lb) clams
2 large, ripe tomatoes
2 tablespoons olive oil
1 small onion, finely chopped
2 cloves garlic, crushed
1 tablespoon chopped fresh flat-leaf
  parsley
pinch of nutmeg
⅓ cup (80 ml/2¾ fl oz) dry white wine

1 Soak the clams in salted water for
1 hour to release any grit. Rinse under
running water and discard any open
clams.
2 Score a cross in the base of each
tomato. Place in a bowl of boiling water
for 10 seconds, then plunge into cold
water and peel away from the cross. Cut
the tomatoes in half and scoop out the
seeds with a teaspoon. Finely chop the
tomatoes.
3 Heat the oil in a large flameproof
casserole and cook the onion over low
heat for 5 minutes, or until softened. Add
the garlic and tomato and cook for
5 minutes. Stir in the parsley and nutmeg
and season with salt and pepper. Add ⅓
cup (80 ml/2¾ fl oz) water.
4 Add the clams and cook over low heat
until they open. Discard any that don't
open. Add the wine and cook over low
heat for 3–4 minutes, until the sauce
thickens, gently moving the casserole
back and forth a few times, rather than
stirring the clams, so that the clams stay
in the shells. Serve at once, with bread.

NOTE: You can use mussels instead of
clams in this recipe.

KOUSA MIHSHI BI LABANO
(STUFFED ZUCCHINI/COURGETTES WITH YOGHURT SAUCE)

Preparation time: 20 minutes
Total cooking time: 1 hour 10 minutes
Serves 4

4 zucchini (courgettes)
1½ cups (375 ml/12 fl oz) chicken stock

Filling
1 tablespoon olive oil
1 onion, finely chopped
1½ tablespoons pine nuts
125 g (4 oz) lamb mince
¼ cup (55 g/2 oz) short-grain rice
1 ripe tomato, seeded and chopped
2 tablespoons chopped fresh flat-leaf
    parsley
½ teaspoon ground allspice
½ teaspoon ground cinnamon

Yoghurt sauce
250 g (8 oz) thick natural yoghurt
1 teaspoon cornflour
1 clove garlic, crushed
1 teaspoon dried mint

1 Cut each zucchini in half lengthways. Scoop out the flesh from each piece, leaving a 2 mm (⅛ inch) border on each shell. This can be done with an apple corer, but be careful not to pierce the skins of the zucchini. Soak the zucchini in salted water for 10 minutes, then drain and pat dry.

2 For the filling, heat the oil in a frying pan, add the onion and cook over medium heat for 5 minutes, or until soft. Add the pine nuts and cook for 3–4 minutes, until golden. Cool slightly, then transfer to a large bowl. Add the remaining filling ingredients and combine well.

3 Spoon filling into each zucchini half and carefully place in a wide, heavy-based saucepan or casserole. Cover with the chicken stock then invert a dinner plate over the top. Gently simmer over low heat for 1 hour.

4 About 15 minutes before the zucchini is ready, make the sauce by warming the yoghurt in a saucepan over medium heat. Stir the cornflour into 1 tablespoon water in a small bowl until smooth, then add to the yoghurt and stir well. Bring to the boil and add the crushed garlic and mint. Season well, then reduce the heat and simmer for 8–10 minutes, stirring regularly.

5 Remove the zucchini from the casserole and serve the yoghurt sauce poured over the top. Serve hot with steamed rice.

BEEF KEUH TEOW

Preparation time: 15 minutes
Total cooking time: 15 minutes
Serves 4

600 g (1¼ lb) fresh flat rice noodles (about
    2 cm/¾ inch wide)
¼ cup (60 ml/2 fl oz) peanut oil
150 g (5 oz) bacon, thinly sliced
300 g (10 oz) beef round, blade or sirloin
    steak, thinly sliced across the grain
3 garlic cloves, crushed
4 small red chillies, seeded and thinly
    sliced
12 spring onions (scallions), thinly sliced
250 g (8 oz) bean sprouts, tailed
¼ cup (55 g/2 oz) sugar
⅓ cup (80 ml/2¾ fl oz) soy sauce
⅓ cup (80 ml/2¾ fl oz) oyster sauce
3 eggs, lightly beaten
4 spring onions (scallions) (green part
    only), thinly sliced, extra

1 Briefly soak the noodles in boiling water, then gently separate the noodles and drain.

2 Heat a wok over high heat, add 1 tablespoon of the oil and swirl to coat. Stir-fry the bacon until crispy. Remove from the wok. Heat another tablespoon of the oil, then stir-fry the beef for 2 minutes. Remove from the wok.

3 Heat the remaining oil in the wok, add the garlic, chilli and spring onion and stir-fry over high heat for 5 seconds. Add the bean sprouts and stir-fry for another 10 seconds, then add the sugar, soy sauce, oyster sauce and noodles and stir-fry for 1–2 minutes, or until the noodles brown slightly. Return the bacon and beef to the wok and toss well until heated through.

4 Push the noodle mixture to one side of the wok, then pour in the egg. Turn the noodle mixture on top of the egg and let it cook, without stirring, for 5 seconds. Invert the noodles and egg in one turn onto a serving dish so a little of the egg is on top of the noodles. Garnish with the extra spring onion and serve.

MEXICAN RICE

Preparation time: 10 minutes
Total cooking time: 30 minutes
Serves 4

1½ tablespoons oil
1½ cups (300 g/10 oz) long-grain rice
1 small onion, chopped
2 garlic cloves, crushed
½ teaspoon ground cumin
½ teaspoon paprika
2 large ripe tomatoes, peeled, seeded and chopped
100 g (3½ oz) sliced mild salami, cut into strips
1 small carrot, diced
2 cups (500 ml/16 fl oz) hot chicken stock
½ cup (80 g/2¾ oz) frozen peas
2 tablespoons chopped coriander (cilantro) leaves

1 Heat the oil in a large saucepan and gently cook the rice, onion and garlic over medium heat for 10 minutes, or until the onion is softened but not browned. Add the spices and cook, stirring frequently, for 30 seconds, or until fragrant.
2 Add the tomato, salami, carrot and stock. Bring to the boil, then reduce the heat and simmer, covered, for 15 minutes. Stir in the peas and coriander and cook, covered, for a further 4 minutes, or until the rice is tender and all the liquid has been absorbed.

GADO GADO
(VEGETABLES WITH PEANUT SAUCE)

Preparation time: 50 minutes
Total cooking time: 20 minutes
Serves 4

250 g (8 oz) potatoes
2 medium carrots
200 g (6½ oz) green beans
¼ cabbage, shredded
3 hard-boiled eggs
200 g (6½ oz) bean sprouts, scraggly ends removed
½ cucumber, sliced
150 g (4¾ oz) firm tofu, cut into small cubes
½ cup (80 g/2⅔ oz) unsalted roasted peanuts, roughly chopped

Peanut Sauce
1 tablespoon oil
1 large onion, very finely chopped
2 cloves garlic, finely chopped
2 red chillies, very finely chopped
1 teaspoon shrimp paste, optional
250 g (8 oz) crunchy peanut butter
1 cup (250 ml/8 fl oz) coconut milk
1 cup (250 ml/8 fl oz) water
2 teaspoons kecap manis
1 tablespoon tomato sauce

1 Cut the potatoes into thick slices; place in a medium pan, cover with cold water and bring to the boil. Reduce the heat and simmer for about 6 minutes or until just tender. Drain and allow to cool.
2 Cut the carrot into thick slices. Top and tail the beans and cut into 4 cm (1½ inch) lengths. Bring a large pan of water to the boil, add the carrots and beans, and cook for 2 to 3 minutes. Remove the vegetables with a sieve and plunge briefly into a bowl of iced water. Drain well.

3 Plunge the shredded cabbage into the boiling water for about 20 seconds. Remove it from the pot and plunge it briefly into the iced water. Drain well.
4 Cut the eggs into quarters or halves. Arrange the eggs, potato, carrot, beans, cabbage, bean sprouts, cucumber and tofu in separate piles on a large serving platter. Cover the platter with plastic wrap and refrigerate while making the Peanut Sauce.
5 To make Peanut Sauce: Heat the oil in a heavy-based pan, add the onion and garlic and cook over low heat for 8 minutes, stirring regularly. Add the chilli and shrimp paste to the pan and cook for another minute. Remove the pan from the heat and mix in the peanut butter. Return the pan to the heat and slowly stir in the combined coconut milk and water. Bring the sauce to the boil, stirring constantly over low heat, and being careful the sauce does not stick and burn. Reduce the heat, add the kecap manis and tomato sauce, and simmer for another minute. Allow to cool.
6 Drizzle a little of the Peanut Sauce over the salad, garnish with the chopped peanuts and serve the remaining sauce in a bowl.

NOTE: Fresh peanut butter, available from health food stores, will give the sauce the best flavour. Be sure not to overcook the vegetables—they should be tender yet still crisp.

KEFTA GHAN' MI BEL' (LAMB KEFTA)

Preparation time: 30 minutes
Total cooking time: 40 minutes
Serves 4

1 kg (2 lb) lamb mince
1 onion, finely chopped
2 cloves garlic, finely chopped
2 tablespoons finely chopped fresh flat-leaf parsley
2 tablespoons finely chopped fresh coriander leaves
½ teaspoon cayenne pepper
½ teaspoon ground allspice
½ teaspoon ground ginger
½ teaspoon ground cardamom
1 teaspoon ground cumin
1 teaspoon paprika

Sauce
2 tablespoons olive oil
1 onion, finely chopped
2 cloves garlic, finely chopped
2 teaspoons ground cumin
½ teaspoon ground cinnamon
1 teaspoon paprika
2 x 400 g (13 oz) cans chopped good-quality tomatoes
2 teaspoons harissa
4 tablespoons chopped coriander leaves

1 Preheat the oven to moderate 180°C (350°F/Gas 4). Lightly grease two baking trays. Place the lamb, onion, garlic, herbs and spices in a bowl and mix well. Season with salt and pepper. Roll tablespoons of mixture into balls and place on the trays. Bake for 20 minutes, or until browned.
2 Meanwhile, for the sauce, heat the oil in a large saucepan, add the onion and cook over medium heat for 5 minutes, or until soft. Add the garlic, cumin, cinnamon and paprika, and cook for 1 minute, or until fragrant. Stir in the tomato and harissa, and bring to the boil. Reduce the heat and simmer for 20 minutes. Add the meatballs and simmer for 10 minutes, or until cooked. Stir in the coriander, season and serve.

VIETNAMESE LETTUCE-WRAPPED SPRING ROLLS

Preparation time: 50 minutes
Total cooking time: 20 minutes
Makes 20

50 g (1⅔ oz) dried mung bean vermicelli
2 tablespoons black fungus
500 g (1 lb) prawns
20 rice paper wrappers
150 g (4¾ oz) pork mince
4 spring onions, chopped
½ cup (45 g/1½ oz) bean sprouts, roughly chopped
1 teaspoon sugar
1 egg, beaten
oil, for deep-frying
20 lettuce leaves
1 cup (90 g/3 oz) bean sprouts, extra, scraggly ends removed
1 cup (20 g/⅔ oz) fresh mint
Vietnamese Dipping Sauce (page 765), to serve

1 Place the vermicelli and fungus in separate heatproof bowls. Cover with hot water and soak for 10 minutes, or until soft. Drain both, and chop the fungus roughly. Peel and devein the prawns; finely chop the prawn meat.
2 Using a pastry brush, brush both sides of each rice paper wrapper liberally with water. Allow to stand for 2 minutes or until they become soft and pliable; stack the wrappers on a plate. Sprinkle over a little extra water and cover the plate with plastic wrap to keep the wrappers moist until needed.
3 Combine the vermicelli, fungus, prawn meat, pork mince, spring onion, bean sprouts, sugar, and salt and pepper to taste in a bowl; stir well. Place 1 tablespoon of the filling along the base of a wrapper. Fold in the sides, roll the wrapper up tightly, and brush the seam with egg. Repeat with the remaining wrappers and filling.
4 Press the rolls with paper towels to remove any excess water. Heat 4 to 5 cm oil in a pan until moderately hot; add the spring rolls in batches and cook for 2 to 3 minutes or until dark golden brown. Drain on paper towels.
5 Place a spring roll in each lettuce leaf, top with 1 tablespoon bean sprouts and 2 mint leaves, and roll up to form a neat parcel. Serve with Vietnamese Dipping Sauce.

CERKES TAVUGU
(CIRCASSIAN CHICKEN)

Preparation time: 25 minutes
Total cooking time: 1 hour
Serves 6

2 teaspoons paprika
¼ teaspoon cayenne pepper
1 tablespoon walnut oil
4 chicken breasts, on the bone
4 chicken wings
1 large onion, chopped
2 sticks celery, coarsely chopped
1 carrot, chopped
1 bay leaf
4 sprigs fresh parsley
1 sprig fresh thyme
6 peppercorns
1 teaspoon coriander seeds
250 g (8 oz) walnuts, toasted (see Note)
2 slices of white bread, crusts removed
1 tablespoon paprika, extra
4 cloves garlic, crushed

1 Place the paprika and the cayenne pepper in a small dry frying pan and heat over low heat for about 2 minutes, or until aromatic, then add the walnut oil to the pan and set aside until ready to use.
2 Put the chicken in a large saucepan with the onion, celery, carrot, bay leaf, parsley, thyme, peppercorns and coriander seeds. Add 1 litre of water and bring to the boil. Reduce the heat to low and simmer for 15–20 minutes, or until the chicken is tender. Remove from the heat and allow to cool in the stock. Remove the chicken and return the stock to the heat. Simmer it for 20–25 minutes, or until reduced by half. Strain, skim off the fat and reserve the stock. Remove the chicken skin and shred the flesh into bite-sized pieces. Season well and ladle some stock over it to moisten it. Set aside.

3 Reserve a few of the walnuts to use as a garnish and blend the rest in a food processor to form a rough paste. Combine the bread with ½ cup (125 ml/ 4 fl oz) stock, add to the food processor and mix in short bursts for several seconds. Add the extra paprika, the garlic and some salt and pepper and process until smooth. Gradually add 1 cup (250 ml/ 8 fl oz) warm chicken stock until the mixture is of a smooth pourable consistency, adding a little more stock if necessary.
4 Mix half the sauce with the chicken and place on a serving platter. Pour the rest over to cover, then sprinkle with spiced oil and the remaining walnuts. Serve at room temperature.

NOTE: Californian walnuts are best for this recipe as they are much less bitter than some.

GINGER CHICKEN WITH
BLACK FUNGUS

Preparation time: 25 minutes +
    15 minutes soaking
Total cooking time: 15 minutes
Serves 4

¼ cup (10 g/⅓ oz) dried black fungus
1 tablespoon oil
3 cloves garlic, chopped
6 cm (2½ inch) piece fresh ginger, cut into fine shreds
500 g (1 lb) chicken breast fillets, sliced
4 spring onions, chopped
1 tablespoon Golden Mountain sauce
1 tablespoon fish sauce
2 teaspoons soft brown sugar
½ red pepper (capsicum), finely sliced
½ cup (15 g/½ oz) fresh coriander leaves
½ cup (25 g/¾ oz) chopped fresh Thai basil

1 Place the fungus in a heatproof bowl, cover with hot water, and leave for 15 minutes until it is soft and swollen; drain and chop roughly.
2 Heat the oil in a large wok, add the garlic and ginger and stir-fry for 1 minute. Add the chicken in batches, stir-frying over high heat until it changes colour. Return all the chicken to the wok. Add the spring onion and Golden Mountain sauce and stir-fry for 1 minute.
3 Add the fish sauce, sugar and fungus to the wok. Stir thoroughly; cover and steam for 2 minutes. Serve immediately with the red pepper, coriander and basil scattered on top.

LAOTIAN DRIED BEEF WITH GREEN PAWPAW SALAD

Preparation time: 30 minutes + 4 hours
    marinating
Total cooking time: 5 hours
Serves 6

1 kg (2 lb) piece of topside steak, partially
    frozen
2 teaspoons salt
¼ teaspoon chilli powder
1 teaspoon ground black pepper
1 tablespoon soft brown sugar
4 cloves garlic, crushed
2 teaspoons sesame oil
1 tablespoon peanut oil

Green Pawpaw Salad
1 small green pawpaw, peeled and
    seeded
1 carrot
2 cloves garlic, crushed
6 cm (2½ inch) piece fresh ginger, grated
2 small red chillies
2 tablespoons fish sauce
4 kaffir lime leaves, finely shredded
1 tablespoon lime juice
2 teaspoons soft brown sugar
1 teaspoon sesame oil
1 cup (30 g/1 oz) fresh coriander leaves
1 cup (160 g/5¼ oz) unsalted roasted
    peanuts

1 Preheat the oven to very slow 120°C
(250°F/Gas 1–2).
2 Trim any excess fat from the steak. Cut
the steak into 2.5 mm (⅛ inch) thick slices,
then into strips. Mix the salt, chilli
powder, pepper, sugar, garlic, sesame oil
and peanut oil in a bowl. Add the steak
and, using your fingertips, toss it in the oil
mixture until coated. Cover and marinate
for 4 hours in the refrigerator.
3 Place the meat on a rack in a large
baking dish and bake for 5 hours, or until
it has dried out.
4 Cook the beef under a hot grill for 3
minutes, then serve with Green Pawpaw
Salad.
5 To make Green Pawpaw Salad: Cut the
pawpaw and carrot into shreds, using a
citrus zester if you have one. Combine the
pawpaw and carrot in a bowl with the
remaining ingredients and toss lightly.

NOTE: The dried beef will keep for 3
weeks in an airtight container or can be
frozen for up to 6 months.

BALINESE FRIED FISH

Preparation time: 25 minutes
Total cooking time: 30 minutes
Serves 4

750 g (1½ lb) firm white fish fillets, such
    as jewfish or ling
½ teaspoon salt
½ teaspoon pepper
oil, for shallow frying
4 red Asian shallots, finely sliced
    lengthways
2.5 cm (1 inch) piece lemon grass (white
    part only), finely chopped
2 red chillies, finely chopped
2 cm (¾ inch) piece fresh ginger, grated
½ teaspoon shrimp paste
½ cup (125 ml/4 fl oz) water
2 tablespoons kecap manis
1 tablespoon grated palm sugar or soft
    brown sugar
2 teaspoons lime juice
3 spring onions, finely chopped

1 Preheat the oven to warm 160°C
(315°F/Gas 2–3). Cut the fish into bite-sized
pieces; sprinkle with the salt and pepper.
2 Heat the oil, about 2 cm (¾ inch) deep,
in a deep frying pan; add the fish 3 or 4
pieces at a time, and fry over moderately
high heat for about 4 minutes, turning the
pieces over, until they are a light golden
brown. Drain the fish on paper towels and
place in the oven to keep warm.
3 In a small pan, heat 2 tablespoons of the
fish frying oil; add the shallots, lemon
grass, chilli, ginger and shrimp paste and
cook for 3 minutes over low heat, stirring
occasionally. Add the water, kecap manis
and sugar, and stir until the sauce boils
and thickens. Stir in the lime juice and
spring onion. Drizzle the sauce over the
fish and serve immediately.

NOTE: The fish must have a solid meaty
texture or it will fall apart during the
frying. Kecap manis is Indonesian soy
sauce, and is slightly thicker and sweeter
than Chinese soy sauce.

SRI LANKAN FISH FILLETS IN TOMATO CURRY

Preparation time: 20 minutes +
  30 minutes marinating
Total cooking time: 20 minutes
Serves 6

¼ cup (60 ml/2 fl oz) lemon juice
¼ cup (60 ml/2 fl oz) coconut vinegar
2 teaspoons cumin seeds
1 teaspoon ground turmeric
1 teaspoon cayenne pepper
1 kg (2 lb) firm white fish fillets (e.g.
  snapper or ling)
¼ cup (60 ml/2 fl oz) vegetable oil
1 large onion, finely chopped
3 large cloves garlic, crushed
2 tablespoons grated fresh ginger
1 teaspoon black mustard seeds
3 x 400 g (13 oz) cans diced tomatoes
3 tablespoons finely chopped coriander
2 small fresh green chillies, seeded and
  finely chopped
2 tablespoons grated palm sugar

1 To make the marinade, put the lemon juice, coconut vinegar, cumin seeds, ground turmeric, cayenne pepper and 1 teaspoon salt in a shallow, non-metallic container and mix together thoroughly.
2 Carefully remove any remaining bones from the fish with tweezers and cut the flesh into 2.5 x 10 cm (1 x 4 inch) pieces. Add the fish pieces to the marinade and gently toss until they are well coated. Cover with plastic wrap and refrigerate for 30 minutes.
3 Heat a non-stick wok over high heat, add the oil and swirl to coat the side of the wok. Reduce the heat to low, add the onion, garlic, ginger and mustard seeds, and cook, stirring frequently, for 5 minutes.
4 Add the fish and marinade, diced tomatoes, coriander, chilli and sugar to the wok and cover with a lid. Simmer gently, stirring occasionally, for 10–15 minutes, or until the fish is cooked and just flakes when tested with the tines of a fork. Serve with basmati rice.

VIETNAMESE CREPES WITH PRAWNS, PORK AND NOODLES

Preparation time: 45 minutes +
  4 hours resting
Total cooking time: 35 minutes
Serves 6

1½ cups (265 g/8 oz) rice flour
1 teaspoon baking powder
1½ teaspoons sugar
½ teaspoon ground turmeric
1 cup (250 ml/8 fl oz) coconut milk
3 teaspoons peanut oil
lime wedges, to serve

Dipping sauce
1 tablespoon fish sauce
2 tablespoons lime juice
1 tablespoon caster sugar
1 small fresh red chilli, thinly sliced

Salad
1 carrot, coarsely grated
120 g (4 oz) iceberg lettuce, shredded
1 Lebanese cucumber, julienned
100 g (3½ oz) bean sprouts, tailed
1 cup (20 g/¾ oz) fresh mint
1 cup (30 g/1 oz) fresh coriander leaves

Filling
75 g (2½ oz) cellophane noodles, broken
1 tablespoon peanut oil
1 large onion, thinly sliced
6 cloves garlic, crushed
300 g (10 oz) lean pork loin fillet, finely
  chopped
150 g (5 oz) raw medium prawns, peeled,
  deveined and chopped
1 small red pepper (capsicum), thinly
  sliced
75 g (2½ oz) button mushrooms, thinly
  sliced
1 tablespoon light soy sauce
¼ teaspoon ground white pepper
4 spring onions, thinly sliced

1 To make the crepe batter, place the rice flour, baking powder, sugar, turmeric, coconut milk, ½ teaspoon salt and 1 cup (250 ml/8 fl oz) water in a blender and blend to a smooth batter. Cover and leave in a warm place for 2–4 hours.
2 Combine all of the dipping sauce ingredients in a small bowl.
3 To make the salad, toss all the salad ingredients together in a large bowl.
4 To make the filling, soak the noodles in boiling water for 3–4 minutes, or until soft. Rinse and drain. Heat a wok over high heat, add the oil and swirl to coat. Add the onion and cook for 2 minutes, then add the garlic and cook for a further 30 seconds. Add the pork and cook for 2 minutes, or until browned. Stir in the prawns, red pepper and mushrooms and cook until the prawns change colour. Stir in the noodles, soy sauce, white pepper and spring onion until combined.
5 To make the crepes, whisk the batter until smooth. Heat ½ teaspoon of the oil in a 30 cm (12 inch) non-stick frying pan. Pour ⅓ cup (80 ml/2¾ fl oz) of the batter into the centre of the pan, and swirl to spread to the edges. Cook over medium heat for 1–2 minutes, or until golden and crispy. Turn and cook for another 1–2 minutes, or until golden and crispy. Repeat with the remaining batter.
6 To assemble, place a portion of the filling on half the crepe, folding the other side on top. Repeat with the remaining crepes and filling to make six in total. Serve with the dipping sauce, salad and lime wedges.

NOTE: The first crepe doesn't usually work; there is enough batter to allow for this.

CHINESE SIZZLING BEEF STIR-FRY

Preparation time: 15 minutes +
   1 hour marinating
Total cooking time: 15 minutes
Serves 4–6

1 tablespoon light soy sauce
1 tablespoon Chinese rice wine
1½ tablespoons peanut oil
750 g (1½ lb) lean beef fillet, thinly sliced
   across the grain
1 large onion, cut into wedges
4 spring onions, cut into 3 cm (1¼ inch)
   lengths
1 green pepper (capsicum), cut into bite-
   sized pieces
3 cloves garlic, crushed
1 tablespoon julienned fresh ginger
1½ tablespoons sesame seeds, lightly
   toasted

Sauce
2 tablespoons hoisin sauce
2 tablespoons tomato sauce
2 tablespoons light soy sauce
2 tablespoons Chinese rice wine
2 teaspoons sesame oil

1 Combine the soy sauce, rice wine,
2 teaspoons of the peanut oil and
¼ teaspoon freshly ground black pepper
in a large non-metallic bowl. Add the
beef, toss together, then cover with
plastic wrap and marinate in the
refrigerator for at least 1 hour.
2 To make the stir-fry sauce, combine all
the ingredients in a small bowl.
3 Heat a wok over high heat, add the
remaining oil and swirl it around to coat the
side of the wok. Stir-fry the beef in two
batches for 2–3 minutes each batch, or until
nicely browned. Remove from the wok.
4 Add the onion and spring onion to the
wok and stir-fry for 2–3 minutes, or until
golden brown, then add the green pepper
and cook for a further minute. Add the
garlic and ginger and stir-fry for a further
30 seconds. Return the beef to the wok,
pour in the stir-fry sauce, and cook,
stirring, for 2 minutes, or until the sauce
reduces slightly and coats the beef and
vegetables. Transfer to a serving bowl,
sprinkle with the sesame seeds and
serve.

SHU MAI

Preparation time: 25 minutes
Total cooking time: 5 minutes
Makes 24

300 g (10 oz) pork mince
300 g (10 oz) prawn mince
3 spring onions, thinly sliced
⅓ cup (60 g/2 oz) chopped water
   chestnuts
1½ teaspoons finely chopped fresh
   ginger
1 tablespoon light soy sauce, plus extra,
   to serve
1 teaspoon caster sugar
24 won ton wrappers
chilli sauce, to serve

1 To make the filling, put the pork and
prawn mince, spring onion, water
chestnuts, ginger, soy sauce and sugar in
large non-metallic bowl and combine
well.
2 Working with one wrapper at a time,
place a heaped tablespoon of the filling in
the centre of the wrapper. Bring the sides
up around the outside, forming pleats to
firmly encase the filling—the top of the
dumpling should be exposed. Pinch
together to enclose the bottom of the
filling, then cover with a damp cloth.
Repeat with the remaining wrappers and
filling to make 24 in total.
3 Line a large double bamboo steamer
with baking paper and arrange the
dumplings on the base so that they don't
touch one another. Cover and steam over
a wok of simmering water for 5 minutes,
or until cooked through. Serve the
dumplings with the soy and chilli sauces,
for dipping.

NOTE: If desired, these dumplings can be
made using just pork mince—just double
the amount.

SALMON NABE

Preparation time: 20 minutes
Total cooking time: 40 minutes
Serves 3–4

12 dried shiitake mushrooms
250 g (8 oz) firm tofu
½ Chinese cabbage
4 salmon cutlets
2 x 5 cm (2 inch) pieces canned bamboo
  shoot
2 litres dashi
⅓ cup (80 ml/2¾ fl oz) Japanese soy
  sauce
¼ cup (60 ml/2 fl oz) mirin or sake
pinch of salt
Sesame Seed Sauce (page 764), to serve

1 Soak the mushrooms in warm water for 15 minutes, then drain. Cut the tofu into 12 squares. Coarsely shred the cabbage into 5 cm (2 inch) wide pieces.
2 Place the mushrooms, tofu, cabbage, salmon, bamboo shoot, dashi, soy sauce, mirin and salt in a large pan and bring to the boil. Reduce the heat, cover and simmer over medium heat for 15 minutes. Turn the salmon pieces over and simmer for a further 15 minutes, or until tender.
3 Pour the Salmon Nabe into a warmed serving bowl and serve with the Sesame Seed Sauce.

NOTE: This dish is traditionally cooked in a clay pot over a burner and served in the same pot. Diners dip the fish and vegetable pieces into the accompanying sauce and the broth is served in small bowls at the end of the meal.

GUN TONG GAU

Preparation time: 40 minutes + 4 hours
  refrigeration + 1 hour standing
Total cooking time: 10 minutes
Makes 24

200 g (6½ oz) pork mince
100 g (3½ oz) peeled raw prawns,
  deveined
2 teaspoons grated fresh ginger
2 cloves garlic, crushed
1 spring onion, finely chopped
3 teaspoons Chinese rice wine
2 teaspoons soy sauce
½ teaspoon sesame oil
pinch of ground white pepper
3 tablespoons beaten egg white
3 teaspoons cornflour
¾ cup (185 ml/6 fl oz) chicken stock
1½ teaspoons gelatine powder
24 won ton wrappers

Dipping sauce
1 tablespoon dark soy sauce
3 teaspoons Chinese black vinegar
1 teaspoon sugar
2½ tablespoons finely shredded fresh
  ginger

1 Put the mince, prawn meat, ginger, garlic, spring onion, rice wine, soy sauce, sesame oil and pepper in a food processor and process until combined. Transfer to a small bowl and fold in the egg white and cornflour. Refrigerate for 4 hours, or overnight if time permits.

2 Meanwhile, pour the stock into a small saucepan over high heat, cover and bring to the boil. Remove from the heat, add the gelatine and stir until dissolved. Transfer to an 8 x 25 cm (3 x 10 inch) bar tin and refrigerate for 1–2 hours or until set. Cut it into 1.5 cm (5/8 inch) cubes.
3 To make the dipping sauce, combine the soy sauce, vinegar, sugar and ½ cup (125 ml/4 fl oz) water and stir until the sugar has dissolved. Add the ginger and allow to stand for 1 hour to allow the flavours to infuse, before serving.
4 Roll 3 teaspoons of filling into a ball with wet fingers and make a deep indentation in the centre of the ball. Place a cube of jelly into the centre and cover completely with the filling. Put in the centre of a won ton wrapper, lightly moisten the edges with water and bring two diagonal corners up to join together and seal. Repeat with the other two corners. Pinch along the seams to seal. Repeat with the remaining ingredients to make 23 more dumplings.
5 Line two bamboo steamers with baking paper. Place a single layer of dumplings in each. Cover and steam over a wok of simmering water for 5–6 minutes, or until cooked through. Serve with the dipping sauce on the side.

CHICKEN DOMBURI

Preparation time: 35 minutes
Total cooking time: 30 minutes
Serves 4

2 cups (440 g/14 oz) short-grain rice
2½ cups (600 ml/20 fl oz) water
2 tablespoons oil
200 g (6½ oz) chicken breast fillet, cut
    into thin strips
2 medium onions, thinly sliced
4 tablespoons water, extra
4 tablespoons Japanese soy sauce
2 tablespoons mirin
1 teaspoon dashi granules
5 eggs, lightly beaten
2 sheets nori
2 spring onions, sliced

1 Wash the rice in a colander under cold running water until the water runs clear. Place the rice in a medium heavy-based pan, add the water and bring to the boil over high heat. Cover the pan with a tight-fitting lid, reduce the heat to as low as possible (otherwise the rice in the bottom of the pan will burn) and cook for 15 minutes. Turn heat to very high for 15 to 20 seconds and remove the pan from heat. Set the pan aside for 12 minutes, without lifting the lid (don't allow steam to escape).

2 Heat the oil in a frying pan over high heat, and stir-fry the chicken until golden and tender; set aside. Reheat the pan, add the onion and cook, stirring occasionally, for 3 minutes or until beginning to soften. Add the extra water, soy sauce, mirin and dashi granules. Stir to dissolve the dashi and bring the stock to the boil. Cook for 3 minutes or until onion is tender.

3 Return the chicken to the pan and pour in the eggs, stirring gently to just break up the eggs. Cover and simmer over very low heat for 2 to 3 minutes or until the eggs are just set. Remove the pan from the heat.

4 Toast the nori by holding it over low heat and moving it back and forward for about 15 seconds; crumble it into small pieces.

5 Transfer the rice to an earthenware dish, carefully spoon over the chicken and egg mixture and sprinkle over the nori. Garnish with the spring onion.

Note: Domburi is actually an earthenware dish, but the food served in the dish has also taken on the name.

SICHUAN CHICKEN

Preparation time: 10 minutes
Total cooking time: 25 minutes
Serves 4

¼ teaspoon five-spice powder
750 g (1½ lb) chicken thigh fillets, halved
2 tablespoons peanut oil
1 tablespoon julienned fresh ginger
1 teaspoon chilli bean paste
1 teaspoon Sichuan peppercorns, crushed
2 tablespoons light soy sauce
1 tablespoon Chinese rice wine
600 g (1¼ lb) baby bok choy, leaves
    separated

1 Rub the five-spice powder over the chicken pieces. Heat a wok to very hot, add half the oil and swirl to coat the side of the wok. Add the chicken and cook for 2 minutes on each side, or until nicely browned. Remove from the wok.

2 Reduce the heat to medium. Add the ginger and cook for 30 seconds. Add the chilli bean paste and crushed peppercorns. Return the chicken to the wok, then add the soy sauce, Chinese rice wine and ½ cup (125 ml/4 fl oz) water and simmer for 15–20 minutes, or until the chicken is cooked through.

3 Meanwhile, heat the remaining oil in a saucepan. Add the bok choy and toss gently and constantly for 1 minute, or until the leaves wilt and the stems are tender. Serve with the chicken and steamed rice.

VIETNAMESE PORK AND PRAWN SALAD

Preparation time: 30 minutes +
    1 hour marinating
Total cooking time: 6 minutes
Serves 6–8

250 g (8 oz) pork fillet
300 g (9⅔ oz) raw prawns
¼ cup (60 ml/2 fl oz) white vinegar
½ cup (125 ml/4 fl oz) water
1 tablespoon sugar
1 carrot, cut into matchsticks
1 Lebanese cucumber, cut into matchsticks
1 red pepper (capsicum), cut into matchsticks
1 Chinese cabbage, finely shredded
1 tablespoon oil
100 g (3⅓ oz) unsalted roasted peanuts, roughly chopped

Dressing
2 red Asian shallots, finely chopped
1 clove garlic, crushed
1 tablespoon fish sauce
1 tablespoon lime juice
1 teaspoon brown sugar
1 teaspoon sesame oil
1 tablespoon chopped Vietnamese mint

1 Cut the pork into thin strips. Peel and devein the prawns, leaving the tails intact.
2 Place the vinegar, water and sugar into a bowl and mix to combine. Add the carrot, cucumber, red pepper and Chinese cabbage and toss to coat in the marinade. Cover and refrigerate for 1 hour.
3 Heat the oil in a wok; stir-fry the pork in 2 batches over high heat for 3 minutes or until browned. Remove the pork from the wok. Add the prawns and stir-fry over high heat for 3 minutes or until bright pink.
4 Remove the vegetables from the marinade and drain thoroughly. Combine the vegetables with the pork, prawns and peanuts and toss well. Pour the Dressing over the salad and toss to coat.
5 Dressing: Combine the shallots, garlic, fish sauce, lime juice, brown sugar and sesame oil. Add the Vietnamese mint and mix well.

SON-IN-LAW EGGS (KAI LEUK KOEY)

Preparation time: 15 minutes
Total cooking time: 15 minutes
Serves 6

6 eggs
oil, for deep-frying
2 tablespoons vegetable oil, extra
2 cloves garlic, thinly sliced
6 red Asian shallots, thinly sliced lengthways
⅓ cup (80 ml/2¾ fl oz) fish sauce
150 g (5 oz) palm sugar, grated
1 teaspoon tamarind purée
1 teaspoon sambal oelek
3 tablespoons chopped fresh coriander leaves

1 Put the eggs in a saucepan of cold water and bring to the boil. Cook for 4 minutes. Rinse in cold water and remove the shells.
2 Fill a wok one-third full of oil and heat to 170°C (325°F), or until a cube of bread browns in 20 seconds. Lower the eggs into the oil with a slotted spoon and deep-fry, turning carefully, for 2–3 minutes, or until lightly golden. Keep warm.
3 Heat the extra oil in a small frying pan. Add the garlic and shallots and fry until golden. Drain on crumpled paper towels. Reduce the heat to low, add the fish sauce, palm sugar, tamarind purée, sambal oelek and ¼ cup (60 ml/2 fl oz) water and cook slowly, stirring, until the sugar dissolves. Cook for 2 minutes, or until the mixture thickens slightly. Stir in the reserved cooked garlic and shallots.
4 Cut the eggs in half and arrange on a plate. Pour on the sauce and garnish with the coriander.

NOTE: This dish is often served at Thai weddings, which may explain its unusual name.

GARITHES ME FETA (BAKED PRAWNS WITH FETA)

Preparation time: 20 minutes
Total cooking time: 30 minutes
Serves 4 as a first course

300 g (10 oz) raw large prawns
2 tablespoons olive oil
2 small red onions, finely chopped
1 large clove garlic, crushed
350 g (11 oz) ripe tomatoes, diced
2 tablespoons lemon juice
2 tablespoons fresh oregano or 1 teaspoon dried
200 g (6½ oz) feta
extra virgin olive oil, for drizzling
cracked black pepper, for sprinkling
chopped fresh flat-leaf parsley, to garnish

1 Peel the prawns, leaving the tails intact. Gently pull out the dark vein from each prawn back, starting at the head end.
2 Preheat the oven to moderate 180°F (350°F/Gas 4). Heat the olive oil in a saucepan over medium heat, add the onion and cook, stirring occasionally for 3 minutes, or until softened. Add the garlic and cook for a few seconds, then add the tomato and cook for 10 minutes, or until the mixture is slightly reduced and thickened. Add the lemon juice and oregano. Season, to taste.
3 Place half the sauce into a 3 cup (750 ml/24 fl oz) baking dish, about 15 cm (6 inches) square. Place the prawns on top. Spoon on the remaining sauce, then crumble the feta over it. Drizzle with extra virgin olive oil and sprinkle with freshly cracked black pepper.
4 Bake for 15 minutes, until the prawns are just cooked. Serve immediately with lightly toasted bread to soak up the juices.

YAKISOBA

Preparation time: 30 minutes +
20 minutes soaking
Total cooking time: 10 minutes
Serves 4

4 dried shiitake mushrooms
600 g (1¼ lb) Hokkien noodles
3 teaspoons finely chopped fresh ginger
2 large cloves garlic, finely chopped
300 g (10 oz) lean beef fillet, thinly sliced
across the grain
6 rashers streaky bacon, cut into 3 cm
(1¼ inch) pieces
2 tablespoons peanut oil
½ teaspoon sesame oil
6 thin spring onions, cut into 3 cm
(1¼ inch) lengths
1 carrot, thinly sliced on the diagonal
1 small green pepper (capsicum), thinly
sliced
220 g (7 oz) wom bok (Chinese cabbage),
shredded
pickled ginger and shredded nori, to
serve (optional)

Sauce
¼ cup (60 ml/2 fl oz) Japanese soy sauce
2 tablespoons Worcestershire sauce
1½ tablespoons Japanese rice vinegar
1 tablespoon sake
1 tablespoon mirin
1 tablespoon tomato sauce
1 tablespoon oyster sauce
2 teaspoons soft brown sugar

1 Soak the mushrooms in boiling water
for 20 minutes, or until soft. Squeeze dry,
reserving 2 tablespoons of the soaking
liquid. Discard the stalks and thinly slice
the caps.

2 Put the noodles in a heatproof bowl,
cover with boiling water and soak for 1
minute. Drain and separate.
3 Combine half the ginger and half the
garlic in a small bowl, then add the beef.
Set aside.
4 To make the sauce, combine all the
ingredients in a bowl with the reserved
mushroom liquid and the remaining
ginger and garlic.
5 Heat a wok over medium–high heat, add
the bacon and cook for 2–3 minutes, or
until softened and just starting to brown.
Transfer to a large bowl. Combine the
peanut and sesame oils. Increase the wok
to high heat, add a little of the oil mixture
and stir-fry the beef very quickly for 1
minute, or until it just changes colour all
over. Add to the bacon.
6 Heat a little more of the oil mixture in
the wok, add the spring onion, carrot and
pepper and stir-fry for 1 minute. Add the
wom bok and mushrooms and cook for
another 30 seconds, or until the
vegetables are just cooked but still
tender, then add to the bowl with the
bacon.
7 Heat the remaining oil in the wok, add
the noodles and stir-fry for 1 minute, then
return the bacon, beef and vegetables to
the wok, pour on the sauce and stir-fry
for 2–3 minutes, or until heated through
(the sauce shouldn't be too runny, it
should be almost completely absorbed
but not dry). Divide the noodles among
four deep bowls and top with pickled
ginger and shredded nori, if desired.

CILBIR
(POACHED EGGS WITH YOGHURT)

Preparation time: 10 minutes
Total cooking time: 20 minutes
Serves 4

60 g (2 oz) butter
1 brown onion, thinly sliced
1 cup (250 g/8 oz) thick natural yoghurt
4 large eggs
1 teaspoon hot paprika

1 Preheat the oven to slow 150°C
(300°F/Gas 2). Melt 20 g (¾ oz) of the
butter in a heavy-based frying pan and
cook the onion over low heat for 15 minutes,
or until golden brown. Remove from the
pan and allow to cool slightly. In a small
bowl, combine the onion, yoghurt and
salt, to taste.
2 Divide the yoghurt mixture among four
ovenproof ramekins, each measuring
about 7.5 cm (3 inches) in diameter and
4 cm (1½ inches) deep. Place on a tray in
the oven to heat gently.
3 Meanwhile, fill a large deep frying pan
three-quarters full of water, add a pinch
of salt and bring to a gentle simmer.
Gently break the eggs one at a time into a
small bowl and slide the eggs into the
water. Reduce the heat so that the water
barely moves. Cook for 2–3 minutes, or
until the eggs are just set. Remove with a
slotted spoon and pat off any excess
water using paper towels. Place an egg in
each ramekin and season with salt and
pepper.
4 Melt the remaining butter in a small
saucepan and add the paprika. Drizzle
over the eggs and serve at once.

NOTE: This dish is perfect for a light
supper or brunch. Instead of, or as well
as, the onions you can use 2 crushed
cloves of garlic cooked gently in the
butter for 1 minute, or until softened.

YUM CHA

MEANING LITERALLY 'TO DRINK TEA', THIS MORNING RITUAL IS ACCOMPANIED IN TEA HOUSES THROUGHOUT CHINA WITH TINY STEAMED OR FRIED PARCELS OF DIM SUM, STUFFED WITH FRESH SEAFOOD, MEATS AND VEGETABLES.

CRABMEAT DIM SIMS

In a bowl, combine 200 g (6½ oz) drained and flaked crabmeat, 250 g (8 oz) raw prawns, peeled, deveined and chopped, 4 finely chopped spring onions, 3 soaked and chopped dried Chinese mushrooms, 3 tablespoons finely chopped bean sprouts, a tablespoon teriyaki sauce, 2 crushed cloves garlic and 2 teaspoons grated fresh ginger. Working with 1 won ton wrapper at a time (you will need about 20), place 1 tablespoon filling in the centre, gather up the corners and pinch together to seal. Keep the other won ton wrappers covered with a damp tea towel until needed. Line the base of a bamboo or metal steamer with a circle of baking paper. Arrange the dim sims on the paper, making sure they are not touching (you may need to cook them in batches). Cover and steam for 8 minutes. Serve immediately.
Makes about 20.

CHICKEN MONEYBAGS

In a bowl, combine 375 g (12 oz) chicken mince, 90 g (3 oz) finely chopped ham, 4 finely chopped spring onions, 1 finely chopped stick of celery, 3 tablespoons chopped bamboo shoots, 1 tablespoon soy sauce, 1 crushed clove garlic and 1 teaspoon grated fresh ginger. Working with 1 won ton wrapper at a time (you will need about 40), place 2 teaspoons filling in the centre, gather up the corners and pinch together to form a pouch, leaving a frill at the top. Cut 15 chives in half and place in a heatproof bowl. Cover with boiling water for 1 minute; rinse and drain. Deep-fry moneybags in hot oil for 4–5 minutes until crisp and golden; drain on paper towels. Tie a chive around each moneybag. Serve immediately.
Makes about 40.

PRAWN GOW GEES

In a bowl, mix 500 g (1 lb) raw prawns, peeled, deveined and chopped, 4 finely sliced spring onions, 1 tablespoon grated fresh ginger and 2 tablespoons chopped water chestnuts. Blend 3 teaspoons cornflour, 2 teaspoons sesame oil, 1 teaspoon soy sauce, ½ teaspoon caster sugar and a little salt and pepper until smooth, and stir into the prawn mixture. Working with 1 gow gee wrapper at a time (you will need about 40), put 1 rounded teaspoon of mixture in the centre and press the edges together to form a semicircle. Twist the corners down to form a crescent shape. Line the base of a bamboo or metal steamer with a circle of baking paper. Arrange the gow gees on the paper, making sure they are not touching (you may need to cook them in batches). Steam, covered, for 8 minutes. Makes about 40.

STUFFED PEPPERS (CAPSICUMS)

Mix together 500 g (1 lb) peeled, deveined and finely chopped raw prawns, 300 g (9⅔ oz) lean pork mince, 1 teaspoon salt, 3 finely chopped spring onions, 3 tablespoons finely chopped water chestnuts, 3 teaspoons soy sauce and 2 teaspoons dry sherry. Cut 3 peppers (capsicums) lengthways into 3–4 segments and remove the seeds and membrane. Fill the pepper wedges with filling and cut in half. Heat 1 tablespoon oil in a wok. Cook the pepper pieces in 2 batches over medium-high heat for 3–4 minutes, or until well browned. Turn over and cook for a further 3 minutes. Repeat with remaining pieces. Serve immediately. Makes about 24.

Clockwise from top left: Prawn Gow Gees; Crabmeat Dim Sims; Stuffed Peppers; Chicken Moneybags

PIROZHKI

Preparation time: 50 minutes +
    1 hour refrigeration + cooling
Total cooking time: 25 minutes
Makes about 20

2½ cups (310 g/10 oz) plain (all-purpose)
    flour
180 g (6 oz) cold butter, cut into cubes
1 egg yolk
¼ cup (60 g/2 oz) sour cream

Filling
150 g (5 oz) mushrooms
50 g (1¾ oz) butter
1 small onion, finely chopped
½ cup (95 g/3 oz) cooked short-grain rice
1 hard-boiled egg, finely chopped
2 tablespoons finely chopped parsley
2 tablespoons finely chopped dill
1 egg, lightly beaten

1 Sift the flour and ½ teaspoon salt into a large bowl and add the butter. Rub the butter into the flour until the mixture resembles fine breadcrumbs. Add the combined egg yolk and sour cream. Cut the liquid in with a flat-bladed knife to form a dough, adding up to 1 tablespoon water, if necessary. Turn onto a lightly floured surface and gather together into a smooth ball. (Do not knead or you will have tough pastry.) Cover with plastic wrap and refrigerate for 30 minutes.

2 To make the filling, blitz the mushrooms in a food processor until finely chopped. Melt the butter in a frying pan, then cook the onion in it for 3 minutes, or until softened but not brown. Add the chopped mushrooms and cook, stirring, for a further 3 minutes. Stir in the rice. Transfer to a bowl and leave to cool. Stir in the chopped egg and herbs and season well.
3 Roll out the pastry thinly, half at a time, on a floured surface. Cut 20 rounds, with an 8 cm (3 inch) plain cutter. Put a tablespoon of filling in the centre of each round. Brush the pastry edges with the egg, then fold in half and pinch the edges to seal. Prick the tops with a fork. Put on a baking tray and refrigerate for 30 minutes. Preheat the oven to moderately hot 190°C (375°F/Gas 5). Brush the pastries with egg and bake for 15 minutes, or until golden. Serve hot as a starter or with soup.

TEPPAN YAKI
(GRILLED STEAK AND VEGETABLES)

Preparation time: 45 minutes
Total cooking time: 25 minutes
Serves 4

350 g (11¼ oz) scotch fillet, partially frozen
4 small slender eggplants (aubergines)
100 g (3⅓ oz) fresh shiitake mushrooms
100 g (3⅓ oz) small green beans
6 baby yellow or green squash
1 red or green pepper (capsicum), seeded
6 spring onions, outside layer removed
200 g (6½ oz) can bamboo shoots, drained
¼ cup (60 ml/2 fl oz) oil
Soy and Ginger Sauce or Sesame Seed
    Sauce (see *Sauces*), to serve

1 Slice the steak into very thin pieces. Place the meat slices in a single layer on a large serving platter and season thoroughly with plenty of salt and freshly ground pepper. Set aside.
2 Trim the ends from the eggplants and cut the flesh into long, very thin diagonal slices. Trim any hard stems from the mushrooms. Top and tail the beans. If the beans are longer than about 7 cm (2¾ inches), cut them in half. Quarter, halve or leave the squash whole, depending on the size. Cut the pepper into thin strips and slice the spring onions into lengths about 7 cm (2¾ inches) long, discarding the tops. Arrange all the vegetables in separate bundles on a plate.
3 When the diners are seated, heat an electric grill or electric frying pan until very hot, and then lightly brush it with the oil. Quickly fry about a quarter of the meat, searing on both sides, and then push it over to the edge of the pan. Add about a quarter of the vegetables and quickly stir-fry, adding a little more oil as needed. Serve a small portion of the meat and vegetables to the diners, who dip the food into a sauce. Repeat the process with the remaining meat and vegetables, cooking in batches as extra helpings are required. Serve with steamed rice.

CHICKEN MASALA

Preparation time: 25 minutes +
    4 hours marinating
Total cooking time: 45 minutes
Serves 4–6

6 chicken thigh cutlets
2 teaspoons ground fenugreek
2 cloves garlic, crushed
1 teaspoon grated fresh ginger
½ cup (10 g/⅓ oz) fresh mint
¼ cup (60 ml/2 fl oz) vinegar
½ cup (15 g/½ oz) fresh coriander leaves
1 teaspoon salt
2 teaspoons ground turmeric
½ teaspoon ground cloves
½ teaspoon ground cardamom

1 Trim the chicken of any excess fat and sinew; cut a few slits in each cutlet.
2 Place the fenugreek, garlic, ginger, mint, vinegar, coriander, salt, turmeric, cloves and cardamom in a food processor and process until a smooth paste is formed.
3 Place the chicken in a shallow non-metallic baking dish and rub it all over with the spice paste. Cover and marinate for at least 4 hours or overnight in the refrigerator.
4 Preheat the oven to moderate 180°C (350°F/Gas 4). Bake the chicken for 45 minutes. Serve with rice.

LAHANO DOLMATHES
(CABBAGE ROLLS)

Preparation time: 30 minutes
Total cooking time: 1 hour 35 minutes
Makes 12 large rolls

1 tablespoon olive oil
1 onion, finely chopped
large pinch of allspice
1 teaspoon ground cumin
large pinch of ground nutmeg
2 bay leaves
1 large head of cabbage
500 g (1 lb) lamb mince
1 cup (250 g/8 oz) short-grain white rice
4 cloves garlic, crushed
⅓ cup (50 g/1¾ oz) toasted pine nuts
2 tablespoons chopped fresh mint
2 tablespoons chopped fresh flat-leaf
    parsley
1 tablespoon chopped currants
1 cup (250 ml/8 fl oz) olive oil, extra
⅓ cup (80 ml/2¾ fl oz) lemon juice
extra virgin olive oil, to drizzle
lemon wedges, for serving

1 Heat the oil in a saucepan, add the onion and cook over medium heat for 10 minutes, or until golden. Add the allspice, cumin and nutmeg, and cook for 2 minutes, or until fragrant. Remove from the pan.
2 Bring a very large saucepan of water to the boil and add the bay leaves. Cut the tough outer leaves and about 5 cm (2 inches) of the core from the cabbage, then carefully add the cabbage to the boiling water. Cook it for 5 minutes, then carefully loosen a whole leaf with tongs and remove. Continue to cook and remove the leaves until you reach the core. Drain, reserving the cooking liquid and set aside to cool.

3 Take 12 leaves of equal size and cut a small 'V' from the core end of each to remove the thickest part. Trim the firm central veins so the leaf is as flat as possible. Place three-quarters of the remaining leaves on the base of a very large saucepan to prevent the rolls catching.
4 Combine the mince, onion mixture, rice, garlic, pine nuts, mint, parsley and currants in a bowl and season well. With the core end of the leaf closest to you, form 2 tablespoons of the mixture into an oval and place in the centre of the leaf. Roll up, tucking in the sides. Repeat with the remaining 11 leaves and filling. Place tightly, in a single layer, in the lined saucepan, seam-side-down.
5 Combine 2½ cups (625 ml/20 fl oz) of the cooking liquid with the extra olive oil, lemon juice and 1 teaspoon salt, and pour over the rolls (the liquid should just come to the top of the rolls). Lay the remaining cabbage leaves over the top. Cover and bring to the boil over high heat, then reduce the heat and simmer for 1 hour 15 minutes, or until the mince and rice are cooked. Carefully remove from the pan with a slotted spoon, then drizzle with extra virgin olive oil. Serve with lemon wedges.

CHINESE BEEF AND GAI LARN (CHINESE BROCCOLI) STIR-FRY

Preparation time: 10 minutes
Total cooking time: 15 minutes
Serves 4

1 kg (2 lb) fresh rice sheet noodles
¼ cup (60 ml/2 fl oz) peanut oil
500 g (1 lb) lean beef fillet, thinly sliced across the grain
1 onion, cut into wedges
4 cloves garlic, chopped
400 g (13 oz) gai larn (Chinese broccoli), cut into 3 cm (1¼ inch) lengths
1 tablespoon soy sauce
¼ cup (60 ml/2 fl oz) kecap manis
1 small fresh red chilli, chopped
½ cup (125 ml/4 fl oz) beef stock

1 Cut the noodles lengthways into 2 cm (¾ inch) wide strips, then cover with boiling water and gently separate the strips.
2 Heat a wok over medium heat, add 2 tablespoons of the peanut oil and swirl to coat the side of the wok. Add the noodles and stir-fry for 2 minutes. Remove from the wok.
3 Reheat the wok over high heat, add the remaining oil and swirl to coat. Add the beef in batches and cook for 3 minutes, or until browned. Remove from the wok. Add the onion and stir-fry for 1–2 minutes, then add the garlic and cook for a further 30 seconds.
4 Return all the beef to the wok and add the gai larn, soy sauce, kecap manis, chilli and beef stock, and cook over medium heat for 2–3 minutes. Divide the noodles among four serving plates and top with the beef mixture. Serve immediately.

NOTE: The noodles may break up during cooking but this will not affect the flavour of the dish.

AFELIA (CYPRIOT PORK AND CORIANDER STEW)

Preparation time: 15 minutes + overnight refrigeration
Total cooking time: 1 hour 20 minutes
Serves 4–6

1½ tablespoons coriander seeds
½ teaspoon cracked black pepper
800 g (1 lb 10 oz) pork fillet, cut into 2 cm (¾ inch) dice
1 tablespoon plain flour
¼ cup (60 ml/2 fl oz) olive oil
1 large onion, thinly sliced
1½ cups (375 ml/12 fl oz) red wine
1 cup (250 ml/8 fl oz) chicken stock
1 teaspoon sugar
fresh coriander sprigs, to garnish

1 Crush the coriander seeds in a mortar and pestle. Transfer to a bowl, add the cracked black pepper and the pork and toss to coat. Cover and refrigerate overnight.
2 Add the flour to the pork and toss. Heat 2 tablespoons oil in a frying pan and cook the pork in batches over high heat for 1–2 minutes, or until brown. Remove from the pan.
3 Heat the remaining oil in the pan, add the onion and cook over medium heat for 2–3 minutes, or until just golden. Return the meat to the pan, add the red wine, stock and sugar. Season, bring to the boil, then reduce the heat and simmer, covered, for 1 hour.
4 Remove the meat. Return the pan to the heat and boil over high heat for 3–5 minutes, or until the sauce is reduced and slightly thickened. Pour over the meat and garnish with coriander sprigs.

GENERAL TSO'S CHICKEN

Preparation time: 10 minutes + 1 hour marinating + 20 minutes soaking
Total cooking time: 10 minutes
Serves 4–6

2 tablespoons Chinese rice wine
1 tablespoon cornflour
⅓ cup (80 ml/2¾ fl oz) dark soy sauce
3 teaspoons sesame oil
900 g (1 lb 13 oz) chicken thigh fillets, cut into 3 cm (1¼ inch) cubes
2 pieces dried citrus peel (2 x 3 cm/ ¾ x 1¼ inch)
½ cup (125 ml/4 fl oz) peanut oil
1½–2 teaspoons chilli flakes
2 tablespoons finely chopped fresh ginger
1 cup (120 g/4 oz) thinly sliced spring onions
2 teaspoons sugar
thinly sliced spring onion, to garnish

1 Combine the Chinese rice wine, cornflour, 2 tablespoons of the dark soy sauce and 2 teaspoons of the sesame oil in a large non-metallic bowl. Toss the chicken, cover and marinate in the fridge for 1 hour.
2 Meanwhile, soak the dried citrus peel in warm water for 20 minutes. Remove from the water and finely chop—you will need 1½ teaspoons chopped peel.
3 Heat the oil in the wok over high heat. Drain the chicken from the marinade using a slotted spoon and stir-fry the chicken in batches for 2 minutes, or until browned and just cooked through. Remove from the oil with a slotted spoon and leave to drain in a colander or sieve.
4 Drain all the oil except 1 tablespoon from the wok. Reheat the wok over high heat, then add the chilli flakes and ginger. Stir-fry for 10 seconds, then return the chicken to the wok. Add the spring onion, sugar, soaked citrus peel, remaining soy sauce and sesame oil and ½ teaspoon salt and stir-fry for a further 2–3 minutes, or until well combined and warmed through. Garnish with spring onion, then serve with rice.

PANANG BEEF

Preparation time: 30 minutes + 20
   minutes soaking
Total cooking time: 1 hour
Serves 4–6

Curry paste
8–10 large dried red chillies
6 red Asian shallots, chopped
6 cloves garlic, chopped
1 teaspoon ground coriander
1 tablespoon ground cumin
1 teaspoon white pepper
2 stems lemon grass, white part only,
   bruised, sliced
1 tablespoon chopped fresh galangal
6 fresh coriander roots
2 teaspoons shrimp paste
2 tablespoons roasted peanuts
400 ml (13 fl oz) can coconut cream (do
   not shake)
1 kg (2 lb) round or blade steak, cut into
   1 cm (½ inch) slices
400 ml (13 fl oz) can coconut milk
⅓ cup (90 g/3 oz) crunchy peanut butter
4 fresh kaffir lime leaves
¼ cup (60 ml/2 fl oz) lime juice
2½ tablespoons fish sauce
3–4 tablespoons grated palm sugar
chopped roasted peanuts, to garnish
fresh Thai basil, to garnish

1 To make the curry paste, put the chillies
in a bowl and cover with boiling water.
Soak them for 20 minutes, or until
softened. Remove the seeds and roughly
chop the flesh. Put the chopped chillies in
a food processor along with the shallots,
garlic, ground coriander, ground cumin,
white pepper, lemon grass, galangal,
coriander roots, shrimp paste and
roasted peanuts and process until a
smooth paste forms—you might need to
add a little water if the paste is too thick.

2 Open the can of coconut cream and
scoop off the really thick cream from the
top. Put this thick cream in a wok and
cook over medium heat for 10 minutes, or
until the oil starts to separate from the
cream. Stir in 8 tablespoons of the curry
paste and cook, stirring often, for
5–8 minutes, or until fragrant.
3 Add the beef, coconut milk, peanut
butter, lime leaves and the remaining
coconut cream to the wok and cook for
8 minutes, or until the beef just starts to
change colour. Reduce the heat to low
and simmer for 30 minutes, or until the
beef is tender, stirring every few minutes
to prevent it from catching on the bottom.
4 Stir in the lime juice, fish sauce and
sugar until they are mixed into the curry.
Serve in bowls, garnished with the
roasted peanuts and basil.

NOTE: Panang curry and Musaman curry
are the two Thai curries with the most
similarities to Indian curries. The
similarity is due to the inclusion of many
of the same dried spices that are used to
make Indian curries. The heavier spice
flavours of these two curries are
traceable to Muslim origins in the south
of Thailand. It is these same spices that
make them more suitable to be made
with red meats, such as beef or lamb,
than poultry or seafood.

THAI SWEET PORK
(MOO WAN)

Preparation time: 10 minutes
Total cooking time: 50 minutes
Serves 4–6

850 g (1 lb 12 oz) pork spareribs
½ cup (125 g/4 oz) grated palm sugar
4 red Asian shallots, sliced
1 tablespoon fish sauce
1 tablespoon kecap manis
½ teaspoon ground white pepper
fresh coriander leaves, to garnish

1 Remove the bone and outer rind from
the ribs. Cut into 1 cm (½ inch) slices.
2 Put the sugar in a wok with
2 tablespoons water and stir over low
heat until the sugar has dissolved.
Increase the heat and boil, without
stirring, for 5 minutes, or until the sugar
turns evenly golden. Stir in the pork and
shallots. Add the fish sauce, kecap manis,
pepper and 1 cup (250 ml/8 fl oz) warm
water. Stir until all the sugar has melted.
3 Cover and cook for 10 minutes, stirring
occasionally, then cook, uncovered,
stirring often, for 20–30 minutes, or until
the sauce is sticky and the meat is
cooked. Garnish with coriander and serve
with rice.

PISSALADIERE

Preparation time: 30 minutes +
   15 minutes standing +
   1 hour 30 minutes rising
Total cooking time: 1 hour 25 minutes
Serves 4–6

7 g (¼ oz) sachet dry yeast
1½ cups (185 g/6 oz) plain flour
1 egg, beaten
1 tablespoon olive oil

Filling
¼ cup (60 ml/2 fl oz) olive oil
2 cloves garlic
1 sprig of fresh thyme
4 large onions, thinly sliced
pinch of ground nutmeg
30 g (1 oz) drained anchovy fillets, halved
   lengthways
16 pitted black olives

1 Place the yeast in a small bowl with
2 tablespoons lukewarm water. Leave in a
warm, draught-free place for 15 minutes,
or until foamy. If your yeast doesn't froth,
it is dead and you will have to start again.
2 Sift the flour and ¼ teaspoon salt into a
large bowl, make a well in the centre and
add the yeast mixture, egg, oil and
2 tablespoons warm water. Bring the
ingredients together with a wooden spoon
and when clumped together, transfer to a
lightly floured surface. Knead to a soft,
pliable dough, adding a little more water
or flour as needed. Continue kneading for
6–8 minutes, or until smooth and elastic.
Lightly oil a clean large bowl and place
the dough in it. Roll the dough around to
coat with oil, cover the bowl with a dry tea
towel and place in a warm place for
1 hour, or until doubled in size.

3 For the filling, heat the oil in a large,
heavy-based frying pan, add the garlic,
thyme and onion and cook, stirring
occasionally, over very low heat for
1 hour, or until the onion is soft and
buttery but not brown. Discard the garlic
and thyme, add the nutmeg and season
well.
4 Brush a 30 cm (12 inch) pizza tray with
oil. Punch down the dough and lightly
knead into a ball. Roll out to a 30 cm
(12 inch) circle and place on the oiled tray.
Spread the onions over the surface
leaving a 1 cm (½ inch) border. Make a
diamond cross-hatch pattern on top with
the anchovies. Intersperse with the olives.
Slide the tray into a large plastic bag and
leave to rise again for 30 minutes.
Preheat the oven to moderately hot 200°C
(400°F/Gas 6).
5 Bake for 20–25 minutes, or until the
dough is cooked and golden. Reduce the
heat to 190°C (375°F/Gas 5) if the crust
starts to overbrown towards the end of
baking. Cut into wedges for serving.

KIM CHI

Preparation time: 9 days
Total cooking time: Nil
Makes about 3 cups

1 large Chinese cabbage
½ cup (160 g/5¼ oz) sea salt
½ teaspoon cayenne pepper
5 spring onions, finely chopped
2 cloves garlic, finely chopped
5 cm (2 inch) piece fresh ginger, grated
3 teaspoons to 3 tablespoons chopped
   fresh chilli (see Note)
1 tablespoon caster sugar
2½ cups (600 ml/20 fl oz) cold water

1 Cut the cabbage in half, then into large
bite-sized pieces. Place a layer of
cabbage in a large bowl and sprinkle with
a little salt. Continue with layers of
cabbage and salt, finishing with a salt
layer. Cover with a dinner plate that will
fit as snugly as possible over the top of
the cabbage. Weigh down the plate with
cans or a small brick and leave the bowl
in a cool place for 5 days.
2 Remove the weights and plate, pour off
any liquid, then rinse the cabbage well
under cold running water. Squeeze out
any excess water and combine the
cabbage with the cayenne pepper, spring
onion, garlic, ginger, chilli and sugar. Mix
well to combine before spooning the
cabbage into a large sterilised jar. Pour
the water over the top and seal with a
tight-fitting lid. Refrigerate for 3 to 4 days
before eating.

NOTE: Kim Chi is an accompaniment
eaten with Korean main meals and with
steamed rice. For an authentic flavour,
use 3 tablespoons of chilli. Bottled
chopped chilli can be used instead of
fresh chilli.

CROSSING-THE-BRIDGE NOODLES

Preparation time: 25 minutes +
    40 minutes soaking
Total cooking time: 10 minutes
Serves 4

100 g (3½ oz) prawns (shrimp)
100 g (3½ oz) skinless chicken breast fillet
100 g (3½ oz) squid tubes
100 g (3½ oz) Chinese ham, thinly sliced
8 dried Chinese mushrooms
125 g (4 oz) bean sprouts, tailed
350 g (11 oz) fresh rice noodles or 250 g
    (8 oz) rice stick noodles
chilli sauce and light soy sauce, to serve
1 litre (32 fl oz) chicken stock
4 spring onions (scallions), finely chopped

1 Peel the prawns, remove the heads, then cut them in half through the back, removing the vein. Slice the prawns and the chicken breast thinly on the diagonal.
2 Open up the squid tubes by cutting down one side, scrub off any soft jelly-like substance and slice thinly on the diagonal. Arrange the prawns, chicken, squid and ham on a plate, cover and refrigerate until needed.
3 Soak the dried mushrooms in boiling water for 30 minutes, then drain and squeeze out any excess water. Remove and discard the stems. Add the mushrooms to the plate. Wash the bean sprouts and drain thoroughly. Add to the plate.
4 Separate the rice noodles into four bundles. If you are using dried rice noodles, soak in hot water for 10 minutes, then drain.
5 Give each guest a small saucer of chilli sauce and a saucer of soy sauce. Place the ingredients and dipping sauces on the table. Heat four soup bowls either in a low oven or by running them under very hot water for a few minutes. Put the chicken stock in a casserole dish or saucepan with the spring onion and bring to the boil. When the stock has reached a rolling boil, fill the bowls.
6 Give each guest a hot bowl filled with stock and let them cook the meat, vegetables and noodles in the stock.

MONEY BAGS
(TOONG NGERN YOUNG)

Preparation time: 30 minutes + cooling
Total cooking time: 15 minutes
Makes 30

1 tablespoon peanut oil
4 red Asian shallots, finely chopped
2 cloves garlic, crushed
1 tablespoon grated fresh ginger
150 g (5 oz) chicken mince
150 g (5 oz) pork mince
2 teaspoons light soy sauce
¼ cup (40 g/1¼ oz) roasted peanuts,
    chopped
2 teaspoons grated palm sugar
2 teaspoons lime juice
3 teaspoons fish sauce
3 tablespoons finely chopped fresh
    coriander leaves
30 won ton wrappers
oil, for deep-frying
garlic chives, for tying

1 Heat a wok over medium heat, add the oil and swirl to coat. Add the shallots, garlic and ginger and cook for 1–2 minutes, or until the shallots are soft. Add the minces and cook for 4 minutes, or until cooked, breaking up the lumps.
2 Stir in the soy sauce, peanuts, palm sugar, lime juice, fish sauce and coriander. Cook, stirring, for 1–2 minutes, or until mixed and dry. Cool.
3 Place 2 teaspoons of the filling in the centre of each won ton wrapper—lightly brush the edges with water. Lift the sides up tightly and pinch around the filling to form a bag. Trim.
4 Fill a clean wok one-third full of oil and heat to 190°C (375°F), or until a cube of bread dropped in the oil browns in 10 seconds. Cook in batches for 30–60 seconds, or until golden and crisp. Drain. Tie with the chives.

PAELLA ANDALUCIA
(CHICKEN AND CHORIZO PAELLA)

Preparation time: 20 minutes +
    10 minutes standing
Total cooking time: 1 hour 15 minutes
Serves 6

¼ cup (60 ml/2 fl oz) olive oil
1 large red capsicum (pepper), seeded
    and cut into 5 mm (¼ inch) strips
600 g (1¼ lb) chicken thigh fillets, cut into
    3 cm (1¼ inch) cubes
200 g (6½ oz) chorizo sausage, cut into
    2 cm (¾ inch) slices
200 g (6½ oz) flat mushrooms, thinly sliced
3 garlic cloves, crushed
1 tablespoon grated lemon zest
700 g (1 lb 6½ oz) ripe tomatoes, chopped
200 g (6½ oz) green beans, trimmed and
    cut into 3 cm (1¼ inch) lengths
1 tablespoon chopped rosemary
2 tablespoons chopped flat-leaf parsley
¼ teaspoon saffron threads soaked in
    ¼ cup (60 ml/2 fl oz) hot water
2 cups (440 g/14 oz) paella rice
3 cups (750 ml/24 fl oz) hot chicken stock
6 lemon wedges, to serve

1 Heat the olive oil in a paella pan, or in a large, deep heavy-based frying pan over medium heat. Add the capsicum and cook, stirring, for about 5 minutes. Remove from the pan. Toss in the chicken and cook for 10 minutes, or until browned all over. Remove from the pan. Add the chorizo to the pan and cook for 5 minutes. Remove from the pan. Add the mushrooms, garlic and lemon zest to the pan, and cook over medium heat for about 5 minutes.
2 Stir in the tomato and capsicum, and cook for another 5 minutes, or until the tomato is soft. Add the beans, rosemary, parsley, saffron mixture, rice, chicken and sausage. Stir briefly and add the stock. Do not stir at this point. Reduce the heat and simmer for 30 minutes. Remove from the heat, cover loosely with foil and leave to stand for 10 minutes. Season to taste with salt and black pepper; serve with lemon wedges.

AROMATIC PANTRY

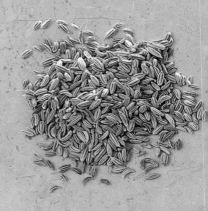

Besan flour: pale yellow, finely milled flour made from dried chickpeas (garbanzo beans). High in protein, it is used in many dishes, including doughs and sauces. Also known as gram flour.

Chilli powder: made by finely grinding whole dried red chillies. Flavour varies from mild to fiery hot, so add sparingly to dishes until the heat of the particular chilli powder has been ascertained. Sometimes available as a blend containing chilli, oregano, cumin and garlic.

Curry leaves: small shiny, bright green pointed leaves from a tree native to India. Fresh leaves are used in many Indian dishes. Much of the flavour is lost from dried leaves.

Fennel seeds: greenish brown seeds from the fennel plant. Have a light licorice taste, not overpowering if used sparingly. Also available ground. Used in both sweet and savoury dishes and to flavour some liqueurs.

Garam masala: a mixture of dry-roasted ground spices, usually including cinnamon, pepper, coriander, cumin, cardamom, cloves and either mace or nutmeg. Some variations contain up to 12 spices.

Kaffir lime leaves: dark, shiny, double leaves with a distinctive citrus flavour and strong perfume rich in aromatic oils. Remove the central thick vein and slice thinly. Dried leaves may need soaking before use.

Coriander seeds: small pale yellow/brown, slightly ridged round seeds with a mild fragrance. Also available ground. Often used in conjunction with fresh coriander. The flavours are completely different.

Lemon grass: The tough exterior leaves are removed and the white interior is used in cooking, sliced or pounded into a paste. The bruised stem can be used in soups or curries and removed before serving.

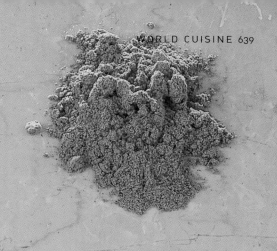

Red lentils: tiny round flat pulses. Can also be deep orange or yellow. Not necessary to soak before cooking. Widely available.

Fresh coriander: a pungent herb, also known as cilantro and Chinese parsley. All parts of the plant are edible. Whole dried seeds or ground coriander also available.

Curry powder: blend of up to 20 spices. Varies depending on the region, but ranges from mild to hot. Will lose flavour after two months and should be bought in small quantities.

Cumin seeds: small, pale brown aromatic seeds which have a warm pungent earthy flavour. Also available ground.

Brown mustard seeds: small golden brown seeds. Hotter and more aromatic than the yellow mustard seeds.

Kalonji/nigella seeds: small black seeds with a slight peppery onion flavour. Available in speciality stores.

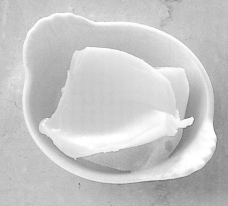

Ghee: pure clarified butter with no milk solids, so it can be heated to a high temperature without burning. Available in tins or the refrigerated section of the supermarket.

Palm sugar: made from the boiled sap of palm trees. Sold in blocks or jars, it is thick and crumbly and is generally grated before use. Soft brown sugar makes a good substitute.

Ground turmeric: dried ground root of fresh turmeric, a member of the ginger family. Has a mild musky flavour and imparts a distinctive yellow colour to food.

PHAD SI-IEW (NOODLES WITH BEEF)

Preparation time: 20 minutes
Total cooking time: 20 minutes
Serves 4–6

500 g (1 lb) fresh rice noodle sheets
2 tablespoons peanut oil
2 eggs, lightly beaten
500 g (1 lb) rump steak, thinly sliced
 across the grain
¼ cup (60 ml/2 fl oz) kecap manis
1½ tablespoons soy sauce
1½ tablespoons fish sauce
300 g (10 oz) Chinese broccoli (gai larn),
 cut into 5 cm (2 inch) lengths
¼ teaspoon ground white pepper
lemon wedges, to serve

1 Cut the noodle sheets lengthways into
2 cm (¾ inch) strips. Cover with boiling
water, then gently separate the strips.
2 Heat a wok over medium heat, add
1 tablespoon of the oil and swirl to coat
the side. Add the egg, swirl to coat and
cook for 1–2 minutes, or until set.
Remove, roll up and cut into shreds.
3 Reheat the wok over high heat, add the
remaining oil and swirl to coat. Stir-fry
the beef in batches for 3 minutes, or until
brown. Remove the beef to a side plate.
4 Reduce the heat to medium, add the
noodles and stir-fry for 2 minutes.
Combine the kecap manis, soy sauce and
fish sauce. Add to the wok with the
broccoli and white pepper, then stir-fry
for a further 2 minutes. Return the egg
and beef to the wok and stir-fry for
another 3 minutes, or until the broccoli
has wilted and the noodles are soft but
not falling apart. Serve with the lemon
wedges on the side.

NOTE: Rice noodles should not be
refrigerated, as they are very difficult to
separate when cold.

TANDOORI CHICKEN

Preparation time: 25 minutes + 4 hours 30
 minutes marinating
Total cooking time: 45 minutes
Serves 4–6

6 chicken thighs
¼ cup (60 ml/2 fl oz) lemon juice
½ small onion, chopped
4 cloves garlic
1 tablespoon grated fresh ginger
3 teaspoons coriander seeds
1 tablespoon cumin seeds
1 tablespoon lemon juice, extra
1 teaspoon salt
¼ teaspoon paprika
pinch chilli powder
1 cup (250 g/8 oz) yoghurt
red food colouring

1 Remove the skin from the chicken
pieces and brush the flesh with lemon
juice; cover and marinate in the
refrigerator for 30 minutes.
2 Place the onion, garlic, ginger,
coriander and cumin seeds, extra lemon
juice and salt in a food processor and
process until a smooth paste is formed.
Combine the spice paste with the paprika,
chilli powder and yoghurt, and mix
together until smooth. Add enough drops
of food colouring to make the mixture a
deep red colour.
3 Place the chicken pieces in a large
shallow dish, and spread liberally with the
spicy yoghurt mixture. Cover with plastic
wrap and refrigerate. Marinate the
chicken for at least 4 hours or overnight.
4 Preheat the oven to moderate 180°C
(350°F/Gas 4). Place the chicken pieces
on a wire rack over a large baking dish.
Bake for 45 minutes, or until the chicken
pieces are tender and cooked through.
Serve with rice.

COCETTE DE LAPIN WITH MUSTARD SAUCE

Preparation time: 30 minutes
Total cooking time: 2 hours
Serves 4–6

2 rabbits (800 g/1 lb 10 oz each)
2 tablespoons olive oil
2 onions, sliced
4 rashers bacon, cut into 3 cm (1¼ inch)
 pieces
2 tablespoons plain flour
1½ cups (375 ml/12 fl oz) chicken stock
½ cup (125 ml/4 fl oz) white wine
1 teaspoon fresh thyme leaves
½ cup (125 ml/4 fl oz) cream
2 tablespoons Dijon mustard
fresh sprigs of thyme, extra, to garnish

1 Preheat the oven to moderate 180°C
(350°F/Gas 4). Remove any fat from the
rabbits and wash the rabbits under cold
water. Pat dry with paper towels. Cut
along both sides of the backbones with
kitchen scissors and discard. Cut each
rabbit into eight even-sized pieces and pat
dry again.
2 Heat half the oil in a 2.5 litre flameproof
casserole dish. Brown the rabbit in
batches, adding oil when necessary, then
remove from the dish.
3 Add the onion and bacon to the
casserole, and cook, stirring, for 5 minutes,
or until lightly browned. Sprinkle the flour
into the pan and mix. Stir with a wooden
spoon to scrape the sediment from the
base. Add the stock and wine, and stir
until the sauce comes to the boil. Return
the rabbit to the casserole dish and add
the thyme.
4 Cover and bake for 1¼ –1½ hours, or
until the rabbit is tender and the sauce
has thickened. Stir in the combined
cream and mustard. Garnish with thyme
sprigs. Delicious with steamed
vegetables.

SIAMESE NOODLES IN SPICY COCONUT SAUCE

Preparation time: 1 hour 10 minutes
Total cooking time: 30 minutes
Serves 6

Spice Paste
10 dried red chillies, soaked in hot water
    until softened
10 red Asian shallots, chopped
1 stalk lemon grass (white part only),
    chopped
1 teaspoon shrimp paste
3 tablespoons peanut oil
1 teaspoon salt
1 tablespoon sugar

1 tablespoon dried tamarind pulp
½ cup (125 ml/4 fl oz) warm water
1.25 litres coconut milk
300 g (9⅔ oz) dried rice vermicelli
400 g (12⅔ oz) fried tofu
oil, for shallow frying
400 g (12⅔ oz) bean sprouts, scraggly
    ends removed
500 g (1 lb) cooked prawns, peeled with
    tails left on
1 cup (125 g/4 oz) chopped garlic chives
3 hard-boiled eggs, shells removed and
    cut into quarters
2 red chillies, seeded and finely sliced,
    optional
3 limes, quartered

1 To make Spice Paste: Drain and seed
the soaked chillies, reserving the water,
and chop. Place the chillies in a food
processor along with the shallots, lemon
grass and shrimp paste. Process until
finely chopped, adding a little of the chilli
water if necessary. Heat the peanut oil in
a small frying pan and fry the paste over
low heat for about 3 minutes. Add the salt
and sugar. Set aside.

2 Soak the tamarind in the warm water
for about 10 minutes.
3 Take half the spice paste and place it in
a pan along with the coconut milk. Strain
the soaked tamarind and water through a
nylon sieve into the coconut milk and
discard any seeds and fibre. Bring the
mixture to the boil and simmer for
3 minutes. Set aside.
4 Soak the vermicelli in boiling water for
5 minutes, and drain. Cut the tofu into
thick slices. Heat the oil in a small frying
pan and fry the slices of tofu until golden
on both sides. Remove and drain on paper
towels.
5 When ready to serve the dish, heat the
remaining spice paste in a large wok and
add the bean sprouts. Turn the heat up
high and cook for about a minute. Add
half the prawns and half the garlic chives.
Add the drained vermicelli to the wok;
toss until heated through. Reheat the
coconut sauce and keep it hot.
6 To serve, transfer the vermicelli
mixture to a large warm serving platter
and arrange the remaining prawns, the
egg quarters and slices of tofu on top.
Scatter over the sliced chilli and
remaining garlic chives. Pour the coconut
sauce into a large warm soup tureen.
Provide deep bowls for diners to fill with
the vermicelli mixture, then ladle over
some coconut sauce and a squeeze of
lime juice.

BALINESE FRIED RICE

Preparation time: 20 minutes
Total cooking time: 20 minutes
Serves 6

500 g (1 lb) raw prawns (shrimp)
2 teaspoons oil
2 eggs
2 onions, chopped
2 garlic cloves
¼ cup (60 ml/2 fl oz) oil, extra
¼ teaspoon shrimp paste
125 g (4 oz) rump steak, thinly sliced
1 cooked chicken breast, thinly sliced
1½ cups (300 g/10 oz) long-grain rice,
    cooked and cooled
1 tablespoon soy sauce
1 tablespoon fish sauce
1 tablespoon sambal oelek
1 tablespoon tomato paste (purée)
6 spring onions (scallions), finely chopped
sliced cucumber, to garnish (optional)

1 Peel and devein the prawns, then chop
the meat.
2 Heat the oil in a wok or large, heavy-
based frying pan. Lightly beat the eggs and
season with salt and freshly ground black
pepper. Add the eggs to the pan and cook
over medium heat for 1–2 minutes, or until
cooked. When set, transfer the omelette to
a plate, cool, and cut into thin strips—this
is easy if you first roll the omelette.
3 Put the onion and garlic in a food
processor and process until finely chopped.
4 Heat the extra oil in the wok, add the
onion mixture and cook over medium heat,
stirring frequently until it has reduced in
volume and is translucent. Add the shrimp
paste and cook for a further minute. Add
the prawns and steak and cook over high
heat for 3 minutes. Add the cooked chicken
and rice and toss until heated.
5 Combine the soy sauce, fish sauce,
sambal oelek, tomato paste and spring
onion and add to the rice mixture. Mix
well. Remove the rice from the heat and
transfer to a serving platter. Top with the
omelette strips and garnish with cucumber.

NORTH VIETNAMESE BRAISED PORK LEG

Preparation time: 30 minutes +
    2 hours marinating
Total cooking time: 1 hour 45 minutes
Serves 4–6

1½ tablespoons vegetable oil
1 kg (2 lb) boned pork leg in one piece,
    skin and fat intact (1.3 kg/2 lb 10 oz with
    bone in)
1 teaspoon shrimp paste
5 cloves garlic, crushed
3 large red Asian shallots, finely chopped
3 teaspoons ground galangal
1 teaspoon ground turmeric
2 teaspoons sugar
2 tablespoons fish sauce
700 ml (23 fl oz) home-made chicken
    stock or 2 cups (500 ml/16 fl oz)
    purchased stock diluted with 200 ml
    (6½ fl oz) water
2 tablespoons Chinese black vinegar
1 teaspoon cornflour
3 spring onions, thinly sliced on the
    diagonal

1 Heat a wok to very hot, add 2 teaspoons
of the oil and swirl to coat. Put the pork in
the wok, skin-side-down, and cook for
2 minutes until well browned. Turn and
cook the other side for a further
2 minutes, or until browned. Remove and
set aside to cool. Cut the pork into 3 cm
(1¼ inch) cubes.

2 Preheat the grill to high, wrap the
shrimp paste in foil, and put under the hot
grill for 5 minutes. Cool, remove the foil,
then put the paste in a large bowl with the
garlic, shallots, galangal, turmeric, sugar
and fish sauce and mix well. Add the pork
to the bowl and coat it in the marinade.
Cover and refrigerate for 1–2 hours.
3 Heat the wok until hot, add the
remaining oil, and swirl to coat. Add the
pork and stir-fry in batches for 1–2 minutes,
or until browned. Pour in the stock and
vinegar, and simmer, covered, over low
heat for 1½ hours, or until very tender.
Skim the surface constantly to remove
any fat and scum that floats to the
surface.
4 Dissolve the cornflour in 1 teaspoon
water. Remove the pork from the liquid
with a slotted spoon and set aside. Bring
the remaining stock to a simmer and
skim the surface. Mix in the cornflour
paste. Simmer for 2 minutes, or until
thickened, then return the pork to the
wok and add the spring onion. Season and
serve.

VEGETABLE DOMBURI

Preparation time: 20 minutes +
    15 minutes soaking
Total cooking time: 35 minutes
Serves 4

2 cups (440 g/14 oz) Japanese short-
    grain rice
10 g (¼ oz) dried whole shiitake
    mushrooms
2 tablespoons oil
1 onion, sliced
2 slender eggplants (aubergines), sliced
    on the diagonal
100 g (3½ oz) green beans, cut into 4 cm
    (1½ inch) lengths
5 spring onions (scallions), cut into 2 cm
    (¾ inch) lengths
100 ml (3½ fl oz) Shoyu (Japanese soy
    sauce)
100 ml (3½ fl oz) mirin
¼ cup (60 g/2 oz) sugar
4 eggs, lightly beaten

1 Wash the rice and place in a saucepan
with 2½ cups (625 ml/20 fl oz) water. Bring
to the boil, reduce the heat and simmer,
covered, for 15 minutes. Leave, covered,
for 10 minutes.
2 Soak the mushrooms in 1⅔ cups
(410 ml/13 fl oz) boiling water for 15
minutes. Drain and reserve the soaking
liquid. Remove the stems and cut the
caps in half.
3 Heat the oil in a deep frying pan. Cook
the onion over medium heat for 4 minutes,
or until softened but not browned. Add the
eggplant and cook for 3–4 minutes, or until
softened. Add the beans, mushrooms and
spring onion and cook for 2–3 minutes, or
until almost cooked. Combine the Shoyu,
mushroom soaking liquid, mirin and sugar,
and stir through the vegetables. Simmer
for 4 minutes.
4 Pour the egg over the vegetables, cover
and simmer for 1 minute, or until partly
cooked. Serve the rice in bowls, spoon on
the vegetable mixture and pour on the
cooking sauce.

STEAMED GLUTINOUS RICE IN LOTUS LEAVES

Preparation time: 30 minutes + overnight
    soaking + 1 hour soaking
Total cooking time: 1 hour 20 minutes
Makes 8

3 cups (600 g/1¼ lb) glutinous rice
4 large lotus leaves (see Note)

Filling
2 tablespoons dried shrimp
4 dried Chinese mushrooms
2 tablespoons oil
360 g (12 oz) skinless chicken breast
    fillet, cut into 1 cm (½ inch) cubes
1 garlic clove, crushed
2 Chinese sausages (lap cheong), thinly
    sliced
2 spring onions (scallions), thinly sliced
1 tablespoon oyster sauce
3 teaspoons light soy sauce
3 teaspoons sugar
1 teaspoon roasted sesame oil
1 tablespoon cornflour (cornstarch)
chilli sauce, to serve

1 Put the rice in a bowl, cover with cold water and leave to soak overnight. Drain in a colander, then put the rice in a steamer lined with greaseproof paper punched with holes. Steam, covered, over simmering water in a wok for 30–40 minutes, or until the rice is cooked. Cool slightly before using.
2 Soak the lotus leaves in boiling water for 1 hour, or until softened. Shake dry and cut the leaves in half to give eight equal pieces.

3 Meanwhile, to make the filling, soak the dried shrimp in boiling water for 1 hour, then drain. Soak the dried mushrooms in boiling water for 30 minutes, then drain and squeeze out any excess water. Remove and discard the stems and finely chop the caps.
4 Heat a wok over high heat, add half the oil and heat until very hot. Stir-fry the chicken for 2–3 minutes, or until browned. Add the shrimp, mushrooms, garlic, sausage and spring onion. Stir-fry for another 1–2 minutes, or until fragrant. Add the oyster sauce, soy sauce, sugar and sesame oil and toss well. Combine the cornflour with 220 ml (7 fl oz) water, add to the sauce and simmer until thickened.
5 With wet hands, divide the rice into 16 balls. Place the lotus leaves on a work surface, put a ball of rice in the centre of each leaf and flatten the ball slightly, making a slight indentation in the middle. Spoon one-eighth of the filling onto each rice ball, top with another slightly flattened rice ball and smooth into one ball. Wrap up firmly by folding the leaves over to form an envelope.
6 Place the parcels in three steamers. Cover and steam over simmering water in a wok, swapping the steamers halfway through, for 30 minutes. To serve, open up each leaf and eat straight from the leaf while hot with some chilli sauce.

NOTE: Lotus leaves are the dried leaves of the lotus. They are sold in packets in Chinese markets.

PORK VINDALOO
(SHIKAR VINDALOO)

Preparation time: 20 minutes
Total cooking time: 1 hour 45 minutes
Serves 4

1 kg (2 lb) pork fillets
¼ cup (60 ml/2 fl oz) vegetable oil
2 onions, finely chopped
4 cloves garlic, finely chopped
1 tablespoon finely chopped fresh ginger
1 tablespoon garam masala
2 teaspoons brown mustard seeds
4 tablespoons vindaloo curry paste (see
    Sauces)
1 tablespoon white vinegar

1 Trim the pork of any excess fat and sinew and cut into bite-sized pieces.
2 Heat a wok over medium heat, add the oil and swirl to coat the side of the wok. Add the meat in small batches and cook for 5–7 minutes, or until browned. Remove from the wok.
3 Add the onion, garlic, ginger, garam masala and mustard seeds to the wok, and cook, stirring, for 5 minutes, or until the onion is soft. Add the vindaloo paste and cook for 2 minutes.
4 Return all the meat to the wok, add 3 cups (750 ml/24 fl oz) water and bring to the boil. Reduce the heat and simmer, covered, for 1½ hours, or until the meat is tender. Stir in the vinegar 15 minutes before serving and season to taste with salt. Serve with rice and poppadoms.

SPANOKOPITA
(SILVERBEET AND CHEESE FILO PIE)

Preparation time: 25 minutes + cooling
Total cooking time: 1 hour
Serves 4–6

1.5 kg (3 lb) silverbeet (Swiss chard)
3 tablespoons olive oil
1 white onion, finely chopped
10 spring onions, chopped (include some green)
1½ tablespoons chopped fresh dill
200 g (6½ oz) Greek feta, crumbled
125 g (4 oz) cottage cheese
3 tablespoons finely grated kefalotyri
¼ teaspoon ground nutmeg
4 eggs, lightly beaten
10 sheets filo pastry
80 g (2¾ oz) butter, melted, for brushing

1 Rinse and drain the silverbeet thoroughly. Discard the stems and shred the leaves. Heat the olive oil in a large frying pan, add the onion and cook, stirring, over medium heat for 5 minutes, or until softened. Add the spring onion and silverbeet and cook, covered, over medium heat for 5 minutes. Add the dill and cook, uncovered, for 3–4 minutes, or until most of the liquid has evaporated. Remove from the heat and cool to room temperature.
2 Preheat the oven to moderate 180°C (350°F/Gas 4) and lightly grease a 20 x 25 cm (8 x 10 inch) 2.5 litre baking dish. Place the feta, cottage and kefalotyri cheeses in a large bowl. Stir in the silverbeet mixture and add the nutmeg. Gradually add the eggs and combine well. Season, to taste.

3 Line the base and sides of the baking dish with a sheet of filo pastry. (Keep the rest covered with a damp tea towel to prevent drying out.) Brush with butter and cover with another sheet of filo. Butter the sheet and repeat in this way, using five sheets of pastry. Spoon the filling into the dish and level the surface. Fold the exposed pastry up and over to cover the top of the filling. Cover with a sheet of pastry, brush with butter and continue until all the sheets are used. Roughly trim the pastry with kitchen scissors then tuck the excess inside the wall of the dish.
4 Brush the top with butter. Using a sharp knife, score the surface into squares. Sprinkle a few drops of cold water on top to discourage the pastry from curling. Bake for 45 minutes, or until puffed and golden. Rest at room temperature for 10 minutes before serving.

NOTE: You can use pecorino cheese if kefalotyri is unavailable.

BURMESE CHICKEN

Preparation time: 15 minutes
Total cooking time: 45 minutes to 1 hour
Serves 4–6

1.5 kg (3 lb) whole chicken or chicken pieces (legs, thighs, wings, breasts)
2 tablespoons ghee or oil
2 medium onions, chopped
3 bay leaves
2 teaspoons ground turmeric
¼ teaspoon chilli powder
½ teaspoon ground cardamom
½ teaspoon ground cumin
½ teaspoon ground coriander
½ teaspoon ground ginger
1 cinnamon stick
2 stems lemon grass (white part only), chopped
6 cloves garlic, crushed
1 tablespoon grated fresh ginger
1 cup (250 ml/8 fl oz) chicken stock

1 If using a whole chicken, cut it into pieces.
2 Heat the ghee in a large pan; add the onion and cook, stirring, until the onion is soft. Add the bay leaves, turmeric, chilli powder, cardamom, cumin, coriander, ginger, cinnamon stick, lemon grass, garlic and fresh ginger. Cook, stirring, for 1 minute or until fragrant.
3 Add the chicken pieces and stir to coat with the mixture. Stir in the stock and simmer, covered, for 45 minutes to 1 hour or until the chicken is tender.

FISH STEW WITH RICE

Preparation time: 20 minutes + overnight
    soaking + 30 minutes refrigeration
Total cooking time: 40 minutes
Serves 4

115 g (4 oz) dried white fish, such as
    salted cod
½ cup (125 ml/4 fl oz) oil
3 tablespoons chopped parsley
1½ teaspoons chilli flakes
5 large garlic cloves, crushed
6 x 150 g (5 oz) mixed white fish steaks
2 onions, chopped
¼ cup (60 g/2 oz) tomato passata
1.5 litres (48 fl oz) well-flavoured fish
    stock
2 cups (400 g/13 oz) long-grain rice
400 g (13 oz) orange sweet potato, peeled
    and cut into chunks
150 g (5 oz) carrot, peeled and cut into
    chunks
1 red capsicum (pepper), seeded and cut
    into chunks
300 g (10 oz) white cabbage, cut into
    chunks

1 Soak the dried fish in water overnight,
changing the water three to four times.
Drain, then put it in a saucepan with clean
water and simmer for 15–20 minutes, or
until soft. Drain and remove any skin and
bones.
2 Mix together ¼ cup (60 ml/2 fl oz) of the
oil, 2 tablespoons of the parsley, ½
teaspoon of the chilli flakes and 3 of the
crushed garlic cloves. Rub into the fresh
fish, transfer to a non-metallic dish, cover
and refrigerate for 30 minutes.

3 Heat a tablespoon of the remaining oil
in a large saucepan and add the onion.
Cook for about 6 minutes, or until the
onion has softened but not browned. Stir
in the remaining garlic and cook for a
further minute. Add the tomato passata
and the remaining chilli flakes to the
cooked onions, then pour in the stock.
Season with salt, bring to the boil, then
gently simmer for 10 minutes.
4 Meanwhile, heat a frying pan with the
remaining 2 tablespoons of oil and cook
the fresh fish for 1 minute on each side.
Transfer to a plate and set aside. Tip the
rice into a saucepan. Add 3½ cups (875
ml/28 fl oz) water and a generous pinch of
salt. Bring the liquid back to the boil, then
reduce the heat to low. Cover and cook for
15 minutes, or until tender.
5 Stir the sweet potato and carrot into the
stew, and simmer for 10 minutes. Add the
capsicum, cabbage and dried fish.
Simmer for 5 minutes, season and add
more chilli flakes, if desired. Put the fish
steaks on top and cook, covered, for 6
minutes, or until the fish is cooked
through. Scatter with the remaining
parsley. Drain the cooked rice and serve
with the fish.

NOTE: Rice culture in much of the
Americas has its roots in Africa.
Plantation slaves from West Africa
brought with them a knowledge of how to
grow and cook rice. This meal can be
traced back to Senegal, West Africa. Fish
stew with rice (diebou dien) is the national
dish there. As it is common for local
fishermen to dry part of their catch, the
stew combines both fresh and dried fish.
If dried fish is unavailable, or you don't
have time to soak it, just leave it out.

YAKHNI PULAO

Preparation time: 20 minutes +
    10 minutes standing
Total cooking time: 20 minutes
Serves 4

225 g (7 oz) basmati rice
2 cups (500 ml/16 fl oz) chicken stock
6 tablespoons ghee or oil
5 cardamom pods
5 cm (2 inch) piece of cinnamon stick
6 cloves
8 black peppercorns
4 Indian bay leaves (cassia leaves)
1 onion, finely sliced

1 Wash the rice in a sieve under cold
running water until the water runs clear.
Drain.
2 Pour the stock into a saucepan and heat
to near boiling point.
3 Meanwhile, heat 2 tablespoons of the
ghee or oil over medium heat in a large,
heavy-based saucepan. Add the
cardamom, cinnamon, cloves,
peppercorns and bay leaves and fry for
1 minute. Reduce the heat to low, add the
rice and stir constantly for 1 minute. Add
the heated stock and some salt to the rice
and bring rapidly to the boil. Cover and
simmer over low heat for 15 minutes.
Leave the rice to stand for 10 minutes
before uncovering. Lightly fluff up the rice
before serving.
4 Meanwhile, heat the remaining ghee or
oil in a frying pan over low heat and fry
the onion until soft. Increase the heat and
fry until the onion is brown. Drain on
paper towels, then use as garnish.

MEDITERRANEAN PANTRY

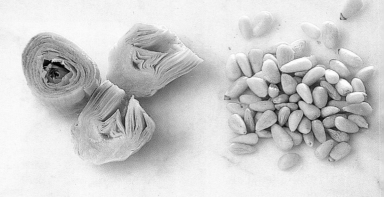

Anchovy fillets: small fish fillets that are salt cured, canned or bottled in oil. The strong flavour and saltiness can be reduced by soaking in milk or water for a short time.

Arborio rice: Italian-grown, short-grain rice, used for making risotto because of the high starch content.

Artichoke hearts: the edible buds from a large plant of the thistle family. Available canned or bottled in brine or oil.

Pine nuts: high-fat nuts from a variety of pine tree. One of the more expensive nuts, due to the labour required to separate the nuts from the cones. Toasting brings out the flavour.

Parmesan: a hard cheese with a crumbly texture and distinctive flavour. Made from skimmed or partly skimmed cow's milk and aged for 2–3 years in large 'wheels'.

Mozzarella: a smooth, mild, white soft cheese. Originally made from buffalo milk, but now made from cow's milk or a mixture. Available sealed in plastic, or loose in whey or water. Bocconcini are small individual mozzarella balls.

Goat's cheese: varies in texture from smooth and creamy to soft and crumbly, depending on the age of the cheese. Available plain or rolled in a variety of coatings from herbs to ash. Has a distinctive sharp taste.

Ricotta: a fresh, white, moist curd cheese, usually made from the whey drained off when making mozzarella. Slightly grainy, but smoother than cottage cheese.

Balsamic vinegar: gets its sweet and syrupy intense flavour and dark colour from being aged in a variety of wooden barrels. Use sparingly as a flavouring as well as a vinegar.

Olive oils: extra virgin olive oil is made from the first pressing of the olives and used mainly in uncooked dishes or dressings. Use a basic olive oil for cooking.

Olives: are black or green and varying sizes. Some are stuffed with anchovies, almonds or pimientos, others are cured in salt or marinated in oil.

Capers: flower buds of a bush native to the Mediterranean and parts of Asia. Sun-dried, then pickled in vinegar or brine. Available in several sizes. Also sold salted in jars.

Sun-dried tomatoes/peppers (capsicums): chewy, intensely flavoured and dark in colour. Available packed in oil or dry. The dry ones must be soaked in oil or other liquid to reconstitute before use.

Rocket: also known as arugula. A bitter, aromatic salad leaf with a peppery mustard tang. Available in bunches, sometimes with roots attached.

Feta: Firm white cheese with a crumbly texture and mild salty flavour. Originally made from goat and sheep's milk, now often made with cow's milk. Pressed into cakes and preserved in brine.

Haloumi: a firm, yet creamy, salty cheese. It is made from sheep's milk and matured in a whey and salt mixture. Smooth and creamy when melted.

Vine leaves: Available in jars or plastic packs in brine. Wash before use to remove saltiness. Fresh vine leaves need to be simmered before use to soften.

Pastrami: a well-seasoned dry-cured, smoked, cooked lean cut of beef, rubbed with a mix which can contain salt, pepper, cumin, paprika and garlic.

Prosciutto: salted and air-dried hind leg of pork. The salt removes some of the moisture. Pancetta is a good substitute.

Roma tomatoes: also known as egg or plum tomatoes. Egg-shaped with thick walls yielding a high flesh to seed ratio, making them great for cooking.

SHABU-SHABU
(BRAISED BEEF AND VEGETABLE STEAMBOAT)

Preparation time: 50 minutes +
   30 minutes refrigeration
Total cooking time: 30 minutes
Serves 4

750 g (1½ lb) scotch fillet, partially frozen
15 spring onions
3 carrots
400 g (12⅔ oz) button mushrooms
½ Chinese cabbage
150 g (4¾ oz) firm tofu
Sesame Seed Sauce (page 764) or ready-
   made shabu-shabu sauce, to serve
1 cup (220 g/7 oz) short-grain rice, cooked
8 cups (2 litres) chicken stock

1 Cut the steak into very thin slices and
set aside. Cut the firm section of the
spring onions into 4 cm (1½ inch) lengths
and discard the dark green tops. Slice the
carrots very thinly. Slice the the
mushrooms. Chop the cabbage into bite-
sized pieces, discarding any tough parts.
Cut the tofu into bite-sized cubes.
2 Arrange the prepared vegetables, tofu and
meat in separate piles on a serving platter;
cover with plastic wrap and refrigerate until
about 30 minutes before cooking time.
3 Set the table with individual place
settings, each with a serving bowl, a bowl
of Sesame Seed Sauce, a bowl of rice,
chopsticks, soup spoons and napkins. Position
the serving platter and cooking vessel so
they are within easy reach of each diner.
4 When all the diners are seated, pour the
stock into the cooking vessel, cover and
bring to a simmer. Each diner then picks
up an ingredient or two with their
chopsticks, and places it in the simmering
stock for about a minute, or until just
cooked. (Do not overcook—the vegetables
should be just tender and the steak still
pink in the centre.) The food is then dipped
into the Sesame Seed Sauce and eaten
with the rice. The remaining stock can be
served as soup at the end of the meal.

STUFFED SHIITAKE

Preparation time: 30 minutes
Total cooking time: 20 minutes
Serves 4–6

300 g (10 oz) raw medium prawns
150 g (5 oz) chicken mince
50 g (1¾ oz) pork fat (ask your butcher),
   very finely chopped
30 g (1 oz) ham, finely chopped
1 spring onion, finely chopped
2 large cloves garlic, crushed
1½ tablespoons finely chopped water
   chestnuts
1½ tablespoons finely chopped bamboo
   shoots
1½ teaspoons grated fresh ginger
1 tablespoon Chinese rice wine
1 tablespoon oyster sauce, plus extra, to
   drizzle
1 tablespoon light soy sauce
2–3 drops of sesame oil
1 egg white, beaten until frothy
¼ teaspoon sugar
pinch of five-spice powder
300 g (10 oz) fresh shiitake mushrooms
   (see Note)
1 litre (32 fl oz) chicken stock
1 star anise
toasted sesame seeds, to garnish
   (optional)

1 To make the stuffing, peel and devein
the prawns. Finely chop the prawn meat
and put it in a bowl with the chicken
mince, pork fat, ham, spring onion, garlic,
water chestnuts, bamboo shoots, ginger,
rice wine, oyster sauce, soy sauce,
sesame oil, egg white, sugar, five-spice
powder and white pepper and mix
together thoroughly.

2 Remove the stalks from the shiitake and
reserve. Generously fill each mushroom
cap with stuffing, rounding the tops
slightly. The amount of stuffing you use
for each mushroom will differ depending
on their size—if the mushrooms are very
small you may have some mixture left
over.
3 Pour the chicken stock and 2 cups
(500 ml/16 fl oz) water into a wok and add
the star anise and reserved mushroom
stalks. Bring to the boil over high heat,
then reduce to a simmer.
4 Line a large bamboo steamer with
baking paper and place the mushrooms in
a single layer on top, filling-side-up.
Cover and simmer over the wok for about
15 minutes, or until the filling and the
mushrooms are cooked through. Place on
a serving platter and pour over a little of
the broth. If desired, you can drizzle with
a little extra oyster sauce and some
toasted sesame seeds. Serve as part of as
Asian banquet or as a light entrée to an
Asian meal.

NOTE: When purchasing fresh shiitake,
choose mushrooms that are plump, with
firm caps that curl under. Ignore any with
shrivelled, dehydrated caps as they are
well past their peak. Choose ones of
similar size so they cook evenly.

KOTOPOULO ME SYKO
(CHICKEN WITH FIGS)

Preparation time: 20 minutes
Total cooking time: 1 hour 10 minutes
Serves 4

1.5 kg (3 lb) chicken, cut into 8 even-sized
   pieces
1 tablespoon olive oil
12 fresh figs (not too big), or 12 dried figs,
   soaked in hot water for 2 hours
10 whole cloves garlic
1 large onion, thinly sliced
½ teaspoon ground coriander
½ teaspoon ground cinnamon
½ teaspoon ground cumin
pinch of cayenne
3 bay leaves
1½ cups (375 ml/12 fl oz) ruby port
1 teaspoon finely grated lemon rind
2 tablespoons lemon juice

1 Preheat the oven to moderate 180°C
(350°F/Gas 4). Remove any excess
chicken fat. Reserve the chicken giblets if
there are any. Lightly season the chicken.
Heat the olive oil in a large heavy-based
frying pan over high heat and cook the
chicken in batches, skin-side-down, for
5 minutes, or until the skin is golden.
2 Remove from the pan and place skin-
side-down in a single layer in a 33 x 23 cm
(13 x 9 inch) baking dish with the giblets.
Place the figs between the chicken
pieces. Scatter the garlic and onion over
the top, carefully pressing them into any
gaps and being careful not to squash the
figs. Sprinkle the spices over the top, tuck
in the bay leaves, then pour in the port.
Cover and bake for 25 minutes, then turn
the chicken. Uncover and bake for
another 20 minutes, or until the chicken is
just tender. Stir in the lemon rind and
juice and bake for another 15 minutes, or
until the chicken is very tender.

SHANGHAI PORK NOODLES

Preparation time: 25 minutes +
  30 minutes marinating
Total cooking time: 20 minutes
Serves 4

½ teaspoon sesame oil
¼ cup (60 ml/2 fl oz) soy sauce
2 tablespoons oyster sauce
250 g (8 oz) pork loin fillet, cut into
   julienne strips
2 tablespoons dried shrimp
8 dried shiitake mushrooms
1 teaspoon sugar
1 cup (250 ml/8 fl oz) chicken stock
300 g (10 oz) fresh Shanghai noodles
2 tablespoons peanut oil
1 clove garlic, thinly sliced
2 teaspoons grated fresh ginger
1 celery stick, julienned
1 leek, white part only, julienned
150 g (5 oz) wom bok (Chinese cabbage),
   shredded
50 g (1¾ oz) bamboo shoots, julienned
8 spring onions, thinly sliced

1 Combine the sesame oil and 1
tablespoon each of the soy sauce and
oyster sauce in a large non-metallic bowl.
Add the pork and toss in the marinade.
Cover and marinate in the refrigerator for
30 minutes.
2 Meanwhile, place the dried shrimp in a
bowl, cover with boiling water and soak
for 20 minutes. Drain and finely chop. At
the same time, soak the shiitake
mushrooms in hot water for 20 minutes.
Drain, discard the stalks and thinly slice
the caps.

3 To make the stir-fry sauce, combine the
sugar, chicken stock, remaining soy and
oyster sauces and 1 teaspoon salt in a
small non-metallic jug. Set aside until
needed.
4 Cook the noodles in a large saucepan of
boiling water for 4–5 minutes, or until
tender. Drain and refresh under cold
water. Toss with 1 teaspoon peanut oil.
5 Heat a wok over high heat, add 1
tablespoon of the peanut oil and swirl to
coat. Add the pork and stir-fry for 1–2
minutes, or until the pork is no longer
pink. Transfer to a plate. Heat the
remaining peanut oil, add the garlic,
ginger, celery, leek and wom bok and stir-
fry for 1 minute, or until softened. Add the
bamboo shoots, spring onion, mushrooms
and shrimp and stir-fry for 1 minute. Add
the noodles and the stir-fry sauce and
toss together for 3–5 minutes, or until the
noodles absorb the sauce. Return the
pork to the wok, with any juices and toss
through for 1–2 minutes, or until
combined and heated through. Serve
immediately.

MU SHU PORK

Preparation time: 30 minutes + 3 hours
    marinating + 30 minutes refrigeration
Total cooking time: 20 minutes
Serves 4

2 cloves garlic, crushed
1 teaspoon finely grated fresh ginger
2½ tablespoons light soy sauce
1½ tablespoons Chinese rice wine
2 tablespoons hoisin sauce
2½ teaspoons cornflour
500 g (1 lb) pork loin fillet, sliced into
    julienne strips
20 g (¾ oz) dried black fungus
20 g (¾ oz) dried lily buds
2 tablespoons chicken stock
3 eggs
2 tablespoons vegetable oil
½ teaspoon sesame oil
2 cups (150 g/5 oz) finely shredded wom
    bok (Chinese cabbage)
¼ cup (40 g/1¼ oz) julienned bamboo shoots
5 spring onions, thinly sliced on the diagonal
white pepper, to taste
spring onion lengths, to garnish (optional)

Pancakes
300 g (10 oz) plain flour
200 ml (6½ fl oz) boiling water
½ teaspoon vegetable oil
plain flour, for dusting

1 Combine the garlic, ginger, 1 tablespoon of
the soy sauce, 1 tablespoon of the Chinese
rice wine, 1 tablespoon of the hoisin sauce
and 1 teaspoon of the cornflour in a large
non-metallic bowl. Add the the pork, toss
well, then cover with plastic wrap and
marinate in the refrigerator for 3 hours.
2 To make the pancake dough, sift the flour
into a large bowl and make a well in the
centre. Slowly pour in the boiling water,
stirring with a wooden spoon, then add the
oil. Mix until a dough forms. Place the dough
on a lightly floured workbench and knead for
5 minutes, or until smooth and elastic—be
careful as the dough will be hot. Transfer
the dough to a clean bowl, cover with plastic

wrap, and refrigerate for 30 minutes.
3 Meanwhile, soak the black fungus and
lily buds separately by covering with
boiling water for 20 minutes. Drain,
remove any hard ends from the lily buds,
julienne the black fungus, and cut the lily
buds into 1 cm (½ inch) pieces.
4 Combine the chicken stock and remaining
soy sauce, rice wine, hoisin sauce and
cornflour in a small jug. Whisk with a fork to
dissolve the cornflour and form a paste.
5 Lightly whisk the eggs. Heat a wok over
high heat, add 1 teaspoon of vegetable oil
and ¼ teaspoon of the sesame oil, and add
the eggs. Stir for about 30 seconds, or
until scrambled. Remove from the wok.
6 Heat the same wok over high heat, add
2 teaspoons of the vegetable oil and the
remaining sesame oil and swirl to coat.
Stir-fry the pork in batches for 2 minutes,
or until browned.
7 Add the remaining oil to the wok, then
add the wom bok, bamboo shoots, spring
onion, black fungus and lily buds and stir-
fry for 3 minutes, or until the wom bok
begins to wilt. Return the pork to the wok,
add the sauce mixture and cook until it
comes to the boil and begins to thicken.
Stir in the reserved scrambled eggs and
season with white pepper. Remove the
wok from direct heat. Keep warm.
8 To make the pancakes, lightly flour a
workbench, then divide the dough into four
even pieces and roll each piece into a long
sausage. Cut each sausage into four.
Flatten each piece with your palm, then roll
each piece out as thinly as possible to a
pancake about 15 cm (6 inch) in diameter. The
dough is quite elastic and you can roll the
dough thin enough to almost see through it.
9 Heat a frying pan over medium heat.
Dry-fry the pancakes on each side for
about 30 seconds, or until some brown
spots appear. Stack the cooked pancakes
on a plate, covered with foil to keep warm
while cooking the remaining pancakes.
Wrap the filling in the pancakes, garnish
with the spring onion lengths then serve.

TONKATSU
(CRUMBED FRIED PORK)

Preparation time: 35 minutes +
    2 hours refrigeration
Total cooking time: 12 minutes
Serves 4

500 g (1 lb) pork loin
½ cup (60 g/2 oz) plain flour
6 egg yolks, beaten with 2 tablespoons water
2 cups (120 g/4 oz) Japanese dried
    breadcrumbs
2 spring onions
pickled ginger and pickled daikon
1 sheet nori
oil, for shallow frying
2 cups (90 g/3 oz) finely shredded
    Chinese cabbage
1 cup (250 ml/8 fl oz) Tonkatsu sauce

1 Trim the pork of any sinew and cut it into
8 thin slices. Sprinkle the slices with a
good pinch of salt and pepper and lightly
coat with flour. Shake off excess flour.
2 Dip each steak into the egg mixture and
then into the breadcrumbs; press the
crumbs on with your fingertips to ensure
an even coating. Place the steaks in a
single layer on a plate and refrigerate,
uncovered, for at least 2 hours.
3 Meanwhile prepare the garnishes. Peel
away the outside layers of the spring
onions, slice the stems very finely and
place them in a bowl of cold water until
serving time. Slice the ginger and daikon.
Using a sharp knife, shred the nori very
finely and then break it into strips about
4 cm (1½ inches) long.
4 Heat 1 cm (½ inch) oil in a heavy-based
frying pan; add the steaks 2 or 3 at a time and
cook over medium heat until golden brown on
both sides, then drain on paper towels.
5 Carefully slice each steak into 1 cm
(½ inch) strips and then reassemble the
strips into the original steak shape. Top
each of the steaks with a small bundle of
the nori strips. Serve with the drained
spring onion, ginger, daikon, cabbage,
Tonkatsu sauce and steamed rice.

CANTONESE LEMON CHICKEN

Preparation time: 15 minutes +
    10 minutes standing
Total cooking time: 25 minutes
Serves 4

500 g (1 lb) chicken breast fillets
1 egg yolk, lightly beaten
1 tablespoon water
2 teaspoons soy sauce
2 teaspoons dry sherry
3 teaspoons cornflour
½ cup (60 g/2 oz) cornflour, extra
2½ tablespoons plain flour
oil, for deep-frying

Lemon Sauce
⅓ cup (80 ml/2¾ fl oz) fresh lemon juice
2 tablespoons water
2 tablespoons sugar
1 tablespoon dry sherry
2 teaspoons cornflour
1 tablespoon water, extra
4 spring onions, very finely sliced

1 Cut the chicken into long strips, about 1 cm (½ inch) wide, and then set aside. Combine the egg, water, soy sauce, sherry and cornflour in a small bowl and mix until smooth. Pour the egg mixture over the chicken, mixing well, and set aside for 10 minutes.
2 Sift the extra cornflour and plain flour together onto a plate. Roll each piece of chicken in the flour, coating each piece evenly, and shake off excess. Place the chicken in a single layer on a plate ready to be fried.

3 Heat the oil for deep-frying in a wok or pan. It is hot enough to use when a cube of bread turns brown in it in 30 seconds. Carefully lower about 4 pieces of chicken into the oil and cook until golden brown. Remove the chicken with a slotted spoon and drain it on paper towels. Repeat with the remaining chicken. Let the chicken stand while preparing the sauce.
4 To make Lemon Sauce: Combine the lemon juice, water, sugar and sherry in a small pan. Bring to the boil over medium heat, stirring until the sugar dissolves. Stir the cornflour into the extra tablespoon water and mix to a smooth paste; add it to the lemon juice mixture, stirring constantly until the sauce boils and thickens. Set the sauce aside.
5 Just before serving, reheat the oil in the wok to very hot; add all the chicken pieces and fry for 2 minutes until very crisp and a rich golden brown. Remove the chicken with a slotted spoon and drain well on paper towels. Pile the chicken onto a serving plate, drizzle over the sauce, sprinkle with spring onion and serve immediately.

NOTE: The first frying can be done several hours in advance.

HOPPIN' JOHN

Preparation time: 10 minutes + overnight
    soaking
Total cooking time: 30 minutes
Serves 4

1½ cups (300 g/10 oz) black-eyed beans
1 tablespoon oil
1 onion, finely chopped
1 red capsicum (pepper), finely chopped
4 back bacon rashers, diced
½ cup (100 g/3½ oz) long-grain rice
Louisiana hot sauce or chilli sauce (see
    Notes)

1 Soak the black-eyed beans in cold water overnight, then drain.
2 Heat the oil in a frying pan over medium heat. Add the onion, capsicum and bacon and cook for 10 minutes, or until the bacon is crisp and the vegetables are soft.
3 Add the beans, rice and 2 cups (500 ml/16 fl oz) water. Cover, bring to the boil and simmer for about 20 minutes, or until the rice is cooked. Season with salt, freshly ground black pepper and some Louisiana hot sauce.

NOTES: Hoppin' John is said to have originated with the African slaves who worked on southern American plantations. The most well known rice dish from the southern American region, it it is traditionally served there on New Year's day with collards (a green leafy vegetable related to kale). The rice is said to bring good luck, and the collards to bring 'greenbacks', or wealth.
  There are hundreds of varieties of Louisiana hot sauce, which come in varying degrees of heat. Made from red peppers or chillies, and sometimes with the addition of garlic, onion and other spices, hot sauce is ubiquitous in southern America and is used to spice up anything from hot dogs to rice dishes.

INDIAN FRIED FISH

Preparation time: 15 minutes
Total cooking time: 20 minutes
Serves 4

500 g (1 lb) firm white fish fillets
¾ cup (80 g/2⅔ oz) besan (chickpea flour)
1 teaspoon salt
1 teaspoon garam masala
¼ teaspoon chilli powder
¼ teaspoon ground turmeric
¼ teaspoon freshly ground black pepper
2 tablespoons chopped fresh coriander leaves
2 eggs, lightly beaten
oil, for shallow-frying

1 Wash the fish fillets, pat them dry, and cut them in half lengthways.
2 Sift the besan, salt, garam masala, chilli powder, turmeric and black pepper into a bowl. Add the coriander and stir to combine, then spread the mixture out on a plate.
3 Dip each fish fillet into the egg, then into the spiced flour, shaking off any excess.
4 Heat 2 cm (¾ inch) oil in a frying pan; fry the coated fish fillets in batches over high heat for 5 minutes or until crisp and golden. Serve with rice and raitas.

LEMPER
(COCONUT RICE IN BANANA LEAVES)

Preparation time: 40 minutes + cooling
Total cooking time: 1 hour 30 minutes
Makes about 12

2–3 young banana leaves, or foil (see Notes)
2 cups (400 g/13 oz) glutinous rice
¾ cup (185 ml/6 fl oz) coconut milk

Chicken filling
2 tablespoons oil
2–3 garlic cloves, crushed
6 curry leaves
1 teaspoon shrimp paste
2 teaspoons ground coriander
2 teaspoons ground cumin
½ teaspoon ground turmeric
250 g (8 oz) minced (ground) chicken
¼ cup (60 ml/2 fl oz) coconut milk, extra
1 teaspoon lemon juice

1 With a sharp knife, cut away the central ribs of the banana leaves. The leaves will split into large pieces—cut into pieces about 15 cm (6 inches) square. Blanch in boiling water briefly to soften them, then spread out on a tea towel and cover.
2 Wash the rice, drain and put in a large heavy-based saucepan with 1¾ cups (440 ml/14 fl oz) water. Bring slowly to the boil, then reduce the heat to very low, cover tightly and cook for 15 minutes.
3 Pour the coconut milk and ½ cup (125 ml/4 fl oz) water into a small saucepan and heat without boiling. Stir through the rice with a fork. Transfer to a bowl and set aside to cool.

4 To make the chicken filling, heat the oil in a large heavy-based frying pan, add the garlic and curry leaves and stir over medium heat for 1 minute. Add the shrimp paste, coriander, cumin and turmeric and cook for another minute. Add the chicken and cook, breaking up with a fork, for 3–4 minutes, or until the chicken changes colour. Add the extra coconut milk and continue to cook over low heat for 5 minutes, or until absorbed. Remove the curry leaves. Add the lemon juice and season to taste with salt and freshly ground black pepper. Cool.
5 Place 1 heaped tablespoon of rice in the centre of each piece of banana leaf and flatten to a 4 cm (1½ inch) square. Top with a heaped teaspoon of the chicken filling. Roll the leaf into a parcel and place, seam-side down, in a steamer lined with leftover banana leaf scraps or baking paper. Steam, in batches, for 15 minutes, or if you have a double-layered steamer, cook with one basket on top of the other, swapping halfway through—you'll need to cook them for a little longer.

NOTES: Banana leaves are used throughout Asia to wrap foods for steaming or baking. They keep the food moist and impart a mild flavour. They can be bought at Asian food stores if you don't have access to fresh leaves from a plant. Lemper is a popular Indonesian snack and can be eaten hot or at room temperature.

INDONESIAN SAMBAL SQUID

Preparation time: 20 minutes +
   10 minutes soaking
Total cooking time: 15 minutes
Serves 6

1 kg (2 lb) cleaned squid hoods
1 tablespoon white vinegar
1 tablespoon tamarind pulp
4 red Asian shallots, finely chopped
8 small fresh red chillies, half of them
   seeded, chopped
6 cloves garlic
1 stem lemon grass, white part only,
   chopped
2 teaspoons grated fresh ginger
½ teaspoon shrimp paste
2½ tablespoons peanut oil
½ teaspoon ground cumin
1½ tablespoons brown sugar

1 Cut each squid hood in half lengthways and open out flat with the inside uppermost. Score a shallow diamond pattern all over the squid hoods, taking care not to cut all the way through. Cut the hoods into 5 cm (2 inch) squares. Put the pieces in a bowl with the vinegar and 1 litre (32 fl oz) water and soak for 10 minutes, then rinse and drain the squid and set aside.
2 Put the tamarind in a bowl and pour in ⅓ cup (80 ml/2¾ fl oz) boiling water. Allow to steep for 5 minutes, breaking up the pulp as it softens. Strain, then discard the solids.

3 Put the shallots, chilli, garlic, lemon grass, ginger, shrimp paste and 1 teaspoon of the oil in a small food processor or mortar and pestle and blend until a smooth paste is formed, then stir in the cumin.
4 Heat a non-stick wok over high heat, add 1 tablespoon of the oil and swirl to coat the side of the wok. Add the paste and cook for 5 minutes, or until it is fragrant, glossy and the liquid has evaporated. Remove from the wok.
5 Reheat the wok to very hot, add the remaining oil and swirl to coat. Add the squid pieces in small batches, stir-frying for 1–2 minutes each batch, or until cooked through. Remove from the wok.
6 Reduce the heat to medium, then add the spice paste, strained tamarind water and sugar. Stir-fry for 2 minutes, or until the sauce ingredients are well combined. Return the squid to the wok and stir-fry for 1 minute, or until the squid is well coated with the sauce and heated through. Serve with steamed rice.

LAMB TAGINE WITH QUINCE

Preparation time: 20 minutes
Total cooking time: 1 hour 40 minutes
Serves 4–6

1.5 kg (3 lb) lamb shoulder, cut into 3 cm
   (1¼ inch) pieces
2 large onions, diced
½ teaspoon ground ginger
½ teaspoon cayenne pepper
¼ teaspoon pulverised saffron threads
1 teaspoon ground coriander
1 cinnamon stick
½ cup (25 g/¾ oz) roughly chopped coriander
40 g (1¼ oz) butter
500 g (1 lb) quinces, peeled, cored and
   quartered
100 g (3½ oz) dried apricots
fresh coriander sprigs, extra, to garnish

1 Place the lamb in a heavy-based, flameproof casserole dish and add half the onion, the ginger, cayenne pepper, saffron, ground coriander, cinnamon stick, fresh coriander and some salt and pepper. Cover with cold water and bring to the boil over medium heat. Lower the heat and simmer, partly covered, for 1½ hours, or until the lamb is tender.
2 While the lamb is cooking, melt the butter in a heavy-based frying pan and cook the remaining onion and the quinces for 15 minutes over medium heat, or until lightly golden.
3 When the lamb has been cooking for 1 hour, add the quinces and apricots.
4 Taste the sauce and adjust the seasoning if necessary. Transfer to a warm serving dish and sprinkle with coriander sprigs. Delicious served with couscous or rice.

NOTE: The word 'tagine' not only refers to the classic stews of Morocco but also the special, often beautifully decorated, earthenware dish, with its distinctive pointed top, in which the stews are cooked. A heavy-based casserole with a tight-fitting lid is a perfect substitute.

VEGETABLE DISHES

CHINESE BROCCOLI IN OYSTER SAUCE

Wash 1 kg (2 lb) Chinese broccoli (gai lan). Discard any tough stems and diagonally cut into 2 cm (¾ inch) pieces through the stem and the leaf. Blanch for 2 minutes, or until just tender, then refresh in cold water and dry. Heat a wok over high heat, add 1½ tablespoons oil and heat until very hot. Stir-fry 2 finely chopped spring onions (scallions), 1½ tablespoons grated ginger and 3 finely chopped garlic cloves for 10 seconds. Add the broccoli and cook until it is heated through. Add a combined mixture of ½ cup (125 ml/4 fl oz) chicken stock, ¼ cup (60 ml/2 fl oz) oyster sauce, 1½ tablespoons light soy sauce, 1 tablespoon Chinese rice wine, 2 teaspoons cornflour (cornstarch), 1 teaspoon sugar and 1 teaspoon roasted sesame oil. Cook until it has thickened, tossing to coat the broccoli.
Serves 6.

TOFU IN YELLOW BEAN SAUCE

Cut 400 g (13 oz) firm, drained tofu into bite-sized pieces. Heat a wok over medium heat, add 2 tablespoons oil and heat until hot. Cook the tofu until golden. Add 1 crushed garlic clove, 1½ tablespoons yellow bean sauce, 2 teaspoons oyster sauce and 2 teaspoons sugar and toss well. Combine 2 teaspoons cornflour (cornstarch) with 170 ml (5½ fl oz) water, add to the sauce with 1 sliced spring onion (scallion) and simmer until the sauce has thickened and the spring onion has softened slightly.
Serves 4.

SICHUAN-STYLE EGGPLANT

Peel 500 g (1 lb) Chinese or thin eggplants (aubergines) and trim off the ends. Cut in half lengthways and cut each half into strips 2 cm (¾ inch) thick. Cut the strips into 5 cm (2 inch) lengths. Put the eggplant in a bowl with ½ teaspoon salt and toss lightly, then leave for 1 hour. Pour off any liquid. Put the eggplant on a heatproof plate and sit in a steamer. Cover and steam over simmering water in a wok for 15 minutes, or until tender. Combine ¼ cup (60 ml/2 fl oz) light soy sauce, 1 tablespoon Chinese rice wine, 1 tablespoon roasted sesame oil, 2 teaspoons clear rice vinegar, 1 teaspoon sugar, 1 finely chopped spring onion (scallion), 2 finely chopped garlic cloves and 1 teaspoon chilli bean paste (toban jiang), then pour the sauce over the eggplant, tossing lightly to coat. Serves 6.

HOT AND SOUR CABBAGE

Separate the leaves from 1 small Chinese cabbage (wom bok) and trim off the stems. Cut the leaves across their length into 1 cm (½ inch) wide strips, separating the stems from the leaves. Combine ⅓ cup (80 ml/2¾ fl oz) Chinese black vinegar, ¼ cup (60 ml/2 fl oz) light soy sauce, 2 tablespoons sugar and ½ teaspoon salt. Heat a wok over high heat, add 1 tablespoon oil and heat until very hot. Stir-fry 1 chopped red chilli and 2½ tablespoons finely chopped ginger for 15 seconds. Add 1½ diced red capsicums (peppers) and stir-fry for 30 seconds, then add 1½ tablespoons Chinese rice wine and stir-fry for 30 seconds. Add the cabbage stems, toss lightly and cook for 1 minute. Add the leaves and toss lightly, then pour in the soy sauce mixture, tossing lightly to coat. Cook for 30 seconds, then add 1 teaspoon roasted sesame oil. Serves 6.

STIR-FRIED WATER SPINACH

Wash and dry 1 kg (2 lb) water spinach. Remove any tough lower stalks and only use the young stems and leaves. Heat a wok over high heat, add 1½ tablespoons oil and heat until very hot. Stir-fry the water spinach for 1 minute, or until it begins to wilt. Drain in a colander. Add another tablespoon of oil to the wok with 2 teaspoons shrimp paste, 3 crushed garlic cloves and 1–2 seeded and chopped red chillies, and toss over medium heat for 1 minute. Add the water spinach, 2 teaspoons oyster sauce and 2 teaspoons sugar and toss for 1 minute. Serves 4.

FROM LEFT: Chinese broccoli in oyster sauce, Tofu in yellow bean sauce, Sichuan-style eggplant, Hot and sour cabbage, Stir-fried water spinach

CHRISTMAS

PEAR-SHAPED POTATO CROQUETTES

Preparation time: 30 minutes +
    1 hour 30 minutes refrigeration
Total cooking time: 20 minutes
Makes 12

600 g (1¼ lb) floury potatoes, peeled and
    chopped
1 egg
1 egg yolk
60 g (2 oz) Parmesan, grated
¼ cup (40 g/1¼ oz) finely chopped ham
3 tablespoons chopped fresh parsley
plain flour, for coating
1 egg, lightly beaten, extra
1 cup (100 g/3½ oz) dry breadcrumbs
2–3 strands raw spaghetti
oil, for deep-frying

1 Cook the potato for 5–10 minutes, or
until tender (pierce with the point of a
small knife—if the potato comes away
easily, it is ready). Drain and mash
thoroughly. While the potato is still hot,
gradually stir or fold in the combined
beaten egg and egg yolk, Parmesan, ham
and parsley. Divide into 12 portions, put on
a tray, cover with plastic wrap and
refrigerate for at least 1 hour.
2 Shape the potato portions into small
pear shapes and coat each in the flour,
egg and then the breadcrumbs. Break the
spaghetti into short lengths and insert
one piece into the top of each pear shape
to represent a stalk. Put on a non-stick
tray or a baking tray covered with baking
paper. Refrigerate for at least 30 minutes,
to firm.
3 Fill a large heavy-based saucepan one
third full of oil and heat to 180°C (350°F),
or until a cube of bread browns in 15
seconds. Cook the potato pears, three or
four at a time so the pan does not
overcrowd, for 2 minutes, or until evenly
browned and heated through. Drain on
crumpled paper towels. Serve hot or
warm.

STEAMED PRAWN WON TONS

Preparation time: 30 minutes
Total cooking time: 10–15 minutes
Makes 24

¾ cup (15 g/½ oz) dried Chinese
    mushrooms, sliced
24 raw prawns
1 tablespoon sake
1 tablespoon grated fresh ginger
1 teaspoon sesame oil
2 teaspoons sweet chilli sauce
24 gow gee wrappers

Dipping sauce
¼ cup (60 ml/2 fl oz) soy sauce
1 tablespoon fish sauce
1 tablespoon lime juice
¼ cup (60 ml/2 fl oz) sweet chilli sauce

1 Put the Chinese mushrooms in a
heatproof bowl, pour boiling water over
and soak for 10 minutes. Drain well and
finely chop. Meanwhile, peel the prawns,
leaving the tails intact. Gently pull out the
dark vein from each prawn back, starting
at the head end. Cut the prawns in half
and set aside the ends with the tails.
Finely chop the remaining prawns.
2 Combine the mushrooms and chopped
prawns with the sake, ginger, sesame oil
and chilli sauce. Put a heaped teaspoon of
the mixture in the centre of each gow gee
wrapper. Place a reserved prawn tail in
the centre of each, standing up. Brush the
edges of the wrappers with water and
gather up to form parcels, leaving the
prawn tails exposed. Steam in batches, in
a bamboo steamer for 5 minutes, or until
the prawns turn pink.
3 Stir together all the dipping sauce
ingredients in a bowl and serve with the
pyramids.

COUSCOUS WITH PEAR AND VEGETABLE TAGINE

Preparation time: 20 minutes
Total cooking time: 1 hour
Serves 4–6

½ preserved lemon
3 tablespoons oil
2 onions, chopped
1 teaspoon ground ginger
2 teaspoons ground paprika
2 teaspoons ground cumin
1 cinnamon stick
pinch of saffron threads
1.5 kg (3 lb) vegetables (eg. carrot, eggplant,
    parsnip, potato, pumpkin), cut into chunks
400 g (13 oz) can peeled tomatoes
1 cup (250 ml/8 fl oz) vegetable stock
100 g (3½ oz) dried pears, halved
50 g (1¾ oz) pitted prunes
2 zucchini (courgettes), cut into large chunks
3 tablespoons chopped fresh flat-leaf parsley
300 g (10 oz) couscous
⅓ cup (30 g/1 oz) flaked or slivered
    almonds, toasted

1 Preheat the oven to 180°C (350°F/Gas 4).
Remove the flesh from the preserved
lemon and thinly slice the lemon rind.
2 Heat 2 tablespoons of the oil in a large
saucepan or ovenproof dish, add the onion
and cook over medium heat for 5 minutes,
or until soft. Add the spices and cook for
3 minutes. Add all the vegetables, except
the zucchini, and stir until coated with the
spices and the outsides begin to soften.
Add the lemon, tomatoes, stock, pears
and prunes. Cover (if using a saucepan
transfer to an ovenproof dish) and bake for
30 minutes. Add the zucchini and cook,
uncovered, for 15 minutes, or until the
vegetables are tender. Remove the
cinnamon stick, then stir in the parsley.
3 Cover the couscous with the remaining
oil and 2 cups (500 ml/16 fl oz) boiling
water and stand until all the water has been
absorbed. Fluff with a fork and serve on the
outside of a platter, with the vegetables in
the centre. Sprinkle with the almonds.

LOBSTER WITH PARSLEY MAYONNAISE

Preparation time: 25 minutes
Total cooking time: Nil
Serves 4

2 cooked medium rock lobsters
mixed lettuce leaves, for serving
lemon wedges, for serving
fresh chives, chopped, for serving

Parsley mayonnaise
2 cups (40 g/1¼ oz) firmly packed fresh
    parsley sprigs, stalks removed
3 teaspoons Dijon mustard
1 teaspoon honey
1 tablespoon lemon juice
¼ cup (60 ml/2 fl oz) cream
¼ cup (60 g/2 oz) whole-egg mayonnaise

1 Using a sharp knife, cut each lobster in half lengthways through the shell. Lift the meat from the tail and body. Crack the legs and prise the meat from them. Remove the cream-coloured vein and soft body matter and discard. Cut the lobster meat into 2 cm (¾ inch) pieces, cover and refrigerate.
2 For the parsley mayonnaise, finely chop the parsley sprigs and put in a food processor with the mustard, honey, lemon juice, cream and mayonnaise. Blend until well combined, then season, to taste, with salt and cracked black pepper. Spoon the mixture into a bowl or jug, cover and refrigerate until required.
3 Place a bed of lettuce on each serving plate, top with slices of lobster and spoon parsley mayonnaise over the top. Serve with wedges of lemon and a sprinkle of chopped fresh chives.

ROAST PORK FILLET WITH APPLE AND MUSTARD SAUCE AND GLAZED APPLES

Preparation time: 30 minutes
Total cooking time: 25 minutes
Serves 4

750 g (1½ lb) pork fillet
30 g (1 oz) butter
1 tablespoon oil
1 clove garlic, crushed
½ teaspoon grated fresh ginger
1 tablespoon seeded mustard
¼ cup (60 ml/2 fl oz) apple sauce
2 tablespoons chicken stock
½ cup (125 ml/4 fl oz) cream
1 teaspoon cornflour

Glazed apples
2 green apples
50 g (1¾ oz) butter
2 tablespoons soft brown sugar

1 Trim the pork fillet, removing any fat or sinew from the outside. Tie the fillet with kitchen string at 3 cm (1¼ inch) intervals to keep in shape.
2 Heat the butter and oil in a frying pan, add the pork fillet and cook until lightly browned all over. Remove and place on a rack in a baking dish. (Retain the cooking oils in the frying pan.) Add ½ cup (125 ml/4 fl oz) water to the baking dish and bake in a moderate 180°C (350°F/Gas 4) oven for 15–20 minutes. Leave in a warm place for 10 minutes before removing the string and slicing.
3 For the sauce, reheat the oils in the frying pan, add the garlic and ginger and stir for 1 minute. Stir in the mustard, apple sauce and stock. Slowly stir in the combined cream and cornflour and stir until the mixture boils and thickens.
4 For the glazed apples, cut the apples into 1 cm (½ inch) slices. Melt the butter in the pan and add the sugar. Stir until the sugar dissolves. Add the apple slices and pan-fry, turning occasionally, until the apples are glazed and lightly browned.
5 Slice the pork and serve the apple and mustard sauce over it. Serve with the glazed apples.

NOTE: Pork fillets can be thick and short or long and thin and the time they take to cook will vary accordingly.

OYSTERS

THERE IS PROBABLY NOTHING MORE DELICIOUS THAN A FRESH OYSTER STRAIGHT FROM THE SHELL, BUT OYSTERS ARE ALSO SUPERB WHEN COMBINED WITH OTHER FLAVOURS. THESE RECIPES ALL USE 24 OYSTERS.

OYSTERS WRAPPED IN CUCUMBER

Trim the ends from a Lebanese cucumber with a vegetable peeler, then carefully peel 24 long thin strips from the entire width of the cucumber. Cut 8–10 chives into lengths 1 cm (½ inch) longer than the width of the cucumber strip. Place an oyster and 3 lengths of chive on one end of each cucumber strip, so the chives stick out the top. Roll up to enclose. Place 24 chives in a small bowl, cover with boiling water, then drain. Tie a chive around each roll to secure. Stand upright and top each with a little sour cream and salmon roe.

OYSTERS WITH PINE NUTS AND BACON

Remove 24 oysters from their shells. Clean and dry the shells. Finely chop 2 rindless rashers of bacon and fry in a frying pan for about 2 minutes, or until just soft. Remove from the pan. Melt 30 g (1 oz) butter in the same pan, add 1 finely chopped small onion and stir until soft. Add 125 g (4 oz) torn rocket leaves to the pan and stir until just wilted. Stir in 2 teaspoons Worcestershire sauce. Divide the rocket among the oyster shells, replace the oysters in the shells and top with the combined bacon and 2 tablespoons roughly chopped toasted pine nuts. Grill under a hot grill for 2–3 minutes, or until the bacon is crisp.

OYSTERS IN POTATOES WITH CHEESE SAUCE

Cook 24 baby new potatoes in boiling water for 5 minutes, or until tender. Drain and cool. Slice a round from the top of each potato and with a melon baller, scoop a ball from the centre of each. Trim the bases to sit flat. Fill a saucepan one third full of oil and heat to 180°C (350°F), or until a cube of bread dropped in the oil turns brown in 15 seconds. Deep-fry the potatoes until golden, then drain on paper towels. Melt 15 g (½ oz) butter in a small saucepan, add 24 oysters and toss quickly to seal. Remove from the pan. Add half a small finely chopped onion to the pan and fry until soft. Add 1 tablespoon brandy and, keeping away from anything flammable, ignite with a match. Allow the flames to die down. Add ½ cup (125 ml/ 4 fl oz) cream, bring to the boil, then reduce the heat and simmer until slightly thickened. Remove from the heat, stir in ¼ cup (30 g/1 oz) grated Cheddar and 2 teaspoons chopped fresh dill. Season. Return the oysters to the sauce, then spoon into the potatoes. Grill until golden brown. Sprinkle with dill.

CRUMBED OYSTERS WITH WASABI CREAM

Remove 24 oysters from their shells. Clean and dry the shells. Toss the oysters in plain flour, then in 1 beaten egg. Toss in ⅔ cup (55 g/2 oz) fresh breadcrumbs, combined with 1 tablespoon sesame seeds and 2 teaspoons black sesame seeds. Fill a saucepan one third full of oil and heat to 180°C (350°F), or until a cube of bread dropped in the oil browns in 15 seconds. Deep-fry the oysters until golden, then drain. Beat 1½ tablespoons cream until thick, then beat in 1 teaspoon wasabi paste and 2 tablespoons mayonnaise. Spoon a little into each dried shell. Top with an oyster and a piece of segmented lime. (Remove the rind and pith with a sharp knife, then cut between the membranes to release the segments.)

OYSTERS WITH BLOODY MARY SAUCE

Remove 24 oysters from their shells. Clean and dry the shells. Combine ¼ cup (60 ml/2 fl oz) tomato juice, 2 teaspoons vodka, 1 teaspoon lemon juice, ½ teaspoon Worcestershire sauce and a few drops of Tabasco sauce in a small bowl. Cut 1 celery stick into very thin julienne strips and place in the bases of the oyster shells. Top with an oyster and drizzle with tomato mixture. Sprinkle with 1–2 teaspoons snipped chives.

FROM LEFT: Oysters wrapped in cucumber; Oysters with pine nuts and bacon; Crumbed oysters with wasabi cream (top); Oysters in potatoes with cheese sauce; Oysters with bloody Mary sauce

DRESSED CRAB

Preparation time: 40 minutes + freezing
Total cooking time: 15 minutes
Serves 1–2

1 kg (2 lb) live mud crab
2–3 teaspoons lemon juice
1½ tablespoons whole-egg mayonnaise
1 cup (80 g/2¾ oz) fresh breadcrumbs
1 teaspoon Worcestershire sauce
2 hard-boiled eggs
2 tablespoons chopped fresh parsley
1 tablespoon chopped fresh chives

1 Freeze the crab for about 1 hour to immobilize it, then drop it into a large pan of boiling water. Reduce the heat and simmer for 10–15 minutes, or until bright orange all over— it should be cooked through by this stage. Drain and cool.
2 Twist the claws off the crab. Pull back the small flap on the underside of the crab and prise off the top shell. Scrape out any creamy brown meat and set aside. Wash and dry the top shell and set aside. Remove the intestines and grey feathery gills from the main body and discard. Scrape out any remaining creamy brown meat and add to the rest. Cut the crab in half and remove the white meat. Crack the claws and remove any meat. Keep the white meat separate.
3 Finely chop the brown crab meat and combine with the lemon juice, mayonnaise and enough of the breadcrumbs to combine. Add the Worcestershire sauce and salt and pepper, to taste.
4 Press the egg yolks and whites separately through a sieve.
5 Place the white crab meat inside the dry crab shell, on both the outside edges. Spoon the brown meat mixture into the centre of the shell and arrange the combined parsley and chives, sieved yolks and whites in rows over the brown crab meat. Can be served with bread, lemon wedges and extra mayonnaise.

POACHED OCEAN TROUT

Preparation time: 50 minutes
Total cooking time: 50 minutes
Serves 8–10

2 litres (64 fl oz) good-quality white wine
¼ cup (60 ml/2 fl oz) white wine vinegar
2 onions
10 whole cloves
4 carrots, chopped
1 lemon, cut in quarters
2 bay leaves
4 stalks fresh parsley
1 teaspoon whole black peppercorns
2.5 kg (5 lb) ocean trout, cleaned, gutted and scaled

Dill mayonnaise
1 egg, at room temperature
1 egg yolk, at room temperature
1 tablespoon lemon juice
1 teaspoon white wine vinegar
1½ cups (375 ml/12 fl oz) light olive oil
1–2 tablespoons chopped fresh dill

1 Combine the wine and vinegar with 2.5 litres (80 fl oz) water in a large heavy-based pan.
2 Stud the onions with the cloves. Add to the pan with the carrot, lemon, bay leaves, parsley and peppercorns. Bring to the boil, reduce the heat and simmer for 30–35 minutes. Cool. Strain into a fish kettle that will hold the trout.

3 Place the whole fish in the fish kettle and add water if necessary, to just cover the fish. Bring to the boil, then reduce the heat to a low simmer, cover and poach gently for 10–15 minutes, until the fish flakes when tested in the thickest part. Remove the kettle from the heat and leave the fish to cool in the liquid.
4 For the dill mayonnaise, process the egg, yolk, lemon juice and wine vinegar in a food processor for 10 seconds, or until blended. With the motor running, add the oil in a thin, steady stream, blending until all the oil is added and the mayonnaise is thick and creamy—it should be thick enough to form peaks. Transfer to a bowl and stir in the dill and salt and pepper, to taste.
5 Remove the cold fish from the liquid, place on a serving platter and peel back the skin. Garnish with watercress and lemon slices. Serve with the dill mayonnaise.

NOTE: Atlantic salmon, snapper, sea bass or red emperor can also be used. If you don't have a fish kettle, use a baking dish big enough to hold the fish, cover and bake in a moderate 180°C (350°F/Gas 4) oven for 20–30 minutes.

SEAFOOD TERRINE

Preparation time: 1 hour
Total cooking time: 35 minutes +
    cooling + chilling
Serves 8

First layer
500 g (1 lb) raw medium prawns, chilled
2 egg whites, chilled
pinch of freshly grated nutmeg
1 cup (250 ml/8 fl oz) cream, chilled
150 g (5 oz) baby green beans

Second layer
250 g (8 oz) skinless salmon or ocean
    trout fillet, chopped
2 egg whites, chilled
2 tablespoons chopped fresh chives
1 cup (250 ml/8 fl oz) cream, chilled

Tomato coulis
750 g (1½ lb) very ripe Roma (egg)
    tomatoes
2 tablespoons extra virgin olive oil
1 onion, very finely chopped
2 tablespoons Grand Marnier (optional)

1 Preheat the oven to moderate 180°C
(350°F/Gas 4). Brush a 1.5 litre (48 fl oz)
capacity loaf tin, measuring 22 x 12 cm
(9 x 5 inches), with oil and line the base
with baking paper.
2 For the first layer, peel the prawns and
gently pull out the dark vein from each
prawn back, starting at the head end.
Finely chop the prawns in a food
processor. Add the egg whites one at a
time, processing until smooth. Season
with salt, pepper and nutmeg. Gradually
add the cream. Don't over-process or it
will curdle. Spoon into the prepared loaf
tin, cover and refrigerate.

3 Cook the beans in boiling water until
tender, then drain and plunge into cold
water. Drain and dry with paper towels.
Arrange lengthways over the prawn
mixture.
4 For the second layer, process the fish
until finely chopped. Add the egg whites
one at a time and process until smooth.
Add the chives. Gradually add the cream.
Do not over-process or it may curdle.
Spread evenly over the beans.
5 Cover the terrine tightly with foil
brushed with oil and place in a baking
dish. Pour cold water into the dish to
come halfway up the side of the tin. Bake
for 35 minutes, or until lightly set in the
centre. Cool before removing the foil.
Cover with plastic wrap and refrigerate
until firm. Serve at room temperature.
6 For the tomato coulis, score a cross in
the base of each tomato. Place in a
heatproof bowl and cover with boiling
water. Leave for 30 seconds, transfer to
cold water, drain and peel away from the
cross. Cut the tomatoes in half, scoop out
the seeds with a teaspoon and chop the
flesh. Heat the oil, add the onion and stir
for 2–3 minutes, or until tender. Add the
tomato and cook over medium heat,
stirring often, for 8 minutes, or until
reduced and thickened slightly. Stir in the
Grand Marnier and cook for 1 minute.
Cool, then process until smooth. Season,
to taste, and serve with slices of terrine.

CHRISTMAS HAM AND CIDER CASSEROLE

Preparation time: 15 minutes
Total cooking time: 25 minutes
Serves 4

40 g (1¼ oz) butter
1 onion, chopped
2 leeks, white part only, finely sliced
2 cloves garlic, crushed
8 slices ham, chopped
100 ml (3½ fl oz) apple cider
300 g (10 oz) can butter beans, rinsed and
    drained
⅓ cup (25 g/¾ oz) fresh breadcrumbs
1 tablespoon grated Parmesan

1 Preheat the oven to moderately hot
200°C (400°F/Gas 6). Melt half the butter
in a heavy-based frying pan, add the onion
and cook over low heat for 2–3 minutes,
or until tender. Add the leek and stir until
cooked through. Stir in the garlic.
2 Transfer the onion mixture to an
ovenproof dish. Scatter the ham over the
top and season with freshly ground black
pepper. Pour in the apple cider. Spoon the
butter beans over and around the ham
and sprinkle with the breadcrumbs and
Parmesan. Dot with the remaining butter
and bake for 20 minutes, or until lightly
golden on top.

NOTE: This can also be cooked in
individual ramekin dishes—check them
after 15 minutes as they may not take as
long to cook. Leftover turkey can be
chopped and used instead of the ham. For
a creamy casserole, stir ½ cup (125 g/4 oz)
sour cream into the leek mixture with the
garlic.

GLAZED HAM

THE SIZE OF HAM WE HAVE USED IS ENOUGH FOR ABOUT 20 PEOPLE. CHOOSE YOUR FAVOURITE GLAZE AND FOLLOW THE DIRECTIONS BELOW. CARVING IS EASIER IF YOU HOLD ONTO THE UNGLAZED SHANK END.

PREPARING, GLAZING AND HEATING LEG HAM

Preheat the oven to moderate 180°C (350°F/Gas 4). Cut a line through the thick rind of a 7 kg (14 lb) smoked, cooked leg ham, 6 cm (2½ inches) from the shank end so you can easily lift the rind. (For an uncooked leg of ham, refer to the note further on.) To remove the rind, run your thumb around the edge, under the rind and carefully pull back, easing your hand under the rind between the fat and the rind. With a sharp knife, lightly score the fat to form a diamond pattern. Do not cut all the way through to the ham or the fat will fall off during cooking. Spread half the glaze of your choice over the ham with a palette knife or the back of a spoon and press a clove into the centre of each diamond. Put the ham on a rack in a deep baking dish and pour 2 cups (500 ml/ 16 fl oz) water into the dish. Cover the ham and dish securely with greased foil and cook for 45 minutes. Remove from the oven and brush or spread the remaining glaze over the ham. Increase the heat to hot 210°C (415°F/Gas 6-7) and bake, uncovered, for 20 minutes, or until the surface is lightly caramelized. Set aside for 15 minutes before carving.

NOTE: If you are using an uncooked leg ham, for a 7 kg (14 lb) leg ham, soak the ham overnight in a large clean bucket or container of cold water, changing the water a couple of times. Preheat the oven to warm 160°C (315°F/Gas 2-3). Tip out

the soaking water and rinse the ham thoroughly under cold running water. Pat dry with paper towels and place in a deep baking dish large enough to hold the ham (the end may stick out slightly). Chop an onion, carrot and stick of celery and place around the baking dish with a couple of bay leaves and a few peppercorns. Pour 2 cups (500 ml/16 fl oz) cold water into the dish and cover the dish completely with foil. Bake for 2 hours 40 minutes (20 minutes per kilo, plus 20 minutes). When cooked, remove the ham from the liquid and discard the liquid and vegetables. Allow the ham to cool (this can be done several days ahead if you wish). When ready to use, prepare, glaze and heat as described for the cooked leg of ham above.

HONEY GLAZE

Mix ⅔ cup (125 g/4 oz) soft brown sugar, 3 tablespoons honey and 1 tablespoon hot English mustard together in a bowl.

ORANGE GLAZE

Stir together 1 cup (250 ml/8 fl oz) orange juice, ¾ cup (140 g/4½ oz) soft brown sugar, 1 tablespoon French mustard, ½ cup (175 g/6 oz) honey, 2 teaspoons soy sauce and 2 tablespoons Grand Marnier in a bowl.

MUSTARD AND REDCURRANT GLAZE

Put ⅓ cup (90 g/3 oz) Dijon mustard, 1 cup (315 g/10 oz) redcurrant jelly, 4 crushed cloves of garlic and 2 tablespoons each of oil and soy sauce into a small saucepan. Stir and gently warm over medium heat for 2–3 minutes, or until the jelly has melted. Take care the glaze doesn't catch on the base of the pan.

ROAST CHICKEN WITH BACON AND SAGE STUFFING

Preparation time: 15 minutes
Total cooking time: 1 hour 10 minutes
Serves 6

2 x 1.2 kg (2 lb 7 oz) chickens
4 rashers bacon
2 tablespoons oil
1 small onion, finely chopped
1 tablespoon chopped fresh sage
1½ cups (125 g/4 oz) fresh breadcrumbs
1 egg, lightly beaten

1 Preheat the oven to moderate 180°C (350°F/Gas 4). Remove the giblets and any large fat deposits from the chickens. Wipe over and pat dry inside and out with paper towels.
2 Finely chop two of the bacon rashers. Heat half the oil in a small frying pan. Add the onion and the finely chopped bacon and cook until the onion is soft and the bacon is starting to brown. Transfer to a bowl and cool. Add the sage, breadcrumbs and egg to the onion, season, to taste, and mix lightly. Spoon some stuffing into each chicken cavity.
3 Fold the wings back and tuck under the chickens. Tie the legs of each chicken together with string. Place the chickens on a rack in a large baking dish, making sure they are not touching, and brush with some of the remaining oil. Pour 1 cup (250 ml/8 fl oz) water into the baking dish.
4 Cut the remaining bacon into long, thin strips and lay across the chicken breasts. Brush the bacon with oil. Bake for 45–60 minutes, or until the juices run clear when a thigh is pierced with a skewer.

NOTE: This chicken dish is delicious served with the Gravy with Wine (see Sauces) and roast vegetables.

ROAST RACK OF VENISON

Preparation time: 30 minutes +
    overnight marinating
Total cooking time: 35 minutes
Serves 6–8

Marinade
1 cup (250 ml/8 fl oz) red wine
¼ cup (60 ml/2 fl oz) olive oil
2 tablespoons brandy
1 spring onion or brown onion, finely chopped
2 cloves garlic, crushed
2 bay leaves
6 juniper berries, crushed
1 tablespoon fresh thyme leaves
8 whole black peppercorns

2 racks of venison (10 chops per rack)
1 cup (250 ml/8 fl oz) beef stock
1 tablespoon redcurrant jelly
2 tablespoons port
40 g (1¼ oz) butter, cut into small cubes
20 whole canned chestnuts
    (about 150 g/5 oz)

1 Stir the marinade ingredients together in a large bowl. Put the venison racks in the bowl and turn them over a few times until coated in the marinade. Cover and marinate in the refrigerator overnight, turning occasionally.

2 Preheat the oven to hot 220°C (425°F/Gas 7). Remove the venison racks from the marinade, reserving the marinade. Roast the racks for 30 minutes for medium, or slightly longer if you prefer well-done meat. Remove from the oven, cover with foil and leave to rest for 10 minutes while you make the sauce.
3 Put the reserved marinade in a small saucepan with the beef stock and bring to the boil over medium heat. Boil until reduced to 1 cup (250 ml/8 fl oz). Reduce the heat, stir in the redcurrant jelly and port and simmer gently. Whisk 30 g (1 oz) butter into the sauce until amalgamated. Remove from the heat.
4 Drain the chestnuts and heat in a small saucepan with the remaining butter. Season with freshly ground black pepper.
5 Carve the racks into chops and serve with the hot chestnuts. Strain the warm sauce through a sieve and serve over the meat. Serve immediately. Bread sauce (see Sauces) is often served with the venison.

ROAST CHICKEN WITH RICE STUFFING

Preparation time: 20 minutes +
   1 hour standing
Total cooking time: 1 hour 35 minutes
Serves 4

½ cup (95 g/3 oz) wild rice
15 pitted prunes, quartered
2 tablespoons port
⅓ cup (45 g/1½ oz) hazelnuts
60 g (2 oz) butter
4 spring onions, finely chopped
½ green apple, coarsely grated
½ teaspoon grated orange rind
½ teaspoon ground cardamom
1 egg, lightly beaten
1.5 kg (3 lb) chicken

1 Measure the rice into a saucepan and add enough boiling water to come 2.5 cm (1 inch) above the rice. Bring to the boil, reduce the heat and simmer for 10 minutes. Remove from the heat, cover and leave for 1 hour, then drain well.
2 Preheat the oven to moderate 180°C (350°F/Gas 4). Combine the prunes and port in a bowl, cover and set aside.
3 Bake the hazelnuts on a baking tray for 8 minutes. Wrap in a tea towel and rub off the skins. Coarsely chop the hazelnuts.
4 Melt half the butter in a pan and add the spring onion. Cook over low heat, stirring, for 2 minutes or until soft. Remove from the heat and mix in the rice, prune and port mixture, hazelnuts, apple, orange rind, cardamom and beaten egg. Season.
5 Wipe the chicken and pat dry inside and out with paper towels. Spoon the stuffing into the cavity and close with a toothpick or skewer. Tuck the wings under the chicken and tie the drumsticks securely together with string. Place on a rack in a baking dish.
6 Melt the remaining butter and brush over the chicken. Bake for 1 hour 15 minutes, or until brown and tender. Cover loosely with foil and leave in a warm place for 10 minutes. Remove the toothpicks and string before carving.

ROAST DUCK

Preparation time: 40 minutes
Total cooking time: 2 hours 15 minutes
Serves 4

2 kg (4 lb) duck, with neck
2 chicken wings, chopped
½ cup (125 ml/4 fl oz) white wine
1 onion, chopped
1 carrot, sliced
1 ripe tomato, chopped
bouquet garni

Orange sauce
2 tablespoons shredded orange rind
⅔ cup (170 ml/5½ fl oz) orange juice
⅓ cup (80 ml/2¾ fl oz) Cointreau
2 teaspoons cornflour

1 Place the duck neck, chicken wings and wine in a pan. Boil over high heat for 5 minutes, or until the wine has reduced by half. Add the onion, carrot, tomato, bouquet garni and 2 cups (500 ml/16 fl oz) water. Bring to the boil and simmer gently for 40 minutes. Strain and set aside 1 cup (250 ml/8 fl oz) of the stock.
2 Preheat the oven to 180°C (350°F/Gas 4). Place the duck in a large saucepan, cover with boiling water, then drain. Dry with paper towels. With a fine skewer, prick all over the outside of the duck, piercing only the skin, not the flesh. Place the duck breast-side-down on a rack in a baking dish and bake for 50 minutes.
3 Drain off any fat, turn the duck over and pour the reserved stock into the pan. Bake for 40 minutes, or until the breast is golden brown. Remove the duck from the pan and leave in a warm place for 15 minutes before carving. Reserve any pan juices for making gravy or orange sauce.
4 For the sauce, skim any fat off the reserved pan juices. Place in a saucepan with the rind, juice and Cointreau and bring to the boil. Reduce the heat and simmer for 5 minutes. Blend the cornflour with 1 tablespoon water, add to the sauce and stir over heat until the mixture boils and thickens.

QUAILS WITH BACON AND ROSEMARY

Preparation time: 30 minutes
Total cooking time: 35 minutes
Serves 4

8 quails
1 onion, chopped
3 rashers bacon, chopped
1 tablespoon fresh rosemary leaves
30 g (1 oz) butter, melted
½ cup (125 ml/4 fl oz) port
½ cup (125 ml/4 fl oz) cream
1 teaspoon cornflour

1 Preheat the oven to moderately hot 200°C (400°F/Gas 6). Wash the quails thoroughly under cold running water, then dry thoroughly inside and out with paper towels. Tuck the wings underneath the quails and tie the legs close to the body with kitchen string.
2 Spread the onion, bacon and rosemary over the base of a baking dish, and add the quails. Brush each quail with melted butter. Combine the port with ¼ cup (60 ml/2 fl oz) of water, then pour ½ cup (125 ml/4 fl oz) of this mixture over the quails.
3 Bake for about 25 minutes, or until the juices run clear when the quails are pierced in the thigh with a skewer. Cover and leave for 10 minutes in a warm place.
4 Carefully strain any juices from the baking dish into a small saucepan, reserving the rosemary and bacon mixture. Add the remaining port and water mixture to the pan, and bring to the boil. Reduce the heat and gradually stir in the blended cream and cornflour, stirring until the mixture boils and is slightly thickened. Serve the quails with the sauce and the reserved rosemary and bacon mixture. Delicious with roast vegetables.

NOTE: This recipe can also be made with chicken thigh cutlets instead of the quails.

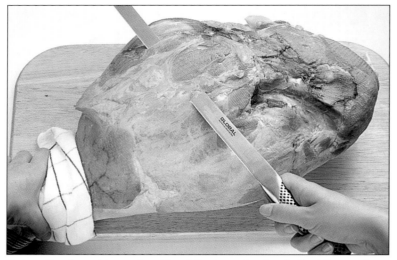

Cut a slice from the underside of the ham to steady it while carving.

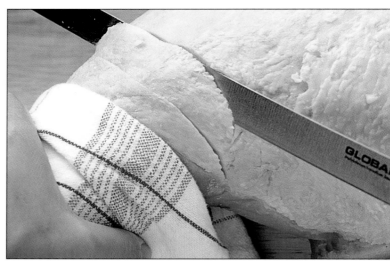

Remove a wedge of ham from the knuckle end before you carve.

Cut thin slices, working away from the knuckle.

Cut the slices away from the bone and serve.

HOW TO CARVE

CARVING A ROAST CAN BE TRICKY, SO FOLLOW THESE INSTRUCTIONS AND EVEN THE MOST INEXPERIENCED CARVER WILL BE ABLE TO SERVE A PERFECT CHRISTMAS ROAST IN A QUICK AND FUSS-FREE MANNER.

Turkey and ham are the most popular Christmas roasts—and the most daunting. They are rarely eaten at other times of the year and can easily confound even the most confident of cooks when it comes to carving and presenting them. Before carving any roast, it is important to let the meat 'rest' for 15 minutes or so. Remove the roast from the oven and cover it with foil so the heat does not escape too quickly and the juices can settle and distribute evenly, moistening and tenderizing the flesh.

Make sure your carving knife is sharp and try to slice rather than saw—the more you hack into the meat, tearing the flesh, the more juices are lost, making the meat dry. Electric knives can make life much easier. A carving fork is also important for holding the meat steady. Do not pierce the meat—try to use the back of the fork to get a good hold. When carving a bird, however, a sharp-pronged fork is needed to dig deep into the carcass (not the flesh) to keep it still.

Always carve on a carving board, not a serving platter. China and metal surfaces can scratch easily and can be quite slippery, causing you to lose control of the knife. It is preferable to use a carving board with a rim around the edges to catch any excess juices—this not only stops the juices from spilling over onto the table but it also means they can be strained off and used in your gravy for an extra boost of flavour. It is also a good idea to place a damp cloth underneath your board to keep it steady while carving.

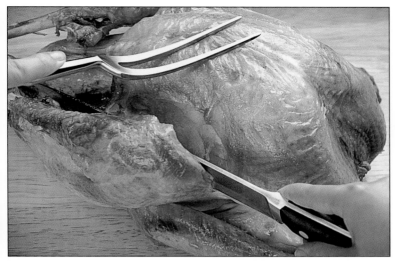

Remove the leg and thigh section from the body of the turkey.

With larger birds it is possible to separate the leg and thigh.

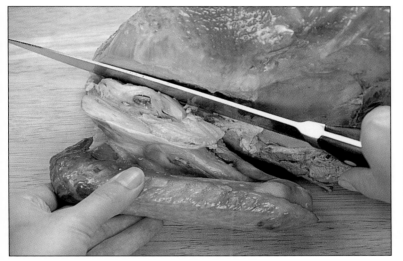

Similarly, remove the turkey wing by cutting through the joint.

Carve the turkey breast, using the fork to keep the bird steady.

HAM

1 After it has rested, place the ham on a cutting board with the bone to the left. Use a clean tea towel to hold the bone firmly while carving. Remember to keep your fingers away from the blade! Slice a piece from the underside of the leg so that it sits flat on the board. Remove this slice and set aside.

2 Slice into the meat about 10 cm (4 inches) from the knuckle. Make another cut at an angle to the first so that it forms a wedge, then remove. Continue cutting to the right, cutting several thin slices right down to the bone. The meat will still be attached to the bone so to release the pieces you must run the knife along the bone, under the meat. Lift off the slices with the flat of the knife. Cut enough slices for serving, covering the slices with foil as you go if the ham is to be served warm.

TURKEY

1 After it has rested, place the turkey on a cutting board, breast-side-up and with the legs facing you.

2 Use a carving fork to steady the bird and cut downward into the skin and meat where the leg meets the breast. Bend the leg outwards with the carving knife until you can see the joint where the thighbone and the backbone connect. Keep cutting at a slight angle towards the joint, then cut down and through it until the leg section (the thigh and drumstick) can be easily removed. Depending on the size of the turkey, you can also cut through the leg at the joint to remove the thigh and have two separate pieces. Set the meat aside on a warm serving dish and keep covered with foil while you are carving the rest of the turkey. This will keep it warm and stop it from drying out.

3 On the same side of the bird, find where the wing meets the body and cut down, again until you meet the joint. You may

need to pull the wing out with your left hand while you are cutting with your right hand to loosen the wing from the bird. Set aside and cover to keep warm.

4 Continuing on the same side, begin to carve the breast. Start at the top of the breast where it attaches to the ridge of bone and carve downwards in even slices, at a slight angle, towards the cutting board. Add to the rest of the meat and cover. Now repeat this process on the other side of the turkey. To remove the wishbone, snip the sinews on either side.

5 Remove the stuffing from the opening of the carcass with a spoon and, depending on the texture of the stuffing, serve it either in slices or in spoonfuls.

ROAST TURKEY WITH STUFFING

Preparation time: 45 minutes +
  making stuffing
Total cooking time: 2 hours
Serves 6–8

3 kg (6 lb) turkey
1 quantity stuffing (see recipes following)
2 tablespoons oil
2 cups (500 ml/16 fl oz) chicken stock
2 tablespoons plain flour

1 Remove the neck and giblets from inside the turkey. Wash the turkey well and pat dry inside and out with paper towels. Preheat the oven to moderate 180°C (350°F/Gas 4).
2 Make the stuffing you prefer and loosely stuff into the turkey cavity. Tuck the wings underneath and join the cavity with a skewer. Tie the legs together. Place on a rack in a baking dish. Roast for 2 hours, basting with the combined oil and ½ cup (125 ml/4 fl oz) of the stock. Cover the breast and legs with foil after 1 hour if the turkey is overbrowning. Remove from the oven, cover and leave to rest for 15 minutes.
3 To make the gravy, drain off all except 2 tablespoons of pan juices from the baking dish. Place the dish on the stove over low heat, add the flour and stir well. Stir over medium heat until browned. Gradually add the remaining stock, stirring until the gravy boils and thickens. Serve the turkey with gravy and roast vegetables.

NOTE: Do not stuff the turkey until you are ready to cook it. Stuffing can be made ahead of time and frozen for up to a month in an airtight container. If you prefer to cook the stuffing separately, press it lightly into a lightly greased ovenproof dish and bake for about 30 minutes, or until golden brown. Small greased muffin tins can also be used (bake for 15–20 minutes). Alternatively, you can form the mixture into balls and fry in a little melted butter or oil, over medium heat, until golden brown all over.

CITRUS STUFFING

Heat 1 tablespoon oil in a small frying pan and cook 1 finely chopped onion until soft. Transfer to a large bowl and cool. Add 200 g (6½ oz) sausage mince, 2 crushed cloves of garlic, 2 cups (160 g/5½ oz) fresh white breadcrumbs, 2 teaspoons each of grated lemon and orange rinds and ½ cup (60 g/2 oz) finely chopped pecans and mix well. Season, to taste, with salt and pepper and mix.

COUNTRY SAGE STUFFING

Melt 45 g (1½ oz) butter in a small saucepan and cook 1 finely chopped onion and 1 sliced celery stick over medium heat for 3 minutes, or until the onion has softened. Transfer to a bowl and add 10 shredded large fresh sage leaves, 2 cups (160 g/5½ oz) fresh white breadcrumbs, 1½ teaspoons dried sage, 4 tablespoons finely chopped fresh parsley, 2 lightly beaten egg whites, 1 teaspoon salt and ½ teaspoon white pepper.

CASHEW STUFFING

Melt 60 g (2 oz) butter in a frying pan and cook 1 chopped onion until golden. Cool, then mix thoroughly with 2 cups (370 g/12 oz) cooked long-grain brown rice, 1 cup (185 g/6 oz) chopped dried apricots, ½ cup (80 g/2¾ oz) unsalted cashews, 3 tablespoons chopped fresh parsley, 2 tablespoons chopped fresh mint and 1 tablespoon lemon juice. Season, to taste, with salt and pepper. (You will need to cook 1 cup/200 g/6½ oz brown rice for this recipe.)

QUAIL STUFFED WITH WILD RICE

Preparation time: 15 minutes
Total cooking time: 1 hour
Serves 4

¼ cup (50 g/1¾ oz) wild rice
1 cup (250 ml/8 fl oz) chicken stock
1 onion, finely chopped
20 g (¾ oz) butter
1 tablespoon finely chopped dried apricots
1 tablespoon finely chopped prunes
1 tablespoon chopped mixed parsley and chervil
4 quails
⅓ cup (80 ml/2¾ fl oz) olive oil

1 Heat the oven to 200°C (400°F/Gas 6). Put the wild rice and chicken stock in a saucepan and bring to the boil. Simmer for 30 minutes, or until tender, then drain.
2 Sauté the onion in the butter for 5 minutes, or until softened but not browned. Then add the apricots, prunes, parsley and chervil. Add the rice and season well.
3 Loosely fill the quails with the prepared rice stuffing and fasten them closed with cocktail sticks or toothpicks.
4 Heat the oil in a frying pan and brown the quails all over—you may need to do this in batches. Transfer to a roasting tin and cook for 15–20 minutes, or until a skewer inserted into the cavity comes out very hot. Serve the quails with a green salad and potatoes.

ROAST GOOSE

Preparation time: 15 minutes
Total cooking time: 1 hour 30 minutes
Serves 6

3 kg (6 lb) fresh or frozen goose
1 tablespoon plain flour
2 tablespoons brandy
1½ cups (375 ml/12 fl oz) chicken stock
bread sauce (see *Sauces*), for serving

1 If using a frozen goose, thaw in the refrigerator—it may take 1–2 days. Preheat the oven to moderate 180°C (350°F/Gas 4). Remove any excess fat from inside the cavity of the goose. Place the goose in a large pan, cover with boiling water, then drain. Dry thoroughly with paper towels.
2 Place the goose breast-side-down on a rack in a very large baking dish. (Make sure the goose doesn't sit directly on the dish or it will be very greasy.) Using a fine skewer, prick the skin of the goose all over, being careful to pierce only the skin, not the flesh.
3 Bake the goose for 1 hour, then remove from the oven and drain off any excess fat. Turn the goose over and bake for another 30 minutes, or until the outside is golden and crisp. Remove from the baking dish, cover loosely with foil and leave for 5–10 minutes.
4 For gravy, drain all except 2 tablespoons of fat from the baking dish and place the dish on the stove over low heat. Add the flour and stir to incorporate all the sediment. Stir constantly over medium heat until well browned, without burning. Remove from the heat and gradually stir in the brandy and chicken stock. Return to the heat and stir constantly, until the gravy boils and thickens. Season with salt and pepper, and serve with bread sauce.

GAME PIE

Preparation time: 40 minutes +
  refrigeration
Total cooking time: 2 hours 30 minutes
Serves 4–6

1 kg (2 lb) rabbit, boned, cut into bite-sized pieces
1.25 kg (2½ lb) venison goulash or diced venison
¼ cup (30 g/1 oz) plain flour
2–3 tablespoons oil
2 rashers bacon, chopped
1 onion, sliced into thin wedges
2 cloves garlic, crushed
150 g (5 oz) button mushrooms, cut in halves
1 cup (250 ml/8 fl oz) red wine
1 cup (250 ml/8 fl oz) beef stock
3 sprigs fresh thyme
2 bay leaves
1½ x 375 g (12 oz) blocks puff pastry, thawed
1 egg yolk
2 tablespoons milk

1 Lightly coat the rabbit and venison in seasoned flour. Heat the oil in a large saucepan and cook the bacon over medium heat until golden. Remove. Brown the meats well in batches, remove and set aside. Add the onion and garlic to the saucepan and cook until browned.
2 Return the bacon and meat to the saucepan and add the mushrooms, wine, stock, thyme and bay leaves. Bring to the boil, then reduce the heat and simmer over low heat, stirring occasionally, for 1½ hours, or until the meat is tender. Transfer to a heatproof bowl. Remove the thyme and bay leaves. Refrigerate until cold.

3 Preheat the oven to moderately hot 200°C (400°F/Gas 6). Spoon the mixture into a 2 litre (64 fl oz) ovenproof dish. Roll the half block of pastry on a lightly floured surface to about 5 mm (¼ inch) thick. Cut strips the width of the pie dish rim and secure to the dish with a little water. Reserve the leftover pastry. Roll the other block of pastry on a lightly floured surface until large enough to fit the top of the pie dish. Brush the edges of the pastry strips with a little combined egg yolk and milk. Drape the pastry over the rolling pin and lower it onto the top of the pie. Trim off any excess pastry using a sharp knife. Score the edges of the pastry with the back of a knife to seal. Use any leftover pastry to decorate the top. Cut two slits in the top of the pastry and brush all over with the remaining egg and milk mixture. Bake for 30–40 minutes, or until puffed and golden.

NOTE: Ask the butcher to bone the rabbit. Order the venison from the butcher or poultry shop.

SLOW-ROASTED LAMB WITH CUMIN AND PAPRIKA

Preparation time: 15 minutes
Total cooking time: 3 hours 30 minutes
Serves 6

2.2 kg (4 lb 6½ oz) leg of lamb
75 g (3 oz) butter, softened at room
    temperature
3 cloves garlic, crushed
2 teaspoons ground cumin
3 teaspoons ground coriander
1 teaspoon paprika
1 tablespoon cumin, extra, for dipping

1 Preheat the oven to hot 220°C (425°F/
Gas 7). With a small sharp knife, cut small
deep slits in the top and sides of the lamb.
2 Mix the butter, garlic, spices and
¼ teaspoon salt in a bowl until a smooth
paste forms.
3 With the back of a spoon rub the paste
all over the lamb, then use your fingers to
spread the paste and make sure all the
lamb is covered.
4 Put the lamb bone-side-down in a deep
baking dish and place on the top shelf of
the oven. Bake for 10 minutes, then baste
and return to the oven. Reduce the
temperature to warm 160°C (315°F/Gas
2–3). Bake for 3 hours 20 minutes, basting
every 20–30 minutes. Basting makes the
lamb tender and flavoursome. Carve the
lamb into chunky pieces. Mix the cumin
with 1½ teaspoons salt and serve on the
side for dipping.

ROAST TURKEY WITH RICE AND CHESTNUT STUFFING

Preparation time: 30 minutes +
    20 minutes soaking
Total cooking time: 3 hours 30 minutes
Serves 6–8

Stuffing
12 prunes, pitted
180 g (6 oz) whole fresh chestnuts
40 g (1¼ oz) butter
1 red onion, finely chopped
2 garlic cloves, crushed
60 g (2 oz) pancetta (including any fat),
    finely chopped
100 g (3½ oz) wild rice blend
¼ cup (60 ml/2 fl oz) chicken stock
3 dried juniper berries, lightly crushed
2 teaspoons finely chopped rosemary
3 teaspoons finely chopped thyme

3 kg (6 lb) turkey
1 large red onion, cut into 4–5 slices
30 g (1 oz) butter, softened
1½ cups (375 ml/12 fl oz) dry white wine
1 carrot, quartered
1 celery stalk, quartered
1 large rosemary sprig
2 teaspoons finely chopped thyme
1 cup (250 ml/8 fl oz) chicken stock
2 tablespoons plain (all-purpose) flour

1 Preheat the oven to warm 170°C
(325°F/Gas 3). Soak the prunes in hot
water for 20 minutes. Meanwhile, to
prepare the chestnuts, make a small cut
in the skin on the flat side, put under a hot
grill (broiler) and cook on both sides until
well browned. Put the hot chestnuts in a
bowl lined with a damp tea towel and
cover with the towel. Leave until cool
enough to handle, then peel. Do not allow
the chestnuts to cool completely before
peeling, as they will become harder to
peel as they cool. Coarsely chop the
prunes and chestnuts and set aside.

2 To make the stuffing, melt the butter in
a large saucepan and add the onion,
garlic and pancetta. Cook over low heat
for 5–6 minutes, or until the onion is
softened but not brown. Add the rice,
stock, juniper berries, prunes and
chestnuts, stir well, then pour in 1½ cups
(375 ml/12 fl oz) water. Bring to the boil
and cook, covered, stirring once or twice,
for 20–25 minutes, or until the rice is
tender and all the liquid has been
absorbed. Remove from the heat, stir in
the rosemary and thyme, then season.
3 Fill the turkey cavity with the stuffing.
Cross the turkey legs and tie them
together, then tuck the wings underneath
the body. Arrange the onion slices in the
centre of a large roasting tin, then sit the
turkey on top, breast-side up. Season well
and dot with butter. Pour 1 cup (250 ml/
8 fl oz) of the wine into the tin and scatter
the carrot, celery, rosemary and 1
teaspoon of the thyme around the turkey.
4 Roast for 2–2½ hours, or until cooked
through and the juices run clear, basting
every 30 minutes. After 1 hour, pour half
the chicken stock into the tin. Once the
skin becomes golden brown, cover with
buttered foil.
5 When cooked, transfer the turkey to a
carving plate, cover with foil and leave to
rest in a warm spot. Meanwhile, pour the
juices into a small saucepan and reduce
for 8–10 minutes. Stir in the flour, then
add a little of the stock at a time, stirring
to form a paste. Slowly add the rest of the
stock and wine, stirring so that no lumps
form. Stir in the remaining thyme. Bring
to the boil and continue to simmer for
6–8 minutes, or until reduced by one-
third, then season to taste. Transfer to a
gravy boat. Carve the turkey and serve
with the stuffing and gravy.

TURKEY ROLL WITH MANDARIN SAUCE

Preparation time: 1 hour +
  30 minutes soaking
Total cooking time: 2 hours
Serves 8

No. 34 (3.4 kg) turkey
90 g (3 oz) dried apricots, chopped
30 g (1 oz) butter
1 onion, finely chopped
1 clove garlic, crushed
400 g (13 oz) chicken mince
1½ cups (120 g/4 oz) fresh breadcrumbs
½ cup (35 g/1¼ oz) currants
½ cup (35 g/1¼ oz) pistachio nuts, toasted
  and chopped
3 tablespoons chopped fresh parsley

Mandarin sauce
2 mandarins
1 tablespoon long thin strips of mandarin
  rind
2 tablespoons sugar
1 tablespoon brandy
1 cup (250 ml/8 fl oz) mandarin juice
⅓ cup (80 ml/2¾ fl oz) chicken stock
3 teaspoons cornflour
1 spring onion, finely sliced

1 To bone the turkey, cut through the skin on the centre back with a sharp knife or pair of scissors. Separate the flesh from the bone down one side to the breast, being careful not to pierce the skin. Follow along the ribcage closely with the knife, gradually easing the meat from the bones. Repeat on the other side, then lift the rib cage away, leaving the flesh in one piece and the drumsticks still attached to the flesh. Cut off the wing tips and scrape all the meat from the drumsticks and wings, discarding the bones. Turn the wing and drumstick flesh inside the turkey and lay the turkey out flat, skin-side-down. Refrigerate.

2 Place the apricots in a small bowl, cover with boiling water and soak for 30 minutes. Preheat the oven to moderate 180°C (350°F/Gas 4).

3 Meanwhile, melt the butter in a frying pan, add the onion and garlic and cook, stirring, for about 5 minutes, or until the onion is soft. Remove from the heat. Combine the mince, onion mixture, breadcrumbs, currants, nuts, parsley and drained apricots in a large bowl and mix well. Season with salt and pepper and fry a little of the mixture to taste for seasoning. Adjust the seasoning if necessary. Place the turkey on the work surface skin-side-down and form the stuffing mixture into a large sausage shape about the same length as the turkey. Fold the turkey over to enclose the stuffing. Secure with toothpicks or skewers and truss with kitchen string at 3 cm (1¼ inch) intervals.

4 Place in a large lightly greased baking tray. Rub with a little extra oil and some salt and pepper. Roast the turkey roll for 1½ –2 hours, or until the juices run clear. Cover and set aside for 10 minutes while preparing the sauce. Carefully remove the string and toothpicks. Cut into slices and serve with the mandarin sauce. If you wish, make a gravy out of the pan juices .

5 For the mandarin sauce, firstly segment the mandarins. Use a sharp knife to remove the rind and white pith, then cut between the membranes to release the segments. Place the strips of mandarin rind in a small pan, cover with water and bring to the boil. Drain and repeat (this removes the bitterness from the rind). Sprinkle the sugar over the base of a saucepan over medium heat and stir gently until all the sugar has dissolved and turned caramel. Remove from the heat, cool slightly, then carefully stir in the brandy, stirring until combined. Return to the heat, stir to dissolve any toffee, then add the combined mandarin juice and chicken stock and stir until heated through. Add the combined cornflour and 1 tablespoon water and stir over heat until the mixture boils and thickens. Add the mandarin segments and rind, stirring until heated through. Stir in the spring onion, then season, to taste.

NOTE: You can ask your butcher or poulterer to bone the turkey. You may have to shop or ring around so leave yourself plenty of time. If time is short, buy a boned and rolled frozen turkey from the supermarket. Defrost according to the instructions, then follow the recipe.

ICE CREAM BOMBE

Preparation time: 20 minutes + overnight
    freezing + 25 minutes refrigeration
Total cooking time: 3 minutes
Serves 8

1 large mango, finely chopped
1 cup (160 g/5½ oz) canned pineapple
    pieces, drained
¼ cup (60 ml/2 fl oz) Grand Marnier
250 g (8 oz) fresh strawberries, puréed
400 g (13 oz) can condensed milk
2½ cups (600 ml/20 fl oz) cream
80 g (2¾ oz) dessert nougat, chopped
¼ cup (35 g/1¼ oz) roughly chopped
    unsalted pistachios
strawberries, extra, halved, to garnish

Toffee bark
⅓ cup (90 g/3 oz) caster sugar

1 Lightly grease a 2 litre (64 fl oz) pudding
basin and line with plastic wrap, allowing
it to hang over the side of the basin. Put in
the freezer until ready to use. Drain the
mango and pineapple in a sieve.
2 Mix the Grand Marnier, strawberry
purée and condensed milk in a large
bowl. Whisk the cream to soft peaks, then
add to the bowl and continue whisking
until thick. Fold in the drained fruits,
nougat and pistachios. Pour the mixture
into the pudding basin, cover with plastic
wrap and freeze overnight, or until firm.
3 To serve, remove the plastic wrap from

the base and invert the pudding onto a
chilled serving plate. Remove the bowl,
but leave the plastic wrap and refrigerate
for 15–25 minutes to soften slightly.
4 For the toffee bark, line a baking tray
with baking paper. Heat the sugar over
low heat in a heavy-based saucepan for
2–3 minutes, or until melted and golden.
Carefully pour onto the tray. Tilt the tray
to get a thin, even layer of toffee over the
paper and cool slightly. While still pliable,
drape the paper over a rolling pin and
allow to cool for 30–60 seconds before
peeling away strips of toffee in large
irregular shapes. Cool. To serve, remove
the plastic and decorate the bombe with
toffee bark and strawberries.

NOTE: Dessert nougat is a soft nougat
available at confectionery shops and
some delicatessens.

SPECULAAS

Preparation time: 20 minutes +
45 minutes refrigeration

Total cooking time: 12 minutes per tray
Makes about 48

3¼ cups (405 g/13 oz) plain flour
1 teaspoon ground cinnamon
¼ teaspoon ground nutmeg
¼ teaspoon ground cloves
¼ teaspoon ground cardamom
160 g (5½ oz) unsalted butter, softened
1⅓ cups (310 g/10 oz) soft brown sugar
1 egg
⅓ cup (80 ml/2¾ fl oz) milk
¼ cup (45 g/1½ oz) ground almonds
milk, extra, for glazing

1 Preheat the oven to moderately hot
200°C (400°F/Gas 6). Cover baking trays
with baking paper. Sift the flour, spices
and ¼ teaspoon salt together into a large
bowl.
2 Beat the butter and sugar together in a
bowl until pale and creamy. Beat in the
egg, mixing well, and then the milk. Fold
in the almonds, then the sifted flour and
spices and mix well. Wrap in plastic and
refrigerate for 45 minutes.
3 Divide the mixture into 4 portions and
roll each portion out on a lightly floured
surface to 4 mm (1/8 inch) thick. Cut into
shapes using Christmas-theme cutters
(stars, trees, candy canes or bells). Place
on the baking trays, leaving room for
spreading. Brush with milk and bake for
12 minutes, or until light brown. Repeat
with the remaining dough, returning any
scraps to the refrigerator to chill before
re-rolling. Cool the biscuits on wire racks.
When cold, store in airtight containers.

NOTE: This Christmas biscuit is from the
Rhine area in Germany and neighbouring
Holland.

FIGS WITH ORANGE CREAM AND RAISINS

Preparation time: 20 minutes + soaking
Total cooking time: 12 minutes
Serves 8

250 g (8 oz) raisins
155 ml (5 fl oz) tawny port
1 tablespoon custard powder
1 cup (250 ml/8 fl oz) skim milk
1 tablespoon sugar
100 g (3½ oz) fresh ricotta
200 g (6½ oz) light French vanilla frûche
   or fromage frais
rind and juice of 1 orange
1 teaspoon ground cinnamon
16 fresh figs

1 Soak the raisins in the tawny port for
1 hour or until plumped up.
2 In a small saucepan, blend the custard
powder with the milk, add the sugar and
stir over low heat until the sugar has
dissolved. Increase the heat and stir
continuously until the custard boils and
thickens. Remove from the heat
immediately, pour into a small bowl and
cover the surface with plastic wrap. Cool.
3 Transfer the completely cooled custard
to the small bowl of an electric mixer, add
the fresh ricotta and the frûche and beat
until smooth.
4 Just before serving, add the orange
rind, juice and cinnamon to the raisin
mixture in a small pan and warm over low
heat for 2–3 minutes. Cover and keep
warm.
5 Starting from the top, cut the figs into
quarters, slicing only two-thirds of the
way down. Place into ramekins or on a
large platter. Place 2 heaped tablespoons
of the orange cream into the centre of
each fig, top with a tablespoon of the
warm raisin mixture and serve at once.

NOTE: Frûche is a type of fromage frais
and is set in the cup.

TROPICAL CHEESECAKE

Preparation time: 50 minutes + chilling
Total cooking time: Nil
Serves 8

145 g (5 oz) plain sweet biscuits
¼ cup (25 g/¾ oz) desiccated coconut
90 g (3 oz) unsalted butter, melted

Filling
½ cup (125 ml/4 fl oz) fresh orange juice
6 teaspoons gelatine
350 g (11 oz) cream cheese, softened
⅓ cup (90 g/3 oz) caster sugar
2 tablespoons lemon juice
425 g (14 oz) can mangoes, drained and
   chopped, or 2 fresh mangoes, chopped
450 g (14 oz) can unsweetened crushed
   pineapple, drained
1¼ cups (315 ml/10 fl oz) cream
extra whipped cream, kiwi fruit and
   mango wedges, to decorate

1 Lightly grease a 20 cm (8 inch) diameter
springform tin and line the base with baking
paper. Put the biscuits in a food processor
and chop until they are finely crushed. Add
the coconut and butter and process until
well combined. Spoon into the tin, press
firmly over the base, then refrigerate.
2 Put the fresh orange juice in a small
heatproof bowl, sprinkle the gelatine in
an even layer over the surface and leave
to go spongy. Bring a large pan filled with
about 4 cm (1½ inches) water to the boil,
then remove from the heat. Carefully
lower the gelatine bowl into the water (it
should come halfway up the side of the
bowl), then stir until the gelatine has
dissolved. Allow to cool.
3 Beat the softened cream cheese and
caster sugar in a bowl for 3 minutes, or
until smooth. Beat in the lemon juice and
gently fold in the mango and crushed
pineapple. Fold in the dissolved gelatine.
4 Whip the cream into peaks. Fold into
the mixture with a metal spoon. Pour into
the tin, smooth and chill overnight. Decorate
with extra cream and slices of fruit.

SUMMER BERRIES IN CHAMPAGNE JELLY

Preparation time: 10 minutes +
   refrigeration
Total cooking time: 5 minutes
Serves 8

1 litre (32 fl oz) Champagne or sparkling
   white wine
1½ tablespoons powdered gelatine
1 cup (250 g/8 oz) sugar
4 strips lemon rind
4 strips orange rind
250 g (8 oz) small strawberries, hulled
250 g (8 oz) blueberries

1 Pour half the Champagne into a bowl
and let the bubbles subside. Sprinkle the
gelatine over the top in an even layer.
Leave until the gelatine is spongy—do not
stir. Pour the remaining Champagne into
a large saucepan, add the sugar and rinds
and heat gently, stirring constantly, until
all the sugar has dissolved.
2 Remove the saucepan from the heat,
add the gelatine mixture and stir until
thoroughly dissolved. Leave to cool
completely, then remove the rind.
3 Divide the berries among eight ½ cup
(125 ml/4 fl oz) stemmed wine glasses
and gently pour the jelly over them.
Refrigerate until set. Remove from the
refrigerator 15 minutes before serving.

FROSTED FRUIT CAKE

Preparation time: 30 minutes + overnight
  soaking + 1–2 hours decorating
Total cooking time: 3 hours 30 minutes
Makes 1

4 cups (640 g /1¼ lb) sultanas
3 cups (480 g/15 oz) raisins, chopped
2 cups (300 g/10 oz) currants
1¼ cups (265 g/8 oz) glacé cherries,
  quartered
1 cup (250 ml/8 fl oz) brandy or rum
250 g (8 oz) unsalted butter, chopped,
  softened
1 cup (230 g/7½ oz) dark brown sugar
2 tablespoons apricot jam
2 tablespoons treacle or golden syrup
1 tablespoon grated lemon or orange rind
4 eggs
2¾ cups (340 g/11 oz) plain flour
1 teaspoon mixed spice
1 teaspoon ground cinnamon
1 teaspoon ground ginger
1 tablespoon brandy or rum, extra

Decorations
selection of seasonal fruits such as white
  and dark cherries, small bunches of
  red, white and black currants, apricots,
  tiny plums or pears
1 egg white
caster sugar

Icing
1 egg white
1–3 teaspoons lemon juice
1 cup (125 g/4 oz) pure icing sugar, sifted

1 Put the fruit in a large bowl with the
brandy and leave to soak overnight.
Preheat the oven to slow 150°C
(300°F/Gas 2). Grease and line an oval
cake tin 18 x 25 cm (7 x 10 inch), or a
23 cm (9 inch) round cake tin, as shown
on pages 836–7.
2 Beat the butter and sugar in a small
bowl with electric beaters until just
combined. Beat in the jam, treacle and
rind. Add the eggs one at a time, beating

well after each addition. Transfer to a
large bowl.
3 Stir the fruit and the combined sifted
flour and spices alternately into the
mixture. Spoon into the tin, tap the tin on
the bench to remove any air bubbles and
smooth the surface with wet fingers.
Wrap newspaper around the outside of
the tin as shown on pages 836–7. Sit the
tin on several layers of newspaper in the
oven and bake for 3¼ –3½ hours, or until a
skewer inserted into the centre comes
out clean. Drizzle with the extra brandy
while hot. Cover the top with baking
paper, cover tightly with foil and wrap the
tin in a clean dry tea towel until the cake
is completely cold.
4 Remove from the tin and store in an
airtight container or wrapped in plastic
wrap for up to 8 months.
5 Wash the fruit to be used for decorating
several hours in advance so it is
completely dry. Line a tray with paper
towels. Place the egg white in a shallow
bowl and whisk until just foamy. Put some
caster sugar on a large plate and working
with one portion of fruit at a time, brush
the egg white lightly all over the fruit.
Sprinkle the sugar over the fruit, shaking
off any excess and leave to dry on the
paper-covered tray for about 1–2 hours,
depending on the humidity. Frost more
fruit than you think you will need so you
have a good selection.
6 For the icing, whisk the egg white until
just foamy, beat in 1 teaspoon of lemon
juice and then gradually beat in the icing
sugar, beating well after each addition.
The icing should be thick and white—add
a little more lemon juice if necessary, but
don't make it too runny. Place the fruit
cake on a serving plate and working
quickly pour the icing over the top. Using
a palette knife smooth the icing to the
edge of the cake, allowing it to run slowly
down the side of the cake. Leave for at
least 10 minutes to let the icing set a little
before arranging the frosted fruits on the
top. The iced cake will keep for up to a
month.

DANISH KLEJNE

Preparation time: 25 minutes +
  1 hour 30 minutes refrigeration
Total cooking time: 15 minutes
Makes about 50

4 cups (500 g/8 oz) plain flour
1¼ teaspoons baking powder
¼ teaspoon bicarbonate of soda
½ teaspoon ground cinnamon
½ cup (125 g/4 oz) caster sugar
1 teaspoon finely grated lemon rind
100 g (3½ oz) butter, melted
1 cup (250 ml/8 fl oz) milk
oil, for deep-frying
icing sugar, for dusting

1 Sift the flour, baking powder, bicarbonate
of soda and cinnamon into a large bowl and
stir in the sugar and lemon rind. Make a
well in the centre and stir in the butter.
Gradually add enough milk to make a soft
dough. Turn onto a lightly floured surface
and press together until the dough comes
together. Pat into a ball, wrap in plastic
wrap and refrigerate for 1 hour to firm.
2 Roll the dough on a lightly floured
surface into a rectangular shape about
5 mm (¼ inch) thick. Trim the edges. Cut
into strips at 3 cm (1¼ inch) intervals, then
cut each strip on the diagonal into
8 cm (3 inch) lengths.
3 Cut a slit in each strip leaving 1 cm
(½ inch) at each end. Poke one end
through the slit and carefully pull out the
other side to form a twist in the pastry.
Take care when pulling through as it may
split. Repeat with the remaining dough.
Place the shapes on a tray covered with
baking paper and refrigerate for 30 minutes.
4 Fill a deep heavy-based saucepan one
third full of oil and heat to 180°C (350°F),
or until a cube of bread dropped into the
oil browns in 15 seconds. Fry the biscuits
in batches until well browned and cooked
through. Drain on paper towels. Place on
a tray covered with baking paper, cool to
warm and dust lightly with icing sugar.
Best eaten warm but can be eaten cold.

WHITE CHOCOLATE LEMON TRUFFLES

Preparation time: 25 minutes +
 4 hours refrigeration
Total cooking time: 2 minutes
Makes about 40

¼ cup (60 ml/2 fl oz) cream
250 g (8 oz) white chocolate melts,
 chopped
1 tablespoon finely grated lemon rind
2 teaspoons lemon juice
½ cup (45 g/1½ oz) desiccated coconut
¾ cup (45 g/1½ oz) toasted shredded
 coconut

1 Heat the cream and white chocolate melts in a saucepan over low heat until the chocolate has just melted. Remove the pan from the heat and stir in the lemon rind, lemon juice and desiccated coconut. Leave to cool, then refrigerate for 1½–2 hours, until firm.
2 Place teaspoons of the mixture on a foil-lined tray and refrigerate for 2 hours, or until very firm. Roll into balls, then coat with toasted shredded coconut. Keep refrigerated until ready to serve.

PROFITEROLES WITH DARK CHOCOLATE SAUCE

Preparation time: 40 minutes + cooling
Total cooking time: 50 minutes
Serves 4–6

60 g (2 oz) butter, chopped
¾ cup (90 g/3 oz) plain flour
3 eggs, lightly beaten

White chocolate filling
¼ cup (30 g/1 oz) custard powder
1 tablespoon caster sugar
1½ cups (375 ml/12 fl oz) milk
150 g (5 oz) white chocolate melts,
 chopped
1 tablespoon Grand Marnier

Dark chocolate sauce
125 g (4 oz) dark chocolate, chopped
½ cup (125 ml/4 fl oz) cream

1 Preheat the oven to hot 210°C (415°F/Gas 6–7). Line a baking tray with baking paper. Put the butter and ¾ cup (185 ml/6 fl oz) water in a pan. Bring to the boil, then remove from the heat. Add the flour all at once. Return to the heat and stir until the mixture forms a smooth ball. Set aside to cool slightly. Transfer to a bowl and, while beating with electric beaters, gradually add the eggs a little at a time, beating well after each addition, to form a thick, smooth, glossy paste.
2 Spoon 2 heaped teaspoons of the mixture onto the tray at 5 cm (2 inch) intervals. Sprinkle lightly with water and bake for 12–15 minutes, or until the dough is puffed. Turn off the oven. Pierce a small hole in the base of each profiterole with the point of a knife and return the profiteroles to the oven. Leave them to dry in the oven for 5 minutes.

3 For the filling, combine the custard powder and sugar in a pan. Gradually add the milk, stirring until smooth, then continue to stir over low heat until the mixture boils and thickens. Remove from the heat and add the white chocolate and Grand Marnier. Stir until the chocolate is melted. Cover the surface with plastic wrap and allow to cool. Stir the custard until smooth, then spoon into a piping bag fitted with a 1 cm (½ inch) plain nozzle. Pipe the filling into each profiterole. Serve with the warm chocolate sauce.
4 For the dark chocolate sauce, combine the chocolate and cream in a small saucepan. Stir over low heat until the chocolate is melted and the mixture is smooth. Serve warm.

NOTE: The profiteroles can be made a day ahead. Fill just before serving. You can also make miniature profiteroles, using 1 teaspoon of the mixture. Dip the tops of the cooked profiteroles in melted chocolate. When set, fill them with whipped cream.

BLACK BUN

Preparation time: 45 minutes +
    30 minutes refrigeration +
    20 minutes standing
Total cooking time: 2 hours 30 minutes
Makes 1

2½ cups (310 g/10 oz) plain flour
½ teaspoon baking powder
150 g (5 oz) butter, chilled and grated
1 egg, beaten

Filling
¾ cup (90 g/3 oz) plain flour
½ teaspoon grated nutmeg
½ teaspoon ground coriander
½ teaspoon mixed spice
1 teaspoon ground cinnamon
1 teaspoon ground ginger
½ cup (115 g/4 oz) soft brown sugar
3⅔ cups (590 g/1¼ lb) raisins, chopped
1½ cups (240 g/7½ oz) sultanas
2⅓ cups (350 g/11 oz) currants
½ cup (95 g/3 oz) mixed peel
⅔ cup (100 g/3½ oz) blanched almonds,
    chopped
2 teaspoons finely grated lemon rind
2 eggs
2 tablespoons brandy
3 tablespoons treacle
2 tablespoons milk

1 Grease a 24 cm (9 inch) springform cake tin. Sift the flour, baking powder and ¼ teaspoon salt into a bowl. Mix the butter into the flour with your fingertips. Make a well, add up to ⅓ cup (80 ml/2¾ fl oz) water and mix with a flat-bladed knife, using a cutting action, until the mixture comes together in clumps (you may need extra water). Gather together and lift onto a lightly floured surface. Press into a ball, cover with plastic wrap and refrigerate for 30 minutes.

2 Divide the dough into 3 portions. Roll out a portion, on a lightly floured surface, to fit the base of the tin. Divide another portion into 3 and roll each piece to line the side of the tin. Refrigerate the tin and the remaining portion of dough while preparing the filling.
3 Preheat the oven to slow 150°C (300°F/Gas 2). For the filling, sift the flour, spices and ¼ teaspoon salt into a large bowl, then stir in the sugar, fruit, peel, almonds and rind. Mix well.
4 Lightly beat the eggs with the brandy, treacle and milk in a bowl, then mix into the fruit. The mixture should come together, but not be too wet.
5 Spoon the mixture into the pastry-lined tin and press into the base. The mixture will only come about three-quarters up the sides. Fold the pastry edges over the filling and brush the pastry with beaten egg. Roll the remaining pastry out, on a lightly floured surface, until large enough to cover the top. Trim to fit and press down firmly to seal. Prick the pastry top a few times with a fork. Brush with beaten egg and bake for 2–2½ hours. The top should be golden brown. If the pastry is over-browning, cover loosely with foil. Place the tin on a wire rack for 20 minutes to cool, then remove the side of the springform tin, and cool completely. When cold, store in an airtight container. Serve thin wedges.

GINGER CHRISTMAS TREE BISCUITS

Preparation time: 20 minutes +
    4 hours refrigeration
Total cooking time: 25 minutes
Makes about 45

1 cup (185 g/6 oz) soft brown sugar
½ cup (175 g/6 oz) molasses
2 teaspoons ground ginger
½ teaspoon ground cinnamon
½ teaspoon ground cloves
185 g (6 oz) unsalted butter, cubed
1 egg, beaten
5 cups (625 g/1¼ lb) plain flour, sifted
2 teaspoons baking powder

1 Put the sugar, molasses, ginger, cinnamon and cloves in a small saucepan and bring to the boil over medium heat. Remove from the heat, add the butter, then pour into a heatproof bowl and stir until the butter melts and the mixture is combined. Cool slightly, then mix in the beaten egg. Stir in the sifted flour and baking powder in two batches, mixing thoroughly. Press together on a lightly floured board for 2 minutes, then wrap in plastic wrap and refrigerate for at least 2–4 hours. Preheat the oven to moderate 180°C (350°/Gas 4).
2 Divide the dough into 3 and roll out 1 portion to a thickness of 3 mm (⅛ inch). Cut into shapes using Christmas-theme cutters. Repeat with the other portions of dough, re-rolling any leftover dough. Place on a baking tray lined with baking paper, then make a hole in the top of each biscuit with a skewer and bake in batches for 5–6 minutes, or until lightly coloured and firm.
3 While the biscuits are still warm reinforce each hole with the skewer (they may have closed during baking). Cool on a wire rack, then thread the biscuits with ribbon and store in an airtight container until ready to hang on your Christmas tree. The biscuits will last hanging on the tree for up to 1 week, after which they will soften.

RUM TRUFFLES

Preparation time: 20 minutes + 50
   minutes refrigeration
Total cooking time: 1 minute
Makes about 25

200 g (6½ oz) dark cooking chocolate,
   finely chopped
¼ cup (60 ml/2 fl oz) cream
30 g (1 oz) butter
½ cup (50 g/1¾ oz) chocolate cake crumbs
2 teaspoons dark rum, brandy or whisky
½ cup (95 g/3 oz) chocolate sprinkles

1 Line a baking tray with foil. Put the
chocolate in a heatproof bowl. Combine
the cream and butter in a small pan and
stir over low heat until the butter melts
and the mixture is just boiling. Pour the
hot cream mixture over the chocolate and
stir until the chocolate melts and the
mixture is smooth.
2 Stir in the cake crumbs and rum.
Refrigerate for 20 minutes, stirring
occasionally, or until firm enough to
handle. Roll heaped teaspoons of the
mixture into balls.
3 Spread the chocolate sprinkles on a
sheet of greaseproof paper. Roll each
truffle in sprinkles, then place on the
baking tray. Refrigerate for 30 minutes, or
until firm. Serve in small paper patty
cups, if desired.

NOTE: Truffles can also be rolled in dark
cocoa powder. They can be made up to a
week in advance and refrigerated in an
airtight container.

NESSELRODE

Preparation time: 25 minutes + freezing
Total cooking time: Nil
Serves 8

5 egg yolks
¾ cup (185 g/6 oz) caster sugar
1 litre (32 fl oz) cream
1 teaspoon vanilla essence
1 tablespoon brandy
½ cup (165 g/5½ oz) chestnut purée
½ cup (75 g/2½ oz) currants
½ cup (80 g/2¾ oz) sultanas
¼ cup (60 g/2 oz) glacé cherries, chopped
½ cup (95 g/3 oz) mixed peel
To decorate
toasted flaked almonds
**selection of glacé cherries (cut in halves),
   angelica, crystallized violets or
   sugared grapes, fresh fruit or sugared
   rose petals**
**1 cup (250 ml/8 fl oz) cream, extra,
   whipped, optional**

1 Beat the egg yolks and sugar together in
a small bowl with electric beaters until
pale, thick and fluffy. Pour half the cream
into a saucepan and heat until almost
boiling. Gradually pour onto the eggs and
sugar, mixing well. Strain the mixture
back into the clean pan and place over
low heat.
2 Using a wooden spoon, stir constantly
around the base and sides of the pan until
the custard thickens slightly and coats
the back of the spoon. Do not boil or the
custard will curdle. Remove from the heat
and stir in the vanilla and brandy. Add the
chestnut purée and beat well to combine.
Strain the mixture and allow to cool.

3 Beat the remaining cream in a bowl
until soft peaks form and fold into the
custard mixture.
4 Put the currants and sultanas in a bowl
and cover completely with warm water.
5 Pour the cream mixture into a shallow
metal tray and freeze for 2–3 hours, or
until the mixture is just starting to freeze.
Transfer to a large bowl or food
processor, beat until smooth, then pour
back into the tray and return to the
freezer. Repeat this step three times.
Before the final freezing, add the glacé
cherries, mixed peel and the well-drained
currants and sultanas, then mix
thoroughly.
6 Lightly oil a 2 litre (64 fl oz) charlotte
mould, line with plastic, then pour in the
cream mixture Cover the surface with a
piece of plastic and freeze for at least
8 hours, or until firm.
7 Invert the pudding onto a serving plate
and carefully peel away the plastic.
Decorate the sides with evenly spaced
lines of toasted almonds, pieces of
angelica, halved glacé cherries,
crystallized violets or sugared fruits.
The nesselrode can be put back in the
freezer after it is decorated. When ready
to serve, pile whipped cream over the top,
then top that with piped whipped cream.

SPICED TREACLE GINGERBREADS

Preparation time: 45 minutes +
25 minutes refrigeration
Total cooking time: 10 minutes per batch
Makes about 36

140 g (4½ oz) unsalted butter, softened
½ cup (115 g/4 oz) dark brown sugar
¼ cup (90 g/3 oz) treacle, preferably black
1 egg
2 cups (250 g/8 oz) plain flour
¼ cup (30 g/1 oz) self-raising flour
3 teaspoons ground ginger
2 teaspoons ground cinnamon
¾ teaspoon ground cloves
¾ teaspoon ground nutmeg
1 teaspoon bicarbonate of soda

Icing
1 egg white
½ teaspoon lemon juice
1 cup (125 g/4 oz) icing sugar, sifted
assorted food colourings

1 Lightly grease two baking trays. Beat the butter and sugar in a bowl with electric beaters until light and creamy, then beat in the treacle and egg. Fold in the combined sifted flours, spices and bicarbonate of soda. Turn out onto a lightly floured surface and knead for 2–3 minutes, or until smooth. Cover with plastic wrap and chill for 10 minutes.

2 Divide the dough in half and roll out between two sheets of baking paper to 4 mm (¼ inch) thick. Lay on the trays and chill for 15 minutes until just firm. Preheat the oven to moderate 180°C (350°F/Gas 4).
3 Cut out the dough using a 7 cm (2¾ inch) heart-shaped cutter (or whatever shapes you prefer). Using a sharp knife, cut out a 1 cm (½ inch) hole at the top of each shape (you can thread ribbon through these holes to hang up the biscuits). Place on the trays and bake for 10 minutes. Remove from the oven and leave on the trays for 5 minutes before transferring to a wire cake rack to cool. When the biscuits are cold, decorate with the icing.
4 For the icing, whisk the egg white until foamy. Add the lemon juice and sugar and stir until glossy. Tint the icing any colour you want, then spoon into paper piping bags or a small plastic bag, seal the end and snip off the tip. When decorated, leave the icing to set.

ICE CREAM CHRISTMAS PUDDING

Preparation time: 1 hour + overnight
standing + 2 nights freezing
Total cooking time: Nil
Serves 10

⅓ cup (50 g/1¾ oz) toasted almonds, chopped
¼ cup (45 g/1½ oz) mixed peel
½ cup (80 g/2¾ oz) raisins, chopped
½ cup (80 g/2¾ oz) sultanas
⅓ cup (50 g/1¾ oz) currants
⅓ cup (80 ml/2¾ fl oz) rum
1 litre (32 fl oz) good-quality vanilla ice cream
½ cup (105 g/3½ oz) red and green glacé cherries, quartered
1 teaspoon mixed spice
1 teaspoon ground cinnamon
½ teaspoon ground nutmeg
1 litre (32 fl oz) good-quality chocolate ice cream

1 Mix the almonds, peel, raisins, sultanas, currants and rum in a bowl, cover with plastic wrap and leave overnight. Chill a 2 litre (64 fl oz) pudding basin in the freezer overnight.
2 Soften the vanilla ice cream slightly and mix in the glacé cherries. Working quickly, press the ice cream around the inside of the chilled basin, spreading it evenly to cover the base and side of the basin. Return the basin to the freezer and leave overnight. Check the ice cream a couple of times and spread it evenly to the top.
3 The next day, mix the spices and chocolate ice cream with the fruit mixture. Spoon it into the centre of the pudding bowl and smooth the top. Freeze overnight, or until very firm. Turn the pudding out onto a chilled plate and decorate. Cut into wedges to serve.

DOUBLE CHOCOLATE MOUSSE

Preparation time: 45 minutes + chilling
Total cooking time: 5 minutes
Serves 6

250 g (8 oz) white chocolate, melted
90 g (3 oz) good-quality dark chocolate, chopped
15 g (½ oz) unsalted butter
2 eggs, separated
1 cup (250 ml/8 fl oz) cream, whipped to soft peaks

1 Cut some freezer wrap into six 16 cm (6½ inch) squares. Place the white chocolate in a heatproof bowl. Half fill a saucepan with water and bring to the boil. Remove from the heat and place the bowl over the pan, making sure the base of the bowl does not touch the water. Stir until the chocolate is melted, then keep it warm by leaving the bowl over the pan. Working with one sheet at a time, spread 6 circles of white chocolate onto the freezer wrap. Drape each piece over the rim of a glass or mould, chocolate-side-up. When set, carefully peel away the freezer wrap, then refrigerate.
2 To make the mousse, melt the dark chocolate with the butter in a double saucepan. (Alternatively, bring a small pan of water to a simmer, remove from the heat and place a heatproof bowl over the pan, making sure you don't let the bottom of the bowl touch the water. Add the chocolate and butter to the bowl.) Stir the mixture over the hot water until melted. Alternatively, melt in the microwave for 1 minute on High (100%), stirring after 30 seconds. Whisk in the egg yolks and allow to cool. Fold in half the cream. Beat the egg whites until soft peaks form and fold lightly into the mousse until well combined. Fold in the remaining cream to make a swirled pattern. Spoon the mousse into the chocolate cups and chill for several hours before serving.

CHOCOLATE PFEFFERNUSSE

Preparation time: 50 minutes +
　2 hours refrigeration
Total cooking time: 15 minutes per tray
Makes 65

200 ml (6½ fl oz) honey
100 ml (3½ fl oz) treacle
⅔ cup (155 g/5 oz) soft brown sugar
150 g (5 oz) unsalted butter
4 cups (500 g/1 lb) plain flour
½ cup (60 g/1¾ oz) cocoa powder
1 teaspoon baking powder
½ teaspoon bicarbonate of soda
1 teaspoon ground white pepper
1 teaspoon ground cinnamon
½ teaspoon ground nutmeg
⅔ cup (100 g/3½ oz) blanched almonds, chopped
1 teaspoon finely grated lemon rind
¼ cup (45 g/1½ oz) mixed peel
2 eggs, lightly beaten
300 g (10 oz) dark chocolate, chopped

1 Cover baking trays with baking paper. Combine the honey, treacle, brown sugar and butter in a small saucepan. Place over medium heat and bring to the boil, stirring occasionally.

2 Remove from the heat and set aside to cool a little. Sift the flour, cocoa, baking powder, bicarbonate of soda, spices and ¼ teaspoon salt into a large bowl. Stir in the almonds, lemon rind and mixed peel and mix thoroughly. Make a well in the centre. Pour in the honey mixture and the eggs and mix until well combined.
3 Cover the mixture and refrigerate for 2 hours. Preheat the oven to moderate 180°C (350°F/Gas 4). Roll level tablespoons of the dough into balls. Place on the trays, allowing room for spreading. Bake for 12–15 minutes, until slightly coloured and firm to the touch. Transfer to a wire rack to cool.
4 To decorate, put the chocolate in a heatproof bowl. Bring a pan of water to the boil, then remove from the heat. Sit the bowl over the pan, making sure the base of the bowl doesn't sit in the water. Stir occasionally until the chocolate melts. Dip the tops of the biscuits in chocolate (up to the base), allow excess to drain off, then place on baking paper to set.

THREE-IN-ONE FRUIT MIX

Preparation time: 20 minutes
Makes enough for 1 cake (use half the mixture), 1 steamed pudding (quarter of the mixture) and 36 mince tarts (quarter of the mixture)

10 cups (1.6 kg/3¼ lb) sultanas
4 cups (640 g/1¼ lb) raisins, chopped
2½ cups (375 g/12 oz) currants
1½ cups (315 g/10 oz) glacé cherries, quartered
2¼ cups (500 g/1 lb) pitted prunes, quartered
1⅓ cups (245 g/7½ oz) mixed peel
2 cups (500 ml/16 fl oz) brandy
½ cup (115 g/4 oz) soft brown sugar
½ cup (160 g/5½ oz) sweet orange marmalade
2 tablespoons cocoa powder
1 tablespoon ground cinnamon
2 teaspoons ground ginger
2 teaspoons mixed spice

Mix the ingredients together in a large bowl, then store in a sterilized jar or airtight container in a cool, dark place for up to 1 month before using. Stir occasionally.

FRUIT CAKE

Preheat the oven to slow 150°C (300°F/Gas 2). Grease and line a 23 cm (9 inch) round or square cake tin as shown on pages 836–7. Beat 250 g (8 oz) softened unsalted butter, 1 cup (230 g/7½ oz) soft brown sugar and 2 teaspoons each of finely grated orange and lemon rind in a small bowl with electric beaters until just combined. Add 4 eggs one at a time, beating well after each addition. Transfer to a large bowl and stir in half of the soaked fruit mix alternately with 2 cups (250 g/8 oz) sifted plain flour and ½ cup (60 g/2 oz) sifted self-raising flour. Mix thoroughly, then spread evenly into the tin and tap the tin on the bench to remove any air bubbles. Dip your fingers in water and level the surface. Decorate the top of the cake with whole blanched almonds in a pattern. Sit the cake on several layers of newspaper on the oven shelf and bake for 3¼–3½ hours, or until a skewer comes out clean. Cover the top with baking paper, seal firmly with foil, then wrap the cake and tin in a clean tea towel and leave to cool.

STEAMED PUDDING

Prepare a 2 litre (64 fl oz) pudding basin as shown on pages 836–7. Beat 150 g (5 oz) softened unsalted butter and 1 cup (230 g/7½ oz) soft brown sugar in a small bowl with electric beaters until light and fluffy. Add 3 eggs, one at a time, beating well after each addition. Transfer to a large bowl and stir in a quarter of the soaked fruit alternately with 1 cup (125 g/4 oz) each of sifted plain flour and self-raising flour. Mix well. Spread into the basin and cover with the lid or as shown on pages 190–1, then follow the cooking directions on the same pages (cook for 5 hours). Replenish the water when necessary with boiling water. Remove the pudding and test with a skewer. If it is not cooked, re-cover and cook until done. Stand the pudding for 5 minutes before turning onto a large plate. If the pudding sticks, ease down the sides a little way with a palette knife to help release it. Serve wedges hot with custard or flavoured butter.

FRUIT MINCE TARTS

Mix a quarter of the soaked fruit mix with 125 g (4 oz) grated frozen butter, 1 grated green apple and ½ cup (115 g/4 oz) soft brown sugar in a large bowl. For the pastry, sift ½ cup (60 g/2 oz) custard powder and 4 cups (500 g/1 lb) plain flour into a large bowl and rub in 360 g (12 oz) chopped chilled butter with your fingertips until the mixture resembles fine breadcrumbs. Stir in ½ cup (60 g/2 oz) icing sugar. Make a well in the centre and add 1 egg yolk and ¼ cup (60 ml/2 fl oz) water and mix with a flat-bladed knife until the mixture comes together in beads. Gently gather the dough together and lift out onto a lightly floured work surface. Press into a ball, flatten slightly into a disc, then wrap in plastic and refrigerate for 30 minutes. Preheat the oven to moderate 180°C (350°F/Gas 4). Lightly grease three 12-hole tartlet tins. Roll two-thirds of the dough out between 2 sheets of baking paper to 3 mm (1/8 inch) thick. Cut 36 rounds from the pastry using a 7 cm (2¾ inch) cutter. Place in the tins and top with spoonfuls of fruit mixture. Roll the remaining pastry out between baking paper and cut 36 rounds with a 6.5 cm (2½ inch) cutter. Brush the edges with lightly beaten egg and press the tops on firmly. Crimp the edges if you wish. Brush with more egg, then bake for 20–25 minutes, or until well browned. Leave in the tins for 5 minutes, then lift onto a wire rack to cool. Dust with icing sugar before serving.

SHORTBREAD BELLS

Preparation time: 30 minutes +
   15 minutes refrigeration
Total cooking time: 25 minutes
Makes about 40

250 g (8 oz) butter, softened
½ cup (125 g/4 oz) caster sugar
2 cups (250 g/8 oz) plain flour
½ cup (90 g/3 oz) rice flour
1 egg white, lightly beaten
edible gold leaf (see Note)

1 Line two baking trays with baking paper. Place the butter and sugar in a bowl and beat with electric beaters until light and creamy.
2 Sift the flours into the butter mixture, and mix together with a flat-bladed knife to make a crumbly dough. Gather together and turn out onto a sheet of baking paper. Press together gently. Cover with another sheet of baking paper and roll out to 7 mm (¼ inch) thick.
3 Peel off the top sheet of baking paper and cut shapes from the dough using bell-shaped cutters of varying sizes. Cut as many as possible, then gently press the leftovers together, re-roll and cut out more. Lift onto the trays and refrigerate for 15 minutes. Preheat the oven to warm 160°C (315°F/Gas 2–3), then bake for 20–25 minutes, or until golden underneath. Cool on a wire rack.
4 Lightly brush the top of some of the biscuits with egg white and lay a piece of gold leaf on top. Rub gently with your finger to transfer the gold leaf from the tissue paper to the biscuit. The gold leaf will give a decorative effect.

NOTE: Edible gold leaf is available from art supply shops and some cake-decorating shops.

BOILED PUDDING

Preparation time: 40 minutes +
   overnight soaking + overnight hanging
Total cooking time: 5 hours
Serves 10–12

1⅔ cups (310 g/10 oz) mixed dried fruit
¼ cup (45 g/1½ oz) mixed peel
4 cups (640 g/1¼ lb) mixed sultanas,
   currants and raisins
½ cup (125 ml/4 fl oz) brown ale
2 tablespoons rum or brandy
2 tablespoons orange juice
2 tablespoons lemon juice
1 tablespoon grated orange rind
1 tablespoon grated lemon rind
225 g (7 oz) suet, grated
1⅓ cups (245 g/7½ oz) soft brown sugar
3 eggs, lightly beaten
2½ cups (200 g/6½ oz) fresh white
   breadcrumbs
¾ cup (90 g/3 oz) self-raising flour
1 teaspoon mixed spice
¼ teaspoon freshly grated nutmeg
⅔ cup (100 g/3½ oz) blanched almonds,
   chopped

1 Finely chop the mixed dried fruit and put in a large bowl with the mixed peel, sultanas, currants, raisins, ale, rum, orange and lemon juice and rind. Cover and leave overnight.
2 Mix the fruit with the remaining ingredients and a pinch of salt. Leave for 10 minutes.
3 Cut an 80 cm (32 inch) square from a clean piece of calico or an old tea towel and follow the instructions on pages 204–5. Cover, place a couple of large cans of fruit or a brick on the lid if possible, and boil the pudding for 5 hours. Replenish with boiling water when necessary. Remove from the water and hang in a well-ventilated, dry place where it will not touch anything. Hook up the calico ends or open up and loosely place on top of the pudding. Leave the pudding hanging overnight to dry.
4 Untie the cloth and, if there are damp patches at the top, spread it out to make sure it dries. When it is dry, re-wrap and tie with a new piece of string. The pudding will store hanging in a cool, dry place for up to 4 months. To serve, boil for 2 hours, hang for 15 minutes, then remove from the cloth and cut into wedges.

STEAMED PUDDING

THESE CAN BE MADE 3 MONTHS AHEAD, WRAPPED IN PLASTIC WRAP AND FOIL AND KEPT IN A COOL, DARK PLACE OR THE FRIDGE. ON THE BIG DAY, STEAM IN A GREASED BASIN FOR 1 HOUR.

PREPARING THE BASIN

It is essential that the capacity of the basin is the correct size for the recipe so the pudding has room to rise and does not expand out of the basin. Check the capacity by filling the basin with water from a measuring jug or cup. Basins are available in many different shapes and sizes and are made of ceramic, glass, steel or aluminium. Ceramic basins let the pudding cook more slowly, so it cooks through without overcooking the edges. Metal basins cook the pudding more quickly, so it should be checked 30 minutes before the cooking time is up. Most metal basins come with a lid but this is not essential and is often used as well as baking paper and foil.

STEAMING THE PUDDING

You need a large saucepan which will hold the basin sitting on a trivet and leave space around the basin and enough room to fit the saucepan lid on properly. If you don't have a trivet (a small round or square metal rack, available at speciality stores), you can use a collapsible metal vegetable steamer (unscrew the handle), or an upturned saucer. Place the empty basin on the trivet in the saucepan and pour water into the saucepan to come halfway up the side of the basin. Remove the basin.

To help prevent the cooked pudding sticking to the basin, brush the basin well with melted butter and line the base with a circle of baking paper (even if your base is very small).

Make the pudding mixture according to the recipe and spoon into the basin, smoothing the top to make it level. Put the saucepan of water on to boil.

To cover the pudding, place a sheet of foil on the bench, top with a piece of baking paper the same size and brush the paper well with melted butter. Fold a pleat across the centre of the foil and paper to allow for expansion. Place the paper and foil, foil-side-up, over the basin (don't press it onto the pudding) and smooth it down the side of the basin. Tie a double length of string firmly around the rim of the basin, then tie a double length of string onto that string to form a handle to lower the pudding into the water. If you have a basin with a lid, clip it on at this stage. The paper/foil lid prevents any moisture getting into the pudding and making it soggy.

Using the handle, carefully lower the pudding into the saucepan and reduce the heat until the water is simmering quickly. Cover the saucepan and cook according to the directions in the recipe. Add more boiling water to the saucepan occasionally to maintain the water level.

WHEN IS IT COOKED?

When the cooking time is up, carefully remove the pudding from the saucepan using the string handles. Remove the lid and paper/foil and test the pudding— a skewer should come out clean when inserted into the centre (if you hit a piece of fruit, the skewer may come out sticky). You can also check by pressing the top gently—the pudding should be firm in the centre, well risen and moist. If the pudding is not cooked, replace the top and continue cooking until done. When the pudding is cooked, leave it in the basin for 5 minutes before gently turning out onto a large plate. Discard the round of baking paper from the base. If the pudding sticks to the basin, gently loosen around the edges with a palette knife to help release it.

PUDDING TOPPINGS

THESE CUSTARDS, BUTTERS AND SAUCES WILL COMPLEMENT YOUR RICH CHRISTMAS PUDDING, WHETHER YOU PREFER CLASSIC TOPPINGS OR SOMETHING DIFFERENT.

VANILLA CUSTARD

Combine 1 cup (250 ml/8 fl oz) milk and ¼ cup (60 ml/2 fl oz) cream in a saucepan. Bring to the boil, then remove from the heat immediately. In a bowl, whisk 3 egg yolks, ½ cup (125 g/4 oz) caster sugar and 2 teaspoons cornflour. Slowly pour the hot milk and cream into the egg mixture, whisking continuously. Return to the saucepan and stir over low heat for 5 minutes, or until thickened—do not boil. Remove from the heat and stir in ½ teaspoon vanilla essence. Serve. Makes 1½ cups (375 ml/12 fl oz).

WHISKY SAUCE

Melt 2 tablespoons butter in a saucepan over low heat. Remove from the heat, add ⅓ cup (40 g/1¼ oz) plain flour and stir until combined. Gradually whisk in 2 cups (500 ml/16 fl oz) milk and 2 tablespoons caster sugar. Return to medium heat. Stir until the sauce boils and thickens. Reduce the heat and simmer for 10 minutes, stirring occasionally. Remove from the heat and stir in ⅓ cup (80 ml/2¾ fl oz) whisky, 2 teaspoons butter and 1 tablespoon thick (double) cream. Cover with plastic wrap until ready to serve. Makes 2½ cups (600 ml/20 fl oz).

CREME A L'ANGLAISE

Whisk 3 egg yolks and 2 tablespoons caster sugar together in a heatproof bowl for 2 minutes, or until light and creamy. Heat 1½ cups (375 ml/12 fl oz) milk until almost boiling, then pour into the bowl, whisking constantly. Return to the clean pan and stir over low heat for 5 minutes, or until thick enough to coat the back of a spoon. Don't let the mixture boil or it will scramble. Remove from the heat. Stir in ½ teaspoon vanilla essence. Transfer to a jug.
Makes 2 cups (500 ml/16 fl oz).

GRAND MARNIER WHIPPED BUTTER

Remove the rind from an orange with a vegetable peeler, avoiding any white pith. Cut the rind into long thin strips, place in a pan of cold water and bring to the boil. Drain and repeat. Return to the pan with ⅓ cup (80 ml/2¾ fl oz) water and 2 tablespoons caster sugar. Stir over low heat until the sugar has dissolved, then boil for 2 minutes until thick and syrupy. Beat 250 g (4 oz) softened unsalted butter in a bowl with electric beaters until light and fluffy. Beat in ⅓ cup (40 g/1¼ oz) icing sugar, ¼ cup (60 ml/2 fl oz) orange juice and 2–3 tablespoons Grand Marnier, to taste, then fold in the orange rind syrup. Don't add the liquid too quickly or the mixture may split. If this happens, beat in enough icing sugar to bring the mixture back together. Dollop on top of hot Christmas pudding.
Makes 1 cup (250 g/8 oz).

BRANDY BUTTER

Beat 250 g (8 oz) softened unsalted butter and 1½ cups (185 g/6 oz) sifted icing sugar with electric beaters until smooth and creamy. Gradually add ¼ cup (60 ml/2 fl oz) brandy, beating thoroughly. Refrigerate until required.
Makes 1 cup (250 g/4 oz).

CHOCOLATE SAUCE

Put 40 g (1½ oz) butter, 30 g (1 oz) sifted cocoa powder and 185g (6½ oz) soft brown sugar in a saucepan and mix well. Add 300ml (10½ fl oz) of thickened cream and stir over a low heat until the sauce come to the boil. Serve hot.
Makes 2 cups (500ml/16 fl oz)

LEFT to right: Vanilla custard; Whisky sauce; Crème à l'Anglaise; Grand Marnier whipped butter; Brandy butter; Chocolate sauce; Vanilla custard (on pudding)

SAGO PLUM PUDDING WITH RUM BUTTER

Preparation time: 35 minutes +
  overnight soaking
Total cooking time: 4 hours
Serves 6–8

⅓ cup (65 g/2¼ oz) sago
1 cup (250 ml/8 fl oz) milk
1 teaspoon bicarbonate of soda
¾ cup (140 g/4½ oz) dark brown sugar
2 cups (160 g/5¼ oz) fresh white
  breadcrumbs
½ cup (80 g/2¾ oz) sultanas
½ cup (75 g/2½ oz) currants
½ cup (80 g/2¾ oz) dried dates, chopped
2 eggs, lightly beaten
60 g (2 oz) unsalted butter, melted and
  cooled
raspberries, for decoration
blueberries, for decoration
icing sugar, for decoration

Rum butter
125 g (4 oz) butter, softened
¾ cup (140 g/4½ oz) dark brown sugar
4 tablespoons rum

1 Combine the sago and milk in a small
bowl, cover and refrigerate overnight.
2 Prepare a 1.5 litre (48 fl oz) pudding
basin as shown on pages 680–1. Place the
empty basin in a large saucepan on a
trivet or upturned saucer and pour in
enough cold water to come halfway up the
side of the basin. Remove the basin and
put the water on to boil.
3 Transfer the soaked sago and milk to a
large bowl and stir in the bicarbonate of
soda until dissolved. Stir in the sugar,
breadcrumbs, dried fruit, beaten eggs
and melted butter and mix well. Spoon
into the basin and smooth the surface
with wet hands.

4 Cover the basin and make a string
handle as shown on pages 680–1. Gently
lower the basin into the boiling water,
reduce to a fast simmer and cover the
saucepan with a tight-fitting lid. Cook for
3½–4 hours, or until a skewer inserted
into the centre of the pudding comes out
clean. Check the water level every hour
and top up with boiling water as
necessary.
5 Carefully remove the pudding basin
from the saucepan, remove the coverings
and leave for 5 minutes before turning the
pudding out onto a large serving plate.
Loosen the edges with a palette knife if
necessary. Serve decorated with
raspberries and blueberries and lightly
dusted with icing sugar. Serve hot with
cold rum butter.
6 For the rum butter, beat together the
butter and sugar with electric beaters for
about 3–4 minutes, or until light and
creamy. Gradually beat in the rum,
1 tablespoon at a time. You can add more
rum, to taste. Transfer to a serving dish,
cover and refrigerate until required.

NOTE: Sago is the starch extracted from
the sago palm. It is dried and formed into
balls by pushing through a sieve. It is
often called pearl sago and is available
from supermarkets or health food stores.
It is white when uncooked but goes
transparent when cooked.

FIG PUDDING

Preparation time: 40 minutes
Total cooking time: 3 hours 40 minutes
Serves 8

500 g (1 lb) dried figs, chopped
1¾ cups (440 ml/14 fl oz) milk
3 cups (240 g/7½ oz) coarse fresh
  breadcrumbs
¾ cup (140 g/4½ oz) soft brown sugar
2 cups (250 g/8 oz) self-raising flour,
  sifted
2 eggs, lightly beaten
150 g (5 oz) unsalted butter, melted and
  cooled

1 Prepare a 2 litre (64 fl oz) pudding basin
as shown on pages 680–1. Place the
empty basin in a large saucepan on a
trivet or upturned saucer and pour in
enough water to come halfway up the side
of the basin. Remove the basin and put
the water on to boil.
2 Put the figs in a small saucepan with
the milk. Bring to a simmer, cover and
cook over low heat for 10 minutes. The
mixture will curdle— stir to combine.
3 Combine the breadcrumbs, sugar and
flour in a large bowl. Stir in the soaked
figs and any liquid, the beaten eggs and
the melted butter. Spoon into the basin.
Cover the basin and make a handle with
string as shown on pages 680–1.
4 Gently lower the basin into the boiling
water, reduce to a fast simmer and cover
the saucepan with a tight-fitting lid. Cook
for 3½ hours, checking the water every
hour and topping up with boiling water as
necessary. The pudding is cooked when a
skewer inserted in the centre comes out
clean. Leave for 5 minutes before turning
out. Serve with custard or cream.

GLUTEN-FREE PUDDING

Preparation time: 30 minutes +
    overnight soaking
Total cooking time: 4 hours
Serves 8–10

2⅔ cups (500 g/1 lb) mixed dried fruit
3 cups (480 g/15 oz) raisins, chopped
1 cup (220 g/7 oz) pitted prunes,
    quartered
1 cup (200 g/6½ oz) dried fruit medley
1⅓ cups (200 g/6½ oz) currants
½ cup (95 g/3 oz) dried figs, chopped
½ cup (125 ml/4 fl oz) sweet sherry
1 tablespoon treacle
1 cup (230 g/7½ oz) soft brown sugar
4 eggs, lightly beaten
250 g (8 oz) unsalted butter, melted and
    cooled
1½ cups (120 g/4 oz) soya flour
¾ cup (90 g/3 oz) rice cereal
¾ cup (90 g/3 oz) maize cornflour
2 teaspoons ground cinnamon
2 teaspoons ground nutmeg
1 teaspoon ground ginger

1 Prepare a 2.5 litre (80 fl oz) pudding
basin as shown on pages 680–1. Place the
empty basin in a large saucepan on a
trivet or upturned saucer and pour in
enough water to come halfway up the side
of the basin. Remove the basin and put
the water on to boil.
2 Mix all the fruit with the sherry in a large
bowl. Cover and leave overnight, stirring
occasionally, until the sherry is absorbed.
3 Mix the treacle, sugar and eggs into the
fruit. Stir in the cooled butter and sifted
dry ingredients until completely
combined. Spoon into the pudding basin.
Cover with a greased circle of foil. Lower
the pudding into the boiling water for
3½–4 hours, or until cooked when tested.
Replenish the water when necessary.
4 Stand the pudding in the basin for
5 minutes before turning out onto a
serving plate. To reheat on the day, steam
the pudding for 1 hour, or until heated
through.

LOW-FAT PUDDING

Preparation time: 20 minutes +
    overnight soaking
Total cooking time: 4 hours 30 minutes
Serves 8–10

2⅔ cups (500 g/1 lb) mixed dried fruit
1 cup (200 g/6½ oz) dried fruit medley
1¼ cups (185 g/6 oz) currants
1 cup (160 g/5½ oz) raisins
½ cup (125 ml/4 fl oz) whisky
½ cup (115 g/4 oz) soft brown sugar
2 eggs, lightly beaten
1 egg white, lightly beaten
1 green apple, peeled, cored and grated
2 bananas, mashed
1½ cups (185 g/6 oz) plain flour
½ cup (60 g/2 oz) self-raising flour
1 teaspoon ground cinnamon
1 teaspoon ground nutmeg
1 teaspoon ground ginger

1 Mix all the fruit with the whisky in a
large bowl. Cover and leave for several
hours, or overnight, stirring occasionally
until the liquid is absorbed.
2 Prepare a 2 litre (64 fl oz) pudding basin
as shown on pages 680–1.
3 Place the basin on a trivet or upturned
saucer in the saucepan and add enough
water to come halfway up the side of the
basin. Remove the basin and put the
water on to boil while preparing the
pudding mixture.
4 Add the sugar, eggs, egg white, apple
and banana to the fruit and mix
thoroughly. Stir in the sifted dry
ingredients. Mix well, then spread evenly
into the basin. Cover the basin and make
a string handle as shown on pages 680–1.

5 Using the handle, lower the pudding
into the pan and lower the water to a fast
simmer. Cover the saucepan with a lid
and cook the pudding for 4–4½ hours. It
may be necessary to replenish the water
with more boiling water occasionally,
making sure the water is always about
halfway up the side of the basin.
6 Remove the pudding from the saucepan
using the string handle. Remove the lid
and paper/foil and test the pudding with a
skewer (it should come out clean when
inserted into the centre). Sometimes it
may come out sticky but this could be due
to the fruit. It should be well risen and
moist. If it is not cooked, cover and cook
until done. When cooked, stand the
pudding for 5 minutes before inverting
onto a large plate. If the pudding sticks,
ease down the sides a little way with a
palette knife to help release it.
7 To reheat, return the pudding to a clean
buttered basin, cover as above and steam
for 2 hours, or until heated through.

NOTE: This pudding looks very attractive
if presented with decorations on top. Use
your favourites, or try a combination of
cassia bark or cinnamon sticks and
sugar-coated leaves.

BOILED PUDDING

WHEN THERE IS A CHRISTMAS PUDDING HANGING IN ITS CLOTH IN THE KITCHEN, EVERYONE KNOWS THAT PLANNING HAS BEGUN AND THE DELICIOUS COUNTDOWN HAS STARTED.

Although a little more skill and patience is required to make traditional boiled Christmas puddings than for steamed ones, many people still enjoy making them. A major factor when making a boiled pudding is to ensure the water is on a constant low boil, otherwise you run the risk of having the pudding absorb water and turning into a soggy mass which unfortunately can't be resurrected.

PREPARING THE CLOTH

You will need a large, deep saucepan with a tight-fitting lid. The pudding must be able to be suspended in the boiling water so it won't touch the base or side of the saucepan during cooking. This helps keep the pudding in shape while it is cooking. Half fill the saucepan with water, cover and bring to the boil. Cut a large square of calico (or follow the directions in the recipe). You can use a clean old tea towel if it is large enough. Add the calico to the saucepan and simmer for 20 minutes. Wearing rubber gloves and using tongs, remove the calico from the boiling water and wring out well. Cover the pan and keep at a constant simmer. Spread the calico out on a work surface. Cover generously with an even layer of plain flour, using about ½ cup (60 g/2 oz), leaving a border around the edge. Spread the flour with your hands to get an even covering (this forms a seal between the pudding and the water and prevents the pudding absorbing water). You will need to cover enough calico with flour so that when the cloth is gathered up the pudding mixture is completely enclosed by the floured calico.

BOILING THE PUDDING

Make the fruit mixture according to the recipe and spoon into the centre of the cloth. Bring the points of the cloth together over the top and gather in all the excess material, easing it in little by little to keep the pleats as small and neat as possible, as these will leave impressions on the pudding when cooked. Pat gently to form a nice round shape. Leaving a small amount of room at the top for expansion, tie the top tightly with string so there is no gap where water can get into the pudding. Tie another length of string around the top, long enough to tie to the handles on either side of the pan to suspend the pudding (if your saucepan doesn't have suitable handles, suspend a wooden spoon across the saucepan and tie the string to that). Gently lower the pudding into the simmering water. The pudding should float, without touching the bottom. Carefully tie the string tautly across the pan to the opposite handles or the spoon. Cover with a lid and place a couple of large cans of fruit or a brick on the lid if possible. The water needs to be maintained on a low boil constantly for

the time stated in the recipe. Replenish the water with boiling water as necessary. When the cooking time is up, remove the pudding from the water and hang it over a bowl (to catch any drips) in a dry, well-ventilated area (make sure it is not touching anything). Hook up the loose calico ends in the string to help them dry. Leave overnight. The next day, remove the string and if the top is slightly wet, open out and allow to dry. When completely dry, tie with a new piece of string and hang in a cool dark place for up to 4 months. In humid weather, you may need to refrigerate the pudding.

REHEATING THE PUDDING

To reheat, boil the pudding as above for 2 hours, hang for 15 minutes to dry slightly, then undo the string and carefully peel away some of the calico. Place a plate over the top and invert the plate, pudding and cloth. Ease the calico away from the pudding skin. Serve with your favourite butter or sauce (pages 682–3).

SUGAR-FREE PUDDING

Preparation time: 30 minutes
Total cooking time: 1 hour 30 minutes
Serves 6–8

6 ripe bananas, mashed
1 egg, lightly beaten
2 cups (370 g/12 oz) mixed dried fruit
1 cup (80 g/3 oz) fresh breadcrumbs

Orange cream
1¼ cups (315 ml/10 fl oz) cream
2 tablespoons orange juice
1 tablespoon grated orange rind
1 teaspoon vanilla essence

1 Prepare a 1.25 litre (40 fl oz) pudding basin as shown on pages 190–1.
2 Place the basin in a large pan, on a trivet or upturned saucer, and pour in enough cold water to come halfway up the side of the basin. Remove the basin and put the water on to boil.
3 Combine the banana, egg, dried fruit and breadcrumbs in a bowl. Spoon into the prepared pudding basin.
4 Cover the basin and make a handle as shown on pages 680–1.
5 Gently lower the basin into the boiling water, reduce the heat to a fast simmer and cover with a tight-fitting lid. Cook for 1½ hours, checking the water after an hour and topping up to the original level with boiling water as needed.
6 For the orange cream, combine the cream, orange juice, rind and vanilla in a bowl and mix well. Serve over the pudding.

CHOC-GINGER PUDDINGS

Preparation time: 45 minutes +
  overnight standing + overnight hanging
Total cooking time: 1 hour 15 minutes
Makes 10

2 cups (320 g/11 oz) raisins, chopped
1⅓ cups (200 g/6½ oz) currants
⅔ cup (110 g/3½ oz) pitted dates, chopped
⅓ cup (75 g/2½ oz) glacé ginger, chopped
1 cup (160 g/5½ oz) sultanas
100 g (3½ oz) dried pears, chopped
100 g (3½ oz) dried apricots, chopped
1 cup (175 g/6 oz) dark chocolate bits
½ cup (75 g/2½ oz) pistachios, chopped
½ cup (125 ml/4 fl oz) brandy
250 g (8 oz) unsalted butter, frozen and grated
1 cup (185 g/6 oz) dark brown sugar
1 tablespoon treacle
⅓ cup (80 ml/2¾ fl oz) orange juice
1 teaspoon finely grated orange rind
⅓ cup (80 ml/2¾ fl oz) lemon juice
1 teaspoon finely grated lemon rind
4 eggs, lightly beaten
1 teaspoon bicarbonate of soda
1½ cups (185 g/6 oz) plain flour
½ cup (60 g/2 oz) self-raising flour
2 teaspoons mixed spice
2 teaspoons ground cinnamon
1 teaspoon ground nutmeg
1 cup (80 g/2¾ oz) fresh breadcrumbs
cream, for serving, optional

1 Put all the fruit, chocolate and pistachios into a large basin and stir in the brandy. Cover with plastic wrap and leave overnight.
2 Bring 2 large saucepans of water to the boil. Cut a piece of calico into ten 30 cm (12 inch) squares. Put the calico in one of the saucepans of boiling water for 15 minutes, then remove with tongs and, with gloved hands, wring out the water.
3 Put the butter in a large bowl and stir in the sugar, treacle, rinds and juices and the eggs. Add the combined sifted bicarbonate of soda, flours and spices in two batches. Stir in the fruit and breadcrumbs.
4 Place a calico square on a flat surface and rub liberally with plain flour, leaving a border of calico. Place a loosely packed cup of the mixture into the centre of the cloth. Gather and tie the cloth into a neat ball, pleating the calico, as shown on pages 686–7. Tie firmly with string around the top and tie the end of the string to enable you to hang the puddings from a wooden spoon. Repeat with all the mixture and calico. Place half the puddings in each saucepan of boiling water, then sit the lids over the spoons to keep most of the steam in. Simmer for 1 hour. Hang overnight in a cool place to dry, then refrigerate in an airtight container. Keep for up to 1 month.
5 To reheat, lower the puddings into a pan of boiling water and boil for 30 minutes. Remove the cloths and serve individually, with cream.

INDIVIDUAL BOURBON CHRISTMAS CAKES

Preparation time: 40 minutes +
  overnight soaking + decorating
Total cooking time: 1 hour 15 minutes
Makes 12

¼ cup (60 g/2 oz) chopped glacé apricots
½ cup (110 g/3½ oz) chopped glacé
  pineapple
½ cup (100 g/3½ oz) chopped glacé figs
2 cups (320 g/11 oz) raisins, chopped
1⅔ cups (250 g/8 oz) currants
¾ cup (180 ml/6 fl oz) bourbon
250 g (8 oz) unsalted butter, chopped
1 cup (230 g/7½ oz) dark brown sugar
½ cup (180 g/6 oz) treacle
4 eggs
2½ cups (310 g/10 oz) pecans, chopped
1½ cups (185 g/6 oz) plain flour
½ cup (60 g/2 oz) self-raising flour
2 teaspoons ground nutmeg
2 teaspoons ground ginger
2 teaspoons ground cinnamon
6 tablespoons bourbon, extra

Holly leaves and berries
60 g (2 oz) ready-made almond icing
pure icing sugar
green and red food colouring

Soft icing-covered cakes
⅓ cup (105 g/3½ oz) apricot jam, warmed,
  sieved
1.2 kg (2 lb 6½ oz) ready-made soft icing
pure icing sugar
thin ribbon

Royal icing-covered cakes
1 egg white
2 cups (250 g/8 oz) pure icing sugar,
  sifted
2–3 teaspoons lemon juice

1 Cut the glacé fruits and raisins into
small pieces. Place in a large bowl with
the currants and bourbon and mix well.
Cover and leave to soak overnight, stirring
occasionally.
2 Preheat the oven to slow 150°C

(300°F/Gas 2). Lightly grease twelve 1 cup
(250 ml/8 fl oz) muffin holes and line the
bases with a circle of baking paper. Beat
the butter, sugar and treacle in a small
bowl until just combined. Add the eggs
one at a time, beating well after each
addition. Transfer to a large bowl, stir in
the soaked fruit mixture, pecans and then
the sifted dry ingredients and mix well.
3 Spoon the mixture evenly into the tins,
and smooth the surface with fingers dipped
in cold water. Bake for 1–1¼ hours, or until
a skewer inserted into the centre comes
out clean. Cover the top of the cakes lightly
with foil if over-browning. Brush the tops of
the cakes with half the extra bourbon while
hot, cover with baking paper, then seal
firmly with foil and cool in the tins before
turning out. Brush with the remaining
bourbon, wrap firmly in plastic and leave
for two weeks before decorating. When
decorating, the base will become the top.
4 To make the holly leaves, knead 50 g (1¾
oz) of the almond icing until it is soft. Roll
out on a surface lightly dusted with icing
sugar until very thin. Cut out the leaves
using a cutter or template. Pinch the
leaves in half, open out and press the
edges gently to curl in different directions.
Dry on baking paper. Brush the edges
with green food colouring. Knead a little
red colouring into the remaining almond
icing and roll into small balls to make
berries. Paint or roll the berries in
colouring to coat thoroughly. Allow to dry.
5 For the soft icing-covered cakes, melt
the jam until runny, strain and brush
some all over each cake. Roll out 100 g
(3½ oz) of the soft icing on a surface
lightly dusted with icing sugar until large
enough to cover one cake. If there are any
holes in the cake, use a little extra icing
to fill the holes and make a smooth

surface. Place the icing over the cake and
ease over the side, pressing lightly, then
trim from around the base. Mix together a
little icing sugar and water into a smooth
paste. Wrap a ribbon around the base of
the cake and seal with a little paste. Use
the paste to secure 2 holly leaves and
berries to the top. Repeat with remaining
cakes and icing.
6 For the royal icing-covered cakes,
lightly beat the egg white with a wooden
spoon just to break down a little.
Gradually add the icing sugar, beating to a
smooth paste. Slowly add the lemon juice
until slightly runny. Spread a tablespoon
of icing over each cake, using a palette
knife to smooth and letting some drizzle
down the sides. Secure holly leaves and
berries on the top just before the icing
sets.

NOTE: Iced cakes can be kept for up to a
month in an airtight container, or un-iced
for up to 8 months.

YULE LOG

Preparation time: 40 minutes
Total cooking time: 15 minutes
Serves 8

½ cup (60 g/2 oz) plain flour
2 tablespoons cocoa powder
3 eggs
⅓ cup (90 g/3 oz) caster sugar
50 g (1¾ oz) unsalted butter, melted and
  cooled
1 tablespoon caster sugar, extra

Filling
125 g white chocolate, chopped
½ cup (125 ml/4 fl oz) cream
50 g (1¾ oz) hazelnuts, toasted and finely
  chopped
Topping
125 g (4 oz) dark chocolate, chopped
½ cup (125 ml/4 fl oz) cream, extra
icing sugar, to dust

1 Preheat the oven to moderate 180°C
(350°F/Gas 4). Brush a 30 x 35 cm
(12 x 14 inch) swiss roll tin with oil or
melted butter and line the base and sides
with baking paper. Sift the flour and cocoa
powder together twice. Using electric
beaters, beat the eggs and sugar for 5
minutes, or until light and fluffy and
increased in volume.
2 Sift the flour over the eggs and pour the
butter around the edge of the bowl. Using
a large metal spoon, gently fold the
mixture together to incorporate the flour
and butter. Take care not to overmix and
lose too much volume.

3 Spread the mixture into the tin and bake
for 12 minutes, or until the sponge springs
back when lightly touched with your
fingertips. Sprinkle the extra caster sugar
over a clean tea towel. Turn the sponge
out onto the tea towel close to one end.
Roll the sponge and tea towel together
lengthways and leave to cool.
4 For the filling, put the white chocolate
in a small heatproof bowl. Bring a small
pan of water to the boil, then remove from
the heat. Add the cream to the chocolate
and stand the bowl over the pan of water,
making sure the base of the bowl does
not touch the water, until the chocolate is
soft. Stir until smooth. Repeat with the
dark chocolate and cream for the topping.
Leave the white chocolate mixture until it
has cooled to room temperature and is
the consistency of cream. Leave the dark
chocolate mixture until it cools to a
spreadable consistency.
5 Beat the white chocolate mixture with
electric beaters until soft peaks form—
do not overbeat or the mixture will curdle.
Unroll the sponge, remove the tea towel
and spread with the filling, finishing 2 cm
(¾ inch) from the end. Sprinkle with the
hazelnuts. Re-roll the sponge and trim
the ends. Cut off one end on the diagonal
and place it alongside the log to create a
branch.
6 Place the yule log on a serving plate and
spread the dark chocolate topping all over
it. Run the tines of a fork along the length
of the roll to give a 'bark' effect. Just
before serving, dust with icing sugar.
Decorate with some fresh green leaves.

MINI FRUIT TRUFFLE PUDDINGS

Preparation time: 40 minutes
Total cooking time: Nil
Makes about 44

500 g (1 lb) fruit cake
2 tablespoons desiccated coconut
⅓ cup (80 ml/2¾ fl oz) dark rum
⅓ cup (30 g/1 oz) flaked almonds, toasted
  and crushed
400 g (13 oz) dark chocolate buttons,
  melted
2 teaspoons oil
150 g (5 oz) white chocolate, melted
1 stick of angelica (see Note), chopped
8 red glacé cherries, chopped

1 Finely chop the fruit cake in a food
processor. Combine in a bowl with the
coconut, rum, almonds and 150 g (5 oz) of
the melted dark chocolate buttons and
mix thoroughly. Roll two teaspoons of the
mixture at a time into balls and place on a
baking tray covered with baking paper.
2 Place the remaining melted dark
chocolate buttons and oil in a small bowl
and stir well. Sit each truffle on a fork and
dip in the chocolate to coat. Carefully
remove, allowing any excess to drain
away. Place back on the paper and leave
to set. Do not refrigerate.
3 When the chocolate is set, spoon the
white chocolate into a small piping bag or
a small plastic bag, snip off the end of the
bag and drizzle chocolate on top of each
pudding and down the sides (to look like
custard). Before the chocolate sets,
decorate with small pieces of angelica
and cherry.

NOTE: Angelica, sold in health-food
stores, is candied stems or leaf ribs of a
parsley-like plant.

GLACE FRUIT AND NUT LOAF

Preparation time: 30 minutes
Total cooking time: 1 hour 45 minutes
Serves 12

50 g (1¾ oz) unsalted butter, softened
¼ cup (55 g/2 oz) soft brown sugar
2 tablespoons breakfast marmalade
2 eggs
1 cup (125 g/4 oz) plain flour
1 teaspoon baking powder
1 teaspoon ground nutmeg
1¼ cups (200 g/6½ oz) pitted dried dates
1½ cups (240 g/7½ oz) raisins, chopped
1 cup (155 g/5 oz) brazil nuts
⅔ cup (140 g/4½ oz) red, yellow and green glacé cherries, quartered
½ cup (120 g/4 oz) chopped glacé pears or pineapple
½ cup (120 g/4 oz) chopped glacé apricots
½ cup (120 g/4 oz) chopped glacé peaches
⅓ cup (120 g/4 oz) chopped glacé figs
1 cup (100 g/3½ oz) walnut halves
⅔ cup (100 g/3½ oz) blanched almonds

Topping
2 teaspoons gelatine
2 tablespoons breakfast marmalade
150 g (5 oz) glacé pineapple or pear rings
100 g (3½ oz) red, yellow and green glacé cherries
¼ cup (40 g/1¼ oz) blanched almonds, toasted

1 Grease a deep 20 x 8 cm (8 x 3 inch) bar tin and line the base and sides with baking paper. Preheat the oven to slow 150°C (300°F/Gas 2).
2 Beat the butter, sugar and marmalade together until pale and creamy. Add the eggs and beat until combined.
3 Sift the flour, baking powder and nutmeg into a large bowl. Add the fruit and nuts and mix until each piece is coated in the flour. Stir into the egg mixture.
4 Put the mixture in the tin, pushing well into each corner. Bake for 1½–1¾ hours, or until a skewer inserted into the centre comes out clean. Cool in the tin for 10 minutes before turning out. Remove the baking paper and transfer to a wire rack to cool.
5 For the topping, sprinkle the gelatine over 2 tablespoons water and the marmalade in a small bowl. Bring a pan of water to the boil, then remove from the heat. Stand the bowl in the pan and stir until the gelatine has dissolved. Brush the top of the cake with some of the gelatine mixture, top with arranged pineapple, cherries and almonds. Brush or drizzle with more gelatine mixture and allow to set.

NOTE: This type of cake is known in some places as an American-style fruit cake, or a stained glass fruit cake.

FRESH FRUIT PAVLOVA

Preparation time: 30 minutes
Total cooking time: 55 minutes
Serves 6–8

6 egg whites
2 cups (500 g/1 lb) caster sugar
1½ tablespoons cornflour
1½ teaspoons vinegar
2 cups (500 ml/16 fl oz) cream, whipped
2 bananas, sliced
500 g (1 lb) strawberries, sliced
4 kiwi fruit, sliced
4 passionfruit, pulped

1 Preheat the oven to slow 150°C (300°F/Gas 2). Line a large baking tray with baking paper and draw a 26 cm (10½ inch) circle on the paper. Turn the paper over and place on the tray. Beat the egg whites with electric beaters in a large dry bowl until soft peaks form. Gradually add all but 2 tablespoons of the sugar, beating well after each addition. Combine the cornflour and vinegar with the last of the sugar and beat for 1 minute before adding it to the bowl. Beat for 5–10 minutes, or until all the sugar has completely dissolved and the meringue is stiff and glossy. Spread onto the paper inside the circle.
2 Shape the meringue evenly, running the flat side of a palette knife along the edge and over the top. Run the palette knife up the edge of the meringue mixture all the way round, making furrows. This strengthens the pavlova and helps prevent the edge from crumbling, as well as being decorative.
3 Bake for 40 minutes, or until pale and crisp. Reduce the heat to very slow 120°C (250°F/Gas ½) and bake for 15 minutes. Turn off the oven and cool the pavlova in the oven, using a wooden spoon to keep the door slightly ajar. When completely cooled, top with cream and fruit. Drizzle with passionfruit pulp and serve.

FRESH FRUIT MINCE TARTS

Preparation time: 1 hour + 30 minutes
 refrigeration
Total cooking time: 50 minutes
Makes 24

1¾ cups (215 g/7 oz) plain flour
150 g (5 oz) butter, chilled and chopped
¾ cup (80 g/2¾ oz) ground hazelnuts
2 tablespoons caster sugar
1–2 tablespoons iced water
icing sugar, for dusting

Filling
¾ cup (115 g/4 oz) blueberries
1 cup (200 g/6½ oz) peeled, finely chopped
 apple
½ cup (80 g/2¾ oz) raisins, chopped
½ cup (75 g/2½ oz) currants
½ cup (80 g/2¾ oz) sultanas
¼ cup (30 g/1 oz) slivered almonds,
 toasted
¼ cup (60 g/2 oz) caster sugar
2 tablespoons mixed peel
½ cup (125 ml/4 fl oz) brandy
1 teaspoon grated lemon rind
½ teaspoon mixed spice
½ teaspoon ground ginger

1 For the pastry, sift the flour into a large
bowl and rub in the butter with your
fingertips until the mixture resembles
fine breadcrumbs. Stir in the nuts and
sugar. Make a well and mix in the water
with a flat-bladed knife until the mixture
comes together in beads. Gather into a
ball and turn out onto a lightly floured
surface. Press into a ball and flatten
slightly into a disc. Cover with plastic
wrap and chill for 30 minutes.

2 Preheat the oven to moderate 180°C
(350°F/Gas 4). Roll out the dough between
sheets of baking paper to 3 mm (⅛ inch)
thick. Using a 7 cm (2¾ inch) round pastry
cutter, cut 24 pastry rounds and line two
deep 12-hole tartlet pans with the rounds.
Line each pastry case with baking paper
and fill with baking beads. Bake for 10
minutes, remove the paper and beads and
bake for another 10 minutes.
3 Meanwhile, press together the pastry
scraps and roll to 3 mm (⅛ inch) thick.
Using 4.5 cm (1¾ inch) star, bell or holly-
shaped cutters, cut 24 shapes from the
pastry for the tart lids.
4 For the filling, put all the ingredients in
a saucepan and simmer, stirring, for
5–10 minutes, or until thick and pulpy.
Cool slightly. Divide among the pastry
cases, then top each with a pastry lid.
Bake for 20 minutes, or until the lids are
golden. Leave in the pans for 5 minutes
before transferring to a wire rack to cool.
Dust with sifted icing sugar before
serving. Store in an airtight container for
up to a week.

STAINED-GLASS WINDOW BISCUITS

Preparation time: 1 hour + 15 minutes
 refrigeration
Total cooking time: 10 minutes
Makes about 20

150 g (5 oz) unsalted butter, cubed,
 softened
½ cup (60 g/3 oz) icing sugar
1 egg
1 teaspoon vanilla essence
⅓ cup (40 g/1¼ oz) custard powder
2 cups (250 g/8 oz) plain flour
¼ cup (30 g/1 oz) self-raising flour
200 g (6½ oz) assorted boiled lollies
beaten egg, to glaze

1 Line two baking trays with baking paper.
Beat the butter and icing sugar until light
and creamy. Add the egg and vanilla and
beat until fluffy, then beat in the custard
powder. Fold in the combined sifted
flours.
2 Turn onto a lightly floured surface and
knead until smooth. Roll between
2 sheets of baking paper to 3 mm (⅛ inch)
thick. Refrigerate for 15 minutes, or until
firm.
3 Preheat the oven to moderately hot
200°C (400°F/Gas 6). Separate the lollies
into their different colours and crush
using a rolling pin. Cut out the dough with
a 9.5 cm (3½ inch) fluted round cutter. Lay
on the trays. Use small cutters to cut
shapes from inside the circles.
4 Glaze the biscuits with the beaten egg
and bake for 5 minutes. Don't let the
glaze drip into the cutout sections of the
biscuits or the stained glass will be
cloudy. Fill each cut-out section with a
different-coloured lolly. Bake for
5–6 minutes, or until the lollies melt.
Leave for 10 minutes, then cool on a wire
rack.

GINGERBREAD HOUSE

MAKING THE MIXTURE

The first thing to do is to make the mixture. Place 250 g (8 oz) softened unsalted butter, ⅔ cup (155 g/5 oz) soft brown sugar and ½ cup (175 ml/6 fl oz) golden syrup in a bowl and beat until light and creamy. Gradually add 2 lightly beaten eggs, beating thoroughly after each addition. Sift 5 cups (625 g/1¼ lb) plain flour, 2 tablespoons ground ginger and 2 teaspoons bicarbonate of soda into the bowl and stir until combined. Bring the dough together with your hands, turn it out onto a well-floured work surface, then knead until smooth. Cover with plastic wrap and refrigerate for 30 minutes.

CUTTING THE SHAPES

Meanwhile, cut a paper pattern for each part of the house (when cutting the gingerbread you will need to cut two pieces of each paper pattern). The pattern for the sides should measure 10 x 20 cm (4 x 8 inches), the roof 15 x 20 cm (6 x 8 inches) and the front/back 16 x 20 cm (6½ x 8 inches). Measure 10 cm (4 inches) down from the centre of the front/back piece and draw a line across the rectangle. Turn the paper so the smaller rectangle is at the top, then draw a diagonal line from the centre of the top of the rectangle to each side, joining with the line already drawn across (this will give you a triangular end to the rectangle), then cut off the corners. Preheat the oven to moderate 180°C (350°F/Gas 4). Roll out the dough between two sheets of baking paper, in two batches if necessary, to 5 mm (¼ inch) thick. Using the paper templates as a

guide, cut out two roof pieces, a front and back piece and two sides of the house. Cut 4 rectangular pieces for the chimney 5 x 4 cm (2 x 1½ inches), then cut a wedge out of 2 of them so they will sit on the roof when joined together. If you would like windows or a door, cut these from the gingerbread. Line four baking trays with baking paper. Lift the pieces onto the trays, refrigerate for 20 minutes, then bake each tray for 12 minutes. Set aside to cool. For stained glass windows, crush assorted coloured boiled lollies and fill the cut-out windows about 5 minutes before the gingerbread is cooked. They will melt together.

ICING AND ASSEMBLY

To make the icing, place 1 egg white in a bowl and gradually add about 2¼ cups (280 g/9 oz) sifted pure icing sugar until you have a smooth mixture which will stay in place when piped—if it is too runny, add more icing sugar. To assemble the house, join the front and sides of the house together with a piped line of icing and leave to dry. Add the back to the house in the same way, hold for a few minutes, then stand up to dry. Decorate the outside seam with more piped icing to strengthen it. Join the chimney pieces together with a little icing. Attach the roof pieces and chimney using more piped icing. Leave everything to dry before decorating. Decorate the roof by attaching sweets with icing or piping decorations such as roof tiles or ivy onto the house.

NOTE: This quantity of mixture is also enough to make about 30 gingerbread people. Extra mixture can be made and cut into tree shapes to decorate the scene.

WHITE CHRISTMAS

Preparation time: 15 minutes +
  30 minutes refrigeration
Total cooking time: 5 minutes
Makes 24 pieces

1½ cups (45 g/1½ oz) puffed rice cereal
1 cup (100 g/3½ oz) milk powder
1 cup (125 g/4 oz) icing (confectioners') sugar
1 cup (90 g/3 oz) desiccated coconut
⅔ cup (160 g/5½ oz) chopped red and green glacé cherries
⅓ cup (55 g/2 oz) sultanas
250 g (8 oz) copha (white vegetable shortening)

1 Line a shallow 18 x 28 cm (7 x 11 inch) tin with foil. Put the puffed rice, milk powder, icing sugar, coconut, glacé cherries and sultanas in a large bowl and stir. Make a well in the centre.
2 Melt the shortening over low heat, cool slightly, then add to the well in the puffed rice mixture. Stir with a wooden spoon until all the ingredients are moistened.
3 Spoon the mixture into the prepared tin and smooth down the surface. Refrigerate for 30 minutes, or until completely set. Remove from the tin, and peel away and discard the foil. Cut into 24 small triangles to serve.

FRESH FROM THE OVEN

MALT BREAD

Preparation time: 45 minutes +
  1 hour 50 minutes standing
Total cooking time: 40 minutes
Makes 1 loaf

1 cup (250 ml/8 fl oz) lukewarm water
7 g (¼ oz) sachet dried yeast
1 teaspoon sugar
2 cups (300 g/9⅔ oz) plain wholemeal
  flour
1 cup (125 g/4 oz) plain flour
2 teaspoons ground cinnamon
½ cup (60 g/2 oz) raisins
30 g (1 oz) butter, melted
1 tablespoon treacle
1 tablespoon liquid malt extract, plus ½
  teaspoon
1 tablespoon hot milk

1 Brush a 21 x 14 x 7 cm (8½ x 5½ x 2¾
inch) loaf tin with oil; line the base with
baking paper. Combine the water, yeast
and sugar in a small bowl. Cover with
plastic wrap and set aside in a warm
place for 10 minutes or until foamy. Sift
the flours and cinnamon into a large
bowl; add raisins and stir. Make a well in
the centre. Add melted butter, treacle,
tablespoon of malt extract and the yeast
mixture.
2 Using a knife, mix to a soft dough. Turn
onto lightly floured surface; knead 10
minutes or until smooth. Shape into a ball
and place in a lightly oiled bowl. Set aside,
covered with plastic wrap, in a warm
place for 1 hour or until well risen. Punch
down. Knead 3 minutes or until smooth.
3 Roll into a 20 cm (8 inch) square and
then roll up. Place in tin, with the seam
underneath, and set aside, covered with
plastic wrap, in a warm place for
40 minutes or until well risen.
4 Preheat oven to moderate 180°C
(350°F/Gas 4). Brush with combined milk
and remaining malt. Bake for 40 minutes
or until a skewer comes out clean. Set
aside for 3 minutes in tin before
transferring to a wire rack to cool.

OLIVE BREAD

Preparation time: 30 minutes +
  2 hours 30 minutes rising
Total cooking time: 35 minutes
Makes 1 loaf

3 cups (375 g/12 oz) plain flour
7 g (¾ oz) sachet dry yeast
2 teaspoons sugar
2 tablespoons olive oil
110 g (3½ oz) Kalamata olives, pitted,
  halved
2 teaspoons plain flour, extra, to coat
1 small sprig of fresh oregano, leaves
  removed and torn into small pieces,
  optional
olive oil, to glaze

1 Place a third of the flour in a large bowl
and stir in 1 teaspoon salt. Place the
yeast, sugar and 1 cup (250 ml/8 fl oz)
warm water in a small bowl and stir well.
Set aside in a warm, draught-free place
for 10 minutes, or until bubbles appear on
the surface. The mixture should be frothy
and slightly increased in volume. If your
yeast doesn't foam, it is dead and you will
have to start again.
2 Add the yeast mixture to the flour and
salt mixture in the bowl and stir to make a
thin, lumpy paste. Cover with a tea towel
and set aside in a warm, draught-free
place for 45 minutes, or until doubled in
size.
3 Stir in the remaining flour and the oil
and ½ cup (125 ml/4 fl oz) warm water. Mix
with a wooden spoon until a rough dough
forms. Transfer to a lightly floured work
surface and knead for 10–12 minutes,
incorporating as little extra flour as
possible to keep the dough soft and moist,
but not sticky. Form into a ball. Oil a clean
large bowl and roll the dough around in it
to lightly coat in the oil. Cut a cross on
top, cover the bowl with a tea towel and
set aside in a warm place for 1 hour, or
until doubled in size.

4 Lightly grease a baking tray and dust
with flour. Punch down the dough on a
lightly floured surface. Roll out to
30 x 25 x 1 cm (12 x 10 x ½ inch). Squeeze
any excess liquid from the olives and toss
to coat in the extra flour. Scatter over the
dough and top with the oregano. Roll up
tightly lengthways, pressing firmly to
expel any air pockets as you roll. Press
the ends together to form an oval loaf
25 cm (10 inches) long. Transfer to the
prepared tray, join-side-down. Make
3 shallow diagonal slashes across the
top. Slide the tray into a large plastic bag
and leave in a warm place for 45 minutes,
or until doubled in bulk.
5 Preheat the oven to hot 220°C
(425°F/Gas 7). Brush the top of the loaf
with olive oil and bake for 30 minutes.
Reduce the heat to moderate 180°C
(350°F/Gas 4) and bake for another
5 minutes. Cool on a wire rack. Serve
warm or cold.

NOTE: Instead of the oregano you can use
2 teaspoons of finely chopped rosemary.
Fold it through the dough and sprinkle
whole leaves on the top after brushing
with olive oil.

TORTILLAS

Preparation time: 30 minutes
Total cooking time: 20 minutes
Makes 16

1½ cups (185 g/6 oz) plain flour, sifted
1 cup (150 g/4¾ oz) maize meal, sifted
1 cup (250 ml/8 fl oz) warm water

1 Combine the flour and maize meal in a large bowl. Make a well in the centre and then gradually add the warm water. Using a knife, mix to a firm dough. Turn out onto a lightly floured surface. Knead the dough for 3 minutes or until smooth.
2 Divide the dough into 16 portions. Roll out one portion on a lightly floured surface to a 20 cm (8 inch) round. Set aside, cover with plastic wrap and repeat with remaining portions.
3 Heat a dry heavy-based frying pan or flatplate. Place one tortilla in the pan. When the edges begin to curl slightly, turn and cook the other side. A few seconds each side is ample cooking time. If residual flour begins to burn in the pan, wipe it out with paper towels.

NOTE: Maize meal is a flour made from corn kernels. The texture varies and this recipe requires a finely ground one. It is not to be confused with polenta or cornmeal which will not work in this recipe. Tortillas (pronounced tor-tee-yah) will remain fresh for a week in an airtight container. Warm quickly in the oven or microwave. Stale tortillas can be torn into bite-sized pieces and fried in oil until crisp.

FOCACCIA
(ITALIAN FLATBREAD)

Preparation time: 30 minutes +
  3 hours 30 minutes rising
Total cooking time: 20 minutes per loaf
Makes two loaves

½ teaspoon caster sugar
7 g (¾ oz) sachet dry yeast
1 kg (2 lb) bread flour
¼ cup (60 ml/2 fl oz) olive oil

1 Put the sugar, yeast and 2 tablespoons warm water in a small bowl, mix well and leave in a warm, draught-free place for 10 minutes, or until bubbles appear on the surface. The mixture should be frothy and slightly increased in volume. If your yeast doesn't foam it is dead and you will have to start again.
2 Place the flour and 2 teaspoons salt in a large bowl and mix well. Add 2 tablespoons of the olive oil, the yeast mixture and 3 cups (750 ml/24 fl oz) warm water. Mix with a wooden spoon until the mixture comes together in a loose dough, then turn out onto a lightly floured surface. Start kneading to form a soft, moist, but non-sticky dough, adding a little extra flour or warm water as needed. Knead for 8 minutes, or until smooth, or until the impression made by a finger springs straight back out.
3 Lightly oil a large bowl. Place the dough in the bowl and roll around to coat. Cut a cross on top with a sharp knife. Cover the bowl with a clean tea towel and leave in a dry, warm place for 1 hour 30 minutes, or until doubled in size.

4 Punch down the dough on a lightly floured surface and divide in half. One or both portions can be frozen at this point. Roll one portion out to 28 x 20 cm (11 x 8 inches). Use the heels of your hands to work from the middle outwards and shape to measure 38 x 28 cm (15 x 11 inches).
5 Lightly oil a baking tray and dust with flour. Place the dough in the centre and slide the tray inside a large plastic bag. Leave in a dry, warm place for 2 hours, or until doubled in size.
6 Preheat the oven to hot 220°C (425°F/Gas 7). Brush the surface of the dough with some of the remaining olive oil and bake for 20 minutes, or until golden. Transfer to a wire rack to cool. Allow plenty of air to circulate under the loaf to keep the crust crisp. Repeat with the remaining dough. Best eaten within 6 hours of baking.

NOTES: When bread flour is unavailable and plain flour must be used, start by adding 1 cup (250 ml/8 fl oz) of the water in step 2, then gradually adding more to give a soft but non-sticky dough. Plain flour requires less water in a dough, and will give a denser textured bread.
  For a simple variation, try the simple toppings given below. Add them when the dough has risen a second time.
 Brush the top with olive oil, scatter 200 g (6½ oz) green olives over the dough and press them down firmly. Sprinkle with sea salt and rosemary sprigs and bake.
  Brush the top with olive oil, scatter 100 g (3½ oz) diced pancetta over the dough and press it down firmly. Sprinkle with 2 tablespoons grated Parmesan and bake.

BREAD

CRUSTY AND FRESH, IN ALL ITS DELIGHTFUL VARIETIES, BREAD IS THE PERFECT ACCOMPANIMENT TO MOST MEALS. SERVE PLAIN, OR DRESS IT UP WITH GARLIC, CHEESE, FRESH BASIL, PARSLEY AND OTHER HERBS.

GARLIC GRISSINI STICKS

Preheat the oven to moderately hot 200°C (400°F/Gas 6). Combine 2 crushed cloves of garlic with 1 tablespoon of olive oil. Brush over 1 packet of grissini sticks and wrap each in paper-thin strips of prosciutto. Bake for 5 minutes, until the ends crisp. Cool on trays before serving. Makes about 25.

CHEESY HERB ROLLS

Preheat the oven to 220°C (425°F/Gas 7). Combine 125 g (4 oz) of softened butter with 1 tablespoon each of chopped fresh basil, parsley and chives and ¼ cup (30 g/1 oz) of grated Cheddar cheese. Season with salt and pepper. Cut 4 crusty rosetta rolls into thin slices, but don't cut all the way through. Spread each side of each slice with flavoured butter. Bake for 15 minutes, or until the rolls are crisp and golden.
Serves 4.

CRISPY FOCACCIA TOASTS WITH PESTO

Cut a square of focaccia, about 20 cm (8 inches) in diameter, in half horizontally. Combine 1 cup (50 g/1¾ oz) of basil leaves, 2 cloves of garlic, 3 tablespoons of toasted pine nuts and 4 tablespoons of freshly grated Parmesan in a food processor until roughly chopped. With the motor running, gradually add ¼ cup (60 ml/2 fl oz) of olive oil and process until the mixture forms a smooth paste. Brush the focaccia squares with olive oil and toast both sides until golden brown. Spread the pesto over the focaccia and cut into small rectangles.
Makes 16–20.

ROASTED PEPPER (CAPSICUM) BRUSCHETTA

Cut a red and a yellow pepper (capsicum) in half, removing the seeds and membrane. Place, skin-side-up, under a hot grill until the skin blackens and blisters. Cover with a damp tea towel and allow to cool. Peel away the skin and cut the flesh into thin strips. Cut 1 loaf of woodfired Italian bread into thin slices and toast lightly until golden. Rub each side of the slices with halved cloves of garlic and brush lightly with extra virgin olive oil. Top with a little of the pepper and sprinkle with fresh lemon thyme.
Makes about 30 slices.

ANCHOVY AND TOMATO CROSTINI

Cut 1 French baguette into thick diagonal slices. Brush lightly with olive oil and toast until golden. Spread with 250 g (8 oz) of sun-dried tomato pesto and sprinkle with 50 g (1¾ oz) of drained, thinly sliced anchovy fillets, 50 g (1¾ oz) of chopped black olives and some shredded fresh basil. Makes about 15 pieces.

ABOVE, FROM LEFT: Garlic grissini sticks; Cheesy herb rolls; Crispy focaccia toasts with pesto; Roasted pepper bruschetta; Anchovy and tomato crostini

LEMON PEPPER BREAD

Preparation time: 20 minutes
Total cooking time: 25 minutes
Serves 8

2 cups (250 g/8 oz) self-raising flour
1 teaspoon salt
2 teaspoons lemon pepper, or 1 teaspoon
   grated lemon rind and 2 teaspoons
   black pepper
45 g (1½ oz) butter, chopped
1 tablespoon chopped fresh chives
¾ cup (90 g/3 oz) grated Cheddar cheese
2 teaspoons white vinegar
¾ cup (185 ml/6 fl oz) milk

1 Preheat the oven to hot 210°C
(415°F/Gas 6–7). Brush two oven trays
with melted butter or oil. Sift the flour and
salt into a large bowl and add the lemon
pepper, or lemon rind and pepper. Using
your fingertips, rub in the butter until the
mixture resembles coarse breadcrumbs.
Stir in the chives and cheese.
2 Stir vinegar into milk (it should look
slightly curdled). Add to flour mixture and
mix to a soft dough, adding more milk if
dough is too stiff.
3 Turn the dough onto a lightly floured
surface and knead until smooth. Divide
dough into two. Place on prepared trays
and press out into a circle approximately
2.5 cm (1 inch) thick. Score each with a
knife into 8 wedges, cutting lightly into
the top of the bread. Dust lightly with
flour. Bake for 20–25 minutes, or until a
deep golden colour and sounds hollow
when tapped on the base. Serve warm
with butter.

WALNUT BREAD

Preparation time: 45 minutes +
   2 hours 30 minutes rising
Total cooking time: 50 minutes
Makes 1 loaf

2½ teaspoons dried yeast
¼ cup (90 g/3 oz) liquid malt
2 tablespoons olive oil
3 cups (300 g/10 oz) walnut halves, lightly
   toasted
4¼ cups (530 g/1 lb 1 oz) white bread flour
1½ teaspoons salt
1 egg, lightly beaten

1 Grease a baking tray. Place the yeast,
liquid malt and 1⅓ cups (350 ml/11 fl oz)
warm water in a small bowl and stir well.
Leave in a warm, draught-free place for
10 minutes, or until bubbles appear on the
surface. The mixture should be frothy and
slightly increased in volume. If your yeast
doesn't foam it is dead, so you will have to
discard it and start again. Stir in the oil.
2 Process 2 cups (200 g/6½ oz) of the
walnuts in a food processor to a coarse
meal. Combine 4 cups (500 g/1 lb) of the
flour and the salt in a large bowl and stir
in the walnut meal. Make a well and add
the yeast mixture. Mix with a large metal
spoon until just combined. Turn out onto a
lightly floured surface and knead for 10
minutes, or until smooth, incorporating
enough of the remaining flour to keep the
dough from sticking—it should be soft
and moist, but it won't become very
springy. Shape the dough into a ball.
Place in a lightly oiled bowl, cover with
plastic wrap or a damp tea towel and
leave in a warm place for up to 1½ hours,
or until doubled.

3 Punch down the dough and turn out
onto a lightly floured surface. With very
little kneading, shape the dough into a
25 x 20 cm (10 x 8 inch) rectangle. Spread
with the remaining walnuts and roll up
firmly from the short end. Place the loaf
on the baking tray, cover with plastic wrap
or a damp tea towel and leave to rise for 1
hour, or until well risen and doubled in
size.
4 Preheat the oven to moderately hot
190°C (375°F /Gas 5). Glaze the loaf with
the egg and bake for 45–50 minutes, or
until golden and hollow sounding when
tapped. Transfer to a wire rack to cool.

NOTE: Use good-quality pale and plump
walnuts as cheaper varieties can be
bitter.

ROSEMARY BREAD TRIOS

Preparation time: 40 minutes +
  1 hour 30 minutes rising
Total cooking time: 15 minutes
Makes 10 trios

7 g (¼ oz) sachet dried yeast
1 teaspoon caster sugar
4 cups (500 g/1 lb) plain flour
1 tablespoon caster sugar, extra
1 teaspoon salt
1 cup (250 ml/8 fl oz) warm milk
¼ cup (60 ml/2 fl oz) vegetable oil
10 small sprigs of rosemary
1 egg yolk
sea salt flakes, to sprinkle

1 Combine the yeast, caster sugar and
½ cup (125 ml/4 fl oz) of warm water in a
small bowl. Cover and set aside in a warm
place for 10 minutes, or until frothy.
2 Sift the flour into a large bowl and stir in
the extra caster sugar and salt. Make a
well in the centre and pour in the warm
milk, oil and frothy yeast. Mix to a soft
dough, gather into a ball then turn out
onto a lightly floured surface and knead
for 10 minutes, or until smooth and
elastic. Add a little extra flour if the dough
becomes too sticky. Place in a large, oiled
bowl, cover loosely with greased plastic
wrap and leave in a warm place for 1 hour,
or until doubled in size.

3 Punch down the dough, then turn out
onto a lightly floured surface and knead
for 1 minute. Lightly grease 2 large
baking trays. Divide the dough into 10
pieces. Form each piece into three balls—
keeping the remaining pieces covered—
and place close together on the prepared
baking tray; add a sprig of rosemary to
the centre of each trio. Repeat with the
remaining pieces of dough, and lay each
set separately on the baking tray.
4 Cover the trios with a damp tea towel
and set aside for 20 minutes, or until well
risen. Preheat the oven to moderate
180°C (350°F/Gas 4). Brush the trios
lightly with the combined egg yolk and
1 teaspoon of water and sprinkle with the
sea salt flakes. Bake for 15 minutes, or
until golden brown. Allow to cool on a
wire rack and replace the rosemary
sprigs with fresh ones, if you want.

PEPPER (CAPSICUM) AND CORN MUFFINS

Preparation time: 15 minutes
Total cooking time: 20 minutes
Makes 12

1 cup (125 g/4 oz) plain flour
¼ teaspoon salt
1 tablespoon baking powder
1 cup (150 g/4¾ oz) fine polenta
  (cornmeal)
1 tablespoon caster sugar
1 egg
⅔ cup (170 ml/5½ fl oz) milk
¼ teaspoon Tabasco sauce (optional)
¼ cup (60 ml/2 fl oz) oil
½ red pepper (capsicum), finely chopped
440 g (14 oz) canned corn kernels,
  drained
3 tablespoons finely chopped fresh
  parsley

1 Preheat the oven to hot 210°C
(415°F/Gas 6–7). Brush a 12-hole muffin
tin with oil or melted butter. Sift flour, salt
and baking powder into a large bowl. Add
the polenta and sugar. Stir thoroughly
until all the ingredients are well mixed.
Make a well in the centre of the mixture.
2 Combine egg, milk, Tabasco and oil in a
separate bowl. Add egg mixture, pepper,
corn and parsley all at once to dry
ingredients. Stir quickly with a wooden
spoon or rubber spatula until all
ingredients are just moistened. (Do not
over-mix—batter should be quite lumpy.)
3 Spoon into tin. Bake 20 minutes or until
golden. Remove from oven, loosen with a
knife but leave in tin 2 minutes; cool on a
wire rack.

PARMESAN AND PROSCIUTTO LOAF

Preparation time: 30 minutes +
  2 hours rising
Total cooking time: 25 minutes
Serves 6

7 g (¼ oz) dried yeast
1 teaspoon caster sugar
½ cup (125 ml/4 fl oz) warm milk
2 cups (250 g/8 oz) plain flour
1 teaspoon salt
1 egg, lightly beaten
30 g (1 oz) butter, melted and cooled
  slightly
1 tablespoon milk, extra
60 g (2 oz) sliced prosciutto, finely
  chopped
½ cup (50 g/1¾ oz) grated Parmesan

1 Mix the yeast, sugar and milk in a bowl.
Cover and set aside in a warm place for
10 minutes, or until frothy.
2 Mix the flour and salt in a bowl. Make a
well in the centre and add the egg, butter
and frothy yeast. Mix to a soft dough and
gather into a ball; turn out onto a floured
surface and knead for 8 minutes, or until
elastic.
3 Put in an oiled bowl, cover loosely with
greased plastic wrap and leave in a warm
place for 1¼ hours, or until doubled in
size.
4 Punch down the dough, turn out onto a
floured surface and knead for 30 seconds,
or until smooth. Roll out to a rectangle,
30 x 20 cm (12 x 8 inches), and brush with
some extra milk. Sprinkle with the
prosciutto and Parmesan, leaving a
border. Roll lengthways into a log shape.
5 Lay on a greased baking tray and brush
with the remaining milk. Slash the loaf at
intervals. Leave to rise in a warm place
for 30 minutes. Bake at 220°C (425°F/
Gas 7) for 25 minutes.

CHEESE AND HERB PULL-APART LOAF

Preparation time: 25 minutes +
  1 hour 40 minutes rising
Total cooking time: 30 minutes
Serves 8

7 g (¼ oz) dried yeast
1 teaspoon sugar
4 cups (500 g/1 lb) plain flour
1½ teaspoons salt
2 tablespoons chopped fresh parsley
2 tablespoons chopped chives
1 tablespoon chopped fresh thyme
60 g (2 oz) Cheddar cheese, grated
milk, to glaze

1 Combine the yeast, sugar and ½ cup
(125 ml/4 fl oz) of warm water in a small
bowl. Cover and set aside in a warm place
for 10 minutes, or until frothy.
2 Sift the flour and salt into a bowl. Make
a well in the centre and pour in 1 cup
(250 ml/8 fl oz) warm water and the frothy
yeast. Mix to a soft dough. Knead on a
lightly floured surface for 10 minutes, or
until smooth. Put the dough in an oiled
bowl, cover loosely with greased plastic
wrap and leave for 1 hour, or until doubled
in size.
3 Punch down and knead for 1 minute.
Divide the dough in half and shape each
half into 10 flat discs, 6 cm (2½ inches) in
diameter. Mix the fresh herbs with the
Cheddar and put 2 teaspoons on a disc.
Press another disc on top. Repeat with
the remaining discs and herb mixture.
4 Grease a 21 x 10.5 x 6.5 cm (8½ x 4¼ x
2½ inch) loaf tin. Stand the filled discs
upright in the prepared tin, squashing
them together. Cover the tin with a damp
tea towel and set aside in a warm place
for 30 minutes, or until well risen.
Preheat the oven to hot 210°C (415°F/
Gas 6–7).
5 Glaze with a little milk and bake for
30 minutes, or until brown and crusty.

DOSAS

Preparation time: 5 minutes +
  overnight soaking + 8 hours standing
Total cooking time: 25 minutes
Makes 20

110 g (3½ oz) urad dal
300 g (10 oz) rice flour
oil, for cooking

1 Put the dal in a bowl and cover with
water. Soak for at least 4 hours or
overnight.
2 Drain, then grind the dal with 1 teaspoon
salt and a little water in a food processor,
blender or mortar and pestle to form a
fine paste. Mix the paste with the rice
flour, add 1 litre (32 fl oz) water and mix
well. Cover with a cloth and leave in a
warm place for 8 hours, or until the batter
ferments and bubbles. The batter will
double in volume.
3 Heat a tava (traditional Indian hot-plate)
or non-stick frying pan over medium heat
and leave to heat up. Don't overheat it—
the heat should always be medium.
Lightly brush the surface with oil. Stir the
batter and pour a ladleful into the middle
of the griddle and quickly spread it out
with the back of the ladle or a palette
knife, to form a thin pancake. Don't worry
if the dosa is not perfect, they are very
hard to get exactly right. Drizzle a little oil
or ghee around the edge to help it crisp
up. Cook until small holes appear on the
surface and the edges start to curl. Turn
over with a spatula and cook the other
side. (The first dosa is often a failure but it
will season the pan.)
4 Repeat with the remaining mixture,
oiling the pan between each dosa. Roll the
dosas into big tubes and keep warm.
Dosas are often filled with potato masala
and served with chutneys, or with curries.

FOUGASSE

Preparation time: 30 minutes +
  1 hour 20 minutes rising
Total cooking time: 35 minutes
Makes 4

7 g (¼ oz) sachet dried yeast
1 teaspoon sugar
4 cups (500 g/1 lb) white bread flour
2 teaspoons salt
¼ cup (60 ml/2 fl oz) olive oil

1 Place the yeast, sugar and ½ cup
(125 ml/4 fl oz) warm water in a small
bowl and stir until dissolved. Leave in a
warm, draught-free place for 10 minutes,
or until bubbles appear on the surface.
The mixture should be frothy and slightly
increased in volume. If your yeast doesn't
foam it is dead, so you will have to discard
it and start again.
2 Sift the flour and salt into a bowl and
make a well in the centre. Add the yeast
mixture, olive oil and ¾ cup (185 ml/6 fl
oz) warm water. Mix to a soft dough and
gather into a ball with floured hands. Turn
out onto a floured surface and knead for
10 minutes, or until smooth.
3 Place in a large, lightly oiled bowl, cover
loosely with plastic wrap or a damp tea
towel and leave in a warm place for
1 hour, or until doubled in size.
4 Punch down the dough and knead for
1 minute. Divide the mixture into four
equal portions. Press each portion into a
large, oval shape 1 cm (½ inch) thick and
make several cuts on either side of all of
them. Lay on large, floured baking trays,
cover with plastic wrap and leave to rise
for 20 minutes.
5 Preheat the oven to hot 210°C
(415°F/Gas 6–7). Bake the fougasse for
35 minutes, or until crisp. To assist the
crust to crispen, after 15 minutes cooking,
spray the oven with water.

BEER BREAD WITH SUN-DRIED TOMATO AND HERBS

Preparation time: 20 minutes
Total cooking time: 45 minutes
Serves 8

1 tablespoon finely chopped fresh
  oregano, or 1½ teaspoons dried
3 tablespoons finely chopped fresh
  parsley
2 tablespoons finely chopped fresh basil
3 tablespoons chopped sun-dried tomato
1 teaspoon cracked black pepper
3 tablespoons grated Parmesan
2 cloves garlic, crushed
3 cups (375 g/12 oz) self-raising flour
1 teaspoon salt
2 teaspoons sugar
1½ cups (375 ml/12 fl oz) beer (not bitter),
  at room temperature
2 teaspoons olive oil

1 Preheat the oven to 210°C (415°C/
Gas 6–7). Brush a 25 x 15 cm (10 x 6 inch)
loaf tin with melted butter. Mix the
oregano, parsley, basil, sun-dried tomato,
pepper, cheese and garlic.
2 Sift the flour, salt and sugar into a large
mixing bowl. Make a well in the centre
and add the herb mixture and beer. Stir
with a wooden spoon for 1 minute. (It
should be very moist—add a little more
beer if necessary.)
3 Spoon into the tin and smooth the
surface. Bake for 10 minutes, then reduce
to 180°C (350°F/Gas 4) and bake for
30 more minutes. Brush the top with oil
and cook for 5 more minutes or until well
browned and cooked through. Turn out
onto a wire rack to cool.

MOROCCAN FLATBREAD

Preparation time: 1 hour + 30 minutes
  rising
Total cooking time: 12 minutes
Makes 16

2½ cups (375 g/12 oz) wholemeal flour
1 teaspoon caster sugar
7 g (¾ oz) sachet dried yeast
½ teaspoon sweet paprika
⅓ cup (50 g/1¾ oz) cornmeal
1 tablespoon oil
1 egg, lightly beaten
2 tablespoons sesame seeds

1 Preheat the oven to moderate 180°C
(350°F/Gas 4). Lightly grease a baking
tray. Put ½ cup (75 g/2½ oz) of the flour,
the sugar, yeast, 1 teaspoon salt and
1¼ cups (315 ml/10 fl oz) tepid water in a
bowl and stir until dissolved. Cover and
leave in a warm place for 10 minutes, or
until bubbles appear. The mixture should
be frothy and slightly increased in
volume. If your yeast doesn't foam, it is
dead and you will have to start again.
2 Sift the paprika, cornmeal and
remaining flour into a bowl. Add the oil,
then stir in the yeast mixture. Mix to a
firm dough and knead until smooth. Cover
and leave in a warm, draught-free place
for 20 minutes.
3 Divide into 16 portions, roll each into a
ball, then flatten into 8 cm (3 inch)
rounds. Place on the baking tray, brush
with egg and sprinkle with sesame seeds.
Cover and set aside for 10 minutes, or
until puffed up. Bake for 12 minutes, or
until golden.

POTATO SKINS

Preparation time:5 minutes
Total cooking time: 1 hour and 10 minutes
Serves 2–4

1 Scrub 5 or 6 large potatoes and pat dry with paper towels but do not peel. Prick each potato with a fork. Bake at hot 210°C (415°F/Gas 6–7) for 1 hour, or until the skins are crisp and the flesh is soft. Turn once during cooking.
2 Leave the potatoes to cool, then halve them and scoop out the flesh, leaving a thin layer of potato in each shell. Cut each half into 3 wedges.
3 Half fill a heavy-based pan with oil and heat to moderately hot. Cook the potato skins in batches for 2–3 minutes, or until crisp. Drain on paper towels. Sprinkle with salt and cracked black pepper and serve with a creamy dip or a salsa.

PITTA BREAD

Preparation time: 20 minutes +
  40 minutes rising
Total cooking time: 5 minutes
Makes 12

7 g (¾ oz) sachet dried yeast
1 teaspoon caster sugar
3½ cups (435 g/14 oz) plain flour
2 tablespoons olive oil

1 Place the yeast, sugar and 1½ cups (375 ml/12 fl oz) lukewarm water in a bowl and stir until dissolved. Leave in a warm place for 10 minutes, or until bubbles appear on the surface. The mixture should be frothy and slightly increased in volume. If your yeast doesn't foam it is dead and you will have to start again.
2 Process the flour, yeast mixture and oil in a food processor for 30 seconds, or until the mixture forms a ball. Or, if you prefer, place the ingredients in a bowl and mix with a wooden spoon, or with your hand, until the mixture forms a smooth dough.
3 Turn the dough onto a well-floured surface and knead until smooth and elastic. Place in a well-oiled bowl, cover with plastic wrap, then a tea towel and leave in a warm place for 20 minutes, or until almost doubled in size.
4 Punch down the dough and divide into twelve equal portions. Roll each portion into a 5 mm (2 inch) thick round. Place on greased baking trays and brush well with water. Stand and allow to rise for another 20 minutes.
5 Preheat the oven to very hot 250°C (500°F/Gas 10). If the dough has dried, brush again with water. Bake for 4–5 minutes. The pitta bread should be soft and pale, slightly swollen, and hollow inside. Eat warm with kebabs or falafel, or cool on wire racks and serve with salad.

ROASTED RED CAPSICUM BUNS

Preparation time: 40 minutes +
  1 hour 40 minutes rising
Total cooking time: 1 hour
Makes 8 buns

2 red capsicums, cut into large flat pieces
7 g (¼ oz) dried yeast
2 teaspoons sugar
4 cups (500 g/1 lb) plain flour
1 teaspoon salt
1 tablespoon olive oil
1 egg, lightly beaten

1 Place the capsicum skin-side-up under a hot grill, until the skins blacken. Cool in a plastic bag, then peel away the skin and dice the flesh.
2 Combine the dried yeast, sugar and ½ cup (125 ml/4 fl oz) of warm water in a bowl and leave in a warm place for 10 minutes, or until frothy.
3 Sift the flour and salt into a bowl, make a well in the centre and pour in the oil, the frothy yeast and 1¼ cups (315 ml/10 fl oz) of warm water. Mix to a soft dough, gather into a ball and knead on a floured surface until smooth. Add a little extra flour if needed. Place in a lightly oiled bowl, cover loosely with greased plastic wrap and leave in a warm place for 1 hour, or until doubled.
4 Punch down the dough, turn out onto a floured surface and knead for 10 minutes, adding the capsicum half-way through. Divide the dough into eight and form into rounds. Lay apart on a greased baking tray. Cover with a damp tea towel and leave for 30 minutes, or until well risen. Preheat the oven to 180°C (350°F/Gas 4). Brush the buns with beaten egg. Bake for 40–45 minutes, or until the bases sound hollow when tapped.

CHAPATTIS

Preparation time: 40 minutes +
  standing time
Total cooking time: 40 minutes
Makes 20

2½ cups (310 g/9¾ oz) fine wholemeal
  flour
1 teaspoon salt
1 tablespoon oil
1 cup (250 ml/8 fl oz) warm water
½ cup (60 g/2 oz) fine wholemeal flour,
  extra

1 Place the flour and salt in a large mixing
bowl; make a well in the centre. Add the
oil and water all at once and use a
wooden spoon, then your hands, to mix to
a firm dough.
2 Turn onto a lightly floured surface and
knead for 15 minutes. Do not incorporate
the extra flour at this stage. Form dough
into a smooth ball and place in a bowl.
Cover with plastic wrap and set aside for
at least 2 hours. The dough can be left
overnight, if desired.
3 Divide the dough into 20 even-sized
pieces. Form each piece into a smooth
ball. With the aid of the extra flour, roll
each ball into a thin, pancake-sized circle.
Cover each chapatti with floured plastic
wrap and leave to rest while rolling the
remaining dough.
4 Heat a heavy-based frying pan until hot.
Cook each chapatti for 1 minute, then turn
and cook the other side for another
minute. Adjust the heat so that the dough
browns but does not burn. While the
chapatti is cooking, press the edges with
a folded tea towel. This will help bubbles
to form and make the chapatti lighter.
5 Stack and wrap the cooked chapattis in
a clean tea towel to keep them warm and
soft. Serve immediately with curry and
vegetable dishes.

ZUCCHINI (COURGETTE) AND CARROT MUFFINS

Preparation time: 20 minutes
Total cooking time: 20 minutes
Makes 12

2 medium zucchinis (courgettes)
2 carrots, peeled
2 cups (250 g/8 oz) self-raising flour
pinch salt
1 teaspoon ground cinnamon
½ teaspoon ground nutmeg
½ cup (60 g/2 oz) chopped pecans
2 eggs
1 cup (250 ml/8 fl oz) milk
90 g (3 oz) butter, melted

1 Preheat the oven to hot 210°C (415°F/
Gas 6–7). Brush a 12-hole muffin tin with
melted butter or oil. Grate the zucchinis
and carrots. Sift the flour, salt, cinnamon
and nutmeg into a large bowl. Add the
carrot, zucchini and chopped pecans.
Stir thoroughly until all the ingredients
are well combined.
2 Combine the eggs, milk and melted
butter in a separate bowl and whisk well
until combined.
3 Make a well in the centre of the flour
mixture; add the egg mixture all at once.
Mix quickly with a fork or rubber spatula
until all the ingredients are just
moistened. (Do not over-mix; the batter
should be quite lumpy.)
4 Spoon the batter evenly into the
prepared tin. Bake for 15–20 minutes or
until golden. Loosen the muffins with a
flat-bladed knife or spatula and leave in
the tin for 2 minutes, before turning out
onto a wire rack to cool.

MINI ONION AND PARMESAN SCONES

Preparation time: 25 minutes
Total cooking time: 12 minutes
Makes 24

30 g (1 oz) butter
1 small onion, finely chopped
2 cups (250 g/8 oz) self-raising flour,
  sifted
pinch salt
½ cup (50 g/1⅔ oz) finely shredded
  Parmesan cheese
½ cup (125 ml/4 oz) milk
½ cup (125 ml/4 oz) water
cayenne pepper, for sprinkling

1 Preheat the oven to hot 210°C
(415°F/Gas 6–7). Brush an oven tray with
melted butter or oil. Melt the butter in a
small pan; add onions and cook, over low
heat, for 2–3 minutes or until soft; cool
slightly.
2 Combine the flour, salt and Parmesan
cheese in a bowl. Make a well in the
centre; add onions and almost all the
combined milk and water. Mix lightly, with
a flat-bladed knife, to a soft dough, adding
more liquid if necessary.
3 Knead dough briefly on a lightly floured
surface until smooth and press out to
2 cm (¾ inch) thickness. Cut dough into
rounds with a floured 3 cm (1¼ inch) plain
round cutter. Place rounds on prepared
tray and sprinkle each lightly with
cayenne pepper. Cook for 10–12 minutes
until golden brown.

NOTE: Treat scone dough with a light
touch. Cut the liquid in with a knife and
then take care not to over-knead or you'll
have tough scones.

SPICY VEGETABLE MUFFINS

Preparation time: 20 minutes
Total cooking time: 25 minutes
Makes 12

2 cups (250 g/8 oz) self-raising flour
3 teaspoons curry powder
salt and freshly ground black pepper
½ cup (80 g/2⅔ oz) grated carrot
½ cup (60 g/2 oz) grated orange sweet
   potato
1 cup (125 g/4 oz) grated Cheddar cheese
90 g (3 oz) butter, melted
1 egg, lightly beaten
¾ cup (185 ml/6 fl oz) milk

1 Preheat oven to moderate 180°C
(350°F/Gas 4). Brush a 12-hole muffin tin
with oil or melted butter. Sift the flour,
curry powder, salt and pepper into a bowl.
Add the carrot, sweet potato and cheese
and mix through with your fingertips until
ingredients are evenly combined. Make a
well in the centre.
2 Add the combined butter, egg and milk
all at once. Using a wooden spoon, stir
until the ingredients are just combined.
(Do not over-mix—batter should be quite
lumpy.)
3 Spoon batter into tin. Bake for
25 minutes or until puffed and golden,
then loosen with a knife and leave in the
tin for 2 minutes before turning out onto a
wire rack to cool.

OLIVE SPIRALS

Preparation time: 25 minutes +
   1 hour 40 minutes rising
Total cooking time: 35 minutes
Makes 12 spirals

7 g (¼ oz) dried yeast
1 teaspoon sugar
4 cups (500 g/1 lb) plain flour
1 teaspoon salt
2 tablespoons olive oil
2 cups (250 g/8 oz) pitted black olives
½ cup (50 g/1¾ oz) finely grated
   Parmesan
3 cloves garlic, chopped
1 tablespoon oil

1 Mix the yeast, sugar and ½ cup (125 ml/
4 fl oz) warm water in a bowl. Cover and
set aside in a warm place for 10 minutes,
or until frothy.
2 Sift the flour and salt into a bowl and
make a well in the centre. Add the frothy
yeast, oil and 1 cup (250 ml/8 fl oz) of
warm water. Mix to a soft dough and
gather into a ball. Turn out onto a floured
surface and knead for 10 minutes, or until
smooth. Cover loosely with greased
plastic wrap and set aside for 1 hour, or
until well risen.
3 Process the olives, Parmesan and garlic
in a food processor until chopped. With
the motor running, add the tablespoon of
oil and process to a paste.
4 Punch down the dough and knead for
1 minute. Roll out to a rectangle 42 x 35 cm
(18 x 14 inches). Spread with the olive
paste, leaving a border along one long
side. Roll up length-ways, ending with the
clear long side.
5 Cut into 12 slices and place close
together on a greased baking tray. Cover
with a damp tea towel and set aside for
30 minutes, or until well risen. Preheat
the oven to moderately hot 200°C
(400°F/Gas 6). Bake for 35 minutes, or
until golden brown.

CHEESE AND CHIVE SCONES

Preparation time: 20 minutes
Total cooking time: 12 minutes
Makes 9

2 cups (250 g/8 oz) self-raising flour
pinch salt
30 g (1 oz) butter, chopped
½ cup (60 g/2 oz) grated Cheddar cheese
3 tablespoons shredded Parmesan
   cheese
2 tablespoons chopped chives
½ cup (125 ml/4 fl oz) milk
½ cup (125 ml/4 fl oz) water
3 tablespoons grated Cheddar cheese,
   extra

1 Preheat the oven to hot 210°C
(415°F/Gas 6–7). Brush an oven tray with
melted butter or oil. Sift the flour and salt
into bowl. Rub in the butter using your
fingertips. Stir in the cheeses and the
chives. Make a well in the centre; add the
milk and almost all of the water. Mix
lightly with a flat-bladed knife to form a
soft dough, adding more liquid if
necessary.
2 Knead the dough briefly on a lightly
floured surface until smooth. Press out
the dough to 2 cm (¾ inch) thickness.
Using a floured 5 cm (2 inch) plain round
cutter, cut rounds from dough. Place the
rounds on prepared tray and sprinkle with
extra cheese. Cook for 12 minutes or until
cheese is golden.

MINI SCONES WITH HAM, LEEK AND PORT FIGS

Preparation time: 40 minutes + chilling
Total cooking time: 45 minutes
Makes about 40

2 cups (250 g/8 oz) plain flour
3 teaspoons baking powder
110 g (3½ oz) chilled butter
100 g (3½ oz) Stilton cheese
2 tablespoons chopped fresh chives
¾ cup (185 ml/6 fl oz) milk

Filling
1 cup (250 ml/8 fl oz) port
6 large dried figs, stems removed
1 teaspoon sugar
1 large leek
1 teaspoon Dijon mustard
2 teaspoons red wine vinegar
1 tablespoon olive oil
150 g (5 oz) shaved ham

1 Sift the flour, baking powder and
¾ teaspoon salt into a large bowl.
Coarsely grate the butter and cheese into
the flour and rub in with your fingertips
until the pieces are the size of coarse
breadcrumbs. Stir in the chives. Pour in
the milk and combine with a fork until
large clumps form. Turn onto a floured
surface and press into a ball.
2 On a floured surface, roll the dough into
a 15 x 25 cm (6 x 10 inch) rectangle. With
the long edge of the dough facing you,
fold in both ends so they meet in the
centre, then fold the dough in half
widthways. Roll again into a 15 x 25 cm (6
x 10 inch) rectangle, about 1 cm (½ inch)
thick. Cut rounds close together with a 3
cm (1¼ inch) cutter. Push the scraps
together and roll and cut as before.
Place 2.5 cm (1 inch) apart on a baking
tray and refrigerate for 20 minutes.
Preheat the oven to hot 220°C (425°F/Gas
7) and bake for 10–12 minutes, or until
lightly browned.

3 In a small pan, heat the port, figs and
sugar. Bring to the boil, reduce the heat
and simmer for 15 minutes. Remove the
figs and, when cooled, roughly chop.
Simmer the liquid for about 3 minutes,
until reduced and syrupy. Put the figs
back in and stir to combine. Set aside.
4 Discard any tough leaves from the leek,
then rinse the leek. Trim off the dark
green tops. Slit the leek lengthways,
almost to the bottom, roll a quarter turn
and slit again. Wash well, drain and
steam for about 10 minutes, or until very
soft. Roughly chop, then combine with the
mustard, vinegar and oil. Season with salt
and pepper.
5 Cut the scones in half. Put a folded
piece of ham on each bottom half, top
with a teaspoon each of leek and fig
mixture, then replace the tops.

POTATO AND OLIVE SCONES

Preparation time: 25 minutes
Total cooking time: 15 minutes
Makes 15

250 g (8 oz) potatoes, peeled and chopped
½ cup (125 ml/4 fl oz) milk
freshly ground black pepper
2 cups (250 g/8 oz) self-raising flour
30 g (1 oz) butter, chopped
3 tablespoons black olives, pitted and
    chopped
3–4 teaspoons chopped fresh rosemary
½ cup (125 ml/4 fl oz) water
milk, extra, for glazing

1 Preheat the oven to hot 210°C
(415°F/Gas 6–7). Brush an oven tray with
melted butter or oil. Boil or microwave
the potatoes until tender. Mash the
potatoes with the milk and season with
pepper.
2 Sift the flour into a large bowl; add the
butter and rub in, using fingertips. Add
the olives and rosemary and stir until just
combined. Make a well in the centre; add
the mashed potato and almost all of the
water. Mix with a flat-bladed knife to a
soft dough, adding more liquid if
necessary.
3 Knead the dough briefly on a lightly
floured surface until smooth. Press out to
a thickness of 2 cm (¾ inch). Using a
floured 5 cm (2 inch) plain round cutter,
cut rounds from the dough and place
them on the prepared tray. Brush the tops
with extra milk and cook for 10–15 minutes
until the scones are golden brown. Serve
hot or cold with butter.

NOTE: The saltiness of the olives means
that no extra salt needs to be added to
this dough.

SIDE DISHES

STEAMED MIXED BEAN BUNDLES

Preparation time: 15 minutes
Total cooking time: 8 minutes
Serves 4

8 long chives
20 green beans
20 butter beans

1 Place the chives in a small bowl, cover with boiling water to soften, then drain. Trim the tops and tails from all the beans, divide into 8 bundles and tie them together with a chive. Place the bundles in a steamer over a medium pan half-filled with simmering water, or, alternatively, place them in a medium pan with 3 tablespoons of water.
2 Cover the steamer and steam the beans over medium heat for 5–8 minutes, or until just tender. Don't allow the water to completely evaporate—add more if necessary. Sprinkle the cooked beans with salt and ground black pepper and serve immediately.

HERBED CARROTS

Preparation time: 15 minutes
Total cooking time: 10 minutes
Serves 6

1 kg (2 lb) carrots
40 g (1¼ oz) butter
2 teaspoons sugar
2 teaspoons lemon juice
2 teaspoons finely chopped fresh flat-leaf parsley

1 Peel the carrots and cut into thick matchsticks. Cook in a saucepan of boiling water for 3–5 minutes, or until tender. Drain well.
2 Melt the butter in the pan and add the sugar. Return the carrots to the saucepan and toss together until the carrots start to colour a little. Add the lemon juice and parsley and toss together until the carrots are well coated.

MARINATED RED PEPPERS (CAPSICUMS)

Preparation time: 20 minutes +
    overnight marinating
Total cooking time: 5 minutes
Serves 6

3 red peppers (capsicums)
3 sprigs of fresh thyme
1 clove garlic, thinly sliced
2 teaspoons coarsely chopped fresh
    flat-leaf parsley
1 bay leaf
1 spring onion, sliced
1 teaspoon paprika
¼ cup (60 ml/2 fl oz) extra virgin olive oil
2 tablespoons red wine vinegar

1 Preheat the grill. Cut the red peppers into quarters and grill, skin-side-up, until the skin blackens and blisters. Cool in a plastic bag, then peel. Slice thinly, then place in a bowl with the thyme, garlic, parsley, bay leaf and spring onion. Mix well.
2 Whisk together the paprika, oil, vinegar and some salt and pepper. Pour over the red pepper mixture and toss to combine. Cover and refrigerate for at least 3 hours, or preferably overnight. Remove from the refrigerator about 30 minutes before serving.

NOTE: These peppers can be refrigerated for up to 3 days.

BABY BAKED POTATOES

Preparation time: 20 minutes +
  1 hour standing
Total cooking time: 30 minutes
Serves 6

750 g (1½ lb) baby potatoes
2 tablespoons olive oil
2 tablespoons fresh thyme leaves
2 teaspoons crushed sea salt

1 Wash the potatoes thoroughly under cold water. Cut any large ones in half so that they are all a uniform size for even cooking. Boil, steam or microwave the potatoes until they are just tender. (Potatoes should remain whole and intact.) Drain and lightly pat them dry with paper towels.
2 Place the potatoes in a large bowl; add the oil and thyme. Toss gently to coat the potatoes and set aside for 1 hour. Preheat the oven to moderate 180°C (350°F/Gas 4).
3 Place the potatoes in a lightly oiled baking dish. Bake for 20 minutes, turning frequently and brushing with the remaining oil and thyme mixture, until golden brown. Place in a serving bowl and sprinkle with salt. Garnish with extra thyme sprigs, if desired.

ORANGE SWEET POTATO CRUMBLE

Preparation time: 25 minutes
Total cooking time: 40 minutes
Serves 6

1 kg (2 lb) orange sweet potato (kumera)
50 g (1¾ oz) butter
⅓ cup (80 ml/2¾ fl oz) milk or cream
¼ teaspoon ground cinnamon
480 g (15 oz) loaf sourdough bread
½ cup (55 g/2 oz) grated Parmesan
1 teaspoon dried thyme leaves

1 Preheat the oven to moderate 180°C (350°F/Gas 4). Cut the orange sweet potato into chunks, put in a saucepan and cook in lightly salted boiling water for 15 minutes, or until tender. Drain and return to the saucepan.
2 Mash with a potato masher, adding the butter, milk and cinnamon. Season, to taste, with salt and freshly ground pepper, then spoon into a shallow 1 litre (32 fl oz) capacity casserole dish and smooth the top.
3 For the crumble topping, remove the crusts from the bread, break the bread into smaller pieces and finely chop in a food processor. Mix in the Parmesan and thyme, then scatter over the mash and bake for 20 minutes, or until the crumble is golden and crispy.

EGGPLANT (AUBERGINE) WITH TOMATO HERB SAUCE

Preparation time: 30 minutes
Total cooking time: 40 minutes
Serves 4

6–8 slender eggplants (aubergines)
olive oil, for frying, plus 2 tablespoons, extra
2 cloves garlic, crushed
1 onion, chopped
1 red pepper (capsicum), seeded and chopped
2 ripe tomatoes, chopped
½ cup (125 ml/4 fl oz) vegetable stock
1 teaspoon finely chopped fresh thyme
1 teaspoon finely chopped fresh marjoram
2 teaspoons finely chopped fresh oregano
1 teaspoon sugar
3–4 teaspoons white wine vinegar
3 tablespoons small black olives
salt and pepper
¼ cup (7 g/¼ oz) fresh basil leaves, shredded

1 Cut the eggplants in half lengthways. Pour enough oil into a large frying pan to cover the base. Heat until the oil is almost smoking. Fry the eggplants in batches over medium-high heat for 2–3 minutes on each side, or until golden brown. Remove from the pan with tongs and drain on paper towels. Add more oil, if necessary, to cook each batch. Cover the eggplants and keep them warm.
2 Heat the extra oil in a pan and add the garlic and onion. Stir over medium heat for 2–3 minutes. Add the red pepper and tomatoes and cook, stirring, for 1–2 minutes or until just softened.
3 Add the stock to the pan. Bring to the boil, reduce heat and simmer, stirring occasionally, for 5–10 minutes or until the liquid reduces and thickens. Stir in the thyme, marjoram, oregano, sugar and vinegar. Cook for another 3–4 minutes. Stir in the olives; season with salt and pepper. Serve the warm eggplants topped with the tomato sauce and the shredded basil.

FESTIVE FRUITY POTATOES

Preparation time: 20 minutes
Total cooking time: 50 minutes
Serves 8

1 kg (2 lb) new potatoes
1 kg (2 lb) orange sweet potato (kumera)
¾ cup (135 g/4½ oz) dried apricots
¾ cup (90 g/3 oz) raisins
⅔ cup (170 ml/5½ fl oz) orange juice
60 g (2 oz) butter, cubed
2 tablespoons chopped fresh chives

1 Preheat the oven to moderate 180°C (350°F/Gas 4). Peel the potato and orange sweet potato and cut into 3 cm (1¼ inch) pieces. Cook in simmering water for 5 minutes, or until tender, then drain.
2 Combine the apricots, raisins and orange juice in a small pan. Cover and bring to the boil, then remove from the heat and leave for 5 minutes.
3 Combine the potato, orange sweet potato and undrained fruit in a shallow ovenproof dish. Dot with butter and bake for 45 minutes, or until lightly browned. Stir occasionally. Garnish with chives before serving.

NOTE: This dish can be prepared up to baking stage 4 hours ahead.

ROASTED BALSAMIC ONIONS

Preparation time: 15 minutes +
    overnight refrigeration
Total cooking time: 1 hour 30 minutes
Serves 8 (as part of an antipasto platter)

1 kg (2 lb) pickling onions, unpeeled (see Note)
¾ cup (185 ml/6 fl oz) balsamic vinegar
2 tablespoons soft brown sugar
¾ cup (185 ml/6 fl oz) olive oil

1 Preheat the oven to warm 160°C (315°F/Gas 2–3). Bake the onions in a baking dish for 1½ hours. When cool enough to handle, trim the stems from the onions and peel away the skin (the outer part of the root should come away but the onions will remain intact). Rinse a 1 litre wide-necked jar with boiling water and dry in a warm oven (do not dry with a tea towel). Add the onions to the jar.
2 Combine the vinegar and sugar in a small screw top jar and stir to dissolve the sugar. Add the oil, seal the jar and shake the jar vigorously until the mixture is combined.
3 Pour the vinegar mixture over the onions, seal, and turn upside-down to coat. Marinate overnight in the refrigerator, turning occasionally. Return to room temperature and shake to combine the dressing before serving.

NOTE: Pickling onions are very small. The ideal size is around 35 g (1¼ oz) each. Sizes will probably range from 20 g (¾ oz) up to 40 g (1¼ oz). The cooking time given is suitable for this range and there is no need to cook the larger ones for any longer. The marinating time given is a minimum time and the onions can be marinated for up to three days in the refrigerator. The marinade may separate after a few hours, which is fine — simply stir occasionally.

BRUSSELS SPROUTS AND CHESTNUTS

Preparation time: 30 minutes
Total cooking time: 20 minutes
Serves 8

500 g (1 lb) fresh chestnuts or
    240 g (7½ oz) can
1 kg (2 lb) Brussels sprouts
30 g (1 oz) butter
grated fresh nutmeg

1 Make slits in the skins of the chestnuts and put them in a saucepan. Cover with cold water and bring to the boil over high heat. Reduce the heat and simmer for 10 minutes. Drain and leave until cool enough to handle. Peel off the skins.
2 Trim the sprouts and cut a cross in the base of each. Bring a pan of water to the boil, add the sprouts and simmer for 5–8 minutes, or until just tender. Melt the butter in a large frying pan and add the chestnuts. Cook until they begin to brown, then add the sprouts and toss together until heated through. Season well with salt, pepper and nutmeg.

MUSHROOMS IN SPRING ONION DRESSING

Preparation time: 15 minutes +
    15 minutes marinating
Total cooking time: Nil
Serves 4

2 cm (¾ inch) piece fresh ginger
500 g (1 lb) button mushrooms
6 spring onions
¼ cup (60 ml/2 fl oz) Japanese rice
    vinegar
¼ cup (60 ml/2 fl oz) Japanese soy sauce
2 tablespoons mirin

1 Cut the ginger into very thin slices, place into a bowl and cover with iced water. Set aside.
2 Wipe the mushrooms with damp paper towels and trim the stalks. Slice the spring onions finely, including most of the green tops. Combine the mushrooms and spring onion in a bowl.
3 Place the vinegar, soy sauce, mirin and salt to taste in a small bowl and mix to combine. Pour the marinade over the mushroom mixture, toss to coat and leave to marinate for 15 minutes.
4 Remove the mushrooms and spring onion from the marinade with a slotted spoon, draining excess liquid. Arrange the mushroom mixture on a platter. Drain the ginger and scatter the slices over the mushrooms.

KHICHHARI

Preparation time: 10 minutes + 2 hours
    soaking + 10 minutes standing
Total cooking time: 25 minutes
Serves 6

¼ cup (60 g/2 oz) yellow lentils
1½ cups (300 g/10 oz) basmati rice
60 g (2 oz) ghee
1 teaspoon cumin seeds
6 cloves
½ cinnamon stick
2 onions, finely chopped
2 garlic cloves, finely chopped
2 cm (¾ inch) piece of ginger, finely
    chopped
1 teaspoon garam masala
¼ cup (60 ml/2 fl oz) lemon juice
1 teaspoon salt

1 Soak the lentils in 2 cups (500 ml/ 16 fl oz) water in a large saucepan for 2 hours. Wash the rice in a sieve under cold water until the water from the rice runs clear. Drain.
2 Heat the ghee in a heavy-based saucepan over low heat and fry the cumin seeds, cloves and cinnamon for a few seconds. Increase the heat to medium, add the onion, garlic and ginger and cook for a few minutes until they soften and begin to brown.
3 Add the rice and lentils and toss to thoroughly coat in ghee. Add the garam masala, lemon juice, salt and 3 cups (750 ml/24 fl oz) boiling water. Bring to the boil, then reduce the heat to very low, cover tightly and cook for 15 minutes. Remove from the heat and gently fluff up with a fork. Cover the pan with a clean cloth and leave for 10 minutes. Fluff up again and season with salt, to taste.

FRIED GREEN TOMATOES

Preparation time: 15 minutes
Total cooking time: 12 minutes
Serves 4–6

¾ cup (90 g/3 oz) plain flour
1 teaspoon salt
½ teaspoon white pepper
¼ cup (35 g/1¼ oz) polenta (cornmeal)
1 egg
¾ cup (185 ml/6 fl oz) milk
4 medium green tomatoes
    (about 500 g/1 lb)
oil, for frying

1 Sift the flour, salt and pepper into a medium bowl. Add the polenta and stir to combine. Make a well in the centre.
2 Combine the egg and milk and add gradually to flour mixture. Whisk the batter until just combined, but do not over-beat.
3 Cut the tomatoes into thick slices. Heat about 1 cm (½ inch) of oil in a frying pan.
4 Dip the tomatoes into the batter; drain excess and fry for 1 minute on each side, turning only once with tongs. Drain on paper towels and serve immediately.

NOTE: Red tomatoes can be also be used.

BROCCOLI WITH ALMONDS

Preparation time: 10 minutes
Total cooking time: 10 minutes
Serves 6

500 g (1 lb) broccoli, cut into small florets
2 teaspoons oil
20 g (¾ oz) butter
1 clove garlic, crushed
1 tablespoon flaked almonds

1 Add the broccoli to a saucepan of boiling water and cook for 1–2 minutes, or until just tender. Drain thoroughly. Heat the oil and butter in a large frying pan, add the garlic and almonds and cook for
1–2 minutes, or until
the almonds are golden. Remove from the pan and set aside.
2 Add the broccoli to the frying pan and toss over medium heat for 2–3 minutes, or until the broccoli is heated through. Return the almonds to the pan and stir until well distributed. Serve hot.

SAUTEED ROSEMARY POTATOES

Preparation time: 15–20 minutes
Total cooking time: 35 minutes
Serves 4–6

750 g (1½ lb) baby new potatoes
30 g (1 oz) butter
2 tablespoons olive oil
black pepper
2 cloves garlic, crushed
1 tablespoon finely chopped fresh rosemary
1 teaspoon coarse rock or sea salt
½ teaspoon cracked black pepper

1 Wash the potatoes, pat dry with paper towels. Cut in half. Lightly boil or steam potatoes until they are just tender. Drain; cool slightly.
2 Heat the butter and oil in a large heavy-based frying pan. When the mixture is foaming, add the potatoes and season with pepper. Cook over medium heat for 5–10 minutes or until golden and crisp, tossing regularly to ensure that the potatoes are evenly coloured.
3 Stir in the garlic, rosemary and salt. Cook for 1 minute or until well coated. Add the cracked pepper and mix well. Serve hot or warm.

NOTE: Fresh thyme would work nicely in this recipe, as would fresh parsley.

FENNEL CRUMBLE

Preparation time: 25 minutes
Total cooking time: 40 minutes
Serves 6

2 fennel bulbs
¼ cup (60 ml/2 fl oz) plus 2 tablespoons lemon juice
salt and freshly ground black pepper
1 tablespoon honey
1 tablespoon plain flour
1¼ cups (315 ml/10 fl oz) cream

Crumble Topping
¾ cup (75 g/2½ oz) rolled oats
½ cup (60 g/2 oz) plain flour
1 cup (110 g/3⅔ oz) black rye breadcrumbs, (made from 3 slices bread)
60 g (2 oz) butter
1 clove garlic, crushed

1 Preheat the oven to moderate 180°C (350°F/Gas 4). Brush a large ovenproof serving dish with melted butter or oil. Trim fennel and cut into thin slices. Wash and drain well. Bring a large pan of water to boil. Add ¼ cup (60 ml/2 fl oz) lemon juice and fennel slices. Cook over medium heat for 3 minutes. Drain; rinse under cold water.
2 Place the fennel in a large bowl. Add the extra lemon juice with the black pepper and honey; toss to combine. Sprinkle with the flour. Spoon into the prepared dish and pour the cream over the top.
3 To make Crumble Topping: Combine the oats, flour and breadcrumbs. Heat the butter in a small pan, add the garlic and cook 30 seconds. Pour over the dry ingredients and mix well. Sprinkle the crumble over the fennel. Bake for 20–30 minutes or until fennel is tender and crumble is browned.

NOTE: White or wholemeal breadcrumbs can be used in place of rye bread. Fennel has an aniseed flavour. Blanching it before use softens the texture slightly and reduces the strong flavour.

SPICY STEAMED CORN COBS

Preparation time: 25 minutes
Total cooking time: 10–20 minutes
Serves 4

4 corn cobs or 15 baby corn cobs
5 cm (2 inch) piece fresh ginger, grated
3 cloves garlic, chopped
1–3 teaspoons chopped fresh red chillies
2 teaspoons green peppercorns, crushed
2 tablespoons water
2 tablespoons fish sauce (optional)

1 Remove the husks and all the silk threads from the corn cobs. In a bowl, place the ginger, garlic, chillies, peppercorns and water; mix well.
2 Roll each cob in the spice mixture and place in a steaming basket, lined with banana leaves or baking paper.
3 Place the basket over a wok or pan of boiling water, cover and steam for 10–20 minutes (depending on the size of the corn), or until the corn is tender; drain. Sprinkle with fish sauce and serve immediately.

NOTE: Bamboo steaming baskets are inexpensive to buy and very handy for steaming vegetables. Always line the base to prevent food falling through. Baby corn cobs are available from speciality fruit and vegetable shops.

SAUTEED SILVERBEET (SWISS CHARD)

Preparation time: 15 minutes
Total cooking time: 10 minutes
Serves 4–6

1 kg (2 lb) silverbeet (Swiss chard)
2 tablespoons olive oil
3 cloves garlic, sliced thinly
extra virgin olive oil, for serving

1 Trim the leaves from the stalks of the silverbeet and rinse them in cold water. Blanch the leaves in a large saucepan of boiling, salted water for 1–2 minutes, or until tender but still firm. Drain well in a colander. Lay out on a tea towel or tray to cool, then, using your hands, gently wring out the excess water from the leaves.
2 Heat the oil in a heavy-based frying pan and cook the garlic over low heat until just starting to turn golden. Add the silverbeet, season with salt and pepper and cook over medium heat for 3–4 minutes, or until warmed through. Transfer to a serving plate and drizzle with extra virgin olive oil. Serve warm or at room temperature.

NOTE: This is delicious eaten warm with meats or fish, or at room temperature with bruschetta, as part of an antipasto platter.

CANDIED PUMPKIN

Preparation time: 20 minutes
Total cooking time: 35 minutes
Serves 4

500 g (1 lb) pumpkin
30 g (1 oz) butter
2 tablespoons cream
1 tablespoon soft brown sugar
fresh chives, chopped, to garnish

1 Preheat the oven to moderate 180°C (350°F/Gas 4). Peel the pumpkin and remove the membrane and seeds. Cut the pumpkin into thin slices and place the slices, overlapping, in a 1 litre (32 fl oz) ovenproof dish. Put the butter, cream and sugar in a small pan over low heat. Stir until smooth, then pour the mixture over the pumpkin. Bake for 35 minutes, or until the pumpkin is tender. Sprinkle with chives.

INDIAN SIDE DISHES

CAULIFLOWER BHAJI

Heat ¼ cup (60 ml/2 fl oz) oil over low heat in a saucepan. Add ¼ teaspoon black mustard seeds and ¾ teaspoon cumin seeds, cover and pop for a few seconds. Uncover, add 250 g (8 oz) diced potato and fry for 1 minute, stirring occasionally. Add 750 g (1½ lb) cauliflower florets, ½ teaspoon ground cumin, ½ teaspoon ground coriander, ¼ teaspoon ground turmeric, ½ teaspoon garam masala, 2 finely chopped garlic cloves, 2 seeded and finely chopped green chillies and 5 curry leaves and stir well. Add ¼ cup (60 ml/2 fl oz) water and bring to the boil. Cover and simmer for 6 minutes, or until the cauliflower is cooked and tender.
Serves 4.

MIXED VEGETABLE CURRY

Bring 2 cups (500 ml/16 fl oz) water to the boil in a saucepan, add ½ teaspoon ground turmeric and 200 g (6½ oz) thickly sliced carrots, reduce the heat and simmer for 5 minutes. Add 200 g (6½ oz) thickly sliced sweet potato and 200 g (6½ oz) halved green beans, return to the boil, then reduce the heat and simmer for 5 minutes, or until the vegetables are almost cooked. Put 50 g (1¾ oz) grated coconut, 2 tablespoons grated ginger and 3 finely chopped green chillies in a blender with a little water, and blend to a paste. Add to the vegetables with 1½ teaspoons ground cumin and some salt and simmer for 2 minutes. Stir in 400 g (13 oz) thick natural yoghurt and heat through. Heat 1 tablespoon oil over low heat in a small saucepan. Add 10 curry leaves and allow to crisp. Pour over the vegetables.
Serves 4.

BALTI OKRA

Remove the stems from 750 g (1½ lb) okra, then cut into 2.5 cm (1 inch) lengths. Heat ⅓ cup (80 ml/2¾ fl oz) oil in a frying pan, add 1 finely chopped onion and cook for 10 minutes, or until golden. Add the okra, 1 teaspoon chilli powder, ½ teaspoon ground turmeric, 2 quartered tomatoes, and salt and cook, covered, stirring often, for 30 minutes, or until the okra is tender. Add 1 tablespoon garam masala, ¼ teaspoon ground cardamom and a pinch of freshly grated nutmeg, and cook, stirring, for 1–2 minutes.
Serves 6.

CHICKPEA CURRY

Soak 1 cup (220 g/7 oz) dried chickpeas in a bowl of water overnight. Drain, rinse and put in a large saucepan. Cover with plenty of water and bring to the boil, then reduce the heat and simmer for 40 minutes, or until soft. Drain. Heat 2 tablespoons oil in a large saucepan, add 2 finely chopped onions and cook over medium heat for 15 minutes, or until golden. Add 2 chopped tomatoes, 1 tablespoon channa (chole) masala, 1 teaspoon each of cumin and chilli powder, ½ teaspoon ground coriander, ¼ teaspoon turmeric and 2 cups (500 ml/16 fl oz) water, and cook for 10 minutes, or until the tomato is soft. Add the chickpeas, season with salt and cook for 7–10 minutes, or until the sauce thickens. Transfer to a serving dish. Put 20 g (¾ oz) ghee or butter on top and allow to melt before serving. Garnish with sliced onion, mint and coriander (cilantro).
Serves 6.

EGG CURRY

Put 8 eggs at room temperature in a saucepan of cold water and bring to the boil. Reduce the heat and simmer for 8 minutes. Remove from the pan and allow to cool in cold water. Peel the eggs. Heat 2 tablespoons oil in a saucepan, add 2 finely chopped onions, 1 teaspoon grated fresh ginger, 2 crushed garlic cloves and 3 bay leaves, and cook for 4 minutes, or until the onion is soft. Add a 400 g (13 oz) tin chopped tomatoes, ¼ teaspoon ground turmeric, ½ teaspoon chilli powder, 1 teaspoon ground cumin, 1 teaspoon ground coriander, 1 teaspoon salt and 1 cup (250 ml/8 fl oz) water. Bring to the boil, then reduce the heat and simmer for 3 minutes. Add 1 tablespoon garam masala and the whole hard-boiled eggs, and simmer for another 1–2 minutes. Garnish with coriander leaves.
Serves 4–6.

CRISP POTATOES IN SPICY TOMATO SAUCE

Preparation time: 15 minutes
Total cooking time: 1 hour
Serves 6

1 kg (2 lb) desiree potatoes
oil, for deep-frying
500 g (1 lb) ripe Roma tomatoes
2 tablespoons olive oil
¼ red onion, finely chopped
2 cloves garlic, crushed
3 teaspoons paprika
¼ teaspoon cayenne pepper
1 bay leaf
1 teaspoon sugar
1 tablespoon chopped fresh flat-leaf
   parsley, to garnish

1 Cut the potatoes into 2 cm (¾ inch) cubes. Rinse, then drain well and pat completely dry. Fill a deepfryer or large heavy-based saucepan one third full of oil and heat to 180°C (350°F), or until a cube of bread dropped into the oil browns in 15 seconds. Cook the potato in batches for 10 minutes, or until golden. Drain well on paper towels. Do not discard the oil.
2 Score a cross in the base of each tomato. Place in a bowl of boiling water for 10 seconds, then plunge into cold water and peel the skin away from the cross. Chop the flesh.

3 Heat the olive oil in a saucepan over medium heat and cook the onion for 3 minutes, or until softened. Add the garlic, paprika and cayenne, and cook for 1–2 minutes, until fragrant.
4 Add the tomato, bay leaf, sugar and 90 ml (3 fl oz) water, and cook, stirring occasionally, for 20 minutes, or until thick and pulpy. Cool slightly and remove the bay leaf. Blend in a food processor until smooth, adding a little water if necessary. Before serving, return the sauce to the saucepan and simmer over low heat for 2 minutes, or until heated though. Season well.
5 Reheat the oil to 180°C (350°F) and cook the potato again, in batches, for 2 minutes, or until very crisp and golden. Drain on paper towels. This second frying makes the potato extra crispy and stops the sauce soaking in immediately. Place on a platter and cover with sauce. Garnish with parsley and serve.

GREEN BEANS WITH TOMATO AND OLIVE OIL

Preparation time: 10 minutes
Total cooking time: 25 minutes
Serves 4

⅓ cup (80 ml/2¾ fl oz) olive oil
1 large onion, chopped
3 cloves garlic, finely chopped
400 g (13 oz) can good-quality chopped
   tomatoes
½ teaspoon sugar
750 g (1½ lb) green beans, trimmed
3 tablespoons chopped fresh flat-leaf
   parsley

1 Heat the olive oil in a large frying pan, add the onion and cook over medium heat for 4–5 minutes, or until softened. Add the garlic and cook for another 30 seconds.
2 Add the tomato, sugar and ½ cup (125 ml/4 fl oz) water, then season with salt and freshly ground black pepper. Bring to the boil, then reduce the heat and simmer for 10 minutes, or until reduced slightly.
3 Add the beans and simmer for another 10 minutes, or until the beans are tender and the tomato mixture is pulpy. Stir in the parsley. Check the seasoning, and adjust according to your taste. Serve immediately, as a side dish.

FESTIVE COCONUT RICE

Preparation time: 25 minutes
Total cooking time: 40 minutes
Serves 4

3 tablespoons oil
1 medium onion, cut into thin wedges
4 cm (1½ inch) piece fresh ginger, grated
2 cloves garlic, finely chopped
2½ cups (500 g/1 lb) long-grain rice
1 teaspoon ground turmeric
4 cups (1 litre) coconut milk
1 teaspoon salt
6 curry leaves

Garnishes
3 hard-boiled eggs, cut into quarters
1 Lebanese cucumber, thinly sliced
2 red chillies, thinly sliced
½ cup (35 g/1¼ oz) crisp fried onion

1 Heat the oil in a large heavy-based pan; add the onion, ginger and garlic and fry over low heat for 5 minutes. Add the rice and turmeric, and cook for 2 minutes, stirring well.
2 Place the coconut milk in a medium pan, and heat until nearly boiling. Pour the milk over the rice, stirring constantly until the mixture comes to the boil. Add the salt and curry leaves. Cover with a tight-fitting lid, reduce the heat to very low and cook for 25 minutes.
3 Remove the lid, stir well and leave to cool for 10 minutes. Remove the curry leaves and pile the rice onto a platter (traditionally lined with banana leaves). Arrange the egg, cucumber and chilli over the rice and scatter the fried onion over the top.

SPICED RED CABBAGE

Preparation time: 20 minutes
Total cooking time: 1 hour 30 minutes
Serves 6

750 g (1½ lb) red cabbage
1 large red onion, chopped
1 green apple, cored and chopped
2 cloves garlic, crushed
¼ teaspoon ground cloves
¼ teaspoon ground nutmeg
1½ tablespoons soft brown sugar
2 tablespoons red wine vinegar
20 g (¾ oz) butter, cubed

1 Preheat the oven to slow 150°C (300°F/Gas 2). Quarter the cabbage and remove the core. Finely slice the cabbage and put it in a large ovenproof casserole dish with the onion and apple. Toss well.
2 Combine the garlic, spices, sugar and vinegar in a small bowl. Pour the mixture over the cabbage, and toss. Dot the top with the butter. Cover and bake for 1½ hours, stirring once or twice. Season, to taste, with salt and freshly ground black pepper, and serve hot.

SPICY EGGPLANT (AUBERGINE) SLICES

Preparation time: 15 minutes +
  15 minutes standing
Total cooking time: 15 minutes
Serves 4–6

2 medium eggplants (aubergines)
salt
⅓ cup (40 g/1⅓ oz) plain flour
2 teaspoons ground cumin
2 teaspoons ground coriander
1 teaspoon chilli powder
oil, for frying
½ cup (125 g/4 oz) plain yoghurt
1 tablespoon chopped fresh mint

1 Cut the eggplants into 1 cm (½ inch) slices. Arrange in a single layer on a tray and cover well with salt. Allow to stand for 15 minutes, then rinse and pat dry thoroughly with paper towels.
2 Sift the flour and spices onto a plate. Dust the eggplant slices with flour mixture; shake off any excess. Heat about 2 cm (¾ inch) oil in a heavy-based pan. Cook the eggplant slices a few at a time, for 2–3 minutes each side or until golden. Drain on paper towels. Combine the yoghurt and mint. Serve with the warm eggplant.

JAMAICAN RICE WITH PEAS

Preparation time: 5 minutes
Total cooking time: 35 minutes
Serves 6–8

2 cups (400 g/13 oz) long-grain rice
3 cups (750 ml/24 fl oz) coconut milk
400 g (13 oz) tin kidney beans, drained and rinsed
2 teaspoons finely chopped thyme
4 garlic cloves, crushed
large pinch of ground allspice
4 whole spring onions (scallions), bruised
1 small red chilli

1 Combine all the ingredients in a large saucepan and add enough water to come about 2.5 cm (1 inch) above the rice. Slowly bring to the boil over medium heat, cover, reduce the heat to low and simmer for about 25 minutes, or until the rice is tender and the liquid has been absorbed.
2 Remove the spring onion and chilli, season well and serve.

NOTES: As a variation, add 1 cup (155 g/5 oz) chopped smoked ham to the other ingredients before you start to cook.

This Jamaican staple is actually rice with beans; however beans are often referred to as peas in Jamaica. Kidney beans are commonly used, though some authentic versions contain hard-to-find gungo or pigeon peas.

BAKED ROOT VEGETABLES WITH SWEET GINGER GLAZE

Preparation time: 25 minutes
Total cooking time: 1 hour 10 minutes
Serves 4–6

150 g (4¾ oz) sweet potato
1 medium potato
1 medium carrot
1 medium parsnip
1 medium turnip
2 tablespoons olive oil
60 g (2 oz) butter
2 tablespoons caster sugar
1 tablespoon finely grated fresh ginger
¼ cup (60 ml/2 fl oz) water

1 Preheat oven to hot 210°C (415°F/Gas 6–7). Brush a large baking tray with oil.
2 Peel the sweet potato, potato, carrot, parsnip and turnip and cut into sticks about 5 cm (2 inches) long and 1 cm (½ inch) thick.
3 Place the vegetables in a single layer on the prepared baking tray and brush them all over with olive oil. Bake for 1 hour or until golden.
4 Melt the butter in a small pan. Add the sugar and stir over low heat until the sugar has dissolved. Add the grated ginger and the water and stir to combine. Bring to the boil, reduce heat to low and simmer, uncovered, for 5 minutes or until the mixture has reduced and thickened slightly. Pour the glaze over the baked vegetables; toss to coat and return the tray to the oven for another 5 minutes. Serve immediately, with steamed green vegetables if you like.

CREAMY POTATO GRATIN

Preparation time: 20 minutes
Total cooking time: 40 minutes
Serves 6

750 g (1½ lb) waxy or all-purpose potatoes
1 onion
1 cup (125 g/4 oz) grated Cheddar
1½ cups (375 ml/12 fl oz) cream
2 teaspoons chicken stock powder

1 Preheat the oven to moderate 180°C (350°F/Gas 4). Thinly slice the potatoes and slice the onion into rings.
2 Arrange a layer of overlapping potato slices in a baking dish and top with a layer of onion rings. Divide the cheese in half and set aside one half for topping. Sprinkle a little of the remaining cheese over the onion. Continue layering in this order until all the potato and the onion have been used, finishing with a little cheese.
3 Pour the cream into a small jug, add the chicken stock powder and whisk gently until thoroughly combined. Pour the mixture over the layered potato and onion and sprinkle the top with the reserved cheese. Bake for 40 minutes, or until the potato is tender, the cheese has melted and the top is golden brown.

NOTES: A gratin is any dish topped with cheese and/or breadcrumbs and cooked until browned. There are many versions of potato gratin—some are creamy like this one, others less so.

If you prefer, you can use different types of stock, including vegetable, to vary the flavour.

Waxy or all-purpose potatoes are best as they hold their shape better when cooked in this way.

If you have a mandolin, use it to cut the potatoes into thin slices. If not, make sure you use a very sharp knife. Peel the skin very thinly.

ROAST VEGETABLE MASH

Preparation time: 30 minutes
Total cooking time: 1 hour 30 minutes
Serves 4–6

2 large pontiac or sebago potatoes
400 g (13 oz) pumpkin
400 g (13 oz) orange sweet potato
　(kumera)
2 large parsnips
1 large onion, chopped
2 ripe tomatoes, quartered
6 cloves garlic, unpeeled
2 tablespoons olive oil
30 g (1 oz) butter, chopped

1 Preheat the oven to moderate 180°C
(375°F/Gas 4). Peel the potatoes,
pumpkin, orange sweet potato and
parsnip, then cut into large pieces and
place in a large baking dish with the
onion, tomato and garlic. Drizzle with oil
and sprinkle with salt and cracked black
pepper.
2 Bake the vegetables for 1½ hours, or
until soft and starting to brown, turning
every 30 minutes. Peel the garlic.
3 Transfer the vegetables to a bowl, add
the butter and mash. Season, to taste,
with salt and freshly ground pepper.

NOTE: You could also substitute swedes,
celeriac or Jerusalem artichoke for the
parsnips, or carrot for pumpkin or orange
sweet potato. Fresh herbs are also a tasty
addition—stir through some chopped
fresh basil or parsley when mashing the
vegetables.

BROAD BEANS WITH HAM

Preparation time: 10 minutes
Total cooking time: 30 minutes
Serves 4

20 g (¾ oz) butter
1 onion, chopped
180 g (6 oz) serrano ham, roughly
　chopped (see Note)
2 cloves garlic, crushed
500 g (1 lb) broad beans, fresh or frozen
½ cup (125 ml/4 fl oz) dry white wine
¾ cup (185 ml/6 fl oz) chicken stock

1 Melt the butter in a large saucepan and
add the onion, ham and garlic. Cook over
medium heat for 5 minutes, stirring often,
until the
onion softens.
2 Add the broad beans and wine and cook
over high heat until reduced by half. Add
the stock, reduce the heat, cover and
cook, for 10 minutes. Uncover and simmer
for another 10 minutes. Serve hot as a
vegetable accompaniment to meat, or
warm as a snack with crusty bread.

NOTE: Instead of serrano ham, you can
use thickly sliced prosciutto, choosing
one which is pink, soft and sweet, not dry
and salty.

BRAISED FENNEL

Preparation time: 15 minutes
Total cooking time: 30 minutes
Serves 8

4 small fennel bulbs
20 g (¾ oz) butter
1 tablespoon sugar
⅓ cup (80 ml/2¾ fl oz) white wine
⅔ cup (160 ml/5 fl oz) chicken stock
1 tablespoon sour cream

1 Slice the fennel bulbs into quarters,
reserving the fronds. Melt the butter in a
frying pan and stir in the sugar. Add the
fennel, and cook for 5–10 minutes, until
lightly browned all over.
2 Pour in the wine and stock and bring to
the boil, then reduce the heat and
simmer, covered, for 10 minutes, or until
tender.
3 Uncover and boil until most of the liquid
has evaporated and the sauce has
become sticky. Remove from the heat and
stir in the sour cream. Garnish with the
reserved fennel fronds.

RISOTTO-STUFFED ONIONS

Preparation time: 15 minutes
Total cooking time: 1 hour 40 minutes
Serves 8

8 onions (about 200 g/6½ oz each)
1 tablespoon oil
20 g (¾ oz) butter
70 g (2¼ oz) mushrooms, chopped
20 g (¾ oz) prosciutto, chopped
½ cup (110 g/3½ oz) arborio rice
2½ cups (600 ml/20 fl oz) hot chicken
   stock
2 tablespoons grated Parmesan
2 tablespoons chopped fresh parsley

1 Preheat the oven to moderately hot
200°C (400°F/Gas 6). Trim the bases of
the onions so they sit flat and cut the tops
off, leaving a wide opening. Place in a
baking dish, drizzle with the oil and bake
for 1–1½ hours, or until golden.
2 Meanwhile, melt the butter in a pan, add
the mushrooms and prosciutto and cook
for 5 minutes, or until the mushrooms
have softened. Add the rice and stir until
well coated with the butter. Gradually stir
in the hot chicken stock, about ½ cup
(125 ml/4 fl oz) at a time, making sure the
liquid has been absorbed before adding
more. When all the stock has been
absorbed, stir in the Parmesan and
parsley.
3 Scoop out the flesh from the middle of
each onion, leaving at least 3 outside
layers on each, to hold the filling. Chop
the scooped flesh and stir through the
risotto mixture. Spoon the filling into the
onion shells, piling a little on top. Bake for
10 minutes to heat through, then serve.

ANDALUCIAN ASPARAGUS

Preparation time: 10 minutes
Total cooking time: 15 minutes
Serves 4

500 g (1 lb) fresh asparagus
¼ cup (60 ml/2 fl oz) extra virgin olive oil
1 thick slice crusty country bread, crusts
   removed and cut into cubes
2–3 cloves garlic
12 blanched almonds
1 teaspoon paprika
1 teaspoon ground cumin
1 tablespoon red wine or sherry vinegar

1 Trim the woody ends from the
asparagus.
2 Heat the oil in a heavy-based frying pan
and cook the bread, garlic and almonds
over medium heat for 2–3 minutes, or
until all the ingredients are golden. Using
a slotted spoon, transfer to a food
processor and add the paprika, cumin,
vinegar, salt and pepper and 1 tablespoon
water. Process until the mixture forms a
coarse meal.
3 Return the frying pan to the heat and
add the asparagus with a little extra oil if
necessary. Cook over medium heat for
3–5 minutes, then add the bread and
almond mixture with 200 ml (6½ fl oz)
water. Simmer for 3–4 minutes, or until
the asparagus is tender but still firm to
the bite and most of the liquid has boiled
away. Serve.

SWEET ROAST BEETROOT

Preparation time: 15 minutes
Total cooking time: 1 hour 30 minutes
Serves 6

12 small fresh beetroot
1½ tablespoons olive oil
20 g (¾ oz) butter
1½ teaspoons ground cumin
1 teaspoon coriander seeds, lightly
   crushed
½ teaspoon mixed spice
1 clove garlic, crushed, optional
3–4 teaspoons soft brown sugar
1 tablespoon balsamic vinegar

1 Preheat the oven to moderate 180°C
(350°F/Gas 4) and brush a baking dish
with melted butter or oil. Trim the leafy
tops from the beetroot (cut about 3 cm/
1¼ inches above the pulp to prevent
bleeding), wash the bulbs thoroughly and
place on the tray. Bake for 1 hour
15 minutes, or until very tender. Set aside
until the bulbs are cool enough to handle.
2 Peel the beetroot and trim the tops and
tails to neaten. Heat the oil and butter in a
frying pan, add the cumin, coriander
seeds, mixed spice and garlic and cook
over medium heat for 1 minute. Add the
sugar and vinegar to the pan and stir for
2–3 minutes, or until the sugar dissolves.
Add the beetroot, reduce the heat to low
and turn the beetroot for 5 minutes, or
until glazed all over. Serve warm or at
room temperature.

NOTE: These are also delicious with some
natural yoghurt stirred through and
served as a salad. When handling
beetroot, take care to prevent them from
bleeding. Wash carefully to prevent the
skin breaking and don't cut them before
cooking.

DUCHESS POTATOES

Preparation time: 20 minutes +
  refrigeration
Total cooking time: 30 minutes
Serves 6

860 g (1 lb 12 oz) floury potatoes,
  quartered
2 eggs
¼ cup (60 ml/2 fl oz) cream
2 tablespoons freshly grated Parmesan
¼ teaspoon grated nutmeg
1 egg yolk, for glazing

1 Boil or steam the potato for 10 minutes,
or until just tender (pierce with the point
of a small knife—if the potato comes away
easily, it is ready). Drain and return to the
pan. Turn the heat to very low and shake
the pan for 1–2 minutes to dry out the
potato. Transfer to a bowl and mash well
until smooth.
2 Beat together the eggs, cream,
Parmesan, nutmeg and some salt and
black pepper. Add to the potato and mash
to combine. Taste for seasoning and
adjust if necessary. Cover and leave for
20 minutes to cool slightly. Preheat the
oven to moderate 180°C (350°F/Gas 4).
3 Put the just warm potato mixture in a
piping bag with a 1.5 cm (5/8 inch) star
nozzle. Pipe the mixture in swirls, not too
close together, onto greased baking trays.
Brush lightly all over with the extra egg
yolk, to give a golden, crisp finish. Bake
for 15–20 minutes, or until golden. Serve
hot, sprinkled with a little paprika if
desired.

NOTE: These can be prepared in advance
and refrigerated, covered with plastic.
Just before serving, brush with egg yolk
and bake.

SUGAR PEAS AND
CARROTS IN LIME BUTTER

Preparation time: 15 minutes
Total cooking time: 10 minutes
Serves 4

125 g (4 oz) carrots
125 g (4 oz) sugar snap peas
60 g (2 oz) butter
2 cloves garlic, crushed
1 tablespoon lime juice (and rind from 1
  lime, to make zest for garnish)
½ teaspoon soft brown sugar

1 Peel the carrots and cut into thin
diagonal slices. Wash and string the
sugar snap peas. Heat the butter in a
large heavy-based frying pan. Add the
garlic, cook over low heat for 1 minute.
Add the lime juice and sugar. Cook,
stirring over low heat, until sugar has
completely dissolved.
2 Add the carrots and peas and cook over
medium heat for 2–3 minutes or until just
cooked. Serve hot. Garnish with lime zest.
3 To make lime zest, peel lime rind into
long strips using a vegetable peeler.
Remove all white pith. Cut into long thin
strips with a sharp knife.

NOTE: Snow peas (mange tout) or green
beans can be used in place of sugar snap
peas. Baby carrots also make an
attractive addition to this recipe—leave a
portion of the green tops on. If limes are
unavailable, substitute lemon juice and
zest. This dish can be adapted to make a
light salad—replace the butter with 2
tablespoons of olive oil and cook
according to the recipe. Cool to room
temperature and sprinkle with finely
chopped cashews or toasted pine nuts.

LAYERED POTATO AND
APPLE BAKE

Preparation time: 30 minutes
Total cooking time: 45 minutes
Serves 6

2 large potatoes
3 medium green apples
1 medium onion
½ cup (60 g/2 oz) finely grated Cheddar
  cheese
1 cup (250 ml/8 fl oz) cream
¼ teaspoon ground nutmeg
freshly ground black pepper

1 Preheat the oven to moderate 180°C
(350°F/Gas 4). Brush a large, shallow
ovenproof dish with melted butter or oil.
Peel the potatoes and cut into thin slices.
Peel, core and quarter the apples. Cut
into thin slices. Slice the peeled onion into
very fine rings.
2 Layer the potatoes, apples and onions in
the prepared dish, ending with a layer of
potatoes. Sprinkle evenly with cheese.
Pour the cream over the top, covering as
evenly as possible.
3 Sprinkle with nutmeg and black pepper,
to taste. Bake for 45 minutes or until
golden brown. Remove from the oven and
allow to stand for 5 minutes before
serving.

NOTE: To prevent potatoes and apples
browning before assembling dish, place
in a bowl of cold water with a squeeze of
lemon juice. Drain and pat dry with paper
towels before using.

PINEAPPLE CURRY

Preparation time: 20 minutes
Total cooking time: 15 minutes
Serves 4

1 medium pineapple
1 teaspoon cardamom seeds
1 teaspoon coriander seeds
1 teaspoon cumin seeds
½ teaspoon whole cloves
2 tablespoons oil
2 spring onions, cut in 2 cm (¾ inch) pieces
2 teaspoons grated fresh ginger
4 candlenuts, roughly chopped
1 cup (250 ml/8 fl oz) water
1 teaspoon sambal oelek
1 tablespoon chopped fresh mint

1 Peel and halve the pineapple, remove the core, and cut the pineapple into 2 cm (¾ inch) chunks.
2 Grind the cardamom seeds, coriander seeds, cumin seeds and cloves in a mortar and pestle.
3 Heat the oil in a medium pan; add the spring onion, ginger, candlenuts and spice mixture, and stir-fry over low heat for 3 minutes.
4 Add the water, sambal oelek, mint and pineapple and bring to the boil. Reduce the heat to low, cover and simmer for 10 minutes, or until the pineapple is tender but still holding its shape. Serve as an accompaniment.

NOTE: If the pineapple is a little tart, add 1 to 2 teaspoons sugar. A 450 g (14⅓ oz) can of drained pineapple pieces can be used instead of fresh pineapple.

PICKLED CAULIFLOWER

Preparation time: 10 minutes
Total cooking time: 10 minutes
Serves 4–6

2 cups (500 ml/16 fl oz) white wine vinegar
1 tablespoon yellow mustard seeds
½ teaspoon cumin seeds
3 bay leaves
¾ cup (185 g/6 oz) caster sugar
400 g (13 oz) cauliflower, cut into florets

1 Put the white wine vinegar, mustard seeds, cumin seeds, bay leaves and sugar into a saucepan. Stir over medium heat until the sugar has dissolved. Bring to the boil, then reduce the heat and add the cauliflower. Simmer for 4 minutes, or until just tender, but still firm. Remove from the heat and leave the cauliflower to cool in the liquid. Can be served chilled or at room temperature.

NOTE: To store the cauliflower, wash a glass jar with a lid in hot soapy water, then rinse thoroughly in hot water. Place the jar in a very slow 120°C (250°F/Gas ½) oven to dry for about 20 minutes, or until you are ready to use it. Don't dry it with a tea towel. Put the hot liquid and cauliflower in the jar and seal while still hot. Will keep unopened for up to three months.

SPINACH WITH RAISINS AND PINE NUTS

Preparation time: 15 minutes
Total cooking time: 15 minutes
Serves 6

500 g (1 lb) English spinach
2 tablespoons pine nuts
1 tablespoon olive oil
1 small red onion, halved and sliced
1 clove garlic, thinly sliced
2 tablespoons raisins
pinch of ground cinnamon

1 Trim the stalks from the spinach and discard. Wash the leaves and shred them.
2 Put the pine nuts in a frying pan and stir over medium heat for 3 minutes, or until lightly brown. Remove from the pan.
3 Heat the oil in the pan, add the onion and cook over low heat, stirring occasionally, for 10 minutes, or until translucent. Increase the heat to medium, add the garlic and cook for 1 minute. Add the spinach with the water clinging to it, the raisins and cinnamon. Cover and cook for 2 minutes, or until the spinach wilts. Stir in the pine nuts, and season, to taste.

NOTE: Silverbeet (Swiss chard) works equally well in this recipe, although it may take a little longer to cook than spinach.

HONEY-ROASTED VEGETABLES

Preparation time: 20 minutes
Total cooking time: 50 minutes
Serves 4

4 parsnips
2 carrots
2 small orange sweet potatoes (kumera)
4 beetroot, cut into wedges
8 cloves garlic, unpeeled
¼ cup (60 ml/2 fl oz) oil
1 tablespoon honey
1 teaspoon cumin seeds
½ teaspoon cracked black pepper
½ teaspoon rock salt

1 Preheat the oven to moderately hot 200°C (400°F/Gas 6). Cut the parsnips, carrots and sweet potatoes into 10 cm (4 inch) lengths. Place the vegetables and the unpeeled garlic in a large baking dish, and drizzle with the oil and honey. Sprinkle with the cumin seeds, pepper and salt. Toss to coat.
2 Bake the vegetables for 40–50 minutes, or until tender inside and golden brown outside.

POTATO CURRY WITH SESAME SEEDS

Preparation time: 20 minutes
Total cooking time: 20 minutes
Serves 4

4 large potatoes
1 tablespoon oil
1 teaspoon cumin seeds
1 teaspoon coriander seeds
2 teaspoons mustard seeds
2 tablespoons sesame seeds
½ teaspoon turmeric
1 teaspoon chopped fresh chilli
2 teaspoons finely grated lemon rind
2 tablespoons lemon juice
salt and pepper

1 Boil, steam or microwave the potatoes until tender. Cool, peel and chop. Heat the oil in a large heavy-based pan over medium heat. Cook the cumin, coriander and mustard seeds for 1 minute, stirring constantly.
2 Add the sesame seeds; cook for 1–2 minutes, stirring until golden. Add the turmeric, chillies, potatoes, lemon rind and juice. Stir until well combined and heated through. Season, to taste, with salt and pepper.

COMBINATION VEGETABLE STEW

Preparation time: 15 minutes
Total cooking time: 10–15 minutes
Serves 4–6

2 teaspoons olive oil
1 small onion, thinly sliced
¼ cup (60 g/2 oz) tomato paste
¼ teaspoon chilli powder
1 teaspoon cumin seeds
½ cup (125 ml/4 fl oz) tomato juice
1 cup (250 ml/8 fl oz) vegetable stock
440 g (14 oz) canned tomatoes, crushed
2 small carrots, sliced
2 medium zucchinis (courgettes), halved and cut into chunks
20 green beans, topped and tailed
315 g (10 oz) cauliflower, cut into small florets

1 Heat the oil in a large pan. Add the onions, tomato paste, chilli, cumin seeds and tomato juice. Stir until well combined.
2 Add the stock and crushed tomatoes. Bring to the boil. Reduce the heat. Add the remaining vegetables. Simmer, uncovered, until soft. Serve with fresh tortillas.

BASIC ROAST POTATOES

Preparation time: 15 minutes
Total cooking time: 55 minutes
Serves 4

4 large floury or all-purpose potatoes
  (eg. spunta, sebago, russet, desiree,
  pontiac)
20 g (¾ oz) butter, melted
1 tablespoon oil

1 Cut the potatoes in half and simmer in a
pan of water for 5 minutes. Drain, then
cool on paper towels. Using a fork, scrape
the rounded side of the potatoes to form a
rough surface. Place on a greased baking
dish and brush with the butter and oil.
Roast for 50 minutes, or until golden,
brushing halfway through the cooking
time with a little more butter and oil.

ROAST ORANGE SWEET POTATO

Preparation time: 10 minutes
Total cooking time: 25 minutes
Serves 4

800 g (1 lb 10 oz) orange sweet potato
  (kumera)
20 g (¾ oz) butter, melted
2 teaspoons sesame seeds
½ teaspoon cracked black pepper

1 Cut the orange sweet potato into 1 cm
(½ inch) thick slices. Combine with the
butter, sesame seeds and pepper. Toss,
then roast in a baking dish for 25 minutes,
or until lightly browned and tender,
turning once. Sprinkle with salt before
serving.

PUMPKIN WITH CHILLI AND AVOCADO

Preparation time: 20 minutes
Total cooking time: 10 minutes
Serves 6

750 g (1½ lb) pumpkin
2 tablespoons olive oil
1 tablespoon chopped fresh coriander
  leaves
1 tablespoon chopped fresh mint
2 teaspoons sweet chilli sauce
1 small red (Spanish) onion, finely
  chopped
2 teaspoons balsamic vinegar
1 teaspoon soft brown sugar
1 large avocado

1 Scrape the seeds from the inside of the
pumpkin. Cut the pumpkin into slices.
Remove the skin. Cook in a large pan of
simmering water until tender but still
firm. Remove from heat; drain well.
2 Mix oil, coriander, mint, chilli sauce,
onion, vinegar and sugar in a small bowl.
Cut the avocado in half. Remove the seed
using a sharp-bladed knife. Peel and
discard the skin from the avocado. Cut the
avocado flesh in thin slices.
3 Combine the warm pumpkin and
avocado in a serving bowl. Gently toss the
coriander dressing through. Serve
immediately.

NOTE: Assemble this dish just before
serving. The dressing can be made up
several hours in advance. Store, covered,
in the refrigerator. Add one small red
chilli, finely chopped, to the dressing if
you want a spicier flavour.

ROAST LEEK WITH BACON

Preparation time: 15 minutes
Total cooking time: 25 minutes
Serves 6

3 leeks
2 rashers bacon
20 g (¾ oz) butter, softened
1 teaspoon chopped fresh thyme

1 Preheat the oven to moderate 180°C (350°F/Gas 4). Discard most of the green part from the top section of the leeks, then cut each leek in half lengthways and wash well.
2 Cut each bacon rasher into 3 long strips and wrap a piece around the middle of each portion of leek.
3 Place the leeks, rounded-side-up, in a greased shallow baking dish. Combine the butter and thyme and spread over the leeks. Bake for 25 minutes, or until lightly browned and tender.

NOTE: Grit tends to stick between the tightly compacted layers of leeks, so rinse carefully.

SPRING ONION AND CELERY BUNDLES

Preparation time: 20 minutes
Total cooking time: 10 minutes
Serves 6

4 celery sticks
24 spring onions
30 g (1 oz) butter
1 teaspoon celery seeds
1 tablespoon honey
½ cup (125 ml/4 fl oz) vegetable stock
1 teaspoon soy sauce
1 teaspoon cornflour
1 teaspoon water

1 Cut the celery into 10 cm (4 inch) lengths, then into strips the same thickness as spring onions. Cut the root from the spring onions. Cut the spring onions into 10 cm (4 inch) lengths. Reserve spring onion tops for ties. Plunge spring onion tops into boiling water for 30 seconds or until they are bright green, then plunge immediately into iced water. Drain and pat dry with paper towels.
2 Combine the spring onions and celery sticks. Divide into six bundles. Tie each bundle firmly with a spring onion top.
3 Heat butter in a frying pan. Fry the bundles quickly over medium-high heat for 1 minute on each side. Remove from pan. Add celery seeds and cook for 30 seconds. Add honey, stock, soy sauce, and blended cornflour and water. Bring to the boil, reduce heat, stirring continuously. Add the spring onion and celery bundles. Simmer gently for 7 minutes, or until bundles are just tender. Serve immediately with cooking liquid.

NOTE: This is a very attractive way to serve vegetables. Try it with bundles of carrot and zucchini sticks, asparagus, pumpkin and parsnip or any vegetable combination that takes about the same amount of cooking.

INDIVIDUAL BAKED ROSTI

Preparation time: 20–25 minutes
Total cooking time: 55 minutes
Makes 12

500 g (1 lb) waxy potatoes, peeled
30 g (1 oz) butter, melted
1 onion

1 Preheat the oven to hot 220°C (425°F/Gas 7). Cook the potatoes in a pan of boiling salted water for 7 minutes, or until just tender (pierce with the point of a sharp knife—if the knife comes away easily, the potato is ready). Drain and cool.
2 Brush twelve ½ cup (125 ml/4 fl oz) capacity muffin holes with a little of the butter. Grate the potatoes and onion, mix in a bowl and add the butter. Season with salt and mix well. Divide the mixture among the holes, gently pressing in. Bake for 45 minutes, or until cooked through and golden brown.
3 With a small palette knife, gently loosen each rosti around the edge and lift out for serving.

WRINKLED POTATOES WITH MOJO SAUCE

Preparation time: 20 minutes
Total cooking time: 20–25 minutes
Serves 4–6

18 baby potatoes
1 tablespoon olive oil
2 teaspoons salt

Mojo Sauce
2 cloves garlic
1 teaspoon cumin seeds
1 teaspoon ground sweet paprika
⅓ cup (80 ml/2¾ fl oz) olive oil
2 tablespoons white wine vinegar
1 tablespoon hot water

1 Preheat oven to hot 210°C (415°F/ Gas 6–7). Place potatoes in a single layer in a baking dish. Pour oil over and shake to distribute evenly. Sprinkle the salt evenly over the potatoes.
2 Bake for 20–25 minutes or until the potatoes are golden brown and slightly wrinkled. Shake the pan twice during cooking time.
3 To make Mojo Sauce: Place the garlic, cumin and paprika in a food processor and blend for 1 minute. With the motor running, add the oil slowly in a thin stream, blending until all the oil is added. Add the vinegar and hot water, blend for another minute.
4 Serve the potatoes hot accompanied by a spoonful of Mojo Sauce.

ORANGE POPPY SEED ROASTED VEGETABLES

Preparation time: 20 minutes
Total cooking time: 50 minutes
Serves 8

500 g (1 lb) new potatoes, halved
6 parsnips, peeled and quartered lengthways
500 g (1 lb) orange sweet potato (kumera), cut into large chunks
330 g (11 oz) baby carrots, some with tops on
6 pickling onions, halved
⅓ cup (80 ml/2¾ fl oz) oil
2 tablespoons poppy seeds
200 g (6½ oz) triple cream Brie, thinly sliced

Orange dressing
½ cup (125 ml/4 fl oz) orange juice
2 cloves garlic, crushed
1 tablespoon Dijon mustard
1 teaspoon white wine vinegar
1 teaspoon sesame oil

1 Preheat the oven to moderately hot 200°C (400°F/Gas 6). Place all the vegetables and the oil in a large deep baking dish. Toss the vegetables to coat with the oil. Bake for 50 minutes, or until the vegetables are crisp and tender, tossing every 15 minutes. Remove from the oven and sprinkle with the poppy seeds.
2 For the orange dressing, whisk the ingredients together in a small jug.
3 Pour the dressing over the warm vegetables and toss. Transfer to a large bowl, top with the Brie and serve immediately while still warm.

SAFFRON RICE

Preparation time: 10 minutes + 30 minutes soaking
Total cooking time: 25 minutes
Serves 6

2 cups (400 g/13 oz) basmati rice
25 g (¾ oz) butter
3 bay leaves
¼ teaspoon saffron threads
2 cups (500 ml/16 fl oz) boiling vegetable stock

1 Wash the basmati rice thoroughly, cover with cold water and soak for 30 minutes. Drain.
2 Heat the butter gently in a frying pan until it melts. Add the bay leaves and washed rice, and cook, stirring, for 6 minutes, or until all the moisture has evaporated.
3 Meanwhile, soak the saffron in 2 tablespoons hot water for a few minutes. Add the saffron, and its soaking liquid, to the rice with the vegetable stock, 1½ cups (375 ml/12 fl oz) boiling water and salt to taste. Bring to the boil, then reduce the heat and cook, covered, for 12–15 minutes, or until all the water is absorbed and the rice is cooked. Serve with curries.

MINTED PEAS

Preparation time: 5 minutes
Total cooking time: 6 minutes
Serves 6

4 cups (620 g/1¼ lb) fresh or frozen peas
4 sprigs fresh mint
30 g (1 oz) butter
2 tablespoons shredded fresh mint

1 Place the peas in a saucepan and pour in water to just cover the peas. Add the mint sprigs.
2 Bring to the boil and simmer for 5 minutes (only 2 minutes if frozen), or until the peas are just tender. Drain and discard the mint. Return to the saucepan, add the butter and shredded mint and stir over low heat until the butter has melted. Season with salt and cracked pepper.

GARLIC MUSHROOMS

Preparation time: 10 minutes
Total cooking time: 15 minutes
Serves 4

6 cloves garlic
1½ tablespoons lemon juice
650 g (1 lb 5 oz) button mushrooms, sliced
¼ cup (60 ml/2 fl oz) olive oil
¼ small fresh red chilli, finely chopped
2 teaspoons chopped fresh flat-leaf parsley

1 Crush four of the garlic cloves and finely slice the rest. Sprinkle the lemon juice over the sliced mushrooms.
2 Heat the oil in a large frying pan and add the crushed garlic and chopped chilli. Stir over medium-high heat for 10 seconds, then add the mushrooms. Season and cook, stirring often, for 8–10 minutes. Stir in the sliced garlic and parsley and cook for another minute. Serve hot.

NOTE: You can also use field, Swiss brown or any wild mushrooms for this recipe, but take care to adjust the cooking times if you use the more fragile wild mushrooms.

ASPARAGUS WITH BUTTER AND PARMESAN

Preparation time: 15 minutes
Total cooking time: 3 minutes
Serves 4–6

300 g (10 oz) fresh asparagus
40 g (1½ oz) butter, melted
fresh Parmesan shavings
cracked black pepper, for serving

1 Snap any thick woody ends from the asparagus and discard. Peel the bottom half of each spear with a vegetable peeler if the skin is very thick.
2 Plunge the asparagus into a pan of boiling water and cook for 2–3 minutes, or until the asparagus is bright-green and just tender. Drain and place on serving plates. Drizzle with a little melted butter. Top with Parmesan shavings and sprinkle with cracked black pepper.

NOTE: You can use green, purple or white asparagus for this recipe, or a combination. Lightly toasted, crushed hazelnuts or pecan nuts can be sprinkled over the top.

TOMATOES

VERSATILE, RELIABLE AND
AVAILABLE YEAR-ROUND,
EATEN SLICED ON ITS OWN OR
USED AS THE BASE FOR A
MYRIAD OF DISHES, VERY FEW
FOODS EVOKE THE SAME
COMMON CHORD OF PLEASURE
AS AN APPEALING, RED-RIPE
TOMATO.

TOMATO SALAD

Arrange sliced egg (Roma) tomatoes on a
platter with sliced bocconcini. Scatter
with shredded basil and drizzle with the
best extra virgin olive oil you can afford.
You can sprinkle with rock salt and
freshly cracked black pepper and serve
with rocket leaves and crusty fresh bread.

HOME-DRIED TOMATOES

Cut 500 g (1 lb) tomatoes, either round or
egg (Roma), in half; place in one layer on
a baking tray, cut-side up. Sprinkle with
salt; put in a preheated very slow 120°C
(250°F/Gas ½) oven for 7–8 hours for egg
(Roma) tomatoes or up to 10 hours for
round. The tomatoes will wrinkle up and
become darker. Allow to cool, then pack
into clean, sterilised jars with a little
chopped fresh parsley; cover with olive
oil. Store in a cool place.

  Roasted Tomatoes are made by the
same method but cooked for only 4 to
5 hours. Serve the same day with cracked
black pepper and olive oil.

TOMATO PIZZETTAS

Spread small home-made or ready-made pizza bases with fresh tomato sauce. Top with sliced ripe tomatoes, halved black olives and slivers of anchovy fillets (optional). Sprinkle with a little shredded mozzarella and crumbled goats cheese; put on a baking tray. Bake 15–20 minutes at hot 220°C (425°F/Gas 7) until crisp. Scatter with oregano leaves to serve.

WARM TOMATO SAUCE

Heat ¼ cup (60 ml/2 fl oz) olive oil in a frying pan; add 6 finely chopped spring onions. Cook over low heat for 5 minutes or until soft, being careful not to allow them to brown. Cut a cross in the bottom of 3 ripe tomatoes; put into a bowl of boiling water for 2 minutes. Plunge into cold water; remove and peel. Chop them finely and add to the pan. Simmer for 5 minutes and add ¼ cup (60 ml/2 fl oz) red wine vinegar, 2 cloves chopped garlic, ⅔ cup (170 ml/5½ fl oz) dry white wine, salt and pepper. Simmer for another 15 minutes or until the sauce has reduced and is quite thick. Just before serving, add 2 tablespoons finely chopped gherkins and 1 tablespoon chopped capers. Serve with fried or grilled zucchinis (courgettes) or eggplants (aubergines), topped with caperberries. Serves 4.

BRUSCHETTA WITH TOMATO

Peel 500 g (1 lb) ripe tomatoes by cutting a cross in the bottom of each and putting them in a bowl of boiling water for 2 minutes. Plunge them into cold water; remove and peel. Cut the tomatoes in half; remove the seeds by squeezing gently; dice the flesh. Put the flesh in a bowl and pour ¼ cup (60 ml/2 fl oz) of olive oil over the top. Add 8 finely chopped fresh basil leaves and salt and freshly ground black pepper, to taste. Toast 8 thick slices of crusty Italian bread and rub both sides with whole cut cloves of garlic. Spoon the tomato over the warm toast and serve. Serves 4.

CLOCKWISE, FROM TOP LEFT: Bruschetta with Tomato; Warm Tomato Sauce (served with grilled eggplant); Tomato Pizzetta; Roasted Tomatoes; Tomato Salad; Home-dried Tomatoes

GREEN BEANS IN ROASTED SESAME SEED SAUCE

Preparation time: 15 minutes
Total cooking time: 8 minutes
Serves 4

500 g (1 lb) slender green beans, trimmed
2 tablespoons Japanese white sesame
  seeds
6 cm (2½ inch) piece fresh ginger
1 tablespoon Japanese soy sauce
1 tablespoon mirin
3 teaspoons sugar
1 teaspoon Japanese white sesame
  seeds, extra

1 Cook the beans in a large pan of boiling water for 2 minutes; drain, plunge into iced water to stop the cooking, drain again and set aside.
2 Toast the sesame seeds in a dry frying pan, over a medium heat, for about 5 minutes shaking the pan constantly until golden brown. Pound the seeds in a mortar and pestle until a paste is formed (the mixture will become damp as oil is released from the seeds).
3 Combine the sesame seed paste with the ginger, soy sauce, mirin and sugar. Pour the sauce over the beans, scatter over the extra sesame seeds and serve.

NOTE: The beans can be marinated in the sauce overnight if desired. Japanese sesame seeds are plump and large, with a fuller flavour than other sesame seeds.

MARINATED BARBECUED VEGETABLES

Preparation time: 40 minutes +
  1 hour marinating
Total cooking time: 5 minutes
Serves 4–6

3 small slender eggplants (aubergines)
2 small red peppers (capsicums)
3 medium zucchinis (courgettes)
6 medium mushrooms

Marinade
¼ cup (60 ml/2 fl oz) olive oil
¼ cup (60 ml/2 fl oz) lemon juice
¼ cup (7 g/¼ oz) shredded fresh basil leaves
1 clove garlic, crushed

1 Cut the eggplants into diagonal slices. Place on a tray in a single layer, sprinkle with salt and let stand for 15 minutes. Rinse thoroughly and pat dry with paper towels. Trim the red peppers, remove the seeds and membrane and cut into long, wide pieces. Cut the zucchinis into diagonal slices. Trim each mushroom stalk so that it is level with the cap. Place all the vegetables in a large, shallow non-metal dish.
2 To make Marinade: Place the oil, juice, basil and garlic in a small screw-top jar. Shake vigorously until well combined. Pour the marinade over the vegetables and stir gently. Store, covered with plastic wrap, in the refrigerator for 1 hour, stirring occasionally. Prepare and heat the barbecue.
3 Place the vegetables on a hot, lightly greased barbecue grill or flatplate. Cook pieces over the hottest part of the fire for 2 minutes on each side. Transfer to a serving dish once browned. Brush the vegetables frequently with any remaining marinade while cooking.

LEEKS IN WHITE SAUCE

Preparation time: 15 minutes
Total cooking time: 15 minutes
Serves 6

2 leeks, trimmed
50 g (1¾ oz) butter
1 tablespoon plain flour
1 cup (250 ml/8 fl oz) milk
2 tablespoons grated Cheddar
1 tablespoon dry breadcrumbs

1 Wash the leeks, cut in half lengthways and then into 5 cm (2 inch) pieces. Heat 30 g (1 oz) of the butter in a heavy-based saucepan, add the leeks and cook for 10 minutes, stirring, until tender. Transfer to an ovenproof serving dish.
2 Melt the remaining butter in a pan over low heat. Stir in the flour and cook for 1 minute, or until pale and foaming. Remove from the heat and gradually stir in the milk. Return to the heat and stir until the sauce boils and thickens. Pour over the leeks. Sprinkle with cheese and crumbs. Grill for 2–3 minutes, or until golden brown.

POTATO AND PEA CURRY

Preparation time: 20 minutes
Total cooking time: 35 minutes
Serves 4

750 g (1½ l b) potatoes, peeled
2 teaspoons brown mustard seeds
2 tablespoons ghee or oil
2 onions, sliced
2 cloves garlic, crushed
2 teaspoons grated fresh ginger
1 teaspoon turmeric
salt and pepper
½ teaspoon chilli powder
1 teaspoon ground cumin
1 teaspoon garam masala
½ cup (125 ml/4 fl oz) water
⅔ cup (110 g/3⅔ oz) fresh or frozen peas
2 tablespoons chopped fresh mint

1 Cut the potatoes into large cubes. Heat the mustard seeds in a large dry pan until they start to pop. Add the ghee, onions, garlic and ginger and cook, stirring, until soft. Add the turmeric, salt, pepper, chilli, cumin, garam masala and potatoes. Stir until the potatoes are coated.
2 Add the water and simmer, covered, for 15–20 minutes, or until the potatoes are just tender. Add the peas and stir; simmer, covered, for 3–5 minutes, or until the potatoes are cooked and the liquid is absorbed. Stir in the mint and serve hot or warm.

PROVENCAL ROAST TOMATOES

Preparation time: 10 minutes
Total cooking time: 40 minutes
Makes 4

60 g (2 oz) fresh breadcrumbs
2 tablespoons chopped fresh flat-leaf parsley
2 tablespoons chopped fresh basil
1 tablespoon chopped fresh oregano
4 large vine-ripened tomatoes,
4–6 cloves garlic, finely chopped
2 tablespoons olive oil

1 Preheat the oven to moderate 180°C (350°F/Gas 4). Combine the breadcrumbs and herbs in a bowl and season with salt and pepper.
2 Halve each tomato horizontally and scoop out the core and seeds with a teaspoon.
3 Sprinkle garlic into each tomato, then top with the breadcrumb mixture. Drizzle with olive oil and bake for 40 minutes, or until soft.

MARINATED TOFU

Preparation time: 10 minutes +
    overnight marinating
Total cooking time: 15 minutes
Serves 4

½ cup (125 ml/4 fl oz) peanut oil
2 cloves garlic, crushed
1 teaspoon grated fresh ginger
2 stems lemon grass, white part only, finely chopped
1 small fresh red chilli, finely chopped
2 tablespoons fish sauce
2 tablespoons lime juice
1 tablespoon soft brown sugar
500 g (1 lb) fried tofu puffs, halved on the diagonal

1 Combine all the ingredients in a flat non-metallic dish. Toss the tofu until coated in the marinade, then cover with plastic wrap and refrigerate overnight.
2 Heat a lightly oiled wok over high heat and stir-fry the tofu in batches for 1–2 minutes, or until browned. Serve hot.

CAULIFLOWER CHEESE

Preparation time: 15 minutes
Total cooking time: 20 minutes
Serves 4

500 g (1 lb) cauliflower, cut into small
   pieces
2 tablespoons fresh breadcrumbs
¼ cup (30 g/1 oz) grated Cheddar

Cheese sauce
30 g (1 oz) butter
30 g (1 oz) plain flour
1¼ cups (315 ml/10 fl oz) warm milk
1 teaspoon Dijon mustard
½ cup (60 g/2 oz) grated Cheddar
½ cup (50 g/1¾ oz) grated Parmesan

1 Lightly grease a 1.5 litre (48 fl oz)
heatproof dish. Cook the cauliflower
pieces in a saucepan of lightly salted
boiling water for 10 minutes, or until just
tender. Drain thoroughly, then transfer to
the prepared dish and keep warm.
2 For the cheese sauce, melt the butter in
a pan over low heat. Stir in the flour and
cook for 1 minute, or until pale and
foaming. Remove from the heat and
gradually stir in the milk and mustard.
Return to the heat and stir constantly
until the sauce boils and thickens. Reduce
the heat and simmer for 2 minutes, then
remove the pan from the heat. Add the
Cheddar and Parmesan and stir until
melted. Do not reheat or the oil will come
out of the cheese. Season with salt and
white pepper, to taste, and pour over the
cauliflower.
3 Combine the breadcrumbs and Cheddar
and sprinkle over the sauce. Grill under
medium heat until the top is brown and
bubbling. Serve immediately.

NOTE: This cheese sauce is also delicious
poured over other vegetables such as
broccoli, asparagus, or a combination of
vegetables.

ROAST ONIONS

Preparation time: 20 minutes
Total cooking time: 1 hour 10 minutes
Serves 6

6 onions
¾ cup (60 g/2 oz) fresh breadcrumbs
¼ cup (25 g/¾ oz) grated Romano or
   Parmesan
1 tablespoon chopped fresh basil
20 g (¾ oz) butter, melted

1 Peel the onions, leaving the root ends
intact. Place in a pan of water, bring to
the boil and simmer gently for 20
minutes. Remove and cool. Cut off and
discard the top quarter of each onion, and
scoop out a third of the inside. Combine
the breadcrumbs, cheese, basil and
butter in a bowl and season. Spoon into
the onions and roast in a lightly greased
baking dish for 50 minutes, or until the
onions are soft.

PANCETTA POTATOES

Preparation time: 20 minutes
Total cooking time: 50 minutes
Serves 4

8 medium floury or all-purpose potatoes
   (eg. sebago, spunta, russet, desiree,
   pontiac)
2 slices pancetta
8 sprigs of fresh rosemary
2 teaspoons butter, softened
oil, for brushing

1 Cut the potatoes and trim the bases so
they sit flat. Cut each pancetta slice
lengthways into 4 pieces. Roll a sprig of
rosemary in each piece of pancetta. Cut a
hole in the centre of the potatoes about
halfway through and insert the pancetta.
Place on a greased baking dish. Top each
potato with ¼ teaspoon of the butter.
Brush with oil and sprinkle with pepper.
Roast for 40–50 minutes, or until golden.

NOTE: The texture of potatoes varies from
waxy to floury or starchy and it is best to
use the type stated in recipes. Sebago and
pontiac are good all-rounders and are
particularly good for baking. Russet and
spunta have a floury texture and are also
good baking varieties.

STUFFED ONIONS

Preparation time: 30 minutes
Total cooking time: 1 hour 5 minutes
Serves 4

8 brown onions, about 125 g (4 oz) each
6 slices bacon, diced
4 cloves garlic, finely chopped
1 tablespoon cream
1 egg, lightly beaten
¼ teaspoon ground nutmeg
3 tablespoons chopped fresh flat-leaf
 parsley
¾ cup (60 g/2 oz) fresh breadcrumbs
2 tablespoons grated Parmesan
40 g (1¼ oz) butter, softened
1 cup (250 ml/8 fl oz) chicken stock

1 Preheat the oven to moderately hot
200°C (400°F/Gas 6). Lightly grease a
shallow earthenware dish.
2 Peel the onions, place in a large
saucepan or stockpot of boiling water and
simmer for 5–6 minutes. Remove the
onions and drain well. Cool slightly and,
using a small sharp knife, hollow out the
centres, leaving a 1 cm (½ inch) rim.
Reserve ½ cup of the onion centres.
Season the onions.
3 Meanwhile, cook the bacon in a small
frying pan over medium heat until the fat
has melted. Chop the reserved onion and
add to the pan with the garlic. Cook for
5 minutes, or until lightly golden. Remove
from the heat, add the cream, egg,
nutmeg, parsley and ½ cup (40 g/1¼ oz) of
the crumbs. Season well and mix.
4 Spoon about 1–1½ tablespoons of the
filling into the onion shells, piling a little
to the top. Combine the remaining
breadcrumbs with the Parmesan,
sprinkle over the onions and dot with
butter. Place in baking dish, and carefully
pour stock around the onions. Bake,
basting occasionally, for 1 hour, or until
the onions are tender.

MEXICAN GREEN RICE

Preparation time: 15 minutes
Total cooking time: 35 minutes
Serves 8

3 large mild green chillies, such as
 poblano or banana
1 small green chilli, chopped
4 garlic cloves, chopped
1 small onion, chopped
1½ cups (45 g/1½ oz) coriander (cilantro)
 leaves
40 g (1¼ oz) butter
2 cups (400 g/13 oz) long-grain white rice
3 cups (750 ml/24 fl oz) hot chicken or
 vegetable stock
2 tablespoons finely chopped coriander
 (cilantro) leaves, extra

1 Grill (broil) the large chillies or hold
over a gas flame until the skin blackens
and blisters. Place on a cutting board,
cover with a tea towel and allow to cool.
Peel the skin off, then deseed and roughly
chop the chillies. Put the flesh in a food
processor with the small chilli, garlic,
onion and coriander leaves and process
until smooth.
2 Melt the butter in a saucepan and, when
sizzling, add the rice and cook, stirring,
over medium heat for about 5 minutes, or
until lightly golden. Add the chilli purée
and mix well.
3 Gradually stir in the stock and bring to
the boil. Cover and reduce the heat to low.
Cook, without lifting the lid, for 20 minutes,
or until all the liquid has been absorbed
and the rice is tender. Fluff with a fork,
stir in the extra coriander and season to
taste.

PLAIN MEXICAN RICE

Preparation time: 10 minutes
Total cooking time: 35 minutes
Serves 8

1 tablespoon olive oil
1 small onion, chopped
1 garlic clove, chopped
1 cup (200 g/6½ oz) long-grain white rice
½ cup (125 g/4 oz) tomato passata
1 cup (250 ml/8 fl oz) chicken stock

1 Heat the oil in a large saucepan, add the
onion and cook for 5 minutes, or until
softened but not browned. Add the garlic
and cook for 1 minute. Add the rice and
stir for 1–2 minutes, or until well coated in
the oil.
2 Add the tomato passata and stock to the
pan and bring to the boil. Reduce the heat
to very low, cover tightly with a lid and
simmer for 25 minutes, or until the liquid
is absorbed and the rice is tender. Fluff
up the grains with a fork, and serve as a
side dish.

POTATO CAKES WITH APPLE SAUCE

Preparation time: 20 minutes
Total cooking time: 30 minutes
Serves 4

4 cups (620 g/1 lb 4⅔ oz) finely grated
   potato
1 large onion, finely chopped
2 teaspoons celery or fennel seeds
3 tablespoons plain flour
2 eggs, beaten
salt and freshly ground black pepper
oil, for frying
1 cup (250 ml/8 fl oz) ready-made apple
   sauce

1 Squeeze the excess liquid from the
potatoes. Combine the potatoes, onions,
celery or fennel seeds, flour, beaten eggs,
salt and pepper in a large bowl; stir until
just mixed.
2 Heat 2 cm (¾ inch) of oil in a large
heavy-based frying pan. Form 2 heaped
tablespoons of mixture at a time into flat
cakes. Cook the cakes for 3 minutes on
each side or until golden brown and
cooked through. Serve immediately with
apple sauce.

NOTE: Squeezing the excess liquid from
grated potato helps to prevent the oil
from spitting during frying. Canned,
puréed baby apple makes a good apple
sauce.

BRAISED BOK CHOY

Preparation time: 10 minutes
Total cooking time: 5 minutes
Serves 4

2 tablespoons peanut oil
1 clove garlic, crushed
1 tablespoon julienned fresh ginger
500 g (1 lb) bok choy, separated, cut into 8
   cm (3 inch) lengths
1 teaspoon sugar
1 teaspoon sesame oil
1 tablespoon oyster sauce

1 Heat a wok over high heat, add the oil
and swirl to coat. Add the garlic and
ginger, and stir-fry for 1–2 minutes, then
add the bok choy and stir-fry for 1 minute.
Add the sugar, a pinch of salt and pepper
and ¼ cup (60 ml/2 fl oz) water. Bring to
the boil, then reduce the heat and
simmer, covered, for 3 minutes, or until
the stems are tender but crisp.
2 Stir in the sesame oil and oyster sauce
and serve immediately.

BROAD BEANS WITH PEAS AND ARTICHOKES

Preparation time: 15 minutes
Total cooking time: 15 minutes
Serves 4–6

2 medium onions
2 tablespoons fresh dill
1 tablespoon fresh mint leaves
¼ cup (60 ml/2 fl oz) olive oil
250 g (8 oz) frozen broad beans, rinsed
   and drained
½ cup (125 ml/4 fl oz) water
2 tablespoons lemon juice
250 g (8 oz) frozen peas
400 g (12⅔ oz) canned artichoke hearts,
   drained, cut in half
4 spring onions, chopped
salt and freshly ground black pepper

1 Slice the onions into rings. Finely chop
the dill and mint.
2 Heat the oil in a large pan. Add the
onions. Stir over low heat for 5 minutes or
until soft and golden.
3 Add the beans, water and lemon juice to
the pan. Bring to the boil, reduce the heat
and simmer, covered, for 5 minutes.
4 Add the peas, artichoke hearts and
herbs. Simmer, covered, for 5 minutes, or
until the peas are just tender, but not soft.
Remove from the heat, stir in the spring
onions, salt and pepper. Serve warm or at
room temperature.

CHINESE FRIED RICE

Preparation time: 15 minutes
Total cooking time: 10 minutes
Serves 4

2 eggs, lightly beaten
1 medium onion
4 spring onions
1 x 250 g (8 oz) piece of ham
2 tablespoons peanut oil
2 teaspoons lard, optional
1⅓ cups (265 g/8½ oz) long-grain rice,
   cooked and cooled (see note)
¼ cup (40 g/1⅓ oz) frozen peas
2 tablespoons soy sauce
250 g (8 oz) cooked small prawns, peeled

1 Season the eggs with salt and pepper.
2 Cut the onion into 8 wedges. Cut the spring onions into short lengths on the diagonal. Cut the ham into very thin strips.
3 Heat 1 tablespoon oil in a wok or large frying pan and add the eggs, pulling the set egg towards the centre and tilting the pan to let the unset egg run to the edges. When the egg is almost set, break it up into large pieces so it resembles scrambled eggs. Transfer to a plate and set aside.
4 Heat the remaining oil and lard in the wok, swirling to coat the base and side. Add the onion and stir-fry over high heat until it starts to turn transparent. Add the ham and stir-fry for 1 minute. Add the rice and peas and stir-fry for 3 minutes until the rice is heated through. Add the eggs, soy sauce, spring onion and prawns. Heat through and serve.

NOTE: If possible, cook the rice a day ahead and refrigerate it overnight. This makes the grains separate and means the fried rice is not gluggy.

MEXICAN-STYLE VEGETABLES

Preparation time: 30 minutes + 2 hours
   refrigeration
Total cooking time: 50 minutes
Serves 4–6

Polenta
1⅓ cups (350 ml/11 fl oz) vegetable stock
1 cup (250 ml/8 fl oz) water
1 cup (150 g/4¾ oz) polenta (cornmeal)
½ cup (50 g/1⅔ oz) freshly grated
   Parmesan cheese
2 tablespoons olive oil

1 large green pepper (capsicum)
1 large red pepper (capsicum)
3 medium tomatoes
6 green button squash
6 yellow button squash
1 cob fresh corn
1 tablespoon oil
1 medium onion, sliced
1 tablespoon ground cumin
½ teaspoon chilli powder
2 tablespoons chopped fresh coriander
   (optional)
salt and freshly ground black pepper

1 Brush a 20 cm (8 inch) round springform (spring-release) tin with oil.
2 To make Polenta: Place the stock and water in a medium pan and bring to the boil. Add the polenta and stir to combine; stir constantly for 10 minutes or until very thick. (Polenta must be stirred for the time given, otherwise it will be gritty.) Remove from the heat and stir in the Parmesan. Spread the mixture into the prepared tin; smooth the surface. Refrigerate for 2 hours. Turn out, cut into six wedges. Brush one side with olive oil, cook under a preheated grill for 5 minutes or until edges are browned. Repeat with other side.

3 Cut the green and red peppers into small squares; chop the tomatoes, cut the squash into quarters and cut the corn into 2 cm (¾ inch) slices, then in quarters.
4 Heat the oil in a large pan. Cook the onion over medium heat for 5 minutes or until soft. Stir in the cumin and chilli powder; cook for 1 minute. Add the vegetables. Bring to the boil and reduce heat. Simmer, covered, over low heat for 30 minutes or until the vegetables are tender, stirring occasionally. Stir in the coriander, if using. Add salt and pepper. Serve with polenta wedges.

NOTE: Vegetables can be cooked up to one day ahead. Polenta can be cooked one day ahead. Grill just before serving. A little crushed garlic can be added to the olive oil before brushing.

SAUCES, DRESSINGS AND CONDIMENTS

CLASSIC WHITE SAUCE (BECHAMEL)

Preparation time: 15 minutes
Total cooking time: 10 minutes
Makes about 250 ml (8 fl oz)

1 cup (250 ml/8 fl oz) milk
1 slice of onion
1 bay leaf
6 peppercorns
30 g (1 oz) butter
1 tablespoon plain flour
salt and white pepper

1 Combine milk, onion, bay leaf and peppercorns in a small pan. Bring to the boil; remove the pan from heat and set aside to infuse for 10 minutes. Strain the milk and discard all the flavourings.
2 Melt the butter in a small pan and add the flour. Stir over medium heat for 1 minute, or until the mixture is golden and bubbling. Remove from heat, add milk very slowly, a little at a time, and stir between each addition until mixture is completely smooth. When all the milk has been added, return to heat, keep stirring over medium heat until mixture boils and thickens.
3 Boil for another minute and remove from the heat. Season with salt and white pepper.

NOTE: Infusing the milk with onion, bay leaves and peppercorns adds flavour. Plain milk may be used, particularly if adding other flavourings.

VARIATION: Parsley sauce: Add 3 tablespoons finely chopped fresh parsley to the finished sauce and stir to combine. Other fresh herbs such as chives, dill or tarragon may be added, or try different combinations of your favourite herbs.

GREEN PEPPERCORN SAUCE

Preparation time: 10 minutes
Total cooking time: 15 minutes
Serves 4

4 steaks or chicken breast fillets
1 cup (250 ml/8 fl oz) beef or chicken stock
1 cup (250 ml/8 fl oz) cream
2–3 teaspoons canned green peppercorns, rinsed and drained
1 tablespoon brandy

1 Pan-fry the steak or chicken in a little oil or butter. Remove from the pan, cover with foil and keep warm.
2 Add the stock to the meat juices in the pan. Stir over low heat until boiling, then add the cream and peppercorns. Boil for 8–10 minutes, stirring constantly until slightly thickened. Add the brandy and boil for 1 minute. Serve with the meat.

TOMATO SAUCE

Preparation time: 15 minutes
Total cooking time: 20 minutes
Serves 4

1.5 kg (3 lb) large ripe tomatoes
1 tablespoon olive oil
1 medium onion, finely chopped
2 cloves garlic, crushed
1 teaspoon dried oregano leaves
2 tablespoons tomato paste
1 teaspoon sugar
salt and pepper

1 Mark a small cross on the base (opposite stem end) of each tomato. Place in a small bowl and cover with boiling water for 2 minutes; drain and cool. Peel the skin down from the cross and discard. Finely chop the flesh.
2 Heat the oil in a medium pan. Add the onion and cook, stirring, over medium heat 3 minutes or until soft. Add garlic and cook for 1 minute. Add tomato, oregano, tomato paste and sugar.
3 Bring to the boil, reduce heat and simmer, uncovered, for about 15 minutes or until the sauce has thickened slightly. Season, to taste.

NOTE: This will keep, covered, for up to 2 days in the refrigerator, or freeze for up to 2 months. Reheat in a pan or in the microwave. Serve hot over pasta, or use as a pizza sauce.

BASIC HOLLANDAISE

Preparation time: 5 minutes
Total cooking time: 10 minutes
Makes about 315 ml (10 fl oz)

175 g (5²⁄₃ oz) butter
2 tablespoons water
4 egg yolks
1 tablespoon lemon juice
salt and white pepper

1 Melt the butter in a small pan. Skim any froth from the top and discard; cool the melted butter. Combine water and egg yolks in another small pan. Using a wire whisk, beat for about 30 seconds until the mixture is pale and creamy.
2 Place the pan over very low heat and continue whisking for 3 minutes or until thick and foamy; remove from the heat. (Make sure the pan does not get too hot or you will end up with scrambled eggs.)
3 Add the cooled butter slowly, a little at a time at first, whisking well between each addition. Keep adding the butter in a thin stream, whisking continuously, until all the butter has been used. Try to avoid using the milky white whey in the bottom of the pan, but don't worry if a little gets in. Stir in the lemon juice and season with salt and white pepper.

VARIATION: Processor method: Use the same quantities of ingredients as for making basic hollandaise, but place the yolks, water and juice in a food processor and blend for 10 seconds. Melt the butter; skim off the froth. With the motor running, add the melted hot butter to the processor in a thin stream. Transfer to a bowl and season, to taste.

BASIC MAYONNAISE

Preparation time: 10 minutes
Total cooking time: Nil
Makes about 250 ml (8 fl oz)

2 egg yolks
1 teaspoon Dijon mustard
4 teaspoons lemon juice
1 cup (250 ml/8 fl oz) light olive oil
salt and white pepper

1 Place egg yolks in a medium bowl. Add mustard and 2 teaspoons of the lemon juice; whisk for 30 seconds until light and creamy.
2 Add olive oil, about a teaspoon at a time, whisking continuously. Increase the amount of oil as the mayonnaise thickens. When all the oil has been added, stir in the remaining 2 teaspoons lemon juice; season with salt and white pepper.

VARIATION: Processor method: Process the yolks, mustard and juice in a food processor for 10 seconds. With the motor running, add the oil in a slow, thin stream until combined. Transfer to a bowl and season, to taste.

AIOLI
(GARLIC MAYONNAISE)

Preparation time: 10 minutes
Total cooking time: Nil
Makes about 250 ml (8 fl oz)

2 egg yolks
3 large cloves garlic, crushed
4 teaspoons lemon juice
1 cup (250 ml/8 fl oz) light olive oil
salt and white pepper

1 Place the egg yolks in a medium bowl. Add the garlic and 2 teaspoons of the lemon juice; whisk for 30 seconds until light and creamy.
2 Add the olive oil, about a teaspoonful at a time, whisking continuously. Increase the amount of oil as the mayonnaise thickens. When all the oil has been added, stir in the remaining 2 teaspoonsful of lemon juice and season, to taste, with salt and white pepper.

SAUCES

THESE DELICIOUS ROAST SAUCES AND GRAVIES CAN BE QUICKLY MADE WHILE THE ROAST IS COOKING OR RESTING. MINT SAUCE WILL DEVELOP IN FLAVOUR IF MADE A DAY IN ADVANCE.

APPLE SAUCE

Peel and core 4 green apples, then roughly chop the flesh. Place the flesh in a pan with 1 tablespoon caster sugar, ½ cup (125 ml/4 fl oz) water, 2 whole cloves and 1 cinnamon stick. Cover and simmer for 10 minutes, or until soft. Remove from the heat and discard the cloves and cinnamon stick. Mash or, for a finer sauce, press through a sieve. Stir in 1–2 teaspoons lemon juice, or to taste. Serve with roast pork or ham.
Makes 1 cup (250 ml/8 fl oz).

GRAVY WITH WINE

Discard all but 2 tablespoons of the pan juices from the baking dish you cooked the roast in. Heat the dish on the stovetop over moderate heat, stir in 2 tablespoons plain flour and cook, stirring, until well browned. Remove from the heat and gradually add 2 teaspoons Worcestershire sauce, 2 tablespoons red or white wine and 2¼ cups (560 ml/ 18 fl oz) beef or chicken stock. Return to the heat, stir until the mixture boils and thickens, then simmer for 2 minutes. Season with salt and pepper, to taste. Suitable for all roast meats.
Makes 1½ cups (375 ml/12 fl oz).

MINT SAUCE

Sprinkle 1 tablespoon caster sugar over ½ cup (10 g/¼ oz) fresh mint leaves on a chopping board, then finely chop the mint. Transfer to a bowl and add 2 tablespoons caster sugar. Cover with ¼ cup (60 ml/ 2 fl oz) boiling water and stir until the sugar has dissolved. Stir in ¾ cup (185 ml/ 6 fl oz) malt vinegar, cover and chill overnight. Traditionally served with roast lamb.
Makes 1½ cups (375 ml/12 fl oz).

CREAMY HORSERADISH

Combine 175 g (6 oz) horseradish cream, 1 finely chopped spring onion and ¼ cup (60 g/2 oz) sour cream in a bowl. Fold in ½ cup (125 ml/4 fl oz) whipped cream. Season. Serve with roast beef or veal.
Makes 1½ cups (375 ml/12 oz).

BREAD SAUCE

Slice 1 small onion and combine in a small pan with 1¼ cups (315 ml/10 fl oz) milk, 1 bay leaf, 4 black peppercorns and 2 whole cloves. Bring to the boil over medium heat, then lower the heat and simmer for 10 minutes. Strain into a large heatproof bowl and discard the onion and flavourings. Add 1¼ cups (100 g/3½ oz) fresh breadcrumbs to the bowl with a pinch of ground nutmeg and 20 g (¾ oz) butter. Stir until smooth, then season with salt and pepper, to taste. Bread sauce is traditionally served with roast goose, turkey or chicken.
Makes 1¼ cups (315 ml/10 fl oz).

RASPBERRY AND CRANBERRY SAUCE

Purée 150 g (5 oz) fresh or frozen raspberries, then press through a sieve to remove the seeds. Combine the purée in a small pan with ¼ cup (60 ml/2 fl oz) orange juice, ½ cup (160 g/5½ oz) cranberry sauce, 2 teaspoons Dijon mustard and 1 teaspoon finely grated orange rind. Stir over heat until smooth. Add ¼ cup (60 ml/2 fl oz) port and simmer for 5 minutes. Remove and allow to cool—the sauce will thicken slightly. Serve with roast turkey, goose, ham or duck.
Makes 1 cup (250 ml/8 fl oz).

FROM LEFT: Apple sauce; Gravy with wine; Mint sauce; Creamy horseradish; Bread sauce; Raspberry and cranberry sauce

VELOUTE SAUCE

Preparation time: 5 minutes
Total cooking time: 10 minutes
Serves 4

30 g (1 oz) butter
3 tablespoons plain flour
1½ cups (375 ml/12 fl oz) chicken, fish or
    veal stock
lemon juice, to taste
1 tablespoon cream

1 Melt the butter in a pan, add the flour
and cook over medium heat for
2 minutes, or until a thick paste has
formed—be careful not to brown the
mixture or it will colour your sauce.
2 Whisk in the stock a little at a time to
prevent the mixture becoming lumpy.
Cook the sauce, whisking continuously,
for 3–5 minutes—it should be quite thick
and not have a floury taste.
3 Season with salt, pepper and lemon
juice, adding a little at a time. Finally, stir
in the cream. Serve immediately, as this
sauce will quickly thicken if left to stand.
If necessary, add a little extra stock to
thin it down.

CUMBERLAND SAUCE

Preparation time: 20 minutes
Total cooking time: 20 minutes
Serves 8

2 oranges
1 lemon
225 g (7 oz) redcurrant jelly
2 teaspoons Dijon mustard
2 tablespoons red wine vinegar
1 cup (250 ml/8 fl oz) port

1 Remove the orange and lemon rind with
a zester. Place the rind in a small pan
with 1 cup (250 ml/8 fl oz) water and bring
to the boil. Cook for 5 minutes, then strain
the liquid, keeping the rind.
2 Squeeze the juice from the oranges and
lemon and place in a pan. Add the jelly,
mustard, vinegar, port and reserved rind.
Slowly bring to the boil, stirring as the
jelly melts. Reduce the heat to simmer
gently for 15 minutes. Season to taste and
serve at room temperature or cover with
plastic wrap and refrigerate for up to a
week.

BASIL PESTO

Preparation time: 10 minutes
Total cooking time: Nil
Makes about 250 ml (8 fl oz)

250 g/8 oz fresh basil
⅓ cup (50 g/1⅔ oz) toasted pine nuts
2 cloves garlic, crushed
⅓ cup (35 g/1¼ oz) finely grated
    Parmesan cheese
⅓ cup (80 ml/2¾ fl oz) olive oil
salt and pepper

1 Remove basil leaves from the stalks.
Wash and dry the leaves and place them
in a food processor with the pine nuts,
garlic and Parmesan cheese. Process
until finely chopped.
2 With the motor running, add the olive oil
in a thin stream and process until well
combined. Season, to taste, with salt and
pepper.

NOTE: To toast pine nuts, either place in a
small pan and stir over low heat until
golden; or grill until golden, stirring to
prevent burning.

BOLOGNESE SAUCE

Preparation time: 15 minutes
Total cooking time: 2 hours 15 minutes
Serves 6

2 tablespoons olive oil
1 large onion, chopped
1 carrot, chopped
1 celery stick, chopped
2 cloves garlic, crushed
500 g (1 lb) beef mince
1 cup (250 ml/8 fl oz) beef stock
2 x 425 g (14 oz) cans chopped tomatoes
1½ cups (375 ml/12 fl oz) red wine
1 teaspoon sugar

1 Heat the olive oil in a large heavy-based pan. Add the onion, carrot and celery and cook, stirring, over medium heat for 5 minutes, or until softened. Add the garlic and cook for 1 minute.
2 Add the mince and cook until well browned. Add the stock, tomatoes, wine and sugar.
3 Bring to the boil, reduce the heat to low and simmer for 2 hours, stirring occasionally. Season to taste with salt and pepper. Serve hot or keep, covered, for up to two days in the refrigerator. Can also be frozen for up to two months.

CHILLI SPICED MANGO SAUCE

Preparation time: 35 minutes
Total cooking time: 20 minutes
Serves 4

1 large ripe mango
1 tablespoon oil
1 red onion, finely sliced
3 cloves garlic, finely chopped
4 cm (1½ inch) piece fresh ginger, finely chopped
2–3 red chillies, seeded and finely chopped
1 tablespoon honey
¼ teaspoon ground cinnamon
pinch of ground cardamom
pinch of ground nutmeg
pinch of ground cloves
¼ cup (60 ml/2 fl oz) dark rum
¼ cup (60 ml/2 fl oz) lime juice
¼ cup (7 g/¼ oz) coriander leaves, chopped

1 Peel the mango and dice the flesh. Heat the oil in a frying pan and add the onion, garlic, ginger and chilli. Cook for about 3–4 minutes, or until the onion is soft.
2 Add the mango, honey, cinnamon, cardamom, nutmeg and cloves. Mix well and bring to the boil. Simmer gently for 5 minutes. Add the rum and simmer for a further 5 minutes. Add the lime juice, coriander and salt and pepper to taste.

PRESERVED LEMONS

Preparation time: 1 hour + 6 weeks standing
Total cooking time: Nil
Fills a 2 litre jar

8–12 small thin-skinned lemons
1 cup (315 g/10 oz) rock salt
2 cups (500 ml/16 fl oz) lemon juice (8–10 lemons)
½ teaspoon black peppercorns
1 bay leaf
olive oil

1 Scrub the lemons under warm running water with a soft bristle brush to remove the wax coating. Cut into quarters, leaving the base attached at the stem end. Gently open each lemon, remove any visible seeds and pack 1 tablespoon of the salt against the cut edges of each lemon. Push the lemons back into shape and pack tightly into a 2 litre jar that has a clip or tight-fitting lid. Depending on the size of the lemons, you may not need all 12. They should be firmly packed and fill the jar.
2 Add 1 cup (250 ml/8 fl oz) of the lemon juice, the peppercorns, bay leaf and remaining rock salt to the jar. Fill the jar to the top with the remaining lemon juice. Seal and shake to combine all the ingredients. Leave in a cool, dark place for 6 weeks, inverting the jar each week. (In warm weather, store the jar in the refrigerator.) The liquid will be cloudy initially, but will clear by the fourth week.
3 To test if the lemons are preserved, cut through the centre of one of the lemon quarters. If the pith is still white, the lemons aren't ready.
In this case, re-seal and leave for another week before testing again. The lemons should be soft-skinned and the pith should be the same colour as the skin.
4 Once the lemons are preserved, cover the brine with a layer of olive oil. Replace the oil each time you remove some of the lemon pieces. Refrigerate after opening.

SEAFOOD SAUCES

A SIMPLE PIECE OF FRESHLY COOKED SEAFOOD BECOMES SIMPLE PERFECTION WHEN TOPPED WITH A GOOD SPOONFUL OF ONE OF THESE FAVOURITE SAUCES.

TARTARE SAUCE

Mix 1 tablespoon finely chopped onion, 1 teaspoon lemon juice, 1 tablespoon chopped gherkins, 1 teaspoon drained, chopped capers, ¼ teaspoon Dijon mustard, 1 tablespoon finely chopped fresh parsley and 1½ cups (375 g/12 oz) mayonnaise. Season, to taste. Cover and refrigerate for up to 1 month.
Makes about 2 cups.

COCKTAIL SAUCE

Mix 1 cup (250 g/8 oz) whole-egg mayonnaise, 3 tablespoons tomato sauce, 2 teaspoons Worcestershire sauce, ½ teaspoon lemon juice and 1 drop of Tabasco sauce. Season with salt and pepper, to taste. Cover and refrigerate for up to 1 month.
Makes about 1 cup.

GREEN GODDESS DRESSING

Mix 1½ cups (375 g/12 oz) whole-egg mayonnaise, 4 mashed anchovy fillets, 4 finely chopped spring onions, 1 crushed clove garlic, 3 tablespoons chopped fresh flat-leaf parsley, 3 tablespoons finely chopped chives and 1 teaspoon tarragon vinegar. Cover and refrigerate for up to 1 month.
Makes about 2 cups.

LEMON CAPER BUTTER

Combine 250 g (8 oz) soft butter in a bowl with 1 tablespoon each of finely grated lemon rind and juice, 1 crushed garlic clove and 1 tablespoon drained, chopped capers. Roll up firmly in foil to form a roll. Refrigerate for up to 1 month. Cut into rounds for serving. Serve at room temperature.
Makes about 1 cup.

MONTPELLIER BUTTER

Beat 250 g (8 oz) softened butter in a bowl until creamy. Blanch 100 g (3½ oz) baby spinach leaves. Drain, refresh in cold water, then squeeze out as much water as possible. Chop roughly, then combine in a food processor with 2 tablespoons chopped fresh parsley leaves, 1 tablespoon chopped fresh tarragon, 2 small chopped gherkins, 1 tablespoon drained bottled capers, 2 drained anchovy fillets, 2 hard-boiled egg yolks, 1 teaspoon lemon juice and 2 tablespoons oil. Process until fine. Add to the butter, mix well, then season with cracked black pepper. Cover and refrigerate for up to 3 days, or freeze. Serve at room temperature. Portions of the butter are placed on top of hot seafood and allowed to melt.
Makes about 1 cup.

WHITE WINE SAUCE

Melt 1 tablespoon butter in a medium pan, add 1 finely chopped spring onion and cook, stirring over medium heat until the onion is soft. Add ½ cup (125 ml/4 fl oz) white wine, bring to the boil and simmer for 5 minutes, or until reduced by half. Add ½ cup (125 ml/4 fl oz) each of cream and milk and bring to the boil. Blend 3 teaspoons each of soft butter and plain flour to form a paste, then whisk into the boiling liquid and boil until thick. Season, to taste, with salt and pepper. If too thick, thin with a little milk to reach a pouring consistency. Cover and refrigerate for up to 3 days.
Makes about 1 cup.

FROM LEFT: Tartare sauce; Cocktail sauce; Green goddess dressing; Lemon caper butter; Montpellier butter; White wine sauce

QUICK AND EASY CRANBERRY SAUCE

Preparation time: 10 minutes
Total cooking time: 5 minutes
Serve 4–6

250 g (8 oz) whole cranberry sauce
1 teaspoon grated orange rind
3 tablespoons orange juice
1 teaspoon ground ginger
½ teaspoon ground
   cardamom
¼ teaspoon ground allspice

1 Mix together the cranberry sauce, grated orange rind and juice, ginger, cardamom and allspice in a small pan.
2 Bring the cranberry mixture to the boil over medium heat, stirring occasionally. Reduce the heat and leave to simmer for 2 minutes. Allow the sauce to cool to room temperature before serving.

CREAMY MUSHROOM SAUCE

Preparation time: 10 minutes
Total cooking time: 15 minutes
Serves 4

4 chicken breasts or steaks
30 g (1 oz) butter
350 g (11 oz) small button mushrooms,
   sliced
2 tablespoons white wine
½ cup (125 ml/4 fl oz) chicken stock
½ cup (125 ml/4 fl oz) cream
1 clove garlic, crushed
1 tablespoon chopped chives

1 Pan-fry the chicken or meat in a little oil or butter. Remove from the pan, cover with foil and keep warm. Add the butter and mushrooms to the pan juices and stir over medium heat for 5 minutes, or until soft and golden.
2 Add the wine, stock, cream and garlic, and bring to the boil. Cook for 5 minutes, stirring constantly, until the sauce thickens slightly. Stir in the chives and serve immediately.

HARISSA

Preparation time: 30 minutes + 1 hour
   soaking
Total cooking time: Nil
Fills a 600 ml (20 fl oz) jar

125 g (4 oz) dried red chillies, stems
   removed
1 tablespoon dried mint
1 tablespoon ground coriander
1 tablespoon ground cumin
1 teaspoon ground caraway seeds
10 cloves garlic, chopped
½ cup (125 ml/4 fl oz) olive oil

1 Roughly chop the chillies, then cover with boiling water and soak for 1 hour. Drain, place in a food processor and add the mint, spices, garlic, 1 tablespoon of oil and ½ teaspoon salt. Process for 20 seconds, scrape down the side of the bowl, then process for another 30 seconds. Add 2 tablespoons oil and process again. Repeat and process until a thick paste forms.
2 Spoon the paste into a clean jar (see Note), cover with a thin layer of olive oil and seal. Label and date.

NOTES: To prepare a storage jar, preheat the oven to very slow 120°C (250°F/Gas ½). Wash the jar and lid in hot soapy water and rinse with hot water. Put the jar in the oven for 20 minutes, or until fully dry. Do not dry with a tea towel.
   This hot pepper sauce will keep in the fridge for up to six months. It is delicious with tagines and couscous, or can be added to salad dressings, marinades and pasta sauces for extra flavour.

AVOCADO SALSA

Preparation time: 15 minutes
Total cooking time: 1 minute
Serves 6

1 medium red (Spanish) onion
2 large avocados
1 tablespoon lime juice
1 medium tomato
1 small red pepper (capsicum)
1 teaspoon ground coriander
1 teaspoon ground cumin
3 tablespoons chopped fresh coriander
   leaves
2 tablespoons olive oil
4–5 drops Tabasco sauce

1 Finely chop the onion. Cut the avocados
in half; remove the seed and carefully
peel. Finely chop the flesh; place in a
medium bowl and toss lightly with lime
juice.
2 Cut the tomato in half horizontally,
squeeze gently to remove seeds; chop
finely. Remove seeds and membrane
from pepper, chop finely.
3 Place the ground coriander and cumin
in a small pan; stir over medium heat for
1 minute to enhance fragrance and
flavour; cool. Add all the ingredients to
the avocado in a bowl and gently combine,
so that the avocado retains its shape and
is not mashed. Refrigerate until required
and serve at room temperature with corn
chips.

ALGERIAN EGGPLANT (AUBERGINE) JAM

Preparation time: 10 minutes + 30
   minutes salting
Total cooking time: 20 minutes
Serves 6–8

2 eggplants (aubergines), about 400 g
   (13 oz), cut into 1 cm (½ inch) slices
olive oil, for frying
2 garlic cloves, crushed
1 teaspoon sweet paprika
1½ teaspoons ground cumin
½ teaspoon sugar
1 tablespoon lemon juice

1 Sprinkle the eggplant slices with salt
and drain in a colander for 30 minutes.
Rinse well, squeeze gently and pat dry.
Heat about 5 mm (¼ inch) of the oil in a
large frying pan and fry the slices in
batches over medium heat until golden
brown on both sides. Drain on paper
towels, then chop finely. Put in a colander
until most of the oil has drained off, then
transfer to a bowl and add the garlic,
paprika, cumin and sugar.
2 Wipe out the pan, add the eggplant
mixture and stir constantly over medium
heat for 2 minutes. Transfer to a bowl, stir
in the lemon juice and season. Serve at
room temperature.

PAWPAW SAUCE

Preparation time: 35 minutes
   + 20 minutes standing
Total cooking time: Nil
Serves 4

250 g (8 oz) ripe pawpaw or papaya
3 tablespoons cream
1 tablespoon dry white wine
2 teaspoons wholegrain mustard
2 spring onions, finely chopped

1 Cut the pawpaw or papaya in half,
discarding the seeds and peel. Chop the
flesh finely and place in a bowl with all of
the juices from the fruit.
2 Add the cream, wine, mustard and
spring onion to the pawpaw. Season to
taste with salt and pepper and whisk well.
Cover and leave to stand for 20 minutes
before serving.

POTATO AND OIL PUREE

Preparation time: 5 minutes
Total cooking time: 20 minutes
Serves 4

1 kg (2 lb) floury potatoes (such as russet, spunta and pontiac), cut into large chunks
200 ml (6/2 fl oz) stock (choose according to the dish the potatoes will be served with)
2 garlic cloves, peeled and bruised
2 sprigs of fresh thyme
150 ml (5 fl oz) extra-virgin olive oil

1 Cook the potatoes in boiling salted water until tender but still firm. While the potatoes are cooking, heat the stock in a small saucepan with the garlic and thyme. Bring to simmering point, then remove from the heat and allow to infuse.
2 Drain the potatoes well and pass them through a mouli or mash with a potato masher. Strain the stock, return to the saucepan, add the olive oil and reheat gently. Place the potato purée in a bowl and add the stock in a thin steady stream, stirring continuously with a flat wooden spoon. Season with salt and pepper, then beat well until the purée is smooth.

SPICED COCONUT SAUCE

Preparation time: 30 minutes
Total cooking time: 5 minutes
Serves 2–4

40 g (1¼ oz) bunch coriander (roots, stems and leaves)
2 teaspoons oil
3 cm (1¼ inch) fresh ginger, peeled and grated
2 stalks lemon grass (white part only), finely chopped
2 small red chillies, finely chopped
1 clove garlic, finely chopped
3 tablespoons coconut cream, plus extra if necessary
2 tablespoons rice vinegar
1 teaspoon soft brown sugar

1 Finely chop the coriander, keeping the roots, stems and leaves separate. Heat the oil in a frying pan over low heat and cook the ginger, lemon grass, chilli, coriander root and garlic, stirring constantly, for 3 minutes, or until aromatic. Add the coconut cream, stirring well. Increase the heat to high and bring the sauce to a rapid boil. Cook for about 1 minute until the mixture looks oily (this is the coconut cream separating or 'cracking'). Do not let the sauce burn. Add another 2 tablespoons of coconut cream if the sauce becomes too thick.
2 Transfer to a bowl and add the coriander stem and leaves, rice vinegar and sugar. Stir well and add salt and more sugar, to taste. Serve at room temperature.

ZABAGLIONE

Preparation time: 10 minutes
Total cooking time: 10 minutes
Serves 10–12

8 egg yolks
⅓ cup (90 g/3 oz) caster sugar
1¼ cups (315 ml/10 fl oz) Marsala

1 Beat the egg yolks and sugar in a heatproof bowl with electric beaters until pale yellow.
2 Put the bowl over a gently simmering pan of water and beat continuously, adding the Marsala gradually. Beat for 5 minutes, or until thick and frothy. To test if it is ready, dip a metal spoon into the Zabaglione, hold it up and if the mixture slides down the back it is not yet thickened enough. If you can draw a line through the Zabaglione with a spoon and leave a trail, it is ready. Serve immediately or keep refrigerated for up to 1 day and serve chilled.

PRALINE CREAM SAUCE

Preparation time: 15 minutes
Total cooking time: 15 minutes
Serves 6

½ cup (80 g/2¾ oz) blanched almonds,
    toasted
½ cup (125 g/4 oz) caster sugar
⅓ cup (100 g/3½ oz) chocolate hazelnut
    spread
300 ml (10 fl oz) chilled cream

1 To make almond praline, line a baking
tray with baking paper and arrange the
almonds on it in a single layer. Mix the
sugar together with 4 tablespoons of
water in a small pan. Stir over low heat,
without boiling, until the sugar has
dissolved. Without stirring, cook the
mixture until it turns golden, then quickly
pour it over the almonds. Allow to set
until hard, then chop in a food processor
until broken down into fine crumbs.
2 Place the hazelnut spread in a
heatproof bowl over a pan of hot water
until the spread softens slightly. Remove
the bowl from the pan and stir in the
cream. Whisk the mixture until smooth
(do not overbeat or it will become grainy),
then fold in the praline crumbs.

HOT CHOCOLATE SAUCE

Preparation time: 10 minutes
Total cooking time: 10 minutes
Serves 8

250 g (8 oz) good-quality dark cooking
    chocolate, chopped
¾ cup (185 ml/6 fl oz) cream
50 g (1¾ oz) butter
1 tablespoon golden syrup
2 tablespoons chocolate or coffee
    liqueur, such as Baileys, Tia Maria or
    Kahlua

1 Place the chocolate, cream, butter and
syrup in a pan and stir over low heat until
the mixture is smooth. Stir in the liqueur
and serve hot or cold.

BERRY COULIS

Preparation time: 10 minutes
Total cooking time: Nil
Serves 6

250 g (8 oz) mixture of berries
    (strawberries, raspberries or
    blackberries)
2–4 tablespoons icing sugar, or to taste
1 tablespoon lemon juice
1–2 tablespoons Cointreau or Grand
    Marnier

1 Hull the berries. Place the fruit in a
food processor and add the sugar and
lemon juice. Blend until smooth. Stir in
the Cointreau or Grand Marnier.

OILS & VINEGARS

GREAT FOR GIFTS, MOST OILS AND VINEGARS WILL KEEP FOR UP TO 6 MONTHS IF YOU STERILIZE THE STORAGE JARS BY WASHING, RINSING WITH BOILING WATER AND DRYING IN A WARM OVEN.

RASPBERRY VINEGAR

Place 2⅓ cups (290 g/10 oz) fresh or thawed frozen raspberries in a non-metallic bowl and crush gently with the back of a spoon. Warm 2 cups (500 ml/16 fl oz) white wine vinegar in a saucepan over low heat. Add the vinegar to the raspberries and mix well. Pour into a 2 cup (500 ml/16 fl oz) sterilized glass bottle and leave in a warm place for about 2 weeks, shaking regularly. Strain through a muslin-lined sieve into a small pan. Add 2 teapoons caster sugar and stir over medium heat until dissolved. Pour into the clean, warm sterilized bottle. Add 2–3 raspberries, if desired, then seal, label and date. Store in a cool, dark place. Makes 2 cups (500 ml/16 fl oz).

TARRAGON VINEGAR

Warm 2 cups (500 ml/16 fl oz) white wine vinegar in a saucepan over low heat. Gently bruise 25 g (¾ oz) fresh tarragon leaves in your hands and put into a 2 cup (500 ml/16 fl oz) sterilized glass bottle. Pour in the vinegar, seal with a non-metallic lid and shake well. Leave to infuse in a warm place for about 2 weeks. Strain and return to the clean, warm sterilized bottle. Add a fresh sprig of tarragon, then seal, label and date. Store in a cool, dark place. Makes 2 cups (500 ml/16 fl oz).

PARMESAN OIL

Combine 2 cups (500 ml/16 fl oz) olive oil and 100 g (3½ oz) finely grated Reggiano Parmesan in a small pan. Stir the oil mixture over low heat for 10–15 minutes, or until the Parmesan starts to melt and clump together. Remove from the heat and allow to cool. Strain into a sterilized 2 cup (500 ml/16 fl oz) bottle and add 20 g (¾ oz) shaved Parmesan. Seal, label and date, then store in a cool, dark place. Makes 2 cups (500 ml/16 fl oz).

CHILLI OIL

Place 6 dried chillies and 1 teaspoon chilli powder in a heavy-based saucepan. Add 3 cups (750 ml/24 fl oz) olive oil and stir over medium heat for 5 minutes (if it gets too hot the oil will change flavour). Remove from the heat. Cover with plastic wrap and leave in a cool, dark place for 3 days. Strain into a 3 cup (750 ml/24 fl oz) sterilized bottle. Discard the chillies and add new chillies. Seal, label and date, then store in a cool, dark place. Makes 3 cups (750 ml/24 fl oz).

SPICED MALT VINEGAR

Pour 2 cups (500 ml/16 fl oz) malt vinegar into a saucepan. Add a 1 cm (½ inch) piece fresh ginger, quartered, 10 whole cloves, 1 cinnamon stick, 2 teaspoons allspice berries, ½ teaspoon black peppercorns, 1 teaspoon brown mustard seeds and warm over low heat. Pour into a warm, sterilized 2 cup (500 ml/16 fl oz) glass bottle and seal with a non-metallic lid. Leave in a warm place for 2 weeks. Strain the vinegar and return to the clean, warm bottle with some black peppercorns. Seal, label and date, then store in a cool, dark place.
Makes 2 cups (500 ml/16 fl oz).

SPICED APPLE AND CINNAMON VINEGAR

Combine 2 cups (500 ml/16 fl oz) white wine vinegar, ⅓ cup (30 g/1 oz) finely chopped dried apple slices, ¼ teaspoon black peppercorns, 2 bay leaves, ¼ teaspoon yellow mustard seeds, 2 cinnamon sticks, 2 sprigs fresh thyme or a sprig of fresh tarragon and 1 peeled garlic clove in a sterilized 2 cup (500 ml/ 16 fl oz) bottle. Seal and leave in a cool, dark place for 2 weeks. Strain the vinegar and return to the warm sterilized bottle. Seal, label and date, then store in a cool, dark place.
Makes 2 cups (500 ml/16 fl oz).

FROM LEFT: Raspberry vinegar (2); Tarragon vinegar (2); Chilli oil; Spiced malt vinegar; Parmesan oil (2); Spiced apple and cinnamon vinegar (with tarragon); Spiced apple and cinnamon vinegar (with thyme)

INDIAN ACCOMPANIMENTS

MANGO CHUTNEY

Slice the flesh of 3 large mangoes and sprinkle with salt. Finely chop 2 seeded red chillies. Blend ½ teaspoon garam masala with 1½ cups (330 g/11 oz) raw sugar and place in a large pan with 1 cup (250 ml/8 fl oz) white vinegar. Bring to the boil, reduce the heat and simmer for 5 minutes. Add the mango, chilli, a finely grated 5 cm (2 inch) piece of fresh ginger and ½ cup (95 g/3¼ oz) finely chopped pitted dates. Simmer for 1 hour, or until the mango is tender. Spoon into warm sterilized jars and seal. Store in the fridge for a week before using. Keeps for up to 1 month.
Fills three 250 ml (8 fl oz) jars.

INDIAN LIME PICKLE

Cut 10 ripe yellowed limes into eight wedges each. Place in a large glass bowl, sprinkle with 2 tablespoons cooking salt and stir well. Cover with plastic wrap and leave for 48 hours in a cool dark place, stirring occasionally. Drain, rinse well and mix with 200 g (6½ oz) raisins and 150 g (5 oz) sultanas. Process in batches in a food processor until coarsely chopped. Heat 3 tablespoons peanut oil in a large heavy-based pan, add 2 teaspoons ground cumin, 1 teaspoon ground coriander, 1 teaspoon black mustard seeds, ½ teaspoon ground chilli powder, ½ teaspoon ground black pepper, 5 finely chopped cloves of garlic and a 5 cm (2½ inch) piece of fresh ginger, grated. Don't overcook the ginger or it will be bitter. Cook over medium heat for 2–3 minutes, or until very aromatic. Add the lime mixture, 1¼ cups (315 ml/10 fl oz) malt vinegar and 500 g (1 lb) soft brown sugar. Bring to the boil, stirring until the sugar dissolves. Reduce the heat and simmer for 1–1½ hours, stirring occasionally. Pour into warm, sterilized jars and seal. Refrigerate after opening.
Makes about 2½ cups (600 ml/20 fl oz).

CUCUMBER WITH YOGHURT

Mix 1 finely diced small tomato, ½ finely chopped onion, ½ coarsely grated cucumber, 1 tablespoon cumin seeds and 1½ tablespoons plain yoghurt. Season, to taste. Cover and refrigerate until ready to use.
Makes about ¾ cup (185 ml/6 fl oz).

BANANA WITH COCONUT

Finely dice 2 bananas, add ⅔ cup (35 g/1¼ oz) flaked coconut and ½ cup (125 ml/4 fl oz) lemon juice and stir well. Cover and refrigerate until ready to use.
Makes about 1 cup (250 ml/8 fl oz).

CUCUMBER AND CORIANDER

Peel a telegraph cucumber, discard the seeds, then dice finely. Mix with 1 tablespoon lemon juice and 2 tablespoons chopped fresh coriander leaves. Season with salt, cover and refrigerate until ready to use.
Makes about ¾ cup (185 ml/6 fl oz).

PAPAYA WITH MINT

Peel a papaya, slice thinly, then cut into small dice. Mix with 3 tablespoons fresh orange juice and 1 tablespoon chopped fresh mint. Cover and chill until ready to use.
Makes about 1 cup (250 ml/8 fl oz).

CHILLI EGGPLANT (AUBERGINE) PICKLE

Slice 3 eggplants (aubergines) into 1 cm (½ inch) thick slices, put in a colander and sprinkle with salt. Leave for 1 hour, then rinse and pat dry. Bring 2 cups (500 ml/16 fl oz) white wine vinegar to the boil, add a few slices of eggplant at a time and cook for 4 minutes each batch. Layer the eggplant, 10 peeled cloves garlic, 2 sliced red chillies, some fresh curry leaves and a sliced lemon, in sterilized jars. Pour in enough olive oil to cover the eggplant. Seal and leave for a week in the fridge before using.
Fills five 250 ml (8 fl oz) jars.

CLOCKWISE, FROM TOP LEFT: Mango chutney; Indian lime pickle; Banana with coconut; Cucumber and coriander; Chilli eggplant pickle (2 jars); Papaya with mint; Cucumber with yoghurt

INDIAN ACCOMPANIMENTS (CONT'D)

CARROT PACHADI

Heat 1 tablespoon oil in a small saucepan or frying pan over medium heat, add 1 teaspoon black mustard seeds and 2–3 dried chillies, then cover the pan with a lid and shake it until the seeds start to pop. Remove the pan from the heat and immediately stir in ¼ teaspoon asafoetida and 1 stalk's worth of curry leaves. Scoop 600 g (1¼ lb) thick natural yoghurt into a bowl and lightly whisk it to remove any lumps. Add 4 finely grated carrots and stir together until combined. Add the spices from the pan, stir well, then season with a little salt. Traditionally this is served with biryani or pulao.
Serves 4.

MANGO SALAD

Put 300 g (10 oz) grated coconut, 2 seeded and chopped dried chillies and 1 tablespoon grated jaggery or soft brown sugar in a blender and add enough water to make a thick, coarse paste. Transfer to a bowl and toss in 300 g (10 oz) cubed ripe mango. Season with salt. Heat a tablespoon of oil in a small frying pan over low heat and add ½ teaspoon each of coriander seeds and mustard seeds and 6 curry leaves. Cover and shake the pan until the seeds start to pop. Pour the oil and seeds over the mango mixture and stir. Serve with any Indian meal.
Serves 4.

MINT AND CORIANDER CHUTNEY

Discard the tough stalks from 30 g (1 oz) each of mint and coriander (cilantro), but keep the soft ones. Blend 1 green chilli, 1 tablespoon tamarind purée, 1½ teaspoons sugar and ½ teaspoon salt with the herbs in a food processor.
Serves 4.

CHURRI

Put 1 teaspoon cumin seeds in a dry frying pan and cook until fragrant. Grind the seeds to a fine powder in a spice grinder or mortar and pestle. Chop ½ cup (10 g/¼ oz) mint, ½ cup (15 g/½ oz) coriander (cilantro) leaves, a 2 cm (¾ inch) piece of ginger and 2 green chillies into a fine paste in a blender, or chop together finely with a knife. Add 300 g (10 oz) thick natural yoghurt and 300 ml (9½ fl oz) buttermilk and a pinch of salt to the mixture and blend until all the ingredients are well mixed. Season to taste, then mix in 1 thinly sliced onion and the ground cumin, reserving a little cumin to sprinkle on top. Traditionally this is served with biryani, but it is cooling when eaten with hot or spicy dishes.
Serves 4.

EGGPLANT SAMBAL

Preheat the oven to moderately hot 200°C (400°F/Gas 6). Slice 2 medium eggplants (aubergines) in half and brush the cut halves with 2 teaspoons oil and ½ teaspoon ground turmeric. Put the eggplants in a roasting tin and roast for 30 minutes, or until they are browned all over and very soft. Scoop the eggplant pulp into a bowl, then mash with ¼ cup (60 ml/2 fl oz) lime juice, 2 seeded and finely diced red chillies and 1 finely diced red onion, reserving some chilli and onion for garnish. Season with salt, then fold in ⅓ cup (80 g/2¾ oz) thick natural yoghurt. Garnish with the remaining onion and chilli. Use as an accompaniment or a dip with bread.
Serves 4.

POTATO MASALA

Heat 2 tablespoons oil in a heavy-based frying pan, add 1 teaspoon black mustard seeds, cover and when they start to pop add 10 curry leaves, ¼ teaspoon ground turmeric, 2 teaspoons grated ginger, 2 finely chopped green chillies and 2 chopped onions and cook, uncovered, until the onion is soft. Add 500 g (1 lb) of cubed waxy potato and 1 cup (250 ml/ 8 fl oz) water, bring to the boil, cover and cook until the potato is tender and almost breaking up. If there is any liquid left in the pan, simmer, uncovered, until it evaporates. Add 1 tablespoon tamarind purée and season with salt. Roll in dosas (page 145) or serve on the side.
Serves 4.

FROM LEFT: Carrot pachadi, Churri, Mint and coriander chutney, Mango salad, Eggplant sambal, Potato masala

ASSORTED CURRY PASTES

BALTI CURRY PASTE

One at a time, dry-fry 4 tablespoons coriander seeds, 2 tablespoons cumin seeds, 2 crumbled cinnamon sticks, 2 teaspoons each of fennel seeds, black mustard seeds and cardamom seeds, 1 teaspoon fenugreek seeds and 6 whole cloves in a small frying pan over medium heat for 2–3 minutes, or until each spice starts to become aromatic.

Transfer the spices to a food processor or mortar and pestle, allow to cool and process or grind to a fine powder. Add 20 fresh curry leaves, 4 fresh bay leaves, 1 tablespoon ground turmeric, 2 crushed cloves garlic, 1 tablespoon grated fresh ginger, 1½ teaspoons chilli powder and ¾ cup (185 ml/6 fl oz) malt vinegar, and mix together well.

Heat ½ cup (125 ml/4 fl oz) vegetable oil in the frying pan, add the paste and cook, stirring, for 5 minutes. Add ¼ cup (60 ml/ 2 fl oz) malt vinegar and mix well. Makes 1 cup.

MUSAMAN CURRY PASTE

Preheat the oven to moderate 180°C (350°F/Gas 4). Put 10 dried red chillies in a heatproof bowl and cover with boiling water. Soak for 20 minutes. Drain, remove the seeds and roughly chop the flesh.

Meanwhile, put 5 chopped red Asian shallots, 1 finely chopped stem lemon grass (white part only), 1 tablespoon chopped fresh galangal, 10 chopped cloves garlic, 3 cardamom pods, 1 tablespoon coriander seeds, 1 teaspoon cumin seeds, 1 teaspoon shrimp paste (wrapped in foil) and ¼ teaspoon black peppercorns in a roasting tin and bake for 5 minutes, or until aromatic. Remove the foil from the shrimp paste.

Transfer the roasted ingredients to a food processor or mortar and pestle, then add the chopped chilli, ½ teaspoon ground nutmeg and ¼ teaspoon each of ground cinnamon and ground cloves. Process or grind to a smooth paste. If the mixture is too dry, add a little white vinegar. Makes ½ cup.

MADRAS CURRY PASTE

Dry-fry 2½ tablespoons coriander seeds and 1 tablespoon cumin seeds separately in a frying pan for 30 seconds–1 minute, or until aromatic, being careful not to burn them. Cool, then grind the seeds in a food processor or mortar and pestle.

Transfer to a small bowl and add 2 crushed cloves garlic, 2 teaspoons grated fresh ginger, 1 teaspoon each of brown mustard seeds, chilli powder, ground turmeric and salt, and ½ teaspoon cracked black peppercorns. Mix together well. Add 3–4 tablespoons white vinegar and mix to a smooth paste.
Makes ½ cup.

VINDALOO CURRY PASTE

Put 2 tablespoons grated fresh ginger, 4 chopped cloves garlic, 4 chopped fresh red chillies, 1 tablespoon each of ground coriander and cumin seeds, 2 teaspoons each of ground turmeric and ground cardamom, 1 teaspoon ground cinnamon, 4 whole cloves, 6 peppercorns and ½ cup (125 ml/4 fl oz) cider vinegar in a food processor and process for 20 seconds, or until well combined and smooth.
Makes ½ cup.

JUNGLE CURRY PASTE

Soak 12 large dried red chillies in boiling water for 20 minutes. Drain and chop. Meanwhile, wrap 1 tablespoon shrimp paste in foil and heat under a hot grill for 1 minute, or until aromatic. Remove the foil from the shrimp paste.

Transfer the shrimp paste to a food processor, add the chopped chilli, 4 red Asian shallots, 4 sliced cloves garlic, 1 sliced stem lemon grass (white part only), 2 chopped small coriander roots, 1 tablespoon each of finely chopped fresh galangal and finely chopped fresh ginger and 1 teaspoon each of ground white pepper and salt, then blend until a smooth paste forms—add a little water, if necessary.
Makes ½ cup.

FROM LEFT: Balti curry paste, Madras curry paste, Vindaloo curry paste, Musaman curry paste, Jungle curry paste.

VEGETABLE PUREES

THESE VERSATILE MIXTURES CAN DOUBLE AS DIPS AND PASTA SAUCES, AND ARE FABULOUS AS FILLINGS FOR PANCAKES AND OMELETTES— BUT NEVER FORGET HOW GREAT THEY ARE ON THEIR OWN.

JERUSALEM ARTICHOKE PUREE

Place 1 kg (2 lb) peeled Jerusalem artichokes and 2 sliced cloves of garlic in a pan, cover with cold water and bring to boil. Cook until artichokes are tender. Process artichokes and garlic in food processor with 60 g (2 oz) butter until smooth, gradually adding ¼ cup (60 ml/ 2 fl oz) extra virgin olive oil. Season with salt and pepper, drizzle with olive oil and sprinkle with sweet paprika.

PARSNIP AND LEEK PUREE

Cook 1 thinly sliced leek and 3 large peeled and chopped parsnips in a pan of boiling salted water until tender. Drain well, purée in blender or food processor. Place purée in a pan, add 2 tablespoons chopped fresh chives, 30 g (1 oz) butter, and salt and pepper, to taste. Cook until the purée is heated through. Remove from the heat and stir through about 3 tablespoons of crème fraîche.

ASPARAGUS PUREE

Heat 30 g (1 oz) butter and 1 tablespoon oil in a pan, add 3 chopped spring onions and 315 g (10 oz) of young, thin chopped asparagus; cook for 3 minutes. Add ½ cup (125 ml/4 fl oz) vegetable stock and ½ cup (125 ml/4 fl oz) cream, cover and simmer until tender. Remove the vegetables from the liquid and process until smooth. Bring liquid to boil and reduce by one quarter. Return purée to pan, stir in 1 tablespoon grated Parmesan cheese. Cook over medium heat for
5 minutes or until the purée thickens slightly. Season with salt and pepper. If the asparagus is stringy, the purée should be passed through a sieve.

RED PEPPER (CAPSICUM) PUREE

Grill 3 large red peppers (capsicums) until the skin blisters and blackens. Place peppers in a plastic bag, cool slightly, then peel, remove seeds and roughly chop the flesh. Place the peppers in a food processor, add 4 chopped spring onions, 2 crushed cloves of garlic and 2 finely chopped small red chillies. Process until smooth, transfer to a pan and stir in 2 tablespoons fish sauce (optional), 2 tablespoons lime juice and 2 tablespoons chopped fresh coriander. Cook over medium heat for 5 minutes, or until thickened slightly.

ROAST TOMATO AND CHICKPEA PUREE

Soak 250 g (8 oz) dried chickpeas in cold water overnight. Cook the chickpeas in boiling salted water with 1 chopped onion and 1 bay leaf for 1½ hours or until tender. Drain, remove the bay leaf and reserve ¼ cup (60 ml/2 fl oz) of liquid. Cut 4 egg (Roma) tomatoes in halves, sprinkle with sea salt and drizzle with olive oil. Bake in a preheated moderately hot 200°C (400°F/Gas 6) oven for 30–40 minutes or until the tomatoes are very tender. Allow the tomatoes and chickpeas to cool a little, place in a food processor, then add 2 crushed cloves of garlic, 2 tablespoons of lime juice, 1 teaspoon sugar, ¼ cup (60 ml/2 fl oz) of olive oil and the reserved liquid; process until smooth. Stir through 2 tablespoons of chopped fresh basil and 1 tablespoon of freshly grated Parmesan cheese.

CLOCKWISE, FROM TOP LEFT: Parsnip and Leek Purée; Asparagus Purée; Red Pepper Purée; Jerusalem Artichoke Purée; Roast Tomato and Chickpea Purée

THAI CURRY PASTES

Curry pastes are great to make in advance and store. They are surprisingly easy to make and they are a great flavour starter for soups and curries, and will also spice up other dishes.

Curry pastes will keep in an airtight container for 2 weeks in the fridge or 2 months in the freezer. To ensure that your container is clean, preheat the oven to very slow 120°C (250°F/Gas ½). Thoroughly wash a glass jar and its lid in hot, soapy water (or preferably a dishwasher) and rinse well with hot water. Put the jar in the oven for 20 minutes, or until completely dried—don't dry it with a tea towel or germs can be transferred to the jar.

CHU CHEE CURRY PASTE

Preheat the oven to moderate 180°C (350°F/Gas 4). Put 10 large dried red chillies in a heatproof bowl, cover with boiling water and soak for 20 minutes. Drain, then remove the seeds and roughly chop the flesh.

Meanwhile, put 1 teaspoon coriander seeds, 1 tablespoon shrimp paste (wrapped in foil) and 1 tablespoon white peppercorns in a roasting tin and bake for 5 minutes, or until aromatic. Remove the foil from the shrimp paste.

Transfer the toasted spices to a food processor or mortar and pestle with the chopped chilli and add 10 finely shredded fresh kaffir lime leaves, 10 chopped red Asian shallots, 2 teaspoons finely grated kaffir lime rind, 1 tablespoon chopped fresh coriander stem and root, 1 finely chopped stem lemon grass (white part only), 3 tablespoons chopped fresh galangal, 1 tablespoon chopped Krachai and 6 chopped cloves garlic. Process or grind to a smooth paste. You may need to add a little lemon juice if the paste is too thick.
Makes ½ cup.

THAI RED CURRY PASTE

Preheat the oven to moderate 180°C (350°F/Gas 4). Put 15 large dried red chillies in a heatproof bowl, cover with boiling water and soak for 20 minutes. Drain, then remove the seeds and roughly chop the flesh.

Meanwhile, place 2 teaspoons shrimp paste (wrapped in foil), 2 teaspoons coriander seeds and 1 teaspoon each of white peppercorns and cumin seeds in a roasting tin and bake for 5–10 minutes, or until aromatic. Remove the foil.

Transfer the shrimp paste to a food processor or mortar and pestle with the chopped chilli, then add 5 chopped red Asian shallots, 10 chopped cloves garlic, 2 thinly sliced stems lemon grass (white part only), 1 tablespoon chopped fresh galangal, 2 tablespoons chopped fresh coriander root and 1 teaspoon finely grated kaffir lime rind. Process or grind until it forms a smooth paste.
Makes 1 cup.

THAI GREEN CURRY PASTE

Preheat the oven to moderate 180°C (350°F/Gas 4). Place 2 tablespoons coriander seeds, 2 teaspoons shrimp paste (wrapped in foil) and 1 teaspoon each of white peppercorns and cumin seeds in a roasting tin and bake for 5–10 minutes, or until aromatic. Remove the foil from the shrimp paste.

Transfer to a food processor or mortar and pestle and add 1 teaspoon sea salt, 4 finely chopped stems lemon grass (white part only), 2 teaspoons each of chopped fresh galangal and finely shredded fresh kaffir lime leaves, 1 tablespoon chopped fresh coriander root, 5 chopped red Asian shallots, 10 chopped cloves garlic and 16 seeded and chopped large green chillies. Process or grind until it forms a smooth paste.
Makes 1 cup.

THAI YELLOW CURRY PASTE

Put 8 small fresh green chillies, 5 roughly chopped red Asian shallots, 1 chopped stem lemon grass (white part only), 2 chopped cloves garlic, 2 tablespoons finely chopped fresh galangal, 1 tablespoon each of lime juice and finely chopped fresh coriander stem and root, 1 teaspoon each of ground coriander and cumin and ½ teaspoon each of ground turmeric and black peppercorns in a food processor or mortar and pestle. Process or grind to a smooth paste.
Makes ½ cup.

FROM LEFT: Thai red curry paste, Thai green curry paste, Chu chee curry paste, Thai yellow curry paste.

DIPPING SAUCES

A SMALL BOWL OF ONE OF THESE DELICIOUS SAUCES WILL ENHANCE THE FLAVOUR OF DISHES RANGING FROM SPRING ROLLS, SATAYS AND FRITTERS, TO NOODLES AND FISH DISHES.

SWEET CHILLI SAUCE

Remove the seeds from 6 large red chillies and soak for 15 minutes in hot water. Process with 1 tablespoon chopped red chilli, ¼ cup (60 ml/2 fl oz) white vinegar, 1 cup (250 g/8 oz) caster sugar, 1 teaspoon salt and 4 chopped cloves garlic until smooth. Transfer to a pan and cook for 15 minutes over medium heat, stirring frequently until thickened. Cool. Stir in 2 teaspoons fish sauce.

SESAME SEED SAUCE

Toast 100 g (3⅓ oz) Japanese white sesame seeds in a dry pan over medium heat for 3–4 minutes, shaking the pan gently, until seeds are golden brown; remove from the pan at once to prevent burning. Grind the seeds in a mortar and pestle until a paste is formed. Add 2 teaspoons oil, if necessary, to assist in forming a paste. Mix the paste with ½ cup (125 ml/4 fl oz) Japanese soy sauce, 2 tablespoons mirin, 3 teaspoons caster sugar, ½ teaspoon instant dashi granules and ½ cup (125 ml/4 fl oz) warm water. Store, covered, in the refrigerator and use within 2 days of preparation.

SOY AND GINGER SAUCE

In a bowl combine 1 tablespoon grated fresh ginger, 2 teaspoons sugar and 1 cup (250 ml/8 fl oz) soy sauce. Mix well and serve immediately.

PEANUT SATAY SAUCE

Place 1 cup (160 g/5¼ oz) unsalted roasted peanuts in a food processor and process until finely chopped. Heat 2 tablespoons oil in a medium pan. Add 1 chopped onion and cook over medium heat for 5 minutes or until softened. Add 2 crushed cloves garlic, 2 teaspoons grated fresh ginger, ½ teaspoon chilli powder, 2 teaspoons curry powder and 1 teaspoon ground cumin, and cook, stirring, for 2 minutes. Add 1⅔ cups (410 ml/13 fl oz) coconut milk, 3 tablespoons soft brown sugar and chopped peanuts. Reduce heat and cook for 5 minutes or until the sauce thickens. Add 1 tablespoon lemon juice, season and serve. (For a smoother sauce, process in a food processor for 30 seconds.)

LEMON AND GARLIC DIPPING SAUCE

In a small bowl, stir ¼ cup (60 ml/2 fl oz) lemon juice, 2 tablespoons fish sauce and 1 tablespoon sugar until the sugar has dissolved. Stir in 2 chopped small red chillies and 3 finely chopped cloves garlic.

VIETNAMESE DIPPING SAUCE

In a bowl, mix together 2 tablespoons fish sauce, 2 tablespoons cold water, 2 tablespoons chopped fresh coriander leaves, 1 teaspoon chopped red chilli and 1 teaspoon soft brown sugar and serve.

THAI DIPPING SAUCE

In a small pan, combine ½ cup (125 g/ 4 oz) sugar, ½ cup (125 ml/4 fl oz) water, ¼ cup (60 ml/2 fl oz) white vinegar, 1 tablespoon fish sauce and 1 small chopped red chilli. Bring to the boil and simmer, uncovered, for 5 minutes or until slightly thickened. Remove from heat and cool slightly. Stir in ¼ small, peeled, seeded and finely chopped cucumber, ¼ small finely chopped carrot, and 1 tablespoon chopped roasted peanuts.

PICKLES & CHUTNEYS

JUST A SPOONFUL OF THESE SPICY RELISHES WILL LIFT AN INDIAN DISH, WHILE THE PICKLED VEGETABLES AND GINGER ARE TRADITIONAL IN JAPANESE AND KOREAN MEALS.

LIME OIL PICKLE

Cut 12 limes into 8 thin wedges each, sprinkle with salt and set aside. In a medium pan, dry roast 3 teaspoons mustard seeds and 2 teaspoons each ground turmeric, cumin seeds, fennel seeds and fenugreek seeds for 1–2 minutes. Remove and grind to a fine powder in a mortar and pestle. Over low heat, fry 5 chopped green chillies, 4 sliced cloves garlic and 2 teaspoons grated fresh ginger in 1 tablespoon oil until golden brown. Add 2 cups (500 ml/16 fl oz) oil, 1 tablespoon sugar, the lime wedges and spices; simmer over low heat for 10 minutes, stirring occasionally. Spoon into warm sterilised jars and seal. Store in the refrigerator.

SWEET MANGO CHUTNEY

Peel 3 large green mangoes, remove stones, chop into large slices, and sprinkle with salt. Seed 2 red chillies; chop finely. Blend ½ teaspoon garam masala with 1½ cups (330 g/10½ oz) raw sugar and place in a large pan with 1 cup (250 ml/8 fl oz) white vinegar; bring to the boil. Reduce heat and simmer for 5 minutes. Add mango, chilli, 1 tablespoon finely grated fresh ginger and ½ cup (95 g/3¼ oz) finely chopped dates. Simmer for 1 hour or until the mango is tender. Pour into warm sterilised jars and seal. Store in the refrigerator.

PICKLED VEGETABLES

Put ⅓ cup (80 ml/2¾ fl oz) rice (or white) vinegar, 2 teaspoons salt and 1 teaspoon sugar into a large non-metallic bowl. Pour over 2 cups (500 ml/16 fl oz) boiling water, mix well and allow to cool until lukewarm. Cut 250 g (8 oz) cabbage into 4 cm (1½ inch) strips, 1 small Lebanese cucumber and 2 medium carrots into matchsticks and 1 medium white onion into thick rings, and add to the warm pickling mixture. Put a flat plate on top of the vegetables. Place a small bowl filled with water on top of the plate to weigh it down and submerge the vegetables. Leave for 3 days. Place into sterilised jars, seal and store in the refrigerator for up to 1 month.

EGGPLANT (AUBERGINE) PICKLE

Cut 1 kg (2 lb) slender eggplants (aubergines) lengthways and sprinkle lightly with salt. In a food processor, place 6 cloves garlic, 2.5 cm (1 inch) piece roughly chopped fresh ginger, 4 teaspoons garam masala, 1 teaspoon ground turmeric, 1 teaspoon chilli powder and 1 tablespoon oil; process until a paste forms. Rinse salt off eggplant and pat dry. Heat ⅓ cup (80 ml/2¾ fl oz) oil in a large pan and fry eggplant for 5 minutes or until golden brown. Add paste and fry for 2 minutes. Stir in 1⅔ cups (410 ml/13 fl oz) oil and cook, uncovered, for 10–15 minutes, stirring occasionally. Spoon into warm sterilised jars and seal. Store in a cool, dark place for up to 2 months.

PICKLED GINGER

Cut 125 g (4 oz) fresh ginger into 2.5 cm (1 inch) pieces. Sprinkle with 2 teaspoons salt, cover and refrigerate for 1 week. With a very sharp knife, cut into paper-thin slices across the grain. Over low heat dissolve 2 tablespoons sugar in ½ cup (125 ml/4 fl oz) rice vinegar and 2 tablespoons water. Bring to the boil and simmer for 1 minute. Place ginger in sterilised jars, cover with the marinade, seal and refrigerate for 1 week before using. The ginger will turn pale pink or it can be coloured using 1 teaspoon grenadine. Store in the refrigerator for up to 3 months.

From left: Lime Oil Pickle; Sweet Mango Chutney; Pickled Vegetables; Eggplant Pickle; Pickled Ginger

RAITAS & RELISHES

ADD INTEREST TO YOUR
CURRIES WITH ONE OF THESE
SPICY RELISHES, THEN COOL
DOWN WITH A CHILLED
VEGETABLE OR HERB YOGHURT
RAITA. ALL THESE SERVE FOUR,
AS AN ACCOMPANIMENT.

CUCUMBER RAITA

Mix 2 peeled, finely chopped Lebanese
cucumbers with 1 cup (250 g /8 oz)
yoghurt. Fry 1 teaspoon each ground
cumin and mustard seeds in a dry pan for
1 minute until fragrant. Add to the yoghurt
mixture with ½ teaspoon grated fresh
ginger. Season well with salt and pepper
and garnish with paprika.
Serve chilled.

CARROT RAITA

Place ¼ cup (35 g/1¼ oz) chopped
pistachio nuts, ⅓ cup (40 g/1⅓ oz) sultanas
and ⅓ cup (80 ml/2¾ fl oz) boiling water in
a small bowl. Soak for 30 minutes, then
drain and pat dry with paper towels. In
another bowl, place 2 grated carrots,
¾ cup (185 g/6 oz) yoghurt, 1 teaspoon
crushed cardamom seeds, 1 teaspoon
ground cumin and ¼ teaspoon chilli
powder and mix well. Chill for 30 minutes.
Stir the pistachio nut mixture into the
yoghurt mixture, keeping a couple of
tablespoons aside to garnish. Serve
chilled.

CORIANDER CHUTNEY

Wash, dry and roughly chop 1 bunch (90 g/3 oz) coriander, including the roots. Place in a food processor with ¼ cup (25 g/¾ oz) desiccated coconut, 1 tablespoon soft brown sugar, 1 teaspoon salt, 1 tablespoon grated fresh ginger, 1 small chopped onion, 2 tablespoons lemon juice and 1–2 small green seeded chillies. Process for about 1 minute, or until finely chopped. Serve chilled.

FRESH MINT RELISH

Finely chop 50 g (1⅔ oz) fresh mint, 2 spring onions and 1 green chilli. Mix with 1 crushed clove garlic, 1 teaspoon caster sugar, ½ teaspoon salt and 2 tablespoons lemon juice. Cover and chill for at least 1 hour. Garnish with fine slices of lemon and spring onion and serve.

FRESH TOMATO RELISH

Mix together 2 diced tomatoes, 3 finely sliced spring onions, 2 tablespoons finely chopped fresh coriander leaves, 1 finely sliced green chilli, 1 tablespoon lemon juice and 1 teaspoon soft brown sugar. Season with salt and pepper. Serve chilled.

COCONUT BANANAS

Peel 2 large bananas and cut into thick slices. Dip into ⅓ cup (80 ml/2¾ fl oz) lemon juice, then toss in enough desiccated coconut to coat each piece. Serve at room temperature.

YOGHURT AND MINT RAITA

Combine 1 cup (250 ml/8 fl oz) yoghurt, ⅓ cup (20 g/⅔ oz) chopped fresh mint and a pinch of cayenne pepper and mix well. Serve chilled.

Clockwise from top left: Fresh Coriander Chutney; Carrot Raita; Fresh Tomato Relish; Yoghurt and Mint Raita; Coconut Bananas; Fresh Mint Relish; Cucumber Raita

SWEET SAUCES

WHAT A MARRIAGE MADE IN HEAVEN... DELICIOUSLY SWEET SAUCES POURED OVER SPONGE PUDDINGS THAT SOAK UP THEIR SYRUP AND SOFTEN INTO IRRESISTIBLE GOOEYNESS.

BUTTERSCOTCH SAUCE

Stir 75 g (2½ oz) butter, 1 cup (185 g/6 oz) soft brown sugar and ¾ cup (185 ml/ 6 fl oz) cream in a small pan over low heat until the butter has melted and the sugar dissolved. Bring to the boil, reduce the heat and simmer for 2 minutes.
Makes 1⅔ cups (410 ml/13 fl oz).

CARAMEL BAR SAUCE

Chop four Snickers® bars. Put in a pan with ¼ cup (60 ml/2 fl oz) milk and ¾ cup (185 ml/6 fl oz) cream and stir over low heat until melted. Add 100 g (3½ oz) chopped milk chocolate and stir until melted. Cool to room temperature.
Makes 2¼ cups (560 ml/18 fl oz).

DARK CHOCOLATE SAUCE

Put 150 g (5 oz) chopped dark chocolate in a bowl. Bring 300 ml (10 fl oz) cream to the boil in a pan. Stir in 2 tablespoons caster sugar, then pour over the chocolate. Leave for 2 minutes, then stir until smooth. Add a spoonful of any liqueur. Serve warm.
Makes 2 cups (500 ml/16 fl oz).

CHOCOLATE FUDGE SAUCE

Put 1 cup (250 ml/8 fl oz) cream, 30 g (1 oz) butter, 1 tablespoon golden syrup and 200 g (6½ oz) chopped dark chocolate in a pan. Stir over low heat until melted and smooth. Serve hot or warm.
Makes 2 cups (500 ml/16 fl oz).

LIQUEUR TOKAY SYRUP

Put 250 g (8 oz) sugar and 250 ml (8 fl oz) water in a medium pan. Slowly bring to the boil, stirring to dissolve the sugar. Add half a vanilla bean and boil, without stirring for 5 minutes. Add 250 ml (8 fl oz) liqueur tokay, liqueur muscat or sauterne and stir. Bring back to the boil and cook for 15 minutes, depending on the thickness desired.
Makes 2 cups (500 ml/16 fl oz).

VANILLA HAZELNUT SAUCE

Pour 300 ml (10 fl oz) cream into a small pan. Split 1 vanilla bean and scrape the seeds into the cream. Add the pod and bring to the boil. Remove from the heat, cover and leave for 10 minutes, then strain. Put 200 g (6½ oz) chopped white chocolate in a bowl, reheat the cream and pour over the chocolate. Leave for 2 minutes, then stir until melted. Stir in 30 g (1 oz) chopped roasted hazelnuts.
Makes 2 cups (500 ml/16 fl oz).

RICH BRANDY SAUCE

Bring 2 cups (500 ml/16 fl oz) cream to the boil in a heavy-based pan. Whisk 4 egg yolks with ½ cup (125 g/4 oz) caster sugar until creamy. Slowly pour the hot cream in, stirring. Return to the pan and stir over low heat for 5–6 minutes, until slightly thickened; do not boil. Stir in 3 tablespoons brandy before serving. Makes 3¼ cups (810 ml/26 fl oz).

CITRUS SYRUP

Cut the rind from an orange, a lemon and a lime. Remove the pith. Cut the rind into fine strips. Put in a pan with the juice from the lime and half the juice from the lemon and orange. Add 125 g (4 oz) sugar and 125 ml (4 fl oz) water. Stir over low heat to dissolve. Add half a vanilla bean. Simmer for 10 minutes; do not stir. Makes 1 cup (250 ml/8 fl oz).

From Left: Butterscotch; Caramel bar; Dark chocolate; Liqueur Tokay; Chocolate fudge; Vanilla hazelnut; Rich brandy; Citrus syrup

FRUIT SAUCES

FRESH FRUITS, HERBS AND SPICES CAN BE USED TO MAKE SUBLIME SAUCES THAT TRANSFORM A BOWL OF ICE CREAM OR SIMPLE DESSERT INTO SOMETHING QUITE OUT OF THE ORDINARY.

RHUBARB SAUCE

Chop 350 g (11 oz) rhubarb and place in a pan with ½ cup (95 g/3 oz) soft brown sugar, 1 cup (250 ml/8 fl oz) water and ¼ teaspoon ground mixed spice. Slowly bring to the boil, stirring to dissolve the sugar. Simmer for 10 minutes, stirring often. Push through a sieve and serve hot or cold.
Makes 1½ cups (375 ml/12 fl oz).

PASSIONFRUIT COULIS

Put ½ cup (125 ml/4 fl oz) fresh passionfruit pulp (canned is not suitable for this recipe), ½ cup (125 ml/4 fl oz) water and 2 tablespoons caster sugar in a small pan. Slowly bring to the boil, stirring to dissolve the sugar. Simmer, without stirring, for 5 minutes.
Makes 1 cup (250 ml/8 fl oz).

LEMON GRASS, LIME AND CORIANDER SYRUP

Finely grate 250 g (8 oz) palm sugar and place in a small pan with 1 cup (250 ml/ 8 fl oz) water. Stir over low heat until the sugar has dissolved. Add 2 finely sliced stems lemon grass (white part only), 1 teaspoon lightly crushed coriander seeds, 1 teaspoon lime rind and 2 teaspoons lime juice. Bring to the boil and simmer for 15–20 minutes, or until syrupy. Strain, if you like, and serve with tropical fruits, ice cream or pancakes.
Makes 1 cup (250 ml/8 fl oz).

HOT BLUEBERRY SAUCE

In a non-metallic bowl, combine 500 g (1 lb) blueberries, ¼ cup (60 g/2 oz) sugar and 1 tablespoon balsamic vinegar. Set aside for 30 minutes. Place in a pan with 2 tablespoons water and stir over low heat to dissolve the sugar. Bring to the boil and simmer for 5 minutes. Serve warm. Delicious on ice cream and good with fresh ricotta or warm chocolate cake. Makes 2 cups (500 ml/16 fl oz).

MANGO COULIS

Chop 2 small mangoes. Blend in a food processor with 3 tablespoons orange juice and 2 teaspoons Cointreau (optional), until smooth. Makes 1⅓ cups (350 ml/11 fl oz).

STRAWBERRY COULIS

Hull 250 g (8 oz) strawberries and place in a food processor with 2 tablespoons icing sugar, 2 teaspoons lemon juice and 1–2 teaspoons Grand Marnier (optional). Process until smooth and strain through a fine sieve, if desired.
Makes 1 cup (250 ml/8 fl oz).

BUMBLEBERRY COULIS

Place 300 g (10 oz) fresh or thawed frozen berries (use a combination of raspberry, strawberry, blueberry and blackberry) and 2 tablespoons icing sugar in a food processor. Blend in short bursts until smooth and glossy. Strain in a fine sieve to remove the seeds. Add 2 teaspoons lemon juice and 3 teaspoons Cassis liqueur (optional) and mix well.
Makes 1 cup (250 ml/8 fl oz).

SPICY PEACH SAUCE

Place 500 g (1 lb) peaches in a bowl, cover with boiling water and leave for 20 seconds. Drain, peel and chop, then put in a pan with 1 cup (250 ml/8 fl oz) water, ½ vanilla bean, 2 cloves and a cinnamon stick. Bring to the boil, reduce the heat and simmer for 15–20 minutes, or until tender. Add 3 tablespoons sugar and stir over low heat until dissolved. Increase the heat and simmer for 5 minutes. Remove the vanilla and spices and cool slightly. Blend in a food processor or blender. Push through a fine sieve before serving.
Makes 1¾ cups (440 ml/14 fl oz).

SAUCES CLOCKWISE, FROM TOP LEFT: Lemon grass, lime and coriander; Mango; Passionfruit; Bumbleberry; Spicy peach; Strawberry; Hot blueberry; Rhubarb

DRINKS
FOR ALL
OCCASIONS

TEAS

IT WAS CHINA WHICH FIRST INTRODUCED TEA TO THE REST OF THE WORLD. WHETHER IT BE BLACK OR GREEN, PLAIN OR HIGHLY SPICED, TEA IS AN IMPORTANT PART OF THE MEAL IN MOST ASIAN COUNTRIES.

BLACK TEA

Mainly produced in India, China and Sri Lanka, black tea leaves undergo fermentation which gives them their characteristic full, aromatic flavour and rich colour and strength.

Assam: Grown in north-east India, this classic tea has a strong, full-flavoured malty taste and is ideal for drinking with milk.

Darjeeling: Grown in the foothills of the Himalayas, this prized tea has a subtle 'muscatel' flavour and a light reddish-brown colour.

Ceylon: Produced in the high-altitude areas of Sri Lanka and widely known for its excellent quality, this tea has a strong rich flavour.

Lapsang Souchong: A famous tea from China and Taiwan, this is rich and full-bodied, with a distinctive smoky, tarry taste due to the unique smoking process it undergoes. Well suited for lemon tea.

Yunnan: Often used in blended teas, this Chinese tea produces a sweet light golden liquid, considered to have health-giving properties.

OOLONG TEA

Semi-fermented oolong teas are stronger than green teas and milder than black. They are often scented with jasmine, gardenia or rose petals and are then known as pouchong. Oolong tea originated in China, but the highest grade is now produced in Taiwan.

Formosa: These Taiwanese leaves produce a dark tea with a natural fruity flavour.

GREEN TEA

A favourite in the East, green tea is served with meals in many Asian restaurants and is believed to aid digestion. It is always made weak: only 1 teaspoon of tea for the whole pot. Sugar and milk are never added.

Gunpowder: A high quality, small Chinese leaf which yields a very pale green, fruity and slightly bitter tea.

Jasmine: This Chinese green tea is scented with jasmine petals and traditionally served with yum cha.

Sencha: A Japanese tea with a delicate, light flavour and colour.

Genmai-cha: This blend of rolled Japanese green tea leaves and toasted, puffed rice is a nutty-flavoured tea.

BLENDED TEA

Blended teas are a combination of 15–20 leaves from different areas. They were introduced to provide tea that was unaffected by fluctuations in price and availability.

English breakfast: A mix of a number of strong Indian leaves and Ceylon tea which produces a full-flavoured, fragrant tea.

Irish breakfast: A strong, fragrant tea which is a combination of Assam and Ceylon leaves.

Russian caravan: Originally transported from India to Russia by camels, this tea is a blend of Keemun, Assam and Chinese green leaves.

Earl grey: Scented with oil of bergamot, this blend of Keemun and Darjeeling leaves produces a pale tea with a citrus flavour.

BREWING THE PERFECT CUP OF TEA

1 Bring cold water to the boil rapidly to prevent the water being de-aerated.
2 Use a china or glazed earthenware teapot that will retain the heat, and warm it by swirling a little hot water around the sides and emptying it out.
3 Measure the tea carefully: 1 heaped teaspoon leaves for each cup and 1 for the pot.
4 Follow the old adage 'bring your teapot to the kettle, not the kettle to the teapot' to ensure the water is still on the boil when it is poured onto the tea leaves. This will agitate the leaves and release the full flavour of the tea.
5 Put the lid on the pot and leave for 5 minutes to infuse the leaves.
6 If using, add milk to the cup before the tea. The scalding tea will slightly cook the milk and blend the flavours.
7 Stir the pot and pour tea through a strainer into each cup. Add sugar to taste and a slice of lemon if desired.

Above: The selection of teas from Asia is colourful and fragrant, vast and varied.

LEMON AND LIME BARLEY WATER

Preparation time: 5 minutes
Total cooking time: 30 minutes
Makes about 4 cups (1 litre)

1 cup (220 g/7 oz) pearl barley
8 cups (2 litres) water
¼ cup (60 ml/2 fl oz) lemon juice
½ cup (125 ml/4 fl oz) lime juice
½ cup (125 g/4 oz) caster sugar

1 Boil barley and water in a large heavy-based pan for 30 minutes, or until liquid has reduced by half. Remove from heat and strain.
2 Add juices and sugar; mix well. Serve chilled with ice, and lemon and lime slices.

HOME-MADE LEMONADE

Preparation time: 10 minutes + overnight
  soaking
Total cooking time: 10–15 minutes
Makes about 5 cups (1.25 litres)

Lemon Syrup
6 large lemons
6 whole cloves
5 cups (1.25 litres) boiling water
2 cups (500 g/1 lb) sugar

ice
soda water

1 To make Lemon Syrup: Slice 6 lemons, place in a large bowl with cloves, cover with the boiling water. Leave to infuse overnight. Strain water into a large pan. Discard lemon slices and cloves. Add sugar and stir over low heat, without boiling, until dissolved. Bring to boil, simmer 10 minutes until reduced and slightly syrupy; cool.
2 To serve, place ice in a highball glass. Pour over 2 tablespoons lemon syrup, top with soda water. Garnish with lemon slices and mint leaves.

ICED TEA

Preparation time: 5 minutes
Total cooking time: Nil
Serves 1

ice
½ cup (125 ml/4 fl oz) cold black tea
1 teaspoon sugar

1 Place ice, cold tea and sugar in a highball glass and stir with a swizzle stick. Garnish with lemon slices and mint leaves. Iced tea may also be made with cold herbal teas.

BANANA EGG FLIP

Preparation time: 5 minutes
Total cooking time: Nil
Makes 2

1½ cups (375 ml/12 fl oz) milk
1 medium-sized banana
1 tablespoon honey
1 egg
2–3 tablespoons yoghurt
2 scoops vanilla ice cream
2 ice cubes

1 Pour the milk into a blender. Add the peeled and roughly chopped banana, honey, egg, yoghurt, ice cream and ice and blend well until the mixture is smooth. Pour into 2 glasses and serve.

SUMMER STRAWBERRY SMOOTHIE

Preparation time: 5 minutes
Total cooking time: Nil
Serves 2

1 tablespoon strawberry flavouring
1 cup (250 ml/8 fl oz) wildberry drinking
  yoghurt
1 cup (250 g/9 oz) strawberries, hulled
4 scoops frozen strawberry yoghurt
few drops vanilla essence
ice cubes

1 Combine the strawberry flavouring, drinking yoghurt, strawberries, frozen yoghurt and vanilla untl smooth.
2 Pour over lots of ice to serve.

FRUIT SALAD SMOOTHIE

Preparation time: 5 minutes
Total cooking time: Nil
Makes 2

2 scoops vanilla ice cream
1 cup (175 g/5⅔ oz) chopped fruit
  (passionfruit, strawberries, banana,
  etc)
3–4 ice cubes
2 tablespoons honey

1 Place all the ingredients in a blender and blend until smooth. Pour into tall glasses to serve.

PEACH DREAM

Preparation time: 5 minutes
Total cooking time: Nil
Serves 4

425 g (13½ oz) canned peach slices
3–4 scoops vanilla ice cream
¼ cup (60 ml/2 fl oz) orange juice
2–3 drops vanilla essence
2 cups (500 ml/16 fl oz) chilled milk
orange slices

1 Drain the peach slices and combine with ice cream, orange juice, vanilla and milk in a blender; blend until smooth. Serve at once in glasses, garnished with orange slices.

ENERGY SHAKE

Preparation time: 5 minutes
Total cooking time: Nil
Makes 2 shakes

1½ cups (375 ml/12 fl oz) skim or soy milk
1 tablespoon skim milk powder
½ cup (125 g/4 oz) yoghurt
1 tablespoon honey
1 banana, peeled
6 strawberries (optional)
ground cinnamon, for sprinkling

1 Blend all the ingredients except the cinnamon until smooth. Pour immediately into tall glasses and serve sprinkled with a little cinnamon.

CLASSIC COCOA FOR TWO

Preparation time: 5 minutes
Total cooking time: 5 minutes
Serves 2

1 tablespoon cocoa powder
1 tablespoon sugar
¼ cup (60 ml/2 fl oz) water
2 cups (500 ml/16 fl oz) hot milk
dash of rum or whisky (optional)

1 Combine cocoa powder and sugar in a small pan. Add water and whisk until smooth. Bring to boil, reduce heat to low and add hot milk, whisking until frothy. Sprinkle with extra cocoa powder. Serve with a dash of rum or whisky.

SPICY COFFEE

Preparation time: 10 minutes
Total cooking time: Nil
Serves 4

½ –1 teaspoon ground cinnamon
1 pot of strong black coffee
   (4 cups/1 litre)
Kahlua
2 cups (500 ml/16 fl oz) cream, whipped
shredded orange rind, for decoration

1 Add the cinnamon to the coffee while it is still in the pot. Add 1–2 tablespoons of Kahlua to each cup or glass.
2 Top with the coffee, spoon or pipe the cream over the top and decorate with orange rind.

VIENNA COFFEE

Preparation time: 10 minutes
Total cooking time: Nil
Serves 4

4 cups (1 litre) milky coffee
80 g (22/3 oz) milk chocolate, grated
2 cups (500 ml/16 fl oz) cream, whipped

1 Stir 1 tablespoon of grated milk chocolate into each cup of milky coffee and top each with a generous dollop of whipped cream. Decorate with extra chocolate and serve immediately.

IRISH COFFEE

Preparation time: 10 minutes
Total cooking time: Nil
Serves 4

1 pot of strong black coffee
   (4 cups/1 litre)
sugar
Irish whiskey
thick cream

1 Pour the coffee into tall, preferably glass, mugs. Add sugar and Irish Whiskey, to taste.
2 Pour thick cream slowly over the back of a spoon onto the coffee to create a 6 mm (¼ inch) thick layer. Serve immediately. As a variation, substitute dark rum for the Irish Whiskey to make Jamaican Coffee.

PARTY PUNCHES

HERE YOU WILL FIND A REFRESHING IDEA FOR A DELICIOUS PUNCH WHETHER YOU WANT ONE WITH OR WITHOUT ALCOHOL. THEY WILL DELIGHT YOUR GUESTS AND ADD COLOUR TO THE TABLE.

PINEAPPLE AND PAWPAW JUICE

Roughly chop the flesh from a 2 kg (4 lb) pineapple. Juice the flesh in a juicer, then pour into a punch bowl. Blend a 1.2 kg (2 lb 6½ oz) peeled pawpaw in a blender until smooth. Add 2 cups (500 ml/16 fl oz) chilled ginger ale. Serve immediately in tall chilled glasses. Garnish the glasses with pineapple slices and fronds. Serves 8.

SANGRIA

Mix 2 tablespoons caster sugar with 1 tablespoon each of lemon and orange juice in a large jug until the sugar has dissolved. Thinly slice an unpeeled orange, a lemon and a lime, discard any pips, and add to the jug with a 750 ml (24 fl oz) bottle of chilled red wine and plenty of ice. Stir well until very cold. Serve in large wine glasses. (Do not strain.) This traditional Spanish drink can be made in large quantities, and its flavour will improve over several hours— it can be made up to a day in advance. Chopped seasonal fruits, such as peaches, pears and pineapples, can be added to this basic recipe. Good-quality wine is not essential in Sangria, so use a table wine or even a cask wine. Serves 6.

BRANDY ALEXANDER PUNCH

Pour 3 cups (750 ml/24 fl oz) brandy, 1½ cups (375 ml/12 fl oz) crème de cacao and six 300 ml (10 fl oz) cartons of cream into a large bowl. Whisk to just combine. Add ice cubes to a 3.5 litre (104 fl oz) punch bowl and pour in the brandy mixture. Sprinkle with grated nutmeg, then serve in cocktail glasses garnished with strawberry halves.
Serves 16.

PINEAPPLE DELIGHT

Roughly chop the flesh from a 1.5 kg (3 lb) pineapple, then blend in a blender until as smooth as possible. Pour 4 cups (1 litre/32 fl oz) lemonade into a jug and gently stir in the pineapple. Add ⅓ cup (80 ml/2¾ fl oz) lime juice and mix well. Pour into serving glasses and garnish with mint leaves.
Serves 8.

SPARKLING PUNCH

Pour 1 cup (250 ml/8 fl oz) chilled pineapple juice and 2 cups (500 ml/16 fl oz) each of chilled orange juice, apple cider and ginger ale into a large jug. Stir them all together, then stir in the flesh from 2 passionfruit. Garnish with halved orange and lemon slices. Ice cubes can be added to the jug or to each individual glass.
Serves 6.

BERRY AND CHERRY PUNCH

Peel the skin from a lemon with a vegetable peeler, avoiding the bitter white pith. Cut into long thin strips. Drain a 425 g (14 oz) can pitted black cherries and place in a large jug. Add 125 g (4 oz) halved strawberries, 600 g (1¼ lb) assorted fresh or frozen berries, 2 cups (500 ml/16 fl oz) lemonade, 3 cups (750 ml/24 fl oz) ginger ale, 1 cup (250 ml/8 fl oz) cold black tea, 10 torn mint leaves and the lemon rind. Cover and chill for at least 3 hours. Add ice cubes when serving. Can be garnished with berries on a toothpick.
Serves 10.

FROM LEFT: Pineapple and pawpaw juice; Berry and cherry punch; Brandy Alexander punch; Sangria; Pineapple delight; Sparkling punch

REFRESHING JUICES

A COLOURFUL ADDITION TO THE DRINKS MENU, THESE FRUITY JUICES WILL BE MUCH APPRECIATED BY THOSE NEEDING A LIFT BUT NOT WISHING TO INDULGE IN ALCOHOL.

FRUIT SPARKLE

Pour 2 cups (500 ml/16 fl oz) chilled apricot nectar, 2 cups (500 ml/16 fl oz) chilled soda water, 1 cup (250 ml/8 fl oz) chilled apple juice and 1 cup (250 ml/ 8 fl oz) chilled orange juice into a large jug and stir well. Stir in about 8 ice cubes, then pour into tall glasses and serve. Serves 4–6.

PASSIONFRUIT LIME CRUSH

Combine ½ cup (125 g/4 oz) passionfruit pulp (you will need about 6 passionfruit), ¾ cup (185 ml/6 fl oz) lime juice cordial and 3 cups (750 ml/24 fl oz) ginger ale in a large jug and mix together well. Pour into large glasses that have been half filled with crushed ice. Serve immediately. Serves 4.

RUBY GRAPEFRUIT AND LEMON SORBET FIZZ

Pour 2 cups (500 ml/16 fl oz) chilled ruby grapefruit juice and 1 cup (250 ml/ 8 fl oz) chilled soda water into a jug. Stir in 1 tablespoon caster sugar, then pour into chilled glasses. Top with a scoop of lemon sorbet. Mix the sorbet in or serve with a parfait spoon. Serves 4.

HAWAIIAN SMOOTHIE

Put 2 cups (500 ml/16 fl oz) chilled apple juice in a blender with 200 g (7 oz) peeled and seeded papaya or pawpaw, 400 g (13 oz) peeled and seeded watermelon and about 20 ice cubes. Blend until smooth. Serves 4.

BLUEBERRY CRUSH

Blend 150 g (5 oz) blueberries in a blender with 1 tablespoon caster sugar until smooth. Mix well with 3 cups (750 ml/ 24 fl oz) apple and blackcurrant juice and 2 cups (500 ml/16 fl oz) soda water. Serve immediately in chilled glasses half filled with ice cubes. If you have a good blender, you may wish to add the ice cubes when blending the blueberries, to make a slushy.
Serves 4–6.

VIRGIN MARY

Stir 3 cups (750 ml/24 fl oz) tomato juice in a large jug with 1 tablespoon Worcestershire sauce, 2 tablespoons lemon juice, ¼ teaspoon ground nutmeg and a few drops of Tabasco sauce until well mixed. Place 12 ice cubes in a blender and blend for 30 seconds, or until the ice is crushed. Spoon the crushed ice into the tomato juice mixture, then carefully pour into tall glasses. Add a celery stick to each glass—this not only adds a delicious subtle flavour to the drink but also serves as an edible swizzle stick. Decorate each glass with some very thin lemon slices. Season with salt and freshly ground black pepper, to taste, before serving.
Serves 4.

MINT JULEP

Roughly chop 2 cups (40 g/1¼ oz) fresh mint leaves, place in a bowl and bruise with a wooden spoon to release the oils. Transfer to a heatproof jug and add 2 tablespoons sugar, 1 tablespoon lemon juice, 2 cups (500 ml/16 fl oz) pineapple juice and 1 cup (250 ml/8 fl oz) boiling water. Mix, cover with plastic wrap and set aside for 30 minutes. Strain, then cover and refrigerate until well chilled. Mix in 2 cups (500 ml/16 fl oz) chilled ginger ale. Put ice cubes in glasses and pour in the drink. Garnish each glass with a few fresh mint leaves.
Serves 4–6.

FROM LEFT: Fruit sparkle; Passionfruit lime crush; Ruby grapefruit and lemon sorbet fizz; Blueberry crush; Hawaiian smoothie; Virgin Mary; Mint julep

COLD DRINKS

THESE DELICIOUS DRINKS ARE MADE FROM FRESH FRUIT JUICES AND CHILLED MILK OR YOGHURT. MIX UP A JUG AS A PERFECT COOLER FOR A HOT AFTERNOON.

GINGERED WATERMELON JUICE

Remove skin and seeds from 500 g (1 lb) watermelon and roughly chop. Place in a blender or food processor with 2 teaspoons grated fresh ginger. Process for 2 minutes. Add 6 ice cubes and process a 1 more minute or until the ice is crushed. Serve garnished with a thin wedge of watermelon.
Makes 2½ cups (600 ml/20 fl oz).

LASSI

Place ¾ cup (185 g/6 oz) yoghurt, 2 cups (250 ml/8 fl oz) water and ¼ teaspoon salt into a blender or food processor. Blend for 1–2 minutes, until smooth and frothy. Serve with ice cubes. Makes 3 cups (750 ml/24 fl oz). Variations: For Mint Lassi, add 8–10 fresh mint leaves before blending. For Sweet Lassi, add 4 teaspoons sugar and ¼ teaspoon rose water before blending and omit the salt.

MINTY MELON JUICE

Roughly chop 1 peeled and cored green apple and ½ small honeydew melon. Place in a blender or food processor with 1 cup (250 ml/8 fl oz) orange juice and 8 fresh mint leaves. Process for 1–2 minutes until smooth. Add ¾ cup (100 g/3⅓ oz) ice cubes and process for 1 minute. Pour into 4 large glasses and garnish with fresh mint leaves.
Makes 1.25 litres.

MANGO FRAPPE

Peel and roughly chop 2 or 3 fresh mangoes. Place ¾ cup (100 g/3⅓ oz) ice cubes in a blender or food processor and process in short bursts for 5 minutes, or until the ice is roughly chopped. Add the mango and process until smooth. Add a little water to thin if you wish.
Makes 2½ cups (600 ml/20 fl oz).

VARIATIONS: Fresh pineapple, guava, carambola or melons can be used to make other tropical frappés.

LIME SODA

Place 1 cup (250 g/8 oz) sugar and 2½ cups (600 ml/20 fl oz) water in a large pan. Dissolve sugar over low heat, stirring occasionally. Bring to the boil and cook, uncovered, for 5 minutes. Add 1½ cups (375 ml/ 12 fl oz) fresh lime juice and boil for 5 minutes more. Cool then chill for 1 hour. Makes 2¼ cups (560 ml/ 18 fl oz) syrup. Dilute about 2–3 tablespoons per glass with soda or sparkling mineral water.

TROPICAL THICKSHAKE

Put ½ cup (80 g/2⅔ oz) chopped fresh pineapple, ½ cup (110 g/3⅔ oz) chopped papaya, 2 chopped bananas, ½ cup (125 ml/4 fl oz) coconut milk and 1 cup (250 ml/8 fl oz) orange juice in a food processor or blender. Blend for 1–2 minutes, or until the fruit is puréed. Add ¾ cup (100 g/3⅓ oz) ice cubes and process in bursts for 5 minutes, or until the ice is crushed. Garnish with banana slices.
Makes 1 litre.

FRAGRANT MILK SHERBET

Place ¾ cup (100 g/3⅓ oz) ice cubes in a blender or food processor and process in bursts for 5 minutes, or until the ice is crushed. Place the ice in 4 tall glasses. Place ½ cup (75 g/ 2½ oz) shelled pistachio nuts, ¼ cup (60 g/2 oz) caster sugar, ½ teaspoon ground cardamom and ½ teaspoon ground cinnamon in the blender. Process for 2 minutes until smooth. Add 1.25 litres milk, process until frothy and pour over the ice. Sprinkle 1 teaspoon roughly chopped shelled pistachios over each sherbet.
Makes 1.5 litres.

From left: Gingered Watermelon Juice; Mint Lassi; Minty Melon Juice; Mango Frappé; Lime Soda; Tropical Thickshake; Fragrant Milk Sherbet

HOT CLASSICS

WHETHER IT'S HOT OR COLD OUTSIDE, WARMING DRINKS CREATE A COMFORTING WELCOME TO ANY GATHERING, WHETHER YOU ARE CELEBRATING CHRISTMAS OR JUST RELAXING IN HOLIDAY MODE.

MULLED WINE

Push 12 cloves into 2 oranges and place in a saucepan with ¼ cup (60 g/2 oz) sugar, 1 whole nutmeg, grated, 4 cinnamon sticks and 2 thinly sliced lemons. Pour in 2 cups (500 ml/16 fl oz) water and bring to the boil, then reduce the heat, cover the pan and simmer for 20 minutes. Allow to cool, then strain and discard the fruit and spices. Pour the mixture into a saucepan, add 3 cups (750 ml/24 fl oz) full-bodied red wine and heat until almost boiling— do not allow to boil or the alcohol will evaporate off. Serve in heatproof glasses. Serves 6.

EGGNOG

Separate 4 eggs and beat the yolks and ⅓ cup (90 g/3 oz) caster sugar in a heatproof bowl until light and fluffy. Add 1¼ cups (315 ml/10 fl oz) hot milk and stir to combine. Bring a saucepan of water to the boil and reduce the heat to simmer. Place the bowl over simmering water and stir with a wooden spoon for about 5–10 minutes until the mixture thickens and lightly coats the back of the spoon. Remove from the heat and allow to cool. Stir in ½ cup (125 ml/4 fl oz) bourbon. Beat ½ cup (125 ml/4 fl oz) cream and the 4 egg whites separately until soft peaks form. Fold the cream, then egg whites into the bourbon in two batches. Pour into glasses and sprinkle with grated nutmeg. Serves 6–8.

HOT TODDY

Put 1 tablespoon soft brown sugar,
4 slices of lemon, 4 cinnamon sticks,
12 whole cloves, ½ cup (125 ml/4 fl oz)
whisky and 4 cups (1 litre/32 fl oz) boiling
water in a heatproof jug. Stir to combine
and leave to infuse for a few minutes,
then strain. Add more sugar, to taste.
Serve in heatproof glasses.
Serves 4.

BUTTERED RUM

Place 1 tablespoon sugar, 1 cup (250 ml/
8 fl oz) rum and 2 cups (500 ml/16 fl oz)
boiling water in a heatproof jug. Stir to
dissolve the sugar, then divide among
4 mugs. Stir 1–2 teaspoons softened
unsalted butter into each mug and serve.
Serves 4.

BRANDIED APPLE CIDER

Thinly slice 2 apples into discs, discarding
the ends—do not core. Place the apple in
a large heavy-based saucepan and add
2 x 375 ml (12 fl oz) bottles alcoholic cider
and 1 cup (250 ml/8 fl oz) brandy or
Calvados. Heat until almost boiling—
do not boil. Serve in heatproof glasses.
Serves 4.

CARAMEL AND VANILLA MILKSHAKE

Slowly heat 1 litre (32 fl oz) milk in a
saucepan—be careful not to boil. Add
100 g (3½ oz) hard caramels and heat over
low heat until melted, stirring
occasionally. Place in a blender with
2–3 scoops vanilla ice cream and blend
briefly until smooth. Pour into 4 tall
heatproof glasses.
Serves 4.

FROM LEFT: Buttered rum; Mulled wine; Eggnog; Hot toddy; Brandied apple cider; Caramel and vanilla milkshake

COCKTAILS

THIS IS A SELECTION OF SIMPLE COCKTAIL DRINKS WITH QUANTITIES SUITABLE FOR ONE PERSON. USE GLASSWARE APPROPRIATE FOR THE STYLE OF DRINK AND REMEMBER TO HAVE PLENTY OF ICE IN THE FREEZER.

CRANBERRY AND VODKA SPARKLE

Combine ½ cup (125 ml/4 fl oz) each of chilled cranberry juice and lemonade or mineral water in a jug with 2 teaspoons lime juice, 30 ml (1 fl oz) vodka and a few ice cubes. Mix well, pour into a tall glass and serve immediately.

BLOODY MARY

Half fill a tall glass with crushed ice. Pour in ¼ cup (60 ml/2 fl oz) vodka, then top up with tomato juice and stir. Stir in a dash of Tabasco sauce, Worcestershire sauce, lemon juice and a little salt and pepper. Traditionally, this drink is served with a celery stick, including leaves, as an edible swizzle stick. For Virgin Mary, a non-alcoholic version, delete the vodka.

BUCK'S FIZZ

Pour ½ cup (125 ml/4 fl oz) fresh orange juice and a dash of Grenadine into a champagne flute. Top slowly with chilled good-quality sparkling white wine.

SPARKLING WINE AND BRANDY COCKTAIL

Place 1–2 sugar cubes in a champagne flute. Add a dash of Angostura bitters over the sugar, then pour in 15 ml (½ fl oz) brandy. Slowly top up the glass with chilled good-quality sparkling white wine.

PINA COLADA

Combine about 6 ice cubes in a drink shaker or jug with 45 ml (1½ fl oz) white rum, 30 ml (1 fl oz) coconut cream, 15 ml (½ fl oz) cream and about ½ cup (125 ml/4 fl oz) pineapple juice and mix well (or blend in a blender). Pour into a tall glass. You can garnish the glass with pineapple leaves and a maraschino cherry. Serve immediately.

BRANDY ALEXANDER

Combine 6 ice cubes in a drink shaker or jug with 30 ml (1 fl oz) each of brandy and crème de cacao and ¼ cup (60 ml/ 2 fl oz) cream. Shake or stir well, then strain into a champagne saucer and serve sprinkled lightly with some grated fresh nutmeg.

MANGO DAIQUIRI

Combine about 6 ice cubes in a blender with 45 ml (1½ fl oz) white rum, 15 ml (½ fl oz) mango liqueur and 30 ml (1 fl oz) each of lemon juice and either Cointreau or Grand Marnier. Add the roughly chopped pulp of 1 mango, or a 400 g (13 oz) can mango slices, drained, and blend until smooth. Pour into a goblet-shaped glass.

STRAWBERRY MARGARITA

Frost the rim of a martini glass by lightly beating an egg white until just frothy, then dipping the rim of the martini glass into the egg, then in salt. Place about 6 ice cubes in a blender with 30 ml (1 fl oz) each of tequila, strawberry liqueur, lime juice cordial and lemon juice and 15 ml (½ fl oz) Cointreau. Blend well, then pour into the martini glass, taking care to avoid touching the rim of the glass.

FROM LEFT: Cranberry and vodka sparkle; Bloody Mary; Buck's fizz; Sparkling wine and brandy cocktail; Pina colada; Brandy Alexander; Mango daiquiri; Strawberry Margarita

SMALL SWEET THINGS

ALMOND SHORTBREADS

Preparation time: 25 minutes +
    10 minutes cooling + 1 hour
    refrigeration
Total cooking time: 15 minutes
Makes 22

250 g (8 oz) unsalted butter
100 g (3½ oz) slivered almonds
2 cups (250 g/8 oz) plain flour
1 teaspoon baking powder
¾ cup (90 g/3 oz) icing sugar, sifted
1 egg yolk
1 teaspoon vanilla essence
1 tablespoon ouzo
4 tablespoons almond meal
½ cup (60 g/2 oz) icing sugar, extra, for
    dusting

1 Gently melt the butter over low heat in a
small heavy-based saucepan, without
stirring or shaking the pan. Carefully pour
the clear butter into another container,
leaving the white sediment in the pan to
be discarded. Refrigerate for 1 hour.
2 Preheat the oven to warm 170°C
(325°F/Gas 3) and line two baking trays
with baking paper. Grind the slivered
almonds to a medium-fine meal. In a bowl,
sift the flour and baking powder together.
3 Using electric beaters, beat the chilled
butter until light and fluffy. Gradually add
the icing sugar and combine well. Add the
egg yolk, vanilla and ouzo and beat until
just combined. Fold in the flour, ground
almonds and the almond meal.
4 Shape heaped tablespoons of mixture
into crescents, place on the baking trays
and bake for 12 minutes, or until lightly
coloured. Remove from the oven and dust
liberally with icing sugar. Leave to cool on
the trays for 10 minutes.
5 Line a baking tray with baking paper
and dust the paper with icing sugar. Lift
the warm biscuits onto this and dust
again with icing sugar. When the biscuits
are cool, dust them once again with icing
sugar before storing them in an airtight
container.

DOUBLE CHOC MUFFINS

Preparation time: 15 minutes
Total cooking time: 12–15 minutes
Makes 6 large muffins

2 cups (250 g/8 oz) plain flour
2½ teaspoons baking powder
¼ cup (30 g/1 oz) cocoa powder
2 tablespoons caster sugar
1 cup (175 g/5⅔ oz) dark choc bits
1 egg, lightly beaten
½ cup (125 g/4 oz) sour cream
¾ cup (185 ml/6 fl oz) milk
90 g (3 oz) butter, melted

1 Preheat the oven to moderate 180°C
(350°F/Gas 4). Brush a 6-hole large
muffin tin with melted butter or oil. Sift
the flour, baking powder and cocoa into a
large mixing bowl. Add the sugar and the
choc bits and stir to mix through. Make a
well in the centre of the mixture. Add the
combined egg, sour cream, milk and
melted butter all at once and stir with a
fork until just combined. (Do not
overbeat—batter should look quite
lumpy.)
2 Spoon the mixture into the tin. Bake for
12–15 minutes or until firm. Loosen the
muffins with a knife before turning out
onto a wire rack to cool.

NOTE: For a delicious topping, combine
50 g (1⅔ oz) chocolate, 1 tablespoon cream
and 10 g (⅓ oz) butter in a pan; stir over
low heat until smooth. Refrigerate until
firm, then pipe or spoon over muffins.
Sprinkle with icing sugar.

CREOLE RICE FRITTERS
(CALAS)

Preparation time: 20 minutes +
    40 minutes resting
Total cooking time: 15 minutes
Makes about 24

¾ cup (90 g/3 oz) plain (all-purpose) flour
½ cup (115 g/4 oz) caster (superfine)
    sugar
½ teaspoon freshly grated nutmeg
1 teaspoon ground cinnamon
1 x 8 g (¼ oz) sachet instant dry yeast
2 eggs, lightly beaten
2 cups (370 g/12 oz) well cooked short-
    grain rice, lightly mashed
1 teaspoon pure vanilla extract
vegetable oil, for deep-frying
icing (confectioners') sugar, to sprinkle

1 Sift the flour into a bowl and add the
sugar, nutmeg, cinnamon, yeast and a
large pinch of salt and combine well.
Gradually stir in ⅓ cup (80 ml/2¾ fl oz) very
hot but not boiling water until you have a
thick paste. Gradually beat in the eggs and
continue beating until you have a smooth
batter, then mix in the rice and vanilla until
well combined. Cover and allow to rise in a
warm, draft-free place for about 20
minutes, or until doubled in size. Stir well,
then rest again for a further 20 minutes.
2 Heat enough oil in a deep-fat fryer or
large saucepan to fully cover the fritters.
Heat the oil to 180°C (350°F), or until a
piece of batter dropped into the oil
browns in 15 seconds. Stir the batter
again, then drop tablespoons of the
mixture (in batches) into the hot oil and
cook, turning occasionally for 2–3 minutes,
or until deeply golden. Drain on paper
towels, sprinkle with icing sugar and
serve immediately.

NOTE: Cooked and sold on the streets of
New Orleans this popular treat is enjoyed
most often as a breakfast food or a snack
but makes a great dessert served with ice
cream.

SCONES

Preparation time: 20 minutes
Total cooking time: 10–12 minutes
Makes 12

2 cups (250 g/8 oz) self-raising flour
pinch salt (optional—see Note)
30 g (1 oz) butter, cut into small pieces
½ cup (125 ml/4 fl oz) milk
⅓ cup (80 ml/2¾ fl oz) water
milk, extra, for glazing

1 Preheat the oven to hot 210°C
(415°F/Gas 6–7). Brush an oven tray with
melted butter or oil. Sift the flour and salt
(if using) into a bowl. Add the chopped
butter and rub in lightly using your
fingertips.
2 Make a well in the centre of the flour.
Add almost all of the combined milk and
water. Mix with a flat-bladed knife to a
soft dough, adding more liquid if
necessary.
3 Turn the dough onto a lightly floured
surface (use self-raising flour). Knead the
dough briefly and lightly until smooth.
Press or roll out the dough to form a
round 1.5 cm (⅝ inch) thick.
4 Cut the dough into rounds using a
floured round 5 cm (2 inch) cutter. Place
the rounds on the prepared tray; glaze
with milk. Bake the scones for
10–12 minutes or until golden brown.
Serve with jam and whipped cream.

NOTE: Use a light touch when kneading
scones or they may turn out heavy and
tough—the dough needs very little
handling. It is usual to add a pinch of salt
to the mixture when making scones, even
the sweet ones, to enhance the flavour.

PINE NUT TARTS

Preparation time: 25 minutes
Total cooking time: 15 minutes
Makes 24

½ cup (60 g/2 oz) plain flour
60 g (2 oz) butter, chopped
40 g (1¼ oz) pine nuts
20 g (¾ oz) butter, melted
½ cup (175 g/6 oz) golden syrup
2 tablespoons soft brown sugar

1 Preheat the oven to moderate 180°C
(350°F/Gas 4). Grease two 12-hole mini
muffin tins.
2 Sift the flour into a bowl and add the
chopped butter. Rub into the flour with
your fingertips until the mixture comes
together. Turn onto a lightly floured
surface and gather together.
3 Roll out on a lightly floured surface to a
thickness of 3 mm (¼ inch). Cut out
rounds with a 5 cm (2 inch) fluted cutter.
Lift gently with a flat-bladed knife and
line each muffin hole with pastry. Spread
the pine nuts onto a flat baking tray and
bake for 2–3 minutes, or until just golden.
Remove from the tray and cool; divide the
nuts among the pastry cases.
4 Combine the melted butter, syrup and
sugar in a jug and whisk with a fork, then
pour over the pine nuts. Bake for
15 minutes, or until golden. Cool in the
trays for 5 minutes before lifting out onto
a wire rack to cool completely. Dust with
icing sugar before serving, if desired.
note: You can use chopped walnuts or
pecans instead of the pine nuts.

IN ADVANCE: The tarts can be made up
to 8 hours ahead. Store in an airtight
container.

PEANUT CHOC-CHIP MUFFINS

Preparation time: 15 minutes
Total cooking time: 20–25 minutes
Makes 12

2 cups (250 g/8 oz) self-raising flour
⅓ cup (80 g/2⅔ oz) raw sugar
1½ cups (240 g/7½ oz) dark choc bits
1 egg
1 cup (250 g/8 oz) crunchy peanut butter
2 tablespoons strawberry jam
60 g (2 oz) butter, melted
1 cup (250 ml/8 fl oz) milk
icing sugar, for dusting

1 Preheat oven to moderate 180°C
(350°F/Gas 4). Brush a 12-hole standard
size muffin tin with melted butter or oil.
2 Sift flour into a large bowl. Add sugar
and choc bits; make a well in centre. Add
combined egg, peanut butter, jam, butter
and milk. Stir until just combined. (Do not
overbeat.)
3 Spoon evenly into muffin cups. Bake for
20–25 minutes or until a skewer comes
out clean when inserted in the centre.
Loosen muffins in the pan and leave for
10 minutes before turning onto a wire
rack to cool. Dust with icing sugar.

CREAMY COCONUT ICE

Preparation time: 20 minutes +
    2 hours refrigeration
Total cooking time: Nil
Makes 30 pieces

2 cups (250 g (8 oz) icing sugar
¼ teaspoon cream of tartar
400 g (13 oz) can condensed milk
3½ cups (315 g/10 oz) desiccated coconut
2–3 drops pink food colouring

1 Grease a 20 cm (8 inch) square cake tin and line the base with baking paper.
2 Sift the icing sugar and cream of tartar into a bowl. Make a well and add the condensed milk. Using a wooden spoon, stir in half the coconut, then the remaining coconut. Mix well with your hands. Divide in half and tint one half pink. Using your hand, knead the colour through evenly.
3 Press the pink mixture over the base of the tin, cover with the white mixture and press down firmly. Refrigerate for 1–2 hours, or until firm. Remove from the tin, remove the paper and cut into pieces. Store in an airtight container in a cool place for up to 3 weeks.

MINI PARIS-BREST

Preparation time: 30 minutes
Total cooking time: 35 minutes
Makes 15

½ cup (60 g/2 oz) plain flour
60 g (2 oz) butter, chopped
2 eggs, lightly beaten

Custard filling
1¼ cups (315 ml/10 fl oz) milk
3 egg yolks
2 tablespoons caster sugar
1 tablespoon plain flour
1 tablespoon custard powder
few drops almond essence, to taste

Toffee
1 cup (250 g/8 oz) caster sugar
⅔ cup (60 g/2 oz) flaked almonds, lightly
    toasted

1 To make choux pastry, sift the flour onto a sheet of baking paper. Put the butter in a pan with ½ cup (125 ml/4 fl oz) water, stir over low heat until melted, then bring to the boil. Remove from the heat, add the flour in one go and quickly beat it into the water with a wooden spoon. Return to the heat and continue beating until the mixture forms a ball and leaves the side of the pan. Transfer to a large clean bowl and cool slightly. Beat with electric beaters to release any more heat. Gradually add the beaten egg, about 3 teaspoons at a time. Beat well after each addition until all the egg has been added and the mixture is smooth and glossy.
2 Preheat the oven to moderately hot 190°C (375°F/Gas 5). Line 3 baking trays with baking paper. Place the choux pastry into a piping bag with a 5 mm (¼ inch) star nozzle. Pipe 3 cm (1¼ inch) circles of choux onto the paper. Bake for 10 minutes then reduce the heat to moderate 180°C (350°F/Gas 4). Bake for 15–20 minutes more, or until well browned and puffed. Pierce the sides to allow the steam to escape and cool on a wire rack.

3 For the filling, heat 1 cup (250 ml/8 fl oz) milk to simmering point in a pan. In a bowl, whisk together the remaining milk, egg yolks, sugar, flour and custard powder and slowly pour on the hot milk, whisking vigorously until well combined. Pour back into the clean pan and stir over medium heat until the mixture boils and thickens. Stir in the essence. Transfer to a bowl, cover and cool.
4 To make the toffee, combine the sugar and ½ cup (125 ml/4 fl oz) water in a small pan, stirring constantly over low heat until the sugar has dissolved. Bring to the boil and boil rapidly without stirring for about 10 minutes, or until just golden. Place the pan immediately over another pan of hot water to stop the toffee setting.
5 Immediately dip the choux tops into the toffee, decorate with a few toasted flaked almonds and place on a wire rack to set. Split the choux rings in half, pipe or spoon the filling in and top with the toffee lids.

SWEET WON TONS

Preparation time: 15 minutes
Total cooking time: 20 minutes
Makes 30

125 g (4 oz) dates, pitted and chopped
2 bananas, finely chopped
½ cup (45 g/1½ oz) flaked almonds, lightly
   crushed
½ teaspoon ground cinnamon
60 won ton wrappers
oil, for deep-frying
icing sugar, to dust

1 Mix together the dates, bananas, almonds and cinnamon. Place 2 teaspoons of the fruit mixture into the centre of a won ton wrapper, and brush the edges lightly with water. Place another won ton wrapper on top at an angle so that the wrappers make a star shape. Place the won tons on a tray lined with baking paper. Repeat with the remaining ingredients, taking care not to stack the won tons on top of each other or they will stick together.
2 Heat the oil in a large pan until moderately hot; add the won tons in small batches and deep-fry for 2 minutes or until crisp and golden. Drain on paper towels. Dust the won tons lightly with icing sugar before serving.

SEMOLINA AND NUT DIAMONDS

Preparation time: 30 minutes +
   30 minutes standing
Total cooking time: 40 minutes
Makes 12

115 g (4 oz) unsalted butter, softened
½ cup (125 g/4 oz) caster sugar
1 cup (125 g/4 oz) semolina
1 cup (110 g/3½ oz) ground roasted
   hazelnuts
2 teaspoons baking powder
3 eggs, lightly beaten
1 tablespoon finely grated orange rind
2 tablespoons orange juice
whipped cream or honey-flavoured
   yoghurt, for serving

Syrup
3 cups (750 g/1½ lb) sugar
4 cinnamon sticks
1 tablespoon thinly julienned orange rind
⅓ cup (80 ml/2¾ fl oz) lemon juice
½ cup (125 ml/4 fl oz) orange blossom
   water

Topping
½ cup (60 g/2¾ oz) slivered almonds
½ cup (70 g/2¼ oz) roasted hazelnuts,
   coarsely chopped

1 Preheat the oven to hot 210°C (415°F/Gas 6–7). Lightly grease a 23 cm (9 inch) square baking tin and line the base with baking paper. Cream the butter and sugar in a medium bowl until light and fluffy. Stir in the semolina, ground hazelnuts and baking powder. Add the eggs, orange rind and juice and fold through until well combined. Spoon into the tin, smooth the surface and bake for 20 minutes, or until golden and just set. Leave in the tin.

2 Meanwhile, for the syrup, place the sugar, cinnamon sticks and 3⅓ cups (830 ml/28 fl oz) water in a saucepan over low heat and stir until the sugar has dissolved. Increase the heat and boil rapidly, without stirring, for 5 minutes. Pour into a heatproof measuring jug then return half to the saucepan. Boil for 15–20 minutes, or until thickened and reduced to about ⅔ cup (170 ml/5½ fl oz). Stir in the orange zest.
3 Add the lemon juice and orange blossom water to the syrup in the jug and pour it over the cake in the tin. When absorbed, turn the cake out onto a large flat plate. Slice into 4 equal strips, then slice each strip diagonally into 3 diamond-shaped pieces. Discard the end scraps but keep the pieces touching together.
4 For the topping, combine the almonds and hazelnuts and scatter over the cake. Pour the thickened syrup and julienned orange rind over the nuts and leave to stand for 30 minutes before serving. Using a cake slice, transfer the diamonds to individual plates and serve with whipped cream or honey-flavoured yoghurt.

GREEK SHREDDED PASTRIES WITH ALMONDS

Preparation time: 45 minutes +
   2 hours standing
Total cooking time: 50 minutes
Makes 40 pieces

500 g (1 lb) kataifi pastry
250 g (8 oz) unsalted butter, melted
1 cup (125 g/4 oz) ground pistachios
2 cups (230 g/7½ oz) ground almonds
2½ cups (625 g/1 lb 5 oz) caster sugar
1 teaspoon ground cinnamon
¼ teaspoon ground cloves
1 tablespoon brandy
1 egg white
1 teaspoon lemon juice
5 cm (2 inch) strip lemon rind
4 cloves
1 cinnamon stick
1 tablespoon honey

1 Allow the kataifi pastry to come to room temperature, still in its packaging. This will take about 2 hours and makes the pastry easier to work with.
2 Preheat the oven to warm 170°C (325°/Gas 3). Brush a 20 x 30 cm (8 x 12 inch) baking dish or tray with some melted butter.
3 Place the nuts in a bowl with ½ cup (125 g/4 oz) caster sugar, the ground cinnamon, cloves and brandy. Lightly beat the egg white with a fork and add to the mixture. Stir to make a paste. Divide the mixture into 8 portions and form each into a sausage shape about 18 cm (7 inches) long.

4 Take a small handful of the pastry strands and spread them out fairly compactly with the strands running lengthways towards you. The pastry should measure 25 x 18 cm (10 x 7 inches). Brush the pastry with melted butter. Place one of the 'nut' sausages along the end of the pastry nearest to you and roll up into a neat sausage shape. Repeat with the other pastry portions.
5 Place the rolls close together in the baking dish and brush them again with melted butter. Bake for 50 minutes, or until golden brown.
6 While the pastries are cooking, place the remaining sugar in a small saucepan with 2 cups (500 ml/16 fl oz) water and stir over low heat until dissolved. Add the lemon juice, rind, cloves and cinnamon and boil together for 10 minutes. Stir in the honey, then set aside until cold.
7 When the pastries come out of the oven, pour the syrup over the top. Leave them to cool completely before cutting each roll into 5 pieces.

NOTES: Kataifi, a shredded pastry, is available from Greek delicatessens and other speciality food stores.
   It is very important that the syrup is cold and the kataifi hot when pouring the syrup over, otherwise the liquid will not be absorbed as well or as evenly.
   These pastries keep for up to a week if you cover them. Don't refrigerate them.

CHOCOLATE-COFFEE CUPS

Preparation time: 40 minutes
Total cooking time: 10 minutes
Makes 20

200 g (6½ oz) dark chocolate melts
20 foil cups
1 tablespoon cream
50 g (1¾ oz) white chocolate, chopped
1 tablespoon Tia Maria
10 coffee beans, halved

1 Put the dark chocolate in a heatproof bowl. Bring a pan of water to the boil, remove from the heat and sit the bowl over the pan, making sure the base of the bowl does not sit in the water. Stir occasionally until the chocolate has melted. Cool slightly.
2 Working with one foil cup at a time, put 1 teaspoon of chocolate in each. Use a small new paintbrush to coat the inside with chocolate, making sure it is thick and there are no gaps. Turn the cups upside down on a wire rack and leave until firm. Set the remaining chocolate aside.
3 Combine the cream, white chocolate and Tia Maria in a heatproof bowl. Stir over a pan of simmering water until smooth. Cool slightly, then spoon into the chocolate cups. Press half a coffee bean into each cup. Allow to set.
4 Remelt the reserved chocolate. Spoon it over the filling and tap to level, then leave to set.

TEARDROP CHOCOLATE CHERRY MOUSSE CUPS

Preparation time: 1 hour
Total cooking time: Nil
Makes about 24

glossy contact paper
200 g (6½ oz) dark chocolate melts or
    buttons
¾ cup (150 g/5 oz) stoneless black
    cherries, well drained

Chocolate mousse
60 g (2 oz) dark cooking chocolate,
    melted
1 tablespoon cream
1 egg yolk
½ teaspoon gelatine
⅓ cup (80 ml/2¾ fl oz) cream, extra
1 egg white

1 Cut glossy contact into 24 rectangles
4 x 11 cm (1½ x 4½ inches). Line a tray with
baking paper.
2 Place the chocolate melts in a small
heatproof bowl. Bring a small pan of
water to the boil and remove from the
heat. Sit the bowl over the pan, making
sure the bowl does not touch the water.
Stir occasionally until the chocolate has
melted and the mixture is smooth. Using
a palette or flat-bladed knife, spread a
little of the chocolate over one of the
contact rectangles. Just before the
chocolate starts to set, bring the short
edges together to form a teardrop shape.
(Leave the contact attached.) Hold
together with your fingers until the shape
holds by itself and will stand up. Repeat
with some of the remaining chocolate and
rectangles. (The chocolate will need to be
re-melted several times. To do this, place
the bowl over steaming water again.)

3 Spoon about 1½ teaspoons of the
remaining chocolate on the tray and
spread into an oval about 5 cm (2 inches)
long. Sit a teardrop in the centre of it and
press down gently. Repeat with the
remaining teardrops. Allow to almost set.
4 Using a sharp small knife or scalpel,
cut around the outer edge of each
teardrop. Allow the cups to set
completely before lifting away from the
baking paper. Carefully break away the
excess chocolate from the bases to form
a neat edge on the base. Carefully peel
away the contact. Set the cups aside. Cut
the cherries into quarters and drain on
crumpled paper towels.
5 For the mousse, mix the chocolate,
cream and yolk in a bowl until smooth.
Sprinkle the gelatine in an even layer over
2 teaspoons water in a small heatproof
bowl and leave until spongy. Bring a
small pan of water to the boil, remove
from the heat and place the bowl over the
pan. The water should come halfway up
the side of the bowl. Stir the gelatine until
clear and dissolved. Stir into the
chocolate mixture.
6 Working quickly, so the gelatine does
not set, beat the extra cream with electric
beaters until soft peaks form; fold into
the chocolate. Using electric beaters,
beat the egg white in a clean dry bowl
until soft peaks form. Fold into the
chocolate.
7 Place a few pieces of cherry inside each
teardrop cup. Spoon the chocolate
mousse over the cherries. (Fill to slightly
over the brim as the mousse will drop
during setting.) Chill until set.

CONTINENTAL SLICE

Preparation time: 30 minutes +
    refrigeration
Total cooking time: 5 minutes
Makes 36

125 g (4 oz) butter
½ cup (125 g/4 oz) caster sugar
¼ cup (30 g/1 oz) cocoa
250 g (8 oz) shredded wheat biscuits, crushed
¾ cup (65 g/2¼ oz) desiccated coconut
¼ cup (30 g/1 oz) chopped hazelnuts
¼ cup (60 g/2 oz) chopped glacé cherries
1 egg, lightly beaten
1 teaspoon vanilla essence

Topping
60 g (2 oz) butter
1¾ cups (215 g/6¾ oz) icing sugar
2 tablespoons custard powder
1 tablespoon hot water
1 tablespoon Grand Marnier
125 g (4 oz) dark chocolate
60 g (2 oz) white vegetable shortening (copha)

1 Line the base and sides of an 18 x 28 cm
(7 x 11 inch) shallow tin with foil. Combine
the butter, sugar and cocoa and stir over
low heat until the butter melts and mixture
is well combined. Cook, stirring, for 1 minute.
Remove from the heat and cool slightly.
2 Combine the biscuit crumbs, coconut,
hazelnuts and cherries in a large bowl.
Make a well in the centre; add the butter
mixture, egg and vanilla all at once and
stir well. Press the mixture firmly into the
prepared tin. Refrigerate until firm.
3 Beat the butter until creamy. Gradually
add the combined icing sugar and custard
powder, alternately with the combined water
and Grand Marnier. Beat the mixture until
light and fluffy. Spread evenly over the base
and then refrigerate until set.
4 Combine the chocolate and shortening in a
heatproof bowl; stand bowl over a pan of
simmering water and stir over low heat until
chocolate melts and mixture is smooth.
Spread over the slice. Refrigerate for 4 hours
or until firm. Cut into squares to serve.

TINY TREATS

THERE IS ONLY ONE THING BETTER THAN A HUGE CHEESECAKE, AND THAT'S A PLATEFUL OF MINIATURE CHEESECAKES... SO YOU CAN SNEAK BACK AND EAT AS MANY AS YOU WANT WITHOUT ANYONE NOTICING.

CHOCOLATE LIQUEUR CHEESECAKES

Grease four deep 12-hole patty tins and place a thin strip of baking paper in the bases, extending up the sides. Finely crush 250 g (8 oz) sweet biscuits, stir in 125 g (4 oz) melted butter, then firmly press 1 heaped teaspoon into each base. Refrigerate. Dissolve 3 teaspoons gelatine in ¼ cup (60 ml/2 fl oz) boiling water. Beat 250 g (8 oz) soft cream cheese with ⅓ cup (90 g/3 oz) caster sugar, then add 150 g (5 oz) melted chocolate, 2 teaspoons grated orange rind and 3 tablespoons Tia Maria and beat until smooth. Stir in the gelatine, spoon onto the bases and refrigerate for 2 hours, or until firm. Whip 300 ml (10 fl oz) cream, spoon over the cheesecakes and garnish with chocolate curls.
Makes 48.

BAKED CHEESECAKES

Preheat the oven to warm 160°C (315°F/ Gas 2–3). Grease three deep 12-hole patty tins and place a thin strip of baking paper in the bases, extending up the sides. Finely crush 250 g (8 oz) sweet biscuits, stir in 125 g (4 oz) melted butter, then firmly press 1 heaped teaspoon into each base. Refrigerate. Beat 250 g (8 oz) soft cream cheese, ½ cup (125 g/4 oz) sour cream and ½ cup (125 g/4 oz) caster sugar, until smooth. Mix in 2 egg yolks, 1 tablespoon lemon juice and 2 teaspoons plain flour. Beat 2 egg whites until stiff peaks form, then fold through the cream cheese mixture. Spoon 1 tablespoon filling into each base and bake for 15–20 minutes, until set. Cool.
Makes 36.

CUSTARD AND FRUIT TARTS

Preheat the oven to moderate 180°C (350°F/Gas 4). Grease three shallow 12-hole patty tins. Using a 7 cm (2¾ inch) round cutter, cut rounds from 4 sheets of ready-rolled sweet shortcrust pastry. Place in the tins and prick the bases several times with a fork. Bake for 12–15 minutes, or until golden brown. Remove and cool. Cut a vanilla pod in half and place in a saucepan with 1¼ cups (315 ml/10 fl oz) milk. Slowly bring to the boil, remove from the heat and cool slightly. In a large heatproof bowl whisk 2 egg yolks and 2 tablespoons sugar until thick and pale. Add 3 tablespoons plain flour, then gradually whisk in the vanilla milk. Return to a clean pan and heat slowly, stirring constantly for 5–10 minutes, or until it boils and thickens. Allow to cool, then spoon evenly into each pastry case and top with some sliced fruit. Glaze with warmed sieved apricot jam.
Makes 36.

MINI LIME MERINGUE PIES

Preheat the oven to moderate 180°C (350°F/Gas 4). Grease three shallow 12-hole patty tins. Cut rounds with a 7 cm (2¾ inch) cutter from 4 sheets of ready-rolled sweet shortcrust pastry. Place in the tins and prick the bases well with a fork. Bake for 12–15 minutes, or until golden brown, then cool. Put ½ cup (125 g/4 oz) caster sugar, ¼ cup (30 g/1 oz) cornflour, 2 teaspoons lime rind, ⅓ cup (80 ml/2¾ fl oz) lime juice and ¾ cup (185 ml/6 fl oz) water in a large pan. Stir over medium heat until the mixture boils and thickens. Remove from the heat and add 30 g (1 oz) butter, then mix. Gradually mix in 2 egg yolks. Spoon heaped teaspoons into each pastry case. Beat 3 egg whites into stiff peaks, gradually add ½ cup (125 g/4 oz) sugar and beat until the sugar dissolves and is glossy. Spoon
1 tablespoon over each tart. Bake for 4–5 minutes, or until lightly golden.
Makes 36.

PEACH AND ALMOND STRUDELS

Preheat the oven to moderate 180°C (350°F/Gas 4). Grease two deep patty tins. Mix a 425 g (14 oz) can pie peaches, 60 g (2 oz) slivered almonds, 60 g (2 oz) sultanas and 1 tablespoon soft brown sugar. Brush a sheet of filo pastry with melted butter, then top with another sheet. Cut into 4 and cut each piece into 4 again. Repeat with another 4 sheets of filo. Place 4 squares in each base and bake for 10 minutes. Place 1 tablespoon of filling in each pastry case, sprinkle with cinnamon and bake for 5–10 minutes, until the pastry is golden.
Makes 24.

FROM LEFT: Chocolate liqueur cheesecakes; Baked cheesecakes; Custard and fruit tarts; Mini lime meringue pies; Peach and almond strudels

CINNAMON STARS

Preparation time: 15 minutes +
setting time

Total cooking time: 10 minutes per batch
Makes about 30

2 egg whites
2¼ cups (280 g/9 oz) icing sugar
1½ cups (145 g/5 oz) ground almonds
1½ tablespoons ground cinnamon

1 Beat the egg whites lightly with a
wooden spoon in a large bowl. Gradually
stir in the sifted icing sugar to form a
smooth paste. Remove ⅓ cup (100 g/
3½ oz), cover and set aside. Add the
almonds and cinnamon to the remaining
icing and gently press together with your
hands. Add 1 teaspoon water if the
mixture is too dry. Press together well
before adding any water as the warmth of
your hands will soften the mixture.
2 Lightly dust a work surface with icing
sugar and roll out the mixture to about
3 mm (⅛ inch) thick. Spread with a thin
layer of the reserved icing. Leave,
uncovered, at room temperature for
30–35 minutes, or until the icing has set.
Preheat the oven to slow 150°C
(300°F/Gas 2).
3 Cut out shapes using a star cutter
(about 45 mm/2 inches across from point
to point). Dip the cutter in icing sugar to
help prevent sticking. Place the stars on a
baking tray covered with baking paper
and cook for 10 minutes, or until just firm.
Turn the tray around after 5 minutes. Cool
on the tray. Store in an airtight container
up to 2 weeks.

MELTING MOMENTS WITH JAM AND CREAM

Preparation time: 15 minutes
Total cooking time: 12 minutes
Makes 20

125 g (4 oz) unsalted butter
½ cup (125 g/4 oz) caster sugar
2 egg yolks
1 teaspoon vanilla essence
¼ cup (30 g/1 oz) custard powder
¾ cup (90 g/3 oz) plain flour
¾ cup (90 g/3 oz) self-raising flour
½ cup (160 g/5¼ oz) strawberry jam
¾ cup (185 ml/6 fl oz) thick cream,
   whipped

1 Preheat oven to moderate 180°C
(350°F/Gas 4). Line two biscuit trays with
baking paper. Using electric beaters, beat
the butter and sugar until light and
creamy. Add the egg yolks one at a time,
beating thoroughly after each addition.
Add the vanilla essence; beat until
combined.
2 Transfer the mixture to a large bowl.
Using a flat-bladed knife, incorporate the
custard powder and sifted flours. Stir
until ingredients are just combined.
Gather the mixture together with
fingertips to form a soft dough.
3 Roll 1 level teaspoonful of mixture at a
time into balls. Arrange about 5 cm
(2 inches) apart on prepared trays. Flatten
slightly with a fork. Bake 12 minutes or
until golden. Stand biscuits on trays for
5 minutes before putting a wire rack to
cool. Spread half the biscuits with
¼ teaspoon of jam on each. Spoon or pipe
cream over jam, sandwich with remaining
biscuits.

THAI STICKY RICE SLICE

Preparation time: 15 minutes +
   overnight soaking
Total cooking time: 1 hour
Makes 25–30

2½ cups (500 g/1 lb) glutinous rice
2½ cups (600 ml/20 fl oz) coconut milk
½ cup (125 g/4 oz) caster sugar

Topping
1 cup (90 g/3 oz) desiccated coconut
¼ cup (60 ml/2 fl oz) coconut milk, heated
90 g (3 oz) palm sugar, grated

1 Put the rice in a large glass bowl and
cover with water. Soak for 8 hours or
overnight; drain. Line a 30 x 20 cm (12 x 8
inch) shallow tin with baking paper,
overlapping the two long sides. Line a
large bamboo steamer with baking paper.
2 Spread the steamer base with rice, cover
and place over a wok. Half-fill the wok with
boiling water. Steam for 45–50 minutes, or
until the grains are softened. Top up the
wok with water when necessary.
3 Put the rice, coconut milk and sugar in a
large heavy-based pan. Stir over low heat
for 10 minutes, or until all the coconut milk
is absorbed. Spoon into the tin and flatten
the surface. Set aside to cool and firm.
4 For the topping, put the coconut in a
small bowl and mix in the coconut milk.
Put the palm sugar and 3 tablespoons
water in a small pan and stir over low heat
for 3 minutes, or until the sugar has
dissolved and the syrup has thickened
slightly. Stir in the coconut and continue to
stir until the mixture holds together. Cover
and set aside to cool. Spread the topping
over the rice base. Cut into diamonds for
serving. Serve at room temperature.

NOTE: These are best eaten on the same
day. Chilling firms the mixture and it loses
its flavour. Glutinous rice and palm sugar
are available from Asian speciality stores.
Palm sugar can be crushed with a rolling
pin.

EASTER WALNUT CAKES

Preparation time: 15 minutes
Total cooking time: 20 minutes
Makes 28

200 g (6½ oz) unsalted butter, softened
½ cup (125 g/4 oz) caster sugar
2 tablespoons orange flower water
2 cups (250 g/8 oz) plain flour, sifted

Walnut filling
½ cup (50 g/1¾ oz) walnuts, chopped
¼ cup (60 g/2 oz) caster sugar
1 teaspoon ground cinnamon

1 Preheat the oven to warm 160°C
(315°F/Gas 2–3). Lightly grease two
baking trays and line with baking paper.
2 Cream the butter and sugar in small
bowl until light and fluffy. Transfer to a
large bowl. Using a metal spoon, fold in
the orange flower water and flour until
well combined. Press with your hands
until the mixture comes together to make
a stiff dough.
3 For the walnut filling, combine all the
ingredients in a bowl and mix well.
4 Roll heaped tablespoons of dough into
balls. Press a hollow in the centre with
your thumb. Place 1 teaspoon of filling
into each hollow. Place on the trays and
flatten slightly without folding dough over
the filling. Bake for 15–20 minutes, or
until golden. Cool on a wire rack and
serve.

VANILLA ALMOND BISCOTTI WITH GERANIUM CREAM

Preparation time: 1 hour + overnight
   standing
Total cooking time: 1 hour
Serves 6–8

½ cup (125 g/4 oz) caster sugar
2 tablespoons caster sugar, extra
1 vanilla bean, split in half
3 rose-scented geranium leaves

Biscotti
125 g (4 oz) blanched almonds
3 egg whites
¾ cup (90 g/3 oz) plain flour

Geranium Cream
1 cup (250 ml/8 fl oz) cream
½ cup (125 ml/4 fl oz) thick (double)
   cream
selection of fruits in season: grapes, kiwi
   fruit, strawberries, blueberries,
   blackberries, raspberries or
   mulberries

1 Preheat oven to moderate 180°C (350 F/
Gas 4). Place each measure of caster
sugar into a separate screw-top jar. Add
vanilla bean to the ½ cup of sugar and
geranium leaves to the 2 tablespoons of
sugar. Shake each jar for 10 seconds,
then set aside for at least 2 hours to allow
flavours to develop.
2 To make Biscotti: Brush a 26 x 8 x
4.5 cm (10½ x 3 x 1¾ inch) bar tin with oil
or melted butter; line the base and sides
with baking paper. Spread the blanched
almonds on a baking tray and bake in the
oven for 4 minutes or until the nuts are
lightly golden; cool.
3 Place the egg whites in a clean, dry
bowl. Using electric beaters, beat until
stiff peaks form. Gradually add the
vanilla-scented sugar, beating constantly
until the mixture is thick and glossy and
the sugar has dissolved.

4 Transfer the mixture to a large bowl.
Add the sifted flour and almonds. Using a
metal spoon, gently fold the ingredients
together. Spread into the prepared tin and
smooth the surface. Bake for 25 minutes;
remove from oven and allow to cool
completely in the tin. Turn the loaf out
and then wrap in aluminium foil.
Refrigerate overnight.
5 Preheat the oven to warm 160°C
(315°F/Gas 2–3). Brush two baking trays
with oil or melted butter. Using a sharp
serrated knife, cut the cooked loaf into
5 mm (¼ inch) slices. Arrange the slices
on the baking trays; bake for 30 minutes
or until lightly golden and crisp.
6 To make Geranium Cream: Using
electric beaters, beat the geranium-
flavoured sugar with cream until firm
peaks form. Using a metal spoon, fold
into thick cream. Trim fruits and serve
with biscotti and cream. Vanilla Almond
Biscotti will keep for up to 2 weeks in an
airtight container. Fruits and cream are
best prepared on the day of serving.
Vanilla and geranium sugars can be
prepared up to 2 weeks in advance.

NOTE: This dessert can be served on
individual plates but would make an
attractive platter for a party or buffet.
Vanilla Almond Biscotti are also delicious
served plain, as an accompaniment to
coffee. As a variation, other nuts can be
used instead of almonds. Roasted
hazelnuts or pistachios are particularly
delicious.

CHOCOLATE MERINGUE KISSES

Preparation time: 20 minutes
Total cooking time: 40 minutes
Makes 25

2 egg whites, at room temperature
½ cup (125 g/4 oz) caster sugar
¼ teaspoon ground cinnamon

Filling
125 g (4 oz) dark chocolate melts or
  buttons
⅓ cup (90 g/3 oz) sour cream

1 Preheat the oven to slow 150°C
(300°F/Gas 2). Line two oven trays with
baking paper.
2 Using electric beaters, beat the egg
whites in a small clean dry bowl until soft
peaks form. Gradually add the sugar,
beating well after each addition until
stiffened and glossy peaks form. Add the
cinnamon and beat until just combined.
3 Transfer the mixture to a piping bag fitted
with a 1 cm (½ inch) fluted nozzle. Pipe
small stars of 1.5 cm (⅝ inch) diameter onto
the trays, 3 cm (1¼ inches) apart. Bake for
30 minutes, or until pale and crisp. Turn off
the oven and leave the meringues to cool in
the oven with the door ajar.
4 To make the filling, place the chocolate
and sour cream in a small heatproof
bowl. Bring a pan of water to the boil,
remove from the heat and sit the bowl
over the pan, making sure the bottom of
the bowl does not sit in the water. Stir
occasionally until the chocolate has
melted. Remove from the heat and cool
slightly. Sandwich the meringues
together with the chocolate filling.

NOTE: You can use white chocolate
instead of dark and other ground spices
such as ground cloves, allspice or
nutmeg. Meringues should be cooked
slowly. The ideal texture is crunchy on the
outside and soft inside.

NOUGAT

Preparation time: 30 minutes +
  4 hours refrigeration
Total cooking time: 15 minutes
Makes 1 kg (2 lb)

2 cups (500 g/1 lb) sugar
1 cup (250 ml/8 fl oz) liquid glucose
½ cup (175 g/6 oz) honey (preferably
  blossom honey)
2 egg whites
1 teaspoon vanilla essence
125 g (4 oz) unsalted butter, softened
60 g (2 oz) almonds, unblanched and toasted
100 g (3½ oz) glacé cherries (not imitation)

1 Grease a 28 x 18 cm (11 x 7 inch) baking
dish and line with baking paper. Place the
sugar, glucose, honey, ¼ cup (60 ml/2 fl oz)
water and ¼ teaspoon salt in a heavy-
based saucepan and stir over low heat
until dissolved. Bring to the boil and cook
at a rolling boil for 8 minutes, or in a small
amount of water or reaches 122°C (225°F)
on a sugar thermometer. The correct
temperature is very important, otherwise
the mixture will not set properly.
2 Beat the egg whites in a bowl with
electric beaters until stiff peaks form.
Slowly pour a quarter of the mixture onto
the egg whites in a thin stream and beat for
up to 5 minutes, or until the mixture holds
its shape. Place the remaining syrup over
the heat and cook for 2 minutes (watch that
it doesn't burn), or until a small amount
forms brittle threads when dropped in cold
water, or reaches 157°C (315°F) on a sugar
thermometer. Pour slowly onto the
meringue mixture with the beaters running
and beat until the mixture is very thick.
3 Add the vanilla and butter and beat for
another 5 minutes. Stir in the almonds
and cherries with a metal spoon. Turn the
mixture into the tin and smooth the top
with a palate knife. Refrigerate for at least
four hours, or until firm. Turn out onto a
large chopping board and with a sharp knife
cut into 4 x 2 cm (1½ x ¾ inch) pieces. Wrap
each piece in cellophane and refrigerate.

LEMON AND LIME BISCUITS

Preparation time: 40 minutes + 1 hour
  refrigeration
Total cooking time: 10–15 minutes
Makes 30

150 g (4¾ oz) butter, softened
¾ cup (185 g/6 oz) caster sugar
1 egg, lightly beaten
1 tablespoon lime juice
2 teaspoons grated lime rind
2 teaspoons grated lemon rind
1 cup (125 g/4 oz) plain flour
½ cup (60 g/2 oz) self-raising flour
60 g (2 oz) marzipan, grated

Lime Icing
1 cup (125 g/4 oz) icing sugar, sifted
1 teaspoon finely grated lime rind
1 tablespoon lime juice
2 teaspoons water

1 Line two oven trays with baking paper.
Using electric beaters, beat the butter
and sugar in a bowl until light and
creamy. Add the egg, juice and rinds,
beating until well combined.
2 Transfer the mixture to a large bowl.
Using a flat-bladed knife, mix the flours
and marzipan until a soft dough forms.
Divide the mixture in two. Turn one
portion out onto a lightly floured surface
and press together until smooth.
3 Form the biscuit dough into a log shape
about 4 cm (1½ inches) in diameter. Wrap
the log in plastic wrap and refrigerate for
1 hour. Repeat the process with the
remaining dough. Preheat the oven to
180°C (350°F/Gas 4). Cut the dough into 1
cm (½ inch) slices. Place the slices on the
prepared trays and bake for 10–15
minutes or until the biscuits are lightly
golden. Leave on the trays until cool. Dip
the biscuits in the icing. Decorate if you like.
4 To make the icing, place the icing sugar,
lime rind, lime juice and water in a bowl.
Stir. Beat the mixture until smooth. If the
mixture is too thick, add a little extra water.

BEIGNETS DE FRUITS

Preparation time: 25 minutes +
    3 hours resting
Total cooking time: 10 minutes
Serves 4

3 Granny Smith or golden delicious
    apples
70 g (2¼ oz) raisins
3 tablespoons Calvados or rum
1½ tablespoons caster sugar
vegetable oil, for frying
2 tablespoons plain flour, for coating
icing sugar, for dusting

Batter
1 egg, separated
3½ tablespoons warm beer
60 g (2 oz) plain flour
1 teaspoon vegetable oil

1 Peel and core the apples and cut into
1 cm (½ inch) cubes. Place in a bowl with
the raisins, Calvados and sugar and
marinate for 3 hours.
2 For the batter, beat the egg yolk and
beer together in a large bowl. Blend in the
flour and oil and add a pinch of salt. Stir
until smooth. The batter will be very thick
at this stage. Cover and leave in a warm
place for 1 hour.
3 Pour the oil into a large saucepan to a
depth of 10 cm (4 inches) and heat to
170°C (325°F), or until a cube of bread
dropped into the oil browns in 20 seconds.
Add 1½ tablespoons of the Calvados
marinade to the batter and stir until
smooth. Whisk the egg white until stiff
and gently fold into the batter. Drain the
apples and raisins, toss with the flour to
coat, then lightly fold them through the
batter. Carefully lower heaped
tablespoons of batter into the oil in
batches and fry for 1–2 minutes, until the
fritters are golden on both sides. Remove
with a slotted spoon and drain on paper
towels. Keep them warm. Dust with icing
sugar and serve.

ISRAELI DOUGHNUTS

Preparation time: 40 minutes +
    10 minutes standing + overnight
    refrigeration + 30 minutes rising
Total cooking time: 25 minutes
Makes 14

¾ cup (185 ml/6 fl oz) lukewarm milk
1 tablespoon dried yeast
2 tablespoons caster sugar
2½ cups (375 g/12 oz) plain flour
2 teaspoons ground cinnamon
1 teaspoon finely grated lemon rind
2 eggs, separated
40 g (1¼ oz) butter, softened
⅓ cup (100 g/3½ oz) plum, strawberry or
    apricot jam or conserve
oil, for deep-frying
caster sugar, extra, for rolling

1 Put the milk in a small bowl, add the
yeast and 1 tablespoon of the sugar and
leave in a warm place for 10 minutes, or
until bubbles appear on the surface. If
your yeast doesn't foam, it is dead and
you will have to start again.
2 Sift the flour into a large bowl and add
the cinnamon, lemon rind, egg yolks,
yeast mixture, remaining sugar, and a
pinch of salt. Mix well, then place the
dough on a lightly floured work surface
and knead for 5 minutes. Work in the
butter, a little at a time, continually
kneading until the dough becomes
elastic. This should take about 10
minutes. Place in a large bowl and cover
with a clean, damp tea towel. Leave to
rise overnight in the refrigerator.
3 Place the dough on a lightly floured
work surface and roll out to 3 mm (⅛ inch)
thickness. Using a 6 cm (2½ inch) cutter,
cut 28 rounds from the dough. Place 14 of
the rounds on a lightly floured tray and
carefully place ¾ teaspoon of the jam or
conserve into the centre of each. Lightly
beat the egg whites, then brush a little
around the outside edges of the rounds,
being careful not to touch the jam at all.
Top with the remaining 14 rounds and
press down firmly around the edges to
seal. Cover with a clean tea towel and
leave to rise for 30 minutes. Make sure
the dough has not separated at the edges.
Press any open edges firmly together.

CRACKLE COOKIES

Preparation time: 20 minutes +
   3 hours refrigeration
Total cooking time: 25 minutes per batch
Makes about 60

125 g (4 oz) unsalted butter, softened
2 cups (370 g/12 oz) soft brown sugar
1 teaspoon vanilla essence
2 eggs
60 g (2 oz) dark chocolate, melted
1/3 cup (80 ml/2¾ fl oz) milk
2¾ cups (340 g/11 oz) plain flour
2 tablespoons cocoa powder
2 teaspoons baking powder
¼ teaspoon ground allspice
2/3 cup (85 g/3 oz) chopped pecans
icing sugar, to coat

1 Lightly grease two baking trays. Beat the butter, sugar and vanilla until light and creamy. Beat in the eggs, one at a time. Stir the chocolate and milk into the butter mixture.
2 Sift the flour, cocoa, baking powder, allspice and a pinch of salt into the butter mixture and mix well. Stir the pecans through. Refrigerate for at least 3 hours, or overnight.
3 Preheat the oven to moderate 180°C (350°F/Gas 4). Roll tablespoons of the mixture into balls and roll each in sifted icing sugar to coat.
4 Place well apart on the trays to allow for spreading. Bake for 20–25 minutes, or until lightly browned and just firm. Leave on the trays for 3–4 minutes, then cool on a wire rack.

RUM-AND-RAISIN TRUFFLES

Preparation time: 30 minutes +
   soaking and chilling
Total cooking time: 5 minutes
Makes about 40

60 g (2 oz) raisins, finely chopped
¼ cup (60 ml/2 fl oz) dark rum
200 g (6½ oz) chocolate-coated
   wheatmeal biscuits, crushed
1/3 cup (60 g/2 oz) soft brown sugar
1 teaspoon ground cinnamon
50 g (1¾ oz) pecans, finely chopped
¼ cup (60 ml/2 fl oz) cream
250 g (8 oz) dark chocolate, chopped
¼ cup (90 g/3 oz) golden syrup
125 g (4 oz) pecans, finely ground

1 Marinate the raisins in the rum in a small bowl for 1 hour. Put the biscuits, sugar, cinnamon and pecans in a large bowl and mix until combined.
2 Stir the cream, chocolate and golden syrup in a pan over low heat until melted. Pour onto the biscuit mixture, add the raisins and rum mixture and stir until well combined. Refrigerate until just firm enough to roll into balls.
3 Roll tablespoons of the mixture into balls, then roll the balls in the ground pecans. Refrigerate until firm.

IN ADVANCE: Truffles can be made up to 2 weeks ahead.

CHURROS

Preparation time: 10 minutes
Total cooking time: 25 minutes
Serves 4

½ cup (125 g/4 oz) sugar
1 teaspoon ground nutmeg
30 g (1 oz) butter
150 g (5 oz) plain flour
½ teaspoon finely grated orange rind
¼ teaspoon caster sugar
2 eggs
1 litre vegetable oil, for deep-frying

1 Combine the sugar and nutmeg and spread out on a plate.
2 Place the butter, flour, orange rind, caster sugar, 2/3 cup (170 ml/5½ fl oz) water and a pinch of salt in a heavy-based saucepan. Stir over low heat until the butter softens and forms a dough with the other ingredients. Keep cooking for 2–3 minutes, stirring constantly, until the dough forms a ball around the spoon and leaves a coating on the base of the pan.
3 Transfer the dough to a food processor and, with the motor running, add the eggs. Do not over-process. If the dough is too soft to snip with scissors, return it to the pan and cook, stirring over low heat until it is firmer. Spoon it into a piping bag fitted with a 5 mm (¼ inch) star nozzle.
4 Heat the oil in a wide saucepan to 180°C (350°F) or when a cube of bread dropped into the oil browns in 15 seconds. Pipe lengths of batter 6–8 cm (2½–3 inches) long into the oil a few at a time. An easy technique is to pipe with one hand and cut the batter off using kitchen scissors in the other hand. Fry for about 3 minutes, until puffed and golden, turning once or twice. Transfer each batch to paper towels to drain. While still hot, toss them in the sugar mixture and serve at once.

NOTE: Churros is a popular breakfast snack in Spain and is usually eaten with hot chocolate.

DATE CANDIES

Preparation time: 10 minutes
Total cooking time: 15 minutes
Serves 6–8

1½ cups (150 g/5 oz) walnut halves
2 tablespoons sesame seeds
100 g (3½ oz) ghee
600 g (1¼ lb) pitted dried dates, coarsely
  chopped

1 Preheat the oven to moderate 180°C
(350°F/Gas 4) and line the base and two
opposite sides of an 18 cm (7 inch) square
slice tin with baking paper. Spread the
walnuts on a baking tray and bake for
5 minutes, until lightly toasted. Chop
coarsely. Bake the sesame seeds until
golden.
2 Melt the ghee in a large heavy-based
saucepan and cook the dates, covered,
over low heat for about 10 minutes,
stirring often, until the dates soften.
Using the back of a spoon dipped in cold
water, spread half in the tin. Scatter the
walnuts on top and press into the dates.
Spread the remaining date mixture over
the walnuts. Smooth the surface with wet
fingers and press down firmly. Sprinkle
with the sesame seeds and press lightly
into the dates. When cool, cut into small
diamonds. Serve at the end of a meal or
as a delicious treat.

CHOCOLATE CARROT SLICE

Preparation time: 20 minutes
Total cooking time: 30 minutes
Makes 32

1 cup (125 g/4 oz) self-raising flour
1 teaspoon ground cinnamon
¾ cup (185 g/6 oz) caster sugar
½ cup (80 g/2⅔ oz) finely grated carrot
1 cup (185 g/6 oz) mixed dried fruit
½ cup (90 g/3 oz) choc bits
⅓ cup (30 g/1 oz) desiccated coconut
2 eggs, lightly beaten
90 g (3 oz) unsalted butter, melted
⅓ cup (40 g/1⅓ oz) chopped walnuts

Cream Cheese Frosting
125 g (4 oz) cream cheese
30 g (1 oz) unsalted butter
1½ cups (185 g/6 oz) icing sugar, sifted
1 teaspoon hot water

1 Preheat the oven to moderate 180°C
(350°F/Gas 4). Brush a shallow 23 cm
(9 inch) square cake tin with melted
butter or oil and line the base and sides
with baking paper.
2 Sift the flour and cinnamon into a large
bowl. Add the caster sugar, grated carrot,
mixed fruit, choc bits and coconut and stir
until just combined. Add the beaten eggs
and butter and then stir until combined.
3 Spread the mixture evenly into the
prepared tin and smooth the surface.
Bake for 30 minutes or until golden. Cool
the cake in the tin and turn out onto a flat
surface.
4 To make Cream Cheese Frosting: Using
electric beaters, beat the cream cheese
and butter in a small bowl until smooth.
Add the icing sugar and beat for 2 minutes
or until the mixture is light and fluffy. Add
the water and beat until well combined.
5 Spread the slice with frosting using a
flat-bladed knife and sprinkle with
walnuts. Cut into 16 squares, then cut
each square into triangles.

PETITS PITHIVIERS

Preparation time: 40 minutes + chilling
Total cooking time: 15 minutes
Makes 26

Almond filling
45 g (1½ oz) butter
⅓ cup (40 g/1¼ oz) icing sugar
1 egg yolk
70 g (2¼ oz) ground almonds
1 teaspoon finely grated orange rind
few drops almond essence

3 sheets puff pastry
1 egg, lightly beaten

1 To make the filling, beat the butter and
icing sugar with electric beaters until
light and creamy. Add the egg yolk and
beat well. Stir in the ground almonds, rind
and essence.
2 Preheat the oven to hot 210°C
(415°F/Gas 6–7) and lightly grease
2 baking trays. Lay the puff pastry on a
work surface and cut into 5 cm (2 inch)
circles with a cutter. Divide the almond
filling among half the circles, using about
1½ teaspoons filling for each. Leave a
5 mm (¼ inch) border. Brush the border
with egg.
3 Place the remaining pastry circles over
the filling and press the edges firmly to
seal. Transfer to the baking trays and chill
for 30 minutes. With a blunt-edged knife,
press up the edges gently at intervals.
Carefully score the tops of the pastries
into wedges, then brush with beaten egg.
Bake on the greased trays for 10 minutes,
or until lightly golden.

SACHER SQUARES

Preparation time: 1 hour
Total cooking time: 40 minutes
Makes 24

Base
1 cup (125 g/4 oz) plain flour
60 g (2 oz) butter, chopped
¼ cup (60 g/2 oz) sugar
2 egg yolks, lightly beaten

Cake
1 cup (125 g/4 oz) plain flour
⅓ cup (40 g/1¼ oz) cocoa powder
1 cup (250 g/4 oz) caster sugar
100 g (3½ oz) butter
2 tablespoons apricot jam
4 eggs, separated
1 cup (315 g/10 oz) apricot jam, extra

Topping
250 g (4 oz) dark chocolate
¾ cup (185 ml/6 fl oz) cream

1 Preheat the oven to moderate 180°C (350°F/Gas 4). To make the base, sift the flour into a large bowl and add the butter. Rub in until the mixture resembles fine breadcrumbs. Stir in the sugar and make a well in the centre. Add the egg yolks and 1½ teaspoons iced water and mix with a flat-bladed knife, using a cutting action, to a firm dough, adding more water if necessary. Gently gather the dough together and lift onto a lightly floured surface. Roll out the pastry to an 18 x 28 cm (7 x 11 inch) rectangle. Bake on a tray covered with baking paper for 10 minutes, or until just golden. Cool completely.
2 To make the cake, keep the oven at moderate 180°C (350°F/Gas 4). Lightly grease a shallow 18 x 28 cm (7 x 11 inch) tin and line the base and side with baking paper, extending over two sides. Sift the flour and cocoa into a large bowl. Make a well in the centre. Combine the sugar, butter and jam in a small pan and stir over low heat until the butter has melted and the sugar has dissolved. Remove from the heat. Add the butter mixture to the dry ingredients and stir until just combined. Mix in the egg yolks.
3 Place the egg whites in a small clean dry bowl and beat with electric beaters until soft peaks form. Using a metal spoon, fold the egg whites into the cake mixture. Pour into the prepared tin and bake for 30 minutes or until a skewer comes out clean when inserted into the centre of cake. Leave in the tin for 15 minutes before turning out onto a wire rack to cool.
4 Warm the extra jam in a microwave or in a small pan, then push through a fine sieve. Brush the pastry base with 3 tablespoons of the jam. Place the cake on the base. Trim the sides evenly, cutting the hard edges from the cake and base. Using a serrated knife, cut into 24 squares.
5 Brush the top and sides of each square with apricot jam. Place the squares on a large wire rack, over a piece of baking paper, leaving at least 4 cm (1½ inches) between each.
6 To make the topping, break the chocolate into small pieces and place in a small bowl. Place the cream in a small pan and bring to the boil. Remove from the heat, pour over the chocolate and leave for 5 minutes, then stir until the mixture is smooth. Cool slightly. Working with one at a time, spoon the topping over each square and use a flat-bladed knife to cover completely. Scrape the excess topping from the paper, with any left over, and spoon into a small paper piping bag. Seal the open end, snip off the tip and pipe an 'S' onto each square.

IN ADVANCE: Store for up to 5 days in an airtight container.

SWEET TWISTS

Preparation time: 40 minutes
Total cooking time: 10 minutes
Makes 45

1 egg
1½ tablespoons sugar
½ cup (125 ml/4 fl oz) milk
2 cups (250 g/8 oz) plain flour
oil, for deep-frying
1¾ cups (215 g/7 oz) icing sugar

1 Beat the egg with the sugar in a bowl, then stir in the milk. Sift the flour with ½ teaspoon salt and mix in to form a stiff dough, adding more milk if necessary. Roll out on a lightly floured work surface. Cut into strips about 10 cm (4 inches) long and 3 cm (1¼ inches) wide. Make a slit along the length, like a buttonhole. Tuck one end through the slit and pull through to make a twist.
2 Fill a deep heavy-based pan one third full of oil and heat the oil to 180°C (350°F). The oil is ready when a cube of bread dropped into the oil turns golden brown in 15 seconds. Fry 3 or 4 khvorst at a time, until golden brown on both sides. Drain on crumpled paper towel. Sift icing sugar over the pastry after it is fried but before it gets cold.

IN ADVANCE: These will keep for up to 2 weeks in a dry airtight container.

STRAWBERRY AND PASSIONFRUIT MUFFINS

Preparation time: 20 minutes
Total cooking time: 10–15 minutes
Makes 12

1¾ cups (215 g/6¾ oz) self-raising flour
pinch salt
1 teaspoon baking powder
½ teaspoon bicarbonate of soda
¼ cup (60 g/2 oz) caster sugar
1 cup (175 g/5⅔ oz) chopped fresh
    strawberries
½ cup (125 g/4 oz) canned (or fresh)
    passionfruit pulp
1 egg
¾ cup (185 ml/6 fl oz) milk
60 g (2 oz) butter, melted

1 Preheat the oven to hot 210°C (415°F/
Gas 6–7). Brush a 12-hole muffin tin with
melted butter or oil.
2 Sift the flour, salt, baking powder, soda
and sugar into a bowl. Add the
strawberries and stir to combine. Make a
well in the centre.
3 Add the passionfruit pulp and the
combined egg and milk. Pour the melted
butter into the flour mixture all at once
and lightly stir with a fork until just
combined. (Do not overbeat; the batter
should be quite lumpy.)
4 Spoon the mixture into the prepared
tins and bake for 10–15 minutes, or until
golden brown. Loosen the muffins with a
flat-bladed knife or spatula and turn out
onto a wire rack to cool. Top with
softened, sweetened cream cheese or
whipped cream and fresh strawberry
halves and sprinkle with icing sugar, if
desired.

EGG TARTS

Preparation time: 30 minutes +
    15 minutes standing
Total cooking time: 15 minutes
Makes 18

Outer Dough
1⅓ cups (165 g/5½ oz) plain flour
2 tablespoons icing sugar
⅓ cup (80 ml/2¾ oz) water
2 tablespoons oil

Inner Dough
1 cup (125 g/4 oz) plain flour
100 g (3⅓ oz) lard, chopped

Custard
⅓ cup (80 ml/2¾ oz) water
¼ cup (60 g/2 oz) caster sugar
2 eggs

1 To make Outer Dough: Sift the flour and
icing sugar into a medium bowl. Make a
well in the centre. Pour in the combined
water and oil. Mix with a knife to form a
rough dough. (If the flour is very dry, add
a little extra water.) Turn out onto a
lightly floured surface and gather
together in a smooth ball. Cover and set
aside for 15 minutes.
2 To make Inner Dough: Sift the flour into
a medium bowl. Using your fingertips, rub
the lard into the flour until the mixture
resembles coarse breadcrumbs. Press
the dough together into a ball, cover and
set aside for 15 minutes.
3 On a lightly floured surface, roll the
Outer Dough into a rectangle about
10 x 20 cm (4 x 8 inches). On a lightly
floured surface, roll the Inner Dough into
a smaller rectangle, one-third the size of
the Outer Dough. Place the Inner Dough
in the centre of the Outer Dough. Fold the
Outer Dough over the Inner Dough so the
short edges overlap and the Inner Dough
is enclosed. Pinch the edges together to
seal.

4 On a lightly floured surface, roll the
dough away from you in one direction into
a long rectangle, until it is about half as
thick as it was previously. Turn the dough
90 degrees so that the long edges are
now horizontal to you. Fold the pastry into
3 layers by taking the left-hand edge over
first, and then folding the right-hand edge
on top. Wrap the dough in plastic wrap
and refrigerate for 30 minutes.
5 Preheat the oven to hot 210°C
(415°F/Gas 6–7). Brush 2 shallow 12-cup
patty tins with melted butter or oil.
6 To make Custard: Place the water and
sugar in a pan and stir without boiling
until the sugar dissolves. Bring to the boil
and simmer without stirring for 1 minute.
Cool the mixture for 5 minutes. Place the
eggs in a bowl and beat lightly with a fork.
Whisk the sugar syrup into the eggs until
just combined. Strain into a jug.
7 Place the pastry on a lightly floured
surface. With one open end towards you,
roll the pastry out to a rectangle about
2.5 mm (⅛ inch) thick. Cut out rounds of
pastry using a 7 cm (2¾ inch) fluted
cutter. Carefully place the pastry rounds
into the prepared patty tins. Fill each
pastry case two-thirds full with the egg
custard mixture. Bake for 15 minutes, or
until just set. Take care not to overcook
the custard.
8 Leave the egg tarts for 3 minutes before
removing them from the tin. Slip a flat-
bladed knife down the side of each tart to
help lift it out. Cool the tarts on a wire
rack, and serve warm or cold.

FRIED HONEY CAKES

Preparation time: 20 minutes +
　1 hour standing
Total cooking time: 20 minutes
Serves 4–6

3 eggs
¼ cup (60 ml/2 fl oz) orange juice
¼ cup (60 ml/2 fl oz) vegetable oil
1 tablespoon grated orange rind
¼ cup (60 g/2 oz) caster sugar
300 g (10 oz) plain flour
1 teaspoon baking powder
about 4 tablespoons flour, extra, for
　rolling

Syrup
2 tablespoons lemon juice
275 g (9 oz) sugar
⅓ cup (115 g/4 oz) honey
1 tablespoon grated orange rind
vegetable oil, for deep-frying

1 Whisk the eggs, orange juice and oil
together in a large bowl. Add the orange
rind and sugar and whisk until frothy. Sift
in the flour and baking powder and mix
with a wooden spoon until smooth, but
still a bit sticky. Cover and set aside for
1 hour.

2 For the syrup, in a saucepan, heat 1¼
cups (315 ml/10 fl oz) cold water with the
lemon juice and sugar, stirring until the
sugar dissolves. Bring to the boil, reduce
the heat and simmer for 5 minutes. Add
the honey and orange rind and simmer
for another 5 minutes. Keep warm.
3 Sprinkle a little of the extra flour onto
the dough and transfer it to a lightly
floured surface. Work in just enough
extra flour to give a dough which doesn't
stick to your hands. Roll it out to a
thickness of 5 mm (¼ inch). It will be very
elastic, so keep rolling and resting it until
it stops shrinking. Using a 5 cm (2 inch)
biscuit cutter, cut out round cakes.
4 Heat the oil in a large deep-sided frying
pan to 170°C (325°F), or until a cube of
bread dropped into the oil browns in
20 seconds. Fry the cakes 3 or 4 at a time
until puffed and golden, about 1 minute on
each side. Remove with tongs and drain
on paper towels.
5 Using tongs, dip each cake into the
warm syrup long enough for it to soak in.
Transfer to a platter. Serve warm or cold.

CHINESE FORTUNE COOKIES

Preparation time: 40 minutes +
　15 minutes standing
Total cooking time: 50 minutes
Makes about 30

3 egg whites
½ cup (60 g/2 oz) icing sugar, sifted
45 g (1½ oz) unsalted butter, melted
½ cup (60 g/2 oz) plain flour

1 Preheat the oven to moderate 180°C
(350°F/Gas 4). Line an oven tray with
baking paper. Draw 3 circles with 8 cm
(3 inch) diameters on the paper.
2 Place the egg whites in a medium bowl
and whisk until just frothy. Add the icing
sugar and butter and stir until smooth.
Add the flour and mix until smooth. Let
stand for 15 minutes.
3 Using a flat-bladed knife, spread
1½ level teaspoons of mixture over each
circle. Bake for 5 minutes or until slightly
brown around the edges. Working quickly,
remove the cookies from the tray by
sliding a flat-bladed knife under each.
Place a written fortune message on each
cookie. Fold the cookie in half to form a
semicircle, then fold it again over a blunt-
edged object like the rim of a glass. Allow
to cool on a wire rack. Repeat with the
remaining mixture.

NOTE: Cook no more than 2 or 3 cookies
at a time, otherwise they will harden too
quickly and break when folding.

MINI PAVLOVAS

Preparation time: 50 minutes
Total cooking time: 50 minutes
Makes 35–40

3 egg whites
1 cup (125 g/4 oz) icing sugar
150 g (5 oz) dark chocolate, melted
1 cup (250 ml/8 fl oz) thick (double) cream
1 tablespoon icing sugar, extra
1 teaspoon finely grated orange rind
assorted fresh fruit for garnish, such as
    strawberries, cut into thin wedges,
    sliced pawpaw and kiwi fruit, and
    passionfruit pulp

1 Preheat the oven to slow 150°C
(300°F/Gas 2). Place the egg whites in a
large bowl and beat until stiff peaks form.
Set the bowl over a large pan of
simmering water and add the icing sugar
to the egg whites while continuing to beat.
Add it carefully or it will fly all over the
place. At this stage it is best to use
electric beaters as you must now beat the
meringue until thick and very solid.
2 Using a cutter as a guide, draw 4 cm
(1½ inch) circles onto two sheets of baking
paper, then invert these sheets onto
baking trays (so the pencil won't come off
on the base of the pavlovas). Spread a
little of the meringue mixture over each
round—this will be the base of the
pavlova. Spoon the remaining meringue
into a piping bag fitted with an 5 mm
(¼ inch) plain piping nozzle.

3 Pipe three small circles on top of each
other on the outer edge of each base,
leaving a small hole in the centre. Bake
for 30 minutes, or until firm to touch.
Leave to cool in the oven with the door
slightly ajar.
4 When cold, dip the bases of the
meringues into the melted chocolate to
come about 2 mm (⅛ inch) up the sides of
the meringues, then place on trays
covered with baking paper and allow to
set.
5 Combine the cream, extra icing sugar
and rind, stirring until just thick. If
necessary, beat slightly. Spoon into a
piping bag fitted with a small plain nozzle
and pipe into the meringues. Top with
fruit and passionfruit pulp.

NOTE: Chocolate-dipped meringues
without the filling can be made up to a
week ahead and stored in an airtight
container. Fill them close to serving time,
otherwise they will soften.

COFFEE KISSES

Preparation time: 40 minutes
Total cooking time: 10 minutes
Makes 30

3 cups (375 g/12 oz) self-raising flour
160 g (5¼ oz) butter, chopped
½ cup (125 g/4 oz) caster sugar
1 egg, lightly beaten
1 tablespoon instant coffee powder
1–2 tablespoons iced water

Coffee Butter Cream
80 g (2⅔ oz) butter
1 cup (125 g/4 oz) icing sugar, sifted
2 teaspoons water
2 teaspoons instant coffee powder
100 g (3⅓ oz) white chocolate, melted

1 Preheat oven to moderate 180°C
(350°F/Gas 4). Brush two biscuit trays
with oil. Line with baking paper. Sift flour
into a bowl. Add butter and rub into flour,
using your fingertips, until mixture
resembles fine breadcrumbs. Add
combined sugar, egg and coffee powder,
dissolved in the water, all at once. Mix
with a knife until the ingredients come
together to form a soft dough. Lightly
knead until smooth.
2 Roll out between two sheets of baking
paper to 5 mm (¼ inch) thickness. Cut into
5 cm (2 inch) rounds, using a fluted biscuit
cutter. Place on prepared trays. Bake 10
minutes or until lightly golden. Transfer
to a wire rack.
3 To make Coffee Butter Cream: Using
electric beaters, beat butter and icing
sugar until light and creamy. Add
combined water and coffee powder and
beat until mixed. Place in a piping bag
fitted with a fluted nozzle and pipe onto
half of the biscuits. Top with another
biscuit; sandwich together. Drizzle or pipe
with melted chocolate. Top each with a
chocolate-coated coffee bean, if desired.

RICH CHOCOLATE TRUFFLES

Preparation time: 40 minutes + chilling
Total cooking time: 5 minutes
Makes about 30

¾ cup (185 ml/6 fl oz) thick (double)
  cream
400 g (13 oz) dark chocolate, grated
70 g (2¼ oz) butter, chopped
2 tablespoons Cointreau
dark cocoa powder, for rolling

1 Place the cream in a small pan and bring to the boil. Remove from the heat and stir in the chocolate until it is completely melted. Add the butter and stir until melted. Stir in the Cointreau. Transfer to a large bowl, cover and refrigerate for several hours or overnight, or until firm enough to roll.
2 Quickly roll tablespoons of the mixture into balls, and refrigerate until firm. Roll the balls in the cocoa, shake off any excess and return to the refrigerator. Serve at room temperature.

IN ADVANCE: Truffle mixture can be made and rolled up to 2 weeks ahead. You will need to roll the balls in cocoa again close to serving time.

PETITS FOURS

Preparation time: 45 minutes
Total cooking time: 20 minutes
Makes 32

2 eggs
¼ cup (60 g/2 oz) caster sugar
⅔ cup (85 g/3 oz) plain flour
30 g (1 oz) butter, melted

Topping
1 cup (315 g/10 oz) apricot jam, warmed
  and strained
2 teaspoons liqueur
200 g (6½ oz) marzipan
400 g (13 oz) ready-made soft icing,
  chopped

1 Preheat the oven to moderate 180°C (350°F/Gas 4). Brush two 26 x 8 x 4.5 cm (10½ x 3 x 1¾ inch) bar tins with melted butter or oil. Line the bases and sides with baking paper.
2 Using electric beaters, beat the eggs and sugar in a bowl for 5 minutes, until very thick and pale. Fold in the sifted flour and melted butter quickly and lightly, using a metal spoon. Divide between the tins and bake for 15 minutes, until lightly golden and springy to the touch. Leave in the tins for 3 minutes before turning out onto a wire rack to cool.

3 Using a 3 cm (1¼ inch) round cutter, cut shapes from the cakes. Brush the top and sides of each with the combined jam and liqueur. Roll the marzipan out to a thickness of 2 mm (⅛ inch) and cut out rounds and strips to cover the top and sides of the cakes.
4 Place the icing and 2 tablespoons water in a heatproof bowl and stand the bowl over a pan of simmering water. Stir until the icing has melted and the mixture is smooth; cool slightly.
5 Place the marzipan-covered cakes on a wire rack over a tray. Spoon the icing over each cake and use a flat-bladed knife to spread evenly over the base and sides. Reheat the icing over the pan if it begins to thicken. Leave the cakes to set. Carefully lift from the rack and place each in a paper petit four case. Decorate with small coloured fondant flowers if desired.

NOTE: Fondant flowers for decorating are found in some supermarkets and in speciality shops.

SAFFRON BUNS (SWEDISH)

Preparation time: 30 minutes + 2 hours
  rising
Total cooking time: 10 minutes per tray
Makes 16

2 x 7 g (¼ oz) sachets dry yeast
2 cups (500 ml/16 fl oz) milk
½ teaspoon saffron threads
150 g (5 oz) unsalted butter, chopped
7 cups (875 g/1 lb 12½ oz) white bread
  flour
1 teaspoon salt
⅔ cup (160 g/5½ oz) sugar
1 cup (160 g/5½ oz) raisins
2 eggs, lightly beaten

1 Combine the yeast with ½ cup (125 ml/4
fl oz) warm milk and the saffron in a
small bowl. Set aside for 5 minutes, or
until foamy. Melt the butter in a small
saucepan, add the saffron and remaining
milk and stir over low heat until warm.
Remove from the heat and cover.
2 Sift the flour into a large bowl, stir in the
frothy yeast, salt, sugar and half the
raisins, then make a well in the centre.
Add the just warm saffron milk mixture
and 1 of the eggs. Mix with a flat-bladed
knife, using a cutting action, until the
mixture comes together to form a soft
dough.

3 Turn the dough onto a lightly floured
work surface and knead for 5–7 minutes,
or until the dough is smooth. Place the
dough in a large, lightly oiled bowl, cover
with plastic wrap or a damp tea towel, and
leave for 1–1½ hours in a warm place or
until doubled in size.
4 Turn out the dough onto a lightly floured
work surface and knead for 5 minutes.
Cut into 16 portions. Roll each portion into
a sausage shape about 20 cm (8 inches)
long and form each into an 'S' shape.
Place on a greased baking tray. Cover
loosely and stand in a warm place for 30
minutes, or until doubled in size. Preheat
the oven to moderately hot 200°C
(400°F/Gas 6).
5 Brush with the remaining beaten egg
and decorate with the remaining raisins,
placing them gently into the 'S' shape,
being careful not to deflate the buns.
Bake for 10 minutes, or until the tops are
brown and the buns feel hollow when
tapped underneath. Transfer to a wire
rack to cool. Serve warm or cold, plain or
buttered.

NOTE: These buns are also popular in
England.

LITTLE LEMON TARTS

Preparation time: 40 minutes +
  refrigeration
Total cooking time: 15 minutes
Makes 24

2 cups (250 g/8 oz) plain flour
125 g (4 oz) butter, chopped
2 teaspoons caster sugar
1 teaspoon grated lemon rind
1 egg yolk

Filling
125 g (4 oz) cream cheese, softened
½ cup (125 g/4 oz) caster sugar
2 egg yolks
2 tablespoons lemon juice
½ cup (160 g/5¼ oz) sweetened condensed
  milk

1 Preheat oven to moderate 180°C
(350°F/Gas 4). Brush two 12-cup shallow
patty tins with oil. Sift flour and a pinch of
salt into a bowl; rub in butter. Add sugar,
rind, egg yolk and 2–3 tablespoons iced
water; mix with a knife. Gently knead on
lightly floured surface until smooth. Cover
in plastic wrap and chill for 10 minutes.
2 To make Filling: Using electric beaters,
beat combined cream cheese, sugar and
egg yolks until smooth and thickened. Add
lemon juice and condensed milk; beat
until well combined.
3 Roll out the dough between sheets of
baking paper to 3 mm (about ⅛ inch)
thickness. Using a 7 cm (2¾ inch) fluted,
round cutter, cut rounds from pastry.
Gently press into patty tins. Lightly prick
each round 3 times with a fork, bake for
10 minutes or until just starting to turn
golden. Remove from oven and spoon
2 teaspoons of filling into each case.
Return to oven for another 5 minutes or
until filling has set. Cool slightly before
removing from tins. Garnish with strips of
candied lemon peel, if desired.

KOEKSISTERS

Preparation time: 20 minutes +
    1 hour resting
Total cooking time: 15 minutes
Makes about 12

Syrup
3½ cups (875 g/1 lb 12½ oz) caster sugar
1 cinnamon stick
2 teaspoons lemon juice

3½ cups (435 g/14 oz) self-raising flour
1 teaspoon ground cinnamon
1 tablespoon caster sugar
50 g (1¾ oz) butter, chopped
2 eggs, lightly beaten
1 cup (250 ml/8 fl oz) milk
oil, for deep-frying

1 Combine the sugar, cinnamon stick, lemon juice and 1½ cups (375 ml/12 fl oz) water in a saucepan and stir over medium heat until the sugar has dissolved. Bring to the boil, then reduce the heat and simmer for 5–7 minutes, or until thick and syrupy. Remove and leave until cold.
2 Sift the flour and cinnamon into a large bowl, stir in the sugar and add the butter. Rub the butter into the flour with your fingertips until the mixture resembles fine breadcrumbs. Make a well in the centre, add the eggs and milk and mix with a flat-bladed knife, using a cutting action, until the mixture comes together in clumps. Gather together and knead on a lightly floured surface for 1 minute, or until smooth. Place in a large lightly oiled bowl, cover and leave for 1 hour.

3 Roll the dough out into a 30 x 40 cm (12 x 16 inch) rectangle. Cut the dough in half crossways, then cut each half into quarters. Cut each quarter into nine 10 cm (4 inch) long strips. Plait 3 strips together, pinching the ends firmly to seal. Repeat with the remaining strips.
4 Fill a deep heavy-based saucepan one third full of oil and heat to 170°C (325°F), or until a cube of bread dropped into the oil browns in 20 seconds. Fry the plaits in several batches for about 2–3 minutes, or until well browned and cooked though. Drain on crumpled paper towels. While still hot, dip each into the cold syrup for about 5 seconds, turning to coat evenly. Drain on a wire cake rack over a baking tray. Although best eaten on the day they are made, they can be eaten the next day, heated and brushed with any remaining syrup.

AMARETTI

Preparation time: 15 minutes + standing
Total cooking time: 20 minutes
Makes 40

1 tablespoon plain flour
1 tablespoon cornflour
1 teaspoon ground cinnamon
⅔ cup (160 g/5½ oz) caster sugar
1 teaspoon grated lemon rind
1 cup (185 g/6 oz) ground almonds
2 egg whites
¼ cup (30 g/1 oz) icing sugar

1 Line two baking trays with baking paper. Sift the plain flour, cornflour, cinnamon and half the caster sugar into a large bowl; add the lemon rind and ground almonds.
2 Place the egg whites in a small, dry bowl. With electric beaters, beat the egg whites until soft peaks form. Add the remaining caster sugar gradually, beating constantly until the mixture is thick and glossy, stiff peaks form and all the sugar has dissolved. Using a metal spoon, fold the egg white into the dry ingredients. Stir until the ingredients are just combined and the mixture forms a soft dough.
3 With oiled or wetted hands, roll 2 level teaspoons of mixture at a time into a ball. Arrange on the prepared tray, allowing room for spreading. Set the tray aside, uncovered, for 1 hour before baking.
4 Heat the oven to moderate 180°C (350°F/Gas 4). Sift the icing sugar liberally over the biscuits. Bake for 15–20 minutes, or until crisp and lightly browned. Transfer to a wire rack to cool.

IN ADVANCE: The biscuits can be stored in an airtight container for up to 2 days.
note: You can use orange rind instead of lemon rind. These biscuits have a chewy texture and are perfect served with coffee.

CHOCOLATE CUPS WITH CARAMEL

Preparation time: 40 minutes
Total cooking time: 5–10 minutes
Makes 24

150 g (5 oz) **dark chocolate melts**
24 **small foil confectionery cups**
80 g (2¾ oz) **Mars® bar, chopped**
¼ cup (60 ml/2 fl oz) **cream**
50 g (1¾ oz) **white chocolate melts**

1 Place the dark chocolate in a small heatproof bowl. Bring a small pan of water to the boil and remove from the heat. Sit the bowl over the pan, making sure the bowl does not touch the water. Stir occasionally until the chocolate has melted and the mixture is smooth.
2 Using a small new paintbrush, brush a thin layer of chocolate inside the foil cases. Stand the cases upside-down on a wire rack to set. (Return the remaining chocolate to the pan of steaming water for later use.)
3 Combine the Mars® bar and cream in a small pan and stir over low heat until the chocolate has melted and the mixture is smooth. Transfer to a bowl and leave until just starting to set, then spoon into each cup leaving about 3 mm (about ¼ inch) of space at the top.
4 Spoon the reserved melted chocolate into the caramel cases and allow the chocolate to set. Melt the white chocolate in the same way as the dark chocolate. Place in a small paper piping bag and drizzle patterns over the cups. Carefully peel away the foil when the chocolate has set.

NOTE: Ensure the chocolate is set before piping the white chocolate on the top.
IN ADVANCE: Caramel cups can be made up to 3 days ahead.

CHOCOLATE PRALINE TRIANGLES

Preparation time: 40 minutes + chilling
Total cooking time: 3 minutes
Makes 36

60 g (2 oz) **slivered almonds**
½ cup (125 g/4 oz) **caster sugar**
150 g (5 oz) **dark chocolate, chopped**
40 g (1¼ oz) **butter**
¼ cup (60 ml/2 fl oz) **cream**
80 g (2¾ oz) **blanched almonds, toasted**
200 g (6½ oz) **dark compound chocolate, melted**
50 g (1¾ oz) **white compound chocolate, optional**

1 Line a baking tray with foil and brush lightly with oil. Line a 20 x 10 cm (8 x 4 inch) loaf tin with foil.
2 Combine the almonds and sugar in a small pan and place over low heat. Watch carefully, without stirring, for 3–5 minutes, until the sugar is melted and golden. (Swirl the pan slightly to dissolve the sugar.) Pour onto the tray and leave until set and completely cold. Break into chunks, place in a plastic bag and crush with a rolling pin, or chop in a food processor until crumbly.
3 Put the chopped chocolate in a heatproof bowl. Combine the butter and cream in a small pan and stir over low heat until the butter melts. Bring to the boil, then remove from the heat. Pour the hot cream mixture over the chocolate. Leave for 2 minutes, then stir until the chocolate is smooth. Cool slightly, then stir in the crushed praline.
4 Spread the mixture into the loaf tin and smooth the surface. Tap gently on the bench to level. Cover with plastic wrap, then refrigerate for 1 hour, or until set. Lift from the tin, peel away the foil and cut into 36 small triangles.
5 Line a tray with foil. Press a whole toasted almond onto each triangle. Using two forks, dip the triangles one at a time into the chocolate to coat. Lift out, drain off the excess chocolate and place on the tray to set. Pipe with white chocolate to decorate, if desired.

NOTE: Refrigerate in warm weather.

PROFITEROLES

Preparation time: 20 minutes
Total cooking time: 50 minutes
Makes 32

Choux pastry
50 g (1¾ oz) unsalted butter
¾ cup (90 g/3 oz) plain flour, sifted twice
3 eggs, lightly beaten

Filling
1½ cups (375 ml/12 fl oz) milk
4 egg yolks
⅓ cup (90 g/3 oz) caster sugar
3 tablespoons plain flour
1 teaspoon vanilla essence

110 g (3½ oz) good-quality dark chocolate
2 teaspoons vegetable oil

1 Preheat the oven to hot 210°C (415°F/Gas 6–7). Put the butter in a large heavy-based pan with ¾ cup (185 ml/6 fl oz) water and stir over medium heat until coming to the boil. Remove from the heat and quickly beat in the flour. Return to the heat and continue beating until the mixture comes together and leaves the side of the pan. Allow to cool slightly.

2 Transfer to a bowl and beat to release any more heat. Gradually add the beaten egg about 3 teaspoons at a time, beating well until all the egg has been added and the mixture is thick and glossy—a wooden spoon should stand upright in it. (If it is too runny, the egg has been added too quickly. Beat for several more minutes, or until thickened.) Spoon the mixture onto two baking trays, leaving room for spreading. A heaped teaspoonful of mixture will make 1 small puff. Sprinkle the baking trays with water—this creates steam, helping the puffs to rise. Bake for 20–30 minutes, or until browned and hollow sounding, then remove and make a small hole in the base of each one. Return to the oven for 5 minutes to dry out. Cool on a wire rack.

3 To make the filling, put the milk into a small pan and bring to the boil. Set aside while quickly whisking the yolks and sugar in a bowl, until light and creamy. Whisk in the flour. Pour the hot milk slowly onto the egg mixture, whisking constantly. Wash out the pan, return the milk mixture and bring to the boil, stirring with a wire whisk. Boil for 2 minutes, stirring often. Transfer to a bowl, stir in the vanilla, cover the surface of the custard with plastic wrap to prevent a skin forming, then refrigerate until cold.

4 Pipe the filling into the profiteroles through the hole in the base, using a piping bag and nozzle. Melt the chocolate and oil gently, stir until smooth and dip the profiterole tops in the chocolate.

WALNUT CHOCOLATES

Preparation time: 30 minutes + chilling
Total cooking time: 2–3 minutes
Makes 30

100 g (3½ oz) walnut pieces
½ cup (60 g/2 oz) icing sugar
2 teaspoons egg white
200 g (6½ oz) dark chocolate
30 walnut halves

1 Chop the walnut pieces in a food processor. Sift the icing sugar and process with the walnuts and egg white until a moist paste forms. Cover and refrigerate for 20 minutes.

2 Roll teaspoons of walnut paste into balls and flatten slightly. Place the chocolate in a heatproof bowl. Bring a pan of water to the boil and remove from the heat. Sit the bowl over the pan, making sure the base of the bowl does not sit in the water. Stir occasionally until the chocolate has melted.

3 Dip the walnut rounds in the chocolate and transfer to a piece of greaseproof paper or foil. Press the walnut halves gently into the top of each round and leave to set.

IN ADVANCE: Can be made 4 days ahead.

BLUEBERRY MUFFINS

Preparation time: 20 minutes
Total cooking time: 20 minutes
Makes 6 large muffins

3 cups (375 g/12 oz) plain flour
1 tablespoon baking powder
¾ cup (140 g/4⅔ oz) soft brown sugar
125 g (4 oz) butter, melted
2 eggs, lightly beaten
1 cup (250 ml/8 fl oz) milk
1 cup (155 g/5 oz) blueberries
icing sugar, for sprinkling

1 Preheat oven to hot 210°C (415°F/Gas 6–7). Brush a 6-hole large muffin tin with melted butter or oil. Sift flour and baking powder into a large bowl. Stir in sugar; make a well in centre.
2 Add combined melted butter, eggs and milk all at once; stir until just blended. (Do not overmix; the batter should look quite lumpy.)
3 Fold in blueberries thoroughly but lightly. Spoon batter into tin. Bake 20 minutes or until golden brown. Loosen with a knife and transfer to a wire rack to cool. Sprinkle with icing sugar.

ANISEED BISCUITS

Preparation time: 15 minutes
Total cooking time: 35 minutes
Makes 16

3 cups (375 g/12 oz) plain flour
½ cup (125 ml/4 fl oz) olive oil
½ cup (125 ml/4 fl oz) beer
3 tablespoons anisette liqueur
½ cup (125 g/4 oz) caster sugar
¼ cup (40 g/1¼ oz) sesame seeds
2 tablespoons aniseeds

1 Preheat the oven to moderately hot 200°C (400°F/Gas 6). Lightly grease a baking tray and line with baking paper.
2 Sift the flour and 1 teaspoon salt into a large bowl and make a well. Add the oil, beer and anisette and mix with a large metal spoon until the dough comes together. Transfer to a lightly floured surface and knead for 3–4 minutes, or until smooth. Divide the dough into two, then divide each portion into eight. In a small bowl, combine the sugar, sesame seeds and aniseeds.
3 Make a small pile of the seed mix on a work surface and roll out each portion of dough over the mix to a 15 cm (6 inch) round with the seeds embedded underneath. Place the rounds on a baking tray with the seeds on top and cook for 5–6 minutes, until the bases are crisp. Place 10 cm (4 inches) below a grill for about 40 seconds, until the sugar caramelizes and the surface is golden. Transfer to a wire rack to cool.

NOTE: If aniseeds are unavailable, you can use 1½ tablespoons fennel seeds instead.

SORBET BALLS

Preparation time: 15 minutes +
  overnight freezing
Total cooking time: 35 minutes
Makes 24

400 g (13 oz) sorbet
250 g (8 oz) dark chocolate melts or
  buttons

1 Soften the sorbet slightly (if you do this step as soon as you get home it will probably be the right consistency and will save having to refreeze it) and spread it out in a shallow container to a depth of about 2.5 cm (1 inch). Put in the freezer until solid.
2 Cover a baking tray with baking paper and place in the freezer. Using a melon baller, scoop out tiny balls of sorbet and place them on the prepared tray. Put a cocktail stick in each sorbet ball. Cover the tray tightly with plastic wrap, ensuring it is completely covered, then refreeze overnight so the balls are solid.
3 Place the chocolate in a heatproof bowl. Bring a pan of water to the boil, then remove the pan from the heat. Sit the bowl over the pan, making sure the base of the bowl does not touch the water. Stir occasionally until the chocolate has melted. Remove the bowl and set aside to cool a little.
4 The next part is quite tricky so you need to be careful. Ladle some of the chocolate into a separate bowl so that if anything goes wrong you won't ruin the whole batch. Work with just a few balls at a time so they do not melt. Dip each sorbet ball in the chocolate, making sure it is thoroughly coated and place it back on the tray. Return to the freezer. Reheat the chocolate if necessary. It must be liquid enough not to coat too thickly. Add more melted chocolate to the bowl when necessary, but if it seizes, start with a new bowl and a new batch. Freeze until you are ready to serve.

BAKLAVA

Preparation time: 30 minutes + cooling
Total cooking time: 1 hour 15 minutes
Makes 18 pieces

2¼ cups (560 g/1 lb 2 oz) caster sugar
1½ teaspoons grated lemon rind
¼ cup (90 g/3 oz) honey
¼ cup (60 ml/2 fl oz) lemon juice
2 tablespoons orange blossom water
200 g (6½ oz) walnuts, finely chopped
200 g (6½ oz) shelled pistachios, finely
    chopped
200 g (6½ oz) almonds, finely chopped
2 tablespoons caster sugar, extra
2 teaspoons ground cinnamon
200 g (6½ oz) unsalted butter, melted
375 g (12 oz) ready-made filo pastry

1 Place the sugar, lemon rind and 1½ cups
(375 ml/12 fl oz) water in a saucepan and
stir over high heat until the sugar has
dissolved, then boil for 5 minutes. Reduce
the heat to low and simmer for 5 minutes,
or until the syrup has thickened slightly
and just coats the back of a spoon. Add
the honey, lemon juice and orange
blossom water and cook for 2 minutes.
Remove from the heat and leave to cool
completely.
2 Preheat the oven to warm 170°C
(325°F/Gas 3). Combine the nuts, extra
sugar and cinnamon in a bowl. Brush the
base and sides of a 30 x 27 cm (12 x 11 inch)
baking dish or tin with the melted butter.
Cover the base with a single layer of filo
pastry, brush lightly with the butter,
folding in any overhanging edges.
Continue layering the filo, brushing each
new layer with butter and folding in the
edges until 10 sheets have been used.
Keep the unused filo under a damp tea
towel.

3 Sprinkle half the nut mixture over the
pastry and pat down evenly. Repeat the
layering and buttering of 5 more filo
sheets, sprinkle with the remaining nuts,
then continue to layer and butter the
remaining sheets, including the top layer.
Press down with your hands so the pastry
and nuts adhere to each other. Using a
large sharp knife, cut into diamond
shapes, ensuring you cut through to the
bottom layer. Pour any remaining butter
evenly over the top and smooth with your
hands. Bake for 30 minutes, then lower
the temperature to slow 150°C (300°F/Gas
2) and cook for another 30 minutes.
4 Immediately cut through the original
diamond markings, then strain the syrup
evenly over the top. Cool completely
before lifting the diamonds out onto a
serving platter.

NOTE: To achieve the right texture, it is
important for the baklava to be piping hot
and the syrup cold when pouring the
syrup.

CHOCOLATE CLUSTERS

Preparation time: 35 minutes
Total cooking time: Nil
Makes about 40

125 g (4 oz) dark chocolate melts
125 g (4 oz) white chocolate melts
⅔ cup (125 g/4 oz) dried mixed fruit
125 g (4 oz) glacé ginger, chopped
30 g (1 oz) each dark chocolate and white
    chocolate melts or buttons, extra,
    melted

1 Put the dark chocolate in a heatproof
bowl. Bring a pan of water to the boil,
remove from the heat. Sit the bowl over
the pan, making sure the base of the bowl
is not touching the water. Stir
occasionally until the chocolate has
melted. Cool slightly. Repeat with the
white chocolate.
2 Stir the mixed fruit into the dark
chocolate. Combine the ginger with the
white chocolate.
3 Drop spoonfuls of the mixtures onto
foil-lined trays, and leave to set at room
temperature. Drizzle with the extra
melted chocolate.

BRANDY SNAPS WITH COFFEE LIQUEUR CREAM

Preparation time: 12 minutes + chilling
Total cooking time: 20 minutes
Makes 25

60 g (2 oz) butter
2 tablespoons golden syrup
⅓ cup (60 g/2 oz) soft brown sugar
¼ cup (30 g/1 oz) plain flour
1½ teaspoons ground ginger
80 g (2¾ oz) dark chocolate, melted

Coffee liqueur cream
⅔ cup (170 ml/5½ fl oz) cream
1 tablespoon icing sugar, sifted
1 teaspoon instant coffee powder
1 tablespoon coffee liqueur

1 Preheat the oven to moderate 180°C (350°F/Gas 4). Line two baking trays with baking paper. Combine the butter, syrup and sugar in a small pan. Stir over low heat until the butter has melted and the sugar has dissolved; remove from the heat. Add the sifted flour and ginger and, using a wooden spoon, stir until well combined; do not overbeat.
2 Drop 1 level teaspoon of mixture at a time onto the trays, about 12 cm (5 inches) apart. (Prepare only three or four biscuits at a time.) Use a palette knife to spread the mixture into 8 cm (3 inch) rounds. Bake for 6 minutes, or until lightly browned. Leave on the trays for 30 seconds, then lift off the tray and wrap around the handle of a wooden spoon while still hot. If the biscuits harden on the trays, return to the oven to soften again, then roll. Set aside to cool. Repeat with the remaining mixture.

3 To make the coffee liqueur cream, combine all the ingredients in a small bowl and stir until just combined. Cover with plastic wrap and refrigerate for 1 hour. Using electric beaters, beat until the mixture is thick and forms stiff peaks. Fill the biscuits. (You can spoon the cream into a small paper icing bag, seal the open end and snip off the tip, then pipe into the snaps.) Pipe or drizzle with melted chocolate before serving.

IN ADVANCE: Store in an airtight container for up to 2 days, or freeze snaps for up to 1 month without filling.

HONEY BISCUITS

Preparation time: 20 minutes + cooling
Total cooking time: 35 minutes
Makes 20

1⅔ cups (210 g/7 oz) plain flour
1 teaspoon baking powder
1 tablespoon finely grated orange rind
1 teaspoon ground cinnamon
½ cup (60 g/2 oz) walnuts, finely chopped
60 g (2 oz) unsalted butter, softened
¼ cup (60 g/2 oz) caster sugar
¼ cup (60 ml/2 fl oz) olive oil
¼ cup (60 ml/2 fl oz) orange juice

Syrup
75 g (3 oz) caster sugar
2 tablespoons runny honey
1 teaspoon ground cinnamon
2 tablespoons orange juice

1 Preheat the oven to moderate 180°C (350°F/Gas 4). Line a baking tray with baking paper. Sift the flour and baking powder into a bowl. Mix in the rind, cinnamon and half the walnuts.
2 Cream the butter and sugar in another bowl with electric beaters until pale and fluffy. Mix the oil and orange juice in a jug and add a little at a time to the butter and sugar mixture, whisking constantly.
3 Mix the flour in two batches into the butter mixture, then bring the dough together with your hands. Shape tablespoons of dough into balls and place on the tray. Flatten slightly and bake for 20–25 minutes, until golden. Cool on the tray.
4 Make the syrup by mixing all the ingredients with ¼ cup (60 ml/2 fl oz) water and the remaining walnuts in a small saucepan. Bring to the boil over medium heat until the sugar dissolves, then reduce the heat to low and simmer for 10 minutes. The syrup will thicken.
5 Using a slotted spoon, dip a few biscuits at a time in the hot syrup. Use another spoon to baste them, then transfer to a plate.

OLIEBOLLEN

Preparation time: 20 minutes +
 30 minutes proving
Total cooking time: 15 minutes
Makes about 48

7 g (¼ oz) sachet dry yeast
1 tablespoon caster sugar
1 cup (250 ml/8 fl oz) milk, warmed
2¼ cups (280 g/9 oz) plain flour
¾ cup (120 g/4 oz) raisins, chopped
1 green apple, peeled and diced
¼ cup (45 g/1½ oz) mixed peel
2 eggs, lightly beaten
2 teaspoons finely grated lemon rind
oil, for deep-frying
caster sugar, for coating

1 Place the yeast, 1 teaspoon of the sugar
and ¼ cup (60 ml/2 fl oz) of the milk in a
bowl and stir. Leave in a warm place for
about 10 minutes, until frothy. (If the yeast
doesn't froth it is dead and you will need
to start again.)
2 Sift the flour into a large bowl and stir in
the remaining sugar, raisins, apple and
peel. Make a well in the centre and pour
in the remaining milk, the yeast mixture,
eggs and lemon rind. Mix with a flat-
bladed knife to a soft sticky batter. Cover
and leave to prove for 30 minutes. Stir the
mixture thoroughly before cooking. It
should drop off the spoon in one thick
blob.
3 Fill a deep heavy-based saucepan one
third full of oil and heat to moderate
180°C (350°F), or until a cube of bread
dropped into the oil browns in 15 seconds.
Drop walnut-sized balls of dough from a
tablespoon into the hot oil. Cook in
several batches until well browned and
cooked through. Drain well on crumpled
paper towels, then toss lightly in caster
sugar. Serve while still warm.

NOTE: For a delicious dessert, you can
make large oliebollen and serve them
with cream or ice cream.

GINGER PECAN BISCOTTI

Preparation time: 30 minutes + cooling
Total cooking time: 1 hour 20 minutes
Makes about 20

1 cup (100 g/3½ oz) pecans
2 eggs
⅔ cup (155 g/5 oz) soft brown sugar
1 cup (125 g/4 oz) self-raising flour
¾ cup (90 g/3 oz) plain flour
100 g (3½ oz) glacé ginger, finely chopped

1 Preheat the oven to warm 160°C
(315°F/Gas 2–3). Spread the pecans on a
baking tray and bake for 10–12 minutes, or
until fragrant. Tip onto a chopping board
to cool, then roughly chop. Cover the
baking tray with baking paper.
2 Put the eggs and sugar in a bowl and
beat with electric beaters until pale and
creamy. Sift the flours into the bowl and
add the nuts and ginger. Mix to a soft
dough, then place on the tray and shape
into a 9 x 23 cm (3½ x 9 inch) loaf.
3 Bake for 45 minutes, or until lightly
golden. Transfer to a wire rack to cool for
about 20 minutes, then carefully cut into
1 cm (½ inch) slices with a large serrated
bread knife. It will be crumbly on the
edges, so work slowly and, if possible, try
to hold the sides as you cut. Arrange the
slices on baking trays and bake again for
about 10 minutes each side. Don't worry if
they don't seem fully dry as they will
become crisp on cooling. Cool completely
before storing in an airtight container.

HARD CARAMELS

Preparation time: 25 minutes + setting
Total cooking time: 15 minutes
Makes 49

1 cup (250 g/8 oz) sugar
90 g (3 oz) butter
2 tablespoons golden syrup
⅓ cup (80 ml/2¾ fl oz) liquid glucose
½ cup (90 ml/3 fl oz) canned condensed
 milk
250 g (8 oz) dark chocolate, chopped

1 Grease the base and sides of a 20 cm
(8 inch) square cake tin, then line with
baking paper and grease the paper.
Combine the sugar, butter, golden syrup,
liquid glucose and condensed milk in a
heavy-based saucepan. Stir over medium
heat without boiling until the butter has
melted and the sugar has dissolved
completely. Brush the sugar crystals
from the sides of the saucepan with a wet
pastry brush.
2 Bring to the boil, reduce the heat
slightly and boil, stirring, for about
10–15 minutes, or until a teaspoon of
mixture dropped into cold water reaches
hard ball stage (forming a firm ball that
holds its shape). If using a sugar
thermometer, the mixture must reach
122°C (250°F). Remove from the heat
immediately. Pour into the tin and leave to
cool. While the caramel is still warm, mark
into 49 squares with an oiled knife. When
cold, cut through completely into squares.
3 Line two baking trays with foil. Place the
chocolate in a small heatproof bowl.
Bring a saucepan of water to the boil,
then remove the saucepan from the heat.
Sit the bowl over the saucepan, making
sure the bowl doesn't touch the water.
Stir until the chocolate has melted.
Remove from the heat and cool slightly.
Using two forks, dip the caramels one at a
time into the chocolate to coat. Lift out,
drain the excess chocolate, then place on
the trays and leave to set.

CHOCOLATE TARTS

Preparation time: 40 minutes + chilling
Total cooking time: 30 minutes
Makes about 45

1¼ cups (155 g/5 oz) plain flour
75 g (2½ oz) butter, chopped
¼ cup (60 g/2 oz) caster sugar
2 egg yolks
250 g (4 oz) dark chocolate, finely
    chopped
1 cup (250 ml/4 fl oz) cream
1 tablespoon orange-flavoured liqueur
1 orange
½ cup (125 g/4 oz) caster sugar, extra

1 Lightly grease two 12-hole tartlet tins. Sift the flour into a large bowl and add the butter. Rub in with your fingertips until the mixture resembles fine breadcrumbs. Stir in the sugar. Make a well and add the egg yolks and up to 2 tablespoons water. Mix with a flat-bladed knife using a cutting action, until the mixture comes together in beads. Gather together and lift out onto a lightly floured work surface. Press into a ball and flatten slightly into a disc. Wrap in plastic and refrigerate for 20 minutes.
2 Preheat the oven to moderate 180°C (350°F/Gas 4). Roll the dough between two sheets of baking paper and cut rounds with a 5 cm (2 inch) cutter. Press into the tins.

3 Bake for about 10 minutes, or until lightly browned. Remove from the tins and cool. Repeat to use all the pastry. Allow to cool.
4 Put the chocolate in a heatproof bowl. Bring the cream to the boil in a small pan and pour over the chocolate. Leave for 1 minute, then stir until the chocolate has melted. Stir in the liqueur. Allow to set, stirring occasionally until thick.
5 Meanwhile, thinly peel the orange, avoiding the bitter white pith, and cut into short thin strips. Combine the extra sugar, rind and ½ cup (125 ml/4 fl oz) water in a small pan, stir over heat until the sugar has dissolved, then simmer for about 5–10 minutes, or until thick and syrupy. Remove the rind with tongs and drain on baking paper; allow to cool.
6 Spoon the chocolate mixture into a piping bag fitted with a 1 cm (½ inch) plain piping nozzle. Pipe three small blobs of ganache into the pastry case, pulling up as you pipe so the ganache forms a point. Dust with cocoa, decorate with the orange rind and refrigerate until ready to serve.

PEACH BAKLAVA

Preparation time: 40 minutes
Total cooking time: 20–25 minutes
Serves 8

6 sheets filo pastry
60 g (2 oz) butter, melted
⅔ cup (85 g/2¾ oz) slivered almonds
1½ teaspoons ground cinnamon
½ cup (95 g/3¼ oz) soft brown sugar
¾ cup (185 ml/6 fl oz) orange juice,
    strained
4 peaches
icing sugar, for dusting

1 Preheat the oven to moderate 180°C (350°F/Gas 4). Cut each sheet of pastry into 8 squares. Line eight 1-cup muffin tins with 3 layers of filo pastry, brush the pieces with melted butter to stick them together and overlap the sheets at angles.
2 Combine the almonds, cinnamon and half the sugar in a small bowl. Sprinkle over the bases then cover with the 3 final squares of filo pastry brushed with butter. Bake for 10–15 minutes.
3 Meanwhile, dissolve the remaining sugar in the orange juice, bring to the boil, reduce the heat and simmer. Halve the peaches and slice thinly, add to the syrup and stir gently to coat the fruit. Simmer for 2–3 minutes; lift from the pan with a slotted spoon. Arrange the peaches on the pastries, dust with icing sugar and serve with clotted cream or ice cream.

NOTE: Peaches can be peeled if you like. Tinned peaches can be used instead of fresh.

CAKES, TARTS AND PIES

DATE AND MASCARPONE TART

Preparation time: 50 minutes + chilling
Total cooking time: 40–45 minutes
Serves 6–8

Coconut pastry
½ cup (90 g/3 oz) rice flour
½ cup (60 g/2 oz) plain flour
100 g (3½ oz) chilled unsalted butter, chopped
2 tablespoons icing sugar
¼ cup (25 g/¾ oz) desiccated coconut
100 g (3½ oz) marzipan, grated

Filling
8 fresh dates (about 200 g/6½ oz), pitted
2 eggs
2 teaspoons custard powder
125 g (4 oz) mascarpone
2 tablespoons caster sugar
⅓ cup (80 ml/2¾ fl oz) cream
2 tablespoons flaked almonds

1 Preheat the oven to moderate 180°C (350°F/Gas 4). Grease a shallow, 10 x 34 cm (4 x 14 inch) fluted loose-bottomed flan tin. Sift the flours into a large bowl. Using just your fingertips, rub in the butter until the mixture resembles breadcrumbs, then press the mixture together gently. Stir in the icing sugar, coconut and marzipan. Turn out onto a lightly floured surface and gather together into a ball. Flatten slightly, cover with plastic wrap and refrigerate for 15 minutes.

2 Roll out the pastry between two sheets of baking paper until large enough to line the tin. Ease the pastry into the tin and trim the edge. Refrigerate for 5–10 minutes. Line the pastry-lined tin with a crumpled sheet of baking paper and spread a layer of baking beads or rice evenly over the paper. Place the tin on a baking tray and bake for 10 minutes. Remove the paper and beads, bake for another 5 minutes, or until just golden, then allow to cool.
3 Cut the dates into quarters lengthways and arrange over the pastry. Whisk together the eggs, custard powder, mascarpone, caster sugar and cream until smooth. Pour the mixture over the dates, then sprinkle with the flaked almonds. Bake for 25–30 minutes, or until golden and just set, then allow to cool slightly. Serve warm. The tart can be decorated if you wish.

BANANA CAKE

Preparation time: 25 minutes
Total cooking time: 1 hour
Makes one 20 cm (8 inch) round cake

125 g (4 oz) butter
½ cup (125 g/4 oz) caster sugar
2 eggs, lightly beaten
1 teaspoon vanilla essence
4 medium ripe bananas, mashed
1 teaspoon bicarbonate of soda
½ cup (125 ml/4 fl oz) milk
2 cups (250 g/8 oz) self-raising flour

Butter Frosting
125 g (4 oz) butter
¾ cup (90 g/3 oz) icing sugar
1 tablespoon lemon juice
¼ cup (15 g/½ oz) flaked coconut, toasted

1 Preheat the oven to moderate 180°C (350°F/Gas 4). Brush a 20 cm (8 inch) round cake tin with oil or melted butter and line the base with baking paper. Using electric beaters, beat butter and sugar in a small bowl until light and creamy. Add the eggs gradually, beating thoroughly after each addition. Add the essence and mashed banana and beat until combined.
2 Transfer the mixture to a large bowl. Dissolve the soda in the milk. Using a metal spoon, fold in the sifted flour alternately with the milk. Stir until all the ingredients are just combined and the mixture is smooth. Spoon into the prepared tin; smooth the surface. Bake for 1 hour or until a skewer comes out clean when inserted into the centre of cake. Leave in the tin for 10 minutes before turning onto a wire rack to cool.
3 To make Frosting: Using electric beaters, beat the butter, icing sugar and lemon juice until smooth and creamy. Spread onto the cooled cake, sprinkle with toasted coconut flakes.

CHOCOLATE HAZELNUT TORTE

Preparation time: 1 hour +
  overnight refrigeration
Total cooking time: 1 hour 15 minutes
Serves 10

500 g (1 lb) dark chocolate, chopped
6 eggs
2 tablespoons Frangelico (see Note)
1½ cups (165 g/5½ oz) ground hazelnuts
1 cup (250 ml/8 fl oz) cream, whipped
12 whole hazelnuts, lightly roasted

Chocolate topping
200 g (6½ oz) dark chocolate, chopped
¾ cup (185 ml/6 fl oz) cream
1 tablespoon Frangelico

1 Preheat the oven to slow 150°C (300°F/Gas 2). Grease a deep 20 cm (8 inch) round cake tin and line with baking paper.
2 Put the chocolate in a heatproof bowl. Half fill a saucepan with water and bring to the boil. Remove from the heat and place the bowl over the pan, making sure it is not touching the water. Stir occasionally until the chocolate is melted.
3 Put the eggs in a large heatproof bowl and add the Frangelico. Place the bowl over a saucepan of barely simmering water over low heat, making sure it does not touch the water. Beat with an electric mixer on high speed for 7 minutes, or until the mixture is light and foamy. Remove from the heat.
4 Using a metal spoon, quickly and lightly fold the melted chocolate and ground nuts into the egg mixture until just combined. Fold in the cream and pour the mixture into the tin. Place the tin in a shallow baking dish. Pour in enough hot water to come halfway up the side of the tin.

5 Bake for 1 hour, or until just set. Remove the tin from the baking dish. Cool to room temperature, cover with plastic wrap and refrigerate overnight.
6 Cut a 17 cm (7 inch) circle from heavy cardboard. Invert the chilled cake onto the disc so that the base of the cake becomes the top. Place on a wire rack over a baking tray and remove the baking paper. Allow the cake to return to room temperature before you start to decorate.
7 To make the topping, combine the chopped chocolate, cream and Frangelico in a small pan. Heat gently over low heat, stirring, until the chocolate is melted and the mixture is smooth.
8 Pour the chocolate mixture over the cake in the centre, tilting slightly to cover the cake evenly. Tap the baking tray gently on the bench so that the top is level and the icing runs completely down the side of the cake. Place the hazelnuts around the edge of the cake. Refrigerate just until the topping has set and the cake is firm. Carefully transfer the cake to a serving plate, and cut into thin wedges to serve.

NOTE: Frangelico is a hazelnut-flavoured liqueur. Brandy or whisky can also be used, if preferred. This is a very rich cake so you only need to serve small portions.

ALMOND FILO SNAKE

Preparation time: 30 minutes
Total cooking time: 40 minutes
Serves 8

⅔ cup (70 g/2¼ oz) ground almonds
⅓ cup (30 g/1 oz) flaked almonds
175 g (6 oz) icing sugar
1 egg, separated
1 teaspoon finely grated lemon rind
¼ teaspoon almond essence
1 tablespoon rosewater
2 tablespoons olive oil
2 tablespoons almond oil
9 sheets filo pastry
pinch of ground cinnamon
icing sugar, extra, to dust

1 Preheat the oven to moderate 180°C (350°F/Gas 4). Lightly grease a 20 cm (8 inch) round springform tin.
2 Place all of the almonds in a bowl with the icing sugar. Put the egg white in a bowl and lightly beat with a fork. Add to the almonds with the lemon rind, essence and rosewater. Mix to a paste.
3 Divide the mixture into 3 and roll each portion into a sausage 45 cm (18 inches) long and 1 cm (½ inch) thick. If the paste is too sticky to roll, dust the bench with icing sugar.
4 Mix the oils in a bowl. Remove 1 sheet of filo and cover the rest with a damp tea towel to prevent it drying out. Brush the filo sheet with the oils, then cover with 2 more oiled sheets. Place 1 almond 'sausage' along the length of the oiled pastry and roll up to enclose the filling. Form into a coil and sit the coil in the centre of the tin. Use oil to join the other sausages and continue shaping to make a large coil.
5 Add the cinnamon to the egg yolk and brush over the snake. Bake for 30 minutes, then remove the side of the tin and turn the snake over. Bake for another 10 minutes to crisp the base. Dust with icing sugar and serve warm.

INDIVIDUAL PANETTONE

Preparation time: 30 minutes + 1 hour
   soaking and 1 hour 40 minutes rising
Total cooking time: 35 minutes
Makes 8

½ cup (95 g/3 oz) chopped dried apricots
½ cup (75 g/2½ oz) currants
½ cup (80 g/2¾ oz) sultanas
½ cup (125 ml/4 fl oz) Marsala
2 x 7 g (¼ oz) sachets dried yeast (see
   Note)
¾ cup (185 ml/6 fl oz) milk, warmed
½ cup (125 g/4 oz) caster sugar
180 g (6 oz) butter, softened
2 teaspoons vanilla essence
3 eggs
2 egg yolks
4 cups (500 g/1 lb) plain flour
1 teaspoon ground aniseed

1 Combine the fruit and Marsala in a bowl,
cover with plastic wrap and stand for 1
hour, or until most of the liquid is
absorbed. Put the yeast, milk and 1
teaspoon of the sugar in a bowl and leave
in a warm place for about 10 minutes,
until foamy.
2 Place the butter, vanilla and the
remaining sugar in a bowl and beat with
electric beaters until light and fluffy. Add
the eggs and yolks one at a time, beating
well after each addition.
3 Sift the flour and aniseed into a bowl,
make a well in the centre and add the yeast
mixture, butter mixture and fruit mixture.
Mix with a flat-bladed knife, until the
mixture forms a soft, sticky dough. Cover
and leave in a warm place for 40 minutes,
or until the dough has doubled in size.

4 Lightly oil the base and sides of eight ½
cup (125 ml/4 fl oz) soufflé dishes. Cut a
strip of brown paper long enough to fit
around the inside of each dish and tall
enough to come 10 cm (4 inches) above
the edge. Fold down a cuff about 2 cm (¾
inch) deep along the length of each strip.
Make diagonal cuts up to the fold line on
each strip, about 1 cm (½ inch) apart. Fit
the strips around the inside of the dishes,
pressing the cuts so they sit flat around
the bottom edge of the dish. Cut circles of
brown paper using the dish as a guide,
place in the base of each dish, and grease
the paper.
5 Turn the dough out onto a floured
surface and knead for 3 minutes, or until
smooth. You will need more flour, up to ½
cup (60 g/2 oz), and the dough should be
soft but not sticky. Divide into eight equal
portions and press into the dishes. Cover
with a tea towel and place in a warm
place for an hour, or until doubled in size.
6 Preheat the oven to moderately hot
200°C (400°F/Gas 6). Bake for 30–35
minutes, or until golden brown and
cooked through when tested with a
skewer. Remove from the soufflé dishes,
leaving the paper attached. Dust with
icing sugar, if desired. Serve warm or
cold.

NOTE: If you are using fresh yeast, you
will need double the amount of the dry
yeast stated in the recipe.

   This special cake from Milan can be
made in various sizes. These individual
ones are delightful to serve but if you
prefer to make a large one and serve it in
portions, you will find a recipe on
page 848.

LEMON ALMOND TART

Preparation time: 40 minutes + chilling
Total cooking time: 1 hour
Serves 6–8

Lemon pastry
2 cups (250 g/8 oz) plain flour, sifted
¼ cup (60 g/2 oz) caster sugar
125 g (4 oz) chilled unsalted butter,
   softened
1 teaspoon finely grated lemon rind
2 egg yolks

Filling
350 g (11 oz) ricotta, sieved
⅓ cup (90 g/3 oz) caster sugar
3 eggs, well beaten
1 tablespoon finely grated lemon rind
80 g (2¾ oz) blanched almonds, chopped
3 tablespoons flaked almonds
icing sugar, to dust

1 Combine the flour, sugar and a pinch of
salt in a large bowl. Make a well in the
centre and add the butter, rind and egg
yolks. Work the flour into the centre with
the fingertips of one hand until a smooth
dough forms (add a little more flour if
necessary). Wrap in plastic wrap, flatten
slightly, then refrigerate for 20 minutes.
2 To make the filling, with electric
beaters, beat the ricotta and sugar
together. Add the eggs gradually, beating
well after each addition. Add the rind,
beating briefly to combine, and then stir
in the chopped almonds.
3 Preheat the oven to moderate 180°C
(350°F/Gas 4). Brush a 20 cm (8 inch)
fluted flan tin with melted unsalted
butter. Roll out the pastry on a lightly
floured surface and line the tin, trimming
away the excess pastry. Pour in the filling
and smooth the top. Sprinkle with the
flaked almonds and bake for 55 minutes
to 1 hour, or until lightly golden and set.
4 Cool to room temperature, then
carefully remove the sides from the tin.
Lightly dust with icing sugar and serve at
room temperature or chilled.

APPLE GALETTES

Preparation time: 45 minutes + chilling
Total cooking time: 30 minutes
Serves 8

2 cups (250 g/8 oz) plain flour
250 g (8 oz) unsalted butter, chopped
8 apples
¾ cup (185 g/6 oz) caster sugar
125 g (4 oz) unsalted butter, chopped

1 Place the flour and butter in a bowl and cut the butter into the flour with two knives until it resembles large crumbs. Gradually add about ½ cup (125 ml/4 fl oz) chilled water, stirring with a knife and pressing together, until a rough dough forms. Turn onto a lightly floured board and roll into a rectangle. The dough will be crumbly and hard to manage at this point. Fold the pastry into thirds; turn it so the hinge is on your left and roll into a large rectangle. Always turn the pastry the same way so the hinge is on the left. Refrigerate in plastic wrap for 30 minutes.
2 Complete two more turns and folds before refrigerating the pastry for another 30 minutes. Repeat the process so that you have completed 6 folds and turns. Wrap the pastry in plastic wrap and refrigerate before use. The pastry can be stored in the refrigerator for 2 days or in the freezer for up to 3 months.
3 Preheat the oven to moderately hot 190°C (375°F/Gas 5). Roll the pastry out on a lightly floured surface until 3 mm (⅛ inch) thick. Cut into eight 10 cm (4 inch) rounds. Peel and core the apples and slice thinly. Arrange the apples in a spiral on the pastry. Sprinkle well with sugar and dot with unsalted butter. Bake on greased baking trays for 20–30 minutes, until the pastry is crisp and golden. Serve warm.

LIGHT FRUIT CAKE

Preparation time: 30 minutes
Total cooking time: 2 hours
Makes 1

185 g (6 oz) unsalted butter, softened
½ cup (125 g/4 oz) caster sugar
3 eggs
1 cup (160 g/5½ oz) sultanas
⅔ cup (100 g/3½ oz) currants
¼ cup (60 g/2 oz) chopped glacé apricots
¼ cup (45 g/1½ oz) chopped glacé figs
1 cup (240 g/7½ oz) coarsely chopped glacé cherries
½ cup (80 g/2¾ oz) macadamia nuts, coarsely chopped
1½ cups (185 g/6 oz) plain flour
½ cup (60 g/2 oz) self-raising flour
½ cup (125 ml/4 fl oz) milk
1 tablespoon sweet sherry
nuts or glacé cherries, for decoration

1 Preheat the oven to 160°C (315°F/Gas 2–3). Grease and line a deep 20 cm (8 inch) round or 18 cm (7 inch) square cake tin.
2 Cream the butter and sugar in a small bowl until just combined. Add the eggs, one at a time, beating well after each addition.
3 Transfer the mixture to a large bowl and stir in the fruit and nuts. Sift in half the flours and half the milk, stir to combine, then stir in the remaining flours and milk, and the sherry. Spoon into the prepared tin and tap the tin on the bench to remove any air bubbles. Smooth the surface with wet fingers and decorate the top with nuts or cherries, or both. Wrap the outside of the tin with paper. Sit the tin on several layers of newspaper in the oven and bake for 1¾–2 hours, or until a skewer inserted into the centre of the cake comes out clean. The top may need to be covered with a sheet of baking paper if it colours too much.
4 Remove from the oven, remove the top baking paper and wrap the tin in a thick tea towel until cool. Remove any remaining paper and wrap the cake well in aluminium foil, or store in an airtight container. Keeps for up to 2 weeks.

RICOTTA POTS WITH RASPBERRIES

Preparation time: 20 minutes
Total cooking time: 25 minutes
Serves 4

4 eggs, separated
½ cup (125 g/4 oz) caster sugar
350 g (11¼ oz) ricotta
35 g (1¼ oz) finely chopped pistachio nuts
1 teaspoon grated lemon rind
2 tablespoons lemon juice
1 tablespoon vanilla sugar (see note)
200 g (6½ oz) raspberries
icing sugar, to dust

1 Preheat the oven to moderate 180°C (350°F/Gas 4). Beat the egg yolks and sugar in a small bowl until thick and pale. Transfer to a large bowl and add the ricotta, pistachio nuts, lemon rind and juice and mix well.
2 In a separate bowl, whisk the egg whites to stiff peaks. Beat in the vanilla sugar, then gently fold into the ricotta mixture, until just combined.
3 Lightly grease four 250 ml (8 fl oz) ramekins. Divide the raspberries among the dishes and spoon the ricotta filling over the top. Place on a baking tray and bake for 20–25 minutes, or until puffed and lightly browned. Serve immediately, dusted with a little icing sugar.

NOTE: You can buy vanilla sugar or make your own. Split a whole vanilla bean in half lengthways and place in a jar of caster sugar (about 1 kg/2 lb). Leave for at least 4 days before using.

TORTE DE LA ALMENDRA
(ALMOND TORTE)

Preparation time: 15 minutes
Total cooking time: 1 hour 20 minutes
Serves 8

450 g (14 oz) blanched whole almonds,
  lightly toasted
150 g (5 oz) unsalted butter, softened
400 g (13 oz) caster sugar
6 eggs
150 g (5 oz) plain flour
2 teaspoons lemon rind
2 tablespoons lemon juice
icing sugar, to dust

1 Preheat the oven to warm 170°C
(325°F/Gas 3). Lightly grease a 24 cm (9
inch) springform cake tin. Grind the
almonds finely in a food processor and
set aside.
2 Using electric beaters, cream the butter
and sugar in a bowl until light and fluffy.
Add the eggs one at a time, beating well
after each addition. Using a large metal
spoon, fold in the flour, ground almonds
and the lemon rind. Stir until just
combined and almost smooth.
3 Pour the batter into the prepared tin
and bake for 1 hour 20 minutes, or until a
skewer inserted in the centre comes out
clean. Allow to cool for 5 minutes, then
brush the top with lemon juice. Remove to
a wire rack and allow to cool completely.
Dust with icing sugar in a cross pattern,
using a stencil if you wish.

HONEY AND PINE NUT TART

Preparation time: 25 minutes +
  15 minutes refrigeration
Total cooking time: 1 hour
Serves 6

Pastry
2 cups (250 g/8 oz) plain flour
1½ tablespoons icing sugar
115 g (4 oz) chilled unsalted butter,
  chopped
1 egg, lightly beaten

1½ cups (235 g/7½ oz) pine nuts
½ cup (175 g/6 oz) honey
115 g (4 oz) unsalted butter, softened
½ cup (125 g/4 oz) caster sugar
3 eggs, lightly beaten
¼ teaspoon vanilla essence
1 tablespoon almond liqueur
1 teaspoon finely grated lemon rind
1 tablespoon lemon juice
icing sugar, for dusting
crème fraîche or mascarpone, to serve

1 Preheat the oven to moderately hot
190°C (375°F/Gas 5) and place a baking
tray on the middle shelf. Lightly grease a
23 cm (9 inch), 3.5 cm (1½ inch) deep
loose-based tart tin. To make the pastry,
sift the flour and icing sugar into a large
bowl and add the butter. Rub the butter
into the flour with your fingertips until it
resembles fine breadcrumbs. Make a well
in the centre and add the egg and 2
tablespoons cold water. Mix with a flat-
bladed knife, using a cutting action, until
the mixture comes together in beads.

2 Gather the dough together and lift out
onto a lightly floured work surface. Press
together into a ball, roll out to a circle
3 mm (⅛ inch) thick and invert into the tin.
Use a small ball of pastry to press the
pastry into the tin, allowing any excess to
hang over the sides. Roll a rolling pin
over the tin, cutting off any excess pastry.
Prick the base all over with a fork and
chill for 15 minutes. Roll out the pastry
scraps and cut out 3 leaves for decoration.
Cover and refrigerate for 15 minutes.
3 Line the pastry with baking paper and
fill with baking beads or uncooked rice.
Bake on the heated tray for 10 minutes,
then remove the tart tin, leaving the tray
in the oven. Reduce the oven to moderate
180°C (350°F/Gas 4).
4 To make the filling, spread the pine
nuts on a baking tray and roast in the
oven for 3 minutes, or until golden. Heat
the honey in a small saucepan until
runny, then allow to cool. Cream the
butter and sugar in a bowl until smooth
and pale. Gradually add the eggs, beating
well after each addition. Mix in the honey,
vanilla, liqueur, lemon rind and juice and
a pinch of salt. Stir in the pine nuts, spoon
into the pastry case and smooth the
surface. Arrange the reserved pastry
leaves in the centre.
5 Place the tin on the hot tray and bake
for 40 minutes, or until golden and set.
Cover the top with foil after 25 minutes.
Serve warm or at room temperature,
dusted with icing sugar. Serve with crème
fraîche or mascarpone.

ORANGE BERRY SPONGE

Preparation time: 1 hour
Total cooking time: 45 minutes
Serves 8–10

½ cup (60 g/2 oz) plain flour
¼ cup (30 g/1 oz) cornflour
1 teaspoon baking powder
¼ cup (60 ml/2 fl oz) milk
50 g (1⅔ oz) butter
¾ cup (185 g/6 oz) caster sugar
3 eggs
3 egg yolks
1 teaspoon finely grated orange rind
1½ cups (375 ml/12 fl oz) cream
3–4 teaspoons icing sugar
1–2 tablespoons Grand Marnier
250 g (8 oz) strawberries, hulled and
   sliced
250 g (8 oz) blueberries
2 tablespoons flaked almonds, toasted
icing sugar, for dusting

1 Preheat the oven to moderate 180°C
(350°F/Gas 4). Brush a 30 x 20 cm
(12 x 8 inch) shallow cake tin with melted
butter or oil. Line the base and sides with
baking paper extending 3 cm (1¼ inches)
over each edge. Sift the flours and baking
powder twice onto a sheet of greaseproof
paper. Place milk and butter in pan. Stir
over medium heat until butter has
melted. (Take care not to boil mixture, but
keep it hot.)
2 Place the sugar, eggs and yolks in a
large heatproof bowl. Stand the bowl over
a pan of simmering water. Using electric
beaters, beat the mixture over heat until
pale yellow, thick and glossy and
increased in volume. Remove bowl from
heat. Stir in rind until well combined.

3 Using a metal spoon, fold in a third of
the flour at a time. Fold in the hot butter
mixture and stir until just smooth. (Do not
over-mix. It is important to keep as much
volume as possible in the mixture.) Spoon
the mixture into the prepared tin. Bake
for 25–30 minutes or until springy to
touch. Leave in the tin to cool.
4 Turn the cake out onto a flat work
surface. Using a sharp serrated knife,
trim away any dark patches. Cut the cake
into three even rectangles, around
10 x 20 cm (4 x 8 inches) each.
5 Beat the cream and icing sugar with
electric beaters until stiff peaks form. Stir
in the Grand Marnier.
6 Spread one quarter of the cream
mixture over one layer of cake. Top with a
third of the berries. Add a second layer of
cake; press down lightly. Repeat the
process with cream and berries,
reserving some berries for the top and
finishing with the third cake layer. Spread
the remaining cream evenly over the top
and sides of the cake. Decorate the cake
with the remaining berries and toasted
flaked almonds. Dust the cake lightly with
icing sugar.

NOTE: To toast almonds, scatter on an
oven tray lined with baking paper. Place in
a preheated moderate 180°C (350°F/Gas
4) oven for 5–10 minutes. Do not use
frozen or canned berries in this recipe as
they are too soggy. If blueberries are
unavailable, substitute any berry in
season, such as blackberries, or omit the
second berry variety entirely, if you
prefer.

GOLDEN GLACE CAKE

Preparation time: 15 minutes
Total cooking time: 1 hour 45 minutes
Makes 1

½ cup (120 g/4 oz) chopped glacé orange
   slices
½ cup (120 g/4 oz) chopped glacé pears
1 cup (240 g/8 oz) chopped glacé apricots
1 cup (240 g/8 oz) chopped glacé pineapple
⅓ cup (60 g/2 oz) chopped mixed peel
½ cup (80 g/2¾ oz) blanched almonds,
   coarsely chopped
1½ cups (185 g/6 oz) plain flour
½ cup (60 g/2 oz) self-raising flour
250 g (8 oz) unsalted butter, softened
1 tablespoon finely grated orange rind
1 tablespoon finely grated lemon rind
1 cup (250 g/8 oz) caster sugar
5 eggs
¼ cup (60 ml/2 fl oz) sweet sherry

1 Preheat the oven to moderate 180°C
(350°F/Gas 4). Grease and line a deep
20 cm (8 inch) square or 23 cm (9 inch)
round cake tin as shown on pages 224–5.
2 Combine the fruits, peel and almonds,
then toss with ¼ cup (30 g/1 oz) of the
plain flour to keep the fruits separate. Sift
together the remaining flours.
3 Beat the butter and rind in a small bowl
with electric beaters, gradually adding the
sugar, until light and fluffy. Beat in the
eggs, one at a time, beating well after each
addition. Transfer to a large bowl, stir in
the flour alternately with sherry, then fold
in the fruit, nut and flour mixture.
4 Spoon into the tin, tap the tin on the
bench to remove any air bubbles and
smooth the surface with wet fingers. Sit
the tin on several layers of newspaper
and bake for 30 minutes. Reduce the heat
to warm 160°C (315°F/Gas 2–3) and bake
for 1–1¼ hours, or until cooked when a
skewer inserted in the centre comes out
clean. Cool completely in the tin, covered
with a clean tea towel, before turning
onto a wire rack to cool. Store in an airtight
container or in plastic wrap for up to 4 weeks.

CASHEW MERINGUE CAKE

Preparation time: 30 minutes + cooling
Total cooking time: 45 minutes
Serves 8–10

Cashew Meringue
300 g (10 oz) cashews
8 egg whites
1½ cups (375 g/12 oz) caster sugar
2 teaspoons vanilla essence
2 teaspoons white vinegar

Fillings
250 g (8 oz) unsalted butter, softened
1 cup (125 g/4 oz) icing sugar
4 tablespoons Crème de Cacao
2 cups (500 ml/16 fl oz) cream
1 tablespoon orange liqueur
2 teaspoons vanilla essence
chocolate curls and cocoa powder, for
    decoration

1 To make Cashew Meringue: Preheat the
oven to moderate 180°C (350°F/Gas 4).
Spread the cashews on a baking tray and
toast them in the oven for 5 minutes or
until golden, stirring occasionally to turn
them over. Check frequently to make sure
they don't burn. Remove the cashews
from the oven and allow to cool. Place the
cashews in a food processor and process
them in short bursts until finely ground.
2 Reduce the oven temperature to slow
150°C (300°F/Gas 2). Line 4 oven trays
with non-stick baking paper and draw a
21 cm (8½ inch) diameter circle on each
piece of paper.

3 Beat the egg whites in a large, clean,
dry bowl until soft peaks form. Gradually
add the sugar to the bowl, beating well
after each addition, until the whites are
thick and glossy. Using a metal spoon,
fold in the vanilla, vinegar and ground
cashews.
4 Divide the mixture evenly among the
4 circles and carefully spread it to the
edge of each circle. Bake the meringues
for 45 minutes or until they are crisp.
Turn the oven off and allow the
meringues to cool in the oven, leaving the
oven door ajar.
5 To make Fillings: Place the butter, icing
sugar and Crème de Cacao in a bowl and
beat until the mixture becomes light and
creamy. Set aside. Place the cream,
orange liqueur and vanilla essence in a
separate bowl and beat until soft peaks
form.
6 Place 1 meringue circle on a serving
plate and carefully spread it with half the
butter mixture. Place a second meringue
circle on top and spread it with half the
orange cream mixture. Repeat with the
remaining meringue circles, butter
mixture and orange cream mixture.
7 The top of the meringue cake can be
decorated with chocolate curls and
dusted lightly with cocoa. Carefully cut
into sections for serving.

CHERRY PIE

Preparation time: 25 minutes + chilling
Total cooking time: 40 minutes
Serves 6–8

Almond pastry
1¼ cups (155 g/5 oz) plain flour
¼ cup (30 g/1 oz) icing sugar
100 g (3½ oz) chilled unsalted butter,
    chopped
60 g (2 oz) ground almonds
3 tablespoons chilled water

2 x 700 g (1 lb 7 oz) jars pitted morello
    cherries, drained
1 egg, lightly beaten
caster sugar, to decorate
cream or ice cream, optional, for serving

1 Sift the flour and icing sugar into a bowl.
Add the butter and rub in with just your
fingertips until the mixture is fine and
crumbly. Stir in the ground almonds, then
add almost all the water and stir into the
flour mixture with a flat-bladed knife until
the mixture forms a dough, adding the
remaining water if necessary.
2 Turn the dough onto a lightly floured
surface and gather together into a ball.
Roll out on a sheet of baking paper into a
circle about 26 cm (10½ inches) in
diameter. Flatten slightly, cover with
plastic wrap and refrigerate for 20 minutes.
Spread the cherries into a 23 cm (9 inch)
round pie dish.
3 Preheat the oven to moderately hot
200°C (400°F/Gas 6). Cover the pie dish
with the pastry and trim the overhanging
edge. Roll out the remaining scraps of
pastry and use a small sharp knife to cut
out decorations. Brush the pastry top all
over with beaten egg and arrange the
decorations on top. Brush these with
beaten egg as well, and then sprinkle
lightly with caster sugar. Place the pie
dish on a baking tray (the cherry juice may
overflow a little) and cook for 35–40 minutes,
or until golden brown. Serve warm or at room
temperature, with cream or ice cream.

HALVAS FOURNO
(SEMOLINA CAKE)

Preparation time: 20 minutes
Total cooking time: 1 hour
Serves 6–8

Syrup
2½ cups (625 g/1 lb 5 oz) sugar
2 tablespoons lemon juice

125 g (4 oz) unsalted butter
¾ cup (185 g/6 oz) caster sugar
2 teaspoons finely grated lemon rind
3 eggs
1½ cups (185 g/6 oz) semolina
1 cup (125 g/4 oz) self-raising flour
½ cup (125 ml/4 fl oz) milk
½ cup (80 g/2¾ oz) blanched almonds,
   toasted and finely chopped
blanched flaked almonds, to decorate

1 Preheat the oven to warm 170°C
(325°F/Gas 3). Grease a 30 x 20 cm
(12 x 8 inch) cake tin.
2 In a saucepan, dissolve the sugar in
3 cups (750 ml/24 fl oz) water over high
heat, add the lemon juice and bring to the
boil. Reduce the heat to medium and
simmer for 20 minutes. Remove from the
heat and leave until cool.
3 While the syrup is cooking, cream the
butter, sugar and lemon rind with electric
beaters until light and fluffy. Add the eggs
one at a time, beating well after each
addition.
4 Sift together the semolina and flour and
fold into butter mixture alternately with
the milk. Mix in the chopped almonds,
then spread the mixture into the tin and
arrange rows of flaked almonds on top.
Bake for 35–40 minutes, or until the cake
is golden and shrinks slightly from the
sides of the tin. Prick the surface with a
fine skewer, then pour the cooled syrup
over the hot cake. When the cake is cool,
cut it into squares or diamonds.

BANANA AND BLUEBERRY TART

Preparation time: 30 minutes
Total cooking time: 25 minutes
Serves 6

cooking oil spray
1 cup (125 g/4 oz) plain flour
½ cup (60 g/2 oz) self-raising flour
1 teaspoon cinnamon
1 teaspoon ground ginger
40 g (1¼ oz) butter, chopped
½ cup (95 g/3 oz) soft brown sugar
½ cup (125 ml/4 fl oz) buttermilk
200 g (6½ oz) blueberries
2 bananas
2 teaspoons lemon juice
1 tablespoon demerara sugar

1 Preheat the oven to moderately hot
200°C (400°F/Gas 6). Spray a baking tray
or pizza tray lightly with oil. Sift both the
flours and the spices into a bowl. Add the
butter and brown sugar, and rub in with
your fingertips until the butter is
combined well with the flour. Make a well
in the centre and add enough buttermilk
to mix to a soft dough.
2 Roll the dough out on a lightly floured
surface to a 23 cm (9 inch) diameter
round. Place on the tray and roll the edge
to form a lip to hold the fruit in.
3 Spread the blueberries over the dough,
keeping them within the lip. Slice the
bananas and toss the slices in the lemon
juice. Arrange the banana evenly over the
top of the blueberries, then sprinkle
with the demerara sugar and bake for
25 minutes, or until the base is browned.
Serve immediately.

NOTE: The dough for this tart can be
made in a food processor if you wish. The
fruit topping can be varied by using
raspberries. Other soft or stoned fruit
also work very well.

BANOFFIE PIE

Preparation time: 35 minutes + chilling
Total cooking time: 30 minutes
Serves 8

Walnut pastry
1¼ cups (155 g/5 oz) plain flour
2 tablespoons icing sugar
85 g (3 oz) ground walnuts
80 g (2¾ oz) chilled unsalted butter,
   chopped

Filling
400 g (13 oz) can condensed milk
30 g (1 oz) unsalted butter
1 tablespoon golden syrup
4 bananas, sliced
1½ cups (375 ml/12 fl oz) cream, whipped
50 g (1¾ oz) dark chocolate, melted

1 To make the walnut pastry, sift the flour
and icing sugar into a large bowl. Add the
walnuts and butter and rub the butter into
the flour, using just your fingertips, until
the mixture resembles breadcrumbs. Mix
in 2–3 tablespoons chilled water with a
flat-bladed knife to form a firm dough. Add
more water if needed. Turn onto a floured
surface and gather together into a ball.
Wrap and chill for 15 minutes. Roll out to fit
a 23 cm (9 inch) flan tin; chill for 20 minutes.
2 Preheat the oven to moderate 180°C
(350°F/Gas 4). Line the pastry base with
crumpled baking paper and spread
baking beads or rice over paper. Bake for
15 minutes, then remove the paper and
beads. Bake the pastry for 10 minutes, or until
lightly golden. Set aside to cool completely.
3 To make the filling, place the condensed
milk, butter and golden syrup in a small
pan. Stir over medium heat for 5 minutes,
until it boils and thickens and turns a light
caramel colour. Cool slightly, then arrange
half the bananas over the pastry and pour
the caramel over the top. Smooth the
surface and chill for 30 minutes.
4 Drop spoonfuls of cream over the caramel
and arrange the remaining banana on top.
Drizzle with melted chocolate.

TOURTE DE BLETTES
(APPLE, SILVERBEET/SWISS CHARD AND PINE NUT PIE)

Preparation time: 30 minutes +
    30 minutes refrigeration
Total cooking time: 50 minutes
Serves 6–8

60 g (2 oz) sultanas
2 tablespoons brandy
400 g (13 oz) plain flour
100 g (3½ oz) icing sugar
250 g (8 oz) unsalted butter, softened and
    chopped
3 eggs
800 g (1 lb 10 oz) silverbeet (Swiss chard),
    stalks removed
100 g (3½ oz) pine nuts, toasted
3 green cooking apples
1 teaspoon grated lemon rind
115 g (4 oz) mild goat's cheese
1 egg yolk, extra, for glazing
icing sugar, extra, for dusting

1 Soak the sultanas in the brandy. Sift the
flour and 1 tablespoon icing sugar into a
large bowl and rub in the butter with your
fingertips until the mixture resembles
fine breadcrumbs. Make a well, add 1 egg
and mix with a flat-bladed knife, using a
cutting action, until the mixture comes
together in beads. Add 1 tablespoon water
if the mixture is a little dry. Gather
together and lift onto a lightly floured
work surface. Press into a ball and flatten
to a disc. Wrap in plastic wrap and
refrigerate for 30 minutes.
2 Preheat the oven to moderate 180°C
(350°F/Gas 4). Heat a baking tray in the
oven.

3 Wash the silverbeet and pat dry. Place
in a food processor with 2 eggs and the
remaining icing sugar. Process to chop
the silverbeet and combine, but don't
overprocess. Transfer to a bowl. Drain
the sultanas and add to the bowl with the
pine nuts. Season with salt and pepper.
4 Bring the pastry to room temperature,
then break into two portions. Roll one half
and use to line a 26 cm (10½ inch) loose-
based tart tin.
5 Peel the apples, slice thinly and toss
with the lemon rind. Place the silverbeet
on the pastry and top with the crumbled
goat's cheese. Spiral the apples on top,
making one or two layers.
6 Roll out the remaining pastry and cover
the pie. Trim off the excess pastry and
seal the edges with a little water. Crimp
the edges.
7 Brush the pie with the egg yolk and
bake for 45–50 minutes, until golden.
Cool slightly. Dust with icing sugar. Serve
warm.

YOGHURT CAKE WITH SYRUP

Preparation time: 20 minutes + cooling
Total cooking time: 50 minutes
Serves 8–10

185 g (6 oz) unsalted butter, softened
1 cup (250 g/8 oz) caster sugar
5 eggs, separated
1 cup (250 g/8 oz) Greek-style yoghurt
2 teaspoons grated lemon rind
½ teaspoon vanilla essence
2¼ cups (280 g/9 oz) plain flour
½ teaspoon bicarbonate of soda
2 teaspoons baking powder
whipped cream, for serving

Syrup
1 cup (250 g/8 oz) caster sugar
1 cinnamon stick
4 cm (1½ inch) strip lemon rind
1 tablespoon lemon juice

1 Preheat the oven to moderate 180°C
(350°F/Gas 4) and lightly grease a 20 x 10
cm (8 x 4 inch) loaf tin.
2 Cream the butter and sugar in a bowl
with electric beaters until light and fluffy.
Add the egg yolks gradually, beating well
after each addition. Stir in the yoghurt,
lemon rind and vanilla essence. Fold in
the sifted flour, bicarbonate of soda and
baking powder with a metal spoon.
3 Whisk the egg whites in a clean, dry
bowl until stiff and gently fold into the
mixture. Spoon into the tin and bake for
50 minutes, or until a skewer comes out
clean when inserted into the centre of the
cake. Cool, then turn out onto a wire rack.
4 Meanwhile, place the sugar and
cinnamon stick in a small saucepan with
¾ cup (185 ml/6 fl oz) cold water. Stir over
medium heat until the sugar has dissolved.
Bring to the boil, add the lemon rind and
juice, then reduce the heat and simmer for
5–6 minutes. Strain, then pour the syrup
over the hot cake and wait for most of it to
be absorbed. Cut into slices and serve
warm with whipped cream.

PINEAPPLE SAVARIN

Preparation time: 40 minutes + rising
Total cooking time: 40 minutes
Serves 6–8

7 g (¼ oz) dried yeast
⅔ cup (170 ml/5½ fl oz) unsweetened
   pineapple juice, warmed
2 teaspoons caster sugar
2 cups (250 g/8 oz) plain flour
3 eggs, lightly beaten
90 g (3 oz) unsalted butter, softened

Rum syrup
1 cup (250 g/8 oz) caster sugar
1½ cups (375 ml/12 fl oz) unsweetened
   pineapple juice
5 cm (2 inch) piece lemon rind
½ cup (125 ml/4 fl oz) dark rum

1 Grease a 25 cm (10 inch) deep savarin ring. Dissolve the yeast in the pineapple juice, then stir in the sugar. Set aside for 5 minutes, or until frothy. Sift the flour and ¼ teaspoon salt into a large bowl. Add the yeast and eggs and beat with a cupped hand for 5 minutes. Add the butter and beat by hand for 5 minutes. Cover and set aside in a warm place for 45 minutes, or until bubbly and well-risen. Press down on the dough to push the air out, and beat by hand for 1–2 minutes.

2 Ladle into the ring and cover loosely with plastic wrap. Set aside in a warm place for 10 minutes. Preheat the oven to moderately hot 190°C (375°F/Gas 5). Bake on a baking tray for 25 minutes, or until firm and golden (it may overflow a little in the centre).
3 Meanwhile, to make the rum syrup, stir the sugar, juice and rind in a small pan over low heat until the sugar has dissolved. Bring to the boil and boil, without stirring, for 10–15 minutes, or until slightly thickened. Remove the rind. Add the rum.
4 When the savarin is cooked, trim to a flat base with a knife. Turn out of the tin and stand on a rack over a tray. Prick all over with a toothpick. While the savarin is still hot, drizzle with rum syrup, pouring the excess back from where it is caught in the tray, until all the syrup is absorbed.

BOILED GINGER FRUIT CAKE

Preparation time: 20 minutes
Total cooking time: 2 hours
Makes 1

1¼ cups (155 g/5 oz) self-raising flour
1¼ cups (155 g/5 oz) plain flour
250 g (8 oz) unsalted butter
1 cup (230 g/7½ oz) dark brown sugar
1 cup (160 g/5½ oz) pitted dried dates,
   chopped
1⅔ cups (270 g/9 oz) raisins, chopped
1⅔ cups (270 g/9 oz) sultanas
½ cup (110 g/3½ oz) chopped glacé ginger
⅔ cup (170 ml/5½ fl oz) green ginger wine
⅓ cup (80 ml/2¾ fl oz) apple juice
2 teaspoons ground ginger
½ teaspoon bicarbonate of soda
2 eggs, lightly beaten
2–3 tablespoons green ginger wine, extra

1 Sift the flours into a large bowl and make a well in the centre. Combine the butter in a large saucepan with the sugar, fruit, green ginger wine, apple juice and ground ginger. Stir over low heat until the butter has melted and the sugar has dissolved. Bring to the boil, then reduce the heat and simmer for 5 minutes. Remove from the heat, stir in the bicarbonate of soda and set aside to cool.
2 Preheat the oven to moderate 180°C (350°F/Gas 4). Grease and line a deep 20 cm (8 inch) square or 23 cm (9 inch) round cake tin.
3 Mix one egg at a time into the fruit, then add the mixture to the well in the flour and stir until just combined—don't overmix. Spoon into the tin, tap the tin on the bench to remove any air bubbles and smooth the surface with wet fingers. Wrap newspaper around the outside of the tin. Sit the tin on several layers of newspaper in the oven and bake for 1½–1¾ hours, or until a skewer comes out clean.
4 Drizzle the hot cake with green ginger wine. Cool in the tin, covered with a clean tea towel, then store in an airtight container or plastic wrap for up to 2 months.

BANANA TART

Preparation time: 40 minutes + chilling
Total cooking time: 35 minutes
Serves 6

Flaky pastry
1¾ cups (215 g/7 oz) plain flour
160 g (5½ oz) unsalted butter (chill 100
g/3½ oz of it)

rind and juice of 2 oranges
4 tablespoons soft brown sugar
¼ teaspoon cardamom seeds
1 tablespoon rum
3–4 ripe bananas

1 For the pastry, sift the flour into a bowl with a pinch of salt and rub in the unchilled butter. Add enough water (about 155 ml/5 fl oz), mixing with a flat-bladed knife to make a dough-like consistency. Turn onto a floured surface and knead until just smooth. Roll into a rectangle 10 x 30 cm (4 x 12 inches), cut a third of the chilled butter into cubes and dot all over the top two-thirds of the pastry, leaving a little room around the edge. Fold the bottom third of the pastry up and the top third down and press the edges down to seal. Now turn the pastry to your left, so the hinge is on your right, and roll and fold as before. Chill for 20 minutes, then with the hinge to your right, roll it out again, cover the top two-thirds of the pastry with another third of the butter and roll and fold. Repeat, using the rest of the butter and then roll and fold once more without adding any butter.

2 Roll the pastry out on a floured surface into a rectangle 25 x 30 cm (10 x 12 inches), cut a 2 cm (¾ inch) strip off each side and use this to make a frame on the pastry by brushing the edges of the pastry with water and sticking the strips onto it. Trim off any excess and put the tart base on a baking tray lined with baking paper, cover with plastic wrap and refrigerate until required.
3 Combine the orange rind, juice, brown sugar and cardamom seeds in a small pan, bring to the boil, simmer for 5 minutes, then remove from the heat and add the rum. Set aside to cool. Preheat the oven to hot 220°C (425°F/Gas 7).
4 Slice the bananas in half lengthways, arrange on the tart in an even layer, cut-side-up and brush with a little syrup. Bake on the top shelf for 20–30 minutes, making sure the pastry does not overbrown. Brush with syrup and serve.

CHERRY CHEESE STRUDEL

Preparation time: 25 minutes
Total cooking time: 35–40 minutes
Serves 8–10

500 g (1 lb) ricotta
2 teaspoons lemon or orange rind
¼ cup (60 g/2 oz) sugar
½ cup (40 g/1¼ oz) fresh breadcrumbs
2 tablespoons ground almonds
2 eggs
425 g (14 oz) can pitted black cherries
2 teaspoons cornflour
8 sheets filo pastry
60 g (2 oz) unsalted butter, melted
2 tablespoons dry breadcrumbs
icing sugar, to dust

1 Preheat the oven to moderate 180°C (350°F/Gas 4). Lightly grease a baking tray with melted butter. Combine the ricotta, rind, sugar, breadcrumbs and almonds in a bowl. Add the eggs and mix well. Drain the cherries, reserving half the juice. Blend the cornflour with the reserved cherry juice in a small pan. Stir over heat until the mixture boils and thickens, then cool slightly.
2 Layer the pastry sheets, brushing between each sheet with melted butter and sprinkling with a few breadcrumbs. Form a large square by placing the second sheet halfway down the first sheet. Alternate layers, brushing with melted butter and sprinkling with breadcrumbs.
3 Place the ricotta mixture along one long edge of the pastry. Shape into a log and top with cherries and cooled syrup. Roll the pastry around the ricotta filling, folding in the edges as you roll. Finish with a pastry edge underneath. Place on the prepared tray and bake for 35–40 minutes, or until the pastry is golden. Serve in slices, warm or cold, heavily dusted with icing sugar. Can be served with cream.

BLACK FOREST GATEAU

Preparation time: 1 hour + standing
Total cooking time: 50–60 minutes
Serves 8–10

125 g (4 oz) unsalted butter
1 cup (250 g/8 oz) caster sugar
2 eggs, lightly beaten
1 teaspoon vanilla essence
⅓ cup (40 g/1¼ oz) self-raising flour
1 cup (125 g/4 oz) plain flour
1 teaspoon bicarbonate of soda
½ cup (60 g/2 oz) cocoa powder
¾ cup (185 ml/6 fl oz) buttermilk

Filling
¼ cup (60 ml/2 fl oz) Kirsch
3 cups (750 ml/24 fl oz) cream, whipped
425 g (14 oz) can pitted morello or black
   cherries, drained

Topping
100 g (3½ oz) good-quality dark chocolate
100 g (3½ oz) milk chocolate
cherries with stalks, to decorate

1 Preheat the oven to moderate 180°C
(350°F/Gas 4). Brush a deep, 20 cm
(8 inch) round cake tin with oil or melted
butter. Line the base and side with
baking paper.
2 Using electric beaters, beat the butter
and sugar until light and creamy. Add the
eggs gradually, beating well after each
addition. Add the vanilla essence and beat
until well combined. Transfer to a large
bowl. Using a metal spoon, fold in the
sifted flours, bicarbonate of soda and
cocoa alternately with the buttermilk.
Mix until combined and the mixture is
smooth.
3 Pour the mixture into the tin and
smooth the surface. Bake for
50–60 minutes, or until a skewer comes
out clean when inserted into the centre.
Leave the cake in the tin for 30 minutes
before turning it onto a wire rack to cool.

When cold, cut horizontally into 3 layers,
using a long serrated knife. The easiest
way to do this is to rest the palm of one
hand lightly on top of the cake while
cutting into it. Turn the cake every few
strokes so the knife cuts in evenly all the
way around the edge. When you have
gone the whole way round, cut through
the middle. Remove the first layer so it
will be easier to see what you are doing
while cutting the next one.
4 To make chocolate shavings, leave the
chocolate in a warm place for
10–15 minutes, or until soft but still firm.
With a vegetable peeler, and using long
strokes, shave curls of chocolate from the
side of the block. If the block is too soft,
chill it to firm it up. Making curls takes a
little practice to perfect (see page 924).
5 To assemble, place one cake layer on a
serving plate and brush liberally with
Kirsch. Spread evenly with one-fifth of the
whipped cream. Top with half the
cherries. Continue layering with the
remaining cake, cream and liqueur
cherries, finishing with the cream on top.
Spread the cream evenly on the outside of
the cake. Coat the side with chocolate
shavings by laying the shavings on a small
piece of greaseproof and then gently
pressing them into the cream. If you use
your hands, they will melt, so the paper
acts as a barrier. Pipe rosettes of cream
around the top edge of the cake and
decorate with fresh or maraschino
cherries on stalks and more chocolate
shavings.

NOTE: Black Forest gateau is probably
one of the most famous cakes in the
world. It originated in Swabia in the Black
Forest region and is always flavoured with
Kirsch, a colourless cherry liqueur.

CHARLOTTE MALAKOFF

Preparation time: 1 hour + chilling
Total cooking time: Nil
Serves 8–12

250 g (8 oz) sponge finger biscuits
½ cup (125 ml/4 fl oz) Grand Marnier
500 g (1 lb) strawberries, hulled and halved
whipped cream and strawberries, for serving

Almond cream
125 g (4 oz) unsalted butter
⅓ cup (90 g/3 oz) caster sugar
¼ cup (60 ml/2 fl oz) Grand Marnier
¼ teaspoon almond essence
¾ cup (185 ml/6 fl oz) cream, whipped
140 g (4½ oz) ground almonds

1 Brush a deep 1–1.5 litre soufflé dish with
melted butter or oil. Line the base with
greaseproof paper and grease the paper.
Trim the sponge finger biscuits to fit the
sides of the dish. Quickly dip the sponge
fingers into the liqueur that has been
mixed with ½ cup (125 ml/4 fl oz) water.
Arrange upright around the side of the
dish, rounded-side-down.
2 To make the almond cream, using
electric beaters, beat the butter and
sugar until light and creamy. Add the
liqueur and almond essence. Continue
beating until the mixture is smooth and
the sugar has dissolved. Using a metal
spoon, fold in the cream and almonds.
3 Spoon one-third of the almond cream
into the base of the dish and cover with
strawberry halves. Top with a layer of
dipped sponge fingers. Continue layering,
finishing with a layer of sponge fingers,
then press down.
4 Cover with foil and place a small plate
and weight on top. Refrigerate for 8
hours, or overnight. Remove the plate and
foil and turn onto a chilled serving plate.
Remove the greaseproof paper. Decorate
with whipped cream and strawberries.

NOTE: This dessert is very rich and should
be served after a light main course.

LINING CAKE TINS

IF YOU PUT A LITTLE EXTRA TIME AND EFFORT INTO THE PREPARATION OF THE TINS, YOU SHOULDN'T END UP WITH MISSHAPEN CAKES OR ROUND EDGES ON SQUARE CAKES.

CHOOSING THE CAKE TIN

Choose and prepare the cake tin well before you make the mixture. Cake tins not only come in the round and square type but also in the shape of bells, flowers, hearts and diamonds. Most tins are aluminium, but some are made of tin, specially treated to make them food safe. The size of tins given in recipes is for the measurement across the base. If you want to use a different tin from the one stated you will need to use a tin with the same capacity. So if the recipe asks for a 20 cm (8 inch) round cake tin, fill a tin this size with water, gradually transfer the water into the chosen tin, and keep doing so until the chosen tin is full. In this way, you can work out how many quantities of mixture are required to fill the tin.

HOW MUCH LINING?

Average-sized cakes or fruit cakes that are not in the oven for extended cooking times only require a single layer of baking paper to line the base and side. However, cakes that are much larger or those that require long cooking times (most fruit cakes) need extra protection from burning, both around the side and under the base of the tin. Extra layers of baking paper are used inside the tin and newspaper is wrapped around the outside. Several layers of newspaper are also put under the tin, on the oven shelf.

SUCCESSFUL LINING

Lightly grease the cake tin with melted butter or a mild-flavoured vegetable oil. This helps keep the paper in place. Cut a double layer of paper into a strip long enough to fit around the outside of the tin and tall enough to come 5 cm (2 inches) above the edge of the tin. Fold down a cuff about 2 cm (¾ inch) deep along the length of the strip, along the folded edges. Make diagonal cuts up to the fold line on each strip about 1 cm (½ inch) apart. Fit the strip around the inside of the tin, with the cuts on the base, pressing the cuts out at right angles so they sit flat around the base. Place the cake tin on a doubled piece of baking paper and draw around the edge. Cut it out and sit it on the base of the tin, over the cuts. Most cake tins

can be lined successfully this way. Before you turn on the oven, prepare your cake tin following these instructions and have the oven shelves in the correct position to accommodate the lined tin. Cakes are normally cooked on the third shelf. Spoon the prepared cake mixture into the tin, ensuring it is pushed well into corners and edges. Tap the tin on the bench to remove any air bubbles. Smooth the top with fingers dipped in water and decorate the top with fruit or nuts if desired. To prevent the cake burning on the outside, fold over several sheets of newspaper long enough to wrap around the side of the cake tin and to come a little higher than the baking paper. Tie around the tin securely with string and sit the tin on several layers of folded newspaper on the oven shelf. Because the oven temperature

is low, it is quite safe to have the paper in the oven. Some people also like to use a layer of brown paper and a layer of baking paper.

When the cake is completely cold, remove it from the tin, then remove the paper. If there is a wet spot on the base of the cake, return the cake to the tin and cook for another hour, or until dried out. If the edges and side of the cake feel a little dry, brush well all over with extra brandy or rum and wrap in plastic wrap. When you are happy with the cake and it is cold, wrap firmly in plastic wrap and store in an airtight container. Most fruit cakes will keep for 8–12 months. Cakes containing nuts only keep for up to 3 months. Fruit cakes can be frozen.

BUTTERSCOTCH TART

Preparation time: 30 minutes + chilling
Total cooking time: 1 hour
Makes one tart

Shortcrust pastry
2 cups (250 g/8 oz) plain flour
125 g (4 oz) chilled unsalted butter, chopped
2 tablespoons caster sugar
1 egg yolk
1 tablespoon chilled water

Butterscotch filling
1 cup (185 g/6 oz) soft brown sugar
⅓ cup (40 g/1¼ oz) plain flour
1 cup (250 ml/8 fl oz) milk
45 g (1½ oz) unsalted butter
1 teaspoon vanilla essence
1 egg yolk

Meringue
2 egg whites
2 tablespoons caster sugar

1 Preheat the oven to moderate 180°C (350°F/Gas 4). Grease a deep, 22 cm (9 inch) flan tin. Sift the flour into a large bowl and rub in the butter with your fingertips until the mixture resembles breadcrumbs. Stir in the sugar, yolk and water. Mix to a soft dough, then gather into a ball. Wrap and chill for 20 minutes.

2 Roll the pastry between two sheets of baking paper, to cover the base and side of the tin. Trim the edge and prick the pastry evenly with a fork. Chill again for 20 minutes. Line the pastry with a sheet of crumpled baking paper and spread baking beads or rice over the paper. Bake for 35 minutes, then remove the paper and beads.
3 For the filling, place the sugar and flour in a small pan. Make a well and gradually whisk in the milk to form a smooth paste. Add the butter and stir with a whisk over low heat for 8 minutes, or until the mixture boils and thickens. Remove from the heat, add the essence and yolk and whisk until smooth. Spread into the pastry case and smooth the surface.
4 Beat the egg whites until firm peaks form. Add the sugar gradually, beating until thick and glossy and all the sugar has dissolved. Spoon over the filling and swirl into peaks with a fork or flat-bladed knife. Bake for 5–10 minutes, or until the meringue is golden. Serve warm or cold.

ALMOND ORANGE SYRUP PUDDING

Preparation time: 45 minutes
Total cooking time: 50 minutes
Serves 6–8

125 g (4 oz) unsalted butter
¾ cup (185 g/6 oz) caster sugar
2 eggs, lightly beaten
3 teaspoons finely grated orange rind
1½ cups (280 g/9 oz) ground almonds
1 cup (125 g/4 oz) semolina
¼ cup (60 ml/2 fl oz) orange juice
250 g (8 oz) blueberries, to decorate
icing sugar, to dust
thick (double) cream, optional, for serving

Syrup
1 cup (250 ml/8 fl oz) orange juice, strained
½ cup (125 g/4 oz) caster sugar

1 Preheat the oven to moderate 180°C (350°F/Gas 4). Lightly brush a 20 cm (8 inch) ring tin with oil or melted butter and line the base with baking paper.
2 Using electric beaters, beat the butter and sugar in a small bowl until light and creamy. Add the eggs gradually, beating well after each addition. Add the rind and beat to combine.
3 Transfer to a large bowl. Using a metal spoon, fold in the almonds and semolina alternately with the juice. Stir until just combined and the mixture is smooth. Spoon into the tin and smooth the surface. Bake for 40 minutes, or until a skewer comes out clean.
4 To make the syrup, stir the juice and sugar in a small pan over low heat, until the sugar completely dissolves. Bring to the boil, reduce the heat slightly and simmer for 10 minutes. Remove from the heat and cool slightly.
5 Pour half the warm syrup over the warm cake while still in the tin. Leave for 3 minutes, then place the cake onto a serving plate. Brush the remaining syrup over the cake, then allow to cool. Fill the centre with blueberries dusted with icing sugar.

CUSTARD TART

Preparation time: 20 minutes + chilling
Total cooking time: 1 hour
Serves 8

1½ cups (185 g/6 oz) plain flour
¼ cup (30 g/1 oz) custard powder
125 g (4 oz) chilled unsalted butter,
    chopped
1½ tablespoons caster sugar
1 egg yolk

Custard
4 eggs, lightly beaten
2 teaspoons vanilla essence
½ cup (125 g/4 oz) caster sugar
1½ cups (375 ml/12 fl oz) milk
¼ teaspoon ground nutmeg

1 Sift the flour and custard powder into a bowl. Using just your fingertips, rub in the butter until the mixture resembles breadcrumbs. Stir in the sugar, then use a flat-bladed knife to mix in the yolk and 1–2 tablespoons water, to form a soft dough. Wrap in plastic and chill for 30 minutes.
2 Preheat the oven to moderately hot 190°C (375°F/Gas 5). Lightly grease a pie plate, about 20 cm (8 inch) diameter. Roll the pastry out between two sheets of baking paper and line the base and side of the plate. Trim the edge with a sharp knife. Make a decorative edge if you wish. Line with crumpled baking paper, fill with baking beads or rice and bake for 10 minutes. Remove the paper and beads and bake for 5 minutes, or until the base is dry (cover the edges with foil if overbrowning). Cool. Reduce the oven to moderate 180°C (350°F/Gas 4).
3 To make the custard, mix together the eggs, vanilla essence and sugar. Bring the milk to the boil, remove from the heat and gradually pour onto the egg mixture. Place the pie plate on a baking tray, strain the egg mixture into the pastry case and sprinkle with ground nutmeg. Bake for 40 minutes, or until just set in the centre. Allow to cool and serve cut into wedges.

REAL LEMON PIE

Preparation time: 30 minutes + standing
Total cooking time: 50–55 minutes
Serves 8–10

Lemon filling
4 thin-skinned lemons
2 cups (500 g/1 lb) caster sugar
4 eggs

Shortcrust pastry
1¾ cups (220 g/7 oz) plain flour
150 g (5 oz) chilled unsalted butter,
    chopped
2 tablespoons caster sugar
milk, for glazing

1 Wash the lemons. Slice 2 unpeeled lemons very thinly and remove the seeds. Peel the other lemons, removing all the pith, and slice the flesh very thinly. Remove the seeds. Put all the lemons in a bowl with the sugar and stir until all the slices are coated. Cover and leave overnight.
2 Preheat the oven to moderate 180°C (350°F/Gas 4). Sift the flour and a pinch of salt into a bowl. Use your fingertips to rub in the butter until crumbly. Stir in the sugar. Gradually add 1–2 tablespoons water, mixing with a knife. Gather the dough together, divide in half and roll each portion into a 25 cm (10 inch) circle. Lightly grease a 23 cm (9 inch) pie dish and line with pastry. Cover and chill the other circle.

3 Beat the eggs and add to the lemon slices, mixing gently but thoroughly. Spoon into the pastry shell and cover with the pastry circle, crimping the edges to seal. Decorate the top with pastry scraps, brush with milk and bake for 50–55 minutes, or until golden brown.

NOTE: To use this pastry for a delicious apple pie, peel, core and slice 5 apples into thin slices, toss the apple slices in 3 tablespoons caster sugar and a large pinch of cinnamon and fill the pie. Cover with the pastry lid and press the edges together to seal. Trim the edges and make two or three slashes in the top of the the the pie. Dust with 1 tablespoon caster sugar and bake in a preheated moderate 180°C (350°F/Gas 4) oven for 50 minutes.

PRUNE AND ALMOND TART

Preparation time: 1 hour + soaking +
    chilling
Total cooking time: 50 minutes
Serves 6–8

375 g (12 oz) pitted prunes
⅔ cup (170 ml/5½ fl oz) brandy
⅓ cup (105 g/3½ oz) redcurrant jelly

Almond pastry
1½ cups (185 g/6 oz) plain flour
125 g (4 oz) chilled unsalted butter,
    chopped
⅓ cup (60 g/2 oz) ground almonds
¼ cup (60 g/2 oz) caster sugar
1 egg yolk
2–3 tablespoons chilled water
50 g (1¾ oz) marzipan, grated

Custard cream
¼ cup (30 g/1 oz) custard powder
1⅔ cups (410 ml/13 fl oz) milk
1 tablespoon caster sugar
½ cup (125 g/4 oz) sour cream
2 teaspoons vanilla essence

1 Put the prunes in a pan with the brandy,
leave to soak for 1 hour, then simmer over
very low heat for 10 minutes, or until the
prunes are tender but not mushy. Remove
the prunes with a slotted spoon and leave
to cool. Add the redcurrant jelly to the pan
and stir over low heat until dissolved.
Cover and set aside.
2 To make the almond pastry, sift the
flour into a large bowl. Rub in the butter
with just your fingertips, until the mixture
resembles breadcrumbs. Stir in the
almonds and sugar using a flat-bladed
knife. Add the egg yolk and water, until
the dough just comes together. Turn out
onto a lightly floured surface and gather
together into a ball. Flatten slightly, cover
with plastic wrap and refrigerate for
15 minutes. Preheat the oven to moderate
180°C (350°F/Gas 4) and heat a baking
tray.

3 Roll out the chilled pastry between
2 sheets of baking paper until large
enough to line the base and side of a
lightly greased 23 cm (9 inch) loose-
bottomed flan tin. Ease the pastry into the
tin and trim the edge. Refrigerate for
15 minutes. Line the pastry with a sheet of
crumpled baking paper and spread a
layer of baking beads or rice evenly over
the paper, then bake on the heated baking
tray for 15 minutes.
4 Remove the paper and beads and bake
the pastry for another 5 minutes. Reduce
the heat to warm 160°C (315°F/Gas 2–3).
Sprinkle marzipan over the pastry base,
then bake for another 5–10 minutes, or
until golden. Leave in the tin to cool.
5 To make the custard cream, in a small
bowl, mix the custard powder with a little
milk until smooth. Transfer to a pan and
add the remaining milk and sugar. Stir
over medium heat for 5 minutes, or until
the mixture boils and thickens. Stir in the
sour cream and vanilla essence, remove
from the heat and cover the surface with
plastic wrap to prevent a skin forming.
Allow to cool slightly.
6 Spread the custard cream, while it is
still warm, evenly over the pastry case.
Cut the prunes in half lengthways and
arrange over the custard. Warm the
redcurrant mixture and carefully spoon
over the tart to cover it completely.
Refrigerate for at least 2 hours to allow
the custard to firm before serving.

CHOCOLATE RICOTTA TART

Preparation time: 20 minutes + chilling
Total cooking time: 1 hour
Serves 8–10

1½ cups (185 g/6 oz) plain flour
100 g (3½ oz) unsalted butter, chopped
2 tablespoons caster sugar

Filling
1.25 kg (2½ lb) ricotta
½ cup (125 g/4 oz) caster sugar
2 tablespoons plain flour
1 teaspoon instant coffee
125 g (4 oz) chocolate, finely chopped
4 egg yolks
40 g (1¼ oz) chocolate, extra
½ teaspoon vegetable oil

1 Sift the flour into a large bowl and adding
the butter. Rub the butter into the flour
with your fingertips, until fine and crumbly.
Stir in the sugar. Add 3 tablespoons cold
water and cut with a knife to form a
dough, adding a little more water if
necessary. Turn out onto a lightly floured
surface and gather together into a ball.
Lightly grease a 25 cm (10 inch) diameter
springform tin. Roll out the dough, then
line the tin so that the pastry comes about
two-thirds of the way up the side. Cover
and refrigerate while making the filling.
2 To make the filling, mix together the
ricotta, sugar, flour and a pinch of salt until
smooth. Dissolve the coffee in 2 teaspoons
hot water. Stir into the ricotta mixture, with
the chocolate and egg yolks, until mixed.
Spoon into the pastry shell and smooth.
Chill for 30 minutes, or until firm. Preheat
the oven to moderate 180°C (350°F/Gas 4).
3 Put the springform tin on a baking tray.
Bake for 1 hour, or until firm. Turn off the
oven and leave to cool with the door
ajar—the tart may crack slightly but this
will not be noticeable when it has been
decorated. To decorate, melt the extra
chocolate and stir in the oil. With a fork,
flick thin drizzles of melted chocolate over
the tart. Cool completely before serving.

SPOTTED DICK

Preparation time: 15 minutes + standing
Total cooking time: 1 hour 30 minutes
Serves 4

1½ cups (185 g/6 oz) plain flour
1½ teaspoons baking powder
½ cup (125 g/4 oz) sugar
1½ teaspoons ground ginger
2 cups (160 g/5½ oz) fresh breadcrumbs
60 g (2 oz) sultanas
110 g (3½ oz) currants
125 g (4 oz) suet, grated
2 teaspoons finely grated lemon rind
2 eggs, lightly beaten
⅔ cup (170 ml/5½ fl oz) milk

1 Sift the flour, baking powder, sugar and ginger into a large bowl. Add the breadcrumbs, sultanas, currants, suet and lemon rind. Mix thoroughly with a wooden spoon.
2 Combine the egg and milk, add to the dry ingredients and mix well. Add a little more milk if necessary, then set aside for 5 minutes.
3 Lay a sheet of baking paper on a work surface and form the mixture into a roll shape about 20 cm (8 inches) long. Roll the pudding in the paper and fold up the ends—do not wrap it too tight as it has to expand as it cooks. Wrap the roll in a tea towel, put it in the top of a bamboo or metal steamer, cover and steam for 1 hour 30 minutes. Do not let the pudding boil dry—replenish with boiling water as the pudding cooks. Unmould the pudding onto a plate and slice. Can be served with custard or cream.

FRUIT TART

Preparation time: 40 minutes + chilling
Total cooking time: 40 minutes
Serves 6

Shortcrust pastry
1¼ cups (155 g/5 oz) plain flour
2 tablespoons caster sugar
90 g (3 oz) chilled unsalted butter, chopped
1 egg yolk
1 tablespoon chilled water

Filling
1 cup (250 ml/8 fl oz) milk
3 egg yolks
¼ cup (60 g/2 oz) caster sugar
2 tablespoons plain flour
1 teaspoon vanilla essence
strawberries, kiwi fruit and blueberries
apricot jam, to glaze

1 Sift the flour into a bowl and stir in the sugar. Add the butter and using just your fingertips, rub into the flour until the mixture resembles breadcrumbs. Make a well in the centre, add the egg yolk and water. Using a knife, mix to a dough. Turn out onto a lightly floured surface and gather together into a ball. Press together gently until smooth, and then roll out to fit a 34 x 10 cm (13½ x 4 inch) loose-bottomed, fluted flan tin. Line the tin with pastry and trim away any excess. Refrigerate for 20 minutes. Preheat the oven to moderately hot 190°C (375°F/Gas 5).

2 Line the pastry-lined tin with a sheet of crumpled baking paper and spread a layer of baking beads or rice evenly over the paper. Bake for 15 minutes, remove the paper and beads and bake for another 20 minutes, until cooked on the base and golden brown around the edge. Set aside to cool completely.
3 To make the filling, put the milk into a small pan and bring to the boil. Set aside while quickly whisking the egg yolks and sugar together in a bowl, until light and creamy. Whisk in the flour. Pour the hot milk slowly onto the egg mixture, whisking constantly. Wash out the pan, return the milk mixture and bring to the boil over medium heat, stirring with a wire whisk. Boil for 2 minutes, stirring occasionally. Transfer to a bowl, stir in the vanilla essence, and leave to cool, stirring frequently to avoid a skin forming. When cooled to room temperature, cover the surface with plastic wrap and refrigerate until cold.
4 Cut the strawberries in half and peel and slice the kiwi fruit. Spoon the cold custard into the cold pastry shell, then arrange the fruit over the custard, pressing in slightly. Heat the jam in the microwave or in a small pan until liquid, sieve to remove any lumps, then, using a pastry brush, glaze the fruit. Serve the tart on the same day, at room temperature. If it is to be left for a while on a hot day, refrigerate it.

NOTE: If you don't have a rectangular tin, this tart may be made in a 23 cm (9 inch) flan tin. You can use different fruits to top the tart, according to taste and season.

FARMHOUSE RHUBARB PIE

Preparation time: 40 minutes + chilling
Total cooking time: 50 minutes
Serves 6

Shortcrust pastry
1½ cups (185 g/6 oz) plain flour, sifted
2 tablespoons icing sugar
125 g (4 oz) chilled unsalted butter,
   chopped
1 egg yolk

1 cup (250 g/8 oz) sugar
750 g (1½ lb) rhubarb, chopped
2 large apples, peeled, cored and
   chopped
2 teaspoons grated lemon rind
3 pieces preserved ginger, sliced
2 teaspoons sugar
sprinkle of ground cinnamon

1 Sift the flour into a large bowl, add the
icing sugar, then use just your fingertips
to rub in the butter until the mixture
resembles breadcrumbs. Add the egg
yolk and 1 tablespoon water and mix with
a knife until the dough comes together.
Turn onto a floured surface, gather into a
ball, flatten slightly and refrigerate in
plastic wrap for 15 minutes. Preheat the
oven to moderately hot 190°C (375°F/
Gas 5). Roll the pastry out to a rough
35 cm (14 inch) circle and line a greased
20 cm (8 inch) pie plate, leaving the extra
pastry to hang over the edge. Refrigerate
while you prepare the filling.
2 Heat the sugar and ½ cup (125 ml/4 fl oz)
water in a pan for 4–5 minutes, or until
syrupy. Add the rhubarb, apple, lemon
rind and ginger, then cover and simmer
for 5 minutes, until the rhubarb is cooked
but still holds its shape.
3 Drain off the liquid and cool the
rhubarb. Spoon into the pastry base and
sprinkle with the sugar and cinnamon.
Fold the overhanging pastry roughly over
the fruit and bake for 40 minutes, or until
golden. Dust with icing sugar. Delicious
with ice cream or custard.

RICE GATEAU

Preparation time: 20 minutes + soaking +
   20 minutes resting + cooling
Total cooking time: 1 hour 25 minutes
Serves 10

1 cup (240 g/7½ oz) finely chopped glacé
   apricots
2 tablespoons very finely chopped glacé
   ginger
2 tablespoons cognac or amaretto
1 cup (250 g/8 oz) arborio rice
2½ cups (625 ml/20 fl oz) milk
300 ml (9½ fl oz) cream
1 teaspoon finely grated orange zest
1 vanilla bean, split
1¾ cups (435 g/14 oz) caster (superfine)
   sugar
300 g (10 oz) crème fraîche
4 egg yolks
¼ cup (25 g/¾ oz) ground almonds, lightly
   toasted

1 Combine the glacé fruit with the cognac
and set aside to soak.
2 Put the rice, milk, cream, orange zest
and vanilla bean in a saucepan over
medium heat and mix together. Stir
occasionally until the mixture comes to
the boil, then reduce the heat a little and
cook, stirring frequently, for 30 minutes,
or until the rice is tender and most of the
liquid has been absorbed—it should look
like a creamy rice pudding or risotto. Set
aside to cool to room temperature, then
discard the vanilla bean. Preheat the oven
to warm 170°C (325°F/Gas 3).

3 While the rice is cooling, put 1 cup
(250 g/8 oz) of the sugar in a small heavy-
based saucepan over low heat. As the
sugar begins to dissolve, swirl the pan
gently to ensure the sugar melts evenly.
Increase the heat to medium and boil,
without stirring, until the caramel turns
dark golden, being careful that the sugar
doesn't burn. Working quickly, pour the
caramel into the base of a 2 litre (64 fl oz)
round ovenproof dish and tilt and swirl
the dish until the entire base and side are
covered; be very careful not to burn
yourself on the hot caramel.
4 Add the crème fraîche, egg yolks,
ground almonds, soaked glacé fruit and
the remaining sugar to the cooled rice
and mix well. Pour the rice mixture into
the caramel-lined dish and smooth the
top. Put the dish in a roasting tin and pour
in enough warm water to come halfway
up the side of the dish. Cook for
45 minutes, or until quite firm and lightly
golden on top.
5 Cool for about 20 minutes before
turning out onto a large serving plate.
Cool completely before cutting. Serve
with some lightly whipped cream and
orange segments, if desired.

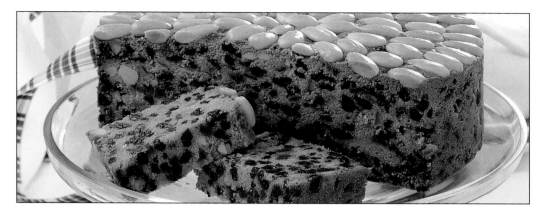

DUNDEE CAKE

Preparation time: 35 minutes
Total cooking time: 2 hours 30 minutes
Makes 1

250 g (8 oz) unsalted butter, softened
1 cup (230 g/7½ oz) soft brown sugar
¼ teaspoon almond essence
2 teaspoons finely grated orange rind
2 teaspoons finely grated lemon rind
4 eggs, lightly beaten
1⅔ cups (250 g/8 oz) currants
2 cups (320 g/11 oz) sultanas
½ cup (80 g/2¾ oz) raisins, chopped
⅓ cup (60 g/2 oz) mixed peel
⅔ cup (100 g/3½ oz) blanched almonds,
    coarsely chopped
¾ cup (75 g/2½ oz) ground almonds
1½ cups (185 g/6 oz) plain flour
½ cup (60 g/2 oz) self-raising flour
½ teaspoon ground cinnamon
2 tablespoons whisky
⅔ cup (100 g/3½ oz) whole blanched
    almonds, for decoration

1 Preheat the oven to slow 150°C
(300°F/Gas 2). Lightly grease a 20 cm
(8 inch) round cake tin and line as shown
on pages 836–7.

2 Beat the butter, sugar, essence and
rinds in a small bowl with electric beaters
until light and fluffy. Add the eggs
gradually, beating well after each
addition. Transfer to a large bowl, stir in
the dried fruits, mixed peel and chopped
nuts, then the ground almonds, sifted
flours, cinnamon and whisky. The batter
should be just soft enough to drop from a
spoon when shaken, so if it is too dry add
1–2 tablespoons milk. Spread into the tin
and smooth the surface. Wrap newspaper
around the tin as shown on pages 224–5.
3 Arrange whole almonds on top of the
cake in a spiral pattern. Place the tin on
several layers of newspaper on the oven
shelf. Bake for 2–2½ hours, or until a
skewer comes out clean when inserted
into centre of the cake. Cover the top with
a sheet of baking paper then cover tightly
with foil and wrap in a thick tea towel.
Cool completely in the tin, then store in
an airtight container for up to 3 months.

BLUEBERRY PIE

Preparation time: 20 minutes +
    10 minutes refrigeration
Total cooking time: 30–35 minutes
Serves 4

1½ cups (185 g/6 oz) plain flour
125 g (4 oz) butter, chopped
½ cup (60 g/2 oz) icing sugar
¼ cup (60 ml/2 fl oz) lemon juice
500 g (1 lb) fresh blueberries
3 tablespoons icing sugar, extra
1 teaspoon finely grated lemon rind
½ teaspoon ground cinnamon
1 egg white, lightly beaten

1 Preheat the oven to moderate 180°C
(350°F/Gas 4). Place the flour, butter and
icing sugar in a food processor. Process
for 15 seconds or until fine and crumbly.
Add almost all the juice and process
briefly until the mixture comes together,
adding more juice if necessary.
2 Turn the dough out onto a sheet of
baking paper and press together until
smooth. Roll out to a circle about 30 cm
(12 inches) in diameter and cover with
plastic wrap. Refrigerate for 10 minutes.
Place blueberries in a bowl and sprinkle
sugar, rind and cinnamon over the top.
3 Place the dough (still on baking paper)
onto an oven tray. Brush the centre lightly
with egg white. Pile blueberry mixture
onto dough in a circle 20 cm (8 inches) in
diameter; fold edges of the pastry over
the filling. Bake for 30–35 minutes or until
golden. Dust the top with icing sugar and
serve.

BEAUTY TIPS

TRADITIONALLY, ONLY SAVOURY PIES WERE DECORATED, TO DISTINGUISH THEM AT A GLANCE FROM SWEET PIES. TODAY WE ARE UNLIKELY TO BAKE MORE THAN ONE PIE IN A DAY, SO CONFUSION SHOULDN'T BE A PROBLEM.

Pies are usually double crusted (with a pastry base and top) or just crusted on the top, whereas tarts are generally open with no pastry on top. Pies or tarts which are made in pie dishes with a lip can all be decorated around the edge.

As well as making pies look attractive, decorating can be practical—it seals the edges of a double crusted pie, uses up pastry trimmings and helps identify the filling of your pie.

DECORATIVE CRUST EDGES

Fork pressed: press a lightly floured fork around the edge of the pie crust.

Fluted: press the pastry edge between your thumbs at a slight angle, to create a ripple effect.

Crimped: press the pastry between thumb and forefinger, while indenting with the other forefinger.

Scalloped: mark or cut out semi-circles with a spoon.

Checkerboard: make cuts in the pastry edge. Turn every other square inward.

Leaves: cut out leaf shapes with a cutter or template and place over the lip of the pie, fixing with water or egg glaze.

Plait: cut three long strips and plait them to the length of the circumference of the tart. Brush the pastry edge with a little water and press gently into place.

Rope: twist two long sausages of pastry together and attach to the edge with water.

Feathering: lift the pastry off the lip so it stands upright and snip diagonally into the edge of the pie. Push one point inwards and one outwards.

DECORATIVE TOPS

When decorating with pastry trimmings, don't make the shapes too thick or they won't cook through. Re-roll the leftover pastry to an even thickness and cut out shapes with small cutters. If you want to make a shape you don't have a cutter for, draw it on a piece of stiff card and cut out to make a template. The shapes can indicate the pie filling, such as cherries or apples, or be purely whimsical, such as hearts or stars. Attach the shapes to the pastry top with the glaze (often egg white, though for a rich colour, you might use a lightly beaten egg), then glaze them as well.

You can place pastry shapes onto an open tart or around the edge. If the filling is quite liquid, cook the shapes separately and arrange on the middle of the tart after it is baked and the filling has set. If your tart cooks for a long time, check that the edges are not over-browning and cover with pieces of foil if necessary.

LATTICE TOP

A lattice makes a very impressive top for a pie, and is actually quite easy to make. On a sheet of baking paper, roll the pastry out to a square or rectangle a little larger than the pie (just as you would to cover normally). Using a fluted pastry wheel, or a small, sharp knife, cut strips of pastry about 1.5 cm (⅝ inch) wide. Use a ruler to make perfect straight lines. Lay half the strips on another sheet of baking paper, all in the same direction, and about 1 cm (½ inch) apart. Fold alternate strips of pastry back away from you (all the way back to start with). Lay a strip of pastry horizontally across the unfolded strips, then fold them back into place. Fold the lower strips back this time, and lay another strip of pastry across. Repeat with all the strips, alternating the vertical strips. If the pastry is very soft, refrigerate it until firm. Invert the lattice onto the pie and peel the paper away.

Press the edges to seal, and trim off the excess pastry. Alternatively, make life easy for yourself and buy a special lattice-cutter, then simply roll out your pastry and roll over it once with your cutter, gently open the lattice out and lift it onto your pie and then trim the edges.

CLOCKWISE, FROM TOP LEFT: Crimped; Checkerboard; Scalloped; Rope; Lattice; Fork pressed; Plait; Leaves; Fluted

ORANGE MACADAMIA TARTS

Preparation time: 40 minutes + chilling
Total cooking time: 45 minutes
Serves 6

Shortcrust pastry
1½ cups (185 g/6 oz) plain flour
100 g (3½ oz) chilled unsalted butter, chopped
3–4 tablespoons chilled water

Filling
1½ cups (240 g/7½ oz) macadamia nuts
¼ cup (45 g/1½ oz) soft brown sugar
2 tablespoons light corn syrup
20 g (¾ oz) unsalted butter, melted
1 egg, lightly beaten
2 teaspoons finely grated orange rind
icing sugar, to dust

1 Preheat the oven to moderate 180°C (350°F/Gas 4). Sift the flour into a bowl, add the butter and, using just your fingertips, rub it in until the mixture resembles breadcrumbs. Add almost all the water and mix in with a flat-bladed knife until the mixture comes together, adding more water if necessary. Turn onto a lightly floured surface and gather together into a ball. Divide into six equal portions, roll out and line six 8 cm (3 inch) fluted flan tins, then refrigerate for 15 minutes. Cut sheets of baking paper to fit the pastry-lined tins, crumple the paper, put in the tins, then spread baking beads or rice evenly over the paper. Put the tins on a baking tray and bake for 15 minutes. Remove the beads and paper. Bake for another 10 minutes, or until the pastry is lightly golden. Cool completely.
2 Spread the macadamia nuts in a single layer on a flat baking tray. Bake for about 8 minutes, until lightly golden. Cool.
3 Divide the macadamia nuts evenly among the pastry shells. With a wire whisk, beat together the brown sugar, light corn syrup, butter, egg, orange rind and a pinch of salt. Pour the mixture over the nuts and bake for 20 minutes, or until set and lightly browned. Dust with icing sugar.

NUTMEG DATE CAKE

Preparation time: 25 minutes
Total cooking time: 55 minutes
Serves 8–10

2 cups (375 g/12 oz) soft brown sugar, plus 2 tablespoons
2 cups (250 g/8 oz) plain flour
2 teaspoons baking powder
125 g (4 oz) cold butter, chopped
1 teaspoon bicarbonate soda
¾ cup (185 ml/6 fl oz) milk
2 eggs, beaten
1½ teaspoons grated fresh nutmeg
375 g (12 oz) dried dates, roughly chopped
icing sugar, for dusting
whipped cream, for serving

1 Preheat the oven to moderate 180°C (350°F/Gas 4). Brush a 22 cm (8¾ inch) springform (spring-release) pan with melted butter or oil; line the base with baking paper.
2 Process the 2 cups of brown sugar with the flour and baking powder in a food processor for 10 seconds. Add butter; process for another 10 seconds until the mixture resembles fine crumbs. Press half the mixture into the base of the prepared tin.
3 Dissolve the soda in the milk; add the eggs and nutmeg and whisk. Pour the mixture into the remaining brown sugar and flour mixture and process for another 10 seconds. Pour into the cake tin and scatter half the dates over the top. Bake for 55 minutes. Remove the cake from the oven and cool in tin for 10 minutes. Remove from tin and cool on a wire rack.
4 Place the remaining dates on top of the cake, sprinkle with the extra brown sugar and place under a very hot grill for about 1 minute, or until the sugar begins to melt; cool. Dust the top with icing sugar and serve with cream.

PECAN AND MAPLE SYRUP PUDDING

Preparation time: 20 minutes
Total cooking time: 2 hours
Serves 8–10

200 g (6½ oz) unsalted butter
1 cup (250 g/8 oz) caster sugar
4 eggs, lightly beaten
1 teaspoon vanilla essence
3 cups (375 g/12 oz) self-raising flour, sifted
200 g (6½ oz) pecans, chopped
½ teaspoon ground cinnamon
grated rind of 1 lemon
¾ cup (185 ml/6 fl oz) milk
1 cup (250 ml/8 fl oz) maple syrup

1 Preheat the oven to moderate 180°C (350°F/Gas 4). Beat the butter and sugar with electric beaters until creamy. Gradually beat in the eggs, then the vanilla. Combine the flour, three-quarters of the pecans, cinnamon and rind and fold in, alternating with spoonfuls of milk, until smooth.
2 Grease a 2.25 litre pudding basin and line the base with a circle of baking paper. Pour three-quarters of the maple syrup into the basin and add the remaining pecans. Fill with mixture and pour the rest of the syrup over.
3 Cover with foil and put in a large baking dish. Pour enough water into the dish to come halfway up the side of the bowl, then bake for 2 hours. Test with a skewer—it should come out clean. Turn out onto a large serving plate. Serve with ice cream or cream, if desired.

FROZEN PRALINE MERINGUE TORTE

Preparation time: 1 hour + freezing
Total cooking time: 1 hour 10 minutes
Serves 8–10

4 egg whites
1½ cups (375 g/12 oz) caster sugar
100 g (3½ oz) blanched almonds
2 litres good-quality vanilla ice cream, softened

Strawberry sauce
500 g (1 lb) strawberries
2 tablespoons lemon juice
¼ cup (30 g/1 oz) icing sugar

1 Preheat the oven to slow 150°C (300°F/Gas 2). Line two baking trays with baking paper and mark a 20 cm (8 inch) circle on each. Brush with oil and dust with a little caster sugar. Beat the egg whites to stiff peaks, then gradually add 1 cup (250 g/8 oz) of the sugar, a tablespoon at a time. Beat until thick and glossy and the sugar has dissolved. Pipe in a spiral into the two circles. Bake for 1 hour, turn off the oven and leave the meringues to cool with the oven door ajar.
2 To make the praline, line a baking tray with baking paper and sprinkle with almonds. Combine the remaining sugar with ⅓ cup (80 ml/2¾ fl oz) water in a pan and stir over low heat until dissolved. Bring to the boil without stirring and, when golden, pour over the almonds. Allow to set and cool before crushing finely in a food processor or with a rolling pin.
3 Process or beat the ice cream until creamy and fold in the praline. Put a meringue circle into a lined 23 cm (9 inch) diameter springform tin, spoon in the ice cream and put the other meringue on top. Freeze until ready to serve.
4 To make the sauce, mix the ingredients in a food processor until smooth. Add a little water if too thick. Serve with the meringue torte.

GALETTE DES ROIS

Preparation time: 25 minutes +
  30 minutes refrigeration
Total cooking time: 35 minutes
Makes 1

2 x 375 g (12 oz) blocks ready-made puff pastry, thawed
¾ cup (75 g/2½ oz) ground almonds
⅓ cup (90 g/3 oz) caster sugar or vanilla sugar
1 tablespoon cornflour
1 teaspoon finely grated orange rind
100 g (3½ oz) unsalted butter, softened
3 egg yolks
½ teaspoon almond essence
1 tablespoon rum or kirsch
1 dried haricot bean or ceramic token
1 egg, lightly beaten, for glazing

1 Roll 1 block of pastry out on a lightly floured surface to 5 mm (¼ inch) thick and cut into a 22 cm (9 inch) circle. Repeat with the other block of pastry. Line a baking tray with baking paper and top with one of the circles.
2 In a bowl, combine the almonds, sugar, cornflour and rind. Add the butter, egg yolks, essence and rum and mix well. Spread over the pastry on the tray, poking in the bean or token and leaving a 2 cm (¾ inch) rim. Brush the rim with some beaten egg, taking care not to brush the cut edges as this will prevent the pastry puffing.
3 Place the second circle of puff pastry over the first, pressing gently around the edge to seal. Using a sharp knife, make swirling patterns from the centre, fanning outwards in the pastry, taking care not to cut all the way through. Brush the top with beaten egg and refrigerate for 30 minutes. Preheat the oven to moderately hot 200°C (400°F/Gas 6). Bake for 30–35 minutes, or until well puffed and golden. Serve warm or cold. Remember to tell everyone about the bean or token in the filling.

STRAWBERRY SWISS ROLL

Preparation time: 25 minutes + standing
Total cooking time: 10 minutes
Serves 6–8

3 eggs, separated
½ cup (125 g/4 oz) caster sugar, plus 1 tablespoon, extra
¾ cup (90 g/3 oz) self-raising flour, sifted
½ cup (160 g/5½ oz) strawberry jam
¾ cup (185 ml/6 fl oz) cream
250 g (8 oz) strawberries, quartered

1 Preheat the oven to moderately hot 200°C (400°F/Gas 6). Sprinkle a tablespoon of sugar over a piece of baking paper 30 x 35 cm (12 x 14 inch), resting on a tea towel. Brush a 25 x 30 cm (10 x 12 inch) swiss roll tin with oil or melted butter and line with baking paper.
2 Beat the egg whites until soft peaks form. Gradually add the sugar and beat until dissolved. Beat in the lightly beaten egg yolks until thick.
3 Fold in the flour and 2 tablespoons hot water. Spread into the tin and bake for 8–10 minutes, or until firm and golden. Turn out onto the sugared paper and peel the paper from the base. Using the tea towel as a guide, roll up loosely from the narrow end. Leave for 20 minutes, or until cooled, then unroll. (This prevents the sponge cracking when rolled with filling.)
4 Beat the cream and extra sugar until soft peaks form. Spread the roll with jam and top with cream and strawberries. Re-roll and chill.

PANETTONE

Preparation time: 30 minutes + 4 hours
   rising
Total cooking time: 50 minutes
Makes 1

½ cup (90 g/3 oz) candied mixed peel
½ cup (80 g/2¾ oz) sultanas
1 teaspoon grated lemon rind
1 teaspoon grated orange rind
1 tablespoon brandy or rum
7 g (¼ oz) sachet dried yeast
220 ml (7 fl oz) warm milk
¼ cup (60 g/2 oz) caster sugar
3¼ cups (400 g/13 oz) white bread flour
2 eggs
1 teaspoon vanilla essence
150 g (5 oz) unsalted butter, softened
20 g (½ oz) unsalted butter, melted, to
   glaze

1 Put the peel, sultanas and grated rind in
a small bowl. Add the alcohol, mix well
and set aside.
2 Put the yeast, warm milk and 1 teaspoon
sugar in a small bowl and leave in a warm
place for 10–15 minutes, or until foamy.
Sift 200 g (6½ oz) flour and ½ teaspoon salt
into a large bowl, make a well in the
centre and add the yeast mixture. Mix
together with a large metal spoon to form
a soft dough. Cover the bowl and leave to
'sponge' and rise in a warm place for
45 minutes, or until frothy and risen.
3 Add the eggs, remaining sugar and
vanilla and mix. Add the butter and stir
until well combined. Stir in the remaining
flour and mix well. Knead well on a
floured surface until the dough is smooth
and elastic. You may need to add up to
½ cup (60 g/2 oz) flour to the dough as you
knead. Place the dough in a lightly
greased bowl, cover with plastic wrap and
leave in a warm place for 1½–2 hours, or
until doubled.

4 Lightly grease a 15 cm (6 inch) round
cake tin and line the base and side with a
double thickness of baking paper,
ensuring the collar extends above the rim
of the tin by 10 cm (4 inches).
5 Knock back the dough and turn out onto
a floured work surface. Roll into a
30 x 20 cm (12 x 8 inch) rectangle. Drain
the fruit mixture and spread half the fruit
over the surface of the dough. Fold over
the short edges like an envelope to cover
the fruit. Roll again and repeat the
process to incorporate all the fruit. Gently
knead the dough for 2–3 minutes and
shape into a neat ball. Place in the tin,
brush with the melted butter, then slash
a cross on the top with a sharp knife and
leave to rise again in a warm place for
45 minutes, or until doubled in size.
6 Preheat the oven to moderately hot
190°C (375°F/Gas 5). Bake for 50 minutes,
or until golden brown and a skewer
inserted into the centre comes out clean.
Leave in the tin for 5 minutes, then
transfer to a wire rack to cool.

NOTE: This yeast cake is a speciality of
Milan but is enjoyed throughout Italy at
festive times such as Christmas and
Easter. It can be made in all different
sizes, ranging from an individual cake to
a large one.

FLOURLESS CHOCOLATE FRUIT AND NUT CAKE

Preparation time: 40 minutes
Total cooking time: 1 hour
Serves 8–10

5 egg whites
¾ cup (185 g/6 oz) caster sugar
100 g (3⅓ oz) glacé apricots, chopped
100 g (3⅓ oz) glacé figs, chopped
80 g (2⅔ oz) glacé ginger, chopped
250 g (8 oz) blanched almonds, finely
   chopped
250 g (8 oz) dark cooking chocolate,
   chopped
60 g (2 oz) dark cooking chocolate, melted
1½ cups (375 ml/12 fl oz) cream

1 Preheat oven to slow 150°C (300°F/
Gas 2). Brush a deep 24 cm (9½ inch)
round springform (spring-release) pan
with melted butter or oil. Line base and
side with baking paper.
2 Using electric beaters, beat egg whites
until soft peaks form. Gradually add
sugar, beating well after each addition;
beat until sugar has dissolved and the
mixture is thick and glossy.
3 Using a metal spoon, fold in fruits,
ginger, almonds, and both the chopped
and melted chocolate. Stir until just
combined. Spread in tin and bake for
1 hour or until a skewer comes out clean
when inserted in centre. Leave in tin for
15 minutes before removing. Cool on a
wire rack. When completely cooled, whip
cream until stiff peaks form. Using a
piping bag with a plain nozzle, pipe swirls
of cream on top of the cake. Decorate
with chocolate leaves, if desired.

TARTE AU CITRON

Preparation time: 1 hour + refrigeration
Total cooking time: 1 hour 40 minutes
Serves 6–8

Pastry
1 cup (125 g/4 oz) plain flour
75 g (2½ oz) unsalted butter, softened
1 egg yolk
2 tablespoons icing sugar, sifted

3 eggs
2 egg yolks
¾ cup (185 g/6 oz) caster sugar
½ cup (125 ml/4 fl oz) cream
¾ cup (185 ml/6 fl oz) lemon juice
1½ tablespoons finely grated lemon rind
3 small lemons, washed and scrubbed
⅔ cup (160 g/5½ oz) sugar

1 For the pastry, sift the flour and a pinch of salt into a large bowl. Make a well and add the butter, egg yolk and icing sugar. Work together the butter, yolk and sugar with your fingertips, then slowly incorporate the flour. Bring together into a ball—you may need to add a few drops of cold water. Flatten the ball slightly, cover with plastic wrap and refrigerate for 20 minutes.
2 Preheat the oven to moderately hot 200°C (400°F/Gas 6). Lightly grease a shallow loose-based flan tin, about 2 cm (¾ inch) deep and 21 cm (8½ inches) across the base.

3 Roll out the pastry between two sheets of baking paper until 3 mm (⅛ inch) thick, to fit the base and side of the tin. Trim the edge. Chill for 10 minutes. Line the pastry with baking paper, fill with baking beads or rice and bake for 10 minutes, or until cooked. Remove the paper and beads and bake for 6–8 minutes, until the pastry looks dry all over. Cool the pastry and reduce the oven to slow 150°C (300°F/Gas 2).
4 Whisk the eggs, yolks and sugar together, add the cream and juice and mix. Strain into a jug and add the rind. Place the flan tin on a baking tray in the centre of the oven and pour in the filling right to the top. Bake for 40 minutes, or until just set—it should wobble in the middle when the tin is tapped. Cool before removing from the tin.
5 Cut the lemons into very thin (about 2 mm/⅛ inch) slices. Blanch in simmering water for 5 minutes. Combine the sugar and 200 ml (6½ fl oz) water in a small frying pan and stir over low heat until the sugar has dissolved. Add the lemon slices and simmer over low heat for 40 minutes, or until the peel is very tender and the pith looks transparent. Lift out of the syrup using a slotted spoon and drain on baking paper. If serving immediately, cover the surface with the lemon. If not, keep the slices covered and decorate the tart when ready to serve. Serve warm or chilled.

HONEY CAKE

Preparation time: 15 minutes
Total cooking time: 1 hour 20 minutes
Makes 1

3 cups (375 g/12 oz) self-raising flour
1 cup (250 g/8 oz) sugar
2 teaspoons ground ginger
1 teaspoon ground cloves
1 teaspoon ground cinnamon
1 teaspoon bicarbonate of soda
1 teaspoon vanilla essence
2 eggs, lightly beaten
1 cup (350 g/11 oz) honey
1 cup (250 ml/8 fl oz) sunflower oil

1 Preheat the oven to warm 170°C (325°F/Gas 3). Lightly grease a 24 x 9 x 10 cm (9 x 3½ x 4 inch) loaf tin and line the base with baking paper.
2 Sift the flour into a large bowl, make a well in the centre and add all the remaining ingredients. Pour in 1 cup (250 ml/8 fl oz) hot water, stir thoroughly to mix, then beat until quite smooth.
3 Spoon the mixture into the prepared loaf tin and lightly tap the tin on the bench to remove any air pockets. Bake for 1 hour 20 minutes, or until a skewer inserted into the centre comes out clean. If the cake starts to brown too much, cover loosely with foil halfway through cooking. Leave to cool in the tin for 20 minutes, then invert onto a wire rack and cool completely.

ICINGS AND FROSTINGS

SWEET OR PIQUANT, COOKED OR UNCOOKED, TOPPINGS LIKE THESE HELP TO CONVERT AN UNADORNED HOME-MADE MUFFIN OR A SIMPLE SWEET SLICE TO AN OUTSTANDING EVENT.

EASY BUTTER CREAM

Using electric beaters, beat 80 g (2⅔ oz) of soft butter with ½ cup (60 g/2 oz) of icing sugar. Flavourings, such as 2 teaspoons of finely grated orange rind, 60 g (2 oz) of melted and cooled chocolate, or a few drops of your favourite flavoured essence and some complementary food colouring, can be added if you wish.

CHOCOLATE ICING

Combine 30 g (1 oz) of melted butter, 2 tablespoons of hot water and 2 tablespoons of sifted cocoa powder in a bowl and stir the mixture until it forms a smooth paste. Add 1 cup (125 g/4 oz) of sifted icing sugar and stir until the ingredients are well combined and the mixture is quite smooth.

HONEY MOCK CREAM

Using electric beaters, beat 125 g (4 oz) butter with ⅓ cup (90 g/3 oz) of caster sugar and 2 tablespoons of honey until the mixture is light and creamy. Pour cold water onto the mixture, swirl around and pour off. Beat again for 2 minutes, then swirl water over the mixture and pour it off again. Repeat this process four more times until the mixture is white and creamy and the sugar has completely dissolved. This cream is a delicious topping for spiced cakes or cupcakes.

CITRUS GLACE ICING

Combine 1 cup (125 g/4 oz) of sifted icing sugar, 10 g (⅓ oz) of unsalted butter and 1 teaspoon finely grated citrus rind in a small heatproof bowl. Add sufficient juice (about 1–2 tablespoons) to make a firm paste. Stand the bowl over a pan of simmering water and stir until the icing is smooth and glossy; remove from heat. Spread onto cake or biscuits with a long palette knife. Orange, lemon or lime rind and juice can be used.

SOFT CITRUS ICING

Make a deliciously simple glacé icing by combining 1¼ cups (155 g/5 oz) sifted icing sugar, 30 g (1 oz) softened butter, a little grated citrus rind and enough hot water to mix to a thick, smooth paste. Spread over cake. This mixture is easy to work with as it doesn't set quickly. The same mixture can also be heated in a small bowl over simmering water. Work quickly with this method, using a hot, wet knife for spreading, as the icing will set very quickly.

CREAM CHEESE FROSTING

Chop 185 g (6 oz) cream cheese into small cubes and, using electric beaters, beat until smooth. Add ⅓ cup (40 g/1⅓ oz) sifted icing sugar and a couple of teaspoons of lemon juice and beat until well combined. Add a little more juice, to taste, if you like but don't make the frosting too runny. This is an excellent topping for carrot or banana cakes.

CHOCOLATE GANACHE

Combine 100 g (3⅓ oz) of chopped dark chocolate, 60 g (2 oz) unsalted butter and a tablespoon of cream in a heatproof bowl. Stand bowl over a pan of simmering water; stir until the mixture is melted and smooth. This mixture can be cooled slightly and poured while still liquid over a very smooth cake. (If the top surface is rough, turn the cake upside down and use the base as the top.) Ganache can also be cooled until it is spreadable, or cooled and then beaten to make a lighter, fluffier topping.

CLOCKWISE, FROM TOP LEFT: Citrus Glacé Icing; Chocolate Ganache; Chocolate Icing (with whipped cream and chocolate lattice); Honey Mock Cream; Soft Citrus Icing; Easy Butter Cream; Cream Cheese Frosting

LEMON MERINGUE PIE

Preparation time: 1 hour + chilling
Total cooking time: 45 minutes
Serves 6

1½ cups (185 g/6 oz) plain flour
2 tablespoons icing sugar
125 g (4 oz) chilled unsalted butter,
    chopped
3 tablespoons iced water

Filling and topping
¼ cup (30 g/1 oz) cornflour
¼ cup (30 g/1 oz) plain flour
1 cup (250 g/8 oz) caster sugar
¾ cup (185 ml/6 fl oz) lemon juice
3 teaspoons grated lemon rind
40 g (1¼ oz) unsalted butter, chopped
6 eggs, separated
1½ cups (375 g/12 oz) caster sugar, extra
½ teaspoon cornflour, extra

1 Sift the flour and icing sugar into a large
bowl. Rub the butter into the flour with
your fingertips until the mixture
resembles breadcrumbs. Add almost all
the water and mix to a firm dough, adding
more liquid if necessary. Turn onto a
lightly floured surface and gather
together into a ball. Roll between two
sheets of baking paper until large enough
to fit a 23 cm (9 inch) pie plate. Line the
pie plate with the pastry, trim the edge
and chill for 20 minutes. Preheat the oven
to moderate 180°C (350°F/Gas 4).

2 Line the pastry with a sheet of crumpled
baking paper and spread a layer of baking
beads or rice evenly over the paper. Bake
for 10 minutes, then remove the paper
and beads. Bake for another 10 minutes,
or until the pastry is lightly golden. Leave
to cool.
3 To make the filling, place the flours and
sugar in a medium pan. Whisk in the
lemon juice, rind and 1½ cups (375 ml/12 oz)
water. Whisk continually over medium
heat until the mixture boils and thickens.
Reduce the heat and cook for another
minute, then whisk in the butter and egg
yolks, one at a time. Transfer to a bowl,
cover the surface with plastic wrap and
allow to cool completely.
4 To make the topping, preheat the oven
to hot 220°C (425°F/Gas 7). Beat the egg
whites in a small, dry bowl with electric
beaters, until soft peaks form. Add the
extra sugar gradually, beating constantly
until the meringue is thick and glossy.
Beat in the extra cornflour. Pour the cold
filling into the cold pastry shell. Spread
with meringue to cover, forming peaks.
Bake for 5–10 minutes, or until lightly
browned. Serve hot or cold.

PINEAPPLE AND BANANA CAKE

Preparation time: 40 minutes
Total cooking time: 1 hour
Serves 8–10

2 medium bananas, mashed
½ cup (130 g/4¼ oz) drained crushed
    pineapple
1¼ cups (310 g/9¾ oz) caster sugar
1⅔ cups (200 g/6½ oz) self-raising flour
2 teaspoons ground cinnamon
⅔ cup (170 ml/5½ fl oz) oil
¼ cup (60 ml/2 fl oz) pineapple juice
2 eggs

Icing
250 g (8 oz) cream cheese
1½ cups (185 g/6 oz) icing sugar
1 small mango, thinly sliced

1 Preheat the oven to moderate 180°C
(350°F/Gas 4). Brush a 23 cm (9 inch)
round cake tin with melted butter or oil
and line the base and side with baking
paper.
2 Place the bananas, pineapple and sugar
in a large bowl. Add the sifted flour and
cinnamon; using a wooden spoon, stir to
combine.
3 Whisk the oil, pineapple juice and eggs
together and add to the banana mixture.
Stir until the ingredients are combined
and the mixture is smooth.
4 Pour into the prepared tin, smooth the
surface and bake for 1 hour, or until a
skewer comes out clean when inserted
into the centre of cake. Leave in the tin for
10 minutes; turn onto a wire rack to cool.
5 To make Icing: Using electric beaters,
beat the cream cheese and icing sugar
until light and fluffy. Using a serrated
knife, cut the cake in half horizontally.
Spread a third of the icing over the bottom
layer of the cake and arrange the mango
slices over the icing. Replace the top layer
and cover the top of the cake with the
remaining icing. Decorate with pieces of
glacé pineapple, if desired.

CHOCOLATE NUT CAKE

Preparation time: 30 minutes + overnight
  refrigeration
Total cooking time: 5–10 minutes
Serves 6–8

250 g (8 oz) stellini
1 cup (140 g/5½ oz) roasted hazelnuts,
  skinned
1½ cups (150 g/4½ oz) walnuts
¾ cup (100 g/3½ oz) blanched almonds
3 tablespoons cocoa powder
1 teaspoon ground cinnamon
⅔ cup (155 g/5 oz) sugar
1 tablespoon mixed peel
grated rind of 1 lemon
1 teaspoon vanilla essence
2 tablespoons Cognac
60 g (2 oz) butter
100 g (3½ oz) dark chocolate, chopped

1 Grease and line the base of a deep
20 cm (8 inch) round springform tin. Cook
the pasta in boiling water until al dente.
Rinse under cold water to cool. Drain
thoroughly.
2 Place the nuts, cocoa powder,
cinnamon, sugar, mixed peel, rind, vanilla
essence and Cognac in a food processor.
Process in short bursts until finely
ground.
3 Melt the butter and chocolate in a small
pan over low heat or in the microwave,
until smooth.
4 Combine the pasta, nut mixture and
melted chocolate and butter. Mix well.
Spoon the mixture into the prepared tin.
Press down firmly with a wet hand.
Smooth the surface with the back of a wet
spoon. Refrigerate overnight to firm.
Remove from the tin and cut into wedges.
Dust with a little cocoa powder and icing
sugar for serving. Delicious with whipped
cream.

ORANGE, LEMON AND WHITE CHOCOLATE GATEAU

Preparation time: 1 hour
Total cooking time: 30 minutes
Serves 8–10

1 cup (125 g/4 oz) plain flour
4 eggs
⅔ cup (160 g/5½ oz) caster sugar
60 g (2 oz) unsalted butter, melted and
  cooled

Filling
2 tablespoons cornflour
⅓ cup (80 ml/2¾ fl oz) lemon juice
⅓ cup (80 ml/2¾ fl oz) orange juice
1 teaspoon finely grated lemon rind
1 teaspoon finely grated orange rind
⅓ cup (90 g/3 oz) caster sugar
2 egg yolks
20 g (¾ oz) unsalted butter

Topping
200 g (6½ oz) white chocolate, chopped
½ cup (125 ml/4 fl oz) cream
60 g (2 oz) unsalted butter
white chocolate curls and candied rind

1 Preheat the oven to 180°C (350°F/Gas 4).
Grease two shallow 20 cm (8 inch) cake
tins and line the base and sides with
baking paper.
2 Sift the flour three times onto a sheet of
greaseproof paper. Beat the eggs and
sugar until thick, pale and increased in
volume.
3 Using a metal spoon, fold in the flour in
two batches, quickly and lightly until just
combined. Add the melted butter with the
second batch, discarding any white
sediment in the butter. Spread into the
tins and bake for 20 minutes, until lightly
golden. Leave for 2 minutes before
turning out onto a wire rack to cool.

4 To make the filling, blend the cornflour
with a tablespoon of water. Place
3 tablespoons water, the juice, rind and
sugar in a small pan and stir over
medium heat, without boiling, until the
sugar has dissolved. Add the cornflour
and stir until the mixture boils and
thickens. Cook, stirring, for another
minute. Remove from the heat, add the
egg yolks and butter and stir well.
Transfer to a bowl, cover the surface with
plastic wrap and cool completely.
5 To make the topping, place the
chocolate, cream and butter in a small
pan and stir over low heat until melted.
Transfer to a bowl, cover with plastic
wrap and allow to cool completely. Do not
refrigerate. Using electric beaters, beat
until fluffy.
6 Using a serrated knife, cut the cakes in
half horizontally. Place one cake layer on
a serving plate and spread evenly with the
filling. Continue layering cake and filling,
ending with a cake layer on top. Spread
the top and sides of the cake with topping.
Decorate with white chocolate curls and
candied lemon rind.

NOTE: To make your own candied lemon
rind, cut each lemon into quarters and
pull out the flesh. Put the lemon rind in a
pan of cold water and bring to the boil.
Reduce the heat, simmer for 2 minutes,
then discard the water and repeat. This
will remove the bitterness from the pith.
Drain. Combine 220 g (7 oz) sugar and
1 cup (250 ml/8 fl oz) water in a pan and
dissolve the sugar over low heat, stirring
constantly. When the sugar has dissolved,
bring to the boil, reduce the heat and
simmer. Add a few drops of lemon juice
and the pieces of lemon peel and cook
over very low heat until the pith and peel
look translucent. Leave to cool in the
syrup, then remove and drain. Cut out
star shapes, using a cutter or sharp knife.
Roll the shapes in caster sugar.

LIME CHIFFON PIE

Preparation time: 30 minutes + chilling
Total cooking time: 1 hour
Serves 12

Almond pastry
1¼ cups (155 g/5 oz) plain flour
90 g (3 oz) ground almonds
90 g (3 oz) chilled unsalted butter,
   chopped
1–2 tablespoons chilled water

Filling
6 egg yolks
½ cup (125 g/4 oz) caster sugar
100 g (3½ oz) unsalted butter, melted
⅓ cup (80 ml/2¾ fl oz) lime juice
2 teaspoons finely grated lime rind
2 teaspoons gelatine
½ cup (125 ml/4 fl oz) cream, whipped
½ cup (125 g/4 oz) sugar
rind of 4 limes, finely shredded

1 Sift the flour into a large bowl and add the almonds and butter. Using just your fingertips, rub in the butter until the mixture resembles breadcrumbs. Add almost all the water and mix to a firm dough, adding more liquid if necessary. Turn onto a lightly floured surface and gather together into a ball. Roll the pastry out to fit a 23 cm (9 inch) fluted flan tin. Line the tin, trim the edges and refrigerate for 20 minutes.
2 Preheat the oven to moderate 180°C (350°F/Gas 4). Line the pastry-lined tin with a sheet of crumpled baking paper and spread a layer of baking beads or rice evenly over the paper. Bake for 20 minutes, remove the paper and beads and bake the pastry for another 20 minutes, or until lightly golden. Allow to cool completely.

3 To make the filling, place the egg yolks, sugar, butter, lime juice and rind in a heatproof bowl. Whisk to combine thoroughly and dissolve the sugar. Stand the bowl over a pan of simmering water and stir constantly for 15 minutes, or until the mixture thickens. Remove from the heat and cool slightly. Put 1 tablespoon water in a small heatproof bowl, sprinkle the gelatine in an even layer over the surface and leave to go spongy. Do not stir. Bring a small pan filled with about 4 cm (1½ inches) water to the boil, remove from the heat and place the bowl into the pan. The water should come halfway up the side of the bowl. Stir the gelatine until clear and dissolved. Cool slightly, add to the lime curd and stir to combine. Cool to room temperature, stirring occasionally.
4 Fold the cream through the lime curd and pour into the pastry case. Refrigerate for 2–3 hours, until set. Leave the pie for 15 minutes at room temperature before serving.
5 To prepare the lime rind, combine the sugar with 1 tablespoon water in a small pan. Stir over low heat until the sugar has dissolved. Bring to the boil, add the rind and simmer for 3 minutes. Drain the rind on a wire rack, then decorate the lime chiffon pie to serve.

APPLE STRUDEL

Preparation time: 20 minutes
Total cooking time: 25–30 minutes
Makes 2 strudels

4 green cooking apples
30 g (1 oz) butter
2 tablespoons orange juice
1 tablespoon honey
¼ cup (60 g/2 oz) sugar
½ cup (60 g/2 oz) sultanas
2 sheets ready-rolled puff pastry
¼ cup (45 g/1½ oz) ground almonds
1 egg, lightly beaten
2 tablespoons soft brown sugar
1 teaspoon ground cinnamon

1 Preheat the oven to hot 220°C (425°F/Gas 7). Brush two oven trays lightly with melted butter or oil. Peel, core and thinly slice the apples. Heat the butter in a medium pan; add the apples and cook for 2 minutes until lightly golden. Add the orange juice, honey, sugar and sultanas. Stir over medium heat until the sugar dissolves and the apples are just tender. Transfer the mixture to a bowl and leave until completely cooled.
2 Place a sheet of the pastry on a flat work surface. Fold it in half; and make small cuts in the folded edge of the pastry at 2 cm (¾ inch) intervals. Open out the pastry and sprinkle with half of the ground almonds. Drain away the liquid from the apples and place half of the mixture in the centre of the pastry. Brush the edges with the lightly beaten egg, and fold together, pressing firmly to seal.
3 Place the strudel on a prepared tray, seam-side down. Brush the top with egg and sprinkle with half of the combined brown sugar and cinnamon. Repeat the process with the other sheet and the remaining filling. Bake for 20–25 minutes or until the pastry is golden and crisp. Serve hot with cream or ice cream, or at room temperature as a teatime treat.

PUMPKIN PIE

Preparation time: 30 minutes + 30
   minutes standing
Total cooking time: 1 hour 15 minutes
Serves 8

1¼ cups (155 g/5 oz) plain flour
100 g (3⅓ oz) butter, chopped
2 teaspoons caster sugar
4 tablespoons chilled water
1 egg yolk, lightly beaten, mixed with
   1 tablespoon milk, for glazing

Filling
2 eggs, lightly beaten
¾ cup (140 g/4⅔ oz) soft brown sugar
500 g (1 lb) pumpkin, cooked, mashed and
   cooled
⅓ cup (80 ml/2¾ fl oz) cream
1 tablespoon sweet sherry
1 teaspoon ground cinnamon
½ teaspoon ground nutmeg
½ teaspoon ground ginger

1 Sift the flour into a large bowl and add
chopped butter. Using your fingertips, rub
the butter into the flour for 2 minutes or
until the mixture is fine and crumbly. Stir
in the caster sugar. Add almost all the
liquid and mix to a firm dough, adding
more liquid if necessary. Turn onto a
lightly floured surface and press together
for 1 minute or until smooth.
2 Roll out the pastry, on a sheet of baking
paper, until it is large enough to cover the
base and side of a 23 cm (9 inch) diameter
pie dish. Line the dish with pastry, trim
away excess and crimp the edges. Roll
out the pastry trimmings to a thickness of
2 mm (¼ inch). Using a sharp knife, cut
out leaf shapes of different sizes. Score
vein markings onto the leaves.
Refrigerate the pastry-lined dish and the
leaf shapes for about 20 minutes.

3 Cut a sheet of greaseproof paper to
cover the pastry-lined dish. Spread a
layer of dried beans or rice over the
paper. Bake for 10 minutes, remove from
oven and discard paper and beans or rice.
Return the pastry to the oven for 10 minutes
or until lightly golden. Meanwhile, place
the leaves on an oven tray lined with
baking paper, brush with egg glaze and
bake for 10–15 minutes, until golden; set
aside to cool.
4 To make Filling: Preheat the oven to
moderate 180°C (350°F/Gas 4). Whisk the
eggs and sugar in a large bowl. Add the
cooled pumpkin, cream, sweet sherry and
spices and stir to combine thoroughly.
Pour the mixture into the pastry shell,
smooth the surface with the back of a
spoon and bake for 40 minutes or until
set. If the pastry edge begins to brown too
much during cooking, cover the edge with
foil. Allow the pie to cool to room
temperature and place the leaves on top
of the filling. Serve with cream or ice
cream, if desired.

NOTE: As an alternative to using the
pastry trimmings to make the decoration,
you can use a sheet of ready-rolled puff
pastry. Cut out some leaf shapes, brush
with egg white and bake on a tray, in a
moderate 180°C (350°F/Gas 4) oven, until
puffed and golden, about 10–15 minutes.

DEEP DISH APPLE PIE

Preparation time: 1 hour + chilling
Total cooking time: 1 hour
Serves 6–8

Shortcrust pastry
1 cup (125 g/4 oz) self-raising flour
1 cup (125 g/4 oz) plain flour
125 g (4 oz) chilled unsalted butter, chopped
2 tablespoons caster sugar
2 eggs
1–2 tablespoons milk

8 large apples, peeled, cored, thickly sliced
2 thick strips lemon rind
6 whole cloves
1 cinnamon stick
½ cup (125 g/4 oz) sugar

1 Grease a deep, 20 cm (8 inch) round
springform tin. Line the base with baking
paper, grease the paper, dust lightly with
flour and shake off the excess.
2 Sift the flours, then rub in the butter
until the mixture resembles breadcrumbs.
Mix in the sugar, add 1 egg and almost all
the milk and mix with a flat-bladed knife
until the mixture comes together, adding
more liquid if necessary. Turn onto a lightly
floured surface and gather together. Roll
two-thirds of the pastry between two
sheets of baking paper to cover the base
and side of the tin. Ease into the tin. Roll
out the remaining pastry large enough to
fit the top of tin. Chill for 20 minutes.
3 Put the apples, rind, cloves, cinnamon,
sugar and 2 cups (500 ml/16 fl oz) water in
a large pan. Cover and simmer for
10 minutes, or until tender. Remove from
the heat, drain and cool. Discard the rind,
cloves and cinnamon.
4 Preheat the oven to moderate 180°C
(350°F/Gas 4). Spoon the filling into the
pie shell. Cover with the pie top, lightly
beat the remaining egg and brush over
the pastry edges to seal. Prick the top
with a fork. Trim the edges and crimp to
seal. Brush with beaten egg and bake for
50 minutes. Leave to cool for 10 minutes.

DESSERTS

MINI TOFFEE PUFFS WITH LIQUEUR CREAM

Preparation time: 30 minutes
Total cooking time: 30 minutes
Serves 4–6

30 g (1 oz) butter
¼ cup (60 ml/2 fl oz) water
¼ cup (30 g/1 oz) plain flour
1 egg, lightly beaten

Liqueur Cream
½ cup (125 ml/4 fl oz) cream
1 tablespoon Grand Marnier

Toffee
1 cup (250 g/8 oz) caster sugar
⅓ cup (80 ml/2¾ fl oz) water

1 Preheat oven to hot 220°C (425°F/Gas 7). Line an oven tray with baking paper. Combine the butter and water in a small pan. Stir over low heat until the butter is melted and the mixture just boils. Remove from heat and add the flour all at once. Using a wooden spoon, beat mixture until smooth. Return to heat and beat until mixture thickens and comes away from the side of the pan. Remove from heat; cool slightly. Transfer to a small bowl. Using electric beaters, add the egg gradually, beating until the mixture is thick and glossy.

2 Drop teaspoonsful of mixture about 4 cm (1½ inches) apart on prepared tray. Bake for 10 minutes, reduce heat to moderate 180°C (350°F/Gas 4) and bake for another 5–10 minutes, or until golden and well puffed. Pierce the side of each puff to release steam. Turn off oven, return puffs to the oven to dry out the inside; allow to cool.
3 To make Liqueur Cream: Using electric beaters, beat cream until soft peaks form. Add Grand Marnier and beat until just combined. Place cream in a piping bag fitted with a small plain nozzle. Pipe into puffs.
4 To make Toffee: Combine sugar and water in a small pan. Stir over low heat until sugar dissolves, brushing down sides of pan occasionally. Bring to boil, reduce heat and simmer until golden. Quickly spoon over the puffs and allow to set.

NOTE: The puffs can be made up to 6 hours in advance; store in an airtight container. Fill and coat with toffee within 1 hour of serving.

FIGS IN HONEY SYRUP

Preparation time: 20 minutes
Total cooking time: 1 hour
Serves 4

100 g (3½ oz) blanched whole almonds
12 whole fresh figs (about 750 g/1½ lb)
½ cup (125 g/4 oz) sugar
⅓ cup (115 g/4 oz) honey
2 tablespoons lemon juice
6 cm (2½ inch) sliver of lemon rind
1 cinnamon stick
1 cup (250 g/8 oz) Greek-style natural yoghurt

1 Preheat the oven to moderate 180°C (350°F/Gas 4). Place the almonds on a baking tray and bake for 5 minutes, or until golden. Leave to cool. Cut the stems off the figs and make a small crossways incision 5 mm (¼ inch) deep on top of each. Push a blanched almond into the base of each fig. Roughly chop the remaining almonds.
2 Place 3 cups (750 ml/24 fl oz) water in a large saucepan, add the sugar and stir over medium heat until the sugar dissolves. Increase the heat and bring to the boil. Stir in the honey, lemon juice, lemon rind and cinnamon stick. Reduce the heat to medium, place the figs in the pan and simmer gently for 30 minutes. Remove with a slotted spoon and place on a large serving dish.
3 Boil the liquid over high heat for about 15–20 minutes, or until thick and syrupy. Remove the cinnamon and rind. Cool the syrup slightly and pour over the figs. Sprinkle with almonds and serve warm or cold with yoghurt.

LEMON LIME SORBET

Preparation time: 25 minutes + freezing
Total cooking time: 10 minutes
Serves 4

1 cup (250 g/8 oz) sugar
¾ cup (185 ml/6 fl oz) lemon juice
¾ cup (185 ml/6 fl oz) lime juice
2 egg whites, lightly beaten

1 Stir 2 cups (500 ml/16 fl oz) water with the sugar in a pan, over low heat, until the sugar has dissolved. Bring to the boil, reduce the heat to low, simmer for 5 minutes, then cool.
2 Add the lemon and lime juice to the syrup and pour into a metal tray. Cover with a piece of greaseproof paper and freeze for 2 hours. Transfer the icy mixture to a food processor or bowl and process or beat with electric beaters to a slush, then return to the freezer. Repeat the beating and freezing twice more.
3 Transfer to a bowl or food processor. With the electric beaters or processor motor running, add the egg whites and blend. Return to the freezer container, cover with a piece of greaseproof paper and freeze until firm.
4 If you are using an ice cream machine, add the egg white when the sorbet is almost churned and the machine is still running.

ITALIAN RICE PUDDING

Preparation time: 10 minutes
Total cooking time: 40 minutes
Serves 4

2½ cups (600 ml/20 fl oz) milk
1 cup (250 ml/8 fl oz) thick (double/heavy) cream
1 vanilla bean, split
50 g (1¾ oz) caster (superfine) sugar
¼ teaspoon ground cinnamon
pinch of freshly grated nutmeg
1 tablespoon grated orange zest
½ cup (80 g/2¾ oz) sultanas
2 tablespoons brandy or sweet Marsala
½ cup (110 g/3½ oz) risotto rice

1 Put the milk, cream and vanilla bean in a heavy-based saucepan and bring just to the boil, then remove from the heat. Stir in the sugar, cinnamon, nutmeg and orange zest and set aside.
2 Soak the sultanas in the brandy. Meanwhile, add the rice to the infused milk and return to the heat. Bring to a simmer and stir slowly for about 35 minutes, or until the rice is creamy. Stir in the sultanas and remove the vanilla bean at the end. Serve warm or cold.

TRIPLE CHOCOLATE TERRINE

Preparation time: 1 hour + freezing
Total cooking time: 15–20 minutes
Serves 8–10

150 g (5 oz) milk chocolate, chopped
6 eggs
¾ cup (90 g/3 oz) icing sugar
60 g (2 oz) unsalted butter
2 cups (500 ml/16 fl oz) cream
150 g (5 oz) white chocolate, chopped
2 teaspoons instant coffee
3–4 teaspoons dark rum
150 g (5 oz) good-quality dark chocolate, chopped

1 Line a 10 x 23 cm (4 x 9 inch) loaf tin with baking paper, extending above the top of the tin. Melt the milk chocolate in a small bowl, over a pan of steaming water, off the heat, making sure the bottom of the bowl does not touch the water, until smooth. Separate 2 of the eggs and beat the whites until soft peaks form. Gradually beat in ¼ cup (30 g/1 oz) of the icing sugar, until thick and glossy. Beat in the 2 egg yolks and the cooled melted chocolate. Melt 20 g (1 oz) of the butter and beat in. Whip ⅔ cup (170 ml/5½ fl oz) of the cream into soft peaks. Fold into the egg white mixture and then spoon into the tin, with the tin tilted on one side lengthways. Put in the freezer on this angle and leave for 1–2 hours, until just firm.
2 Repeat the same method with the white chocolate. Spoon this mixture into the other side of the tin so that the terrine becomes level. Put the tin flat in the freezer to set.
3 Repeat the same method with the remaining ingredients, folding in the coffee dissolved in 1 tablespoon of water, and rum, with the dark chocolate. Spoon into the tin and smooth the surface. Freeze for several hours. Turn out onto a plate, then cut into thin slices to serve. Can be garnished with chocolate leaves.

STICKY RICE WITH MANGOES

Preparation time: 40 minutes +
    12 hours soaking
Total cooking time: 1 hour
Serves 4

2 cups (400 g/12⅔ oz) glutinous rice
1 tablespoon white sesame seeds, to
    serve
1 cup (250 ml/8 fl oz) coconut milk
½ cup (90 g/3 oz) grated palm sugar or
    soft brown sugar
¼ teaspoon salt
2–3 mangoes, peeled, seeded and sliced
3 tablespoons coconut cream
fresh mint sprigs, to garnish

1 Place the rice in a sieve and wash it under running water until the water runs clear. Place the rice in a glass or ceramic bowl, cover it with water and leave it to soak overnight, or for a minimum of 12 hours. Drain the rice.
2 Line a metal or bamboo steamer with muslin. Place the rice on top of the muslin and cover the steamer with a tight-fitting lid. Place the steamer over a pot of boiling water and steam over moderately low heat for 50 minutes, or until the rice is cooked. Transfer the rice to a large bowl and fluff it up with a fork.

3 Toast the sesame seeds in a dry pan over medium heat for 3 to 4 minutes, shaking the pan gently, until the seeds are golden brown; remove from the pan at once to prevent burning.
4 Pour the coconut milk into a small pan; add the sugar and salt. Slowly bring the mixture to the boil, stirring constantly until the sugar has dissolved. Lower the heat and simmer for 5 minutes, or until the mixture has thickened slightly. Stir the mixture often while it is simmering, and take care that it does not stick to the bottom of the pan.
5 Slowly pour the coconut milk over the top of the rice. Use a fork to lift and fluff the rice. Do not stir the liquid through, otherwise the rice will become too gluggy. Let the rice mixture rest for 20 minutes before carefully spooning it into the centre of 4 warmed serving plates. Arrange the mango slices around the rice mounds. Spoon a little coconut cream over the rice, sprinkle over the sesame seeds, and garnish with the mint leaves.

STRAWBERRIES WITH BALSAMIC VINEGAR

Preparation time: 10 minutes +
    1 hour marinating
Total cooking time: Nil
Serves 4

750 g (1½ lb) ripe small strawberries
¼ cup (60 g/2 oz) caster sugar
2 tablespoons good-quality balsamic
    vinegar
½ cup (125 g/4 oz) mascarpone, to serve

1 Wipe the strawberries with a clean damp cloth and hull them. Halve large strawberries.
2 Place the strawberries in a glass bowl, sprinkle the sugar evenly over the top and toss gently to coat. Leave for 30 minutes to macerate. Sprinkle the vinegar over the strawberries, toss and refrigerate for 30 minutes.
3 Spoon the strawberries into four glasses, drizzle with the syrup and top with a dollop of mascarpone.

NEW YEAR SWEET DUMPLINGS

Preparation time: 40 minutes
Total cooking time: 15 minutes
Makes 24

60 g (2 oz) black sesame paste, red bean
    paste or smooth peanut butter
⅓ cup (80 g/2¾ oz) caster (superfine)
    sugar
250 g (8 oz) glutinous rice flour
30 g (1 oz) rock sugar (see Note)

1 Combine the sesame paste with the
caster sugar in a small bowl.
2 Sift the rice flour into a bowl and stir in
220 ml (7 fl oz) boiling water. Knead
carefully (the dough will be very hot) to
form a soft, slightly sticky dough. Dust
your hands with extra rice flour, roll the
dough into a cylinder, then divide it into
cherry-size pieces. Cover the dough with
a tea towel and, using one piece at a time,
form each piece of dough into a flat
round, then gather it into a cup shape.
The dough should be fairly thin.
3 Fill each cup shape with 1 teaspoon of
paste and fold the top over, smoothing the
dough so you have a round ball with no
visible joins.
4 Bring 1 litre (32 fl oz) water to the boil,
add the rock sugar and stir until
dissolved. Return to the boil, add the
dumplings in batches and simmer for
5 minutes, or until they rise to the
surface. Serve warm with a little of the
syrup.

NOTE: Yellow rock sugar comes as
uneven lumps of sugar, which may need
to be further crushed before use if very
big. It is a pure sugar that produces a
clear syrup and makes sauces shiny and
clear. You can use sugar cubes instead.

LEMON GRANITA

Preparation time: 15 minutes +
    2 hours freezing
Total cooking time: 5 minutes
Serves 4–6

1¼ cups (275 ml) lemon juice
1 tablespoon grated lemon rind
200 g (6½ oz) caster sugar

1 Place the lemon juice, rind and sugar in
a small saucepan and stir over low heat
for 5 minutes, or until the sugar is
dissolved. Allow to cool.
2 Add 2 cups (500 ml/16 fl oz) water to the
lemon mixture and mix well. Pour into
a shallow 30 x 20 cm (12 x 8 inch) metal
container or tray and cool completely.
Freeze for 30 minutes, then scrape with a
fork to distribute the ice crystals evenly.
Return to the freezer for 30 minutes.
3 Using a fork, scrape the granita into fine
crystals and return to the freezer for
1 hour before serving. Spoon into chilled
glasses and serve immediately.

STUFFED FIGS

Preparation time: 30 minutes +
    3 hours soaking
Total cooking time: 30 minutes
Makes 18

½ cup (175 g/6 oz) honey
½ cup (125 ml/4 fl oz) sweet dark sherry
¼ teaspoon ground cinnamon
18 large dried figs
18 whole blanched almonds
100 g (3½ oz) dark chocolate, cut into
    shards
butter, for greasing
thick (double) cream for serving, optional

1 Combine the honey, sherry, cinnamon
and figs with 1½ cups (375 ml/12 fl oz)
water in a large saucepan over high heat.
Bring to the boil then reduce the heat and
simmer for 10 minutes. Remove the pan
from the heat and set aside for 3 hours.
Remove the figs with a slotted spoon,
reserving the liquid.
2 Preheat the oven to moderate 180°C
(350°F/Gas 4). Return the pan of liquid to
the stove and boil over high heat for
5 minutes, or until syrupy, then set aside.
Snip the stems from the figs with scissors
then cut a slit in the top of each fig with
small sharp knife. Push an almond and a
few shards of chocolate into each slit.
Place the figs in a lightly buttered dish
and bake for 15 minutes or until the
chocolate has melted.
3 Serve three figs per person with a little
of the syrup and a dollop of cream.

ALL ABOUT CREAM

MILK IS AMAZING—IT CONTAINS NOURISHING PROTEINS, SUGARS, FATS, VITAMINS AND MINERALS AND IT CAN BE TRANSFORMED INTO A HOST OF OTHER DAIRY PRODUCTS.

CREAM

If fresh milk is left to stand, a layer of cream will form on top as the butterfat rises. So cream is simply a form of milk in which the butterfat is more concentrated. It is either skimmed off the top after rising naturally or removed by the use of centrifugal force. Cream varies in thickness and richness, according to how much butterfat it contains—the thicker the cream, the higher the percentage of butterfat. But cream labelled 'thickened cream' has had thickening agents such as gelatine added to help it hold its shape. Cream for whipping must have at least 35% butterfat to trap the air bubbles and hold them in place. Reduced fat cream has a maximum of 25% fat and light cream around 18%. Pouring cream has a butterfat content higher than both English single cream and American light cream, neither of which can be whipped—it varies between 35% and 48%. Thick cream ('double' in England and 'heavy' in America) has a minimum butterfat content of 48%. Clotted, scalded or Devonshire cream is the thickest and yellowest of all. All cream should be well chilled before whipping and should be refrigerated when not in use.

SOUR CREAM

Originally made by leaving cream at room temperature to sour, today it is made by adding a culture to cream. It is thickened and slightly acidic because the milk sugar (lactose) converts to lactic acid. Low-fat varieties are now available.

CREME FRAICHE

This French version of cultured sour cream is smooth, rich and slightly acidic, with a higher fat content than thick cream. Its mild acidity complements the sweetness of chocolate and fruit.

RICOTTA

This was originally made from the whey of milk but nowadays is often made from milk. It is low in fat, has a slight sweetness and short shelf life. It should look moist and white, not dry and discoloured.

QUARK/FROMAGE FRAIS/FROMAGE BLANC/CREAM CHEESE

These are soft curd cheeses made from both full-fat and non full-fat milk. Fromage frais and fromage blanc have been homogenized to give a smoother texture and have a slightly acidic edge. Cream cheese is also sold as Neufchatel.

BUTTERMILK

Butter is produced by churning cream until the fat comes together and, traditionally, buttermilk was the liquid remaining after this process. However, cultured buttermilk is made from skim milk which has a bacterial culture added to ripen and thicken it slightly. It becomes slightly acidic as the lactose turns to lactic acid. It activates bicarbonate of soda, so is often used in baking to give a light texture.

YOGHURT

This is made by adding a culture of Lactobacillus bulgaricus, Lactobacillus acidophilus or Streptococcus thermophilus to warm milk. The bacilli create acidity which ferments and thickens the milk and destroys some of the intrinsic bacteria, giving it a longer 'edible' life and making it an easily digested food.

MASCARPONE

This rich creamy cheese originated in Italy. Traditional in tiramisu, it also works well in cheesecakes and ice cream.

CLOCKWISE, FROM TOP LEFT: Double (thick) cream, cream, buttermilk, milk, mascarpone, ricotta, yoghurt, (on plate: fromage blanc, quark, cream cheese), crème fraîche, sour cream, clotted cream

SWEET COUSCOUS

Preparation time: 10 minutes + 10 minutes
standing
Total cooking time: 5 minutes standing
Serves 4–6

80 g (2¾ oz) combined pistachio nuts,
pine nuts and blanched almonds
45 g (1½ oz) dried apricots
½ cup (90 g/3 oz) pitted dried dates
250 g (8 oz) instant couscous
¼ cup (60 g/2 oz) caster sugar
1 cup (250 ml/8 fl oz) boiling water
90 g (3 oz) unsalted butter, softened

For serving
2 tablespoons caster sugar
½ teaspoon ground cinnamon
1½ cups (375 ml/12 fl oz) hot milk

1 Preheat the oven to warm 160°C
(315°F/Gas 2–3). Spread the nuts on a
baking tray and bake for about 5 minutes,
until light golden. Allow to cool, then chop
coarsely and place in a bowl. Slice the
apricots into matchstick-sized pieces and
quarter the dates lengthways. Add both to
the bowl and toss to combine.
2 Put the couscous and sugar in a large
bowl and cover with the boiling water. Stir
well, then add the butter and a pinch of
salt. Stir until the butter melts. Cover with
a tea towel and set aside for 10 minutes.
Fluff with a fork, then toss half the fruit
and nut mixture through.
3 To serve, pile the warm couscous in the
centre of a platter. Arrange the remaining
nut mixture around the base. Combine the
sugar and cinnamon in a small bowl and
serve separately for sprinkling. Pass
around the hot milk in a jug for guests to
help themselves.

NOTE: This can be made up to 4 days
ahead. Spoon it into an earthenware
baking dish, cover with foil and
refrigerate. To reheat, bring to room
temperature, then place in a moderate
180°C (350°F/Gas 4) oven for 20 minutes.

CHOCOLATE ECLAIRS

Preparation time: 20 minutes
Total cooking time: 40 minutes
Makes 18

1 cup (250 ml/8 fl oz) water
125 g (4 oz) butter
1 cup (125 g/4 oz) plain flour, sifted
4 eggs
315 ml (10 fl oz) cream, whipped
150 g (4¾ oz) dark chocolate, melted

1 Preheat oven to hot 210°C (415°F/
Gas 6–7). Brush two baking trays with oil.
Combine water and butter in pan. Stir
over medium heat until butter melts.
Bring to boil, remove from heat.
2 Add flour all at once. Return to heat and
stir with a wooden spoon until mixture
leaves side of pan and forms a ball
around the spoon. Transfer to a large
bowl; cool slightly. Add eggs one at a
time, beating well after each addition until
mixture is thick, smooth and shiny.
3 Spoon into a piping bag fitted with a
1.5 cm (⅝ inch) plain nozzle. Pipe 15 cm
(6 inch) lengths onto trays, leaving room
for expansion.
4 Bake for 10–15 minutes. Reduce heat to
moderate 180°C (350°F/Gas 4). Bake
another 15 minutes or until golden and
firm. Split each éclair, removing
uncooked dough. Fill with cream. Coat the
tops with melted chocolate.

INDIVIDUAL BAKED RICE PUDDINGS

Preparation time: 10 minutes
Total cooking time: 1 hour
Serves 4–6

¼ cup (55 g/2 oz) short- or medium-grain
rice
1⅔ cups (410 ml/13 fl oz) milk
1½ tablespoons caster (superfine) sugar
¾ cup (185 ml/6 fl oz) cream, plus extra,
to serve
¼ teaspoon natural vanilla extract
¼ teaspoon freshly grated nutmeg

1 Preheat the oven to slow 150°C
(300°F/Gas 2) and grease four 1 cup
(250 ml/8 fl oz) ramekins or six smaller
ones. In a bowl, mix together the rice,
milk, sugar, cream and vanilla extract,
and pour into the greased dishes. Dust
the surface of each one with grated
nutmeg.
2 Bake the rice puddings for about 1 hour,
or until the rice has absorbed most of the
milk, the texture is creamy and a brown
skin has formed on top. Serve hot with
fresh cream.

MASCARPONE TRIFLE

Preparation time: 40 minutes + chilling
Total cooking time: 10 minutes
Serves 4–6

175 g (6 oz) plain sponge cake
½ cup (125 ml/4 fl oz) Tia Maria or Kahlua
70 g (2¼ oz) dark chocolate, grated
500 g (1 lb) strawberries, hulled
cocoa powder and icing sugar, to dust

Custard
4 egg yolks
2 tablespoons sugar
2 teaspoons cornflour
½ cup (125 ml/4 fl oz) cream
½ cup (125 ml/4 fl oz) milk
2 teaspoons vanilla essence
1⅓ cups (350 ml/11 fl oz) cream, extra
250 g (4 oz) mascarpone

1 Cut the cake into chunks and put in the base of a 1.75 litre dish. Spoon the liqueur over the cake and sprinkle with half the grated chocolate. Slice a third of the strawberries and sprinkle over the top. Cover and refrigerate.
2 To make the custard, whisk together the yolks, sugar and cornflour until thick and pale. Heat the cream and milk in a pan until almost boiling, then gradually whisk into the yolk mixture. Pour into a clean pan and return to low heat, until the custard thickens and coats the back of a spoon. Remove from the heat and stir in the vanilla essence and remaining grated chocolate until smooth. Cover the surface with plastic wrap, to stop a skin forming, and allow to cool.

3 Whip a third of the extra cream until soft peaks form and gently fold this and the mascarpone into the cooled custard. Spoon over the cake and strawberries, cover with plastic wrap and then refrigerate until needed. When you are ready to serve, whip the remaining cream until stiff peaks form and spoon over the trifle. Cut the remaining strawberries in half and arrange on top. Dust with a mixture of cocoa powder and icing sugar to serve.

NOTE: Mascarpone is made with cream and looks more like cream than cheese. Slightly sweet with an acidic edge, it is softer than cream cheese.

ALMOND CREAM PUDDING

Preparation time: 15 minutes +
  1 hour refrigeration
Total cooking time: 40 minutes
Serves 4

2 cups (500 ml/16 fl oz) milk
75 g (2½ oz) caster sugar
2 tablespoons cornflour
2 tablespoons ground rice
75 g (2½ oz) ground blanched almonds
1 teaspoon rosewater
2 tablespoons flower blossom honey
2 tablespoons shelled pistachio nuts, chopped

1 Place the milk and sugar in a saucepan and heat over medium heat, stirring until the sugar has dissolved.
2 Combine the cornflour and ground rice with ¼ cup (60 ml/2 fl oz) water and mix to a paste. Add to the milk and cook, stirring occasionally, over low heat for 20 minutes. Add the almonds and cook for 15 minutes, then add the rosewater. Spoon into shallow serving dishes and refrigerate for 1 hour. Serve drizzled with a little honey and sprinkled with pistachios.

STUFFED PEACHES

Preparation time: 15 minutes
Total cooking time: 25 minutes
Serves 6

6 ripe peaches
60 g (2 oz) amaretti biscuits, crushed
1 egg yolk
2 tablespoons caster sugar
20 g (¾ oz) almond meal
1 tablespoon amaretto
¼ cup (60 ml/2 fl oz) white wine
1 teaspoon caster sugar, extra
20 g (¾ oz) unsalted butter

1 Preheat the oven to moderate 180°C
(350°/Gas 4) and lightly grease a
30 x 25 cm (12 x 10 inch) ovenproof dish
with butter.
2 Cut each peach in half and carefully
remove the stones. Scoop a little of the
pulp out from each and combine in a
small bowl with the crushed biscuits, egg
yolk, caster sugar, almond meal and
amaretto.
3 Spoon some of the mixture into each
peach and place them cut-side-up in the
dish. Sprinkle with the white wine and the
extra sugar. Place a dot of butter on the
top of each and bake for 20–25 minutes,
until golden.

NOTE: When they are in season, you can
also use ripe apricots or nectarines for
this recipe.

SWEET CHEESE IN LEMON PASTA

Preparation time: 1 hour + standing
Total cooking time: 25 minutes
Serves 4–6

2 cups (250 g/8 oz) plain flour
½ teaspoon salt
1 teaspoon caster sugar
grated rind of 2 lemons
2 tablespoons fresh lemon juice
2 eggs, lightly beaten
1 tablespoon currants
1 tablespoon brandy
600 g (1¼ lb) ricotta cheese
5 tablespoons icing sugar
¾ teaspoon grated lemon rind
¾ teaspoon vanilla essence
beaten egg, for glazing
4 tablespoons flaked almonds, toasted
vegetable oil, for frying
1 cup (250 ml/8 fl oz) cream, flavoured
   with brandy, to taste
mint leaves and thin strips of lemon rind
   or candied lemon peel, to garnish,
   optional

1 Pile the combined flour, salt, sugar and
lemon rind on a work surface and make a
well in the centre. Add 1–2 tablespoons of
water, the lemon juice and egg and
gradually blend them into the flour, using
a fork. The dough can be made in a
processor up to this point. When a loosely
combined dough forms, use your hands
and begin kneading. Incorporate a little
extra flour if the dough feels moist.
Knead for 5–8 minutes, or until smooth
and elastic. Cover with plastic and set
aside for 15 minutes.
2 Soak the currants in the brandy in a
bowl. In a larger bowl, combine the
ricotta cheese, icing sugar, lemon rind
and vanilla. Set aside.
3 Divide the dough into eight equal
portions. Roll each out to a thin sheet
about 18 cm (7 inches) square. Cover each
as it is completed.
4 Trim the pasta into neat squares.
Working with a few at a time, brush
around the edges with beaten egg. Add
the currants and toasted almonds to the
ricotta filling, then put one-eighth of the
filling in the middle of each square of
dough. Fold the edges over to completely
enclose the filling. Press the edges down
to seal.
5 Heat oil in a pan to 1–2 cm (about ½
inch) depth. Drop a piece of scrap pasta in
to check that it turns golden without
burning. Fry the parcels, two or three at a
time, until golden. Remove with a slotted
spoon, drain on paper towels and keep
warm. Serve with brandy cream,
sprinkled with icing sugar and garnished
with mint leaves and lemon rind.

STUFFED FRIED PANCAKES

Preparation time: 20 minutes +
   1 hour rising
Total cooking time: 1 hour
Makes about 16

Batter
7 g (¾ oz) sachet dry yeast
1 teaspoon sugar
1½ cups (185 g/6 oz) plain flour

Syrup
500 g (1 lb) sugar
2 teaspoons lemon juice
2 tablespoons rosewater

Filling
1 cup (250 g/8 oz) ricotta

oil, for brushing
peanut oil, for deep-frying

1 Place the yeast and sugar in a small bowl with ¼ cup (60 ml/fl oz) warm water and stir until dissolved. Leave in a warm place for 10 minutes or until bubbles appear on the surface. The mixture should be frothy and slightly increased in volume. If your yeast doesn't foam it is dead and you will have to start again. Sift the flour into a large bowl, make a well in the centre and add the yeast mixture and 1½ cups (375 ml/12 fl oz) warm water. Using a wooden spoon, gradually stir in the flour and mix until smooth. Cover the bowl with a cloth and leave in a warm place for 1 hour, or until the batter has risen and the surface is bubbly.

2 Meanwhile, for the syrup, dissolve the sugar in 1¼ cups (315 ml/10 fl oz) water in a heavy-based saucepan over medium heat, stirring occasionally. Bring to the boil, add the lemon juice and simmer for 8–10 minutes, until the syrup is thick enough to coat the back of a spoon. It should be the consistency of thin honey. Add the rosewater and cook for another minute. Allow to cool completely.
3 To make the pancakes, lightly grease a heavy-based frying pan and place over medium heat. Stir ¼ cup (60 ml/fl oz) water into the batter. Pour 1½ tablespoons batter into the pan, tilting it a little so the batter spreads to about 10 cm (4 inches). If the batter is too thick, add a little extra water. Cook the pancakes for about 3 minutes, or until golden on the underside and bubbles appear on the surface. Remove them from the pan, stack them on a plate and allow to cool slightly.
4 Place 1 tablespoon of the ricotta on the unfried side of each pancake. Fold each in half and pinch the edges together to seal into a half moon shape.
5 Heat the peanut oil in a deep-fryer or heavy-based saucepan to 190°C (375°F), or until a cube of bread dropped into the oil browns in 10 seconds. Fry the stuffed pancakes 3 or 4 at a time for 2–3 minutes, until golden. Remove with a slotted spoon and drain on paper towels. Dip the hot pancakes into the cooled syrup and serve warm or cold stacked on a large flat plate.

FROZEN HONEY CHEESECAKE WITH PRALINE CRUST

Preparation time: 1 hour + freezing
Total cooking time: 25 minutes
Serves 8–10

100 g (3½ oz) flaked almonds
¾ cup (185 g/6 oz) sugar
225 g (7 oz) plain sweet biscuits
100 g (3½ oz) unsalted butter, melted

Filling
250 g (8 oz) mascarpone cheese
250 g (8 oz) cream cheese, softened to
   room temperature
400 g (13 oz) can condensed milk
¼ cup (60 ml/2 fl oz) honey
1¼ cups (315 ml/10 fl oz) cream
2 teaspoons ground cinnamon

1 Preheat the oven to slow 150°C (300°F/Gas 2). To make the praline, spread the almonds on a foil-lined, greased baking tray. Put the sugar in a pan with ½ cup (125 ml/4 fl oz) water and stir over low heat until the sugar has dissolved. Bring to the boil, then simmer without stirring until the toffee is golden brown. Pour over the almonds, then set aside to cool and harden before breaking into pieces.
2 Lightly grease a 23 cm (9 inch) diameter springform tin and line the base with baking paper. Reserve about half the praline and finely chop the rest with the biscuits in a food processor. Stir in the butter, spoon into the base and press firmly on the side of the tin. Bake for 15 minutes and then leave to cool.
3 To make the filling, process the mascarpone and cream cheese together until soft and creamy. Add the condensed milk and honey. Whip the cream until soft peaks form and then fold in. Pour into the tin, sprinkle with cinnamon and swirl gently with a skewer. Do not overmix. Freeze for several hours, or until firm, and decorate with the remaining praline.

TORTA DI RISO
(ITALIAN RICE TART)

Preparation time: 25 minutes +
1 hour 30 minutes refrigeration
Total cooking time: 1 hour 35 minutes
Serves 8–10

Pastry

1¼ cups (155 g/5 oz) plain (all-purpose)
    flour
¼ cup (60 g/2 oz) caster (superfine) sugar
125 g (4 oz) cold unsalted butter, cut into
    1 cm (½ inch) dice
2 egg yolks
1 teaspoon vanilla extract

Filling

½ cup (110 g/3½ oz) arborio rice
½ cup (60 g/2 oz) raisins
2 tablespoons cognac or brandy
3 cups (750 ml/24 fl oz) cream
1 vanilla bean, split
2 cinnamon sticks
6 egg yolks
¾ cup (180 g/6 oz) caster (superfine)
    sugar
⅓ cup (50 g/1¾ oz) pine nuts, toasted
1½ teaspoons finely grated lemon zest

1 To make the pastry, sift the flour into a
bowl and add the sugar and a pinch of
salt. Add the butter and toss to coat in the
flour mix. Rub the butter into the flour
with your fingertips for about 5 minutes or
until it resembles fine breadcrumbs, then
make a well in the centre.
2 Mix the egg yolks, vanilla and 3
tablespoons of cold water together, then
pour into the well. Using a flat-bladed
knife, cut into the mixture while you turn
the bowl until it is well combined and
comes together in small beads. Pinch a
small amount of dough together to see if
it holds; if it still crumbles add 1 more
teaspoon of water.

3 Gather the dough together, press into a
ball then flatten into a 2 cm (¾ inch) thick
disc. Cover with plastic wrap and
refrigerate for 30 minutes.
4 Roll the pastry out between two sheets
of baking paper or plastic wrap until it is
36 cm (14 inches) in diameter. Remove the
top layer of baking paper and invert the
pastry onto a 28 cm (11 inch) fluted tart
dish or tin with 4 cm (1½ inch) sides.
Remove the final layer of paper and
carefully press the pastry into the dish,
allowing any extra to hang over the sides,
then trim the edges using a small sharp
knife. Prick the base all over with a fork
then put in the fridge for 1 hour or the
freezer for 30 minutes.
5 Meanwhile, preheat the oven to moderate
180°C (350°F/Gas 4). Toss the raisins and
cognac together and set aside to soak.
Cook the rice in boiling water for 15
minutes, or until tender—there will still be
some give. Drain, rinse with cold water and
leave to drain and cool thoroughly. Place
the cream, vanilla bean and cinnamon
sticks in a saucepan and bring almost to
the boil over medium heat. Remove from
the heat and set aside to infuse and cool.
6 Remove the tart from the fridge, line
with lightly crumpled baking paper and
pour in some baking beads and spread
evenly over the base. Bake for 15 minutes
then remove the paper and beads and
cook for a further 10–15 minutes, or until
lightly golden all over. Remove from the
oven and set aside. Reduce the
temperature to slow 150°C (300°F/Gas 2).
7 Beat the egg yolks and sugar together
until thick and creamy. Strain the cream
mixture and stir into the eggs until well
combined. Combine the cold rice with the
raisins and pine nuts.
8 When the tart shell is at room
temperature evenly spread the rice
mixture over the base, then gently pour
over the custard. Bake for 45 minutes, or
until the centre has just set. Allow the tart
to cool completely as it will break up if
you try to cut it while it is still warm.
Serve with lightly whipped cream.

STRAWBERRY AND
BANANA ICE

Preparation time: 10 minutes + freezing
Total cooking time: Nil
Serves 4

300 g (10 oz) silken tofu, chopped
250 g (4 oz) strawberries, chopped
2 ripe bananas, chopped
¼ cup (60 g/2 oz) caster sugar

1 Blend the tofu, strawberries, bananas
and caster sugar in a blender or
processor until smooth.
2 Freeze in a shallow cake tin until almost
frozen, then chop roughly using a fork.
Transfer to a large bowl and beat until
smooth. Pour into a 15 x 25 cm (6 x 10
inch) loaf tin, cover and freeze again, until
firm. Alternatively, freeze in an ice cream
machine until thick and creamy.
Refrigerate for about 30 minutes before
serving to allow the ice to soften slightly.

HOT FRUIT SOUFFLE

Preparation time: 15 minutes
Total cooking time: 30 minutes
Serves 4

unsalted butter, melted, for greasing
caster sugar, for sprinkling
60 g (2 oz) unsalted butter, extra
½ cup (60 g/2 oz) plain flour
1½ cups (375 ml/12 fl oz) puréed fruit (see Note)
¼ cup (60 g/2 oz) caster sugar, extra
4 egg whites
icing sugar, to dust

1 Prepare a 1.25 litre soufflé dish by brushing melted butter evenly and generously over the dish, especially at the rim. Sprinkle with caster sugar, shake to coat evenly, then tip out any excess. Preheat the oven to moderately hot 200°C (400°F/Gas 6) and put a baking tray on the top shelf to heat.
2 Melt the extra butter in a saucepan, add the flour and mix well. Remove from the heat, stir until smooth, then stir in the fruit purée. Return the saucepan to the heat, bring the mixture to the boil and simmer for 2 minutes. Add the extra sugar a little at a time, tasting for sweetness as you go. Add a little extra sugar if necessary. Leave to cool.

3 Whisk the egg whites in a large clean bowl until soft peaks form, add 1 tablespoon to the fruit mixture and mix well. Fold in the remaining whites, being careful not to lose too much volume. Fill the soufflé dish to three-quarters full.
4 Put the soufflé dish on the hot baking tray and bake for 20–25 minutes, until risen well and golden. Serve immediately, dusted with icing sugar.

NOTE: To ensure success when making soufflés, make sure you fold the egg whites into the basic soufflé mixture as gently as possible. It is better to leave a few pieces of egg white unmixed than to end up with a flat soufflé.
 Suitable fruits to use are those that make a good purée, such as raspberries, strawberries, mangoes, peaches, apricots and passionfruit. Bananas are a little too heavy. You could use apples or plums, or dried fruit, but you'd have to cook them into a purée first.

CHOCOLATE RUM MOUSSE

Preparation time: 20 minutes + chilling
Total cooking time: 5 minutes
Serves 4

250 g (8 oz) good-quality dark chocolate, chopped
3 eggs
¼ cup (60 g/2 oz) caster sugar
2 teaspoons dark rum
1 cup (250 ml/8 fl oz) cream, softly whipped

1 Put the chocolate in a heatproof bowl. Half fill a saucepan with water and bring to the boil. Remove from the heat and place the bowl over the pan, making sure it is not touching the water. Stir occasionally until the chocolate has melted. Set aside to cool.
2 Using electric beaters, beat the eggs and sugar in a small bowl for 5 minutes, or until thick, pale and increased in volume.
3 Transfer the mixture to a large bowl. Using a metal spoon, fold in the melted chocolate with the rum, leave the mixture to cool, then fold in the whipped cream until just combined.
4 Spoon into four 250 ml (8 fl oz) ramekins or dessert glasses. Refrigerate for 2 hours, or until set. This dessert can be decorated with chocolate leaves.

SOUFFLE SECRETS

SOUFFLES ARE HELD UP BY BEATEN EGG WHITES AND HOT AIR. AS THE SOUFFLE COOKS, THE AIR WITHIN IT EXPANDS AND PUSHES IT UPWARDS, SOMETIMES AS MUCH AS DOUBLING ITS HEIGHT.

Soufflés are, technically, always hot. Although iced or cold soufflés are actually mousses, they are sometimes called soufflés—they are held up by gelatine and beaten egg whites and will not collapse like hot soufflés. The lightness in a cold soufflé comes from the egg whites themselves, rather than the expansion of hot air. Soufflés can be made on a custard-type base, a roux base, or, for a really light result, a fruit purée.

MAKING A PERFECT SOUFFLE

To get the best rise out of a soufflé, you will need a straight-sided ovenproof glass or ceramic soufflé dish (a metal dish will give a quicker cooking time, but be careful as some fruits react with metal and turn the soufflé grey around the edge). If the mixture comes more than two-thirds of the way up the dish, you will need to make a collar. The following instructions are for a soufflé based on a fruit purée. You will need about 250 g (8 oz) of fruit (we've used 2 mangoes and the pulp from 4 passionfruit), 4 egg whites and 3 tablespoons caster sugar. Separate the eggs one by one into a smaller bowl, just in case one of them breaks.

1 To make a collar, wrap a double layer of non-stick baking paper around a 1.5 litre soufflé dish so that it extends 5 cm (2 inches) above the rim. Fix it firmly in place with a piece of string.

2 Lightly grease the inside of the dish and collar with melted butter or flavourless oil and sprinkle with a little caster sugar. Turn the dish so the sugar coats the entire surface of the dish and collar, then turn the dish upside down and tap to loosen any excess sugar. The sugar will help the soufflé grip and climb up the side of the dish as it cooks. Preheat the oven to hot 220°C (425°F/Gas 7) and put a baking tray on the middle shelf.

3 Purée the mango in a food processor and then add the passionfruit (leave the seeds in if you wish but do not process).

4 Place the egg whites in a large, very clean, dry stainless steel or glass bowl—any hint of grease will prevent them foaming. (Traditionally, egg whites are beaten in copper bowls as the copper and whites react to form a more stable foam. If you use a copper bowl, you must clean it with 2 tablespoons salt mixed with 2 tablespoons lemon juice or vinegar, and rinse and dry it thoroughly JUST before you use it.) Leave the whites for a few minutes to reach room temperature, then beat with a balloon whisk or electric beaters. A balloon whisk gives better volume than electric beaters as each sweep of the whisk passes through the whole amount of whites, but make sure you use a large enough whisk—a small one will not give you enough volume. Beat slowly until the whites start to become a frothy foam, then increase your speed until the bubbles in the foam have become small and evenly-sized. When the foam forms stiff peaks, add the sugar little by little. Continue beating until the mixture is glossy—don't overbeat or it will become grainy and not rise well.

5 Fold two spoonfuls of the whites into the fruit purée and mix well to loosen and lighten the mixture. Fold in the remaining whites with a large metal spoon, being careful not to lose any volume. Pour into the dish and run your finger around the edge to loosen the mixture from the side of the dish. Place on the baking tray in the oven—unless it's an emergency, don't open the oven door until the cooking time is up. It should take 20–25 minutes to cook. If the soufflé is rising more on one side than the other, carefully rotate the dish. Some fruit may have a higher sugar content and cause the top of the soufflé to brown too quickly. If so, rest a piece of foil on top of the soufflé to prevent over-browning. When the soufflé is ready, it should have a pale gold crust and not wobble too much. It should be served immediately, as soufflés wait for no-one. Traditionally, you would make a hole in the centre and pour in a contrasting fruit sauce or cream.

CRANBERRY KISEL

Preparation time: 15 minutes +
   2 hours refrigeration
Total cooking time: 15 minutes
Serves 4

2 lemons
1½ cups (375 g/12 oz) caster sugar
2 cinnamon sticks
600 g (1¼ lb) cranberries (fresh or frozen)
2 teaspoons cornflour
2 teaspoons orange juice

Yoghurt cream
1 cup (250 ml/8 fl oz) cream
½ cup (125 ml/4 fl oz) natural yoghurt
½ cup (115 g/4 oz) soft brown sugar

1 Remove the peel from the lemons in
large strips with a vegetable peeler,
avoiding the white pith. Place the peel,
sugar, cinnamon sticks and 1½ cups (375
ml/12 fl oz) water into a saucepan and stir
over low heat until the sugar has
dissolved. Bring to the boil, reduce the
heat and simmer for 5 minutes.
2 Rinse the cranberries (not necessary if
frozen) and remove any stems. Add the
cranberries to the hot syrup, return to the
boil and simmer for 10 minutes, or until
the skins have split. Remove from the
heat and set aside to cool.
3 When cool, remove and discard the peel
and cinnamon sticks. Remove about ½ cup
of the berries and reserve. Blend or
process the remaining mixture until
smooth, return to the saucepan and add
the reserved whole berries. Blend the
cornflour and orange juice in a small
bowl, add to the purée then stir over
medium heat for 5 minutes, or until the
mixture boils and thickens. Serve cold or
warm with yoghurt cream.
4 For the yoghurt cream, beat the cream
in a bowl until soft peaks form, then fold
the yoghurt through. Transfer to a small
bowl and sprinkle with the sugar.
Refrigerate, covered, for 2 hours.

CHOCOLATE COLLAR CHEESECAKE

Preparation time: **1 hour** 30 minutes +
   chilling
Total cooking time: 50 minutes
Serves 8–10

200 g (6½ oz) plain chocolate biscuits,
   crushed
70 g (2¼ oz) unsalted butter, melted

Filling
500 g (1 lb) cream cheese, softened
⅓ cup (90 g/3 oz) sugar
2 eggs
1 tablespoon cocoa powder
300 g (10 oz) sour cream
250 g (8 oz) good-quality dark chocolate,
   melted
⅓ cup (80 ml/2¾ fl oz) Bailey's Irish
   Cream

Collar
50 g (1¾ oz) white chocolate, melted
150 g (5 oz) good-quality dark chocolate,
   melted

1¼ cups (315 ml/10 fl oz) cream, whipped
cocoa powder and icing sugar, to dust

1 Brush a 23 cm (9 inch) round springform
tin with melted butter or oil and line the
base and side with baking paper. Mix
together the biscuit crumbs and butter,
press firmly into the base of the tin and
refrigerate for 10 minutes. Preheat the
oven to moderate 180°C (350°F/Gas 4).
2 Beat the cream cheese and sugar with
electric beaters until smooth and creamy.
Add the eggs, one at a time, beating well
after each addition. Beat in the cocoa and
sour cream until smooth. Beat in the
cooled melted dark chocolate. Beat in the
liqueur and pour over the base. Smooth
the surface and bake for 45 minutes. The
cheesecake may not be fully set, but will
firm up. Refrigerate, overnight if possible,
until cold.
3 Remove the cheesecake from the tin
and put it on a board. Measure the height
and add 5 mm (¼ inch). Cut a strip of
baking paper this wide and 75 cm (30
inches) long. Pipe or drizzle the melted
white chocolate in a figure eight pattern
along the paper. When just set, spread the
dark chocolate over the entire strip of
paper. Allow the chocolate to set a little,
but you need to be able to bend the paper
without it cracking.
4 Wrap the paper around the cheesecake
with the chocolate inside. Seal the ends
and hold the paper in place until the
chocolate is completely set. Peel away the
paper. Spread the top with cream. Dust
with cocoa powder and icing sugar.

CHILLED BERRY SOUFFLE

Preparation time: 35 minutes + chilling
Total cooking time: Nil
Serves 6

3 teaspoons gelatine
300 g (10 oz) raspberries
1¼ cups (315 ml/10 fl oz) cream
4 egg whites
2–3 tablespoons caster sugar

1 Prepare six 125 ml (4 fl oz) soufflé dishes by wrapping a double strip of baking paper around the outside of each, extending 2 cm (¾ inch) above the rim, then tying with string. Brush the collar and dish with oil or butter, sprinkle with sugar, shake to coat evenly, then tip out any excess.
2 Place 3 tablespoons water in a small heatproof bowl. Sprinkle evenly with the gelatine and leave to go spongy. Bring a large pan filled with about 4 cm (1½ inches) water to the boil, remove from the heat and carefully lower the gelatine bowl into the water. Stir until dissolved; cool slightly.
3 Purée half the raspberries and push through a sieve. Mash the other half and mix both lots together. Fold in the cooled gelatine mixture. Beat the cream into soft peaks. In a separate bowl, beat the egg whites into stiff peaks. Gradually beat in 2 tablespoons of the sugar until dissolved—if the raspberries are tart, add the remaining sugar. Fold the cream into the raspberries, followed by the egg white, using a large metal spoon. Spoon into the dishes and chill for several hours, until set. Remove the collars to serve. Can be served with cream and raspberries.

FEUILLETE WITH CHERRIES JUBILEE

Preparation time: 15 minutes + chilling
Total cooking time: 25 minutes
Serves 4

375 g (12 oz) puff pastry
1 egg, lightly beaten
20 g (¾ oz) unsalted butter
20 g (¾ oz) sugar
500 g (1 lb) cherries, pitted
300 ml (9 fl oz) thick (double) cream
½ cup (125 ml/4 fl oz) brandy or Kirsch
icing sugar, to dust

1 Roll the pastry out on a floured work surface and cut out four rectangles of 10 x 12 cm (4 x 5 inches) each. Put them on a baking tray and brush with the egg glaze, being careful not to let any drip down the sides of the pastry. Refrigerate for 30 minutes. Preheat the oven to hot 220°C (425°F/Gas 7).
2 Melt the butter and sugar together in a saucepan and add the pitted cherries. Cook over high heat for about 1 minute, then reduce the heat and simmer for about 3 minutes, or until the cherries are tender. Reduce the heat to low and keep the cherries warm.
3 Bake the feuilleté on the top shelf of the oven for 15 minutes until golden and puffed, then cut them in half horizontally and gently pull any doughy bits out of the centre. Turn the oven off and and put the feuilleté back in the oven and allow to dry out for a couple of minutes.
4 When you are ready to serve, whisk the cream until it reaches stiff peaks. Place a warm feuilleté base on each serving plate. Heat the brandy or Kirsch in a small saucepan and set it alight, then pour it over the cherries (keep a saucepan lid nearby in case the flames get too high). Spoon some cherries into each feuilleté and top with a little cream. Put the lids on and dust with icing sugar before serving.

CHOCOLATE PUDDING

Preparation time: 20 minutes
Total cooking time: 1 hour 20 minutes
Serves 6

90 g (3 oz) unsalted butter
½ cup (95 g/3 oz) soft brown sugar
3 eggs, separated
125 g (4 oz) dark chocolate, melted and cooled
1 teaspoon vanilla essence
1 cup (125 g/4 oz) self-raising flour
1 tablespoon cocoa powder
½ teaspoon bicarbonate of soda
¼ cup (60 ml/2 fl oz) milk
2 tablespoons brandy

Chocolate sauce
125 g (4 oz) dark chocolate, broken
¼ cup (60 ml/2 fl oz) cream
1 tablespoon brandy

1 Grease a 1.25 litre pudding basin and line the base with a circle of baking paper. Preheat the oven to moderate 180°C (350°F/Gas 4). Cream the butter and half the sugar until light and creamy. Beat in the egg yolks, chocolate and vanilla. Sift together the flour, cocoa and bicarbonate of soda. Fold into the mixture, alternating with spoonfuls of the combined milk and brandy. Beat the egg whites until soft peaks form. Gradually beat in the remaining sugar, until stiff and glossy. Fold into the chocolate mix.
2 Pour into the pudding basin. Cover tightly with foil. Secure with string, put in a deep ovenproof tray and pour in enough hot water to come halfway up the side of the basin. Bake for 1¼ hours, or until a skewer comes out clean. Unmould onto a serving plate.
3 To make the chocolate sauce, combine the ingredients in a heatproof bowl set over a pan of steaming water and stir until smooth. Serve the pudding with the sauce and cream.

SICILIAN CANNOLI

Preparation time: 30 minutes + 30
   minutes refrigeration
Total cooking time: 5 minutes
Makes 12

Filling
500 g (1 lb) ricotta
1 teaspoon orange flower water
½ cup (100 g/3 oz) cedro, diced
60 g (2 oz) bittersweet chocolate,
   coarsely grated or chopped
1 tablespoon grated orange rind
½ cup (60 g/2 oz) icing sugar

300 g (10 oz) plain flour
1 tablespoon caster sugar
1 teaspoon ground cinnamon
40 g (1¼ oz) unsalted butter
3 tablespoons Marsala
vegetable oil, for deep-frying
icing sugar, for dusting

1 For the filling, combine all the
ingredients in a bowl and mix. Add
2–3 tablespoons water and mix well to
form a dough. Cover with plastic wrap and
refrigerate.
2 Combine the flour, sugar and cinnamon
in a bowl, rub in the butter and add the
Marsala. Mix until the dough comes
together in a loose clump, then knead on
a lightly floured surface for 4–5 minutes,
or until smooth. Wrap in plastic wrap and
refrigerate for at least 30 minutes.

3 Cut the dough in half and roll each
portion on a lightly floured surface into a
thin sheet about 5 mm (¼ inch) thick. Cut
each dough half into six 9 cm (3½ inch)
squares. Place a metal tube (see Note)
diagonally across the middle of each
square. Fold the sides over the tube,
moistening the overlap with water, then
press together.
4 Heat the oil in a large deep frying pan to
180°C (350°F), or until a cube of bread
dropped into the oil browns in 15 seconds.
Drop one or two tubes at a time into the
hot oil. Fry gently until golden brown and
crisp. Remove from the oil, gently remove
the moulds and drain on crumpled paper
towels. When they are cool, fill a piping
bag with the ricotta mixture and fill the
shells. Dust with icing sugar and serve.

NOTE: Cannoli tubes are available at
kitchenware shops. You can also use 2
cm (¾ inch) diameter wooden dowels cut
into 12 cm (5 inch) lengths.

LAVENDER ICE CREAM

Preparation time: 15 minutes + freezing
Total cooking time: 15 minutes
Serves 6–8

8 stems English lavender (or 4–6 if the
   lavender is in full flower as it has a
   stronger flavour)
2½ cups (600 ml/20 fl oz) thick (double)
   cream
1 small piece lemon rind
⅔ cup (160 g/5½ oz) sugar
4 egg yolks, lightly whisked

1 Wash and dry the English lavender, then
put it in a saucepan with the cream and
lemon rind. Heat until almost boiling,
then stir in the sugar until dissolved.
Strain through a fine sieve, then gradually
pour onto the egg yolks in a bowl, return
to the pan and stir over low heat until
thick enough to coat the back of a spoon
— do not boil. Pour into a chilled metal
tray to cool, or freeze in an ice cream
machine, following the manufacturer's
instructions. Freeze until frozen around
the edge, but not in the centre.
2 In a food processor or bowl, beat until
smooth. Freeze again and repeat this
process twice more. Cover with
greaseproof paper and freeze.

CREAMY FRESH STRAWBERRY ROLLS

Preparation time: 40 minutes
Total cooking time: 50 minutes
Serves 6

250 g (8 oz) strawberries, hulled
60 g (2 oz) butter
2 egg yolks
⅓ cup (80 ml/2¾ fl oz) cream
⅓ cup (90 g/3 oz) sugar
1 teaspoon lemon juice
6 sheets fresh lasagne, 16 cm x 21 cm (6½ x 8½ inches)
⅓ cup (40 g/1¼ oz) toasted slivered almonds, plus 1 tablespoon for decoration
icing sugar, for dusting

1 Preheat the oven to moderate 180°C (350°F/Gas 4) and grease a gratin dish. Halve the strawberries, slicing from top to bottom. Melt 20 g (¾ oz) of butter in a pan and lightly toss the strawberries for 20 seconds. Remove from the pan. Melt another 20 g (¾ oz) of butter in the pan. Mix the egg yolks with the cream, then add to the pan with the sugar and lemon juice. Cook, stirring often, until very thick. Remove from the heat and stir in the strawberries. Cool.
2 Cook the fresh lasagne sheets, two at a time, in plenty of boiling water for 3 minutes, or until al dente. Transfer to a bowl of cold water and leave for 1 minute before placing on tea towels to dry.

3 Divide the strawberry mixture and the almonds among the pasta sheets, leaving a 3 cm (1¼ inch) border all around. Fold in the long edges first, then carefully fold up the end closest to you and roll. As the mixture begins to ooze, bring the top end over and towards you. Carefully place, seam-side-down, in the prepared dish. Position the rolls closely side-by-side.
4 Dot the top with pieces of the remaining butter. Sprinkle with extra almonds and 2 teaspoons of sifted icing sugar. Bake for 15 minutes, then place under a preheated grill for 5 minutes or until lightly browned.

NOTE: This dessert is delicious accompanied by vanilla ice cream and a strawberry coulis. For a change, you can use fresh raspberries when they are in season. They will not need to be cooked, so just add them to the prepared cream mixture. Blueberries can also be used and should be prepared the same way as the strawberries, but not sliced. You can use dry lasagne sheets instead of fresh, but they are often thicker, less pliable and slippery to handle. If you use them, cook them as they come from the packet, then trim to the dimensions above.

BAKED RISSONI PUDDING

Preparation time: 15 minutes
Total cooking time: 1 hour
Serves 4–6

¼ cup (50 g/1¾ oz) rissoni
2 eggs, lightly beaten
⅓ cup (80 ml/2¾ fl oz) maple syrup
2 cups (500 ml/16 fl oz) cream
¼ cup (30 g/1 oz) sultanas
1 teaspoon vanilla essence
pinch of nutmeg
¼ teaspoon ground cinnamon

1 Preheat the oven to slow 150°C (300°F/Gas 2). Cook the rissoni in a large pan of rapidly boiling water for 3–4 minutes, or until al dente. Drain well.
2 Whisk together the eggs, maple syrup and cream in a bowl.
3 Stir in the rissoni, sultanas, vanilla essence, nutmeg and cinnamon. Pour the mixture into a deep round or oval ovenproof dish. Sit the dish in a large baking dish and pour enough water into the baking dish to come halfway up the sides of the ovenproof dish. Bake for 50–55 minutes, or until a knife comes out clean when inserted into the centre.
note: As a variation, replace the sultanas with chopped dried apricots or raisins. Or, use fresh pitted and chopped dates or whole raspberries and blueberries. The cooking time may need to be a little longer with the fresh fruit, because some of the juice will ooze out.

BERRIES

A TANGY SUMMER EXPLOSION OF GLORIOUS COLOUR AND BITTERSWEET JUICES, BERRIES MAKE THE PERFECT PARTNER FOR CRISPY SWEET MERINGUE, BUT DON'T STOP THERE—THEY HAVE MYRIAD OTHER ROLES IN THE DESSERT WORLD.

BLACKBERRIES

This slightly tart fruit is delicious in pies, crumbles and cobblers and is an essential ingredient in summer pudding. Refrigerate, then wash just before use. Blackberries are delicious with crème fraîche, brandy and apple.

BLUEBERRIES

Blueberries have a blue exterior but are white or pale green inside. Available most of the year, they keep in the refrigerator for up to 7 days. Don't store in a metal container as they react and cause dark stains. Rinse before use. Great in baked desserts, pies and cheesecakes, blueberries taste good with port, cinnamon and cream.

CURRANTS

Available in red, white and black. White currants are a variety of the red and look similar. Leave on the stalk until ready to use, then remove the stalks by gently loosening the berries between the tines of a fork. Often frosted and used as a cake decoration, moulded in jellies or used in fruit tarts. Redcurrants are often used with almonds, cherries and oranges. Blackcurrants are an excellent source of Vitamin C and are the basic ingredient in the liqueur Cassis. Blackcurrants are good with pears, apples and red wine.

MULBERRIES

The fruit of a tree, mulberries are available in black, red and white, the black having the best flavour. They have a rich, winey flavour and their juice stains very badly. They go well with cream and brandy and can be used in pastries, cakes and crumbles.

PHYSALIS (CAPE GOOSEBERRIES)

A summer fruit that enjoys a relatively short season, this small orange or greeny yellow berry is enclosed in a papery calyx. Peel away the calyx and eat the sharp tasting berry raw, or dipped in caramel or fondant. They make a wonderful garnish for cheesecakes, desserts and fruit platters.

RASPBERRIES

A true summer berry, the red ones are the most common but a golden variety is sometimes available. Store this delicate fruit covered in the refrigerator and get rid of any mouldy ones immediately. Eat them on their own or puréed as part of a cold mousse or hot soufflé.

STRAWBERRIES

Strawberries are available all year round but vary vastly in flavour, size and colour. When they are in season, they have a wonderful aroma and flavour. Store them in the refrigerator and rinse them just before using. They are delicious on their own, with cream or ice cream, or used in traditional recipes such as strawberries romanoff, summer pudding and shortcake.

CLOCKWISE, FROM LEFT: Raspberries, Blackberries, Red, black and white currants, Blueberries, Strawberries, Mulberries, Physalis

SOFT FRUIT

THE SIMPLE PERFECTION OF NATURE IS IMPOSSIBLE TO SURPASS. WHEN IN SEASON, A FRESH RIPE PIECE OF FRUIT WITH TANGY FLESH AND SWEET JUICES IS ONE OF LIFE'S SMALL JOYS.

APRICOTS

These soft, sweet fruits are available late spring and summer. To ripen, leave in a paper bag at room temperature. Apricots taste good with honey, almonds, vanilla and Amaretto. Delicious raw, they can also be poached, puréed, used in desserts and ice creams or baked in pies and tarts.

CHERRIES

Available briefly in summer, in both sweet and sour varieties, cherries can be preserved in liqueur before use in cooking, or added fresh to baked dishes such as clafoutis. Cherries are perfect with cream cheese, almonds and chocolate and poached cherries can be used in cheesecakes, trifles and tarts, as well as in fillings for pancakes and pastries.

FIGS

Available in summer and autumn, figs vary from green to black. They have a delicate, sweet flesh and a soft skin which may need to be peeled. Versatile, they can be eaten raw as part of a dessert or baked, poached and grilled. Figs taste good with vanilla, mascarpone, orange and toffee.

GRAPES

Best known for wine making properties, the grape is one of the first cultivated fruits and the world's largest fruit crop. Refrigerate unwashed and rinse before serving. Grapes go with brown sugar, cream and soft cheeses. Usually eaten raw, grapes can be added to fresh fruit mincemeats and tarts and grilled in gratins.

MANGOES

Available in many shapes and colours, ripe mangoes have a wonderful aroma and a rich, sweet delicious flesh. Ripen at room temperature, then store in the vegetable crisper in the refrigerator. They can be puréed to make ice creams and fools or cooked in crumbles and cobblers, and taste good with lime and coconut.

NECTARINES

A member of the peach family, available in summer, nectarines have a smooth skin and are usually redder than peaches. Press gently along the seam to check that they are ripe. Nectarines can be used in a similar way to peaches in cooking.

PEACHES

Available in summer, there are over 2,000 varieties worldwide. Peaches can be broken into two categories: clingstone or slipstone (freestone). They can be poached, baked and grilled and complement almonds, cinnamon, vanilla and ginger. Peaches can be preserved in alcohol. Peach purée makes delicious ice creams and sorbets.

PLUMS

Available in summer and early autumn, plums vary from white, yellow and green to dark purple. Cooking plums have a drier flesh and sharper taste than the sweet, juicy dessert plums. Plums go well with marzipan and almonds, cinnamon, vanilla, nutmeg and red wine. They are traditional in pies, cobblers and cakes and certain varieties are divine poached in red wine.

FROM TOP LEFT: Apricots, nectarines, mangoes, peaches, plums, nectarines, grapes, cherries.IN FRONT: Figs (left); peaches (in paper).

BUTTERMILK CHEESECAKE WITH RASPBERRY SAUCE

Preparation time: 35 minutes + chilling
Total cooking time: 1 hour 20 minutes
Serves 8

250 g (8 oz) plain sweet biscuits
125 g (4 oz) unsalted butter, melted
3 teaspoons grated lemon rind

Filling
750 g (1½ lb) ricotta
4 eggs, lightly beaten
1 cup (250 ml/8 fl oz) buttermilk
2 tablespoons cornflour
½ cup (125 ml/4 fl oz) honey
1 tablespoon lemon juice
icing sugar, to dust

Raspberry sauce
300 g (10 oz) fresh or frozen raspberries
¼ cup (30 g/1 oz) icing sugar
1 teaspoon lemon juice

1 Grease a 23 cm (9 inch) diameter springform tin and line the base with baking paper. Preheat the oven to warm 160°C (315°F/Gas 2–3). Finely crush the biscuits in a processor and stir in the butter and 2 teaspoons of rind, until combined. Spoon into the tin and press firmly over the base. Refrigerate while preparing the filling.
2 Beat the ricotta with electric beaters for 2 minutes, or until smooth. Add the beaten egg gradually, beating well after each addition. Whisk together the buttermilk and cornflour until smooth and add gradually to the ricotta mixture. Beat in the honey, remaining lemon rind and the lemon juice. Pour into the tin and bake for 1 hour 20 minutes, or until set. Cool, then refrigerate for at least 6 hours.
3 To make the raspberry sauce, defrost the raspberries, reserve a few as garnish, and process the rest with the icing sugar for 20 seconds, or until smooth. Add lemon juice, to taste. Serve at room temperature with raspberry sauce. Dust with icing sugar.

DEEP-FRIED FRUIT WITH GOLDEN NUT SAUCE

Preparation time: 55 minutes + chilling
Total cooking time: 30 minutes
Serves 6

1¾ cups (215 g/7 oz) plain flour, sifted
2½ teaspoons baking powder
2 tablespoons oil
2 tablespoons caster sugar
2 eggs, separated
oil, for deep-frying
800 g (1 lb 10 oz) fresh fruit, such as pitted cherries, pineapple pieces, banana pieces, apple wedges and pear wedges
ice cream or cream, for serving

Golden nut sauce
125 g (4 oz) unsalted butter
1¼ cups (230 g/7½ oz) soft brown sugar
½ cup (125 ml/4 fl oz) thick (double) cream
2 teaspoons lemon juice
2 tablespoons chopped roasted macadamias

1 Sift the flour and baking powder into a large bowl and make a well in the centre. Add the oil, sugar, egg yolks and 1 cup (250 ml/8 fl oz) warm water. Whisk until smooth, cover and refrigerate for 2 hours. (You will add the egg white later.)
2 To make the golden nut sauce, melt the butter in a small pan over low heat. Add the sugar and stir until dissolved. Add the cream and lemon juice. Bring to the boil, stirring. Add the nuts and keep warm.
3 Whisk the egg whites until stiff peaks form and fold into the batter. Heat the oil in a large heavy-based pan or deep-fryer to 180°C (350°F), or until a cube of bread will brown in 15 seconds. Turn the heat down. Dip the fruit in the batter, shaking off any excess. Deep-fry in small batches, draining on paper towels. Serve immediately, drizzled with the golden nut sauce. Serve with ice cream or cream.

PAVLOVA ROLL WITH RASPBERRY COULIS

Preparation time: 25 minutes
Total cooking time: 15 minutes
Serves 8–10

4 egg whites
1 cup (250 g/8 oz) caster sugar
1 teaspoon cornflour
2 teaspoons lemon juice or vinegar
⅔ cup (170 ml/5½ fl oz) cream, whipped
¼ cup (55 g/1¾ oz) chopped fresh berries

Raspberry Coulis
2 tablespoons brandy
250 g (8 oz) fresh raspberries, washed and hulled
1 tablespoon icing sugar

1 Brush a 25 x 30 cm (10 x 12 inch) Swiss roll tin with oil and line with non-stick baking paper extending up 2 sides. Preheat the oven to moderate 180°C (350°F/Gas 4). Beat the egg whites into soft peaks. Gradually add ¾ cup sugar and beat until thick and glossy. Combine 1 tablespoon sugar with the cornflour. Fold into the meringue with the lemon juice or vinegar. Spoon into the tin and smooth. Bake for 12–15 minutes until springy.
2 Put a large sheet of baking paper on top of a tea towel and generously sprinkle with the rest of the sugar. Turn the pavlova onto this, peel off the lining paper and leave for 3 minutes. Roll up pavlova from the long side using the tea towel to assist; cool. Fold berries into whipped cream.
3 Unroll the pavlova, fill with the cream mixture and re-roll without the tea towel and baking paper. Transfer to a plate and refrigerate.
4 To make Raspberry Coulis: Put the brandy, raspberries and icing sugar in a food processor and process until well blended. Serve Pavlova Roll in slices with Raspberry Coulis.

MARINATED FIGS WITH RASPBERRY SAUCE

Preparation time: 20 minutes + standing
Total cooking time: 5–10 minutes
Serves 4

6 fresh figs, halved
1¼ cups (315 ml/10 fl oz) dessert wine
1 cinnamon stick
1 tablespoon soft brown sugar
315 g (10 oz) fresh raspberries
¼ cup (60 g/2 oz) caster sugar
1 teaspoon lemon juice
½ cup (110 g/3⅔ oz) mascarpone

1 Place figs in a glass or ceramic bowl. Combine wine, cinnamon and sugar in a small pan and warm over low heat. When sugar has dissolved, pour over figs. Cover; allow to stand for 2 hours.
2 Set aside a few raspberries for garnishing, if you wish, and blend the rest with the caster sugar in a food processor. Sieve, then stir in the lemon juice.
3 Drain the figs; strain and reserve the marinade. Grill the figs until golden. Pour a little raspberry sauce onto each dessert plate (enough to cover the base). Arrange 3 fig halves on each plate and serve with a spoonful of mascarpone.

EIGHT-TREASURE RICE

Preparation time: 20 minutes +
    30 minutes soaking
Total cooking time: 3 hours
Serves 8

12 whole blanched lotus seeds (see Notes)
12 jujubes (dried Chinese dates) (see Notes)
20 fresh or tinned gingko nuts, shelled (see Notes)
225 g (7 oz) glutinous rice
2 tablespoons sugar
2 teaspoons oil
30 g (1 oz) slab sugar (see Notes)
8 glacé cherries
6 dried longans, pitted (see Notes)
4 almonds or walnuts
225 g (7 oz) red bean paste (see Notes)

1 Soak the lotus seeds and jujubes in bowls of cold water for 30 minutes, then drain. Remove the seeds from the jujubes. If using fresh gingko nuts, blanch in a saucepan of boiling water for 5 minutes, then refresh in cold water and dry thoroughly.
2 Put the glutinous rice and 300 ml (9½ fl oz) water in a heavy-based saucepan and bring to the boil. Reduce the heat to low and simmer for 10–15 minutes. Stir in the sugar and oil.
3 Dissolve the slab sugar in 220 ml (7 fl oz) water and bring to the boil. Add the lotus seeds, jujubes and gingko nuts and simmer for 1 hour, or until the lotus seeds are soft. Drain, reserving the liquid.
4 Grease a 1 litre (32 fl oz) heatproof bowl and decorate the base with the lotus seeds, jujubes, gingko nuts, cherries, longans and almonds. Smooth two-thirds of the rice over this to form a shell on the surface of the bowl. Fill with the bean paste, cover with the remaining rice and smooth the surface.
5 Cover the rice with a piece of greased foil and put the bowl in a steamer. Cover and steam over simmering water in a wok for 1–1½ hours, replenishing with boiling water during cooking.
6 Turn the pudding out onto a plate and pour the reserved sugar liquid over the top. Serve hot.

NOTES: Eight-treasure rice is a Chinese rice pudding. It is a favourite at banquets and Chinese New Year. The eight treasures vary, but can also include other preserved fruits. You will need access to a Chinese grocer to obtain most of the ingredients.

PREMIUM CHOCOLATE AND CINNAMON ICE CREAM

Preparation time: 20 minutes + chilling + freezing
Total cooking time: 30 minutes
Serves 6–8

2 cups (500 ml/16 fl oz) milk
200 g (6½ oz) good-quality dark chocolate, chopped
4 cinnamon sticks
¾ cup (185 g/6 oz) caster sugar
1½ teaspoons ground cinnamon
4 egg yolks
2 cups (500 ml/16 fl oz) cream

1 Heat the milk, chocolate and cinnamon sticks in a heavy-based pan, stirring occasionally, over low heat for 15 minutes, or until the chocolate has melted and the mixture is well mixed. Do not allow to boil. Remove the cinnamon sticks.
2 Mix the sugar and cinnamon in a large heatproof bowl. Add the egg yolks and place the bowl over a pan of simmering water. Whisk until the mixture is thick and pale.
3 Gradually whisk the chocolate mixture into the eggs and sugar. Cook, whisking all the time, for 5 minutes or until the mixture coats the back of a spoon.
4 Chill for 30 minutes in the refrigerator, strain and slowly stir in the cream. Pour into a shallow metal container. Freeze for 2 hours (the edges will be frozen and the centre soft). Transfer to a large bowl and beat with electric beaters until smooth. Repeat this step twice more. Freeze in a 2 litre plastic container, covered with a piece of baking paper or plastic wrap, then a lid, for 7–8 hours, or until solid.

BANANA AND COCONUT PANCAKES

Preparation time: 10 minutes
Total cooking time: 30 minutes
Serves 4–6

1 tablespoon shredded coconut, to serve
⅓ cup (40 g/1⅓ oz) plain flour
2 tablespoons rice flour
¼ cup (60 g/2 oz) caster sugar
¼ cup (25 g/¾ oz) desiccated coconut
1 cup (250 ml/8 fl oz) coconut milk
1 egg, lightly beaten
butter, for frying
4 large bananas
60 g (2 oz) butter, extra
⅓ cup (60 g/2 oz) lightly packed soft brown sugar
⅓ cup (80 ml/2¾ fl oz) lime juice
strips of lime rind, to serve

1 Spread the shredded coconut on an oven tray and toast it in a slow 150°C (300°F/Gas 2) oven for 10 minutes or until it is dark golden, shaking the tray occasionally. Remove the coconut from the tray to prevent it from burning and set aside.

2 Sift the plain and rice flour into a medium bowl. Add the sugar and desiccated coconut and mix through with a spoon. Make a well in the centre of the flour, pour in the combined coconut milk and egg, and beat until smooth.
3 Melt a little butter in a non-stick frying pan or crepe pan. Pour 3 tablespoons of the pancake mixture into the pan and cook over medium heat until the underside is golden. Turn the pancake over and cook the other side. Transfer to a plate and cover with a tea towel to keep warm. Repeat with the remaining pancake batter, buttering the pan when necessary.
4 Cut the bananas diagonally into thick slices. Heat the butter in the pan; add the banana, toss until coated, and cook over medium heat until the banana starts to soften and brown. Sprinkle with the brown sugar and shake the pan gently until the sugar has melted. Stir in the lime juice. Divide the banana among the pancakes and fold over to enclose. Sprinkle with the toasted coconut and strips of lime rind.

BREAD AND BUTTER PUDDING

Preparation time: 20 minutes + soaking + chilling
Total cooking time: 40 minutes
Serves 4

60 g (2 oz) mixed raisins and sultanas
2 tablespoons brandy or rum
30 g (1 oz) unsalted butter
4 slices good-quality white bread or brioche loaf
3 eggs
3 tablespoons caster sugar
3 cups (750 ml/24 fl oz) milk
¼ cup (60 ml/2 fl oz) cream
¼ teaspoon vanilla essence
¼ teaspoon ground cinnamon
1 tablespoon demerara sugar

1 Soak the raisins and sultanas in the brandy or rum for about 30 minutes. Butter the slices of bread or brioche and cut each piece into 8 triangles. Arrange the bread in a 1 litre ovenproof dish.
2 Mix the eggs with the sugar, add the milk, cream, vanilla and cinnamon and mix well. Drain the raisins and sultanas and add any liquid to the custard.
3 Scatter the soaked raisins and sultanas over the bread and pour the custard over the top. Cover with plastic wrap and refrigerate for 1 hour.
4 Preheat the oven to moderate 180°C (350°F/Gas 4). Remove the pudding from the refrigerator and sprinkle with the demerara sugar. Bake for 35–40 minutes, or until the custard is set and the top crunchy and golden.

NOTE: It is very important that you use good-quality bread for this recipe. Ordinary sliced white bread will tend to go a bit claggy when it soaks up the milk.

OAXACAN RICE PUDDING

Preparation time: 15 minutes + soaking
Total cooking time: 1 hour 20 minutes
Serves 6

⅓ cup (40 g/1¼ oz) raisins
2 tablespoons white rum
1½ cups (330 g/11 oz) paella or arborio rice
1 cinnamon stick
1 strip lime zest
1 vanilla bean, split
1 cup (250 ml/8 fl oz) milk
300 ml (9½ fl oz) cream
395 g (13 oz) tin condensed milk
3 egg yolks, beaten
20 g (¾ oz) butter
ground cinnamon, to serve

1 Soak the raisins in the rum in a small bowl until needed.
2 Combine the rice with 2½ cups (625 ml/20 fl oz) water, the cinnamon stick, lime zest and the split vanilla bean and seeds in a large saucepan and bring to the boil over medium heat. Cook, stirring frequently so it doesn't catch on the bottom of the pan, for about 10 minutes, or until the water has almost absorbed, then reduce the heat to very low.
3 Combine the milk, cream, condensed milk and gradually stir into the pan until well combined with the rice. Cook over a gentle heat for 1 hour, stirring frequently until the rice is very tender and most of the liquid has been absorbed—it should be a creamy consistency. Again, be careful not to let the mixture catch.
4 Carefully remove the vanilla, lime and cinnamon stick, then add the beaten yolks, butter and the raisins and stir for 2 minutes before pouring into a serving platter or individual dishes. Sprinkle with a little ground cinnamon before serving. This dish is delicious served warm or chilled.

CHILLED ORANGE CREAMS

Preparation time: 30 minutes + chilling
Total cooking time: 5 minutes
Serves 6

½ cup (125 ml/4 fl oz) juice of blood oranges
3 teaspoons gelatine
4 egg yolks
½ cup (125 g/4 oz) caster sugar
1¼ cups (315 ml/10 fl oz) milk
1 teaspoon finely grated rind of blood oranges
1 cup (250 ml/8 fl oz) cream

1 Chill a large bowl in the freezer. Lightly grease six 125 ml (4 fl oz) ramekins or dariole moulds with flavourless oil. Pour the orange juice into a small heatproof bowl, sprinkle the gelatine in an even layer over the surface and leave until spongy. Bring a large pan filled with about 4 cm (1½ inches) water to the boil, remove from the heat, carefully lower the gelatine bowl into the water (it should come halfway up the side of the bowl), then stir until dissolved. Cool slightly.
2 Whisk the egg yolks and sugar in a small bowl until thick. Heat the milk and grated orange rind in a pan and gradually pour onto the egg mixture while whisking. Return to the pan and stir until the custard coats the back of the spoon. Do not allow to boil. Add the gelatine mixture and stir.
3 Pour the mixture immediately through a strainer into the chilled bowl. Cool, stirring occasionally, until beginning to thicken.
4 Whip the cream into soft peaks and fold gently into the custard. Spoon into the greased ramekins and chill to set. Can be served with wedges of blood orange or thin strips of rind.

PERFECT CUSTARD

STREAMING SMOOTHLY OVER A PUDDING, BAKED IN THE OVEN OR CHILLED IN RAMEKINS, CUSTARD COMES IN A MYRIAD OF DIFFERENT GUISES—ALL OF THEM A PERFECT SPOONFUL OF CREAMINESS.

Custard forms the basis of many desserts, either in its purest form as crème anglaise, with a wine base as zabaglione or sabayon, or thickened with flour and cornflour as crème patisserie. Pouring custard (home-made or even out of a packet) is a deliciously traditional accompaniment to pies, tarts and steamed puddings. Custard can create a base for ice creams, soufflés, baked puddings, and desserts set with gelatine, like bavarois. As the name crème anglaise suggests, custard is of English origin.

There are two types of custard, pouring (made on the stovetop) and baked. The main ingredients of both are eggs, which are better if brought to room temperature first, and milk. To make a perfect smooth velvety custard, of whichever type, the golden rule is to keep the heat low. Never let custard overcook or you will end up with a pan full of scrambled eggs. Custards made with whole eggs will set more quickly, as the egg white sets at a lower temperature.

POURING CUSTARD

To make a perfect pouring custard, separate 3 eggs, put the yolks in a bowl with 2 tablespoons caster sugar and beat with a balloon whisk until light and fluffy. When properly beaten, the mixture will fall in a ribbon which will hold its shape for a few seconds. Pour 1½ cups (375 ml/ 12 fl oz) milk into a saucepan and bring to scalding point— small bubbles will appear around the edge. Stir if a skin appears to be forming. Pour into the egg mixture, stirring with the balloon whisk until well combined. If there is any milk protein on the base of the saucepan, rinse it out as this may cause the custard to catch on the bottom. Return the custard to the pan and stir over low heat.

If you have a double boiler, you can use

it for custard making. Alternatively, use a metal bowl set over a pan of simmering water (don't let the bowl touch the water) for a more gentle heat. However, a pan over gentle heat is quite adequate. Keep the custard below simmering point as the egg yolks will thicken evenly if heated slowly. To prevent lumps forming, stir continuously. There is even a technique for efficient stirring. Make sure the wooden spoon passes through the middle of the pan and around the edge, where the custard is hottest and so will thicken quickest. Keep stirring to ensure the custard thickens evenly. (If the custard curdles a little, try removing it from the heat, adding a teaspoon of iced water and beating well. This will prevent further curdling but will not make a smooth custard.) The custard is ready when it forms a coating on the back of a spoon that you can draw a line through which will hold its shape. When ready, either pour it quickly through a sieve into a bowl or plunge the base of the saucepan into iced water to stop the cooking process. If chilling the custard, lay a piece of baking paper or plastic wrap directly over the surface to prevent a skin forming. If keeping the custard warm, put it in a bowl over a pan of hot water. For a vanilla custard, add a split vanilla bean to the milk when you scald it and leave to infuse for 5–30 minutes, depending on the strength of flavour required. Remove the bean before adding the milk to the eggs. Alternatively, add 2 teaspoons of vanilla essence to the finished custard. If you add it earlier, it will evaporate.

BAKED CUSTARD

Baked custard should be cooked in a bain-marie or water bath to ensure a gentle heat, so the mixture does not curdle. The ramekins or moulds should be placed in a baking dish with enough water to come halfway up their sides. To prevent water bubbling around the edges, you can sit the moulds on a tea towel inside the dish. The custard is cooked when the centre is set but still wobbles when the mould is shaken. The custard will stiffen as it cools. The texture should be smooth and creamy.

NEW YORK CHEESECAKE

Preparation time: 1 hour + chilling
Total cooking time: 1 hour 50 minutes
Serves 10–12

½ cup (60 g/2 oz) self-raising flour
1 cup (125 g/4 oz) plain flour
¼ cup (60 g/2 oz) caster sugar
1 teaspoon grated lemon rind
80 g (2¾ oz) unsalted butter, chopped
1 egg
1½ cups (375 ml/12 fl oz) cream, for
  serving

Filling
750 g (1½ lb) cream cheese, softened
1 cup (250 g/8 oz) caster sugar
¼ cup (30 g/1 oz) plain flour
2 teaspoons grated orange rind
2 teaspoons grated lemon rind
4 eggs
⅔ cup (170 ml/5½ fl oz) cream

Candied rind
finely shredded rind of 3 limes, 3 lemons
  and 3 oranges
1 cup (250 g/8 oz) caster sugar

1 Combine the flours, sugar, lemon rind and unsalted butter for about 30 seconds in a food processor, until crumbly. Add the egg and process briefly until the mixture just comes together. Turn out onto a lightly floured surface and gather together into a ball. Refrigerate in plastic wrap for about 20 minutes, or until the mixture is firm.

2 Preheat the oven to hot 210°C (415°F/Gas 6–7). Lightly grease a 23 cm (9 inch) diameter springform tin. Roll the pastry between 2 sheets of baking paper until large enough to fit the base and side of the tin. Ease into the tin and trim the edges. Cover the pastry with baking paper, then rice or dried beans. Bake for 10 minutes, then remove the baking paper and rice. Flatten the pastry lightly with the back of a spoon and bake for another 5 minutes. Set aside to cool.
3 To make the filling, reduce the oven to slow 150°C (300°F/Gas 2). Beat the cream cheese, sugar, flour and rinds until smooth. Add the eggs, one at a time, beating after each addition. Beat in the cream, pour over the pastry and bake for 1 hour 25–35 minutes, or until almost set. Turn off the oven and leave to cool with the door ajar. When cool, refrigerate.
4 To make the candied rind, place a little water in a pan with the rind, bring to the boil and simmer for 1 minute. Drain the rind and repeat with fresh water. This will get rid of any bitterness in the rind and syrup. Put the sugar in a pan with ¼ cup (60 ml/2 fl oz) water and stir over low heat until dissolved. Add the rind, bring to the boil, reduce the heat and simmer for 5–6 minutes, or until the rind looks translucent. Allow to cool, drain the rind and place on baking paper to dry (you can save the syrup to serve with the cheesecake). Whip the cream, spoon over the cold cheesecake and top with candied rind.

NOTE: To make the cheesecake easier to cut, heap the rind in mounds, then cut between the mounds of rind.

CHOCOLATE WHISKY LOAF

Preparation time: 10 minutes + freezing
Total cooking time: 10 minutes
Serves 6

250 g (8 oz) good-quality dark chocolate,
  roughly chopped
60 g (2 oz) unsalted butter, softened
4 egg yolks
1¼ cups (315 ml/10 fl oz) cream
2 teaspoons vanilla essence
2 tablespoons whisky
3 tablespoons cocoa, to dust

1 Line a 21 x 14 x 7 cm (8½ x 5½ x 2¾ inch) loaf tin with plastic wrap. Put the chocolate in a heatproof bowl. Bring a small pan of water to a simmer, remove from the heat and place the bowl over the pan, being careful not to let the bottom of the bowl touch the water. Stir the chocolate over the hot water until melted. Alternatively, melt the chocolate in the microwave for 1 minute on High (100%), stirring after 30 seconds. Allow to cool.
2 Beat the butter and egg yolks in a small bowl until thick and creamy, then beat in the cooled chocolate mixture. In a medium bowl, using clean beaters, beat the cream and vanilla essence until soft peaks form. Fold in the whisky. Using a metal spoon, fold the cream and chocolate mixtures together until just combined.
3 Pour the mixture into the prepared loaf tin, cover the surface with plastic wrap and freeze for 2–3 hours or overnight, or until firm. Remove from the freezer, unmould and carefully peel away the plastic wrap. Smooth the wrinkles on the surface of the loaf using a flat-bladed knife. Place on a serving plate and dust with cocoa. If not serving immediately, return to the freezer for up to 1 week. Cut into slices to serve. Can be served with extra cream and dessert wafers.

LEMON PASSIONFRUIT SYLLABUB WITH BERRIES

Preparation time: 40 minutes +
   standing + chilling
Total cooking time: Nil
Serves 8–10

2 teaspoons grated lemon rind
⅓ cup (80 ml/2¾ fl oz) lemon juice
½ cup (125 g/4 oz) caster sugar
½ cup (125 ml/4 fl oz) dry white wine
8 passionfruit
2 cups (500 ml/16 fl oz) thick (double) cream
500 g (1 lb) blueberries
500 g (1 lb) raspberries
2 tablespoons icing sugar
500 g (1 lb) strawberries, halved
icing sugar, extra, to dust

1 Stir the rind, juice, sugar and white wine together in a jug and set aside for 10 minutes. Cut the passionfruit in half and push the pulp through a sieve to remove the seeds. Add half the passionfruit pulp to the lemon, sugar and wine mixture.
2 Beat the cream with electric beaters until soft peaks form. Gradually beat in the lemon and passionfruit syrup until all the syrup is added (mixture will have the consistency of softly whipped cream). Stir in the remaining passionfruit, cover and refrigerate for 1 hour.
3 Combine the blueberries, raspberries and icing sugar and place in a 2.5–3 litre serving bowl. Spoon the cream mixture over the top, decorate with strawberries, dust with icing sugar and serve immediately.

NOTE: This thick, custardy dessert was originally made by beating milk or cream with wine, sugar, lemon juice and possibly spices, the acid curdling and thickening the mixture. Some versions were based on cider while others were further fortified with brandy. Syllabub was sometimes used in place of cream on desserts such as trifle, and instead of meringue for floating islands.

DECADENT WHITE CHOCOLATE MOUSSE

Preparation time: 40 minutes + chilling
Total cooking time: 5 minutes
Serves 6

60 g (2 oz) good-quality dark chocolate, melted
4 egg yolks
½ cup (125 g/4 oz) caster sugar
1 tablespoon honey
1 teaspoon instant coffee powder, optional
200 g (6½ oz) white chocolate, melted
125 g (4 oz) unsalted butter
⅔ cup (170 ml/5½ fl oz) thick (double) cream

Praline
80 g (2¾ oz) blanched almonds, lightly toasted
½ cup (125 g/4 oz) sugar

1 Place the chocolate in a small paper piping bag and pipe in a swirling pattern over the inside surface of six dessert glasses. Refrigerate until set.
2 To make the praline, line a baking tray with baking paper and spread the almonds over it. Combine the sugar with ⅓ cup (80 ml/2¾ fl oz) water in a small pan and stir over low heat, without boiling, until the sugar has dissolved. Brush the edges of the pan with water. Bring to the boil, reduce the heat and simmer, without stirring, until golden brown. Remove from the heat immediately and pour carefully over the almonds. Allow to set until hard. Break half into pieces for topping. Chop or process the remainder into fine crumbs.
3 Using electric beaters, beat the egg yolks, sugar, honey and the coffee blended with 1 teaspoon of hot water in a small bowl until very thick. Beat in the white chocolate until smooth. In a medium bowl, beat the butter with electric beaters until light and creamy. Add the egg yolk mixture and beat until smooth.
4 Beat the cream until soft peaks form. Using a metal spoon, gently fold the cream into the chocolate mixture. Fold in the finely chopped or processed praline. Spoon the mixture into dessert glasses. Refrigerate for 2–3 hours. Serve decorated with large praline pieces and perhaps whipped cream.

ORANGE SPANISH CREAM

Preparation time: 20 minutes + chilling
Total cooking time: 10 minutes
Serves 6

3 eggs, separated
²/₃ cup (160 g/5½ oz) caster sugar
2 teaspoons finely grated orange rind
½ cup (125 ml/4 fl oz) fresh orange juice
1½ tablespoons gelatine
3 cups (750 ml/24 fl oz) milk

1 Beat the egg yolks, sugar and orange rind in a small bowl with electric beaters or a balloon whisk for about 5 minutes, or until thick and creamy.
2 Pour the orange juice into a small heatproof bowl, sprinkle the gelatine in an even layer over the surface and leave to go spongy. Do not stir. Bring a large pan filled with about 4 cm (1½ inches) water to the boil, remove from the heat, carefully lower the gelatine bowl into the water (it should come halfway up the side of the bowl), then stir the gelatine until it has dissolved.
3 Combine the gelatine mixture with the milk in a saucepan and bring almost to the boil—do not boil or the gelatine will lose its setting properties. Remove from the heat and gradually pour onto the egg yolk mixture, mixing continually as you pour.

4 Beat the egg whites in a metal or glass bowl until stiff peaks form, then gently fold them into the milk mixture with a large metal spoon. Pour carefully into a 1.5 litre glass serving dish or six 250 ml (8 fl oz) dishes and cover with plastic wrap. Refrigerate for several hours, or overnight, until set.

NOTE: Spanish cream is also known as Honeycomb mould, Snow cream and New England quaking custard. This recipe appears in old English and American recipe books including Shaker recipes. It is a custard which separates into two or three layers—a bubbly layer on top and smooth layers underneath, created by folding the egg whites into a warm mixture rather than a cold one. If the custard mixture is cold when the egg whites are folded in, they will stay suspended by the gelatine and not separate out.

BERRIES AND CREAM PASTA STACK

Preparation time: 15 minutes
Total cooking time: 15 minutes
Serves 4

4 fresh or dried lasagne sheets
oil, for deep-frying
2 cups (500 ml/16 fl oz) cream
250 g (8 oz) punnet strawberries
250 g (8 oz) punnet blueberries
250 g (8 oz) punnet raspberries
4 passionfruit
icing sugar, for dusting

1 Cook the lasagne sheets two at a time in a large pan of rapidly boiling water until al dente. Add a little oil to the water to prevent the pasta from sticking together. Drain, then carefully rinse the pasta sheets under cold running water. Carefully cut each sheet into three, crossways. Pat dry with a tea towel.
2 Half fill a medium pan with oil. Heat the oil until moderately hot. Cook the pasta pieces one at a time until crisp and golden. Drain on paper towels.
3 Whip the cream until soft peaks form. Place one piece of fried lasagne sheet on each serving plate. Top with some cream, berries and passionfruit pulp. Dust with a little icing sugar. Continue layering once more for each, finishing with a lasagne sheet. Dust again with icing sugar and serve immediately.

NOTE: Any fruits in season are suitable to use for this dessert. Chop or slice the way you like. If you prefer, you can add a little sugar and vanilla to the whipped cream to sweeten.

PEANUT BRITTLE PARFAIT

Preparation time: 40 minutes + freezing
Total cooking time: 15 minutes
Serves 8

1½ cups (375 g/12 oz) caster sugar
2 cups (500 ml/16 fl oz) milk
6 egg yolks
1 tablespoon instant coffee powder
2½ cups (600 ml/20 fl oz) cream
120 g (4 oz) chocolate-coated peanut
   brittle, roughly chopped

1 Stir 1 cup (250 g/8 oz) sugar with ⅓ cup
(80 ml/2¾ fl oz) water in a pan over low
heat, without boiling, until the sugar
dissolves. Brush down the sides of the
pan with water to dissolve the sugar
crystals. Bring to the boil, reduce the heat
and simmer without stirring for 4 minutes,
or until caramel. Remove from the heat
and allow to cool slightly before stirring in
the milk. Be careful as the mixture will
splutter. Return to the heat and stir until
the toffee dissolves.
2 Line a 15 x 23 cm (6 x 9 inch) loaf tin with
plastic wrap. Whisk the remaining sugar
with the egg yolks in a metal or heatproof
bowl. Beat in the milk mixture and the
coffee blended with 1 teaspoon water.
Stand the bowl over a pan of simmering
water (or mix in the top of a double
boiler). Whisk until the mixture thickens
and coats the back of a spoon.
3 Cool the mixture, then add the cream.
Pour into a large shallow tin and freeze
until just firm. Transfer to a large bowl.
Using electric beaters, beat until light and
fluffy. Return to the tin and freeze until
just firm. Repeat the beating process
twice more. Fold the chopped peanut
brittle through, spread the mixture into
the loaf tin, cover the surface with a piece
of greaseproof paper, then freeze until
firm. Cut into slices to serve. Can be
decorated with pieces of toffee.

CROQUEMBOUCHE

Preparation time: 1 hour 30 minutes
Total cooking time: 1 hour 30 minutes
Serves 10–12

Choux pastry
100 g (3½ oz) unsalted butter
1½ cups (185 g/6 oz) plain flour, sifted
6 eggs, beaten
4 cups (1 kg/2 lb) sugar

Filling
1½ cups (375 ml/12 fl oz) milk
1 vanilla bean
3 egg yolks
¼ cup (60 g/2 oz) caster sugar
2 tablespoons plain flour
¼ cup (60 ml/2 fl oz) Grand Marnier
1½ cups (375 ml/12 fl oz) cream

1 Preheat the oven to hot 210°C
(415°F/Gas 6–7). Put the butter in a large
heavy-based pan with 1½ cups (375 ml/12
fl oz) water and stir over medium heat
until the mixture comes to the boil.
Remove from the heat and quickly beat in
the flour. Return to the heat and continue
beating until the mixture comes together
and leaves the side of the pan. Allow to
cool slightly.
2 Beat the mixture to release any more
heat. Gradually add the beaten egg, about
3 teaspoons at a time. Beat well between
each addition until all the egg has been
added and the mixture is thick and
glossy—a wooden spoon should stand
upright in it. (If it is too runny, the egg has
been added too quickly. Beat for several
more minutes, or until thickened.)
Sprinkle 3 baking trays with water—this
creates steam, helping the puffs to rise.
Spoon the mixture onto the trays, leaving
plenty of room for spreading. You will
need about eight large puffs (use 1
tablespoon mixture for each). Vary the
remainder, gradually reducing the size.
One small puff is equal to about 1 heaped
teaspoonful of mixture. Bake for

20–30 minutes, or until browned and
hollow sounding when the base is tapped.
Turn the oven off and leave the puffs
inside to dry out. (You may need to
prepare and cook them in two batches.)
3 To make the filling, put the milk and
vanilla bean in a pan. Heat gently until the
milk almost boils. Remove from the heat
and cool slightly. Beat the yolks, sugar
and flour until thick and pale. Gradually
whisk in the warm milk. Stir over medium
heat until the custard boils and thickens.
Remove from the heat and stir in the
liqueur. Discard the vanilla bean. Cover
the surface of the custard with plastic
wrap to prevent a skin forming and cool
completely.
4 Whip the cream into stiff peaks and fold
into the custard. Put into a piping bag with
a nozzle less than 1 cm (½ inch). Poke a
small hole in the base of each puff and fill
with custard.
5 Put 2 cups of the sugar in a pan with
1 cup (250 ml/8 fl oz) of water. Stir over
low heat, without boiling, until dissolved.
Bring to the boil and cook until lightly
golden. Remove from the heat and plunge
the base of the pan in cold water.
6 To assemble, begin with the large puffs.
Dip the bases in enough toffee to coat and
arrange in a large circle, with the sides
touching—you don't need to have any in
the centre. Build up into a cone shape,
using smaller puffs nearer the top.
7 Make the rest of the toffee and then dip
two forks in it. Rub the backs of the forks
together until tacky, then gently pull them
apart. Spin toffee around the
Croquembouche.

FROZEN CHOCOLATE PARFAIT

Preparation time: 40 minutes + freezing
Total cooking time: 25 minutes
Serves 8

6 egg yolks
½ cup (125 g/4 oz) caster sugar
150 g (5 oz) dark chocolate, finely chopped
150 g (5 oz) milk chocolate, finely chopped
1 vanilla bean, split lengthways
1 cup (250 ml/8 fl oz) milk
1⅓ cups (350 ml/11 fl oz) cream

1 Lightly grease a 1.25 litre terrine mould and line the entire mould with two layers of plastic wrap, allowing the plastic to extend over the sides. (This will help when removing the parfait once it has set.) Place the egg yolks in a bowl and gradually whisk in the sugar. Continue to whisk until the sugar has dissolved and the mixture is thick and pale. Place the chopped dark and milk chocolate in separate bowls and set aside.
2 Put the vanilla bean in a small pan with the milk. Slowly bring to the boil, then remove from the heat and scrape the seeds out of the vanilla bean and into the milk. Discard the empty bean. Gently pour the milk onto the egg yolks, whisking constantly. Return the mixture to a clean pan and cook over low heat, stirring constantly, until the custard coats the back of a wooden spoon. This will take about 20 minutes. Do not overcook or the egg will curdle.

3 Divide the hot custard evenly between the bowls of chocolate. Using a wooden spoon, quickly mix in the custard, stirring until the chocolate is completely melted. Allow to cool completely. Beat the cream with electric beaters until soft peaks form. Divide evenly between the cooled chocolate mixtures, and gently fold in. Carefully pour the dark chocolate mixture into the base of the terrine dish. Freeze for 30 minutes, or until firm. Pour the milk chocolate mixture over the back of a spoon to form an even layer, and smooth the top with the back of a spoon. Cover with a piece of greaseproof paper and freeze overnight, or until the terrine is completely frozen.
4 Just before serving, carefully remove the plastic wrap and parfait from the dish. Slice the parfait and immediately return the remaining portion to the freezer.

FRUIT COVERED WITH MERINGUE

Preparation time: 25 minutes
Total cooking time: 20 minutes
Serves 4

4 ripe peaches or nectarines
40 g (1¼ oz) marzipan
3 egg whites
⅔ cup (160 g (5½ oz) caster sugar
demerara sugar, to sprinkle

1 Preheat the oven to moderately hot 200°C (400°F/Gas 6). Cut the peaches in half and remove the stone. To remove the skin, place the peaches cut-side-down on a plate, put the plate in the sink and pour boiling water over, followed by cold water. Drain immediately and peel. Roll the marzipan into 4 small balls, put them in the gaps left by the peach stones, then put the halves back together. Stand the peaches in a shallow ovenproof dish.
2 Whisk the egg whites in a large, clean, dry bowl until stiff peaks form, gradually add the sugar and whisk until thick and glossy. Cover the fruit with a layer of meringue, making sure there are no gaps. Using a fork, rough up the surface of the meringue. Sprinkle with demerara sugar and bake for 15–20 minutes, until the meringue is lightly browned. Gently lift out. These can be served with cream or ice cream.

POACHED PEARS WITH CHOCOLATE SHORTBREAD FLOWERS

Preparation time: 50 minutes + chilling
Total cooking time: 1 hour 10 minutes
Serves 6

6 medium pears
1½ cups (375 ml/12 fl oz) sweet dessert wine
1 vanilla bean, split lengthways

Cardamom custard
1 cup (250 ml/8 fl oz) milk
½ cup (125 ml/4 fl oz) cream
6 cardamom pods, crushed
3 egg yolks
2 tablespoons caster sugar

Chocolate shortbread flowers
60 g (2 oz) unsalted butter, chopped
2 tablespoons soft brown sugar
1 egg yolk
1 tablespoon cocoa powder
½ cup (60 g/2 oz) plain flour
¼ cup (30 g/1 oz) cornflour

Toffee fingers
1 cup (250 g/8 oz) caster sugar

1 Peel the pears and remove the cores with a melon baller. Place in a saucepan large enough to hold all the pears. Add the wine and vanilla bean, cover and simmer for 20–25 minutes, or until soft (cooking time will depend on the ripeness of the pears). Remove the pan from the heat and allow the pears to cool in the syrup.
2 To make the cardamom custard, combine the milk, cream and cardamom pods in a small pan, bring to the boil and remove from the heat. Beat the egg yolks and sugar in a heatproof bowl for about 5 minutes, or until light and fluffy, then gradually pour in the hot milk mixture. Place the bowl over a pan of simmering water and stir with a wooden spoon for 10–15 minutes, or until the mixture coats the back of a wooden spoon. Strain and cool.

3 To make the chocolate shortbread flowers, preheat the oven to moderate 180°C (350°F/Gas 4). Beat the butter and sugar in a small bowl with electric beaters until light and creamy. Add the egg yolk, then the sifted cocoa and flours. Press together to form a soft dough. Wrap in plastic wrap and refrigerate for 30 minutes. Roll the dough out between two sheets of baking paper to 4 mm (¼ inch) thick. Cut 42 rounds from the pastry, using a 3 cm (1¼ inch) round cutter. Cut the remaining pastry into 12 small leaves. For each flower, use 7 rounds, slightly overlapping, to form a flower on a baking tray lined with baking paper. Decorate with the leaves. Bake for 10–15 minutes, or until the pastry is firm to touch. Remove from the tray and cool on a wire rack.
4 To make the toffee fingers, line two or three baking trays with baking paper. Sprinkle the sugar over the base of a heavy-based frying pan, then stir gently until the sugar has dissolved and is light golden brown. Remove from the heat (the toffee will continue to darken away from the heat). Use a spoon to drizzle 12 cm (5 inch) lengths of toffee onto the prepared trays, about 5 mm (¼ inch) wide, and allow to set until cold.
5 To assemble for serving, dust the shortbread flowers very lightly with icing sugar, place in the centre of a serving plate and position a well-drained pear on top. Spoon cardamom custard around the outside of the shortbread. Stand the toffee strips up around the outside of the pear like a tepee.

NOTE: The cardamom custard can be made three days ahead. Pears and shortbread rounds can be made a day ahead and the shortbread can be frozen

STICKY DATE PUDDING

Preparation time: 35 minutes
Total cooking time: 55 minutes
Serves 6–8

200 g (6½ oz) dates, pitted and chopped
1 cup (250 ml/8 fl oz) water
1 teaspoon bicarbonate of soda
100 g (3⅓ oz) butter
⅔ cup (160 g/5¼ oz) caster sugar
2 eggs, lightly beaten
1 teaspoon vanilla essence
1½ cups (185 g/6 oz) self-raising flour

Sauce
1 cup (185 g/6 oz) soft brown sugar
½ cup (125 ml/4 fl oz) cream
100 g (3⅓ oz) butter

1 Preheat the oven to moderate 180°C (350°F/Gas 4). Brush a 20 cm (8 inch) square cake tin with oil or melted butter. Line the base with baking paper. Combine the dates and water in a small pan. Bring to the boil and remove from heat. Stir in soda and set aside to cool to room temperature.
2 Using electric beaters, beat the butter and sugar in a small bowl until light and creamy. Add the eggs gradually, beating thoroughly after each addition. Add the essence and beat until combined. Transfer to a large bowl.
3 Using a metal spoon, fold in the flour and dates with the liquid and stir until just combined—do not over-beat. Pour into prepared tin and bake for 50 minutes, until a skewer comes out clean when inserted into centre of pudding. Leave in tin for 10 minutes before turning out.
4 To make Sauce: Combine sugar, cream and butter in a small pan; stir until butter melts and sugar dissolves. Bring to boil, reduce heat and simmer for 2 minutes. Cut the pudding into wedges and place on serving plates. Pour hot sauce over. Serve immediately, with extra cream and raspberries, if desired.

STRAWBERRY GRANITA

Preparation time: 15 minutes + freezing
Total cooking time: 10 minutes
Serves 4

½ cup (125 g/4 oz) sugar
500 g (1 lb) strawberries
2 tablespoons lemon juice

1 Stir the sugar and ½ cup (125 ml/4 fl oz) water together in a pan over low heat until the sugar has dissolved. Bring to the boil and simmer for 5 minutes. Leave to cool.
2 Hull the strawberries and chop in a food processor or blender with the lemon juice for 30 seconds, or until smooth. Add the cooled sugar syrup and process to combine.
3 Sieve the purée to remove the seeds. Pour into a shallow metal container, cover and freeze for 2 hours, or until the granita around the edge of the tray is frozen. Stir with a fork to break up the ice crystals. Return to the freezer for 1 hour and stir again with a fork. Repeat this until the mixture is a smooth consistency of ice crystals, then pour into a storage container, cover with greaseproof paper and return to the freezer for 3–4 hours, or until set.
4 To serve, soften the frozen mixture in the refrigerator for 15–20 minutes and stir again with a fork to break up the ice crystals and freeze again.

NOTE: If you have stored the granita for a few days, you may need to fork and freeze it again more than once until you to get it to the correct consistency for serving. It is delicious with a dollop of cream.

SAGO PUDDING

Preparation time: 20 minutes + 1 hour
  soaking + 2 hours refrigeration
Total cooking time: 20 minutes
Serves 6

1 cup (195 g/6⅓ oz) sago
3 cups (750 ml/24 fl oz) water
1 cup (185 g/6 oz) lightly packed soft
  brown sugar
1 cup (250 ml/8 fl oz) water, extra
1 cup (250 ml/8 fl oz) coconut cream, well
  chilled

1 Soak the sago in the water for 1 hour. Pour into a pan, add 2 tablespoons of the sugar and bring to the boil over low heat, stirring constantly. Reduce the heat and simmer, stirring occasionally, for 8 minutes. Cover and cook for 2 to 3 minutes, until the mixture becomes thick and the sago grains are translucent.
2 Half fill 6 wet ½ cup (125 ml/4 fl oz) moulds with the sago mixture. Refrigerate for 2 hours, or until set.
3 Combine the remaining sugar with the extra water in a small pan and cook over low heat, stirring constantly, until the sugar dissolves. Simmer for 5 to 7 minutes, until the syrup thickens. Remove from the heat and cool. To serve, unmould the sago and top with a little of the sugar syrup and coconut cream.

PAPAYA LIME FOOL

Preparation time: 15 minutes + chilling
Total cooking time: Nil
Serves 4

2 red pawpaw or papaya, about 1 kg
1–2 tablespoons lime juice
3 tablespoons vanilla sugar
1¼ cups (315 ml/10 fl oz) cream

1 Peel the pawpaw, remove the seeds and mash the flesh until smooth. Do not do this in a food processor or the fruit will be too runny.
2 Add the lime juice and vanilla sugar, to taste—the amount will vary according to the sweetness of the fruit.
3 Whisk the cream until soft peaks form, then fold through the mashed pawpaw. Spoon into serving glasses and chill until ready to serve.

NOTE: 500 g (1 lb) stewed rhubarb can be substituted for the pawpaw.

BERRY TRIFLE

Preparation time: 35 minutes + overnight
  refrigeration
Total cooking time: 5 minutes
Serves 8–10

1½ cups (2 x 225 g/7 oz jars) redcurrant jelly
⅔ cup (170 ml/5½ fl oz) fresh orange juice
2½ cups (600 ml/20 fl oz) cream
250 g (8 oz) mascarpone
¼ cup (30 g/1 oz) icing sugar
1 teaspoon vanilla essence
¼ teaspoon ground cinnamon
250 g (8 oz) thin sponge finger biscuits
1½ cups (375 ml/12 fl oz) Marsala
400 g (13 oz) fresh raspberries
250 g (8 oz) large fresh strawberries,
  hulled and quartered
400 g (13 oz) fresh blueberries

1 Melt the redcurrant jelly in a small
saucepan over medium heat. Remove from
the heat, stir in the orange juice and set aside
until the mixture reaches room temperature.
2 Put the cream, mascarpone, icing
sugar, vanilla essence and cinnamon in a
bowl and beat with electric beaters until
soft peaks form.
3 Cut each biscuit in half crossways and
dip each piece in the Marsala. Arrange
half over the base of a 3.25 litre (104 fl oz)
serving bowl.
4 Sprinkle a third of the combined berries
over the biscuits and drizzle with half the
remaining Marsala and a third of the
redcurrant sauce. Spoon half the cream
mixture over the sauce. Repeat the layering
with the remaining half of the dipped
biscuits and Marsala, a third of the berries
and sauce, and the remaining cream.
5 Arrange the remaining berries over the
cream in a mound in the centre of the
bowl. Reserve the final third of the
redcurrant sauce, cover and refrigerate.
Cover the trifle with plastic wrap and
refrigerate overnight. Before serving,
pour the reserved redcurrant sauce over
the berries to glaze. (Gently reheat the
sauce if it is too thick.)

STRAWBERRY MERINGUE STACKS

Preparation time: 25 minutes
Total cooking time: 40 minutes
Serves 6

4 egg whites
1 cup (250 g/8 oz) caster sugar
500 g (1 lb) strawberries, hulled
1¼ cups (315 ml/10 fl oz) cream, whipped

1 Preheat oven to slow 150°C (300°F/
Gas 2). Brush two 32 x 28 cm (13 x 11 inch)
oven trays with melted butter or oil. Cut
non-stick baking paper to fit trays. Using
an 8 cm (3 inch) round cutter as a guide,
mark 12 circles onto paper, and place
pencil-side down on trays.
2 Place egg whites in a medium, clean dry
bowl. Using electric beaters, beat until
soft peaks form. Add the sugar gradually,
beating constantly until mixture is thick
and glossy and all the sugar has
dissolved. Spread meringue into rounds
on the prepared trays. Bake for 40 minutes
then turn off heat and allow meringues to
cool in oven.
3 Place half the strawberries into a food
processor or blender and blend until
completely liquid. Slice the remaining
strawberries and fold through whipped
cream. To serve, sandwich two meringue
rounds together with cream mixture and
place on each plate. Pour some
strawberry sauce around base of the
meringue.

NOTE: The meringues can be made up to
two days in advance and stored in an
airtight container. Strawberry sauce can
be made up to one day ahead. Make the
strawberry cream mixture up to two
hours in advance. Store the sauce and
cream, covered, in the refrigerator. After
assembling, serve immediately. If you
prefer a sweeter sauce, a little caster
sugar can be added. Garnish with
strawberry leaves to serve, if you wish.

DANISH CREAMED RICE WITH DARK CHERRY SAUCE

Preparation time: 15 minutes + cooling
Total cooking time: 50 minutes
Serves 6

1 cup (220 g/7 oz) short-grain rice
1 litre (32 fl oz) milk
1 tablespoon vanilla sugar (see Note)
2 tablespoons caster (superfine) sugar
1¼ cups (310 ml/10 fl oz) cream
2 tablespoons whole blanched almonds

Dark cherry sauce
3 teaspoons cornflour (cornstarch)
425 g (14 oz) tin stoneless black cherries
  in syrup

1 Put the rice and milk in a saucepan,
cover and cook over low heat for
40–45 minutes, or until the rice is cooked
and the mixture is thick and creamy. Stir
occasionally to prevent the rice forming
lumps and sticking to the pan. Remove
from the heat and stir in both the sugars.
Spoon into a large bowl, cover the top of
the rice with plastic wrap and allow to
cool at room temperature, stirring
occasionally.
2 When the rice is cool, stir to separate
the grains. Beat the cream in a bowl with
electric beaters until soft peaks form.
Fold into the creamed rice. Reserve one
whole almond and roughly chop the rest.
Fold into the creamy rice and stir in the
whole almond. Refrigerate the rice while
preparing the sauce.
3 To make the sauce, blend the cornflour
with 2 tablespoons water in a small bowl.
Pour the cherries and their juice into a
small saucepan, add the cornflour
mixture and stir over medium heat until
the mixture boils and thickens. Remove
from the heat. Spoon the rice into serving
bowls and top with the hot sauce.

VANILLA BAVAROIS

Preparation time: 40 minutes + standing + chilling
Total cooking time: 10–15 minutes
Serves 4

2¾ cups (685 ml/22 fl oz) milk
1 vanilla bean
1 cinnamon stick
6 egg yolks
⅔ cup (160 g/5½ oz) caster sugar
3 teaspoons gelatine
¾ cup (185 ml/6 fl oz) cream

1 Gently heat the milk, vanilla bean and cinnamon stick in a pan until almost boiling. Remove from the heat and set aside to infuse for 5 minutes. Remove the cinnamon stick and vanilla bean.
2 Whisk together the egg yolks and sugar until thick and pale. Gradually whisk in the milk. Pour into a large clean pan and stir continuously over low heat until the mixture thickens. Do not boil. Remove from the heat. Cover the surface with plastic wrap to prevent a skin forming.
3 Place 2 tablespoons water in a small heatproof bowl, sprinkle the gelatine in an even layer over the surface and leave to go spongy. Bring a large pan filled with about 4 cm (1½ inches) water to the boil, remove from the heat, carefully lower the gelatine bowl into the water (it should come halfway up the side of the bowl) and stir until dissolved. Whisk into the custard. Cover as before and leave to cool.
4 Beat the cream until soft peaks form and fold into the cold custard. Spoon into four 250 ml (8 fl oz) ramekins or moulds, tap the bases gently on a worktop to remove air bubbles, then refrigerate overnight.
5 To unmould, tilt each ramekin slightly on its side. Use your finger to gently pull the bavarois away from the edge, allowing air to enter and break the suction. Turn the bavarois out onto a plate. If it does not come out straight away, wipe a cloth dipped in hot water over the outside of the mould. Garnish with pieces of fresh fruit if you wish.

JAM PUDDING

Preparation time: 30 minutes
Total cooking time: 50 minutes
Serves 6

185 g (6 oz) unsalted butter, softened
¾ cup (185 g/6 oz) caster sugar
1 teaspoon vanilla essence
3 eggs, lightly beaten
½ cup (60 g/2 oz) plain flour
1 cup (125 g/4 oz) self-raising flour
½ cup (160 g/5½ oz) berry jam

1 Preheat the oven to moderate 180°C (350°F/Gas 4). Lightly grease six 250 ml (8 fl oz) fluted or plain heatproof moulds.
2 Beat the butter, sugar and vanilla essence with electric beaters for 1–2 minutes, or until light and creamy. Add the eggs gradually, beating well after each addition. Using a metal spoon, fold in the combined sifted flour, a quarter at a time.
3 Spoon the mixture evenly into the moulds and smooth the surface. Cover each with a piece of greased foil, pleated in the middle. Secure with string. Place in a large deep baking dish filled with enough boiling water to come halfway up the sides of the moulds. Bake for 45 minutes, or until a skewer comes out clean. Put the jam in a small pan and warm over low heat for 3–4 minutes, or until liquid. Leave the puddings for 5 minutes before loosening the sides with a knife and turning out. Top with the jam. Can be served with custard, cream or ice cream.

SPANISH RICE PUDDING

Preparation time: 5 minutes
Total cooking time: 1 hour
Serves 6

1.25 litres (40 fl oz) milk
1 cup (220 g/7 oz) arborio rice
1 large strip of orange zest, pith removed
1 cinnamon stick
1 teaspoon natural vanilla extract
⅔ cup (145 g/5 oz) caster (superfine) sugar
orange zest, to garnish (optional)

1 Put the milk, rice, orange zest, cinnamon stick, vanilla, sugar and a pinch of salt in a large saucepan and stir over high heat until the sugar is dissolved. Allow to just come to the boil, then reduce the heat to a simmer.
2 Cook the rice mixture over low heat, stirring regularly, for 50 minutes, or until the rice is tender but not mushy. Stirring not only helps to ensure the rice mixture does not stick to the bottom of the pan but it also helps to produce a very creamy texture.
3 Lift out the zest and cinnamon stick from the pan with some tongs and serve the rice pudding warm or cold, garnished with some thin strips of orange zest.

NOTE: In Spanish, this dish is called Arroz con leche and it is found not only in Spain but also in Spanish influenced countries. The Spanish often dust the surface of the pudding with cinnamon just before serving—use only a little or you risk overpowering the subtle flavour.

COCONUT ICE CREAM

Preparation time: 10 minutes + freezing
Total cooking time: 15 minutes
Serves 6

1¾ cups (440 ml/14 fl oz) coconut cream
1½ cups (375 ml/12 fl oz) cream
2 eggs
2 egg yolks
½ cup (125 g/4 oz) caster sugar
¼ teaspoon salt
1 teaspoon vanilla essence
¼ cup (15 g/½ oz) shredded coconut
fresh mint, to garnish

1 Place the coconut cream and cream in a medium pan. Stir over medium heat, without boiling, for 2 to 3 minutes. Remove from the heat, cover and keep warm.
2 Place the eggs, egg yolks, sugar, salt and vanilla in a large heatproof bowl. Using electric beaters, beat the mixture for 2 to 3 minutes until frothy and thickened.
3 Place the bowl over a pan of simmering water. Continue to beat the egg mixture while gradually adding the warm coconut mixture, ¼ cup (60 ml/2 fl oz) at a time, until all the coconut mixture is added and the custard has thickened. This process will take about 10 minutes. The mixture will be the consistency of thin cream and should easily coat the back of a spoon. Do not allow to boil or it will curdle.

4 Transfer the mixture to a cold bowl, cover and set aside to cool; stir it occasionally while it is cooling. When cool, pour the mixture into a shallow cake tin, cover and freeze for about 1½ hours or until half-frozen.
5 Quickly spoon the ice cream into a food processor and process for 30 seconds, or until smooth. Return the ice cream to the cake tin or place it in a plastic container, and cover and freeze completely.
6 Spread the coconut on an oven tray and toast it in a slow 150°C (300°F/Gas 2) oven for 10 minutes or until it is dark golden, shaking the tray occasionally. Remove the coconut from the tray to prevent it from burning and set aside to cool. Serve the ice cream in scoops with the coconut sprinkled over and garnished with the mint.

NOTE: Before serving the ice cream, leave to stand at room temperature for 10 to 15 minutes or until it has softened slightly.

STICKY ORANGE AND PASSIONFRUIT PUDDING

Preparation time: 35 minutes + chilling
Total cooking time: 55 minutes
Serves 6

3 cups (375 g/12 oz) plain flour
1½ teaspoons baking powder
200 g (6½ oz) chilled unsalted butter, chopped
½ cup (45g/1½ oz) desiccated coconut
300 ml (9½ fl oz) cream
½ cup (160 g/5¼ oz) orange marmalade
2 tablespoons passionfruit pulp

Passionfruit syrup
½ cup (125 ml/4 fl oz) orange juice
¾ cup (185 g/6 oz) caster sugar
¼ cup (60 g/2 oz) passionfruit pulp

1 Sift the flour, baking powder and a pinch of salt into a bowl. Rub in the butter with just your fingertips until fine and crumbly. Stir in the coconut. With a flat-bladed knife, mix in most of the cream. Add the rest, if needed, to bring the mixture together. Press together into a soft dough and roll between 2 sheets of baking paper to make a 25 x 40 cm (10 x 16 inch) rectangle.
2 Spread marmalade over the dough and drizzle with passionfruit pulp. Roll up lengthways like a swiss roll. Chill for 20 minutes, or until firm.
3 Preheat the oven to 180°C (350°F/Gas 4). Brush a deep 20 cm (8 inch) round cake tin with melted butter or oil; line the base with baking paper. Cut the rolled dough into 2 cm (¾ inch) slices; arrange half over the base of the tin. Place a second layer over the gaps where the bottom slices join. Place the tin on a baking tray.
4 To make the passionfruit syrup, put all the ingredients with ¼ cup (60 ml/2 fl oz) water in a pan. Stir over low heat, without boiling, until the sugar has dissolved. Bring to the boil, then pour over the pudding. Bake for 50 minutes, or until a skewer comes out clean. Leave for 15 minutes before turning out.

CARAMEL

FOR CREATING REAL SHOW STOPPING DESSERTS CARAMEL IS AN INVALUABLE AND DELICIOUS ACCESSORY. GLAZE, DIP, OR SPIN IT INTO GOLDEN THREADS, SET NUTS IN CARAMEL TO MAKE PRALINE, OR LET IT HARDEN INTO A TOFFEE TOPPING.

There are two different ways to make caramel. The wet method involves dissolving the sugar in water and then boiling the sugar syrup; the dry method means melting the sugar on its own. The wet method is more complicated as the syrup can crystallize, but it is easier to keep an eye on as it starts to darken. The dry method needs a bit more practice to avoid burning the sugar as it melts. For either method, use a heavy-based pan which gives an even heat all over the base. Non-stick pans and those with dark linings are harder to use as you cannot easily see the colour of the caramel. Use a coarser grade of sugar so you get less scum—granulated sugar is good as it dissolves easily and is not too refined.

WET METHOD

Put the water and sugar in a pan and stir over low heat until all the sugar has dissolved, then bring to the boil. If you boil before the sugar has completely dissolved, it will crystallize. Do not stir the syrup as it boils or crystals will form on the spoon. Do not allow any crystals to form on the side of the pan from splashes—if they do, dip a clean dry pastry brush in cold water and brush down the side of the pan.

As the water evaporates off the syrup, the temperature will start to rise. Be very careful as the hot syrup can cause serious burns. Once the syrup reaches 160°C–175°C (315°F–335°F), all the water will have evaporated and the molten sugar which is left will start to caramelize. The syrup will be thicker and the bubbles will be bigger and break

more slowly. At this point, the sugar will start to colour quite quickly, so keep an eye on it and remove from the heat the moment it reaches the colour you want. Swirl the pan to keep the colour of the caramel even, otherwise patches may darken and burn before the rest has coloured. To stop the caramel continuing to cook in the pan after you've removed it from the heat, plunge the base of the pan into a sink of cold water. You can then remelt the caramel over low heat as you need it.

DRY METHOD

Sprinkle the sugar in an even layer over the base of the pan and place over low heat. Melt the sugar slowly, tipping the pan from side to side so that it melts evenly—keep the sugar moving or it might start to colour on one side before the other side has melted. When the caramel starts to colour, keep swirling until you have an even colour and then remove the pan from the heat. Stop the cooking by plunging the base of the pan into a sink of cold water.

If you find your caramel isn't dark enough, simply remelt it and cook until it reaches the colour you want— if it gets too dark, there is no magic remedy and you will have to start again, so be careful. The darkest stage of caramel is known as black jack—this has a strong flavour and

is used in very small amounts as a colouring for desserts, but is inedible on its own.

If the sugar syrup starts to crystallize, rescue it by adding a tablespoon of honey, a squeeze of lemon juice or a pinch of cream of tartar—these all slow down the crystallization by breaking down the sucrose into fructose and glucose. If you only have a few crystals, take your pan off the stove to allow it to cool a little, then add some more water and redissolve the crystals. If you are worried about crystallization, you can add a few drops of lemon juice to the sugar at the beginning.

CARAMEL DECORATIONS

THINGS TO MAKE

Caramel decorations must be made and used quickly—they do not store well and will soften in humidity. They will also soften and become sticky if refrigerated. The sugar in caramel will liquefy when it comes into contact with cream, ice creams, custard etc., so don't make your decorations sit too long before being served. If possible, add them just before serving. Make your caramel as described on the previous page. When the caramel reaches the colour you want, stop it cooking and colouring further and keep liquid by reheating gently when necessary.

Caramel sheets If you are making sheets of caramel, pour the caramel onto an oiled baking sheet and leave to cool (be careful as the baking sheet will become extremely hot). The sheets of caramel can then be broken into different shapes and sizes for decoration. It is easiest to break the caramel by hand, but don't stab yourself with a sharp piece. You can also pour the caramel into freeform threads or shapes, or pour it into a template cut from plasticine brushed with a little oil. The caramel can be coloured with food colouring and you can create whole pictures using different colours.

Spun sugar Caramel can be spun into fine threads using two forks or a balloon whisk with the ends cut off. Keep the caramel liquid by standing the pan in a pan of hot water while you work. It will need to be thick enough to run in continuous streams from the ends of the forks. Oil the handle of a broom or long

handled wooden spoon and place it between two chairs. Lay some newspaper on the floor under the handle. Hold two forks back to back and dip them in the caramel. Flick them backwards and forwards across the broom handle—sugar threads will form across the broom handle and hang down on each side. Re-dip the forks as necessary until you have enough threads draped over the handle. Form the threads into decorative shapes by gently moulding them with your hands. Use immediately.

Caramel baskets Make caramel baskets by drizzling the caramel backwards and forwards across the bowl of a well oiled ladle or mould and leave to harden before carefully sliding the basket off the ladle. Lengths of caramel or crisscross patterns for decoration can be made by drizzling the caramel in patterns on a well oiled baking tray or any metal mould. Remember, the thicker the threads, the

less likely they are to break, although with practice you should be able to make thinner more delicate decorations.

Praline Add toasted whole, flaked or slivered blanched almonds to a golden caramel made with an equal quantity of sugar to the weight of the nuts. Mix well, quickly tip out onto a marble surface or oiled baking sheet, then spread out into a single layer and cool. The praline can then either be broken into pieces or crushed in a plastic bag with a rolling pin or in a food processor. Store in an airtight container. Sheets of praline made with chopped almonds can be moulded into cup shapes by reheating the praline gently, then pressing it down onto an upturned mould.

Lining a mould Pour the liquid caramel into the bases of moulds used for desserts such as crème caramel and swirl them to coat the mould evenly. Be

careful as the mould will get hot. Dipping fruit Whole fruit or nuts can be dipped in pale caramel to give a glossy sheen. Use a fork or skewer or hold the fruit by its stalk. Place on a piece of baking paper until completely cool.

Caramel bark Sprinkle a foil-lined baking tray with a thin layer of sugar and place under a preheated grill. Watch carefully until the sugar melts and turns to caramel. Leave to set and then carefully lift the caramel off the foil and break into pieces.

Toffee glazes Pour liquid caramel onto crème brulées and other similar desserts to make a hard toffee topping. Pour the caramel over the surface and carefully tip from side to side to coat evenly. The caramel will harden quickly so work fast.

CLASSIC KHEER

Preparation time: 10 minutes +
   30 minutes soaking
Total cooking time: 2 hours 5 minutes
Serves 6

155 g (5 oz) basmati rice
20 cardamom pods
2.5 litres (80 fl oz) milk
⅓ cup (30 g/1 oz) flaked almonds
175 g (6 oz) sugar
30 g (1 oz) sultanas

1 Wash the rice, then soak for 30 minutes in cold water. Drain well. Remove the seeds from the cardamom pods and lightly crush them in a spice grinder or mortar and pestle.
2 Bring the milk to the boil in a large heavy-based saucepan and add the rice and cardamom. Reduce the heat and simmer for 1½–2 hours,
or until the rice has a creamy consistency. Stir occasionally to stop the rice sticking to the pan.
3 Dry-fry the almonds in a frying pan for a few minutes over medium heat. Add the sugar, almonds and sultanas to the rice, reserving some for a garnish. Mix, then divide among bowls. Serve warm, garnished with almonds and sultanas.

BAKED CHEESECAKE WITH SOUR CREAM

Preparation time: 30 minutes + chilling
Total cooking time: 50 minutes
Serves 8–10

250 g (8 oz) plain sweet biscuits
1 teaspoon mixed spice
100 g (3½ oz) unsalted butter, melted

Filling
500 g (1 lb) cream cheese, softened
⅔ cup (160 g/5½ oz) caster sugar
1 teaspoon vanilla essence
1 tablespoon lemon juice
4 eggs

Topping
1 cup (250 g/8 oz) sour cream
½ teaspoon vanilla essence
3 teaspoons lemon juice
1 tablespoon caster sugar
nutmeg, for sprinkling

1 Lightly grease a 20 cm (8 inch) diameter springform tin and line the base with baking paper. Finely crush the biscuits in a food processor or place them in a sealed plastic bag and crush them with a rolling pin. Transfer to a bowl, add the spice and butter and stir until the crumbs are all moistened. Press firmly over the base and up the side of the tin to create an even shell. Refrigerate for 20 minutes, or until firm. Preheat the oven to moderate 180°C (350°F/Gas 4).

2 To make the filling, beat the cream cheese with electric beaters, until smooth. Add the sugar, vanilla essence and lemon juice, then beat until smooth. Add the eggs, one at a time, beating well after each addition. Pour carefully over the crumbs and bake for 45 minutes, or until just firm to touch.
3 To make the topping, combine the sour cream, vanilla essence, lemon juice and sugar in a bowl. Spread over the hot cheesecake. Sprinkle with nutmeg and return to the oven for another 7 minutes. Turn off the oven and leave to cool with the door ajar. When cool, refrigerate until firm. Can be decorated with strawberries.

NOTE: Cheesecake tends to be quite heavy and will be easier to cut using a knife dipped in hot water and dried between each slice.

RICE PUDDING WITH LEMON THYME AND BALSAMIC STRAWBERRIES

Preparation time: 20 minutes + standing
Total cooking time: 1 hour 15 minutes
Serves 6–8

500 g (1 lb) strawberries
2 tablespoons good-quality balsamic vinegar
⅓ cup (90 g/3 oz) caster (superfine) sugar
¾ cup (150 g/5 oz) long-grain rice
3 cups (750 ml/24 fl oz) milk
6 x 3 cm (1¼ inch) lemon thyme sprigs
⅓ cup (90 g/3 oz) sugar
3 egg yolks
1 egg

1 Trim the stalks from the strawberries and cut the strawberries in half. Put in a bowl with the vinegar. Sprinkle the caster sugar over the top and stir well. Set aside, turning occasionally.
2 Preheat the oven to warm 160°C (315°F/Gas 2–3). Lightly grease a 1.5 litre (48 fl oz) ovenproof dish.
3 Thoroughly rinse the rice and put it in a medium saucepan with 1½ cups (375 ml/ 12 fl oz) water. Bring to the boil, cover and cook over low heat for 8–10 minutes. Remove from the heat and leave the pan with the lid on for 5 minutes, until the liquid is absorbed and the rice is soft.
4 Heat the milk with the lemon thyme and sugar in a small saucepan. When bubbles form at the edge, remove from the heat and set aside for 10 minutes so that it absorbs flavour from the lemon thyme. Strain. Beat the egg yolks and egg in a large bowl, add the rice and gradually stir in the warm milk. Pour into the prepared ovenproof dish. Place the dish in a baking dish and carefully pour in enough warm water to come halfway up the side of the pudding dish. Bake for 50–60 minutes, or until the pudding is just set (timing may vary according to the dish used). Remove from the oven and allow to stand for 10 minutes. Serve warm or cold with the balsamic strawberries.

POACHED PEARS WITH GINGER ZABAGLIONE

Preparation time: 30 minutes
Total cooking time: 1 hour
Makes 6

2 cups (500 ml/16 fl oz) good-quality red wine
4 pieces crystallized ginger
½ cup (125 g/4 oz) sugar
6 pears, peeled

Ginger zabaglione
8 egg yolks
⅓ cup (90 g/3 oz) caster sugar
1 teaspoon ground ginger
1¼ cups (315 ml/10 fl oz) Marsala

1 Put the wine, ginger and sugar in a large pan with 1 litre water and stir over medium heat until the sugar has dissolved. Add the pears, cover and simmer for 45 minutes, or until tender.
2 To make the zabaglione, put a large pan half filled with water on to boil. When boiling, remove from the heat. Beat the egg yolks, sugar and ginger in a metal or heatproof bowl, using electric beaters, until pale yellow. Set the bowl over the pan of steaming water, making sure the bowl does not touch the water, and beat continuously, adding the Marsala gradually. Beat for 5 minutes, or until very thick and foamy and like a mousse.
3 Remove the pears from the pan with a slotted spoon. Arrange on plates and pour ginger zabaglione over each. Serve immediately.

NOTE: Use as good a quality wine for cooking as you would for drinking.

POACHED APPLES WITH CLOVES, MINT AND BASIL

Preparation time: 15 minutes
Total cooking time: 30 minutes
Serves 4

4 large or 6 small green apples
2½ cups (600 ml/20 fl oz) water
2 tablespoons lemon juice
½ cup (125 g/4 oz) sugar
4 whole cloves
4 sprigs fresh mint
6 leaves fresh basil
cream or yoghurt, for serving

1 Peel apples, remove cores and cut apples into quarters. Place water, juice, sugar, cloves and mint in a pan. Stir over low heat without boiling until sugar dissolves. Bring to the boil.
2 Add apples to pan. Cook over low heat with lid tilted to let steam escape, for 10 minutes or until apples are soft but not breaking up. Add basil. Remove from heat, set aside until cold.
3 Carefully remove apples and place in a bowl; pour syrup through a sieve over top of apples. Serve chilled with berries and cream or yoghurt.

CUSTARD PUDDING WITH STEWED APPLE

Preparation time: 25 minutes
Total cooking time: 1 hour 5 minutes
Serves 6

Custard
1½ tablespoons custard powder
½ cup (125 ml/4 fl oz) milk
1 tablespoon sugar
⅓ cup (90 g/3 oz) sour cream

180 g (5¾ oz) unsalted butter
½ cup (125 g/4 oz) caster sugar
2 eggs
1¼ cups (155 g/5 oz) self-raising flour
¼ cup (30 g/1 oz) custard powder
¼ cup (45 g/1½ oz) ground almonds
1 cup (250 ml/8 fl oz) cream
4 cooking apples
2 tablespoons sugar
icing sugar, to dust

1 To make the custard, combine the custard powder and a little of the milk in a bowl and mix until smooth. Add the remaining milk and mix together. Pour into a pan, add the sugar and sour cream and stir over medium heat until the custard thickens and boils. Remove from the heat and cover the surface with plastic wrap to prevent a skin forming.

2 Preheat the oven to moderate 180°C (350°F/Gas 4). Beat the butter and sugar together until light and creamy. Add the eggs one at a time, beating well after each addition. Fold in the sifted flour, custard powder and ground almonds alternately with the cream.
3 Place half the pudding mixture in a 2 litre ovenproof dish and spoon the custard over it. Top with the remaining pudding mixture. The mixture will be a little stiff, pile it on top of the custard and smooth it out gently with the back of a spoon. Bake for 45–50 minutes, or until the pudding is firm to the touch. Dust with icing sugar.
4 Meanwhile, peel, core and thinly slice the apples and place in a pan with the sugar and 2 tablespoons water. Bring to the boil, reduce the heat and simmer, covered, for 10 minutes, until the apples are tender. Serve the pudding from the dish, accompanied by the warm apples.

APRICOT COMPOTE

Preparation time: 15 minutes + cooling
Total cooking time: 30 minutes
Serves 4–6

1 orange
1 lemon
1 small vanilla bean, split
½ cup (125 g/4 oz) sugar
1 kg (2 lb) ripe, firm apricots, halved and seeded
1–2 tablespoons caster sugar

1 Peel two strips of rind about 5 cm (2 inches) long from both the orange and lemon. Squeeze all the juice from the orange (about 4 tablespoons) and 1 tablespoon from the lemon.
2 Place 3 cups (750 ml/24 fl oz) water in a saucepan, add the rind, vanilla bean and sugar and bring to the boil. Boil rapidly for 5 minutes.
3 Place the apricots in a wide saucepan and pour the hot syrup over the top. Gently bring to the boil and simmer until the apricots are tender. This can take from 2–10 minutes, depending on the fruit. Do not damage the apricots by over-cooking. Transfer the apricots to a bowl, using a slotted spoon, and boil the syrup for 10 minutes, or until it thickens. Remove from the heat, allow to cool for 15 minutes, then stir in the juices. Taste for sweetness and add more sugar if necessary. Strain the sauce over the apricots. Serve warm or at room temperature.

COCONUT SAGO PUDDINGS

Preparation time: 10 minutes + chilling
Total cooking time: 1 hour
Serves 8

220 ml (7 fl oz) coconut milk
¼ cup (90 g/3 oz) grated palm sugar
1 stem lemon grass, bruised
250 g (8 oz) sago
1 teaspoon grated lime rind
1 egg white, lightly beaten
4 guavas, thinly sliced

Lime syrup
2 cups (500 g/1 lb) caster sugar
1 tablespoon finely shredded fresh ginger
rind of 2 limes

1 Lightly grease eight 125 ml (4 fl oz) dariole moulds. Put the coconut milk, palm sugar and lemon grass in a pan with 3 cups (750 ml/24 fl oz) water. Bring just to the boil. Add the sago and lime rind and cook over low heat, stirring, for 35–40 minutes, until the sago is thick and clear.
2 Remove from the heat and cool slightly. Remove the lemon grass. Whisk the egg white into stiff peaks and gently fold into the sago. Spoon the mixture in the moulds, cover with plastic wrap and chill for 3 hours, or until firm. Stand the moulds in hot water for 20 seconds before turning out.
3 To make the lime syrup, put the sugar and 1 cup (250 ml/8 fl oz) water in a pan and stir over low heat until the sugar is dissolved. Bring to the boil and cook for 10 minutes, without stirring, until the syrup thickens. Add the ginger and lime rind and cook for another 5 minutes. Arrange the sliced guava on a plate, pour over the lime syrup and serve with the puddings.

BAKED ALASKA

Preparation time: 40 minutes + freezing
Total cooking time: 8 minutes
Serves 6–8

2 litres good-quality vanilla ice cream
250 g (8 oz) mixed glacé fruit, finely
chopped
¼ cup (125 ml/4 fl oz) Grand Marnier or
Cointreau
2 teaspoons grated orange rind
60 g (2 oz) toasted almonds, finely
chopped
60 g (2 oz) dark chocolate, finely chopped
1 sponge or butter cake, cut into 3 cm (1¼
inch) slices
3 egg whites
¾ cup (185 g/6 oz) caster sugar

1 Line a 2 litre pudding basin with damp muslin. Soften 1 litre of ice cream enough to enable the glacé fruit to be folded in with 2 tablespoons liqueur and 1 teaspoon orange rind. Spoon into the basin, smooth over the base and up the sides, then put in the freezer until frozen. Soften the remaining ice cream and fold in the almonds, chocolate, remaining liqueur and orange rind. Spoon into the frozen shell and level the surface.
2 Work quickly to evenly cover the ice cream with a 3 cm (1¼ inch) thick layer of cake. Cover with foil and freeze for at least 2 hours. Preheat the oven to hot 220°C (425°F/Gas 7). Using electric beaters, beat the egg whites in a dry bowl until soft peaks form. Gradually add the sugar, beating well after each addition. Beat for 4–5 minutes, until thick and glossy.
3 Unmould the ice cream onto an ovenproof dish and remove the muslin. Quickly spread the meringue over the top to cover the ice cream completely. Bake for 5–8 minutes, or until lightly browned. Cut into wedges and serve at once.
note: Partly bury an upturned half egg shell in the top of the meringue before baking. Fill with warmed brandy and set alight to serve.

CREMA CATALANA (CATALAN BURNT CREAM)

Preparation time: 15 minutes + overnight
refrigeration
Total cooking time: 20 minutes
Serves 6

1 litre milk
1 vanilla bean
1 cinnamon stick
zest of 1 small lemon, sliced into strips
2 strips orange zest, 4 x 2 cm (1½ x ¾
inches)
8 egg yolks
½ cup (125 g/4 oz) caster sugar
4 tablespoons cornflour
3 tablespoons soft brown sugar

1 Place the milk, scraped vanilla bean, cinnamon stick and lemon and orange zests in a saucepan and bring to the boil. Simmer for 5 minutes, then strain and set aside.
2 Whisk the egg yolks with the caster sugar in a bowl for about 5 minutes, until pale and creamy. Add the cornflour and mix well. Slowly add the warm milk mixture to the egg and whisk continuously. Return to the saucepan and cook over low to medium heat, stirring constantly, for 5–10 minutes, or until the mixture is thick and creamy. Do not boil as it will curdle. Pour into six 1-cup (250 ml/8 fl oz) ramekins and refrigerate for 6 hours, or overnight.
3 When ready to serve, sprinkle evenly with brown sugar and grill for 3 minutes, or until it caramelizes.

PEAR DUMPLINGS

Preparation time: 40 minutes + cooling
Total cooking time: 40 minutes
Serves 4

1 cup (250 g/8 oz) caster sugar
2 cinnamon sticks
2 cloves
4 pears
2 cups (250 g/8 oz) plain flour
150 g (5 oz) chilled unsalted butter,
    chopped
⅔ cup (85 g/3 oz) icing sugar
⅓ cup (80 ml/2¾ fl oz) lemon juice
1 egg, lightly beaten

1 Stir the sugar with 1.5 litres water in a
large pan over low heat until the sugar
has completely dissolved. Add the
cinnamon sticks and cloves and bring to
the boil.
2 Peel the pears, leaving the stems intact.
Add to the pan, cover and simmer for
about 10 minutes, until just tender when
tested with the point of a sharp knife.
Remove the pears, drain thoroughly and
cool completely. Remove the pear cores
using a melon baller—leave the stem
attached.
3 Sift the flour into a large bowl and rub in
the butter until it resembles fine
breadcrumbs. Stir in the icing sugar. Add
almost all the juice and mix with a flat-
bladed knife until the mixture comes
together, adding more juice if necessary.
Turn onto a lightly floured work surface
and gather together into a ball. Chill for
20 minutes.

4 Preheat the oven to moderate 180°C
(350°F/Gas 4). Line a flat baking tray with
baking paper. Divide the dough into 4
equal portions and roll one portion out to
a 23 cm (9 inches) diameter circle. Place a
pear in the centre of the pastry, cut the
pastry into a wide cross and set cut-out
sections aside. Carefully fold one section
of pastry at a time up the side of the pear,
trimming and pressing the edges together
to neatly cover. Repeat with the remaining
pears.
5 Cut leaf shapes from the leftover pastry.
Brush the pears all over with egg and
attach the leaves, then brush the leaves
with egg. Put the pears on the tray and
bake for 30 minutes, or until golden
brown. Serve warm with custard or
cream.

BANANA AND RASPBERRY YOGHURT PUDDING

Preparation time: 10 minutes + chilling
Total cooking time: Nil
Serves 4

2 large ripe bananas
125 g (4 oz) fresh raspberries
1 teaspoon caster sugar
2 cups (500 g/1 lb) low-fat natural
    yoghurt
4 tablespoons soft brown sugar

1 Combine the bananas, raspberries and
caster sugar in a large bowl and mash
them well. Divide among four individual
serving dishes.
2 Divide the yoghurt among the dishes,
making a smooth layer over the fruit.
Sprinkle each with a layer of soft brown
sugar. Cover the dishes with plastic wrap
and leave in the refrigerator for at least 1
hour. The sugar on top should form a
fudgy layer.

MOCHA ICE CREAM

Preparation time: 20 minutes + freezing
Total cooking time: 10–15 minutes
Serves 4–6

½ cup (40 g/1¼ oz) espresso coffee beans
3 cups (750 ml/24 fl oz) cream
250 g (8 oz) good-quality dark cooking
    chocolate, chopped
¾ cup (185 g/6 oz) caster sugar
6 egg yolks
1 cup (250 ml/8 fl oz) milk

1 Line a rectangular tin with plastic wrap and freeze. Combine the coffee beans and cream in a pan. Stir over medium heat until the mixture just starts to boil. Add the chocolate, remove from the heat and set aside for 1 minute before stirring.
2 Combine the sugar and egg yolks in a large bowl, whisk until slightly thickened, then whisk in the milk. Gradually add the coffee mixture with the beans and whisk until smooth. Strain the mixture and discard the beans.
3 Return the mixture to the pan and stir over low heat until the mixture thickens and will coat the back of a spoon. Do not boil. Remove from the heat and set aside to cool.
4 Put the mixture into the prepared tin and freeze until just firm. Transfer to a large chilled bowl and beat with electric beaters until thick. Return to the tin and cover with plastic wrap and freeze again until firm. Repeat, beating once more before transferring to a container for storage in the freezer. Cover the surface with plastic wrap or baking paper. Serve in scoops with frosted rose petals (see Note) or store in the freezer for up to 7 days.

NOTE: To frost rose petals, lightly whisk 1 egg white, dip clean dry petals in egg white (or brush lightly with a paintbrush), then sprinkle with sugar. Shake off the excess sugar and place on a paper-lined tray to dry.

CREME BRULEE

Preparation time: 30 minutes + standing +
    chilling
Total cooking time: 30 minutes
Serves 6

3 cups (750 ml/24 fl oz) cream
2 vanilla beans
8 egg yolks
½ cup (125 g/4 oz) sugar
3 teaspoons sugar

1 Gently heat the cream and vanilla beans in a large, heavy-based pan until almost boiling. Remove from the heat and set aside to infuse for 30 minutes. Remove the vanilla beans.
2 Beat or whisk the egg yolks and sugar in a large bowl until thick and pale. Add the cream, then pour into a clean pan over low heat and stir until the mixture thickens slightly and coats the back of a wooden spoon. Do not boil or you will curdle the mixture. Remove from the heat and divide among six 170 ml (5½ fl oz) ramekins. Cover with plastic wrap and refrigerate for at least 3 hours, or overnight.
3 Just before serving, preheat the grill to very hot. Sprinkle a layer of sugar about 3 mm (⅛ inch) thick over the surface of the brûlées. To do this, put the ramekins on a sheet of baking paper and sift the sugar over—you can pour the dry sugar off the baking paper back into your container.
4 Place the ramekins in a large baking dish and pack ice around the sides to prevent the custards being heated. Place under the grill until the sugar caramelizes into an even sheet. Keep watching or you may burn the caramel. The sugar needs to caramelize quickly so that the custard doesn't have time to melt. If your grill does not get particularly hot (restaurants use special hot grills called salamanders) you might want to invest in a mini blowtorch which also does the job well. Play the flame evenly over the surface. Do not put too much sugar on or the crust will be too thick to break with a spoon.
5 Chill the crème brûlées until you serve them but not for longer than an hour or the crust will soften. This dessert can be garnished with fresh fruit such as blueberries.

MAKING JELLY

JELLIES DON'T HAVE TO BE GREEN AND YELLOW AND REMINISCENT OF CHILDREN'S PARTIES. WELCOME TO GROWN-UP JELLIES—SPARKLING, TRANSLUCENT AND TANGY WITH FRESH FRUIT.

Gelatine is best known as a setting agent for jellies, but it is also used in just about any dessert that needs to be moulded or turned out, such as light jellies, creamy bavarois or cheesecakes. Gelatine is available as powder or granules and in clear sheets or leaves. As a rule, 6 sheets of gelatine is equal to 3 teaspoons of powdered gelatine or a 10 g (¼ oz) sachet. This is enough to soft-set 2 cups (500 ml/ 16 fl oz) of liquid. Agar-agar, a vegetarian alternative to gelatine, is found in health food shops—use 1 teaspoon agar-agar to set 1 cup (250 ml/8 fl oz) liquid.

Jellies should be firm enough to hold their shape and be turned out without collapsing but, of course, the whole point of a jelly is that it should wobble! If your jelly is too firm to wobble, it may simply be too cold. Jellies become very firm on chilling and may need to be brought back to room temperature. Gelatine does not freeze well and separates when thawed.

FRUIT JELLIES

Fruit jellies can be made with a variety of fruits. But some fruits just don't work well in jellies—pineapple, papaya, kiwi fruit and figs all contain enzymes which prevent the jelly setting. Fruit juices and purées can both be set, though juices give clearer, more sparkling jellies.

Cut the fruit into whatever size pieces you think would look best in the jelly. Your spoon should be able to slide through the jelly and cut through the fruit easily, so pieces of fruit which are too big will make it harder to cut and eat if you are making a terrine.

Make up a quantity of jelly using the gelatine as follows. To dissolve powdered gelatine, sprinkle it in an even layer over the surface of a little cold water (about 2 tablespoons) and leave it to become spongy. For it to dissolve properly, it is important that the gelatine lies on top of the water and not underneath. Put a large pan filled with about 4 cm (1½ inches) water on to boil. When it boils, remove from the heat and carefully lower the gelatine bowl into the water (the water should come halfway up the side of the bowl). Stir until the gelatine has dissolved, then leave to cool slightly. Leaf gelatine must be soaked in a large bowl of cold water until floppy, then remove it and squeeze out any excess water. It can then be stirred straight into a hot liquid or melted like powdered gelatine. Gelatine sets at 20°C (68°F) so, if you are incorporating melted gelatine into a liquid or purée, make sure it is not too cold or it will form lumps or strings. Leave the jelly to cool.

Rinse out the mould you are using and shake it dry. Make sure the mould is not too big for the jelly or it will be difficult to turn out. Pour a small layer of jelly into the mould and refrigerate until set—this gives a nice shiny surface when the jelly is turned out and ensures the fruit doesn't stick out of the top. Carefully place the fruit in the mould and pour the rest of the jelly over it. Give the whole thing a sharp tap on the work surface to dislodge any air bubbles, cover and refrigerate until set.

To turn out the jelly, use a wet finger to pull it away from the mould all the way around. Invert onto a plate and give the whole thing a firm shake to break the airlock—you should hear a squelching noise. If this fails, wrap a warm cloth around the mould for a few seconds and try again. If the jelly seems to have melted too much, refrigerate it again until it sets. If you are turning the jelly out onto a plate, remember that unless you wet the plate first, the jelly will stick and you won't be able to move it.

You can, of course, eat jelly out of the dish it is made in. Jellies also look lovely set in wine or champagne glasses.

CHAMPAGNE BERRY TERRINE

Preparation time: 15 minutes + cooling + chilling
Total cooking time: 5 minutes
Serves 4–6

75 g (2½ oz) caster sugar
rind of 1 orange
3 teaspoons or 6 sheets gelatine
2½ cups (600 ml/20 fl oz) pink Champagne
300 g (10 oz) mixed berries, fresh or frozen

1 Put the sugar and orange rind in a pan with 1⅓ cups (350 ml/11 fl oz) water. Bring to the boil, stirring over low heat until the sugar dissolves. When dissolved, remove the pan from the heat and cool for 1 hour.
2 Strain the rind out of the syrup. Put about ¼ cup (60 ml/2 fl oz) syrup in a small heatproof bowl, sprinkle the gelatine in an even layer over the top and leave to go spongy. Put a large pan filled with about 4 cm (1½ inches) water on to boil. When it boils, remove from the heat and carefully lower the gelatine bowl into the water (it should come halfway up the side of the bowl), then stir until dissolved. If you want to use sheets of gelatine, follow the steps shown. Cool slightly, add to the rest of the syrup and mix. Add the Champagne, then pour a little of the jelly into the base of a 1.25 litre loaf tin and refrigerate to set. Do not leave too long or the next layer will not stick.
3 Arrange the fruit in the tin, pour in a little more jelly up to the top of the fruit, set in the refrigerator, then pour the rest of the jelly in and set completely. Setting in layers will ensure a smooth surface on top and stop the fruit floating.
4 When you are ready to serve, unmould by wiping the tin with a cloth dipped in hot water and inverting the terrine onto a plate. Bring the terrine to room temperature before serving. It should not be stiff and should sag very slightly. Can be served with cream or ice cream.

PASTA CASES WITH FRUITY RICOTTA FILLING

Preparation time: 35 minutes
Total cooking time: 30 minutes
Serves 4

oil, for deep-frying
6 dried lasagne sheets

Ricotta fruit filling
350 g (11 oz) fresh ricotta cheese
1 tablespoon caster sugar
60 g (2 oz) mixed candied fruit (cherries, orange and lemon peel), chopped
30 g (1 oz) dark chocolate shavings

1 Heat the oil. It will need to be at least 10 cm (4 inches) deep. Cook the lasagne sheets one at a time in plenty of boiling salted water until al dente. Remove with a sieve and place in a bowl of cold water for a minute or two, then transfer to a tea towel and dry both sides. Trim the end of each sheet to make a square.
2 For the next step you will need 3 implements able to withstand boiling oil: a soup ladle of approximately 9 cm (3½ inch) diameter or a wire scoop of the same dimensions; a utensil such as an egg whisk or a mixmaster beater which fits into the scoop to hold the pasta in shape; a pair of tongs. Take one pasta square and gently push it into the ladle by hand. Form a cup shape, with the corners sticking out and with flutes between them.

3 Test the oil for frying by dropping in a piece of scrap pasta. It should bubble immediately and rise to the top. Lower the ladle into the oil. Use tongs to lift the pasta away from the ladle to prevent it sticking initially, then use the egg whisk to maintain the shape. The cases are quite sturdy so don't be afraid to manhandle them. They are ready when crisp and golden with bubbles forming on the surface. Practise with the first two, as these are spares.
4 As each case is ready, remove from the oil and drain upside-down on paper towels. Allow to cool before serving.
5 To make the sweet ricotta filling, mix the ricotta with the sugar until combined. Don't use a food processor as it will make the texture too smooth. Fold in the fruit and chocolate. Spoon into the pasta shells just before serving. Top with shaved curls of chocolate.

NOTE: If the cases become limp or have spots of surface oil, put them in a hot oven to crisp up again. These cases are perfect for turning a humble dessert such as ice cream or fruit salad into an elegant course. Dress the dish up further with a simple sauce and finish off with a dusting of icing sugar. Wire gaufrette baskets, suitable for making the pastry cases, are available from speciality kitchenware shops.

CINNAMON ICE CREAM

Preparation time: 15 minutes + freezing
Total cooking time: 15 minutes
Serves 6

1 litre milk
2 pieces lemon rind
3 cinnamon sticks
1½ cups (375 g/12 oz) caster sugar
6 egg yolks
1 teaspoon ground cinnamon

1 Put the milk, rind, cinnamon sticks and half the sugar in a saucepan and heat to just below boiling. Set aside for 10 minutes.
2 Using a wire whisk, combine the yolks, remaining sugar and ground cinnamon in bowl until thick and pale. Pour in the milk in a steady stream, whisking constantly.
3 Wash the pan, pour in the mixture and stir over very low heat for 5–10 minutes, until thickened. To test, run a finger through the mixture across the back of a wooden spoon. If it leaves a clear line, the custard is ready. Strain it into a bowl and leave to cool to room temperature. Pour it into a 1.25 litre shallow metal container. Freeze for 2 hours, or until firm.
4 When half frozen around the edges, beat well then freeze again. Repeat the beating and freezing process twice more.

PASSIONFRUIT BAVAROIS

Preparation time: 10 minutes + chilling
Total cooking time: Nil
Serves 8

2 x 170 g (5½ oz) cans passionfruit syrup
300 g (10 oz) silken tofu, drained and chopped
600 ml (20 fl oz) buttermilk
2 tablespoons caster sugar
1 teaspoon vanilla essence
6 teaspoons gelatine
8 strawberries, to garnish
¾ cup (185 ml/6 fl oz) passionfruit pulp

1 Push the canned passionfruit syrup through a sieve, discard the seeds, then blend on high for 90 seconds, with the tofu, buttermilk, caster sugar and vanilla essence. Leave in the blender.
2 Sprinkle the gelatine in an even layer onto 1 tablespoon water in a small bowl and leave to go spongy. Bring a small pan of water to the boil, remove from the heat and place the bowl into the pan. The water should come halfway up the side of the bowl. Stir the gelatine until dissolved. Leave to cool.
3 Place eight 200 ml (6½ fl oz) dariole moulds in a baking dish. Add the gelatine to the blender and mix on high for 1 minute. Pour into the moulds, cover the dish with plastic wrap and refrigerate overnight.
4 Cut the strawberries in half. When ready to serve, carefully run a spatula around the edge of each mould and dip the bases into hot water for 2 seconds to make removal easier. Place each on a plate and spoon the passionfruit pulp around the bases. Garnish and serve.

CHOCOLATE HAZELNUT OMELETTE

Preparation time: 20 minutes
Total cooking time: 15 minutes
Serves 4

3 tablespoons finely chopped hazelnuts
60 g (2 oz) dark chocolate, roughly chopped
4 egg yolks
3 tablespoons caster sugar
5 egg whites
salt
30 g (1 oz) unsalted butter
1 tablespoon cocoa powder

1 Stir hazelnuts in a dry pan over medium heat until golden. Set aside.
2 Place the chocolate in a small heatproof bowl over a pan of simmering water. Stir until melted. Allow to cool slightly.
3 Using electric beaters, beat the egg yolks and sugar for 1 minute or until thick. Add the melted chocolate and beat well.
4 Beat the whites with a pinch of salt until stiff peaks form. Fold a third at a time into chocolate mixture. Fold through the hazelnuts. Preheat grill.
5 Melt the butter in a medium frying pan. When butter is foaming pour in the chocolate mixture. Swirl pan until mixture evenly covers base. Cook over low heat for 1–2 minutes or until set half-way through and bubbles have formed on top. Place under grill, cook until golden. Divide into 4 wedges and place on serving plates. Dust with sifted cocoa. Serve with vanilla ice cream and fresh or frozen berries.

VANILLA ICE CREAM

Preparation time: 30 minutes + chilling +
 freezing
Total cooking time: 15 minutes
Serves 4

1 cup (250 ml/8 fl oz) milk
1 cup (250 ml/8 fl oz) cream
1 vanilla bean, split lengthways
6 egg yolks
½ cup (125 g/4 oz) caster sugar

1 Combine the milk and cream in a pan
and add the vanilla bean. Bring to the boil,
then remove from the heat and set aside
for 10 minutes.
2 Using a wire whisk, beat the yolks and
sugar together in a bowl for 2–3 minutes,
until thick and pale, then whisk in the
warm milk mixture. Scrape the seeds
from the vanilla bean into the mixture.
Discard the bean.
3 Wash the pan, and pour the mixture into
it. Stir over very low heat until thickened.
This will take about 5–10 minutes. To test,
run a finger through the mixture across
the back of the wooden spoon—if it leaves
a clear line, the custard is ready.
4 Pour the custard into a bowl and cool to
room temperature, stirring frequently to
hasten cooling.

5 Pour into a shallow metal container,
cover the surface of the custard with
plastic wrap or baking paper and freeze
for about 2 hours, until almost frozen.
Scoop into a chilled bowl and beat with
electric beaters until smooth, then return
to the tray and freeze again. Repeat this
step twice more before transferring to a
storage container. Cover the surface with
baking paper or plastic wrap to stop ice
crystals forming on the surface, then a
lid.
6 To serve, transfer the ice cream to the
refrigerator for about 30 minutes, to
soften slightly. Ice cream will keep, well
sealed, in the freezer for up to 1 month.
Note: This recipe can also be made using
an ice cream machine.

VARIATIONS: To make strawberry ice
cream, chop 250 g (8 oz) strawberries in a
food processor just until smooth. Stir into
the custard mixture when it is well chilled
(end of step 4). Freeze the ice cream as
directed.
To make banana ice cream, thoroughly
mash 3 ripe bananas (or for a finer
texture, purée in a food processor). Stir
into the custard mixture when it is well
chilled, along with 1 tablespoon lemon
juice. Freeze as directed. Makes 1.5 litres.

PLUM COBBLER

Preparation time: 15 minutes
Total cooking time: 45 minutes
Serves 6–8

750 g (1½ lb) blood plums, or other plums
¼ cup (60 g/2 oz) caster sugar

Topping
1 cup (125 g/4 oz) self-raising flour
½ cup (60 g/2 oz) plain flour
¼ cup (60 g/2 oz) caster sugar
125 g (4 oz) unsalted butter, chopped
1 egg
½ cup (125 ml/4 fl oz) milk
icing sugar, to dust

1 Preheat the oven to moderate 180°C
(350°F/Gas 4). Lightly grease a 2 litre
ovenproof dish. Cut the blood plums into
quarters, discarding the stones.
2 Put the plums in a pan with the sugar
and 1 tablespoon water. Stir over low heat
for 5 minutes, or until the sugar dissolves
and the fruit softens slightly. Spread the
plum mixture in the prepared dish.
3 Sift the flours into a bowl, add the sugar
and stir. Rub in the butter, using just your
fingertips, until the mixture is fine and
crumbly. Combine the egg and milk and
whisk until smooth. Stir into the flour
mixture.
4 Place large spoonfuls of mixture on top
of the plums. Bake for 30–40 minutes, or
until the top is golden and cooked
through. Dust with icing sugar before
serving.

APPLE COBBLER

Preparation time: 30 minutes
Total cooking time: 1 hour 15 minutes
Serves 6

1 kg (2 lb) cooking apples, peeled and
   cored
¼ cup (60 g/2 oz) caster sugar
25 g (¾ oz) unsalted butter, melted
1 teaspoon grated orange rind
2 tablespoons fresh orange juice

Topping
⅔ cup (85 g/3 oz) self-raising flour
⅓ cup (40 g/1¼ oz) plain flour
50 g (1¾ oz) unsalted butter, chopped
2 tablespoons caster sugar
1 egg, lightly beaten
2–3 tablespoons milk
1 teaspoon raw sugar

1 Preheat the oven to moderate 180°C
(350°F/Gas 4). Cut the apples into
8–12 wedges and combine them with the
caster sugar, butter and orange rind and
juice in a large bowl. Mix well until all the
apple pieces are thoroughly coated.
Transfer to a 1.5 litre ovenproof dish
about 5 cm (2 inches) deep, cover with foil
and bake for 40 minutes, or until the
apples are tender, stirring once during
cooking.
2 When the apples have been cooking for
about 30 minutes, start to prepare the
topping. Sift the flours into a bowl and rub
the butter into the mixture until it
resembles fine breadcrumbs. Stir in the
sugar and make a well in the centre of the
mixture. Using a flat-bladed knife, stir in
the egg and enough milk to make a
mixture of thick dropping consistency.
3 Remove the foil and drop spoonfuls of
the mixture onto the surface of the
cooked apples, covering the surface.
Sprinkle with the raw sugar and return to
the oven. Bake for 35 minutes or until a
skewer inserted into the topping comes
out clean. Serve hot. Cobbler can be
served with cream or custard.

STRAWBERRY RICOTTA CREPES WITH ORANGE LIQUEUR SAUCE

Preparation time: 40 minutes + standing
Total cooking time: 30 minutes
Makes about 12 crepes

¾ cup (90 g/3 oz) plain flour
1 egg, plus 1 egg yolk
¾ cup (185 ml/6 fl oz) milk
20 g (¾ oz) unsalted butter, melted
fresh berries, for serving

Ricotta cream filling
350 g (11 oz) ricotta
¼ cup (60 ml/2 fl oz) cream
1 tablespoon caster sugar
1 teaspoon vanilla essence
300 g (10 oz) strawberries, sliced

Orange liqueur sauce
½ teaspoon grated orange rind
¾ cup (185 ml/6 fl oz) fresh orange juice
2 tablespoons caster sugar
2 tablespoons Grand Marnier or
   Cointreau
1 tablespoon cornflour
30 g (1 oz) unsalted butter

1 Sift the flour into a large bowl and make
a well in the centre. Gradually whisk in
the combined egg, egg yolk and milk until
the batter is smooth and free of lumps.
Mix in the melted butter and transfer the
batter to a jug for easy pouring. Cover and
set aside for 30 minutes.
2 To make the ricotta cream filling, beat
together the ricotta, cream, sugar and
vanilla essence until smooth. Fold in the
strawberries, cover and refrigerate.

3 To make the orange liqueur sauce,
place the orange rind, juice, sugar and
liqueur in a small pan. Mix the cornflour
with 3 tablespoons water in a small bowl
until smooth, add to the pan and stir over
low heat for 3–4 minutes, or until the
mixture boils and thickens. Add the butter
and stir for another minute. Cover and set
aside.
4 Heat a small crepe pan or non-stick
frying pan and brush lightly with melted
butter. Pour a little batter into the pan,
swirling, to thinly coat the base. Pour any
excess batter back into the jug. If the
batter is too thick, add a little more milk.
Cook for about 30 seconds, or until the
edges just begin to curl, then turn and
cook the other side until lightly browned.
Transfer to a plate and cover with a tea
towel. Repeat with the remaining batter,
greasing the pan when necessary. Stack
the crepes between greaseproof paper to
prevent them sticking together.
5 Place a crepe on a serving plate and
spread evenly with filling. Fold the crepe
in half, then in half again. Pour the sauce
over the top and scatter with berries. Do
the same with the remaining crepes.
Note: The crepes can be made ahead of
time and frozen until needed. Wrap in foil
and reheat in a moderate 180°C
(350°F/Gas 4) oven before use.

CARROT MILK PUDDING

Preparation time: 5 minutes
Total cooking time: 1 hour
Serves 6

4 cups (1 litre) milk
1½ cups (240 g/7½ oz) grated carrot
⅓ cup (40 g/1⅓ oz) sultanas
½ cup (125 g/4 oz) caster sugar
¼ teaspoon ground cinnamon
¼ teaspoon ground cardamom
⅓ cup (80 ml/2¾ oz) cream
2 tablespoons unsalted chopped
   pistachios

1 Pour the milk into a large heavy-based
pan and stir over medium heat until it
comes to the boil. Reduce the heat to low
and simmer until reduced by half, stirring
occasionally to prevent it from catching
on the base of the pan.
2 Add the carrot and sultanas and cook
for a further 15 minutes.
3 Add the sugar, cinnamon, cardamom
and cream and cook, stirring, until the
sugar has dissolved. Serve the pudding
warm in small dishes, and sprinkle over
the pistachios.

PASHKA

Preparation time: 30 minutes +
   draining + soaking + chilling
Total cooking time: Nil
Serves 8–10

750 g (1½ lb) ricotta
100 g (3½ oz) glacé pineapple, chopped
100 g (3½ oz) glacé ginger, chopped
60 g (2 oz) mixed peel
60 g (2 oz) sultanas
2 tablespoons white or dark rum
100 g (3½ oz) unsalted butter, softened
½ cup (125 g/4 oz) caster sugar
2 egg yolks
60 g (2 oz) slivered almonds, toasted
2 teaspoons finely grated lemon rind
2 teaspoons finely grated orange rind
2 tablespoons lemon juice
½ cup (125 g/4 oz) sour cream
slivered almonds and glacé fruits, to
   decorate

1 Drain the ricotta overnight in a sieve. In
a bowl, soak the pineapple, ginger, mixed
peel and sultanas in the rum for 2 hours.
Thoroughly wet a piece of muslin in
boiling water, wring out the excess water
and use to line a 2 litre pudding basin or
charlotte mould.
2 Beat the butter and sugar in a bowl until
light and creamy, then beat in the egg
yolks one at a time. Add the almonds,
rinds and lemon juice and mix well.
Transfer to a large bowl and fold in the
ricotta, sour cream and fruit mixture.
3 Press into the basin and fold the edges
of the cloth over the top. Cover the top
with plastic wrap, place a saucer on top
and weigh down with a can placed on top
of the saucer. Place the bowl on a plate
and refrigerate overnight. Turn out of the
basin and peel away the muslin. Transfer
to a serving plate with the smaller end
facing up. Decorate with almonds and
glacé fruits and serve in small wedges.

SUMMER PUDDING

Preparation time: 30 minutes + chilling
Total cooking time: 5 minutes
Serves 4–6

150 g (5 oz) blackcurrants
150 g (5 oz) redcurrants
150 g (5 oz) raspberries
150 g (5 oz) blackberries
200 g (6½ oz) strawberries, hulled and
   quartered or halved
caster sugar, to taste
6–8 slices good-quality white bread,
   crusts removed
cream, for serving, optional

1 Put all the berries except the
strawberries in a large pan with ½ cup
(125 ml/4 fl oz) water and heat gently until
the berries begin to collapse. Add the
strawberries and turn off the heat. Add
sugar, to taste (how much you need will
depend on how ripe the fruit is). Set aside
to cool.
2 Line six 150 ml (5 fl oz) moulds or a
1 litre pudding basin with the bread. For
the small moulds, use 1 slice of bread for
each, cutting a circle to fit the bottom and
strips to fit the sides. For the large mould,
cut a large circle out of 1 slice for the
bottom and cut the rest of the bread into
fingers. Drain a little juice off the fruit
mixture. Dip one side of each piece of
bread in the juice before fitting it, juice-
side-down, into the mould, leaving no
gaps. Do not squeeze it or flatten it or it
will not absorb the juices as well.
3 Fill the centre of the mould with the
fruit and add a little juice. Cover the top
with a layer of dipped bread, juice-side-
up, and cover with plastic wrap. Place a
plate which fits inside the dish onto the
plastic wrap, then weigh it down. Stack
the small ones on top of each other to
weigh them down. Refrigerate overnight.
Carefully turn out the pudding and serve
with any extra mixture and cream.

ALMOND SEMIFREDDO

Preparation time: 30 minutes + 4 hours
  freezing
Total cooking time: 10 minutes
Serves 8–10

1¼ cups (315 ml/10 fl oz) cream
4 eggs, room temperature, separated
⅔ cup (85 g/3 oz) icing sugar
¼ cup (60 ml/2 fl oz) amaretto
½ cup (80 g/2¾ oz) toasted almonds,
  chopped
8 amaretti biscuits, crushed
fresh fruit or extra amaretto, for serving

1 Whip the cream until firm peaks form,
then cover and refrigerate. Line a
10 x 21 cm (4 x 8½ inch) loaf tin with plastic
wrap so that it overhangs the two long
sides.
2 Beat the egg yolks and icing sugar in a
large bowl until pale and creamy. Whisk
the egg whites in a separate bowl until
firm peaks form. Stir the amaretto,
almonds and amaretti biscuits into the
egg yolk mixture, then carefully fold in
the chilled cream and the egg whites until
well combined. Carefully pour or spoon
into the lined loaf tin and cover with the
overhanging plastic. Freeze for 4 hours,
or until frozen but not rock hard. Serve
slices with fresh fruit or a sprinkling of
amaretto. The semifreddo can also be
frozen in individual moulds or serving
dishes.

NOTE: Semifreddo means semi frozen, so
if you leave it in the freezer overnight,
place it in the refrigerator for 30 minutes
before serving.

PETITS POTS AU CHOCOLAT

Preparation time: 20 minutes + chilling
Total cooking time: 1 hour
Serves 8

⅔ cup (170 ml/5½ fl oz) thick (double) cream
½ vanilla bean, split lengthways
150 g (5 oz) good-quality dark bittersweet
  chocolate, chopped
⅓ cup (80 ml/2¾ fl oz) milk
2 egg yolks
¼ cup (60 g/2 oz) caster sugar
whipped cream and cocoa powder, for
  serving

1 Lightly brush eight 80 ml (2¾ fl oz)
moulds or ramekins with melted butter
and put them in a deep baking dish.
Preheat the oven to very slow 140°C
(275°F/Gas 1). Heat the cream in a small
pan with the vanilla bean until the cream
is warm, then leave to infuse.
2 Combine the chocolate and milk in a
small pan. Stir constantly over low heat
until the chocolate has just melted.
3 Place the egg yolks in a small bowl, and
slowly whisk in the sugar. Continue
whisking until the sugar has dissolved
and the mixture is light and creamy.
Scrape the seeds out of the vanilla bean
into the cream, and discard the empty
bean. Add the vanilla cream and the
melted chocolate mixture to the beaten
egg yolks, and mix until well combined.
4 Pour the mixture into the ramekins,
filling approximately two-thirds of the
way. Fill the baking dish with enough
boiling water to come halfway up the pots.
Bake for 45 minutes, or until the
chocolate pots have puffed up slightly and
feel spongy. Remove from the baking dish
and cool completely. Cover with plastic
wrap and refrigerate for 6 hours before
serving. Serve with a dollop of cream and
a sprinkle of sifted cocoa powder.

NOTE: The pots will have a slight crust on
the top when they first come from the oven.

COINTREAU BREAD PUDDINGS WITH ORANGE CREAM

Preparation time: 40 minutes + soaking
Total cooking time: 30 minutes
Serves 4

60 g (2 oz) muscatels or sultanas
⅓ cup (80 ml/2¾ fl oz) Cointreau
5 eggs
⅓ cup (115 g/4 oz) honey
1 cup (250 ml/8 fl oz) milk
1 cup (250 ml/8 fl oz) cream
1 loaf crusty white bread

Orange cream
1 cup (250 ml/8 fl oz) cream
2 teaspoons icing sugar
2 teaspoons Cointreau
grated rind of 1 orange
sprinkle of ground nutmeg

1 Soak the muscatels or sultanas in
Cointreau for 2 hours, or overnight. Drain,
reserving the liquid. Preheat the oven to
moderate 180°C (350°F/Gas 4). Beat
together the eggs, honey, milk, cream and
reserved Cointreau. Grease four 250 ml
(8 fl oz) ramekins and divide half the
muscatels among the ramekins.
2 Slice the bread thickly. Remove the
crusts. Put a slice in each ramekin,
trimming to fit. Sprinkle the remaining
muscatels over the bread, then top with
another slice of bread. Pour the egg
mixture over the top, giving it time to soak
in. Put the ramekins in a baking dish and
pour water into the dish to come halfway
up the sides of the ramekins. Bake for
25–30 minutes, or until set. Leave for
5 minutes before turning out.
3 To make the orange cream, whip
together the cream and icing sugar until
peaks form. Fold in the Cointreau, rind
and nutmeg. Serve with the puddings.

CASSATA ALLA SICILIANA

Preparation time: 25 minutes +
 overnight refrigeration
Total cooking time: 2 minutes
Serves 6

60 g (2 oz) blanched almonds, halved
650 g (1 lb 5 oz) fresh ricotta
½ cup (80 g/2¾ oz) icing sugar
1½ teaspoons vanilla essence
2 teaspoons finely grated lemon rind
60 g (2 oz) cedro, chopped
60 g (2 oz) glacé orange, chopped
60 g (2 oz) red glacé cherries, halved
30 g (1 oz) shelled pistachios
375 g (12 oz) ready-made round sponge
 cake, unfilled
½ cup (125 ml/4 fl oz) Madeira
6 blanched almonds, extra
red glacé cherries, extra, halved
icing sugar, for dusting
sweetened whipped cream, to serve

1 Place the almonds in a small frying pan
and dry-fry, tossing, over medium heat
for 2 minutes, or until just starting to
change colour. Remove and cool.
2 Press the ricotta through a sieve over a
bowl. Stir in the icing sugar, vanilla,
lemon rind, cedro, glacé orange, glacé
cherries, almonds and pistachios. Mix.
3 Grease a 1.5 litre pudding basin. Cut the
cake horizontally into 1 cm (½ inch) thick
slices. Set aside 1 round and cut the
remaining rounds into wedges, trimming
the base to make triangles. Lightly sprinkle
the cut side of the triangles with Madeira
and arrange around the base and side of the
bowl, cut-side-down, trimming if necessary
to fit. Spoon the ricotta mixture into the
centre. Top with a layer of sponge cake.
Press down firmly and neaten the rough
edges, if necessary. Refrigerate overnight.
4 Carefully unmould onto a serving plate.
Arrange the extra almonds and cherries
on top and dust with icing sugar just
before serving. Serve with the cream,
which can be piped in patterns over the
cassata for a true Sicilian look.

DATE PANCAKES WITH CARAMEL SAUCE

Preparation time: 40 minutes + standing
Total cooking time: 30 minutes
Makes 10–12 pancakes

185 g (6 oz) pitted dates, chopped
1 teaspoon bicarbonate of soda
2 cups (250 g/8 oz) self-raising flour, sifted
½ cup (95 g/3 oz) soft brown sugar
1 cup (250 g/8 oz) sour cream
3 eggs, separated
ice cream, for serving

Caramel sauce
1 cup (185 g/6 oz) soft brown sugar
1 cup (250 ml/8 fl oz) cream
200 g (6½ oz) unsalted butter

1 Put the dates with 1 cup (250 ml/8 fl oz)
water in a small pan and bring to the boil.
Remove from the heat, stir in the
bicarbonate of soda and cool for 5 minutes.
Purée in a food processor until smooth. Cool.
2 Mix the flour and sugar in a large bowl.
Stir in the date purée and make a well in
the centre.
3 Whisk the sour cream and egg yolks
together and pour into the well, stirring
until the batter is just smooth. Set aside
for 15 minutes. Beat the egg whites in a
clean, dry bowl until soft peaks form. Stir
a heaped tablespoon of egg white into the
batter to loosen it, then fold in the
remainder until just combined.
4 Heat a frying pan and brush lightly with
melted butter or oil. Pour ¼ cup (60 ml/
2 fl oz) batter into the pan. Cook for 2–3
minutes, or until bubbles form on the
surface. Turn over and cook the other
side. Transfer to a plate and cover with a
tea towel while cooking the remaining
batter. Grease the pan when necessary.
Stack the pancakes between greaseproof
paper to prevent them sticking together.
5 For the sauce, stir all the ingredients in a
pan over medium heat, without boiling, until
dissolved, then simmer gently for 3 minutes.
Serve over the pancakes, with ice cream.

PEACHES AND CREAM TRIFLE

Preparation time: 20 minutes + chilling
Total cooking time: Nil
Serves 6–8

1 day-old sponge cake, cut into cubes
825 g (1 lb 11 oz) can sliced peaches
¼ cup (60 ml/2 fl oz) Marsala, peach
 schnapps liqueur or Grand Marnier
1 cup (250 ml/8 fl oz) cream
200 g (6½ oz) mascarpone
25 g (¾ oz) flaked almonds, toasted

1 Put the cake cubes in a 2 litre dish and
press down firmly. Drain the peaches,
reserving ½ cup (125 ml/4 fl oz) of juice.
Mix the Marsala with the juice and drizzle
over the cake.
2 Arrange the peach slices over the cake.
Beat the cream until soft peaks form. Add
the mascarpone and beat briefly, to just
mix. Spread over the peaches. Refrigerate
for 1 hour to allow the flavours to develop.
Sprinkle with almonds just before
serving.

CAPPUCCINO ICE CREAM CAKES

Preparation time: 1 hour 45 minutes
Total cooking time: 30 minutes
Serves 10

Chocolate cake
185 g (6 oz) unsalted butter
330 g (11 oz) caster sugar
2½ teaspoons vanilla essence
3 eggs
75 g (2½ oz) self-raising flour
225 g (7 oz) plain flour
1½ teaspoons bicarbonate of soda
¾ cup (90 g/3 oz) cocoa powder
280 ml (9 fl oz) buttermilk

1 tablespoon instant coffee powder
1 litre vanilla ice cream, softened
1 cup (250 ml/8 fl oz) thick (double)
  cream
1 tablespoon icing sugar
125 g (4 oz) dark chocolate melts, melted
cocoa powder, to dust

1 Lightly grease ten muffin holes (with
250 ml/8 fl oz capacity). Preheat the oven
to moderate 180°C (350°F/Gas 4).
2 To make the cake, beat the butter and
sugar with electric beaters until light and
creamy. Beat in the vanilla essence. Add
the eggs, one at a time, beating well after
each addition.
3 Using a metal spoon, fold in the
combined sifted flours, bicarbonate of
soda and cocoa powder alternately with
the buttermilk. Stir until the mixture is
just combined.
4 Divide the mixture evenly among the
muffin holes and bake for 25 minutes, or
until a skewer comes out clean. Cool in
the tins for 5 minutes before turning onto
a wire cake rack to cool.

5 Dissolve the coffee powder in
2 tablespoons boiling water, then cool.
Roughly break up the vanilla ice cream in
a large bowl and stir until smooth. Stir in
the coffee mixture and freeze until
required.
6 Beat the cream and icing sugar
together in a small bowl with an electric
mixer until soft peaks form. Refrigerate
until ready to use.
7 Draw the outline of a small spoon, ten
times, on a piece of baking paper, then
turn the paper over. Spoon the melted
chocolate into a paper piping bag. Snip
the end off the bag and draw a chocolate
outline around the spoons, then fill in with
melted chocolate. Allow the chocolate to
set.
8 Cut the top off each cake, leaving a 1 cm
(½ inch) border around the top edge of
each cake and reserving the tops. Use a
spoon to scoop out some of the cake,
leaving a 1 cm (½ inch) shell of cake.
(Leftover cake can be frozen for another
use.)
9 Soften the coffee ice cream with a
spoon and pile into the cakes so it comes
slightly above the top. Replace the tops
and press gently. Spread cream mixture
roughly over the top of each cake to
represent the froth. Dust the tops with
cocoa and serve with a chocolate spoon
tucked into the cream.

LEMON DELICIOUS

Preparation time: 20 minutes
Total cooking time: 40 minutes
Serves 4

60 g (2 oz) unsalted butter
¾ cup (185 g/6 oz) caster sugar
3 eggs, separated
1 teaspoon grated lemon rind
⅓ cup (40 g/1¼ oz) self-raising flour,
  sifted
¼ cup (60 ml/2 fl oz) lemon juice
¾ cup (185 ml/6 fl oz) milk
icing sugar, to dust

1 Preheat the oven to moderate 180°C
(350°F/Gas 4). Brush a 1 litre ovenproof
dish with oil. Using electric beaters, beat
the butter, sugar, egg yolks and rind in a
small bowl until the mixture is light and
creamy. Transfer to a medium bowl.
2 Add the flour and stir with a wooden
spoon until just combined. Add the juice
and milk and stir to combine.
3 Place the egg whites in a small, dry
bowl. Using electric beaters, beat until
firm peaks form. Fold in the pudding
mixture with a metal spoon until just
combined.
4 Spoon into the ovenproof dish and place
the dish in a deep baking dish. Pour in
boiling water to come one-third of the way
up the side of the pudding dish. Bake for
40 minutes. Dust with icing sugar. Spoon
some sauce on each serving.

CHINESE ALMOND PUDDING

Preparation time: 5 minutes + 3 hours chilling
Total cooking time: 1 hour 15 minutes
Serves 6

1 cup (100 g/3½ oz) ground almonds
½ cup (90 g/3 oz) glutinous rice flour
2½ cups (625 ml/20 fl oz) milk
½ cup (115 g/4 oz) caster (superfine) sugar

1 Combine the ground almonds and rice flour in a heavy-based saucepan and mix in about ⅓ cup (80 ml/2¾ fl oz) cold water to form a thick, smooth paste. Add a little more water if necessary. Then stir in the milk until smooth.
2 Place the pan over low heat and cook, stirring almost constantly so that it does not catch, for about 1¼ hours, or until thick and smooth. Gradually add the sugar, stirring until dissolved.
3 Pour the mixture into six small Chinese rice bowls. You can either serve the pudding warm, or allow to cool slightly, then refrigerate for 3 hours, or until firm. When chilled, it is nice served with fresh mango.

VARIATION: Stir in 50 g (1¾ oz) pitted and chopped jujubes (Chinese dates).

CHOCOLATE MUD CAKE

Preparation time: 30 minutes + chilling
Total cooking time: 1 hour 55 minutes
Serves 8–10

250 g (8 oz) unsalted butter
250 g (8 oz) dark chocolate, broken
2 tablespoons instant espresso coffee powder or granules
150 g (5 oz) self-raising flour
150 g (5 oz) plain flour
½ cup (60 g/2 oz) cocoa powder
½ teaspoon bicarbonate of soda
550 g (1 lb 2 oz) sugar
4 eggs
2 tablespoons oil
½ cup (125 ml/4 fl oz) buttermilk

Glaze
250 g (8 oz) good-quality dark cooking chocolate, chopped
½ cup (125 ml/4 fl oz) cream
⅔ cup (160 g/5½ oz) caster sugar

1 Preheat the oven to moderately slow 160°C (315°F/Gas 2–3). Brush a deep 22 cm (8¾ inch) round cake tin with melted butter or oil. Line the base and side with baking paper, extending at least 2 cm (1 inch) above the rim.
2 Stir the butter, chocolate and coffee in a pan with 185 ml (6 oz) hot water, over low heat, until the butter and chocolate have melted and the mixture is smooth. Remove from the heat.
3 Sift the flours, cocoa and bicarbonate of soda into a large bowl. Stir in the sugar and make a well. Add the combined eggs, oil and buttermilk and, using a large metal spoon, slowly stir in the dry ingredients, then the melted chocolate mix until combined.
4 Spoon the mixture into the tin and bake for 1 hour 40 minutes. Test with a skewer and, if it does not come out clean, cook for another 5–10 minutes. Cool in the tin. When completely cold, remove from the tin.
5 To make the glaze, stir all the ingredients in a pan over low heat until melted. Bring to the boil, reduce the heat and simmer for 4–5 minutes. Remove from the heat and cool slightly. Put a cooling rack on a baking tray and transfer the cake to the rack. Pour the glaze over the cake, making sure the sides are evenly covered. Decorate with chocolate.

FRUIT KEBABS WITH HONEY CARDAMOM SYRUP

Preparation time: 20 minutes + marinating
Total cooking time: 5 minutes
Makes 8 kebabs

¼ small pineapple or 2 rings canned pineapple
1 peach
1 banana
16 strawberries
cream or yoghurt, for serving, optional

Honey cardamom syrup
2 tablespoons honey
20 g (¾ oz) unsalted butter, melted
½ teaspoon ground cardamom
1 tablespoon rum or brandy, optional
1 tablespoon soft brown sugar

1 Soak eight wooden skewers in cold water for 20 minutes. Cut the pineapple into 8 bite-sized pieces. Cut the peach into 8 wedges and slice the banana. Thread the fruit alternately on skewers and place in a shallow dish.
2 To make the honey cardamom syrup, combine the honey, butter, cardamom, rum and sugar in a bowl. Pour the mixture over the kebabs and brush to coat. Cover and leave to stand at room temperature for 1 hour. Prepare and heat a barbecue or griller.
3 Cook the kebabs on a hot, lightly greased barbecue flatplate or under the griller, for 5 minutes. Brush with syrup occasionally during cooking. Serve drizzled with the remaining syrup. Can also be served with fresh cream or natural yoghurt.

LEMON ICE CREAM

Preparation time: 20 minutes + freezing
Total cooking time: 15 minutes
Serves 4–6

6 egg yolks
1 cup (250 g/8 oz) caster sugar
2 teaspoons grated lemon rind
⅓ cup (80 ml/2¾ fl oz) lemon juice
2 cups (500 ml/16 fl oz) cream, lightly whipped
lemon rind strips, for serving

1 Whisk or beat the egg yolks in a heatproof bowl. Stand the bowl over a pan of steaming water, off the heat, and whisk until light and fluffy and increased in volume. Add the sugar, lemon rind and juice, and continue whisking until thick and pale. Allow to cool.
2 Using a metal spoon, fold the cream into the lemon mixture. Pour into a 1.25 litre capacity shallow metal container and freeze for 2 hours, or until firm. When half frozen around the edges, beat well, then freeze again. Repeat the beating and freezing twice more. Garnish with lemon rind strips.

NOTE: This recipe can also be made using an ice cream machine.

TIRAMISU

Preparation time: 30 minutes + chilling
Total cooking time: Nil
Serves 6–8

3 cups (750 ml/24 fl oz) strong black coffee, cooled
3 tablespoons brandy or Kahlua
2 eggs, separated
3 tablespoons caster sugar
250 g (8 oz) mascarpone
1 cup (250 ml/8 fl oz) cream, whipped
16 large sponge finger biscuits
2 teaspoons dark cocoa powder

1 Put the coffee and liqueur in a bowl. Using electric beaters, beat the egg yolks and sugar in a small bowl for 3 minutes, or until thick and pale. Add the mascarpone and beat until just combined. Fold in the cream with a metal spoon.
2 Beat the egg whites until soft peaks form. Fold quickly and lightly into the cream mixture with a metal spoon, trying not to lose the volume.
3 Quickly dip half the biscuits, one at a time, into the coffee mixture. Drain off any excess and arrange the biscuits in the base of a deep serving dish. Spread half the cream mixture over the biscuits.
4 Dip the remaining biscuits and repeat the layers. Smooth the surface and dust liberally with cocoa powder. Refrigerate for 2 hours, or until firm, to allow the flavours to develop.

CHOCOLATE

IT WAS THE AZTECS WHO DISCOVERED THE DELIGHTS OF THE COCOA BEAN AND INDULGED THEMSELVES WITH CHOCOLATE DRINKS, AND SIXTEENTH CENTURY SPANISH EXPLORERS WHO INTRODUCED THE BEAN TO EUROPE.

Chocolate comes from cocoa beans which grow in pods on the cacao tree. It is made up of several different components which are extracted from the bean and then reformed. The beans are roasted and their shells removed to leave the nibs, which are then ground to produce chocolate liquor (a bitter chocolate). It is this liquor that forms the base for all chocolate products. It is pressed to extract the cocoa butter, leaving a dry substance which is ground into cocoa powder. Cocoa liquor then has varying amounts of cocoa butter and flavouring added to produce different types of chocolate. Next, the chocolate is 'conched' or stirred and rolled until smooth. Good quality chocolate is glossy and smooth with a slightly reddish colour. It breaks cleanly, melts easily (cocoa butter melts at body temperature) and has a high percentage of cocoa solids and real vanilla extract as a flavouring. The golden rule for cooking with chocolate is to always use the best-quality that you can afford. The white powdery bloom that sometimes appears on chocolate is caused either by sugar forming crystals on the surface when it is humid or the cocoa butter forming crystals on the surface when it gets too hot. If chocolate is not wrapped tightly in the fridge, it will appear to sweat and as the water evaporates, it will leave behind the sugar crystals. Bloom does not affect the taste.

TO MELT CHOCOLATE...

Chocolate needs to be handled carefully. Water will make it seize and go clumpy, as will overheating. Always make sure you use a clean dry heatproof bowl and don't try to hurry the process—only melt as much chocolate as you need at any one time. Chop the chocolate finely, place it in the bowl and set the bowl over a pan with about 4 cm (1½ inches) water that has been boiled and taken off the heat. The bottom of the bowl should not touch the water and should fit the pan tightly so that no moisture can get into the bowl and seize the chocolate. Leave the chocolate to soften, then stir until smooth. Either remove the bowl from the pan to cool the chocolate slightly or leave in place if you want to keep it liquid. Do not overheat chocolate or it will scorch, seize and taste bitter. Chocolate can also be melted in a microwave: place in a microwave safe bowl and cook in 15-second bursts on Medium (50%), stirring after every burst until smooth. The chocolate may keep its shape but it will become shiny and sag slightly around the edges as it melts. If it seizes, try adding a few drops of vegetable oil or shortening and stir until smooth.

TEMPERING CHOCOLATE

Cocoa butter is made up of several different fats which melt and set at different temperatures. We temper chocolate to stabilise the fats—this gives moulded or dipped chocolate a lovely shiny surface, as well as ensuring that it sets properly. Tempering is a process that involves heating and cooling the chocolate to exact temperatures—a process usually too complicated to do at home, although there is a quick method which helps stabilise the chocolate before use. Grate the chocolate and melt two-thirds of it as above. Then stir in the remaining chocolate in batches until it has all melted. The chocolate should now be tempered and its temperature should be about 88–90°F for dark chocolate and 85–88°F for milk chocolate.

THINGS TO MAKE

Chocolate collar Collars are beautiful decorations for cheesecakes or cakes. Remove the cheesecake or cake from the tin and put it on a board. Measure the height and add 1 cm (½ inch). Cut a strip of baking paper or mat contact this wide and long enough to easily go round the dessert. Spread a thin even layer of melted chocolate over the paper or shiny side of the contact, allow to set a little (but the chocolate must still be pliable) and wrap round the cake, paper-side-out. Fix in place and chill until set, then peel off the paper. Make spotted or patterned collars by piping white, dark or milk chocolate spots or lines on the paper first, allowing them to set a little, then spreading all over with a different coloured chocolate.

Chocolate curls Pour melted chocolate onto a marble work surface or a heavy chopping board. When it has cooled and just set, scrape off curls by pulling a knife set at a 45° angle across the chocolate. If the chocolate hardens too much it will splinter and crack, so work quickly once it has reached the right temperature. Make striped curls by pouring melted chocolate onto the surface and making ridges through it with a fork or comb scraper. Leave this layer to set, then pour a layer of different coloured melted chocolate over the top. Scrape off curls as above. Or pour lines of different coloured chocolate side by side and make curls as above. Small chocolate curls or shavings can be made by pulling a potato peeler over a block of chocolate.

Chocolate cups Spread a circle of chocolate onto a piece of freezer wrap or plastic wrap and drape it over a mould. Allow it to harden completely before removing the chocolate cup and pulling out the plastic wrap. Cups can also be made by lining a mould with plastic wrap, filling it with water, then freezing it until you have a solid block of ice. Remove the ice-filled plastic wrap from the mould and dip it in the melted chocolate. It should set immediately. The insides of moulds can also be brushed with oil and then with chocolate. The chocolate shrinks as it cools—a few minutes in the refrigerator helps and the chocolate cup should pull away from the inside of the mould. This gives a smooth shiny surface.

Chocolate boxes Melt chocolate and spread it in a thin, even layer on a piece of baking paper. When it has begun to set, cut it into equal squares with a sharp knife (heat the knife if the chocolate has set too much). Use more melted chocolate to glue the squares together to make into a box.

Piped shapes Put melted chocolate into a piping bag and pipe shapes onto a piece of baking paper. Peel the shapes off the baking paper and stick them together with a little more melted chocolate to give three-dimensional effects, or use them flat to pattern surfaces.

Chocolate leaves Wash the underside of non-toxic, unsprayed leaves such as rose or camellia, and dry well. Brush each leaf with a thin layer of melted chocolate, leave until set, then carefully peel the leaf away from the chocolate shape.

TYPES OF CHOCOLATE

Semi-sweet and bitter-sweet chocolate have vanilla, sugar and cocoa butter added. They are interchangeable. Milk chocolate was developed on a large scale by the Swiss (who had little chocolate and sugar but lots of milk) in the 1870s.

White chocolate is not strictly chocolate as it does not contain cocoa liquor. It is a mixture of cocoa butter, sugar and milk.

Compound or baking chocolate is used for cooking and decorations. It contains vegetable fat instead of cocoa butter. It does not need to be tempered. Also available as 'melts', 'buttons' and 'drops'. Known as 'summer coating' in America.

Couverture has a higher percentage of cocoa butter and is not as stable as ordinary chocolate. It needs to be tempered before use. It is used mainly by the catering industry as it melts and coats easily.

PEAR AND GINGER CHEESECAKE

Preparation time: 50 minutes + chilling
Total cooking time: 1 hour 10 minutes
Serves 10

250 g (8 oz) plain sweet biscuits
2 tablespoons ground ginger
100 g (3½ oz) unsalted butter, melted

Filling
3–4 firm ripe pears
1 cup (250 g/8 oz) caster sugar
2 tablespoons lemon juice
500 g (1 lb) cream cheese, softened
2 eggs
2 tablespoons ground ginger
300 g (10 oz) sour cream

1 Lightly grease a 23 cm (9 inch) diameter springform tin and line the base with baking paper. Sprinkle with flour and shake off excess.
2 Finely crush the biscuits with the ginger in a food processor. Add the butter and mix well. Spoon into the tin and press firmly onto the base and up the side. Refrigerate for 10 minutes. Preheat the oven to slow 150°C (300°F/Gas 2).
3 To make the filling, peel, core and thinly slice the pears and put them with half the sugar, the lemon juice and 1½ cups (375 ml/12 fl oz) water in a pan. Bring to the boil, lower the heat and simmer until the pears are tender but not breaking up. Strain and set aside to cool.
4 Process the cream cheese and remaining sugar in a food processor until light and smooth. Mix in the eggs and ginger. Add the sour cream and process to combine. Arrange the pears over the crust, pour the filling over the top and bake for 1 hour, or until set. Cool in the tin, then refrigerate overnight. Can be served with cream.

NOTE: For a stronger ginger flavour, use gingernuts instead of plain biscuits for the base.

CHOCOLATE TART WITH ESPRESSO CONES

Preparation time: 1 hour + chilling +
 freezing
Total cooking time: 5–10 minutes
Serves 8

¼ cup (20 g/¾ oz) instant coffee powder
1 litre good-quality vanilla ice cream,
 softened

Tart base
100 g (3½ oz) pecans
100 g (3½ oz) dark chocolate-flavoured
 biscuits
1 tablespoon cocoa powder
3 teaspoons soft brown sugar
1 tablespoon overproof rum
30 g (1 oz) unsalted butter, melted
40 g (1¼ oz) good-quality dark chocolate,
 melted

Filling
200 g (6½ oz) good-quality dark chocolate
30 g (1 oz) unsalted butter
½ cup (125 ml/4 fl oz) cream
3 egg yolks, lightly beaten
1 cup (250 ml/8 fl oz) cream, whipped

1 To mould the ice cream into shape for the espresso cones, first prepare the moulds. Cover 8 large cream horn moulds with baking paper and secure with sticky tape. Pull the paper off the moulds and transfer the paper cones to the inside of the moulds. Stand the lined cream horn moulds, points down, in mugs to make it easier to spoon in the ice cream.
2 Using a metal spoon, mix the coffee powder with 1 tablespoon hot water and fold through the ice cream in a bowl. Stir until smooth, then spoon into the paper inside the moulds, before freezing overnight.
3 To make the tart base, grease a shallow, 23 cm (9 inch) round fluted flan tin. Process all the ingredients in short bursts in a food processor for 30 seconds, or until even and crumbly. Press into the base and side of the tin. Refrigerate until firm.
4 To make the filling, stir the chocolate, butter and cream together in a heavy-based pan over low heat until melted and smooth. Remove from the heat, whisk in the egg yolks and transfer to a bowl. Cool slightly. Using a metal spoon, fold in the cream. Stir until smooth, pour into the tart base, then refrigerate until set.
5 Serve a wedge of chocolate tart with each espresso cone.

HOT PASSIONFRUIT SOUFFLE

Preparation time: 20 minutes
Total cooking time: 20–25 minutes
Serves 4

2 egg yolks
½ cup (125 g/4 oz) passionfruit pulp
   (about 6 passionfruit)
2 tablespoons lemon juice
¾ cup (90 g/3 oz) icing sugar
6 egg whites
icing sugar, for decorating

1 Preheat oven to hot 210°C (415°F/Gas 6–7). Place a collar of baking paper to come about 3 cm above the sides of 4 small ramekins. Tie securely with string. Lightly grease base and side of ramekins (including the paper) and sprinkle with caster sugar; shake out excess.
2 Combine yolks, pulp, lemon juice and half the icing sugar in a large bowl. Whisk until well combined. With electric beaters, beat egg whites in a large bowl until soft peaks form. Gradually add the remaining icing sugar, beating well after each addition.
3 Using a large metal spoon, fold the egg white mixture in batches through the passionfruit mixture. Spoon into dishes. Using a flat-bladed knife, cut through the mixture in a circular motion 2 cm (¾ inch) from the edge. Place the dish on a large oven tray and bake for 20–25 minutes or until the soufflé is well-risen and cooked through. Cut the collars from the dishes and serve the soufflés immediately, sprinkled with sifted icing sugar.

LEMON POSSET

Preparation time: 5 minutes + chilling
Total cooking time: 5 minutes
Serves 4

110 g (3½ oz) caster sugar
1¼ cups (315 ml/10 fl oz) thick (double)
   cream
juice of 2 lemons (about 100 ml/3½ fl oz)

1 Place the sugar and cream in a saucepan over low heat and bring to the boil slowly, stirring so the sugar dissolves and the cream does not boil over. Boil for 2–3 minutes, then add the lemon juice and mix well.
2 Pour the mixture into four 100 ml (3½ fl oz) ramekins, cover with plastic wrap and chill well for at least 2 hours or overnight. Serve with biscuits such as tuiles.

RICH CHOCOLATE SELF-SAUCING PUDDING

Preparation time: 20 minutes
Total cooking time: 45–50 minutes
Serves 6

1½ cups (185 g/6 oz) self-raising flour
¼ cup (30 g/1 oz) cocoa powder
¾ cup (185 g/6 oz) caster sugar
90 g (3 oz) butter, melted
¾ cup (185 ml/6 fl oz) milk
2 eggs, lightly beaten

Sauce
1½ cups (375 ml/12 fl oz) milk
1 cup (250 ml/8 fl oz) water
185 g (6 oz) dark chocolate, chopped

1 Preheat oven to moderate 180°C (350°F/Gas 4). Brush a 9-cup capacity deep ovenproof dish with oil or melted butter.
2 Sift flour and cocoa into a large bowl; add sugar, make a well in the centre. Add butter and combined milk and eggs. Using a wooden spoon, stir until just combined and smooth; do not over-beat. Pour into prepared dish.
3 To make Sauce: Place the milk, water and chocolate in a small pan; stir over low heat until melted and smooth. Pour slowly over the pudding mixture. Bake for 45–50 minutes, until firm to the touch. Serve with cream or ice cream and fresh fruit, if desired.

BLUEBERRY CHEESECAKE

Preparation time: 40 minutes +
refrigeration
Total cooking time: 45–50 minutes
Serves 8–10

125 g (4 oz) butter
1 cup (100 g/3⅓ oz) rolled oats
100 g (3⅓ oz) wheatmeal biscuits, finely
crushed
2 tablespoons soft brown sugar

Filling
375 g (12 oz) light cream cheese
100 g (3⅓ oz) fresh ricotta cheese
⅓ cup (90 g/3 oz) caster sugar
½ cup (125 g/4 oz) sour cream
2 eggs
1 tablespoon finely grated orange rind
1 tablespoon plain flour

Topping
250 g (8 oz) fresh blueberries
¾ cup (240 g/7½ oz) spreadable
blackberry fruit or conserve
¼ cup (60 ml/2 fl oz) cherry brandy

1 Brush a 20 cm (8 inch) round deep
springform tin with melted butter or oil
and line the base with non-stick baking
paper. Melt the butter in a pan, add the
oats and biscuit crumbs and mix well. Stir
in the sugar. Press half the biscuit
mixture into the base of the tin and
gradually press the remainder around the
sides, using a glass to firm it into place,
but not all the way up to the rim.
Refrigerate for 10–15 minutes. Preheat
oven to moderate 180°C (350°F/Gas 4).

2 To make Filling: Beat the cream cheese,
ricotta, sugar and sour cream with
electric beaters until smooth. Beat in the
eggs, orange rind and flour until smooth.
Put the tin on a flat oven tray to catch any
drips, pour the filling into the crust and
bake for 40–45 minutes, or until the filling
is just set. Remove from the oven but
leave in the tin to cool.
3 To make Topping: Scatter the
blueberries on top of the cheesecake.
Sieve the spreadable fruit or conserve
into a small pan with the brandy. Stir over
medium heat until smooth and then
simmer for 2–3 minutes. Carefully brush
over the blueberries. Refrigerate for
several hours or overnight, until well
chilled.

ZUCCOTTO

Preparation time: 1 hour + chilling
Total cooking time: Nil
Serves 6–8

1 slab sponge cake
⅓ cup (80 ml/2¾ fl oz) Kirsch
¼ cup (60 ml/2 fl oz) Cointreau
⅓ cup (80 ml/2¾ fl oz) rum, Cognac,
Grand Marnier or maraschino
2 cups (500 ml/16 fl oz) cream
90 g (3 oz) dark roasted almond
chocolate, chopped
175 g (6 oz) finely chopped mixed glacé
fruit
100 g (3½ oz) good-quality dark chocolate,
melted
70 g (2¼ oz) hazelnuts, roasted and
chopped
cocoa powder and icing sugar, to
decorate

1 Line a 1.5 litre pudding basin with damp
muslin. Cut the cake into curved pieces
with a sharp knife (you will need about 12
pieces). Work with one strip of cake at a
time, lightly brushing it with the combined
liqueurs and arranging the pieces closely
in the basin. Put the thin ends in the
centre so the slices cover the base and
side of the basin. Brush with the
remaining liqueur to soak the cake. Chill.
2 Beat the cream until stiff peaks form,
then divide in half. Fold the almond
chocolate and glacé fruit into one half and
spread evenly over the cake in the basin,
leaving a space in the centre.
3 Fold the cooled melted chocolate and
hazelnuts into the remaining cream and
spoon into the centre cavity, packing it in
firmly. Smooth the surface, cover and
chill for 8 hours to allow the cream to
firm slightly.
4 Turn out onto a serving plate and
decorate by dusting generously with
cocoa powder and icing sugar. You can
make a cardboard template to help you
dust separate wedges neatly—you may
need help holding it in place.

KULFI

Preparation time: 20 minutes + freezing
Total cooking time: 50 minutes
Serves 6

1½ litres milk
8 cardamom pods
4 tablespoons caster sugar
20 g (¾ oz) blanched almonds, finely
    chopped
20 g (¾ oz) pistachios, finely chopped

1 Put the milk and cardamom pods in a
large heavy-based pan, bring to the boil,
reduce the heat and simmer, stirring
often until it has reduced by about one-
third, to 1 litre—this will take some time.
Keep stirring or it will stick.
2 Add the sugar and cook for 2–3 minutes.
Strain out the cardamom pods and add
the nuts. Pour the kulfi into a shallow
metal or plastic container, cover the
surface with a sheet of baking paper and
freeze for 1 hour. Remove from the
freezer and beat to break up any ice
crystals, freeze again and repeat twice
more.
3 Line 6 cream horn moulds with baking
paper or lightly brush six 250 ml (8 fl oz)
pudding basins with flavourless oil and
divide the kulfi among them, then freeze
overnight. To serve, unmould each kulfi
and cut a cross ½ cm (¼ inch) deep in the
top.

CHOCOLATE ROULADE

Preparation time: 35 minutes + chilling
Total cooking time: 12 minutes
Serves 6–8

3 eggs
½ cup (125 g/4 oz) caster sugar
¼ cup (30 g/1 oz) plain flour
2 tablespoons cocoa powder
1 cup (250 ml/8 fl oz) cream
1 tablespoon icing sugar
½ teaspoon vanilla essence
icing sugar, extra, to dust

1 Preheat the oven to 200°F (400°F/Gas
6). Lightly grease the base and sides of a
25 x 30 cm (10 x 12 inch) swiss roll tin. Line
the base with paper and grease the paper.
Place the eggs in a small bowl with ⅓ cup
(90 g/3 oz) of the caster sugar. Beat with
electric beaters for about 8 minutes, or
until the mixture is thick and pale.
2 Sift the flour and cocoa together and
gently fold into the egg mixture with a
metal spoon. Spread the mixture evenly
into the prepared tin. Bake for about
12 minutes, or until the cake is just set.
3 Meanwhile, place a clean tea towel on a
work surface, top with a sheet of baking
paper and sprinkle with the remaining
caster sugar. When the cake is cooked,
turn it out immediately onto the prepared
paper and sugar. Trim off any crispy
edges. Roll the cake up from the long
side, rolling the paper inside the roll and
using the tea towel as a guide. Stand the
rolled cake on a wire cake rack for
5 minutes, then carefully unroll the cake
and allow it to cool to room temperature.
4 Beat the cream, icing sugar and vanilla
essence until stiff peaks form. Spread the
cream over the cooled cake, leaving a
1 cm (½ inch) border around each edge.
Roll the cake again, using the paper as a
guide. Place the roll, seam-side-down, on
a tray and refrigerate, covered, for about
30 minutes. Dust the top of the chocolate
roulade with icing sugar before carefully
cutting into slices to serve.

PRALINE ICE CREAM WITH CARAMEL BARK

Preparation time: 25 minutes + freezing
Total cooking time: 7 minutes
Serves 4

70 g (2¼ oz) blanched almonds, toasted
¼ cup (60 g/2 oz) caster sugar
¾ cup (185 ml/6 fl oz) cream
250 g (8 oz) mascarpone
125 g (4 oz) white chocolate, melted and
    cooled
2 tablespoons sugar
fresh figs and dessert wafers, for
    serving, optional

1 Line a flat baking tray with foil, brush
the foil lightly with oil and put the
almonds on the foil. Place the caster
sugar in a small pan over low heat. Tilt
the pan slightly (do not stir) and watch
until the sugar melts and turns golden—
this should take about 3–5 minutes.
2 Pour the caramel over the almonds and
leave until set and cold. Break into
chunks, put in a plastic bag and crush
with a rolling pin, or process briefly in a
food processor until crumbly.
3 Whip the cream until stiff peaks form.
Stir the mascarpone and chocolate in a
large bowl to combine. Using a metal
spoon, fold in the whipped cream and
crushed praline. Transfer to a 1 litre
metal tray, cover the surface with a piece
of greaseproof paper and freeze for
6 hours, or overnight. Remove from the
freezer 15 minutes before serving, to
soften slightly.
4 To make the caramel bark, line a baking
tray with foil and brush lightly with oil.
Sprinkle the sugar evenly onto the tray
and place under a hot grill for 2 minutes,
until the sugar is melted and golden.
Check frequently towards the end of
cooking time, as the sugar may burn
quickly. Remove from the heat, leave until
set and completely cold, then break into
shards. Serve with the ice cream, perhaps
with fresh figs and dessert wafers.

SPICY COCONUT CUSTARD

Preparation time: 20 minutes
Total cooking time: 1 hour
Serves 8

2 cinnamon sticks
1 teaspoon ground nutmeg
2 teaspoons whole cloves
1¼ cups (315 ml/10 fl oz) cream
90 g (3 oz) palm sugar, chopped, or soft
   brown sugar
280 ml (9 fl oz) coconut milk
3 eggs, lightly beaten
2 egg yolks, lightly beaten

1 Preheat the oven to warm 160°C
(315°F/Gas 2–3). Combine the spices,
cream and 1 cup (250 ml/8 fl oz) water in a
pan, bring to simmering point, reduce the
heat to very low and leave for 5 minutes to
allow the spices to flavour the liquid. Add
the sugar and coconut milk, return to low
heat and stir until the sugar has
dissolved.
2 Whisk the eggs and egg yolks in a bowl
until combined. Stir in the spiced mixture,
strain into a jug, then discard the whole
spices. Pour into eight 125 ml (4 fl oz)
ramekins. Place in a baking dish and pour
in hot water to come halfway up the sides
of the ramekins. Bake for 40–45 minutes,
until set. The custards should be no
longer liquid and should wobble slightly
when the dish is shaken lightly. Remove
the custards from the baking dish. Serve
hot or chilled. Can be served with whipped
cream and toasted coconut shreds.

CRANACHAN

Preparation time: 30 minutes + chilling
Total cooking time: 10 minutes
Serves 6

2 tablespoons medium oatmeal
1 cup (250 ml/8 fl oz) cream
2 tablespoons honey
1 tablespoon whisky
500 g (1 lb) raspberries or strawberries
2 tablespoons rolled oats, toasted

1 Put the oatmeal in a small pan. Stir over
low heat for 5 minutes, or until lightly
toasted. Remove from the heat and cool
completely.
2 Using electric beaters, beat the cream
in a small bowl until soft peaks form. Add
the honey and whisky and beat until just
combined.
3 Fold the cooled, toasted oatmeal into
the cream mixture with a metal spoon.
4 Begin layering the raspberries and
cream evenly into six tall dessert glasses,
ending with the cream. Refrigerate for
2 hours and serve sprinkled with toasted
oats.

NOTE: In Scotland, charms are placed
into cranachan at Halloween, somewhat
like the customary coins in English
Christmas puddings. This dessert is also
known as cream crowdie.

MANGO ICE CREAM

Preparation time: 20 minutes + freezing
Total cooking time: Nil
Serves 6

400 g (12⅔ oz) fresh mango flesh
½ cup (125 g/4 oz) caster sugar
3 tablespoons mango or apricot nectar
1 cup (250 ml/8 fl oz) cream
extra mango slices, optional

1 Place the mango in a food processor
and process until smooth. Transfer the
mango purée to a bowl and add the sugar
and nectar. Stir until the sugar has
dissolved.
2 Beat the cream in a small bowl until
stiff peaks form and then gently fold it
through the mango mixture.
3 Spoon the mixture into a shallow cake
tin, cover and freeze for 1½ hours or until
half-frozen. Quickly spoon the mixture
into a food processor and process for
30 seconds, or until smooth. Return the
mixture to the tin or a plastic container,
cover and freeze completely. Remove the
ice cream from the freezer 15 minutes
before serving to allow it to soften a little.
Serve the ice cream in scoops with some
extra fresh mango if desired.

NOTE: Frozen or canned mango can be
used if fresh mango is not available.

ALMOND MASCARPONE CREPES WITH SUMMER FRUIT

Preparation time: 40 minutes + standing
Total cooking time: 35 minutes
Makes about 12 crepes

Almond mascarpone
60 g (2 oz) slivered almonds
½ cup (125 g/4 oz) caster sugar
500 g (1 lb) mascarpone

250 g (8 oz) fresh strawberries, sliced
1 tablespoon caster sugar
1 cup (125 g/4 oz) plain flour
2 eggs
½ cup (125 ml/4 fl oz) milk
30 g (1 oz) unsalted butter, melted
4 kiwi fruit, thinly sliced
200 g (6½ oz) raspberries
250 g (8 oz) blueberries

1 To make the almond mascarpone, grill the almonds under a low heat until lightly golden, then place on an oiled baking tray. Put the caster sugar in a small heavy-based pan with ½ cup (125 ml/ 4 fl oz) water and stir, without boiling, until the sugar has dissolved. Bring to the boil, then reduce the heat and simmer, without stirring, for 15 minutes, or until the liquid turns golden brown. Quickly pour over the almonds and leave to set. Finely grind in a food processor, transfer to a bowl, then stir in the mascarpone, cover and refrigerate.

2 Place the strawberries in a large bowl and sprinkle with the caster sugar. Refrigerate.
3 Mix the flour, eggs and milk in a food processor for 10 seconds. Add ½ cup (125 ml/4 fl oz) water and the butter and process until smooth. Pour into a jug and set aside for 30 minutes.
4 Heat a small crepe pan or non-stick frying pan and brush lightly with melted butter. Pour ¼ cup (60 ml/2 fl oz) batter into the pan, swirling to cover the base thinly. Cook for about 30 seconds, or until the edges just begin to curl, turn the crepe over and cook the other side until lightly browned. Transfer to a plate and cover with a tea towel while cooking the remaining batter.
5 Spread each warm crepe with almond mascarpone and fold into quarters. Serve with macerated strawberries and some kiwi fruit, raspberries and blueberries.

RED WINE JELLY WITH FROSTED FRUITS

Preparation time: 20 minutes + chilling
Total cooking time: 5 minutes
Serves 4

2½ cups (600 ml/20 fl oz) good-quality red wine
rind of 1 lemon
rind and juice of 1 orange
2 cinnamon sticks
½ cup (125 g/4 oz) caster sugar
5 teaspoons gelatine
1 egg white
caster sugar, for frosting
200 g (6½ oz) blackcurrants and redcurrants or mixed seedless grapes

1 Combine the wine, rinds, cinnamon and sugar in a small pan. Heat gently until the sugar has dissolved. Put the orange juice in a small heatproof bowl, sprinkle the gelatine in an even layer over the surface and leave it to go spongy. Put a large pan filled with about 4 cm (1½ inches) water on to boil. When it boils, remove from the heat and carefully lower the gelatine bowl into the water (it should come halfway up the side of the bowl), then stir until dissolved. Cool slightly.
2 Stir the gelatine into the wine mixture. Pour through a muslin-lined strainer into a wetted 1.5 litre mould. Refrigerate until set (about 3 hours).
3 Whisk the egg white lightly in a bowl. Put the caster sugar in another bowl. Dip the fruit first into the egg, then into the caster sugar, shaking off the excess. Leave to dry on non-stick paper. Turn out the jelly and serve with the frosted fruit.

PEARS POACHED IN WINE

Preparation time: 20 minutes
Total cooking time: 45 minutes
Serves 4

4 firm pears
3 cups (750 ml/24 fl oz) good-quality red
  wine
¾ cup (185 g/6 oz) caster sugar
1 cinnamon stick
¼ cup (60 ml/2 fl oz) orange juice
5 cm (2 inch) piece of orange rind
200 g (6½ oz) mascarpone, for serving

1 Peel the pears, being careful to keep the
pears whole with the stalks still attached.
2 Place the wine, sugar, cinnamon stick,
orange juice and rind in a saucepan that
is large enough for the pears to be able to
stand upright. Stir over medium heat until
sugar is dissolved. Add the pears to the
saucepan and stir gently to coat. The
pears should be almost covered with wine
mixture. Cover the pan and simmer for
20–25 minutes, or until pears are cooked.
Allow to cool in syrup.
3 Remove the pears with a slotted spoon.
Bring the liquid to the boil and boil rapidly
until about ¾ cup (185 ml/6 fl oz) of liquid
remains. Serve the pears with a little
syrup and some mascarpone.

HOT MOCHA SOUFFLE

Preparation time: 25 minutes
Total cooking time: 45 minutes
Serves 20

3 tablespoons caster sugar
40 g (1¼ oz) unsalted butter
2 tablespoons plain flour
¾ cup (185 ml/6 fl oz) milk
1 tablespoon instant espresso-style
  coffee powder
100 g (3½ oz) good-quality dark chocolate,
  melted
4 eggs, separated
icing sugar, to dust

1 Preheat the oven to moderate 180°C
(350°F/Gas 4). Wrap a double thickness of
baking paper around a 1.25 litre soufflé
dish extending 3 cm (1¼ inches) above the
rim, then tie securely with string. Brush
with oil or melted butter, sprinkle
1 tablespoon of the sugar into the dish,
shake the dish to coat the base and side
evenly, then shake out the excess.
2 Melt the butter in a pan, add the flour
and stir over low heat for 2 minutes, or
until lightly golden. Add the milk
gradually, stirring until smooth. Stir over
medium heat until the mixture boils and
thickens; boil for another minute, then
remove from the heat. Transfer to a large
bowl.
3 Dissolve the coffee in 1 tablespoon hot
water, add to the milk with the remaining
sugar, melted chocolate and egg yolks,
then beat until smooth.
4 Beat the egg whites in a clean dry bowl
until stiff peaks form and then fold a little
into the chocolate mixture to loosen it
slightly. Gently fold in the remaining egg
white, then spoon the mixture into the
soufflé dish and bake for 40 minutes, or
until well risen and just firm. Remove the
collar, dust the soufflé with icing sugar
and serve immediately.

GREEN TEA ICE CREAM

Preparation time: 15 minutes + freezing
Total cooking time: 30 minutes
Serves 4

4 tablespoons Japanese green tea leaves
2 cups (500 ml/16 fl oz) milk
6 egg yolks
½ cup (125 g/4 oz) caster sugar
2 cups (500 ml/16 fl oz) cream

1 Combine the green tea leaves with the
milk in a saucepan and slowly bring to
simmering point. This step should not be
rushed—the longer the milk takes to
come to a simmer, the better the infusion
of flavour. Set aside for 5 minutes before
straining.
2 Whisk the egg yolks and sugar in a
heatproof bowl until thick and pale, then
add the infused milk. Place the bowl over
a saucepan of simmering water, making
sure that the base of the bowl is not
touching the water.
3 Stir the custard until it is thick enough
to coat the back of spoon, then remove
from the heat and allow to cool slightly
before adding the cream.
4 Pour the mixture into a metal tray and
freeze for 3–4 hours, or until just frozen
around the edges. Transfer the mixture to
a bowl, beat with electric beaters until
thick and creamy, then return to the
metal tray. Repeat the freezing and
beating twice more. Transfer to a storage
container, cover the surface with
greaseproof paper and freeze overnight.

NOTE: If you want your green tea ice
cream green, add a few drops of food
colouring.

ZERDE (TURKISH SWEET SAFFRON RICE)

Preparation time: 10 minutes +
　30 minutes soaking
Total cooking time: 45 minutes
Serves 6

1 teaspoon saffron threads
½ cup (125 g/4 oz) medium-grain rice
1 cup (250 g/8 oz) caster (superfine)
　sugar
2 tablespoons rosewater
¼ cup (40 g/1¾ oz) pine nuts, lightly
　toasted
¼ cup (35 g/1¼ oz) pistachios, chopped
pomegranate seeds, to garnish
thick natural yoghurt, to serve

1 Crush the saffron threads with your
fingers and soak in 2 tablespoons of
boiling water for 30 minutes.
2 Bring 1.25 litres (40 fl oz) water to the
boil in a large saucepan, then add the
rice. Reduce to a simmer and cook,
stirring occasionally, for 20 minutes. Stir
in the sugar, rosewater and the saffron
with the soaking liquid and simmer for
another 10 minutes.
3 Add the pine nuts and chopped
pistachios and simmer for another
10 minutes. The mixture should be thick
and soupy. If it is too thick, add a little
more water. Serve either hot or cold (it
will thicken as it cools). Garnish with
pomegranate seeds. Serve with thick
natural yoghurt.

NOTE: This delectable rice pudding from
Turkey is unusual in that is made without
any milk, cream or butter. If serving it
cold, top it with the pomegranate seeds
just before serving.

CHILLED LIME SOUFFLE

Preparation time: 35 minutes + chilling
Total cooking time: Nil
Serves 4

5 eggs, separated
1 cup (250 g/8 oz) caster sugar
2 teaspoons finely grated lime rind
¾ cup (185 ml/6 fl oz) lime juice, strained
1 tablespoon gelatine
1¼ cups (315 ml/10 fl oz) cream, lightly
　whipped

1 Cut four strips of baking paper or foil
long enough to fit around 250 ml (8 fl oz)
soufflé dishes. Fold each in half
lengthways, wrap one around each dish,
extending 4 cm (1½ inches) above the rim,
then secure with string. Brush the inside
of the collar with melted butter, sprinkle
with caster sugar, shake to coat, then tip
out excess.
2 Using electric beaters, beat the egg
yolks, sugar and lime rind in a small bowl
for 3 minutes, until the sugar has
dissolved and the mixture is thick and
pale. Heat the lime juice in a small pan,
then gradually add to the yolk mixture
while beating, until well mixed.

3 Pour ¼ cup (60 ml/2 fl oz) water into a
small heatproof bowl, sprinkle the
gelatine in an even layer over the surface
and leave to go spongy. Bring a large pan
filled with about 4 cm (1½ inches) water to
the boil, remove from the heat, carefully
lower the gelatine bowl into the water (it
should come halfway up the side of the
bowl), then stir until dissolved. Cool
slightly, then add gradually to the lime
mixture, beating on low speed until
combined. Transfer to a large bowl, cover
with plastic wrap and refrigerate for 15
minutes, or until thickened but not set.
Using a metal spoon, fold the cream into
the lime mixture until almost combined.
4 Using electric beaters, beat the egg
whites in a clean, dry bowl until soft peaks
form. Fold the egg white quickly and
lightly into the lime mixture, using a large
metal spoon, until just combined with no
lumps of egg white remaining. Spoon
gently into the soufflé dishes and chill
until set. Remove the collars when ready
to serve. Can be served with whipped
cream.

LIQUEUR FRUITS

THESE LIQUEUR-INFUSED FRUITS ARE LUSCIOUS WITH CREAM OR ICE CREAM, WAFFLES OR CREPES. THEY ARE ALSO GREAT WITH BRIOCHE OR PANETTONE SPREAD WITH RICOTTA OR MASCARPONE.

PEARS IN MULLED WINE

Put 2 cups (500 g/1 lb) sugar and 3 cups (750 ml/24 fl oz) red wine in a large pan. Stir over low heat until the sugar has dissolved. Add 1.25 kg (2½ lb) peeled, halved and cored small pears, 1 cinnamon stick, 6 cloves, 6 whole allspice and 2 strips each of orange and lemon rind. Cover with a plate to keep the pears submerged. Bring to the boil (at least 90°C), then reduce the heat and simmer for 10 minutes. Arrange the pears in a heatproof, warm, sterilized 1 litre (32 fl oz) jar. Boil the syrup for 15 minutes, then mix ½ cup (125 ml/4 fl oz) syrup with ½ cup (125 ml/4 fl oz) brandy and 3 cloves. Pour over the pears to cover, seal and invert for 2 minutes. Store in a cool, dark place for up to a month before using. Refrigerate after opening.
Fills a 1 litre (32 fl oz) jar.

DRUNKEN PRUNES

Put 750 g (1½ lb) pitted prunes in a heatproof, warm sterilized 1 litre (32 fl oz) jar. Cut a vanilla bean in half lengthways and add to the jar. Add 2 cups (500 ml/ 16 fl oz) tawny port to cover the prunes, seal and invert for 2 minutes. Leave for at least 1 month before using. Store for up to 6 months. Refrigerate after opening.
Fills a 1 litre (32 fl oz) jar.

CLEMENTINES OR CUMQUATS IN LIQUEUR

Cut a cross in the tops of 500 g (1 lb) cumquats or clementines and pack into heatproof, warm sterilized jars. Place 1 cup (250 g/8 oz) sugar and ¾ cup (185 ml/6 fl oz) water in a saucepan and boil for 1 minute. Stir in ¼ cup (60 ml/ 2 fl oz) orange liqueur, then pour over the fruit. Screw on the lids loosely—do not tighten. Place layers of cloth on the base of a deep, heavy-based saucepan. Put the jars on top and cover with hot water to reach the shoulders of the jars. Bring the water slowly to simmering point, then reduce the heat and simmer for 20 minutes, or until the fruit starts to look clear. Remove the jars. Immediately tighten the lids fully with a tea towel. Cool, label and date. Store in a cool, dark place for 2 months before using, turning the jars upside-down every 2 weeks. Will keep for 6 months. Refrigerate after opening.
Fills a 750 ml (24 fl oz) jar.

PEACHES IN SPICED SAUTERNES

Cut 4–6 kg (8–12 lb) ripe freestone peaches in half, discard the stones and pack the peaches, with 1 cinnamon stick and 1 star anise into a heatproof, warm sterilized 2 litre (64 fl oz) jar. Place 2 cups (500 g/1 lb) sugar in a large saucepan, add 2 cups (500 ml/16 fl oz) water and stir over low heat until all the sugar has dissolved. Bring to the boil (at least 90°C) and boil for 5 minutes, then pour the hot syrup over the peaches and top with 1 cup (250 ml/4 fl oz) Sauternes. Following the cumquat instructions, simmer in the jar for 10 minutes, or until the peach syrup reaches 90° (check with a thermometer). Keep in a cool, dark place for at least 2 weeks before using. Will keep for 6 months. Refrigerate after opening.
Fills a 2 litre (64 fl oz) jar.

CHERRIES IN VANILLA BRANDY

Prick the skins of 750 g (1½ lb) cherries with a fine skewer. Heat 1½ cups (375 g/ 12 oz) sugar with ½ cup (125 ml/4 fl oz) each of brandy and water in a pan, stirring until all the sugar has dissolved. Add the cherries and a vanilla bean and heat until boiling (90°C). Place the cherries and syrup in a heatproof, warm, sterilized jar, seal while hot and invert for 2 minutes. Store in a cool place for 6 weeks, turning every couple of days for the first 2 weeks. Serve the cherries in the liqueur. Refrigerate after opening.
Fills a 1 litre (32 fl oz) jar.

FROM LEFT: Pears in mulled wine; Drunken prunes; Clementines in liqueur; Peaches in spiced Sauternes; Cherries in vanilla brandy

ZUPPA INGLESE

Preparation time: 35 minutes + chilling
Total cooking time: 10 minutes
Serves 6

2 cups (500 ml/16 fl oz) milk
1 vanilla bean, split lengthways
4 egg yolks
½ cup (125 g/4 oz) caster sugar
2 tablespoons plain flour
300 g (10 oz) Madeira cake, cut into 1 cm
    (½ inch) slices
⅓ cup (80 ml/2¾ fl oz) rum
30 g (1 oz) chocolate, grated or shaved
50 g (1¾ oz) flaked almonds, toasted

1 Grease a 1.5 litre serving dish with
flavourless oil or melted butter. Place the
milk and vanilla bean in a pan and slowly
heat until bubbles appear around the
edge of the pan. Whisk the egg yolks,
sugar and flour together in a bowl, until
thick and pale.
2 Discard the vanilla bean, whisk the
warm milk slowly into the egg mixture
and blend well. Return the custard
mixture to a clean pan and stir over
medium heat until the custard boils and
thickens.
3 Line the base of the prepared dish with
one-third of the cake slices and brush
well with the rum combined with
1 tablespoon of water. Spread one-third of
the custard over the cake, top with cake
slices and brush with rum mixture.
Repeat this process, finishing with a layer
of custard. Cover and refrigerate for at
least 3 hours. Sprinkle with grated or
shaved chocolate and toasted flaked
almonds just before serving.

VANILLA BEAN CUSTARD BRULEE

Preparation time: 10 minutes +
    3 hours refrigeration
Total cooking time: 55 minutes
Serves 4

1 cup (250 ml/8 fl oz) cream
1 cup (250 ml/8 fl oz) milk
1 whole vanilla bean
2 eggs
2 egg yolks
¼ cup (60 g/2 oz) caster sugar
⅓ cup (60 g/2 oz) soft brown sugar
½ teaspoon ground cinnamon

1 Preheat oven to warm 160°C (315 F/Gas
2–3). Brush four 185 ml (6 fl oz) ramekins
with oil or melted butter. Place cream,
milk and vanilla bean in small pan. Stir
over low heat until almost boiling.
Remove from heat; cool. Remove vanilla
bean and cut in half. Scrape out inside of
one half of bean (save the other half for
later use) and add the seeds to the milk
mixture.
2 Beat the eggs, yolks and caster sugar in
a small bowl and gradually add the cream
mixture. Pour into the prepared
ramekins. Stand the ramekins in a baking
dish and pour in enough hot water to
come halfway up the sides of the
ramekins. Place a piece of foil lightly over
baking dish to cover the ramekins.
3 Bake for 45 minutes, or until the
custard is set and a knife comes out clean
when inserted into the centre. Remove
the ramekins from the water bath and set
aside to cool. Refrigerate for several
hours or overnight.
4 Preheat the grill to high heat. Sprinkle
the combined brown sugar and cinnamon
over the top of each custard. Place the
custards under the grill until tops are
dark brown and bubbling. Remove from
the grill and refrigerate for 5 minutes
before serving.

BANANA FRITTERS IN COCONUT BATTER

Preparation time: 15 minutes +
    1 hour standing
Total cooking time: 20 minutes
Serves 6

100 g (3½ oz) glutinous rice flour
100 g (3½ oz) freshly grated coconut or
    ⅔ cup (60 g/2 oz) desiccated coconut
50 g (1¾ oz) sugar
1 tablespoon sesame seeds
¼ cup (60 ml/2 fl oz) coconut milk
6 sugar bananas
oil, for deep-frying

1 Combine the flour, coconut, sugar,
sesame seeds, coconut milk and ¼ cup
(60 ml/2 fl oz) water in a large bowl.
Whisk to a smooth batter—add more
water if the batter is too thick. Set aside
to rest for 1 hour.
2 Peel the bananas and cut in half
lengthways (cut each portion in half again
crossways if the bananas are large).
3 Fill a wok or deep-fat fryer one-third
full of oil and heat to 180°C (350°F), or
until a cube of bread dropped into the oil
browns in 15 seconds. Dip each piece of
banana into the batter, then drop gently
into the hot oil. Cook in batches for
4–6 minutes, or until golden brown all
over. Remove with a slotted spoon and
drain on crumpled paper towels. Serve
hot with vanilla ice cream and a
sprinkling of extra toasted sesame seeds,
if desired.

CHERRY CLAFOUTIS (FRENCH BATTER PUDDING)

Preparation time: 15 minutes
Total cooking time: 40 minutes
Serves 6–8

500 g (1 lb) fresh cherries (see Note)
¾ cup (90 g/3 oz) plain flour
2 eggs, lightly beaten
⅓ cup (90 g/3 oz) caster sugar
1 cup (250 ml/8 fl oz) milk
¼ cup (60 ml/2 fl oz) thick cream
60 g (2 oz) unsalted butter, melted
icing sugar, for dusting

1 Preheat the oven to moderate 180°C (350°F/Gas 4). Lightly grease a 1.5 litre ovenproof dish with melted butter.
2 Pit the cherries and spread into the dish in a single layer.
3 Sift the flour into a bowl, add the eggs and whisk until smooth. Add the sugar, milk, cream and butter, whisking until just combined. Do not overbeat.
4 Pour the batter over the cherries and bake for 30–40 minutes, or until a skewer comes out clean when inserted into the centre. Dust generously with icing sugar before serving. Serve warm, straight from the oven.

NOTE: You can use a 720 g (1½ lb) jar of cherries if fresh ones aren't available. Make sure you drain it thoroughly before using the cherries.

SPEARMINT CITRUS SORBET

Preparation time: 25 minutes + freezing
Total cooking time: 35 minutes
Serves 4

1½ cups (375 g/12 oz) caster sugar
2 cups (50 g/1¾ oz) spearmint leaves
¾ cup (185 ml/6 fl oz) lemon or grapefruit juice
1¼ cups (315 ml/10 fl oz) orange juice
½ cup (125 ml/4 fl oz) dry white wine
½ cup (15 g/½ oz) finely sliced spearmint leaves

1 Put the sugar, spearmint leaves and 3 cups (750 ml/24 fl oz) water in a pan. Stir over low heat until the sugar dissolves. Bring to the boil, reduce the heat and simmer for 30 minutes. Strain and discard the spearmint leaves.
2 Stir in the juices and wine. Pour into a metal container and, when cool, stir in the finely sliced spearmint leaves. Freeze until just firm.
3 Transfer to a bowl or food processor and beat with electric beaters, or process, until smooth. Return to the freezer. Repeat the beating and freezing twice more. Cover with greaseproof paper. Freeze overnight, or until firm. Allow to soften slightly before scooping out.

CREME CARAMEL

Preparation time: 25 minutes + chilling
Total cooking time: 35 minutes
Serves 8

¾ cup (185 g/6 oz) sugar

Custard
3 cups (750 ml/24 fl oz) milk
⅓ cup (90 g/3 oz) caster sugar
4 eggs
1 teaspoon vanilla essence

1 Preheat the oven to warm 160°C (315°F/Gas 2–3). Brush eight 125 ml (4 fl oz) ramekins or moulds with melted butter.
2 Place the sugar and ¼ cup (60 ml/2 fl oz) water in a pan. Stir over low heat until the sugar dissolves. Bring to the boil, reduce the heat and simmer until the mixture turns golden and starts to caramelize. Remove from the heat immediately and pour enough hot caramel into each ramekin to cover the base. The caramel will continue cooking in the pan so work quickly and be careful not to burn yourself.
3 To make the custard, heat the milk in a pan over low heat until almost boiling. Remove from the heat. Whisk together the sugar, eggs and vanilla essence for 2 minutes, then stir in the warm milk. Strain the mixture into a jug and pour into the ramekins.
4 Place the ramekins in a baking dish and pour in enough boiling water to come halfway up the sides of the ramekins. Bake for 30 minutes, or until the custard is set. The custards should be no longer liquid and should wobble slightly when the dish is shaken lightly. Allow to cool, then refrigerate for at least 2 hours, or until set. To unmould, run a knife carefully around the edge of each custard and gently upturn onto serving plates. Shake gently to assist removal, if necessary. Crème caramel can be served by itself or with fresh berries, whipped cream and wafers.

GRILLED ORANGES WITH CARAMEL MINT BUTTER

Preparation time: 20 minutes + chilling
Total cooking time: 20 minutes
Serves 4

6 oranges
⅓ cup (90 g/3 oz) sugar
¼ cup (60 ml/2 fl oz) cream
45 g (1½ oz) unsalted butter, chopped
2 teaspoons grated orange rind
2 tablespoons finely chopped fresh mint
cream or mascarpone, for serving
ground nutmeg, for serving

1 Cut the base off each orange to steady it, then cut the skin away in a downward motion, cutting only deep enough to remove all the white membrane. Slice the oranges thinly.
2 Cook the sugar and 3 tablespoons water in a small pan over very low heat, without boiling, until the sugar has dissolved (shake occasionally, but do not stir). Increase the heat, bring to the boil and cook until deep golden or caramel. Remove from the heat and gradually add the cream (the mixture will become lumpy and may spit, so be careful). Return to the heat and stir until the caramel dissolves. Add the butter, orange rind and mint and whisk until blended. Transfer to a bowl and refrigerate.
3 Preheat the grill. Arrange the orange slices slightly overlapping in a 24 cm (9½ inch) diameter shallow ovenproof gratin or pie dish. Dot the top of the oranges with the caramel butter, then grill until the butter has melted and the oranges are hot. Serve with cream or mascarpone. Sprinkle with nutmeg to serve.

NOTE: Caramel mint butter can be prepared ahead and refrigerated for 24 hours.

HAZELNUT PRALINE CREPES WITH CHOCOLATE SAUCE

Preparation time: 1 hour + standing
Total cooking time: 45 minutes
Makes about 10 crepes

100 g (3½ oz) hazelnuts
⅓ cup (90 g/3 oz) caster sugar, plus 2
  tablespoons
90 g (3 oz) unsalted butter, at room
  temperature
1 cup (125 g/4 oz) plain flour
1 egg, plus 1 egg yolk
1¼ cups (315 ml/10 fl oz) milk
125 g (4 oz) dark chocolate, chopped
50 g (1¾ oz) unsalted butter
2 tablespoons sifted icing sugar
½ cup (125 g/4 oz) sour cream
2 tablespoons Kahlua or Tia Maria
ice cream, for serving

1 Toast the hazelnuts under a low grill, watching them carefully to ensure they don't burn, then rub off the skins with a tea towel. Roughly chop a third of the nuts, set aside and put the remaining nuts on an oiled baking tray. To make the praline, put ⅓ cup (90 g/3 oz) sugar with 2 tablespoons water in a heavy-based pan. Stir over low heat, without boiling, until the sugar has completely dissolved. Do not boil until the sugar has dissolved or it will crystallize. Bring to the boil and cook without stirring, until golden brown. If the caramel darkens in patches, swirl the pan until you have an even colour. Dip a pastry brush in cold water and brush down the side of the pan if crystals start to form. Be very careful at this stage as the caramel can cause burns. Quickly pour the caramel over the whole nuts and allow to set. (The heat of the caramel will cause the tray to become very hot.) Finely chop the praline in a food processor or crush it with a rolling pin or in a mortar and pestle.

2 Beat the unsalted butter and remaining sugar with electric beaters until creamy. Stir in two-thirds of the praline, cover and keep cool.
3 Sift the flour into a large bowl and make a well in the centre. Gradually whisk in the combined egg, egg yolk and milk until the batter is smooth and free of lumps. Transfer to a jug for easy pouring, cover and set aside for 30 minutes. Heat a medium crepe pan or non-stick frying pan and brush with melted butter. Pour ¼ cup (60 ml/2 fl oz) batter into the pan, swirling to cover the base. Pour any excess batter back into the jug. Cook for 30 seconds, or until the edges just begin to curl, then turn and cook the other side. Transfer to a plate and cover with a tea towel. Repeat with the remaining batter, greasing the pan when necessary. Stack the crepes between greaseproof paper to prevent them sticking together.
4 Preheat the oven to warm 160°C (315°F/Gas 2–3). Spread each crepe with a tablespoon of the praline butter. Roll up into cigar shapes and place in a greased ovenproof dish in a single layer. Bake for 10 minutes, or until warm.
5 Meanwhile, heat the chocolate and the remaining butter in a heatproof bowl over a pan of simmering water. When it has melted, add the icing sugar, sour cream and liqueur. Stir the mixture until smooth and glossy.
6 To serve, sprinkle the crepes with the chopped hazelnuts and the remaining praline. Serve with warm chocolate sauce and ice cream.

NOTE: The praline can be made a day in advance and stored in an airtight jar in the refrigerator. It may become sticky but will still have the same flavour.

PEACH CHARLOTTES WITH MELBA SAUCE

Preparation time: 30 minutes + 20
  minutes standing
Total cooking time: 40 minutes
Serves 4

1 cup (250 g/8 oz) sugar
4 cups (1 litre) water
6 medium peaches
⅓ cup (80 ml/2¾ fl oz) peach liqueur
2 loaves brioche
100 g (3⅓ oz) butter, melted
½ cup (160 g/5¼ oz) apricot jam, warmed
  and sieved

Melba Sauce
315 g (10 oz) fresh or thawed frozen
  raspberries
2 tablespoons icing sugar

1 Preheat the oven to moderate 180°C
(350°F/Gas 4). Brush four 1-cup capacity
ovenproof ramekins or moulds with
melted butter. Combine the sugar and
water in large, heavy-based pan. Stir over
medium heat until the sugar completely
dissolves. Bring to the boil, reduce heat
slightly and add the whole peaches.
Simmer, covered for 20 minutes. Drain
and cool. Peel the skins and slice the
flesh thickly. Place in a bowl, sprinkle
with liqueur and set aside for 20 minutes.

2 Cut the brioche into 1 cm (½ inch) thick
slices; remove the crusts. With a scone-
cutter, cut rounds to fit the tops and
bases of each dish. Cut the remaining
slices into 2 cm (¾ inch) wide fingers and
trim to fit the height of the dish. Dip the
first round into melted butter and place in
the base of the dish. Dip brioche fingers
into melted butter and press around the
sides of dish, overlapping slightly. Line all
the dishes in this manner.
3 Fill the lined dishes evenly with peach
slices and top with the last round of
brioche dipped in melted butter. Press to
seal. Place the dishes on a baking tray
and bake for 20 minutes. Turn onto
serving plates, brush with jam and pour
Melba Sauce alongside. Serve with fresh
berries, if desired.
4 To make Melba Sauce: Process the
berries in a food processor and add icing
sugar, to taste. Push through a fine sieve.

NOTE: The peaches can be cooked, the
dishes lined with brioche and the sauce
made, up to 6 hours ahead. Refrigerate
the charlottes, then fill and bake them
close to serving time.

SUMMER FRUIT COMPOTE

Preparation time: 40 minutes
Total cooking time: 30 minutes
Serves 8

5 apricots, halved
4 nectarines, halved
4 blood plums or other plums, stoned
4 peaches, quartered
200 g (6½ oz) can pitted cherries
1 cup (250 ml/8 fl oz) good-quality claret
⅓ cup (80 ml/2¾ fl oz) dry sherry
¾ cup (185 g/6 oz) caster sugar
whipped cream, optional, for serving

1 Gently plunge the fruit in small batches
into boiling water for 30 seconds. Remove
with a slotted spoon and place in a bowl of
iced water. Peel all the fruit except the
cherries.
2 Combine the claret, sherry, sugar and
1 cup (250 ml/8 fl oz) water in a large
heavy-based pan. Stir over low heat
without boiling until the sugar has
dissolved. Bring to the boil, reduce the
heat and simmer for 5 minutes.
3 Add the drained fruits to the syrup in
small batches and simmer each batch for
5 minutes. Remove with a slotted spoon.
Pile the fruit into a bowl. Bring the syrup
to the boil, reduce the heat and simmer
for another 5 minutes. Remove from the
heat and allow to cool slightly—it should
be the consistency of a syrup. Pour over
the fruit. Serve with a dollop of freshly
whipped cream.

NOTE: Blood plum is a generic term
covering some Japanese varieties of dark
flesh plums such as satsuma and
mariposa. Other plum varieties can be
substituted.

CHOCOLATE CHESTNUT BLISS

Preparation time: 50 minutes + chilling
Total cooking time: 30 minutes
Serves 6

100 g (3½ oz) unsalted butter, chopped
80 g (2¾ oz) dark chocolate, chopped
½ cup (125 ml/4 fl oz) milk
½ cup (125 g/4 oz) caster sugar
¼ cup (25 g/¾ oz) desiccated coconut
¼ cup (30 g/1 oz) cocoa powder
½ cup (60 g/2 oz) self-raising flour
2 eggs, lightly beaten

Amaretto syrup
2 tablespoons caster sugar
¼ cup (60 ml/2 fl oz) Amaretto

Chestnut filling
30 g (1 oz) unsalted butter, softened
1 cup (260 g/8 oz) unsweetened chestnut
   purée
¼ cup (30 g/1 oz) icing sugar

Chocolate topping
75 g (2½ oz) unsalted butter
150 g (5 oz) dark chocolate, chopped
2 tablespoons light corn syrup

Raspberry sauce
150 g (5 oz) frozen raspberries, thawed
2 tablespoons caster sugar

Chocolate swirls
60 g (2 oz) dark chocolate

1 Preheat the oven to 180°C (350°F/Gas 4). Lightly grease a 30 x 25 cm (12 x 10 inch) swiss roll tin and cover the base and side with baking paper. Combine the butter, chocolate, milk and sugar in a pan and stir over low heat until the sugar and chocolate dissolve. Remove from the heat and allow to cool slightly. Combine the coconut, cocoa and flour in a bowl, pour in the chocolate mixture and the beaten eggs and mix well. Pour into the tin and bake for 15 minutes, or until just firm to touch. Leave for 5 minutes before turning onto a rack to cool.

2 To make the Amaretto syrup, combine the sugar and ¼ cup (60 ml/2 fl oz) water in a small pan and stir over low heat until the sugar has dissolved. Remove from the heat, stir in the Amaretto and allow to cool.
3 To make the chestnut filling, beat the butter, chestnut purée and icing sugar in a bowl until smooth. Cut rounds from the chocolate cake using 3 cm (1¼ inch), 5 cm (2 inch), 7 cm (2¾ inch) cutters, making six of each size. (Any leftover chocolate cake can be frozen and made into rum balls if it doesn't get eaten first.)
4 Reserve ½ cup (125 ml/4 fl oz) of the chestnut cream. Place large rounds of cake on a baking paper covered baking tray, brush well with some of the syrup and spread with a layer of the chestnut cream. Top with another round of cake, slightly smaller than the first, brush well with syrup and top with some chestnut cream. Top with the remaining round of cake and brush with remaining syrup. Spread the reserved chestnut cream as thinly and smoothly as possible over the outside of each cake, to form smooth sides. Refrigerate for 1 hour, or until the chestnut cream has firmed slightly.
5 To make the topping, combine the butter, chocolate and corn syrup in a bowl, place over a pan of simmering water and stir until melted. Lift the cakes onto a wire rack over a baking tray, spoon topping over each cake to completely cover, then refrigerate until just set.
6 Meanwhile, to make the raspberry sauce, combine the raspberries and sugar in a small saucepan, then simmer for 5 minutes. Strain through a plastic sieve and allow to cool.
7 To make the chocolate swirls, melt the dark chocolate and spoon into a paper piping bag or small plastic bag. Snip off a corner and drizzle chocolate into concentric circles, about 7 cm in diameter, on a baking paper covered baking tray, then refrigerate until firm. Decorate with the swirls, dust the top with icing sugar and serve with sauce.

PASSIONFRUIT AND ORANGE SORBET

Preparation time: 15 minutes + freezing
Total cooking time: Nil
Serves 4

3 cups (750 ml/24 fl oz) orange juice
¾ cup (185 ml/6 fl oz) passionfruit pulp
½ cup (125 g/4 oz) caster sugar
2 egg whites, lightly beaten

1 Mix the orange juice, passionfruit pulp and sugar in a large bowl. Pour into a metal tray and freeze until just firm around the edges. Do not allow to become too firm. Transfer to a bowl or food processor and beat with an electric whisk or process. Refreeze. Repeat this step twice more, adding the egg white the final time, with the beaters or motor running. Return to the tray, cover with greaseproof paper and freeze for 3 hours, or until firm.
2 Alternatively, pour the mixture into an ice cream machine and churn for about 30 minutes.

CHOCOLATE BAVAROIS

Preparation time: 30 minutes + chilling
Total cooking time: 5 minutes
Serves 6

200 g (6½ oz) good-quality dark
    chocolate, chopped
1½ cups (375 ml/12 fl oz) milk
4 egg yolks
⅓ cup (90 g/3 oz) caster sugar
1 tablespoon gelatine
1¼ cups (315 ml/10 fl oz) cream

1 Combine the chocolate and milk in a
small pan. Stir over low heat until the
chocolate has melted and the milk just
comes to the boil. Remove from the heat.
2 Beat the egg yolks and sugar until
combined. Gradually add the hot
chocolate milk, whisking until combined.
Return to a clean pan and cook over low
heat until the mixture thickens enough to
coat the back of a wooden spoon. Do not
allow to boil. Remove from the heat.
3 Put 2 tablespoons water in a small
heatproof bowl, sprinkle the gelatine in
an even layer over the surface and leave
to go spongy. Stir into the hot chocolate
mixture until dissolved.
4 Refrigerate until the mixture is cold but
not set, stirring occasionally. Beat the
cream until soft peaks form, then fold into
the chocolate mixture in two batches.
Pour into six 250 ml (8 fl oz) glasses and
refrigerate for several hours or overnight,
or until set.

CARAMEL BREAD PUDDING

Preparation time: 40 minutes + standing +
    chilling
Total cooking time: 1 hour
Serves 6–8

⅔ cup (160 g/5½ oz) caster sugar
500 g (1 lb) panettone or brioche
½ cup (125 g/4 oz) caster sugar, extra
2 cups (500 ml/16 fl oz) milk
2 wide strips lemon rind, white pith
    removed
3 eggs, lightly beaten
fresh fruit and cream, optional, for
    serving

1 Preheat the oven to moderate 180°C
(350°F/Gas 4). Lightly brush a 23 x 13 x
7 cm (9 x 5 x 2¾ inch), 1.25 litre loaf tin
with oil or melted butter.
2 Place the caster sugar with 2
tablespoons water in a small pan over
medium heat and stir, without boiling,
until the sugar has completely dissolved.
Bring to the boil, reduce the heat slightly
and simmer, without stirring, for about
10 minutes, until the syrup becomes a rich
golden colour. Watch carefully towards
the end of cooking to prevent burning. As
soon as it reaches the colour you desire,
pour into the loaf tin and leave to cool.
3 Using a large serrated knife, cut the
panettone or brioche into 2 cm (¾ inch)
thick slices and remove the crusts. Trim
into large pieces to fit the tin in three
layers, filling any gaps with panettone cut
to size.

4 Stir the extra caster sugar, milk and
lemon rind in a pan over low heat until
the sugar has dissolved. Bring just to the
boil, remove from the heat and transfer to
a jug to allow the lemon flavour to be
absorbed and the mixture to cool.
Remove the lemon rind and whisk in the
beaten eggs. Pour the mixture gradually
into the tin, allowing it to soak into the
panettone after each addition. Set aside
for 20 minutes to let the panettone soak
up the liquid.
5 Place the loaf tin into a large baking
dish and pour in enough hot water to
come halfway up the sides of the tin.
Bake the pudding for 50 minutes, until
just set. Carefully remove the tin from the
baking dish and set aside to cool.
Refrigerate the pudding overnight.
6 When ready to serve, turn out onto a
plate and cut into slices. Serve with fresh
fruit and cream, if desired.

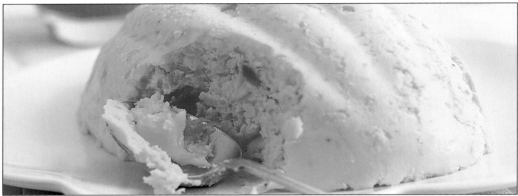

STICKY BLACK RICE PUDDING

Preparation time: 10 minutes + overnight
   soaking + 15 minutes standing
Total cooking time: 30 minutes
Serves 6–8

2 cups (400 g/13 oz) black rice
3 fresh pandan leaves (see Notes)
2 cups (500 ml/16 fl oz) coconut milk
80 g (2¾ oz) palm sugar, grated
¼ cup (55 g/2 oz) caster (superfine) sugar
coconut cream, to serve
mango or papaya cubes, to serve

1 Put the rice in a large glass or ceramic
bowl and cover with water. Leave to soak
for at least 8 hours, or preferably
overnight. Drain, then put in a saucepan
with 1 litre (32 fl oz) water and slowly
bring to the boil. Cook at a low boil,
stirring frequently, for 20 minutes, or
until tender. Drain.
2 Pull your fingers through the pandan
leaves to shred them and then tie them in
a knot. Pour the coconut milk into a large
saucepan and heat until almost boiling.
Add the palm sugar, caster sugar and
pandan leaves and stir until the sugars
have dissolved.
3 Add the cooked rice to the pan of
coconut milk and cook, stirring, for 8
minutes without boiling. Turn off the heat,
cover and leave for 15 minutes to absorb
the flavours. Remove the pandan leaves.
4 Spoon into bowls and serve warm with
coconut cream and fresh mango.

NOTES: The long flat leaves of the
pandanus are crushed and used as a
flavouring in many Thai sweets. They are
sold fresh, frozen, dried or as a flavouring
essence or paste.
   Don't refrigerate the black rice pudding
or it will dry out and harden.

VARIATION: Any fresh tropical fruit, such
as banana, pineapple or lychee is also
delicious served with this dish.

EMPRESS RICE

Preparation time: 45 minutes +
   refrigeration
Total cooking time: 1 hour
Serves 6–8

⅔ cup (140 g/4½ oz) short-grain rice
2 cups (500 ml/16 fl oz) milk
½ teaspoon natural vanilla extract
¼ cup (60 g/2 oz) caster (superfine) sugar
30 g (1 oz) unsalted butter
½ cup (125 g/4 oz) chopped mixed glacé
   fruit
2 tablespoons Kirsch (see Note)

Custard
1 tablespoon gelatine
4 egg yolks
¼ cup (60 g/2 oz) caster (superfine) sugar
1 teaspoon cornflour (cornstarch)
1 cup (250 ml/8 fl oz) milk
300 ml (9½ fl oz) cream

Apricot sauce
⅔ cup (125 g/4 oz) dried apricots
2 tablespoons Kirsch
1–2 tablespoons caster (superfine) sugar

1 Lightly grease a 2 litre (64 fl oz)
decorative mould with oil. Put the rice in a
saucepan with 2 cups (500 ml/16 fl oz)
cold water. Bring slowly to the boil and
cook for 2 minutes, then drain. Return the
rice to the pan with the milk and vanilla
extract. Cook, stirring frequently, over low
heat for 25 minutes, or until the rice is
tender and the milk has been absorbed.
Stir in the sugar and butter while hot.
Cover and cool completely. Put the glacé
fruit in a bowl, add the Kirsch and soak.

2 To make the custard, put 2 tablespoons
water in a small heatproof bowl, sprinkle
with gelatine and leave over hot water
until dissolved. Put the egg yolks, caster
sugar and cornflour in a large bowl and
whisk for 3 minutes, or until the mixture
is pale and thickened. In a pan, heat the
milk to scalding point. Pour the milk,
whisking continuously, into the egg
mixture, then return to the pan. Whisk
over low heat until thickened to a thin
custard that coats the back of a spoon
(take care not to overheat and curdle).
Stir in the dissolved gelatine. Cover and
cool a little.
3 Combine the cooled rice and cooled
custard. Beat the cream until firm peaks
form. Gently fold the glacé fruit and
cream into the rice custard. Spoon into
the mould and flatten the surface. Cover
and refrigerate for several hours until
firm.
4 While the rice pudding is cooling, make
the apricot sauce. Put the apricots in a
small saucepan and cover with water.
Leave to soak for 30 minutes, then cook
gently for 10 minutes, or until softened.
Drain, reserving the liquid. Cool, then
purée the apricots in a food processor,
adding enough cooking liquid to reach
sauce consistency. Add Kirsch and sugar
to taste.
5 Unmould the rice pudding—the easiest
way to do this is to briefly dip the mould in
hot water, wipe it dry and then invert onto
a serving plate. Serve with some of the
apricot sauce.

NOTE: Kirsch is a clear brandy distilled
from fermented black cherries. The
brandy has a bitter almond flavour and is
often used in desserts.

COCONUT CREPES WITH LIQUEUR FIGS

Preparation time: 30 minutes
Total cooking time: 50 minutes
Serves 4

Liqueur figs
375 g (12 oz) dried figs
1 tablespoon soft brown sugar
1 cup (250 ml/8 fl oz) orange juice
¼ cup (60 ml/2 fl oz) brandy
1 bay leaf
3 cloves
1 cinnamon stick

Mascarpone cream
150 g (5 oz) mascarpone
2 tablespoons soft brown sugar
2 tablespoons thick (double) cream

½ cup (60 g/2 oz) plain flour
2 eggs
2 teaspoons oil
¾ cup (185 ml/6 fl oz) milk
1 cup (60 g/2 oz) shredded coconut,
  toasted

1 To make the liqueur figs, place the figs, sugar, orange juice, brandy, bay leaf, cloves and cinnamon stick in a pan. Simmer for 20 minutes, or until the figs are plump and the liquid has reduced by two-thirds.

2 To make the mascarpone cream, gently mix together the mascarpone, sugar and cream.

3 Sift the flour and a pinch of salt into a large bowl and make a well in the centre. Gradually whisk in the combined eggs, oil and milk until just smooth and free of lumps. Mix in the coconut.

4 Heat a small crepe or non-stick frying pan and brush lightly with melted butter. Add ¼ cup (60 ml/2 fl oz) batter to the pan and spread with the back of a spoon. Cook over moderate heat for 1 minute, or until the underside is golden, then turn over and cook the other side. Transfer to a plate and cover with a tea towel while cooking the remaining crepes. Stack the crepes between greaseproof paper to prevent them sticking together.

5 Place a few drained figs in the centre of each crepe. Fold the crepes up and around the figs to form bags and tie with string. Dust lightly with icing sugar and serve with mascarpone cream.

PANFORTE

Preparation time: 20 minutes
Total cooking time: 40 minutes
Makes 1

⅔ cup (100 g/3½ oz) blanched almonds
¾ cup (105 g/3½ oz) roasted, skinned
  hazelnuts
½ cup (95 g/3 oz) candied peel, chopped
½ cup (100 g/3½ oz) chopped candied
  pineapple
¼ cup (30 g/1 oz) cocoa powder
½ cup (60 g/2 oz) plain flour
½ teaspoon ground cinnamon
¼ teaspoon mixed spice
⅓ cup (90 g/3 oz) sugar
⅓ cup (115 g/4 oz) honey
icing sugar, for dusting

1 Line a 20 cm (8 inch) springform tin with baking paper and grease well with butter. Toast the almonds under a hot grill until brown, then leave to cool. Put the nuts in a bowl with the peel, pineapple, cocoa powder, flour and spices and toss them all together. Preheat the oven to slow 150°C (300°F/Gas 2).

2 Put the sugar and honey in a saucepan and melt them together over low heat. Cook the syrup until a little of it dropped into cold water forms a soft ball when moulded between your finger and thumb. The colour will turn from golden to brown.

3 Pour the syrup into the nut mixture and mix well, working fast before it stiffens too much. Spoon straight into the tin, press firmly and smooth the surface. Bake for 35 minutes. Unlike other cakes this will neither firm up nor colour as it cooks at all so you need to time it carefully.

4 Cool in the tin until the cake firms enough to enable you to remove the side of the tin. Peel off the paper, turn the cake over onto another piece of paper and leave to cool completely. Dust the top heavily with icing sugar before serving.

PARFAITS

THESE ARE AMERICAN STYLE PARFAITS WITH LAYERS OF ICE CREAM, FRUIT AND SAUCES MADE TO CLASSIC 'SODA FOUNTAIN' FORMULAE. THE ORIGINAL FRENCH PARFAIT WAS A TYPE OF ICE CREAM MADE WITH EGGS, SUGAR AND CREAM.

VANILLA AND CARAMEL PARFAIT

Heat 90 g (3 oz) unsalted butter in a heavy-based pan. Add ¾ cup (140 g/4½ oz) soft brown sugar and stir over low heat, without boiling, until the sugar is dissolved. Increase the heat and simmer, without boiling, for 3 minutes, or until golden. Remove from the heat and cool slightly. Stir in ⅔ cup (170 ml/5½ fl oz) cream, allow to cool, then whisk until smooth. Layer 500 g (1 lb) vanilla ice cream, halved chocolate-coated malt balls and the caramel sauce into four parfait glasses and top with some more halved malt balls. Serve immediately. Serves 4.

STRAWBERRY AND RASPBERRY PARFAIT

Stir an 85 g (3 oz) packet strawberry-flavoured jelly crystals in 2 cups boiling water until the crystals have dissolved, then refrigerate until set. Process 125 g (4 oz) chopped strawberries in a food processor for 30 seconds. Layer 500 g (1 lb) vanilla ice cream, the jelly, 125 g (4 oz) chopped strawberries, 100 g (3½ oz) raspberries and the strawberry purée in six parfait glasses. Serve immediately. Serves 6.

CARAMEL NUT PARFAIT

Put 100 g (3½ oz) butter, 2 tablespoons golden syrup, ½ cup (95 g/3 oz) soft brown sugar and 1 cup (250 ml/8 fl oz) cream in a pan and stir over low heat until dissolved. Do not boil. Cool slightly. Layer 1 litre of vanilla ice cream and the warm sauce in parfait glasses. Sprinkle with chopped nuts.
Serves 4–6.

SPICED CHERRY BRANDY PARFAIT

Place 3 tablespoons sugar, 2 tablespoons soft brown sugar, 1 teaspoon mixed spice and 3 tablespoons brandy in a pan with 1 cup of water and stir without boiling until all the sugar has dissolved, then bring
to the boil. Add 500 g (1 lb) pitted cherries and reduce the heat, simmer for 10 minutes, remove from the heat and cool. Layer the cherries with 1 litre vanilla ice cream in tall glasses and top with some of the cherry syrup. Serve with brandy snaps.
Serves 6.

CHOCOLATE KAHLUA PARFAIT

Combine 125 g (4 oz) chopped chocolate and vanilla cream biscuits with
2 tablespoons Kahlua in a bowl. Set aside for 5 minutes. Layer 500 g (1 lb) chocolate ice cream, the biscuit mixture, 1 cup (250 ml/8 fl oz) cream, whipped, and 60 g (2 oz) choc-bits, alternately, in four parfait glasses. Finish with whipped cream, sprinkle with choc-bits.
Serves 4.

BANANA SPLIT

Put 200 g (6½ oz) good-quality dark chocolate, ¾ cup (185 ml/6 fl oz) cream and 30 g (1 oz) butter in a pan and stir over low heat until smooth. Cool slightly. Split 4 ripe bananas lengthways, and place one half on each side of a glass dish. Place 3 scoops of ice cream between the bananas and pour the chocolate sauce over the top. Sprinkle chopped nuts over the banana splits.
Serves 4.

FROM LEFT: Vanilla and caramel parfait; Strawberry and raspberry parfait; Spiced cherry brandy parfait; Chocolate Kahlua parfait; Caramel nut parfait; Banana split

CHILDREN'S
FARE

MINI QUICHES LORRAINES

Preparation time: 20 minutes
Total cooking time: 25 minutes
Makes 24

3 sheets ready-rolled shortcrust pastry,
   thawed
60 g (2 oz) Gruyère cheese, grated
30 g (1 oz) butter
2 rashers bacon, finely chopped
1 onion, finely chopped
2 eggs
¾ cup (185 ml/6 fl oz) cream
½ teaspoon ground nutmeg
fresh chives, cut into short strips, to
   garnish

1 Lightly grease two 12-hole round-based
patty tins. Preheat the oven to moderately
hot 190°C (375°F/Gas 5). Using a plain 8
cm (3 inch) cutter, cut rounds of pastry
and fit in the tins. Divide the cheese
evenly among the pastry bases. Cover and
refrigerate while making the filling.
2 Heat the butter in a small pan and cook
the bacon and onion for 2–3 minutes, until
tender. Drain on paper towels. When cool,
divide the mixture evenly among the
bases. Whisk the eggs in a bowl with the
cream, nutmeg and freshly ground black
pepper. Pour or spoon carefully over the
bacon mixture.
3 Place 2–3 strips of chive on top of each
quiche to decorate. Bake for 20 minutes,
or until lightly browned and set. Serve hot
or warm.
in advance: These quiches can be cooked
up to 2 days ahead and stored in an
airtight container in the refrigerator. They
can be frozen in single layers for up to
2 months. Reheat in a moderate 180°C
(350°F/Gas 4) oven.

FISH CROQUETTES

Preparation time: 30 minutes +
   1½ hours chilling
Total cooking time: 30 minutes
Makes 16

1½ cups (375 ml/12 fl oz) milk
500 g (1 lb) skinless white fish fillets (eg.
   ling, flake, hake, coley, flathead)
90 g (3 oz) butter
4 spring onions, finely chopped
¾ cup (90 g/3 oz) plain flour
½ teaspoon ground nutmeg
2 teaspoons grated lemon rind
1 tablespoon lemon juice
4 tablespoons chopped fresh parsley
½ cup (60 g/2 oz) plain flour, for dusting
2 eggs, lightly beaten
1½ cups (150 g/5 oz) dry breadcrumbs
oil, for deep-frying

1 Heat the milk in a large frying pan and
add the fish fillets in a single layer. Cook
over low heat for 3–4 minutes, or until the
fish flakes easily when tested with a fork.
Transfer to a plate with a slotted spoon.
Reserve the milk. Flake the fish well with
a fork and set aside.
2 Melt the butter in a large heavy-based
pan, add the spring onion and cook for
2 minutes, or until soft. Add the flour and
nutmeg and stir for 1 minute, or until pale
and foaming. Remove from the heat and
add 1 cup (250 ml/8 fl oz) of the reserved
milk all at once. Whisk until smooth, then
return to the heat. Stir over medium heat
until the mixture thickens. Continue to
stir for 2 minutes over medium heat. The
mixture will be very thick.

3 Add the flaked fish, lemon rind, juice
and parsley. Season, to taste. Transfer to
a bowl, cover and refrigerate for at least
1 hour.
4 Form into 16 croquette shapes 8 x 3 cm
(3 x 11/4 inches). Dust each with plain
flour, then dip in the egg and coat with
breadcrumbs. Refrigerate again for at
least 20 minutes.
5 Fill a deep, heavy-based pan one third
full of oil and heat to 180°C (350°F), or
until a cube of bread dropped into the oil
browns in 15 seconds. Cook a few
croquettes at a time for 2–3 minutes, or
until golden brown. Drain on crumpled
paper towels. Serve hot.

NOTE: You can freeze uncooked
croquettes for up to 1 month.

STUFFED PRAWNS IN CRISPY WON TON

Preparation time: 40 minutes
Total cooking time: 10 minutes
Makes 12

15 won ton wrappers
12 raw large prawns
400 g (13 oz) raw medium prawns, peeled and finely chopped
4 spring onions, very finely chopped
1 egg white
½ cup (60 g/2 oz) cornflour
1 egg, lightly beaten
oil, for deep-frying

1 Using a very sharp knife, thinly shred the won ton wrappers. Peel the large prawns and gently pull out the dark vein from each prawn back, starting at the head end. Cut an incision along the inside of each prawn, to form a pocket.
2 Combine the chopped prawns and spring onion in a bowl and mix well. Add the egg white, 3 teaspoons of the cornflour, and salt and pepper, to taste, and mix together well with your fingertips.
3 Using a flat-bladed knife, spread about 1 tablespoon of the prawn mixture along each large prawn, pressing as much mixture as possible into the pocket. With wet hands, press any remaining mixture around the prawn. Toss each prawn in the remaining cornflour and shake off the excess. Dip in the egg, then loosely sprinkle with won ton shreds, pressing very firmly so they stick.
4 Fill a deep, heavy-based pan or wok one third full of oil and heat to 180°C (350°F), or until a cube of bread dropped into the oil browns in 15 seconds. Cook the prawns in batches for 4 minutes, or until golden brown all over. You may need to turn them with tongs or a long-handled slotted metal spoon. Drain on crumpled paper towels and serve immediately.

BAKED PASTA AND MINCE

Preparation time: 20 minutes
Total cooking time: 2 hours
Serves 8

2 tablespoons olive oil
1 large onion, chopped
1 kg (2 lb) beef mince
¼ cup (60 ml/2 fl oz) red wine
700 ml (23 fl oz) chunky tomato pasta sauce
2 chicken stock cubes, crumbled
2 tablespoons finely chopped fresh parsley
500 g (1 lb) bucatini
2 egg whites, lightly beaten
2 tablespoons dry breadcrumbs

Cheese sauce
50 g (1¾ oz) butter
2 tablespoons plain flour
2½ cups (600 ml/20 fl oz) milk
2 egg yolks, lightly beaten
1 cup (125 g/4 oz) grated Cheddar cheese

1 Heat the oil in a heavy-based pan. Add the onion and cook over medium heat for 2 minutes, or until soft. Add the mince and stir over high heat until well browned and almost all the liquid has evaporated.
2 Add the wine, sauce and stock cubes and bring to the boil. Reduce to a simmer and cook, covered, for 1 hour, stirring occasionally. Remove from the heat. Add the parsley and allow to cool.
3 To make the cheese sauce, heat the butter in a medium pan over low heat, add the flour and stir for 1 minute, or until golden and smooth. Remove from the heat and gradually stir in the milk. Return to the heat and stir constantly over medium heat for 5 minutes, or until the sauce boils and begins to thicken. Simmer for another minute. Remove from the heat, allow to cool slightly and stir in the egg yolks and cheese.
4 Preheat the oven to moderate 180°C (350°F/Gas 4). Cook the bucatini in a large pan of rapidly boiling salted water until al dente. Drain, rinse under cold water and drain thoroughly, then mix with the egg whites. Place half the bucatini over the base of a lightly oiled, deep ovenproof dish. Cover with the mince mixture.
5 Combine the remaining bucatini with the cheese sauce and spread over the mince. Sprinkle with the dry breadcrumbs. Bake in the oven for 45 minutes, or until the top is lightly golden.

SPAGHETTI CARBONARA
(SPAGHETTI WITH CREAMY EGG AND BACON SAUCE)

Preparation time: 10 minutes
Total cooking time: 20 minutes
Serves 6

500 g (1 lb) spaghetti
8 bacon rashers
4 eggs
½ cup (50 g/1¾ oz) freshly grated
    Parmesan
1¼ cups (315 ml/10 fl oz) cream

1 Cook the spaghetti in a large pan of rapidly boiling salted water until al dente. Drain and return to the pan.
2 While the pasta is cooking, discard the bacon rind and cut the bacon into thin strips. Cook in a heavy-based pan over medium heat until crisp. Remove and drain on paper towels.
3 Beat the eggs, Parmesan and cream in a bowl until well combined. Add the bacon and pour the sauce over the warm pasta. Toss gently until pasta is well coated.
4 Return the pan to the heat and cook over very low heat for ½–1 minute, or until slightly thickened. Serve seasoned with freshly ground pepper. Garnish with herb sprigs if you wish.

PRAWN FRITTERS

Preparation time: 20 minutes
Total cooking time: 10 minutes
Makes about 30

⅔ cup (85 g/3 oz) plain flour
⅓ cup (40 g/1¼ oz) self-raising flour
2 spring onions, chopped
2 tablespoons chopped fresh flat-leaf
    parsley
pinch of cayenne pepper
¾ cup (185 ml/6 fl oz) soda water
125 g (4 oz) small cooked prawns, peeled
    and chopped
olive oil, for deep-frying

1 Sift the flours into a large bowl. Add the spring onion, parsley, cayenne pepper and some salt and mix well. Make a well in the centre and gradually add the soda water, whisking to form a smooth lump-free batter. Add enough soda water to form a batter that will drop from a spoon. Add the prawns and stir until combined.
2 Fill a deep heavy-based pan one third full of oil and heat to 180°C (350°F), or until a cube of bread dropped into the oil browns in 15 seconds. Drop half tablespoons of the batter into the hot oil in batches and cook for 1–2 minutes, turning, until puffed and evenly browned all over. Remove with a slotted spoon and drain on crumpled paper towels. Serve hot.

HAM AND PINEAPPLE PIZZA WHEELS

Preparation time: 25 minutes
Total cooking time: 20 minutes
Makes 16

2 cups (250 g/8 oz) self-raising flour
40 g (1¼ oz) butter, chopped
½ cup (125 ml/4 fl oz) milk
4 tablespoons tomato paste (tomato
    purée)
2 small onions, finely chopped
4 pineapple slices, finely chopped
200 g (6½ oz) sliced ham, shredded
80 g (2¾ oz) Cheddar, grated
2 tablespoons finely chopped fresh
    parsley

1 Preheat the oven to moderate 180°C (350°F/Gas 4). Brush 2 baking trays with oil. Sift the flour into a bowl, add the butter and rub into the flour with your fingertips until the mixture resembles fine breadcrumbs. Make a well and add almost all the milk. With a flat-bladed knife, mix with a cutting action until the mixture comes together in beads. Gather into a ball and turn onto a lightly floured surface. Divide the dough in half. Roll out each half on baking paper to a 20 x 30 cm (8 x 12 inch) rectangle, about 5 mm (¼ inch) thick. Spread the tomato paste over each rectangle, leaving a 1 cm (½ inch) border.
2 Mix the onion, pineapple, ham, Cheddar and parsley. Spread evenly over the tomato paste, leaving a 2 cm (¾ inch) border. Using the paper as a guide, roll up the dough from the long side.
3 Cut each roll into 8 even slices. Place on the tray and bake for 20 minutes, or until golden. Serve warm.

IN ADVANCE: The wheels can be made in advance and gently reheated.

BASIC SAUSAGE ROLLS

Preparation time: 30 minutes
Total cooking time: 15 minutes
Makes 36

3 sheets ready-rolled puff pastry
2 eggs, lightly beaten
750 g (1½ lb) sausage mince
1 onion, finely chopped
1 clove garlic, crushed
1 cup (80 g/2¾ oz) fresh breadcrumbs
3 tablespoons chopped fresh parsley
3 tablespoons chopped fresh thyme
½ teaspoon each ground sage, nutmeg, black pepper and cloves

1 Preheat the oven to 200°C (400°F/Gas 6). Cut the pastry sheets in half and lightly brush the edges with some of the beaten egg.
2 Mix half the remaining egg with the remaining ingredients in a large bowl, then divide into six even portions. Pipe or spoon the filling down the centre of each piece of pastry, then brush the edges with some of the egg. Fold the pastry over the filling, overlapping the edges and placing the join underneath. Brush the rolls with more egg, then cut each into 6 short pieces.
3 Cut two small slashes on top of each roll and place on lightly greased baking trays and bake for 15 minutes, then reduce the oven temperature to moderate 180°C (350°F/Gas 4) and bake for another 15 minutes, or until puffed and golden.

For a different flavour, select a filling from the recipes below and follow the method outlined for the basic sausage roll.

CURRIED PORK AND VEAL

Soak 3 dried Chinese mushrooms in hot water for 30 minutes, squeeze dry and chop finely. Cook 4 finely chopped spring onions, 1 crushed clove garlic, 1 finely chopped small red chilli and 2–3 teaspoons curry powder in 1 tablespoon oil. Transfer to a bowl and mix with 750 g (1½ lb) pork and veal mince, 1 cup (90 g/3 oz) fresh breadcrumbs, the dried mushrooms, 1 lightly beaten egg, 3 tablespoons chopped coriander and 1 tablespoon each soy and oyster sauce.

SPICY LAMB

Mix 750 g (1½ lb) lamb mince, 1 cup (90 g/ 3 oz) fresh breadcrumbs, 1 small grated onion, 1 tablespoon soy sauce, 2 teaspoons each of grated fresh ginger and soft brown sugar, 1 teaspoon ground coriander, ½ teaspoon each of ground cumin and sambal oelek. Lightly sprinkle the pastry rolls with poppy seeds after glazing and before baking.

SAUCY BEEF

Cook 1 finely chopped onion and 1–2 crushed cloves garlic in 20 g (⅔ oz) butter until the onion is softened. Mix 750 g (1½ lb) lean beef mince, the sautéed onion and garlic, 3 tablespoons finely chopped fresh parsley, 3 tablespoons plain flour, 3 tablespoons tomato sauce, 1 tablespoon each of Worcestershire and soy sauces and 2 teaspoons ground allspice until well combined.

CHUTNEY CHICKEN

Mix 750 g (1½ lb) chicken mince, 4 finely chopped spring onions, 1 cup (80 g/2¾ oz) fresh breadcrumbs, 1 finely grated carrot, 2 tablespoons fruit chutney and 1 tablespoon each of sweet chilli sauce and grated ginger. Sprinkle the pastry with sesame seeds after glazing, before baking.

PENNE WITH CHICKEN AND MUSHROOMS

Preparation time: 30 minutes
Total cooking time: 25 minutes
Serves 4

30 g (1 oz) butter
1 tablespoon olive oil
1 onion, sliced
1 clove garlic, crushed
60 g (2 oz) prosciutto, chopped
250 g (8 oz) chicken thigh fillets, trimmed and sliced
125 g (4 oz) mushrooms, sliced
1 tomato, peeled, halved and sliced
1 tablespoon tomato paste (tomato purée, double concentrate)
½ cup (125 ml/4 fl oz) white wine
1 cup (250 ml/8 fl oz) cream
500 g (1 lb) penne
freshly grated Parmesan, for serving

1 Heat the butter and oil in a large frying pan. Add the onion and garlic and stir over low heat until the onion is tender. Add the prosciutto to the pan and fry until crisp.
2 Add the chicken and cook over medium heat for 3 minutes. Add the mushrooms and cook for another 2 minutes. Add the tomato and tomato paste and stir until combined. Stir in the wine and bring to the boil. Reduce the heat and simmer until the liquid is reduced by half.
3 Stir in the cream and salt and pepper, to taste, and bring to the boil. Reduce the heat and simmer until the sauce begins to thicken.
4 While the sauce is cooking, cook the penne in a large pan of rapidly boiling salted water until al dente. Drain well and return to the pan. Add the sauce to the pasta and toss to combine. Serve immediately, sprinkled with Parmesan.
note: If you prefer, you can use chicken mince in this recipe instead of the sliced chicken thigh fillets.

MINI CORN DOGS

Preparation time: 10 minutes
Total cooking time: 8–10 minutes
Makes 16

8 large frankfurts
8 wooden skewers
cornflour, for dusting
oil, for deep-frying
tomato sauce, for dipping

Batter
1¾ cups (220 g/7 oz) self-raising flour
¼ cup (35 g/1¼ oz) cornmeal
1 egg, lightly beaten
1 tablespoon oil

1 Cut the frankfurts in half crossways. Cut 8 wooden skewers in half and insert one half through each frankfurt, leaving some of the skewer sticking out for a handle. Dust the frankfurts with a little cornflour.
2 To make the batter, sift the flour into a large bowl, stir in the cornmeal and make a well in the centre. Gradually add the combined egg, oil and 1½ cups (375 ml/ 12 fl oz) water, whisking to make a smooth, lump-free batter.
3 Fill a deep heavy-based pan one third full of oil and heat to 180°C (350°F). The oil is ready when a cube of bread dropped into the oil turns golden brown in 15 seconds. Dip the frankfurts into the batter a few at a time; drain off the excess batter. Using tongs, gently lower the frankfurts into the oil. Cook over medium-high heat for 1–2 minutes, or until golden and crisp and heated through. Carefully remove from the oil. Drain on crumpled paper towels and keep warm. Repeat with the remaining frankfurts. Serve with tomato sauce.

NOTE: You can add a teaspoon of chopped fresh chilli or a pinch of chilli powder to the batter.

BACON AND MUSHROOM CREAM BITES

Preparation time: 15 minutes
Total cooking time: 45 minutes
Makes 18

1 egg yolk, lightly beaten
2 sheets ready-rolled shortcrust pastry
2 tablespoons oil
375 g (12 oz) mushrooms, finely chopped
4 bacon rashers, finely chopped
4 spring onions, finely chopped
15 g (½ oz) fresh parsley, finely chopped
250 g (8 oz) cream cheese, softened
4 eggs

1 Preheat the oven to hot 210°C (415°F/Gas 6–7). Brush a shallow 23 cm (9 inch) square cake tin with melted butter or oil.
2 Brush egg yolk over one sheet of pastry. Place the other sheet over the top and gently press together. Trim the edges to fit the tin. Prick the pastry evenly with a fork and bake for 15 minutes, or until golden brown. Reduce the oven to moderate 180°C (350°F/Gas 4).
3 Heat the oil in a heavy-based pan. Add the mushrooms and stir over medium heat for 5 minutes, or until well browned. Remove from the heat and stir in the bacon, spring onion and parsley. Season with salt and pepper, to taste, and allow to cool.
4 Using electric beaters, beat the cream cheese and eggs in a small bowl for 5 minutes. Add the cooled mushrooms and stir to combine. Pour the mixture onto the cooked pastry base. Bake for 25 minutes, or until firm and lightly browned. Cool in the tin. Cut into triangles when cool.

NOTE: These bites are best eaten on the day they are made.

FISH AND CHIPS

Preparation time: 25 minutes + soaking
Total cooking time: 25 minutes
Serves 4

1¼ cups (155 g/5 oz) plain flour
1½ cups (375 ml/12 fl oz) beer
4 floury potatoes (desiree, spunta or russet)
oil, for deep-frying
4 firm white fish fillets (eg. bream, cod, coley, flake, flathead, pollack, snapper)
cornflour, for coating
lemon wedges, for serving

1 Sift the flour into a large bowl and make a well. Gradually add the beer, whisking to make a smooth lump-free batter. Cover and set aside.
2 Peel the potatoes and cut into chips 1 cm (¾ inch) thick. Soak for 10 minutes in cold water. Drain and pat dry. Fill a deep heavy-based pan one third full of oil and heat to 160°C (315°F), or until a cube of bread browns in 30 seconds. Cook batches of chips for 4–5 minutes, or until pale golden. Remove with tongs or a slotted spoon. Drain on crumpled paper towels.
3 Just before serving, reheat the oil to moderate 180°C (350°F), or until a cube of bread browns in 15 seconds. Cook the chips again, in batches, until crisp and golden. Drain on crumpled paper towels. Keep hot in the oven. Serve with the fish.
4 Pat the fish dry with paper towels. Dust with cornflour, dip into the batter and drain off excess. Deep-fry in batches for 5–7 minutes, or until cooked. Turn with tongs if necessary. Drain on crumpled paper towels. Serve with lemon wedges.

CHICKEN STRIPS WITH SWEET AND SOUR SAUCE

Preparation time: 30 minutes + chilling
Total cooking time: 30 minutes
Makes 35–40

½ cup (60 g/2 oz) plain flour
1 tablespoon chicken seasoning salt
4 chicken breast fillets, cut into 2 cm (¾ inch) wide strips
2 eggs
1½ cups (150 g/5 oz) dry breadcrumbs
oil, for shallow-frying

Sweet and sour sauce
1 cup (250 ml/8 fl oz) pineapple juice
3 tablespoons white wine vinegar
2 teaspoons soy sauce
2 tablespoons soft brown sugar
2 tablespoons tomato sauce
1 tablespoon cornflour

1 Combine the flour and seasoning in a plastic bag and toss with the chicken strips to coat; remove and shake off excess.
2 Beat the eggs lightly in a shallow bowl, and put the breadcrumbs in a plastic bag.
3 Working with a few chicken strips at a time, dip into the beaten egg, then toss in the breadcrumbs. Transfer to a baking tray covered with baking paper and refrigerate for about 30 minutes.
4 Heat 3 cm (1¼ inches) oil in a large frying pan to 180°C (350°F/Gas 4), or until a cube of bread dropped into the oil turns golden brown in 15 seconds. Fry the strips in batches for 3–5 minutes, or until golden brown. Drain on crumpled paper towels. Serve with the sauce.
5 For the sauce, combine the juice, vinegar, soy sauce, sugar and tomato sauce in a small pan. Stir over low heat until the sugar has dissolved. Blend the cornflour with 1 tablespoon water, add to the pan and stir constantly, until the mixture boils and thickens. Reduce the heat and simmer for 2 minutes.

HAM AND MUSHROOM CROQUETTES

Preparation time: 35 minutes + cooling + chilling
Total cooking time: 20 minutes
Makes 36

90 g (3 oz) butter
1 small onion, finely chopped
110 g (3½ oz) cap mushrooms, finely chopped
¾ cup (90 g/3 oz) plain flour
1 cup (250 ml/8 fl oz) milk
¾ cup (185 ml/6 fl oz) chicken stock
110 g (3½ oz) ham, finely chopped
½ cup (60 g/2 oz) plain flour, extra
2 eggs, lightly beaten
½ cup (50 g/1¾ oz) dry breadcrumbs
olive oil, for deep-frying

1 Melt the butter in a pan over low heat and cook the onion for 5 minutes, or until translucent. Add the mushrooms and cook, stirring occasionally, over low heat for 5 minutes. Add the flour and stir over medium–low heat for 1 minute, or until the mixture is dry and crumbly and begins to change colour.
2 Remove the pan from the heat and gradually stir in the milk and stock. Return to the heat, stirring constantly until the mixture boils and becomes very thick. Stir in the ham and some black pepper, then transfer to a bowl to cool for about 2 hours.

3 When completely cool, roll tablespoons of the mixture into croquette shapes. Place the extra flour, beaten eggs and breadcrumbs in three shallow bowls. Toss the croquettes in the flour, then in the eggs, allowing the excess to drip away, then toss in the breadcrumbs. Place on a baking tray covered with paper and refrigerate for about 30 minutes.
4 Fill a deep heavy-based pan one third full of oil and heat to 180°C (350°F), or until a cube of bread dropped into the oil browns in 15 seconds. Deep-fry the croquettes, in batches, for about 3 minutes each batch, until they are browned all over and heated through. Drain each batch on crumpled paper towels. Serve the croquettes warm or hot.

SPAGHETTI BOLOGNESE

Preparation time: 20 minutes
Total cooking time: 1 hour 40 minutes
Serves 4–6

2 tablespoons olive oil
2 cloves garlic, crushed
1 large onion, chopped
1 carrot, chopped
1 celery stick, chopped
500 g (1 lb) beef mince
2 cups (500 ml/16 fl oz) beef stock
1½ cups (375 ml/12 fl oz) red wine
2 x 425 g (14 oz) cans crushed tomatoes
1 teaspoon sugar
¼ cup (7 g/¼ oz) fresh parsley, chopped
500 g (1 lb) spaghetti
freshly grated Parmesan, for serving

1 Heat the olive oil in a large deep pan. Add the garlic, onion, carrot and celery and stir for 5 minutes over low heat until the vegetables are golden.
2 Increase the heat, add the mince and brown well, stirring and breaking up any lumps with a fork as it cooks. Add the stock, wine, tomato, sugar and parsley.
3 Bring the mixture to the boil, reduce the heat and simmer for 1½ hours, stirring occasionally. Season, to taste.
4 While the sauce is cooking and shortly before serving, cook the pasta in a large pan of rapidly boiling salted water until al dente. Drain and then divide among serving bowls. Serve the sauce over the top of the pasta and sprinkle with the freshly grated Parmesan.

CORN FRITTERS

Preparation time: 20 minutes
Total cooking time: 20 minutes
Serves 4–6

1¼ cups (155 g/5 oz) plain flour
1½ teaspoons baking powder
½ teaspoon ground coriander
¼ teaspoon ground cumin
130 g (4¼ oz) canned corn kernels, well-drained
130 g (4¼ oz) canned creamed-style corn
½ cup (125 ml/4 fl oz) milk
2 eggs, lightly beaten
2 tablespoons chopped fresh chives
salt and pepper
½ cup (125 ml/4 fl oz) olive oil

Dipping sauce
1 tablespoon brown vinegar
3 teaspoons soft brown sugar
1 teaspoon sambal oelek or chilli sauce
1 tablespoon chopped fresh chives
½ teaspoon soy sauce

1 Sift the flour, baking powder, coriander and cumin into a bowl; make a well in the centre. Add the corn kernels, creamed corn, milk, eggs, chives, salt and pepper. Stir until combined.
2 Heat the oil in a large non-stick pan. Lower heaped tablespoonsful of the mixture into the pan about 2 cm (¾ inch) apart, flatten slightly. Cook over medium-high heat 2 minutes or until underside is golden. Turn over, cook other side. Remove and drain on paper towels; repeat with the remaining mixture. Serve with dipping sauce.
3 To make Dipping Sauce: Heat vinegar, sugar, sambal oelek, chives and soy in small pan for 1–2 minutes until sugar is dissolved.

MACARONI CHEESE

Preparation time: 20 minutes
Total cooking time: 35 minutes
Serves 4

2 cups (500 ml/16 fl oz) milk
1 cup (250 ml/8 fl oz) cream
1 bay leaf
1 whole clove
½ cinnamon stick
60 g (2 oz) butter
2 tablespoons plain flour
2 cups (250 g/8 oz) freshly grated Cheddar cheese
½ cup (50 g/1¾ oz) freshly grated Parmesan
375 g (12 oz) elbow macaroni
1 cup (80 g/2¾ oz) fresh breadcrumbs
2 rashers rindless bacon, chopped and fried until crisp

1 Preheat the oven to moderate 180°C (350°F/Gas 4). Pour the milk and cream into a medium pan with the bay leaf, clove and cinnamon stick. Bring to the boil, then remove from the heat and set aside for 10 minutes. Strain into a jug; remove and discard the flavourings.
2 Melt the butter in a medium pan over low heat. Add the flour and stir for 1 minute. Remove from the heat and gradually add the milk and cream mixture, stirring until smooth. Return to the heat and stir constantly until the sauce boils and thickens. Simmer for 2 minutes, then remove from the heat and add half the Cheddar cheese, half the Parmesan and salt and pepper, to taste. Set aside.
3 Cook the macaroni in a large pan of rapidly boiling salted water until al dente. Drain and return to the pan. Add the sauce and mix well. Spoon into a deep casserole dish. Sprinkle with combined breadcrumbs, bacon and remaining cheeses. Bake for 15–20 minutes, or until golden. Serve.

FISH BURGERS AND WEDGES

Preparation time: 30 minutes + 1 hour
  chilling
Total cooking time: 25 minutes
Serves 4

500 g (1 lb) skinless white fish fillets (eg.
  flake, ling, redfish, warehou)
2 tablespoons finely chopped fresh
  parsley
2 tablespoons finely chopped fresh dill
2 tablespoons lemon juice
1 tablespoon drained bottled capers,
  chopped
2 bottled gherkins, finely chopped
350 g (11 oz) potatoes, cooked and
  mashed
plain flour, for dusting
1 tablespoon olive oil
4 hamburger buns, split into halves
lettuce leaves
2 Roma (egg) tomatoes, sliced
tartare sauce

Crunchy potato wedges
6 potatoes, unpeeled, cut into wedges
1 tablespoon oil
½ teaspoon chicken or vegetable stock
  powder
¼ cup (25 g/¾ oz) dry breadcrumbs
2 teaspoons chopped fresh chives
1 teaspoon celery salt
¼ teaspoon garlic powder
½ teaspoon chopped fresh rosemany

1 Place the fish in a frying pan and just
cover with water. Slowly heat, making
sure the water doesn't boil. Cover and
cook over low heat until just cooked.
Drain the fish on paper towels, transfer to
a bowl and flake with a fork, removing
any bones. Add the parsley, dill, juice,
capers, gherkins and potato, season with
cracked pepper and salt and mix well.
Shape into 4 patties. Dust with flour and
refrigerate on a plate for 1 hour.
2 Heat the oil in a large non-stick
frying pan, add the patties and cook for
5–6 minutes on each side, or until well
browned and cooked through.
3 Grill the buns and butter if you wish. On
each base, put some lettuce, tomato, a
patty and some tartare sauce. Top and
serve.
4 For the wedges, preheat the oven to
moderately hot 200°C (400°F/Gas 6). Pat
the potato dry with paper towels and toss
with the oil. Combine the remaining
wedge ingredients and toss with the
wedges. Spread on greased baking trays
and bake for 40 minutes, or until golden.

EMPANADAS

Preparation time: 45 minutes + cooling
Total cooking time: 1 hour
Makes 48

oil, for frying
1 small onion, finely chopped
1 small green pepper (capsicum), finely
  chopped
1 clove garlic, crushed
350 g (11 oz) beef mince
200 g (6½ oz) pork mince
¾ cup (185 ml/6 fl oz) tomato passata, or
  chopped canned tomatoes
110 g (3¾ oz) pitted green olives, chopped
8 frozen sheets shortcrust pastry,
  thawed

1 Heat a little oil in a frying pan and cook
the onion over low heat for 3 minutes, or
until soft. Add the green pepper, cook for
3 minutes, then add the garlic and cook
for another minute. Add the minces and
cook, breaking up any lumps with a fork,
until browned.
2 Stir in the tomato passata and green
olives and bring to the boil. Reduce the
heat and simmer for 10 minutes, stirring
occasionally, or until most of the liquid
has evaporated. Remove from the heat,
season to taste, and allow to cool
completely.
3 Cut six 8 cm (3 inch) rounds from each
sheet of pastry. Place 2 heaped teaspoons
of the filling onto each round and fold
over to enclose. Press the edges down
with a fork to seal.
4 Heat 2 cm (¾ inch) of oil in a deep frying
pan to 180°C (350°F). The oil is ready
when a cube of bread dropped into the oil
turns golden brown in 15 seconds. Cook
the empanadas in batches until crisp and
golden, then drain well on crumpled
paper towels. Alternatively, bake in a
moderately hot 200°C (400°F/Gas 6) oven
for 20–25 minutes, or until puffed and
golden.

MACARONI EGGPLANT (AUBERGINE) CAKE

Preparation time: 1 hour
Total cooking time: 1 hour
Serves 6

¾ cup (115 g/4 oz) macaroni
2–3 eggplant (aubergine), sliced thinly
   lengthways
1 onion, chopped
1 clove garlic, crushed
500 g (1 lb) pork, beef or chicken mince
425 g (14 oz) can crushed tomatoes
2 tablespoons tomato paste (tomato
   purée, double concentrate)
½ cup (80 g/2¾ oz) frozen peas
1 cup (150 g/5 oz) freshly grated
   mozzarella cheese
½ cup (60 g/2 oz) freshly grated Cheddar
   cheese
1 egg, beaten
½ cup (50 g/1¾ oz) freshly grated
   Parmesan

1 Lightly brush a deep 23 cm (9 inch)
round springform tin with oil or butter
and line it with baking paper. Cook the
macaroni in a large pan of rapidly boiling
salted water until al dente. Drain and set
aside.
2 Arrange the eggplant on trays, sprinkle
with salt and allow to stand for 20 minutes.
Rinse well and pat dry with paper towels.
Heat 2 tablespoons of oil in a frying pan,
add the eggplant and cook, in batches, in
a single layer, until golden on each side.
Add more oil as required. Drain on paper
towels.

3 Add the onion and garlic to the same
pan and stir over low heat until the onion
is tender. Add the mince and brown,
breaking up any lumps with a spoon or
fork as it cooks. Add the tomato, tomato
paste and salt and pepper, to taste, and
stir well. Bring to the boil. Reduce the
heat and simmer for 15–20 minutes. Set
aside.
4 In a bowl, mix together the peas,
macaroni, mozzarella and Cheddar
cheeses, egg and half the Parmesan. Set
aside.
5 Preheat the oven to moderate 180°C
(350°F/Gas 4). Place a slice of eggplant in
the centre on the base of the prepared tin.
Arrange three-quarters of remaining
eggplant in an overlapping pattern to
completely cover the base and sides of
the tin. Sprinkle with half the remaining
Parmesan.
6 Combine the mince mixture with the
macaroni mixture. Carefully spoon the
filling into the eggplant case, packing
down well. Arrange the remaining
eggplant slices, overlapping, over the
filling. Sprinkle with the remaining
Parmesan.
7 Bake, uncovered, for 25–30 minutes, or
until golden. Allow to rest for 5 minutes
before unmoulding onto a serving plate.
Serve with salad, if desired.

NOTE: You can omit the mince and add
chopped cooked Italian sausage and
chopped cooked chicken to the tomato
mixture.

CRUMBED CALAMARI WITH CHILLI PLUM SAUCE

Preparation time: 25 minutes
Total cooking time: 12 minutes
Serves 4

500 g (1 lb) squid hoods
¼ cup (30 g/1 oz) plain flour, seasoned
1–2 eggs, lightly beaten
3 cups (240 g/7½ oz) fresh white
   breadcrumbs
oil, for deep-frying

Chilli plum sauce
1 teaspoon oil
1 clove garlic, crushed
1 cup (315 g/10 oz) dark plum jam
⅓ cup (80 ml/2¾ fl oz) white vinegar
1–2 tablespoons sweet chilli sauce

1 Pat the squid with paper towels. Remove
the quill and any skin. Cut into 1 cm
(½ inch) rings.
2 Put the flour in a plastic bag, add the
rings and toss. Dip each ring in beaten
egg, drain off excess, then coat in
breadcrumbs. Pat the crumbs lightly onto
the rings and shake off any excess
crumbs.
3 Fill a deep deavy-based pan one third
full of oil and heat to 180°C (350°F), or
until a cube of bread dropped into the oil
turns golden brown in 15 seconds. Cook
batches of rings for 3 minutes, or until
golden. Drain on crumpled paper towels.
Keep warm. Skim crumbs from the
surface of the oil between batches. Serve
hot, with the sauce.
4 For the sauce, heat the oil in a small
pan over low heat and cook the garlic
until softened. Stir in the jam, vinegar and
chilli over medium heat until combined.

PRAWN CUTLETS

Preparation time: 30 minutes +
 15 minutes chilling
Total cooking time: 10 minutes
Serves 4–6

1 kg (2 lb) raw large prawns
4 eggs
2 tablespoons soy sauce
cornflour, for coating
2 cups (200 g/6½ oz) dry breadcrumbs
oil, for deep-frying
tartare sauce, for serving
lemon wedges, for serving

1 Peel the prawns, leaving the tails intact. Slit them all open down the backs, remove the veins and then gently flatten open with your fingers.
2 Beat the eggs and soy sauce in a small bowl. Coat the prawns in cornflour, shake off the excess, then dip in the egg mixture and finally press in the breadcrumbs. Chill for 15 minutes.
3 Fill a deep, heavy-based pan one third full of oil and heat to 180°C (350°F), or until a cube of bread browns in 15 seconds. Deep-fry the prawns in batches until lightly golden. Drain on crumpled paper towels, then serve with tartare sauce and lemon wedges.

CHICKEN TORTELLINI WITH TOMATO SAUCE

Preparation time: 1 hour + resting of
 dough
Total cooking time: 30 minutes
Serves 4

Pasta
2 cups (250 g/8 oz) plain flour
3 eggs
1 tablespoon olive oil

Filling
20 g (¾ oz) butter
90 g (3 oz) chicken breast fillet, cubed
2 slices pancetta, chopped
½ cup (50 g/1¾ oz) freshly grated
 Parmesan
½ teaspoon nutmeg
1 egg, lightly beaten

Tomato sauce
⅓ cup (80 ml/2¾ fl oz) olive oil
1½ kg (3 lb) very ripe tomatoes, peeled
 and chopped
¼ cup (7 g/¼ oz) chopped fresh oregano
½ cup (50 g/1¾ oz) freshly grated
 Parmesan

100 g (3½ oz) bocconcini, thinly sliced, for
 serving

1 To make the pasta, sift the flour and a pinch of salt into a bowl and make a well in the centre. In a jug, whisk together the eggs, oil and 1 tablespoon of water. Add the egg mixture gradually to the flour, mixing to a firm dough. Gather together into a ball, adding a little extra water if necessary.
2 Knead on a lightly floured surface for 5 minutes, or until the dough is smooth and elastic. Put in a lightly oiled bowl, cover with plastic wrap and set aside for 30 minutes.

3 To make the filling, heat the butter in a frying pan, add the chicken cubes and cook, stirring, until golden brown. Drain and allow to cool slightly. Process the chicken and pancetta in a food processor or mincer until finely chopped. Transfer to a bowl and add the Parmesan, nutmeg, egg and salt and pepper, to taste. Set aside.
4 Roll out the dough very thinly on a lightly floured surface. Using a floured cutter, cut into 5 cm (2 inch) rounds and spoon ½ teaspoon of filling into the centre of each. Brush the edges with a little water. Fold in half to form semi-circles, pressing the edges together. Wrap each around your finger to form a ring and then press the ends of the dough together firmly.
5 To make the tomato sauce, put the oil, tomato and oregano in a frying pan and cook over high heat for 10 minutes. Stir the Parmesan through and set aside.
6 Cook the tortellini in two batches in a large pan of rapidly boiling water for about 6 minutes each batch, or until al dente. Drain and return to the pan. Reheat the tomato sauce, add to the tortellini and toss to combine. Divide the tortellini among individual bowls, top with bocconcini and allow the cheese to melt a little before serving.

CHEESE SOUFFLE OMELETTE

Preparation time: 10 minutes
Total cooking time: 5 minutes
Serves 2–4

5 eggs, separated
2 teaspoons water
2 teaspoons lemon juice
salt and pepper
20 g (²/₃ oz) butter
²/₃ cup (85 g/2¾ oz) coarsely grated
   Cheddar cheese

1 Place the egg yolks, water, juice, salt and pepper in a small bowl. Using electric beaters, beat on high for 2 minutes or until the mixture is pale and creamy.
2 Place the egg whites in a small, dry, bowl. Using electric beaters or a wire whisk, beat the egg whites until firm peaks form. Using a metal spoon, gently fold the egg whites into the yolk mixture. Preheat the grill to high.
3 Place the butter in a deep, non-stick pan and heat over high heat. When the butter is foaming, add the omelette mixture and swirl the pan to spread evenly over the base. Cook over high heat for 1 minute without stirring. Remove from heat and sprinkle with cheese.
4 Place under a hot grill for 2–3 minutes, or until the omelette is puffed and golden. Cut the omelette into serving portions and serve immediately as it may deflate quickly. Sprinkle with chopped fresh herbs, if desired.

NOTE: This is delicious accompanied by grilled or pan-fried mushrooms, or tomatoes which have been halved, sprinkled with cheese and then grilled.

POTATO AND PUMPKIN PANCAKES

Preparation time: 25 minutes
Total cooking time: 25 minutes
Makes 10

250 g (8 oz) potato, cooked and mashed
250 g (8 oz) pumpkin, cooked and mashed
30 g (1 oz) butter
3 spring onions, finely chopped
2 eggs, lightly beaten
¼ cup (30 g/1 oz) plain flour
2 tablespoons self-raising flour
¼ teaspoon ground nutmeg
pinch cayenne pepper
¼ teaspoon salt
30 g (1 oz) butter, extra

1 Place the potato and pumpkin in a food processor and add the butter. Process until smooth. Transfer to a bowl and add the spring onions and eggs.
2 Sift flours, spices and salt into a bowl. Add to the pumpkin mixture and stir well to combine.
3 Heat extra butter in a non-stick frying pan. Cook heaped tablespoons of mixture for 2 minutes. Turn and cook approximately 2–3 minutes or until golden. Drain on paper towels.
4 Repeat process with the remaining mixture. Keep warm in the oven. Serve plain, or with yoghurt or butter.

GNOCCHI CHEESE BAKE

Preparation time: 10 minutes
Total cooking time: 15 minutes
Serves 4

500 g (1 lb) fresh potato gnocchi
30 g (1 oz) butter, chopped
1 tablespoon chopped fresh parsley
100 g (3½ oz) fontina cheese, sliced
100 g (3½ oz) provolone cheese, sliced

1 Preheat the oven to moderately hot 200°C (400°F/Gas 6). Cook the fresh gnocchi, in batches, in a large pan of boiling water for about 2 minutes, or until the gnocchi rise to the surface. Carefully remove from the pan with a slotted spoon and drain well.
2 Put the gnocchi in a lightly greased ovenproof dish. Scatter with the butter and parsley. Lay the fontina and provolone cheeses over the top of the gnocchi. Season with sea salt and cracked black pepper. Bake for 10 minutes, or until the cheese has melted.

PASSIONFRUIT FLUMMERY

Preparation time: 15 minutes + chilling
Total cooking time: Nil
Serves 6

85 g (3 oz) passionfruit jelly crystals
375 g (12 oz) can well-chilled evaporated
   milk
3 passionfruit

1 Stir the jelly crystals into 1 cup (250 ml/
8 fl oz) boiling water until dissolved. Pour
into a shallow metal tray and refrigerate
until the consistency of unbeaten egg
white.
2 Transfer the jelly to a bowl, add the
evaporated milk and beat with electric
beaters, on high, for 5–8 minutes, or until
doubled in volume. Using a large metal
spoon, fold in the pulp from 2
passionfruit.
3 Spoon into six 1 cup (250 ml/8 fl oz)
capacity glasses, or a serving bowl, cover
loosely with plastic wrap and chill for
1 hour, or until set. Top with pulp from the
remaining passionfruit.

NOTE: Different fruit jellies can be used
and decorated with the appropriate fruit.

BANANA FRITTERS WITH CARAMEL SAUCE

Preparation time: 10 minutes
Total cooking time: 15 minutes
Serves 4

Caramel sauce
1¼ cups (230 g/7½ oz) soft brown sugar
½ cup (125 ml/4 fl oz) cream
100 g (3½ oz) unsalted butter, chopped

1 cup (125 g/4 oz) self-raising flour
1 egg, beaten
¾ cup (185 ml/6 fl oz) soda water
oil, for deep-frying
4 bananas, each cut into quarters
ice cream, for serving

1 To make the caramel sauce, combine all
the ingredients in a small pan and stir
until the sugar has dissolved and the
butter has melted. Bring to the boil,
reduce the heat and simmer for 2 minutes.
2 Sift the flour into a bowl. Make a well in
the centre and add the egg and soda
water all at once. Stir until all the liquid is
incorporated and the batter is free of
lumps.
3 Heat the oil in a deep heavy-based pan,
to 180°C (350°F), or until a cube of bread
browns in 15 seconds. Dip the bananas in
batter a few pieces at a time, then drain
off any excess batter. Gently lower the
bananas into the oil and cook for
2 minutes, or until golden, crisp and
warmed through. Carefully remove from
the oil with a slotted spoon. Drain on
paper towels and keep warm. Repeat with
the remaining bananas. Serve the fritters
immediately with ice cream and caramel
sauce.

BAKED SPAGHETTI FRITTATA

Preparation time: 30 minutes
Total cooking time: 35 minutes
Serves 4

30 g (1 oz) butter
125 g (4 oz) mushrooms, sliced
1 green pepper (capsicum), seeded and
   chopped
125 g (4 oz) ham, sliced
½ cup (80 g/2¾ oz) frozen peas
6 eggs
1 cup (250 ml/8 fl oz) cream or milk
100 g (3½ oz) spaghetti, cooked and
   chopped
2 tablespoons chopped fresh parsley
¼ cup (25 g/¾ oz) freshly grated
   Parmesan

1 Preheat the oven to moderate 180°C
(350°F/Gas 4). Lightly brush a 23 cm
(9 inch) flan dish with oil or melted butter.
2 Melt the butter in a frying pan, add the
mushrooms and cook over low heat for
2–3 minutes. Add the pepper and cook for
1 minute. Stir in the ham and peas.
Remove the pan from the heat and allow
the mixture to cool slightly.
3 In a small bowl, whisk the eggs, cream
and salt and pepper, to taste. Stir in the
spaghetti, parsley and mushroom mixture
and pour into the prepared dish. Sprinkle
with Parmesan and bake for 25–30 minutes.

NOTE: Serve with chargrilled vegetables
and leafy salad greens.

WAFFLES WITH HOT CHOCOLATE SAUCE

Preparation time: 20 minutes + standing
Total cooking time: 20–25 minutes
Makes 8 waffles

2 cups (250 g/8 oz) self-raising flour
1 teaspoon bicarbonate of soda
2 teaspoons sugar
2 eggs
90 g (3 oz) unsalted butter, melted
1¾ cups (440 ml/14 fl oz) buttermilk

Chocolate sauce
50 g (1¾ oz) unsalted butter
200 g (6½ oz) good-quality dark
    chocolate, chopped
½ cup (125 ml/4 fl oz) cream
1 tablespoon golden syrup

1 Sift the flour, bicarbonate of soda, sugar and a pinch of salt into a large bowl and make a well in the centre. Whisk the eggs, melted butter and the buttermilk in a jug and gradually pour into the well, whisking until the batter is just smooth. Set aside for 10 minutes. Preheat the waffle iron.
2 To make the chocolate sauce, put the butter, chopped chocolate, cream and golden syrup in a pan and stir over low heat until smooth. Remove from the heat and keep warm.
3 Brush the waffle iron with melted butter. Pour about ½ cup (125 ml/4 fl oz) batter (the amount will vary according to your waffle iron) into the centre and spread almost to the corners of the grid.
4 Cook the waffle for about 2 minutes, or until golden and crisp. Keep the cooked waffles warm while cooking the remaining mixture. Serve with vanilla ice cream and the hot chocolate sauce.

STRIPED FRUIT JELLY

Preparation time: 35 minutes + chilling
Total cooking time: 30 minutes
Serves 6–8

200 g (6½ oz) caster sugar
rind and juice of 2 limes
6 teaspoons gelatine
¼ cup (125 ml/4 fl oz) thick (double)
    cream
1 tablespoon caster sugar, extra
½ cup (125 g/4 oz) natural yoghurt
400 g (13 oz) can pitted cherries, drained
    and syrup reserved

1 Stir the sugar with 1¼ cups (315 ml/10 fl oz) water in a pan over low heat until the sugar dissolves. Bring slowly to the boil. Simmer for 15 minutes, then remove from the heat. You should have 200 ml (6½ fl oz) liquid—tip half into a jug and reserve. Return the pan to the heat, add the lime rind and juice and cook very gently for 5 minutes. Strain into a bowl. Discard the rind. Put 2 tablespoons water in a small bowl, sprinkle 2 teaspoons gelatine over the surface in an even layer and leave to go spongy. Put a large pan filled with about 4 cm (1½ inches) water on to boil. When it boils, remove from the heat and carefully lower the gelatine bowl into the water (it should come halfway up the side of the bowl), then stir until dissolved. Cool slightly, then add to the lime syrup. Rinse a 3 cup (750 ml/24 fl oz) mould. Pour in the lime syrup and chill until set. Don't leave too long or the next layer won't stick.

2 Place 2 tablespoons water in a small bowl, sprinkle on 2 teaspoons gelatine and leave to go spongy. Put the cream and extra sugar in a small pan and heat slowly, stirring until the sugar is dissolved. Add to the gelatine mixture and stir until dissolved. Whisk in the yoghurt. Cover and cool in the refrigerator (be careful not to leave it too long or it will set). Pour carefully onto the lime layer, then refrigerate until set.
3 Place 2 tablespoons of the cherry liquid in a small bowl, sprinkle on 2 teaspoons gelatine, leave to go spongy, then add to the remaining sugar syrup, which should still be warm. Add to this another 150 ml (5 fl oz) cherry juice, stir to dissolve, cover and cool.
4 When the yoghurt layer has set, spoon in the cherries and pour the cherry juice over them. Chill until set. To unmould, gently pull the jelly away from the sides of the mould with wet fingers and invert onto a plate, shaking to loosen.

CHOCOLATE SHORTBREADS

Preparation time: 25 minutes
Total cooking time: 10 minutes
Serves 6

1½ cups (185 g/6 oz) plain flour
⅓ cup (40 g/1¼ oz) cocoa powder
¾ cup (90 g/3 oz) icing sugar
225 g (7¼ oz) chilled unsalted butter,
  chopped
2 egg yolks
1 teaspoon vanilla essence
1 cup (250 ml/8 fl oz) cream, whipped
250 g (8 oz) strawberries, quartered

Berry sauce
250 g (8 oz) fresh strawberries, or frozen,
  thawed
1 tablespoon caster sugar

1 Preheat the oven to hot 210°C
(415°F/Gas 6–7). Line two baking trays
with baking paper. Sift the flour, cocoa
and icing sugar into a large bowl. Rub in
the butter, using just your fingertips, until
the mixture resembles breadcrumbs. Add
the yolks and vanilla and mix with a knife
until the mixture comes together. Turn
onto a lightly floured surface and gather
together into a ball.
2 Roll the pastry between two layers of
baking paper to 5 mm (¼ inch) thick.
Using a 7 cm (2¾ inch) fluted round
cutter, cut 18 rounds from the pastry.
Place on the prepared trays and bake for
8 minutes, or until cooked through.
Transfer to a wire rack to cool.
3 Place a biscuit on a serving plate, top
with a little cream and some
strawberries. Top with a second biscuit,
cream and strawberries, then a third
biscuit. Repeat to make another five
stacks. Dust each with a little sifted cocoa
and icing sugar. For the sauce, process
the strawberries and sugar until smooth
and stir in 1–2 tablespoons water, until
pourable. Serve with the shortbreads.

RASPBERRY SWIRL CHEESECAKE

Preparation time: 40 minutes + chilling
Total cooking time: Nil
Serves 8–10

250 g (8 oz) plain sweet biscuits
90 g (3 oz) unsalted butter, melted

Filling
2 tablespoons gelatine
500 g (1 lb) light cream cheese, softened
⅓ cup (80 ml/2¾ fl oz) lemon juice
½ cup (125 g/4 oz) caster sugar
1¼ cups (315 ml/10 fl oz) cream, whipped
250 g (8 oz) frozen raspberries
2 tablespoons caster sugar, extra

1 Lightly grease a 23 cm (9 inch) diameter
springform tin and line the base with
baking paper. Finely crush the biscuits in
a food processor, then mix in the butter.
Spoon into the tin, press firmly over the
base and up the side and refrigerate for
20 minutes, or until firm.
2 Put ¼ cup (60 ml/2 fl oz) water in a
small heatproof bowl, sprinkle evenly
with the gelatine and leave to go spongy.
Bring a large pan filled with about 4 cm
(1½ inches) water to the boil, remove from
the heat, carefully lower the gelatine bowl
into the water (it should come halfway up
the side of the bowl), then stir until
dissolved. Allow to cool.
3 Using electric beaters, beat the cream
cheese until creamy, add the juice and
sugar and beat until smooth. Gently fold
in the whipped cream and half the gelatine.
4 Process the raspberries and extra sugar in
a food processor until smooth. Push the
purée through a fine-meshed nylon sieve
to remove any pips. Fold the remaining
gelatine into the raspberry mixture. Place
blobs of cheesecake mixture into the tin
and fill the gaps with the raspberry. Swirl
the two mixtures together, using a
skewer or the point of a knife. Refrigerate
for 4 hours, or until set. Can be decorated
with whipped cream and raspberries.

CHOCOLATE MALLOW FUDGE

Preparation time: 20 minutes +
  overnight refrigeration
Total cooking time: 10 minutes
Makes about 40 pieces

70 g (2¼ oz) butter, chopped
150 g (5 oz) dark chocolate, chopped
250 g (8 oz) white marshmallows
1 teaspoon vanilla essence
50 g (1¾ oz) milk chocolate, melted

1 Line the base and two long sides of an
8 x 26 cm (3 x 10½ inch) bar tin with foil.
2 Put the chopped butter, dark chocolate
and white marshmallows in a saucepan.
Stir constantly over low heat until the
chocolate and marshmallows are melted.
Remove the saucepan from the heat and
stir in the vanilla essence.
3 Pour the mixture into the tin and
refrigerate for several hours, or
overnight, until firm. Remove the fudge
from the tin and remove the foil. Cut into
2 cm (¾ inch) slices, then cut each slice
into 3 pieces. Drizzle the fudge with the
melted milk chocolate, then set aside
until set.

LICORICE ALL-SORT ICE CREAM

Preparation time: 1 hour + freezing
Total cooking time: 30 minutes
Serves 6–8

Coconut meringue
2 egg whites
½ cup (125 g/4 oz) caster sugar
1 cup (90 g/3 oz) desiccated coconut
1 tablespoon cornflour

Raspberry ice cream
200 g (6½ oz) fresh or frozen raspberries
⅔ cup (170 ml/5½ fl oz) milk
⅓ cup (90 g/3 oz) caster sugar
½ cup (125 ml/4 fl oz) cream

Licorice ice cream
60 g (2 oz) soft eating licorice, chopped
1 cup (250 ml/8 fl oz) milk
¾ cup (185 ml/6 fl oz) cream
¼ cup (60 g/2 oz) caster sugar
black food colouring

Mango ice cream
1 large mango
⅔ cup (170 ml/5½ fl oz) milk
⅓ cup (90 g/3 oz) caster sugar
½ cup (125 ml/4 fl oz) cream

1 Preheat the oven to slow 150°C (300°F/Gas 2). Cover two baking trays with baking paper and draw six 25 x 7 cm (10 x 2¾ inch) rectangles. For the coconut meringues, beat the egg whites in a small bowl, with electric beaters, until stiff peaks form. Gradually add the sugar, beating well after each addition until the sugar has dissolved. Stir in the combined coconut and cornflour. Spread evenly over the rectangles. Bake for about 20 minutes, or until just firm to touch. Turn the oven off and leave to cool in the oven with the door slightly ajar.
2 Lightly grease two 25 x 7.5 cm (10 x 3 inch), 4 cm (1½ inches) deep bar tins and line completely with plastic wrap. Trim the edges of all the meringues to fit neatly into the bar tins.

3 To make the raspberry ice cream, purée the raspberries and press through a plastic strainer to remove the seeds (do not use a metal strainer or the raspberries will discolour). You will need ⅔ cup (170 ml/5½ fl oz) of purée. Combine the milk and sugar in a small pan, stir over heat without boiling, until the sugar has dissolved, remove from heat, stir in the cream and allow to cool. When cool, stir in the purée, pour into a shallow metal container and freeze until semi-frozen. Chop the mixture and beat in a large bowl with electric beaters until thick and creamy, then divide between the prepared tins. Top each with a trimmed coconut meringue and freeze.
4 To make the licorice ice cream, stir the licorice, milk and cream together in a small pan over low heat, stirring gently until the licorice is soft and melting. Press through a strainer to remove any remaining lumps. Add the sugar, stir until dissolved, then allow to cool. Tint a deeper colour with food colouring if desired. Pour the mixture into a shallow metal container and freeze until firm. Chop the mixture, beat in a large bowl with electric beaters until thick and creamy, then spread over the meringues and top each with another meringue. Freeze.
5 To make the mango ice cream, purée the mango until smooth. You will need ⅔ cup (180 ml/5½ fl oz) purée. Follow the same method as for the raspberry ice cream. Spread over the meringues, top the mango ice cream with the remaining meringues, cover and freeze until firm. When ready to serve, invert the ice cream onto a cutting board, remove the plastic and cut into slices.

NOTE: The ice creams can also be made in an ice cream machine. You can freeze the three ice creams at once, to save on preparation time.

SHORTBREAD STARS WITH LEMON GLAZE

Preparation time: 20 minutes
Total cooking time: 15 minutes
Makes 35

2 cups (250 g/8 oz) plain flour
2 tablespoons rice flour
200 g (6½ oz) unsalted butter
⅓ cup (40 g/1¼ oz) icing sugar
1 teaspoon finely grated lemon rind
2 tablespoons lemon juice
silver cachous, to decorate

Lemon glaze
1 cup (125 g/4 oz) pure icing sugar
2 tablespoons lemon juice, strained
yellow or orange food colouring

1 Preheat the oven to 180°C (350°F/Gas 4). Line two baking trays with baking paper. Place the flours, butter and sugar in a food processor and process for 30 seconds or until the mixture is fine and crumbly. Add the lemon rind and juice and process for 20 seconds or until the mixture forms a soft dough.
2 Turn out onto a lightly floured surface and knead for 20 seconds or until smooth. Roll the dough out to 7 mm (¼ inch) thickness. Using a 6 cm (2½ inch) star cutter, cut out shapes. Bake for 15 minutes. Transfer to wire rack to cool.
3 To make the lemon glaze, place the icing sugar and lemon juice in a heatproof bowl over a pan of hot water. Stir until smooth. Dip the biscuits face down in glaze and drain any excess. Dip a skewer into food colouring and draw lines into icing before it sets. Decorate with a cachou.

ROCKY ROAD

Preparation time: 20 minutes + several
hours refrigeration
Total cooking time: 5 minutes
Makes about 30 pieces

250 g (8 oz) pink and white
marshmallows, halved
1 cup (160 g/5½ oz) unsalted peanuts,
roughly chopped
½ cup (105 g/3½ oz) glacé cherries, halved
1 cup (60 g/2 oz) shredded coconut
350 g (11 oz) dark chocolate, chopped

1 Line the base and two opposite sides of
a shallow 20 cm (8 inch) square cake tin
with foil.
2 Put all the marshmallows, peanuts,
cherries and coconut into a large bowl
and mix until well combined.
3 Put the chocolate in a heatproof bowl.
Half fill a saucepan with water and bring
to the boil. Remove from the heat and
place the bowl over the pan, making sure
it is not touching the water. Stir
occasionally until the chocolate is melted.
4 Add the chocolate to the marshmallow
mixture and toss until well combined.
Spoon into the cake tin and press evenly
over the base. Refrigerate for several
hours, or until set. Carefully lift out of the
tin, then peel away the foil and cut the
rocky road into small pieces. Store in an
airtight container in the refrigerator.

CUSTARD ROLLS

Preparation time: 35 minutes
Total cooking time: 20 minutes
Makes 18 rolls

1½ cups (375 ml/12 fl oz) milk
½ cup (125 g/4 oz) caster sugar
½ cup (60 g/2 oz) semolina
1 teaspoon grated lemon rind
1 egg, lightly beaten
12 sheets filo pastry
125 g (4 oz) unsalted butter, melted
2 tablespoons icing sugar
½ teaspoon ground cinnamon

1 Put the milk, caster sugar, semolina and
lemon rind in a pan and stir until coming
to the boil. Reduce the heat and simmer
for 3 minutes.
2 Remove from the heat and gradually
whisk in the egg. Pour into a bowl, cover
the surface with plastic wrap and set
aside to cool. Preheat the oven to
moderate 180°C (350°F/Gas 4). Lightly
brush two baking trays with melted
butter.
3 Work with 2 sheets of filo at a time.
Cover the rest with a tea towel. Brush one
with butter, then top with another. Cut
lengthways into three strips. Brush the
edges with melted butter.
4 Spoon about a tablespoon of custard
5 cm (2 inches) in from the short edge of
each pastry strip. Roll the pastry over the
filling, fold the ends in, then roll up.
Repeat with the remaining pastry and
custard. Arrange on the trays 2 cm
(¾ inch) apart. Brush with the remaining
butter. Bake for 12–15 minutes, or until
crisp and golden. Cool on a wire rack.
Dust with a little combined icing sugar
and cinnamon.

BANANA CUSTARD

Preparation time: 15 minutes
Total cooking time: 5 minutes
Serves 4

1 egg, lightly beaten
2 tablespoons custard powder
2 tablespoons sugar
1 cup (250 ml/8 fl oz) milk
½ cup (125 ml/4 fl oz) thick (double)
cream
2 bananas, sliced diagonally

1 Combine the beaten egg, custard
powder, sugar, milk and cream in a
heatproof bowl and whisk until smooth.
2 Pour into a pan and stir constantly over
low heat for 5 minutes, or until the
custard thickens slightly and coats the
back of a wooden spoon.
3 Remove the bowl from the heat and
gently stir in the banana. Serve hot or
cold.

MERINGUE BASKET

Preparation time: 30 minutes
Total cooking time: 2 hours
Serves 6

8 egg whites
450 g (14 oz) pure icing sugar, sifted
1½ cups (375 ml/12 fl oz) cream, whipped
450 g (14 oz) fresh fruit

1 Preheat the oven to very slow 140°C (275°/Gas 1). Place 4 egg whites in a large metal or heatproof bowl, leave for a few minutes to come to room temperature, then beat them until stiff peaks form. Set the bowl over a large pan of simmering water and add half the icing sugar while continuing to beat the mixture. Add it carefully or it will fly all over the place. At this stage it is best to use electric beaters as you must now beat the meringue mixture until it is thick and very solid—beyond stiff peak. Set this batch aside and cover with plastic wrap.
2 Line two baking trays with baking paper and draw four 18 cm (7 inch) circles on the paper. If you use pencil, remember to turn the paper over or it will mark the meringue. Stir the meringue a couple of times, fill a piping bag fitted with a 1 cm (½ inch) nozzle with the meringue, and pipe concentric circles into one of the rings, filling it out to the marked line—this will be the base. Pipe a single circle onto the other 3 drawn circles up to the edge of the marked line—these will form the sides of the basket. Bake for 45–50 minutes, until dry and crisp. Cool on wire racks.

3 Make up another batch of meringue as before. Place the base of the basket back on the baking paper and, using a little of the uncooked meringue mixture, 'glue' the circles one on top of the other onto the base. Fit a 1 cm (½ inch) star-shaped nozzle into the piping bag and, with the remaining mixture, pipe the meringue in strips up the edges of the basket all the way around. Finish the basket by tidying up the edges with piped rosettes of meringue. Bake for 50–60 minutes, until dry and crisp and leave to cool before filling with whipped cream and fresh fruit.

NOTE: This meringue is called meringue cuite or cooked meringue. It is very stable and does not lose its shape when cooked, so it works very well for piping into shapes. It can also be left in a covered bowl in the fridge overnight.

GOLDEN SYRUP DUMPLINGS

Preparation time: 15 minutes
Total cooking time: 30 minutes
Serves 4

1 cup (125 g/4 oz) self-raising flour
40 g (1¼ oz) unsalted butter, chopped
1 egg
1 tablespoon milk

Syrup
1 cup (250 g/8 oz) sugar
40 g (1¼ oz) unsalted butter
2 tablespoons golden syrup
¼ cup (60 ml/2 fl oz) lemon juice

1 Sift the flour and a pinch of salt into a bowl. Rub in the butter until fine and crumbly, and make a well. Using a flat-bladed knife, stir in the combined egg and milk to form a soft dough.
2 Put the syrup ingredients in a pan with 2 cups (500 ml/16 fl oz) water and stir over medium heat until the sugar has dissolved. Bring to the boil, then gently drop dessertspoons of dough into the syrup. Cover and reduce the heat to simmer for 20 minutes, or until a knife inserted into a dumpling comes out clean. Spoon onto plates; drizzle with syrup. Can be served with cream.

APPLE TRIFLE

Preparation time: 35 minutes + chilling
Total cooking time: 20 minutes
Serves 6

Custard
3 egg yolks
2 tablespoons sugar
1 tablespoon cornflour
1½ cups (375 ml/12 fl oz) milk
½ teaspoon vanilla essence

1 kg (2 lb) apples
¾ cup (185 g/6 oz) sugar
½ teaspoon nutmeg
1 teaspoon grated lime or lemon rind
6 sponge finger biscuits
½ cup (125 ml/4 fl oz) cream, whipped
1 tablespoon icing sugar
1 teaspoon ground mixed spice

1 To make the custard, whisk the egg yolks, sugar and cornflour together in a small bowl. Pour the milk into a small pan, bring it almost to the boil, then pour the milk over the egg mixture. Stir well, then pour back into a clean pan and bring to the boil, stirring constantly. Add the vanilla essence and pour the custard into a bowl. Cover the surface with a layer of plastic wrap and leave to cool.
2 Peel and slice the apples and cook in 2 tablespoons water in a large heavy-based pan over low heat for 10–15 minutes, or until the apples are tender. Remove from the heat and mash with a fork. Stir in the sugar, nutmeg and lime or lemon rind.
3 Break the sponge finger biscuits into even-sized pieces and use them to line the base of six glass dessert dishes. Top with a layer of apple and then a layer of custard. Cover and refrigerate for 3–4 hours.
4 Decorate with piped whipped cream. Dust lightly with the combined icing sugar and spice.

RASPBERRY RIPPLE

Preparation time: 30 minutes + freezing
Total cooking time: Nil
Serves 8–10

250 g (8 oz) raspberries
1 litre good-quality vanilla ice cream
1 cup (250 ml/8 fl oz) cream
raspberries, extra, for serving

1 Line the base and sides of a 1.75 litre loaf tin with plastic or foil.
2 Purée the raspberries in a food processor until smooth. Remove the ice cream from the freezer and allow to soften. Beat the cream until soft peaks form. Using a metal spoon, gently fold the cream into the raspberry purée. Pour the mixture into a metal freezer tray and put in the freezer until cool but not frozen solid. Stir occasionally until thick. When half frozen, remove from the freezer and beat well.
3 Spoon blobs of softened vanilla ice cream over the base of the prepared loaf tin. Spoon the raspberry mixture between the vanilla blobs. Using a sharp knife or skewer, swirl the two together, being careful not to dig into the foil.
4 Freeze for 2 hours, or until half frozen, then smooth the edges of the ice cream. Freeze overnight. When ready, it may be served in scoops or removed from the tin and cut in slices. Garnish with extra raspberries.

NURSERY RICE PUDDING

Preparation time: 5 minutes + 10 minutes standing
Total cooking time: 45 minutes
Serves 4–6

⅔ cup (140 g/4½ oz) arborio or short-grain rice
1 litre (32 fl oz) milk
⅓ cup (80 g/2¾ oz) caster (superfine) sugar
1 teaspoon natural vanilla extract
½ cup (125 ml/4 fl oz) cream

1 Rinse the rice in a colander until the water runs clear. Drain well and place in a heavy-based pan with the milk, sugar and vanilla.
2 Bring to the boil while stirring, then reduce the heat to the lowest setting and cook for about 45 minutes, stirring frequently, until the rice is thick and creamy.
3 Remove the pan from the heat and leave to stand for 10 minutes. Stir in the cream. Serve warm with stewed fruit, if desired.

VARIATIONS: Add a cinnamon stick and a strip of lemon zest to the rice in place of vanilla extract. Or add a small sprig of washed lavender to the rice while cooking.

BEFORE YOU START

GOOD COOKING BEGINS WITH SENSIBLE SHOPPING, CORRECT STORAGE OF INGREDIENTS, HANDLING FOOD SAFELY AND ENTHUSIASM FOR THE TASK AT HAND.

WHAT TO COOK

The first decision you will make is 'what to cook?'. To a certain extent this question should be answered by what is in season. Make friends with your greengrocer, butcher and fish-monger and don't be afraid to ask 'what's good today?' Ideally, shop for fresh fruit and vegetables regularly, if not daily. This prevents waste and ensures that you are using the fresh-est possible produce. Of course this is not always possible, so if you need to shop less frequently, try to plan your meals to make the best use of your fresh ingredients. Produce which is in season is better value and quality. Don't try to make asparagus hollandaise for eight dinner guests if there are no good-quality fresh aspara-gus available. Choose another recipe.

RECIPE RULES

The golden commonsense rule of cooking is *always read the recipe before you start*. Don't rush in at step 1 and work your way through blind, only to discover in step 4 that you need a food processor which you don't have. Even more serious, don't start working through a recipe for a dinner party that starts in 2 hours, only to get to the end and discover your fabulous centrepiece needs to be chilled overnight.
Read through the recipe and get together all the ingredients and equipment required. Preheat the oven and prepare the cooking dish.

Prepare as much as you can before-hand, so you are not caught out dur-ing cooking. If you are making a stew, or a slow-cooking dish, you can prob-ably get away with leaving some ingredients to cook by themselves while you prepare others as you go along. However, don't try this if you are making a stir-fry! There is noth-ing more panic-inducing that having a sizzling wok, burning onions and a pile of ingredients that need chop-ping. So, always anticipate what you are going to have to do next.

If the recipe states to use a large bowl, do so, even if at first you're only mixing two ingredients. Later on you might need to add a large quantity of other ingredients.

FOLLOW THE INSTRUCTIONS!

We employ some basic common-sense rules in our recipes... If the recipe doesn't state to 'cover' the pan or dish, then it is to be cooked uncovered. We assume basic prepa-ration of ingredients, such as wash-ing and trimming, and peeling of veg-etables such as potatoes and onions—the recipe will, however, state if these are to be left unpeeled. With well-known vegetables such as leeks, we assume that the reader knows to use the white part of the leek only. But with less familiar ingredients such as lemon grass, we will state 'white part only' where nec-essary. These are best stored in a cool, dark dry pantry. Most will keep for at least 3, if not 6, months.

It is best to buy whole spices and grind them yourself, as needed—they stay fresher than the jars. Make sure bottles of oil are kept out of direct light, as they can become rancid; however, if you keep them in the fridge the oil will thicken and appear cloudy—it will return to normal once it has reached room temperature again. Most bottles of sauces and condiments should be refrigerated once opened: check the label.

Keep potatoes and onions in a cool, dark place—though not without adequate ventilation. Tomatoes, like most fruit, are best kept at room temperature, unless the weather is very hot or they are very ripe.

IN THE FRIDGE
Your fridge is somewhere where important hygiene rules come into play. When you get home with your shopping, unwrap meat or chicken and place on a plate large enough to prevent drips falling on to other food. Cover loosely with foil or plastic wrap.

Bacteria in food is killed by cooking, but take care not to put cooked food back into the fridge touching raw food, which could contaminate it. For example, never let raw meat drip onto cooked dishes. The same goes for when you are preparing food: if you chop raw meat, don't then use the same, unwashed chopping board and knife to prepare salad, or slice the cooked meat.

Store vegetables unwashed (unless they are dried thoroughly, the moisture contributes to deterioration) in the crisper compartment of the fridge.

Many recipes will instruct you to cook something, then 'cool and refrigerate'. When you are doing this, cool the food as quickly as possible before refrigerating. Transfer it from the cooking pan to a wide bowl and stir frequently to release the heat. It is not necessary for the food to be completely cold before it is refrigerated, just cooled. Don't put hot food in the fridge or freezer or it will raise the temperature inside, putting other foods at risk of deterioration.

The remaining contents of half-used cans should be transferred to a bowl or plastic container and refrigerated. Use within 2–3 days or discard.

Thaw frozen food in the fridge, not at room temperature and never in a sink full of water. If you haven't removed food from the freezer in enough time, thaw in the microwave, or have something else.

Never refreeze thawed food. (Of course, you can thaw something, cook it and then freeze again—for instance frozen chicken that you might casserole and then freeze.)

Clean out your fridge, freezer and storecupboard regularly and remember—if you ever have any doubts about the freshness of a product, throw it out.

COOKERY TERMS

MOST TERMS ARE EXPLAINED WITHIN THE RECIPES BUT IF THERE ARE ANY TERMS WHICH AREN'T FAMILIAR YOU SHOULD FIND THEM HERE.

AL DENTE Italian phrase meaning 'to the tooth'. Refers to pasta and sometimes vegetables. Means slightly underdone, so still with some 'bite'.

BAIN-MARIE Also called a 'water bath'. Usually a baking dish half-filled with water so delicate food is protected from direct heat. Often used for custards.

BAKE BLIND To bake an empty pastry case before the filling is added. Ensures the pastry is cooked through and not soggy. Usually lined with baking paper and baking beads or rice or beans so it keeps its shape.

BASTE To spoon or brush cooking juices or other fat over food during cooking.

BOIL To cook liquid, or food in liquid, at 100°C. Large bubbles will break on the surface.

BOUQUET GARNI
A small bunch of herbs used to flavour stocks, soups and stews. Removed before serving.

BROWN To fry food (usually meat) quickly so the outside is cooked and has changed colour.

CREAM To beat butter or butter and sugar together until light and creamy.

CUBE To chop food into even cubes. Usually bite-sized and for use in soups or stews so the size is not overly important.

DICE To chop food into very small even cubes.

DRAIN To remove liquid from food (usually with a colander or sieve). The food is kept and the liquid discarded unless specified.

EN CROUTE Cooked entirely encased in pastry. Usually refers to meat.

ESCALOPE Very thin slice of meat, such as veal or chicken.

FILLET To cut meat from the bones.

FLAMBE To pour liqueur over food (usually in the pan, over heat) and set fire to it.

FOLD To mix one ingredient into another very gently (usually flour or egg whites) with a metal spoon or plastic spatula. The idea is to combine the mixture without losing the air. To fold properly, cut through the centre of the mixture, then run the edge of the spoon or spatula around the outer edge of the bowl, turning the bowl as you go.

GLAZE A substance (often warmed jam or beaten egg) brushed over food to give it shine and colour.

GREASE To lightly coat a tin or dish with oil or melted butter to prevent food sticking.

INFUSE To flavour a liquid by heating it with aromatic ingredients (often spices) and leaving to let the flavour develop.

JULIENNE To cut into uniform thin matchsticks for quick cooking. Often used for stir-fries or in French cuisine.

KNEAD To stretch and fold dough to make it firm and smooth. This stretches the gluten in the flour and gives elasticity. Used for bread making but not for pastry making (over-handling will make pastry tough).

MARINATE To tenderize and flavour food (usually meat) by leaving it in an acidulated seasoned liquid (a marinade).

PARBOIL To partially cook in boiling water before some other form of cooking. Most commonly used for roast potatoes which are parboiled before being added to the roasting meat.

PINCH A small amount of something—as much as can be held between your thumb and forefinger.

POACH To cook food immersed in a gently simmering liquid.

PUNCH DOWN THE DOUGH A term used in bread making. A yeast dough which is left to rise is then punched with one firm blow of the fist, to remove the air from it.

PUREE Food blended or processed to a pulp.

REDUCE To boil or simmer liquid in an uncovered pan so that the liquid evaporates and the mixture becomes thicker and more concentrated in flavour. Most soups and stews are reduced—this should usually be done at a simmer so the flavour of the dish is not impaired by long hard boiling.

ROUX The basic mixture of many sauces—fat (usually melted butter) and flour. Used to thicken. Liquid is added to make a sauce.

RUB IN To mix together flour and butter with your fingertips, usually for pastry. It will resemble fine breadcrumbs.

SCORE To ensure even cooking. Make incisions with a knife (usually into fish or meat) that do not cut all the way through.

SIFT To shake dry ingredients (usually flour) through a sieve to aerate and remove lumps.

SIMMER To cook liquid, or food in liquid, over low heat, below boiling point. The surface of the liquid will be moving with a few small bubbles.

SKIM To remove fat or scum that comes to the surface of a liquid.

SOFT PEAKS A term used when egg whites are whipped. The peak will fold over on itself when the beater is lifted.

STIFF PEAKS A term used when egg whites are whipped. The peak will hold its shape when the beater is lifted.

STIR-FRY To quickly fry (usually in a wok) over high heat while stirring.

STRAIN To remove solids from a liquid by pouring through a sieve. The solids are discarded, unless specified.

WHISK To beat rapidly with a wire whisk, to incorporate air and add volume.

ZEST The coloured skin of citrus fruits. Avoid the bitter white pith below.

INDEX

A

abbacchio, 455
accompaniments, Indian, 758-61
afelia, 634
aioli
    garlic mayonnaise, 745
    roasted red pepper, 321
Algerian eggplant jam, 753
almejas a la marinera, 618
almonds
    almond cream pudding, 867
    almond filo snake, 827
    almond mascarpone crepes with
        summer fruit, 929
    almond orange syrup pudding, 840
    almond pastry, 856
    almond ricotta cream with fresh fruits
        and berries, 145
    almond semifreddo, 915
    almond sesame soya burgers, 518
    almond shortbreads, 796
    almond torte, 830
    broccoli with almonds, 718
    chicken and almond pilaff, 373
    Chinese almond pudding, 918
    Greek shredded pastries with
        almonds, 800
    lemon almond tart, 828
    petits pithiviers, 809
    tamari roasted almonds with spicy
        green beans, 262
    trout with almonds, 327
    vanilla almond biscotti with geranium
        cream, 805
almonds, flaked, toasting, 519
amaretti, 816
amchoor powder, 611
amok trei, 618
anchovies
    anchovy fillets, 646
    anchovy and tomato crostini, 703
    tomato and anchovy toasts, 168
Andalucian asparagus, 726
andhra-style chicken pulao, 382
angelica, 694
aniseed biscuits, 819
antipasto, 122-3
ants climbing trees, 587

apples
    apple cobbler, 912
    apple galettes, 829
    apple mousseline mayonnaise, 137
    apple sauce, 746
    apple, silverbeet and pine nut pie, 834
    apple strudel, 856
    apple trifle, 963
    beignets de fruits, 807
    brandied apple cider, 791
    caramelized apples on
        pumpernickel, 194
    chicken and apple curry, 388
    curried apple and onion mini
        quiche, 175
    deep-dish apple pie, 857
    goat's cheese and apple tarts, 178
    hot apple chutney, 108
    layered potato and apple bake, 727
    poached apples with cloves, mint and
        basil, 903
    potato cakes with apple sauce, 740
    roast pork fillet with apple and mustard
        sauce and glazed apples, 659
    spiced apple and cinnamon vinegar, 757
    Waldorf salad, 82
apricots, 880
    apricot compote, 904
    apricot and onion marinade, 495
    apricot sauce, 940
arancini, 583
arborio rice, 646
arroz con mariscos, 358
arroz con pollo, 412
artichokes
    artichoke dip, 102
    artichoke, egg and sorrel pasta, 238
    artichoke frittata, 217
    artichoke hearts, 646
    artichokes in aromatic vinaigrette, 120
    baked chicken and artichoke
        pancakes, 391
    broad beans with peas and
        artichokes, 740
    Florentine scones with mortadella and
        artichoke, 147
    Jerusalem artichoke purée, 764
    lamb and artichoke fricassee, 426
    polenta sticks with artichokes, feta and
        peppers, 209
    ravioli with peas and artichokes, 246
    Roman-style artichokes, 582
    Russian salad, 84
    Tuscan warm pasta salad, 86
arugula, 647
Asian basil, 589
Asian greens with teriyaki tofu
    dressing, 541
Asian marinade, 504
Asian mushroom risotto, 532
Asian peppered beef, 447

Asian shallots, 589
Asian-style seafood soup, 41
asparagus
    Andalucian asparagus, 726
    asparagus with butter and parmesan,
        733
    asparagus and mint frittata, 552
    asparagus and mushroom salad, 68
    asparagus and prosciutto rolls, 143
    asparagus purée, 765
    asparagus and red capsicum salad, 79
        asparagus spears, 183
    borek of asparagus, 197
    chargrilled spring onions and
        asparagus, 123
    chicken and asparagus gratin, 369
    Chinese beef and asparagus with
        oyster sauce, 442
    conchiglie salad with bocconcini,
        asparagus and oregano, 55
    creamy asparagus linguine, 519
    mustard chicken and asparagus
        quiche, 392
    spaghettini with asparagus and rocket,
        254
    tagliatelle with asparagus and fresh
        herbs, 568
aubergine *see* eggplant
avgolemono soup with chicken, 12
avocado
    avocado and black bean salad, 84
    avocado and herb dip, 109
    avocado salsa, 753
    avocado sauce, 118, 490
    chicken and guacamole squares, 151
    citrus and avocado salad, 89
    crab cakes with avocado salsa, 226
    cucumber rounds with avocado and
        turkey, 121
    guacamole, 106
    hot corn cakes with avocado and
        prawns, 118
    Mexican layered dip, 107
    pumpkin with chilli and avocado, 730
    spinach and avocado salad with warm
        mustard vinaigrette, 71

B

baba ghannouj, 98
baby squash with rice stuffing, 140
bacon
    bacon and mushroom cream bites,
        950
    bacon and pea soup, 16
    bacon-wrapped chicken, 503
    basil tortellini with bacon and tomato
        sauce, 473
    chicken and bacon gougäre, 395
    hoppin' John, 651
    meatloaf, 461
    bacon continues...

ba-be

be-br

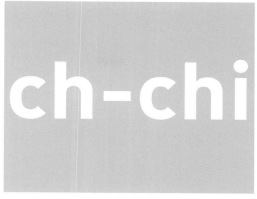

CO-CU

de-dr

fe-fr

ho-la

la–le

le-me

mu-on

on-pa

pe-po

po-pr

pr-pu

ri-sa

sa-sal

si-so

so-sp

sp-st

te–tr

tu-ve

ve-vi

ALTERNATIVE NAMES

aubergine — eggplant
besan flour — chickpea flour
bicarbonate of soda — baking soda
bok choy — Napa cabbage
capsicum — red or green bell pepper
caster sugar — superfine sugar
chickpeas — garbanzo beans
coriander — cilantro
cornflour — cornstarch
courgette — zucchini
flat-leaf parsley — Italian parsley
grill — broil
hazelnut — filbert
icing sugar — confectioners' sugar
mangetout — snow pea
minced beef — ground beef
plain flour — all-purpose flour
polenta — cornmeal
prawn — shrimp
Roma tomato — plum or egg tomato
sambal oelek — chilli paste
single cream — cream
spring onion — scallion
thick cream — heavy cream
tomato purée — tomato paste
witloof — belgian endive

LIQUID CUP MEASUREMENTS

¼ cup	60 ml	2 fluid oz
⅓ cup	80 ml	2¾ fluid oz
½ cup	125 ml	4 fluid oz
¾ cup	180 ml	6 fluid oz
1 cup	250 ml	8 fluid oz

SPOON MEASUREMENTS

¼ teaspoon	1.25 ml
½ teaspoon	2.5 ml
1 teaspoon	5 ml
1 tablespoon	20 ml

WEIGHT

10 g	¼ oz
125 g	4 oz
150 g	5 oz
220 g	7 oz
250 g	8 oz
275 g	9 oz
300 g	10 oz
330 g	11 oz
375 g	12 oz
400 g	13 oz
425 g	14 oz
475 g	15 oz
500 g	1 lb
1 kg	2 lb

NOTES

The recipes in this book were developed using a tablespoon measure of 20 ml. In some other countries the tablespoon is 15 ml. For most recipes this difference will not be noticeable but, for recipes using baking powder, gelatine, bicarbonate of soda, small amounts of flour and cornflour, we suggest that, if you are using the smaller tablespoon, you add an extra teaspoon for each tablespoon.

The recipes in this book are written using convenient cup measurements. You can buy special measuring cups in the supermarket or use an ordinary household cup: first you need to check it holds 250 ml (8 fl oz) by filling it with water and measuring the water (pour it into a measuring jug or a carton that you know holds 250 ml). This cup can then be used for both liquid and dry cup measurements.

OVEN TEMPERATURES

You may find cooking times vary depending on the oven you are using. For fan-forced ovens, as a general rule, set the oven temperature to 20°C (35°F) lower than indicated in the recipe.

IMPORTANT

Those who might be at risk from the effects of salmonella poisoning (the elderly, pregnant women, young children and those suffering from immune deficiency diseases) should consult their doctor with any concerns about eating raw eggs.

IMPRINT

Published in 2008 by Bay Books, an imprint of Murdoch Books Pty Limited.

Murdoch Books Australia
Pier 8/9, 23 Hickson Road
Millers Point NSW 2000
Phone: + 61 (0) 2 8220 2000
Fax: + 61 (0) 2 8220 2558
www.murdochbooks.com.au

Chief Executive: Juliet Rogers
Publishing Director: Kay Scarlett

Concept: James Mills-Hicks
Editorial: Karen Gee, Victoria Fisher
Layout: David Fairs, SASO Content and Design
Indexer: Jo Rudd
Production: Kita George

ISBN-10: 0-681-53387-0
ISBN-13: 978-0-681-53387-5

Printed by i-Book Printing Ltd in 2008.
PRINTED IN CHINA.